IRB
WORLD RUGBY
YEARBOOK
2013

This book is dedicated to the memory of
Andrea Wiggins

IRB
WORLD RUGBY
YEARBOOK
2013

EDITED BY KAREN BOND, ALEX MORTON AND JOHN GRIFFITHS

VSP

Vision Sports Publishing
19-23 High Street
Kingston upon Thames
Surrey, KT1 1LL

www.visionsp.co.uk

Published by Vision Sports Publishing in 2012

Copyright © International Rugby Board 2012

ISBN 13: 978-1-907637-67-4

All pictures by Getty Images unless otherwise stated.

Typeset by Palimpsest Book Production Limited, Falkirk, Stirlingshire

Printed and bound in the UK by Ashford Colour Press Ltd

The IRB World Rugby Yearbook is an independent publication supported by the
International Rugby Board but the views throughout, expressed by the different
authors, do not necessarily reflect the policies and opinions of the IRB.

International Rugby Board
Huguenot House
35-38 St Stephen's Green
Dublin 2, Ireland

t +353-1-240-9200
f +353-1-240-9201

www.irb.com

Contents

England 2015 Set to be Nationwide Festival

A message from Bernard Lapasset, Chairman of the International Rugby Board

Welcome to the seventh edition of the *IRB World Rugby Yearbook*. It is hard to believe that a year has passed since New Zealand captain Richie McCaw held aloft the Webb Ellis Cup to cap an exceptional Rugby World Cup that exceeded all sporting and cultural expectations, not to mention firmly established the tournament as one of the world's premier sporting events.

The baton has been passed to England, where sports mania abounds after the successful hosting of the London 2012 Olympic Games and we look ahead to 2015 with excitement, anticipation and what promises to be the biggest Rugby World Cup to date – a seven-week nationwide festival that will showcase the sport and England's culture, heritage, innovation and hospitality the length and breadth of the land.

I know that England 2015 will be a resounding success. All the foundations are in place. A strong and dynamic Organising Committee headed by Andy Cosslett and Debbie Jevans is delivering exciting plans for what will be a special event and at the time of the Yearbook going to press, the list of potential match venues has been announced and the Pool Allocation Draw is looming fast on the horizon and will reveal the mouth-watering match-ups that fans throughout the world can look forward to in three years' time.

The global qualification process for England 2015 will deliver thrills and drama in equal measure as 80 nations across all continents compete to claim one of the eight available places. It all kicked off in Mexico in March, and who can forget Madagascar defeating RWC 2011 participants Namibia in dramatic circumstances in front of an astonishing 40,000 strong crowd earlier this year, or India's nail-biting 18-16 victory over Guam? There are sure to be more thrills along the way and it will be fascinating to see whether we will have a new nation at RWC 2015.

Of course, Rugby World Cup is more than just 48 matches. Even in this commercial world, this event is firmly rooted in development. Without the Rugby World Cup and its success, we would not be able to invest unprecedented sums into the development and growth of Rugby worldwide at all levels. Indeed, the tournament has enabled the IRB to pump £150 million into the Game between 2009 and 2012 to deliver new tournaments, support Unions, promote participation and deliver player welfare, training and education programmes in order that the Game we all love can continue to flourish.

I am confident that we have in place the processes and platform to do just that. Tournaments such as the IRB Americas Rugby Championship, IRB Nations Cup and IRB Pacific Nations Cup, coupled with the beginning of an expanded Tours and Test schedule, mean that the second tier of nations are able to continually benchmark their performances against the world's best teams.

On and off the field it has been a fantastic year for Rugby. Indeed it has been an historic year. On the field, we welcomed Argentina into The Rugby Championship and a rightful place at the top table and they performed admirably against the world's top three ranked teams. Fiji and Samoa welcomed Scotland for the first Tier One tour to the Pacific Islands since 2003. A spectacular IRB Junior World Championship in South Africa saw the host nation break New Zealand's grip on the trophy with a remarkable 35,000 fans packed into Newlands.

Sevens continues to go from strength to strength. We are three years on from the Olympic decision and the positive effect of inclusion is being felt across our 118 Member Unions. Sevens has gone mainstream and, propelled by being in the Rio Olympic Games cycle, the profile and prestige will only grow. London gave us a unique insight into what to expect, from the atmosphere in the stadium to the excellence of the volunteers and the inclusivity of the athletes village and all our players are excited about their journey over the next four years. Whether the road leads to a gold medal or not is irrelevant, the Olympics will be positive for Rugby and Rugby will bring a special atmosphere to the Olympics.

As we continue to prepare for Rio, perhaps the most significant and exciting development has been in Women's Rugby. The Women's Game is our fastest area of growth. The appetite across all our Unions is impressive and we are working hard to ensure that they have the tools they need to embrace

x the opportunity created by the Olympics. This year we have launched the inaugural IRB Women's Sevens World Series with events taking place in four exciting markets for Rugby. The Series provides a regular competitive pathway to the Olympics and, while plans are afoot to expand, we need to ensure that we start by delivering an exceptional Series that players and Unions can be proud of.

The catalyst has been the *IRB Women's Rugby Plan* which is the blueprint for growth and high performance excellence. The indications are that it is working and, with the likes of Tunisia qualifying for Rugby World Cup Sevens 2013 in Moscow, the Game is certainly expanding beyond its traditional boundaries. We are also committed to ensuring that women have the same opportunity as men to engage, to participate and to contribute to major decisions in Rugby.

The HSBC Sevens World Series continues to go from strength to strength with its winning blend of extreme competitiveness, high-quality entertainment and broadcast and commercial appeal reaching out to new audiences year on year. New Zealand were deserved champions, but a whole host of nations are capable of winning and that is good for Sevens.

Off the field we remain committed to investment in the sport at all levels, but it is not just about money. Players are at the very heart of our Game and we continue to ensure that player welfare is central to all that we do. The new pitch-side concussion assessment trials are a positive innovation and are certainly delivering what was intended of them – to protect the player. And while it is impossible to implement at community level where there are no match doctors, the message to players, coaches and referees is simple – do not take a risk with your head. If there is any doubt, sit it out.

The good news is that, contrary to popular belief, injury rates in Rugby are falling. There is, of course, more that we can be doing and we are committed to working in partnership with our Unions to deliver best-practice models and practices across the spectrum of medical and player welfare areas.

This year also saw the implementation of Law trials and so far the feedback has been encouraging from players and coaches. It is important that we continually take stock and review trends in the Game, the way it is played at all levels to ensure that Rugby retains its unique character and is as enjoyable to play, coach, officiate and watch as possible. There is, of course, one anomaly – the scrum. We are committed to addressing this issue in order that collapses that are prevalent at the elite level are reduced and that the scrum remains a fair contest for possession.

Next year promises to be just as exciting as we all look forward to RWC Sevens 2013 and an indication of progress ahead of Rio 2016. We also look forward to announcements regarding ticketing, venues and the match schedule for RWC 2015. It will be a big year!

The Front
Row

How do You Make the Lions Roar?

Greg Thomas talks to Sir Ian McGeechan

Ian McGeechan made two tours as a player with the British & Irish Lions and played seven Tests, including all four on the unbeaten tour of South Africa in 1974. The Scot went on to coach the Lions on five subsequent tours, including the winning series of 1989 in Australia and 1997 in South Africa. There is nothing he doesn't understand about the Lions and their place in the Rugby landscape.

Is there a place in today's burgeoning Rugby calendar for the Lions?

In 125 years the Lions have won only eight or so series, and with professionalism in the mid-1990s there was a thought that the Lions concept would die. But the 1997 tour to South Africa proved this wrong when we beat the then world champions, and I think it showed how important the Lions are to the Rugby brand. Then we had the 2001 Australia and 2009 South Africa tours, which were also great series, despite narrow losses. And ironically you can say that despite these disappointments the support for the Lions has grown and grown. The Lions cannot now be separated from their supporters and they are arguably the best-supported rugby team in the world. It is a phenomenon that cannot be ignored and tours are now also about the engagement with the supporters from four different countries who unite in their tens of thousands and travel together to create fervent support.

Funnily enough the Lions tour used to mirror the traditional tours by most national teams, with 30 players hitting the road for two or three months. Then everything turned professional and tours changed and teams ended

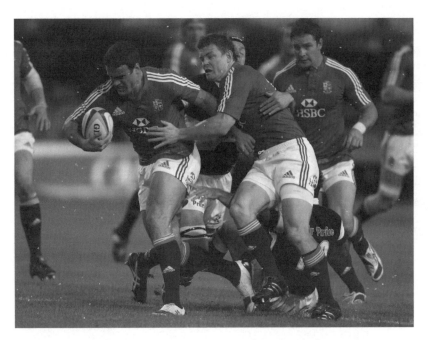

Jamie Roberts and Brian O'Driscoll combine well against the Sharks in 2009.

up flying in, playing one or two Test matches, and flying out. But interestingly the Lions tour, although shorter, has endured – everyone has realised that more traditional tours are the best environment to develop talent. Nothing like playing twice a week to develop character, combinations and playing patterns!

For me the best part of it is to see the best players from the four countries combining together. In 2009 Brian O'Driscoll and Jamie Roberts were the Test centre pairing and they turned out to be the best pair in the world that year. This is the magic of the Lions, drawing players together who react in amazing ways when challenged. This is what attracts such support.

Are the Lions getting a fair go in terms of tour preparation and assembly?

In this professional age I do not think that the club administrators understand what being a Lion means to the players. They do not want to go out of their way to ensure the timing is right for the players, and this is where it is undervalued. In 2009, and indeed next year, the Lions will probably not assemble as a complete unit prior to heading overseas. In practical terms a week together with everybody available would make a big difference – you would arrive in the country having had that week with all the basic things in place. Then you can be upfront with players about the unique challenges and spend a bit more time developing combinations and the chemistry within the squad that is vital.

Training and preparation is vital for the Lions to develop a good chemistry.

However, the short build up and the relatively short time to develop a Test side means you are very focused. You cannot afford to get too complicated with things, which can be an advantage. You spend the hours available simplifying things so that you have a fighting chance, tactically, of being able to shape a game you can play. Also the biggest challenge is getting everybody thinking along the same lines. Motivation is not an issue as the players all want to be Lions and to play in the Test side.

So how do you go about selecting the right squad? Because it is such a challenge over a short period of time, chemistry within the group is important. You need to find players who will not be afraid of the immense challenge, and they have got to come with an open mind. Talent is important but attitude is just as important as you have to accept that things will be done differently on a Lions tour. When the chemistry is right that is when the team performs. You need experienced players on tour, but I have always had some younger players in the squad because it helps draw the squad together. The older players do look after the younger ones, who in turn are being challenged to step up. They then challenge the older players to adjust and do things differently. Everyone is learning, which adds to the chemistry. Playing twice in a week is something they are not used to, but they rise to it and then realise they can do it. It is amazing how this prepares them physically and mentally. That said, some adapt quicker than others and the coaching staff have to allow for this.

In terms of squad size it is easy to pick too many. I believe around 34-36 is about right as everyone has to be involved. It doesn't work when you think you have a Test team in your mind from the outset and play it on the weekend matches with everyone else playing midweek. You have to create a competitive environment where everybody is part of the tour and has an opportunity to fight for a place in the Test match team. It's important that the management team buys into this as well as it is against the norm. Having a team that is constantly changing is a challenge for the coaches, with combinations continually assessed and the Test side not put together until the week of the first Test.

Selecting the squad is a long process involving discussions with national coaches and viewing matches taking place during the preceding November and the Six Nations. It is important to get a feel for how the players react to challenges, what character they have, can they handle the pressure, and of course how well they are playing. You have to think about injuries and ensure that the squad is well balanced.

So what would be the minimum number of matches for a Lions tour? As many as possible, but the playing calendar does not allow for it! Ten matches with six before the first Test is the absolute minimum. Ideally it should be 12 games with three Tests at the end. We have learned lessons over the last few tours such as not having a match between the last two Tests because of attrition. The host country has to understand the nature of the tour and come to the party in assisting in the tour planning to give the Lions the best opportunity to be competitive in the Test series. Otherwise the Lions concept does not work. New Zealand is incredibly intense in terms of the rugby, Australia presents travel challenges due to distances and in South Africa you have altitude to consider, so all of this has to be part of the planning. The 2013 tour fits into the current model of 10 matches, but Australia cannot offer enough quality provincial matches, hence the first match in Hong Kong. What will be interesting is if the top Australian players play for their Super Rugby provinces in the lead up to Test matches. You need matches with intensity prior to the Test series and it is always disappointing when the host country holds back most of its best players for the Test series.

Another part of the equation is that the squad must engage with the host country. The players must get out, be seen and enjoy the country and be ambassadors for rugby. In 2009 we opened new playing fields and dressing rooms and

Lions players make an effort to engage with the local community in 2009.

interacted with communities. We also engaged fully with the media and made them part of the tour. We were told this wouldn't work. Well it did and helped create a really powerful environment around the team and the tour. This was all highlighted by the third Test win in 2009. Everything was against us having lost the first two. We had played quality rugby to that point and I was really proud of the victory, which showed huge character.

I was a player in 1977 and we got it wrong in terms of all of this, but I learnt a hell of a lot on that tour in terms of the Lions concept and what was needed on tour. I was determined to use those lessons and eradicate the mistakes when I took up the coaching reins.

Facing the Challenge of the Lions

with John Eales

The unpredictable nature of the British & Irish Lions represents the greatest threat to Australia's hopes of a series victory when the tourists arrive Down Under in 2013, according to former Wallaby captain John Eales.

The second row was capped 86 times by Australia and led his country to an historic first series win over the Lions in 2001 and believes the current Wallabies team must be prepared for another leap into the unknown when the tourists return after a 12-year hiatus.

"Each Lions squad arrives with a different collective personality, a different outlook on how they want to play," Eales says. "The make-up of the touring party in terms of the different nationalities, the philosophy of the head coach and the balance of power in the northern hemisphere at that time all make it difficult to confidently predict the style of a Lions team.

"We got it wrong in the first Test in 2001. We had been building up for the series for three years, but the Lions still surprised us in Brisbane. We anticipated they would be more conservative, but they came out to attack and outscored us four tries to two. We didn't adapt quickly enough in terms of our defence and as a result we lost the game.

John Eales led Australia to victory against the Lions in 2001.

"We put things right for the second and third Tests, but we were caught cold in that first game. When Australia play a side like the All Blacks, we know what to expect in terms of their patterns and systems because of the frequency of the fixtures, but it's always harder to accurately second guess what the Lions will do.

"More specifically, it's hard to know how the important partnerships will go. It's rare for the Lions to have a back row with three players from the same country, and it's not unusual for the half backs to come from different Test sides, and so you don't always have previous performances to analyse."

Despite a one-Test triumph over the Lions back in 1930, Australia had never beaten the Lions in a series before 2001, but after their 29-13 reverse in Brisbane a 35-14 win in Melbourne followed by their 29-23 victory in Sydney in Rod Macqueen's last game as head coach ensured they finally claimed a famous scalp.

Thousands of fans made the journey Down Under to cheer on Martin Johnson's team, and Eales admits the huge travelling support the tourists traditionally command makes a Lions game a unique occasion.

"We knew they would bring a lot of fans, but we were still surprised by just how many. The atmosphere at the Tests was absolutely amazing and there was a real sense that the games were something special. I think the sheer number of Lions supporters gave our own fans a shot in the arm.

"The atmosphere in the Docklands Stadium for the second Test in Melbourne in particular was unforgettable. There was a record crowd of more than 56,000 for the game, the roof was closed and

Lions captain Martin Johnson shakes hands with John Eales after the final Test in 2001.

you could literally feel the noise seeping through the cracks in the dressing room before kick-off.

"We knew it was make or break after the defeat in Brisbane. We were the reigning world and Tri-Nations champions at the time and, although we had achieved a lot as a team, we knew there was a huge level of expectation and pressure on us to keep the series alive.

"The rarity of Test matches against the Lions ensures the games are unique. They're different in nature to a Bledisloe Cup match with New Zealand for example, but both are stand-out memories of my international career."

THE LIONS

British & Irish Lions Tour to Australia 2013 Fixtures

The British & Irish Lions return to Australia in 2013 looking to avenge their defeat to the Wallabies in 2001 and register a first series victory since they stunned the Springboks in 1997.

The Lions lost Down Under despite claiming a convincing 29-13 win in the first Test in Brisbane against the reigning world champions but were overhauled in the next two games, losing the pivotal third Test 29-23 in Sydney in one of the most dramatic denouements to a series in the tourists' history.

Much, however, has changed for both teams since they last crossed swords and the 2013 tour will be a relatively new experience for the Lions with four of the stadiums on the nine-match itinerary not having hosted matches in 2001.

After a warm-up against the Barbarians in Hong Kong, the Lions open up against Western Force in the unfamiliar surroundings of Patersons Stadium in Perth. They continue to break new ground against the Reds at the 52,500 capacity Suncorp Stadium in Brisbane before facing a combined New South Wales-Queensland Country XV in midweek at Newcastle's Hunter Stadium.

The fourth match of the tour finally sees the Lions return to an old haunt when they tackle the Waratahs at Sydney Football Stadium, the scene of an entertaining 41-24 victory 12 years earlier.

The clash with the Brumbies will take Warren Gatland's side to Canberra Stadium which, under the guise of Bruce Stadium, was the venue for a narrow 30-28 triumph for the previous tourists while the final midweek clash is against the Melbourne Rebels at the AAMI Stadium in Melbourne, a 30,000 capacity stadium built in 2010.

The three-Test series against the Wallabies begins in late June back at the Suncorp Stadium but the final two games of the tour see the Lions return to familiar, if renamed, venues. The second Test takes in place in Melbourne at the Etihad Stadium. In 2001 it went by the name of the Colonial Stadium and was the setting for the second Test, a match in which the Wallabies crushed the Lions 35-14 in front of a crowd of 56,605. The potentially decisive third Test will be staged at the ANZ Stadium in Sydney. In 2001 it was called Stadium Australia and witnessed a titanic struggle between the two sides which famously finished in favour of the Wallabies.

Date	Opposition	Location	Stadium
Saturday 1 June	Barbarians	Hong Kong	
Wednesday 5 June	Western Force	Perth	Patersons Stadium
Saturday 8 June	Queensland Reds	Brisbane	Suncorp Stadium
Wednesday 12 June	Comb NSW-Queensland County	Newcastle	Hunter Stadium
Saturday 15 June	NSW Waratahs	Sydney	Sydney Football Stadium
Tuesday 18 June	ACT Brumbies	Canberra	Canberra Stadium
Saturday 22 June	Australia	Brisbane	Suncorp Stadium
Tuesday 25 June	Melbourne Rebels	Melbourne	AAMI Stadium
Saturday 29 June	Australia	Melbourne	Etihad Stadium
Saturday 6 July	Australia	Sydney	ANZ Stadium

① **Perth** Patersons Stadium
Capacity: 43,500

② **Brisbane** Suncorp Stadium
Capacity: 52,500

③ **Newcastle** Hunter Stadium
Capacity: 33,000

④ **Sydney** Sydney Football Stadium
Capacity: 45,500

Sydney ANZ Stadium
Capacity: 84,000

⑤ **Canberra**
Canberra Stadium
Capacity: 25,000

⑥ **Melbourne** AAMI Stadium
Capacity: 51,500

Melbourne Etihad Stadium
Capacity: 56,300

THE RUGBY
CHAMPIONSHIP

Reflections on a First Rugby Championship

By Agustín Pichot

Now that the inaugural Rugby Championship has finished, I can only feel an incredible sense of relief, pride and achievement. It was much bigger than I had personally anticipated, but a joy to live through. I am convinced the way the Argentine public got captured by its intensity, by the way Los Pumas performed, will bring huge benefits to the game.

Having spoken with many foreigners that travelled to our three venues and enjoyed the Argentine hospitality, our country, our food, sampled our culture and watched games at three great venues, we also fulfilled part of the vision and ambition we had as a nation: to be great hosts of an incredible tournament.

The team performed to a level that confounded critics. It seemed that at times we put the top three teams in the world under serious pressure and, even if we finished with one draw in six games, the players left no gas in the tank and earned the respect of the Rugby community. We will get better, which is great for us.

I felt proud to be present at the launch of The Rugby Championship.

The number of messages and e-mails I received during and after The Rugby Championship ensured that all the hard work we put in at the Unión Argentina de Rugby to make this happen was well worth it. For me, it was a road that I would take again with no hesitation as it was one that taught me a lot and helped me be a better person and rounded me in my new role as an official.

When I look back to where it all started, I remember that as a player I was always complaining about the lack of opportunities my team had. I must have cornered many administrators and officials about this, but then I also had to focus on playing the Game at the highest level and hoping that message would soon filter and we, Los Pumas, would be given an opportunity with a regular calendar.

After what was an incredible and never-to-be-forgotten Rugby World Cup in 2007, I felt like I had played my last game of rugby, even if I announced my international retirement much later. The International Rugby Board, incredible allies in all of this, invited me as one of two international players – the other being a certain Richie McCaw – to the Game's Forum in Woking, England, in December 2007. It was clear then that if Argentina wanted competition, we had to look to the southern hemisphere.

The UAR had offered me the Pumas coaching job, but I wasn't yet decided on what I was going to do with my future, and anyway I was still an active player, at least for a few more months, so they asked me to help them with this new process. I jumped at the chance; what was supposedly going to be part-time became four years of my life. And what a ride it has been! With the inestimable help of Morgan Buckley, who became a close friend, and Mark Egan, another good friend from the IRB, we sat down to draw strategic plans for the Game in Argentina.

To create our own plan, we were fortunate to look at every different model and how it worked for every country. Ours is different and our club scene is very big and important. I played for the same club as my father and, even if I

It was great to see Los Pumas perform well in our first Rugby Championship.

was a professional player in Europe, the Club Atlético San Isidro was always "my" club. My older brother coaches the first XV, I help out at the club and so does my younger brother. It is the same at every club in the country. This is something very unique to us and we had to preserve that.

These plans were approved in Argentina in December 2008, and on Monday 2 February 2009 the High Performance Units (PlaDAR) opened in five centres in Argentina. That was an important day as it was the kick-start to what was to come. IRB Chairman Bernard Lapasset came to Argentina to underpin our plan and offer support. He was a great fighter for the Argentina and Puma cause.

Internally, we had a lot of convincing to do. We had to ensure we had the support of all the provinces that make up our Union; some took longer than others, but the long-term benefits were eventually understood. And internationally, it was meetings and more meetings all over the world, with the IRB, with SANZAR, with European clubs.

I remember two that were crucial. One in Wellington in 2008 that set the tone of what was to come and the second in Sydney a year later in which they told us that if we complied with a number of items – a long and difficult list – we might be invited to what ended up being The Rugby Championship. The light appeared at the end of the very long tunnel.

The assistance – structural, financial and moral – from the IRB was great and we managed to slowly convince the world to include The Rugby Championship into Regulation 9 and the clubs also helped with the release of players. We are extremely thankful to all of them.

South Africa were always good friends of Argentine rugby and they invited our home-based team, the Pampas XV, to play in the Vodacom Cup for the past three years. That helped enormously and a number of current Test players were in that team.

Last November we launched the tournament in Buenos Aires and it has been a whirlwind ever since, more so after the team got together on 1 July to prepare for this exciting new chapter.

It was fitting that the first two games were against South Africa, and the opening day was one in which a lot of emotions went through me. I thought a lot about my family – my wife and two daughters knew how much I had been fighting for the cause – about my friends and former teammates and for all those who once played for Argentina. This current team is the beneficiary of a century-long international history.

I found a corner in the changing room, where I wasn't intruding, and seeing what was about to happen I cried. It was tears of joy for what had finally come to fruition. For what was to start, for the future. Some of my closest friends were in that team and it was great that they could enjoy it. It wasn't my time and I was at peace with that.

Hosting three games of this calibre at home was also very important for the Union. The three venues looked superb and a lot of lessons will be carried into next year, but the overall feeling is that we achieved something very unique. One of the luxuries of The Rugby Championship is that we will be able to work on our mistakes in the next three seasons.

Thousands of Argentine fans turned out to watch a fantastic tournament.

The way the team performed was also something that made all of us very proud. They played with their hearts on their sleeves and the whole community in my country was enthralled with their performances. They showed that, with passion and commitment, everything is possible.

There are a lot of people who deserve mention as I close this article; far too many to list everyone. Of course the IRB and SANZAR; those clubs with Pumas who kindly released them and, we hope, received better players for that; the local communities of Mendoza, La Plata and Rosario; the visiting fans; those who hosted our fans in South Africa, New Zealand and Australia.

This was a team effort and having been part of a team that managed to perform to the standard we did in the inaugural Rugby Championship is something that made me very proud of being Argentine.

Richie McCaw's New Zealand remain at the top of the IRB World Rankings.

Getty Images

IRB World Rankings

By Karen Bond

The IRB World Rankings took on extra significance in 2012 with the fact that they would be used to seed the 12 teams directly qualified for Rugby World Cup 2015 into three bands for the Pool Allocation Draw in London on 3 December 2012.

This division will take place at the end of a busy month of internationals in Europe and will see the countries ranked one to four on that day form band one and therefore unable to be drawn in the same pool for England 2015. The teams ranked five to eight will form band two and the remaining four teams band three. The teams will then be randomly drawn by band into the four pools that will comprise Rugby's showcase event in England in 2015. The eight qualification places will then be placed into bands four and five according to strength.

This means that, if the rankings stay as they are at the end of The Rugby Championship, there will be no chance of a pool match between hosts England and defending champions New Zealand, but the two finalists at RWC 2011 could be drawn together for the second tournament in a row, as could the Six Nations and Rugby Championship winners.

New Zealand continue to sit atop the rankings, as they have done since November 2009, and have actually increased their advantage over Australia to 7.43 points after a perfect record of nine wins from nine in 2012. The series win over Ireland and emphatic clean sweep in The Rugby Championship have taken the All Blacks' unbeaten run to 16 matches and within touching distance of the record 18 achieved by Lithuania between 2006 and 2010.

The All Blacks, who have occupied top spot for almost 80 per cent of the time since the rankings were introduced in October 2003, are one of only two teams to remain stationary for the last year, the other being Canada in 13th position. Canada played only three matches in this timeframe, beating USA and Georgia and losing to Italy.

Eight other nations have ended the 12-month period since RWC 2011 in the same position as they began it, although unlike New Zealand and Canada they did move up or down during this time. They are Australia (2), USA (17), Romania (18), Chile (24), Sweden (38), Cook Islands (54), Jamaica (83) and Bosnia & Herzegovina (87).

Mexico are one of three new nations in the IRB World Rankings.

In total 36 nations improved their ranking in this time, while 50 ended the year lower than they began it. This is in contrast to last year when more nations enjoyed climbs than falls, although it can easily be explained by the introduction of Mexico, Pakistan and the Philippines to the IRB World Rankings. The trio entered the rankings in March with a rating of 40.00, putting them equal 71st and resulting in all the sides below this falling three places.

Mexico and Pakistan had both slipped from their initial entry position by October, unlike the Philippines who sit 16 places higher in 55th as a result of victories over Singapore, Chinese Taipei and Sri Lanka in the HSBC Asian 5 Nations Division I in April. This tournament in Manila marked the start of Rugby World Cup 2015 qualifying in Asia, and by winning it the Philippines will now take their place alongside Japan, Korea, Hong Kong and UAE in the top echelon of Asian rugby in 2013, an impressive achievement for a country who played in the bottom tier in 2008.

This 16-place gain means that the Philippines share the honour of being the biggest climbers in the IRB World Rankings over the last 12 months with

Colombia, a side who sit just two places lower in 57th. Colombia's gain came in the space of seven days in September when they beat the higher ranked Peru and Venezuela in the South American B Championship, the first RWC 2015 qualifying matches in the region. The Colombians have been something of a yo-yo nation in the rankings in recent years, this gain coming on the back of a 20-place plummet in the previous 12 months and a 12-place elevation the year before.

These two were not alone in profiting from success in RWC 2015 qualifiers as Madagascar jumped 13 places to 42nd on the back of beating Morocco and RWC 2011 participants Namibia – the latter 57-54 before 40,000 vocal fans in Antananarivo in July – to earn promotion to next year's Africa Cup Division 1A. This position is the highest Madagascar have been since the first week of the IRB World Rankings in October 2003.

Losses in qualifiers also proved costly with Venezuela and Peru both suffering falls into double figures after defeats in the South American B Championship. Four other sides with similarly large falls were Hungary, Latvia, Slovenia and St Vincent & The Grenadines, but it was Singapore who suffered the biggest fall in the last 12 months, slumping 17 places to 66th and also suffering relegation from the Asian 5 Nations Division I to end their involvement in the RWC 2015 qualifying process.

Other nations worth a mention include Korea, who were the surprise package on their return to the Asian 5 Nations Top 5 and have climbed seven places to 25th as a result, and Zimbabwe who continue to rise up the rankings and will soon be putting Namibia under threat as Africa's second best team behind the Springboks.

There was also some movement among the 12 nations who already know they will play at England 2015 with France and Tonga suffering the biggest falls, the RWC 2011 runners-up slipping two to fifth and the Ikale Tahi three to 12th after losing two of their three matches at the IRB Pacific Nations Cup in June. Scotland, meanwhile, fell to their lowest ever ranking of 12th after picking up the Six Nations wooden spoon, but by the end of June had returned to ninth after beating Australia, Fiji and Samoa. Wales were the biggest climbers in the top 10, rising two places to sixth after their Grand Slam success.

The IRB World Rankings are published every Monday on www.irb.com. They are calculated using a points exchange system in which teams take points off each other based on the match result. Whatever one team gains, the other team loses. The exchanges are determined by the match result, the relative strength of the team and the margin of victory. There is also an allowance for home advantage.

Ninety-six of the IRB's Member Unions have a rating, typically between 0 and 100 with the top side in the world usually having a rating above 90 – New Zealand's was 93.35 at the time of writing. Any match that is not a full international between two countries or a Test against the Lions does not count towards the rankings. Likewise neither does a match against a country that is not an IRB Full Member Union. For more details, visit www.irb.com.

IRB WORLD RANKINGS 31/10/11 – 08/10/12

POSITION	MEMBER UNION	RATING	POINTS
1	New Zealand	93.35	
2	Australia	85.92	
3	South Africa	84.69	Up 1
4	England	83.09	Up 1
5	France	83.03	Down 2
6	Wales	82.26	Up 2
7	Ireland	79.85	Down 1
8	Argentina	78.63	Down 1
9	Scotland	77.97	Up 1
10	Samoa	76.23	Up 1
11	Italy	76.03	Up 1
12	Tonga	74.79	Down 3
13	Canada	72.30	
14	Fiji	70.60	Up 2
15	Georgia	67.95	Down 1
16	Japan	67.93	Down 1
17	USA	66.61	
18	Romania	64.54	
19	Russia	62.05	Up 2
20	Spain	61.63	Up 3
21	Uruguay	61.13	Up 1
22	Namibia	59.24	Down 3
23	Belgium	59.17	Up 2
24	Chile	58.32	
25	Korea	56.72	Up 7
26	Portugal	56.58	Down 6
27	Poland	56.38	Up 3
28	Hong Kong	55.49	Down 1
29	Zimbabwe	54.70	Up 6
30	Ukraine	53.95	Up 3
31	Germany	53.33	Up 6
32	Morocco	52.35	Down 6
33	Brazil	51.57	Down 5
34	Moldova	51.28	Down 5
35	Kazakhstan	51.28	Down 4
36	Lithuania	50.90	Up 3
37	Paraguay	50.67	Up 4
38	Sweden	50.41	
39	Kenya	50.28	Up 1
40	Czech Republic	48.96	Down 6
41	Uganda	48.76	Up 2
42	Madagascar	48.19	Up 13
43	Tunisia	48.18	Down 7
44	Croatia	48.06	Up 6
45	Malta	47.97	Up 8
46	Ivory Coast	47.67	Down 2
47	Netherlands	47.66	Down 5
48	Sri Lanka	47.60	Down 3
49	Senegal	47.14	Up 3

IRB WORLD RANKINGS 31/10/11 – 08/10/12

POSITION	MEMBER UNION	RATING	POINTS
50	Bermuda	46.78	Down 3
51	Papua New Guinea	46.55	Down 5
52	Switzerland	45.88	Up 4
53	Trinidad & Tobago	44.68	Down 5
54	Cook Islands	44.61	
55	Philippines	44.34	* Up 16
56	Israel	43.90	Up 5
57	Colombia	43.65	Up 16
58	Guyana	43.56	Up 2
59	Thailand	43.44	Up 6
60	Chinese Taipei	43.19	Down 3
61	Denmark	42.51	Up 7
62	Andorra	42.21	Down 4
63	Venezuela	41.83	Down 12
64	Malaysia	41.37	Down 1
65	Cayman Islands	41.27	Up 1
66	Singapore	41.19	Down 17
67	Barbados	41.01	Up 9
68	India	40.81	Up 7
69	China	40.73	Down 7
70	Solomon Islands	40.70	Up 7
71	Niue Islands	40.45	Down 4
72	Latvia	40.16	Down 13
73	Serbia	40.14	Down 4
74	Peru	39.67	Down 10
75	Mexico	39.38	* Down 4
76	Zambia	38.87	Down 4
77	Botswana	38.65	Up 5
78	Pakistan	38.38	* Down 7
79	Cameroon	38.33	Down 1
80	Slovenia	37.76	Down 10
81	Hungary	37.66	Down 10
82	Bulgaria	37.49	Down 3
83	Jamaica	37.08	
84	St Vincent & The Grenadines	36.84	Down 10
85	Austria	36.84	Down 5
86	Tahiti	36.25	Down 1
87	Bosnia & Herzegovina	36.18	
88	Guam	35.70	Down 2
89	Bahamas	35.68	Down 5
90	Swaziland	35.63	Down 9
91	Nigeria	35.29	Down 3
92	Monaco	35.17	Down 3
93	Norway	34.33	Down 3
94	Vanuatu	34.77	Down 3
95	Luxembourg	33.62	Down 3
96	Finland	26.29	Down 3

* Mexico, Pakistan and Philippines entered the IRB World Rankings at 40.00 in March so climb is based on entry ranking of joint 71st.

The Numbers Game

850 million
Estimated global audience of HSBC Sevens World Series 2011/12

21
Number of games New Zealand went unbeaten in the Junior World Championship before the 9-6 loss to Wales in the 2012 pool stages

66
New JWC graduates since end of RWC 2011 and climax of The Rugby Championship

44
Tries scored in The Rugby Championship (12 matches)

1
First titles won in 2012 by Harlequins (Aviva Premiership), Chiefs (Super Rugby), South Africa (IRB Junior World Championship) and Romania (IRB Nations Cup)

2,127
Tries scored across the HSBC Sevens World Series 2011/12

10
Sevens World Series won by New Zealand

400,000

The number of international fans expected to visit England for RWC 2015

15

Women's teams qualified for RWC Sevens 2013 so far (one remaining)

46

Tries scored in the Six Nations (15 matches)

547,500

Record attendance for HSBC Sevens World Series in 2011/12

7

Consecutive Six Nations titles won by England's women with 2012 success

68

Points scored by Mexico in winning the first RWC 2015 qualifying match against Jamaica

23

Men's teams qualified for RWC Sevens 2013 so far (one remaining)

45

Caps won by the most capped JWC graduate David Pocock

17

Number of venues on shortlist to host RWC 2015 matches

265

Number of Test matches since RWC 2011 to end of The Rugby Championship

Roll of Honour

RBS 6 Nations: Wales

The Rugby Championship: New Zealand

IRB Pacific Nations Cup: Samoa

IRB Pacific Rugby Cup: Fiji Warriors

HSBC Asian 5 Nations: Japan

IRB Nations Cup: Romania

IRB Junior World Championship: South Africa

IRB Junior World Rugby Trophy: USA

HSBC Sevens World Series: New Zealand

RBS Women's 6 Nations: England

Aviva Premiership: Harlequins

Top 14: Toulouse

RaboDirect PRO12: Ospreys

Heineken Cup: Leinster

Amlin Challenge Cup: Biarritz

Super Rugby: Chiefs

International
Tournaments

THE ROAD TO RUGBY WORLD CUP 2015

By Karen Bond

Mexico City may be nearly 9,000 kilometres from London but it was here that the road to Rugby World Cup 2015 began on 24 March when Mexico met Jamaica in the opening match of the 2012 NACRA Caribbean Championship.

Less than six months after Richie McCaw held aloft the Webb Ellis Cup at Eden Park, the coveted trophy was in Mexico with England Rugby 2015 Ambassador Lawrence Dallaglio among the record crowd as RWC 2011 Final referee Craig Joubert took charge of the first qualification match.

Mexico ran out 68–14 winners at La Ibero Santa Fe in the first match of a qualification process that will involve 80 nations and 184 matches across the globe in order to determine the eight nations to join the 12 direct qualified teams at England 2015.

"You could see how much it meant to them to be singing their national anthems, at an official World Cup encounter. They knew that having the IRB World Cup logo on the sleeve of their shirts meant they were very much part of the global rugby family," admitted Dallaglio.

"They were clearly very humbled and honoured by the occasion, especially having the actual Webb Ellis Cup there. You could see that it brought home to the players that this was not something out of their reach; they might not reach the 2015 finals themselves, but when they could touch the trophy, they knew that they were a part of it."

This is a hugely important aspect with the road to RWC 2015 a clearly defined pathway, using regional tournaments which give every IRB Member Union a clear vision as to how they can move onwards and upwards, all the time aspiring to play on the sport's greatest stage.

For some, Mexico and Jamaica included, their involvement in the RWC 2015 qualification process has already ended, for others it is yet to begin, but reality is that the dream is there to be lived.

There will be many twists and turns to be played out before we know

the identity of the Africa 1, Americas 1 and 2, Asia 1, Europe 1 and 2 **25**
and Oceania 1 qualifiers or the Repechage winner, but follow it all at
www.rugbyworldcup.com.

AFRICA (CAR)

(One direct place – Africa 1 – and one Repechage place)

An incredible 40,000 fans witnessed the start of Africa's road to England
2015 in Madagascar, a country where rugby is the number one sport,
highlighting the potential that exists for rugby in the continent.
Madagascar hosted Senegal, Morocco and Namibia in the Confédération
Africaine de Rugby (CAR) Division 1B in July and gave their passionate
fans something to cheer about by claiming the title with a remarkable
57–54 win over RWC 2011 participants Namibia.

The Mahamasina Stadium crowd in Antananarivo were treated to a
rollercoaster ride as Madagascar raced into a 19–0 lead only to then
find themselves trailing 43–29 with 10 minutes remaining. Roared on
by their vociferous fans, Madagascar forced the match into extra-time
and then snatched victory from the jaws of defeat in the dying seconds
to secure promotion to Division 1A.

Namibia now face an uphill task to qualify for RWC 2015 – they
must win Division 1B in 2013 to be part of Division 1A in 2014 when
the Africa 1 qualifier will be determined. They will have to overcome
Tunisia, Senegal and Botswana in 2013, the latter winning Division 1C
on home soil to remain in the qualification process.

AMERICAS (NACRA/CONSUR)

(Two direct places – Americas 1 and Americas 2 – and one Repechage place)

The honour of hosting the first qualifier this time fell on the NACRA
(North America Caribbean Rugby Association) in Mexico City with the
hosts one of nine Unions competing in the Caribbean Championship in
March to June 2012.

Split into two zones, the teams stepped their way through the competition until only Bermuda and Guyana remained, the two sides meeting
in the final to determine who would progress to the next stage and a
meeting with the winner of the CONSUR B tournament in September.

Bermuda, buoyed by a training session with former England international
Lewis Moody, which was "a real tonic for the lads" in the words of coach
Lawrence Bird, ran out 18–0 winners to set up a meeting with Paraguay,
who impressively swept aside Colombia, Peru and hosts Venezuela to

win the second tier title in South America a few months later.

Paraguay stole the show and kept their RWC 2015 dream alive but Colombia also deserve mention for upsetting Venezuela and Peru to climb 17 places in the IRB World Rankings in the space of seven days. Paraguay would also prove too strong for Bermuda, running out 29–14 winners in Asunción to earn a play-off with Brazil, who had finished bottom of the South American Championship earlier in the year.

The Americas progress will gather momentum in 2013 when Canada, Chile, Uruguay and USA enter the fray. The two powers of North American rugby will play each other home and away with the winner qualifying for RWC 2015 as Americas 1. The loser will have a second chance to qualify as Americas 2, facing the South America Championship winners in another two-legged play-off, the team missing out will enter the Repechage.

ASIA (ARFU)

(One direct place – Asia 1 – and one Repechage place)

Japan will be favourites to claim the Asia 1 place and remain the continent's only side to grace the Rugby World Cup stage, but the qualification process began in the Philippines in April with Division I of the HSBC Asian 5 Nations 2012.

The Philippines are an inspiration to other developing rugby nations, having entered the bottom of the A5N pyramid in 2008 and now looking forward to their debut in the top tier in 2014 alongside the Brave Blossoms after winning the title on home soil. The country are falling in love with rugby and the matches were shown live on free-to-air television as the Volcanoes beat Singapore, Sri Lanka and Chinese Taipei.

"Today was a win for the Filipino people. The people came out in numbers and the guys went out and won for their country. It was a beautiful thing," insisted Philippines coach Expo Mejia after their title success. "This team definitely has the talent to stay in the Top 5 next season. We need to work on our structures a bit more and make sure we have all of our players available but we have started something here in the Philippines and we plan to build on that."

The teams in Divisions II and III also had their moment in the spotlight with the two winners to play-off for the right to play in Division I in 2013. Thailand claimed the Division II title with a 22–5 defeat of hosts Malaysia in the final, while India edged Guam 18–16 to win Division III. The two champions met under a blazing Bangkok sun in late July with Thailand living up to their billing as favourites by winning 42–29.

The Top 5 and Division I will double as RWC 2015 qualifiers in 2013 with the Asian 5 Nations champions in 2014 qualifying as Asia

1 and the runner-up entering the Repechage for a second chance to book their passage to England.

EUROPE (FIRA-AER)

(Two direct places – Europe 1 and Europe 2 – and one Repechage place)

European nations were the latest to embark on the road to RWC 2015 with Hungary given the honour of hosting the first match, against Bulgaria, on 6 October. The occasion was marked by a week-long journey from Rugby School in England to the match venue in Kecskemét with the Webb Ellis Cup joined by ER 2015 Ambassadors Will Greenwood, Jonny Wilkinson and Lawrence Dallaglio along the way.

RWC 2003 winner Dallaglio was present to see another regional process begin with a record crowd for a rugby match in Hungary cheering the home side to a 29–26 win over Bulgaria in their European Nations Cup 2014 Division 2C encounter.

"We are proud of what we have achieved today on and off the field. The Rugby World Cup has given us the opportunity to put Rugby in the spotlight in this country and we intend to keep it there. Our journey continues and we dream that one day we will be competing for the Webb Ellis Cup on Rugby's greatest stage," said Hungary Rugby Union President Pal Turi.

The European Nations Cup runs over two years and the top six divisions will all double as RWC 2015 qualification matches. In 2012/13, 20 nations across Divisions 2A to 2D will be part of the process with the winner of each division then progressing to a series of play-offs. The team emerging from these play-offs will then meet the Division 1B winner in 2014 for the right to play the third place team in Division 1A for a place in the Repechage. The top two teams in Division 1A – featuring Georgia, Russia, Romania, Portugal, Spain and newcomers Belgium – when the competition concludes in 2013/14 will qualify directly as Europe 1 and 2.

OCEANIA (FORU)

(One direct place – Oceania 1)

This will again be the last region to enter the qualification fray and also the shortest process. The Oceania Cup 2013 will kick-off the process with the winner progressing to a one-off match with Fiji to identify the Oceania 1 qualifier for RWC 2015. Fiji will undoubtedly be favourites to join the region's direct qualifiers New Zealand, Australia, Tonga and Samoa at England 2015.

RUGBY WORLD CUP RECORDS 1987–2011

(FINAL STAGES ONLY)

OVERALL RECORDS

MOST MATCHES WON IN FINAL STAGES

37	New Zealand
33	Australia
30	France
29	England

MOST OVERALL PENALTIES IN FINAL STAGES

58	J P Wilkinson	England	1999–2011
36	A G Hastings	Scotland	1987–95
35	G Quesada	Argentina	1999–2003
33	M P Lynagh	Australia	1987–95
33	A P Mehrtens	New Zealand	1995–99

MOST OVERALL POINTS IN FINAL STAGES

277	J P Wilkinson	England	1999–2011
227	A G Hastings	Scotland	1987–95
195	M P Lynagh	Australia	1987–95
170	G J Fox	New Zealand	1987–91
163	A P Mehrtens	New Zealand	1995–99

MOST OVERALL DROP GOALS IN FINAL STAGES

14	J P Wilkinson	England	1999–2011
6	J H de Beer	South Africa	1999
5	C R Andrew	England	1987–95
5	G L Rees	Canada	1987–99
4	J M Hernández	Argentina	2003–07

MOST OVERALL TRIES IN FINAL STAGES

15	J T Lomu	New Zealand	1995–99
13	D C Howlett	New Zealand	2003–07
11	R Underwood	England	1987–95
11	J T Rokocoko	New Zealand	2003–07
11	C E Latham	Australia	1999–2007
11	V Clerc	France	2007–11

MOST MATCH APPEARANCES IN FINAL STAGES

22	J Leonard	England	1991–2003
20	G M Gregan	Australia	1995–2007
19	M J Catt	England	1995–2007
19	J P Wilkinson	England	1999–2011
18	M O Johnson	England	1995–2003
18	B P Lima	Samoa	1991–2007
18	R Ibañez	France	1999–2007
18	M E Ledesma	Argentina	1999–2011
18	L W Moody	England	2003–11

MOST OVERALL CONVERSIONS IN FINAL STAGES

39	A G Hastings	Scotland	1987–95
37	G J Fox	New Zealand	1987–91
36	M P Lynagh	Australia	1987–95
35	D W Carter	New Zealand	2003–11
28	J P Wilkinson	England	1999–2011
27	P J Grayson	England	1999–2003
27	S M Jones	Wales	1999–2011

MOST POINTS IN ONE COMPETITION

126	G J Fox	New Zealand	1987
113	J P Wilkinson	England	2003
112	T Lacroix	France	1995
105	P C Montgomery	South Africa	2007
104	A G Hastings	Scotland	1995
103	F Michalak	France	2003
102	G Quesada	Argentina	1999
101	M Burke	Australia	1999

MOST TRIES IN ONE COMPETITION

8	J T Lomu	New Zealand	1999
8	B G Habana	South Africa	2007
7	M C G Ellis	New Zealand	1995
7	J T Lomu	New Zealand	1995
7	D C Howlett	New Zealand	2003
7	J M Muliaina	New Zealand	2003
7	D A Mitchell	Australia	2007

MOST CONVERSIONS IN ONE COMPETITION

30	G J Fox	New Zealand	1987
22	P C Montgomery	South Africa	2007
20	S D Culhane	New Zealand	1995
20	M P Lynagh	Australia	1987
20	L R MacDonald	New Zealand	2003
20	N J Evans	New Zealand	2007

MOST PENALTY GOALS IN ONE COMPETITION

31	G Quesada	Argentina	1999
26	T Lacroix	France	1995
23	J P Wilkinson	England	2003
21	G J Fox	New Zealand	1987
21	E J Flatley	Australia	2003
20	C R Andrew	England	1995

MOST DROP GOALS IN ONE COMPETITION

8	J P Wilkinson	England	2003
6	J H de Beer	South Africa	1999
5	J P Wilkinson	England	2007
4	J M Hernández	Argentina	2007

RUGBY WORLD CUP RECORDS

MOST POINTS IN A MATCH
BY A TEAM

145	New Zealand v Japan	1995
142	Australia v Namibia	2003
111	England v Uruguay	2003
108	New Zealand v Portugal	2007
101	New Zealand v Italy	1999
101	England v Tonga	1999

BY A PLAYER

45	S D Culhane	New Zealand v Japan	1995
44	A G Hastings	Scotland v Ivory Coast	1995
42	M S Rogers	Australia v Namibia	2003
36	T E Brown	New Zealand v Italy	1999
36	P J Grayson	England v Tonga	1999
34	J H de Beer	South Africa v England	1999
33	N J Evans	New Zealand v Portugal	2007
32	J P Wilkinson	England v Italy	1999

MOST CONVERSIONS IN A MATCH
BY A TEAM

20	New Zealand v Japan	1995
16	Australia v Namibia	2003
14	New Zealand v Portugal	2007
13	New Zealand v Tonga	2003
13	England v Uruguay	2003

BY A PLAYER

20	S D Culhane	New Zealand v Japan	1995
16	M S Rogers	Australia v Namibia	2003
14	N J Evans	New Zealand v Portugal	2007
12	P J Grayson	England v Tonga	1999
12	L R MacDonald	New Zealand v Tonga	2003

MOST TRIES IN A MATCH
BY A TEAM

22	Australia v Namibia	2003
21	New Zealand v Japan	1995
17	England v Uruguay	2003
16	New Zealand v Portugal	2007
14	New Zealand v Italy	1999

BY A PLAYER

6	M C G Ellis	New Zealand v Japan	1995
5	C E Latham	Australia v Namibia	2003
5	O J Lewsey	England v Uruguay	2003
4	I C Evans	Wales v Canada	1987
4	C I Green	New Zealand v Fiji	1987
4	J A Gallagher	New Zealand v Fiji	1987
4	B F Robinson	Ireland v Zimbabwe	1991
4	A G Hastings	Scotland v Ivory Coast	1995
4	C M Williams	South Africa v Western Samoa	1995
4	J T Lomu	New Zealand v England	1995
4	K G M Wood	Ireland v United States	1999
4	J M Muliaina	New Zealand v Canada	2003
4	B G Habana	South Africa v Samoa	2007
4	V Goneva	Fiji v Namibia	2011
4	Z R Guildford	New Zealand v Canada	2011

MOST PENALTY GOALS IN A MATCH
BY A TEAM

8	Australia v South Africa	1999
8	Argentina v Samoa	1999
8	Scotland v Tonga	1995
8	France v Ireland	1995

BY A PLAYER

8	M Burke	Australia v South Africa	1999
8	G Quesada	Argentina v Samoa	1999
8	A G Hastings	Scotland v Tonga	1995
8	T Lacroix	France v Ireland	1995

MOST DROP GOALS IN A MATCH
BY A TEAM

5	South Africa v England	1999
3	Fiji v Romania	1991
3	England v France	2003
3	Argentina v Ireland	2007
3	Namibia v Fiji	2011

BY A PLAYER

5	J H de Beer	South Africa v England	1999
3	J P Wilkinson	England v France	2003
3	J M Hernández	Argentina v Ireland	2007
3	T A W Kotze	Namibia v Fiji	2011

Holders New Zealand will defend the Webb Ellis Cup in England in 2015.

Getty Images

FIRST TOURNAMENT: 1987
IN AUSTRALIA & NEW ZEALAND

POOL 1

Australia	19	England	6
USA	21	Japan	18
England	60	Japan	7
Australia	47	USA	12
England	34	USA	6
Australia	42	Japan	23

	P	W	D	L	F	A	Pts
Australia	3	3	0	0	108	41	6
England	3	2	0	1	100	32	4
USA	3	1	0	2	39	99	2
Japan	3	0	0	3	48	123	0

POOL 3

New Zealand	70	Italy	6
Fiji	28	Argentina	9
New Zealand	74	Fiji	13
Argentina	25	Italy	16
Italy	18	Fiji	15
New Zealand	46	Argentina	15

	P	W	D	L	F	A	Pts
New Zealand	3	3	0	0	190	34	6
Fiji	3	1	0	2	56	101	2
Argentina	3	1	0	2	49	90	2
Italy	3	1	0	2	40	110	2

POOL 2

Canada	37	Tonga	4
Wales	13	Ireland	6
Wales	29	Tonga	16
Ireland	46	Canada	19
Wales	40	Canada	9
Ireland	32	Tonga	9

	P	W	D	L	F	A	Pts
Wales	3	3	0	0	82	31	6
Ireland	3	2	0	1	84	41	4
Canada	3	1	0	2	65	90	2
Tonga	3	0	0	3	29	98	0

POOL 4

Romania	21	Zimbabwe	20
France	20	Scotland	20
France	55	Romania	12
Scotland	60	Zimbabwe	21
France	70	Zimbabwe	12
Scotland	55	Romania	28

	P	W	D	L	F	A	Pts
France	3	2	1	0	145	44	5
Scotland	3	2	1	0	135	69	5
Romania	3	1	0	2	61	130	2
Zimbabwe	3	0	0	3	53	151	0

QUARTER-FINALS

New Zealand	30	Scotland	3
France	31	Fiji	16
Australia	33	Ireland	15
Wales	16	England	3

SEMI-FINALS

| France | 30 | Australia | 24 |
| New Zealand | 49 | Wales | 6 |

THIRD PLACE MATCH

| Wales | 22 | Australia | 21 |

First Rugby World Cup Final, Eden Park, Auckland, 20 June 1987

NEW ZEALAND 29 (1G 2T 4PG 1DG)

FRANCE 9 (1G 1PG)

NEW ZEALAND: J A Gallagher; J J Kirwan, J T Stanley, W T Taylor, C I Green; G J Fox, D E Kirk (*captain*); S C McDowell, S B T Fitzpatrick, J A Drake, M J Pierce, G W Whetton, A J Whetton, W T Shelford, M N Jones **SCORERS:** *Tries:* Jones, Kirk, Kirwan *Conversion:* Fox *Penalty Goals:* Fox (4) *Drop Goal:* Fox

FRANCE: S Blanco; D Camberabero, P Sella, D Charvet, P Lagisquet; F Mesnel, P Berbizier; P Ondarts, D Dubroca (*captain*), J-P Garuet, A Lorieux, J Condom, E Champ, L Rodriguez, D Erbani

SCORERS: *Try:* Berbizier *Conversion:* Camberabero *Penalty Goal:* Camberabero

REFEREE: K V J Fitzgerald (Australia)

SECOND TOURNAMENT: 1991
IN BRITAIN, IRELAND & FRANCE

POOL 1

New Zealand	18	England	12
Italy	30	USA	9
New Zealand	46	USA	6
England	36	Italy	6
England	37	USA	9
New Zealand	31	Italy	21

	P	W	D	L	F	A	Pts
New Zealand	3	3	0	0	95	39	9
England	3	2	0	1	85	33	7
Italy	3	1	0	2	57	76	5
USA	3	0	0	3	24	113	3

POOL 2

Scotland	47	Japan	9
Ireland	55	Zimbabwe	11
Ireland	32	Japan	16
Scotland	51	Zimbabwe	12
Scotland	24	Ireland	15
Japan	52	Zimbabwe	8

	P	W	D	L	F	A	Pts
Scotland	3	3	0	0	122	36	9
Ireland	3	2	0	1	102	51	7
Japan	3	1	0	2	77	87	5
Zimbabwe	3	0	0	3	31	158	3

POOL 3

Australia	32	Argentina	19
Western Samoa	16	Wales	13
Australia	9	Western Samoa	3
Wales	16	Argentina	7
Australia	38	Wales	3
Western Samoa	35	Argentina	12

	P	W	D	L	F	A	Pts
Australia	3	3	0	0	79	25	9
Western Samoa	3	2	0	1	54	34	7
Wales	3	1	0	2	32	61	5
Argentina	3	0	0	3	38	83	3

POOL 4

France	30	Romania	3
Canada	13	Fiji	3
France	33	Fiji	9
Canada	19	Romania	11
Romania	17	Fiji	15
France	19	Canada	13

	P	W	D	L	F	A	Pts
France	3	3	0	0	82	25	9
Canada	3	2	0	1	45	33	7
Romania	3	1	0	2	31	64	5
Fiji	3	0	0	3	27	63	3

QUARTER-FINALS

England	19	France	10
Scotland	28	Western Samoa	6
Australia	19	Ireland	18
New Zealand	29	Canada	13

SEMI-FINALS

| England | 9 | Scotland | 6 |
| Australia | 16 | New Zealand | 6 |

THIRD PLACE MATCH

| New Zealand | 13 | Scotland | 6 |

RUGBY WORLD CUP TOURNAMENTS

Second Rugby World Cup Final, Twickenham, London, 2 November 1991

AUSTRALIA 12 (1G 2PG) ENGLAND 6 (2PG)

AUSTRALIA: M C Roebuck; D I Campese, J S Little, T J Horan, R H Egerton; M P Lynagh, N C Farr-Jones (*captain*); A J Daly, P N Kearns, E J A McKenzie, R J McCall, J A Eales, S P Poidevin, T Coker, V Ofahengaue

SCORERS *Try:* Daly *Conversion:* Lynagh *Penalty Goals:* Lynagh (2)

ENGLAND: J M Webb; S J Halliday, W D C Carling (*captain*), J C Guscott, R Underwood; C R Andrew, R J Hill; J Leonard, B C Moore, J A Probyn, P J Ackford, W A Dooley, M G Skinner, M C Teague, P J Winterbottom

SCORER: *Penalty Goals:* Webb (2)

REFEREE: W D Bevan (Wales)

THIRD TOURNAMENT: 1995
IN SOUTH AFRICA

POOL A

South Africa	27	Australia	18
Canada	34	Romania	3
South Africa	21	Romania	8
Australia	27	Canada	11
Australia	42	Romania	3
South Africa	20	Canada	0

	P	W	D	L	F	A	Pts
South Africa	3	3	0	0	68	26	9
Australia	3	2	0	1	87	41	7
Canada	3	1	0	2	45	50	5
Romania	3	0	0	3	14	97	3

POOL B

Western Samoa	42	Italy	18
England	24	Argentina	18
Western Samoa	32	Argentina	26
England	27	Italy	20
Italy	31	Argentina	25
England	44	Western Samoa	22

	P	W	D	L	F	A	Pts
England	3	3	0	0	95	60	9
Western Samoa	3	2	0	1	96	88	7
Italy	3	1	0	2	69	94	5
Argentina	3	0	0	3	69	87	3

POOL C

Wales	57	Japan	10
New Zealand	43	Ireland	19
Ireland	50	Japan	28
New Zealand	34	Wales	9
New Zealand	145	Japan	17
Ireland	24	Wales	23

	P	W	D	L	F	A	Pts
New Zealand	3	3	0	0	222	45	9
Ireland	3	2	0	1	93	94	7
Wales	3	1	0	2	89	68	5
Japan	3	0	0	3	55	252	3

POOL D

Scotland	89	Ivory Coast	0
France	38	Tonga	10
France	54	Ivory Coast	18
Scotland	41	Tonga	5
Tonga	29	Ivory Coast	11
France	22	Scotland	19

	P	W	D	L	F	A	Pts
France	3	3	0	0	114	47	9
Scotland	3	2	0	1	149	27	7
Tonga	3	1	0	2	44	90	5
Ivory Coast	3	0	0	3	29	172	3

QUARTER-FINALS

France	36	Ireland	12
South Africa	42	Western Samoa	14
England	25	Australia	22
New Zealand	48	Scotland	30

SEMI-FINALS

South Africa	19	France	15
New Zealand	45	England	29

THIRD PLACE MATCH

France	19	England	9

SOUTH AFRICA 15 (3PG 2DG)
NEW ZEALAND 12 (3PG 1DG) *

SOUTH AFRICA: A J Joubert; J T Small, J C Mulder, H P Le Roux, C M Williams; J T Stransky, J H van der Westhuizen; J P du Randt, C L C Rossouw, I S Swart, J J Wiese, J J Strydom, J F Pienaar (*captain*), M G Andrews, R J Kruger

SUBSTITUTIONS: G L Pagel for Swart (68 mins); R A W Straeuli for Andrews (90 mins); B Venter for Small (97 mins)

SCORER: *Penalty Goals:* Stransky (3) *Drop Goals:* Stransky (2)

NEW ZEALAND: G M Osborne; J W Wilson, F E Bunce, W K Little, J T Lomu; A P Mehrtens, G T M Bachop; C W Dowd, S B T Fitzpatrick (*captain*), O M Brown, I D Jones, R M Brooke, M R Brewer, Z V Brooke, J A Kronfeld

SUBSTITUTIONS: J W Joseph for Brewer (40 mins); M C G Ellis for Wilson (55 mins); R W Loe for Dowd (83 mins); A D Strachan for Bachop (temp 66 to 71 mins)

SCORER: *Penalty Goals:* Mehrtens (3) *Drop Goal:* Mehrtens

REFEREE: E F Morrison (England)

* after extra time: 9–9 after normal time

AFP/Getty Images

Springbok captain Francois Pienaar brandishes the Webb Ellis Cup and salutes the home crowd.

RUGBY WORLD CUP TOURNAMENTS

FOURTH TOURNAMENT: 1999
IN BRITAIN, IRELAND & FRANCE

POOL A

Spain	15	Uruguay	27
South Africa	46	Scotland	29
Scotland	43	Uruguay	12
South Africa	47	Spain	3
South Africa	39	Uruguay	3
Scotland	48	Spain	0

	P	W	D	L	F	A	Pts
South Africa	3	3	0	0	132	35	9
Scotland	3	2	0	1	120	58	7
Uruguay	3	1	0	2	42	97	5
Spain	3	0	0	3	18	122	3

POOL B

England	67	Italy	7
New Zealand	45	Tonga	9
England	16	New Zealand	30
Italy	25	Tonga	28
New Zealand	101	Italy	3
England	101	Tonga	10

	P	W	D	L	F	A	Pts
New Zealand	3	3	0	0	176	28	9
England	3	2	0	1	184	47	7
Tonga	3	1	0	2	47	171	5
Italy	3	0	0	3	35	196	3

POOL C

Fiji	67	Namibia	18
France	33	Canada	20
France	47	Namibia	13
Fiji	38	Canada	22
Canada	72	Namibia	11
France	28	Fiji	19

	P	W	D	L	F	A	Pts
France	3	3	0	0	108	52	9
Fiji	3	2	0	1	124	68	7
Canada	3	1	0	2	114	82	5
Namibia	3	0	0	3	42	186	3

POOL D

Wales	23	Argentina	18
Samoa	43	Japan	9
Wales	64	Japan	15
Argentina	32	Samoa	16
Wales	31	Samoa	38
Argentina	33	Japan	12

	P	W	D	L	F	A	Pts
Wales	3	2	0	1	118	71	7
Samoa	3	2	0	1	97	72	7
Argentina	3	2	0	1	83	51	7
Japan	3	0	0	3	36	140	3

POOL E

Ireland	53	United States	8
Australia	57	Romania	9
United States	25	Romania	27
Ireland	3	Australia	23
Australia	55	United States	19
Ireland	44	Romania	14

	P	W	D	L	F	A	Pts
Australia	3	3	0	0	135	31	9
Ireland	3	2	0	1	100	45	7
Romania	3	1	0	2	50	126	5
United States	3	0	0	3	52	135	3

PLAY-OFFS FOR QUARTER-FINAL PLACES

England	45	Fiji	24
Scotland	35	Samoa	20
Ireland	24	Argentina	28

QUARTER-FINALS

Wales	9	Australia	24
South Africa	44	England	21
France	47	Argentina	26
Scotland	18	New Zealand	30

SEMI-FINALS

South Africa	21	Australia	27
New Zealand	31	France	43

THIRD PLACE MATCH

South Africa	22	New Zealand	18

AUSTRALIA 35 (2G 7PG) FRANCE 12 (4PG)

AUSTRALIA: M Burke; B N Tune, D J Herbert, T J Horan, J W Roff; S J Larkham, G M Gregan; R L L Harry, M A Foley, A T Blades, D T Giffin, J A Eales (*captain*), M J Cockbain, R S T Kefu, D J Wilson

SUBSTITUTIONS: J S Little for Herbert (46 mins); O D A Finegan for Cockbain (52 mins); M R Connors for Wilson (73 mins); D J Crowley for Harry (75 mins); J A Paul for Foley (85 mins); C J Whitaker for Gregan (86 mins); N P Grey for Horan (86 mins)

SCORERS: *Tries:* Tune, Finegan *Conversions:* Burke (2) *Penalty Goals:* Burke (7)

FRANCE: X Garbajosa; P Bernat Salles, R Dourthe, E Ntamack, C Dominici; C Lamaison, F Galthié; C Soulette, R Ibañez (*captain*), F Tournaire, A Benazzi, F Pelous, M Lièvremont, C Juillet, O Magne

SUBSTITUTIONS: O Brouzet for Juillet (HT); P de Villiers for Soulette (47 mins); A Costes for Magne (temp 19 to 22 mins) and for Lièvremont (67 mins); U Mola for Garbajosa (67 mins); S Glas for Dourthe (temp 49 to 55 mins and from 74 mins); S Castaignède for Galthié (76 mins); M Dal Maso for Ibañez (79 mins)

SCORER: *Penalty Goals:* Lamaison (4)

REFEREE: A J Watson (South Africa)

Australian Joe Roff drinks from the Webb Ellis Cup, having shed blood to help Australia beat France in the final.

FIFTH TOURNAMENT: 2003
IN AUSTRALIA

POOL A

Australia	24	Argentina	8
Ireland	45	Romania	17
Argentina	67	Namibia	14
Australia	90	Romania	8
Ireland	64	Namibia	7
Argentina	50	Romania	3
Australia	142	Namibia	0
Ireland	16	Argentina	15
Romania	37	Namibia	7
Australia	17	Ireland	16

	P	W	D	L	F	A	Pts
Australia	4	4	0	0	273	32	18
Ireland	4	3	0	1	141	56	15
Argentina	4	2	0	2	140	57	11
Romania	4	1	0	3	65	192	5
Namibia	4	0	0	4	28	310	0

POOL C

South Africa	72	Uruguay	6
England	84	Georgia	6
Samoa	60	Uruguay	13
England	25	South Africa	6
Samoa	46	Georgia	9
South Africa	46	Georgia	19
England	35	Samoa	22
Uruguay	24	Georgia	12
South Africa	60	Samoa	10
England	111	Uruguay	13

	P	W	D	L	F	A	Pts
England	4	4	0	0	255	47	19
South Africa	4	3	0	1	184	60	15
Samoa	4	2	0	2	138	117	10
Uruguay	4	1	0	3	56	255	4
Georgia	4	0	0	4	46	200	0

POOL B

France	61	Fiji	18
Scotland	32	Japan	11
Fiji	19	United States	18
France	51	Japan	29
Scotland	39	United States	15
Fiji	41	Japan	13
France	51	Scotland	9
United States	39	Japan	26
France	41	United States	14
Scotland	22	Fiji	20

	P	W	D	L	F	A	Pts
France	4	4	0	0	204	70	20
Scotland	4	3	0	1	102	97	14
Fiji	4	2	0	2	98	114	10
United States	4	1	0	3	86	125	6
Japan	4	0	0	4	79	163	0

POOL D

New Zealand	70	Italy	7
Wales	41	Canada	10
Italy	36	Tonga	12
New Zealand	68	Canada	6
Wales	27	Tonga	20
Italy	19	Canada	14
New Zealand	91	Tonga	7
Wales	27	Italy	15
Canada	24	Tonga	7
New Zealand	53	Wales	37

	P	W	D	L	F	A	Pts
New Zealand	4	4	0	0	282	57	20
Wales	4	3	0	1	132	98	14
Italy	4	2	0	2	77	123	8
Canada	4	1	0	3	54	135	5
Tonga	4	0	0	4	46	178	1

QUARTER-FINALS

New Zealand	29	South Africa	9
Australia	33	Scotland	16
France	43	Ireland	21
England	28	Wales	17

SEMI-FINALS

Australia	22	New Zealand	10
England	24	France	7

THIRD PLACE MATCH

New Zealand	40	France	13

INTERNATIONAL TOURNAMENTS

Fifth Rugby World Cup Final, Telstra Stadium, Sydney, 22 November 2003

ENGLAND 20 (1T 4PG 1DG)
AUSTRALIA 17 (4PG 1T) *

ENGLAND: J T Robinson; O J Lewsey, W J H Greenwood, M J Tindall, B C Cohen; J P Wilkinson, M J S Dawson; T J Woodman, S G Thompson, P J Vickery, M O Johnson (*captain*), B J Kay, R A Hill, L B N Dallaglio, N A Back

SUBSTITUTIONS: M J Catt for Tindall (78 mins); J Leonard for Vickery (80 mins); I R Balshaw for Lewsey (85 mins); L W Moody for Hill (93 mins)

SCORERS: *Try:* Robinson *Penalty Goals:* Wilkinson (4) *Dropped Goal:* Wilkinson

AUSTRALIA: M S Rogers; W J Sailor, S A Mortlock, E J Flatley, L Tuqiri; S J Larkham, G M Gregan (*captain*); W K Young, B J Cannon, A K E Baxter, J B Harrison, N C Sharpe, G B Smith, D J Lyons, P R Waugh

SUBSTITUTIONS: D T Giffin for Sharpe (48 mins); J A Paul for Cannon (56 mins); M J Cockbain for Lyons (56 mins); J W Roff for Sailor (70 mins); M J Dunning for Young (92 mins); M J Giteau for Larkham (temp 18 to 30 mins; 55 to 63 mins; 85 to 93 mins)

SCORERS: *Try*: Tuqiri *Penalty Goals*: Flatley (4)

REFEREE: A J Watson (South Africa)

* after extra time: 14–14 after normal time

Getty Images

Jonny Wilkinson kicks the winning drop goal in England's extra-time win over Australia.

SIXTH TOURNAMENT: 2007
IN FRANCE, WALES & SCOTLAND

POOL A

England	28	USA	10
South Africa	59	Samoa	7
USA	15	Tonga	25
England	0	South Africa	36
Samoa	15	Tonga	19
South Africa	30	Tonga	25
England	44	Samoa	22
Samoa	25	USA	21
England	36	Tonga	20
South Africa	64	USA	15

	P	W	D	L	F	A	Pts
South Africa	4	4	0	0	189	47	19
England	4	3	0	1	108	88	14
Tonga	4	2	0	2	89	96	9
Samoa	4	1	0	3	69	143	5
USA	4	0	0	4	61	142	1

POOL C

New Zealand	76	Italy	14
Scotland	56	Portugal	10
Italy	24	Romania	18
New Zealand	108	Portugal	13
Scotland	42	Romania	0
Italy	31	Portugal	5
Scotland	0	New Zealand	40
Romania	14	Portugal	10
New Zealand	85	Romania	8
Scotland	18	Italy	16

	P	W	D	L	F	A	Pts
New Zealand	4	4	0	0	309	35	20
Scotland	4	3	0	1	116	66	14
Italy	4	2	0	2	85	117	9
Romania	4	1	0	3	40	161	5
Portugal	4	0	0	4	38	209	1

POOL B

Australia	91	Japan	3
Wales	42	Canada	17
Japan	31	Fiji	35
Wales	20	Australia	32
Fiji	29	Canada	16
Wales	72	Japan	18
Australia	55	Fiji	12
Canada	12	Japan	12
Australia	37	Canada	6
Wales	34	Fiji	38

	P	W	D	L	F	A	Pts
Australia	4	4	0	0	215	41	20
Fiji	4	3	0	1	114	136	15
Wales	4	2	0	2	168	105	12
Japan	4	0	1	3	64	210	3
Canada	4	0	1	3	51	120	2

POOL D

France	12	Argentina	17
Ireland	32	Namibia	17
Argentina	33	Georgia	3
Ireland	14	Georgia	10
France	87	Namibia	10
France	25	Ireland	3
Argentina	63	Namibia	3
Georgia	30	Namibia	0
France	64	Georgia	7
Ireland	15	Argentina	30

	P	W	D	L	F	A	Pts
Argentina	4	4	0	0	143	33	18
France	4	3	0	1	188	37	15
Ireland	4	2	0	2	64	82	9
Georgia	4	1	0	3	50	111	5
Namibia	4	0	0	4	30	212	0

QUARTER-FINALS

Australia	10	England	12
New Zealand	18	France	20
South Africa	37	Fiji	20
Argentina	19	Scotland	13

SEMI-FINALS

France	9	England	14
South Africa	37	Argentina	13

BRONZE FINAL

France	10	Argentina	34

Sixth Rugby World Cup Final, Stade de France, Paris, 20 October 2007

SOUTH AFRICA 15 (5PG) ENGLAND 6 (2PG)

SOUTH AFRICA: P C Montgomery; J-P R Pietersen, J Fourie, F P L Steyn, B G Habana; A D James, P F du Preez; J P du Randt, J W Smit (*captain*), C J van der Linde, J P Botha, V Matfield, J H Smith, D J Rossouw, S W P Burger

SUBSTITUTIONS: J L van Heerden for Rossouw (72 mins); B W du Plessis for Smit (temp 71 to 76 mins)

SCORERS: *Penalty Goals*: Montgomery (4), Steyn

ENGLAND: J T Robinson; P H Sackey, M J M Tait, M J Catt, M J Cueto; J P Wilkinson, A C T Gomarsall; A J Sheridan, M P Regan, P J Vickery (*captain*), S D Shaw, B J Kay, M E Corry, N J Easter, L W Moody

SUBSTITUTIONS: M J H Stevens for Vickery (40 mins); D J Hipkiss for Robinson (46 mins); T G A L Flood for Catt (50 mins); G S Chuter for Regan (62 mins); J P R Worsley for Moody (62 mins); L B N Dallaglio for Easter (64 mins); P C Richards for Worsley (70 mins)

SCORER: *Penalty Goals*: Wilkinson (2)

REFEREE: A C Rolland (Ireland)

Getty Images

Bryan Habana, Jake White and John Smit celebrate with the Webb Ellis Cup.

SEVENTH TOURNAMENT: 2011
IN NEW ZEALAND

POOL A

New Zealand	41	Tonga	10
France	47	Japan	21
Tonga	20	Canada	25
New Zealand	83	Japan	7
France	46	Canada	19
Tonga	31	Japan	18
New Zealand	37	France	17
Canada	23	Japan	23
France	14	Tonga	19
New Zealand	79	Canada	15

	P	W	D	L	F	A	Pts
New Zealand	4	4	0	0	240	49	20
France	4	2	0	2	124	96	11
Tonga	4	2	0	2	80	98	9
Canada	4	1	1	2	82	168	6
Japan	4	0	1	3	69	184	1

POOL C

Australia	32	Italy	6
Ireland	22	USA	10
Russia	6	USA	13
Australia	6	Ireland	15
Italy	53	Russia	17
Australia	67	USA	5
Ireland	62	Russia	12
Italy	27	USA	10
Australia	68	Russia	22
Ireland	36	Italy	6

	P	W	D	L	F	A	Pts
Ireland	4	4	0	0	135	34	17
Australia	4	3	0	1	173	48	15
Italy	4	2	0	2	92	95	10
USA	4	1	0	3	38	122	4
Russia	4	0	0	4	57	196	1

POOL B

Scotland	34	Romania	24
Argentina	9	England	13
Scotland	15	Georgia	6
Argentina	43	Romania	8
England	41	Georgia	10
England	67	Romania	3
Argentina	13	Scotland	12
Georgia	25	Romania	9
England	16	Scotland	12
Argentina	25	Georgia	7

	P	W	D	L	F	A	Pts
England	4	4	0	0	137	34	18
Argentina	4	3	0	1	90	40	14
Scotland	4	2	0	2	73	59	11
Georgia	4	1	0	3	48	90	4
Romania	4	0	0	4	44	169	0

POOL D

Fiji	49	Namibia	25
South Africa	17	Wales	16
Samoa	49	Namibia	12
South Africa	49	Fiji	3
Wales	17	Samoa	10
South Africa	87	Namibia	0
Fiji	7	Samoa	27
Wales	81	Namibia	7
South Africa	13	Samoa	5
Wales	66	Fiji	0

	P	W	D	L	F	A	Pts
South Africa	4	4	0	0	166	24	18
Wales	4	3	0	1	180	34	15
Samoa	4	2	0	2	91	49	10
Fiji	4	1	0	3	59	167	5
Namibia	4	0	0	4	44	266	0

QUARTER-FINALS

Ireland	10	Wales	22
England	12	France	19
South Africa	9	Australia	11
New Zealand	33	Argentina	10

SEMI-FINALS

Wales	8	France	9
Australia	6	New Zealand	20

BRONZE FINAL

Australia	21	Wales	18

NEW ZEALAND 8 (1T 1PG) FRANCE 7 (1G)

NEW ZEALAND: I J A Dagg; C S Jane, C G Smith, M A Nonu, R D Kahui; A W Cruden, P A T Weepu; T D Woodcock, K F Mealamu, O T Franks, B C Thorn, S L Whitelock, J Kaino, K J Read, R H McCaw (*captain*)

SUBSTITUTIONS: S R Donald for Cruden (33 mins); A J Williams for Whitelock (48 mins); A K Hore for Mealamu (48 mins); A M Ellis for Weepu (49 mins); S Williams for Nonu (75 mins)

SCORERS: *Try*: Woodcock *Penalty Goal*: Donald

FRANCE: M Médard; V Clerc, A Rougerie, M Mermoz, A Palisson; M Parra, D Yachvili; J-B Poux, W Servat, N Mas, P Papé, L Nallet, T Dusautoir (*captain*), I Harinordoquy, J Bonnaire

SUBSTITUTIONS: F Trinh-Duc for Parra (temp 11 to 17 mins and 22 mins); D Traille for Clerc (45 mins); D Szarzewski for Servat (64 mins); F Barcella for Poux (64 mins); J Pierre for Papé (69 mins); J-M Doussain for Yachvili (75 mins)

SCORERS: *Try*: Dusautoir *Conversion:* Trinh-Duc

REFEREE: C Joubert (South Africa)

AFP/Getty Images

Richie McCaw holds aloft the Webb Ellis Cup after New Zealand beat France in the final on home soil.

RUGBY WORLD CUP TOURNAMENTS

Their future is in your hands.

Your donation can make all the difference
to these children.

Every year, the United Nations World Food
Programme provides meals to millions of children
around the world.

Together with partners like the International Rugby
Board, WFP can change young lives forever.

**Help us to tackle hunger:
wfp.org/donate/tacklehunger**

TACKLE
HUNGER

WFP

wfp.org

INTERNATIONAL
RUGBY BOARD

The United Nations
World Food Programme
is the humanitarian
partner of the IRB

ALL-CONQUERING WALES WIN ANOTHER GRAND SLAM

By Sam Warburton

Getty Images

Captain Sam Warburton and his Welsh teammates celebrate their Grand Slam success.

It is every player's dream to win a Grand Slam, let alone captain the team to the trophy, and it was without doubt the highlight of my career to achieve both in the 2012 RBS Six Nations. I wasn't involved with the Wales teams that won the Grand Slam in 2005 and again in 2008 and it was an almost indescribable feeling to play a part in another Championship clean sweep.

I think a lot of people were curious to see how Wales would react to the disappointment of losing to France in the Rugby World Cup semi-final in New Zealand three months earlier, but we genuinely didn't go into the Six Nations with a sense of regret or looking for any kind of redemption.

Of course we were upset not to reach the final, and I was obviously unhappy to have picked up a red card in the semi, but as a group we felt we had expressed ourselves, we'd played to the best of our ability and all the talk before the Six Nations was about making small changes to our game plan rather than ripping the whole thing up and starting again. There was no hangover from what had happened in New Zealand.

In particular, we discussed improving our accuracy and improving our conversion rate once we'd broken the line, but there was no revolution. In fact, a lot of the meetings focused on the team's disappointing three successive fourth place finishes in the Six Nations since the 2008 Slam rather than looking back at the Rugby World Cup.

Our campaign began against Ireland at the Aviva Stadium, and I suppose our big concern was producing a rusty performance at the start of the tournament and getting punished in Dublin. We were under no illusions that Ireland would be powerful and well organised, and to come away with a 23–21 win was a huge relief.

It was touch-and-go, however. Ryan Jones was denied a try early on by the TMO, although he was adamant he got the ball down, and although we scored three tries, Tommy Bowe scored for Ireland late in the second half when we were down to 14 men and we were 21–15 behind.

They say adversity reveals a team's true character and, although I was on the sidelines with an injury by that stage, I was incredibly proud of the way the boys dug deep, scored the third try through George North and won thanks to Leigh Halfpenny's kick in the last minute.

I could see the look of disappointment on the faces of the Ireland players at the final whistle and I could understand why. It was a tight contest that could have gone the other way, and I don't mind admitting the ball carriers in the Irish back row – the likes of Sean O'Brien and Jamie Heaslip – gave us a bruising afternoon.

A week later it was Scotland in Cardiff. I was forced to sit it out with a dead leg and, although we came away with a 27–3 victory, there was a feeling we should have won by a bigger margin. That's no disrespect to Scotland but we did feel as a group that we hadn't been clinical enough.

Scotland were very physical at the contact area, which disrupted some of our patterns, but there was a collective acknowledgement after the match that we hadn't produced a particularly satisfactory performance.

It was a tough tournament for the Scots. They finished with the wooden spoon but they've got some exciting young players coming through, players like Lee Jones, Richie Gray, David Denton and Greg Laidlaw, and they proved by beating the Wallabies in Australia later in the year that the potential is there.

Unbeaten England at Twickenham was the next match. Luckily, I was fit for the game and, having lost a couple of times to them at senior level and taken a few beatings at schoolboy level as well, I was desperate for a good result.

The first 75 minutes turned out to be a battle between the boots of Leigh Halfpenny and Owen Farrell, but Scott Williams's brilliant individual try 15 minutes from time was decisive and we were 17–12 up.

There was, though, still time for a bit of drama when David Strettle dived over in injury-time, and it took the TMO three or four minutes to decide that he hadn't grounded the ball. I remember standing there waiting for the decision, but I was at a funny angle to the big screen at Twickenham and couldn't see the replays properly. I had no idea whether he'd got the ball down, but funnily enough I wasn't feeling tense at all. We knew time was up, we knew a converted try would level the scores and we knew that if the TMO said yes, there was absolutely nothing we could do about it. All the boys seemed quite philosophical as we waited.

It was very satisfying to stop England scoring a try on their own patch and nothing makes Shaun Edwards, our defensive coach, happier than the team keeping a clean sheet. He may be an Englishman, but he was very happy after the game.

England finished as runners-up and, considering they had a new backroom set-up with Stuart Lancaster as caretaker head coach and a new captain in Chris Robshaw, I thought they had a strong tournament. For a fifteen that hadn't played a lot of rugby, they seemed very together and united.

Beating England made it three from three, but while the media and some supporters might have begun talking about the Grand Slam, the mantra inside the squad and from the coaches was one step at a time. It sounds clichéd, but there really was no one who let their thoughts stray beyond the Italy game.

There are two things you can confidently say about any Italy side. They are hard to break down and they are always capable of producing a big performance. They'd beaten France in Rome in 2011, and going into the game we were conscious that they would be dangerous opponents.

We didn't score a try in the first half in Cardiff but, while some of the crowd might have been getting a little anxious, the dressing room was calm despite our slender 9–3 lead. We'd spoken about the need for patience before kick-off and nothing had really changed in the first 40 minutes.

The match reminded me of our World Cup group game with Samoa in Hamilton. We stayed patient then, getting the decisive try from Shane Williams late on, and we stayed patient against Italy and the tries came from Jamie Roberts and Alex Cuthbert in the second half.

I didn't feel any pressure in the build-up to the France game and the 80 minutes that would decide whether we'd win the Grand Slam or not. I was struggling with a knee ligament injury and was only passed fit after coming through training on the Thursday before the match, so I have to admit I was distracted.

The French have always enjoyed a reputation for playing with flair, but they seemed to be praying for rain because they wanted the roof open at the Millennium Stadium and I think that did send a message that they wouldn't be unhappy if it was wet and windy.

To be honest, I don't remember much about the first half because I was in a lot of pain after a knock to my shoulder. We scored the only try of the game through Cuthbert, but we couldn't put any real distance between ourselves and the French, and it was a nervous second half as Halfpenny and Dimitri Yachvili and Lionel Beauxis traded penalties. It

Getty Images

Fabio Ongaro is lifted up as Italy celebrate victory over Scotland at Stadio Olimpico.

wasn't a classic, it wasn't always pretty but we got the job done and held on for a 16–9 win.

After the victory, a lot of people began talking about the 2012 Grand Slam in relation to the 2005 and 2008 successes, but comparisons are difficult. I spoke to JPR Williams a couple of months after beating France and he said that the current team could only be compared to the great sides of the Seventies when we'd beaten England nine times out of 10, as he did, and I'm not going to argue with a legend like him.

I spoke earlier about three disappointing Six Nations for Wales after 2008 and the challenge now is to ensure we are more consistent over the next two or three seasons. The euphoria of the Grand Slam will subside very quickly if we don't build on our achievement and allow our level of performance to drop off.

From a personal point of view, I can't deny I was frustrated that injuries limited me to 160 of the 400 minutes of Championship action. Injury is obviously an occupational hazard, but I would have loved to have been out on the pitch for far, far longer.

I've got to pay tribute to Warren Gatland's role. He's been a huge influence on me personally and has improved my game almost beyond recognition, but it is his effect on the squad, the way he keeps the players calm but focused, that has been the bedrock of the team's success.

His rugby knowledge is staggering, but I think it's the atmosphere he creates that is most important. Obviously he's not backward in pulling us up if things aren't done right, but he chooses his moments very carefully and his philosophy is all about getting the best out of the squad with the carrot rather than the stick.

RBS 6 NATIONS 2012
FINAL TABLE

	P	W	D	L	For	Against	Pts
Wales	5	5	0	0	109	58	**10**
England	5	4	0	1	98	71	**8**
Ireland	5	2	1	2	121	94	**5**
France	5	2	1	2	101	86	**5**
Italy	5	1	0	4	53	121	**2**
Scotland	5	0	0	5	56	108	**0**

Points: Win 2; Draw 1; Defeat 0.

There were 538 points scored at an average of 35.9 a match. The Championship record (803 points at an average of 53.5 a match) was set in 2000. Leigh Halfpenny was the leading individual points scorer with 66, 23 points shy of the Championship record Jonny Wilkinson set in 2001. Tommy Bowe was the Championship's leading try-scorer with five, three short of the all-time record shared between England's Cyril Lowe (1914) and Scotland's Ian Smith (1925).

New England captain Chris Robshaw led his side to a second-place finish.

FRANCE 30 (2G 2T 2PG) ITALY 12 (3PG 1DG)

FRANCE: M Médard; V Clerc, A Rougerie, W Fofana, J Malzieu; F Trinh-Duc, D Yachvili; V Debaty, W Servat, N Mas, P Papé, L Nallet, T Dusautoir (*captain*), L Picamoles, J Bonnaire

SUBSTITUTIONS: Y Maestri for Nallet (50 mins); D Szarzewski for Servat (54 mins); J-B Poux for Debaty (62 mins); M Parra for Yachvili (62 mins); I Harinordoquy for Picamoles (64 mins); L Beauxis for Trinh-Duc (75 mins); M Mermoz for Rougerie (75 mins); V Debaty back for Mas (75 mins)

SCORERS: *Tries:* Rougerie, Malzieu, Clerc, Fofana *Conversions:* Yachvili (2) *Penalty Goals:* Yachvili (2)

ITALY: A Masi; G Venditti, T Benvenuti, A Sgarbi, L McLean; K Burton, E Gori; A Lo Cicero, L Ghiraldini, M-L Castrogiovanni, Q Geldenhuys, C van Zyl, A Zanni, S Parisse (*captain*), R Barbieri

SUBSTITUTIONS: M Bortolami for Van Zyl (55 mins); T Botes for Burton (55 mins); G-J Canale for Sgarbi (55 mins); L Cittadini for Lo Cicero (62 mins); S Favaro for Barbieri (67 mins); T D'Apice for Ghiraldini (75 mins); F Semenzato for Gori (75 mins)

SCORERS: *Penalty Goals:* Burton (2), Botes *Drop Goal:* Burton

YELLOW CARD: Q Geldenhuys (70 mins)

REFEREE: N Owens (Wales)

SCOTLAND 6 (2PG) ENGLAND 13 (1G 2PG)

SCOTLAND: R P Lamont; L Jones, N J de Luca, S F Lamont, M B Evans; D A Parks, C P Cusiter; A F Jacobsen, R W Ford (*captain*), E A Murray, R J Gray, J L Hamilton, A K Strokosch, D K Denton, R M Rennie

SUBSTITUTIONS: M R L Blair for Cusiter (58 mins); A D Kellock for Hamilton (58 mins); G D Laidlaw for Parks (58 mins); J A Barclay for Strokosch (59 mins); S Lawson for Ford (74 mins); G D S Cross for Murray (74 mins)

SCORER: *Penalty Goals:* Parks (2)

ENGLAND: B J Foden; D Strettle, B M Barritt, O A Farrell, C J Ashton; C C Hodgson, B R Youngs; A R Corbisiero, D M Hartley, D R Cole, M J Botha, T P Palmer, T R Croft, P D A Dowson, C D C Robshaw (*captain*)

SUBSTITUTIONS: G M W Parling for Palmer (58 mins); J Turner-Hall for Hodgson (62 mins); L A W Dickson for Youngs (62 mins); M J H Stevens for Corbisiero (62 mins); B Morgan for Dowson (68 mins); M N Brown for Barritt (71 mins)

SCORERS: *Try:* Hodgson *Conversion:* Farrell *Penalty Goals:* Farrell (2)

REFEREE: G Clancy (Ireland)

5 February, Aviva Stadium, Dublin

IRELAND 21 (1G 1T 3PG) WALES 23 (1G 2T 2PG)

IRELAND: R D J Kearney; T J Bowe, F L McFadden, G W D'Arcy, A D Trimble; J J Sexton, C Murray; C E Healy, R D Best, M R Ross, D P O'Callaghan, P J O'Connell (*captain*), S Ferris, J P R Heaslip, S K O'Brien

SUBSTITUTIONS: D C Ryan for O'Callaghan (62 mins); T G Court for Healy (73 mins); R J R O'Gara for Sexton (76 mins); E G Reddan for Murray (76 mins)

SCORERS: *Tries:* Best, Bowe *Conversion:* Sexton *Penalty Goals:* Sexton (3)

YELLOW CARD: S Ferris (79 mins)

WALES: S L Halfpenny; A C G Cuthbert, J J V Davies, J H Roberts, G P North; R Priestland, W M Phillips; I A R Gill, H Bennett, A R Jones, B S Davies, I R Evans, R P Jones, T T Faletau, S K Warburton (*captain*)

SUBSTITUTIONS: J C Tipuric for Warburton (40 mins); J W Hook for Cuthbert (40 mins); P James for A R Jones (70 mins)

SCORERS: *Tries:* J J V Davies (2), North *Conversion:* Halfpenny *Penalty Goals:* Halfpenny (2)

YELLOW CARD: B S Davies (64 mins)

REFEREE: W Barnes (England)

11 February, Stadio Olimpico, Rome

ITALY 15 (1G 1T 1PG) ENGLAND 19 (1G 4PG)

ITALY: A Masi; G Venditti, T Benvenuti, G-J Canale, L McLean; K Burton, E Gori; A Lo Cicero, L Ghiraldini, M-L Castrogiovanni, Q Geldenhuys, M Bortolami, A Zanni, S Parisse (*captain*), R Barbieri

SUBSTITUTIONS: L Cittadini for Castrogiovanni (33 mins); T Botes for Burton (47 mins); A Pavanello for Geldenhuys (57 mins); F Semenzato for Gori (57 mins); T D'Apice for Ghiraldini (58 mins); L Morisi for Canale (63 mins); Mauro Bergamasco for Barbieri (75 mins)

SCORERS: *Tries:* Venditti, Benvenuti *Conversion:* Burton *Penalty Goal:* Burton

ENGLAND: B J Foden; D Strettle, B M Barritt, O A Farrell, C J Ashton; C C Hodgson, B R Youngs; A R Corbisiero, D M Hartley, D R Cole, M J Botha, T P Palmer, T R Croft, P D A Dowson, C D C Robshaw (*captain*)

SUBSTITUTIONS: B Morgan for Dowson (51 mins); L A W Dickson for Youngs (51 mins); G M W Parling for Palmer (58 mins); M J H Stevens for Cole (74 mins); R W Webber for Hartley (74 mins); J Turner-Hall for Hodgson (77 mins)

SCORERS: *Try:* Hodgson *Conversion:* Farrell *Penalty Goals:* Farrell (4)

REFEREE: J Garces (France)

12 February, Millennium Stadium, Cardiff

WALES 27 (3G 2PG) SCOTLAND 13 (1G 2PG)

WALES: S L Halfpenny; A C G Cuthbert, J J V Davies, J H Roberts, G P North; R Priestland, W M Phillips; G D Jenkins, H Bennett, A R Jones, R P Jones (*captain*), I R Evans, D J Lydiate, T T Faletau, A C Shingler

SUBSTITUTIONS: J W Hook for North (39 mins); K J Owens for Bennett (temp 9 to 18 mins and 40 mins); P James for A R Jones (72 mins); A T Powell for Lydiate (72 mins); L D Williams for Phillips (73 mins); L Reed for R P Jones (74 mins); M S Williams for Roberts (77 mins)

SCORERS: *Tries:* Halfpenny (2), Cuthbert *Conversions:* Halfpenny (3) *Penalty Goals:* Halfpenny (2)

YELLOW CARD: G D Jenkins (77 mins)

SCOTLAND: R P Lamont; M B Evans, N J de Luca, S F Lamont, L Jones; G D Laidlaw, C P Cusiter; A F Jacobsen, R W Ford (*captain*), G D S Cross, R J Gray, J L Hamilton, A K Strokosch, D K Denton, R M Rennie

SUBSTITUTIONS: S W Hogg for Evans (15 mins); J A Barclay for Strokosch (43 mins); M R L Blair for Cusiter (48 mins); E D Kalman for Cross (56 mins); A D Kellock for Hamilton (57 mins); S Lawson for Ford (71 mins)

SCORER: *Try:* Laidlaw *Conversion:* Laidlaw *Penalty Goals:* Laidlaw (2)

YELLOW CARDS: N J de Luca (44 mins); R P Lamont (53 mins)

REFEREE: R Poite (France)

25 February, Aviva Stadium, Dublin

IRELAND 42 (4G 1T 3PG) ITALY 10 (1G 1PG)

IRELAND: R D J Kearney; T J Bowe, K G Earls, G W D'Arcy, A D Trimble; J J Sexton, C Murray; C E Healy, R D Best, M R Ross, D P O'Callaghan, P J O'Connell (*captain*), S Ferris, J P R Heaslip, S K O'Brien

SUBSTITUTIONS: E G Reddan for Murray (53 mins); D C Ryan for O'Callaghan (58 mins); P O'Mahony for O'Brien (58 mins); F L McFadden for Earls (67 mins); S M Cronin for Best (69 mins); T G Court for Healy (69 mins); R J R O'Gara for D'Arcy (69 mins)

SCORERS: *Tries:* Bowe (2), Earls, Court, Trimble *Conversions:* Sexton (4) *Penalty Goals:* Sexton (3)

ITALY: A Masi; G Venditti, T Benvenuti, A Sgarbi, L McLean; T Botes, E Gori; M Rizzo, L Ghiraldini, L Cittadini, Q Geldenhuys, M Bortolami, A Zanni, S Parisse (*captain*), R Barbieri

SUBSTITUTIONS: K Burton for Botes (58 mins); A Pavanello for Geldenhuys (58 mins); G-J Canale for Sgarbi (62 mins); S Favaro for Barbieri (62 mins); F Staibano for Cittadini (67 mins); F Semenzato for Gori (71 mins); T D'Apice for Ghiraldini (71 mins)

SCORERS: *Try:* Parisse *Conversion:* Botes *Penalty Goal:* Botes

REFEREE: C Joubert (South Africa)

25 February, Twickenham, London

ENGLAND 12 (4PG) WALES 19 (1G 4PG)

ENGLAND: B J Foden; D Strettle, E M Tuilagi, B M Barritt, C J Ashton; O A Farrell, L A W Dickson; A R Corbisiero, D M Hartley, D R Cole, M J Botha, G M W Parling, T R Croft, B Morgan, C D C Robshaw (*captain*)

SUBSTITUTIONS: C L Lawes for Botha (60 mins); B R Youngs for Dickson (60 mins); T G A L Flood for Farrell (65 mins); M J H Stevens for Corbisiero (65 mins); P D A Dowson for Morgan (72 mins); R W Webber for Hartley (72 mins); M N Brown for Foden (77 mins)

SCORER: *Penalty Goals:* Farrell (4)

WALES: S L Halfpenny; A C G Cuthbert, J J V Davies, J H Roberts, G P North; R Priestland, W M Phillips; G D Jenkins, K J Owens, A R Jones, A-W Jones, I R Evans, D J Lydiate, T T Faletau, S K Warburton (*captain*)

SUBSTITUTIONS: M S Williams for Roberts (40 mins); R P Jones for A-W Jones (53 mins)

SCORERS: *Try:* Williams *Conversion:* Halfpenny *Penalty Goals:* Halfpenny (4)

YELLOW CARD: R Priestland (44 mins)

REFEREE: S R Walsh (Australia)

26 February, Murrayfield, Edinburgh

SCOTLAND 17 (2G 1PG)
FRANCE 23 (2G 2PG 1DG)

SCOTLAND: S W Hogg; R P Lamont, S F Lamont, G A Morrison, L Jones; G D Laidlaw, M R L Blair; A F Jacobsen, R W Ford (*captain*), G D S Cross, R J Gray, J L Hamilton, J A Barclay, D K Denton, R M Rennie

SUBSTITUTIONS: N J de Luca for R P Lamont (30 mins); C P Cusiter for Blair (30 mins); D Weir for Laidlaw (48 mins); R J Vernon for Denton (51 mins); E D Kalman for Cross (61 mins); A D Kellock for Hamilton (68 mins); S Lawson for Ford (68 mins)

SCORERS: *Tries:* Hogg, Jones *Conversions:* Laidlaw, Weir *Penalty Goal:* Laidlaw

FRANCE: M Médard; V Clerc, A Rougerie, W Fofana, J Malzieu; F Trinh-Duc, M Parra; J-B Poux, D Szarzewski, N Mas, P Papé, Y Maestri, T Dusautoir (*captain*), L Picamoles, I Harinordoquy

SUBSTITUTIONS: W Servat for Szarzewski (49 mins); V Debaty for Poux (50 mins); J Bonnaire for Picamoles (56 mins); L Beauxis for Médard (61 mins); L Nallet for Maestri (65 mins); J Dupuy for Parra (74 mins)

SCORERS: *Tries:* Fofana, Médard *Conversions:* Parra (2) *Penalty Goals:* Parra (2) *Drop Goal:* Beauxis

REFEREE: W Barnes (England)

4 March, Stade de France, Paris

FRANCE 17 (1T 4PG) IRELAND 17 (2G 1PG)

FRANCE: C Poitrenaud; V Clerc, A Rougerie, W Fofana, J Malzieu; F Trinh-Duc, M Parra; J-B Poux, D Szarzewski, N Mas, P Papé, Y Maestri, T Dusautoir (*captain*), I Harinordoquy, J Bonnaire

SUBSTITUTIONS: W Servat for Szarzewski (51 mins); V Debaty for Poux (51 mins); L Nallet for Papé (60 mins); L Beauxis for Poitrenaud (67 mins); L Picamoles for Bonnaire (70 mins)

SCORERS: *Try:* Fofana *Penalty Goals:* Parra (4)

IRELAND: R D J Kearney; T J Bowe, K G Earls, G W D'Arcy, A D Trimble; J J Sexton, C Murray; C E Healy, R D Best, M R Ross, D P O'Callaghan, P J O'Connell (*captain*), S Ferris, J P R Heaslip, S K O'Brien

SUBSTITUTIONS: D C Ryan for O'Callaghan (57 mins); E G Reddan for Murray (58 mins); P O'Mahony for O'Brien (65 mins); R J R O'Gara for D'Arcy (70 mins); F L McFadden for Trimble (72 mins); T G Court for Healy (74 mins); Cronin for Best (74 mins)

SCORERS: *Tries:* Bowe (2) *Conversions:* Sexton (2) *Penalty Goal:* Sexton

REFEREE: D J Pearson (England)

10 March, Millennium Stadium, Cardiff

WALES 24 (1G 1T 4PG) ITALY 3 (1PG)

WALES: S L Halfpenny; A C G Cuthbert, J J V Davies, J H Roberts, G P North; R Priestland, W M Phillips; G D Jenkins (*captain*), M Rees, A R Jones, A-W Jones, I R Evans, D J Lydiate, T T Faletau, J C Tipuric

SUBSTITUTIONS: K J Owens for Rees (62 mins); L C Charteris for A-W Jones (62 mins); R P Jones for Faletau (65 mins); M S Williams for Davies (68 mins); P James for A R Jones (70 mins); R Webb for Phillips (70 mins); J W Hook for Halfpenny (73 mins)

SCORERS: *Tries:* Roberts, Cuthbert *Conversion:* Halfpenny *Penalty Goals:* Halfpenny (3), Priestland

YELLOW CARD: S L Halfpenny (61 mins)

ITALY: A Masi; Mirco Bergamasco, G-J Canale, A Sgarbi, L McLean; K Burton, F Semenzato; A Lo Cicero, L Ghiraldini, L Cittadini, Q Geldenhuys, C van Zyl, A Zanni, S Parisse (*captain*), S Favaro

SUBSTITUTIONS: F Staibano for Cittadini (50 mins); M Bortolami for Van Zyl (51 mins); T D'Apice for Ghiraldini (52 mins); R Barbieri for Favaro (62 mins); T Botes for Semenzato (65 mins); T Benvenuti for Canale (65 mins); G Toniolatti for Masi (70 mins); Cittadini back for Lo Cicero (71 mins)

SCORER: *Penalty Goal:* Bergamasco

REFEREE: G Clancy (Ireland)

10 March, Aviva Stadium, Dublin

IRELAND 32 (3G 1T 2PG) SCOTLAND 14 (1T 3PG)

IRELAND: R D J Kearney; T J Bowe, K G Earls, G W D'Arcy, A D Trimble; J J Sexton, E G Reddan; C E Healy, R D Best (*captain*), M R Ross, D P O'Callaghan, D C Ryan, S Ferris, J P R Heaslip, P O'Mahony

SUBSTITUTIONS: S M Cronin for Best (53 mins); T G O'Leary for Reddan (53 mins); R J R O'Gara for D'Arcy (53 mins); S Jennings for O'Mahony (61 mins); F L McFadden for Kearney (72 mins); T G Court for Healy (temp 50 to 58 mins) and for Ross (77 mins); M P McCarthy for O'Callaghan (77 mins)

SCORERS: *Tries:* Best, Reddan, Trimble, McFadden *Conversions:* Sexton (3) *Penalty Goals:* Sexton (2)

SCOTLAND: S W Hogg; S F Lamont, M B Evans, G A Morrison, L Jones; G D Laidlaw, M R L Blair; A F Jacobsen, R W Ford (*captain*), G D S Cross, R J Gray, J L Hamilton, J A Barclay, D K Denton, R M Rennie

SUBSTITUTIONS: E A Murray for Cross (45 mins); C P Cusiter for Blair (49 mins); R J H Jackson for Laidlaw (55 mins); R J Vernon for Rennie (58 mins); A D Kellock for Hamilton (58 mins); M C M Scott for Jones (61 mins)

SCORERS: *Try:* Gray *Penalty Goals:* Laidlaw (3)

YELLOW CARD: M B Evans (72 mins)

REFEREE: C J Pollock (New Zealand)

11 March, Stade de France, Paris

FRANCE 22 (1G 5PG) ENGLAND 24 (3G 1PG)

FRANCE: C Poitrenaud; V Clerc, A Rougerie, W Fofana, J Malzieu; L Beauxis, J Dupuy; J-B Poux, D Szarzewski, N Mas, P Papé, Y Maestri, T Dusautoir (*captain*), I Harinordoquy, J Bonnaire

SUBSTITUTIONS: M Mermoz for Clerc (36 mins); W Servat for Szarzewski (49 mins); V Debaty for Poux (49 mins); M Parra for Dupuy (49 mins); L Nallet for Maestri (54 mins); L Picamoles for Bonnaire (66 mins); F Trinh-Duc for Beauxis (73 mins); Poux back for Mas (75 mins)

SCORERS: *Try:* Fofana *Conversion:* Parra *Penalty Goals:* Beauxis (3), Dupuy, Parra

ENGLAND: B J Foden; C J Ashton, E M Tuilagi, B M Barritt, C D J Sharples; O A Farrell, L A W Dickson; A R Corbisiero, D M Hartley, D R Cole, M J Botha, G M W Parling, T R Croft, B Morgan, C D C Robshaw (*captain*)

SUBSTITUTIONS: T P Palmer for Botha (55 mins); P D A Dowson for Morgan (62 mins); M J H Stevens for Cole (68 mins); B R Youngs for Dickson (71 mins); R W Webber for Dowson (73 mins)

SCORERS: *Tries:* Tuilagi, Foden, Croft *Conversions:* Farrell (3) *Penalty Goal:* Farrell

YELLOW CARD: C D J Sharples (52 mins)

REFEREE: A C Rolland (Ireland)

17 March, Stadio Olimpico, Rome

ITALY 13 (1G 1PG 1DG) SCOTLAND 6 (2PG)

ITALY: A Masi; G Venditti, T Benvenuti, G-J Canale, Mirco Bergamasco; K Burton, E Gori; A Lo Cicero, F Ongaro, M-L Castrogiovanni, Q Geldenhuys, M Bortolami, A Zanni, S Parisse (*captain*), R Barbieri

SUBSTITUTIONS: L Cittadini for Lo Cicero (51 mins); T D'Apice for Ongaro (56 mins); M Vosawai for Barbieri (56 mins); Lo Cicero back for Castrogiovanni (66 mins); T Botes for Gori (66 mins); G Toniolatti for Canale (68 mins); S Favaro for Botes (71 mins); J Furno for Geldenhuys (75 mins)

SCORERS: *Try:* Venditti *Conversion:* Burton *Penalty Goal:* Mirco Bergamasco *Dropped Goal:* Burton

YELLOW CARD: A Zanni (65 mins)

SCOTLAND: S W Hogg; S F Lamont, N J de Luca, G A Morrison, M B Evans; G D Laidlaw, M R L Blair; J Welsh, R W Ford (*captain*), G D S Cross, R J Gray, J L Hamilton, J A Barclay, D K Denton, R M Rennie

SUBSTITUTIONS: E A Murray for Cross (49 mins); A D Kellock for Gray (53 mins); R J Vernon for Barclay (68 mins); R J H Jackson for Laidlaw (68 mins)

SCORER: *Penalty Goals:* Laidlaw (2)

YELLOW CARDS: N J de Luca (38 mins); J L Hamilton (54 mins)

REFEREE: A C Rolland (Ireland)

17 March, Millennium Stadium, Cardiff

WALES 16 (1G 3PG) FRANCE 9 (3PG)

WALES: S L Halfpenny; A C G Cuthbert, J J V Davies, J H Roberts, G P North; R Priestland, W M Phillips; G D Jenkins, M Rees, A R Jones, A-W Jones, I R Evans, D J Lydiate, T T Faletau, S K Warburton (*captain*)

SUBSTITUTIONS: R P Jones for Warburton (40 mins); K J Owens for Rees (63 mins); L C Charteris for A-W Jones (63 mins); L D Williams for Phillips (63 mins); M S Williams for Davies (temp 53 to 59 mins)

SCORERS: *Try:* Cuthbert *Conversion:* Halfpenny *Penalty Goals:* Halfpenny (3)

FRANCE: C Poitrenaud; W Fofana, A Rougerie, F Fritz, A Palisson; L Beauxis, D Yachvili; J-B Poux, W Servat, D Attoub, P Papé, Y Maestri, T Dusautoir (*captain*), I Harinordoquy, J Bonnaire

SUBSTITUTIONS: J-M Buttin for Poitrenaud (35 mins); D Szarzewski for Servat (44 mins); V Debaty for Poux (44 mins); F Trinh-Duc for Palisson (53 mins); L Picamoles for Bonnaire (60 mins); J Pierre for Papé (67 mins); M Parra for Beauxis (71 mins)

SCORERS: *Penalty Goals:* Yachvili (2), Beauxis

REFEREE: C Joubert (South Africa)

17 March, Twickenham, London

ENGLAND 30 (1G 1T 6PG) IRELAND 9 (3PG)

ENGLAND: B J Foden; C J Ashton, E M Tuilagi, B M Barritt, D Strettle; O A Farrell, L A W Dickson; A R Corbisiero, D M Hartley, D R Cole, M J Botha, G M W Parling, T R Croft, B Morgan, C D C Robshaw (*captain*)

SUBSTITUTIONS: B R Youngs for Dickson (48 mins); T P Palmer for Botha (55 mins); M N Brown for Foden (70 mins); M J H Stevens for Cole (74 mins); P D A Dowson for Morgan (74 mins); L A Mears for Hartley (74 mins)

SCORERS: *Tries:* Penalty try, Youngs *Conversion:* Farrell *Penalty Goals:* Farrell (6)

IRELAND: R D J Kearney; T J Bowe, K G Earls, G W D'Arcy, A D Trimble; J J Sexton, E G Reddan; C E Healy, R D Best (*captain*), M R Ross, D P O'Callaghan, D C Ryan, S Ferris, J P R Heaslip, S K O'Brien

SUBSTITUTIONS: T G Court for Ross (36 mins); T G O'Leary for Reddan (48 mins); R J R O'Gara for D'Arcy (48 mins); M P McCarthy for O'Callaghan (66 mins); P O'Mahony for O'Brien (69 mins); F L McFadden for Trimble (73 mins); S M Cronin for Best (77 mins)

SCORER: *Penalty Goals:* Sexton (3)

REFEREE: N Owens (Wales)

Getty Images

Irish wing Tommy Bowe scores against Wales, but ended up on the losing side.

INTERNATIONAL CHAMPIONSHIP RECORDS 1883–2012

PREVIOUS WINNERS:

1883 England	1884 England	1885 Not completed
1886 England & Scotland	1887 Scotland	1888 Not completed
1889 Not completed	1890 England & Scotland	1891 Scotland
1892 England	1893 Wales	1894 Ireland
1895 Scotland	1896 Ireland	1897 Not completed
1898 Not completed	1899 Ireland	1900 Wales
1901 Scotland	1902 Wales	1903 Scotland
1904 Scotland	1905 Wales	1906 Ireland & Wales
1907 Scotland	1908 Wales	1909 Wales
1910 England	1911 Wales	1912 England & Ireland
1913 England	1914 England	1920 England & Scotland & Wales
1921 England	1922 Wales	1923 England
1924 England	1925 Scotland	1926 Scotland & Ireland
1927 Scotland & Ireland	1928 England	1929 Scotland
1930 England	1931 Wales	1932 England & Ireland & Wales
1933 Scotland	1934 England	1935 Ireland
1936 Wales	1937 England	1938 Scotland
1939 England & Ireland & Wales	1947 England & Wales	1948 Ireland
1949 Ireland	1950 Wales	1951 Ireland
1952 Wales	1953 England	1954 England & Wales & France
1955 Wales & France	1956 Wales	1957 England
1958 England	1959 France	1960 England & France
1961 France	1962 France	1963 England
1964 Scotland & Wales	1965 Wales	1966 Wales
1967 France	1968 France	1969 Wales
1970 Wales & France	1971 Wales	1972 Not completed
1973 Five Nations tie	1974 Ireland	1975 Wales
1976 Wales	1977 France	1978 Wales
1979 Wales	1980 England	1981 France
1982 Ireland	1983 Ireland & France	1984 Scotland
1985 Ireland	1986 Scotland & France	1987 France
1988 Wales & France	1989 France	1990 Scotland
1991 England	1992 England	1993 France
1994 Wales	1995 England	1996 England
1997 France	1998 France	1999 Scotland
2000 England	2001 England	2002 France
2003 England	2004 France	2005 Wales
2006 France	2007 France	2008 Wales
2009 Ireland	2010 France	2011 England
2012 Wales		

England have won the title outright 26 times; Wales 25; France 17; Scotland 14; Ireland 11; Italy 0.

TRIPLE CROWN WINNERS:

England (23 times) 1883, 1884, 1892, 1913, 1914, 1921, 1923, 1924, 1928, 1934, 1937, 1954, 1957, 1960, 1980, 1991, 1992, 1995, 1996, 1997, 1998, 2002, 2003

Wales (20 times) 1893, 1900, 1902, 1905, 1908, 1909, 1911, 1950, 1952, 1965, 1969, 1971, 1976, 1977, 1978, 1979, 1988, 2005, 2008, 2012

Scotland (10 times) 1891, 1895, 1901, 1903, 1907, 1925, 1933, 1938, 1984, 1990

Ireland (10 times) 1894, 1899, 1948, 1949, 1982, 1985, 2004, 2006, 2007, 2009

GRAND SLAM WINNERS:

England (12 times) 1913, 1914, 1921, 1923, 1924, 1928, 1957, 1980, 1991, 1992, 1995, 2003

Wales (11 times) 1908, 1909, 1911, 1950, 1952, 1971, 1976, 1978, 2005, 2008, 2012

France (Nine times) 1968, 1977, 1981, 1987, 1997, 1998, 2002, 2004, 2010

Scotland (Three times) 1925, 1984, 1990

Ireland (Twice) 1948, 2009

THE SIX NATIONS CHAMPIONSHIP 2000–2012:

COMPOSITE TABLE

	P	W	D	L	Pts
France	65	46	1	18	93
Ireland	65	44	1	20	89
England	65	43	1	21	87
Wales	65	33	2	30	68
Scotland	65	16	2	47	34
Italy	65	9	1	55	19

INTERNATIONAL CHAMPIONSHIP
RECORDS

61

RECORD	DETAIL		SET
Most team points in season	229 by England	in five matches	2001
Most team tries in season	29 by England	in five matches	2001
Highest team score	80 by England	80–23 v Italy	2001
Biggest team win	57 by England	80–23 v Italy	2001
Most team tries in match	12 by Scotland	v Wales	1887
Most appearances	61 for Ireland	R J R O'Gara	2000–2012
Most points in matches	551 for Ireland	R J R O'Gara	2000–2012
Most points in season	89 for England	J P Wilkinson	2001
Most points in match	35 for England	J P Wilkinson	v Italy, 2001
Most tries in matches	25 for Ireland	B G O'Driscoll	2000–2011
Most tries in season	8 for England	C N Lowe	1914
	8 for Scotland	I S Smith	1925
Most tries in match	5 for Scotland	G C Lindsay	v Wales, 1887
Most cons in matches	89 for England	J P Wilkinson	1998–2011
Most cons in season	24 for England	J P Wilkinson	2001
Most cons in match	9 for England	J P Wilkinson	v Italy, 2001
Most pens in matches	107 for Ireland	R J R O'Gara	2000–2012
Most pens in season	18 for England	S D Hodgkinson	1991
	18 for England	J P Wilkinson	2000
	18 for France	G Merceron	2002
Most pens in match	7 for England	S D Hodgkinson	v Wales, 1991
	7 for England	C R Andrew	v Scotland, 1995
	7 for England	J P Wilkinson	v France, 1999
	7 for Wales	N R Jenkins	v Italy, 2000
	7 for France	G Merceron	v Italy, 2002
	7 for Scotland	C D Paterson	v Wales, 2007
Most drops in matches	11 for England	J P Wilkinson	1998–2011
Most drops in season	5 for France	G Camberabero	1967
	5 for Italy	D Dominguez	2000
	5 for Wales	N R Jenkins	2001
	5 for England	J P Wilkinson	2003
	5 for Scotland	D A Parks	2010
Most drops in match	3 for France	P Albaladejo	v Ireland, 1960
	3 for France	J-P Lescarboura	v England, 1985
	3 for Italy	D Dominguez	v Scotland 2000
	3 for Wales	N R Jenkins	v Scotland 2001

Bryan Habana makes a break during The Rugby Championship match against New Zealand.

Getty Images

McCAW'S ALL BLACKS WIN INAUGURAL RUGBY CHAMPIONSHIP

By Greg Thomas

Richie McCaw led the All Blacks to a clean sweep of The Rugby Championship.

The **All Blacks** were deserved winners of the inaugural 2012 Rugby Championship, a new tournament created through the inclusion of Argentina into the existing Tri-Nations. Yet again they proved to be far too strong for their southern hemisphere cousins and continue to sit at the top of world rugby following their Rugby World Cup 2011 victory.

New Zealand remained unbeaten in an impressive clean sweep and, despite a change in coaching staff, captain Richie McCaw believes his side proved their world champion status after winning The Rugby Championship by beating Argentina in round five, prior to their last match against the Springboks.

The surprisingly easy 54–15 victory in La Plata stretched their winning run to 15 matches. "It was one of our best performances this season. When we started out in the Championship the goal was to put last year behind us. We have got the tag of world champions and we needed to play like them," McCaw said after the triumph.

"To secure The Rugby Championship was obviously the big goal and it is nice to be able to do that. We gave a performance the guys are pretty happy with. It is the manner in which we did it that was so satisfying."

Head coach Steve Hansen, who took over the reins in December 2011, said his unbeaten team still needed to improve certain parts of their game despite the All Blacks' pace and power hurting the Pumas.

"To be able to attack like that you must have a platform to work off so the forwards can be very proud. Our rucking was also much better. We can pat ourselves on the back and enjoy the moment, but there are still areas to improve on and one of them is the connection between the forwards and backs," he said.

And improve they did to give probably their best display of the Championship in beating South Africa 32–16 at the FNB Stadium in Soweto, the four tries to one bonus point victory highlighting their dominance. Indeed the All Blacks were head and shoulders ahead of the other teams and, despite not hitting top gear in the early stages, were too smart, clinical and polished. They finished 14 points clear in the final standings with a points differential of 111 points.

Remarkably the victory over the Springboks was McCaw's 100th Test win in the famous black jersey. "It's definitely pretty special," McCaw said after his 75th match as captain. "I don't often put personal stuff ahead of what you're trying to do out on the field but after a performance like that, I'm thankful just to be out there. To get to 100 wins you've got to be a part of a special team."

For Australia, who pipped South Africa to second spot having won more matches, it was largely a very disappointing Rugby Championship primarily due to the fact that injuries decimated its squad prior to the start and during the tournament itself. The 2011 Tri-Nations champions won just three of their six matches but found themselves without a number of front line players for the start of the Championship, including captain James Horwill, Quade Cooper, James O'Connor and Wycliff Palu.

As the Championship progressed the Wallabies were further badly disrupted with a raft of injuries to forwards David Pocock, Scott Higginbottom and Sekope Kepu, and backs Will Genia, Drew Mitchell, Cooper, Rob Horne, Berrick Barnes and Adam Ashley-Cooper. The overstretched squad managed wins at home against the Springboks and Pumas but struggled on the road in New Zealand and South Africa.

By the time of the last match in Argentina, nine of the Wallabies who took the field against Wales in the third Test in Sydney in June were missing. Several others were nursing sore bodies and essentially a 'B' team took the field.

The backline was one of the most inexperienced in Wallaby history. Nonetheless the Wallabies showed great courage to prevail 25–19. So satisfied was Deans with the result that he hailed it as one of the most satisfying wins of his tenure.

"I think tonight was evidence of how much the match meant to them and obviously we've experienced a fair amount of adversity. However, we'll get the benefit of this in time as many new players have gained Test experience.

"One of our focal points was not to let the crowd in, and particularly early. They silenced the crowd early [leading 15–6] and they didn't allow the Pumas to get a leg-up. This is a fantastic experience for these blokes . . . it was genuine old-school stuff."

On top of this horrendous injury toll fly half Cooper, who regained fitness for the home match against Argentina, only to then suffer further injury, used social media to describe the Wallaby set up as toxic post-match and that he couldn't continue to play in such an environment. One that was so conservative that it was affecting his game. This put more pressure on Deans who came under constant scrutiny for the performances.

To be fair the injury toll was horrific and most pundits were prepared to wait until the third Bledisloe Cup Test in late October to determine if he should survive and take the Wallabies on their November tour to Europe.

Under new coach Heyneke Meyer and captain Jean de Villiers a relatively 'new look' South Africa also disappointed, winning just two matches and drawing with Argentina in Mendoza. In fact they were lucky to escape with that draw which denied the Pumas a maiden win in their debut season.

Injury also affected the Springboks although not quite to the extent of the Wallabies. Notable absentees being Schalk Burger and JP Pietersen, while Bismarck du Plessis was lost to injury early in the tournament. On top of this the Bok squad was in a rebuilding phase due to the retirement of such stalwarts as Victor Matfield, Bakkies Botha and John Smit, while Fourie du Preez, Danie Rossouw and Jaque Fourie were playing in Japan.

Fly half Morné Steyn lost form and confidence during the Championship and was dropped by Meyer towards the latter stages to be replaced by 20-year-old Cheetahs No.10 Johan Goosen, while young Lions fly half Elton Jantjies moved onto the bench. A few highlights for South Africa was the emergence of young second row Eben Etzebeth, the growing stature of flanker Francois Louw and the return to form of top try scorer Bryan Habana.

The Boks' best win was the 31–8 demolition of the understrength Wallabies in Pretoria at Loftus Versfeld. However, the subsequent 32–16 loss to the All Blacks put the earlier win in perspective. Following the match Meyer felt inexperience was costly.

"The All Blacks are a really quality team and I have to take my hat off to them and particularly to Dan Carter for the way he controlled the game once they were ahead. Up until half-time we played the right type of game but the turning point came when they scored after half-time.

"Suddenly they were ahead, and we had to play catch-up, which you can't do against the All Blacks. But while it is easy to make excuses, we also have to be realistic and we have six Under 21 players in this team.

"If you look at previous teams in recent years, when the defence has been a strong point, you will notice that those sides all had settled combinations and really experienced players playing for them. Guys like Jean de Villiers and Jaque Fourie played more than 50 Test matches together. We have had to make a lot of changes for various reasons. So what we ended up with was a lot of inexperience against the best back-line in the world and they punished us."

Argentina brought a breath of fresh air to what was becoming a stale formula in the Tri-Nations. The Pumas brought colour, commitment, passion, wonderful support and some great rugby to the Championship. Although they only managed one draw they came close to upsetting both the Wallabies and the Springboks, and in Wellington made the All Blacks work incredibly hard for a 21–5 victory.

The Pumas' introduction made a mockery of those who said they were not good enough to be included. They should have beaten South

Africa in Mendoza but tired to concede a try to a charge-down and ended with a 16–16 draw, while on the Gold Coast they fell four points short of victory over the Wallabies.

With fly half Juan Martín Hernández back in the side steering a pack containing stalwarts Juan Martín Fernández Lobbe, Juan Manuel Leguizamón, Patricio Albacete and Rodrigo Roncero around the field they were very competitive. And unlike previous years the Pumas showed a lot more enterprise behind the scrum where Lucas González Amorosino, Gonzalo Camacho and centres Santiago Fernández and Marcelo Bosch, in particular, showed growing confidence with the ball in hand.

For world rugby the Pumas playing in a tournament such as The Rugby Championship for the first time is very exciting as it will allow their rugby to develop on a more sustainable basis. Until now the Pumas only had the Rugby World Cup to focus on every four years.

For one Puma, 35-year-old prop Roncero who has six Test tries to his name, the Championship marked the end of a remarkable career. "Looking back, my career has been extremely positive. I'm just missing the plum of beating one of the three powers – New Zealand, South Africa and Australia. I played at three World Cups and I managed to play the first Rugby Championship. I retire content, the Pumas jersey gave me some of the best moments in my life."

THE RUGBY CHAMPIONSHIP

THE RUGBY CHAMPIONSHIP 2012 FINAL STANDINGS

	P	W	D	L	F	A	BP	PTS
New Zealand	6	6	0	0	177	66	2	26
Australia	6	3	0	3	101	137	0	12
South Africa	6	2	1	3	120	109	2	12
Argentina	6	0	1	5	80	166	2	4

Points: win 4; draw 2; four or more tries, or defeat by seven or fewer points 1

Australia finished second ahead of South Africa on superior win rule

Getty Images

Argentina players look on as New Zealand perform the haka during The Rugby Championship.

AUSTRALIA 19 (1G 4PG) NEW ZEALAND 27 (1G 1T 5PG)

AUSTRALIA: K Beale; A Ashley-Cooper, R Horne, A Faingaa, D Ioane; B Barnes, W Genia; B Robinson, T Polota-Nau, S Kepu, S Timani, N Sharpe, D Dennis, D Pocock (captain), S Higginbotham

SUBSTITUTIONS: R Simmons for Timani (temp for 41–45 mins); S Moore for Polota-Nau (60 mins); R Samo for Dennis (65 mins); Simmons for Timani (temp 67–70 mins); J Slipper for Robinson (69 mins)

SCORERS: *Try*: Sharpe *Conversion*: Barnes *Penalty Goals*: Barnes (4)

NEW ZEALAND: I Dagg; C Jane, M Nonu, SB Williams, H Gear; D Carter, A Smith; T Woodcock, K Mealamu, O Franks, L Romano, S Whitelock, L Messam, R McCaw (captain), K Read

SUBSTITUTIONS: B Retallick for Romano (53 mins); B Franks for Woodcock (65 mins); A Hore for Mealamu (68 mins); P Weepu for A Smith (80 mins)

SCORERS: *Tries:* Dagg, Jane *Conversion:* Carter *Penalty Goals:* Carter (5)

REFEREE: A Rolland (Ireland)

SOUTH AFRICA 27 (3G 2PG) ARGENTINA 17 (2PG)

SOUTH AFRICA: Z Kirchner; B Habana, J de Villiers (captain), F Steyn, L Mvovo; M Steyn, F Hougaard; T Mtwarira, B du Plessis, J du Plessis, E Etzebeth, A Bekker, M Coetzee, W Alberts, K Daniel

SUBSTITUTIONS: A Strauss for B du Plessis (5 mins); P Cilliers for J du Plessis (temp 32–36 mins); J Potgieter for Daniel (52 mins); F van der Merwe for Bekker (58 mins); R Pienaar for Mvovo (61 mins); P Cilliers for J du Plessis (67 mins); JJ Engelbrecht for Habana (71 mins)

SCORERS: *Tries:* Kirchner, Coetzee, Habana *Conversions:* M Steyn (3) *Penalty Goal:* M Steyn (2)

ARGENTINA: L González Amorosino; G Camacho, M Bosch, S Fernández, H Agulla; JM Hernández, N Vergallo; R Roncero, E Guiñazu, J Figallo, M Carizza, P Albacete, J Farias Cabello, A Galindo, JM Fernández Lobbe (captain)

SUBSTITUTIONS: T Leonardi for Galindo (43 mins); JP Orlandi for Figallo (61 mins); M Ayerza for Roncero (61 mins); M Landajo for Vergallo (67 mins); M Rodríguez for Fernández (71 mins); L Senatore for Farias Cabello (71 mins)

SCORERS: *Penalty Goals:* Hernández (2)

REFEREE: S Walsh (Australia)

25 August 2012, Eden Park, Auckland

NEW ZEALAND 22 (1G 5PG) AUSTRALIA 0

NEW ZEALAND: I Dagg; C Jane, M Nonu, SB Williams, H Gear; D Carter, A Smith; W Crockett, K Mealamu, O Franks, L Romano, S Whitelock, L Messam, R McCaw (captain), K Read

SUBSTITUTIONS: A Hore for Mealamu (47 mins); B Retallick for Romano (47 mins); B Franks for Crockett (55 mins); B Smith for Nonu (55 mins); V Vito for Messam (65 mins); P Weepu for A Smith (65 mins); A Cruden for Dagg (70 mins)

SCORERS: *Tries*: Dagg *Conversion*: Carter *Penalty Goals*: Carter (5)

AUSTRALIA: A Ashley-Cooper; D Mitchell, R Horne, B Barnes, D Ioane; Q Cooper, W Genia (captain); B Robinson, S Moore, B Alexander, S Timani, N Sharpe, D Dennis, M Hooper, S Higginbotham

SUBSTITUTIONS: K Beale for Mitchell (35 mins); A Faingaa for Horne (41 mins); J Slipper for B Robinson (43 mins); R Samo for Higginbotham (47 mins); L Gill for Dennis (55 mins); S Faingaa for Moore (72 mins)

YELLOW CARD: Genia (29 mins)

REFEREE: N Owens (Wales)

25 August 2012, Estadio Malvinas Argentinas, Mendoza

ARGENTINA 16 (1G 3PG) SOUTH AFRICA 16 (1G 3PG)

ARGENTINA: M Rodríguez; G Camacho, M Bosch, S Fernández, H Agulla; N Sanchez, N Vergallo; R Roncero, E Guiñazu, J Figallo, M Carizza, P Albacete, J Farias Cabello, A Galindo, JM Fernández Lobbe (captain)

SUBSTITUTIONS: T Leonardi for Galindo (36 mins); L González Amorosino for Sanchez (55 mins); M Landajo for Vergallo (58 mins); M Ayerza for Roncero (58 mins); L Senatore for Farias Cabello (75 mins)

SCORERS: *Try*: Fernández *Conversion*: Rodríguez *Penalty Goals*: Rodríguez (3)

SOUTH AFRICA: Z Kirchner; B Habana, J de Villiers (captain), F Steyn, L Mvovo; M Steyn, F Hougaard; T Mtwarira, A Strauss, J du Plessis, E Etzebeth, A Bekker, M Coetzee, J Potgieter; W Alberts

SUBSTITUTIONS: F van der Merwe for Bekker (50 mins); R Pienaar for Habana (59 mins); K Daniel for Coetzee (66 mins); P Cilliers for J du Plessis (69 mins); T Liebenberg for A Strauss (75 mins)

SCORERS: *Try*: F Steyn *Conversion*: M Steyn *Penalty Goal*: M Steyn (3)

REFEREE: S Walsh (Australia)

8 September 2012, Westpac Stadium, Wellington

NEW ZEALAND 21 (1G 1T 3PG) ARGENTINA 5 (1T)

NEW ZEALAND: I Dagg; C Jane, C Smith, M Nonu, J Savea; A Cruden, A Smith; T Woodcock, K Mealamu, O Franks, L Romano, B Retallick, V Vito, R McCaw (captain), K Read

SUBSTITUTIONS: L Messam for Vito (44 mins); A Hore for Mealamu (50 mins); P Weepu for A Smith (62 mins); S Whitelock for Retallick (65 mins); C Faumuina for Franks (73 mins); B Barrett for Cruden (76 mins); B Smith for C Smith (76 mins)

SCORERS: *Tries*: Savea, Jane *Conversion*: Cruden *Penalty Goals*: Cruden (3)

ARGENTINA: M Rodríguez ; G Camacho, M Bosch, S Fernández, H Agulla; JM Hernández, N Vergallo; R Roncero, E Guiñazu, J Figallo, M Carizza, P Albacete, J Farias Cabello, JM Leguizamón, JM Fernández Lobbe (captain)

SUBSTITUTIONS: T Leonardi for Leguizamón (42 mins); M Ayerza for Roncero (52 mins); JP Orlandi for Figallo (52 mins); L González Amorosino for Rodríguez (68 mins); L Senatore for Farias Cabello (74 mins); M Landajo for Bosch (77 mins)

SCORERS: *Try:* Roncero

YELLOW CARD: Farias Cabello (59 mins)

REFEREE: R Poite (France)

8 September 2012, Patersons Stadium, Perth

AUSTRALIA 26 (2G 4PG) SOUTH AFRICA 19 (1G 4PG)

AUSTRALIA: K Beale; D Shipperley, A Ashley-Cooper, B Barnes, D Ioane; Q Cooper, W Genia (captain); B Robinson, T Polota-Nau, B Alexander, S Timani, N Sharpe, D Dennis, M Hooper, R Samo

SUBSTITUTIONS: J Slipper for Robinson (31 mins); S Higginbotham for Samo (54 mins); L Gill for Timani (66 mins); N Phipps for Genia (71 mins); A Faingaa for Beale (71 mins); M Harris for Barnes (72 mins); Robinson for Alexander (75 mins); S Faingaa for Polota-Nau (75 mins)

SCORERS: *Tries*: Higginbotham, Alexander *Conversions*: Barnes (2) *Penalty Goals*: Barnes (4)

SOUTH AFRICA: Z Kirchner; B Habana, J de Villiers (captain), F Steyn, F Hougaard; M Steyn, R Pienaar; T Mtawarira, A Strauss, J du Plessis, E Etzebeth, J Kruger, M Coetzee, W Alberts, D Vermeulen

SUBSTITUTIONS: P Cilliers for Vermeulen (temp 35–44 mins); L Mvovo for Habana (53 mins); Cilliers for du Plessis (53 mins); F Louw for Coetzee (58 mins); F van der Merwe for Etzebeth (60 mins); P Lambie for Kirchner (71 mins); J Goosen for M Steyn (71 mins); T Liebenberg for Strauss (75 mins)

SCORERS: *Try:* Habana *Conversion*: M Steyn *Penalty Goals*: M Steyn (2), F Steyn (2)

YELLOW CARD: T Mtawarira (34 mins)

REFEREE: N Owens (Wales)

THE RUGBY CHAMPIONSHIP

15 September 2012, Forsyth Barr Stadium, Dunedin

NEW ZEALAND 21 (1G 1T 3PG) SOUTH AFRICA 11 (1T 2PG)

NEW ZEALAND: I Dagg; C Jane, C Smith, M Nonu, J Savea; A Cruden, P Weepu; T Woodcock, A Hore, O Franks, L Romano, S Whitelock, L Messam, R McCaw (captain), K Read

SUBSTITUTIONS: A Smith for Weepu (41 mins); K Mealamu for Hore (50 mins); B Retallick for Romano (50 mins); C Faumuina for Franks (70 mins)

SCORERS: *Tries*: Dagg, A Smith *Conversions*: Cruden *Penalty Goals*: Cruden (3)

SOUTH AFRICA: Z Kirchner; B Habana, J de Villiers (captain); F Steyn, F Hougaard; M Steyn, R Pienaar; T Mtawarira, A Strauss, J du Plessis, F van der Merwe, J Kruger, F Louw, W Alberts, D Vermeulen

SUBSTITUTIONS: A Bekker for Van der Merwe (temp 40–43 mins); D Greyling for Mtawarira (51 mins); Bekker for Kruger (54 mins); J Goosen for M Steyn (59 mins); M Coetzee for Alberts (61 mins); T Liebenberg for Strauss (75 mins); P Lambie for Kirchner (75 mins)

SCORERS: *Try*: Habana *Penalty Goals*: M Steyn, Goosen

YELLOW CARD: Greyling (64 mins)

REFEREE: G Clancy (Ireland)

15 September 2012, Skilled Park, Robina

AUSTRALIA 23 (2G 3PG) ARGENTINA 19 (2T 3PG)

AUSTRALIA: B Barnes; D Shipperley, A Ashley-Cooper, P McCabe, D Ioane; Q Cooper, N Phipps; B Robinson, T Polota-Nau, B Alexander, K Douglas, N Sharpe (captain), D Dennis, M Hooper, R Samo

SUBSTITUTIONS: J Slipper for Robinson (30 mins); K Beale for Shipperley (temp from 31–41); S Higginbotham for Samo (53 mins); Beale for Shipperley (66 mins); A Faingaa for Barnes (71 mins); L Gill for Dennis (76 mins); Robinson for Alexander (79 mins)

SCORERS: *Tries*: McCabe, Ioane *Conversions*: Barnes (2) *Penalty Goals*: Barnes (2), Beale

YELLOW CARD: McCabe (12 mins)

ARGENTINA: L González Amorosino; G Camacho, M Bosch, S Fernández, H Agulla; JM Hernández, M Landajo; R Roncero, E Guiñazu, J Figallo, M Carizza, P Albacete, J Farias Cabello, JM Leguizamón, JM Fernández Lobbe (captain)

SUBSTITUTIONS: JJ Imhoff for Camacho (40 mins); JP Orlandi for Figallo (41 mins); T Leonardi for Leguizamón (49 mins); A Creevy for Guiñazu (61 mins); N Vergallo for Landajo (61 mins); L Sentaore for Farias Cabello (74 mins); Figallo for Roncero (74 mins)

SCORERS: *Tries*: Leonardi, Farias Cabello *Penalty Goals*: Hernández (3)

REFEREE: W Barnes (England)

29 September 2012, Loftus Versfeld, Pretoria

SOUTH AFRICA 31 (3G 2T) AUSTRALIA 8 (1T 1PG)

SOUTH AFRICA: Z Kirchner; B Habana, J Taute, J de Villiers (captain), F Hougaard; J Goosen, R Pienaar; T Mtawarira, A Strauss, J du Plessis, E Etzebeth, A Bekker, F Louw, W Alberts, D Vermeulen

SUBSTITUTIONS: P Lambie for Kirchner (56 mins); F van der Merwe for Etzebeth (59 mins); M Coetzee for Alberts (59 mins); P Cilliers for Du Plessis (71 mins); T Liebenberg for Strauss (76 mins); E Jantjies for Goosen (76 mins); J de Jongh for Taute (76 mins)

SCORERS: *Tries*: Kirchner, Habana (3), Louw *Conversions*: Pienaar (3)

AUSTRALIA: B Barnes; D Shipperley, A Ashley-Cooper, P McCabe, D Ioane; K Beale, N Phipps; B Robinson, T Polota-Nau, B Alexander, K Douglas, N Sharpe (captain), D Dennis, M Hooper, R Samo

SUBSTITUTIONS: A Faingaa for McCabe (temp 6–14 mins); A Faingaa for Ioane (temp 19–24 mins); J Slipper for Robinson (31 mins); A Faingaa for Barnes (31 mins); M Harris for Ashley-Cooper (39 mins); R Simmons for Douglas (51 mins); L Gill for Samo (55 mins); B Sheehan for Ioane (63 mins); Robinson for Alexander (68 mins)

SCORERS: *Try*: Harris *Penalty Goal*: Beale

YELLOW CARD: Slipper (53 mins)

REFEREE: A Rolland (Ireland)

29 September 2012, Estadio Ciudad de La Plata, La Plata

ARGENTINA 15 (1G 1T 1PG) NEW ZEALAND 54 (5G 2T 3PG)

ARGENTINA: L González Amorosino; G Camacho, M Bosch, S Fernández, H Agulla; JM Hernández, M Landajo; R Roncero, E Guiñazu, J Figallo, M Carizza, P Albacete, J Farias Cabello, JM Leguizamón, JM Fernández Lobbe (captain)

SUBSTITUTIONS: JJ Imhoff for Agulla (48 mins); T Leonardi for Leguizamón(52 mins); T Vallejos for Carizza (59 mins); A Creevy for Guiñazu (59 mins); M Rodríguez for González Amorosino (66 mins); JP Orlandi for Figallo (67 mins); N Vergallo for Landajo (76 mins)

SCORERS: *Tries*: Landajo, Camacho *Conversion:* Hernández *Penalty Goal*: Hernández

NEW ZEALAND: I Dagg; C Jane, C Smith, M Nonu, J Savea; D Carter, A Smith; T Woodcock, A Hore, O Franks, L Romano, S Whitelock, L Messam, R McCaw (captain), K Read

SUBSTITUTIONS: B Retallick for Romano (temp 6–16 mins); Retallick for Romano (37 mins); K Mealamu for Hore (49 mins); B Smith for C Smith (54 mins); C Faumuina for Franks (59 mins); A Cruden for Carter (59 mins) S Cane for McCaw (59 mins), P Weepu for A Smith (59 mins)

SCORERS: *Tries*: Jane (3), Savea (2), Nonu, A Smith *Conversions*: Carter (3), Cruden (2) *Penalty Goals*: Carter (2), Cruden

REFEREE: J Peyper (South Africa)

6 October 2012, FNB Stadium, Soweto

SOUTH AFRICA 16 (1G 3PG) NEW ZEALAND 32 (3G 1T 1PG 1DG)

SOUTH AFRICA: Z Kirchner; B Habana, J Taute, J de Villiers (captain), F Hougaard; J Goosen, R Pienaar; T Mtawarira, A Strauss, J du Plessis, E Etzebeth, A Bekker, F Louw, W Alberts, D Vermeulen

SUBSTITUTIONS: E Jantjies for Goosen (35 mins); M Coetzee for Louw (temp 37–41 mins); C Oosthuizen for Du Plessis (53 mins); F Van der Merwe for Etzebeth (60 mins); Coetzee for Alberts (60 mins); P Lambie for Kirchner (65 mins); T Liebenberg for Strauss (73 mins); J De Jongh for Taute (77 mins)

SCORERS: *Try*: Habana *Conversions*: Goosen *Penalty Goals*: Goosen, Jantjies (2)

NEW ZEALAND: I Dagg; C Jane, C Smith, M Nonu, H Gear; D Carter, A Smith; T Woodcock, A Hore, O Franks, B Retallick, S Whitelock, L Messam, R McCaw (captain), K Read

SUBSTITUTIONS: K Mealamu for Hore (52 mins); L Romano for Retallick (58 mins); B Franks for O Franks (63 mins); T Ellison for Nonu (63 mins); P Weepu for A Smith (66 mins); A Thomson for Messam (66 mins); Messam for McCaw (temp 70–74 mins); A Cruden for Carter (77 mins)

SCORERS: *Tries*: Whitelock, A Smith, Nonu, C Smith *Conversions*: Carter (3) *Penalty Goals*: Carter *Drop Goal:* Carter

YELLOW CARD: Dagg (67 mins)

REFEREE: A Rolland (Ireland)

6 October 2012, Estadio Gigante de Arroyito, Rosario

ARGENTINA 19 (1G 4PG) AUSTRALIA 25 (1G 6P)

ARGENTINA: L González Amorosino; G Camacho, M Bosch, S Fernández, H Agulla; JM Hernández, M Landajo; R Roncero, E Guiñazu, J Figallo, M Carizza, P Albacete, J Farias Cabello, JM Leguizamón, JM Fernández Lobbe (captain)

SUBSTITUTIONS: N Sanchez for Fernández (temp 46–53 mins); T Leonardi for Leguizamón (47 mins); Sanchez for Hernández (60 mins); A Creevy for Guiñazu (63 mins); JJ Imhoff for Agulla (67 mins); JP Orlandi for Figallo (70 mins); L Senatore for Farias Cabello (74 mins); Guiñazu for Roncero (76 mins)

SCORERS: *Try*: Imhoff *Conversion*: Bosch *Penalty Goals*: Hernández (3), Bosch

YELLOW CARD: Albacete (65 mins)

AUSTRALIA: M Harris; N Cummins, B Tapuai, P McCabe, D Ioane; K Beale, N Phipps; J Slipper, T Polota-Nau, B Alexander, K Douglas, N Sharpe (captain), S Timani, M Hooper, R Samo

SUBSTITUTIONS: S Higginbotham for Douglas (49 mins); B Robinson for Slipper (41 mins); D Dennis for Samo (63 mins); L Gill for Timani (70 mins); B Sheehan for Phipps (74 mins)

SCORERS: *Try*: Ioane *Conversion*: Harris *Penalty Goals*: Harris (6)

YELLOW CARD: Sheehan (75 mins)

REFEREE: C Joubert (South Africa)

RUGBY CHAMPIONSHIP (FORMERLY TRI-NATIONS) RECORDS 1996–2012

PREVIOUS WINNERS

1996 New Zealand	1997 New Zealand	1998 South Africa	1999 New Zealand
2000 Australia	2001 Australia	2002 New Zealand	2003 New Zealand
2004 South Africa	2005 New Zealand	2006 New Zealand	2007 New Zealand
2008 New Zealand	2009 South Africa	2010 New Zealand	2011 Australia
2012 New Zealand			

GRAND SLAM WINNERS

New Zealand (Five times) 1996, 1997, 2003, 2010 and 2012
South Africa (Once) 1998

TEAM RECORD	DETAIL		SET
Most team points in season	184 by N Zealand	in six matches	2010
Most team tries in season	22 by N Zealand	in six matches	2010
Highest team score	61 by S Africa	61–22 v Australia (h)	1997
Biggest team win	49 by Australia	49–0 v S Africa (h)	2006
Most team tries in match	8 by S Africa	v Australia	1997
	8 by S Africa	v Australia	2008

THE RUGBY CHAMPIONSHIP

INDIVIDUAL RECORD	DETAIL		SET
Most appearances	48 for Australia	G M Gregan	1996 to 2007
Most points in matches	519 for N Zealand	D W Carter	2003 to 2012
Most points in season	99 for N Zealand	D W Carter	2006
Most points in match	31 for S Africa	M Steyn	v N Zealand (h) 2009
Most tries in matches	16 for N Zealand	C M Cullen	1996 to 2002
Most tries in season	7 for N Zealand	C M Cullen	2000
	7 for S Africa	B G Habana	2012
Most tries in match	4 for S Africa	J L Nokwe	v Australia (h) 2008
Most cons in matches	69 for N Zealand	D W Carter	2003 to 2012
Most cons in season	14 for N Zealand	D W Carter	2006
Most cons in match	6 for S Africa	J H de Beer	v Australia (h),1997
Most pens in matches	113 for N Zealand	D W Carter	2003 to 2012
Most pens in season	23 for S Africa	M Steyn	2009
Most pens in match	9 for N Zealand	A P Mehrtens	v Australia (h) 1999
Most drops in matches	4 for S Africa	A S Pretorius	2002 to 2006
	4 for S Africa	M Steyn	2009 to 2012
	4 for N Zealand	D W Carter	2003 to 2012
Most drops in season	3 for S Africa	M Steyn	2009
Most drops in match	2 for S Africa	J H de Beer	v N Zealand (h) 1997
	2 for S Africa	F P L Steyn	v Australia (h) 2007

From 1996 to 2005 inclusive, each nation played four matches in a season. The nations have played six matches since, except in 2007 and 2011 (World Cup years) when they reverted to four.

SAMOA BEGIN NEW ERA WITH SUCCESS

By Rich Freeman

Samoa players celebrate winning the Pacific Nations Cup for a second time in three years.

Samoa deservedly claimed the IRB Pacific Nations Cup 2012 following an exhilarating tournament, based mainly in Japan.

Just a single score separated the teams in all five matches played in Nagoya and Tokyo, as the four nations fielded new teams as they began the build-up to Rugby World Cup 2015.

"I am lost for words," said Samoa coach Stephen Betham, after his side had clinched the trophy with a thrilling 27–26 win over Japan at Tokyo's Prince Chichibu Memorial Rugby Ground.

"We knew Japan wouldn't just give us the cup. We knew we had to win it off them. They played very well and forced us into making mistakes. They sure gave us a good fight."

Betham had only been given the job a few weeks before the tournament and the Samoan coach paid tribute to his players and coaching staff.

"I sort of got thrown in at the deep end three weeks before we came here," he said of his move from Samoa Sevens coach to head coach of the national team.

"It was a big shock and it's been a big learning curve, but I am thankful I have a great management group and we have helped each other get through."

Having opted to ditch a number of senior players, Betham picked nine new caps for Samoa's opening game against Tonga at Mizuho Park Rugby Ground in Nagoya.

In a game riddled with errors, two mistakes from Tongan full back Viliame Iongi early in the second half gifted tries to Galuefa Falamore and David Lemi as Samoa made the most of the limited opportunities that came their way.

Kurt Morath's boot kept the Tongans in touch, but an inability to take their try-scoring opportunities cost them the game.

"Obviously we are very disappointed with the result," said coach Toutai Kefu. "But you saw the game, we didn't deserve to win."

Tonga captain Taniela Moa agreed. "We had the opportunities to score but didn't take them," he said.

In the second game in Nagoya, Fiji held on to beat the hosts and defending champions 25–19 to hand Eddie Jones his first loss as Japan coach.

Ayumu Goromaru had given Japan an early lead courtesy of three penalties, but the Fijians' ability to make the most of Japanese turnovers saw Isake Katonibau and Waisea Nayacalevu both cross.

Vereniki Goneva's try in the second half proved to be the killer blow as the Fiji defence held firm, allowing Japan just a penalty try.

"That was by far the best lesson we've had this year," said Jones. "They scored three tries from turnovers. So, while I am disappointed by the result, I am encouraged by the performance."

Fiji coach Inoke Male said the result was the perfect start as his side looks to bounce back from a disappointing season in 2011.

"We are here to rebuild Fiji rugby," Male said. "We all know what happened in the last World Cup and the boys all put in a great performance. The team morale was high and we did really good today."

The second round of matches saw all four teams move to the nation's capital for a doubleheader at the Prince Chichibu Memorial Rugby Ground.

In the opening match, Samoa captain Lemi led by example, crossing twice as his side downed Fiji 29–26 to move within a game of claiming the title, having previously won it in 2010.

"Both teams gave it their all today," said Betham. "The last few minutes were very competitive as Fiji never gave up, so I am very proud of my players."

The two sides shared six tries between them and once again it was Samoan discipline that saw them through.

"We played some good rugby for the first 20 minutes, but then made too many unforced errors," rued Male.

In the second game, Tonga outscored Japan three tries to two to win 24–20 and ensure former Wallaby number 8 Kefu got the better of his former coach Jones.

"It's good to get the win, but whether we played well or not [I don't know]," Kefu said. "But it's good to finish on the right side of the scoreboard."

Goromaru scored 15 of Japan's 20 points, but Paula Kaho's try in the 61st minute eventually proved to be the difference between the two sides.

"We made some elementary errors at crucial times in the game," said Jones. "We gave them some ridiculously easy points and created enough opportunities to win the game."

With Fiji and Tonga not playing their final game until 23 June – to allow the Fijians the chance to play a one-off Test with Scotland – Samoa went into the final game in Tokyo knowing their fate was in their own hands.

A win, draw or even a two-bonus-point loss would hand them the silverware, while a big loss would see the trophy being shipped to Lautoka for either Fiji or Tonga to claim.

For the first 20 minutes, it seemed the unlikely might actually happen as Japan opened up a 16–0 lead, only for the Samoans to respond with 27 unanswered points of their own following a change in tactics.

"They [Japan] disrupted us at first when we tried to maul, so that's why we changed our plan and sucked them in before driving," said Lemi.

Kahn Fotuali'i crossed for Samoa's first try before Faatiga Lemalu grabbed a brace as the Islanders looked to have wrapped things up midway through the second half.

A tremendous fightback by the hosts saw Takashi Kikutani and Toshiaki Hirose cross for five-pointers, but Ryan Nicholas's conversion of Hirose's last-minute try drifted right, handing the Samoans the game and the title.

"Full credit to Japan," said Lemi. "Even though they didn't win their three games they have performed well. We were lucky and had the bounce of the ball today, but they gave us a lesson. But hats off to my guys, they dug in and that's what got us the result."

Japan coach Jones was left to ponder what might have been. "We have lost three games in the PNC by six, four and one point," he said. "We were playing the strongest side Samoa could have put out, with the exception of Tusi Pisi. They knew exactly how we would play, but we put ourselves in a fantastic position at the start of the game to win it and then put ourselves in a fantastic position at the end of the game to win it. But the reality of it was we weren't good enough to win."

With nothing but pride to play for, Fiji and Tonga brought the curtain down on the 2012 tournament at Churchill Park in Lautoka with the home side securing the biggest winning margin in the six games played. Three second-half tries saw Fiji win 29–17 and finish as runners-up with Tonga third and Japan fourth.

IRB PACIFIC NATIONS CUP 2012 RESULTS

05/06/2012	**Samoa** 20–18 **Tonga**	Mizuho Park Rugby Ground, Nagoya
05/06/2012	**Fiji** 25–19 **Japan**	Mizuho Park Rugby Ground, Nagoya
10/06/2012	**Fiji** 26–29 **Samoa**	Prince Chichibu Memorial Rugby Ground, Tokyo
10/06/2012	**Japan** 20–24 **Tonga**	Prince Chichibu Memorial Rugby Ground, Tokyo
17/06/2012	**Samoa** 27–26 **Japan**	Prince Chichibu Memorial Rugby Ground, Tokyo
23/06/2012	**Tonga** 17–29 **Fiji**	Churchill Park, Lautoka

FINAL STANDINGS

	P	W	D	L	F	A	BP	PTS
Samoa	3	3	0	0	76	70	0	**12**
Fiji	3	2	0	1	80	65	2	**10**
Tonga	3	1	0	2	59	69	1	**5**
Japan	3	0	0	3	65	76	4	**4**

FOUR IN A ROW FOR FIJI WARRIORS

By Karen Bond

Digicel Tonga

Fiji Warriors players celebrate winning the Pacific Rugby Cup.

The **IRB Pacific** Rugby Cup trophy had a familiar name engraved on it in 2012 after the Fiji Warriors won the title for the fourth successive year, being crowned champions without even taking to the Teufaiva Stadium pitch after Tonga A beat Samoa A 20–18 in the first match of the concluding Pacific Island Series on 11 October.

Fiji Warriors had travelled to the Tongan capital Nuku'alofa needing just one point from their final two matches to retain the title after winning an impressive five from six against Super Rugby Academy sides in Australia and New Zealand in February and March.

With Samoa A's defeat, they didn't even need that and they could complete the competition without the pressure to secure the title. This they duly did, scoring 10 points in the last two minutes to beat Samoa

A 42–34 and then edging past Tonga A 25–16 in the final match despite the presence of King Tupou VI inspiring the home side.

This was in stark contrast to last year when the Warriors had been the ones hunting down table-toppers Samoa A in the final series. Ironically it was also a Tongan victory over Samoa A that confirmed the Warriors as 2011 champions after they had beaten both sides in the battle of the core teams in the new-look competition.

This victory on home soil was the first in 2012 for Tonga A, who had lost all five matches played earlier in the year, their only points coming as a result of their match with the Brumby Runners being declared a 0–0 draw after inclement weather forced its cancellation.

The Warriors, though, were undoubtedly worthy winners having bounced back from an opening 36–24 loss to Queensland A in late February to win seven matches in a row – two in Australia, three in New Zealand and two in Tonga – in the key development competition, much to the delight of Sale Sorovaki who was in charge for the concluding series.

"I was happy that we won the game and finished the Pacific leg undefeated," said Sorovaki. "It is a relatively inexperienced team with quite a few changes from the team that toured Australia and New Zealand so it was a good test of the depth of our Academy programme."

This unbeaten run was all the more impressive given the fact that New Zealand teams won eight of nine matches in that phase of the competition in 2011, often by big margins, and PRC 2012 would feature all five of the country's Super Rugby franchise development teams with the Blues and Highlanders entering the fray.

The Warriors had lost all three of their matches in New Zealand in 2011, but full of confidence after their performances in Australia this time they went unbeaten to storm to the top of the Pacific Rugby Cup standings, the only one of the core teams to win a match in the second of three series that make up the competition.

Three points had separated Samoa A and the Warriors in the standings after the Australian Series, but the sides had swapped places after one round in New Zealand with the defending champions edging the Crusader Knights 17–13 in Christchurch and their rivals losing 71–17 to the Chiefs Development XV in Pukekohe.

The Fijians had to survive a nervy last 20 minutes at Rugby Park to hang on to beat the Crusader Knights, their defence standing firm amid intense pressure. The Samoans, meanwhile, were caught out by the intensity of the Chiefs Development XV, a team they had edged 18–17 a year earlier. This time Samoa A conceded 11 tries with prop Heroshi Tea admitting afterwards they "were not expecting the high intensity from the development teams but it was a good experience for the boys to play at this level."

Tonga A suffered a third defeat of the competition, 40–3 at the hands of the Blues Development XV on their tournament debut, a side the Fijian Warriors would edge 16–14 a few days later to pull further ahead in the standings.

The Blues Development XV had Tony Woodcock in their ranks, playing his first match since his try-scoring exploits in the Rugby World Cup 2011 Final, but they were unable to halt the Fijians' winning streak with Jonetani Ralulu's penalty proving the match-winner.

Samoa A and Tonga A both suffered second defeats in round five against the Highlanders Development XV (39–27) and Crusader Knights (58–6) respectively, the latter team fielding a number of players with Super Rugby experience.

The final round of matches in New Zealand saw the Warriors scrape a win by an even smaller margin, beating the Chiefs Development XV 35–34 in a thrilling encounter witnessed by All Black legend Colin Meads, who was in attendance at his Waitete club in Te Kuiti. Once again, the Warriors had to survive a tense last quarter as their hosts battled back from 35–22 down with one of their try scorers being Dominiko Waqaniburotu, who had played for Fiji at RWC 2011.

There was no such success for Tonga A, who suffered a 62–8 mauling at the hands of the Highlanders Development XV with Marshall Suckling scoring four tries, or Samoa A after they saw a half-time lead turn into a 29–12 loss against the Hurricanes Development XV to leave them with an almost impossible task of denying the Warriors another title.

When the tournament had kicked off in February it had been the Samoans setting the early pace and seemingly determined to avoid a repeat of missing out on the title in 2012. They made the perfect start with a 30–24 victory over the Brumby Runners, handing the Canberra team their first PRC loss.

The opening round also saw an impressive fight-back from Queensland A to overturn a 24–18 deficit against the Warriors, Mitchell Felsman scoring three of his side's tries at Ballymore, and a 27–11 loss for Tonga A against the Junior Waratahs in Sydney.

The Warriors bounced back from this defeat to beat the Brumby Runners 16–3 in driving rain at Viking Park, giving new national coach Inoke Male cause to smile after witnessing "a very big improvement in our defence" and seeing his players make "some progress" with their scrum in the difficult conditions.

Tonga A slipped to another defeat, this time 23–8 to Queensland A, so it was Samoa A who remained atop the standings after a 25–5 triumph over the Junior Waratahs, the Samoans having too much speed and power for their opponents.

This set up an Australian Series decider between Samoa A and Queensland A, the only unbeaten teams after two rounds. It was expected to be a tight battle, but Samoa A stamped their authority on the match at Ballymore and led 18–3 at half-time after tries from Misioka Timoteo and Maselino Paulino.

The loss of two players to the sin-bin within a minute of each other early in the second half could have proved costly for Samoa A, but they held on to win 24–8 and move to 12 points, three more than the Warriors who signed off in Australia with a 30–15 win over the Junior Waratahs in Sydney after recovering from a slow start.

IRB PACIFIC RUGBY CUP 2012 RESULTS:

AUSTRALIA SERIES

24/02/12 – Brumby Runners 24–30 Samoa A – Canberra Stadium
26/02/12 – Junior Waratahs 27–11 Tonga A – Foreshaw Rugby Park
26/02/12 – Queensland A 36–24 Fiji Warriors – Ballymore
29/02/12 – Brumby Runners 3–16 Fiji Warriors – Viking Park
01/03/12 – Junior Waratahs 5–25 Samoa A – Foreshaw Rugby Park
01/03/12 – Queensland A 23–8 Tonga A – Ballymore
04/03/12 – Brumby Runners 0–0 Tonga A – Griffith Oval *
05/03/12 – Junior Waratahs 15–30 Fiji Warriors – Foreshaw Rugby Park
05/03/12 – Queensland A 8–24 Samoa A – Ballymore

* match postponed due to weather – result declared a 0–0 draw

NEW ZEALAND SERIES

09/03/12 – Crusaders Knights 13–17 Fiji Warriors – Rugby Park
09/03/12 – Blues Development XV 40–3 Tonga A – Bell Park
10/03/12 – Chiefs Development XV 71–17 Samoa A – ECOLight Stadium
13/03/12 – Blues Development XV 14–16 Fiji Warriors – Bell Park
15/03/12 – Highlanders Development XV 39–27 Samoa A – Logan Park
15/03/12 – Crusaders Knights 58–6 Tonga A – Rugby Park
17/03/12 – Chiefs Development XV 34–35 Rugby Park
19/03/12 – Highlanders Development XV 62–8 Tonga A – Logan Park
19/03/12 – Hurricanes Development XV 29–16 Samoa A – Porirua Park

PACIFIC ISLAND SERIES

11/10/12 – Tonga A 20–18 Samoa A – Teufaiva Stadium
15/10/12 – Fiji Warriors 42–34 Samoa A – Teufaiva Stadium
19/10/12 – Tonga A 16–25 Fiji Warriors – Teufaiva Stadium

FINAL STANDINGS (CORE TEAMS)

	P	W	D	L	F	A	BP	PTS
Fiji Warriors	8	7	0	1	205	165	3	31
Samoa A	8	3	0	5	191	238	0	13
Tonga A	8	1	1	6	72	253	0	6

JAPAN MAKE IT FIVE IN A ROW

By Tom Chick

ARFU

Japan celebrate winning their fifth consecutive HSBC Asian 5 Nations.

The fifth edition of the HSBC Asian 5 Nations took on extra significance in 2012 as it marked the beginning of the region's qualification process for Rugby World Cup 2015.

While Japan powered past Hong Kong to secure a fifth successive Asian 5 Nations title, the sides in Divisions I, II and III all entered the respective competitions hoping to fulfil their dream of competing amongst the elite at England 2015.

It would take a brave man to bet against Japan – who recorded their 20th consecutive bonus-point win in the competition with victory over Hong Kong – winning the title in 2014 to qualify for RWC 2015 as

Asia 1. However, the runner-up will again move into the Répechage so there is the possibility that Asia could have two representatives at a Rugby World Cup for the first time.

Playing in their first competition under the guidance of Eddie Jones, who took charge of the Brave Blossoms after John Kirwan's tenure came to an end following RWC 2011, Japan played a brand of rugby that the new coach believes could get them into the world's top 10.

"That was our best performance of the HSBC Asian 5 Nations," said Jones after their victory against Hong Kong. "We had the game won by half-time. We played with a fair bit of discipline and control and I'm really pleased with the growth of the team. We are learning how to manipulate defences and take teams into one area and then attack where they are not."

Japan began their title defence in the opening round by defeating Kazakhstan 87–0 to open the Jones era in style, with the side including no fewer than 10 debutants as Jones concentrated on players who would be around come RWC 2015.

The Brave Blossoms continued their good form in round two with a 106–3 victory against the United Arab Emirates, a match which saw Jones field Japan's youngest-ever international in Yoshikazu Fujita, the 18-year-old repaying his coach's faith by scoring a record six tries on his debut.

It was Korea, though, who provided perhaps the biggest surprise of the year, the Division I champions finishing second behind Japan on their return to the Top 5. Waiting until round two to begin their campaign, they got off to an impressive start with a 21–19 victory away to Hong Kong, who had defeated the UAE 85–10 a week earlier.

The eventual top two sides met in round three, with Japan recording another bit of history in their 52–8 defeat of Korea with Hirotoki Onozawa moving ahead of Rory Underwood into fourth on the all-time try scoring charts after taking his Test tally to 50 with a hat-trick in Seoul.

A day earlier in the UAE, an equally important match had taken place, one which would ultimately determine who was relegated to Division I for 2013. The UAE ran out 46–31 winners over Kazakhstan, who failed to win a match only two years after finishing as runners-up to Japan.

The 67 points scored by Japan against Hong Kong in the fourth round meant Jones ended his first campaign in charge with a record of 312 points scored and 11 conceded. Korea would also return to winning ways to inflict a third defeat on Kazakhstan, by a dominant 87–17 margin.

Korea ended their impressive campaign with a 47–21 victory against the UAE, a result that gave Kazakhstan a slim chance of avoiding relegation, but Hong Kong proved too strong in the final match of the Top 5, winning 55–0 against Kazakhstan.

The top two divisions next year will form part of the region's qualification process, but the Asian road to Rugby World Cup 2015 actually began in Manila on 15 April when the Philippines hosted Sri Lanka, Chinese Taipei and Singapore in Division I.

The Philippines continued their march up the Asian rugby ladder, beating Sri Lanka 28–18 in the final to propel themselves into the Top 5 in 2013, five years after they were competing at the bottom of the A5N pyramid.

Having only become a member of the International Rugby Board in late 2008, the Philippines' rise has been nothing short of astonishing and in front of a 4,000 strong crowd the Volcanoes roared into a 23–0 lead with first-half tries from captain Michael Letts and wing Joseph Matthews.

Full back Rizah Mubarak finally got Sri Lanka on the board with a penalty, and in the second half they scored 15 unanswered points before Justin Coveney sent the home crowd wild and secured the victory.

"Today was a win for the Filipino people. The people came out in numbers and the guys went out and won for their country. It was a beautiful thing," insisted Philippines coach Expo Mejia.

Sri Lanka and Chinese Taipei can still dream of playing at RWC 2015 as the winner of next year's Division I will be promoted to the Top 5 in 2014, but the same hopes ended for Singapore after their 49–31 defeat to Chinese Taipei resulted in relegation to Division II.

It wasn't until the end of May that the process continued, with Divisions II and III taking centre stage in Asia and the winners from the respective divisions meeting in a unique play-off to determine who was promoted to Division I in 2013. Thailand and India were the respective champions and they met on 14 July under a blazing Bangkok sun at the Thephasadin Stadium, with the former winning 42–29 in front of a partisan crowd thanks to 21 points from Walongkorn Khamkoet.

Thailand had set up the match with India after edging out Malaysia 22–19 to win Division II, which included a further 17 points from the boot of the impressive Khamkoet. China were relegated to Division III after a 52–3 defeat to Iran.

Having been relegated from Division II in 2011, India earned the play-off with Thailand and the unique opportunity to jump two divisions with an 18–16 victory over Guam in the final. India had earlier met their fierce rivals Pakistan in the semi-finals. Pakistan lost that 34–5 and were then relegated to Division IV after a 13–7 defeat to Indonesia.

In the lower two divisions, Qatar scored an impressive 50 unanswered points against Lebanon to be crowned Division IV champions and continue their unbeaten run in the A5N, having earlier beaten Uzbekistan 74–13. Laos were also in dominant mood, beating Brunei 70–7 and Cambodia 58-7 to win Division V.

HSBC ASIAN 5 NATIONS 2012 RESULTS

TOP 5

UAE 10–85 Hong Kong, Kazakhstan 0–87 Japan, Hong Kong 19–21 Korea, Japan 106–3 UAE, UAE 46–31 Kazakhstan, Korea 8–52 Japan, Japan 67–0 Hong Kong, Kazakhstan 17–87 Korea, Korea 47–21 UAE, Hong Kong 55–0 Kazakhstan

DIVISION I

Sri Lanka 36–8 Chinese Taipei, Singapore 20–37 Philippines, Sri Lanka 35–10 Singapore, Philippines 34–12 Chinese Taipei, Sri Lanka 18–28 Philippines, Singapore 24–49 Chinese Taipei

DIVISION II

Thailand 37–17 Iran, Malaysia 89–0 China, Iran 52–3 China, Thailand 22–19 Malaysia

DIVISION III

Guam 38–17 Indonesia, India 34–5 Pakistan, Indonesia 13–7 Pakistan, Guam 16–18 India

DIVISION IV

Lebanon 25–19 Jordan, Qatar 74–13 Uzbekistan, Jordan 19–15 Uzbekistan, Lebanon 0–50 Qatar

DIVISION V

Cambodia 15–19 Brunei, Laos 70–7 Brunei, Laos 58–7 Cambodia

TOP 5 STANDINGS

Team	P	W	L	D	F	A	BP	PTS
Japan	4	4	0	0	312	11	4	24
Korea	4	3	1	0	163	109	2	17
Hong Kong	4	2	2	0	159	98	3	13
UAE	4	1	3	0	86	269	1	6
Kazakhstan	4	0	4	0	48	275	1	1

INTERNATIONAL TOURNAMENTS

ROMANIAN DREAM BECOMES A REALITY WITH NATIONS CUP SUCCESS

By Karen Bond

IRB

Romania players celebrate winning a first IRB Nations Cup title on home soil.

There was more at stake than just the IRB Nations Cup title when six teams converged on the Romanian capital of Bucharest in June, with the tournament regarded as an important stepping stone on the road to Rugby World Cup 2015.

Portugal, Romania, Russia and Uruguay all hope to emerge through the global qualifying process to take their place in England, while for the players of Emerging Italy and Argentina Jaguars it was an opportunity to show their respective national coaches that they can be stars of the future.

Romania, hosting the key IRB strategic tournament for the sixth year in a row, would ultimately be crowned champions, but only after edging tight battles with Argentina Jaguars and Emerging Italy at the Stadionul National Arcul de Triumf to succeed South African Kings as champions.

All three sides had entered the final day with a mathematical chance of lifting the trophy, although the Jaguars needed a bonus-point win over Russia and then the unbeaten Romania and Emerging Italy to draw their winner-takes-all encounter to be crowned champions.

The South Americans came up one try short of their target as they turned a slender 12–9 half-time advantage into a comfortable-looking 33–9 win. In reality they had been fortunate that Russia were unable to convert their first-half dominance of the set pieces into points.

That left Romania and Emerging Italy, the youngest team in the tournament, comprising Under 25 players from the Italian domestic championship, to battle it out for the title. For a while it looked as though Romania would be their own worst enemies as chance after chance went begging, although the young Italians never buckled despite long periods of dominance by their hosts.

Romania's new fly half Dorin Manole ensured his side went in leading 10–3 at half-time after adding a converted try to his earlier penalty, but he was also guilty of missing three penalty attempts. Emerging Italy cut the deficit with a penalty, and four points remained the margin until Romania were awarded a penalty try with 10 minutes left as their pressure finally told.

The Italians again refused to give up but could only manage a try by Alberto Chiesa, the fly half rounding off a sweeping backline move, and so it was Romania left celebrating a first piece of silverware since the European Nations Cup success of 2006.

"This was a dream that became a reality today," admitted coach Haralambie Dumitras. "This was achieved by a group of determined players who strongly believed in this dream. We have almost forgotten what it is like to lift a trophy. We are going to celebrate this, but this is not going to last long. As they say, you are only as good as your last match and we must prepare for the next round of international matches."

Emerging Italy ended up finishing third, behind the Jaguars on point differential, but for head coach Gianluca Guidi the placing was almost irrelevant because the experience his young charges had gained was invaluable for both their individual careers and the future of Italian rugby.

"I have to say that I am enormously proud of my team," Guidi admitted. "We left Italy with 15 boys and we go back with 15 men. They proved that the future of Italian rugby is secure and I will not be surprised if some of them will go all the way."

The other match on the final day saw Uruguay finish with a flourish as they blew Portugal away to lead 28–0 at half-time, fly half Felipe Berchesi orchestrating wave after wave of attack. Trying to play catch-up rugby did not suit Portugal's structured style and coach Errol Brain labelled the 35–7 loss as "without doubt our worst performance since I took over."

The Nations Cup had signalled a new focus for Romania, backs and defence coach Neil Kelly admitting in the build up to the tournament a desire to play a more expansive game than traditionally associated with the Oaks.

"By its very nature Eastern European rugby has always been very forwards-orientated, but the Rugby World Cup showed that only gets you so far," he explained.

"We're on the four-year cycle to RWC 2015 and we want to develop some backs that can complement the forwards. It's going to be a bit of a challenge, but I am sure we can do it."

Romania had kicked off with this new approach against Uruguay, the side they had beaten over two legs in November 2010 to secure the last qualification place at RWC 2011, in this year's opening Nations Cup match played in intense heat in Bucharest on 8 June.

Under the watchful eye of new Romanian Prime Minister Victor Ponta, the Oaks ran out 29–9 winners in a physical but mostly forgettable match, defensive errors from the tiring Uruguayans allowing wings Madalin Lemnaru and Catalin Fercu to score tries in the final quarter.

The second match, between Russia and Emerging Italy, was a complete contrast with both sides eager to play running rugby. Russia recovered from conceding an early try to cross three times for a 17–5 lead after half an hour as they dominated the set pieces and held firm in defence. However, two Andrea Bacchetti tries in the five minutes before half-time swung the match in Emerging Italy's favour and they never relinquished the lead, growing in belief and putting the gloss on the victory with further tries by Gabriele Morelli and Chiesa.

Argentina Jaguars also made an impressive start in Bucharest, avenging a narrow loss by Portugal in last year's competition with a comprehensive 41–9 victory, captain Santiago González Iglesias directing the play impressively from fly half.

Four days later the Jaguars almost made it two wins from two after fighting back from 23–9 down approaching the hour mark to end up losing 23–21 to Romania. The hosts should have been further ahead, but had somehow managed at least twice to knock the ball on after crossing the Jaguars' try-line. Fortunately for Romania, the errors didn't prove costly and they could look forward to the winner-takes-all encounter with Emerging Italy, who had earlier shown great composure and smart counter-attacking rugby against the gallant Portuguese. The sides had gone in level at 11–11 at half-time, but an intercept try from

Gonçalo Uva – younger brother of captain Vasco – gave Portugal an 18–14 advantage with half an hour remaining.

Portugal's confidence was high, but the young Italians simply refocused and within minutes Alberto Chillon had given them a lead they would not surrender, the scrum half finishing with 18 points in the 28–21 win that had coach Guidi proclaiming "this is the face of Italian rugby and I am happy to show how many talented players we have in the country, ready to make the step to a higher level, to help the work of (national coach) Jacques Brunel."

The final match on day two was also decided by a single score, Russia beating Uruguay 19–13 after a tough and uncompromising match between two sides who fought to the bitter end in search of a first win in the tournament. Uruguay had raced into a 10–0 lead, but Russia regrouped and tries by debutant Innokentiy Zykov and Ivan Kotov gave them a half-time lead they never relinquished.

IRB NATIONS CUP 2012 RESULTS

08/06/12	Romania 29–9 Uruguay	Stadionul National Arcul de Triumf
08/06/12	Russia 17–33 Emerging Italy	Stadionul National Arcul de Triumf
08/06/12	Portugal 9–41 Argentina Jaguars	Stadionul National Arcul de Triumf
12/06/12	Portugal 21–28 Emerging Italy	Stadionul National Arcul de Triumf
12/06/12	Romania 23–21 Argentina Jaguars	Stadionul National Arcul de Triumf
12/06/12	Russia 19–13 Uruguay	Stadionul National Arcul de Triumf
17/06/12	Russia 9–33 Argentina Jaguars	Stadionul National Arcul de Triumf
17/06/12	Portugal 7–35 Uruguay	Stadionul National Arcul de Triumf
17/06/12	Romania 17–13 Emerging Italy	Stadionul National Arcul de Triumf

FINAL STANDINGS

	P	W	D	L	F	A	BP	PTS
Romania	3	3	0	0	69	43	0	12
Argentina Jaguars	3	2	0	1	95	41	2	10
Emerging Italy	3	2	0	1	74	55	2	10
Uruguay	3	1	0	2	57	55	2	6
Russia	3	1	0	2	45	79	0	4
Portugal	3	0	0	3	37	104	1	1

BABY BOKS MAKE HISTORY ON HOME SOIL

By Karen Bond

Getty Images

South Africa players celebrate after winning the IRB Junior World Championship for the first time.

The form book was well and truly ripped up at IRB Junior World Championship 2012 as not only did New Zealand's unbeaten run finally come to an end after 21 matches, but the Baby Blacks also relinquished their grip on the distinctive trophy with hosts South Africa denying their traditional rivals a fifth successive title following a hard-fought 22–16 victory before a record crowd of 35,000 at Newlands Stadium in Cape Town on 22 June.

Some might say it was fated that Wian Liebenberg would lift the trophy, given the flanker had worn six on his back, the same number that Francois Pienaar had worn when leading the Springboks to Rugby World Cup glory on home soil in 1995.

It had been billed as "the dream final", bringing together the hosts and defending champions, both of whom had endured a rocky road to the title decider, which for the first time would be contested by teams who had lost in the pool stages, South Africa at the hands of Ireland and New Zealand to Wales.

It lived up to all expectations from the moment the sides emerged into a cauldron of noise, the Baby Blacks determined not to be the first team to return home without the trophy and the Baby Boks equally motivated to create another piece of South African rugby history.

South Africa were instantly on the front foot with the rare sight of a New Zealand pack being driven back at will, but the Baby Blacks somehow kept their line intact, restricting their hosts to three penalties from the boot of Handre Pollard, the 18-year-old fly half called up after Johan Goosen – a standout player in Super Rugby for the Cheetahs – injured his shoulder days after the squad announcement in late April.

New Zealand scored the only try of the first half through Milford Keresoma, but the destiny of the title was anyone's guess at half-time. Two things tipped the scales South Africa's way as first they overpowered a New Zealand scrum five metres from their own line and then scored a try of their own two minutes later, and then enjoyed a five-minute spell with a drop goal and Jan Serfontein – who was named IRB Junior Player of the Year after the final – try to put one hand on the trophy.

The Baby Blacks refused to surrender their title without a huge fight, but could only manage another Ihaia West penalty.

"That's what we spoke about the whole week, to never give up," admitted captain Bryn Hall. "It's our last opportunity to wear the black jersey, and whether you die or leave some blood or tears out here, you make sure you leave it all on the field and you make sure you don't leave any 'what ifs' or 'buts'. You make sure that you just put everything out here and just leave it all here on the field."

His counterpart Liebenberg admitted it was "a dream come true", while coach Dawie Theron insisted it was "the best rugby experience of my life and I played for the Springboks for 13 Tests. I must say that was very, very special, but this moment . . . words just can't describe it."

JWC 2012 Ambassador and RWC 2007 winner Ashwin Willemse was also caught up in the moment. "I think the best way to describe the final is to say it was supercalifragilisticexpialidocious! It is one of those things where I don't think words will do justice to the entire atmosphere, the way in which the game was played by both teams."

South Africa had been forced to overcome some big hurdles along the way after their shock 23–19 opening loss to Ireland. Few people gave Ireland a chance of beating a Baby Boks side brimming with Super Rugby and Sevens stars in their own backyard, particularly having elected to leave star players Shane Layden and captain Paddy Jackson at home.

But the Irish came with a plan – tackle low, put them under pressure at the ruck and deny them quick ball – and it worked to perfection, JJ Hanrahan stepping into the fly half jersey vacated by Jackson with aplomb, steering them to a fully-deserved victory and making them "the talk of the team room" in New Zealand according to Brian O'Driscoll.

Ireland would ultimately rue the one that got away against England, Shane Buckley's yellow card resulting in 14 unanswered points and a 20–15 loss, one which cost Mike Ruddock's charges a first-ever JWC semi-final. Had they beaten England then South Africa would have been facing the prospect of missing the semi-finals for a second year in succession.

After Ireland swept Italy aside, South Africa needed to beat England and score four tries to avoid losing top spot to the Irish on the head-to-head rule. A scintillating second-half display at Cape Town Stadium – a venue for the FIFA World Cup in 2010 – saw them achieve that goal, meaning three-time runners-up England missed out on the semi-finals for the first time.

Ireland would still record their best-ever finish of fifth after avenging their loss to England and then beating France, Hanrahan showing why he was nominated for the IRB Junior Player of the Year award with another impressive display.

England finished a disappointing seventh after another second-half comeback, this time against Australia on the final day. Australia on paper were arguably the strongest squad at JWC 2012, led by Queensland Reds flanker Liam Gill and featuring a raft of Tokyo Sevens winners, but their 67–12 rout of Scotland on day one proved a false dawn with defeats by Argentina, France (twice) and England following.

Argentina were the surprise package of JWC 2012, edging France 18–15 on day one and then proving that was no fluke by beating Australia 15–3 amid the pouring rain at Danie Craven Stadium. Australia simply had no answer to Los Pumitas, flanker Pablo Matera winning the race to touch down for the decisive second try.

They had toured South Africa in April and lost all three matches, but laid the foundations for an amazing team spirit and belief which carried Argentina to their first-ever semi-final. Argentina insisted they were there "to win the title", but they had no answer to a dominant South African forward pack in the semi-finals, losing 35–3 and then 25–17 to Wales in the third place play-off.

By finishing third Wales bettered the fourth place of the 2008 team led by Sam Warburton. Their finest hour, though, had come on day two when they became the first to beat New Zealand on the JWC stage, avenging a 92–0 humiliation a year earlier. This may have been a New Zealand without any Super Rugby players, but Wales had the right game plan for the difficult conditions and three penalties from the boot of wing Tom Prydie secured a tense 9–6 victory, setting them on the road to the semi-finals with a 74–3 rout of Samoa making them the top seeds.

New Zealand had to dig deep against a spirited Fijian side to secure the try bonus point and the best runner-up spot in the semi-finals, meaning they would again face Wales. The Welsh again started brightly, leading 6–0 with Prydie's penalties, but once New Zealand hit the front just before half-time there was only ever going to be one winner, the Baby Blacks triumphing 30–6.

Despite their exploits against New Zealand, Fiji ended up facing Italy in the 11th place play-off after losing 29–20 to Samoa on day four. Samoa had scored just six points in the pool stages, but suddenly came alive with four tries to avenge their earlier loss. Fiji had recorded their best-ever finish of sixth last year, but had to survive a late rally from Italy to win 19–17 to avoid relegation to the IRB Junior World Rugby Trophy, a fate that had befallen Samoa and Tonga in the last two years. Instead, Italy will travel to Chile next year, hoping to win the Trophy as they did in 2010 to rejoin the elite nations.

IRB JUNIOR WORLD CHAMPIONSHIP 2012 RESULTS

POOL A

Round One: **Wales** 44–18 **Fiji**, **New Zealand** 63–0 **Samoa**. Round Two: **Fiji** 15–3 **Samoa**, **New Zealand** 6–9 **Wales**. Round Three: **Wales** 74–3 **Samoa**, **New Zealand** 33–12 **Fiji**

POOL B

Round One: **England** 64–5 **Italy**, **South Africa** 19–23 **Ireland**. Round Two: **South Africa** 52–3 **Italy**, **England** 20–15 **Ireland**. Round Three: **Ireland** 41–12 **Italy**, **South Africa** 28–15 **England**

Round One: **Australia** 67–12 **Scotland**, **France** 15–18 **Argentina**. Round Two: **Australia** 3–15 **Argentina**, **France** 30–29 **Scotland**. Round Three: **Argentina** 17–12 **Scotland**, **France** 31–7 **Australia**

POOL TABLES

POOL A

	P	W	D	L	F	A	BP	PTS
Wales	3	3	0	0	127	27	2	14
New Zealand	3	2	0	1	102	21	3	11
Fiji	3	1	0	2	45	80	0	4
Samoa	3	0	0	3	6	152	0	0

POOL B

	P	W	D	L	F	A	BP	PTS
South Africa	3	2	0	1	99	41	3	11
Ireland	3	2	0	1	79	51	2	10
England	3	2	0	1	99	48	1	9
Italy	3	0	0	3	20	157	0	0

POOL C

	P	W	D	L	F	A	BP	PTS
Argentina	3	3	0	0	50	30	0	12
France	3	2	0	1	76	54	3	11
Australia	3	1	0	2	77	58	1	5
Scotland	3	0	0	3	53	114	2	2

PLAY-OFFS FIRST PHASE

Ninth Place Semi-Finals	**Scotland** 34–17 Italy
	Fiji 20–29 **Samoa**
Fifth Place Semi-Finals	**France** 19–17 **Australia**
	Ireland 27–12 **England**
Semi-Finals	Wales 6–30 **New Zealand**
	Argentina 3–35 **South Africa**

PLAY-OFFS SECOND PHASE

11th Place Play-off	Italy 17–19 **Fiji**
Ninth Place Play-off	**Scotland** 62–28 **Samoa**
Seventh Place Play-off	**England** 17–13 **Australia**
Fifth Place Play-off	**Ireland** 18–7 **France**

THIRD PLACE PLAY-OFF

22 June 2012, Newlands Stadium, Cape Town

ARGENTINA 17 (2G 1PG) WALES 25 (1G 6PG)

ARGENTINA: G Ruiz; R Finco, JI Brex, J Cappiello, S Cordero; S Poet (captain), R Ambrosio; S Garcia Botta, S Iglesias, M Diaz; L Ramella, JC Guillemaín; J Camacho, P Matera, F Isa

SUBSTITUTIONS: R Gonzalez for Iglesias (41 mins); J Paz for Poet (55 mins); F Nougues for Ruiz (55 mins); M Sambran for Diaz (62 mins); M Sanchez for Garcia Botta (65 mins); F Ezcurra for Ambrosio (65 mins); L Uriburu for Ramella (67 mins); L Casado for Isa (77 mins)

SCORERS: *Tries:* Isa, Cappiello *Conversions:* Paz (2) *Penalty Goal:* Poet

YELLOW CARDS: Camacho (21 mins); Guillemaín (27 mins)

WALES: R Jones; T Prydie, C Allen, T Pascoe, L Morgan; M Morgan, T Habberfield; R Evans, K Myhill (captain), S Lee; R Hughes, M Screech; L Hamilton, E Jenkins, D Baker

SUBSTITUTIONS: D Thomas for Baker (41 mins); W John for Lee (50 mins); I Jones for Jenkins (60 mins); J Evans for Habberfield (62 mins); O Williams for Pascoe (62 mins); G Thomas for Evans (69 mins); I Evans for L Morgan (77 mins)

SCORERS: *Try:* Penalty *Conversion:* Prydie *Penalty Goals:* Prydie (6)

YELLOW CARD: G Thomas (73 mins)

REFEREE: M Raynal (France)

SOUTH AFRICA 22 (2T 3PG 1DG)
NEW ZEALAND 16 (1G 3PG)

SOUTH AFRICA: D Leyds; R Rhule, K Van Wyk, J Serfontein, T Mbovane; H Pollard, V Van der Watt; S Kitshoff, M Pretorius, N Van Dyk; P Willemse, R Botha; W Liebenberg (captain), PS Du Toit, F Booysen

SUBSTITUTIONS: A Dell for Van Dyk (67 mins)

SCORERS: *Tries:* Van der Watt, Serfontein *Penalty Goal:* Pollard *Drop Goal:* Pollard

RED CARD: Willemse (58 mins)

NEW ZEALAND: M McKenzie; P Ahki, J Emery, O Peleseuma, M Keresoma; I West, B Hall (captain); O Tu'ungafasi, N Harris, F Armstrong; J Latta, N Ross; J Tupou, H Blake, J Taufua

SUBSTITUTIONS: E Sione for Amstrong (48 mins); J Heenan for Latta (52 mins); R Marshall for Harris (63 mins); T Raimona for Ross (66 mins); A Curtis for Keresoma (67 mins); S Eade for Hall (69 mins); M Hanley for Peleseuma (74 mins)

SCORERS: *Try:* Keresoma *Conversion:* West *Penalty Goals:* West (3)

RED CARD: Tu'ungafasi (58 mins)

REFEREE: G Garner (England)

FINAL STANDINGS

1 South Africa	2 New Zealand
3 Wales	4 Argentina
5 Ireland	6 France
7 England	8 Australia
9 Scotland	10 Samoa
11 Fiji	12 Italy

TOP POINTS SCORERS

Name	Pts
Tom Prydie (Wales)	61
Harry Leonard (Scotland)	54
JJ Hanrahan (Ireland)	53
Handre Pollard (South Africa)	42
Ihaia West (New Zealand)	40
Eric Escande (France)	35
Tom Heathcote (England)	35
Jamie Farndale (Scotland)	30
Fomai Ah Ki (Samoa)	28
Kyle Godwin (Australia)	21

TOP TRY SCORERS

Name	Tries
Jamie Farndale (Scotland)	6
Milford Keresoma (New Zealand)	4
Jan Serfontein (South Africa)	4
Jason Emery (New Zealand)	3
Mitch Eadie (Scotland)	3
Gael Fickou (France)	3
Samu Kerevi (Fiji)	3
Aca Simolo (Fiji)	3
Robert Lilomaiava (Samoa)	3

IRB JUNIOR WORLD CHAMPIONSHIP

USA won a thrilling Junior World Rugby Trophy on home soil.

IRB/Dave Brinton

ATTITUDE, HUSTLE AND AGGRESSION THE KEY TO USA VICTORY

By Jon Newcombe

USA became the first host nation to win the IRB Junior World Rugby Trophy on home soil after a thrilling victory over Japan at Murray Rugby Park Stadium in Salt Lake City, Utah.

The JWRT 2012 final was typical of the nail-biting drama evident throughout a tournament that has done much to boost rugby's appeal in the US. In an epic match that saw the lead change hands seven times, USA withstood one last onslaught from Japan to cling on for a 37–33 win in front of a sell-out partisan crowd.

Having lost the two previous finals, it was a case of more disappointment for Japan who were christened the 'Cardiac Kids' because of their involvement in a series of heart-stopping matches. Pool fixtures against Zimbabwe, Canada and Georgia went right down to the wire, with only a single score separating the teams. The final was no different.

Trailing by 14 points to the free-scoring Japanese in the first half, the USA managed to get a foothold in the final when Tua Laei broke away to score a memorable try just before half-time. The Junior All-Americans pressed on thereafter and secured a 15–14 interval lead thanks to the first of three tries for hat-trick hero Noah Tarrant and the trusty boot of Madison Hughes who ended the tournament level with Romania's Stefan Patrascu at the top of the all-time JWRT points scoring list.

The drama was far from over with a converted try from Shunsuke Nunomaki proving the catalyst for a see-saw second half. Japan added two further tries, but two more Tarrant touchdowns and one from fellow wing Kingsley McGowan ensured Japan's wait for JWRT glory will go on for at least another year.

For the USA promotion to the IRB Junior World Championship 2013 in France is the reward for upsetting all the odds in Utah. Ranked seventh going into the tournament after finishing second from bottom in Georgia the year before, the USA faced the toughest of opening matches against much-fancied Tonga.

Tonga enjoyed the support of Salt Lake City's large Polynesian community, but after a tight first half the hosts went on to record a 22–11 win thank to tries from Hughes and Cameron Falcon after the break.

"As soon as we got off the bus we knew we had three things – attitude, hustle, and aggression – and you saw those all the time during the game. We never let up," said USA captain Will Magie.

Comfortable victories followed over Chile (54–25) and Russia (36–13) to confirm the USA's place in the final on 30 June, while Tonga – relegated from the Junior World Championship the year before – were left to battle it out with Georgia for third place.

Another dramatic finale saw Tonga erase a 12-point deficit in the final six minutes to stun Georgia 31–29. With the win, the Tongans denied the eastern Europeans a third consecutive third place finish.

There was no less excitement in the fifth place play-off as 2008 runners-up Chile defeated Canada 43–31 for their second win of the tournament. In the seventh place play-off, Zimbabwe ended JWRT 2012 on a positive note with a 22–10 victory over Russia, who finished without a win to their name.

With an average of nine tries per match and a 25 per cent increase on the overall total compared to the year before, JWRT 2012 will certainly take some beating in the entertainment stakes when the tournament returns to Chile next year.

IRB JUNIOR WORLD RUGBY TROPHY 2012 RESULTS

POOL A

Round One: **Chile** 53–19 **Russia**, **USA** 22–11 **Tonga**. Round Two: **Tonga** 62–7 Russia, **USA** 54–25 **Chile**. Round Three: **Tonga** 41–14 Chile, **USA** 36–13 **Russia**

POOL B

Round One: **Japan** 39–36 **Zimbabwe**, **Georgia** 31–17 **Canada**. Round Two: **Georgia** 43–7 **Zimbabwe**, **Japan** 38–35 **Canada**. Round Three: **Canada** 66–45 **Zimbabwe**, **Japan** 36–29 **Georgia**

PLAY-OFFS

Seventh place play-off	Russia 10–22 **Zimbabwe**
Fifth place play-off	**Chile** 43–31 **Canada**
Third place play-off	**Tonga** 31–29 Georgia
Final	**USA** 37–33 **Japan**

FINAL STANDINGS

1 USA	2 Japan
3 Tonga	4 Georgia
5 Chile	6 Canada
7 Zimbabwe	8 Russia

Sevens

OLYMPIC CYCLE BECKONS FOR MAGNIFICENT SEVENS

By Seb Lauzier

AFP/Getty Images

New Zealand coach Gordon Tietjens was this year inducted into the IRB Hall of Fame.

Late in 2011 all of New Zealand was popping champagne corks as the All Blacks won the country's first Rugby World Cup in 24 years. Just six months later there was more cause for celebration with yet another HSBC Sevens World Series captured.

Such was the scrutiny and anticipation around the Rugby World Cup win in 2011 that the levels of elation and relief almost transcended sport in New Zealand. By contrast, such is the weight of expectation around Gordon Tietjens's Sevens side that news of another success received far more muted applause, but their feats in the Olympic form of the game should be admired in much the same way.

Across the nine rounds of the 2011/12 HSBC Sevens World Series no fewer than five nations won Cup titles, underlining just how competitive and global the international Sevens game has become. Indeed, even on the final day of the season, while the Kiwis lifted the Series trophy, they were denied the Cup final appearance they craved by their closest challengers Fiji.

And yet overall the men in black – now officially to be referred to as 'All Blacks Sevens' – still came out on top, beating off the stiff challenge of the Fijians as well as England, Samoa and Australia, each of whom won Cup titles during the season, and the likes of South Africa, Argentina, Wales and many others.

Six Cup final appearances out of nine and three Cup titles bear testament to New Zealand's potent blend of talent, work ethic, mental strength and physical toughness that is still unparalleled in the abbreviated form. In short, they are still the benchmark.

"It's not about one person in our side, it's not about relying on those players with the X-factor. I have a favourite saying and that is 'whoever plays will do the job'," said Tietjens, who has been in charge of the country's men's Sevens programme since 1994 and intends to bow out only after the sport's first Olympic Games in 2016.

"We've probably got the fittest rugby players in New Zealand. They work harder than any rugby player in New Zealand and that unifies them. My training sessions are probably harder than any game they'll ever play, and that's a real key to that unity as it brings us close.

"We enjoy ourselves, but the jersey means everything and it's the fear of losing that is instilled into them as well.

"I test them every time that they come into camp but, more importantly, they need to work hard in their own environments so that when they come to camp they're where they need to be. That work ethic and togetherness creates a culture that's second to none."

And a strong culture is paramount when you're on the road as long as they are. It's easy to forget that international Sevens players are now rugby's most prolific tourists. In the 2011/12 season they chalked up countless air miles en route to nine global destinations across five continents. Never has the term 'World Series' seemed more appropriate.

Back in 2006, Fiji became the first country to take the World Series crown from New Zealand, and in 2009 and 2010 South Africa and Samoa followed suit by winning respective Series titles, but Tietjens and his various sides have otherwise held sway over the 13 years.

Such is his status in the game that it came as no great surprise that the IRB honoured Tietjens by inducting him into the IRB Hall of Fame this year, shining light on his undeniable and incomparable achievements to date. Having not missed a single tournament since the inception of the Series back in 1999, Tietjens and his players have won 10 World

SEVENS OVERVIEW

Series titles. Under his watch, New Zealand has also won a Rugby World Cup Sevens in 2001 and all four Commonwealth Games gold medals contested. No fewer than 39 All Blacks have graduated from his Sevens regime, most of whom pay generous tribute to their time in his 'care'.

On receiving his Hall of Fame cap at Twickenham, an emotional Tietjens was quick to return the compliment.

"It's just really humbling and quite special really. I'm shocked to be recognised for my contribution to Sevens Rugby. I can only thank the players that have been a big part of my life, the players that have contributed to the successes in the game that I have had," he said.

"In the game of Sevens you've got to be mentally very, very strong. There are a lot of players out there who are gifted, talented but haven't got the work ethic and have gone away from Sevens because it's too tough for them. But there are those players who are mentally tough, incredibly fit and they are the ones who want to make it. And often they are also the ones who will go on and also become All Blacks."

Above all, it is clear that Tietjens still has a passion for the game of Rugby Sevens, even after 18 years as his country's head Sevens coach. His eyes still twinkle at the mention of certain tournaments, finals or players, or when asked about his latest scouting success.

"I love watching players in space expressing themselves. I remember back to Christian Cullen playing for me on a Sevens pitch, and he went on to become a wonderful All Black of course, but to see the step, the acceleration, the vision, the ball skills off both hands, everything you'd expect from a rugby player he could express in the game of Sevens.

"Christian was probably the most outstanding talent I saw in all that time. Eighteen tries in Hong Kong in his second year was incredible."

Ironically, it is that same enthusiasm and dedication that has also helped pave the way for a new generation of Sevens specialist coaches, whose job it is to make Tietjens's life increasingly difficult.

Across the Tasman former dual-code international Michael O'Connor is putting his talent for player identification and coaching to good use. Two seasons ago nine of his players graduated to Super Rugby contracts and, more recently, he enjoyed Cup success with another new crop of youngsters in Tokyo. In Samoa, Stephen Betham won the World Series in 2010 and has since been given the Manu Samoa top job, passing on the Sevens reins to his former manager, Faamoni Lalomilo.

Further afield, Paul Treu was the first coach to instigate a full-time centrally-contracted national Sevens squad in South Africa. Based in Stellenbosch, the team's facilities would be the envy of many an Olympic athlete and his set-up has acted as a blueprint for the other countries.

In Europe, England's head coach Ben Ryan was the first to follow

Treu's lead and now has a full-time squad of Sevens players, victorious in Dubai and building steadily towards Rio 2016, while Paul John led Wales to Rugby World Cup Sevens success in 2009 and is also quietly building a formidable unit.

And crucially now Sevens teams are also finding themselves welcomed for the first time by National Olympic Committees, as the sport enters its maiden Olympic cycle. This fact may just prove to spark the biggest sea change of all. The USA's side now trains regularly out of USOC's stunning Chula Vista facility just outside of San Diego, tapping into untold resources, while new core team Spain are also benefiting from access to superb Olympic facilities and infrastructure they might only have dreamt about a few years ago.

Arguably even more exciting is the attention now being heaped on the women's game of Sevens. Scenting medals opportunities in both 2016 and 2020, National Olympic Committees are already investing heavily in women's programmes in Canada, USA, Netherlands and China, while Brazil's women's Sevens team is the pride of a nation increasingly infatuated by rugby, albeit forever in love with soccer.

The women will have a brand new IRB Series in 2012/13, while for the men the season ahead promises to be their toughest ever assignment with 15 core teams set to compete in each and every tournament, up from 12 last year.

"I've said it many times over the past few seasons and I still don't think people have ever properly believed me: there really are no easy matches anymore in the game of Sevens. And with 15 teams basically full-time on the Series now it's going to go up another notch," said Tietjens.

"In years gone by I could maybe afford to rest a few of my top players for one or even two pool games, and still expect to top the group, or certainly proceed to the Cup quarter-finals. For the past couple of years that really hasn't been the case. Everyone knows about Samoa, Fiji and South Africa, all Series winners, and the likes of England who've done very well for a number of years now, and Australia who are now back to being the same formidable opponent that they were when the Series began.

"Most people also know that Kenya, Wales and Argentina can knock you over if you're not at your best. But it's the other teams who've also raised their level – teams like France who now have full-time players, and Spain, Canada and Portugal, all of whom are now there at every event as the so-called fourth-ranked side in the pool.

"We take our foot off the pedal in a pool match and we can easily lose that match. Knowing that has an effect in the short term because you're asking so much more of your senior players so that element of fatigue can become a much bigger factor, but also in the longer term across an entire season. With more events now, it means we're needing to build in more rest time and my players are also now reaching a stage where they are having to decide whether they can still come back to New Zealand, pack away the Sevens kit and go out and play big 15-a-side matches in our National Provincial Competition.

"I believe Sevens is taking off to such an extent, and has the potential to become such a major force in so many of these countries, that I really do think it's at a tipping point. Players will soon have to decide: do I want to play Fifteens or Sevens? In many ways Fifteens is the easy option and they can always go back to that afterwards, but for the sacrifices you make in Sevens you do now have that possibility of doing something that very few sportsmen and women achieve in their careers – go on to represent your country at an Olympic Games.

"That is incredibly enticing for me as a coach and I believe also for rugby players in New Zealand, and all over the world. That first Olympic cycle now starts for us and in lots of ways we have to be even better than we've been up to now because no country is going to take a backwards step, they're only going to improve and the 2012/13 HSBC Sevens World Series will be the first step for us on that Road to Rio."

IRB SEVENS ROLL OF HONOUR

1999/2000: New Zealand	2006/2007: New Zealand
2000/2001: New Zealand	2007/2008: New Zealand
2001/2002: New Zealand	2008/2009: South Africa
2002/2003: New Zealand	2009/2010: Samoa
2003/2004: New Zealand	2010/2011: New Zealand
2004/2005: New Zealand	2011/2012: New Zealand
2005/2006: Fiji	

COMMONWEALTH GAMES SEVENS ROLL OF HONOUR

1998: Kuala Lumpur, Malaysia	New Zealand	2006: Melbourne, Australia	New Zealand
2002: Manchester, UK	New Zealand	2010: Delhi, India	New Zealand

RWC SEVENS ROLL OF HONOUR

1993: England	2005: Fiji
1997: Fiji	2009: Wales
2001: New Zealand	

NEW ZEALAND STORM TO 10TH WORLD SERIES TITLE

By Nigel Starmer-Smith

Getty Images

Captain DJ Forbes leads the haka as New Zealand celebrates another Sevens World Series title.

As we've now grown accustomed to expect, the 2011/12 season provided us with yet another enthralling season of the HSBC Sevens World Series, the most competitive yet. Twenty-seven countries took part across the nine rounds with five different Cup winners underlining the constant edge, while 2016 Olympic hosts Brazil made a long awaited and significant return.

Four new venues each brought a fresh flavour and vibrancy, as well as new challenges for the players. Skilled Park on Australia's Gold Coast provided a new starting point, while the Nelson Mandela Bay Stadium in Port Elizabeth quickly announced itself as South Africa's new home for

Sevens. One week after the drama of Hong Kong, the Prince Chichibu Memorial Rugby Ground in Tokyo returned to the Series after a decade and Glasgow provided a new Scottish backdrop for the penultimate round.

The opening weeks included tournaments on three consecutive weekends – unprecedented in the 13-year history of the World Series. Skilled Park played host to the inaugural Gold Coast Sevens Fever Pitch and Queensland's 'Famous for Fun' slogan was very apt, those golden beaches proving irresistible for some of the surf-loving players!

Fun was had on the pitch and in the stands too as Fiji, who had not won a Cup title since Wellington 2010, responded to the demands of their Union's Chairman, Mosese Tikoitoga, by reverting to "continuous attack and our traditional running, handling rugby". With a new squad under coaches Alifereti Dere and assistant Etuate Waqa they obliged and in new captain Setefano Cakau had the tournament's outstanding player. Having seen his side lose convincingly in the pool stages to New Zealand, Cakau, now 33 and in his ninth season, was the inspiration on finals day as Fiji put Wales and South Africa to the sword and then in the final avenged their earlier defeat by beating the reigning Series champions New Zealand 26–12.

The teams then headed to the Middle East and one of the cornerstone events of world Sevens, the Emirates Airline Dubai Rugby Sevens. This time the key transformation came from England, coach Ben Ryan inspired in opting for former Marine Greg Barden as captain and revelling in the return from injury of another military man, Isoa Damu. With Rob Vickerman also switching back to Sevens, the stage was set for a tour de force performance in what has always been a second home for England. They revelled in the ex-pat support and in Dan Norton and Mat Turner had two of the most electric players on show. Turner's seven tries in the last five matches helped England to dramatic knockout wins over both New Zealand and Fiji, while the first ever northern hemisphere final was more one-sided, a 29–12 win over France, who were playing in their first Cup final since Paris 2005.

With two tournaments behind them, the show moved on to another new event in Port Elizabeth. For 10 years the kind folk of George had been generous hosts in that stunning setting on the Garden Route, but in truth the advance of the Sevens game, including in South Africa, was clamouring for a larger capacity and the stunning Nelson Mandela Bay Stadium delivered it.

In the opening tournaments New Zealand had blown hot and cold – Cup finalists in Gold Coast and Plate semi-finalists in Dubai, where for the first time they had lost three games in a row. No surprise, then, that when they arrived in PE the tables turned. Whatever words or actions stemmed from perennial coach Gordon Tietjens prior to that South African event I do not know, but his new call-ups, including Charles Piutau and 18-year-old schoolboy Joe Webber, blended with the experienced campaigners to produce an irresistible force. Alongside captain DJ Forbes stood the likes of Tim Mikkelson, Lote Raikabula, Solomon King and Tomasi Cama, a quintet with a total of 182 tournaments under their belts, and it was no surprise that on day one they scored 21 tries and conceded just one. Meanwhile, hosts South Africa were equally determined to repeat their only previous triumph at home, in George in 2008. After not conceding a try in pool play, and with impressive knockout wins, the stage was set for an epic final as the home favourites took on New Zealand. In one of the most extraordinary atmospheres in recent times, 30,000 willed on the home team and, although the Kiwis led 17–14 at the break, the crowd sensed an upset. Steven Hunt and Cecil Afrika answered by giving them the lead but, in a sensational finish, Frank Halai broke through again before the brilliant Cama combined with Toby Arnold to kick and chase to score the winning try: New Zealand 31, South Africa 26. On that initial evidence, the stadium will be spilling over with spectators in 2012.

Recently Wellington has proved a happy hunting ground for New Zealand – five Cup wins in the past nine years – and local confidence and expectation was rampant when the sides arrived in February for round four. Surprise came when Tietjens rung the changes, introducing 18-year-old Ardie Savea, All Black Hosea Gear and debutant Mark Jackman. Things did not begin too auspiciously: Raikabula withdrew injured and Arnold damaged cruciate ligaments in their opening match. But apart from a tough encounter with England, seldom were New Zealand on the rack. Fiji were the opposing finalists and in Waisea Nayacalevu, Levani Botia and Metuisela Talebula they unearthed some remarkable new talent, but by the last match they seemed a spent force in the face of Cama's magic. The Fijian-born maestro called the tune and Halai outgunned the wilting defence, scoring two of his six tries, and New Zealand won convincingly 24–7.

Las Vegas may not be known as a centre for rugby, but once a year the Sam Boyd Stadium marries the Sevens with a superbly enthusiastic and international crowd. Significantly, too, broadcast giants NBC opted to transmit the whole tournament live from coast to coast, giving rugby a bigger audience and profile Stateside than ever before. Suggestions have been made that the narrow gridiron pitch offers an advantage to the more physical teams. In 2011 fleet-footed South Africa made a mockery of such claims, but this time it was one of the powerhouses, Samoa, who hit form. The fact that this coincided with the return of forward Alafoti Fa'osiliva came as no surprise and with Paul Perez also in sparkling form the former World Series winners proved an awesome proposition. Having lost narrowly to red-hot New Zealand early on, the tables were turned when they met again in the final. An inspired Perez made two tries and scored another, and man mountain Fa'osiliva crashed through the defence to win a thrilling contest 26–19, Samoa becoming the fourth different Cup winners in five events.

The next stop was Hong Kong. In unique circumstances Asia's biggest rugby event comprised not one but two tournaments. In one the 12 'core teams' contested the Cup, while in the other 12 more nations went all out for the Shield, and more significantly for three additional core team berths on the 2012/13 HSBC Sevens World Series.

In the Cup event at least five nations were in the mix. Reigning champions New Zealand had injury concerns but Tietjens had back-up ready to step in from the 10s, and some entrance Jack Wilson made. Wins over Wales and South Africa augured well and took them to the Cup final, but at the same time an even less experienced Fiji were clicking into overdrive. New coach Dere had wielded the axe by dropping five after Vegas, but what an inspired transformation. Cakau set the standard as they romped through their pool, then beat Argentina and England to face New Zealand in a repeat of last year's final.

What transpired was an utterly absorbing 20 minutes, swaying one way then the other with the Fijians throwing caution to the wind, only to be pegged back by the battling New Zealanders. In the end Fiji won 35–28, after which co-commentator and former Scotland captain Andy Nicol calmly asserted that it was the "best 20 minutes of rugby he had ever witnessed". It was also Fiji's first win over New Zealand in a World Series Cup final in Hong Kong.

The battle for core team status was proving just as exciting. Inevitably, there was heartbreak for some, Zimbabwe, Japan and Hong Kong coming so close to glory, but it was unbounded joy for winners Canada, runners-up Spain and Portugal, whose experience and guile was too much for Japan. The Japanese did, though, have something on their minds. A week later round seven of the Series took us back to Tokyo after a decade away. Horizontal rain on day one turned the ball into a bar of soap at times but the quality was sustained, and so too the spirits. Australia beat Hong Kong 17–14, Portugal lost to Samoa 21–20 and South Africa 12–7, while Wales overcame Russia 10–7 on a highly competitive day. Day two also provided several knife-edge matches, England beating Fiji 14–7 and South Africa 21–17, while Samoa overcame Fiji 24–21 and New Zealand 17–12. But the real surprise came from Michael O'Connor's Australia, whose young-sters had not shone since their Cup semi on the Gold Coast. Where other captains had so often inspired their sides, this time it was Ed Jenkins who urged his squad to the Cup final against Samoa. Another thriller ensued with the lead changing hands on numerous occasions and superb tries by Australian newcomer Shannon Walker. All hinged on the final try and conversion and appropriately it was Jenkins's try that levelled the scores in the final minute to leave 20-year-old Matt Lucas, making only his second appearance, to kick the winning conversion from near the touchline.

If the conditions in Tokyo were unseasonably wintry, so too were they in Glasgow when the teams arrived for the penultimate round at a new Scottish venue, Scotstoun Stadium. Other than in Dubai, New Zealand had been in contention for every Cup title and were determined and poised to win their 10th overall Series title. England had also been in the mix, although they now had a new captain in Vickerman following Barden's retirement. The two were destined to meet for the seventh time in the season, England looking to deny the Kiwis that Series swansong, and knowing that throughout the season there had never been more than a converted try between them. New Zealand beat Samoa by a single point on day one, but looked imperious as they dispatched Argentina and Australia on the way to another final. England had a tough run – just five-point wins over Australia, South Africa and Fiji – but in Turner had a star performer. In the final, though, New Zealand were to dominate and underline the sheer excellence of their experienced core. Forbes clinched the win with two second-half tries and with it his side had an impressive 11-point lead in the Series and one hand on the trophy.

The teams reconvened in London, where blue skies welcomed them and a world record single-day crowd of 60,000 for day one of the season finale, the Marriott London Sevens at Twickenham. Mathematically, Fiji could still overhaul New Zealand and they did their level best. Indeed, New Zealand did not have everything their way. It was nervy early on as they overcame Argentina 15–10, but with a semi-final target in mind they came out like greyhounds on day two and blew away South Africa 36–0 to win another World Series. Thereafter Fiji made their point, firstly overcoming England and then trouncing New Zealand 32–7 in the semi-final, perhaps pointing at what is to come next season. Fittingly for the Series-ending match, the final was riveting with the subtle skills, pace and lightning breaks of the Fijians juxtaposed against the forceful power and experience of Samoa. On this occasion Samoa and 34-year-old playmaker Uale Mai couldn't cope with their great rivals, Fiji running out 38–15 winners to finish just six points adrift of New Zealand in the final standings

So five Cup winners, seven different Cup final combinations and a 10th Series title for New Zealand. Once again they were far and away the most consistent performers across a season that attracted record broadcast figures around the world, a staggering 152 countries airing action in 374 million homes! And for the New Zealanders, a perfect

HSBC SEVENS WORLD SERIES

ending when Cama was named IRB Sevens Player of the Year and, perhaps more significantly, Tietjens became the 49th inductee into the IRB Hall of Fame. Reward indeed, and richly deserved.

HSBC SEVENS WORLD SERIES 2011/12 RESULTS

AUSTRALIA: 25–26 NOVEMBER

Fiji (22), New Zealand (19), South Africa (17), Australia (15), Wales (13), Samoa (12), England (10), France (10), Argentina (8), Scotland (7), USA (5), Tonga (5), Papua New Guinea (3), Japan (2), Kenya (1), Niue (1)

DUBAI: 2–3 DECEMBER

England (22), France (19), Fiji (17), Argentina (15), Australia (13), South Africa (12), New Zealand (10), Wales (10), Scotland (8), USA (7), Canada (5), Portugal (5), Samoa (3), Kenya (2), Zimbabwe (1), UAE (1)

SOUTH AFRICA: 9–10 DECEMBER

New Zealand (22), South Africa (19), Samoa (17), England (15), Wales (13), Fiji (12), Australia (10), France (10), Scotland (8), Canada (7), USA (5), Argentina (5), Zimbabwe (3), Kenya (2), Portugal (1), Morocco (1)

NEW ZEALAND: 3–4 FEBUARY

New Zealand (22), Fiji (19), England (17), Samoa (15), South Africa (13), Tonga (12), France (10), Canada (10), Kenya (8), Australia (7), Argentina (5), Wales (5), Scotland (3), Cook Islands (2), Japan (1), USA (1)

USA: 10–12 FEBUARY

Samoa (22), New Zealand (19), Fiji (17), South Africa (15), Kenya (13), Argentina (12), England (10), Wales (10), Canada (8), Australia (7), USA (5), Japan (5), France (3), Scotland (2), Brazil (1), Uruguay (1)

HONG KONG: 23–25 MARCH

Fiji (22), New Zealand (19), South Africa (17), England (15), Samoa (13), Argentina (12), Australia (10), Wales (10), Kenya (8), USA (7), Scotland (5), France (5), Canada (3), Spain (2), Portugal (1), Japan (1)

Australia (22), Samoa (19), New Zealand (17), England (15), Fiji (13), South Africa (12), Argentina (10), Wales (10), France (8), USA (7), Portugal (5), Hong Kong (5), Scotland (3), Kenya (2), Japan (1), Russia (1)

SCOTLAND: 5–6 MAY

New Zealand (22), England (19), Fiji (17), Australia (15), Samoa (13), Wales (12), South Africa (10), Argentina (10), Russia (8), Spain (7), France (5), Scotland (5), Kenya (3), USA (2), Portugal (1), Zimbabwe (1)

ENGLAND: 12–13 MAY

Fiji (22), Samoa (19), New Zealand (17), Argentina (15), Australia (13), England (12), South Africa (10), (10), Wales (8), Scotland (7), Portugal (5), Zimbabwe (5), France (3), USA (2), Kenya (1), Russia (1)

FINAL STANDINGS

New Zealand – 167	Portugal – 18
Fiji – 161	Tonga – 17
England – 135	Japan – 10
Samoa – 133	Russia – 10
South Africa – 125	Zimbabwe – 10
Australia – 112	Hong Kong – 5
Argentina – 92	Papua New Guinea – 3
Wales – 91	Cook Islands – 2
France – 73	Brazil – 1
Scotland – 48	Morocco – 1
USA – 41	Niue – 1
Kenya – 40	UAE – 1
Canada – 33	Uruguay – 1
Spain – 19	

PREVIOUS WINNERS

1999/2000 – New Zealand	2006/2007 – New Zealand
2000/2001 – New Zealand	2007/2008 – New Zealand
2001/2002 – New Zealand	2008/2009 – South Africa
2002/2003 – New Zealand	2009/2010 – Samoa
2003/2004 – New Zealand	2010/2011 – New Zealand
2004/2005 – New Zealand	2011/2012 – New Zealand
2005/2006 – Fiji	

HSBC SEVENS WORLD SERIES

SEVENS AROUND THE WORLD

By Seb Lauzier

With the 2016 Olympic cycle on the horizon and the carnival city of Rio de Janeiro promising untold riches for those who reach that stage in rugby's newest journey, more countries are turning their attentions to Sevens. With that, the requirement for Sevens competition at both a national and international level is constantly growing.

While the nine rounds of the HSBC Sevens World Series provided the pinnacle for the men's game in 2011/12, many other tournaments were contested across the IRB Regional Associations, acting as satellite events, qualifying for the Series and also for Rugby World Cup Sevens 2013 in Moscow, Russia.

ASIA

The Sevens landscape is fast changing in the region, and the HSBC Asian Sevens Series now provides a fitting annual showcase. In the first round of the 2011 Series, Korea captured a third consecutive Shanghai title, edging Hong Kong 22–17 in sudden-death extra-time, while Japan beat Kazakhstan to third.

In the final ranking event regional powerhouse Japan won in Borneo, a triumph that proved enough to claim the overall Series title with Hong Kong winning the third Cup title, a non-ranking event in Goa, India.

The Series has also shone a light on the many rapidly-developing nations who have quickly adopted Sevens. The UAE continue to make bold progress along with the likes of Iran, Singapore and India, all of whom have a chance to qualify for RWC Sevens through the 2012 Series, which runs from September to November and has seen Japan and Hong Kong win the first two events.

AFRICA

Of the continents where rugby is still developing, Africa arguably possesses the greatest potential in Sevens with so many countries boasting magnificent athletes, and in 2011 it was the North Africans who held sway in Sevens.

Morocco edged Tunisia 14–12 in the final on home soil in Marrakech, while there were strong signs of development from Nigeria, Ivory Coast, Senegal, Burkina Faso and Mali.

In 2012, the tournament doubled as Africa's regional qualifier for RWC Sevens with Zimbabwe and Tunisia booking their places in Moscow by reaching the final. With the pressure off, Zimbabwe cut loose and ran out 33–12 winners in Morocco.

OCEANIA

Of all the regions playing Sevens, Oceania has arguably the strongest pedigree with New Zealand, Australia, Fiji and Samoa all world beaters and Tonga being pushed by the likes of PNG in catching up those heavyweights.

Hosts Samoa won the 2011 Oceania Sevens title by defeating great rivals Fiji 19–7. Held only days before the start of the World Series, the showpiece was missing New Zealand from its line-up but provided the two former Series champions, Australia and Tonga with a chance to shake off any rustiness and renew local bragging rights.

The 2012 Oceania Sevens took place in Sydney in August with the added prize of RWC Sevens qualification. With Fiji, New Zealand and Samoa pre-qualified as quarter-finalists in 2009, the two places on offer went to champions Australia and Tonga, who edged the Cook Islands for third place.

THE AMERICAS

A major landmark was reached in the Americas in 2011 when Sevens made its debut at the Pan American Games. This wasn't the first time for Sevens in a multi-sport arena – it has proved hugely successful at four Commonwealth Games, the Asian Games and the World Games with the promise of more to come – but with Rio set to host the Olympics in 2016 and the USA such a powerhouse of the summer Games, the Pan Ams held special significance.

Eight teams – four each from CONSUR (South America) and NACRA (North America/Caribbean) – competed over two days and gave the biggest crowd in the history of Mexican rugby, some 5,000 spectators, a scintillating glimpse of what Sevens will bring to the Olympics. In the last medal match of the 26th edition of the Games in Guadalajara, Canada defeated Argentina 26–24 to strike gold. USA claimed the bronze after beating Uruguay 21–17 with a try at the death.

Elsewhere in the Americas, while Canada's men proved too strong at the Pan American Games, Guyana retained their NACRA Sevens title, defeating Cayman Islands 31–0 in the final. As well as strengthening their Sevens grip over the Caribbean, Guyana also earned a place at the Hong Kong Sevens for the first time.

The 2012 edition doubled as the regional qualifier for the Moscow showpiece. Held in Ottawa in late August, the tournament was hard-fought with hosts Canada emerging victorious and USA qualifying as runners-up.

However, it was South America's tournament which provided arguably the biggest shock of the regional calendar in 2012, with Uruguay's men winning their first CONSUR title by beating Argentina 17–14 in the final. With Rio hosting its first international Sevens tournament, Argentina lost their first ever South American Championship and only their second match ever at this level.

With Brazil's women also competing and winning alongside the men, the tournament proved a success for Rio and was attended by members of the Rio 2016 Organising Committee. Next year's event in Rio, which will complete the RWC Sevens 2013 field, has a lot to live up to!

EUROPE

For two seasons now, FIRA-AER's newly branded Sevens 'Grand Prix' Series has provided an added impetus to competition in Europe with all of the major nations competing and many World Series stars on show.

Having lost out the previous year to Portugal and finished as Series runners-up, England's full-time Sevens players showed renewed vigour in winning the opening rounds in Lyon and Moscow.

Those successes set up a strong position and, although France played supremely well to win the last round in Denmark, beating Portugal in the final, England had done enough to finish top of the standings and be crowned European champions.

The top 12 in Europe – save for the three pre-qualified teams England, Wales and Russia – then headed to the Algarve Sevens in Portugal for the region's RWC Sevens qualifier. Portugal once again proved themselves in beating Spain to top spot, while France, Georgia and Scotland also qualified for Moscow.

Women's
Rugby

WORLD CUP WIN IS THE AIM

Ali Donnelly speaks to Michaela Staniford

Michaela Staniford holds the IRB Women's Sevens Challenge Cup after England's win at Twickenham.

A **whirlwind year** for Michaela Staniford was perfectly capped when she was named "best player" of the IRB Women's Sevens Challenge Cup events.

The experienced international campaigner, who has more than 50 Test caps, had once been England's youngest-ever player at the age of 17, but she has now grown into one of her country's most reliable and senior leaders.

At just 25, Staniford is recognised as a true cross-Sevens and Fifteens star, but as the short form of the Game continues to grow exponentially it's in Sevens she is predominantly expected to feature in the years to come.

Of all of England's leading players, Staniford is the one who has had the busiest season, kick-started when she turned out against the world champion Black Ferns in November 2011 at Twickenham and topped off fittingly when she helped England secure their Rugby World Cup Sevens 2013 spot in Moscow and lift the European title at the same time.

"I wasn't expecting to play in the New Zealand Tests to be honest and was expecting to be focusing on going to Dubai to play Sevens with a younger developmental squad in December. But when Gary [Street] spoke to me after a couple of games in France and said he wanted me to play in the first two Test games, one of which was at Twickenham, I didn't hesitate," recalls Staniford.

England's three Tests against New Zealand were historic – the first time they have beaten the world champions in successive games and doing so in superb style to banish the ghosts of the Women's Rugby World Cup 2010 Final.

Staniford believes it marked a big turning point for the senior side. "The Test series was fantastic, and mentally it was vital in proving that the steps we've made since the last World Cup have been very positive."

Having played back-to-back Tests in a four-day period, Staniford jetted out to Dubai to join a young squad who surpassed all expectations in reaching the final and beating the reigning Sevens world champions Australia along the way.

Losing to the then dominant Canada in the final was no disgrace, with a number of new faces such as Joanne Watmore and Leanne Riley putting their hands up for selection for the bigger tournaments later in the season.

For Staniford, beating Australia was a highlight. "The last time I had played them they had knocked us out of the World Cup in 2009, also in Dubai. That was a horrible memory, so to banish that somewhat felt pretty good. That Dubai tournament really set the tone for the rest of the season."

Heading into the new year, Staniford was in the unenviable position of juggling her fitness and training to suit both a Sevens and Fifteens programme, given her hopes of playing in the Women's Six Nations and then focusing on major Sevens tournament such as Hong Kong and London.

"It isn't as tough as you think because the way I look at it is that the fitness work I do for Sevens is only going to benefit the rest of my rugby. In Sevens the training is more compact and intense because you're preparing to play a lot of games in two days and there is no hiding on

WOMEN'S RUGBY

that big pitch so you have got to be pretty sharp. Over the last few years, I have been looking at more repeated speeds and circuit weights as opposed to just power so there has been a slight shift but we have fantastic conditioning coaches who help me balance it out."

Another successful Women's Six Nations came and went for England, with Staniford being handed the honour of running out first against France to mark her 50th cap. It's a memory she savours.

"It was nerve-wracking and I made a few basic errors in the game, but it was a very proud moment for me. I was presented my cap in a ceremony after the game with the men's senior side there so it was special. Getting 50 caps for England isn't easy. We have so many good young players and there is plenty of rotation, but there is still an awful lot more I want to achieve in that set-up. We still haven't won a World Cup and that's a huge aim for us."

On the Sevens front, the next big tournament was Hong Kong, with Staniford and teammates heading there right after the end of the Six Nations. What ensued was a superb women's tournament played in front of huge crowds, and a final which, broadcast live on TV around the world, was one of the highlights of the entire season.

A lung-busting effort saw England prevail 15–10 over Australia and Staniford says it was definitely as hard as it looked.

"I have never, ever experienced fatigue like in that final. We were up against a very good Australian side who are very rugby savvy so we knew it was going to be tough. But we hadn't bargained for the ball staying in play for over nine minutes in the first half. The pitch was massive and that never happens! Jo [Watmore] scored before half-time and you look around and both sets of players had their hands on their knees just chewing the air."

The success of Hong Kong was quickly followed by more at Twickenham as Staniford led England to a big win against the Netherlands, who had stunned Australia in the semi-final. "It was great to play at home and as we went a few scores up early I think we were able to enjoy it a bit more."

At the post-match function she was stunned to receive her 'best player' accolade. "I had no idea that there even was an award. They showed a montage of the women's tournament which was nice and then they mentioned some names and I was called up. It was a complete shock and I was more nervous to have to speak in front of everyone than winning it!"

As England headed off to take part in the Amsterdam Sevens and then to Ameland for the first leg of the European Championships, Staniford was understandably rested after a heavy season of action, saving herself for the second leg of the Europeans and the RWC Sevens 2013 qualifier in Moscow.

The rest also allowed her to focus on her work as a PE teacher at Rickmansworth, her old school who have been so supportive in her quest to reach the top of the Women's Game.

"It had been such a full-on year to that point that I understood I needed a rest and that it was a time to give other people a go. It was a good time for me to give my work and day-job a bit of attention too. They have been so fantastic in giving me time off, I cannot imagine how I would be able to do what I do in the rugby world without them."

Staniford was back in time to head to Moscow and secure England's place at RWC Sevens 2013 and is now looking forward to another huge season of rugby.

England will again play New Zealand in three Tests in November and December, the International Rugby Board are set to launch the first ever Women's Sevens World Series and, of course, there is the small matter of the RWC Sevens in Moscow next year. Staniford hopes to be involved in everything. "I would love to do it all again, but it is World Cup year so that decision will be down to the coaches."

Staniford also professes delight with the progress women's rugby has made in recent years, particularly at Sevens level. "People used to view Sevens as a bit more of an end-of-season thing and it is now going in the right direction. The World Series next year will be massive and Sevens is already changing stereotypes and is shifting ignorance on the Women's Game. I can't wait for next season."

THE FUTURE IS BRIGHT FOR WOMEN'S RUGBY

By Ali Donnelly, editor of scrumqueens.com

WOMEN'S RUGBY

Getty Images

Nathalie Marchino of the USA hands off Australia's Debby Hodgkinson during the IRB Women's Challenge Cup quarter-final at Twickenham.

The explosion of Sevens has been the real story in women's rugby over the past year as the lure of Olympic participation has seen the short form of the Game boom around the world.

The finals of the three IRB Women's Sevens Challenge Cup tournaments in Dubai, Hong Kong and London were played in front of huge crowds and broadcast audiences, giving the sport a regular major global window. The breath-taking final in Hong Kong in particular, between England and Australia, will live long in the memory, with Rugby World Cup-winning coach Sir Clive Woodward describing it afterwards as the best game of the entire tournament.

The growing interest in Sevens has also seen a parallel rise in the number of major tournaments showcasing the Women's Game as the International Rugby Board prepares to launch its first ever Women's Sevens World Series.

By the end of August a huge round of qualifying for Women's Rugby World Cup Sevens 2013 had taken place with involvement from almost every European country and an increase in participation in Asia, South America and Oceania – and there is more to come.

The IRB Women's Sevens World Series is set to be launched in time for the start of the 2012/13 season, with selection to participate in the Series linked to performances in IRB-funded regional women's Sevens tournaments and other international women's Sevens events.

In the first Challenge Cup in Dubai in December 2011, eight of the world's leading sides competed in Australia, Canada, Spain, Brazil, England, USA, China and South Africa. Canada had been the side who had set all the early running in international women's Sevens, and it was no huge surprise that they capped a superb few months with a display full of pace, power and commitment to beat a young England side 26–7 to lift the trophy.

That first IRB sanctioned tournament heralded a key landmark in the evolution of the Women's Game en route to the 2016 Olympics in Rio as all eyes turned to Hong Kong for the second Challenge Cup.

This time four extra teams took part, and in a fantastic finale to a great tournament England's Jo Watmore grabbed the limelight with two well-taken tries, the second late in the game to secure the win over the reigning world champions Australia.

The final IRB Women's Sevens Challenge Cup was held in London in May and England were again crowned victors following an emphatic 34–7 win over a brave Netherlands outfit who had made their first major final.

A record number of European sides were then in action in an effort to grab one of the region's places at RWC Sevens 2013. Twenty-two sides began the process with pre-qualifiers in Sofia and Ghent with Ireland, Wales, Scotland and Croatia coming through to join the top 12 seeds in the finale in Moscow.

With five spots up for grabs – not to mention a European title – it was a tense weekend for the 16 teams taking part. In the end England were crowned European Sevens champions with a 27–7 win over Spain in the final. Both sides had already qualified for RWC Sevens and would be joined by the Netherlands, Ireland and France.

By the end of August, Canada had also confirmed their place in Moscow through the NACRA qualifier, joining the European quintet and automatic qualifiers, defending champions Australia, New Zealand, USA, South Africa and hosts Russia. Tunisia created a piece of history by winning the African qualifier in Morocco at the end of September, beating both Uganda and Kenya in the knockout stages. A week later Fiji won the Asian qualifier to book their place at RWC Sevens 2013 along with China and Japan. Fiji impressed through the tournament in India, having joined the Asian qualifier after finishing as the best placed team behind New Zealand and Australia at the Oceania qualifier in August. This leaves only one place remaining, for the South American champions who will be known in late February.

Elsewhere in Sevens, there has been news from all corners of the globe in the growth of the Game, with a number of Asian and South American tournaments becoming more popular and coverage growing with every tournament.

Brazil continue to reign in South America after winning their eighth consecutive South American title in March. The Brazilians also played in the IRB Women's Sevens Challenge Cup events and, as hosts of the 2016 Olympic Games in Rio de Janeiro, there is no question they will continue to make strides in Sevens.

Initial fears that the lure of Olympic medals would mean that countries would start to move away from 15-a-side rugby have so far proven groundless. Over the past year more than 30 nations played Test rugby and the Game continued to grow and expand into new territories. A number of developing nations made their Test debuts in Switzerland, Laos and the Philippines, while several others, including China, Thailand and Uzbekistan, returned to Fifteens after a break of several years.

Away from Sevens, the major news was the world champion Black Ferns' tour to England in November 2011 which pitted the world's top two teams against each other for the first time since the Women's Rugby World Cup 2010 final. New Zealand had had limited preparation time, but the three matches were expected to be extremely tight and so it proved first up at Twickenham where England won 10–0.

Three days later a younger England side enjoyed a more emphatic 21–7 win before the tour wrapped up with an 8–8 stalemate as the effort of three matches in a week took its toll. England, though, had dismissed the idea that the world champions were unbeatable.

The season's other major tournament – the RBS Women's Six Nations – was also dominated once again by England who, led by captain Katy McLean, swept to a sixth Grand Slam in seven years, this time without conceding a single try across the five games.

The 2012 European Cup was slightly more subdued than usual, with most sides opting to focus on their RWC Sevens qualification programme. **127**

Just four sides entered the oldest tournament in women's rugby with usual attendees Wales, Ireland and Scotland choosing not to take part. Perhaps the most telling impact of Sevens on the nations with smaller playing numbers was with Spain, who, with a side devoid of Sevens stars, suffered heavy losses at the tournament. The final was a thriller nonetheless with England crowned champions after scoring a late try to seal a 29–25 win over France.

Looking ahead to the next 12 months it is likely that Sevens will take centre stage in this RWC Sevens year. But before then New Zealand will be back in London in November and teams will try to end England's dominance of the Six Nations.

The challenge for most nations, certainly those qualified for RWC Sevens 2013, will be the balance of competing in both Sevens and Fifteens. Women's rugby has come a long way, and participation at Rio 2016 for many will be the ultimate, but it is not a sport which commandeers the huge playing numbers needed just yet to rely on two completely different sets of players per country.

The key word, however, is "yet". Numbers are growing across the sport and it won't be long before Sevens specialists focus on just that, particularly as the clamber to secure spots on the World Series grows each year.

There is much to look forward to.

WOMEN'S RUGBY

Leanne Thompson of Auckland Blues passes during a Regional Women's Sevens tournament match.

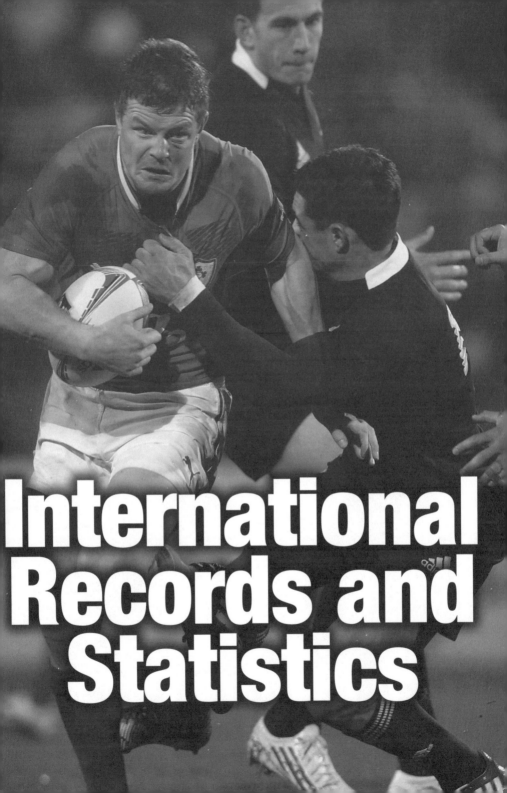

International
Records and
Statistics

INTERNATIONAL RUGBY BOARD

In partnership with

 WORLD ANTI-DOPING AGENCY
play true

Sam Warburton, Wales
IRB Anti-Doping Ambassador

Doping can ruin you and Rugby.
Join us in the fight against doping –
Keep Rugby Clean!

KEEP RUGBY CLEAN
IRB ANTI-DOPING

INTERNATIONAL RECORDS

RESULTS OF INTERNATIONAL MATCHES

UP TO 10 OCTOBER 2012

Cap matches involving senior executive council member unions only. Years for International Championship matches are for the second half of the season: eg 1972 means season 1971–72. Years for matches against touring teams from the Southern Hemisphere refer to the actual year of the match.

Points-scoring was first introduced in 1886, when an International Board was formed by Scotland, Ireland and Wales. Points values varied among the countries until 1890, when England agreed to join the Board, and uniform values were adopted.

Northern Hemisphere seasons	Try	Conversion	Penalty goal	Dropped goal	Goal from mark
1890–91	1	2	2	3	3
1891–92 to 1892–93	2	3	3	4	4
1893–94 to 1904–05	3	2	3	4	4
1905–06 to 1947–48	3	2	3	4	3
1948–49 to 1970–71	3	2	3	3	3
1971–72 to 1991–92	4	2	3	3	3*
1992–93 onwards	5	2	3	3	–

The goal from mark ceased to exist when the free-kick clause was introduced, 1977–78.

WC indicates a fixture played during the Rugby World Cup finals. LC indicates a fixture played in the Latin Cup. TN indicates a fixture played in the Tri Nations. RC indicates a fixture played in the Rugby Championship.

ENGLAND v SCOTLAND

Played 130 England won 70, Scotland won 42, Drawn 18
Highest scores England 43–3 in 2001 and 43–22 in 2005, Scotland 33–6 in 1986
Biggest wins England 43–3 in 2001, Scotland 33–6 in 1986

1871	Raeburn Place (Edinburgh) **Scotland** 1G 1T to 1T		1911	Twickenham **England** 13–8
1872	The Oval (London) **England** 1G 1DG 2T to 1DG		1912	Inverleith **Scotland** 8–3
1873	Glasgow **Drawn** no score		1913	Twickenham **England** 3–0
1874	The Oval **England** 1DG to 1T		1914	Inverleith **England** 16–15
1875	Raeburn Place **Drawn** no score		1920	Twickenham **England** 13–4
1876	The Oval **England** 1G 1T to 0		1921	Inverleith **England** 18–0
1877	Raeburn Place **Scotland** 1 DG to 0		1922	Twickenham **England** 11–5
1878	The Oval **Drawn** no score		1923	Inverleith **England** 8–6
1879	Raeburn Place **Drawn** Scotland 1DG England 1G		1924	Twickenham **England** 19–0
1880	Manchester **England** 2G 3T to 1G		1925	Murrayfield **Scotland** 14–11
1881	Raeburn Place **Drawn** Scotland 1G 1T England 1DG 1T		1926	Twickenham **Scotland** 17–9
			1927	Murrayfield **Scotland** 21–13
1882	Manchester **Scotland** 2T to 0		1928	Twickenham **England** 6–0
1883	Raeburn Place **England** 2T to 1T		1929	Murrayfield **Scotland** 12–6
1884	Blackheath (London) **England** 1G to 1T		1930	Twickenham **Drawn** 0–0
1885	No Match		1931	Murrayfield **Scotland** 28–19
1886	Raeburn Place **Drawn** no score		1932	Twickenham **England** 16–3
1887	Manchester **Drawn** 1T each		1933	Murrayfield **Scotland** 3–0
1888	No Match		1934	Twickenham **England** 6–3
1889	No Match		1935	Murrayfield **Scotland** 10–7
1890	Raeburn Place **England** 1G 1T to 0		1936	Twickenham **England** 9–8
1891	Richmond (London) **Scotland** 9–3		1937	Murrayfield **England** 6–3
1892	Raeburn Place **England** 5–0		1938	Twickenham **Scotland** 21–16
1893	Leeds **Scotland** 8–0		1939	Murrayfield **England** 9–6
1894	Raeburn Place **Scotland** 6–0		1947	Twickenham **England** 24–5
1895	Richmond **Scotland** 6–3		1948	Murrayfield **Scotland** 6–3
1896	Glasgow **Scotland** 11–0		1949	Twickenham **England** 19–3
1897	Manchester **England** 12–3		1950	Murrayfield **Scotland** 13–11
1898	Powderhall (Edinburgh) **Drawn** 3–3		1951	Twickenham **England** 5–3
1899	Blackheath **Scotland** 5–0		1952	Murrayfield **England** 19–3
1900	Inverleith (Edinburgh) **Drawn** 0–0		1953	Twickenham **England** 26–8
1901	Blackheath **Scotland** 18–3		1954	Murrayfield **England** 13–3
1902	Inverleith **England** 6–3		1955	Twickenham **England** 9–6
1903	Richmond **Scotland** 10–6		1956	Murrayfield **England** 11–6
1904	Inverleith **Scotland** 6–3		1957	Twickenham **England** 16–3
1905	Richmond **Scotland** 8–0		1958	Murrayfield **Drawn** 3–3
1906	Inverleith **England** 9–3		1959	Twickenham **Drawn** 3–3
1907	Blackheath **Scotland** 8–3		1960	Murrayfield **England** 21–12
1908	Inverleith **Scotland** 16–10		1961	Twickenham **England** 6–0
1909	Richmond **Scotland** 18–8		1962	Murrayfield **Drawn** 3–3
1910	Inverleith **England** 14–5		1963	Twickenham **England** 10–8
			1964	Murrayfield **Scotland** 15–6
			1965	Twickenham **Drawn** 3–3
			1966	Murrayfield **Scotland** 6–3

1967	Twickenham **England** 27–14		1990	Murrayfield **Scotland** 13–7
1968	Murrayfield **England** 8–6		1991	Twickenham **England** 21–12
1969	Twickenham **England** 8–3		1991	Murrayfield WC **England** 9–6
1970	Murrayfield **Scotland** 14–5		1992	Murrayfield **England** 25–7
1971	Twickenham **Scotland** 16–15		1993	Twickenham **England** 26–12
1971	Murrayfield **Scotland** 26–6		1994	Murrayfield **England** 15–14
Special centenary match – non-championship			1995	Twickenham **England** 24–12
1972	Murrayfield **Scotland** 23–9		1996	Murrayfield **England** 18–9
1973	Twickenham **England** 20–13		1997	Twickenham **England** 41–13
1974	Murrayfield **Scotland** 16–14		1998	Murrayfield **England** 34–20
1975	Twickenham **England** 7–6		1999	Twickenham **England** 24–21
1976	Murrayfield **Scotland** 22–12		2000	Murrayfield **Scotland** 19–13
1977	Twickenham **England** 26–6		2001	Twickenham **England** 43–3
1978	Murrayfield **England** 15–0		2002	Murrayfield **England** 29–3
1979	Twickenham **Drawn** 7–7		2003	Twickenham **England** 40–9
1980	Murrayfield **England** 30–18		2004	Murrayfield **England** 35–13
1981	Twickenham **England** 23–17		2005	Twickenham **England** 43–22
1982	Murrayfield **Drawn** 9–9		2006	Murrayfield **Scotland** 18–12
1983	Twickenham **Scotland** 22–12		2007	Twickenham **England** 42–20
1984	Murrayfield **Scotland** 18–6		2008	Murrayfield **Scotland** 15–9
1985	Twickenham **England** 10–7		2009	Twickenham **England** 26–12
1986	Murrayfield **Scotland** 33–6		2010	Murrayfield **Drawn** 15–15
1987	Twickenham **England** 21–12		2011	Twickenham **England** 22–16
1988	Murrayfield **England** 9–6		2011	Auckland WC **England** 16–12
1989	Twickenham **Drawn** 12–12		2012	Murrayfield **England** 13–6

ENGLAND v IRELAND

Played 126 England won 72, Ireland won 46, Drawn 8
Highest scores England 50–18 in 2000, Ireland 43–13 in 2007
Biggest wins England 46–6 in 1997, Ireland 43–13 in 2007

1875	The Oval (London) **England** 1G 1DG 1T to 0		1891	Dublin **England** 9–0
1876	Dublin **England** 1G 1T to 0		1892	Manchester **England** 7–0
1877	The Oval **England** 2G 2T to 0		1893	Dublin **England** 4–0
1878	Dublin **England** 2G 1T to 0		1894	Blackheath **Ireland** 7–5
1879	The Oval **England** 2G 1DG 2T to 0		1895	Dublin **England** 6–3
1880	Dublin **England** 1G 1T to 1T		1896	Leeds **Ireland** 10–4
1881	Manchester **England** 2G 2T to 0		1897	Dublin **Ireland** 13–9
1882	Dublin **Drawn** 2T each		1898	Richmond (London) **Ireland** 9–6
1883	Manchester **England** 1G 3T to 1T		1899	Dublin **Ireland** 6–0
1884	Dublin **England** 1G to 0		1900	Richmond **England** 15–4
1885	Manchester **England** 2T to 1T		1901	Dublin **Ireland** 10–6
1886	Dublin **England** 1T to 0		1902	Leicester **England** 6–3
1887	Dublin **Ireland** 2G to 0		1903	Dublin **Ireland** 6–0
1888	No Match		1904	Blackheath **England** 19–0
1889	No Match		1905	Cork **Ireland** 17–3
1890	Blackheath (London) **England** 3T to 0		1906	Leicester **Ireland** 16–6
			1907	Dublin **Ireland** 17–9

1908	Richmond	**England** 13–3
1909	Dublin	**England** 11–5
1910	Twickenham	**Drawn** 0–0
1911	Dublin	**Ireland** 3–0
1912	Twickenham	**England** 15–0
1913	Dublin	**England** 15–4
1914	Twickenham	**England** 17–12
1920	Dublin	**England** 14–11
1921	Twickenham	**England** 15–0
1922	Dublin	**England** 12–3
1923	Leicester	**England** 23–5
1924	Belfast	**England** 14–3
1925	Twickenham	**Drawn** 6–6
1926	Dublin	**Ireland** 19–15
1927	Twickenham	**England** 8–6
1928	Dublin	**England** 7–6
1929	Twickenham	**Ireland** 6–5
1930	Dublin	**Ireland** 4–3
1931	Twickenham	**Ireland** 6–5
1932	Dublin	**England** 11–8
1933	Twickenham	**England** 17–6
1934	Dublin	**England** 13–3
1935	Twickenham	**England** 14–3
1936	Dublin	**Ireland** 6–3
1937	Twickenham	**England** 9–8
1938	Dublin	**England** 36–14
1939	Twickenham	**Ireland** 5–0
1947	Dublin	**Ireland** 22–0
1948	Twickenham	**Ireland** 11–10
1949	Dublin	**Ireland** 14–5
1950	Twickenham	**England** 3–0
1951	Dublin	**Ireland** 3–0
1952	Twickenham	**England** 3–0
1953	Dublin	**Drawn** 9–9
1954	Twickenham	**England** 14–3
1955	Dublin	**Drawn** 6–6
1956	Twickenham	**England** 20–0
1957	Dublin	**England** 6–0
1958	Twickenham	**England** 6–0
1959	Dublin	**England** 3–0
1960	Twickenham	**England** 8–5
1961	Dublin	**Ireland** 11–8
1962	Twickenham	**England** 16–0
1963	Dublin	**Drawn** 0–0
1964	Twickenham	**Ireland** 18–5
1965	Dublin	**Ireland** 5–0
1966	Twickenham	**Drawn** 6–6
1967	Dublin	**England** 8–3
1968	Twickenham	**Drawn** 9–9

1969	Dublin	**Ireland** 17–15
1970	Twickenham	**England** 9–3
1971	Dublin	**England** 9–6
1972	Twickenham	**Ireland** 16–12
1973	Dublin	**Ireland** 18–9
1974	Twickenham	**Ireland** 26–21
1975	Dublin	**Ireland** 12–9
1976	Twickenham	**Ireland** 13–12
1977	Dublin	**England** 4–0
1978	Twickenham	**England** 15–9
1979	Dublin	**Ireland** 12–7
1980	Twickenham	**England** 24–9
1981	Dublin	**England** 10–6
1982	Twickenham	**Ireland** 16–15
1983	Dublin	**Ireland** 25–15
1984	Twickenham	**England** 12–9
1985	Dublin	**Ireland** 13–10
1986	Twickenham	**England** 25–20
1987	Dublin	**Ireland** 17–0
1988	Twickenham	**England** 35–3
1988	Dublin	**England** 21–10
		Non-championship match
1989	Dublin	**England** 16–3
1990	Twickenham	**England** 23–0
1991	Dublin	**England** 16–7
1992	Twickenham	**England** 38–9
1993	Dublin	**Ireland** 17–3
1994	Twickenham	**Ireland** 13–12
1995	Dublin	**England** 20–8
1996	Twickenham	**England** 28–15
1997	Dublin	**England** 46–6
1998	Twickenham	**England** 35–17
1999	Dublin	**England** 27–15
2000	Twickenham	**England** 50–18
2001	Dublin	**Ireland** 20–14
2002	Twickenham	**England** 45–11
2003	Dublin	**England** 42–6
2004	Twickenham	**Ireland** 19–13
2005	Dublin	**Ireland** 19–13
2006	Twickenham	**Ireland** 28–24
2007	Dublin	**Ireland** 43–13
2008	Twickenham	**England** 33–10
2009	Dublin	**Ireland** 14–13
2010	Twickenham	**Ireland** 20–16
2011	Dublin	**Ireland** 24–8
2011	Dublin	**England** 20–9
		Non-championship match
2012	Twickenham	**England** 30–9

ENGLAND v WALES

Played 123 England won 56 Wales won 55, Drawn 12
Highest scores England 62–5 in 2007, Wales 34–21 in 1967
Biggest wins England 62–5 in 2007, Wales 25–0 in 1905

1881	Blackheath (London) **England** 7G 1DG 6T to 0	1929	Twickenham **England** 8–3
1882	No Match	1930	Cardiff **England** 11–3
1883	Swansea **England** 2G 4T to 0	1931	Twickenham **Drawn** 11–11
1884	Leeds **England** 1G 2T to 1G	1932	Swansea **Wales** 12–5
1885	Swansea **England** 1G 4T to 1G 1T	1933	Twickenham **Wales** 7–3
1886	Blackheath **England** 1GM 2T to 1G	1934	Cardiff **England** 9–0
1887	Llanelli **Drawn** no score	1935	Twickenham **Drawn** 3–3
1888	No Match	1936	Swansea **Drawn** 0–0
1889	No Match	1937	Twickenham **England** 4–3
1890	Dewsbury **Wales** 1T to 0	1938	Cardiff **Wales** 14–8
1891	Newport **England** 7–3	1939	Twickenham **England** 3–0
1892	Blackheath **England** 17–0	1947	Cardiff **England** 9–6
1893	Cardiff **Wales** 12–11	1948	Twickenham **Drawn** 3–3
1894	Birkenhead **England** 24–3	1949	Cardiff **Wales** 9–3
1895	Swansea **England** 14–6	1950	Twickenham **Wales** 11–5
1896	Blackheath **England** 25–0	1951	Swansea **Wales** 23–5
1897	Newport **Wales** 11–0	1952	Twickenham **Wales** 8–6
1898	Blackheath **England** 14–7	1953	Cardiff **England** 8–3
1899	Swansea **Wales** 26–3	1954	Twickenham **England** 9–6
1900	Gloucester **Wales** 13–3	1955	Cardiff **Wales** 3–0
1901	Cardiff **Wales** 13–0	1956	Twickenham **Wales** 8–3
1902	Blackheath **Wales** 9–8	1957	Cardiff **England** 3–0
1903	Swansea **Wales** 21–5	1958	Twickenham **Drawn** 3–3
1904	Leicester **Drawn** 14–14	1959	Cardiff **Wales** 5–0
1905	Cardiff **Wales** 25–0	1960	Twickenham **England** 14–6
1906	Richmond (London) **Wales** 16–3	1961	Cardiff **Wales** 6–3
1907	Swansea **Wales** 22–0	1962	Twickenham **Drawn** 0–0
1908	Bristol **Wales** 28–18	1963	Cardiff **England** 13–6
1909	Cardiff **Wales** 8–0	1964	Twickenham **Drawn** 6–6
1910	Twickenham **England** 11–6	1965	Cardiff **Wales** 14–3
1911	Swansea **Wales** 15–11	1966	Twickenham **Wales** 11–6
1912	Twickenham **England** 8–0	1967	Cardiff **Wales** 34–21
1913	Cardiff **England** 12–0	1968	Twickenham **Drawn** 11–11
1914	Twickenham **England** 10–9	1969	Cardiff **Wales** 30–9
1920	Swansea **Wales** 19–5	1970	Twickenham **Wales** 17–13
1921	Twickenham **England** 18–3	1971	Cardiff **Wales** 22–6
1922	Cardiff **Wales** 28–6	1972	Twickenham **Wales** 12–3
1923	Twickenham **England** 7–3	1973	Cardiff **Wales** 25–9
1924	Swansea **England** 17–9	1974	Twickenham **England** 16–12
1925	Twickenham **England** 12–6	1975	Cardiff **Wales** 20–4
1926	Cardiff **Drawn** 3–3	1976	Twickenham **Wales** 21–9
1927	Twickenham **England** 11–9	1977	Cardiff **Wales** 14–9
1928	Swansea **England** 10–8	1978	Twickenham **Wales** 9–6
		1979	Cardiff **Wales** 27–3

1980	Twickenham **England** 9–8	2001	Cardiff **England** 44–15
1981	Cardiff **Wales** 21–19	2002	Twickenham **England** 50–10
1982	Twickenham **England** 17–7	2003	Cardiff **England** 26–9
1983	Cardiff **Drawn** 13–13	2003	Cardiff **England** 43–9
1984	Twickenham **Wales** 24–15		Non-championship match
1985	Cardiff **Wales** 24–15	2003	Brisbane WC **England** 28–17
1986	Twickenham **England** 21–18	2004	Twickenham **England** 31–21
1987	Cardiff **Wales** 19–12	2005	Cardiff **Wales** 11–9
1987	Brisbane WC **Wales** 16–3	2006	Twickenham **England** 47–13
1988	Twickenham **Wales** 11–3	2007	Cardiff **Wales** 27–18
1989	Cardiff **Wales** 12–9	2007	Twickenham **England** 62–5
1990	Twickenham **England** 34–6		Non-championship match
1991	Cardiff **England** 25–6	2008	Twickenham **Wales** 26–19
1992	Twickenham **England** 24–0	2009	Cardiff **Wales** 23–15
1993	Cardiff **Wales** 10–9	2010	Twickenham **England** 30–17
1994	Twickenham **England** 15–8	2011	Cardiff **England** 26–19
1995	Cardiff **England** 23–9	2011	Twickenham **England** 23–19
1996	Twickenham **England** 21–15		Non-championship match
1997	Cardiff **England** 34–13	2011	Cardiff **Wales** 19–9
1998	Twickenham **England** 60–26		Non-championship match
1999	Wembley **Wales** 32–31	2012	Twickenham **Wales** 19–12
2000	Twickenham **England** 46–12		

ENGLAND v FRANCE

Played 96 England won 52, France won 37, Drawn 7
Highest scores England 48–19 in 2001, France 37–12 in 1972
Biggest wins England 37–0 in 1911, France 37–12 in 1972 and 31–6 in 2006

1906	Paris **England** 35–8	1931	Paris **France** 14–13
1907	Richmond (London) **England** 41–13	1947	Twickenham **England** 6–3
1908	Paris **England** 19–0	1948	Paris **France** 15–0
1909	Leicester **England** 22–0	1949	Twickenham **England** 8–3
1910	Paris **England** 11–3	1950	Paris **France** 6–3
1911	Twickenham **England** 37–0	1951	Twickenham **France** 11–3
1912	Paris **England** 18–8	1952	Paris **England** 6–3
1913	Twickenham **England** 20–0	1953	Twickenham **England** 11–0
1914	Paris **England** 39–13	1954	Paris **France** 11–3
1920	Twickenham **England** 8–3	1955	Twickenham **France** 16–9
1921	Paris **England** 10–6	1956	Paris **France** 14–9
1922	Twickenham **Drawn** 11–11	1957	Twickenham **England** 9–5
1923	Paris **England** 12–3	1958	Paris **England** 14–0
1924	Twickenham **England** 19–7	1959	Twickenham **Drawn** 3–3
1925	Paris **England** 13–11	1960	Paris **Drawn** 3–3
1926	Twickenham **England** 11–0	1961	Twickenham **Drawn** 5–5
1927	Paris **France** 3–0	1962	Paris **France** 13–0
1928	Twickenham **England** 18–8	1963	Twickenham **England** 6–5
1929	Paris **England** 16–6	1964	Paris **England** 6–3
1930	Twickenham **England** 11–5	1965	Twickenham **England** 9–6

INTERNATIONAL RECORDS

1966	Paris **France** 13–0		1995	Pretoria WC **France 19–9**
1967	Twickenham **France** 16–12		1996	Paris **France** 15–12
1968	Paris **France** 14–9		1997	Twickenham **France** 23–20
1969	Twickenham **England** 22–8		1998	Paris **France** 24–17
1970	Paris **France** 35–13		1999	Twickenham **England** 21–10
1971	Twickenham **Drawn** 14–14		2000	Paris **England** 15–9
1972	Paris **France** 37–12		2001	Twickenham **England** 48–19
1973	Twickenham **England** 14–6		2002	Paris **France** 20–15
1974	Paris **Drawn** 12–12		2003	Twickenham **England** 25–17
1975	Twickenham **France** 27–20		2003	Marseilles **France** 17–16
1976	Paris **France** 30–9			Non-championship match
1977	Twickenham **France** 4–3		2003	Twickenham **England** 45–14
1978	Paris **France** 15–6			Non-championship match
1979	Twickenham **England** 7–6		2003	Sydney WC **England** 24–7
1980	Paris **England** 17–13		2004	Paris **France** 24–21
1981	Twickenham **France** 16–12		2005	Twickenham **France** 18–17
1982	Paris **England** 27–15		2006	Paris **France** 31–6
1983	Twickenham **France** 19–15		2007	Twickenham **England** 26–18
1984	Paris **France** 32–18		2007	Twickenham **France** 21–15
1985	Twickenham **Drawn** 9–9			Non-championship match
1986	Paris **France** 29–10		2007	Marseilles **France** 22–9
1987	Twickenham **France** 19–15			Non-championship match
1988	Paris **France** 10–9		2007	Paris WC **England** 14–9
1989	Twickenham **England** 11–0		2008	Paris **England** 24–13
1990	Paris **England** 26–7		2009	Twickenham **England** 34–10
1991	Twickenham **England** 21–19		2010	Paris **France** 12–10
1991	Paris WC **England** 19–10		2011	Twickenham **England** 17–9
1992	Paris **England** 31–13		2011	Auckland WC **France** 19–12
1993	Twickenham **England** 16–15		2012	Paris **England** 24–22
1994	Paris **England** 18–14			
1995	Twickenham **England** 31–10			

ENGLAND v SOUTH AFRICA

Played 35 England won 12, South Africa won 21, Drawn 2
Highest scores England 53–3 in 2002, South Africa 58–10 in 2007
Biggest wins England 53–3 in 2002, South Africa 58–10 in 2007

1906	Crystal Palace (London) **Drawn** 3–3		1994	1 Pretoria **England** 32–15
1913	Twickenham **South Africa** 9–3			2 Cape Town **South Africa** 27–9
1932	Twickenham **South Africa** 7–0			Series drawn 1–1
1952	Twickenham **South Africa** 8–3		1995	Twickenham **South Africa** 24–14
1961	Twickenham **South Africa** 5–0		1997	Twickenham **South Africa** 29–11
1969	Twickenham **England** 11–8		1998	Cape Town **South Africa** 18–0
1972	Johannesburg **England** 18–9		1998	Twickenham **England** 13–7
1984	1 Port Elizabeth **South Africa** 33–15		1999	Paris WC **South Africa** 44–21
	2 Johannesburg **South Africa** 35–9		2000	1 Pretoria **South Africa** 18–13
	South Africa won series 2–0			2 Bloemfontein **England** 27–22
1992	Twickenham **England** 33–16			Series drawn 1–1

138

2000	Twickenham **England** 25–17		South Africa won series 2–0
2001	Twickenham **England** 29–9	2007	Paris WC **South Africa** 36–0
2002	Twickenham **England** 53–3	2007	Paris WC **South Africa** 15–6
2003	Perth WC **England** 25–6	2008	Twickenham **South Africa** 42–6
2004	Twickenham **England** 32–16	2010	Twickenham **South Africa** 21–11
2006	1 Twickenham **England** 23–21	2012	1 Durban **South Africa** 22–17
	2 Twickenham **South Africa** 25–14		2 Johannesburg **South Africa** 36–27
	Series drawn 1–1		3 Port Elizabeth **Drawn** 14–14
2007	1 Bloemfontein **South Africa** 58–10		South Africa won series 2–0 with
	2 Pretoria **South Africa** 55–22		one drawn

ENGLAND v NEW ZEALAND

Played 34 England won 6, New Zealand won 27, Drawn 1
Highest scores England 31–28 in 2002, New Zealand 64–22 in 1998
Biggest wins England 13–0 in 1936, New Zealand 64–22 in 1998

1905	Crystal Palace (London) **New Zealand** 15–0	1997	1 Manchester **New Zealand** 25–8
1925	Twickenham **New Zealand** 17–11		2 Twickenham **Drawn** 26–26
1936	Twickenham **England** 13–0		New Zealand won series 1–0, with 1 draw
1954	Twickenham **New Zealand** 5–0	1998	1 Dunedin **New Zealand** 64–22
1963	1 Auckland **New Zealand** 21–11		2 Auckland **New Zealand** 40–10
	2 Christchurch **New Zealand** 9–6		New Zealand won series 2–0
	New Zealand won series 2–0	1999	Twickenham WC **New Zealand** 30–16
1964	Twickenham **New Zealand** 14–0	2002	Twickenham **England** 31–28
1967	Twickenham **New Zealand** 23–11	2003	Wellington **England** 15–13
1973	Twickenham **New Zealand** 9–0	2004	1 Dunedin **New Zealand** 36–3
1973	Auckland **England** 16–10		2 Auckland **New Zealand** 36–12
1978	Twickenham **New Zealand** 16–6		New Zealand won series 2–0
1979	Twickenham **New Zealand** 10–9	2005	Twickenham **New Zealand** 23–19
1983	Twickenham **England** 15–9	2006	Twickenham **New Zealand** 41–20
1985	1 Christchurch **New Zealand** 18–13	2008	1 Auckland **New Zealand** 37–20
	2 Wellington **New Zealand** 42–15		2 Christchurch **New Zealand** 44–12
	New Zealand won series 2–0		New Zealand won series 2–0
1991	Twickenham WC **New Zealand** 18–12	2008	Twickenham **New Zealand** 32–6
1993	Twickenham **England** 15–9	2009	Twickenham **New Zealand** 19–6
1995	Cape Town WC **New Zealand 45–29**	2010	Twickenham **New Zealand** 26–16

ENGLAND v AUSTRALIA

Played 40 England won 16, Australia won 23, Drawn 1
Highest scores England 35–18 in 2010, Australia 76–0 in 1998
Biggest wins England 20–3 in 1973, 23–6 in 1976 & 35–18 in 2010, Australia 76–0 in 1998

1909	Blackheath (London) **Australia** 9–3		1997	Twickenham **Drawn** 15–15
1928	Twickenham **England** 18–11		1998	Brisbane **Australia** 76–0
1948	Twickenham **Australia** 11–0		1998	Twickenham **Australia** 12–11
1958	Twickenham **England** 9–6		1999	Sydney **Australia** 22–15
1963	Sydney **Australia** 18–9		2000	Twickenham **England** 22–19
1967	Twickenham **Australia** 23–11		2001	Twickenham **England** 21–15
1973	Twickenham **England** 20–3		2002	Twickenham **England** 32–31
1975	1 Sydney **Australia** 16–9		2003	Melbourne **England** 25–14
	2 Brisbane **Australia** 30–21		2003	Sydney WC **England** 20–17 (aet)
	Australia won series 2–0		2004	Brisbane **Australia** 51–15
1976	Twickenham **England** 23–6		2004	Twickenham **Australia** 21–19
1982	Twickenham **England** 15–11		2005	Twickenham **England** 26–16
1984	Twickenham **Australia** 19–3		2006	1 Sydney **Australia** 34–3
1987	Sydney WC **Australia** 19–6			2 Melbourne **Australia** 43–18
1988	1 Brisbane **Australia** 22–16			Australia won series 2–0
	2 Sydney **Australia** 28–8		2007	Marseilles WC **England** 12–10
	Australia won series 2–0		2008	Twickenham **Australia** 28–14
1988	Twickenham **England** 28–19		2009	Twickenham **Australia** 18–9
1991	Sydney **Australia** 40–15		2010	1 Perth **Australia** 27–17
1991	Twickenham WC **Australia** 12–6			2 Sydney **England** 21–20
1995	Cape Town WC **England** 25–22			Series drawn 1–1
1997	Sydney **Australia** 25–6		2010	Twickenham **England** 35–18

ENGLAND v NEW ZEALAND NATIVES

Played 1 England won 1
Highest score England 7–0 in 1889, NZ Natives 0–7 in 1889
Biggest win England 7–0 in 1889, NZ Natives no win

1889	Blackheath **England** 1G 4T to 0

ENGLAND v RFU PRESIDENT'S XV

Played 1 President's XV won 1
Highest score England 11–28 in 1971, RFU President's XV 28–11 in 1971
Biggest win RFU President's XV 28–11 in 1971

1971	Twickenham **President's XV** 28–11

ENGLAND v ARGENTINA

Played 16 England won 11, Argentina won 4, Drawn 1
Highest scores England 51–0 in 1990, Argentina 33–13 in 1997
Biggest wins England 51–0 in 1990, Argentina 33–13 in 1997

1981	1 Buenos Aires **Drawn** 19–19			2 Buenos Aires **Argentina** 33–13
	2 Buenos Aires **England** 12–6			Series drawn 1–1
	England won series 1–0 with 1 draw		2000	Twickenham **England** 19–0
1990	1 Buenos Aires **England** 25–12		2002	Buenos Aires **England** 26–18
	2 Buenos Aires **Argentina** 15–13		2006	Twickenham **Argentina** 25–18
	Series drawn 1–1		2009	1 Manchester **England** 37–15
1990	Twickenham **England** 51–0			2 Salta **Argentina** 24–22
1995	Durban WC **England** 24–18			Series drawn 1–1
1996	Twickenham **England** 20–18		2009	Twickenham **England** 16–9
1997	1 Buenos Aires **England** 46–20		2011	Dunedin WC **England** 13–9

ENGLAND v ROMANIA

Played 5 England won 5
Highest scores England 134–0 in 2001, Romania 15–22 in 1985
Biggest win England 134–0 in 2001, Romania no win

1985	Twickenham **England** 22–15		2001	Twickenham **England** 134–0
1989	Bucharest **England** 58–3		2011	Dunedin WC **England** 67–3
1994	Twickenham **England** 54–3			

ENGLAND v JAPAN

Played 1 England won 1
Highest score England 60–7 in 1987, Japan 7–60 in 1987
Biggest win England 60–7 in 1987, Japan no win

1987	Sydney WC **England** 60–7

ENGLAND v UNITED STATES

Played 5 England won 5
Highest scores England 106–8 in 1999, United States 19–48 in 2001
Biggest win England 106–8 in 1999, United States no win

1987	Sydney WC **England** 34–6		2001	San Francisco **England** 48–19
1991	Twickenham WC **England** 37–9		2007	Lens WC **England** 28–10
1999	Twickenham **England** 106–8			

ENGLAND v FIJI

Played 4 England won 4
Highest scores England 58–23 in 1989, Fiji 24–45 in 1999
Biggest win England 58–23 in 1989, Fiji no win

1988	Suva **England** 25–12	1991	Suva **England** 28–12
1989	Twickenham **England** 58–23	1999	Twickenham WC **England** 45–24

ENGLAND v ITALY

Played 18 England won 18
Highest scores England 80–23 in 2001, Italy 23–80 in 2001
Biggest win England 67–7 in 1999, Italy no win

1991	Twickenham WC **England** 36–6	2004	Rome **England** 50–9
1995	Durban WC **England** 27–20	2005	Twickenham **England** 39–7
1996	Twickenham **England** 54–21	2006	Rome **England** 31–16
1998	Huddersfield **England** 23–15	2007	Twickenham **England** 20–7
1999	Twickenham WC **England** 67–7	2008	Rome **England** 23–19
2000	Rome **England** 59–12	2009	Twickenham **England** 36–11
2001	Twickenham **England** 80–23	2010	Rome **England** 17–12
2002	Rome **England** 45–9	2011	Twickenham **England** 59–13
2003	Twickenham **England** 40–5	2012	Rome **England** 19–15

ENGLAND v CANADA

Played 6 England won 6
Highest scores England 70–0 in 2004, Canada 20–59 in 2001
Biggest win England 70–0 in 2004, Canada no win

1992	Wembley **England** 26–13		2 Burnaby **England** 59–20
1994	Twickenham **England** 60–19		England won series 2–0
1999	Twickenham **England** 36–11	2004	Twickenham **England** 70–0
2001	1 Markham **England** 22–10		

ENGLAND v SAMOA

Played 6 England won 6
Highest scores England 44–22 in 1995 and 44–22 in 2007, Samoa 22–44 in 1995, 22–35 in 2003 and 22–44 in 2007
Biggest win England 40–3 in 2005, Samoa no win

1995	Durban WC **England** 44–22	2005	Twickenham **England** 40–3
1995	Twickenham **England** 27–9	2007	Nantes WC **England** 44–22
2003	Melbourne WC **England** 35–22	2010	Twickenham **England** 26–13

ENGLAND v THE NETHERLANDS

Played 1 England won 1
Highest scores England 110–0 in 1998, The Netherlands 0–110 in 1998
Biggest win England 110–0 in 1998, The Netherlands no win

1998	Huddersfield **England** 110–0	

ENGLAND v TONGA

Played 2 England won 2
Highest scores England 101–10 in 1999, Tonga 20–36 in 2007
Biggest win England 101–10 in 1999, Tonga no win

1999	Twickenham WC **England** 101–10	2007	Paris WC **England** 36–20

ENGLAND v GEORGIA

Played 2 England won 2
Highest scores England 84–6 in 2003, Georgia 10–41 in 2011
Biggest win England 84–6 in 2003, Georgia no win

2003	Perth WC **England** 84–6	2011	Dunedin WC **England** 41–10

ENGLAND v URUGUAY

Played 1 England won 1
Highest scores England 111–13 in 2003, Uruguay 13–111 in 2003
Biggest win England 111–13 in 2003, Uruguay no win

2003	Brisbane WC **England** 111–13	

ENGLAND v PACIFIC ISLANDS

Played 1 England won 1
Highest scores England 39–13 in 2008, Pacific Islands 13–39 in 2008
Biggest win England 39–13 in 2008, Pacific Islands no win

2008	Twickenham **England** 39–13	

Played 127 Scotland won 64, Ireland won 57, Drawn 5, Abandoned 1
Highest scores Scotland 38–10 in 1997, Ireland 44–22 in 2000
Biggest wins Scotland 38–10 in 1997, Ireland 36–6 in 2003

1877 Belfast **Scotland** 4G 2DG 2T to 0	1923 Dublin **Scotland** 13–3
1878 No Match	1924 Inverleith **Scotland** 13–8
1879 Belfast **Scotland** 1G 1DG 1T to 0	1925 Dublin **Scotland** 14–8
1880 Glasgow **Scotland** 1G 2DG 2T to 0	1926 Murrayfield **Ireland** 3–0
1881 Belfast **Ireland** 1DG to 1T	1927 Dublin **Ireland** 6–0
1882 Glasgow **Scotland** 2T to 0	1928 Murrayfield **Ireland** 13–5
1883 Belfast **Scotland** 1G 1T to 0	1929 Dublin **Scotland** 16–7
1884 Raeburn Place (Edinburgh) **Scotland** 2G 2T to 1T	1930 Murrayfield **Ireland** 14–11
	1931 Dublin **Ireland** 8–5
1885 Belfast **Abandoned** Ireland 0 Scotland 1T	1932 Murrayfield **Ireland** 20–8
1885 Raeburn Place **Scotland** 1G 2T to 0	1933 Dublin **Scotland** 8–6
1886 Raeburn Place **Scotland** 3G 1DG 2T to 0	1934 Murrayfield **Scotland** 16–9
	1935 Dublin **Ireland** 12–5
1887 Belfast **Scotland** 1G 1GM 2T to 0	1936 Murrayfield **Ireland** 10–4
1888 Raeburn Place **Scotland** 1G to 0	1937 Dublin **Ireland** 11–4
1889 Belfast **Scotland** 1DG to 0	1938 Murrayfield **Scotland** 23–14
1890 Raeburn Place **Scotland** 1DG 1T to 0	1939 Dublin **Ireland** 12–3
1891 Belfast **Scotland** 14–0	1947 Murrayfield **Ireland** 3–0
1892 Raeburn Place **Scotland** 2–0	1948 Dublin **Ireland** 6–0
1893 Belfast **Drawn** 0–0	1949 Murrayfield **Ireland** 13–3
1894 Dublin **Ireland** 5–0	1950 Dublin **Ireland** 21–0
1895 Raeburn Place **Scotland** 6–0	1951 Murrayfield **Ireland** 6–5
1896 Dublin **Drawn** 0–0	1952 Dublin **Ireland** 12–8
1897 Powderhall (Edinburgh) **Scotland** 8–3	1953 Murrayfield **Ireland** 26–8
1898 Belfast **Scotland** 8–0	1954 Belfast **Ireland** 6–0
1899 Inverleith (Edinburgh) **Ireland** 9–3	1955 Murrayfield **Scotland** 12–3
1900 Dublin **Drawn** 0–0	1956 Dublin **Ireland** 14–10
1901 Inverleith **Scotland** 9–5	1957 Murrayfield **Ireland** 5–3
1902 Belfast **Ireland** 5–0	1958 Dublin **Ireland** 12–6
1903 Inverleith **Scotland** 3–0	1959 Murrayfield **Ireland** 8–3
1904 Dublin **Scotland** 19–3	1960 Dublin **Scotland** 6–5
1905 Inverleith **Ireland** 11–5	1961 Murrayfield **Scotland** 16–8
1906 Dublin **Scotland** 13–6	1962 Dublin **Scotland** 20–6
1907 Inverleith **Scotland** 15–3	1963 Murrayfield **Scotland** 3–0
1908 Dublin **Ireland** 16–11	1964 Dublin **Scotland** 6–3
1909 Inverleith **Scotland** 9–3	1965 Murrayfield **Ireland** 16–6
1910 Belfast **Scotland** 14–0	1966 Dublin **Scotland** 11–3
1911 Inverleith **Ireland** 16–10	1967 Murrayfield **Ireland** 5–3
1912 Dublin **Ireland** 10–8	1968 Dublin **Ireland** 14–6
1913 Inverleith **Scotland** 29–14	1969 Murrayfield **Ireland** 16–0
1914 Dublin **Ireland** 6–0	1970 Dublin **Ireland** 16–11
1920 Inverleith **Scotland** 19–0	1971 Murrayfield **Ireland** 17–5
1921 Dublin **Ireland** 9–8	1972 No Match
1922 Inverleith **Scotland** 6–3	1973 Murrayfield **Scotland** 19–14

INTERNATIONAL RECORDS

144

1974	Dublin **Ireland** 9–6	1996	Dublin **Scotland** 16–10
1975	Murrayfield **Scotland** 20–13	1997	Murrayfield **Scotland** 38–10
1976	Dublin **Scotland** 15–6	1998	Dublin **Scotland** 17–16
1977	Murrayfield **Scotland** 21–18	1999	Murrayfield **Scotland** 30–13
1978	Dublin **Ireland** 12–9	2000	Dublin **Ireland** 44–22
1979	Murrayfield **Drawn** 11–11	2001	Murrayfield **Scotland** 32–10
1980	Dublin **Ireland** 22–15	2002	Dublin **Ireland** 43–22
1981	Murrayfield **Scotland** 10–9	2003	Murrayfield **Ireland** 36–6
1982	Dublin **Ireland** 21–12	2003	Murrayfield **Ireland** 29–10
1983	Murrayfield **Ireland** 15–13		Non-championship match
1984	Dublin **Scotland** 32–9	2004	Dublin **Ireland** 37–16
1985	Murrayfield **Ireland** 18–15	2005	Murrayfield **Ireland** 40–13
1986	Dublin **Scotland** 10–9	2006	Dublin **Ireland** 15–9
1987	Murrayfield **Scotland** 16–12	2007	Murrayfield **Ireland** 19–18
1988	Dublin **Ireland** 22–18	2007	Murrayfield **Scotland** 31–21
1989	Murrayfield **Scotland** 37–21		Non-championship match
1990	Dublin **Scotland** 13–10	2008	Dublin **Ireland** 34–13
1991	Murrayfield **Scotland** 28–25	2009	Murrayfield **Ireland** 22–15
1991	Murrayfield WC **Scotland** 24–15	2010	Dublin **Scotland** 23–20
1992	Dublin **Scotland** 18–10	2011	Murrayfield **Ireland** 21–18
1993	Murrayfield **Scotland** 15–3	2011	Murrayfield **Scotland** 10–6
1994	Dublin **Drawn** 6–6		Non-championship match
1995	Murrayfield **Scotland** 26–13	2012	Dublin **Ireland** 32–14

SCOTLAND v WALES

Played 117 Scotland won 48, Wales won 66, Drawn 3
Highest scores Scotland 35–10 in 1924, Wales 46–22 in 2005
Biggest wins Scotland 35–10 in 1924, Wales 46–22 in 2005

1883	Raeburn Place (Edinburgh) **Scotland** 3G to 1G	1901	Inverleith **Scotland** 18–8
1884	Newport **Scotland** 1DG 1T to 0	1902	Cardiff **Wales** 14–5
1885	Glasgow **Drawn** no score	1903	Inverleith **Scotland** 6–0
1886	Cardiff **Scotland** 2G 1T to 0	1904	Swansea **Wales** 21–3
1887	Raeburn Place **Scotland** 4G 8T to 0	1905	Inverleith **Wales** 6–3
1888	Newport **Wales** 1T to 0	1906	Cardiff **Wales** 9–3
1889	Raeburn Place **Scotland** 2T to 0	1907	Inverleith **Scotland** 6–3
1890	Cardiff **Scotland** 1G 2T to 1T	1908	Swansea **Wales** 6–5
1891	Raeburn Place **Scotland** 15–0	1909	Inverleith **Wales** 5–3
1892	Swansea **Scotland** 7–2	1910	Cardiff **Wales** 14–0
1893	Raeburn Place **Wales** 9–0	1911	Inverleith **Wales** 32–10
1894	Newport **Wales** 7–0	1912	Swansea **Wales** 21–6
1895	Raeburn Place **Scotland** 5–4	1913	Inverleith **Wales** 8–0
1896	Cardiff **Wales** 6–0	1914	Cardiff **Wales** 24–5
1897	No Match	1920	Inverleith **Scotland** 9–5
1898	No Match	1921	Swansea **Scotland** 14–8
1899	Inverleith (Edinburgh) **Scotland** 21–10	1922	Inverleith **Drawn** 9–9
1900	Swansea **Wales** 12–3	1923	Cardiff **Scotland** 11–8
		1924	Inverleith **Scotland** 35–10

1925	Swansea **Scotland** 24–14		1974	Cardiff **Wales** 6–0	
1926	Murrayfield **Scotland** 8–5		1975	Murrayfield **Scotland** 12–10	
1927	Cardiff **Scotland** 5–0		1976	Cardiff **Wales** 28–6	
1928	Murrayfield **Wales** 13–0		1977	Murrayfield **Wales** 18–9	
1929	Swansea **Wales** 14–7		1978	Cardiff **Wales** 22–14	
1930	Murrayfield **Scotland** 12–9		1979	Murrayfield **Wales** 19–13	
1931	Cardiff **Wales** 13–8		1980	Cardiff **Wales** 17–6	
1932	Murrayfield **Wales** 6–0		1981	Murrayfield **Scotland** 15–6	
1933	Swansea **Scotland** 11–3		1982	Cardiff **Scotland** 34–18	
1934	Murrayfield **Wales** 13–6		1983	Murrayfield **Wales** 19–15	
1935	Cardiff **Wales** 10–6		1984	Cardiff **Scotland** 15–9	
1936	Murrayfield **Wales** 13–3		1985	Murrayfield **Wales** 25–21	
1937	Swansea **Scotland** 13–6		1986	Cardiff **Wales** 22–15	
1938	Murrayfield **Scotland** 8–6		1987	Murrayfield **Scotland** 21–15	
1939	Cardiff **Wales** 11–3		1988	Cardiff **Wales** 25–20	
1947	Murrayfield **Wales** 22–8		1989	Murrayfield **Scotland** 23–7	
1948	Cardiff **Wales** 14–0		1990	Cardiff **Scotland** 13–9	
1949	Murrayfield **Scotland** 6–5		1991	Murrayfield **Scotland** 32–12	
1950	Swansea **Wales** 12–0		1992	Cardiff **Wales** 15–12	
1951	Murrayfield **Scotland** 19–0		1993	Murrayfield **Scotland** 20–0	
1952	Cardiff **Wales** 11–0		1994	Cardiff **Wales** 29–6	
1953	Murrayfield **Wales** 12–0		1995	Murrayfield **Scotland** 26–13	
1954	Swansea **Wales** 15–3		1996	Cardiff **Scotland** 16–14	
1955	Murrayfield **Scotland** 14–8		1997	Murrayfield **Wales** 34–19	
1956	Cardiff **Wales** 9–3		1998	Wembley **Wales** 19–13	
1957	Murrayfield **Scotland** 9–6		1999	Murrayfield **Scotland** 33–20	
1958	Cardiff **Wales** 8–3		2000	Cardiff **Wales** 26–18	
1959	Murrayfield **Scotland** 6–5		2001	Murrayfield **Drawn** 28–28	
1960	Cardiff **Wales** 8–0		2002	Cardiff **Scotland** 27–22	
1961	Murrayfield **Scotland** 3–0		2003	Murrayfield **Scotland** 30–22	
1962	Cardiff **Scotland** 8–3		2003	Cardiff **Wales** 23–9	
1963	Murrayfield **Wales** 6–0			Non-championship match	
1964	Cardiff **Wales** 11–3		2004	Cardiff **Wales** 23–10	
1965	Murrayfield **Wales** 14–12		2005	Murrayfield **Wales** 46–22	
1966	Cardiff **Wales** 8–3		2006	Cardiff **Wales** 28–18	
1967	Murrayfield **Scotland** 11–5		2007	Murrayfield **Scotland** 21–9	
1968	Cardiff **Wales** 5–0		2008	Cardiff **Wales** 30–15	
1969	Murrayfield **Wales** 17–3		2009	Murrayfield **Wales** 26–13	
1970	Cardiff **Wales** 18–9		2010	Cardiff **Wales** 31–24	
1971	Murrayfield **Wales** 19–18		2011	Murrayfield **Wales** 24–6	
1972	Cardiff **Wales** 35–12		2012	Cardiff **Wales** 27–13	
1973	Murrayfield **Scotland** 10–9				

INTERNATIONAL RECORDS

SCOTLAND v FRANCE

Played 85 Scotland won 34, France won 48, Drawn 3
Highest scores Scotland 36–22 in 1999, France 51–16 in 1998 and 51–9 in 2003
Biggest wins Scotland 31–3 in 1912, France 51–9 in 2003

1910	Inverleith (Edinburgh) **Scotland** 27–0	1974	Murrayfield **Scotland** 19–6
1911	Paris **France** 16–15	1975	Paris **France** 10–9
1912	Inverleith **Scotland** 31–3	1976	Murrayfield **France** 13–6
1913	Paris **Scotland** 21–3	1977	Paris **France** 23–3
1914	No Match	1978	Murrayfield **France** 19–16
1920	Paris **Scotland** 5–0	1979	Paris **France** 21–17
1921	Inverleith **France** 3–0	1980	Murrayfield **Scotland** 22–14
1922	Paris **Drawn** 3–3	1981	Paris **France** 16–9
1923	Inverleith **Scotland** 16–3	1982	Murrayfield **Scotland** 16–7
1924	Paris **France** 12–10	1983	Paris **France** 19–15
1925	Inverleith **Scotland** 25–4	1984	Murrayfield **Scotland** 21–12
1926	Paris **Scotland** 20–6	1985	Paris **France** 11–3
1927	Murrayfield **Scotland** 23–6	1986	Murrayfield **Scotland** 18–17
1928	Paris **Scotland** 15–6	1987	Paris **France** 28–22
1929	Murrayfield **Scotland** 6–3	1987	Christchurch WC **Drawn** 20–20
1930	Paris **France** 7–3	1988	Murrayfield **Scotland** 23–12
1931	Murrayfield **Scotland** 6–4	1989	Paris **France** 19–3
1947	Paris **France** 8–3	1990	Murrayfield **Scotland** 21–0
1948	Murrayfield **Scotland** 9–8	1991	Paris **France** 15–9
1949	Paris **Scotland** 8–0	1992	Murrayfield **Scotland** 10–6
1950	Murrayfield **Scotland** 8–5	1993	Paris **France** 11–3
1951	Paris **France** 14–12	1994	Murrayfield **France** 20–12
1952	Murrayfield **France** 13–11	1995	Paris **Scotland** 23–21
1953	Paris **France** 11–5	1995	Pretoria WC **France** 22–19
1954	Murrayfield **France** 3–0	1996	Murrayfield **Scotland** 19–14
1955	Paris **France** 15–0	1997	Paris **France** 47–20
1956	Murrayfield **Scotland** 12–0	1998	Murrayfield **France** 51–16
1957	Paris **Scotland** 6–0	1999	Paris **Scotland** 36–22
1958	Murrayfield **Scotland** 11–9	2000	Murrayfield **France** 28–16
1959	Paris **France** 9–0	2001	Paris **France** 16–6
1960	Murrayfield **France** 13–11	2002	Murrayfield **France** 22–10
1961	Paris **France** 11–0	2003	Paris **France** 38–3
1962	Murrayfield **France** 11–3	2003	Sydney WC **France** 51–9
1963	Paris **Scotland** 11–6	2004	Murrayfield **France** 31–0
1964	Murrayfield **Scotland** 10–0	2005	Paris **France** 16–9
1965	Paris **France** 16–8	2006	Murrayfield **Scotland** 20–16
1966	Murrayfield **Drawn** 3–3	2007	Paris **France** 46–19
1967	Paris **Scotland** 9–8	2008	Murrayfield **France** 27–6
1968	Murrayfield **France** 8–6	2009	Paris **France** 22–13
1969	Paris **Scotland** 6–3	2010	Murrayfield **France** 18–9
1970	Murrayfield **France** 11–9	2011	Paris **France** 34–21
1971	Paris **France** 13–8	2012	Murrayfield **France** 23–17
1972	Murrayfield **Scotland** 20–9		
1973	Paris **France** 16–13		

SCOTLAND v SOUTH AFRICA

Played 21 Scotland won 5, South Africa won 16, Drawn 0
Highest scores Scotland 29–46 in 1999, South Africa 68–10 in 1997
Biggest wins Scotland 21–6 in 2002, South Africa 68–10 in 1997

1906	Glasgow **Scotland** 6–0	2003	1 Durban **South Africa** 29–25
1912	Inverleith **South Africa** 16–0		2 Johannesburg **South Africa**
1932	Murrayfield **South Africa** 6–3		28–19
1951	Murrayfield **South Africa** 44–0		South Africa won series 2–0
1960	Port Elizabeth **South Africa** 18–10	2004	Murrayfield **South Africa** 45–10
1961	Murrayfield **South Africa** 12–5	2006	1 Durban **South Africa** 36–16
1965	Murrayfield **Scotland** 8–5		2 Port Elizabeth **South Africa**
1969	Murrayfield **Scotland** 6–3		29–15
1994	Murrayfield **South Africa** 34–10		South Africa won series 2–0
1997	Murrayfield **South Africa** 68–10	2007	Murrayfield **South Africa** 27–3
1998	Murrayfield **South Africa** 35–10	2008	Murrayfield **South Africa** 14–10
1999	Murrayfield WC **South Africa** 46–29	2010	Murrayfield **Scotland** 21–17
2002	Murrayfield **Scotland** 21–6		

SCOTLAND v NEW ZEALAND

Played 28 Scotland won 0, New Zealand won 26, Drawn 2
Highest scores Scotland 31–62 in 1996, New Zealand 69–20 in 2000
Biggest wins Scotland no win, New Zealand 69–20 in 2000

1905	Inverleith (Edinburgh) **New Zealand**		New Zealand won series 2–0
	12–7	1991	Cardiff WC **New Zealand** 13–6
1935	Murrayfield **New Zealand** 18–8	1993	Murrayfield **New Zealand** 51–15
1954	Murrayfield **New Zealand** 3–0	1995	Pretoria WC **New Zealand** 48–30
1964	Murrayfield **Drawn** 0–0	1996	1 Dunedin **New Zealand** 62–31
1967	Murrayfield **New Zealand** 14–3		2 Auckland **New Zealand** 36–12
1972	Murrayfield **New Zealand** 14–9		New Zealand won series 2–0
1975	Auckland **New Zealand** 24–0	1999	Murrayfield WC **New Zealand** 30–18
1978	Murrayfield **New Zealand** 18–9	2000	1 Dunedin **New Zealand** 69–20
1979	Murrayfield **New Zealand** 20–6		2 Auckland **New Zealand** 48–14
1981	1 Dunedin **New Zealand** 11–4		New Zealand won series 2–0
	2 Auckland **New Zealand** 40–15	2001	Murrayfield **New Zealand** 37–6
	New Zealand won series 2–0	2005	Murrayfield **New Zealand** 29–10
1983	Murrayfield **Drawn** 25–25	2007	Murrayfield WC **New Zealand** 40–0
1987	Christchurch WC **New Zealand** 30–3	2008	Murrayfield **New Zealand** 32–6
1990	1 Dunedin **New Zealand** 31–16	2010	Murrayfield **New Zealand** 49–3
	2 Auckland **New Zealand** 21–18		

SCOTLAND v AUSTRALIA

Played 27 Scotland won 9, Australia won 18, Drawn 0
Highest scores Scotland 24–15 in 1981, Australia 45–3 in 1998
Biggest wins Scotland 24–15 in 1981, Australia 45–3 in 1998

1927	Murrayfield **Scotland** 10–8		1996	Murrayfield **Australia** 29–19
1947	Murrayfield **Australia** 16–7		1997	Murrayfield **Australia** 37–8
1958	Murrayfield **Scotland** 12–8		1998	1 Sydney **Australia** 45–3
1966	Murrayfield **Scotland** 11–5			2 Brisbane **Australia** 33–11
1968	Murrayfield **Scotland** 9–3			Australia won series 2–0
1970	Sydney **Australia** 23–3		2000	Murrayfield **Australia** 30–9
1975	Murrayfield **Scotland** 10–3		2003	Brisbane WC **Australia** 33–16
1981	Murrayfield **Scotland** 24–15		2004	1 Melbourne **Australia** 35–15
1982	1 Brisbane **Scotland** 12–7			2 Sydney **Australia** 34–13
	2 Sydney **Australia** 33–9			Australia won series 2–0
	Series drawn 1–1		2004	1 Murrayfield **Australia** 31–14
1984	Murrayfield **Australia** 37–12			2 Glasgow **Australia** 31–17
1988	Murrayfield **Australia** 32–13			Australia won series 2–0
1992	1 Sydney **Australia** 27–12		2006	Murrayfield **Australia** 44–15
	2 Brisbane **Australia** 37–13		2009	Murrayfield **Scotland** 9–8
	Australia won series 2–0		2012	Newcastle (Aus) **Scotland** 9–6

SCOTLAND v SRU PRESIDENT'S XV

Played 1 Scotland won 1
Highest scores Scotland 27–16 in 1972, SRU President's XV 16–27 in 1973
Biggest win Scotland 27–16 in 1973, SRU President's XV no win

1973	Murrayfield **Scotland** 27–16

SCOTLAND v ROMANIA

Played 13 Scotland won 11 Romania won 2, Drawn 0
Highest scores Scotland 60–19 in 1999, Romania 28–55 in 1987 & 28–22 in 1984
Biggest wins Scotland 48–6 in 2006 and 42–0 in 2007, Romania 28–22 in 1984 & 18–12 in 1991

1981	Murrayfield **Scotland** 12–6		1999	Glasgow **Scotland** 60–19
1984	Bucharest **Romania** 28–22		2002	Murrayfield **Scotland** 37–10
1986	Bucharest **Scotland** 33–18		2005	Bucharest **Scotland** 39–19
1987	Dunedin WC **Scotland** 55–28		2006	Murrayfield **Scotland** 48–6
1989	Murrayfield **Scotland** 32–0		2007	Murrayfield WC **Scotland** 42–0
1991	Bucharest **Romania** 18–12		2011	Invercargill WC **Scotland** 34–24
1995	Murrayfield **Scotland** 49–16			

SCOTLAND v ZIMBABWE

Played 2 Scotland won 2
Highest scores Scotland 60–21 in 1987, Zimbabwe 21–60 in 1987
Biggest win Scotland 60–21 in 1987 & 51–12 in 1991, Zimbabwe no win

1987	Wellington WC **Scotland** 60–21	1991	Murrayfield WC **Scotland** 51–12

SCOTLAND v FIJI

Played 6 Scotland won 5, Fiji won 1
Highest scores Scotland 38–17 in 1989, Fiji 51–26 in 1998
Biggest wins Scotland 38–17 in 1989, Fiji 51–26 in 1998

1989	Murrayfield **Scotland** 38–17	2003	Sydney WC **Scotland** 22–20
1998	Suva **Fiji** 51–26	2009	Murrayfield **Scotland** 23–10
2002	Murrayfield **Scotland** 36–22	2012	Lautoka **Scotland** 37–25

SCOTLAND v ARGENTINA

Played 13 Scotland won 4, Argentina won 9, Drawn 0
Highest scores Scotland 49–3 in 1990, Argentina 31–22 in 1999
Biggest wins Scotland 49–3 in 1990, Argentina 31–22 in 1999 and 25–16 in 2001

1990	Murrayfield **Scotland** 49–3	2008	1 Rosario **Argentina** 21–15
1994	1 Buenos Aires **Argentina** 16–15		2 Buenos Aires **Scotland** 26–14
	2 Buenos Aires **Argentina** 19–17		Series drawn 1–1
	Argentina won series 2–0	2009	Murrayfield **Argentina** 9–6
1999	Murrayfield **Argentina** 31–22	2010	1 Tucumán **Scotland** 24–16
2001	Murrayfield **Argentina** 25–16		2 Mar del Plata **Scotland** 13–9
2005	Murrayfield **Argentina** 23–19		Scotland won series 2–0
2007	Paris WC **Argentina** 19–13	2011	Wellington WC **Argentina** 13–12

SCOTLAND v JAPAN

Played 3 Scotland won 3
Highest scores Scotland 100–8 in 2004, Japan 11–32 in 2003
Biggest win Scotland 100–8 in 2004, Japan no win

1991	Murrayfield WC **Scotland** 47–9	2004	Perth **Scotland** 100–8
2003	Townsville WC **Scotland** 32–11		

INTERNATIONAL RECORDS

SCOTLAND v SAMOA

Played 8 Scotland won 7, Drawn 1
Highest scores Scotland 38–3 in 2004, Samoa 20–35 in 1999
Biggest win Scotland 38–3 in 2004, Samoa no win

1991	Murrayfield WC **Scotland** 28–6	2004	Wellington (NZ) **Scotland** 38–3
1995	Murrayfield **Drawn** 15–15	2005	Murrayfield **Scotland** 18–11
1999	Murrayfield WC **Scotland** 35–20	2010	Aberdeen **Scotland** 19–16
2000	Murrayfield **Scotland** 31–8	2012	Apia **Scotland** 17–16

SCOTLAND v CANADA

Played 3 Scotland won 2, Canada won 1
Highest scores Scotland 41–0 in 2008, Canada 26–23 in 2002
Biggest wins Scotland 41–0 in 2008, Canada 26–23 in 2002

1995	Murrayfield **Scotland** 22–6	2008	Aberdeen **Scotland** 41–0
2002	Vancouver **Canada** 26–23		

SCOTLAND v IVORY COAST

Played 1 Scotland won 1
Highest scores Scotland 89–0 in 1995, Ivory Coast 0–89 in 1995
Biggest win Scotland 89–0 in 1995, Ivory Coast no win

1995	Rustenburg WC **Scotland** 89–0

SCOTLAND v TONGA

Played 2 Scotland won 2
Highest scores Scotland 43–20 in 2001, Tonga 20–43 in 2001
Biggest win Scotland 41–5 in 1995, Tonga no win

1995	Pretoria WC **Scotland** 41–5	2001	Murrayfield **Scotland** 43–20

SCOTLAND v ITALY

Played 19 Scotland won 12, Italy won 7
Highest scores Scotland 47–15 in 2003, Italy 37–17 in 2007
Biggest wins Scotland 47–15 in 2003, Italy 37–17 in 2007

1996	Murrayfield **Scotland** 29–22		2006	Rome **Scotland** 13–10
1998	Treviso **Italy** 25–21		2007	Murrayfield **Italy** 37–17
1999	Murrayfield **Scotland** 30–12		2007	Saint Etienne WC **Scotland** 18–16
2000	Rome **Italy** 34–20		2008	Rome **Italy** 23–20
2001	Murrayfield **Scotland** 23–19		2009	Murrayfield **Scotland** 26–6
2002	Rome **Scotland** 29–12		2010	Rome **Italy** 16–12
2003	Murrayfield **Scotland** 33–25		2011	Murrayfield **Scotland** 21–8
2003	Murrayfield **Scotland** 47–15		2011	Murrayfield **Scotland** 23–12
	Non-championship match			Non-championship match
2004	Rome **Italy** 20–14		2012	Rome **Italy** 13–6
2005	Murrayfield **Scotland** 18–10			

SCOTLAND v URUGUAY

Played 1 Scotland won 1
Highest scores Scotland 43–12 in 1999, Uruguay 12–43 in 1999
Biggest win Scotland 43–12 in 1999, Uruguay no win

1999	Murrayfield WC **Scotland** 43–12

SCOTLAND v SPAIN

Played 1 Scotland won 1
Highest scores Scotland 48–0 in 1999, Spain 0–48 in 1999
Biggest win Scotland 48–0 in 1999, Spain no win

1999	Murrayfield WC **Scotland** 48–0

SCOTLAND v UNITED STATES

Played 3 Scotland won 3
Highest scores Scotland 65–23 in 2002, United States 23–65 in 2002
Biggest win Scotland 53–6 in 2000, United States no win

2000	Murrayfield **Scotland** 53–6		2003	Brisbane WC **Scotland** 39–15
2002	San Francisco **Scotland** 65–23			

SCOTLAND v PACIFIC ISLANDS

Played 1 Scotland won 1
Highest scores Scotland 34–22 in 2006, Pacific Islands 22–34 in 2006
Biggest win Scotland 34–22 in 2006, Pacific Islands no win

2006	Murrayfield **Scotland** 34–22

SCOTLAND v PORTUGAL

Played 1 Scotland won 1
Highest scores Scotland 56–10 in 2007, Portugal 10–56 in 2007
Biggest win Scotland 56–10 in 2007, Portugal no win

2007	Saint Etienne WC **Scotland** 56–10

SCOTLAND v GEORGIA

Played 1 Scotland won 1
Highest scores Scotland 15–6 in 2011, Georgia 6–15 in 2011
Biggest win Scotland 15–6 in 2011, Georgia no win

2011	Invercargill WC **Scotland** 15–6

IRELAND v WALES

Played 118 Ireland won 47, Wales won 65, Drawn 6
Highest scores Ireland 54–10 in 2002, Wales 34–9 in 1976
Biggest wins Ireland 54–10 in 2002, Wales 29–0 in 1907

1882	Dublin **Wales** 2G 2T to 0		1898	Limerick **Wales** 11–3
1883	No Match		1899	Cardiff **Ireland** 3–0
1884	Cardiff **Wales** 1DG 2T to 0		1900	Belfast **Wales** 3–0
1885	No Match		1901	Swansea **Wales** 10–9
1886	No Match		1902	Dublin **Wales** 15–0
1887	Birkenhead **Wales** 1DG 1T to 3T		1903	Cardiff **Wales** 18–0
1888	Dublin **Ireland** 1G 1DG 1T to 0		1904	Belfast **Ireland** 14–12
1889	Swansea **Ireland** 2T to 0		1905	Swansea **Wales** 10–3
1890	Dublin **Drawn** 1G each		1906	Belfast **Ireland** 11–6
1891	Llanelli **Wales** 6–4		1907	Cardiff **Wales** 29–0
1892	Dublin **Ireland** 9–0		1908	Belfast **Wales** 11–5
1893	Llanelli **Wales** 2–0		1909	Swansea **Wales** 18–5
1894	Belfast **Ireland** 3–0		1910	Dublin **Wales** 19–3
1895	Cardiff **Wales** 5–3		1911	Cardiff **Wales** 16–0
1896	Dublin **Ireland** 8–4		1912	Belfast **Ireland** 12–5
1897	No Match		1913	Swansea **Wales** 16–13

1914	Belfast **Wales** 11–3
1920	Cardiff **Wales** 28–4
1921	Belfast **Wales** 6–0
1922	Swansea **Wales** 11–5
1923	Dublin **Ireland** 5–4
1924	Cardiff **Ireland** 13–10
1925	Belfast **Ireland** 19–3
1926	Swansea **Wales** 11–8
1927	Dublin **Ireland** 19–9
1928	Cardiff **Ireland** 13–10
1929	Belfast **Drawn** 5–5
1930	Swansea **Wales** 12–7
1931	Belfast **Wales** 15–3
1932	Cardiff **Ireland** 12–10
1933	Belfast **Ireland** 10–5
1934	Swansea **Wales** 13–0
1935	Belfast **Ireland** 9–3
1936	Cardiff **Wales** 3–0
1937	Belfast **Ireland** 5–3
1938	Swansea **Wales** 11–5
1939	Belfast **Wales** 7–0
1947	Swansea **Wales** 6–0
1948	Belfast **Ireland** 6–3
1949	Swansea **Ireland** 5–0
1950	Belfast **Wales** 6–3
1951	Cardiff **Drawn** 3–3
1952	Dublin **Wales** 14–3
1953	Swansea **Wales** 5–3
1954	Dublin **Wales** 12–9
1955	Cardiff **Wales** 21–3
1956	Dublin **Ireland** 11–3
1957	Cardiff **Wales** 6–5
1958	Dublin **Wales** 9–6
1959	Cardiff **Wales** 8–6
1960	Dublin **Wales** 10–9
1961	Cardiff **Wales** 9–0
1962	Dublin **Drawn** 3–3
1963	Cardiff **Ireland** 14–6
1964	Dublin **Wales** 15–6
1965	Cardiff **Wales** 14–8
1966	Dublin **Ireland** 9–6
1967	Cardiff **Ireland** 3–0
1968	Dublin **Ireland** 9–6
1969	Cardiff **Wales** 24–11
1970	Dublin **Ireland** 14–0
1971	Cardiff **Wales** 23–9
1972	No Match
1973	Cardiff **Wales** 16–12
1974	Dublin **Drawn** 9–9
1975	Cardiff **Wales** 32–4
1976	Dublin **Wales** 34–9
1977	Cardiff **Wales** 25–9
1978	Dublin **Wales** 20–16
1979	Cardiff **Wales** 24–21
1980	Dublin **Ireland** 21–7
1981	Cardiff **Wales** 9–8
1982	Dublin **Ireland** 20–12
1983	Cardiff **Wales** 23–9
1984	Dublin **Wales** 18–9
1985	Cardiff **Ireland** 21–9
1986	Dublin **Wales** 19–12
1987	Cardiff **Ireland** 15–11
1987	Wellington WC **Wales** 13–6
1988	Dublin **Wales** 12–9
1989	Cardiff **Ireland** 19–13
1990	Dublin **Ireland** 14–8
1991	Cardiff **Drawn** 21–21
1992	Dublin **Wales** 16–15
1993	Cardiff **Ireland** 19–14
1994	Dublin **Wales** 17–15
1995	Cardiff **Ireland** 16–12
1995	Johannesburg WC **Ireland** 24–23
1996	Dublin **Ireland** 30–17
1997	Cardiff **Ireland** 26–25
1998	Dublin **Wales** 30–21
1999	Wembley **Ireland** 29–23
2000	Dublin **Wales** 23–19
2001	Cardiff **Ireland** 36–6
2002	Dublin **Ireland** 54–10
2003	Cardiff **Ireland** 25–24
2003	Dublin **Ireland** 35–12
2004	Dublin **Ireland** 36–15
2005	Cardiff **Wales** 32–20
2006	Dublin **Ireland** 31–5
2007	Cardiff **Ireland** 19–9
2008	Dublin **Wales** 16–12
2009	Cardiff **Ireland** 17–15
2010	Dublin **Ireland** 27–12
2011	Cardiff **Wales** 19–13
2011	Wellington WC **Wales** 22–10
2012	Dublin **Wales** 23–21

INTERNATIONAL RECORDS

IRELAND v FRANCE

Played 90 **Ireland won** 29, **France won** 55, **Drawn** 6
Highest scores Ireland 31–43 in 2006, France 45–10 in 1996
Biggest wins Ireland 24–0 in 1913, France 44–5 in 2002

1909	Dublin	**Ireland** 19–8
1910	Paris	**Ireland** 8–3
1911	Cork	**Ireland** 25–5
1912	Paris	**Ireland** 11–6
1913	Cork	**Ireland** 24–0
1914	Paris	**Ireland** 8–6
1920	Dublin	**France** 15–7
1921	Paris	**France** 20–10
1922	Dublin	**Ireland** 8–3
1923	Paris	**France** 14–8
1924	Dublin	**Ireland** 6–0
1925	Paris	**Ireland** 9–3
1926	Belfast	**Ireland** 11–0
1927	Paris	**Ireland** 8–3
1928	Belfast	**Ireland** 12–8
1929	Paris	**Ireland** 6–0
1930	Belfast	**France** 5–0
1931	Paris	**France** 3–0
1947	Dublin	**France** 12–8
1948	Paris	**Ireland** 13–6
1949	Dublin	**France** 16–9
1950	Paris	**Drawn** 3–3
1951	Dublin	**Ireland** 9–8
1952	Paris	**Ireland** 11–8
1953	Belfast	**Ireland** 16–3
1954	Paris	**France** 8–0
1955	Dublin	**France** 5–3
1956	Paris	**France** 14–8
1957	Dublin	**Ireland** 11–6
1958	Paris	**France** 11–6
1959	Dublin	**Ireland** 9–5
1960	Paris	**France** 23–6
1961	Dublin	**France** 15–3
1962	Paris	**France** 11–0
1963	Dublin	**France** 24–5
1964	Paris	**France** 27–6
1965	Dublin	**Drawn** 3–3
1966	Paris	**France** 11–6
1967	Dublin	**France** 11–6
1968	Paris	**France** 16–6
1969	Dublin	**Ireland** 17–9
1970	Paris	**France** 8–0
1971	Dublin	**Drawn** 9–9
1972	Paris	**Ireland** 14–9
1972	Dublin	**Ireland** 24–14
		Non-championship match
1973	Dublin	**Ireland** 6–4
1974	Paris	**France** 9–6
1975	Dublin	**Ireland** 25–6
1976	Paris	**France** 26–3
1977	Dublin	**France** 15–6
1978	Paris	**France** 10–9
1979	Dublin	**Drawn** 9–9
1980	Paris	**France** 19–18
1981	Dublin	**France** 19–13
1982	Paris	**France** 22–9
1983	Dublin	**Ireland** 22–16
1984	Paris	**France** 25–12
1985	Dublin	**Drawn** 15–15
1986	Paris	**France** 29–9
1987	Dublin	**France** 19–13
1988	Paris	**France** 25–6
1989	Dublin	**France** 26–21
1990	Paris	**France** 31–12
1991	Dublin	**France** 21–13
1992	Paris	**France** 44–12
1993	Dublin	**France** 21–6
1994	Paris	**France** 35–15
1995	Dublin	**France** 25–7
1995	Durban WC	**France** 36–12
1996	Paris	**France** 45–10
1997	Dublin	**France** 32–15
1998	Paris	**France** 18–16
1999	Dublin	**France** 10–9
2000	Paris	**Ireland** 27–25
2001	Dublin	**Ireland** 22–15
2002	Paris	**France** 44–5
2003	Dublin	**Ireland** 15–12
2003	Melbourne WC	**France** 43–21
2004	Paris	**France** 35–17
2005	Dublin	**France** 26–19
2006	Paris	**France** 43–31
2007	Dublin	**France** 20–17
2007	Paris WC	**France** 25–3
2008	Paris	**France** 26–21
2009	Dublin	**Ireland** 30–21

2010	Paris **France** 33–10
2011	Dublin **France** 25–22
2011	Bordeaux **France** 19–12
	Non-championship match

2011	Dublin **France** 26–22
	Non-championship match
2012	Paris **Drawn** 17–17

IRELAND v SOUTH AFRICA

Played 20 Ireland won 4, South Africa won 15, Drawn 1
Highest scores Ireland 32–15 in 2006, South Africa 38–0 in 1912
Biggest wins Ireland 32–15 in 2006, South Africa 38–0 in 1912

1906	Belfast **South Africa** 15–12
1912	Dublin **South Africa** 38–0
1931	Dublin **South Africa** 8–3
1951	Dublin **South Africa** 17–5
1960	Dublin **South Africa** 8–3
1961	Cape Town **South Africa** 24–8
1965	Dublin **Ireland** 9–6
1970	Dublin **Drawn** 8–8
1981	1 Cape Town **South Africa** 23–15
	2 Durban **South Africa** 12–10
	South Africa won series 2–0
1998	1 Bloemfontein **South Africa** 37–13

	2 Pretoria **South Africa** 33–0
	South Africa won series 2–0
1998	Dublin **South Africa** 27–13
2000	Dublin **South Africa** 28–18
2004	1 Bloemfontein **South Africa** 31–17
	2 Cape Town **South Africa** 26–17
	South Africa won series 2–0
2004	Dublin **Ireland** 17–12
2006	Dublin **Ireland** 32–15
2009	Dublin **Ireland** 15–10
2010	Dublin **South Africa** 23–21

IRELAND v NEW ZEALAND

Played 27 Ireland won 0, New Zealand won 26, Drawn 1
Highest scores Ireland 29–40 in 2001, New Zealand 66–28 in 2010
Biggest win Ireland no win, New Zealand 60–0 in 2012

1905	Dublin **New Zealand** 15–0
1924	Dublin **New Zealand** 6–0
1935	Dublin **New Zealand** 17–9
1954	Dublin **New Zealand** 14–3
1963	Dublin **New Zealand** 6–5
1973	Dublin **Drawn** 10–10
1974	Dublin **New Zealand** 15–6
1976	Wellington **New Zealand** 11–3
1978	Dublin **New Zealand** 10–6
1989	Dublin **New Zealand** 23–6
1992	1 Dunedin **New Zealand** 24–21
	2 Wellington **New Zealand** 59–6
	New Zealand won series 2–0
1995	Johannesburg WC **New Zealand** 43–19
1997	Dublin **New Zealand** 63–15

2001	Dublin **New Zealand** 40–29
2002	1 Dunedin **New Zealand** 15–6
	2 Auckland **New Zealand** 40–8
	New Zealand won series 2–0
2005	Dublin **New Zealand** 45–7
2006	1 Hamilton **New Zealand** 34–23
	2 Auckland **New Zealand** 27–17
	New Zealand won series 2–0
2008	Wellington **New Zealand** 21–11
2008	Dublin **New Zealand** 22–3
2010	New Plymouth **New Zealand** 66–28
2010	Dublin **New Zealand** 38–18
2012	1 Auckland **New Zealand** 42–10
	2 Christchurch **New Zealand** 22–19
	3 Hamilton **New Zealand** 60–0
	New Zealand won series 3–0

INTERNATIONAL RECORDS

IRELAND v AUSTRALIA

Played 30 Ireland won 9, Australia won 20, Drawn 1
Highest scores Ireland 27–12 in 1979, Australia 46–10 in 1999
Biggest wins Ireland 27–12 in 1979 & 21–6 in 2006, Australia 46–10 in 1999

1927	Dublin **Australia** 5–3		Australia won series 2–0
1947	Dublin **Australia** 16–3	1996	Dublin **Australia** 22–12
1958	Dublin **Ireland** 9–6	1999	1 Brisbane **Australia** 46–10
1967	Dublin **Ireland** 15–8		2 Perth **Australia** 32–26
1967	Sydney **Ireland** 11–5		Australia won series 2–0
1968	Dublin **Ireland** 10–3	1999	Dublin WC **Australia** 23–3
1976	Dublin **Australia** 20–10	2002	Dublin **Ireland** 18–9
1979	1 Brisbane **Ireland** 27–12	2003	Perth **Australia** 45–16
	2 Sydney **Ireland** 9–3	2003	Melbourne WC **Australia** 17–16
	Ireland won series 2–0	2005	Dublin **Australia** 30–14
1981	Dublin **Australia** 16–12	2006	Perth **Australia** 37–15
1984	Dublin **Australia** 16–9	2006	Dublin **Ireland** 21–6
1987	Sydney WC **Australia** 33–15	2008	Melbourne **Australia** 18–12
1991	Dublin WC **Australia** 19–18	2009	Dublin **Drawn** 20–20
1992	Dublin **Australia** 42–17	2010	Brisbane **Australia** 22–15
1994	1 Brisbane **Australia** 33–13	2011	Auckland WC **Ireland** 15–6
	2 Sydney **Australia** 32–18		

IRELAND v NEW ZEALAND NATIVES

Played 1 New Zealand Natives won 1
Highest scores Ireland 4–13 in 1888, Zew Zealand Natives 13–4 in 1888
Biggest win Ireland no win, New Zealand Natives 13–4 in 1888

1888	Dublin **New Zealand Natives** 4G 1T to 1G 1T

IRELAND v IRU PRESIDENT'S XV

Played 1 Drawn 1
Highest scores Ireland 18–18 in 1974, IRFU President's XV 18–18 in 1974

1974	Dublin **Drawn** 18–18

IRELAND v ROMANIA

Played 8 Ireland won 8
Highest scores Ireland 60–0 in 1986, Romania 35–53 in 1998
Biggest win Ireland 60–0 in 1986, Romania no win

1986	Dublin **Ireland** 60–0	2001	Bucharest **Ireland** 37–3
1993	Dublin **Ireland** 25–3	2002	Limerick **Ireland** 39–8
1998	Dublin **Ireland** 53–35	2003	Gosford WC **Ireland** 45–17
1999	Dublin WC **Ireland** 44–14	2005	Dublin **Ireland** 43–12

IRELAND v CANADA

Played 5 Ireland won 4 Drawn 1
Highest scores Ireland 55–0 in 2008, Canada 27–27 in 2000
Biggest win Ireland 55–0 in 2008, Canada no win

1987	Dunedin WC **Ireland** 46–19		2008	Limerick **Ireland** 55–0
1997	Dublin **Ireland** 33–11		2009	Vancouver **Ireland** 25–6
2000	Markham **Drawn** 27–27			

IRELAND v TONGA

Played 2 Ireland won 2
Highest scores Ireland 40–19 in 2003, Tonga 19–40 in 2003
Biggest win Ireland 32–9 in 1987, Tonga no win

1987	Brisbane WC **Ireland** 32–9		2003	Nuku'alofa **Ireland** 40–19

IRELAND v SAMOA

Played 5 Ireland won 4, Samoa won 1, Drawn 0
Highest scores Ireland 49–22 in 1988, Samoa 40–25 in 1996
Biggest wins Ireland 49–22 in 1988 and 35–8 in 2001, Samoa 40–25 in 1996

1988	Dublin **Ireland** 49–22		2003	Apia **Ireland** 40–14
1996	Dublin **Samoa** 40–25		2010	Dublin **Ireland** 20–10
2001	Dublin **Ireland** 35–8			

IRELAND v ITALY

Played 21 Ireland won 18, Italy won 3, Drawn 0
Highest scores Ireland 61–6 in 2003, Italy 37–29 in 1997 & 37–22 in 1997
Biggest wins Ireland 61–6 in 2003, Italy 37–22 in 1997

1988	Dublin **Ireland** 31–15		2005	Rome **Ireland** 28–17
1995	Treviso **Italy** 22–12		2006	Dublin **Ireland** 26–16
1997	Dublin **Italy** 37–29		2007	Rome **Ireland** 51–24
1997	Bologna **Italy** 37–22		2007	Belfast **Ireland** 23–20
1999	Dublin **Ireland** 39–30			Non-championship match
2000	Dublin **Ireland** 60–13		2008	Dublin **Ireland** 16–11
2001	Rome **Ireland** 41–22		2009	Rome **Ireland** 38–9
2002	Dublin **Ireland** 32–17		2010	Dublin **Ireland** 29–11
2003	Rome **Ireland** 37–13		2011	Rome **Ireland** 13–11
2003	Limerick **Ireland** 61–6		2011	Dunedin WC **Ireland** 36–6
	Non-championship match		2012	Dublin **Ireland** 42–10
2004	Dublin **Ireland** 19–3			

IRELAND v ARGENTINA

Played 12 Ireland won 7 Argentina won 5
Highest scores Ireland 32–24 in 1999, Argentina 34–23 in 2000
Biggest win Ireland 29–9 in 2010, Argentina 16–0 in 2007

1990	Dublin **Ireland** 20–18	2007	1 Santa Fé **Argentina** 22–20
1999	Dublin **Ireland** 32–24		2 Buenos Aires **Argentina** 16–0
1999	Lens WC **Argentina** 28–24		Argentina won series 2–0
2000	Buenos Aires **Argentina** 34–23	2007	Paris WC **Argentina** 30–15
2002	Dublin **Ireland** 16–7	2008	Dublin **Ireland** 17–3
2003	Adelaide WC **Ireland** 16–15	2010	Dublin **Ireland** 29–9
2004	Dublin **Ireland** 21–19		

IRELAND v NAMIBIA

Played 4 Ireland won 2, Namibia won 2
Highest scores Ireland 64–7 in 2003, Namibia 26–15 in 1991
Biggest win Ireland 64–7 in 2003, Namibia 26–15 in 1991

1991	1 Windhoek **Namibia** 15–6	2003	Sydney WC **Ireland** 64–7
	2 Windhoek **Namibia** 26–15	2007	Bordeaux WC **Ireland** 32–17
	Namibia won series 2–0		

IRELAND v ZIMBABWE

Played 1 Ireland won 1
Highest scores Ireland 55–11 in 1991, Zimbabwe 11–55 in 1991
Biggest win Ireland 55–11 in 1991, Zimbabwe no win

1991	Dublin WC **Ireland** 55–11

IRELAND v JAPAN

Played 5 Ireland won 5
Highest scores Ireland 78–9 in 2000, Japan 28–50 in 1995
Biggest win Ireland 78–9 in 2000, Japan no win

1991	Dublin WC **Ireland** 32–16	2005	1 Osaka **Ireland** 44–12
1995	Bloemfontein WC **Ireland** 50–28		2 Tokyo **Ireland** 47–18
2000	Dublin **Ireland** 78–9		Ireland won series 2–0

Played 7 Ireland won 7
Highest scores Ireland 83–3 in 2000, United States 18–25 in 1996
Biggest win Ireland 83–3 in 2000, United States no win

1994	Dublin **Ireland** 26–15	2004	Dublin **Ireland** 55–6
1996	Atlanta **Ireland** 25–18	2009	Santa Clara **Ireland** 27–10
1999	Dublin WC **Ireland** 53–8	2011	New Plymouth WC **Ireland** 22–10
2000	Manchester (NH) **Ireland** 83–3		

IRELAND v FIJI

Played 3 Ireland won 3
Highest scores Ireland 64–17 in 2002, Fiji 17–64 in 2002
Biggest win Ireland 64–17 in 2002, Fiji no win

1995	Dublin **Ireland** 44–8	2009	Dublin **Ireland** 41–6
2002	Dublin **Ireland** 64–17		

IRELAND v GEORGIA

Played 3 Ireland won 3
Highest scores Ireland 70–0 in 1998, Georgia 14–63 in 2002
Biggest win Ireland 70–0 in 1998, Georgia no win

1998	Dublin **Ireland** 70–0	2007	Bordeaux WC **Ireland** 14–10
2002	Dublin **Ireland** 63–14		

IRELAND v RUSSIA

Played 2 Ireland won 2
Highest scores Ireland 62–12 in 2011, Russia 12–62 in 2011
Biggest win Ireland 62–12 in 2011, Russia no win

2002	Krasnoyarsk **Ireland** 35–3	2011	Rotorua WC **Ireland** 62–12

IRELAND v PACIFIC ISLANDS

Played 1 Ireland won 1
Highest scores Ireland 61–17 in 2006, Pacific Islands 17–61 in 2006
Biggest win Ireland 61–17 in 2006, Pacific Islands no win

2006	Dublin **Ireland** 61–17

INTERNATIONAL RECORDS

WALES v FRANCE

Played 90 Wales won 44, France won 43, Drawn 3
Highest scores Wales 49–14 in 1910, France 51–0 in 1998
Biggest wins Wales 47–5 in 1909, France 51–0 in 1998

1908	Cardiff **Wales** 36–4	
1909	Paris **Wales** 47–5	
1910	Swansea **Wales** 49–14	
1911	Paris **Wales** 15–0	
1912	Newport **Wales** 14–8	
1913	Paris **Wales** 11–8	
1914	Swansea **Wales** 31–0	
1920	Paris **Wales** 6–5	
1921	Cardiff **Wales** 12–4	
1922	Paris **Wales** 11–3	
1923	Swansea **Wales** 16–8	
1924	Paris **Wales** 10–6	
1925	Cardiff **Wales** 11–5	
1926	Paris **Wales** 7–5	
1927	Swansea **Wales** 25–7	
1928	Paris **France** 8–3	
1929	Cardiff **Wales** 8–3	
1930	Paris **Wales** 11–0	
1931	Swansea **Wales** 35–3	
1947	Paris **Wales** 3–0	
1948	Swansea **France** 11–3	
1949	Paris **France** 5–3	
1950	Cardiff **Wales** 21–0	
1951	Paris **France** 8–3	
1952	Swansea **Wales** 9–5	
1953	Paris **Wales** 6–3	
1954	Cardiff **Wales** 19–13	
1955	Paris **Wales** 16–11	
1956	Cardiff **Wales** 5–3	
1957	Paris **Wales** 19–13	
1958	Cardiff **France** 16–6	
1959	Paris **France** 11–3	
1960	Cardiff **France** 16–8	
1961	Paris **France** 8–6	
1962	Cardiff **Wales** 3–0	
1963	Paris **France** 5–3	
1964	Cardiff **Drawn** 11–11	
1965	Paris **France** 22–13	
1966	Cardiff **Wales** 9–8	
1967	Paris **France** 20–14	
1968	Cardiff **France** 14–9	
1969	Paris **Drawn** 8–8	
1970	Cardiff **Wales** 11–6	
1971	Paris **Wales** 9–5	
1972	Cardiff **Wales** 20–6	
1973	Paris **France** 12–3	
1974	Cardiff **Drawn** 16–16	
1975	Paris **Wales** 25–10	
1976	Cardiff **Wales** 19–13	
1977	Paris **France** 16–9	
1978	Cardiff **Wales** 16–7	
1979	Paris **France** 14–13	
1980	Cardiff **Wales** 18–9	
1981	Paris **France** 19–15	
1982	Cardiff **Wales** 22–12	
1983	Paris **France** 16–9	
1984	Cardiff **France** 21–16	
1985	Paris **France** 14–3	
1986	Cardiff **France** 23–15	
1987	Paris **France** 16–9	
1988	Cardiff **France** 10–9	
1989	Paris **France** 31–12	
1990	Cardiff **France** 29–19	
1991	Paris **France** 36–3	
1991	Cardiff **France** 22–9	
	Non-championship match	
1992	Cardiff **France** 12–9	
1993	Paris **France** 26–10	
1994	Cardiff **Wales** 24–15	
1995	Paris **France** 21–9	
1996	Cardiff **Wales** 16–15	
1996	Cardiff **France** 40–33	
	Non-championship match	
1997	Paris **France 27–22**	
1998	Wembley **France** 51–0	
1999	Paris **Wales** 34–33	
1999	Cardiff **Wales** 34–23	
	Non-championship match	
2000	Cardiff **France** 36–3	
2001	Paris **Wales** 43–35	
2002	Cardiff **France** 37–33	
2003	Paris **France** 33–5	
2004	Cardiff **France** 29–22	
2005	Paris **Wales** 24–18	
2006	Cardiff **France** 21–16	
2007	Paris **France** 32–21	
2007	Cardiff **France** 34–7	
	Non-championship match	
2008	Cardiff **Wales** 29–12	
2009	Paris **France** 21–16	
2010	Cardiff **France** 26–20	
2011	Paris **France** 28–9	
2011	Auckland WC **France** 9–8	
2012	Cardiff **Wales** 16–9	

WALES v SOUTH AFRICA

Played 26 Wales won 1, South Africa won 24, Drawn 1
Highest scores Wales 36–38 in 2004, South Africa 96–13 in 1998
Biggest win Wales 29–19 in 1999, South Africa 96–13 in 1998

1906	Swansea **South Africa** 11–0	
1912	Cardiff **South Africa** 3–0	
1931	Swansea **South Africa** 8–3	
1951	Cardiff **South Africa** 6–3	
1960	Cardiff **South Africa** 3–0	
1964	Durban **South Africa** 24–3	
1970	Cardiff **Drawn** 6–6	
1994	Cardiff **South Africa** 20–12	
1995	Johannesburg **South Africa** 40–11	
1996	Cardiff **South Africa** 37–20	
1998	Pretoria **South Africa** 96–13	
1998	Wembley **South Africa** 28–20	
1999	Cardiff **Wales** 29–19	
2000	Cardiff **South Africa** 23–13	

2002	1 Bloemfontein **South Africa** 34–19	
	2 Cape Town **South Africa** 19–8	
	SA won series 2–0	
2004	Pretoria **South Africa** 53–18	
2004	Cardiff **South Africa** 38–36	
2005	Cardiff **South Africa** 33–16	
2007	Cardiff **South Africa** 34–12	
2008	1 Bloemfontein **South Africa** 43–17	
	2 Pretoria **South Africa** 37–21	
	SA won series 2–0	
2008	Cardiff **South Africa** 20–15	
2010	Cardiff **South Africa** 34–31	
2010	Cardiff **South Africa** 29–25	
2011	Wellington WC **South Africa** 17–16	

WALES v NEW ZEALAND

Played 28 Wales won 3, New Zealand won 25, Drawn 0
Highest scores Wales 37–53 in 2003, New Zealand 55–3 in 2003
Biggest wins Wales 13–8 in 1953, New Zealand 55–3 in 2003

1905	Cardiff **Wales** 3–0
1924	Swansea **New Zealand** 19–0
1935	Cardiff **Wales** 13–12
1953	Cardiff **Wales** 13–8
1963	Cardiff **New Zealand** 6–0
1967	Cardiff **New Zealand** 13–6
1969	1 Christchurch **New Zealand** 19–0
	2 Auckland **New Zealand** 33–12
	New Zealand won series 2–0
1972	Cardiff **New Zealand** 19–16
1978	Cardiff **New Zealand** 13–12
1980	Cardiff **New Zealand** 23–3
1987	Brisbane WC **New Zealand** 49–6
1988	1 Christchurch **New Zealand** 52–3
	2 Auckland **New Zealand** 54–9
	New Zealand won series 2–0

1989	Cardiff **New Zealand** 34–9
1995	Johannesburg WC **New Zealand** 34–9
1997	Wembley **New Zealand** 42–7
2002	Cardiff **New Zealand** 43–17
2003	Hamilton **New Zealand** 55–3
2003	Sydney WC **New Zealand** 53–37
2004	Cardiff **New Zealand** 26–25
2005	Cardiff **New Zealand** 41–3
2006	Cardiff **New Zealand** 45–10
2008	Cardiff **New Zealand** 29–9
2009	Cardiff **New Zealand** 19–12
2010	1 Dunedin **New Zealand** 42–9
	2 Hamilton **New Zealand** 29–10
	New Zealand won series 2–0
2010	Cardiff **New Zealand** 37–25

INTERNATIONAL RECORDS

WALES v AUSTRALIA

Played 35 Wales won 10, Australia won 24, Drawn 1
Highest scores Wales 29–29 in 2006, Australia 63–6 in 1991
Biggest wins Wales 28–3 in 1975, Australia 63–6 in 1991

1908 Cardiff **Wales** 9–6	1996 Cardiff **Australia** 28–19
1927 Cardiff **Australia** 18–8	1999 Cardiff WC **Australia** 24–9
1947 Cardiff **Wales** 6–0	2001 Cardiff **Australia** 21–13
1958 Cardiff **Wales** 9–3	2003 Sydney **Australia** 30–10
1966 Cardiff **Australia** 14–11	2005 Cardiff **Wales** 24–22
1969 Sydney **Wales** 19–16	2006 Cardiff **Drawn** 29–29
1973 Cardiff **Wales** 24–0	2007 1 Sydney **Australia** 29–23
1975 Cardiff **Wales** 28–3	2 Brisbane **Australia** 31–0
1978 1 Brisbane **Australia** 18–8	Australia won series 2–0
2 Sydney **Australia** 19–17	2007 Cardiff WC **Australia** 32–20
Australia won series 2–0	2008 Cardiff **Wales** 21–18
1981 Cardiff **Wales** 18–13	2009 Cardiff **Australia** 33–12
1984 Cardiff **Australia** 28–9	2010 Cardiff **Australia** 25–16
1987 Rotorua WC **Wales** 22–21	2011 Auckland WC **Australia** 21–18
1991 Brisbane **Australia** 63–6	2011 Cardiff **Australia** 24–18
1991 Cardiff WC **Australia** 38–3	2012 1 Brisbane **Australia** 27–19
1992 Cardiff **Australia** 23–6	2 Melbourne **Australia** 25–23
1996 1 Brisbane **Australia** 56–25	3 Sydney **Australia** 20–19
2 Sydney **Australia** 42–3	Australia won series 3–0
Australia won series 2–0	

WALES v NEW ZEALAND NATIVES

Played 1 Wales won 1
Highest scores Wales 5–0 in 1888, New Zealand Natives 0–5 in 1888
Biggest win Wales 5–0 in 1888, New Zealand Natives no win

1888 Swansea **Wales** 1G 2T to 0

WALES v NEW ZEALAND ARMY

Played 1 New Zealand Army won 1
Highest scores Wales 3–6 in 1919, New Zealand Army 6–3 in 1919
Biggest win Wales no win, New Zealand Army 6–3 in 1919

1919 Swansea **New Zealand Army** 6–3

WALES v ROMANIA

Played 8 Wales won 6, Romania won 2
Highest scores Wales 81–9 in 2001, Romania 24–6 in 1983
Biggest wins Wales 81–9 in 2001, Romania 24–6 in 1983

1983	Bucharest **Romania** 24–6	2001	Cardiff **Wales** 81–9
1988	Cardiff **Romania** 15–9	2002	Wrexham **Wales** 40–3
1994	Bucharest **Wales** 16–9	2003	Wrexham **Wales** 54–8
1997	Wrexham **Wales** 70–21	2004	Cardiff **Wales** 66–7

WALES v FIJI

Played 9 Wales won 7, Fiji won 1, Drawn 1
Highest scores Wales 66–0 in 2011, Fiji 38–34 in 2007
Biggest win Wales 66–0 in 2011, Fiji 38–34 in 2007

1985	Cardiff **Wales** 40–3	2005	Cardiff **Wales** 11–10
1986	Suva **Wales** 22–15	2007	Nantes WC **Fiji** 38–34
1994	Suva **Wales** 23–8	2010	Cardiff **Drawn** 16–16
1995	Cardiff **Wales** 19–15	2011	Hamilton WC **Wales** 66–0
2002	Cardiff **Wales** 58–14		

WALES v TONGA

Played 6 Wales won 6
Highest scores Wales 51–7 in 2001, Tonga 20–27 in 2003
Biggest win Wales 51–7 in 2001, Tonga no win

1986	Nuku'Alofa **Wales** 15–7	1997	Swansea **Wales** 46–12
1987	Palmerston North WC **Wales** 29–16	2001	Cardiff **Wales** 51–7
1994	Nuku'Alofa **Wales** 18–9	2003	Canberra WC **Wales** 27–20

WALES v SAMOA

Played 8 Wales won 5, Samoa won 3, Drawn 0
Highest scores Wales 50–6 in 2000, Samoa 38–31 in 1999
Biggest wins Wales 50–6 in 2000, Samoa 34–9 in 1994

1986	Apia **Wales** 32–14	1999	Cardiff WC **Samoa** 38–31
1988	Cardiff **Wales** 28–6	2000	Cardiff **Wales** 50–6
1991	Cardiff WC **Samoa** 16–13	2009	Cardiff **Wales** 17–13
1994	Moamoa **Samoa** 34–9	2011	Hamilton WC **Wales** 17–10

WALES v CANADA

Played 12 Wales won 11, Canada won 1, Drawn 0
Highest scores Wales 61–26 in 2006, Canada 26–24 in 1993 & 26–61 in 2006
Biggest wins Wales 60–3 in 2005, Canada 26–24 in 1993

1987	Invercargill WC **Wales** 40–9		2003	Melbourne WC **Wales** 41–10
1993	Cardiff **Canada** 26–24		2005	Toronto **Wales** 60–3
1994	Toronto **Wales** 33–15		2006	Cardiff **Wales** 61–26
1997	Toronto **Wales** 28–25		2007	Nantes WC **Wales** 42–17
1999	Cardiff **Wales** 33–19		2008	Cardiff **Wales** 34–13
2002	Cardiff **Wales** 32–21		2009	Toronto **Wales** 32–23

WALES v UNITED STATES

Played 7 Wales won 7
Highest scores Wales 77–3 in 2005, United States 23–28 in 1997
Biggest win Wales 77–3 in 2005, United States no win

1987	Cardiff **Wales** 46–0			Wales won series 2–0
1997	Cardiff **Wales** 34–14		2000	Cardiff **Wales** 42–11
1997	1 Wilmington **Wales** 30–20		2005	Hartford **Wales** 77–3
	2 San Francisco **Wales** 28–23		2009	Chicago **Wales** 48–15

WALES v NAMIBIA

Played 4 Wales won 4
Highest scores Wales 81–7 in 2011, Namibia 30–34 in 1990
Biggest win Wales 81–7 in 2011, Namibia no win

1990	1 Windhoek **Wales** 18–9		1993	Windhoek **Wales** 38–23
	2 Windhoek **Wales** 34–30		2011	New Plymouth WC **Wales** 81–7
	Wales won series 2–0			

WALES v BARBARIANS

Played 4 Wales won 2, Barbarians won 2
Highest scores Wales 31–10 in 1996, Barbarians 31–24 in 1990 and 31–28 in 2011
Biggest wins Wales 31–10 in 1996, Barbarians 31–24 in 1990

1990	Cardiff **Barbarians** 31–24		2011	Cardiff **Barbarians** 31–28
1996	Cardiff **Wales** 31–10		2012	Cardiff **Wales** 30–21

WALES v ARGENTINA

Played 13 Wales won 9, Argentina won 4
Highest scores Wales 44–50 in 2004, Argentina 50–44 in 2004
Biggest win Wales 33–16 in 2009, Argentina 45–27 in 2006

1991	Cardiff WC **Wales** 16–7		2 Buenos Aires **Wales** 35–20
1998	Llanelli **Wales** 43–30		Series drawn 1–1
1999	1 Buenos Aires **Wales** 36–26	2006	1 Puerto Madryn **Argentina** 27–25
	2 Buenos Aires **Wales** 23–16		2 Buenos Aires **Argentina** 45–27
	Wales won series 2–0		Argentina won series 2–0
1999	Cardiff WC **Wales** 23–18	2007	Cardiff **Wales** 27–20
2001	Cardiff **Argentina** 30–16	2009	Cardiff **Wales** 33–16
2004	1 Tucumán **Argentina** 50–44	2011	Cardiff **Wales** 28–13

WALES v ZIMBABWE

Played 3 Wales won 3
Highest scores Wales 49–11 in 1998, Zimbabwe 14–35 in 1993
Biggest win Wales 49–11 in 1998, Zimbabwe no win

1993	1 Bulawayo **Wales** 35–14		Wales won series 2–0
	2 Harare **Wales** 42–13	1998	Harare **Wales** 49–11

WALES v JAPAN

Played 7 Wales won 7
Highest scores Wales 98–0 in 2004, Japan 30–53 in 2001
Biggest win Wales 98–0 in 2004, Japan no win

1993	Cardiff **Wales** 55–5		2 Tokyo **Wales** 53–30
1995	Bloemfontein WC **Wales** 57–10		Wales won series 2–0
1999	Cardiff WC **Wales** 64–15	2004	Cardiff **Wales** 98–0
2001	1 Osaka **Wales** 64–10	2007	Cardiff WC **Wales** 72–18

WALES v PORTUGAL

Played 1 Wales won 1
Highest scores Wales 102–11 in 1994, Portugal 11–102 in 1994
Biggest win Wales 102–11 in 1994, Portugal no win

1994	Lisbon **Wales** 102–11

WALES v SPAIN

Played 1 Wales won 1
Highest scores Wales 54–0 in 1994, Spain 0–54 in 1994
Biggest win Wales 54–0 in 1994, Spain no win

1994	Madrid **Wales** 54–0	

WALES v ITALY

Played 19 Wales won 16, Italy won 2, Drawn 1
Highest scores Wales 60–21 in 1999, Italy 30–22 in 2003
Biggest wins Wales 60–21 in 1999 and 47–8 in 2008, Italy 30–22 in 2003

1994	Cardiff **Wales** 29–19	2004	Cardiff **Wales** 44–10
1996	Cardiff **Wales** 31–26	2005	Rome **Wales** 38–8
1996	Rome **Wales** 31–22	2006	Cardiff **Drawn** 18–18
1998	Llanelli **Wales** 23–20	2007	Rome **Italy** 23–20
1999	Treviso **Wales** 60–21	2008	Cardiff **Wales** 47–8
2000	Cardiff **Wales** 47–16	2009	Rome **Wales** 20–15
2001	Rome **Wales** 33–23	2010	Cardiff **Wales** 33–10
2002	Cardiff **Wales** 44–20	2011	Rome **Wales** 24–16
2003	Rome **Italy** 30–22	2012	Cardiff **Wales** 24–3
2003	Canberra WC **Wales** 27–15		

WALES v PACIFIC ISLANDS

Played 1 Wales won 1
Highest scores Wales 38–20 in 2006, Pacific Islands 20–38 in 2006
Biggest win Wales 38–20 in 2006, Pacific Islands no win

2006	Cardiff **Wales** 38–20	

BRITISH/IRISH ISLES v SOUTH AFRICA

Played 46 British/Irish won 17, South Africa won 23, Drawn 6
Highest scores British/Irish 28–9 in 1974 & 2009, South Africa 35–16 in 1997
Biggest wins British/Irish 28–9 in 1974 & 2009, South Africa 34–14 in 1962

1891	1 Port Elizabeth **British/Irish** 4–0		British/Irish won series 3–1
	2 Kimberley **British/Irish** 3–0	1903	1 Johannesburg **Drawn** 10–10
	3 Cape Town **British/Irish** 4–0		2 Kimberley **Drawn** 0–0
	British/Irish won series 3–0		3 Cape Town **South Africa** 8–0
1896	1 Port Elizabeth **British/Irish** 8–0		South Africa won series 1–0, with
	2 Johannesburg **British/Irish** 17–8		two drawn
	3 Kimberley **British/Irish** 9–3	1910	1 Johannesburg **South Africa** 14–10
	4 Cape Town **South Africa** 5–0		2 Port Elizabeth **British/Irish** 8–3

3 Cape Town **South Africa** 21–5
South Africa won series 2–1
1924　1 Durban **South Africa** 7–3
　　　2 Johannesburg **South Africa** 17–0
　　　3 Port Elizabeth **Drawn** 3–3
　　　4 Cape Town **South Africa** 16–9
South Africa won series 3–0, with 1
draw
1938　1 Johannesburg **South Africa** 26–12
　　　2 Port Elizabeth **South Africa** 19–3
　　　3 Cape Town **British/Irish** 21–16
South Africa won series 2–1
1955　1 Johannesburg **British/Irish** 23–22
　　　2 Cape Town **South Africa** 25–9
　　　3 Pretoria **British/Irish** 9–6
　　　4 Port Elizabeth **South Africa** 22–8
Series drawn 2–2
1962　1 Johannesburg **Drawn** 3–3
　　　2 Durban **South Africa** 3–0
　　　3 Cape Town **South Africa** 8–3
　　　4 Bloemfontein **South Africa** 34–14
South Africa won series 3–0, with 1
draw
1968　1 Pretoria **South Africa** 25–20
　　　2 Port Elizabeth **Drawn** 6–6

3 Cape Town **South Africa** 11–6
4 Johannesburg **South Africa** 19–6
South Africa won series 3–0, with 1
draw
1974　1 Cape Town **British/Irish** 12–3
　　　2 Pretoria **British/Irish** 28–9
　　　3 Port Elizabeth **British/Irish** 26–9
　　　4 Johannesburg **Drawn** 13–13
British/Irish won series 3–0, with 1
draw
1980　1 Cape Town **South Africa** 26–22
　　　2 Bloemfontein **South Africa** 26–19
　　　3 Port Elizabeth **South Africa**
12–10
　　　4 Pretoria **British/Irish** 17–13
South Africa won series 3–1
1997　1 Cape Town **British/Irish** 25–16
　　　2 Durban **British/Irish** 18–15
　　　3 Johannesburg **South Africa**
35–16
British/Irish won series 2–1
2009　1 Durban **South Africa** 26–21
　　　2 Pretoria **South Africa** 28–25
　　　3 Johannesburg **British/Irish** 28–9
South Africa won series 2–1

BRITISH/IRISH ISLES v NEW ZEALAND

Played 35 British/Irish won 6, New Zealand won 27, Drawn 2
Highest scores British/Irish 20–7 in 1993, New Zealand 48–18 in 2005
Biggest wins British/Irish 20–7 in 1993, New Zealand 38–6 in 1983

1904　Wellington **New Zealand** 9–3
1930　1 Dunedin **British/Irish** 6–3
　　　2 Christchurch **New Zealand** 13–10
　　　3 Auckland **New Zealand** 15–10
　　　4 Wellington **New Zealand** 22–8
New Zealand won series 3–1
1950　1 Dunedin **Drawn** 9–9
　　　2 Christchurch **New Zealand** 8–0
　　　3 Wellington **New Zealand** 6–3
　　　4 Auckland **New Zealand** 11–8
New Zealand won series 3–0, with 1
draw
1959　1 Dunedin **New Zealand** 18–17
　　　2 Wellington **New Zealand** 11–8
　　　3 Christchurch **New Zealand** 22–8
　　　4 Auckland **British/Irish** 9–6
New Zealand won series 3–1

1966　1 Dunedin **New Zealand** 20–3
　　　2 Wellington **New Zealand** 16–12
　　　3 Christchurch **New Zealand** 19–6
　　　4 Auckland **New Zealand** 24–11
New Zealand won series 4–0
1971　1 Dunedin **British/Irish** 9–3
　　　2 Christchurch **New Zealand** 22–12
　　　3 Wellington **British/Irish** 13–3
　　　4 Auckland **Drawn** 14–14
British/Irish won series 2–1, with 1
draw
1977　1 Wellington **New Zealand** 16–12
　　　2 Christchurch **British/Irish** 13–9
　　　3 Dunedin **New Zealand** 19–7
　　　4 Auckland **New Zealand** 10–9
New Zealand won series 3–1
1983　1 Christchurch **New Zealand** 16–12

2 Wellington **New Zealand** 9–0
3 Dunedin **New Zealand** 15–8
4 Auckland **New Zealand** 38–6
New Zealand won series 4–0
1993 1 Christchurch **New Zealand** 20–18
2 Wellington **British/Irish** 20–7

3 Auckland **New Zealand** 30–13
New Zealand won series 2–1
2005 1 Christchurch **New Zealand** 21–3
2 Wellington **New Zealand** 48–18
3 Auckland **New Zealand** 38–19
New Zealand won series 3–0

ANGLO-WELSH v NEW ZEALAND

Played 3 New Zealand won 2, Drawn 1
Highest scores Anglo Welsh 5–32 in 1908, New Zealand 32–5 in 1908
Biggest win Anglo Welsh no win, New Zealand 29–0 in 1908

1908 1 Dunedin **New Zealand** 32–5
2 Wellington **Drawn** 3–3
3 Auckland **New Zealand** 29–0

New Zealand won series 2–0 with one
drawn

BRITISH/IRISH ISLES v AUSTRALIA

Played 20 British/Irish won 15, Australia won 5, Drawn 0
Highest scores: British/Irish 31–0 in 1966, Australia 35–14 in 2001
Biggest wins: British/Irish 31–0 in 1966, Australia 35–14 in 2001

1899 1 Sydney **Australia** 13–3
2 Brisbane **British/Irish** 11–0
3 Sydney **British/Irish** 11–10
4 Sydney **British/Irish** 13–0
British/Irish won series 3–1
1904 1 Sydney **British/Irish** 17–0
2 Brisbane **British/Irish** 17–3
3 Sydney **British/Irish** 16–0
British/Irish won series 3–0
1930 Sydney **Australia** 6–5
1950 1 Brisbane **British/Irish** 19–6
2 Sydney **British/Irish** 24–3
British/Irish won series 2–0
1959 1 Brisbane **British/Irish** 17–6

2 Sydney **British/Irish** 24–3
British/Irish won series 2–0
1966 1 Sydney **British/Irish** 11–8
2 Brisbane **British/Irish** 31–0
British/Irish won series 2–0
1989 1 Sydney **Australia** 30–12
2 Brisbane **British/Irish** 19–12
3 Sydney **British/Irish** 19–18
British/Irish won series 2–1
2001 1 Brisbane **British/Irish** 29–13
2 Melbourne **Australia** 35–14
3 Sydney **Australia** 29–23
Australia won series 2–1

BRITISH/IRISH ISLES v ARGENTINA

Played 1 British/Irish won 0, Argentina won 0, Drawn 1
Highest scores British/Irish 25–25 in 2005, Argentina 25–25 in 2005
Biggest wins British/Irish no win to date, Argentina no win to date

2005 Cardiff **Drawn** 25–25

FRANCE v SOUTH AFRICA

169

Played 38 France won 11, South Africa won 21, Drawn 6
Highest scores France 36–26 in 2006, South Africa 52–10 in 1997
Biggest wins France 30–10 in 2002, South Africa 52–10 in 1997

1913	Bordeaux **South Africa** 38–5
1952	Paris **South Africa** 25–3
1958	1 Cape Town **Drawn** 3–3
	2 Johannesburg **France** 9–5
	France won series 1–0, with 1 draw
1961	Paris **Drawn** 0–0
1964	Springs (SA) **France** 8–6
1967	1 Durban **South Africa** 26–3
	2 Bloemfontein **South Africa** 16–3
	3 Johannesburg **France** 19–14
	4 Cape Town **Drawn** 6–6
	South Africa won series 2–1, with 1 draw
1968	1 Bordeaux **South Africa** 12–9
	2 Paris **South Africa** 16–11
	South Africa won series 2–0
1971	1 Bloemfontein **South Africa** 22–9
	2 Durban **Drawn** 8–8
	South Africa won series 1–0, with 1 draw
1974	1 Toulouse **South Africa** 13–4
	2 Paris **South Africa** 10–8
	South Africa won series 2–0
1975	1 Bloemfontein **South Africa** 38–25
	2 Pretoria **South Africa** 33–18
	South Africa won series 2–0
1980	Pretoria **South Africa** 37–15

1992	1 Lyons **South Africa** 20–15
	2 Paris **France** 29–16
	Series drawn 1–1
1993	1 Durban **Drawn** 20–20
	2 Johannesburg **France** 18–17
	France won series 1–0, with 1 draw
1995	Durban WC **South Africa** 19–15
1996	1 Bordeaux **South Africa** 22–12
	2 Paris **South Africa** 13–12
	South Africa won series 2–0
1997	1 Lyons **South Africa** 36–32
	2 Paris **South Africa** 52–10
	South Africa won series 2–0
2001	1 Johannesburg **France** 32–23
	2 Durban **South Africa** 20–15
	Series drawn 1–1
2001	Paris **France** 20–10
2002	Marseilles **France** 30–10
2005	1 Durban **Drawn** 30–30
	2 Port Elizabeth **South Africa** 27–13
	South Africa won series 1–0, with 1 draw
2005	Paris **France** 26–20
2006	Cape Town **France** 36–26
2009	Toulouse **France** 20–13
2010	Cape Town **South Africa** 42–17

FRANCE v NEW ZEALAND

Played 51 France won 12, New Zealand won 38, Drawn 1
Highest scores France 43–31 in 1999, New Zealand 61–10 in 2007
Biggest wins France 22–8 in 1994, New Zealand 61–10 in 2007

1906	Paris **New Zealand** 38–8
1925	Toulouse **New Zealand** 30–6
1954	Paris **France** 3–0
1961	1 Auckland **New Zealand** 13–6
	2 Wellington **New Zealand** 5–3
	3 Christchurch **New Zealand** 32–3
	New Zealand won series 3–0
1964	Paris **New Zealand** 12–3
1967	Paris **New Zealand** 21–15

1968	1 Christchurch **New Zealand** 12–9
	2 Wellington **New Zealand** 9–3
	3 Auckland **New Zealand** 19–12
	New Zealand won series 3–0
1973	Paris **France** 13–6
1977	1 Toulouse **France** 18–13
	2 Paris **New Zealand** 15–3
	Series drawn 1–1
1979	1 Christchurch **New Zealand** 23–9

2 Auckland **France** 24–19
Series drawn 1–1
1981 1 Toulouse **New Zealand** 13–9
2 Paris **New Zealand** 18–6
New Zealand won series 2–0
1984 1 Christchurch **New Zealand** 10–9
2 Auckland **New Zealand** 31–18
New Zealand won series 2–0
1986 Christchurch **New Zealand** 18–9
1986 1 Toulouse **New Zealand** 19–7
2 Nantes **France** 16–3
Series drawn 1–1
1987 Auckland WC **New Zealand** 29–9
1989 1 Christchurch **New Zealand** 25–17
2 Auckland **New Zealand** 34–20
New Zealand won series 2–0
1990 1 Nantes **New Zealand** 24–3
2 Paris **New Zealand** 30–12
New Zealand won series 2–0
1994 1 Christchurch **France** 22–8
2 Auckland **France** 23–20
France won series 2–0
1995 1 Toulouse **France** 22–15
2 Paris **New Zealand** 37–12

Series drawn 1–1
1999 Wellington **New Zealand** 54–7
1999 Twickenham WC **France** 43–31
2000 1 Paris **New Zealand** 39–26
2 Marseilles **France** 42–33
Series drawn 1–1
2001 Wellington **New Zealand** 37–12
2002 Paris **Drawn** 20–20
2003 Christchurch **New Zealand** 31–23
2003 Sydney WC **New Zealand** 40–13
2004 Paris **New Zealand** 45–6
2006 1 Lyons **New Zealand** 47–3
2 Paris **New Zealand** 23–11
New Zealand won series 2–0
2007 1 Auckland **New Zealand** 42–11
2 Wellington **New Zealand** 61–10
New Zealand won series 2–0
2007 Cardiff WC **France** 20–18
2009 1 Dunedin **France** 27–22
2 Wellington **New Zealand** 14–10
Series drawn 1–1
2009 Marseilles **New Zealand** 39–12
2011 Auckland WC **New Zealand** 37–17
2011 Auckland WC **New Zealand** 8–7

FRANCE v AUSTRALIA

Played 41 France won 16, Australia won 23, Drawn 2
Highest scores France 34–6 in 1976, Australia 59–16 in 2010
Biggest wins France 34–6 in 1976, Australia 59–16 in 2010

1928 Paris **Australia** 11–8
1948 Paris **France** 13–6
1958 Paris **France** 19–0
1961 Sydney **France** 15–8
1967 Paris **France** 20–14
1968 Sydney **Australia** 11–10
1971 1 Toulouse **Australia** 13–11
2 Paris **France** 18–9
Series drawn 1–1
1972 1 Sydney **Drawn** 14–14
2 Brisbane **France** 16–15
France won series 1–0, with 1 draw
1976 1 Bordeaux **France** 18–15
2 Paris **France** 34–6
France won series 2–0
1981 1 Brisbane **Australia** 17–15
2 Sydney **Australia** 24–14

Australia won series 2–0
1983 1 Clermont-Ferrand **Drawn** 15–15
2 Paris **France** 15–6
France won series 1–0, with 1 draw
1986 Sydney **Australia** 27–14
1987 Sydney WC **France** 30–24
1989 1 Strasbourg **Australia** 32–15
2 Lille **France** 25–19
Series drawn 1–1
1990 1 Sydney **Australia** 21–9
2 Brisbane **Australia** 48–31
3 Sydney **France** 28–19
Australia won series 2–1
1993 1 Bordeaux **France** 16–13
2 Paris **Australia** 24–3
Series drawn 1–1
1997 1 Sydney **Australia** 29–15

	2 Brisbane **Australia** 26–19		2005	Brisbane **Australia** 37–31
	Australia won series 2–0		2005	Marseilles **France** 26–16
1998	Paris **Australia** 32–21		2008	1 Sydney **Australia** 34–13
1999	Cardiff WC **Australia** 35–12			2 Brisbane **Australia** 40–10
2000	Paris **Australia** 18–13			Australia won series 2–0
2001	Marseilles **France** 14–13		2008	Paris **Australia** 18–13
2002	1 Melbourne **Australia** 29–17		2009	Sydney **Australia** 22–6
	2 Sydney **Australia** 31–25		2010	Paris **Australia** 59–16
	Australia won series 2–0			
2004	Paris **France** 27–14			

FRANCE v UNITED STATES

Played 7 France won 6, United States won 1, Drawn 0
Highest scores France 41–9 in 1991 and 41–14 in 2003, United States 31–39 in 2004
Biggest wins France 41–9 in 1991, United States 17–3 in 1924

1920	Paris **France** 14–5			*Abandoned after 43 mins
1924	Paris **United States** 17–3			France won series 2–0
1976	Chicago **France** 33–14		2003	Wollongong WC **France** 41–14
1991	1 Denver **France** 41–9		2004	Hartford **France** 39–31
	2 Colorado Springs **France** 10–3*			

FRANCE v ROMANIA

Played 49 France won 39, Romania won 8, Drawn 2
Highest scores France 67–20 in 2000, Romania 21–33 in 1991
Biggest wins France 59–3 in 1924, Romania 15–0 in 1980

1924	Paris **France** 59–3		1975	Bordeaux **France** 36–12
1938	Bucharest **France** 11–8		1976	Bucharest **Romania** 15–12
1957	Bucharest **France** 18–15		1977	Clermont-Ferrand **France** 9–6
1957	Bordeaux **France** 39–0		1978	Bucharest **France** 9–6
1960	Bucharest **Romania** 11–5		1979	Montauban **France** 30–12
1961	Bayonne **Drawn** 5–5		1980	Bucharest **Romania** 15–0
1962	Bucharest **Romania** 3–0		1981	Narbonne **France** 17–9
1963	Toulouse **Drawn** 6–6		1982	Bucharest **Romania** 13–9
1964	Bucharest **France** 9–6		1983	Toulouse **France** 26–15
1965	Lyons **France** 8–3		1984	Bucharest **France** 18–3
1966	Bucharest **France** 9–3		1986	Lille **France** 25–13
1967	Nantes **France** 11–3		1986	Bucharest **France** 20–3
1968	Bucharest **Romania** 15–14		1987	Wellington WC **France** 55–12
1969	Tarbes **France** 14–9		1987	Agen **France** 49–3
1970	Bucharest **France** 14–3		1988	Bucharest **France** 16–12
1971	Béziers **France** 31–12		1990	Auch **Romania** 12–6
1972	Constanza **France** 15–6		1991	Bucharest **France** 33–21
1973	Valence **France** 7–6		1991	Béziers WC **France** 30–3
1974	Bucharest **Romania** 15–10		1992	Le Havre **France** 25–6

INTERNATIONAL RECORDS

1993	Bucharest **France** 37–20	1997	Lourdes LC **France 39–3**
1993	Brive **France** 51–0	1999	Castres **France** 62–8
1995	Bucharest **France** 24–15	2000	Bucharest **France** 67–20
1995	Tucumán LC **France 52–8**	2003	Lens **France** 56–8
1996	Aurillac **France** 64–12	2006	Bucharest **France** 62–14
1997	Bucharest **France** 51–20		

FRANCE v NEW ZEALAND MAORI

Played 1 New Zealand Maori won 1
Highest scores France 3–12 in 1926, New Zealand Maori 12–3 in 1926
Biggest win France no win, New Zealand Maori 12–3 in 1926

1926	Paris **New Zealand Maori** 12–3	

FRANCE v GERMANY

Played 15 France won 13, Germany won 2, Drawn 0
Highest scores France 38–17 in 1933, Germany 17–16 in 1927 & 17–38 in 1933
Biggest wins France 34–0 in 1931, Germany 3–0 in 1938

1927	Paris **France** 30–5	1934	Hanover **France** 13–9
1927	Frankfurt **Germany** 17–16	1935	Paris **France** 18–3
1928	Hanover **France** 14–3	1936	1 Berlin **France** 19–14
1929	Paris **France** 24–0		2 Hanover **France** 6–3
1930	Berlin **France** 31–0		France won series 2–0
1931	Paris **France** 34–0	1937	Paris **France** 27–6
1932	Frankfurt **France** 20–4	1938	Frankfurt **Germany** 3–0
1933	Paris **France** 38–17	1938	Bucharest **France** 8–5

FRANCE v ITALY

Played 33 France won 31, Italy won 2, Drawn 0
Highest scores France 60–13 in 1967, Italy 40–32 in 1997
Biggest wins France 60–13 in 1967, Italy 40–32 in 1997

1937	Paris **France** 43–5	1962	Brescia **France** 6–3
1952	Milan **France** 17–8	1963	Grenoble **France** 14–12
1953	Lyons **France** 22–8	1964	Parma **France** 12–3
1954	Rome **France** 39–12	1965	Pau **France** 21–0
1955	Grenoble **France** 24–0	1966	Naples **France** 21–0
1956	Padua **France** 16–3	1967	Toulon **France** 60–13
1957	Agen **France** 38–6	1995	Buenos Aires LC **France 34–22**
1958	Naples **France** 11–3	1997	Grenoble **Italy** 40–32
1959	Nantes **France** 22–0	1997	Auch LC **France 30–19**
1960	Treviso **France** 26–0	2000	Paris **France** 42–31
1961	Chambéry **France** 17–0	2001	Rome **France** 30–19

INTERNATIONAL RECORDS

2002	Paris **France** 33–12	2008	Paris **France** 25–13
2003	Rome **France** 53–27	2009	Rome **France** 50–8
2004	Paris **France** 25–0	2010	Paris **France** 46–20
2005	Rome **France** 56–13	2011	Rome **Italy** 22–21
2006	Paris **France** 37–12	2012	Paris **France** 30–12
2007	Rome **France** 39–3		

FRANCE v BRITISH XVs

Played 5 France won 2, British XVs won 3, Drawn 0
Highest scores France 27–29 in 1989, British XV 36–3 in 1940
Biggest wins France 21–9 in 1945, British XV 36–3 in 1940

1940	Paris **British XV** 36–3	1946	Paris **France** 10–0
1945	Paris **France** 21–9	1989	Paris **British XV** 29–27
1945	Richmond **British XV** 27–6		

FRANCE v WALES XVs

Played 2 France won 1, Wales XV won 1
Highest scores France 12–0 in 1946, Wales XV 8–0 in 1945
Biggest wins France 12–0 in 1946, Wales XV 8–0 in 1945

1945	Swansea **Wales XV** 8–0	1946	Paris **France** 12–0

FRANCE v IRELAND XVs

Played 1 France won 1
Highest scores France 4–3 in 1946, Ireland XV 3–4 in 1946
Biggest win France 4–3 in 1946, Ireland XV no win

1946	Dublin **France** 4–3

FRANCE v NEW ZEALAND ARMY

Played 1 New Zealand Army won 1
Highest scores France 9–14 in 1946, New Zealand Army 14–9 in 1946
Biggest win France no win, New Zealand Army 14–9 in 1946

1946	Paris **New Zealand Army** 14–9

INTERNATIONAL RECORDS

FRANCE v ARGENTINA

Played 46 France won 33, Argentina won 12, Drawn 1
Highest scores France 49–10 in 2012, Argentina 41–13 in 2010
Biggest wins France 49–10 in 2012, Argentina 41–13 in 2010

1949 1 Buenos Aires **France** 5–0	1988 1 Nantes **France** 29–9
2 Buenos Aires **France** 12–3	2 Lille **France** 28–18
France won series 2–0	France won series 2–0
1954 1 Buenos Aires **France** 22–8	1992 1 Buenos Aires **France** 27–12
2 Buenos Aires **France** 30–3	2 Buenos Aires **France** 33–9
France won series 2–0	France won series 2–0
1960 1 Buenos Aires **France** 37–3	1992 Nantes **Argentina** 24–20
2 Buenos Aires **France** 12–3	1995 Buenos Aires LC **France** 47–12
3 Buenos Aires **France** 29–6	1996 1 Buenos Aires **France** 34–27
France won series 3–0	2 Buenos Aires **France** 34–15
1974 1 Buenos Aires **France** 20–15	France won series 2–0
2 Buenos Aires **France** 31–27	1997 Tarbes LC **France** 32–27
France won series 2–0	1998 1 Buenos Aires **France** 35–18
1975 1 Lyons **France** 29–6	2 Buenos Aires **France** 37–12
2 Paris **France** 36–21	France won series 2–0
France won series 2–0	1998 Nantes **France** 34–14
1977 1 Buenos Aires **France** 26–3	1999 Dublin WC **France** 47–26
2 Buenos Aires **Drawn** 18–18	2002 Buenos Aires **Argentina** 28–27
France won series 1–0, with 1 draw	2003 1 Buenos Aires **Argentina** 10–6
1982 1 Toulouse **France** 25–12	2 Buenos Aires **Argentina** 33–32
2 Paris **France** 13–6	Argentina won series 2–0
France won series 2–0	2004 Marseilles **Argentina** 24–14
1985 1 Buenos Aires **Argentina** 24–16	2006 Paris **France** 27–26
2 Buenos Aires **France** 23–15	2007 Paris WC **Argentina** 17–12
Series drawn 1–1	2007 Paris WC **Argentina** 34–10
1986 1 Buenos Aires **Argentina** 15–13	2008 Marseilles **France** 12–6
2 Buenos Aires **France** 22–9	2010 Buenos Aires **Argentina** 41–13
Series drawn 1–1	2010 Montpellier **France** 15–9
1988 1 Buenos Aires **France** 18–15	2012 1 Cordoba **Argentina** 23–20
2 Buenos Aires **Argentina** 18–6	2 Tucuman **France** 49–10
Series drawn 1–1	Series drawn 1–1

FRANCE v CZECHOSLOVAKIA

Played 2 France won 2
Highest scores France 28–3 in 1956, Czechoslovakia 6–19 in 1968
Biggest win France 28–3 in 1956, Czechoslovakia no win

1956 Toulouse **France** 28–3	1968 Prague **France** 19–6

FRANCE v FIJI

Played 8 France won 8
Highest scores France 77–10 in 2001, Fiji 19–28 in 1999
Biggest win France 77–10 in 2001, Fiji no win

1964	Paris France 21–3	1999	Toulouse WC France 28–19
1987	Auckland WC France 31–16	2001	Saint Etienne France 77–10
1991	Grenoble WC France 33–9	2003	Brisbane WC France 61–18
1998	Suva France 34–9	2010	Nantes France 34–12

FRANCE v JAPAN

Played 3 France won 3
Highest scores France 51–29 in 2003, Japan 29–51 in 2003
Biggest win France 51–29 in 2003, Japan no win

1973	Bordeaux France 30–18	2011	Albany WC France 47–21
2003	Townsville WC France 51–29		

FRANCE v ZIMBABWE

Played 1 France won 1
Highest scores France 70–12 in 1987, Zimbabwe 12–70 in 1987
Biggest win France 70–12 in 1987, Zimbabwe no win

1987	Auckland WC France 70–12

FRANCE v CANADA

Played 8 France won 7, Canada won 1, Drawn 0
Highest scores France 50–6 in 2005, Canada 20–33 in 1999
Biggest wins France 50–6 in 2005, Canada 18–16 in 1994

1991	Agen WC France 19–13	2002	Paris France 35–3
1994	Nepean Canada 18–16	2004	Toronto France 47–13
1994	Besançon France 28–9	2005	Nantes France 50–6
1999	Béziers WC France 33–20	2011	Napier WC France 46–19

FRANCE v TONGA

Played 4 France won 2, Tonga won 2
Highest scores France 43–8 in 2005, Tonga 20–16 in 1999
Biggest win France 43–8 in 2005, Tonga 19–14 in 2011

1995	Pretoria WC France 38–10	2005	Toulouse France 43–8
1999	Nuku'alofa Tonga 20–16	2011	Wellington WC Tonga 19–14

FRANCE v IVORY COAST

Played 1 France won 1
Highest scores France 54–18 in 1995, Ivory Coast 18–54 in 1995
Biggest win France 54–18 in 1995, Ivory Coast no win

1995 Rustenburg WC **France** 54–18	

FRANCE v SAMOA

Played 2 France won 2
Highest scores France 43–5 in 2009, Samoa 22–39 in 1999
Biggest win France 43–5 in 2009, Samoa no win

1999 Apia **France** 39–22	2009 Paris **France** 43–5

FRANCE v NAMIBIA

Played 2 France won 2
Highest scores France 87–10 in 2007, Namibia 13–47 in 1999
Biggest win France 87–10 in 2007, Namibia no win

1999 Bordeaux WC **France** 47–13	2007 Toulouse WC **France** 87–10

FRANCE v GEORGIA

Played 1 France won 1
Highest scores France 64–7 in 2007, Georgia 7–64 in 2007
Biggest win France 64–7 in 2007, Georgia no win

2007 Marseilles WC **France** 64–7	

FRANCE v PACIFIC ISLANDS

Played 1 Wales won 1
Highest scores France 42–17 in 2008, Pacific Islands 17–42 in 2008
Biggest win France 42–17 in 2008, Pacific Islands no win

2008 Sochaux **France** 42–17	

SOUTH AFRICA v NEW ZEALAND

Played 85 **New Zealand won 48, South Africa won 34, Drawn 3**
Highest scores New Zealand 55–35 in 1997, South Africa 46–40 in 2000
Biggest wins New Zealand 52–16 in 2003, South Africa 17–0 in 1928

1921 1 Dunedin **New Zealand** 13–5	1981 1 Christchurch **New Zealand** 14–9
2 Auckland **South Africa** 9–5	2 Wellington **South Africa** 24–12
3 Wellington **Drawn** 0–0	3 Auckland **New Zealand** 25–22
Series drawn 1–1, with 1 draw	New Zealand won series 2–1
1928 1 Durban **South Africa** 17–0	1992 Johannesburg **New Zealand** 27–24
2 Johannesburg **New Zealand** 7–6	1994 1 Dunedin **New Zealand** 22–14
3 Port Elizabeth **South Africa** 11–6	2 Wellington **New Zealand** 13–9
4 Cape Town **New Zealand** 13–5	3 Auckland **Drawn** 18–18
Series drawn 2–2	New Zealand won series 2–0, with
1937 1 Wellington **New Zealand** 13–7	1 draw
2 Christchurch **South Africa** 13–6	1995 Johannesburg WC **South Africa** 15–12
3 Auckland **South Africa** 17–6	(aet)
South Africa won series 2–1	1996 Christchurch TN **New Zealand** 15–11
1949 1 Cape Town **South Africa** 15–11	1996 Cape Town TN **New Zealand** 29–18
2 Johannesburg **South Africa** 12–6	1996 1 Durban **New Zealand** 23–19
3 Durban **South Africa** 9–3	2 Pretoria **New Zealand** 33–26
4 Port Elizabeth **South Africa** 11–8	3 Johannesburg **South Africa**
South Africa won series 4–0	32–22
1956 1 Dunedin **New Zealand** 10–6	New Zealand won series 2–1
2 Wellington **South Africa** 8–3	1997 Johannesburg TN **New Zealand** 35–32
3 Christchurch **New Zealand** 17–10	1997 Auckland TN **New Zealand** 55–35
4 Auckland **New Zealand** 11–5	1998 Wellington TN **South Africa** 13–3
New Zealand won series 3–1	1998 Durban TN **South Africa** 24–23
1960 1 Johannesburg **South Africa** 13–0	1999 Dunedin TN **New Zealand** 28–0
2 Cape Town **New Zealand** 11–3	1999 Pretoria TN **New Zealand** 34–18
3 Bloemfontein **Drawn** 11–11	1999 Cardiff WC **South Africa** 22–18
4 Port Elizabeth **South Africa** 8–3	2000 Christchurch TN **New Zealand** 25–12
South Africa won series 2–1, with 1 draw	2000 Johannesburg TN **South Africa** 46–40
1965 1 Wellington **New Zealand** 6–3	2001 Cape Town TN **New Zealand** 12–3
2 Dunedin **New Zealand** 13–0	2001 Auckland TN **New Zealand** 26–15
3 Christchurch **South Africa** 19–16	2002 Wellington TN **New Zealand** 41–20
4 Auckland **New Zealand** 20–3	2002 Durban TN **New Zealand** 30–23
New Zealand won series 3–1	2003 Pretoria TN **New Zealand** 52–16
1970 1 Pretoria **South Africa** 17–6	2003 Dunedin TN **New Zealand** 19–11
2 Cape Town **New Zealand** 9–8	2003 Melbourne WC **New Zealand** 29–9
3 Port Elizabeth **South Africa** 14–3	2004 Christchurch TN **New Zealand** 23–21
4 Johannesburg **South Africa** 20–17	2004 Johannesburg TN **South Africa** 40–26
South Africa won series 3–1	2005 Cape Town TN **South Africa** 22–16
1976 1 Durban **South Africa** 16–7	2005 Dunedin TN **New Zealand** 31–27
2 Bloemfontein **New Zealand** 15–9	2006 Wellington TN **New Zealand** 35–17
3 Cape Town **South Africa** 15–10	2006 Pretoria TN **New Zealand** 45–26
4 Johannesburg **South Africa**	2006 Rustenburg TN **South Africa** 21–20
15–14	2007 Durban TN **New Zealand** 26–21
South Africa won series 3–1	2007 Christchurch TN **New Zealand** 33–6

INTERNATIONAL RECORDS

2008 Wellington TN **New Zealand** 19–8	2010 Wellington TN **New Zealand** 31–17
2008 Dunedin TN **South Africa** 30–28	2010 Soweto TN **New Zealand** 29–22
2008 Cape Town TN **New Zealand** 19–0	2011 Wellington TN **New Zealand** 40–7
2009 Bloemfontein TN **South Africa** 28–19	2011 Port Elizabeth TN **South Africa** 18–5
2009 Durban TN **South Africa** 31–19	2012 Dunedin RC **New Zealand** 21–11
2009 Hamilton TN **South Africa** 32–29	2012 Soweto RC **New Zealand** 32–16
2010 Auckland TN **New Zealand** 32–12	

SOUTH AFRICA v AUSTRALIA

Played 76 South Africa won 42, Australia won 33, Drawn 1
Highest scores South Africa 61–22 in 1997, Australia 49–0 in 2006
Biggest wins South Africa 53–8 in 2008, Australia 49–0 in 2006

1933	1 Cape Town **South Africa** 17–3		3 Sydney **South Africa** 18–6
	2 Durban **Australia** 21–6		South Africa won series 3–0
	3 Johannesburg **South Africa** 12–3	1992	Cape Town **Australia** 26–3
	4 Port Elizabeth **South Africa** 11–0	1993	1 Sydney **South Africa** 19–12
	5 Bloemfontein **Australia** 15–4		2 Brisbane **Australia** 28–20
	South Africa won series 3–2		3 Sydney **Australia** 19–12
1937	1 Sydney **South Africa** 9–5		Australia won series 2–1
	2 Sydney **South Africa** 26–17	1995	Cape Town WC **South Africa** 27–18
	South Africa won series 2–0	1996	Sydney TN **Australia** 21–16
1953	1 Johannesburg **South Africa** 25–3	1996	Bloemfontein TN **South Africa** 25–19
	2 Cape Town **Australia** 18–14	1997	Brisbane TN **Australia** 32–20
	3 Durban **South Africa** 18–8	1997	Pretoria TN **South Africa** 61–22
	4 Port Elizabeth **South Africa** 22–9	1998	Perth TN **South Africa** 14–13
	South Africa won series 3–1	1998	Johannesburg TN **South Africa** 29–15
1956	1 Sydney **South Africa** 9–0	1999	Brisbane TN **Australia** 32–6
	2 Brisbane **South Africa** 9–0	1999	Cape Town TN **South Africa** 10–9
	South Africa won series 2–0	1999	Twickenham WC **Australia** 27–21
1961	1 Johannesburg **South Africa** 28–3	2000	Melbourne **Australia** 44–23
	2 Port Elizabeth **South Africa** 23–11	2000	Sydney TN **Australia** 26–6
	South Africa won series 2–0	2000	Durban TN **Australia** 19–18
1963	1 Pretoria **South Africa** 14–3	2001	Pretoria TN **South Africa** 20–15
	2 Cape Town **Australia** 9–5	2001	Perth TN **Drawn** 14–14
	3 Johannesburg **Australia** 11–9	2002	Brisbane TN **Australia** 38–27
	4 Port Elizabeth **South Africa** 22–6	2002	Johannesburg TN **South Africa** 33–31
	Series drawn 2–2	2003	Cape Town TN **South Africa** 26–22
1965	1 Sydney **Australia** 18–11	2003	Brisbane TN **Australia** 29–9
	2 Brisbane **Australia** 12–8	2004	Perth TN **Australia** 30–26
	Australia won series 2–0	2004	Durban TN **South Africa** 23–19
1969	1 Johannesburg **South Africa** 30–11	2005	Sydney **Australia** 30–12
	2 Durban **South Africa** 16–9	2005	Johannesburg **South Africa** 33–20
	3 Cape Town **South Africa** 11–3	2005	Pretoria TN **South Africa** 22–16
	4 Bloemfontein **South Africa** 19–8	2005	Perth TN **South Africa** 22–19
	South Africa won series 4–0	2006	Brisbane TN **Australia** 49–0
1971	1 Sydney **South Africa** 19–11	2006	Sydney TN **Australia** 20–18
	2 Brisbane **South Africa** 14–6	2006	Johannesburg TN **South Africa** 24–16

2007 Cape Town TN **South Africa** 22–19	2010 Brisbane TN **Australia** 30–13
2007 Sydney TN **Australia** 25–17	2010 Pretoria TN **South Africa** 44–31
2008 Perth TN **Australia** 16–9	2010 Bloemfontein TN **Australia** 41–39
2008 Durban TN **Australia** 27–15	2011 Sydney TN **Australia** 39–20
2008 Johannesburg TN **South Africa** 53–8	2011 Durban TN **Australia** 14–9
2009 Cape Town TN **South Africa** 29–17	2011 Wellington WC **Australia** 11–9
2009 Perth TN **South Africa** 32–25	2012 Perth RC **Australia** 26–19
2009 Brisbane TN **Australia** 21–6	2012 Pretoria RC **South Africa** 31–8

SOUTH AFRICA v WORLD XVs

Played 3 South Africa won 3
Highest scores South Africa 45–24 in 1977, World XV 24–45 in 1977
Biggest win South Africa 45–24 in 1977, World XV no win

1977 Pretoria **South Africa** 45–24	2 Johannesburg **South Africa** 22–16
1989 1 Cape Town **South Africa** 20–19	South Africa won series 2–0

SOUTH AFRICA v SOUTH AMERICA

Played 8 South Africa won 7, South America won 1, Drawn 0
Highest scores South Africa 50–18 in 1982, South America 21–12 in 1982
Biggest wins South Africa 50–18 in 1982, South America 21–12 in 1982

1980 1 Johannesburg **South Africa** 24–9	2 Bloemfontein **South America**
2 Durban **South Africa** 18–9	21–12
South Africa won series 2–0	Series drawn 1–1
1980 1 Montevideo **South Africa** 22–13	1984 1 Pretoria **South Africa** 32–15
2 Santiago **South Africa** 30–16	2 Cape Town **South Africa** 22–13
South Africa won series 2–0	South Africa won series 2–0
1982 1 Pretoria **South Africa** 50–18	

SOUTH AFRICA v UNITED STATES

Played 3 South Africa won 3
Highest scores South Africa 64–10 in 2007, United States 20–43 in 2001
Biggest win South Africa 64–10 in 2007, United States no win

1981 Glenville **South Africa** 38–7	2007 Montpellier WC **South Africa** 64–10
2001 Houston **South Africa** 43–20	

SOUTH AFRICA v NEW ZEALAND CAVALIERS

Played 4 South Africa won 3, New Zealand Cavaliers won 1, Drawn 0
Highest scores South Africa 33–18 in 1986, New Zealand Cavaliers 19–18 in 1986
Biggest wins South Africa 33–18 in 1986, New Zealand Cavaliers 19–18 in 1986

1986 1 Cape Town **South Africa** 21–15	4 Johannesburg **South Africa**
2 Durban **New Zealand Cavaliers**	24–10
19–18	South Africa won series 3–1
3 Pretoria **South Africa** 33–18	

SOUTH AFRICA v ARGENTINA

Played 15 South Africa won 14, Drawn 1
Highest scores South Africa 63–9 in 2008, Argentina 33–37 in 2000
Biggest wins South Africa 63–9 in 2008, Argentina no win

1993	1 Buenos Aires **South Africa** 29–26	2000	Buenos Aires **South Africa** 37–33
	2 Buenos Aires **South Africa** 52–23	2002	Springs **South Africa** 49–29
	South Africa won series 2–0	2003	Port Elizabeth **South Africa** 26–25
1994	1 Port Elizabeth **South Africa** 42–22	2004	Buenos Aires **South Africa** 39–7
	2 Johannesburg **South Africa** 46–26	2005	Buenos Aires **South Africa** 34–23
	South Africa won series 2–0	2007	Paris WC **South Africa** 37–13
1996	1 Buenos Aires **South Africa** 46–15	2008	Johannesburg **South Africa** 63–9
	2 Buenos Aires **South Africa** 44–21	2012	Cape Town RC **South Africa** 27–6
	South Africa win series 2–0	2012	Mendoza RC **Drawn** 16–16

SOUTH AFRICA v SAMOA

Played 7 South Africa won 7
Highest scores South Africa 60–8 in 1995, 60–18 in 2002 and 60–10 in 2003, Samoa 18–60 in 2002
Biggest win South Africa 60–8 in 1995 and 59–7 in 2007, Samoa no win

1995	Johannesburg **South Africa** 60–8	2007	Johannesburg **South Africa** 35–8
1995	Johannesburg WC **South Africa** 42–14	2007	Paris WC **South Africa** 59–7
2002	Pretoria **South Africa** 60–18	2011	Albany WC **South Africa** 13–5
2003	Brisbane WC **South Africa** 60–10		

SOUTH AFRICA v ROMANIA

Played 1 South Africa won 1
Highest score South Africa 21–8 in 1995, Romania 8–21 in 1995
Biggest win South Africa 21–8 in 1995, Romania no win

1995	Cape Town WC **South Africa** 21–8

Played 2 South Africa won 2
Highest scores South Africa 51–18 in 2000, Canada 18–51 in 2000
Biggest win South Africa 51–18 in 2000, Canada no win

1995	Port Elizabeth WC **South Africa** 20–0	2000	East London **South Africa** 51–18

SOUTH AFRICA v ITALY

Played 10 South Africa won 10
Highest scores South Africa 101–0 in 1999, Italy 31–62 in 1997
Biggest win South Africa 101–0 in 1999, Italy no win

1995	Rome **South Africa** 40–21	2001	Genoa **South Africa** 54–26
1997	Bologna **South Africa** 62–31	2008	Cape Town **South Africa** 26–0
1999	1 Port Elizabeth **South Africa** 74–3	2009	Udine **South Africa** 32–10
	2 Durban **South Africa** 101–0	2010	1 Witbank **South Africa** 29–13
	South Africa won series 2–0		2 East London **South Africa** 55–11
2001	Port Elizabeth **South Africa** 60–14		South Africa won series 2–0

SOUTH AFRICA v FIJI

Played 3 South Africa won 3
Highest scores South Africa 49–3 in 2011, Fiji 20–37 in 2007
Biggest win South Africa 49–3 in 2011, Fiji no win

1996	Pretoria **South Africa** 43–18	2011	Wellington WC **South Africa** 49–3
2007	Marseilles WC **South Africa** 37–20		

SOUTH AFRICA v TONGA

Played 2 South Africa won 2
Higest scores South Africa 74–10 in 1997, Tonga 25–30 in 2007
Biggest win South Africa 74–10 in 1997, Tonga no win

1997	Cape Town **South Africa** 74–10	2007	Lens WC **South Africa** 30–25

SOUTH AFRICA v SPAIN

Played 1 South Africa won 1
Highest scores South Africa 47–3 in 1999, Spain 3–47 in 1999
Biggest win South Africa 47–3 in 1999, Spain no win

1999	Murrayfield WC **South Africa** 47–3

SOUTH AFRICA v URUGUAY

Played 3 South Africa won 3
Highest scores South Africa 134–3 in 2005, Uruguay 6–72 in 2003
Biggest win South Africa 134–3 in 2005, Uruguay no win

1999	Glasgow WC **South Africa** 39–3		Perth WC **South Africa** 72–6
2003	Glasgow WC **South Africa** 39–3	2005	East London **South Africa** 134–3

SOUTH AFRICA v GEORGIA

Played 1 South Africa won 1
Highest scores South Africa 46–19 in 2003, Georgia 19–46 in 2003
Biggest win South Africa 46–19 in 2003, Georgia no win

2003	Sydney WC **South Africa** 46–19

SOUTH AFRICA v PACIFIC ISLANDS

Played 1 South Africa won 1
Highest scores South Africa 38–24 in 2004, Pacific Islands 24–38 in 2004
Biggest win South Africa 38–24 in 2004, Pacific Islands no win

2004	Gosford (Aus) **South Africa** 38–24

SOUTH AFRICA v NAMIBIA

Played 2 South Africa won 2
Highest scores South Africa 105–13 in 2007, Namibia 13–105 in 2007
Biggest win South Africa 105–13 in 2007, Namibia no win

2007	Cape Town **South Africa** 105–13	2011	Albany WC **South Africa** 87–0

NEW ZEALAND v AUSTRALIA

Played 145 New Zealand won 99, Australia won 41, Drawn 5
Highest scores New Zealand 50–21 in 2003, Australia 35–39 in 2000
Biggest wins New Zealand 43–6 in 1996, Australia 28–7 in 1999

1903	Sydney **New Zealand** 22–3	1910	1 Sydney **New Zealand** 6–0
1905	Dunedin **New Zealand** 14–3		2 Sydney **Australia** 11–0
1907	1 Sydney **New Zealand** 26–6		3 Sydney **New Zealand** 28–13
	2 Brisbane **New Zealand** 14–5		New Zealand won series 2–1
	3 Sydney **Drawn** 5–5	1913	1 Wellington **New Zealand** 30–5
	New Zealand won series 2–0, with 1		2 Dunedin **New Zealand** 25–13
	draw		3 Christchurch **Australia** 16–5

New Zealand won series 2–1

1914 1 Sydney **New Zealand** 5–0
      2 Brisbane **New Zealand** 17–0
      3 Sydney **New Zealand** 22–7
      New Zealand won series 3–0
1929 1 Sydney **Australia** 9–8
      2 Brisbane **Australia** 17–9
      3 Sydney **Australia** 15–13
      Australia won series 3–0
1931 Auckland **New Zealand** 20–13
1932 1 Sydney **Australia** 22–17
      2 Brisbane **New Zealand** 21–3
      3 Sydney **New Zealand** 21–13
      New Zealand won series 2–1
1934 1 Sydney **Australia** 25–11
      2 Sydney **Drawn** 3–3
      Australia won series 1–0, with 1 draw
1936 1 Wellington **New Zealand** 11–6
      2 Dunedin **New Zealand** 38–13
      New Zealand won series 2–0
1938 1 Sydney **New Zealand** 24–9
      2 Brisbane **New Zealand** 20–14
      3 Sydney **New Zealand** 14–6
      New Zealand won series 3–0
1946 1 Dunedin **New Zealand** 31–8
      2 Auckland **New Zealand** 14–10
      New Zealand won series 2–0
1947 1 Brisbane **New Zealand** 13–5
      2 Sydney **New Zealand** 27–14
      New Zealand won series 2–0
1949 1 Wellington **Australia** 11–6
      2 Auckland **Australia** 16–9
      Australia won series 2–0
1951 1 Sydney **New Zealand** 8–0
      2 Sydney **New Zealand** 17–11
      3 Brisbane **New Zealand** 16–6
      New Zealand won series 3–0
1952 1 Christchurch **Australia** 14–9
      2 Wellington **New Zealand** 15–8
      Series drawn 1–1
1955 1 Wellington **New Zealand** 16–8
      2 Dunedin **New Zealand** 8–0
      3 Auckland **Australia** 8–3
      New Zealand won series 2–1
1957 1 Sydney **New Zealand** 25–11
      2 Brisbane **New Zealand** 22–9
      New Zealand won series 2–0
1958 1 Wellington **New Zealand** 25–3
      2 Christchurch **Australia** 6–3
      3 Auckland **New Zealand** 17–8

New Zealand won series 2–1

1962 1 Brisbane **New Zealand** 20–6
      2 Sydney **New Zealand** 14–5
      New Zealand won series 2–0
1962 1 Wellington **Drawn** 9–9
      2 Dunedin **New Zealand** 3–0
      3 Auckland **New Zealand** 16–8
      New Zealand won series 2–0, with
      1 draw
1964 1 Dunedin **New Zealand** 14–9
      2 Christchurch **New Zealand** 18–3
      3 Wellington **Australia** 20–5
      New Zealand won series 2–1
1967 Wellington **New Zealand** 29–9
1968 1 Sydney **New Zealand** 27–11
      2 Brisbane **New Zealand** 19–18
      New Zealand won series 2–0
1972 1 Wellington **New Zealand** 29–6
      2 Christchurch **New Zealand** 30–17
      3 Auckland **New Zealand** 38–3
      New Zealand won series 3–0
1974 1 Sydney **New Zealand** 11–6
      2 Brisbane **Drawn** 16–16
      3 Sydney **New Zealand** 16–6
      New Zealand won series 2–0, with
      1 draw
1978 1 Wellington **New Zealand** 13–12
      2 Christchurch **New Zealand** 22–6
      3 Auckland **Australia** 30–16
      New Zealand won series 2–1
1979 Sydney **Australia** 12–6
1980 1 Sydney **Australia** 13–9
      2 Brisbane **New Zealand** 12–9
      3 Sydney **Australia** 26–10
      Australia won series 2–1
1982 1 Christchurch **New Zealand** 23–16
      2 Wellington **Australia** 19–16
      3 Auckland **New Zealand** 33–18
      New Zealand won series 2–1
1983 Sydney **New Zealand** 18–8
1984 1 Sydney **Australia** 16–9
      2 Brisbane **New Zealand** 19–15
      3 Sydney **New Zealand** 25–24
      New Zealand won series 2–1
1985 Auckland **New Zealand** 10–9
1986 1 Wellington **Australia** 13–12
      2 Dunedin **New Zealand** 13–12
      3 Auckland **Australia** 22–9
      Australia won series 2–1
1987 Sydney **New Zealand** 30–16

1988 1 Sydney **New Zealand** 32–7	2002 Christchurch TN **New Zealand** 12–6
2 Brisbane **Drawn** 19–19	2002 Sydney TN **Australia** 16–14
3 Sydney **New Zealand** 30–9	Series drawn 1–1
New Zealand won series 2–0, with 1	2003 Sydney TN **New Zealand** 50–21
draw	2003 Auckland TN **New Zealand** 21–17
1989 Auckland **New Zealand** 24–12	New Zealand won series 2–0
1990 1 Christchurch **New Zealand** 21–6	2003 Sydney WC **Australia** 22–10
2 Auckland **New Zealand** 27–17	2004 Wellington TN **New Zealand** 16–7
3 Wellington **Australia** 21–9	2004 Sydney TN **Australia** 23–18
New Zealand won series 2–1	Series drawn 1–1
1991 1 Sydney **Australia** 21–12	2005 Sydney TN **New Zealand** 30–13
2 Auckland **New Zealand** 6–3	2005 Auckland TN **New Zealand** 34–24
1991 Dublin WC **Australia** 16–6	New Zealand won series 2–0
1992 1 Sydney **Australia** 16–15	2006 Christchurch TN **New Zealand** 32–12
2 Brisbane **Australia** 19–17	2006 Brisbane TN **New Zealand** 13–9
3 Sydney **New Zealand** 26–23	2006 Auckland TN **New Zealand** 34–27
Australia won series 2–1	New Zealand won series 3–0
1993 Dunedin **New Zealand** 25–10	2007 Melbourne TN **Australia** 20–15
1994 Sydney **Australia** 20–1	2007 Auckland TN **New Zealand** 26–12
1995 Auckland **New Zealand** 28–16	Series drawn 1–1
1995 Sydney **New Zealand** 34–23	2008 Sydney TN **Australia** 34–19
1996 Wellington TN **New Zealand** 43–6	2008 Auckland TN **New Zealand** 39–10
1996 Brisbane TN **New Zealand** 32–25	2008 Brisbane TN **New Zealand** 28–24
New Zealand won series 2–0	2008 Hong Kong **New Zealand** 19–14
1997 Christchurch **New Zealand** 30–13	New Zealand won series 3–1
1997 Melbourne TN **New Zealand** 33–18	2009 Auckland TN **New Zealand** 22–16
1997 Dunedin TN **New Zealand** 36–24	2009 Sydney TN **New Zealand** 19–18
New Zealand won series 3–0	2009 Wellington TN **New Zealand** 33–6
1998 Melbourne TN **Australia** 24–16	2009 Tokyo **New Zealand** 32–19
1998 Christchurch TN **Australia** 27–23	New Zealand won series 4–0
1998 Sydney Australia 19–14	2010 Melbourne TN **New Zealand** 49–28
Australia won series 3–0	2010 Christchurch TN **New Zealand** 20–10
1999 Auckland TN **New Zealand** 34–15	2010 Sydney TN **New Zealand** 23–22
1999 Sydney TN **Australia** 28–7	2010 Hong Kong **Australia** 26–24
Series drawn 1–1	New Zealand won series 3–1
2000 Sydney TN **New Zealand** 39–35	2011 Auckland TN **New Zealand** 30–14
2000 Wellington TN **Australia** 24–23	2011 Brisbane TN **Australia** 25–20
Series drawn 1–1	2011 Auckland WC **New Zealand** 20–6
2001 Dunedin TN **Australia** 23–15	2012 Sydney RC **New Zealand** 27–19
2001 Sydney TN **Australia** 29–26	2012 Auckland RC **New Zealand** 22–0
Australia won series 2–0	

NEW ZEALAND v UNITED STATES

Played 2 New Zealand won 2
Highest scores New Zealand 51–3 in 1913, United States 6–46 in 1991
Biggest win New Zealand 51–3 in 1913, United States no win

1913 Berkeley **New Zealand** 51–3	
1991 Gloucester WC **New Zealand** 46–6	

Played 2 New Zealand won 2
Highest scores New Zealand 85–8 in 2007, Romania 8–85 in 2007
Biggest win New Zealand 85–8 in 2007, Romania no win

1981	Bucharest **New Zealand** 14–6		2007	Toulouse WC **New Zealand** 85–8

NEW ZEALAND v ARGENTINA

Played 16 New Zealand won 15, Drawn 1
Highest scores New Zealand 93–8 in 1997, Argentina 21–21 in 1985
Biggest win New Zealand 93–8 in 1997, Argentina no win

1985	1 Buenos Aires **New Zealand** 33–20	1997	1 Wellington **New Zealand** 93–8
	2 Buenos Aires **Drawn** 21–21		2 Hamilton **New Zealand** 62–10
	New Zealand won series 1–0, with 1		New Zealand won series 2–0
	draw	2001	Christchurch **New Zealand** 67–19
1987	Wellington WC **New Zealand** 46–15	2001	Buenos Aires **New Zealand** 24–20
1989	1 Dunedin **New Zealand** 60–9	2004	Hamilton **New Zealand** 41–7
	2 Wellington **New Zealand** 49–12	2006	Buenos Aires **New Zealand** 25–19
	New Zealand won series 2–0	2011	Auckland WC **New Zealand** 33–10
1991	1 Buenos Aires **New Zealand** 28–14	2012	Wellington RC **New Zealand** 21–5
	2 Buenos Aires **New Zealand** 36–6	2012	La Plata RC **New Zealand** 54–15
	New Zealand won series 2–0		

NEW ZEALAND v ITALY

Played 11 New Zealand won 11
Highest scores New Zealand 101–3 in 1999, Italy 21–31 in 1991
Biggest win New Zealand 101–3 in 1999, Italy no win

1987	Auckland WC **New Zealand** 70–6	2003	Melbourne WC **New Zealand** 70–7
1991	Leicester WC **New Zealand** 31–21	2004	Rome **New Zealand** 59–10
1995	Bologna **New Zealand** 70–6	2007	Marseilles WC **New Zealand** 76–14
1999	Huddersfield WC **New Zealand** 101–3	2009	Christchurch **New Zealand** 27–6
2000	Genoa **New Zealand** 56–19	2009	Milan **New Zealand** 20–6
2002	Hamilton **New Zealand** 64–10		

NEW ZEALAND v FIJI

Played 5 New Zealand won 5
Highest scores New Zealand 91–0 in 2005, Fiji 18–68 in 2002
Biggest win New Zealand 91–0 in 2005, Fiji no win

1987	Christchurch WC **New Zealand** 74–13	2005	Albany **New Zealand** 91–0
1997	Albany **New Zealand** 71–5	2011	Dunedin **New Zealand** 60–14
2002	Wellington **New Zealand** 68–18		

INTERNATIONAL RECORDS

NEW ZEALAND v CANADA

Played 5 New Zealand won 5
Highest scores New Zealand 79–15 in 2011, Canada 15–79 in 2011
Biggest win New Zealand 73–7 in 1995, Canada no win

1991	Lille WC **New Zealand** 29–13		2007	Hamilton **New Zealand** 64–13
1995	Auckland **New Zealand** 73–7		2011	Wellington WC **New Zealand** 79–15
2003	Melbourne WC **New Zealand** 68–6			

NEW ZEALAND v WORLD XVs

Played 3 New Zealand won 2, World XV won 1, Drawn 0
Highest scores New Zealand 54–26 in 1992, World XV 28–14 in 1992
Biggest wins New Zealand 54–26 in 1992, World XV 28–14 in 1992

1992	1 Christchurch **World XV** 28–14		3 Auckland **New Zealand** 26–15
	2 Wellington **New Zealand** 54–26		New Zealand won series 2–1

NEW ZEALAND v SAMOA

Played 5 New Zealand won 5
Highest scores New Zealand 101–14 in 2008, Samoa 14–101 in 2008
Biggest win New Zealand 101–14 in 2008, Samoa no win

1993	Auckland **New Zealand** 35–13		2001	Albany **New Zealand** 50–6
1996	Napier **New Zealand** 51–10		2008	New Plymouth **New Zealand** 101–14
1999	Albany **New Zealand** 71–13			

NEW ZEALAND v JAPAN

Played 2 New Zealand won 2
Highest scores New Zealand 145–17 in 1995, Japan 17–145 in 1995
Biggest win New Zealand 145–17 in 1995, Japan no win

1995	Bloemfontein WC **New Zealand** 145–17		2011	Hamilton WC **New Zealand** 83–7

NEW ZEALAND v TONGA

Played 4 New Zealand won 4
Highest scores New Zealand 102–0 in 2000, Tonga 10–41 in 2011
Biggest win New Zealand 102–0 in 2000, Tonga no win

1999	Bristol WC **New Zealand** 45–9		2003	Brisbane WC **New Zealand** 91–7
2000	Albany **New Zealand** 102–0		2011	Auckland WC **New Zealand** 41–10

Played 1 New Zealand won 1
Highest scores New Zealand 41–26 in 2004, Pacific Islands 26–41 in 2004
Biggest win New Zealand 41–26 in 2004, Pacific Islands no win

2004	Albany **New Zealand**	41–26

NEW ZEALAND v PORTUGAL

Played 1 New Zealand won 1
Highest scores New Zealand 108–13 in 2007, Portugal 13–108 in 2007
Biggest win New Zealand 108–13 in 2007, Portugal no win

2007	Lyons WC **New Zealand**	108–13

AUSTRALIA v UNITED STATES

Played 7 Australia won 7
Highest scores Australia 67–9 in 1990 and 67–5 in 2011, United States 19–55 in 1999
Biggest win Australia 67–5 in 2011, United States no win

1912	Berkeley **Australia** 12–8	1990	Brisbane **Australia** 67–9
1976	Los Angeles **Australia** 24–12	1999	Limerick WC **Australia** 55–19
1983	Sydney **Australia** 49–3	2011	Wellington WC **Australia** 67–5
1987	Brisbane WC **Australia** 47–12		

AUSTRALIA v NEW ZEALAND XVs

Played 24 Australia won 6, New Zealand XVs won 18, Drawn 0
Highest scores Australia 26–20 in 1926, New Zealand XV 38–11 in 1923 and 38–8 in 1924
Biggest wins Australia 17–0 in 1921, New Zealand XV 38–8 in 1924

1920	1 Sydney **New Zealand XV** 26–15	1924	1 Sydney **Australia** 20–16
	2 Sydney **New Zealand XV** 14–6		2 Sydney **New Zealand XV** 21–5
	3 Sydney **New Zealand XV** 24–13		3 Sydney **New Zealand XV** 38–8
	New Zealand XV won series 3–0		New Zealand XV won series 2–1
1921	Christchurch **Australia** 17–0	1925	1 Sydney **New Zealand XV** 26–3
1922	1 Sydney **New Zealand XV** 26–19		2 Sydney **New Zealand XV** 4–0
	2 Sydney **Australia** 14–8		3 Sydney **New Zealand XV** 11–3
	3 Sydney **Australia** 8–6		New Zealand XV won series 3–0
	Australia won series 2–1	1925	Auckland **New Zealand XV** 36–10
1923	1 Dunedin **New Zealand XV** 19–9	1926	1 Sydney **Australia** 26–20
	2 Christchurch **New Zealand XV** 34–6		2 Sydney **New Zealand XV** 11–6
	3 Wellington **New Zealand XV** 38–11		3 Sydney **New Zealand XV** 14–0
	New Zealand XV won series 3–0		4 Sydney **New Zealand XV** 28–21

New Zealand XV won series 3–1	3 Christchurch **Australia** 11–8
1928 1 Wellington **New Zealand XV** 15–12	New Zealand XV won series 2–1
2 Dunedin **New Zealand XV** 16–14	

AUSTRALIA v SOUTH AFRICA XVs

Played 3 South Africa XVs won 3
Highest scores Australia 11–16 in 1921, South Africa XV 28–9 in 1921
Biggest win Australia no win, South Africa XV 28–9 in 1921

1921 1 Sydney **South Africa XV** 25–10	3 Sydney **South Africa XV** 28–9
2 Sydney **South Africa XV** 16–11	South Africa XV won series 3–0

AUSTRALIA v NEW ZEALAND MAORIS

Played 16 Australia won 8, New Zealand Maoris won 6, Drawn 2
Highest scores Australia 31–6 in 1936, New Zealand Maoris 25–22 in 1922
Biggest wins Australia 31–6 in 1936, New Zealand Maoris 20–0 in 1946

1922 1 Sydney **New Zealand Maoris** 25–22	1946 Hamilton **New Zealand Maoris** 20–0
2 Sydney **Australia** 28–13	1949 1 Sydney **New Zealand Maoris** 12–3
3 Sydney **New Zealand Maoris** 23–22	2 Brisbane **Drawn** 8–8
New Zealand Maoris won series 2–1	3 Sydney **Australia** 18–3
1923 1 Sydney **Australia** 27–23	Series drawn 1–1, with 1 draw
2 Sydney **Australia** 21–16	1958 1 Brisbane **Australia** 15–14
3 Sydney **Australia** 14–12	2 Sydney **Drawn** 3–3
Australia won series 3–0	3 Melbourne **New Zealand Maoris**
1928 Wellington **New Zealand Maoris** 9–8	13–6
1931 Palmerston North **Australia** 14–3	Series drawn 1–1, with 1 draw
1936 Palmerston North **Australia** 31–6	

AUSTRALIA v FIJI

Played 19 Australia won 16, Fiji won 2, Drawn 1
Highest scores Australia 66–20 in 1998, Fiji 28–52 in 1985
Biggest wins Australia 49–0 in 2007, Fiji 17–15 in 1952 & 18–16 in 1954

1952 1 Sydney **Australia** 15–9	Australia won series 2–0, with 1 draw
2 Sydney **Fiji** 17–15	1972 Suva **Australia** 21–19
Series drawn 1–1	1976 1 Sydney **Australia** 22–6
1954 1 Brisbane **Australia** 22–19	2 Brisbane **Australia** 21–9
2 Sydney **Fiji** 18–16	3 Sydney **Australia** 27–17
Series drawn 1–1	Australia won series 3–0
1961 1 Brisbane **Australia** 24–6	1980 Suva **Australia** 22–9
2 Sydney **Australia** 20–14	1984 Suva **Australia** 16–3
3 Melbourne **Drawn** 3–3	1985 1 Brisbane **Australia** 52–28

2 Sydney **Australia** 31–9	2007 Perth **Australia** 49–0
Australia won series 2–0	2007 Montpellier WC **Australia** 55–12
1998 Sydney **Australia** 66–20	2010 Canberra **Australia** 49–3

AUSTRALIA v TONGA

Played 4 Australia won 3, Tonga won 1, Drawn 0
Highest scores Australia 74–0 in 1998, Tonga 16–11 in 1973
Biggest wins Australia 74–0 in 1998, Tonga 16–11 in 1973

1973 1 Sydney **Australia** 30–12	1993 Brisbane **Australia** 52–14
2 Brisbane **Tonga** 16–11	1998 Canberra **Australia** 74–0
Series drawn 1–1	

AUSTRALIA v JAPAN

Played 4 Australia won 4
Highest scores Australia 91–3 in 2007, Japan 25–50 in 1973
Biggest win Australia 91–3 in 2007, Japan no win

1975 1 Sydney **Australia** 37–7	1987 Sydney WC **Australia** 42–23
2 Brisbane **Australia** 50–25	2007 Lyons WC **Australia** 91–3
Australia won series 2–0	

AUSTRALIA v ARGENTINA

Played 19 Australia won 14, Argentina won 4, Drawn 1
Highest scores Australia 53–7 in 1995 & 53–6 in 2000, Argentina 27–19 in 1987
Biggest wins Australia 53–6 in 2000, Argentina 18–3 in 1983

1979 1 Buenos Aires **Argentina** 24–13	1995 1 Brisbane **Australia** 53–7
2 Buenos Aires **Australia** 17–12	2 Sydney **Australia** 30–13
Series drawn 1–1	Australia won series 2–0
1983 1 Brisbane **Argentina** 18–3	1997 1 Buenos Aires **Australia** 23–15
2 Sydney **Australia** 29–13	2 Buenos Aires **Argentina** 18–16
Series drawn 1–1	Series drawn 1–1
1986 1 Brisbane **Australia** 39–19	2000 1 Brisbane **Australia** 53–6
2 Sydney **Australia** 26–0	2 Canberra **Australia** 32–25
Australia won series 2–0	Australia won series 2–0
1987 1 Buenos Aires **Drawn** 19–19	2002 Buenos Aires **Australia** 17–6
2 Buenos Aires **Argentina** 27–19	2003 Sydney WC **Australia** 24–8
Argentina won series 1–0, with 1 draw	2012 Robina RC **Australia** 23–19
1991 Llanelli WC **Australia** 32–19	2012 Rosario RC **Australia** 25–19

AUSTRALIA v SAMOA

Played 5 Australia won 4, Samoa won 1
Highest scores Australia 74–7 in 2005, Samoa 32–23 in 2011
Biggest win Australia 73–3 in 1994, Samoa 32–23 in 2011

1991	Pontypool WC **Australia** 9–3		2005	Sydney **Australia** 74–7
1994	Sydney **Australia** 73–3		2011	Sydney **Samoa** 32–23
1998	Brisbane **Australia** 25–13			

AUSTRALIA v ITALY

Played 14 Australia won 14
Highest scores Australia 69–21 in 2005, Italy 21–69 in 2005
Biggest win Australia 55–6 in 1988, Italy no win

1983	Rovigo **Australia** 29–7		2005	Melbourne **Australia** 69–21
1986	Brisbane **Australia** 39–18		2006	Rome **Australia** 25–18
1988	Rome **Australia** 55–6		2008	Padua **Australia** 30–20
1994	1 Brisbane **Australia** 23–20		2009	1 Canberra **Australia** 31–8
	2 Melbourne **Australia** 20–7			2 Melbourne **Australia** 34–12
	Australia won series 2–0			Australia won series 2–0
1996	Padua **Australia** 40–18		2010	Florence **Australia** 32–14
2002	Genoa **Australia** 34–3		2011	Albany WC **Australia** 32–6

AUSTRALIA v CANADA

Played 6 Australia won 6
Highest scores Australia 74–9 in 1996, Canada 16–43 in 1993
Biggest win Australia 74–9 in 1996, Canada no win

1985	1 Sydney **Australia** 59–3		1995	Port Elizabeth WC **Australia** 27–11
	2 Brisbane **Australia** 43–15		1996	Brisbane **Australia** 74–9
	Australia won series 2–0		2007	Bordeaux WC **Australia** 37–6
1993	Calgary **Australia** 43–16			

AUSTRALIA v KOREA

Played 1 Australia won 1
Highest scores Australia 65–18 in 1987, Korea 18–65 in 1987
Biggest win Australia 65–18 in 1987, Korea no win

1987	Brisbane **Australia** 65–18	

AUSTRALIA v ROMANIA

Played 3 Australia won 3
Highest scores Australia 90–8 in 2003, Romania 9–57 in 1999
Biggest win Australia 90–8 in 2003, Romania no win

1995	Stellenbosch WC **Australia** 42–3		2003	Brisbane WC **Australia** 90–8
1999	Belfast WC **Australia** 57–9			

AUSTRALIA v SPAIN

Played 1 Australia won 1
Highest scores Australia 92–10 in 2001, Spain 10–92 in 2001
Biggest win Australia 92–10 in 2001, Spain no win

2001	Madrid **Australia** 92–10

AUSTRALIA v NAMIBIA

Played 1 Australia won 1
Highest scores Australia 142–0 in 2003, Namibia 0–142 in 2003
Biggest win Australia 142–0 in 2003, Namibia no win

2003	Adelaide WC **Australia** 142–0

AUSTRALIA v PACIFIC ISLANDS

Played 1 Australia won 1
Highest scores Australia 29–14 in 2004, Pacific Islands 14–29 in 2004
Biggest win Australia 29–14 in 2004, Pacific Islands no win

2004	Adelaide **Australia** 29–14

AUSTRALIA v RUSSIA

Played 1 Australia won 1
Highest scores Australia 68–22 in 2011, Russia 22–68 in 2011
Biggest win Australia 68–22 in 2011, Russia no win

2011	Nelson WC **Australia** 68–22

WORLD RECORDS

The match and career records cover official Test matches played up to 10 October 2012.

MATCH RECORDS

MOST CONSECUTIVE TEST WINS

18 by Lithuania	2006 *Hun, Nor, Bul* 2007 *Aus, Hun, Bul* 2008 *Lat, Aus, Hun, Nor, And, Swi* 2009 *Ser, Arm, Isr, Hol, And* 2010 *Ser*
17 by N Zealand	1965 *SA* 4, 1966 *BI* 1,2,3,4, 1967 *A, E, W, F, S,* 1968 *A* 1,2, *F* 1,2,3, 1969 *W* 1,2
17 by S Africa	1997 *A* 2, *It, F* 1,2, *E, S,* 1998 *I* 1,2, *W* 1, *E* 1, *A* 1, *NZ* 1,2, *A* 2, *W* 2, *S, I* 3

MOST CONSECUTIVE TESTS WITHOUT DEFEAT

Matches	Wins	Draws	Period
23 by N Zealand	22	1	1987 to 1990
18 by Lithuania	18	0	2006 to 2010
17 by N Zealand	15	2	1961 to 1964
17 by N Zealand	17	0	1965 to 1969
17 by S Africa	17	0	1997 to 1998

MOST POINTS IN A MATCH
BY A TEAM

Pts	Opponents	Venue	Year
164 by Hong Kong	Singapore	Kuala Lumpur	1994
155 by Japan	Chinese Taipei	Tokyo	2002
152 by Argentina	Paraguay	Mendoza	2002
147 by Argentina	Venezuela	Santiago	2004
145 by N Zealand	Japan	Bloemfontein	1995
144 by Argentina	Paraguay	Montevideo	2003
142 by Australia	Namibia	Adelaide	2003
135 by Korea	Malaysia	Hong Kong	1992
134 by Japan	Chinese Taipei	Singapore	1998
134 by England	Romania	Twickenham	2001
134 by S Africa	Uruguay	East London	2005

BY A PLAYER

Pts	Player	Opponents	Venue	Year
60 for Japan	T Kurihara	Chinese Taipei	Tainan	2002
50 for Argentina	E Morgan	Paraguay	San Pablo	1973
50 for H Kong	A Billington	Singapore	Kuala Lumpur	1994
45 for N Zealand	S D Culhane	Japan	Bloemfontein	1995
45 for Argentina	J-M Nuñez-Piossek	Paraguay	Montevideo	2003
44 for Scotland	A G Hastings	Ivory Coast	Rustenburg	1995
44 for England	C C Hodgson	Romania	Twickenham	2001
42 for Australia	M S Rogers	Namibia	Adelaide	2003
41 for Sweden	J Hagstrom	Luxembourg	Cessange	2001
40 for Argentina	G M Jorge	Brazil	Sao Paulo	1993
40 for Japan	D Ohata	Chinese Taipei	Tokyo	2002
40 for Scotland	C D Paterson	Japan	Perth	2004

MOST TRIES IN A MATCH
BY THE TEAM

Tries	Opponents	Venue	Year
26 by Hong Kong	Singapore	Kuala Lumpur	1994
25 by Fiji	Solomon Is	Port Moresby	1969
24 by Argentina	Paraguay	Mendoza	2002
24 by Argentina	Paraguay	Montevideo	2003
23 by Japan	Chinese Taipei	Tokyo	2002
23 by Argentina	Venezuela	Santiago	2004
22 by Australia	Namibia	Adelaide	2003
21 by Fiji	Niue Island	Apia	1983
21 by N Zealand	Japan	Bloemfontein	1995
21 by S Africa	Uruguay	East London	2005

BY A PLAYER

Tries	Player	Opponents	Venue	Year
11 for Argentina	U O'Farrell	Brazil	Buenos Aires	1951
10 for H Kong	A Billington	Singapore	Kuala Lumpur	1994
9 for Argentina	J-M Nuñez-Piossek	Paraguay	Montevideo	2003
8 for Argentina	G M Jorge	Brazil	Sao Paulo	1993
8 for Japan	D Ohata	Chinese Taipei	Tokyo	2002
6 for Argentina	E Morgan	Paraguay	San Pablo	1973
6 for Fiji	T Makutu	Papua New Guinea	Suva	1979
6 for Argentina	G M Jorge	Brazil	Montevideo	1989
6 for Namibia	G Mans	Portugal	Windhoek	1990
6 for N Zealand	M C G Ellis	Japan	Bloemfontein	1995
6 for Japan	T Kurihara	Chinese Taipei	Tainan	2002
6 for S Africa	T Chavhanga	Uruguay	East London	2005
6 for Japan	D Ohata	Hong Kong	Tokyo	2005
6 for Japan	Y Fujita	UAE	Fukuoka	2012
6 for Argentina	F Barrea	Brazil	Santiago	2012

MOST CONVERSIONS IN A MATCH
BY THE TEAM

Cons	Opponents	Venue	Year
20 by N Zealand	Japan	Bloemfontein	1995
20 by Japan	Chinese Taipei	Tokyo	2002
19 by Fiji	Solomon Islands	Port Moresby	1969
18 by Fiji	Niue Island	Apia	1983
17 by Hong Kong	Singapore	Kuala Lumpur	1994
17 by Japan	Chinese Taipei	Singapore	1998
17 by Tonga	Korea	Nuku'alofa	2003
16 by Argentina	Paraguay	Mendoza	2002
16 by Australia	Namibia	Adelaide	2003
16 by Argentina	Venezuela	Santiago	2004

BY A PLAYER

Cons	Player	Opponents	Venue	Year
20 for New Zealand	S D Culhane	Japan	Bloemfontein	1995
18 for Fiji	S Koroduadua	Niue Island	Apia	1983
17 for Hong Kong	J McKee	Singapore	Kuala Lumpur	1994
17 for Tonga	P Hola	Korea	Nuku'alofa	2003
16 for Argentina	J-L Cilley	Paraguay	Mendoza	2002
16 for Australia	M S Rogers	Namibia	Adelaide	2003
15 for England	P J Grayson	Netherlands	Huddersfield	1998
15 for Japan	T Kurihara	Chinese Taipei	Tainan	2002
14 for England	C C Hodgson	Romania	Twickenham	2001
14 for Wales	G L Henson	Japan	Cardiff	2004
14 for New Zealand	N J Evans	Portugal	Lyon	2007

WORLD RECORDS

MOST PENALTIES IN A MATCH
BY THE TEAM

Penalties	Opponents	Venue	Year
9 by Japan	Tonga	Tokyo	1999
9 by N Zealand	Australia	Auckland	1999
9 by Wales	France	Cardiff	1999
9 by Portugal	Georgia	Lisbon	2000
9 by N Zealand	France	Paris	2000
8 by many countries			

BY A PLAYER

Penalties	Player	Opponents	Venue	Year
9 for Japan	K Hirose	Tonga	Tokyo	1999
9 for N Zealand	A P Mehrtens	Australia	Auckland	1999
9 for Wales	N R Jenkins	France	Cardiff	1999
9 for Portugal	T Teixeira	Georgia	Lisbon	2000
9 for N Zealand	A P Mehrtens	France	Paris	2000
8 by many players				

MOST DROP GOALS IN A MATCH
BY THE TEAM

Drops	Opponents	Venue	Year
5 by South Africa	England	Paris	1999
4 by Romania	W Germany	Bucharest	1967
4 by Uruguay	Chile	Montevideo	2002
4 by South Africa	England	Twickenham	2006
3 by several nations			

BY A PLAYER

Drops	Player	Opponents	Venue	Year
5 for S Africa	J H de Beer	England	Paris	1999
4 for Uruguay	J Menchaca	Chile	Montevideo	2002
4 for S Africa	A S Pretorius	England	Twickenham	2006
3 for several nations				

CAREER RECORDS

MOST TEST APPEARANCES

Tests	Player	Career Span
139	G M Gregan (Australia)	1994 to 2007
126 (6)	B G O'Driscoll (Ireland/Lions)	1999 to 2012
126 (2)	R J R O'Gara (Ireland/Lions)	2000 to 2012
119 (5)	J Leonard (England/Lions)	1990 to 2004
118	F Pelous (France)	1995 to 2007
112	R H McCaw (N Zealand)	2001 to 2012
111	P Sella (France)	1982 to 1995
111	J W Smit (S Africa)	2000 to 2011
111	N C Sharpe (Australia)	2002 to 2012
110	G B Smith (Australia)	2000 to 2009
110	V Matfield (S Africa)	2001 to 2011
110 (6)	S M Jones (Wales/Lions)	1998 to 2011
109	C D Paterson (Scotland)	1999 to 2011
107 (2)	J J Hayes (Ireland/Lions)	2000 to 2011
104 (4)	M E Williams (Wales/Lions)	1996 to 2012
103 (3)	Gareth Thomas (Wales/Lions)	1995 to 2007
102	S J Larkham (Australia)	1996 to 2007
102	P C Montgomery (S Africa)	1997 to 2008
101	D I Campese (Australia)	1982 to 1996
101	A Troncon (Italy)	1994 to 2007
100	J M Muliaina (N Zealand)	2003 to 2011
99	K F Mealamu (N Zealand)	2002 to 2012
98	R Ibañez (France)	1996 to 2007
98	P A Stringer (Ireland)	2000 to 2011
97 (6)	J P Wilkinson (England/Lions)	1998 to 2011
96 (2)	C L Charvis (Wales/Lions)	1996 to 2007

The figures include Test appearances for the British/Irish Lions which are shown in brackets. Thus 126 (6) for Brian O'Driscoll (Ireland/Lions) indicates 120 caps for Ireland and six Tests for the Lions.

MOST CONSECUTIVE TESTS

Tests	Player	Career Span
63	S B T Fitzpatrick (N Zealand)	1986 to 1995
62	J W C Roff (Australia)	1996 to 2001
53	G O Edwards (Wales)	1967 to 1978
52	W J McBride (Ireland)	1964 to 1975
51	C M Cullen (N Zealand)	1996 to 2000

MOST TESTS AS CAPTAIN

Tests	Captain	Career Span
84 (1)	B G O'Driscoll (Ireland/Lions)	2002 to 2012
83	J W Smit (S Africa)	2003 to 2011
75*	R H McCaw (N Zealand)	2004 to 2012
59	W D C Carling (England)	1988 to 1996
59	G M Gregan (Australia)	2001 to 2007
55	J A Eales (Australia)	1996 to 2001
51	S B T Fitzpatrick (N Zealand)	1992 to 1997

The figures include Test captaincies of the British/Irish Lions which are shown in brackets. Thus 84 (1) for Brian O'Driscoll (Ireland/Lions) indicates 83 captaincies for Ireland and one in Tests for the Lions.
* McCaw's figure includes the world record of 67 Test wins as captain.

Getty Images

Brian O'Driscoll has made the most Test appearances as captain.

MOST POINTS IN TESTS

Points	Player	Tests	Career Span
1342	D W Carter (N Zealand)	91	2003 to 2012
1246 (67)	J P Wilkinson (England/Lions)	97 (6)	1998 to 2011
1090 (41)	N R Jenkins (Wales/Lions))	91 (4)	1991 to 2002
1075 (0)	R J R O'Gara (Ireland/Lions)	126 (2)	2000 to 2012
1010 (27)	D Dominguez (Italy/Argentina)	76 (2)	1989 to 2003
970 (53)	S M Jones (Wales/Lions)	110 (6)	1998 to 2011
967	A P Mehrtens (N Zealand)	70	1995 to 2004
911	M P Lynagh (Australia)	72	1984 to 1995
893	P C Montgomery (S Africa)	102	1997 to 2008
878	M C Burke (Australia)	81	1993 to 2004
809	C D Paterson (Scotland)	109	1999 to 2011
733 (66)	A G Hastings (Scotland/Lions)	67 (6)	1986 to 1995
684	M J Giteau (Australia)	92	2002 to 2011
670	N J Little (Fiji)	71	1996 to 2011

The figures include Test appearances for the British/Irish Lions or a second nation which are shown in brackets. Thus 1246 (67) for Jonny Wilkinson (England/Lions) indicates 1179 points for England and 67 in Tests for the Lions.

MOST TRIES IN TESTS

Tries	Player	Tests	Career Span
69	D Ohata (Japan)	58	1996 to 2006
64	D I Campese (Australia)	101	1982 to 1996
60 (2)	S M Williams (Wales/Lions)	91 (4)	2000 to 2011
51	H Onozawa (Japan)	74	2001 to 2012
50 (1)	R Underwood (England/Lions)	91 (6)	1984 to 1996
49	D C Howlett (N Zealand)	62	2000 to 2007
47	B G Habana (South Africa)	83	2004 to 2012
46	C M Cullen (N Zealand)	58	1996 to 2002
46	J T Rokocoko (N Zealand)	68	2003 to 2010
46 (1)	B G O'Driscoll (Ireland/Lions)	126 (6)	1999 to 2012
44	J W Wilson (N Zealand)	60	1993 to 2001
41 (1)	Gareth Thomas (Wales/Lions)	103 (3)	1995 to 2007
40	C E Latham (Australia)	78	1998 to 2007

The figures include Test appearances for the British/Irish Lions which are shown in brackets. Thus 60 (2) for Shane Williams (Wales/Lions) indicates 58 tries for Wales and two in Tests for the Lions.

Dan Carter has scored the most points in Test rugby.

MOST PENALTY GOALS IN TESTS

Pens	Player	Tests	Career Span
255 (16)	J P Wilkinson (England/Lions)	97 (6)	1998 to 2011
248 (13)	N R Jenkins (Wales/Lions)	91 (4)	1991 to 2002
235	D W Carter (N Zealand)	91	2003 to 2012
214 (5)	D Dominguez (Italy/Argentina)	76 (2)	1989 to 2003
200 (0)	R J R O'Gara (Ireland/Lions)	126 (2)	2000 to 2012
198 (12)	S M Jones (Wales/Lions)	110 (6)	1998 to 2011
188	A P Mehrtens (N Zealand)	70	1995 to 2004
177	M P Lynagh (Australia)	72	1984 to 1995
174	M C Burke (Australia)	81	1993 to 2004
170	C D Paterson (Scotland)	109	1999 to 2011
160 (20)	A G Hastings (Scotland/Lions)	67 (6)	1986 to 1995

The figures include Test appearances for the British/Irish Lions or a second nation which are shown in brackets. Thus 255 (16) for Jonny Wilkinson (England/Lions) indicates 239 penalties for England and 16 in Tests for the Lions.

MOST CONVERSIONS IN TESTS

Cons	Player	Tests	Career Span
237	D W Carter (N Zealand)	91	2003 to 2012
175 (0)	R J R O'Gara (Ireland/Lions)	126 (2)	2000 to 2012
169	A P Mehrtens (N Zealand)	70	1995 to 2004
169 (7)	J P Wilkinson (England/Lions)	97 (6)	1998 to 2011
160 (7)	S M Jones (Wales/Lions)	110 (6)	1998 to 2011
153	P C Montgomery (S Africa)	102	1997 to 2008
140	M P Lynagh (Australia)	72	1984 to 1995
133 (6)	D Dominguez (Italy/Argentina)	76 (2)	1989 to 2003
131 (1)	N R Jenkins (Wales/Lions))	91 (4)	1991 to 2002
118	G J Fox (N Zealand)	46	1985 to 1993

The figures include Test appearances for the British/Irish Lions or a second nation which are shown in brackets. Thus 169 (7) for Jonny Wilkinson (England/Lions) indicates 162 conversions for England and seven in Tests for the Lions.

MOST DROP GOALS IN TESTS

Drops	Player	Tests	Career Span
36 (0)	J P Wilkinson (England/Lions)	97 (6)	1998 to 2011
28 (2)	H Porta (Argentina/Jaguars)	68 (8)	1971 to 1999
23 (2)	C R Andrew (England/Lions)	76 (5)	1985 to 1997
19 (0)	D Dominguez (Italy/Argentina)	76 (2)	1989 to 2003
18	H E Botha (S Africa)	28	1980 to 1992
17	S Bettarello (Italy)	55	1979 to 1988
17	D A Parks (Scotland)	67	2004 to 2012
15	J-P Lescarboura (France)	28	1982 to 1990
15 (0)	R J R O'Gara (Ireland/Lions)	118 (2)	2000 to 2011

The figures include Test appearances for the British/Irish Lions, South American Jaguars or a second nation shown in brackets. Thus 28 (2) for Hugo Porta (Argentina/ Jaguars) indicates 26 dropped goals for Argentina and two in Tests (against South Africa in the 1980s) for the South American Jaguars.

RUGBY'S VALUES

INTERNATIONAL RUGBY BOARD

integrity
Integrity is central to the fabric of the Game and is generated through honesty and fair play.

respect
Respect for team mates, opponents, match officials and those involved in the Game is paramount.

solidarity
Rugby provides a unifying spirit that leads to life long friendships, camaraderie, teamwork and loyalty which transcends cultural, geographic, political and religious differences.

passion
Rugby people have a passionate enthusiasm for the Game. Rugby generates excitement, emotional attachment and a sense of belonging to the global Rugby Family.

discipline
Discipline is an integral part of the Game both on and off the field and is reflected through adherence to the Laws, the Regulations and Rugby's core values.

www.irb.com

The Countries

Agustín Creevy is tackled during Argentina's away
Rugby Championship match against Australia.

ARGENTINA

ARGENTINA'S 2012 TEST RECORD

OPPONENTS	DATE	VENUE	RESULT
Uruguay	20 May	N	Won 40–5
Brazil	23 May	N	Won 111–0
Chile	26 May	A	Won 59–6
Italy	9 Jun	H	Won 37–22
France	16 Jun	H	Won 23–20
France	23 Jun	H	Lost 10–49
South Africa	18 Aug	A	Lost 27–6
South Africa	25 Aug	H	Drew 16–16
New Zealand	8 Sep	A	Lost 21–5
Australia	15 Sep	A	Lost 23–19
New Zealand	29 Sep	H	Lost 15–54
Australia	6 Oct	H	Lost 19–25

PASSION AND PRIDE SHINES THROUGH IN HISTORIC YEAR

By Frankie Deges

Juan Martin Fernandez Lobbe is tackled by Tatafu Polota-Nau during The Rugby Championship

Over the last few years, the Argentina chapter of the Yearbook contained paragraphs on the Pumas' need for international competition. It was a constant plea which finally came to fruition in 2012 with the country taking part in the inaugural Rugby Championship, playing home and away against the top three ranked teams in the world.

The luxury of having regular Test matches against the All Blacks, Wallabies and Springboks is something that Pumas' fans quickly got accustomed to; a minimum of three seasons are left of this event which confirmed that Argentina has the muscle to mix it with the best in the world. By the end of this calendar year, Argentina will have played 12 Test matches against Tier One nations.

Despite not being able to produce what would certainly have been a deserved win – a 16–16 draw against the Springboks in Mendoza the best result in six matches – The Rugby Championship generated a level of interest in the Game that will bear fruit in the near future.

Rugby World Cup 2011 had kick-started a season that will be among the busiest in history. Los Pumas returned home after losing in the quarter-finals to eventual world champions New Zealand, but confirmation that they were in the best eight at a second successive Rugby World Cup was very important.

Within a month of RWC 2011 drawing to a close in New Zealand, SANZAR met in Buenos Aires and the new tournament, to be called The Rugby Championship, was officially launched. The name may not have met with universal acclaim, but the tournament was well received by the international rugby community.

A combination of a team that had performed in previous years and a well-thought-out and achievable strategic plan had gained the support of both the IRB and SANZAR and the Unión Argentina de Rugby were given four years to perform at the highest level. The IRB's assistance – moral, financial and strategic – was applauded in Argentina.

By now, the High Performance plans in place since 2009 were proving a success. The Pampas XV played in its third Vodacom Cup in South Africa in 2012 over a two-month period and the experience was invaluable. Despite not being able to reach the heady heights of 2011 when they won that tournament, it did provide a mid-level competition for a group of ambitious players headed by RWC 2011 veteran Julio Farías.

The defending champions were based in Stellenbosch and some 30 players were treated to a High Performance tournament programme. The number of players to have earned caps for the Pumas having played in this tournament has topped 20, and later in the year Pampas XV player Martín Landajo would finish as first-choice scrum half for the last three rounds of The Rugby Championship. Their season finished against losing finalists, the Griquas 26–18.

Many of the Pampas XV were included in the South American Championship squad that played in Santiago, Chile, in May. As has become customary, the competition was won by Argentina with ease. The standard of rugby in Argentina has increased exponentially in the past few years and their regional rivals are finding it tough to keep pace.

The 40–6 win over Uruguay showed that this team, despite missing all their European based star players, was too good. Brazil, a team that had pushed Chile hard before losing 19–6 in the opening round, had no answer as Argentina scored 17 tries in a 110–0 win with wings Facundo Barrea and Manuel Montero touching down six and three times respectively. The pair would score three more between them in the 59–6 win over Chile in a rainstorm, to again claim the trophy.

In the June Test window a number of these players were elevated to the Pumas and the rest travelled with the Jaguars to Romania for the IRB Nations Cup. With what could be described as a national third XV, the Argentina Jaguars came within two points of winning the six-team tournament.

After beating Portugal 41–9, the Jaguars came close to beating Romania at home, but the 23–21 loss would cost them the title after they finished with another conclusive win, 33–9 against Russia. No player in the Jaguars squad would feature in The Rugby Championship, but they were back for the IRB Americas Rugby Championship in Canada from 12–20 October.

The three June Tests showed the best and the worst of the Pumas. After reaching a gentlemen's agreement that those players involved in the 45 days preparation and The Rugby Championship would not be selected for the June window, it was a mixture of local talent, untried players from Europe and two of the best servants of Puma rugby in the last 15 years. Felipe Contepomi led the team, while prop Rodrigo Roncero was coming to the end of his career but enjoyed playing for Argentina so much in the win against Italy that he postponed retirement plans for four months.

The Italians were beaten 37–22 in San Juan, with Contepomi scoring 22 points. Next came France in Córdoba and it took 76 minutes for Montero, in his first Test season after a representative ladder that included Argentina Under 20s and Sevens, to score after a long run to turn the game and secure the 23–20 win.

Any hopes of a series win were soon dispelled by a French team set on gaining revenge, with the 49–10 win by Pascal Pape's side hard for Argentina to swallow. But there wasn't much time for coach Santiago Phelan to dwell on as a week after the Tucumán loss he was flying to America for the start of the Pumas' preparation for The Rugby Championship.

June was a busy month, and Argentine rugby was delighted to also celebrate important wins in the IRB Junior World Championship in South Africa. After languishing in the second group of teams in the previous four tournaments – sixth being their best finish on home soil in 2010 – victories against France (18–15), Australia (15–3) and Scotland (17–12) left them top of Pool C. They ultimately ran out of steam, with a 35–3 loss to eventual champions South Africa followed by a closer 25–17 defeat by Wales to finish fourth.

Off the field, the UAR moved offices to new premises more fitting for a thriving Union. It was also announced that Argentina would host a round of the HSBC Sevens World Series, although this was later postponed until the 2013/14 season due to operational issues. The 2011/12 Series saw Argentina Sevens finish seventh overall with a Dubai semi-final their best result.

The best Argentine players were then put through the toughest preparation ahead of The Rugby Championship. Commitment from players and clubs was paramount and every effort was made to ensure they were ready. A two-match series against French club Stade Français – yielding a loss and a win – was not too encouraging, but many players were only making their first outing of the season.

Fittingly, the first Rugby Championship match was played in South Africa, a country that has been so instrumental in Argentina's coming of age. The Springboks were not that friendly, however, and at Newlands the 27–6 loss was a lesson in itself.

A week later, both teams reconvened in Argentina, in the beautiful city of Mendoza, and, sooner than many had expected, Los Pumas showed they fitted into this company. The 16–16 draw saw Argentina squander a lead, after a very good Puma try by Santiago Fernández and outstanding defence that confounded the Springboks. Only a charged-down kick broke the Puma defensive lines with Frans Steyn touching down for the visitors.

This was followed by the second long-haul trip for Argentina and Wellington, a happy hunting ground after the RWC 2011 win over Scotland, brought fond memories. The team stayed at the same hotel and felt at home. The storm that hit the windy city on match day played into the Pumas' hands, and after Roncero scored in the 12th minute the All Blacks knew it wouldn't be an easy match. Only when flanker Farías was sin-binned in the 58th minute did New Zealand make a dent, scoring two tries in the final 15 minutes to win 21–5.

Their huge defensive effort, considered the best in the world by All Black coach Steve Hansen, was again present a week later on the Gold Coast, when the Wallabies and Pumas played for the first time since RWC 2003. Two tries within three minutes put Argentina 19–6 ahead with 20 minutes left, but the strength of the Wallabies and the tiredness of four matches and so much travelling saw Los Pumas concede two tries as Australia ran out 23–19 winners.

Back at home, a lot was expected from Argentina. Only 17 players started for the Pumas in The Rugby Championship – in total only 24 players took the field – and the team was soundly beaten by the All Blacks hitting their peak in La Plata, the newest Test venue and a great stadium. A seventh-minute try from Landajo was the perfect start but was followed by seven All Black tries for the 54–15 title-clinching win.

The final match was in Rosario and brought another frustrating loss. Australia, with nine changes to the starting XV that opened the tournament following an injury-hit campaign, showed adversity to win 25–19 and deny Argentina victory to send off their great warrior Roncero.

No wins was hard to swallow, but the team grew as the Championship progressed and the many lessons they will take with them means that the future bodes very well for rugby in Argentina.

The level of support – internally and from neighbouring countries – was incredible. The standard the Pumas achieved, even with the lack of a win, spoke volumes for their commitment and their hunger. With Rugby World Cup 2015 as the final goal, Argentina are on a road that will make them better, and sooner rather than later.

ARGENTINA INTERNATIONAL STATISTICS

MATCH RECORDS UP TO 10 OCTOBER 2012

WINNING MARGIN

Date	Opponent	Result	Winning Margin
01/05/2002	Paraguay	152–0	152
27/04/2003	Paraguay	144–0	144
01/05/2004	Venezuela	147–7	140
02/10/1993	Brazil	114–3	111
23/05/2012	Brazil	111–0	111

MOST POINTS IN A MATCH
BY THE TEAM

Date	Opponent	Result	Points
01/05/2002	Paraguay	152–0	152
01/05/2004	Venezuela	147–7	147
27/04/2003	Paraguay	144–0	144
02/10/1993	Brazil	114–3	114
23/05/2012	Brazil	111–0	111

BY A PLAYER

Date	Player	Opponent	Points
14/10/1973	Eduardo Morgan	Paraguay	50
27/04/2003	José María Nuñez Piossek	Paraguay	45
02/10/1993	Gustavo Jorge	Brazil	40
24/10/1977	Martin Sansot	Brazil	36
13/09/1951	Uriel O'Farrell	Brazil	33

MOST TRIES IN A MATCH
BY THE TEAM

Date	Opponent	Result	Tries
01/05/2002	Paraguay	152–0	24
27/04/2003	Paraguay	144–0	24
01/05/2004	Venezuela	147–7	23
08/10/1989	Brazil	103–0	20

BY A PLAYER

Date	Player	Opponent	Tries
13/09/1951	Uriel O'Farrell	Brazil	11
27/04/2003	José María Nuñez Piossek	Paraguay	9
02/10/1993	Gustavo Jorge	Brazil	8
23/05/2012	Facundo Barrea	Brazil	6
08/10/1989	Gustavo Jorge	Brazil	6
14/10/1973	Eduardo Morgan	Paraguay	6

MOST CONVERSIONS IN A MATCH
BY THE TEAM

Date	Opponent	Result	Cons
01/05/2002	Paraguay	152–0	16
01/05/2004	Venezuela	147–7	16
09/10/1979	Brazil	109–3	15
21/09/1985	Paraguay	102–3	13
14/10/1973	Paraguay	98–3	13

BY A PLAYER

Date	Player	Opponent	Cons
01/05/2002	Jose Cilley	Paraguay	16
21/09/1985	Hugo Porta	Paraguay	13
14/10/1973	Eduardo Morgan	Paraguay	13
25/09/1975	Eduardo de Forteza	Paraguay	11

MOST PENALTIES IN A MATCH
BY THE TEAM

Date	Opponent	Result	Pens
10/10/1999	Samoa	32–16	8
10/03/1995	Canada	29–26	8
17/06/2006	Wales	45–27	8

BY A PLAYER

Date	Player	Opponent	Pens
10/10/1999	Gonzalo Quesada	Samoa	8
10/03/1995	Santiago Meson	Canada	8
17/06/2006	Federico Todeschini	Wales	8

MOST DROP GOALS IN A MATCH
BY THE TEAM

Date	Opponent	Result	DGs
27/10/1979	Australia	24–13	3
02/11/1985	New Zealand	21–21	3
26/05/2001	Canada	20–6	3
21/09/1975	Uruguay	30–15	3
07/08/1971	SA Gazelles	12–0	3
30/09/2007	Ireland	30–15	3

BY A PLAYER

Date	Player	Opponent	DGs
27/10/1979	Hugo Porta	Australia	3
02/11/1985	Hugo Porta	New Zealand	3
07/08/1971	Tomas Harris-Smith	SA Gazelles	3
26/05/2001	Juan Fernández Miranda	Canada	3
30/09/2007	Juan Martín Hernández	Ireland	3

MOST CAPPED PLAYERS

Name	Caps
Lisandro Arbizu	86
Rolando Martin	86
Mario Ledesma	84
Pedro Sporleder	78
Felipe Contepomi	75

LEADING PENALTY SCORERS

Name	Penalties
Felipe Contepomi	128
Gonzalo Quesada	103
Hugo Porta	101
Santiago Meson	63
Federico Todeschini	54

LEADING TRY SCORERS

Name	Tries
José María Nuñez Piossek	29
Diego Cuesta Silva	28
Gustavo Jorge	24
Facundo Soler	18
Rolando Martin	18

LEADING DROP GOAL SCORERS

Name	DGs
Hugo Porta	26
Lisandro Arbizu	11
Gonzalo Quesada	7
Tomas Harris-Smith	6
Juan Martín Hernández	6

LEADING CONVERSIONS SCORERS

Name	Conversions
Hugo Porta	84
Gonzalo Quesada	68
Santiago Meson	68
Felipe Contepomi	64
Juan Fernández Miranda	41

LEADING POINTS SCORERS

Name	Points
Hugo Porta	590
Felipe Contepomi	588
Gonzalo Quesada	486
Santiago Meson	370
Federico Todeschini	256

ARGENTINA INTERNATIONAL PLAYERS
UP TO 10 OCTOBER 2012

A Abadie 2007 *CHL*, 2009 *E, W, S*
A Abella 1969 *Ur, CHL*
C Abud 1975 *Par, Bra, CHL*
H Achaval 1948 *OCC*
J Aguilar 1983 *CHL, Ur*
A Aguirre 1997 *Par, CHL*
ME Aguirre 1990 *E, S*, 1991 *Sa*
B Agulla 2010 *Ur, CHL*, 2011 *CHL, Ur*, 2012 *It, F*
H Agulla 2005 *Sa*, 2006 *Ur, E, It*, 2007 *It, F, Nm, I, S, SA, F*, 2008 *S, It, SA, F, It, I*, 2009 *E, E, E, W, S*, 2010 *Ur, CHL, S, S, F, I*, 2011 *W, E, R, S, Geo, NZ*, 2012 *SA, SA, NZ, A, NZ, A*
L Ahaulli 2012 *Ur, CHL*
P Albacete 2003 *Par, Ur, F, SA, Ur, C, A, R*, 2004 *W, W, NZ, F, I*, 2005 *It, It*, 2006 *E, It, F*, 2007 *W, F, Geo, Nm, I, S, SA, F*, 2008 *SA, F, It, I*, 2009 *E, E, E, W, S*, 2010 *S, S, F, F, I*, 2011 *W, E, R, S, Geo, NZ*, 2012 *SA, SA, NZ, A, NZ, A*
DL Albanese 1995 *Ur, C, E, F*, 1996 *Ur, F, SA, E*, 1997 *NZ, Ur, R, It, F, A, A*, 1998 *F, F, R, US, C, It, F, W*, 1999 *W, W, S, I, W, Sa, J, I, F*, 2000 *I, A, A, SA*, 2001 *NZ, It, W, S, NZ*, 2002 *F, E, SA, A, It, I*, 2003 *F, F, SA, US, C, A, Nm, I*

F Albarracin 2007 *CHL*
M Albina 2001 *Ur, US*, 2003 *Par, Ur, Fj*, 2004 *CHL, Ven, W, W*, 2005 *J*
C Aldao 1961 *CHL, Bra, Ur*
P Alexenicer 1997 *Par, CHL*
H Alfonso 1936 *BI, CHL*
G Allen 1977 *Par*
JG Allen 1981 *C*, 1985 *F, F, Ur, NZ, NZ*, 1986 *F, F, A, A*, 1987 *Ur, Fj, It, NZ, Sp, A, A*, 1988 *F, F, F, F*, 1989 *Bra, CHL, Par, Ur, US*
L Allen 1951 *Ur, Bra, CHL*
M Allen 1990 *C, E, S*, 1991 *NZ, CHL*
F Allogio 2011 *CHL, Ur*
A Allub 1997 *Par, Ur, It, F, A, A*, 1998 *F, F, US, C, J, It, F, W*, 1999 *W, W, S, I, W, Sa, J, I, F*, 2000 *I, A, A, SA, E*, 2001 *NZ*
M Alonso 1973 *R, R, S*, 1977 *F, F*
A Altberg 1972 *SAG, SAG*, 1973 *R, R, Par*
J Altube 1998 *Par, CHL, Ur*
C Alvarez 1958 *Ur, Per, CHL*, 1959 *JSB, JSB*, 1960 *F*
GM Alvarez 1975 *Ur, Par, CHL*, 1976 *NZ*, 1977 *Bra, Ur, Par, CHL*

R Álvarez Kairelis 1998 *Par, CHL, Ur,* 2001 *Ur, US, C, W, S, NZ,* 2002 *F, E, SA, A, It, I,* 2003 *F, SA, Fj, Ur, C, Nm, I,* 2004 *F, I,* 2006 *W, W, NZ, CHL, Ur,* 2007 *I, It, W, F, Geo, Nm, I, S, SA, F,* 2008 *SA, F, It, I,* 2009 *E*
S Ambrosio 2012 *Ur, Bra*
F Amelong 2007 *CHL*
A Amuchastegui 2002 *Ur, Par, CHL*
GP Angaut 1987 *NZ, Ur, CHL,* 1990 *S,* 1991 *NZ, Sa*
JJ Angelillo 1987 *Ur, CHL, A,* 1988 *F, F, F,* 1989 *It, Bra, CHL, Par, Ur, US,* 1990 *C, US, E, E,* 1994 *US, S, S, US,* 1995 *Par, CHL, R, F*
W Aniz 1960 *F*
R Annichini 1983 *CHL, Ur,* 1985 *F, CHL, Par*
A Anthony 1965 *OCC, CHL,* 1967 *Ur, CHL,* 1968 *W, W,* 1969 *S, S, Ur, CHL,* 1970 *I, I,* 1971 *SAG, SAG, OCC,* 1972 *SAG, SAG,* 1974 *F, F*
F Aranguren 2007 *CHL,* 2011 *CHL, Ur*
G Aráoz 2012 *Bra, CHL*
L Arbizu 1990 *I, S,* 1991 *NZ, NZ, CHL, A, W, Sa,* 1992 *F, F, Sp, Sp, R, F,* 1993 *J, J, Bra, CHL, Par, Ur, SA, SA,* 1995 *Ur, A, A, E, Sa, It, Par, CHL, Ur, R, It, F,* 1996 *Ur, US, Ur, C, SA, SA, E,* 1997 *E, E, NZ, NZ, R, It, F, A, A,* 1998 *F, F, R, US, C, It, F, W,* 1999 *W, W, S, I, W, Sa, J, I, F,* 2000 *A, A, SA, E,* 2001 *NZ, It, W, S, NZ,* 2002 *F, A, It, I,* 2003 *F, F, US, C,* 2005 *It, It*
F Argerich 1979 *Ur*
G Aristide 1997 *E*
J Arocena Messones 2005 *Sa*
E Arriaga 1936 *CHL, CHL*
S Artese 2004 *SA*
G Ascarate 2007 *CHL,* 2010 *CHL,* 2012 *It, F*
M Avellaneda 1948 *OCC, OCC,* 1951 *Bra, CHL*
M Avramovic 2005 *J, Sa,* 2006 *CHL, Ur, E, It,* 2007 *I,* 2008 *It, SA, I,* 2009 *E*
M Ayerra 1927 *GBR*
MI Ayerza 2004 *SA,* 2005 *J, It, Sa,* 2006 *W, W, CHL, Ur, E, It, F,* 2007 *I, I, Geo, F,* 2008 *S, S, SA, F, It, I,* 2009 *E, E, E, W, S,* 2010 *S, S, F, It, F, I,* 2011 *Geo, NZ,* 2012 *SA, SA, NZ*
N Azorin 2012 *Ur, Bra*
M Azpiroz 1956 *OCC,* 1958 *Ur, Per, CHL,* 1959 *JSB, JSB*
J Bach 1975 *Par, Bra, CHL*
A Badano 1977 *Bra, Ur, Par, CHL*
J Baeck 1983 *Par*
M Baeck 1985 *Ur, CHL, Par,* 1990 *US, E, E*
DR Baetti Sabah 1980 *WXV, Fj, Fj,* 1981 *E, E, C,* 1983 *WXV,* 1987 *Ur, Par, CHL,* 1988 *F, F,* 1989 *It, NZ, NZ*
R Baez 2010 *CHL,* 2011 *CHL, Ur,* 2012 *F, F*
L Balfour 1977 *Bra, Ur, Par, CHL*
T Baravalle 2011 *Ur*
C Barrea 1996 *Ur, C, SA*
F Barrea 2012 *Ur, Bra, CHL, F*
O Bartolucci 1996 *US, C, SA,* 1998 *CHL, Ur,* 1999 *W, W, S, I, W, Sa,* 2000 *I, A, A, SA, E,* 2001 *US, C,* 2003 *Par, Ur*
E Basile 1983 *CHL, Ur*
JL Basile 2011 *CHL, Ur*
L Bavio 1954 *F*
R Bazan 1951 *Ur, Bra, CHL,* 1956 *OCC*
D Beccar Varela 1975 *F, F,* 1976 *W, NZ,* 1977 *F, F*
M Beccar Varela 1965 *Rho, OCC, OCC*
G Begino 2007 *CHL*
J Benzi 1965 *Rho,* 1969 *S, Ur, CHL*
E Bergamaschi 2001 *US*
O Bernacchi 1954 *F,* 1956 *OCC, OCC,* 1958 *Ur, Per, CHL*
G Bernardi 1997 *CHL*
O Bernat 1932 *JSB*
MM Berro 1964 *Ur, Bra, CHL*
MJS Bertranou 1989 *It, NZ, NZ, CHL, Par,* 1990 *C, US, C, E, I, E, S,* 1993 *SA*
E Bianchetti 1959 *JSB, JSB*
G Blacksley 1971 *SAG*
T Blades 1938 *CHL*
G Bocca 1998 *J, Par*
C Bofelli 1997 *Ur,* 1998 *Par,* 2004 *CHL, Ur, Ven*
A Bordoy 2012 *F, F*
L Borges 2003 *Par, CHL, Ur,* 2004 *CHL, Ur, Ven, W, W, NZ, F, I, SA,* 2005 *SA, S,* 2006 *W, W, CHL, Ur,* 2007 *W, F, Geo, I, S, SA,* 2008 *S, It,* 2009 *E, W, S,* 2010 *W, S, I*

C Bori 1975 *F*
F Bosch 2004 *CHL, SA,* 2005 *J, Sa*
MA Bosch 1991 *A, Sa,* 1992 *F, F*
MT Bosch 2007 *It,* 2008 *It,* 2010 *F, I,* 2011 *W, E, R, S, Geo, NZ,* 2012 *SA, SA, NZ, A, NZ, A*
N Bossicovich 1995 *Ur, C*
CA Bottarini 1973 *Par, Ur, Bra, I,* 1974 *F,* 1975 *F, F,* 1979 *Ur, CHL, Bra,* 1983 *CHL, Par, Ur*
R Botting 1927 *GBR, GBR, GBR*
S Bottini 2011 *CHL, Ur*
L Bouza 1992 *Sp*
M Bouza 1966 *SAG, SAG,* 1967 *Ur, CHL*
P Bouza 1996 *Ur, F, F, E,* 1997 *E, NZ, NZ, Ur, R,* 1998 *Ur,* 2002 *Ur, Par, CHL,* 2003 *Par, CHL, Ur, US, Ur, Nm, R,* 2004 *CHL, Ur, Ven, W, NZ, SA,* 2005 *J, It, It, SA, S, It,* 2006 *CHL, Ur,* 2007 *I, I*
A Bovet 1910 *GBR*
N Bozzo 1975 *Bra*
JG Braceras 1971 *Bra, Par,* 1976 *W, NZ,* 1977 *F*
W Braddon 1927 *GBR*
EN Branca 1976 *W, NZ, NZ,* 1977 *F, F,* 1980 *Fj,* 1981 *E, E, C,* 1983 *WXV, A, A,* 1985 *F, F, Ur, CHL, Par, NZ, NZ,* 1986 *F, F, A, A,* 1987 *Ur, Fj, It, NZ, Sp, A, A,* 1988 *F, F, F, F,* 1989 *Bra, Par, Ur,* 1990 *E, E*
M Brandi 1997 *Par, CHL,* 1998 *Par, CHL, Ur*
J Bridger 1932 *JSB*
J Brolese 1998 *CHL, Ur*
E Brouchou 1975 *Ur, Par, Bra, CHL*
R Bruno 2010 *Ur, CHL,* 2012 *Bra, CHL, F*
F Buabse 1991 *Ur, Par, Bra,* 1992 *Sp*
PM Buabse 1989 *NZ, US,* 1991 *Sa,* 1993 *Bra,* 1995 *Ur, C, A*
E Buckley 1938 *CHL*
R Bullrich 1991 *Ur, Bra,* 1992 *R,* 1993 *Bra, CHL, SA,* 1994 *SA, SA*
S Bunader 1989 *US,* 1990 *C*
K Bush 1938 *CHL*
E Bustamante 1927 *GBR, GBR, GBR, GBR*
F Bustillo 1977 *F, F, Bra, Ur, Par, CHL*
G Bustos 2003 *Par, Ur,* 2004 *CHL, Ven*
CJ Cáceres 2010 *Ur, CHL*
E Caffarone 1949 *F, F,* 1951 *Bra, CHL,* 1952 *I, I,* 1954 *F, F*
M Caldwell 1956 *OCC*
GO Camacho 2009 *E, E,* 2010 *It, F,* 2011 *W, E, R, S, NZ,* 2012 *SA, SA, NZ, A, NZ, A*
GF Camardon 1990 *E,* 1991 *NZ, CHL, A, W, Sa,* 1992 *F, F, Sp, R, F,* 1993 *J, Par, Ur, SA, SA,* 1995 *A,* 1996 *Ur, US, Ur, C, SA, E,* 1999 *W, W, Sa, J, I, F,* 2001 *US, C, NZ, It, W, S, NZ,* 2002 *F, E, SA, It, I*
PJ Camerlinckx 1989 *Bra, Par, Ur,* 1990 *C, US,* 1994 *S,* 1995 *CHL,* 1996 *Ur, F, F, US, Ur, C, SA, SA, E,* 1997 *E, E, NZ, NZ, Ur, R, It, F, A, A,* 1998 *R, US, C, F, W,* 1999 *W*
A Cameron 1936 *BI, CHL, CHL,* 1938 *CHL*
R Cameron 1927 *GBR, GBR*
J Caminotti 1987 *Ur, Par, CHL*
M Campo 1978 *E, It,* 1979 *NZ, NZ, A, A,* 1980 *WXV, Fj,* 1981 *E, E, C,* 1982 *F, F, Sp,* 1983 *WXV, A, A,* 1987 *Ur, Fj, NZ*
AT Campos 2007 *CHL,* 2008 *S, It, F, It,* 2009 *E, W, S,* 2010 *Ur, S, F,* 2011 *W, E, R, NZ*
A Canalda 1999 *S, I, F,* 2000 *A,* 2001 *Ur, US, C*
R Cano 1997 *Par*
J Capalbo 1975 *Bra,* 1977 *Bra, Ur, CHL*
AE Capelletti 1977 *F, F,* 1978 *E, It,* 1979 *NZ, NZ, A, A,* 1980 *WXV, Fj, Fj,* 1981 *E, E*
R Carballo 2006 *W, CHL, Ur,* 2008 *SA, It, I,* 2010 *S, F*
N Carbone 1969 *Ur, CHL,* 1971 *SAG,* 1973 *I, S*
PF Cardinali 2001 *US,* 2002 *Ur, Par,* 2004 *W,* 2007 *I*
M Carizza 2004 *SA,* 2005 *J, SA, S, It,* 2006 *W, CHL, Ur,* 2007 *It,* 2008 *It,* 2009 *E, E, W, S,* 2010 *S, S, F, It,* 2011 *W, E, R, S, NZ,* 2012 *SA, SA, NZ, A, NZ, A*
J Carlos Galvalisi 1983 *Par, Ur*
MA Carluccio 1973 *R, R, Ur, Bra, I,* 1975 *F, F,* 1976 *NZ,* 1977 *F, F*
M Carmona 1997 *Par, CHL*
SC Carossio 1985 *Ur,* 1987 *It, NZ*
J Carracedo 1971 *CHL, Bra, Par,* 1972 *SAG, SAG,* 1973 *R, R, Par, Ur, Bra, CHL, I, S,* 1975 *F,* 1976 *W, NZ, NZ,* 1977 *F*
M Carreras 1987 *Par,* 1991 *NZ, NZ, CHL, A, W, Sa,* 1992 *F*

M Carrique 1983 *Par, Ur*
J Casanegra 1959 *JSB, JSB*, 1960 *F, F*
GF Casas 1971 *OCC*, 1973 *Par, CHL, I*, 1975 *F, F*
DM Cash 1985 *F, F, Ur, CHL, NZ, NZ*, 1986 *F, F, A, A*, 1987 *Ur, Fj, It, NZ, Sp, A, A*, 1988 *F, F, F, F*, 1989 *It, NZ, NZ, US*, 1990 *C, US, C, E, I, E, S*, 1991 *NZ, NZ, CHL, A, Sa*, 1992 *F, F*
R Castagna 1977 *F*
A Castellina 2004 *CHL, Ur, Ven*
R Castro 1971 *CHL, Bra, Par*
J Cato 1975 *Ur, Par*
R Cazenave 1965 *Rho, JSB, OCC, CHL*, 1966 *SAG, SAG*
N Centurion 2011 *CHL, Ur*
A Cerioni 1975 *F*, 1978 *E, It*, 1979 *CHL, Bra*
G Cernegoy 1938 *CHL*
H Cespedes 1997 *Ur, CHL*
M Chesta 1966 *SAG, SAG*, 1967 *Ur, CHL*, 1968 *W, W*
W Chiswell 1949 *F*
V Christianson 1954 *F, F*, 1956 *OCC*
E Cilley 1932 *JSB, JSB*
J Cilley 1936 *BI, CHL, CHL*, 1938 *CHL*
JL Cilley 1994 *SA*, 1995 *Sa, It, Par, CHL*, 1996 *Ur, F, F, SA, SA*, 1999 *W*, 2000 *A*, 2002 *Par*
J Clement 1987 *Par*, 1989 *Bra*
R Cobelo 1987 *Ur, Par, CHL*
I Comas 1951 *Bra, CHL*, 1958 *Per, CHL*, 1960 *F*
MA Comuzzi 2009 *E, W*, 2011 *CHL, Ur*
J Conrard 1927 *GBR, GBR*
CA Contepomi 1964 *Bra, CHL*
F Contepomi 1998 *CHL, Ur, F, W*, 1999 *W, S, I, J, I, F*, 2000 *I, A, A, SA, E*, 2001 *Ur, US, C, NZ, It, W, S, NZ*, 2002 *F, E, SA, A, It, I*, 2003 *F, SA, US, C, A, Nm, I*, 2004 *W, W, F, I*, 2005 *It, It, SA, S, It*, 2006 *W, NZ, E, F*, 2007 *I, W, F, Geo, Nm, I, S, SA, F*, 2008 *S, S, SA, F, It, F, I*, 2010 *S, S, F, It, F, I*, 2011 *W, E, S, Geo, NZ*, 2012 *It, F, F*
M Contepomi 1998 *US, C, It, F, W*, 1999 *S, I, W, Sa, F*, 2003 *Ur, F, Fj, Ur, A, R*, 2004 *CHL, Ur, Ven, W, W, NZ, F, I, SA*, 2005 *SA, S*, 2006 *It, F*, 2007 *I, It, W, F, Nm, I, S, SA, F*
F Conti 1988 *F*
GEF Cooke 1927 *GBR*
KAM Cookson 1932 *JSB*
N Cooper 1936 *BI, CHL, CHL*
R Cooper 1927 *GBR, GBR, GBR, GBR*
J Copello 1975 *Ur, Bra*
C Cordeiro 1983 *Par*
J Coria 1987 *Ur, Par, CHL*, 1989 *Bra*
I Corleto 1998 *J, F, W*, 1999 *I, J, I, F*, 2000 *I, A, SA, E*, 2001 *W, S, NZ*, 2002 *F, E, SA, A, It, I*, 2003 *F, Fj, US, Ur, C, A, I*, 2006 *It, F*, 2007 *W, F, Geo, Nm, I, S, SA, F*
ME Corral 1993 *J, Bra, Par, Ur, SA, SA*, 1994 *US, S, SA, SA*, 1995 *Ur, C, A, A, E, Sa, It*
RG Cortes 2011 *CHL, Ur*, 2012 *Ur, CHL*
M Cortese 2005 *Sa*, 2010 *Ur, CHL*
F Cortopasso 2003 *CHL, Ur*
A Costa Repetto 2005 *Sa*
JD Constante 1971 *OCC, OCC, CHL, Bra, Par, Ur*, 1976 *W, NZ*, 1977 *F*
AF Courreges 1979 *Ur, Par, Bra*, 1982 *F, F, Sp*, 1983 *WXV, A, A*, 1987 *Sp, A, A*, 1988 *F*
PH Cox 1938 *CHL*
S Craig 2012 *Bra, CHL*
A Creevy 2005 *J, Sa*, 2006 *Ur*, 2009 *S*, 2010 *S, S, F, It, F, I*, 2011 *W, E, R, S, Geo, NZ*, 2012 *A, NZ, A*
P Cremaschi 1993 *J, J*, 1995 *Par, CHL, Ur, It*
RH Crexell 1990 *I, S*, 1991 *Par*, 1992 *Sp*, 1993 *J*, 1995 *Ur, C, A, E, Sa, It, Par, CHL, Ur*
L Criscuolo 1992 *F, F*, 1993 *Bra, SA*, 1996 *Ur, F, F*
V Cruz 2012 *Ur, Bra, CHL*
J Cruz Legora 2002 *Par, CHL*
J Cruz Meabe 1997 *Par*
AG Cubelli 1977 *Bra, Ur, CHL*, 1978 *E, It*, 1979 *A, A*, 1980 *WXV, Fj*, 1983 *Par*, 1985 *F, F, Ur, Par, NZ, NZ*, 1990 *S*
TM Cubelli 2010 *Ur, CHL*, 2011 *CHL, Ur*, 2012 *Ur, Bra, CHL, It, F, F*
D Cuesta Silva 1983 *CHL, Ur*, 1985 *F, F, Ur, CHL, NZ, NZ*, 1986 *F, F, A, A*, 1987 *Ur, Fj, It, Sp, A, A*, 1988 *F, F, F, F*, 1989

It, NZ, NZ, 1990 *C, E, E, I, E, S*, 1991 *NZ, NZ, CHL, A, W, Sa*, 1992 *F, F, Sp, R, F*, 1993 *J, J, Bra, Par, Ur, SA, SA*, 1994 *US, S, S, US*, 1995 *Ur, C, E, Sa, It, Par, R, It, F*
J Cuesta Silva 1927 *GBR, GBR, GBR, GBR*
B Cuezzo 2007 *CHL*
M Cutler 1969 *Ur*, 1971 *CHL, Bra, Par, Ur*
A Da Milano 1964 *Bra, CHL*
F D'Agnillo 1975 *Ur, Bra*, 1977 *Bra, Ur, Par, CHL*
JL Damioli 1991 *Ur, Par, Bra*
H Dande 2001 *Ur, C*, 2004 *CHL, Ven*
J Dartiguelongue 1964 *Bra, CHL*, 1968 *W, W*
S Dassen 1983 *CHL, Par, Ur*
R de Abelleyra 1932 *JSB, JSB*
M De Achaval 2010 *It, F*
L de Chazal 2001 *Ur, C*, 2004 *SA*
E de Forteza 1975 *Ur, Par, Bra, CHL*
R de la Arena 1992 *F, Sp*
T De La Vega 2011 *CHL, Ur*, 2012 *It, F, F*
JC De Pablo 1948 *OCC*
G De Robertis 2005 *Sa*, 2006 *CHL, Ur*, 2011 *CHL*
R de Vedia 1982 *F, Sp*
T de Vedia 2007 *I, I*, 2008 *S*
R del Busto 2007 *CHL*
F del Castillo 1994 *US, SA*, 1995 *Ur, C, A*, 1996 *Ur, F*, 1997 *Par, Ur*, 1998 *Ur*
GJ del Castillo 1991 *NZ, NZ, CHL, A, W*, 1993 *J*, 1994 *S, S, US, SA*, 1995 *C, A*
L del Chazal 1983 *CHL, Par, Ur*
R Dell'Acqua 1956 *OCC*
S Dengra 1982 *F, Sp*, 1983 *WXV, A, A*, 1986 *A*, 1987 *It, NZ, Sp, A, A*, 1988 *F, F, F, F*, 1989 *It, NZ, NZ*
C Derkheim 1927 *GBR*
M Devoto 1975 *Par, Bra*, 1977 *Par*
PM Devoto 1982 *F, F, Sp*, 1983 *WXV*
R Devoto 1960 *F*
M Diaz 1997 *Par, CHL*, 1998 *J, Par, CHL*
F Diaz Alberdi 1997 *Ur*, 1999 *S, I*, 2000 *A, A*
J Diez 1956 *OCC*
R Dillon 1956 *OCC*
P Dinisio 1989 *NZ*, 1990 *C, US*
M Dip 1979 *Par, Bra*
D Dominguez 1989 *CHL, Par*
E Dominguez 1949 *F, F*, 1952 *I, I*, 1954 *F, F*
A Donnelly 1910 *GBR*
L Dorado 1949 *F*
J Dumas 1973 *R, R, Ur, Bra, S*
M Dumas 1966 *SAG, SAG*
MA Durand 1997 *Par*, 1998 *Par, CHL, Ur, It, F, W*, 2000 *SA*, 2001 *Ur, US, C, It, NZ*, 2002 *F, SA, A, It, I*, 2003 *CHL, Ur, Fj, US, Ur, C, A, Nm, R*, 2004 *CHL, Ur, Ven, W, W, NZ, F, I, SA*, 2005 *SA, S, It*, 2006 *W, NZ, CHL, Ur, It, F*, 2007 *I, It, W, F, Geo, I, F*, 2008 *S, S, It, SA, F, It, I*
C Echeverria 1932 *JSB*
G Ehrman 1948 *OCC*, 1949 *F, F*, 1951 *Ur, Bra, CHL*, 1952 *I, I*, 1954 *F, F*
O Elia 1954 *F*
R Elliot 1936 *BI*, 1938 *CHL*
J Escalante 1975 *Ur, Par, CHL*, 1978 *It*, 1979 *Ur, CHL, Par, Bra*
N Escary 1927 *GBR, GBR*, 1932 *JSB, JSB*
R Espagnol 1971 *SAG*
AM Etchegaray 1964 *Ur, Bra, CHL*, 1965 *Rho, JSB, CHL*, 1967 *Ur, CHL*, 1968 *W, W*, 1969 *S, S*, 1971 *SAG, OCC, OCC*, 1972 *SAG, SAG*, 1973 *Par, Bra, I*, 1974 *F, F*, 1976 *W, NZ, NZ*
R Etchegoyen 1991 *Ur, Par, Bra*
C Ezcurra 1958 *Ur, Per, CHL*
E Ezcurra 1990 *I, E, S*
JA Farias Cabello 2010 *F, I*, 2011 *W, E, S, Geo, NZ*, 2012 *It, F, F, SA, SA, NZ, A, NZ, A*
R Fariello 1973 *Par, Ur, CHL, S*
M Farina 1968 *W, W*, 1969 *S, S*
D Farrell 1951 *Ur*
P Felisari 1956 *F*
JJ Fernandez 1971 *SAG, CHL, Bra, Par, Ur*, 1972 *SAG, SAG*, 1973 *R, R, Par, Ur, CHL, I, S*, 1974 *F, F*, 1975 *F*, 1976 *W, NZ, NZ*, 1977 *F, F*

S Fernández 2008 *It, I,* 2009 *E, E, E, W, S,* 2010 *S, S, F, It, F,* 2011 *W, E, R, S, Geo, NZ,* 2012 *SA, SA, NZ, A, NZ, A*
Pablo Fernandez Bravo 1993 *SA, SA*
E Fernandez del Casal 1951 *Ur, Bra, CHL,* 1952 *I, I,* 1956 *OCC, OCC*
CI Fernandez Lobbe 1996 *US,* 1997 *E, E,* 1998 *F, F, R, US, Ur, C, J, It, F,* 1999 *W, W, S, I, W, Sa, J, I, F,* 2000 *I, A, A, SA, E,* 2001 *NZ, It, W, S, NZ,* 2002 *F, E, SA, A, It, I,* 2003 *F, F, SA, US, C, A, Nm, I,* 2004 *W, W, NZ,* 2005 *SA, S, It,* 2006 *W, W, NZ, E, F,* 2007 *It, W, F, Nm, I, S, SA,* 2008 *S, S*
JM Fernandez Lobbe 2004 *Ur, Ven,* 2005 *S, It, Sa,* 2006 *W, W, NZ, E, It, F,* 2007 *I, I, It, W, F, Geo, Nm, I, S, SA, F,* 2008 *S, S, SA, F, It, I,* 2009 *E, E, E, W, S,* 2010 *S, S, F, It, F, I,* 2011 *W, E, R, S,* 2012 *SA, SA, NZ, A, NZ, A*
JC Fernández Miranda 1997 *Ur, R, It,* 1998 *Ur, It,* 2000 *I,* 2001 *US, C,* 2002 *Ur, Par, CHL, It, I,* 2003 *Par, CHL, Ur, Fj, US, Nm, R,* 2004 *W, NZ, SA,* 2005 *J, Sa,* 2006 *CHL, Ur,* 2007 *It*
N Fernandez Miranda 1994 *US, S, S, US,* 1995 *CHL, Ur,* 1996 *F, SA, SA, E,* 1997 *E, E, NZ, NZ, Ur, R,* 1998 *R, US, C, It,* 1999 *I, F,* 2002 *Ur, CHL, It,* 2003 *CHL, Ur, F, F, SA, US, Ur, Nm, R,* 2004 *W, NZ,* 2005 *J, It, It,* 2006 *W, It,* 2007 *It, Geo, Nm*
N Ferrari 1992 *Sp, Sp*
G Fessia 2007 *I,* 2009 *E,* 2010 *S, S, F, It, F, I,* 2011 *R, S, Geo,* 2012 *It*
JG Figallo 2010 *F, It, I,* 2011 *W, E, R, S, Geo, NZ,* 2012 *SA, SA, NZ, A, NZ, A*
A Figuerola 2008 *It, I,* 2009 *E, W, S,* 2010 *S, S*
R Follett 1948 *OCC, OCC,* 1952 *I, I,* 1954 *F*
G Foster 1971 *CHL, Bra, Par, Ur*
R Foster 1965 *Rho, JSB, OCC, OCC, CHL,* 1966 *SAG, SAG,* 1970 *I, I,* 1971 *SAG, SAG, OCC,* 1972 *SAG, SAG*
P Franchi 1987 *Ur, Par, CHL*
JL Francombe 1932 *JSB, JSB,* 1936 *BI*
J Freixas 2003 *CHL, Ur*
R Frigerio 1948 *OCC, OCC,* 1954 *F*
J Frigoli 1936 *BI, CHL, CHL*
C Fruttero 2012 *Ur, Bra, CHL*
P Fuselli 1998 *J, Par*
E Gahan 1954 *F, F*
M Gaitán 1998 *Ur,* 2002 *Par, CHL,* 2003 *Fj, US, Nm, R,* 2004 *W,* 2007 *It, W*
MT Galarza 2010 *S, F, It, F, I,* 2011 *W, E, R, Geo*
AM Galindo 2004 *Ur, Ven,* 2008 *S, It, SA, F, It,* 2009 *E,* 2010 *Ur, It, F,* 2012 *SA, SA*
R Gallo 1964 *Bra*
P Gambarini 2006 *W, CHL, Ur,* 2007 *I, It, CHL,* 2008 *S*
E Garbarino 1992 *Sp, Sp*
FL Garcia 1994 *SA,* 1995 *A, A, Par, CHL,* 1996 *Ur, F, F,* 1997 *NZ,* 1998 *R, Ur, J*
J Garcia 1998 *Par, Ur,* 2000 *A*
PT Garcia 1948 *OCC*
E Garcia Hamilton 1993 *Bra*
P Garcia Hamilton 1998 *CHL*
HM García Simon 1990 *I,* 1992 *F*
M Garcia Veiga 2012 *Ur, Bra, CHL*
G Garcia-Orsetti 1992 *R, F*
PA Garreton 1987 *Sp, Ur, CHL, A, A,* 1988 *F, F, F, F,* 1989 *It, NZ, Bra, CHL, Ur, US,* 1990 *C, E, E, I, E, S,* 1991 *NZ, NZ, CHL, A, W, Sa,* 1992 *F, F,* 1993 *J, J*
P Garzon 1990 *C,* 1991 *Par, Bra*
G Gasso 1983 *CHL, Par*
JM Gauweloose 1975 *F, F,* 1976 *W, NZ, NZ,* 1977 *F, F,* 1981 *C*
E Gavina 1956 *OCC, OCC,* 1958 *Ur, Per, CHL,* 1959 *JSB, JSB,* 1960 *F, F,* 1961 *CHL, Bra, Ur*
OST Gebbie 1910 *GBR*
FA Genoud 2004 *CHL, Ur, Ven,* 2005 *J, It*
J Genoud 1952 *I, I,* 1956 *OCC, OCC*
M Gerosa 1987 *Ur, CHL*
D Giannantonio 1996 *Ur,* 1997 *Par, Ur, It, A, A,* 1998 *F, F,* 2000 *A,* 2002 *E*
MC Giargia 1973 *Par, Ur, Bra,* 1975 *Par, CHL*
R Giles 1948 *OCC,* 1949 *F, F,* 1951 *Ur,* 1952 *I, I*
C Giuliano 1959 *JSB, JSB,* 1960 *F*

L Glastra 1948 *OCC, OCC,* 1952 *I, I*
M Glastra 1979 *Ur, CHL,* 1981 *C*
FE Gomez 1985 *Ur,* 1987 *Ur, Fj, It, NZ,* 1989 *NZ,* 1990 *C, E, E*
JF Gomez 2006 *It,* 2008 *S, S, It*
N Gomez 1997 *Par, CHL*
PM Gomez Cora 2004 *NZ, SA,* 2005 *Sa,* 2006 *E*
F Gómez Kodela 2011 *CHL, Ur,* 2012 *It, F*
D Gonzalez 1987 *Par,* 1988 *F, F*
T Gonzalez 1975 *Ur, CHL*
LP Gonzalez Amorosino 2007 *CHL,* 2009 *E, E,* 2010 *S, S, F, It, F, I,* 2011 *R, S, Geo, NZ,* 2012 *SA, SA, NZ, A, NZ, A*
S Gonzalez Bonorino 2001 *Ur, US, C,* 2002 *Par, CHL,* 2003 *F, SA,* 2007 *I, I, It, W, F, Geo,* 2008 *S, S*
E Gonzalez del Solar 1960 *F,* 1961 *CHL, Bra, Ur*
N Gonzalez del Solar 1964 *Ur, Bra, CHL,* 1965 *Rho, JSB, OCC, OCC, CHL*
S Gonzalez Iglesias 2011 *CHL*
AO Gosio 2011 *Geo,* 2012 *It, F*
H Goti 1961 *CHL, Bra, Ur,* 1964 *Ur, Bra, CHL,* 1965 *Rho,* 1966 *SAG*
LM Gradin 1965 *OCC, OCC, CHL,* 1966 *SAG, SAG,* 1969 *CHL,* 1970 *I, I,* 1973 *R, R, Par, Ur, CHL, S*
P Grande 1998 *Par, CHL, Ur*
RD Grau 1993 *J, Bra, CHL,* 1995 *Par, CHL,* 1996 *F, F, US, Ur, C, SA, SA, E,* 1997 *E, E, NZ, NZ, A, A,* 1998 *F, It, F,* 1999 *W, W, S, I, W, F,* 2000 *A, SA, E,* 2001 *NZ, W, S, NZ,* 2002 *F, E, SA, A, It,* 2003 *F, SA, US, Ur, C, A, I*
L Gravano 1997 *CHL,* 1998 *CHL, Ur*
LH Gribell 1910 *GBR*
B Grigolon 1948 *OCC,* 1954 *F, F*
V Grimoldi 1927 *GBR, GBR*
J Grondona 1990 *C*
R Grosse 1952 *I, I,* 1954 *F, F*
P Guarrochena 1977 *Par*
A Guastella 1956 *OCC,* 1959 *JSB, JSB,* 1960 *F*
J Guidi 1958 *Ur, Per, CHL,* 1959 *JSB,* 1960 *F,* 1961 *CHL, Bra, Ur*
MR Guidone 2011 *CHL, Ur*
E Guiñazu 2003 *Par, CHL, Ur,* 2004 *CHL, Ur, Ven, W, W, SA,* 2005 *J, It,* 2007 *I, It, F,* 2009 *E,* 2012 *It, F, F, SA, SA, NZ, A, NZ, A*
JA Guzman 2007 *CHL,* 2010 *Ur, CHL*
SN Guzmán 2010 *S, I,* 2012 *Ur, Bra, CHL, It*
D Halle 1989 *Bra, CHL, Ur, US,* 1990 *US*
R Handley 1966 *SAG, SAG,* 1968 *W, W,* 1969 *S, S, Ur, CHL,* 1970 *I, I,* 1971 *SAG, SAG,* 1972 *SAG, SAG*
G Hardie 1948 *OCC*
TA Harris-Smith 1969 *S, S,* 1971 *SAG, OCC, OCC,* 1973 *Par, Ur*
O Hasan Jalil 1995 *Ur,* 1996 *Ur, C, SA, SA,* 1997 *E, E, NZ, R, It, F, A,* 1998 *F, F, R, US, C, It, F, W,* 1999 *W, W, S, W, Sa, J, I,* 2000 *SA, E,* 2001 *NZ, It, W, S, NZ,* 2002 *F, E, SA, A, It, I,* 2003 *US, C, A, R,* 2004 *W, W, NZ, F, I,* 2005 *It, It, SA, S, It,* 2006 *NZ, E, F,* 2007 *It, Geo, Nm, I, S, SA, F*
WM Hayman 1910 *GBR*
BH Heatlie 1910 *GBR*
P Henn 2004 *CHL, Ur, Ven,* 2005 *J, It,* 2007 *It,* 2012 *F*
F Henrys 1910 *GBR*
F Heriot 1910 *GBR*
JM Hernández 2003 *Par, Ur, F, F, SA, C, A, Nm, R,* 2004 *F, I, SA,* 2005 *SA, S, It,* 2006 *W, W, NZ, E, It, F,* 2007 *F, Geo, I, S, SA, F,* 2008 *It, F, It,* 2009 *E, E,* 2012 *SA, NZ, A, NZ, A*
M Hernandez 1927 *GBR, GBR, GBR*
L Herrera 1991 *Ur, Par*
FA Higgs 2004 *Ur, Ven,* 2005 *J*
D Hine 1938 *CHL*
C Hirsch 1960 *F*
C Hirsch 1960 *F*
E Hirsch 1954 *F,* 1956 *OCC*
R Hogg 1958 *Ur, Per, CHL,* 1959 *JSB, JSB,* 1961 *CHL, Bra, Ur*
S Hogg 1956 *OCC, OCC,* 1958 *Ur, Per, CHL,* 1959 *JSB, JSB*
E Holmberg 1948 *OCC*
B Holmes 1949 *F, F*
E Holmgren 1958 *Ur, Per, CHL,* 1959 *JSB, JSB,* 1960 *F, F*

G Holmgren 1985 *NZ, NZ*
E Horan 1956 *OCC*
L Hughes 1936 *CHL*
M Hughes 1954 *F, F*
M Hughes 1949 *F, F*
CA Huntley Robertson 1932 *JSB, JSB*
A Iachetti 1975 *Ur, Par,* 1977 *Ur, Par, CHL,* 1978 *E, It,* 1979 *NZ, NZ, A, A,* 1980 *WXV, Fj, Fj,* 1981 *E, E,* 1982 *F, F, Sp,* 1987 *Ur, Par, A, A,* 1988 *F, F, F, F,* 1989 *It, NZ,* 1990 *C, E, E*
A Iachetti 1977 *Bra,* 1987 *CHL*
ME Iachetti 1979 *NZ, NZ, A, A*
M Iglesias 1973 *R,* 1974 *F, F*
G Illia 1965 *Rho*
JJ Imhoff 2010 *CHL,* 2011 *W, E, R, Geo, NZ,* 2012 *A, NZ, A*
JL Imhoff 1967 *Ur, CHL*
V Inchausti 1936 *BI, CHL, CHL*
F Insua 1971 *CHL, Bra, Par, Ur,* 1972 *SAG, SAG,* 1973 *R, R, Bra, CHL, I, S,* 1974 *F, F,* 1976 *W, NZ, NZ,* 1977 *F, F*
R Iraneta 1974 *F,* 1976 *W, NZ*
FJ Irrazabal 1991 *Sa,* 1992 *Sp, Sp*
S Irazoqui 1993 *J, CHL, Par, Ur,* 1995 *E, Sa, Par*
A Irigoyen 1997 *Par*
C Jacobi 1979 *CHL, Par*
AG Jacobs 1927 *GBR, GBR*
AGW Jones 1948 *OCC*
GM Jorge 1989 *Bra, CHL, Par, Ur,* 1990 *I, E,* 1992 *F, F, Sp, Sp, R, F,* 1993 *J, J, Bra, CHL, Ur, SA, SA,* 1994 *US, S, S, US*
E Jurado 1995 *A, A, E, Sa, It, Par, CHL, Ur, R, It, F,* 1996 *SA, E,* 1997 *E, E, NZ, NZ, Ur, R, It, F, A, A,* 1998 *F, Ur, C, It,* 1999 *W*
E Karplus 1959 *JSB, JSB,* 1960 *F, F, F*
A Ker 1936 *CHL,* 1938 *CHL*
E Kossler 1960 *F, F, F*
EH Laborde 1991 *A, W, Sa*
G Laborde 1979 *CHL, Bra*
J Lacarra 1989 *Par, Ur*
R Lagarde 1956 *OCC*
A Lalanne 2008 *SA,* 2009 *E, E, W, S,* 2010 *S, I,* 2011 *R, Geo, NZ*
M Lamas 1998 *Par, CHL*
M Landajo 2010 *Ur, CHL,* 2012 *Ur, Bra, CHL, It, F, SA, SA, NZ, A, NZ, A*
TR Landajo 1977 *F, Bra, Ur, CHL,* 1978 *E,* 1979 *A, A,* 1980 *WXV, Fj, Fj,* 1981 *E, E*
M Lanfranco 1991 *Ur, Par, Bra*
AR Lanusse 1932 *JSB*
M Lanusse 1951 *Ur, Bra, CHL*
J Lanza 1985 *F, Ur, Par, NZ, NZ,* 1986 *F, F, A, A,* 1987 *Ur, Fj, It, NZ*
P Lanza 1983 *CHL, Par, Ur,* 1985 *F, F, Ur, CHL, Par, NZ, NZ,* 1986 *F, F, A, A,* 1987 *It, NZ*
J Lasalle 1964 *Ur*
J Lavayen 1961 *CHL, Bra, Ur*
CG Lazcano Miranda 1998 *CHL,* 2004 *CHL, Ur, Ven,* 2005 *J*
RA le Fort 1990 *I, E,* 1991 *NZ, NZ, CHL, A, W,* 1992 *R, F,* 1993 *J, SA, SA,* 1995 *Ur, It*
F Lecot 2003 *Par, Ur,* 2005 *J,* 2007 *CHL*
P Ledesma 2008 *It, SA*
ME Ledesma Arocena 1996 *Ur, C,* 1997 *NZ, NZ, Ur, R, It, F, A, A,* 1998 *F, F, Ur, C, J, Ur, F, W,* 1999 *W, Sa, J, I, F,* 2000 *SA,* 2001 *It, W, NZ,* 2002 *F, E, SA, A, It, I,* 2003 *F, SA, Fj, US, C, A, Nm, R,* 2004 *W, NZ, F, I,* 2005 *It, It, SA, S, It,* 2006 *W, W, NZ, CHL, Ur, E, It, F,* 2007 *W, F, Geo, I, S, SA,* 2008 *SA, F, It, I,* 2009 *E, E, W,* 2010 *S, S, F, It, F, I,* 2011 *W, E, R, S, Geo, NZ*
J Legora 1996 *F, F, US, Ur,* 1997 *CHL,* 1998 *Par*
JM Leguizamón 2005 *J, It, It, SA, S, It,* 2006 *W, NZ, CHL, Ur, E, It, F,* 2007 *I, I, It, W, F, Geo, Nm, S, SA, F,* 2008 *S, S, It, SA, I,* 2009 *E, E,* 2010 *S, S, F,* 2011 *W, E, R, S, Geo, NZ,* 2012 *NZ, A, NZ, A*
GP Lennon 1973 *Bra, I*
C Lennon 1958 *Ur, Per*
TC Leonardi 2009 *E, W, S,* 2012 *It, F, F, SA, SA, NZ, A, NZ, A*
FJ Leonelli Morey 2001 *Ur,* 2004 *Ur, Ven,* 2005 *J, It, SA, S, It,* 2006 *W, W,* 2007 *I, I, It,* 2008 *F, I,* 2009 *E*
M Lerga 1995 *Par, CHL, Ur*

Lesianado 1948 *OCC*
I Lewis 1932 *JSB*
GA Llanes 1990 *I, E, S,* 1991 *NZ, NZ, CHL, A, W,* 1992 *F, F, Sp, R, F,* 1993 *Bra, CHL, SA, SA,* 1994 *US, S, S, SA, SA,* 1995 *A, A, E, Sa, It, R, It, F,* 1996 *SA, SA, E,* 1997 *E, E, NZ, NZ, R, It, F,* 1998 *F,* 2000 *A*
MA Lobato 2010 *Ur, CHL*
L Lobrauco 1996 *US,* 1997 *CHL,* 1998 *J, CHL, Ur*
MH Loffreda 1978 *E,* 1979 *NZ, NZ, A, A,* 1980 *WXV, Fj, Fj,* 1981 *E, E, C,* 1982 *F, F, Sp,* 1983 *WXV, A, A,* 1985 *Ur, CHL, Par,* 1987 *Ur, Par, CHL, A, A,* 1988 *F, F, F, F,* 1989 *It, NZ, Bra, CHL, Par, Ur, US,* 1990 *C, US, E, E,* 1994 *US, S, S, US, SA, SA*
G Logan 1936 *BI*
GM Longo Elía 1999 *W, W, S, I, W, Sa, I, F,* 2000 *I, A, A, SA, E,* 2001 *US, NZ, It, W, S, NZ,* 2002 *F, E, SA, A, It, I,* 2003 *F, F, SA, Fj, C, A, I,* 2004 *W, W, NZ, F, I,* 2005 *It, It, SA,* 2006 *W, W, NZ, E, It, F,* 2007 *W, Nm, I, S, SA, F*
L Lopez Fleming 2004 *Ur, Ven, W,* 2005 *Sa*
A Lopresti 1997 *Par, CHL*
J Loures 1954 *F*
R Loyola 1964 *Ur, CHL,* 1965 *Rho, JSB, OCC, OCC, CHL,* 1966 *SAG, SAG,* 1968 *W, W,* 1969 *S, S,* 1970 *I, I,* 1971 *CHL, Bra, Par, Ur*
E Lozada 2006 *E, It,* 2007 *I, I, Geo, F,* 2008 *S, S, It, SA, F, It, I,* 2009 *E, E, E,* 2010 *It,* 2012 *F, F*
F Lucioni 1927 *GBR*
R Lucke 1975 *Ur, Par, Bra, CHL,* 1981 *C*
FD Luna 2011 *Ur*
J Luna 1995 *Par, CHL, Ur, R, It, F,* 1997 *Par, CHL*
P Macadam 1949 *F, F*
AM Macome 1990 *I, E,* 1995 *Ur, C*
B Macome 2012 *Ur, Bra, CHL, It, F, F*
B Madero 2011 *CHL, Ur*
RM Madero 1978 *E, It,* 1979 *NZ, NZ, A, A,* 1980 *WXV, Fj, Fj,* 1981 *E, E, C,* 1982 *F, F, Sp,* 1983 *WXV, A, A,* 1985 *F, NZ,* 1986 *A, A,* 1987 *Ur, It, NZ, Sp, Ur, Par, CHL, A, A,* 1988 *F, F, F,* 1989 *It, NZ, NZ,* 1990 *E, E*
M Maineri 2011 *CHL, Ur*
L Makin 1927 *GBR*
A Mamanna 1991 *Par,* 1997 *Par*
J Manuel Belgrano 1956 *OCC*
A Marguery 1991 *Ur, Bra,* 1993 *CHL, Par*
R Martin 1938 *CHL*
RA Martin 1994 *US, S, S, US, SA, SA,* 1995 *Ur, C, A, A, E, Sa, It, CHL, Ur, R, It, F,* 1996 *Ur, F, F, Ur, C, SA, SA, E,* 1997 *E, E, NZ, NZ, It, F, A, A,* 1998 *F, F, R, US, Ur, J, Par, CHL, Ur, It, W,* 1999 *W, W, S, I, W, Sa, J, I, F,* 2000 *I, A, A, SA, E,* 2001 *Ur, US, C, NZ, It, W, S, NZ,* 2002 *Ur, Par, CHL, F, E, SA, A, It, I,* 2003 *Par, CHL, Ur, F, SA, Ur, C, A, R, I*
F Martin Aramburu 2004 *CHL, Ven, W, NZ, F, I,* 2005 *It, SA, S, It,* 2006 *NZ,* 2007 *Geo, F,* 2008 *S, SA, F, It, I,* 2009 *E, S*
J Martin Copella 1989 *CHL, Par*
C Martinez 1969 *Ur, CHL,* 1970 *I, I*
E Martinez 1971 *CHL, Bra, Ur*
O Martinez Basante 1954 *F*
M Martinez Mosquera 1971 *CHL*
RC Mastai 1975 *F,* 1976 *W, NZ, NZ,* 1977 *F, F, Bra, Ur, Par, CHL,* 1980 *WXV*
R Matarazzo 1971 *SAG, SAG, Par, Ur,* 1972 *SAG, SAG,* 1973 *R, R, Par, Ur, CHL, I, S,* 1974 *F, F*
H Maurer 1932 *JSB, JSB*
L Maurette 1948 *OCC, OCC*
C Mazzini 1977 *F, F*
CJ McCarthy 1910 *GBR*
G McCormick 1964 *Bra, CHL,* 1965 *Rho, OCC, OCC, CHL,* 1966 *SAG, SAG*
M McCormick 1927 *GBR*
A Memoli 1979 *Ur, Par, Bra*
FE Méndez 1990 *I, E,* 1991 *NZ, NZ, CHL, A, W,* 1992 *F, F, Sp, Sp, R, F,* 1994 *S, US, SA, SA,* 1995 *Ur, C, A, A, E, Sa, It, Par, CHL, Ur, R, It, F,* 1996 *SA, SA,* 1997 *E, 1998 *F, F, R, US, Ur, C, It, F, W,* 1999 *W, W,* 2000 *I, A, A, SA, E,* 2001 *NZ, It, W, S, NZ,* 2002 *Ur, CHL, F, E, SA, A,* 2003 *F, F, SA, Fj, Ur, Nm, I,* 2004 *CHL, Ur, W, W, NZ, SA*

B Postiglioni 2012 *Ur, Bra, CHL, It, F, F*
C Promanzio 1995 *C,* 1996 *Ur, F, F, E,* 1997 *E, E, NZ, Ur,* 1998 *R, J*
U Propato 1956 *OCC*
L Proto 2010 *Ur, CHL*
A Puccio 1979 *CHL, Par, Bra*
M Puigdeval 1964 *Ur, Bra*
J Pulido 1960 *F*
JC Queirolo 1964 *Ur, Bra, CHL*
G Quesada 1996 *US, Ur, C, SA, E,* 1997 *E, E, NZ, NZ,* 1998 *F, R, US, C, It,* 1999 *W, S, I, W, Sa, J, I, F,* 2000 *I, SA, E,* 2001 *NZ, It, NZ,* 2002 *F, E, SA,* 2003 *F, SA, Ur, C, Nm, R, I*
E Quetglas 1965 *CHL*
G Quinones 2004 *Ur, Ven*
R Raimundez 1959 *JSB, JSB*
C Ramallo 1979 *Ur, CHL, Par*
S Ratcliff 1936 *CHL*
F Rave 1997 *Par*
M Reggiardo 1996 *Ur, F, F, E,* 1997 *E, E, NZ, NZ, R, F, A, A,* 1998 *F, F, R, US, Ur, C, It, W,* 1999 *W, W, S, I, W, Sa, J, I, F,* 2000 *I, SA,* 2001 *NZ, It, W, S, NZ,* 2002 *F, E, SA, A, It, I,* 2003 *F, SA, Fj, US, Ur, A, Nm, I*
A Reid 1910 *GBR*
C Reyes 1927 *GBR, GBR, GBR*
M Ricci 1987 *Sp*
A Riganti 1927 *GBR, GBR, GBR*
MA Righentini 1989 *NZ*
J Rios 1960 *F, F*
G Rivero 1996 *Ur, US, Ur*
G Roan 2010 *Ur, CHL*
T Roan 2007 *CHL*
F Robson 1927 *GBR*
M Roby 1992 *Sp,* 1993 *J*
A Rocca 1989 *US,* 1990 *C, US, C, E,* 1991 *Ur, Bra*
O Rocha 1974 *F, F*
D Rodriguez 1998 *J, Par, CHL, Ur*
D Rodriguez 2002 *Ur, Par, CHL*
EE Rodriguez 1979 *NZ, NZ, A, A,* 1980 *WXV, Fj, Fj,* 1981 *E, E, C,* 1983 *WXV, A, A*
F Rodriguez 2007 *CHL*
M Rodriguez 2009 *E, W, S,* 2010 *S, S, F, It, F, I,* 2011 *W, E, R, S, Geo,* 2012 *SA, SA, NZ, NZ*
A Rodriguez Jurado 1965 *JSB, OCC, OCC, CHL,* 1966 *SAG, SAG,* 1968 *W, W,* 1969 *S, CHL,* 1970 *I,* 1971 *SAG,* 1973 *R, Par, Bra, CHL, I, S,* 1974 *F, I,* 1975 *F, F*
A Rodriguez Jurado 1927 *GBR, GBR, GBR, GBR,* 1932 *JSB, JSB,* 1936 *CHL, CHL*
M Rodriguez Jurado 1971 *SAG, OCC, CHL, Bra, Par, Ur*
J Rojas 2012 *Ur, Bra, CHL*
L Roldan 2001 *Ur, C*
AS Romagnoli 2004 *CHL, Ur, Ven*
R Roncero 1998 *J,* 2002 *Ur, Par, CHL,* 2003 *Fj, US, Nm, A,* 2004 *W, W, NZ, F, I,* 2005 *It, SA, S, It,* 2006 *W, W, NZ,* 2007 *W, F, Nm, I, S, SA, F,* 2008 *It, SA, F, It, I,* 2009 *E, E, W, S,* 2010 *S, S, F, It, F, I,* 2011 *W, E, R, S, NZ,* 2012 *It, SA, SA, NZ, A, NZ, A*
S Rondinelli 2005 *Sa*
T Rosati 2011 *CHL, Ur*
S Rosatti 1977 *Par, CHL*
M Rospide 2003 *Par, CHL, Ur*
F Rossi 1991 *Ur, Par, Bra,* 1998 *F*
D Rotondo 1997 *Par, CHL*
MA Ruiz 1997 *NZ, CHL, R, It, F, A, A,* 1998 *F, F, R, US, Ur, C, J, It, F, W,* 1999 *W, Sa, J, F,* 2002 *Ur, Par, CHL*
I Saenz Lancuba 2012 *Ur, Bra*
JE Saffery 1910 *GBR*
CMS Sainz Trapaga 1979 *Ur, Par, Bra*
A Salinas 1954 *F,* 1956 *OCC,* 1958 *Ur, CHL,* 1960 *F, F*
S Salvat 1987 *Ur, Fj, It,* 1988 *F,* 1989 *It, NZ,* 1990 *C, US, C, E, E,* 1991 *Ur, Par, Bra,* 1992 *Sp, F,* 1993 *Bra, CHL, Par, Ur, SA, SA,* 1994 *SA, SA,* 1995 *Ur, C, A, A, E, Sa, It, Par, CHL, Ur, R, It, F*
T Salzman 1936 *BI, CHL, CHL*
M Sambucetti 2001 *Ur, US, C,* 2002 *Ur, CHL,* 2003 *Par, CHL, Fj,* 2005 *It, Sa,* 2009 *W*
HA San Martin 2009 *W, S*

FN Sanchez 2010 *Ur, CHL,* 2011 *R,* 2012 *SA, A*
T Sanderson 1932 *JSB*
D Sanes 1985 *CHL, Par,* 1986 *F, F,* 1987 *Ur, Par, CHL,* 1989 *Bra, CHL, Ur*
EJ Sanguinetti 1975 *Ur, Par, CHL,* 1978 *It,* 1979 *A,* 1982 *F, F, Sp*
G Sanguinetti 1979 *Ur, CHL, Par, Bra*
J Sansot 1948 *OCC*
M Sansot 1975 *F, F,* 1976 *W, NZ, NZ,* 1977 *Bra, CHL,* 1978 *E, It,* 1979 *NZ, NZ, A, A,* 1980 *WXV, Fj,* 1983 *WXV*
Jm Santamarina 1991 *NZ, NZ, CHL, A, W, Sa,* 1992 *F, Sp, R, F,* 1993 *J, J,* 1994 *US, S, US,* 1995 *A, A, E, Sa, It, Ur, R, It, F*
J Santiago 1948 *OCC,* 1952 *I, I*
JR Sanz 1973 *Par, Ur, Bra, CHL,* 1974 *F, F,* 1977 *F, F*
S Sanz 2003 *Ur,* 2004 *CHL, Ven,* 2005 *It, Sa,* 2007 *CHL*
M Sarandon 1948 *OCC, OCC,* 1949 *F, F,* 1951 *Ur, Bra, CHL,* 1952 *I, I,* 1954 *F*
J Sartori 1979 *CHL, Par, Bra*
R Sauze 1983 *Par*
FW Saywer 1910 *GBR*
MA Scelzo 1996 *US, SA,* 1997 *R, It, F, A,* 1998 *F, US, Ur, C, CHL, F,* 1999 *I, Sa, I, F,* 2000 *I, A, A,* 2003 *F, F, Fj, Ur, C, Nm, R, I,* 2005 *SA, S, It,* 2006 *W, W, NZ, CHL, Ur, E, It, F,* 2007 *W, F, Nm, I, S, SA,* 2009 *E, W, S,* 2010 *S, S, F, It, F, I,* 2011 *W, E, R, S, Geo, NZ*
F Schacht 1989 *Bra, CHL, Par, Ur, US,* 1990 *C*
E Scharemberg 1961 *CHL, Bra, Ur,* 1964 *Ur, Bra,* 1965 *Rho, JSB, OCC, OCC,* 1967 *Ur, CHL*
AM Schiavio 1983 *CHL, Ur,* 1986 *A,* 1987 *Fj, It, NZ*
E Schiavio 1936 *BI, CHL, CHL*
H Schierano 2011 *CHL, Ur*
R Schmidt 1960 *F, F, F,* 1961 *Bra,* 1964 *Ur,* 1965 *JSB*
G Schmitt 1964 *Ur, CHL*
M Schusterman 2003 *Par, Fj,* 2004 *W, W, NZ, F,* 2005 *It, It, SA, S,* 2006 *W, CHL, Ur, E,* 2007 *I, It, Geo*
AA Scolni 1983 *CHL, Par, Ur,* 1985 *Par, SA, A,* 1988 *F, F, F, F,* 1989 *NZ, US,* 1990 *C, US, E, E, I, E, S*
J Seaton 1968 *W, W,* 1969 *Ur, CHL*
R Seaton 1967 *Ur, CHL*
LV Senatore 2011 *Geo, NZ,* 2012 *Ur, Bra, CHL, It, F, SA, SA, NZ, A, A*
H Senillosa 2002 *Ur, Par, CHL,* 2003 *Par, CHL, Ur, F, SA, Fj, US, Nm, R,* 2004 *CHL, Ur, Ven, W, W, NZ, F, I,* 2005 *It, It,* 2006 *CHL, It, F,* 2007 *I, I, F, Geo, Nm, I, S, F,* 2008 *It*
R Serra 1927 *GBR, GBR, GBR*
F Serra Miras 2003 *CHL,* 2005 *J,* 2006 *W, CHL, Ur,* 2007 *I, It, W, Nm,* 2008 *S*
C Serrano 1978 *It,* 1980 *Fj,* 1983 *CHL, Par, Ur*
R Sharpe 1948 *OCC*
HL Silva 1965 *JSB, OCC,* 1967 *Ur, CHL,* 1968 *W, W,* 1969 *S, S, Ur, CHL,* 1970 *I, I,* 1971 *SAG, SAG, OCC, OCC, Ur,* 1978 *E,* 1979 *NZ, NZ, A, A,* 1980 *WXV*
R Silva 1998 *J*
F Silvestre 1988 *F,* 1989 *Bra, Par, Ur, US,* 1990 *C, US*
D Silvetti 1993 *J*
J Simes 1989 *Bra, CHL,* 1990 *C, US,* 1993 *J, J,* 1996 *Ur, F, F, US, C*
HG Simon 1991 *NZ, NZ, A, W, Sa*
E Simone 1996 *US, SA, SA, E,* 1997 *E, E, NZ, NZ, R, F, A, A,* 1998 *F, F, US, Ur, C, J, It, F, W,* 1999 *W, S, I, W, Sa, J, I, F,* 2000 *I, SA,* 2001 *Ur, US, It,* 2002 *Ur, CHL*
A Smidt 2010 *Ur, CHL*
A Soares-Gache 1978 *It,* 1979 *NZ, NZ,* 1981 *C,* 1982 *F, Sp,* 1983 *WXV, A, A,* 1987 *Sp, A, A,* 1988 *F*
T Solari 1996 *Ur, C, SA,* 1997 *E, E, NZ, NZ*
F Soler 1996 *Ur, F, F, SA, SA,* 1997 *E, E, NZ, NZ, Ur, R, It, F,* 1998 *F, F, R, US, C, It, W,* 2001 *Ur, US,* 2002 *Ur, Par, CHL*
JS Soler Valls 1989 *It, Bra, Par, Ur*
H Solveira 1951 *Ur*
J Sommer 1927 *GBR*
E Sorhaburu 1958 *Ur, Per,* 1960 *F,* 1961 *CHL, Ur*
E Spain 1965 *JSB, OCC, OCC, CHL,* 1967 *Ur, CHL*
PL Sporleder 1990 *I, E, S,* 1991 *NZ, NZ, CHL, A, W, Sa,* 1992 *F, F, Sp, Sp, R, F,* 1993 *J, J, Bra, CHL, Par, Ur, SA, SA,* 1994 *US, S, US, SA, SA,* 1995 *A, A, E, Sa, It,* 1996

Ur, F, F, Ur, C, SA, SA, E, 1997 E, E, NZ, NZ, Par, Ur, R, It, F, A, A, 1998 F, R, US, Ur, C, Ur, It, F, W, 1999 W, W, J, 2002 Ur, Par, CHL, It, I, 2003 Par, CHL, Ur, F, Fj, US, Nm, R

J Stanfield 1932 JSB

J Stewart 1932 JSB, JSB

BM Stortoni 1998 J, Par, 2001 Ur, US, C, NZ, It, NZ, 2002 Ur, Par, CHL, 2003 F, Fj, US, 2005 It, It, S, It, 2007 I, 2008 S, S, It, SA, F, It, I

J Stuart 2007 CHL, 2008 S, It

M Sugasti 1995 Par, CHL

W Sutton 1936 CHL

C Swain 1948 OCC, 1949 F, F, 1951 Ur, Bra, CHL, 1952 I, I

J Tagliabue 1936 CHL, CHL

L Tahier 1964 Ur, CHL

F Talbot 1936 BI, 1938 CHL

H Talbot 1936 BI, CHL, CHL, 1938 CHL

HF Talbot 1910 GBR

A Tejeda 2008 S, S, It

RE Tejerizo 2011 CHL, Ur, 2012 Ur, Bra, CHL

EG Teran 1977 Bra, Ur, Par, CHL, 1979 CHL, Par, Bra

G Teran 1988 F

MJ Teran 1991 NZ, NZ, CHL, A, W, Sa, 1992 F, Sp, R, F, 1993 J, J, Ur, SA, SA, 1994 US, S, S, US, SA, SA, 1995 A, A, E, Sa, It, Ur, R, It, F

FN Tetaz Chaparro 2010 CHL, 2012 It, F

GP Tiesi 2004 SA, 2005 J, It, Sa, 2006 W, W, NZ, CHL, Ur, E, 2007 Geo, Nm, SA, 2008 S, S, F, It, 2009 E, E, E, W, S, 2010 S, S, F, It, F, I, 2011 E

FJ Todeschini 1998 R, Ur, 2005 J, It, It, S, 2006 W, W, NZ, CHL, Ur, E, It, F, 2007 I, W, Geo, Nm, 2008 S, S

A Tolomei 1991 Par, Bra, 1993 Bra, CHL, Par

N Tompkins 1948 OCC, 1949 F, F, 1952 I, I

JA Topping 1938 CHL

E Torello 1983 Par, 1989 CHL

F Torino 1927 GBR, GBR

NC Tozer 1932 JSB, JSB

AA Travaglini 1967 Ur, CHL, 1968 W, 1969 S, S, 1970 I, I, 1971 SAG, SAG, OCC, OCC, 1972 SAG, SAG, 1973 R, Par, Ur, Bra, CHL, I, S, 1974 F, F, 1975 F, F, 1976 W, NZ, NZ

G Travaglini 1978 E, It, 1979 NZ, NZ, A, A, 1980 WXV, Fj, Fj, 1981 E, E, 1982 F, F, Sp, 1983 WXV, A, 1987 Ur, Fj, It, NZ

R Travaglini 1996 US, Ur, C, 1997 NZ, R, F, 1998 Ur, C

J Trucco 1977 Bra, Ur, Par, CHL

J Tuculet 2012 It, F, F

A Turner 1932 JSB, JSB

FA Turnes 1985 F, F, Ur, NZ, NZ, 1986 F, F, A, A, 1987 Ur, Fj, NZ, Sp, A, A, 1988 F, F, F, F, 1989 It, NZ, NZ, 1997 Ur, F, A, A

G Ugartemendia 1991 Ur, 1993 J, CHL, Par, Ur, SA, SA, 1994 US, SA, SA, 1997 Ur, 1998 Par, 2000 E

M Urbano 1991 Ur, Bra, 1995 Par, CHL, R, It, F

B Urdapilleta 2007 CHL, 2008 SA, 2009 W, 2010 Ur, 2012 F, F

EM Ure 1980 WXV, Fj, Fj, 1981 E, E, 1982 F, F, Sp, 1983 A, 1985 F, F, NZ, NZ, 1986 F, F, A

J Uriarte 1986 A, 1987 Par

E Valesani 1986 A, A

MR Valesani 1989 It, NZ, NZ, CHL, Par, Ur, US, 1990 C, US, C

T Vallejos 2011 Geo, 2012 NZ

GB Varela 1976 W, NZ, NZ, 1977 F, F, 1979 Ur, CHL

L Varela 1961 CHL, Bra, Ur

F Varella 1960 F

GM Varone 1982 F

C Vazquez 1927 GBR, GBR, GBR

A Velazquez 1971 CHL, Par

R Ventura 1975 Ur, Bra, CHL, 1977 Bra, Ur, 1978 It, 1979 Ur, CHL, Par, 1983 CHL, Par, Ur

E Verardo 1958 CHL, 1959 JSB, JSB, 1964 Ur, Bra, CHL, 1967 Ur, CHL

N Vergallo 2005 Sa, 2006 CHL, Ur, 2007 I, I, CHL, 2008 S, S, It, SA, F, It, I, 2009 E, 2010 F, It, F, I, 2011 W, E, R, S, Geo, NZ, 2012 SA, SA, NZ, A, NZ

AV Vernet Basualdo 2004 SA, 2005 J, 2006 It, 2007 I, Geo, Nm, I, F, 2008 SA, It, 2009 E, E, S

G Veron 1997 Par

M Viazzo 2010 Ur, CHL

J Vibart 1960 F

H Vidou 1987 Par, 1990 C, US, E, E, 1991 NZ

H Vidou 1960 F, 1961 Bra

C Viel Temperley 1993 Bra, CHL, Par, Ur, 1994 US, S, S, US, SA, SA, 1995 Ur, C, A, A, E, Sa, It, Par, Ur, R, It, F, 1996 SA, 1997 E, NZ

E Vila 1975 Ur, Par, CHL

JJ Villar 2001 Ur, US, C, 2002 Par, CHL

D Villen 1998 J, Par

M Viola 1993 Bra

J Virasoro 1973 R, R, Ur, Bra, CHL, S

JL Visca 1985 Par

J Walther 1971 OCC

M Walther 1967 Ur, CHL, 1968 W, W, 1969 S, S, Ur, CHL, 1970 I, I, 1971 SAG, OCC, OCC, 1973 Bra, CHL, 1974 F, F

WA Watson 1910 GBR

W Weiss 2011 Ur

F Werner 1996 US, 1997 Ur

Wessek 1960 F

R Wilkins 1936 CHL, CHL

J Wittman 1971 SAG, SAG, OCC, OCC, Ur, 1972 SAG, SAG, 1973 R

L Yanez 1965 Rho, JSB, OCC, OCC, CHL, 1966 SAG, SAG, 1968 W, W, 1969 S, S, Ur, CHL, 1970 I, I, 1971 SAG, OCC, OCC, Ur

EP Yanguela 1956 OCC

M Yanguela 1987 It

B Yustini 1954 F, 1956 OCC

R Zanero 1990 C

E Zapiola 1998 Par

A Zappa 1927 GBR

AUSTRALIA

AUSTRALIA'S 2011/12 TEST RECORD

OPPONENTS	DATE	VENUE	RESULT
Wales	3 Dec	A	Won 24–18
Scotland	5 Jun	H	Lost 6–9
Wales	9 Jun	H	Won 27–19
Wales	16 Jun	H	Won 25–23
Wales	23 Jun	H	Won 20–19
New Zealand	18 Aug	H	Lost 19–27
New Zealand	25 Aug	A	Lost 22–0
South Africa	8 Sep	H	Won 26–19
Argentina	15 Sep	H	Won 23–19
South Africa	29 Sep	A	Lost 31–8
Argentina	6 Oct	A	Won 25–19

MIXED YEAR FOR INJURY-HIT WALLABIES

By Tim Horan

The Australian players are jubilant after Mike Harris kicked the winning penalty in the second Test against Wales.

Although Australia remain second in the IRB World Rankings, a chronic injury toll and a dark black shadow hung heavily over the Wallabies' efforts in the aftermath of an unfulfilling Rugby World Cup 2011. The promise shown by two excellent performances on the brief British tour which closed 2011 – a record 60–11 demolition of the Barbarians at Twickenham and an equally impressive 24–18 success against a Grand Slam-bound Wales in Cardiff – quickly gave way to sobering reality as the 2012 programme began.

There was much angst when the expectations raised by a gritty 3–0 series win over Wales in June dissipated as soon as the inaugural Rugby Championship began.

Australia has not held the Bledisloe Cup since an All Black side ironically co-coached by current Wallabies mentor Robbie Deans whisked it away with a 2–0 series triumph in 2003. A three-Test series for 2012, with two matches to be played in Australia, seemed an opportune time to regain the silverware. But those hopes were dashed within seven days.

While it was expected that New Zealand could be vulnerable first up in Sydney – and were – a serious case of stage fright got the better of the Wallabies. Although not without a high error count themselves, the All Blacks made fewer mistakes than their opponents and were more comfortable victors than the final 27–19 scoreline suggests, despite a commendable if futile second-half resurgence by the home side.

Worse was to follow in Auckland a week later, where Australia haven't now won for 26 years. Despite dominating the game to the tune of a 65 per cent possession share, the All Blacks scored just one try, but it was all they needed to keep Australia scoreless – 22–0 – for the first time in 50 years.

While the effort, and courage in defence, couldn't be faulted – as was highlighted when the Dan Carter-inspired All Blacks later cut loose to shred the Argentine and South African defences for a combined 12 tries during their away tour – you have to score points to win games and the Wallabies never looked like achieving that at Eden Park.

The loss not only handed New Zealand the Bledisloe Cup for a 10th straight year, it also surrendered Australia's hopes of winning The Rugby Championship, after the Wallabies had ended the 16-year Tri-Nations era by winning just their third title in 2011.

So to the matches against South Africa and Argentina. These were played amidst a back drop of discontent with the now fifth-year coach, and a soaring injury count that saw Australia end the competition with a fourth captain of the year in Nathan Sharpe. It is to the Wallabies' credit that the side didn't implode as the casualties and the off-field distractions grew.

Australia's come-from-behind 26–19 win over South Africa in Perth retained the Nelson Mandela Challenge Plate for the third straight year, while also registering a record fifth successive win against the Springboks.

As had been the trend, however, this win wasn't achieved without enormous cost, as then captain Will Genia was sidelined for the rest of the year after blowing ligaments in his knee.

Genia followed predecessors James Horwill and David Pocock to the injury ward. At the time of his misfortune, the Wallabies were left with a staggering 27 players who had been involved over the previous 12 months, sidelined by injury. Many of these had been first-choice players at the time of their mishaps.

Further disaster beckoned a week later as Argentina's first appearance in Australia since RWC 2003 threatened the first major upset of The Rugby Championship.

Los Pumas, who proved a super addition to the tournament, far exceeding pre-competition predictions with regards to their competitiveness, led 19–6 with 25 minutes left as Sharpe gathered his shell-shocked troops behind the goal posts following the concession of a second breakaway try.

Sharpe, who had grown up locally, implored his men to stay calm, focus on what they did well and give it everything they had. The Wallabies did just that, scoring the final two tries to conclude the first ever Test to be played on the Gold Coast with a 23–19 win.

It was not to be the last time the men in gold responded to a rallying call from Sharpe. Two weeks later, amid a tempestuous background at home following an extraordinary public outburst and self-exile by fly half Quade Cooper, the Wallabies faced further adversity in South Africa during a 31–8 defeat.

The scoreboard looks bad, and it could have been so much worse, but for some extraordinary courage on a night where Australia lost one player to injury during the warm-up and five more during the game, with centre Adam Ashley-Cooper knocked out cold and full back Berrick Barnes later diagnosed with a punctured lung.

By the final whistle, Australia had just 14 men and required uncontested scrums, after injury and a sideline match official team bungle removed hooker Tatafu Polota-Nau from the contest. At one point, Australia had just 12 upright players to defend against waves of South African assault.

A 20-hour trip to Rosario followed, reinforcements were flown in, and another rallying call was issued. Sharpe demanded his boys become men. They did.

Amid a passionate atmosphere of the like that none of the Australian players had experienced before, the Wallabies prevailed.

Later cited as one of the most against-the-odds Australian victories of modern times, the 25–19 success carried significance far beyond the dousing of an Argentine side which had scented victory.

It restored Australia to second in the IRB World Rankings, a position briefly conceded to South Africa the week before. The win also allowed Australia to finish second in The Rugby Championship – a meritorious achievement given the adversity the team faced.

Yet the efforts of June had promised so much more.

Although the Wallabies were ambushed by a last-minute penalty for a 9–6 loss to Scotland in the treacherous weather conditions that gate-crashed Newcastle's debut as a Test venue – the conditions were so bad, the Australia captain was treated for hypothermia post-match – Pocock and his team bounced back.

Wales arrived in Australia intent on securing a major southern hemisphere scalp to add to their Six Nations dominance. The welcome return of a three-Test series also offered Wales the opportunity to wind up a four-match losing streak against the Wallabies.

After the loss to Scotland, where Australia had had just two days of preparation together as a full squad and suffered the consequences, the Welsh were understandably upbeat leading into the first Test in Brisbane.

Resilience got the Wallabies through. Inspired by brilliance from Genia, on the back of a commanding performance by the Australian forwards, the Wallabies won 27–19 to set the series alight.

Public interest in the game soared, and supporters were rewarded with two more thrilling contests as Australia triumphed 25–23 in Melbourne and 20–19 during a rare but hugely successful day-time Test in Sydney, to round out the series.

Arguably the individual performance of the year by a Wallaby was reserved for Melbourne. Berrick Barnes produced a Man of the Match performance, having almost missed the game after rushing back to Sydney the night before to witness the birth of his first child.

When he is old enough to understand, Archie Barnes will have a story to tell his schoolmates, about how his Dad rushed back for his birth, then jumped on a plane back to Victoria, reaching the ground just in time for kick-off, before playing the lead hand as Australia won.

It was another notable performance by a player renowned for his courage, although ironically the winning touch was provided by another, former New Zealand Under 20 representative Mike Harris.

The now Queensland-based Harris, who had been on stand-by to start the match had the first choice not made it back in time, was required anyway when Barnes succumbed to cramps eight minutes from the end.

Australia trailed by a point at the time and were still behind when awarded a penalty in their own half as the final siren sounded in the background. The decision to kick for a lineout, as opposed to a panicky tap and go, reflected the growing maturity in a combination far closer to full strength than was to be the case during The Rugby Championship. So too did the outcome. After securing possession, the Australian forwards formed a powerful maul that sucked Wales into conceding another penalty closer to the posts.

Harris, who'd had a difficult Test initiation in the appalling Newcastle conditions, calmly slotted the goal to secure the win, the series, and the hope that the All Blacks' supremacy was about to be challenged.

At full strength, this Australian side is unquestionably capable of doing just that, but it will have to wait for another year, and until after another showpiece assignment is negotiated. The British and Irish Lions visit next year . . . the excitement Down Under is already building.

AUSTRALIA

AUSTRALIA INTERNATIONAL STATISTICS

MATCH RECORDS UP TO 10 OCTOBER 2012

MOST CONSECUTIVE TEST WINS

10 1991 *Arg, WS, W, I, NZ, E,* 1992 *S 1,2, NZ 1,2*
10 1998 *NZ 3, Fj, Tg, Sm, F, E 2,* 1999 *I 1,2, E, SA 1*
10 1999 *NZ 2, R, I 3, US, W, SA 3, F,* 2000 *Arg 1,2,SA 1*

MOST CONSECUTIVE TESTS WITHOUT DEFEAT

Matches	Wins	Draws	Period
10	10	0	1991 to 1992
10	10	0	1998 to 1999
10	10	0	1999 to 2000

MOST POINTS IN A MATCH
BY THE TEAM

Pts	Opponents	Venue	Year
142	Namibia	Adelaide	2003
92	Spain	Madrid	2001
91	Japan	Lyons	2007
90	Romania	Brisbane	2003
76	England	Brisbane	1998
74	Canada	Brisbane	1996
74	Tonga	Canberra	1998
74	W Samoa	Sydney	2005
73	W Samoa	Sydney	1994
69	Italy	Melbourne	2005
68	Russia	Nelson	2011
67	USA	Brisbane	1990
67	USA	Wellington	2011

BY A PLAYER

Pts	Player	Opponents	Venue	Year
42	M S Rogers	Namibia	Adelaide	2003
39	M C Burke	Canada	Brisbane	1996
30	E J Flatley	Romania	Brisbane	2003
29	S A Mortlock	South Africa	Melbourne	2000
29	J D O'Connor	France	Paris	2010
28	M P Lynagh	Argentina	Brisbane	1995
27	M J Giteau	Fiji	Montpellier	2007
25	M C Burke	Scotland	Sydney	1998
25	M C Burke	France	Cardiff	1999
25	M C Burke	British/Irish Lions	Melbourne	2001
25	E J Flatley*	Ireland	Perth	2003
25	C E Latham	Namibia	Adelaide	2003
24	M P Lynagh	USA	Brisbane	1990
24	M P Lynagh	France	Brisbane	1990
24	M C Burke	New Zealand	Melbourne	1998
24	M C Burke	South Africa	Twickenham	1999

* includes a penalty try

MOST TRIES IN A MATCH
BY THE TEAM

Tries	Opponents	Venue	Year
22	Namibia	Adelaide	2003
13	South Korea	Brisbane	1987
13	Spain	Madrid	2001
13	Romania	Brisbane	2003
13	Japan	Lyons	2007
12	USA	Brisbane	1990
12	Wales	Brisbane	1991
12	Tonga	Canberra	1998
12	Samoa	Sydney	2005
11	Western Samoa	Sydney	1994
11	England	Brisbane	1998
11	Italy	Melbourne	2005
11	USA	Wellington	2011

BY A PLAYER

Tries	Player	Opponents	Venue	Year
5	C E Latham	Namibia	Adelaide	2003
4	G Cornelsen	New Zealand	Auckland	1978
4	D I Campese	USA	Sydney	1983
4	J S Little	Tonga	Canberra	1998
4	C E Latham	Argentina	Brisbane	2000
4	L D Tuqiri	Italy	Melbourne	2005

MOST CONVERSIONS IN A MATCH
BY THE TEAM

Cons	Opponents	Venue	Year
16	Namibia	Adelaide	2003
12	Spain	Madrid	2001
11	Romania	Brisbane	2003
10	Japan	Lyons	2007
9	Canada	Brisbane	1996
9	Fiji	Parramatta	1998
9	Russia	Nelson	2011
8	Italy	Rome	1988
8	United States	Brisbane	1990
7	Canada	Sydney	1985
7	Tonga	Canberra	1998
7	Samoa	Sydney	2005
7	Italy	Melbourne	2005
7	Fiji	Canberra	2010

BY A PLAYER

Cons	Player	Opponents	Venue	Year
16	M S Rogers	Namibia	Adelaide	2003
11	E J Flatley	Romania	Brisbane	2003
10	M C Burke	Spain	Madrid	2001
9	M C Burke	Canada	Brisbane	1996
9	J A Eales	Fiji	Parramatta	1998
9	J D O'Connor	Russia	Nelson	2011
8	M P Lynagh	Italy	Rome	1988
8	M P Lynagh	United States	Brisbane	1990
7	M P Lynagh	Canada	Sydney	1985
7	S A Mortlock	Japan	Lyons	2007

MOST DROP GOALS IN A MATCH
BY THE TEAM

Drops	Opponents	Venue	Year
3	England	Twickenham	1967
3	Ireland	Dublin	1984
3	Fiji	Brisbane	1985

BY A PLAYER

Drops	Player	Opponents	Venue	Year
3	P F Hawthorne	England	Twickenham	1967
2	M G Ella	Ireland	Dublin	1984
2	D J Knox	Fiji	Brisbane	1985

MOST PENALTIES IN A MATCH
BY THE TEAM

Pens	Opponents	Venue	Year
8	South Africa	Twickenham	1999
7	New Zealand	Sydney	1999
7	France	Cardiff	1999
7	Wales	Cardiff	2001
7	England	Twickenham	2008
6	New Zealand	Sydney	1984
6	France	Sydney	1986
6	England	Brisbane	1988
6	Argentina	Buenos Aires	1997
6	Ireland	Perth	1999
6	France	Paris	2000
6	British/Irish Lions	Melbourne	2001
6	New Zealand	Sydney	2004
6	Italy	Padua	2008
6	New Zealand	Sydney	2009
6	South Africa	Brisbane	2010
6	Italy	Florence	2010
6	Wales	Melbourne	2012
6	Argentina	Rosario	2012

BY A PLAYER

Pens	Player	Opponents	Venue	Year
8	M C Burke	South Africa	Twickenham	1999
7	M C Burke	New Zealand	Sydney	1999
7	M C Burke	France	Cardiff	1999
7	M C Burke	Wales	Cardiff	2001
6	M P Lynagh	France	Sydney	1986
6	M P Lynagh	England	Brisbane	1988
6	D J Knox	Argentina	Buenos Aires	1997
6	M C Burke	France	Paris	2000
6	M C Burke	British/Irish Lions	Melbourne	2001
6	M J Giteau	England	Twickenham	2008
6	M J Giteau	New Zealand	Sydney	2009
6	B S Barnes	Italy	Florence	2010
6	M J Harris	Argentina	Rosario	2012

AUSTRALIA

CAREER RECORDS

MOST CAPPED PLAYERS

Caps	Player	Career Span
139	G M Gregan	1994 to 2007
111	N C Sharpe	2002 to 2012
110	G B Smith	2000 to 2009
102	S J Larkham	1996 to 2007
101	D I Campese	1982 to 1996
92	M J Giteau	2002 to 2011
86	J A Eales	1991 to 2001
86	J W C Roff	1995 to 2004
81	M C Burke	1993 to 2004
80	T J Horan	1989 to 2000
80	S A Mortlock	2000 to 2009
79	D J Wilson	1992 to 2000
79	P R Waugh	2000 to 2009
78	C E Latham	1998 to 2007
75	J S Little	1989 to 2000
75	R D Elsom	2005 to 2011
72	M P Lynagh	1984 to 1995
72	J A Paul	1998 to 2006
72	A P Ashley-Cooper	2005 to 2012
72	S T Moore	2005 to 2012
69	A K E Baxter	2003 to 2009
67	P N Kearns	1989 to 1999
67	D J Herbert	1994 to 2002
67	L D Tuqiri	2003 to 2008
63	N C Farr Jones	1984 to 1993
63	M J Cockbain	1997 to 2003
63	D J Vickerman	2002 to 2011
60	R S T Kefu	1997 to 2003

MOST CONSECUTIVE TESTS

Tests	Player	Span
62	J W C Roff	1996 to 2001
46	P N Kearns	1989 to 1995
44	G B Smith	2003 to 2006
42	D I Campese	1990 to 1995
37	P G Johnson	1959 to 1968

MOST TESTS AS CAPTAIN

Tests	Captain	Span
59	G M Gregan	2001 to 2007
55	J A Eales	1996 to 2001
36	N C Farr Jones	1988 to 1992
29	S A Mortlock	2006 to 2009
24	R D Elsom	2009 to 2011
19	A G Slack	1984 to 1987
16	J E Thornett	1962 to 1967
16	G V Davis	1969 to 1972

MOST POINTS IN TESTS

Points	Player	Tests	Career
911	M P Lynagh	72	1984 to 1995
878	M C Burke	81	1993 to 2004
684	M J Giteau	92	2002 to 2011
489	S A Mortlock	80	2000 to 2009
315	D I Campese	101	1982 to 1996
260	P E McLean	30	1974 to 1982
249*	J W Roff	86	1995 to 2004
208	J D O'Connor	37	2008 to 2011
200	C E Latham	78	1998 to 2007
187*	E J Flatley	38	1997 to 2005
174	B S Barnes	46	2007 to 2012
173	J A Eales	86	1991 to 2001

* Roff and Flatley's totals include a penalty try

MOST TRIES IN TESTS

Tries	Player	Tests	Career
64	D I Campese	101	1982 to 1996
40	C E Latham	78	1998 to 2007
31*	J W Roff	86	1995 to 2004
30	T J Horan	80	1989 to 2000
30	L D Tuqiri	67	2003 to 2008
30	D A Mitchell	59	2005 to 2012
29	M C Burke	81	1993 to 2004
29	S A Mortlock	80	2000 to 2009
29	M J Giteau	92	2002 to 2011
25	S J Larkham	102	1996 to 2007
24	B N Tune	47	1996 to 2006
22	A P Ashley-Cooper	72	2005 to 2012
21	J S Little	75	1989 to 2000

* Roff's total includes a penalty try

MOST CONVERSIONS IN TESTS

Cons	Player	Tests	Career
140	M P Lynagh	72	1984 to 1995
104	M C Burke	81	1993 to 2004
103	M J Giteau	92	2002 to 2011
61	S A Mortlock	80	2000 to 2009
38	J D O'Connor	37	2008 to 2011
31	J A Eales	86	1991 to 2001
30	E J Flatley	38	1997 to 2005
27	P E McLean	30	1974 to 1982
27	M S Rogers	45	2002 to 2006
20	J W Roff	86	1995 to 2004
19	D J Knox	13	1985 to 1997

MOST PENALTY GOALS IN TESTS

Pens	Player	Tests	Career
177	M P Lynagh	72	1984 to 1995
174	M C Burke	81	1993 to 2004
107	M J Giteau	92	2002 to 2011
74	S A Mortlock	80	2000 to 2009
62	P E McLean	30	1974 to 1982
34	J A Eales	86	1991 to 2001
34	E J Flatley	38	1997 to 2005
27	B S Barnes	46	2007 to 2012
24	J D O'Connor	37	2008 to 2011
23	M C Roebuck	23	1991 to 1993

MOST DROP GOALS IN TESTS

Drops	Player	Tests	Career
9	P F Hawthorne	21	1962 to 1967
9	M P Lynagh	72	1984 to 1995
8	M G Ella	25	1980 to 1984
7	B S Barnes	46	2007 to 2012
4	P E McLean	30	1974 to 1982
4	M J Giteau	92	2002 to 2011

RUGBY CHAMPIONSHIP (FORMERLY TRI-NATIONS) RECORDS

RECORD	DETAIL	HOLDER	SET
Most points in season	162	in six matches	2010
Most tries in season	17	in six matches	2010
Highest Score	49	49-0 v S Africa (h)	2006
Biggest win	49	49-0 v S Africa (h)	2006
Highest score conceded	61	22-61 v S Africa (a)	1997
Biggest defeat	45	8-53 v S Africa (a)	2008
Most appearances	48	G M Gregan	1996 to 2007
Most points in matches	271	M C Burke	1996 to 2004
Most points in season	72	M J Giteau	2009
Most points in match	24	M C Burke	v N Zealand (h) 1998
Most tries in matches	9	J W C Roff	1996 to 2003
	9	S A Mortlock	2000 to 2009
	9	L D Tuqiri	2003 to 2008
Most tries in season	4	S A Mortlock	2000
	4	J D O'Connor	2010
Most tries in match	2	B N Tune	v S Africa (h) 1997
	2	S J Larkham	v N Zealand (a) 1997
	2	M C Burke	v N Zealand (h) 1998
	2	J W C Roff	v S Africa (h) 1999
	2	S A Mortlock	v N Zealand (h) 2000
	2	C E Latham	v S Africa (h) 2002
	2	M J Giteau	v S Africa (h) 2006
	2	L D Tuqiri	v N Zealand (a) 2006
	2	M J Giteau	v S Africa (h) 2009
	2	J D O'Connor	v S Africa (a) 2010
Most cons in matches	36	M J Giteau	2003 to 2010
Most cons in season	12	S A Mortlock	2006
Most cons in match	5	S A Mortlock	v S Africa (h) 2006

AUSTRALIA

Most pens in matches	65	M C Burke	1996 to 2004
Most pens in season	14	M C Burke	2001
	14	M J Giteau	2009
	14	M J Giteau	2010
Most pens in match	7	M C Burke	v N Zealand (h) 1999

MISCELLANEOUS RECORDS

Record	Holder	Detail
Longest Test Career	G M Cooke	1932-1948
Youngest Test Cap	B W Ford	18 yrs 90 days in 1957
Oldest Test Cap	A R Miller	38 yrs 113 days in 1967

CAREER RECORDS OF AUSTRALIAN INTERNATIONAL PLAYERS

UP TO 10 OCTOBER 2012

PLAYER BACKS:	Debut	Caps	T	C	P	D	Pts
A P Ashley-Cooper	2005 v SA	72	22	0	0	0	110
B S Barnes	2007 v J	46	8	16	27	7	174
K J Beale	2009 v W	31	9	0	4	0	57
L Burgess	2008 v I	37	1	0	0	0	5
Q S Cooper	2008 v It	38	6	7	7	1	68
N M Cummins	2012 v Arg	1	0	0	0	0	0
A S Faingaa	2010 v NZ	23	2	0	0	0	10
S W Genia	2009 v NZ	41	7	0	0	0	35
M J Harris	2012 v S	5	1	1	9	0	34
R G Horne	2010 v Fj	14	3	0	0	0	15
D A N Ioane	2007 v W	31	11	0	0	0	55
P J McCabe	2010 v It	17	4	0	0	0	20
D A Mitchell	2005 v SA	59	30	0	0	0	150
L J Morahan	2012 v S	1	0	0	0	0	0
J D O'Connor	2008 v It	37	12	38	24	0	208
N J Phipps	2011 v Sm	7	0	0	0	0	0
B R Sheehan	2006 v SA	5	0	0	0	0	0
D P Shipperley	2012 v SA	3	0	0	0	0	0
B N L Tapuai	2011 v W	2	0	0	0	0	0
J Tomane	2012 v S	1	0	0	0	0	0
L D Turner	2008 v F	15	4	0	0	0	20
K C Vuna	2012 v W	2	0	0	0	0	0

B E Alexander	2008 v F	45	4	0	0	0	20
R N Brown	2008 v NZ	23	1	0	0	0	5
D A Dennis	2012 v S	10	0	0	0	0	0
K P Douglas	2012 v Arg	3	0	0	0	0	0
S M Faingaa	2010 v Fj	18	0	0	0	0	0
L B Gill	2012 v NZ	5	0	0	0	0	0
S Higginbotham	2010 v F	20	2	0	0	0	10
M Hooper	2012 v S	8	0	0	0	0	0
J E Horwill	2007 v Fj	35	6	0	0	0	30
S M Kepu	2008 v It	18	0	0	0	0	0
R S L Ma'afu	2010 v Fj	14	1	0	0	0	5
B J McCalman	2010 v SA	21	2	0	0	0	10
S T Moore	2005 v Sm	72	5	0	0	0	25
D P Palmer	2012 v S	1	0	0	0	0	0
W L Palu	2006 v E	41	1	0	0	0	5
D W Pocock	2008 v NZ	45	4	0	0	0	20
S U T Polota-Nau	2005 v E	40	2	0	0	0	10
B A Robinson	2006 v SA	51	2	0	0	0	10
U R Samo	2004 v S	22	2	0	0	0	10
N C Sharpe	2002 v F	111	8	0	0	0	40
R A Simmons	2010 v SA	22	0	0	0	0	0
J A Slipper	2010 v E	29	0	0	0	0	0
S Timani	2011 v Sm	7	0	0	0	0	0

AUSTRALIA INTERNATIONAL PLAYERS
UP TO 10 OCTOBER 2012

Entries in square brackets denote matches played in RWC Finals.

Abrahams, A M F (NSW) 1967 NZ, 1968 NZ 1, 1969 W
Adams, N J (NSW) 1955 NZ 1
Adamson, R W (NSW) 1912 US
Alexander, B E (ACT) 2008 F1(R), 2(R), It, F3, 2009 It1(R), 2, F(R), NZ1(R), SA1(R), NZ2(t&R), SA2, 3, NZ3, 4, E, I, S, W, 2010 Fj, NZ4, W, E3, It, F, 2011 Sm, SA1, NZ1, SA2, NZ2, [It, I, US, SA, NZ, W(R)], W(R), 2012 S(R), W1(R), 2(R), 3(R), NZ2, SA1, Arg1, SA2, Arg2
Allan, T (NSW) 1946 NZ 1, M, NZ 2, 1947 NZ 2, S, I, W, 1948 E, F, 1949 M 1,2,3, NZ 1,2
Anderson, R P (NSW) 1925 NZ 1
Anlezark, E A (NSW) 1905 NZ
Armstrong, A R (NSW) 1923 NZ 1,2
Ashley-Cooper, A P (ACT, NSW) 2005 SA4(R), 2007 W1, 2, Fj, SA1(R), NZ1, SA2, NZ2, [J, Fj, C, E], 2008 F1(R), 2, SA1, NZ1, 2, SA3, NZ3, 4, It, E, F3, 2009It1(R), 2(t&R), F, NZ1, SA1, NZ2, SA2, 3, NZ3, 4, E, I, S, W, 2010 Fj, E2(R), I, SA1, NZ1, 2, SA2, 3, NZ3, 4, W, E3, It, F, 2011 Sm, SA1,NZ1, SA2, NZ2, [It, I, US, Ru, SA, NZ, W], W, 2012 W1, 2, 3, NZ1, 2, SA1, Arg1, SA2

Austin, L R (NSW) 1963 E

Baker, R L (NSW) 1904 Bl 1,2
Baker, W H (NSW) 1914 NZ 1,2,3
Ballesty, J P (NSW) 1968 NZ 1,2, F, I, S, 1969 W, SA 2,3,4, 1970 S
Bannon, D P (NSW) 1946 M
Bardsley, E J (NSW) 1928 NZ 1,3, M (R)
Barker, H S (NSW) 1952 Fj 1,2, NZ 1,2, 1953 SA 4, 1954 Fj 1,2
Barnes, B S (Q, NSW) 2007 [J(R), W, Fj], 2008 I, F1, 2, SA1, NZ1, 2, SA2, NZ4(R), It, 2009 It1, 2, F, NZ1, SA1, NZ2, SA3, NZ3, 2010 E1, SA1(R), SA3(R), NZ3(t&R), 4(R), W(R), E3(R), It, F, 2011 [US(R), Ru, SA(R), NZ(t&R), W], W, 2012 S, W1, 2, 3, NZ1, 2, SA1, Arg1, SA2
Barnett, J T (NSW) 1907 NZ 1,2,3, 1908 W, 1909 E
Barry, M J (Q) 1971 SA 3
Bartholomeusz, M A (ACT) 2002 It (R)
Barton, R F D (NSW) 1899 Bl 3
Batch, P G (Q) 1975 S, W, 1976 E, Fj 1,2,3, F 1,2, 1978 W 1,2, NZ 1,2,3, 1979 Arg 2
Batterham, R P (NSW) 1967 NZ, 1970 S

AUSTRALIA

Dixon, E J (Q) 1904 BI 3
Donald, K J (Q) 1957 NZ 1, 1958 W, I, E, S, M 2,3, 1959 BI 1,2
Dore, E (Q) 1904 BI 1
Dore, M J (Q) 1905 NZ
Dorr, R W (V) 1936 M, 1937 SA 1
Douglas, J A (V) 1962 NZ 3,4,5
Douglas, K P (NSW) 2012 Arg1,SA2,Arg2
Douglas, W A (NSW) 1922 NZ 3(R)
Dowse, J H (NSW) 1961 Fj 1,2, SA 1,2
Dunbar, A R (NSW) 1910 NZ 1,2,3, 1912 US
Duncan, J L (NSW) 1926 NZ 4
Dunlop, E E (V) 1932 NZ 3, 1934 NZ 1
Dunn, P K (NSW) 1958 NZ 1,2,3, 1959 BI 1,2
Dunn, V A (NSW) 1920 NZ 1,2,3, 1921 SA 1,2,3, NZ
Dunning, M J (NSW, WF) 2003 [Nm,E(R)], 2004 S1(R), 2(R), E1(R), NZ1(R), SA1(R), NZ2(t&R), SA2(R), S3(R), F(R), S4(R), E2(R), 2005 Sm, It(R), F1(t&R), SA1(R), 2(R), 3, NZ1(t&R), SA4(t&R), NZ2(R), F2, E, W, 2007 W1, 2(R), Fj, SA1, NZ1, SA2, NZ2, [J, W, Fj, E], 2008 I, SA1(R), NZ1(R), SA2, 3, NZ4(R), It, 2009 E(R), W(R)
Dunworth, D A (Q) 1971 F 1,2, 1972 F 1,2, 1976 Fj 2
Dwyer, L J (NSW) 1910 NZ 1,2,3, 1912 US, 1913 NZ 3, 1914 NZ 1,2,3
Dyson, F J (Q) 2000 Arg 1,2, SA 1, NZ 1, SA 2, NZ 2, SA 3, F, S, E

Eales, J A (Q) 1991 W, E, NZ 1,2, [Arg, WS, W, I, NZ, E], 1992 S 1,2, NZ 1,2,3, SA, I, 1994 I 1,2, It 1,2, WS, NZ, 1995 Arg 1,2, [SA, C, R, E], NZ 1,2, 1996 W 1,2, C, NZ 1, SA 1, NZ 2, SA 2, It, S, I, 1997 F 1,2, NZ 1, E 1, NZ 2, SA 1, Arg 1,2, E 2, S, 1998 E 1, S 1,2, NZ 1, SA 1, NZ 2, SA 2, NZ 3, Fj, Tg, WS, F, E 2, 1999 [R, I 3, W, SA 3, F], 2000 Arg 1,2, SA 1, NZ 1, SA 2, NZ 2, SA 3, F, S, E, 2001 BI 1,2,3, SA 1, NZ 1, SA 2, NZ 2
Eastes, C C (NSW) 1946 NZ 1,2, 1947 NZ 1,2, 1949 M 1,2
Edmonds, H (ACT) 2010 Fj, E1(R), 2(R), W(R)
Edmonds, M H M (NSW) 1998 Tg, 2001 SA 1(R)
Egerton, R H (NSW) 1991 W, E, NZ 1,2, [Arg, W, I, NZ, E]
Ella, G A (NSW) 1982 NZ 1,2, 1983 F 1,2, 1988 E 2, NZ 1
Ella, G J (NSW) 1982 S 1, 1983 It, 1985 C 2(R), Fj 2
Ella, M G (NSW) 1980 NZ 1,2,3, 1981 F 2, S, 1982 E, S 1, NZ 1,2,3, 1983 US, Arg 1,2, NZ, It, F 1,2, 1984 Fj, NZ 1,2,3, E, I, W, S
Ellem, M A (NSW) 1976 Fj 3(R)
Elliott, F M (NSW) 1957 NZ 1
Elliott, R E (NSW) 1920 NZ 1, 1921 NZ, 1922 M 1,2, NZ 1(R),2,3, 1923 M 1,2,3, NZ 1,2,3
Ellis, C S (NSW) 1899 BI 1,2,3,4
Ellis, K J (NSW) 1958 NZ 1,2,3, 1959 BI 1,2
Ellwood, B J (NSW) 1958 NZ 1,2,3, 1961 Fj 2,3, SA 1, F, 1962 NZ 1,2,3,4,5, 1963 SA 1,2,3,4, 1964 NZ 3, 1965 SA 1,2, 1966 BI 1
Elsom, R D (NSW, ACT) 2005 Sm, It, F1, SA1, 2, 3(R), 4, NZ2, F2, 2006 E1, 2, I1, NZ1, SA2, NZ2, SA3, SA3, W, It, I2, S, 2007 W1, 2, SA1, NZ1, SA2, NZ2, [J, W, Fj, E], 2008 I, F1, 2, SA1, NZ1, SA2, 3, NZ3, 2009 NZ2, SA2, 3, NZ3, 4, E, I, S, W, 2010 Fj, E1, 2, I, SA1, NZ1, 2, SA2, 3, NZ3, 4, W, E3, It, F, 2011 Sm, SA1, NZ1, SA2, NZ2, [It, I, US, Ru(R), SA, NZ]
Emanuel, D M (NSW) 1957 NZ 2, 1958 W, I, E, S, F, M 1,2,3
Emery, N A (NSW) 1947 NZ 2, S, I, W, 1948 E, F, 1949 M 2,3, NZ 1,2
Erasmus, D J (NSW) 1923 NZ 1,2
Erby, A B (NSW) 1923 M 1,2, NZ 2,3, 1925 NZ 2
Evans, L J (Q) 1903 NZ, 1904 BI 1,3
Evans, W T (Q) 1899 BI 1,2

Fahey, E J (NSW) 1912 US, 1913 NZ 1,2, 1914 NZ 3
Faingaa, A S (Q) 2010 NZ1(R), 2, SA3(R), NZ3(R), 2011 SA1(R), 2(R), NZ2, [It, I, US, SA(R), NZ], 2012 SA1, W1(t&R), 2(R), 3(R), NZ1, 2(R), SA1(R), Arg1(R), SA2(t&R)
Faingaa, S M (Q) 2010 Fj(R), E1, 2, I, SA1, NZ1(R), 2, SA2, 3(R), NZ4(R), W, 2011 SA1(R), NZ1(R), 2(R), [Ru(R), W(R)], 2012 NZ2(R), SA1(R)
Fairfax, R L (NSW) 1971 F 1,2, 1972 F 1,2, NZ 1, Fj, 1973 W, E

Farmer, E H (Q) 1910 NZ 1
Farquhar, C R (NSW) 1920 NZ 2
Farr-Jones, N C (NSW) 1984 E, I, W, S, 1985 C 1,2, NZ, Fj 1,2, 1986 It, F, Arg 1,2, NZ 1,2,3, 1987 SK, [E, I, F, W (R)], NZ, Arg 2, 1988 E 1,2, NZ 1,2,3, E, S, It, 1989 BI 1,2,3, NZ, F 1,2, 1990 F 1,2,3, US, NZ 1,2,3, 1991 W, E, NZ 1,2, [Arg, WS, I, NZ, E], 1992 S 1,2, NZ 1,2,3, SA, 1993 NZ, SA 1,2,3
Fava, S G (ACT, WF) 2005 E(R),I(R), 2006 NZ1(R),SA1,NZ2
Fay, G (NSW) 1971 SA 2, 1972 NZ 1,2,3, 1973 Tg 1,2, W, E, 1974 NZ 1,2,3, 1975 E 1,2, J 1, S, W, 1976 I, US, 1978 W 1,2, NZ 1,2,3, 1979 I 1
Fenwicke, P T (NSW) 1957 NZ 1, 1958 W, I, E, 1959 BI 1,2
Ferguson, R T (NSW) 1922 M 3, NZ 1, 1923 M 3, NZ 3
Fihelly, J A (Q) 1907 NZ 2
Finau, S F (NSW) 1997 NZ 3
Finegan, O D A (ACT) 1996 W 1,2, C, NZ 1, SA 1(t), S, W 3, 1997 SA 1, NZ 3, SA 2, Arg 1,2, E 2, S, 1998 E 1(R), S 1(t + R),2(t + R), NZ 1(R), SA 1(t),2(R), NZ 3(R), Fj (R), Tg, WS (t + R), F (R), E 2(R), 1999 NZ 2(R), [R, I 3(R), US, W (R), SA 3(R), F (R)], 2001 BI 1,2,3, SA 1, NZ 1, SA 2, NZ 2, Sp, E, F, W, 2002 F 1,2, NZ 1, SA 1, NZ 2, SA 2, I, 2003 SA 1(t&R), NZ 1(R), SA 2(R), NZ 2(R)
Finlay, A N (NSW) 1926 NZ 1,2,3, 1927 I, W, S, 1928 E, F, 1929 NZ 1,2,3, 1930 BI
Finley, F G (NSW) 1904 BI 3
Finnane, S C (NSW) 1975 E 1, J 1,2, 1976 E, 1978 W 1,2
Fitter, D E S (ACT) 2005 I,W
FitzSimons, P (NSW) 1989 F 1,2, 1990 F 1,2,3, US, NZ 1
Flanagan, P (Q) 1907 NZ 1,2
Flatley, E J (Q) 1997 E 2, S, 2000 S (R), 2001 BI 1(R),2(R),3, SA 1, NZ 1(R),2(R), Sp (R), F (R), W, 2002 F 1(R),2(R), NZ 1(t+R), SA 1(R), NZ 2(t), Arg (R), I (R), E, It, 2003 I, W, SA 1, NZ 1, SA 2, NZ 2, [Arg, R, I, S, NZ, E], 2004 S3(R), F(R), S4(R), E2, 2005 NZ1(R)
Flett, J A (NSW) 1990 US, NZ 2,3, 1991 [WS]
Flynn, J P (Q) 1914 NZ 1,2
Fogarty, J R (Q) 1949 M 2,3
Foley, M A (Q) 1995 [C (R), R], 1996 W 2(R), NZ 1, SA 1, NZ 2, SA 2, It, S, I, W 3, 1997 NZ 1(R), SA 1, NZ 3, SA 2, Arg 1, E 2, S, 1998 Tg (R), F (R), E 2(R), 1999 NZ 2(R), [US, W, SA 3, F], 2000 Arg 1,2, SA 1, NZ 1, SA 2, NZ 2, SA 3, F, S, E, 2001 BI 1(R),2,3, SA 1, NZ 1, SA 2, NZ 2, Sp, E, F, W
Foote, R H (NSW) 1924 NZ 2,3, 1926 NZ 2
Forbes, C F (Q) 1953 SA 2,3,4, 1954 Fj 1, 1956 SA 1,2
Ford, B (Q) 1957 NZ 2
Ford, E E (NSW) 1927 I, W, S, 1928 E, F, 1929 NZ 1,3
Ford, J A (NSW) 1925 NZ 4, 1926 NZ 1, 2, 1927 I, W, S, 1928 E, 1929 NZ 1, 2, 3, 1930 BI
Forman, T R (NSW) 1968 I, S, 1969 W, SA 1,2,3,4
Fowles, D G (NSW) 1921 SA 1,2,3, 1922 M 2, 3, 1923 M 2,3
Fox, C L (NSW) 1920 NZ 1, 2, 3, 1921 SA 1, NZ, 1922 M 1,2, NZ 1, 1924 NZ 1, 2, 3, 1925 NZ 1,2,3, 1926 NZ 1, 3, 1928 BI 1
Fox, O G (NSW) 1958 F
Francis, E (Q) 1914 NZ 1,2
Frawley, D (Q, NSW) 1986 Arg 2(R), 1987 Arg 1,2, 1988 E 1,2, NZ 1,2,3, S, It
Freedman, J E (NSW) 1962 NZ 3,4,5, 1963 SA 1
Freeman, E (NSW) 1946 NZ 1(R), M
Freier, A L (NSW) 2002 Arg (R), I, E (R), It, 2003 SA 1(R), NZ 1(t), 2005 NZ2(R), 2006 E2, 2007 W1(R), 2(R), Fj, SA1(R), NZ1(R), SA2, NZ2(R), [J(R), W(R), Fj(R), C, E(R)], 2008 I(R), F1(R), 2(R), NZ3(R), W(t&R)
Freney, M E (Q) 1972 NZ 1,2,3, 1973 Tg 1, W, E (R)
Friend, W S (NSW) 1920 NZ 3, 1921 SA 1,2,3, 1922 NZ 1,2,3, 1923 M 1,2,3
Furness, D C (NSW) 1946 M
Futter, F C (NSW) 1904 BI 3

Gardner, J M (Q) 1987 Arg 2, 1988 E 1, NZ 1, E
Gardner, W C (NSW) 1950 BI 1
Garner, R L (NSW) 1949 NZ 1,2
Gavin, K A (NSW) 1909 E
Gavin, T B (NSW) 1988 NZ 2,3, S, It (R), 1989 NZ (R), F 1,2, 1990 F 1,2,3, US, NZ 1,2,3, 1991 W, E, NZ 1, 1992 S 1,2,

Hipwell, J N B (NSW) 1968 NZ 1(R), 2, F, I, S, 1969 W, SA 1,2,3,4, 1970 S, 1971 SA 1,2, F 1,2, 1972 F 1,2, 1973 Tg 1, W, E, 1974 NZ 1,2,3, 1975 E 1,2, J 1, S, W, 1978 NZ 1,2,3, 1981 F 1,2, I, W, 1982 E

Hirschberg, W A (NSW) 1905 NZ

Hodgins, C H (NSW) 1910 NZ 1,2,3

Hodgson, A J (NSW) 1933 SA 2,3,4, 1934 NZ 1, 1936 NZ 1,2, M, 1937 SA 2, 1938 NZ 1,2,3

Hodgson, M J (WF) 2010 Fj(R),E1(R),NZ2(R),It(R), 2011 Sm,SA1(R)

Hoiles, S A (NSW, ACT) 2004 S4(R), E2(R), 2006 W(R), 2007 W1(R), 2(R), Fj(R), SA1(R), NZ1(R), SA2, NZ2, [J(R), W(R), Fj(R), C(R), E(R)], 2008 F2

Holbeck, J C (ACT) 1997 NZ 1(R), E 1, NZ 2, SA 1, NZ 3, SA 2, 2001 BI 3(R)

Holdsworth, J W (NSW) 1921 SA 1,2,3, 1922 M 2,3, NZ 1(R)

Holmes, G S (Q) 2005 F2(R), E(t&R), I, 2006 E1, 2, I1, NZ1, SA1, NZ2, SA2, NZ3, 2007 [F(R), C]

Holt, N C (Q) 1984 Fj

Honan, B D (Q) 1968 NZ 1(R), 2, F, I, S, 1969 SA 1,2,3,4

Honan, R E (Q) 1964 NZ 1,2

Hooper, M (ACT) 2012 S(R),W1(R),2(R),NZ2,SA1,Arg1,SA2,Arg2

Horan, T J (Q) 1989 NZ, F 1,2, 1990 F 1, NZ 1,2,3, 1991 W, E, NZ 1,2, [Arg, WS, W, I, NZ, E], 1992 S 1,2, NZ 1,2,3, SA, I, W, 1993 Tg, NZ, SA 1,2,3, C, F 1,2, 1995 [C, R, E], NZ 1,2, 1996 W 1,2, C, NZ 1, SA 1, It, S, I, W 3, 1997 F 1,2, NZ 1, E 1, NZ 2, Arg 1,2, E 2, S, 1998 E 1, S 1,2, NZ 1, SA 1, NZ 2, SA 2, NZ 3, Fj, Tg, WS, 1999 I 1,2, E, SA 1, NZ 1, SA 2, NZ 2, [R, I 3, W, SA 3, F], 2000 Arg 1

Horne, R G (NSW) 2010 Fj, E1, 2, I, SA1, NZ1, 2011 [US, NZ(R), W(R)], 2012 W1, 2, 3, NZ1, 2

Horodam, D J (Q) 1913 NZ 2

Horsley, G R (Q) 1954 Fj 2

Horton, P A (NSW) 1974 NZ 1,2,3, 1975 E 1,2, J 1,2, S, W, 1976 E, F 1,2, 1978 W 1,2, NZ 1,2,3, 1979 NZ, Arg 1

Horwill, J E (Q) 2007 Fj, 2008 I, F1, 2, SA1, NZ1, 2, SA2, 3, NZ3, 2009 It1, 2, F, NZ1, SA1, NZ2, SA2, 3, NZ3, 4, E, I, S, W, 2011 SA1, NZ1, SA2, NZ2, [It, I, Ru, SA, NZ, W], W

Hoskins, J E (NSW) 1924 NZ 1,2,3

How, R A (NSW) 1967 I 2

Howard, J (Q) 1938 NZ 1,2

Howard, J L (NSW) 1970 S, 1971 SA 1, 1972 F 1(R), NZ 2, 1973 Tg 1,2, W

Howard, P W (Q, ACT) 1993 NZ, 1994 WS, NZ, 1995 NZ 1(R), 2(t), 1996 W 1,2, SA 1, NZ 2, SA 2, It, S, W 3, 1997 F 1,2, NZ 1, Arg 1,2, E 2, S

Howell, M L (NSW) 1946 NZ 1(R), 1947 NZ 1, S, I, W

Hughes, B D (NSW) 1913 NZ 2,3

Hughes, J C (NSW) 1907 NZ 1,3

Hughes, N McL (NSW) 1953 NZ 1,2,3,4, 1955 NZ 1,2,3, 1956 SA 1,2, 1958 W, I, E, S, F

Humphreys, O W (NSW) 1920 NZ 3, 1921 NZ, 1922 M 1,2,3, 1925 NZ 1

Hutchinson, E E (NSW) 1937 SA 1,2

Hutchinson, F E (NSW) 1936 NZ 1,2, 1938 NZ 1,3

Huxley, J L (ACT) 2007 W1, 2, Fj, SA1, NZ1, SA2, [W(R), Fj(R), C]

Hynes, P J (Q) 2008 I, F1, 2, SA1, NZ1, 2, SA2, 3, NZ3, 4, E, F3, W, 2009 It2, NZ2(R), SA2, 3(R), NZ4, E, I, S, W

Ide, W P J (Q) 1938 NZ 2,3

Ioane, D A N (WF, Q) 2007 W2, 2008 It, F3, W, 2009 NZ4, E, I, W, 2010 Fj, E1, 2, 2011 Sm, SA1, NZ1, SA2, NZ2, [It, SA, NZ, W], W, 2012 S, W1, 2, 3, NZ1, 2, SA1, Arg1, SA2, Arg2

Ives, W N (NSW) 1926 NZ 1,2,3,4, 1929 NZ 3

James, P M (Q) 1958 M 2,3

James, S L (NSW) 1987 SK (R), [E (R)], NZ, Arg 1,2, 1988 NZ 2(R)

Jamieson, A E (NSW) 1925 NZ 3(R)

Jaques, T (ACT) 2000 SA 1(R), NZ 1(R)

Jessep, E M (V) 1934 NZ 1,2

Johansson, L D T (Q) 2005 NZ2(R),F2(R),E(R)

Johnson, A P (NSW) 1946 NZ 1, M

Johnson, B B (NSW) 1952 Fj 1,2, NZ 1,2, 1953 SA 2,3,4, 1955 NZ 1,2

Johnson, P G (NSW) 1959 BI 1,2, 1961 Fj 1,2,3, SA 1,2, F, 1962 NZ 1,2,3,4,5, 1963 E, SA 1,2,3,4, 1964 NZ 1,2,3, 1965 SA 1,2, 1966 BI 1,2, W, S, 1967 E, I 1, F, I 2, NZ, 1968 NZ 1,2, F, I, S, 1970 S, 1971 SA 1,2, F 1,2

Johnstone, B (Q) 1993 Tg (R)

Jones, G G (Q) 1952 Fj 1,2, 1953 SA 1,2,3,4, 1954 Fj 1,2, 1955 NZ 1,2,3, 1956 SA 1

Jones, H (NSW) 1913 NZ 1,2,3

Jones, P A (NSW) 1963 E, SA 1

Jorgensen, P (NSW) 1992 S 1(R), 2(R)

Joyce, J E (NSW) 1903 NZ

Judd, H A (NSW) 1903 NZ, 1904 BI 1,2,3, 1905 NZ

Judd, P B (NSW) 1925 NZ 4, 1926 NZ 1,2,3,4, 1927 I, W, S, 1928 E, 1931 M, NZ

Junee, D K (NSW) 1989 F 1(R), 2(R), 1994 WS (R), NZ (R)

Kafer, R B (ACT) 1999 NZ 2, [R, US (R)], 2000 Arg 1(R),2, SA 1, NZ 1(t&R), SA 2(R),3(R), F, S, E

Kahl, P R (Q) 1992 W

Kanaar, A (NSW) 2005 NZ2(R)

Kassulke, N (Q) 1985 C 1,2

Kay, A R (V) 1958 NZ 2, 1959 BI 2

Kay, P (NSW) 1988 E 2

Kearney, K H (NSW) 1947 NZ 1,2, S, I, W, 1948 E, F

Kearns, P N (NSW) 1989 NZ, F 1,2, 1990 F 1,2,3, US, NZ 1,2,3, 1991 W, E, NZ 1,2, [Arg, WS, W, I, NZ, E], 1992 S 1,2, NZ 1,2,3, SA, I, W, 1993 Tg, NZ, SA 1,2,3, C, F 1,2, 1994 I 1,2, It 1,2, WS, NZ, 1995 Arg 1,2, [SA, C, E], NZ 1,2, 1998 E 1, S 1,2, NZ 1, SA 1, NZ 2, SA 2, NZ 3, Fj, WS, F, E 2, 1999 I 2(R), SA 1(R),2, NZ 2, [R, I 3]

Kefu, R S T (Q) 1997 SA 2(R), 1998 E 1, S 1,2, NZ 1, SA 1, NZ 2, SA 2, NZ 3, Fj (R), Tg, WS (R), F, E 2, 1999 I 1,2, E, SA 1, NZ 1(R), SA 2, NZ 2, [R, I 3, SA 3, F], 2000 SA 1(t&R), NZ 1(R), SA 2(R), NZ 2, SA 3(R), F, S, E, 2001 BI 1,2,3, SA 1, NZ 1, SA 2, NZ 2, Sp, E, F, W, 2002 F 1, NZ 1, SA 1, NZ 2, SA 2, Arg, I, E, It, 2003 I, W, E, SA 1, NZ 1, SA 2, NZ 2

Kefu, S (Q) 2001 W (R), 2003 I, W, E, SA 1, NZ 1(R)

Kelaher, J D (NSW) 1933 SA 1,2,3,4,5, 1934 NZ 1, 1936 NZ 1,2, M, 1937 SA 1,2, 1938 NZ 3

Kelaher, T P (NSW) 1992 NZ 1, I (R), 1993 NZ

Kelleher, R J (Q) 1969 SA 2,3

Keller, D H (NSW) 1947 NZ 1, S, I, W, 1948 E, F

Kelly, A J (NSW) 1899 BI 1

Kelly, R L F (NSW) 1936 NZ 1,2, M, 1937 SA 1,2, 1938 NZ 1,2

Kent, A (Q) 1912 US

Kepu, S M (NSW) 2008 It(R), F3(R), 2009 S(R), 2011 Sm, SA1, NZ1, SA2, NZ2, [It, I, US(R), Ru, SA, NZ], 2012 W1, 2, 3, NZ1

Kerr, F R (V) 1938 NZ 1

Kimlin, P J (ACT) 2009 It1(R),2

King, S C (NSW) 1926 NZ 1,2,3,4(R), 1927 W, S, 1928 E, F, 1929 NZ 1,2,3, 1930 BI, 1932 NZ 1,2

Knight, M (NSW) 1978 W 1,2, NZ 1

Knight, S O (NSW) 1969 SA 2,4, 1970 S, 1971 SA 1,2,3

Knox, D J (NSW, ACT) 1985 Fj 1,2, 1990 US (R), 1994 WS, NZ, 1996 It, S, I, 1997 SA 1, NZ 3, SA 2, Arg 1,2

Kraefft, D F (NSW) 1947 NZ 2, S, I, W, 1948 E, F

Kreutzer, S D (Q) 1914 NZ 2

Lamb, J S (NSW) 1928 NZ 1,2, M

Lambie, J K (NSW) 1974 NZ 1,2,3, 1975 W

Lane, R E (NSW) 1921 SA 1

Lane, T A (Q) 1985 C 1,2, NZ

Lang, C W P (V) 1938 NZ 2,3

Langford, J F (ACT) 1997 NZ 3, SA 2, E 2, S

Larkham, S J (ACT) 1996 W 2(R), 1997 F 1,2, NZ 1,2(R), SA 1, NZ 3, SA 2, Arg 1,2, E 2, S, 1998 E 1, S 1,2, NZ 1, SA 1, NZ 2, SA 2, NZ 3, Fj, Tg (t), WS, F, E 2, 1999 [I 3, US, W, SA 3, F], 2000 Arg 1,2, SA 1, NZ 1, SA 2, NZ 2, SA 3, 2001 BI 1,2, NZ 1, SA 2, Sp, E, F, W, 2002 F 1,2, NZ 1, SA 1, NZ 2, SA 2, Arg, I, E, 2003 SA 1(R), NZ 1, SA 2, NZ 2, [Arg, R, I, S, NZ, E], 2004 S1, 2, E1, PI, NZ1, SA1, NZ2, SA2, S3, F, S4, 2005 Sm(R), It, F1, SA1, 2, 3, 2006 E1, 2, I1, NZ1, SA1, NZ2, SA2, NZ3, SA3, W, It, I2, S, 2007 W2, Fj, SA1, NZ1, SA2, NZ2, [J]

Larkin, E R (NSW) 1903 NZ

231

AUSTRALIA

Perrin, T D (NSW) 1931 M, NZ
Phelps, R (NSW) 1955 NZ 2,3, 1956 SA 1,2, 1957 NZ 1,2, 1958 W, I, E, S, F, M 1, NZ 1,2,3, 1961 Fj 1,2,3, SA 1,2, F, 1962 NZ 1,2
Phipps, J A (NSW) 1953 SA 1,2,3,4, 1954 Fj 1,2, 1955 NZ 1,2,3, 1956 SA 1,2
Phipps, N J (MR) 2011 Sm, SA1(R), [Ru(R)], 2012 SA1(R), Arg1, SA2, Arg2
Phipps, W J (NSW) 1928 NZ 2
Piggott, H R (NSW) 1922 M 3(R)
Pilecki, S J (Q) 1978 W 1,2, NZ 1,2, 1979 I 1,2, NZ, Arg 1,2, 1980 Fj, NZ 1,2, 1982 S 1,2, 1983 US, Arg 1,2, NZ
Pini, M (Q) 1994 I 1, It 2, WS, NZ, 1995 Arg 1,2, [SA, R (t)]
Piper, B J C (NSW) 1946 NZ 1, M, NZ 2, 1947 NZ 1, S, I, W, 1948 E, F, 1949 M, 1,2,3
Pocock, D W (WF) 2008 NZ4(R), It(R), 2009 It1(R), 2, F(R), NZ1(R), SA1(R), NZ2(R), SA2(R), 3, NZ3, 4, E(R), I, W, 2010 Fj, E1, 2, I, SA1, NZ1, 2, SA2, 3, NZ3, 4, W, E3, It, F, 2011 SA1, NZ1, SA2, NZ2, [It, Ru, SA, NZ, W], W, 2012 S, W1, 2, 3, NZ1
Poidevin, S P (NSW) 1980 Fj, NZ 1,2,3, 1981 F 1,2, I, W, S, 1982 E, NZ 1,2,3, 1983 US, Arg 1,2, NZ, It, F 1,2, 1984 Fj, NZ 1,2,3, E, I, W, S, 1985 C 1,2, NZ, Fj 1,2, 1986 It, F, Arg 1,2, NZ 1,2,3, 1987 SK, [E, J, I, F, W], Arg 1, 1988 NZ 1,2,3, 1989 NZ, 1991 E, NZ 1,2, [Arg, W, I, NZ, E]
Polota-Nau, S U T (NSW) 2005 E(R), I(R), 2006 S(R), 2008 SA1(R), NZ1(R), 2(R), SA2(R), 3, It(R), E(R), 2009 It1(R), 2, F(R), SA1(R), NZ2(t&R), SA2(R), 3, NZ3, 4(R), E(R), I(R), S(R), W(R), 2010 It(R), F(R), 2011 It(R), I, US, SA(R), NZ(R), W], W, 2012 W1, 2, 3, NZ1, SA1, Arg1, SA2, Arg2
Pope, A M (Q) 1968 NZ 2(R)
Potter, R T (Q) 1961 Fj 2
Potts, J M (NSW) 1957 NZ 1,2, 1958 W, I, 1959 BI 1
Prentice, C (NSW) 1914 NZ 3
Prentice, W S (NSW) 1908 W, 1909 E, 1910 NZ 1,2,3, 1912 US
Price, R A (NSW) 1974 NZ 1,2,3, 1975 E 1,2, J 1,2, 1976 US
Primmer, C J (Q) 1951 NZ 1,3
Proctor, I J (NSW) 1967 NZ
Prosser, R B (NSW) 1967 E, I 1,2, NZ, 1968 NZ 1,2, F, I, S, 1969 W, SA 1,2,3,4, 1971 SA 1,2,3, F 1,2, 1972 F 1,2, NZ 1,2,3, Fj
Pugh, G H (NSW) 1912 US
Purcell, M P (Q) 1966 W, S, 1967 I 2
Purkis, E M (NSW) 1958 S, M 1
Pym, J E (NSW) 1923 M 1

Rainbow, A E (NSW) 1925 NZ 1
Ramalli, C (NSW) 1938 NZ 2,3
Ramsay, K M (NSW) 1936 M, 1937 SA 1, 1938 NZ 1,3
Rankin, R (NSW) 1936 NZ 1,2, M, 1937 SA 1,2, 1938 NZ 1,2
Rathbone, C (ACT) 2004 S1, 2(R), E1, PI, NZ1, SA1, NZ2, S3, F, S4, 2005 Sm, NZ1(R), SA4, NZ2, 2006E1(R), 2(R), I1(R), SA1(R), NZ2(R), SA2(R), NZ3, SA3, W, It, I2
Rathie, D S (Q) 1972 F 1,2
Raymond, R L (NSW) 1920 NZ 1,2, 1921 SA 2,3, NZ, 1922 M 1,2,3, NZ 1,2,3, 1923 M 1 2
Redwood, C (Q) 1903 NZ, 1904 BI 1,2,3
Reid, E J (NSW) 1925 NZ 2,3,4
Reid, T W (NSW) 1961 Fj 1,2,3, SA 1, 1962 NZ 1
Reilly, N P (Q) 1968 NZ 1,2, F, I, S, 1969 W, SA 1,2,3,4
Reynolds, L J (NSW) 1910 NZ 2(R), 3
Reynolds, R J (NSW) 1984 Fj, NZ 1,2,3, 1985 Fj 1,2, 1986 Arg 1,2, NZ 1, 1987 [J]
Richards, E W (Q) 1904 BI 1,3, 1905 NZ, 1907 NZ 1(R), 2
Richards, G (NSW) 1978 NZ 2(R), 3, 1981 F 1
Richards, T J (Q) 1908 W, 1909 E, 1912 US
Richards, V S (NSW) 1936 NZ 1,2(R), M, 1937 SA 1, 1938 NZ 1 1,2, W
Richardson, G C (Q) 1971 SA 1,2,3, 1972 NZ 2,3, Fj, 1973 Tg 1,2, W
Rigney, W A (NSW) 1925 NZ 2,4, 1926 NZ 4
Riley, S A (NSW) 1903 NZ
Ritchie, E V (NSW) 1924 NZ 1,3, 1925 NZ 2,3
Roberts, B T (NSW) 1956 SA 2
Roberts, H F (Q) 1961 Fj 1,3, SA 2, F
Robertson, I J (NSW) 1975 J 1,2
Robinson, B A (NSW) 2006 SA3, I2(R), S, 2007 W1(R), 2, Fj(R), 2008 I, F1, 2, SA1, NZ1, 2, SA2, 3, NZ3, 4, E, W, 2009 It1,

F, NZ1, SA1, NZ2, SA2, 3, NZ3, 4, E, I, S, W, 2010 SA1, NZ1, 2, SA2, 3, NZ3, 4, W, E3, It(R), F(t&R), 2012 W1, 2, 3, NZ1, 2, SA1, Arg1, SA2, Arg2(R)
Robinson, B J (ACT) 1996 It (R), S (R), I (R), 1997 F 1,2, NZ 1, E 1, NZ 2, SA 1(R), NZ 3(R), SA 2(R), Arg 1,2, E 2, S, 1998 Tg
Robinson, B S (Q) 2011 Sm(R)
Roche, C (Q) 1982 S 1,2, NZ 1,2,3, 1983 US, Arg 1,2, NZ, It, F 1,2, 1984 Fj, NZ 1,2,3, I
Rodriguez, E E (NSW) 1984 Fj, NZ 1,2,3, E, I, W, S, 1985 C 1,2, NZ, Fj 1, 1986 It, F, Arg 1,2, NZ 1,2,3, 1987 SK, [E, J, W (R)], NZ, Arg 1,2
Roe, J A (Q) 2003 [Nm(R)], 2004 E1(R), SA1(R), NZ2(R), SA2(t&R), S3, F, 2005 Sm(R), It(R), F1(R), SA1(R), 3, NZ1, SA4(t&R), NZ2(R), F2(R), E, I, W
Roebuck, M C (NSW) 1991 W, E, NZ 1,2, [Arg, WS, W, I, NZ, E], 1992 S 1, 2, NZ 2, 3, SA, I, W, 1993 Tg, SA 1, 2, 3, C, F 2
Roff, J W (ACT) 1995 [C, R], NZ 1,2, 1996 W 1,2, NZ 1, SA 1, NZ 2, SA 2(R), S, I, W 3, 1997 F 1,2, NZ 1, E 1, NZ 2, SA 1, NZ 3, SA 2, Arg 1,2, E 2, S, 1998 E 1, S 1,2, NZ 1, SA 1, NZ 2, SA 2, NZ 3, Fj, Tg, WS, F, E 2, 1999 I 1,2, E, SA 1, NZ 1, SA 2, NZ 2(R), [R (R), I 3, US (R), W, SA 3, F], 2000 Arg 1,2, SA 1, NZ 1, SA 2, NZ 2, SA 3, F, S, E, 2001 BI 1,2,3, SA 1, NZ 1, SA 2, NZ 2, Sp, E, F, W, 2003 I, W, E, SA 1, [Arg, R, I, S(R), NZ(t&R), E(R)], 2004 S1, 2, E1, PI
Rogers, M S (NSW) 2002 F 1(R), 2(R), NZ 1(R), SA 1(R), NZ 2(R), SA 2(t&R), Arg, 2003 E (R), SA 1, NZ 1, SA 2, NZ 2, [Arg, R, Nm, I, S, NZ, E], 2004S3(R), F(R), S4(R), E2(R), 2005 Sm(R), It, F1(R), SA1, 4, NZ2, F2, E, I, W, 2006 E1, 2, I1, NZ1, SA1(R), NZ2(R), SA2(R), NZ3(R), W, It, I2(R), S(R)
Rose, H A (NSW), 1967 I 2, NZ, 1968 NZ 1,2, F, I, S, 1969 W, SA 1,2,3,4, 1970 S
Rosenblum, M E (NSW) 1928 NZ 1,2,3, M
Rosenblum, R G (NSW) 1969 SA 1,3, 1970 S
Rosewell, J S H (NSW) 1907 NZ 1,3
Ross, A W (NSW) 1925 NZ 1,2,3, 1926 NZ 1,2,3, 1927 I, W, S, 1928 E, F, 1929 NZ 1, 1930 BI, 1931 M, NZ, 1932 NZ 2,3, 1933 SA 5, 1934 NZ 1,2
Ross, W S (Q) 1979 I 1,2, Arg 2, 1980 Fj, NZ 1,2,3, 1982 S 1,2, 1983 US, Arg 1,2, NZ
Rothwell, P R (NSW) 1951 NZ 1,2,3, 1952 Fj 1
Row, F L (NSW) 1899 BI 1,3,4
Row, N E (NSW) 1907 NZ 1,3, 1909 E, 1910 NZ 1,2,3
Rowles, P G (NSW) 1972 Fj, 1973 E
Roxburgh, J R (NSW) 1968 NZ 1,2, F, 1969 W, SA 1,2,3,4, 1970 S
Ruebner, G (NSW) 1966 BI 1,2
Russell, C J (NSW) 1907 NZ 1,2,3, 1908 W, 1909 E
Ryan, J R (NSW) 1975 J 2, 1976 I, US, Fj 1,2,3
Ryan, K J (Q) 1958 E, M 1, NZ 1,2,3
Ryan, P F (NSW) 1963 E, SA 1, 1966 BI 1,2
Rylance, M H (NSW) 1926 NZ 4(R)

Sailor, W J (Q) 2002 F 1,2, Arg (R), I, E, It, 2003 I, W, E, SA 1, NZ 1, SA 2, NZ 2, [Arg, R, I, S, NZ, E], 2004 S1, 2, NZ1(R), 2(R), SA2(R), S3(R), F(R), S4(R), E2, 2005 Sm, It, F1, SA1, 2, 3, F2, I(R), W(R)
Samo, U R (ACT,Q) 2004 S1, 2, E1, PI, NZ1, S4(R), 2011 SA2(R), NZ2, [It, I, US(R), Ru, SA, NZ, W(t&R)], W(R), 2012 NZ1(R), 2(R), SA1, Arg1, SA2, Arg2
Sampson, J H (NSW) 1899 BI 4
Sayle, J L (NSW) 1967 NZ
Schulte, B G (Q) 1946 NZ 1, M
Scott, P R I (NSW) 1962 NZ 1,2
Scott-Young, S (Q) 1990 F 2,3(R), US, NZ 3, 1992 NZ 1,2,3
Shambrook, G G (Q) 1976 Fj 2,3
Sharpe, N C (Q, WF) 2002 F 1,2, NZ 1, SA 1, NZ 2, SA 2, 2003 I, W, E, SA 1, NZ 1(R), SA 2(R), NZ 2(R), [Arg, R, Nm, I, S, NZ, E], 2004 S1, 2, E1, PI, NZ1, SA1, NZ2, SA2, 2005 Sm, It, F1, SA1, 2, 3, NZ1, SA4, NZ2, F2, E, I, W, 2006 E1, 2, I1, NZ1, SA1, NZ2, SA2, NZ3, W, It, I2, S, 2007 W1, 2, SA1, NZ1, SA2, NZ2, [J, W, C, E], 2008 I, F1, SA1, NZ1, 2, 3, 4, E, F3, W, 2009 It1, F, NZ1, SA1, NZ2, 2010 Fj, E1, 2, SA1, NZ1, 2, SA2, 3, NZ3, 4, W, E3, It, F, 2011

233

AUSTRALIA

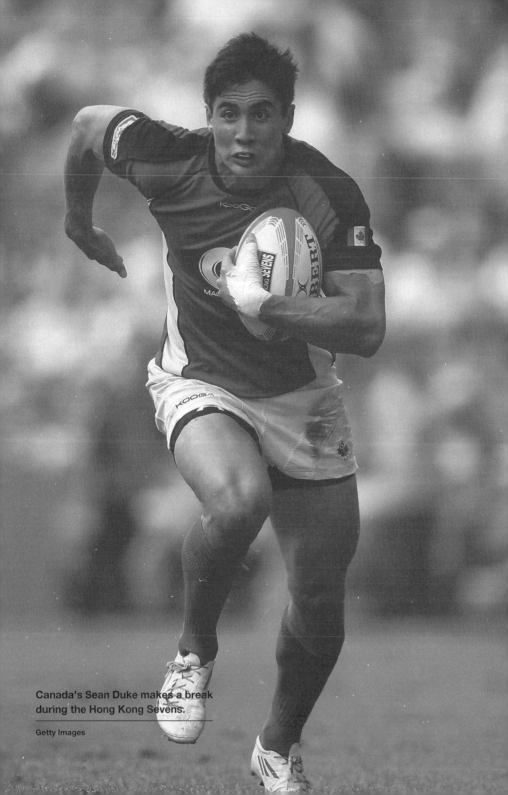

Canada's Sean Duke makes a break during the Hong Kong Sevens.

CANADA

CANADA'S 2012 TEST RECORD

OPPONENTS	DATE	VENUE	RESULT
USA	9 Jun	H	**Won** 28–25
Italy	15 Jun	H	**Lost** 16–25
Georgia	23 Jun	H	**Won** 31–12

CARPENTER'S CAPTAINCY OFF TO SUCCESSFUL START

By Ian Gilbert

Jose Lagman

Canada flanker Nanyak Dala hands off an American opponent during their first Test of 2012.

Keen observers of Super Rugby may have noticed a certain Stormers forward during 2012. Canada's Jebb Sinclair was signed on loan by the Cape Town side as injury cover and reminded onlookers of the forceful play that won him many fans during Rugby World Cup 2011.

Canada has exported more than the occasional tidy player to top-flight rugby over the years, with players such as Gareth Rees, Mike James and Jamie Cudmore excelling. With Sinclair joined in the national team by the likes of Glasgow Warriors' DTH van der Merwe, Canada have the personnel with the big-match nous to close out tight games. And that resolve was required in the Canucks' first international of the year, against neighbours USA in June.

Canada maintained their winning ways against the Americans (their success rate is a shade under 75 per cent), but victory was not without a fight as the game went down to the wire, 28–25.

Although coach Kieran Crowley said his players "left a lot of points out there," his Kiwi pragmatism must be rubbing off on his players if they are able to close out such games. Canada began their international season with a new skipper after 43-cap hooker Pat Riordan – who had led the side through the World Cup – stepped down.

Number 8 Aaron Carpenter assumed the captaincy and set about imposing his own leadership style in a subtly effective way. Carpenter is the type of player who prefers to lead by example, so it was fitting that the 29-year-old should score the winning try against the USA.

"I am not the greatest at pre-match speeches, but I am happy to do them when they are needed to fire the team up," he said.

Crowley had little hesitation in entrusting the role to Carpenter.

"Aaron's always been a leader, all the way through the time I've been here," he said. "Now he's been given the opportunity, he's certainly stepped up and he's developed his own methods."

As introductions to international captaincy go, the June Tests – Canada also played Italy and Georgia – were not so much a baptism of fire as a useful yardstick by which to measure Canada's standing.

Of the three visiting sides, only Italy were higher in the IRB World Rankings, and the Canadians took plenty of confidence into that game to lead the Azzurri 13–9 at the interval.

However, this time it was Italy's turn to show their big-match temperament. Led by wily veteran Martin Castrogiovanni, who captained his country for the first time in his 87th Test appearance, Italy silenced the home crowd with their second-half comeback.

Kris Burton kicked 20 points as the tourists ran out 25–16 winners, leaving Canada without a win against them since their 2000 success in Rovigo. The Italy Test was played in Toronto, in the new captain's home province of Ontario.

Canada's final fixture of the June Test schedule came against Georgia, whom they had previously played only twice before, with honours even.

The Canucks made amends for losing the sides' most recent encounter, in 2010, by winning 31–12 in Burnaby, on the outskirts of Vancouver. Full back James Pritchard weighed in with 21 points to take second place on the country's all-time points list after Gareth Rees.

Carpenter is another of the Test team who plays overseas, featuring in England's second-tier Championship with Plymouth Albion. He advocates the importance of a professional approach. "At the World Cup we made strides towards professionalism, which isn't about making money but about treating rugby as our full-time jobs," he said.

Crowley says a professional league will be the key to further expansion. "It's something that Canada needs," says the former All Black. "It's a little while away, and I don't think we could do it on our own. I think it would have to be a North American league."

The Canadians won plenty of admirers in the most recent World Cup, rising to the challenge of being drawn in a tough pool with eventual finalists New Zealand and France. "The more people we get exposed to the game, the better," says Crowley. "The World Cup was on major TV here – that had a massive impact."

Outside of World Cup years, however, the game needs to find other ways to garner attention, and something that promises to help the profile is the rise of Sevens.

The men's squad are under the tutelage of Welshman Geraint John and have already scored a notable achievement by qualifying to play as a core team in the HSBC Sevens World Series 2012/13.

"Sevens is a big avenue for participation and to get people involved," says Crowley.

Given the cost of equipment for Canada's prevalent domestic sports, Sevens has an advantage of requiring comparatively little kit.

"For schools that don't have the finances for hockey and football, Sevens is a cost-effective way for kids to play sport at school," says Crowley.

The schools factor tallies with Rugby Canada's blueprint for the game, the Long Term Rugby Development (LTRD), which outlines a structured way for the sport, for all ages. The idea is that talented players have a clear progression from junior to senior – and hopefully embrace rugby for life.

With the men's and women's Sevens squads firmly focused on the chance of Olympic gold at Rio 2016, the women are already reaping the benefits of their commitment at the Centre of Excellence in British Columbia.

The team, who train full-time from January to June, won the Las Vegas invitational event in February. Their efforts were further rewarded with the Amsterdam Sevens title in May, banishing the disappointment of semi-final defeats by eventual winners England in the IRB Women's Sevens Challenge Cup events in Hong Kong and London.

The Canadians showed their mettle in the Netherlands despite a tough draw, which pitted them against the powerful Dutch and English sides. Both teams were duly beaten and the Canadians won the final by seeing off the USA 26–19.

On the domestic front, Ontario snared the National Women's League title with a 26–12 victory over British Columbia in the decider.

CANADA INTERNATIONAL STATISTICS

MATCH RECORDS UP TO 10 OCTOBER 2012

WINNING MARGIN

Date	Opponent	Result	Winning Margin
24/06/2006	Barbados	69–3	66
14/10/1999	Namibia	72–11	61
12/08/2006	USA	56–7	49
06/07/1996	Hong Kong	57–9	48

MOST POINTS IN A MATCH
BY THE TEAM

Date	Opponent	Result	Points
14/10/1999	Namibia	72–11	72
24/06/2006	Barbados	69–3	69
15/07/2000	Japan	62–18	62
13/11/2010	Spain	60–22	60
06/07/1996	Hong Kong	57–9	57

BY A PLAYER

Date	Player	Opponent	Points
12/08/2006	James Pritchard	USA	36
24/06/2006	James Pritchard	Barbados	29
14/10/1999	Gareth Rees	Namibia	27
13/07/1996	Bobby Ross	Japan	26
25/05/1991	Mark Wyatt	Scotland	24

MOST TRIES IN A MATCH
BY THE TEAM

Date	Opponent	Result	Tries
24/06/2006	Barbados	69–3	11
14/10/1999	Namibia	72–11	9
11/05/1991	Japan	49–26	8
15/07/2000	Japan	62–18	8
13/11/2010	Spain	60–22	8

BY A PLAYER

Date	Player	Opponent	Tries
15/07/2000	Kyle Nichols	Japan	4
24/06/2006	James Pritchard	Barbados	3
12/08/2006	James Pritchard	USA	3
10/05/1987	Steve Gray	USA	3

MOST CONVERSIONS IN A MATCH
BY THE TEAM

Date	Opponent	Result	Cons
14/10/1999	Namibia	72–11	9
15/07/2000	Japan	62–18	8

BY A PLAYER

Date	Player	Opponent	Cons
14/10/1999	Gareth Rees	Namibia	9
15/07/2000	Jared Barker	Japan	8

MOST PENALTIES IN A MATCH
BY THE TEAM

Date	Opponent	Result	Pens
25/05/1991	Scotland	24–19	8
22/08/1998	Argentina	28–54	7

BY A PLAYER

Date	Player	Opponent	Pens
25/05/1991	Mark Wyatt	Scotland	8
22/08/1998	Gareth Rees	Argentina	7

MOST DROP GOALS IN A MATCH
BY THE TEAM

Date	Opponent	Result	DGs
08/11/1986	USA	27–16	2
04/07/2001	Fiji	23–52	2
08/06/1980	USA	16–0	2
24/05/1997	Hong Kong	35–27	2
18/09/2011	France	19–46	2

BY A PLAYER

Date	Player	Opponent	DGs
04/07/2001	Bobby Ross	Fiji	2
24/05/1997	Bobby Ross	Hong Kong	2
18/09/2011	Ander Monro	France	2

CANADA

MOST CAPPED PLAYERS

Name	Caps
Al Charron	76
Winston Stanley	66
Scott Stewart	64
Rod Snow	62

LEADING TRY SCORERS

Name	Tries
Winston Stanley	24
Morgan Williams	13
DTH van der Merwe	13
James Pritchard	13

LEADING CONVERSION SCORERS

Name	Conversions
James Pritchard	79
Bobby Ross	52
Gareth Rees	51
Jared Barker	24
Mark Wyatt	24

LEADING PENALTY SCORERS

Name	Penalties
Gareth Rees	110
Bobby Ross	84
James Pritchard	74
Mark Wyatt	64
Jared Barker	55

LEADING DROP GOAL SCORERS

Name	DGs
Bobby Ross	10
Gareth Rees	9
Mark Wyatt	5

LEADING POINT SCORERS

Name	Points
Gareth Rees	491
James Pritchard	445
Bobby Ross	421
Mark Wyatt	263
Jared Barker	226

THE COUNTRIES

AD Abrams 2003 *US, NZ, Tg*, 2004 *US, J, EngA, US, F, It, E*, 2005 *US, J, W, EngA, US, Ar, F, R*, 2006 *S, E, US, It*

MJ Alder 1976 *Bb*

P Aldous 1971 *W*

TJ Ardron 2012 *US, It, Geo*

AS Arthurs 1988 *US*

M Ashton 1971 *W*

F Asselin 1999 *Fj*, 2000 *Tg, US, SA*, 2001 *Ur, Ar, Fj*, 2002 *S, US, US, Ur, Ur, CHL, W, F*

O Atkinson 2005 *J, Ar*, 2006 *E, US, It*

S Ault 2006 *W, It*, 2008 *US, Pt*, 2009 *Geo, US, US*

JC Bain 1932 *J*

RG Banks 1999 *J, Fj, Sa, US, Tg, W, E, F, Nm*, 2000 *US, SA, I, J, It*, 2001 *US, Ur, Ar, E, Fj, J*, 2002 *S, US, US, Ur, CHL, Ur, CHL, W, F*, 2003 *EngA, US, M, M, Ur, NZ, It*

S Barber 1973 *W*, 1976 *Bb*

M Barbieri 2006 *E, US*

B Barker 1966 *Bl*, 1971 *W*

J Barker 2000 *Tg, J, It*, 2002 *S, US, US, Ur, CHL, CHL, W*, 2003 *US, NZ, It*, 2004 *US, J, F, It*

T Bauer 1977 *US, E*, 1978 *US, F*, 1979 *US*

DR Baugh 1998 *J, HK, US, HK, J, Ur, Ar*, 1999 *J, Fj, Sa, US, Tg, W, E, F, Fj, Nm*, 2000 *US, SA, I, It*, 2001 *E, E*, 2002 *S, US, Ur, CHL*

BG Beukeboom 2012 *US, Geo*

A Bianco 1966 *Bl*

AJ Bibby 1979 *US, F*, 1980 *W, US, NZ*, 1981 *US, Ar*

R Bice 1996 *US, A*, 1997 *US, J, HK, US, W, I*, 1998 *US, US, HK, J, Ur, US, Ar*, 1999 *J, Fj, Sa, US, Tg, W, F*

P Bickerton 2004 *US, J*

D Biddle 2006 *S, E, Bar*, 2007 *W, Fj, A*

JM Billingsley 1974 *Tg*, 1977 *US*, 1978 *F*, 1979 *US*, 1980 *W*, 1983 *US, It, It*, 1984 *US*

WG Bjarneson 1962 *Bb*

TJH Blackwell 1973 *W*

N Blevins 2009 *J, J*, 2010 *Bel, Sp, Geo, Pt*

B Bonenberg 1983 *US, It, It*

J Boone 1932 *J, J*

T Bourne 1967 *E*

CJ Braid 2010 *Bel, Geo*

R Breen 1986 *US*, 1987 *W*, 1990 *US*, 1991 *J, S, US, R*, 1993 *E, US*

R Breen 1983 *E*, 1987 *US*

R Brewer 1967 *E*

STT Brown 1989 *I, US*

N Browne 1973 *W*, 1974 *Tg*

S Bryan 1996 *Ur, US, Ar*, 1997 *HK, J, US, W*, 1998 *HK, J, US, Ar*, 1999 *Fj, Sa, US, Tg, W, E, F, Fj, Nm*

M Burak 2004 *US, J, EngA, US, F, It, E*, 2005 *EngA, US, Ar, F, R*, 2006 *US, Bar, W*, 2007 *NZ, Pt, W, Fj, J, A*, 2008 *I, W, S*, 2009 *I, W, Geo, US, US*

C Burford 1970 *Fj*

D Burgess 1962 *Bb, W23*

D Burleigh 2001 *Ur, Ar, E, E*

JB Burnham 1966 *Bl*, 1967 *E*, 1970 *Fj*, 1971 *W*

HAW Buydens 2006 *E, Bar*, 2008 *US*, 2011 *Rus, US, US, Tg, F, J, NZ*, 2012 *US, It*

GE Cameron 1932 *J*

JWD Cannon 2001 *US, Ar, E, E, Fj, J*, 2002 *S, US, Ur, CHL, Ur, CHL, W, F*, 2003 *EngA, US, M, M, Ur, US, Ar, NZ, It*, 2004 *US, F, It, E*, 2005 *W, EngA, US, F*

R Card 1996 *US, A, Ur, US, Ar*, 1997 *US, J, HK*

ME Cardinal 1986 *US*, 1987 *US, Tg, I, US*, 1991 *S*, 1993 *A*, 1994 *US, F, E, F*, 1995 *S, Fj, NZ, R, SA*, 1996 *US, US,*

HK, J, A, HK, J, 1997 *US, US, W, I*, 1998 *US, US, HK*, 1999 *Fj, US, W, E, Fj, Nm*

LAG Carlson 2002 *Ur, W*, 2003 *EngA*

A Carpenter 2005 *US, J, EngA, US, Ar, F, R*, 2006 *S, E, US, W, It*, 2007 *US, NZ, Pt, W, Fj, J, A*, 2008 *US, Pt, I, W, S*, 2009 *I, W, Geo, US, J, J, Rus*, 2010 *Ur, Sp, Geo, Pt*, 2011 *Rus, US, US, Tg, F, J, NZ*, 2012 *US, It, Geo*

NS Carr 1985 *A, A*

DJ Carson 1980 *W, US, NZ*, 1981 *US, Ar*, 1982 *J, E, US*, 1983 *It, It*

SFB Carson 1977 *E*

MP Chambers 1962 *Bb, W23*, 1966 *Bl*

AJ Charron 1990 *Ar, US, Ar*, 1991 *J, S, Fj, F, NZ*, 1992 *US*, 1993 *E, E, US, A, W*, 1994 *US, F, W*, 1995 *Fj, NZ, R, A, SA, US*, 1996 *US, US, A, HK, J, Ur, US, Ar*, 1997 *US, J, HK, HK, J, US, W, I*, 1998 *US, HK, J, Ur, US, Ar*, 1999 *Fj, Sa, US, Tg, W, E, F, Fj, Nm*, 2000 *Tg, US, SA, Sa, Fj, J, It*, 2001 *Ur, Ar, E, E*, 2002 *S, US, Ur, CHL, Ur, CHL, F*, 2003 *W, It, Tg*

L Chung 1978 *F*

N Clapinson 1995 *US*, 1996 *US*

RM Clark 1962 *Bb*

D Clarke 1996 *A*

ME Clarkin 1985 *A, A*

B Collins 2004 *US, J*

W Collins 1977 *US, E*

GG Cooke 2000 *Tg, US*, 2001 *Fj, J*, 2003 *EngA, US, M, M, Ur, US, Ar, W, NZ, Tg*, 2004 *EngA, US, It, E*, 2005 *US, J, W, Ar, F, R*, 2006 *US*

I Cooper 1993 *W*

JA Cordle 1998 *HK, J*, 1999 *J, Fj, Sa*, 2001 *J*

GER Cox 1932 *J*

S Creagh 1988 *US*

JN Cudmore 2002 *US, CHL, W, F*, 2003 *EngA, US, W, NZ, It, Tg*, 2004 *US, F, It, E*, 2005 *W, F*, 2006 *US*, 2007 *Pt, W, Fj*, 2011 *Rus, US, US, Tg, F, J, NZ*

L Cudmore 2008 *US*

C Culpan 2006 *E*, 2007 *US, NZ, Pt, W, Fj, J*

TJ Cummings 1966 *Bl*, 1973 *W*

Z Cvitak 1983 *E*

N Dala 2007 *US*, 2008 *US*, 2009 *I, W, Geo, US, US, J, J*, 2010 *Ur*, 2011 *Rus, Tg, F, NZ*, 2012 *US, It, Geo*

MJW Dandy 1977 *E, E*

M Danskin 2001 *J*, 2004 *EngA, F*

D Daypuck 2004 *EngA, F, It, E*, 2005 *US, J, W, EngA, Ar, F, R*, 2006 *US, US, W, It*, 2007 *A*

H de Goede 1974 *Tg*, 1976 *Bb*, 1977 *US, E, E*, 1978 *US*, 1979 *US, F*, 1980 *W, US, NZ*, 1981 *US*, 1982 *J, J, E, US*, 1984 *US*, 1985 *US*, 1986 *J, US*, 1987 *US, Tg, I, W*

F Deacy 1973 *W*

J Delaney 1983 *E*

P Densmore 2005 *EngA*

JD Devlin 1985 *US*, 1986 *US*

M di Girolamo 2001 *Ar*, 2002 *US, Ur, CHL, Ur, W, F*, 2003 *US, M, M, Ur, W, NZ, It, Tg*, 2004 *EngA, US, F, It, E*

GA Dixon 2000 *US, SA, I, Sa, Fj, J, It*, 2001 *US, Ar, E, E*

D Docherty 1973 *W*

TJ Dolezel 2009 *Rus*, 2010 *Ur, Bel, Sp, Geo, Pt*, 2011 *Rus*, 2012 *US, It, Geo*

WJ Donaldson 1978 *F*, 1979 *W, US, NZ*, 1981 *US, F*, 1982 *E, US*, 1983 *US, It, It*, 1984 *US*

A Douglas 1974 *Tg*

JT Douglas 2003 *M, M, Ur, US, Ar, NZ, It*, 2004 *US, F*

A du Temple 1932 *J, J*

MJ **Kokan** 1984 *US*, 1985 *US*
P **Kyle** 1984 *US*
JA **Kyne** 2010 *Bel*, 2011 *J*
A **La Carte** 2004 *US, J*
M **Langley** 2004 *EngA*, 2005 *Ar*
MJ **Lawson** 2002 *US, Ur, CHL, Ur, CHL, F*, 2003 *EngA, US, M, M, Ur, US, Ar, W, It, Tg*, 2004 *F, It, E*, 2005 *US, J, F, R*, 2006 *Bar, US, W*
P **le Blanc** 1994 *F*, 1995 *Ur, Fj, NZ*
CE **le Fevre** 1976 *Bb*
J **Lecky** 1962 *Bb, W23*
JL **Lecky** 1982 *J, US*, 1983 *US, It, It*, 1984 *US*, 1985 *A, US*, 1986 *J, US*, 1987 *I, W, US*, 1991 *J, S, Fj, R*
GB **Legh** 1973 *W*, 1974 *Tg*, 1976 *Bb*
LSF **Leroy** 1932 *J*
J **Lorenz** 1966 *Bl*, 1970 *Fj*, 1971 *W*
DC **Lougheed** 1990 *Ar*, 1991 *J, US*, 1992 *US, E*, 1993 *E, E, US*, 1994 *F, W, E, F*, 1995 *Fj, NZ, R, A, SA*, 1996 *A, HK*, 1997 *J, W, I*, 1998 *US, Ar*, 1999 *US, Tg, W, E, F, Fj, Nm*, 2003 *W, It*
J **Loveday** 1993 *E, E, US, A*, 1996 *HK, J*, 1998 *J, Ur*, 1999 *Sa, US*
B **Luke** 2004 *US, J*
M **Luke** 1974 *Tg*, 1976 *Bb*, 1977 *US, E, E*, 1978 *US, F*, 1979 *US, F*, 1980 *W, US, NZ*, 1981 *US*, 1982 *J, US*
S **Lytton** 1995 *Ur, Ar, US*, 1996 *US, HK, J, J, US, Ar*
G **MacDonald** 1970 *Fj*
GDT **MacDonald** 1998 *HK*
P **Mack** 2009 *I, W, Geo, US, US, J, J, Rus*
I **MacKay** 1993 *A, W*
JL **Mackenzie** 2010 *Bel, Sp*, 2011 *US*
PW **Mackenzie** 2008 *Pt, I*, 2010 *Ur, Sp, Geo, Pt*, 2011 *Rus, US, US, Tg, F, J, NZ*, 2012 *US, It, Geo*
GI **MacKinnon** 1985 *US*, 1986 *J*, 1988 *US*, 1989 *I, US*, 1990 *Ar, Ar*, 1991 *J, S, Fj, R, F, NZ*, 1992 *US, E*, 1993 *E*, 1994 *US, F, W, E, F*, 1995 *S, Ur, Ar, Fj, NZ, A, SA*
S **MacKinnon** 1992 *US*, 1995 *Ur, Ar, Fj*
C **MacLachlan** 1981 *Ar*, 1982 *J, E*
P **Maclean** 1983 *US, It, It, E*
I **Macmillan** 1981 *Ar*, 1982 *J, J, E, US*
M **MacSween** 2009 *Rus*
B **Major** 2001 *Fj, J*
D **Major** 1999 *E, Fj, Nm*, 2000 *Tg, US, SA, I, Fj*, 2001 *Ur, E, E*
A **Marshall** 1997 *J*, 1998 *Ur*
JA **Marshall** 2008 *S*, 2010 *Ur, Bel, Sp, Geo, Pt*, 2011 *US, US, Tg, F, J, NZ*, 2012 *US, It, Geo*
P **Mason** 1974 *Tg*
B **McCarthy** 1996 *US, Ar*, 1998 *J, HK, J*
J **McDonald** 1974 *Tg*
RN **McDonald** 1966 *Bl*, 1967 *E*, 1970 *Fj*
AG **McGann** 1985 *A, A*
R **McGeein** 1973 *W*
RI **McInnes** 1979 *F*, 1980 *NZ*, 1981 *US, Ar*, 1982 *J, J, E, US*, 1983 *US, It, It*, 1984 *US*, 1985 *US*
B **McKee** 1962 *Bb, W23*
B **Mckee** 1966 *Bl*, 1970 *Fj*
SS **McKeen** 2004 *US, J, EngA, US, F, It, E*, 2005 *US, J, W, EngA, F, R*, 2006 *S, US, US, W, It*, 2007 *US, NZ*
JR **McKellar** 1985 *A, A*, 1986 *J*, 1987 *W*
JH **McKenna** 1967 *E*
C **McKenzie** 1992 *US, E*, 1993 *E, US, A, W*, 1994 *US, F, W, E, F*, 1995 *S, Ur, Ar, Fj, NZ, R, SA*, 1996 *US, HK, J, J*, 1997 *J, HK, I*
SG **McTavish** 1970 *Fj*, 1971 *W*, 1976 *Bb*, 1977 *US, E, E*, 1978 *US, F*, 1979 *US, F*, 1980 *W, US*, 1981 *US, Ar*, 1982 *J, J, E, US*, 1985 *US*, 1987 *US, Tg, I*
R **McWhinney** 2005 *F, R*
J **Mensah-Coker** 2006 *S, E, US, Bar, US, W, It*, 2007 *US, NZ, Pt, J, A*, 2008 *US, I, W, S*, 2009 *US, US, J, J, Rus*, 2010 *Ur, Sp, Geo, Pt*, 2011 *Rus*
C **Michaluk** 1995 *SA*, 1996 *US, J*, 1997 *US, HK*
N **Milau** 2000 *US, J*
DRW **Milne** 1966 *Bl*, 1967 *E*
AB **Mitchell** 1932 *J, J*
P **Monaghan** 1982 *J*
AHB **Monro** 2006 *E, US, Bar, US, W, It*, 2007 *W, A*, 2008

US, Pt, I, W, 2009 *I, W, Geo, US, US, J, J, Rus*, 2010 *Ur, Bel, Pt*, 2011 *Rus, US, US, Tg, F, J, NZ*
D **Moonlight** 2003 *EngA*, 2004 *EngA, E*, 2005 *US*
JI **Moonlight** 2009 *Geo*
DL **Moore** 1962 *Bb, W23*
K **Morgan** 1997 *HK, HK, J, W*
VJP **Moroney** 1962 *Bb*
B **Mosychuk** 1996 *Ur*, 1997 *J*
J **Moyes** 1981 *Ar*, 1982 *J, J, E, US*
PT **Murphy** 2000 *Tg, US, SA, I, Sa, Fj, J*, 2001 *Fj, J*, 2002 *S, US, US, Ur, CHL, W, F*, 2003 *US, M, M*, 2004 *F*
WA **Murray** 1932 *J*
K **Myhre** 1970 *Fj*
J **Newton** 1962 *W23*
GN **Niblo** 1932 *J, J*
K **Nichols** 1996 *Ur*, 1998 *J, HK, US, US, Ur*, 1999 *J, Fj, Sa, US, Tg, Fj, Nm*, 2000 *Tg, US, SA, I, Sa, Fj, J, It*, 2001 *Ur, E, Fj, J*, 2002 *S*
D **Nikas** 1995 *Ur, Ar*
S **O'Leary** 2004 *US, J, EngA, E*, 2005 *US, J*
C **O'Toole** 2009 *I, US, J, J, Rus*, 2010 *Ur, Bel, Sp, Geo, Pt*, 2011 *Rus, US, US, Tg, F, J, NZ*, 2012 *US, It*
S **Pacey** 2005 *W*
C **Pack** 2006 *S, US*
J **Pagano** 1997 *I*, 1998 *J, HK, US, HK, J, US*, 1999 *J, Fj, Nm*
DV **Pahl** 1971 *W*
P **Palmer** 1983 *E*, 1984 *US*, 1985 *A*, 1986 *J, US*, 1987 *Tg, I, W*, 1988 *US*, 1990 *Ar, US*, 1991 *J, US, Fj, R, F*, 1992 *US*
K **Parfrey** 2005 *J*
TF **Paris** 2010 *Bel, Sp, Pt*
A **Pasutto** 2004 *US, J*
K **Peace** 1978 *F*, 1979 *US, F*, 1980 *W, US*
J **Penaluna** 1996 *Ur*
DN **Penney** 1995 *US*, 1996 *US, A, US, Ar*, 1997 *HK*, 1999 *E*
J **Phelan** 2010 *Bel, Sp, Pt*, 2012 *It, Geo*
JM **Phelan** 1980 *NZ*, 1981 *Ar*, 1982 *J, J*, 1985 *A, A*
M **Phinney** 2006 *S, E*
EC **Pinkham** 1932 *J*
C **Plater** 2003 *EngA*
D **Pletch** 2004 *US, J, EngA, It, E*, 2005 *US, J, W, EngA*, 2006 *S, E, US, Bar, US, W, It*, 2007 *US, NZ, Pt, W, Fj, J, A*, 2009 *US, US, J, J, Rus*, 2010 *Bel, Sp, Pt*
MT **Pletch** 2005 *Ar*, 2006 *S, E, US, Bar, W, It*, 2007 *US, NZ, Pt, W, J, A*, 2008 *US, Pt, I, W, S*, 2009 *W, Geo, US, US, J, Rus*, 2012 *It, Geo*
JG **Pritchard** 2003 *M, M, Ur, US, Ar, W, Tg*, 2006 *S, US, Bar, US, W*, 2007 *US, NZ, Pt, W, Fj, J, A*, 2008 *US, Pt, I, W, S*, 2009 *I, W, Geo, US, US, J, J, Rus*, 2010 *Ur, Sp, Geo, Pt*, 2011 *Rus, US, US, Tg, F, J*, 2012 *US, It, Geo*
G **Puil** 1962 *Bb, W23*
M **Pyke** 2004 *US, J, US, It*, 2005 *US, F, R*, 2006 *S, E, US, Bar, US, W, It*, 2007 *US, NZ, Pt, W, Fj, J, A*, 2008 *US*
DLJ **Quigley** 1976 *Bb*, 1979 *F*
RE **Radu** 1985 *A*, 1986 *US*, 1987 *US, Tg, I, US*, 1988 *US*, 1989 *I, US*, 1990 *Ar, Ar*, 1991 *US*
D **Ramsey** 2005 *US*
GL **Rees** 1986 *US*, 1987 *US, Tg, I, W, US*, 1989 *I, US*, 1990 *Ar, Ar*, 1991 *J, S, US, Fj, R, F, NZ*, 1992 *US, E*, 1993 *E, E, US, W*, 1994 *US, F, W, E, F*, 1995 *S, Fj, NZ, R, A, SA*, 1996 *HK, J*, 1997 *US, J, HK, W, I*, 1998 *US, US, Ur, US, Ar*, 1999 *Sa, Tg, W, E, F, Fj, Nm*
J **Reid** 2003 *M, US, Ar, NZ, Tg*
G **Relph** 1974 *Tg*
S **Richmond** 2004 *EngA, US, F, It, E*, 2005 *US, W, EngA, US*
PD **Riordan** 2003 *EngA*, 2004 *J, EngA, US*, 2006 *S, E, US, Bar, US, W, It*, 2007 *US, NZ, Pt, W, Fj, J, A*, 2008 *US, Pt, I, W, S*, 2009 *I, J, Rus*, 2010 *Ur, Bel, Sp, Geo, Pt*, 2011 *Rus, US, US, Tg, F, J, NZ*
JR **Robertsen** 1985 *A, A, US*, 1986 *US*, 1987 *US*, 1989 *I, US*, 1990 *Ar, US, Ar*, 1991 *Fj, F*
C **Robertson** 1997 *HK*, 1998 *US, US, HK, J, Ur*, 2001 *Ur*
AK **Robinson** 1998 *HK*
G **Robinson** 1966 *Bl*

247

CANADA

TOTAL RUGBY

Around the world in 30 minutes

The IRB's weekly
television and
radio programmes
broadcast in over
150 countries

ENGLAND

ENGLAND'S 2012 TEST RECORD

OPPONENTS	DATE	VENUE	RESULT
Scotland	4 Feb	A	Won 13–6
Italy	11 Feb	A	Won 19–15
England	25 Feb	H	Lost 12–19
France	11 Mar	A	Won 24–22
Ireland	17 Mar	H	Won 30–9
South Africa	9 Jun	A	Lost 22–17
South Africa	16 Jun	A	Lost 36–27
South Africa	23 Jun	A	Drew 14–14

ENGLAND REGAIN THE FEEL-GOOD FACTOR

By Will Greenwood

Stuart Lancaster has been key to the improvement of a young England side.

England began 2012 in a state of disarray after a difficult Rugby World Cup in New Zealand and the subsequent resignation of Martin Johnson as team manager, but by the end of the summer tour of South Africa I felt the team had put the setbacks behind them and genuinely looked in rude health.

England didn't win the Six Nations, or a Test against the Springboks, but Stuart Lancaster and his players did succeed in restoring a much-needed feel-good factor to English rugby. They reconnected with the fans and, with the foundations of the RFU firmly in place after a couple of years of political upheaval, the future is looking bright.

England as a team are still embroiled in a learning process at Test level, but I believe that as a group of players they are on the cusp of achieving something special. They will make mistakes along the way, but the current squad does remind me of the England set-up I was a part of back in 2000 as we built towards the Rugby World Cup three years later. The current England squad has its sights set on RWC 2015 and if they can achieve continuity in terms of both selection and results, they will be serious contenders on home soil.

It remains a long journey, but the sense of a fresh and exciting new start was palpable once Lancaster took up the reins.

The story of what was a turbulent few months for England began before Christmas when Johnson resigned. Personally, I was surprised he decided to step down, but there was a sense of inevitability about it all as the media clamour grew in the wake of events on and off the pitch at the Rugby World Cup. As a former team-mate of Johnno, I make no apologies for my bias and I thought he should have stayed on. It wasn't to be, though, and I thought he handled his departure with the same degree of dignity he showed throughout his playing career.

The decision to promote Lancaster from the Saxons set-up, initially as interim head coach, was the logical one. The names of Jim Mallinder and Nick Mallett were floated as possible replacements, but I felt Stuart was arguably the only man in a position to take the job and, if possession is nine tenths of the law, it wasn't a great shock when it was announced he had been appointed permanent head coach after what was a creditable and encouraging Six Nations campaign.

The news broke 12 days after England had comprehensively dismantled Ireland 30-9 at Twickenham, but I suspect it was his side's victory against the French in Paris a week earlier which actually sealed the deal.

I remember sitting inside the Stade de France about two hours before kick-off. It was a beautiful sunny day and I saw Stuart standing out in the middle with a big grin on his face and I texted him, asking if he was enjoying the atmosphere. He replied with something along the lines of there was nowhere else he wanted to be, and I think that positive attitude rubbed off on his players.

I thought Stuart hardly put a foot wrong from the moment he took the job. His decision to prepare for the Six Nations at West Park in Yorkshire rather than fly out to Portugal was a statement of intent and also I felt got the England fans back on side. It showed humility and was an intelligent move from both a rugby and PR perspective.

He handled the media with great assurance, but his most astute decision was the appointment of Chris Robshaw as his new captain. He was outstanding for England and more than justified Stuart's faith in him.

I know Chris from his playing days at Harlequins. He was coming through the Academy as I was coming to the end of my career at The Stoop and, although he was a quiet, understated youngster, there was definitely something about him. You could say I'm something of a long-term Robshaw cheerleader and I wrote a piece in 2009 in which I argued he was worth a place in the Lions squad for the tour of New Zealand that year.

It took him a little longer to make the breakthrough at Test level but his leadership, handling and distribution were superb and he looked every inch the man Stuart can build a team around going forward.

Some people have already anointed Sam Warburton as the Lions captain for the Australia tour in 2013, but if Chris continues to play like he did in 2012 Warren Gatland is going to have a pleasant dilemma when it comes to selecting his skipper.

In terms of the Six Nations, England could perhaps have won the Grand Slam had it not been for Scott Williams's steal from Courtney Lawes in the Wales game at Twickenham for the decisive try. England's luck ran out that day, but you could argue that they should have lost to Scotland at Murrayfield so I don't believe there was any great injustice overall.

The two standout performances were the victories over France and Ireland. They scored three tries in Paris to prove there was an attacking edge to their game, while the way they demolished Ireland was all about power up front. If England can put those two elements together on a consistent basis they will become very difficult to beat.

The tour to South Africa was something of a reality check in terms of the team's development, but it was not without positives. England learned that being a big fish in the northern hemisphere pond means absolutely nothing when you face the southern hemisphere in their own backyard but, however chastening, it's an important lesson nonetheless.

Beating Australia, New Zealand or South Africa away from home is the acid test for a Test side, and England showed in the summer that it is something they can achieve in the future.

England paid a heavy price for failing to get some of the basics right in the first Test in Durban and if you do that, the Springboks will steamroll you. It's brutal, ruthless rugby but you have to deal with it.

They looked dead and buried in the second Test at 25-10 down at half-time in Johannesburg, but their second-half fight-back will have given Stuart a lot of encouragement. England were supposed to roll over in the second 40 minutes, but the team showed a lot of character to eventually run South Africa close.

The 14-14 third Test draw was the highlight of the tour and was earned because England got themselves on a level footing early on. This time they didn't allow the Springboks to pull away and England showed in Port Elizabeth they had the skills and the nerve to compete in a tight, tense and low-scoring contest.

The other big plus of the tour was the number of new faces who came in and banked some invaluable experience in a hostile atmosphere. The likes of Joe Marler, Tom Johnson, Jonathan Joseph and Alex Goode are the future for England and they'll all be better, wiser players for their involvement on the tour.

The one criticism made of England under Lancaster has been their perceived inability to put together 80 minutes of rugby. That was probably particularly true in South Africa, but it's a confidence issue and the longer this group of players stay together and the more victories they record, the easier it will become.

I think Stuart's biggest dilemma moving forward is the No.10 issue. The fly half is the heartbeat of the side, the player who pulls all the strings and I'm not convinced England know whether Toby Flood or Owen Farrell is the man to go with.

Farrell's mental strength, his strong defence and his superb kicking put him in pole position during the Six Nations, but Flood was the man in possession by the end of the South Africa series. I think Flood is an underrated player and his awareness of space, his decision making and the way he instinctively knows when to release early and when to hang onto the ball are great attributes. They're contrasting talents but at some stage, fitness permitting, Stuart will have to decide who his number one is.

What I also like about the current England squad is the increasing competition for places. For example, at full back they have the option of Ben Foden, Mike Brown or Goode, who are all talented and exciting players. It's a coach's dream to have that flexibility and, speaking from my own experience, competition and rivalry within a squad is essential if you're going to achieve anything. England seem to have that now.

No doubt Stuart will happily nurture that sense of competition for another year or so and probably chop and change in terms of selection, but as the World Cup looms larger I expect he will have a much clearer idea of his strongest XV and we will see a more familiar starting line-up on a match-to-match basis.

It was overall a positive first seven months for the new regime. It wasn't faultless, but Stuart and his coaching staff have enough time to mould a young squad with plenty of potential for 2015 and ensure England are a team to be feared.

Will Greenwood is an England Rugby 2015 Ambassador

ENGLAND INTERNATIONAL STATISTICS

MATCH RECORDS UP TO 10 OCTOBER 2012

MOST CONSECUTIVE TEST WINS

14 2002 *W, It, Arg, NZ, A, SA*, 2003 *F1, W1, It, S, I, NZ, A, W2*
11 2000 *SA 2, A, Arg, SA3*, 2001 *W, It, S, F, C1, 2, US*
10 1882 *W*, 1883 *I, S*, 1884 *W, I, S*, 1885 *W, I*, 1886 *W, I*
10 1994 *R,C*, 1995 *I, F, W, S, Arg, It, WS, A*
10 2003 *F, Gg, SA, Sm, U, W, F, A*, 2004 *It, S*

MOST CONSECUTIVE TESTS WITHOUT DEFEAT

Matches	Wins	Draws	Period
14	14	0	2002 to 2003
12	10	2	1882 to 1887
11	10	1	1922 to 1924
11	11	0	2000 to 2001

MOST POINTS IN A MATCH
BY THE TEAM

Pts	Opponents	Venue	Year
134	Romania	Twickenham	2001
111	Uruguay	Brisbane	2003
110	Netherlands	Huddersfield	1998
106	USA	Twickenham	1999
101	Tonga	Twickenham	1999
84	Georgia	Perth	2003
80	Italy	Twickenham	2001

BY A PLAYER

Pts	Player	Opponents	Venue	Year
44	C Hodgson	Romania	Twickenham	2001
36	P J Grayson	Tonga	Twickenham	1999
35	J P Wilkinson	Italy	Twickenham	2001
32	J P Wilkinson	Italy	Twickenham	1999
30	C R Andrew	Canada	Twickenham	1994
30	P J Grayson	Netherlands	Huddersfield	1998
30	J P Wilkinson	Wales	Twickenham	2002
29	D J H Walder	Canada	Burnaby	2001
27	C R Andrew	South Africa	Pretoria	1994
27	J P Wilkinson	South Africa	Bloemfontein	2000
27	C C Hodgson	South Africa	Twickenham	2004
27	J P Wilkinson	Scotland	Twickenham	2007
26	J P Wilkinson	USA	Twickenham	1999

MOST TRIES IN A MATCH
BY THE TEAM

Tries	Opponents	Venue	Year
20	Romania	Twickenham	2001
17	Uruguay	Brisbane	2003
16	Netherlands	Huddersfield	1998
16	USA	Twickenham	1999
13	Wales	Blackheath	1881
13	Tonga	Twickenham	1999
12	Georgia	Perth	2003
12	Canada	Twickenham	2004
10	Japan	Sydney	1987
10	Fiji	Twickenham	1989
10	Italy	Twickenham	2001
10	Romania	Dunedin	2011

BY A PLAYER

Tries	Player	Opponents	Venue	Year
5	D Lambert	France	Richmond	1907
5	R Underwood	Fiji	Twickenham	1989
5	O J Lewsey	Uruguay	Brisbane	2003
4	G W Burton	Wales	Blackheath	1881
4	A Hudson	France	Paris	1906
4	R W Poulton	France	Paris	1914
4	C Oti	Romania	Bucharest	1989
4	J C Guscott	Netherlands	Huddersfield	1998
4	N A Back	Netherlands	Huddersfield	1998
4	J C Guscott	USA	Twickenham	1999
4	J Robinson	Romania	Twickenham	2001
4	N Easter	Wales	Twickenham	2007
4	C J Ashton	Italy	Twickenham	2011

MOST CONVERSIONS IN A MATCH
BY THE TEAM

Cons	Opponents	Venue	Year
15	Netherlands	Huddersfield	1998
14	Romania	Twickenham	2001
13	USA	Twickenham	1999
13	Uruguay	Brisbane	2003
12	Tonga	Twickenham	1999
9	Italy	Twickenham	2001
9	Georgia	Perth	2003
8	Romania	Bucharest	1989
8	Italy	Twickenham	2011
7	Wales	Blackheath	1881
7	Japan	Sydney	1987
7	Argentina	Twickenham	1990
7	Wales	Twickenham	1998
7	Wales	Twickenham	2007
7	Romania	Dunedin	2011

BY A PLAYER

Cons	Player	Opponents	Venue	Year
15	P J Grayson	Netherlands	Huddersfield	1998
14	C Hodgson	Romania	Twickenham	2001
13	J P Wilkinson	USA	Twickenham	1999
12	P J Grayson	Tonga	Twickenham	1999
11	P J Grayson	Uruguay	Brisbane	2003
9	J P Wilkinson	Italy	Twickenham	2001
8	S D Hodgkinson	Romania	Bucharest	1989
7	J M Webb	Japan	Sydney	1987
7	S D Hodgkinson	Argentina	Twickenham	1990
7	P J Grayson	Wales	Twickenham	1998
7	J P Wilkinson	Wales	Twickenham	2007

MOST PENALTIES IN A MATCH
BY THE TEAM

Penalties	Opponents	Venue	Year
8	South Africa	Bloemfontein	2000
7	Wales	Cardiff	1991
7	Scotland	Twickenham	1995
7	France	Twickenham	1999
7	Fiji	Twickenham	1999
7	South Africa	Paris	1999
7	South Africa	Twickenham	2001
7	Australia	Twickenham	2010
6	Wales	Twickenham	1986
6	Canada	Twickenham	1994
6	Argentina	Durban	1995
6	Scotland	Murrayfield	1996
6	Ireland	Twickenham	1996
6	South Africa	Twickenham	2000
6	Australia	Twickenham	2002
6	Wales	Brisbane	2003
6	Ireland	Twickenham	2012

BY A PLAYER

Penalties	Player	Opponents	Venue	Year
8	J P Wilkinson	South Africa	Bloemfontein	2000
7	S D Hodgkinson	Wales	Cardiff	1991
7	C R Andrew	Scotland	Twickenham	1995
7	J P Wilkinson	France	Twickenham	1999
7	J P Wilkinson	Fiji	Twickenham	1999
7	J P Wilkinson	South Africa	Twickenham	2001
7	T G A L Flood	Australia	Twickenham	2010
6	C R Andrew	Wales	Twickenham	1986
6	C R Andrew	Canada	Twickenham	1994
6	C R Andrew	Argentina	Durban	1995
6	P J Grayson	Scotland	Murrayfield	1996
6	P J Grayson	Ireland	Twickenham	1996
6	P J Grayson	South Africa	Paris	1999
6	J P Wilkinson	South Africa	Twickenham	2000
6	J P Wilkinson	Australia	Twickenham	2002
6	J P Wilkinson	Wales	Brisbane	2003
6	O A Farrell	Ireland	Twickenham	2012

ENGLAND

MOST DROP GOALS IN A MATCH
BY THE TEAM

Drops	Opponents	Venue	Year
3	France	Sydney	2003
2	Ireland	Twickenham	1970
2	France	Paris	1978
2	France	Paris	1980
2	Romania	Twickenham	1985
2	Fiji	Suva	1991
2	Argentina	Durban	1995
2	France	Paris	1996
2	Australia	Twickenham	2001
2	Wales	Cardiff	2003
2	Ireland	Dublin	2003
2	South Africa	Perth	2003
2	Samoa	Nantes	2007
2	Tonga	Paris	2007
2	Wales	Twickenham	2011
2	Argentina	Manchester	2009

BY A PLAYER

Drops	Player	Opponents	Venue	Year
3	J P Wilkinson	France	Sydney	2003
2	R Hiller	Ireland	Twickenham	1970
2	A G B Old	France	Paris	1978
2	J P Horton	France	Paris	1980
2	C R Andrew	Romania	Twickenham	1985
2	C R Andrew	Fiji	Suva	1991
2	C R Andrew	Argentina	Durban	1995
2	P J Grayson	France	Paris	1996
2	J P Wilkinson	Australia	Twickenham	2001
2	J P Wilkinson	Wales	Cardiff	2003
2	J P Wilkinson	Ireland	Dublin	2003
2	J P Wilkinson	South Africa	Perth	2003
2	J P Wilkinson	Samoa	Nantes	2007
2	J P Wilkinson	Tonga	Paris	2007
2	A J Goode	Argentina	Manchester	2009
2	J P Wilkinson	Wales	Twickenham	2011

CAREER RECORDS

MOST CAPPED PLAYERS

Caps	Player	Career Span
114	J Leonard	1990 to 2004
91	J P Wilkinson	1998 to 2011
85	R Underwood	1984 to 1996
85	L B N Dallaglio	1995 to 2007
84	M O Johnson	1993 to 2003
78	J P R Worsley	1999 to 2011
77	M J S Dawson	1995 to 2006
75	M J Catt	1994 to 2007
75	M J Tindall	2000 to 2011
73	P J Vickery	1998 to 2009
73	S G Thompson	2002 to 2011
72	W D C Carling	1988 to 1997
71	C R Andrew	1985 to 1997
71	R A Hill	1997 to 2004
71	L W Moody	2001 to 2011
71	S D Shaw	1996 to 2011
69	D J Grewcock	1997 to 2007
66	N A Back	1994 to 2003
65	J C Guscott	1989 to 1999
64	B C Moore	1987 to 1995
64	M E Corry	1997 to 2007
62	B J Kay	2001 to 2009
58	P J Winterbottom	1982 to 1993
57	B C Cohen	2000 to 2006
57	S W Borthwick	2001 to 2010
55	W A Dooley	1985 to 1993
55	W J H Greenwood	1997 to 2004
55	O J Lewsey	1998 to 2007
55	M J Cueto	2004 to 2011
54	G C Rowntree	1995 to 2006
51	A S Healey	1997 to 2003
51	K P P Bracken	1993 to 2003
51	J T Robinson	2001 to 2007
51	J M White	2000 to 2009

MOST CONSECUTIVE TESTS

Tests	Player	Span
44	W D C Carling	1989 to 1995
40	J Leonard	1990 to 1995
36	J V Pullin	1968 to 1975
33	W B Beaumont	1975 to 1982
30	R Underwood	1992 to 1996

MOST TESTS AS CAPTAIN

Tests	Captain	Span
59	W D C Carling	1988 to 1996
39	M O Johnson	1998 to 2003
22	L B N Dallaglio	1997 to 2004
21	W B Beaumont	1978 to 1982
21	S W Borthwick	2008 to 2010
17	M E Corry	2005 to 2007
15	P J Vickery	2002 to 2008
13	W W Wakefield	1924 to 1926
13	N M Hall	1949 to 1955
13	E Evans	1956 to 1958
13	R E G Jeeps	1960 to 1962
13	J V Pullin	1972 to 1975

MOST POINTS IN TESTS

Points	Player	Tests	Career
1179	J P Wilkinson	91	1998 to 2011
400	P J Grayson	32	1995 to 2004
396	C R Andrew	71	1985 to 1997
296	J M Webb	33	1987 to 1993
269	C C Hodgson	38	2001 to 2012
243	T G A L Flood	50	2006 to 2012
240	W H Hare	25	1974 to 1984
210	R Underwood	85	1984 to 1996

MOST TRIES IN TESTS

Tries	Player	Tests	Career
49	R Underwood	85	1984 to 1996
31	W J H Greenwood	55	1997 to 2004
31	B C Cohen	57	2000 to 2006
30	J C Guscott	65	1989 to 1999
28	J T Robinson	51	2001 to 2007
24	D D Luger	38	1998 to 2003
22	O J Lewsey	55	1998 to 2007
20	M J Cueto	55	2004 to 2011
18	C N Lowe	25	1913 to 1923
17	L B N Dallaglio	85	1995 to 2007
16	N A Back	66	1994 to 2003
16	M J S Dawson	77	1995 to 2006
15	A S Healey	51	1997 to 2003
15	C J Ashton	26	2010 to 2012
14	M J Tindall	75	2000 to 2011
13	T Underwood	27	1992 to 1998
13	I R Balshaw	35	2000 to 2008

MOST CONVERSIONS IN TESTS

Cons	Player	Tests	Career
162	J P Wilkinson	91	1998 to 2011
78	P J Grayson	32	1995 to 2004
44	C C Hodgson	38	2001 to 2012
41	J M Webb	33	1987 to 1993
35	S D Hodgkinson	14	1989 to 1991
35	T G A L Flood	50	2006 to 2012
33	C R Andrew	71	1985 to 1997
17	L Stokes	12	1875 to 1881

MOST PENALTY GOALS IN TESTS

Penalties	Player	Tests	Career
239	J P Wilkinson	91	1998 to 2011
86	C R Andrew	71	1985 to 1997
72	P J Grayson	32	1995 to 2004
67	W H Hare	25	1974 to 1984
66	J M Webb	33	1987 to 1993
50	T G A L Flood	50	2006 to 2012
44	C C Hodgson	38	2001 to 2012
43	S D Hodgkinson	14	1989 to 1991

MOST DROP GOALS IN TESTS

Drops	Player	Tests	Career
36	J P Wilkinson	91	1998 to 2011
21	C R Andrew	71	1985 to 1997
6	P J Grayson	32	1995 to 2004
4	J P Horton	13	1978 to 1984
4	L Cusworth	12	1979 to 1988
4	A J Goode	17	2005 to 2009

ENGLAND

INTERNATIONAL CHAMPIONSHIP RECORDS

RECORD	DETAIL	HOLDER	SET
Most points in season	229	in five matches	2001
Most tries in season	29	in five matches	2001
Highest Score	80	80–23 v Italy	2001
Biggest win	57	80–23 v Italy	2001
Highest score conceded	43	13–43 v Ireland	2007
Biggest defeat	30	13–43 v Ireland	2007
Most appearances	54	J Leonard	1991–2004
Most points in matches	546	J P Wilkinson	1998–2011
Most points in season	89	J P Wilkinson	2001
Most points in match	35	J P Wilkinson	v Italy, 2001
Most tries in matches	18	C N Lowe	1913–1923
	18	R Underwood	1984–1996
Most tries in season	8	C N Lowe	1914
Most tries in match	4	R W Poulton	v France, 1914
	4	C J Ashton	v Italy, 2011
Most cons in matches	89	J P Wilkinson	1998–2011
Most cons in season	24	J P Wilkinson	2001
Most cons in match	9	J P Wilkinson	v Italy, 2001
Most pens in matches	105	J P Wilkinson	1998–2011
Most pens in season	18	S D Hodgkinson	1991
	18	J P Wilkinson	2000
Most pens in match	7	S D Hodgkinson	v Wales, 1991
	7	C R Andrew	v Scotland, 1995
	7	J P Wilkinson	v France, 1999
Most drops in matches	11	J P Wilkinson	1998–2011
Most drops in season	5	J P Wilkinson	2003
Most drops in match	2	R Hiller	v Ireland, 1970
	2	A G B Old	v France, 1978
	2	J P Horton	v France, 1980
	2	P J Grayson	v France, 1996
	2	J P Wilkinson	v Wales, 2003
	2	J P Wilkinson	v Ireland, 2003

RECORD	HOLDER	DETAIL
Longest Test Career	S D Shaw	1996 to 2011
Youngest Test Cap	H C C Laird	18 yrs 134 days in 1927
Oldest Test Cap	F Gilbert	38 yrs 362 days in 1923

CAREER RECORDS OF ENGLAND INTERNATIONAL PLAYERS

UP TO 10 OCTOBER 2012

PLAYER BACKS:	DEBUT	CAPS	T	C	P	D	PTS
A O Allen	2006 v NZ	2	0	0	0	0	0
D A Armitage	2008 v PI	26	7	0	2	1	44
C J Ashton	2010 v F	26	15	0	0	0	75
M A Banahan	2009 v Arg	16	4	0	0	0	20
B M Barritt	2012 v S	7	0	0	0	0	0
M N Brown	2007 v SA	7	0	0	0	0	0
D S Care	2008 v NZ	33	4	0	0	1	23
L A W Dickson	2012 v S	7	0	0	0	0	0
O A Farrell	2012 v S	8	0	6	23	0	81
T G A L Flood	2006 v Arg	50	4	35	50	1	243
B J Foden	2009 v It	30	7	0	0	0	35
D A V Goode	2012 v SA	2	0	0	0	0	0
S E Hape	2010 v A	13	2	0	0	0	10
C C Hodgson	2001 v R	38	8	44	44	3	269
J B A Joseph	2012 v SA	3	0	0	0	0	0
Y C C Monye	2008 v PI	13	1	0	0	0	5
C D J Sharples	2011 v W	2	0	0	0	0	0
J P M Simpson	2011 v Gg	1	0	0	0	0	0
D Strettle	2007 v I	12	1	0	0	0	5
E M Tuilagi	2011 v W	13	5	0	0	0	25
J Turner-Hall	2012 v S	2	0	0	0	0	0
R E P Wigglesworth	2008 v It	12	1	0	0	0	5
B R Youngs	2010 v S	24	6	0	0	0	30

ENGLAND

FORWARDS:

D M J Attwood	2010 v NZ	2	0	0	0	0	0
M J Botha	2011 v W	9	0	0	0	0	0
D R Cole	2010 v W	31	1	0	0	0	5
A R Corbisiero	2011 v It	16	0	0	0	0	0
T R Croft	2008 v F	36	4	0	0	0	20
L P Deacon	2005 v Sm	29	0	0	0	0	0
P P L Doran-Jones	2009 v Arg	4	0	0	0	0	0
P D A Dowson	2012 v S	7	0	0	0	0	0
C H Fourie	2010 v NZ	8	0	0	0	0	0
D M Hartley	2008 v PI	42	1	0	0	0	5
J A W Haskell	2007 v W	43	4	0	0	0	20
T A Johnson	2012 v SA	3	0	0	0	0	0
C L Lawes	2009 v A	14	0	0	0	0	0
J W G Marler	2012 v SA	3	0	0	0	0	0
L A Mears	2005 v Sm	42	1	0	0	0	5
B J Morgan	2012 v S	7	0	0	0	0	0
M J Mullan	2010 v It	1	0	0	0	0	0
T P Palmer	2001 v US	40	0	0	0	0	0
G M W Parling	2012 v S	8	0	0	0	0	0
C D C Robshaw	2009 v Arg	8	0	0	0	0	0
M J H Stevens	2004 v NZ	44	0	0	0	0	0
T R Waldrom	2012 v SA	2	0	0	0	0	0
R W Webber	2012 v It	3	0	0	0	0	0

ENGLAND INTERNATIONAL PLAYERS
UP TO 10 OCTOBER 2012

Note: Years given for International Championship matches are for second half of season; eg 1972 means season 1971-72. Years for all other matches refer to the actual year of the match. Entries in square brackets denote matches played in RWC Finals.

Aarvold, C D (Cambridge U, W Hartlepool, Headingley, Blackheath) 1928 A, W, I, F, S, 1929 W, I, F, 1931 W, S, F, 1932 SA, W, I, S, 1933 W

Abbott, S R (Wasps, Harlequins) 2003 W2, F3, [Sm, U, W(R)], 2004 NZ1(t&R), 2, 2006 I, A2(R)

Abendanon, N A (Bath) 2007 SA2(R),F2

Ackford, P J (Harlequins) 1988 A, 1989 S, I, F, W, R, Fj, 1990 I, F, W, S, Arg 3, 1991 W, S, I, F, A, [NZ, It, F, S, A]

Adams, A A (London Hospital) 1910 F

Adams, F R (Richmond) 1875 I, S, 1876 S, 1877 I, 1878 S, 1879 S, I

Adebayo, A A (Bath) 1996, It, 1997 Arg 1,2, A 2, NZ 1, 1998 S

Adey, G J (Leicester) 1976 I, F

Adkins, S J (Coventry) 1950 I, F, S, 1953 W, I, F, S

Agar, A E (Harlequins) 1952 SA, W, S, I, F, 1953 W, I

Alcock, A (Guy's Hospital) 1906 SA

Alderson, F H R (Hartlepool R) 1891 W, I, S, 1892 W, S, 1893 W

Alexander, H (Richmond) 1900 I, S, 1901 W, I, S, 1902 W, I

Alexander, W (Northern) 1927 F

Allen, A O (Gloucester) 2006 NZ,Arg

Allison, D F (Coventry) 1956 W, I, S, F, 1957 W, 1958 W, S

Allport, A (Blackheath) 1892 W, 1893 I, 1894 W, I, S

Anderson, S (Rockcliff) 1899 I

Anderson, W F (Orrell) 1973 NZ 1

Anderton, C (Manchester FW) 1889 M

Andrew, C R (Cambridge U, Nottingham, Wasps, Toulouse, Newcastle) 1985 R, F, S, I, W, 1986 W, S, I, F, 1987 I, F, W, [J (R), US], 1988 S, I 1,2, A 1,2, Fj, A, 1989 S, I, F, W, R, Fj, 1990 I, F, W, S, Arg 3, 1991 W, S, I, F, Fj, A, [NZ, It, US, F, S, A], 1992 S, I, F, W, C, SA, 1993 F, W, NZ, 1994 S, I, F, W, SA 1,2, R, C, 1995 I, F, W, S, [Arg, It, A, NZ, F], 1997 W (R)

Appleford, G N (London Irish) 2002 Arg

Archer, G S (Bristol, Army, Newcastle) 1996 S, I, 1997 A 2, NZ 1, SA, NZ 2, 1998 F, W, S, I, A 1, NZ 1, H, It, 1999 Tg, Fj, 2000 I, F, W, It, S

Archer, H (Bridgwater A) 1909 W, F, I

Armitage, D A (London Irish) 2008 PI, A, SA, NZ3, 2009 It, W, I, F, S, Arg 1, 2, 2010 W, It, I, S, A2(R), NZ(R), A3(R), Sm(R), 2011 W2, 3(t&R), I2(R), [Arg, Gg, R(R), S]

Armitage, S E (London Irish) 2009 It,Arg 1,2, 2010 W(R),It(R)

Armstrong, R (Northern) 1925 W

Arthur, T G (Wasps) 1966 W, I

Ashby, **R C** (Wasps) 1966 I, F, 1967 A
Ashcroft, **A** (Waterloo) 1956 W, I, S, F, 1957 W, I, F, S, 1958 W, A, I, F, S, 1959 I, F, S
Ashcroft, **A H** (Birkenhead Park) 1909 A
Ashford, **W** (Richmond) 1897 W, I, 1898 S, W
Ashton, **C J** (Northampton) 2010 F, A1, 2, NZ, A3, Sm, SA, 2011 W1, It, F, S, I1, 2, [Arg, Gg, R, S, F], 2012 S, It, W, F, I, SA 1, 2, 3
Ashworth, **A** (Oldham) 1892 I
Askew, **J G** (Cambridge U) 1930 W, I, F
Aslett, **A R** (Richmond) 1926 W, I, F, S, 1929 S, F
Assinder, **E W** (O Edwardians) 1909 A, W
Aston, **R L** (Blackheath) 1890 S, I
Attwood, **D M J** (Gloucester) 2010 NZ(R),Sm(R)
Auty, **J R** (Headingley) 1935 S

Back, **N A** (Leicester) 1994 S, I, 1995 [Arg (t), It, WS], 1997 NZ 1(R), SA, NZ 2, 1998 F, W, S, I, H, It, A 2, SA 2, 1999 S, I, F, W, A, US, C, [It, NZ, Fj, SA], 2000 I, F, W, It, S, SA 1,2, A, Arg, SA 3, 2001 W, It, S, F, I, A, R, SA, 2002 S, I, F, W, It, NZ (t + R), A, SA, 2003 F 1, W 1, S, I, NZ, A, F 3, [Gg, SA, Sm, W, F, A]
Bailey, **M D** (Cambridge U, Wasps) 1984 SA 1,2, 1987 [US], 1989 Fj, 1990 I, F, S (R)
Bainbridge, **S** (Gosforth, Fylde) 1982 F, W, 1983 F, W, S, I, NZ, 1984 S, I, F, W, 1985 NZ 1,2, 1987 F, W, S, [J, US]
Baker, **D G S** (OMTs) 1955 W, I, F, S
Baker, **E M** (Moseley) 1895 W, I, S, 1896 W, I, S, 1897 W
Baker, **H C** (Clifton) 1887 W
Balshaw, **I R** (Bath, Leeds, Gloucester) 2000 I (R), F (R), It (R), S (R), A (R), Arg, SA 3(R), 2001 W, It, S, F, I, 2002 S (R), I (R), 2003 F2,3, [Sm, U, A(R)], 2004 It, S, I, 2005 It, S, 2006 A1, 2, NZ,Arg, 2007 It,SA1, 2008 W,It,F,S,I
Banahan, **M A** (Bath) 2009 Arg 1,2,A,Arg 3,NZ, 2010 Sm, SA(R), 2011 It(R), F(R), S(R), I1, W2, 3, [Gg(R), S(R), F(R)]
Bance, **J F** (Bedford) 1954 S
Barkley, **O J** (Bath) 2001 US (R), 2004 It(R), I(t), W, F, NZ2(R), A1(R), 2005 W(R), F, I, It, S, A(R), Sm(R), 2006 A1, 2(R), 2007 F2,3(R), [US,Sm,Tg], 2008 NZ1,2(R)
Barley, **B** (Wakefield) 1984 I, F, W, A, 1988 A 1,2, Fj
Barnes, **S** (Bristol, Bath) 1984 A, 1985 R (R), NZ 1,2, 1986 S (R), F (R), 1987 I (R), 1988 Fj, 1993 S, I
Barr, **R J** (Leicester) 1932 SA, W, I
Barrett, **E I M** (Lennox) 1903 S
Barrington, **T J M** (Bristol) 1931 W, I
Barrington-Ward, **L E** (Edinburgh U) 1910 W, I, F, S
Barritt, **B M** (Saracens) 2012 S,It,W,F,I,SA 1,3(t&R)
Barron, **J H** (Bingley) 1896 S, 1897 W, I
Bartlett, **J T** (Waterloo) 1951 W
Bartlett, **R M** (Harlequins) 1957 W, I, F, S, 1958 I, F, S
Barton, **J** (Coventry) 1967 I, F, W, 1972 F
Batchelor, **T B** (Oxford U) 1907 F
Bates, **S M** (Wasps) 1989 R
Bateson, **A H** (Otley) 1930 W, I, F, S
Bateson, **H D** (Liverpool) 1879 I
Batson, **T** (Blackheath) 1872 S, 1874 S, 1875 I
Batten, **J M** (Cambridge U) 1874 S
Baume, **J L** (Northern) 1950 S
Baxendell, **J J N** (Sale) 1998 NZ 2, SA 1
Baxter, **J** (Birkenhead Park) 1900 W, I, S
Bayfield, **M C** (Northampton) 1991 Fj, A 1992 S, I, F, W, C, SA, 1993 F, W, S, I, 1994 S, I, SA 1,2, R, C, 1995 I, F, W, S, [Arg, It, A, NZ, F], SA, WS, 1996 F, W
Bazley, **R C** (Waterloo) 1952 I, F, 1953 W, I, F, S, 1955 W, I, F, S
Beal, **N D** (Northampton) 1996 Arg, 1997 A 1, 1998 NZ 1,2, SA 1, H (R), SA 2, 1999 S, F (R), A (t), C (R), [It (R), Tg (R), Fj, SA]
Beaumont, **W B** (Fylde) 1975 I, A 1(R),2, 1976 A, W, S, I, F, 1977 S, I, F, W, 1978 F, W, S, I, NZ, 1979 S, I, F, W, NZ, 1980 I, F, W, S, 1981 W, S, I, F, Arg 1,2, 1982 A, S
Bedford, **H** (Morley) 1889 M, 1890 S, I
Bedford, **L L** (Headingley) 1931 W, I
Beer, **I D S** (Harlequins) 1955 F, S
Beese, **M C** (Liverpool) 1972 W, I, F
Beim, **T D** (Sale) 1998 NZ 1(R),2
Bell, **D S C** (Bath) 2005 It(R), S, 2009 A(R),Arg 3,NZ
Bell, **F J** (Northern) 1900 W
Bell, **H** (New Brighton) 1884 I
Bell, **J L** (Darlington) 1878 I
Bell, **P J** (Blackheath) 1968 W, I, F, S
Bell, **R W** (Northern) 1900 W, I, S
Bendon, **G J** (Wasps) 1959 W, I, F, S
Bennett, **N O** (St Mary's Hospital, Waterloo) 1947 W, S, F, 1948 A, W, I, S
Bennett, **W N** (Bedford, London Welsh) 1975 S, A1, 1976 S (R), 1979 S, I, F, W

Bennetts, **B B** (Penzance) 1909 A, W
Bentley, **J** (Sale, Newcastle) 1988 I 2, A 1, 1997 A 1, SA
Bentley, **J E** (Gipsies) 1871 S, 1872 S
Benton, **S** (Gloucester) 1998 A 1
Berridge, **M J** (Northampton) 1949 W, I
Berry, **H** (Gloucester) 1910 W, I, F, S
Berry, **J** (Tyldesley) 1891 W, I, S
Berry, **J T W** (Leicester) 1939 W, I, S
Beswick, **E** (Swinton) 1882 I, S
Biggs, **J M** (UCH) 1878 S, 1879 I
Birkett, **J G G** (Harlequins) 1906 S, F, SA, 1907 F, W, S, 1908 F, W,I , S, 1910 W, I, S, 1911 W, F, I , S, 1912 W, I , S, F
Birkett **L** (Clapham R) 1875 S, 1877 I, S
Birkett, **R H** (Clapham R) 1871 S, 1875 S, 1876 S, 1877 I
Bishop, **C C** (Blackheath) 1927 F
Black, **B H** (Blackheath) 1930 W, I, F, S, 1931 W, I, S, F, 1932 S, 1933 W
Blacklock, **J H** (Aspatria) 1898 I, 1899 I
Blakeway, **P J** (Gloucester) 1980 I, F, W, S, 1981 W, S, I, F, 1982 I, F, W, 1984 I, F, W, SA 1, 1985 R, F, S, I
Blakiston, **A F** (Northampton) 1920 S, 1921 W, I, S, F, 1922 W, 1923 S, F, 1924 W, I, F, S, 1925 NZ, W, I, S, F
Blatherwick, **T** (Manchester) 1878 I
Body, **J A** (Gipsies) 1872 S, 1873 S
Bolton, **C A** (United Services) 1909 F
Bolton, **R** (Harlequins) 1933 W, 1936 S, 1937 S, 1938 W, I
Bolton, **W N** (Blackheath) 1882 I, S, 1883 W, I, S, 1884 W, I, S, 1885 I, 1887 I, S
Bonaventura, **M S** (Blackheath) 1931 W
Bond, **A M** (Sale) 1978 NZ, 1979 S, I, NZ, 1980 I, 1982 I
Bonham-Carter, **E** (Oxford U) 1891 S
Bonsor, **F** (Bradford) 1886 W, I, S, 1887 W, S, 1889 M
Boobbyer, **B** (Rosslyn Park) 1950 W, I, F, S, 1951 W, F, 1952 S, I, F
Booth, **L A** (Headingley) 1933 W, I, S, 1934 S, 1935 W, I, S
Borthwick, **S W** (Bath, Saracens) 2001 F, C 1,2(R), US, R, 2003 A(t), W 2(t), F 2, 2004 I, F(R), NZ1(R), 2, A1, C, SA, A2, 2005 W(R), It(R), S(R), A, NZ, Sm, 2006 W, It, S, F, I, 2007 W2,F3, [SA1(t&R),Sm(R),Tg], 2008 W,It,F,S,I,NZ1,2,PI,A,SA,NZ3, 2009 It,W,I,F,S,Arg 1,2,A,Arg 3,NZ, 2010 W,It,I,S
Botha, **M J** (Saracens) 2011 W2(R), 2012 S,It,W,F,I,SA 1,2,3(R)
Botting, **I J** (Oxford U) 1950 W, I
Boughton, **H J** (Gloucester) 1935 W, I, S
Boyle, **C W** (Oxford U) 1873 S
Boyle, **S B** (Gloucester) 1983 W, S, I
Boylen, **F** (Hartlepool R) 1908 F, W, I, S
Bracken, **K P P** (Bristol, Saracens) 1993 NZ, 1994 S, I, C, 1995 I, F, W, S, [It, WS (t)], SA, 1996 It (R), 1997 Arg 1,2, A 2, NZ 1,2, 1998 F, W, 1999 S(R), I, F, A, 2000 SA 1,2, A, 2001 It (R), S (R), F (R), C 1,2, US, I (R), A, R (R), SA, 2002 S, I, F, W, It, 2003 W 1, It(R), I(t), NZ, A, F3, [SA, U(R), W(R), F(t&R)]
Bradby, **M S** (United Services) 1922 I, F
Bradley, **R** (W Hartlepool) 1903 W
Bradshaw, **H** (Bramley) 1892 S, 1893 W, I, S, 1894 W, I, S
Brain, **S E** (Coventry) 1984 SA 2, A (R), 1985 R, F, S, I, W, NZ 1,2, 1986 W, S, I, F
Braithwaite, **J** (Leicester) 1905 NZ
Braithwaite-Exley, **B** (Headingley) 1949 W
Brettargh, **A T** (Liverpool OB) 1900 W, 1903 I, S, 1904 W, I, S, 1905 I, S
Brewer, **J** (Gipsies) 1876 I
Briggs, **A** (Bradford) 1892 W, I, S
Brinn, **A** (Gloucester) 1972 W, I, S
Broadley, **T** (Bingley) 1893 W, S, 1894 W, I, S, 1896 S
Bromet, **W E** (Richmond) 1891 W, I, 1892 W, I, S, 1893 W, I, S, 1895 W, I, S, 1896 I
Brook, **P W P** (Harlequins) 1930 S, 1931 F, 1936 S
Brooke, **T J** (Richmond) 1968 F, S
Brooks, **F G** (Bedford) 1906 SA
Brooks, **M** (Oxford U) 1874 S
Brophy, **T J** (Liverpool) 1964 I, F, S, 1965 W, I, 1966 W, I, F
Brough, **J W** (Silloth) 1925 NZ, W
Brougham, **H** (Harlequins) 1912 W, I, S, F
Brown, **A A** (Exeter) 1938 S
Brown **A T** (Gloucester) 2006 A1, 2007 SA1,2
Brown, **L G** (Oxford U, Blackheath) 1911 W, F, I, S, 1913 SA, W, F, I, S, 1914 W, I, S, F, 1921 W, I, S, F, 1922 W
Brown, **M N** (Harlequins) 2007 SA1,2, 2008 NZ1, 2012 S(R),W(R),I(R),SA 1
Brown **S P** (Richmond) 1998 A 1, SA 1
Brown, **T W** (Bristol) 1928 S, 1929 W, I, S, F, 1932 S, 1933 W, I, S
Brunton, **J** (N Durham) 1914 W, I, S
Brutton, **E B** (Cambridge U) 1886 S

Cranmer, P (Richmond, Moseley) 1934 W, I, S, 1935 W, I, S, 1936 NZ, W, I, S, 1937 W, I, S, 1938 W, I, S

Creed, R N (Coventry) 1971 P

Cridlan, A G (Blackheath) 1935 W, I, S

Croft, T R (Leicester) 2008 F(R),S,I,NZ2(R),PI,A,SA(R),NZ3(R), 2009 It(R),W(R), I(R), F, S, A, Arg 3, NZ(R), 2010 A1, 2, NZ, A3, Sm(R), SA, 2011 S(R), I1(R), W2, I2, [Arg, Gg(R), R, S, F], 2012 S, It, W, F, I

Crompton, C A (Blackheath) 1871 S

Crompton, D E (Bristol) 2007 SA1(R)

Crosse, C W (Oxford U) 1874 S, 1875 I

Cueto, M J (Sale) 2004 C, SA, A2, 2005 W, F, I, It, S, A, NZ, Sm, 2006 W, It, S, F, I, SA1,2, 2007 W1,F3, [US,Sm,Tg,SA2], 2009 It,W,I,F,S,Arg 1,2,A,Arg 3,NZ, 2010 W, It, I, S, F, A1, 2, NZ, A3, Sm, SA, 2011 W1, It, F, S, I1, W2, 3, I2, [R,F]

Cumberlege, B S (Blackheath) 1920 W, I, S, 1921 W, I, S, F, 1922 W

Cumming, D C (Blackheath) 1925 S, F

Cunliffe, F L (RMA) 1874 S

Currey, F I (Marlborough N) 1872 S

Currie, J D (Oxford U, Harlequins, Bristol) 1956 W, I, S, F, 1957 W, I, F, S, 1958 W, A, I, F, S, 1959 W, I, F, S, 1960 W, I, F, S, 1961 SA, 1962 W, I, F

Cusani, D A (Orrell) 1987 I

Cusworth, L (Leicester) 1979 NZ, 1982 F, W, 1983 F, W, NZ, 1984 S, I, F, W, 1988 F, W

D'Aguilar, F B G (Royal Engineers) 1872 S

Dallaglio, L B N (Wasps) 1995 SA (R), WS, 1996 F, W, S, I, It, Arg, 1997 S, I, F, A 1,2, NZ 1, SA, NZ 2, 1998 F, W, S, I, A 2, SA 2, 1999 S, I, F, W, US, C, [It, NZ, Tg, Fj, SA], 2000 I, F, W, S, SA 1,2, A, Arg, SA 3, 2001 W, It, S, F, 2002 It (R), NZ, A (t), SA(R), 2003 F 1 (R), W 1, It, S, I, NZ, A, [Gg, SA, Sm, U, W, F, A], 2004 It, S, I, W, F, NZ1, 2, A1,2006 W(t&R), It(R), S(R), F(R), 2007 W2(R), F2, 3(R), [US, Tg(R), A(R), F(R), SA2(R)]

Dalton, T J (Coventry) 1969 S(R)

Danby, T (Harlequins) 1949 W

Daniell, J (Richmond) 1899 W, 1900 I, S, 1902 I, S, 1904 I, S

Darby, A J L (Birkenhead Park) 1899 I

Davenport, A (Ravenscourt Park) 1871 S

Davey, J (Redruth) 1908 S, 1909 W

Davey, R F (Teignmouth) 1931 W

Davidson, Jas (Aspatria) 1897 S, 1898 S, W, 1899 I, S

Davidson, Jos (Aspatria) 1899 W, S

Davies, G H (Cambridge U, Coventry, Wasps) 1981 S, I, F, Arg 1,2, 1982 A, S, I, 1983 F, W, S, 1984 S, SA 1,2, 1985 R (R), NZ 1,2, 1986 W, S, I, F

Davies, P H (Sale) 1927 I

Davies, V G (Harlequins) 1922 W, 1925 NZ

Davies, W J A (United Services, RN) 1913 SA, W, F, I, S, 1914 I, S, F, 1920 F, I, S, 1921 W, I, S, F, 1922 I, F, S, 1923 W, I, S, F

Davies, W P C (Harlequins) 1953 S, 1954 NZ, I, 1955 W, I, F, S, 1956 W, 1957 F, S, 1958 W

Davis, A M (Torquay Ath, Harlequins) 1963 W, I, S, NZ 1,2, 1964 NZ, W, I, F, S, 1966 W, 1967 A, 1969 SA, 1970 I, W, S

Dawe, R G R (Bath) 1987 I, F, W, [US], 1995 [WS]

Dawson, E F (RIEC) 1878 I

Dawson, M J S (Northampton, Wasps) 1995 WS, 1996 F, W, S, I, 1997 A 1, SA, NZ 2, 1998 W (R), S, I, NZ 1,2, SA 1, H, It, A 2, SA 2, 1999 S, F(R), W, A(R), US, C, [It, NZ, Tg, Fj (R), SA], 2000 I, F, W, It, S, A (R), Arg, SA 3, 2001 F, S, I, F, W, 2002 W (R), It (R), NZ, A, SA, 2003 It, S, I, A(R), F3(R), [Gg, Sm, W, F, A], 2004It(R), S(R), I, W, F, NZ1, 2(R), A1(R), 2005 W, F(R), I(R), It(R), S(R), A, NZ, 2006 W(R), It(R), S(t&R), F, I(R)

Day, H L V (Leicester) 1920 W, 1922 W, F, 1926 S

Deacon, L P (Leicester) 2005 Sm, 2006 A1, 2(R), 2007 S,It,I,F1(R),W1(R), 2009 Arg 1,2,A,Arg 3,NZ(R), 2010 W(R), It(R), I(R), S, F, 2011 W1, It, F, S, I1, W3, I2, [Arg, R, S, F]

Dean, G J (Harlequins) 1931 I

Dee, J M (Hartlepool R) 1962 S, 1963 NZ 1

Devitt, Sir T G (Blackheath) 1926 I, F, 1928 A, W

Dewhurst, J H (Richmond) 1887 W, I, S, 1890 W

De Glanville, P R (Bath) 1992 SA (R), 1993 W, NZ, 1994 S, I, F, W, SA 1,2, C (R), 1995 [Arg (R), It, WS], SA (R), 1996 W (R), I (R), It, 1997 S, I, F, W, Arg 1,2, A 1,2, NZ 1,2 1998 W (R), S (R), I (R), A 2, SA 2, 1999 A (R), US, [It, NZ, Fj (R), SA]

De Winton, R F C (Marlborough N) 1893 W

Dibble, R (Bridgwater A) 1906 S, F, SA, 1908 F, W, I, S, 1909 A, W, F, I, S, 1910 S, 1911 W, F, S, 1912 W, I, S

Dicks, J (Northampton) 1934 W, I, S, 1935 W, I, S, 1936 S, 1937 I

Dickson, L A W (Northampton) 2012 S(R),It(R),W,F,I,SA 1(R),2(R)

Dillon, E W (Blackheath) 1904 W, I, S, 1905 W

Dingle, A J (Hartlepool R) 1913 I, 1914 S, F

Diprose, A J (Saracens) 1997 Arg 1,2, A 2, NZ 1, 1998 W (R), S (R), I, A 1, NZ 2, SA 1

Dixon, P J (Harlequins, Gosforth) 1971 P, 1972 W, I, F, S, 1973 I, F, S, 1974 S, I, F, W, 1975 I, 1976 F, 1977 S, I, F, W, 1978 F, S, I, NZ

Dobbs, G E B (Plymouth Albion) 1906 W, I

Doble, S A (Moseley) 1972 SA, 1973 NZ 1, W

Dobson, D D (Newton Abbot) 1902 W, I, S, 1903 W, I, S

Dobson, T H (Bradford) 1895 S

Dodge, P W (Leicester) 1978 W, S, I, NZ, 1979 S, I, F, W, 1980 W, S, 1981 W, S, I, F, Arg 1,2, 1982 A, S, F, W, 1983 F, W, S, I, NZ, 1985 R, F, S, I, W, NZ 1,2

Donnelly, M P (Oxford U) 1947 I

Dooley, W A (Preston Grasshoppers, Fylde) 1985 R, F, S, I, W, NZ 2(R), 1986 W, S, I, F, 1987 F, W, [A, US, W], 1988 F, W, S, I 1,2 A 1,2, Fj, A, 1989 S, I, F, W, R, Fj, 1990 I, F, W, S, Arg 1,2,3, 1991 W, S, I, F, [NZ, US, F, S, A], 1992 S, I, F, W, C, SA, 1993 W, S, I

Doran-Jones, P P L (Gloucester, Northampton) 2009 Arg 3(R), 2011 S(R),I1(R), 2012 SA 1(R)

Dovey, B A (Rosslyn Park) 1963 W, I

Down, P J (Bristol) 1909 A

Dowson, A O (Moseley) 1899 S

Dowson, P D A (Northampton) 2012 S,It,W(R),F(R),I(R),SA 1(R),3(R)

Drake-Lee, N J (Cambridge U, Leicester) 1963 W, I, F, S, 1964 NZ, W, I, 1965 W

Duckett, H (Bradford) 1893 I, S

Duckham, D J (Coventry) 1969 I, F, S, W, SA, 1970 I, W, S, F, 1971 W, I, F, S (2[1C]), P, 1972 W, I, F, S, 1973 NZ 1, W, I, F, S, NZ 2, A, 1974 S, I, F, W, 1975 I, F, W, 1976 A, W, S

Dudgeon, H W (Richmond) 1897 S, 1898 I, S, W, 1899 W, I, S

Dugdale, J M (Ravenscourt Park) 1871 S

Dun, A F (Wasps) 1984 W

Duncan, R F H (Guy's Hospital) 1922 I, F, S

Duncombe, N S (Harlequins) 2002 S (R), I (R)

Dunkley, P E (Harlequins) 1931 I, S, 1936 NZ, W, I, S

Duthie, J (W Hartlepool) 1903 W

Dyson, J W (Huddersfield) 1890 S, 1892 S, 1893 I, S

Easter, N J (Harlequins) 2007 It, F1, SA1, 2, W2, F3, [SA1, Sm, Tg, A, F, SA2], 2008 It, F, S, I, PI, A, SA, NZ3, 2009 It, W, I, F, S, Arg 1, 2, 2010 W, It, I, S, F, A1, 2, NZ, A3, Sm, SA, 2011 W1,It, F, S, I1, W3, [Arg, S(t&R), F]

Ebdon, P J (Wellington) 1897 W, I

Eddison, J H (Headingley) 1912 W, I, S, F

Edgar, C S (Birkenhead Park) 1901 S

Edwards, R (Newport) 1921 W, I, S, F, 1922 W, F, 1923 W, 1924 W, F, S, 1925 NZ

Egerton, D W (Bath) 1988 I 2, A 1, Fj (R), A, 1989 Fj, 1990 I, Arg 2(R)

Elliot, C H (Sunderland) 1886 W

Elliot, E W (Sunderland) 1901 W, I, S, 1904 W

Elliot, W (United Services, RN) 1932 I, S, 1933 W, I, S, 1934 W, I

Elliott, A E (St Thomas's Hospital) 1894 S

Ellis, H A (Leicester) 2004 SA(R), A2(R), 2005 W(R), F, I, It, S, Sm, 2006 W, It, S, F(R), I, 2007 S, It, I, F1, W1, 2008 PI(R), A(R), SA(R), NZ3(R), 2009 It, W, I, F, S

Ellis, J (Wakefield) 1939 S

Ellis, S S (Queen's House) 1880 I

Emmott, C (Bradford) 1892 W

Enthoven, H J (Richmond) 1878 I

Erinle, A O (Biarritz) 2009 A(R),NZ

Estcourt, N S D (Blackheath) 1955 S

Evans, B J (Leicester) 1988 A 2, Fj

Evans, E (Sale) 1948 A, 1950 W, 1951 I, F, S, 1952 SA, W, S, I, F, 1953 I, F, S, 1954 W, I, F, 1956 W, I, S, F, 1957 W, I, F, S, 1958 W, A, I, F, S

Evans, G W (Coventry) 1972 S, 1973 W (R), F, S, NZ 2, 1974 S, I, F, W

Evans, N L (RNEC) 1932 W, I, S, 1933 W, I

Evanson, A M (Richmond) 1883 W, I, S, 1884 S

Evanson, W A D (Richmond) 1875 S, 1877 S, 1878 S, 1879 S, I

Evershed, F (Blackheath) 1889 M, 1890 W, S, I, 1892 W, I, S, 1893 W, I, S

Eyres, W C T (Richmond) 1927 I

Fagan, A R St L (Richmond) 1887 I

Fairbrother, K E (Coventry) 1969 I, F, S, W, SA, 1970 I, W, S, F, 1971 W, I, F

Faithfull, C K T (Harlequins) 1924 I, 1926 F, S

Fallas, H (Wakefield T) 1884 I

Farrell, A D (Saracens) 2007 S,It,I,W2,F3, [US(R),SA1,Tg(R)]

THE COUNTRIES

Farrell, O A (Saracens) 2012 S,It,W,F,I,SA 1,2(R),3(R)
Fegan, J H C (Blackheath) 1895 W, I, S
Fernandes, C W L (Leeds) 1881 I, W, S
Fidler, J H (Gloucester) 1981 Arg 1,2, 1984 SA 1,2
Fidler, R J (Gloucester) 1998 NZ 2, SA 1
Field, E (Middlesex W) 1893 W, I
Fielding, K J (Moseley, Loughborough Colls) 1969 I, F, S, SA, 1970 I, F, 1972 W, I, F, S
Finch, R T (Cambridge U) 1880 S
Finlan, J F (Moseley) 1967 I, F, S, W, NZ, 1968 W, I, 1969 I, F, S, W, 1970 F, 1973 NZ 1
Finlinson, H W (Blackheath) 1895 W, I, S
Finney, S (RIE Coll) 1872 S, 1873 S
Firth, F (Halifax) 1894 W, I, S
Flatman, D L (Saracens) 2000 SA 1(t),2(t+R), A (t), Arg (t+R), 2001 F (t), C 2(t+R), US (t+R), 2002 Arg
Fletcher, N C (OMTs) 1901 W, I, S, 1903 S
Fletcher, T (Seaton) 1897 W
Fletcher, W R B (Marlborough N) 1873 S, 1875 S
Flood, T G A L (Newcastle, Leicester) 2006 Arg(R),SA2(R), 2007 S(R), It(R), F1, W1, SA1, 2, W2(t), [A(R), F(R), SA2(R)], 2008 W, It, F, S, I, NZ2, PI(R), A(R), SA(R), NZ3, 2009 W, S(R), F, A1, 2,NZ, A3, Sm, SA, 2011 W1, It, F, S, I1, W3, I2(R), [Gg, R(R), S(R), F], 2012 W(R), SA 1(R), 2, 3
Flutey, R J (Wasps, Brive) 2008 PI, A, SA, NZ3, 2009 It, W, I, F, S, 2010 It, I, S, F, 2011 W2
Foden, B J (Northampton) 2009 It(R), 2010 I(R), S(R), F, A1, 2, NZ, A3, Sm, SA, 2011 W1, It, F, S, I1, W3, I2, [Arg, Gg, R, S, F], 2012 S, It, W, F, I, SA 1, 2, 3
Fookes, E F (Sowerby Bridge) 1896 W, I, S, 1897 W, I, S, 1898 I, W, 1899 I, S
Ford, P J (Gloucester) 1964 W, I, F, S
Forrest, J W (United Services, RN) 1930 W, I, F, S, 1931 W, I, S, F, 1934 I, S
Forrest, R (Wellington) 1899 W, 1900 S, 1902 I, S, 1903 I, S
Forrester, J (Gloucester) 2005 W(t), Sm(t&R)
Foulds, R T (Waterloo) 1929 W, I
Fourie, C H (Leeds, Sale) 2010 NZ(R), A3(R), Sm, SA(R), 2011 It(R), F(R), W3, I2
Fowler, F D (Manchester) 1878 S, 1879 S
Fowler, H (Oxford U) 1878 S, 1881 W, S
Fowler, R H (Leeds) 1877 I
Fox, F H (Wellington) 1890 W, S
Francis, T E S (Cambridge U) 1926 W, I, F, S
Frankcom, G P (Cambridge U, Bedford) 1965 W, I, F, S
Fraser, E C (Blackheath) 1875 I
Fraser, G (Richmond) 1902 W, I, S, 1903 W, I
Freakes, H D (Oxford U) 1938 W, 1939 W, I
Freeman, H (Marlborough N) 1872 S, 1873 S, 1874 S
French, R J (St Helens) 1961 W, I, F, S
Freshwater, P T (Perpignan) 2005 v Sm(R), 2006 S(t&R), I(R), Arg, 2007 S, It, I, F3, [SA1(R), Sm(R)]
Fry, H A (Liverpool) 1934 W, I, S
Fry, T W (Queen's House) 1880 I, S, 1881 W
Fuller, H G (Cambridge U) 1882 I, S, 1883 W, I, S, 1884 W

Gadney, B C (Leicester, Headingley) 1932 I, S, 1933 I, S, 1934 W, I, S, 1935 I, S, 1936 NZ, W, I, S, 1937 S, 1938 W
Gamlin, H T (Blackheath) 1899 W, S, 1900 W, I, S, 1901 S, 1902 W, I, S, 1903 W, I, S, 1904 W, I, S
Gardner, E R (Devonport Services) 1921 W, I, S, 1922 W, I, F, 1923 W, I, S, F
Gardner, H P (Richmond) 1878 I
Garforth, D J (Leicester) 1997 W (R), Arg 1,2, A 1, NZ 1, SA, NZ 2, 1998 F, W (R), S, I, H, It, A 2, SA 2, 1999 S, I, F, W, A, C (R), [It (R), NZ (R), Fj], 2000 It
Garnett, H W T (Bradford) 1877 S
Gavins, M N (Leicester) 1961 W
Gay, D J (Bath) 1968 W, I, F, S
Gent, D R (Gloucester) 1905 NZ, 1906 W, I, 1910 W, I
Genth, J S M (Manchester) 1874 S, 1875 S
George, J T (Falmouth) 1947 S, F, 1949 I
Geraghty, S J J (London Irish, Northampton) 2007 F1(R), W1(R), 2009 It(R), A, Arg 3, NZ(R)
Gerrard, R A (Bath) 1932 SA, W, I, S, 1933 W, I, S, 1934 W, I, S, 1936 NZ, W, I, S
Gibbs, G A (Bristol) 1947 F, 1948 I
Gibbs, J C (Harlequins) 1925 NZ, W, 1926 F, 1927 W, I, S, F
Gibbs, N (Harlequins) 1954 S, F
Giblin, L F (Blackheath) 1896 W, I, 1897 S
Gibson, A S (Manchester) 1871 S
Gibson, C O P (Northern) 1901 W
Gibson, G R (Northern) 1899 W, 1901 S

Gibson, T A (Northern) 1905 W, S
Gilbert, F G (Devonport Services) 1923 W, I
Gilbert, R (Devonport A) 1908 W, I, S
Giles, J L (Coventry) 1935 W, I, 1937 W, I, 1938 I, S
Gittings, W J (Coventry) 1967 NZ
Glover, P B (Bath) 1967 A, 1971 F, P
Godfray, R E (Richmond) 1905 NZ
Godwin, H O (Coventry) 1959 F, S, 1963 S, NZ 1,2, A, 1964 NZ, I, F, S, 1967 NZ
Gomarsall, A C T (Wasps, Bedford, Gloucester, Harlequins) 1996 It, Arg, 1997 S, I, F, Arg 2(R) 2000 It (R), 2002 Arg, SA(R), 2003 F 1, W 1(R),2, F2(R), [Gg(R), U], 2004 It, S, NZ1(R), 2, A1, C, SA, A2, 2007 SA1,2,F2(R),3(R), [SA1(R),Sm,Tg,A,F,SA2], 2008 W,It
Goode, A J (Leicester, Brive) 2005 It(R), S(R), 2006 W(R), F(R), I, A1(R), 2, SA1(R),2, 2009 It,W,I(R),F(R),S(R),Arg1,2,3(R)
Goode, D A V (Saracens) 2012 SA2(R),3
Gordon-Smith, G W (Blackheath) 1900 W, I, S
Gotley, A L H (Oxford U) 1910 F, S, 1911 W, F, I, S
Graham, D (Aspatria) 1901 W
Graham, H J (Wimbledon H) 1875 I, S, 1876 I, S
Graham, J D G (Wimbledon H) 1876 I
Gray, A (Otley) 1947 W, I, S
Grayson, P J (Northampton) 1995 WS, 1996 F, W, S, I, 1997 S, I, F, A 2(t), SA (R), NZ 2, 1998 F, W, S, I, H, It, A 2, 1999 I, [NZ (R), Tg, Fj, SA], 2003 S(R), I(t), F2, 3(R), [Gg(R), U], 2004 It, S, I
Green, J (Skipton) 1905 I, 1906 S, F, SA, 1907 F, W, I, S
Green, J F (West Kent) 1871 S
Green, W R (Wasps) 1997 A 2, 1998 NZ 1(t+R), 1999 US (R), 2003 W 2(R)
Greening, P B T (Gloucester, Wasps) 1996 It (R), 1997 W (R), Arg 1 1998 NZ 1(R),2(R), 1999 A (R), US, C, [It (R), NZ (R), Tg, Fj, SA], 2000 I, F, W, It, S, SA 1,2, A, 2001 F, I
Greenstock, N J J (Wasps) 1997 Arg 1,2, A 1, SA
Greenwell, J H (Rockcliff) 1893 W, I
Greenwood, J E (Cambridge U, Leicester) 1912 F, 1913 SA, W, F, I, S, 1914 W, S, F, 1920 W, F, I, S
Greenwood, J R H (Waterloo) 1966 I, F, S, 1967 A, 1969 I
Greenwood, W J H (Leicester, Harlequins) 1997 A 2, NZ 1, SA, NZ 2, 1998 F, W, S, I, H, It, 1999 C, [It, Tg, Fj, SA], 2000 Arg (R), SA 3, 2001 W, It, S, F, I, A, R, SA, 2002 S, I, F, W, It, NZ, A, SA, 2003 F 1, W 1, It, S, I(R), I (t), W 2, F 2, [U], 2004 It, S, W, F, NZ1, 2(R), C, SA, A2(R)
Greg, W (Manchester) 1876 I, S
Gregory, G G (Bristol) 1931 I, S, F, 1932 SA, W, I, S, 1933 W, I, S, 1934 W, I, S
Gregory, J A (Blackheath) 1949 W
Grewcock, D J (Coventry, Saracens, Bath) 1997 Arg 2, SA, 1998 W (R), I (R), A 1, NZ 1, NZ 2(R), 1999 S (R), A (R), US, C, [It, NZ, Tg (R), SA], 2000 SA 1,2, A, Arg, SA 3, 2001 W, It, S, I, A, R, SA 2002 S, A, 2003 F 1, W 1, It, S, I (R), W 2, F 2, [U], 2004 It, S, W, F, NZ1, 2, C, A, 2005 W, F, I, It, S, A2, 2006 W, F, 1 (R), W 1, It, S (R), I (t), 2, F 2, [U], 2004 It, S, W, F, NZ1, 2(R), C, SA, A2(R)
Grylls, W M (Redruth) 1905 I
Guest, R H (Waterloo) 1939 W, I, S, 1947 W, I, S, F, 1948 A, W, I, S, 1949 F, S
Guillemard, A G (West Kent) 1871 S, 1872 S
Gummer, C H A (Plymouth A) 1929 F
Gunner, C R (Marlborough N) 1876 I
Gurdon, C (Richmond) 1880 I, S, 1881 I, W, S, 1882 I, S, 1883 S, 1884 W, S, 1885 I, 1886 W, I, S
Gurdon, E T (Richmond) 1878 S, 1879 I, 1880 S, 1881 I, W, S, 1882 S, 1883 W, I, S, 1884 W, I, S, 1885 W, I, 1886 S
Guscott, J C (Bath) 1989 R, Fj, 1990 I, F, W, S, Arg 3, 1991 W, S, I, F, [NZ, It, F, S, A], 1992 S, I, F, W, C, SA, 1993 F, W, S, I, 1994 S, I, F, W, C (R), SA 1,2, R, 1995 I, F, W, S, [Arg, It, WS, A, NZ, F], SA, WS, 1996 F, W, S, I, 1997 S, I, F, W, A 1, 2, 1999 S, I, F, A, US, C, [It (R), NZ, Tg]

Haag, M (Bath) 1997 Arg 1,2
Haigh, L (Manchester) 1910 W, I, S, 1911 W, F, I, S
Hale, P M (Moseley) 1969 SA, 1970 I, W
Hall, C (Gloucester) 1901 I, S
Hall, J (N Durham) 1894 W, I, S
Hall, J P (Bath) 1984 S (R), I, F, SA 1,2, A, 1985 R, F, S, I, W, NZ 1,2, 1986 W, S, 1987 I, F, W, S, 1990 Arg 3, 1994 S
Hall, N M (Richmond) 1947 W, I, S, F, 1949 W, I, 1952 SA, W, S, I, F, 1953 W, I, F, S, 1955 W, I
Halliday, S J (Bath, Harlequins) 1986 W, S, 1987 S, 1988 S, I 1,2, A 1, A, 1989 S, I, F, W, R, Fj (R), 1990 W, S, 1991 [US, S, A], 1992 S, I, F, W
Hamersley, A St G (Marlborough N) 1871 S, 1872 S, 1873 S, 1874 S

Hyde, J P (Northampton) 1950 F, S
Hynes, W B (United Services, RN) 1912 F

Ibbitson, E D (Headingley) 1909 W, F, I, S
Imrie, H M (Durham City) 1906 NZ, 1907 I
Inglis, R E (Blackheath) 1886 W, I, S
Irvin, S H (Devonport A) 1905 W
Isherwood, F W (Ravenscourt Park) 1872 S

Jackett, E J (Leicester, Falmouth) 1905 NZ, 1906 W, I, S, F, SA, 1907 W, I, S, 1909 W, F, I, S
Jackson, A H (Blackheath) 1878 I, 1880 I
Jackson, B S (Broughton Park) 1970 S (R), F
Jackson, P B (Coventry) 1956 W, I, F, 1957 W, I, F, S, 1958 W, A, F, S, 1959 W, I, F, S, 1961 S, 1963 W, I, F, S
Jackson, W J (Halifax) 1894 S
Jacob, F (Cambridge U) 1897 W, I, S, 1898 I, S, W, 1899 W, I
Jacob, H P (Blackheath) 1924 W, I, F, S, 1930 F
Jacob, P G (Blackheath) 1898 I
Jacobs, C R (Northampton) 1956 W, I, S, F, 1957 W, I, F, S, 1958 W, A, I, F, S, 1960 W, I, F, S, 1961 SA, W, I, F, S, 1963 NZ 1,2, A, 1964 W, I, F, S
Jago, R A (Devonport A) 1906 W, I, SA, 1907 W, I
Janion, J P A G (Bedford) 1971 W, I, F, S (2[1C]), P, 1972 W, S, SA, 1973 A, 1975 A 1,2
Jarman, J W (Bristol) 1900 W
Jeavons, N C (Moseley) 1981 S, I, F, Arg 1,2, 1982 A, S, I, F, W, 1983 F, W, S, I
Jeeps, R E G (Northampton) 1956 W, 1957 W, I, F, S, 1958 W, A, I, F, S, 1959 I, 1960 W, I, F, S, 1961 SA, W, I, F, S, 1962 W, I, F, S
Jeffery, G L (Blackheath) 1886 W, I, S, 1887 W, I, S
Jennins, C R (Waterloo) 1967 A, I, F
Jewitt, J (Hartlepool R) 1902 W
Johns, W A (Gloucester) 1909 W, F, I, S, 1910 W, I, F
Johnson, M O (Leicester) 1993 F, NZ, 1994 S, I, F, W, R, C, 1995 I, F, W, S, [Arg, It, WS, A, NZ, F], SA, WS, 1996 F, W, S, I, It, Arg, 1997 S, I, F, W, A 2, NZ 1,2, 1998 F, W, S, I, H, It, A 2, SA 2, 1999 S, I, F, W, A, US, C, [It, NZ, Tg, Fj, SA], 2000 SA 1,2, A, Arg, SA 3, 2001 W, It, S, F, SA, 2002 S, I, F, It (t+R), NZ, A, SA, 2003 F 1, W 1, S, I, NZ, A, F 3, [Gg, SA, Sm, U(R),W, F, A]
Johnson, T A (Exeter) 2012 SA 1,2,3
Johnston, J B (Saracens) 2002 Arg, NZ (R)
Johnston, W R (Bristol) 1910 W, I, S, 1912 W, I, S, F, 1913 SA, W, F, I, S, 1914 W, I, S, F
Jones, C M (Sale) 2004 It(R), S, I(R), W, NZ1, 2005 W, 2006 A1(R), 2, SA1(R),2, 2007 SA1, 2(R)
Jones, F P (New Brighton) 1893 S
Jones, H A (Barnstaple) 1950 W, I, F
Jorden, A M (Cambridge U, Blackheath, Bedford) 1970 F, 1973 I, F, S, 1974 F, 1975 W, S
Joseph, J B A (London Irish) 2012 SA 1(R),2,3
Jowett, D (Heckmondwike) 1889 M, 1890 S, I, 1891 W, I, S
Judd, P E (Coventry) 1962 W, I, F, S, 1963 S, NZ 1,2, A, 1964 NZ, 1965 I, F, S, 1966 W, I, F, S, 1967 A, I, F, S, W, NZ

Kay, B J (Leicester) 2001 C 1,2, A, R, SA (t+R), 2002 S, I, F, W, It, Arg, NZ (R), A, SA, 2003 F 1, W 1, It, S, I, NZ, A, F 3, [Gg, SA, Sm, W, F, A], 2004 It, S, I, W, F, C(R), SA(R), 2005 W, F, I, It, S, 2006 A2, NZ, Arg, SA1,2(R), 2007 F2, [US,SA1,Sm,Tg,A,F, SA2], 2008 W(R), It(R), F(R), S(R), I(R), NZ1(R), 2(R), 2009 Arg 1(R), 2(t&R)
Kayll, H E (Sunderland) 1878 S
Keeling, J H (Guy's Hospital) 1948 A, W
Keen, B W (Newcastle U) 1968 W, I, F, S
Keeton, G H (Leicester) 1904 W, I, S
Kelly, G A (Bedford) 1947 W, I, S, 1948 W
Kelly, T S (London Devonians) 1906 W, I, S, F, SA, 1907 F, W, I, S, 1908 F, I, S
Kemble, A T (Liverpool) 1885 W, I, 1887 I
Kemp, D T (Blackheath) 1935 W
Kemp, T A (Richmond) 1937 W, I, 1939 S, 1948 A, W
Kendall, P D (Birkenhead Park) 1901 S, 1902 W, 1903 S
Kendall-Carpenter, J MacG K (Oxford U, Bath) 1949 I, F, S, 1950 W, I, F, S, 1951 I, F, S, 1952 SA, W, S, I, F, 1953 W, I, F, S, 1954 W, NZ, I, F
Kendrew, D A (Leicester) 1930 W, I, 1933 I, S, 1934 S, 1935 W, I, 1936 NZ, W, I
Kennedy, N J (London Irish) 2008 PI,NZ3, 2009 It,W,I,F(R),S(R)
Kennedy, R D (Camborne S of M) 1949 I, F, S
Kent, C P (Rosslyn Park) 1977 S, I, F, W, 1978 F (R)
Kent, T (Salford) 1891 W, I, S, 1892 W, I, S
Kershaw, C A (United Services, RN) 1920 W, F, I, S, 1921 W, I, S, F, 1922 W, I, F, S, 1923 W, I, S, F

Kewley, E (Liverpool) 1874 S, 1875 S, 1876 I, S, 1877 I, S, 1878 S
Kewney, A L (Leicester) 1906 W, I, S, F, 1909 A, W, F, I, S, 1911 W, F, I, S, 1912 I, S, 1913 SA
Key, A (O Cranleighans) 1930 I, 1933 W
Keyworth, M (Swansea) 1976 A, W, S, I
Kilner, B (Wakefield T) 1880 I
Kindersley, R S (Exeter) 1883 W, 1884 S, 1885 W
King, A D (Wasps) 1997 Arg 2(R), 1998 SA 2(R), 2000 It (R), 2001 C 2(R), 2003 W2
King, I (Harrogate) 1954 W, NZ, I
King, J A (Headingley) 1911 W, F, I, S, 1912 W, I, S, 1913 SA, W, F, I, S
King, Q E M A (Army) 1921 S
Kingston, P (Gloucester) 1975 A 1,2, 1979 I, F, W
Kitching, A E (Blackheath) 1913 I
Kittermaster, H J (Harlequins) 1925 NZ, W, I, 1926 W, I, F, S
Knight, F (Plymouth) 1909 A
Knight, P M (Bristol) 1972 F, S, SA
Knowles, E (Millom) 1896 S, 1897 S
Knowles, T C (Birkenhead Park) 1931 S
Krige, J A (Guy's Hospital) 1920 W

Labuschagne, N A (Harlequins, Guy's Hospital) 1953 W, 1955 W, I, F, S
Lagden, R O (Richmond) 1911 S
Laird, H C C (Harlequins) 1927 W, I, S, 1928 A, W, I, F, S, 1929 W, I
Lambert, D (Harlequins) 1907 F, 1908 F, W, S, 1911 W, F, I
Lampkowski, M S (Headingley) 1976 A, W, S, I
Lapage, W N (United Services, RN) 1908 F, W, I, S
Larter, P J (Northampton, RAF) 1967 A, NZ, 1968 W, I, F, S, 1969 I, F, S, W, SA, 1970 I, W, F, S, 1971 W, I, F, S (2[1C]), P, 1972 SA, 1973 NZ 1, W
Law, A F (Richmond) 1877 S
Law, D E (Birkenhead Park) 1927 I
Lawes, C L (Northampton) 2009 A(R), 2010 S(R), A1(R), 2, NZ, A3, Sm, SA, 2011 W3, I2, [Arg,S,F(R)], 2012 W(R)
Lawrence, Hon H A (Richmond) 1873 S, 1874 S, 1875 I, S
Lawrie, P W (Leicester) 1910 S, 1911 S
Lawson, R G (Workington) 1925 I
Lawson, T M (Workington) 1928 A, W
Leadbetter, M M (Broughton Park) 1970 F
Leadbetter, V H (Edinburgh Wands) 1954 S, F
Leake, W R M (Harlequins) 1891 W, I, S
Leather, G (Liverpool) 1907 I
Lee, F H (Marlborough N) 1876 S, 1877 I
Lee, H (Blackheath) 1907 F
Le Fleming, J (Blackheath) 1887 W
Leonard, J (Saracens, Harlequins) 1990 Arg 1,2,3, 1991 W, S, I, F, Fj, A, [NZ, It, US, F, S, A], 1992 S, I, F, W, C, SA, 1993 F, W, S, I, NZ, 1994 S, I, F, W, SA 1,2, R, C, 1995 I, F, W, S, [Arg, It, A, NZ, F], SA, WS, 1996 F, W, S, I, It, Arg, 1997 S, I, F, W, A 2, NZ 1, SA, NZ 2, 1998 F, W, S, I, H, It, A 2 SA 2, 1999 S, I, F, W, A, C (R), [It, NZ, Fj, SA], 2000 I, F, W, It, S, SA 1,2, A, Arg, SA 3, 2001 W, It, S, F, I, R, 2002 S (R), I (R), F (R), It (R), A, SA 2003 F 1, S, I, NZ, W 2, F 2(t+R), 3(R), [Gg(t&R), SA(R), Sm, U, W, F(t&R), A(R)], 2004 It(R)
Leslie-Jones, F A (Richmond) 1895 W, I
Lewis, A O (Bath) 1952 SA, W, S, I, F, 1953 W, I, F, S, 1954 F
Lewsey, O J (Wasps) 1998 NZ 1,2, SA 1, 2001 C 1,2, US, 2003 It, S, I, NZ, A, F2, 3(t+R), [Gg, SA, U, F, A], 2004 It, S, I, W, F, NZ1, 2, A1, C, SA, A2, 2005 W, F, I, It, S, A, NZ, Sm, 2006 W, S, F,Arg(R), SA1,2, 2007 S,It,I,F1,2,3, [US,SA1,Sm,Tg,A,F]
Leyland, R (Waterloo) 1935 W, I, S
Linnett, M S (Moseley) 1989 Fj
Lipman, M R (Bath) 2004 NZ2(R), A1(R), 2006 A2, 2008 It,F,S,I,PI(R),A(R),NZ3
Livesay, R O'H (Blackheath) 1898 W, 1899 W
Lloyd, L D (Leicester) 2000 SA 1(R),2(R), 2001 C 1,2, US
Lloyd, R H (Harlequins) 1967 NZ, 1968 W, I, F, S
Locke, H M (Birkenhead Park) 1923 S, F, 1924 W, F, S, 1925 W, I, S, F, 1927 W, I, S, 1928 A, F, S
Lockwood, R E (Heckmondwike) 1887 W, I, S, 1889 M, 1891 W, I, S, 1892 W, I, S, 1893 W, I, 1894 W, I
Login, S H M (RN Coll) 1876 I
Lohden, F C (Blackheath) 1893 W
Long, A E (Bath) 1997 A 2, 2001 US (R)
Longland, R J (Northampton) 1932 S, 1933 W, S, 1934 W, I, S, 1935 W, I, S, 1936 NZ, W, I, S, 1937 W, I, S, 1938 W, I, S
Lowe, C N (Cambridge U, Blackheath) 1913 SA, W, F, I, S, 1914 W, I, S, F, 1920 W, F, I, S, 1921 W, I, S, F, 1922 W, I, F, S, 1923 W, I, S, F

Lowrie, F W (Wakefield T) 1889 M, 1890 W
Lowry, W M (Birkenhead Park) 1920 F
Lozowski, R A P (Wasps) 1984 A
Luddington, W G E (Devonport Services) 1923 W, I, S, F, 1924 W, I, F, S, 1925 W, I, S, F, 1926 W
Luger, D D (Harlequins, Saracens) 1998 H, It, SA 2, 1999 S, I, F, W, A, US, C, [It, NZ, Tg, Fj, SA], 2000 SA 1, A, Arg, SA 3, 2001 W, I, A, R, SA, 2002 F (R), W, It, 2003 F 1, W 1, It, S (R), I (R), NZ(R), W 2, [Gg(R), SA(R), U, W]
Lund, M B (Sale) 2006 A1, 2(R), NZ(R), Arg(t&R), 2007 S, It, I, F1(R),W1(R), SA2
Luscombe, F (Gipsies) 1872 S, 1873 S, 1875 I, S, 1876 I, S
Luscombe, J H (Gipsies) 1871 S
Luxmoore, A F C C (Richmond) 1900 S, 1901 W
Luya, H F (Waterloo, Headingley) 1948 W, I, S, F, 1949 W
Lyon, A (Liverpool) 1871 S
Lyon, G H d'O (United Services, RN) 1908 S, 1909 A

McCanlis, M A (Gloucester) 1931 W, I
McCarthy, N (Gloucester) 1999 I (t), US (R), 2000 It (R)
McFadyean, C W (Moseley) 1966 I, F, S, 1967 A, I, F, S, W, NZ, 1968 W, I
MacIlwaine, A H (United Services, Hull & E Riding) 1912 W, I, S, F, 1920 I
Mackie, O G (Wakefield T, Cambridge U) 1897 S, 1898 I
Mackinlay, J E H (St George's Hospital) 1872 S, 1873 S, 1875 I
MacLaren, W (Manchester) 1871 S
MacLennan, R R F (OMTs) 1925 I, S, F
McLeod, N F (RIE Coll) 1879 S, I
Madge, R J P (Exeter) 1948 A, W, I, S
Malir, F W S (Otley) 1930 W, I, S
Mallett, J A (Bath) 1995 [WS (R)]
Mallinder, J (Sale) 1997 Arg 1,2
Mangles, R H (Richmond) 1897 W, I
Manley, D C (Exeter) 1963 W, I, F, S
Mann, W E (United Services, Army) 1911 W, F, I
Mantell, N D (Rosslyn Park) 1975 A 1
Mapletoft, M S (Gloucester) 1997 Arg 2
Markendale, E T (Manchester R) 1880 I
Marler, J W G (Harlequins) 2012 SA 1,2,3
Marques, R W D (Cambridge U, Harlequins) 1956 W, I, S, F, 1957 W, I, F, S, 1958 W, A, I, F, S, 1959 W, I, F, S, 1960 W, I, F, S, 1961 SA, W
Marquis, J C (Birkenhead Park) 1900 I, S
Marriott, C J B (Blackheath) 1884 W, I, S, 1886 W, I, S, 1887 I
Marriott, E E (Manchester) 1876 I
Marriott, V R (Harlequins) 1963 NZ 1,2, A, 1964 NZ
Marsden, G H (Morley) 1900 W, I, S
Marsh, H (RIE Coll) 1873 S
Marsh, J (Swinton) 1892 I
Marshall, H (Blackheath) 1893 W
Marshall, M W (Blackheath) 1873 S, 1874 S, 1875 I, S, 1876 I, S, 1877 I, S, 1878 S, I
Marshall, R M (Oxford U) 1938 I, S, 1939 W, I, S
Martin, C R (Bath) 1985 F, S, I, W
Martin, N O (Harlequins) 1972 F (R)
Martindale, S A (Kendal) 1929 F
Massey, E J (Leicester) 1925 W, I, S
Mather, B-J (Sale) 1999 W
Mathias, J L (Bristol) 1905 W, I, S, NZ
Matters, J C (RNE Coll) 1899 S
Matthews, J R C (Harlequins) 1949 F, S, 1950 I, F, S, 1952 SA, W, S, I, F
Maud, P (Blackheath) 1893 W, I
Maxwell, A W (New Brighton, Headingley) 1975 A 1, 1976 A, W, S, I, F, 1978 F
Maxwell-Hyslop, J E (Oxford U) 1922 I, F, S
May, T A (Newcastle) 2009 Arg 1,2
Maynard, A F (Cambridge U) 1914 W, I, S
Mears, L A (Bath) 2005 Sm(R), W(R), It(R), F(R), I, A1, 2(R), NZ(R), Arg(R), SA1(R), 2, 2007 S(R), It(R), I(R), W1(R), F2(R), 3(R), [Tg(R)], 2008 W(R), It(R), F(R), S, I, NZ1, 2, PI, A, SA, NZ3, 2009 It, W, I, F, S, 2010 I(R), 2011 W2(R), 3(R), [R(R)], 2012 I(R), SA 1(R), 2(R), 3(t)
Meikle, G W C (Waterloo) 1934 W, I, S
Meikle, S S C (Waterloo) 1929 S
Mellish, F W (Blackheath) 1920 W, F, I, S, 1921 W, I
Melville, N D (Wasps) 1984 A, 1985 I, W, NZ 1,2, 1986 W, S, I, F, 1988 F, W, S, I 1
Merriam, L P B (Blackheath) 1920 W, F
Michell, A T (Oxford U) 1875 I, S, 1876 I
Middleton, B B (Birkenhead Park) 1882 I, 1883 I
Middleton, J A (Richmond) 1922 S

Miles, J H (Leicester) 1903 W
Millett, H (Richmond) 1920 F
Mills, F W (Marlborough N) 1872 S, 1873 S
Mills, S G F (Gloucester) 1981 Arg 1,2, 1983 W, 1984 SA 1, A
Mills, W A (Devonport A) 1906 W, I, S, F, SA, 1907 F, W, I, S, 1908 F, W
Milman, D L K (Bedford) 1937 W, 1938 W, I, S
Milton, C H (Camborne S of M) 1906 I
Milton, J G (Camborne S of M) 1904 W, I, S, 1905 S, 1907 I
Milton, W H (Marlborough N) 1874 S, 1875 I
Mitchell, F (Blackheath) 1895 W, I, S, 1896 W, I, S
Mitchell, W G (Richmond) 1890 W, S, I, 1891 W, I, S, 1893 S
Mobbs, E R (Northampton) 1909 A, W, F, I, S, 1910 I, F
Moberley, W O (Ravenscourt Park) 1872 S
Monye, Y C C (Harlequins) 2008 PI,A,SA,NZ3, 2009 F,S,A,Arg 3,NZ, 2010 W,It,I,S
Moody, L W (Leicester, Bath) 2001 C 1,2, US, I (R), R, SA (R), 2002 I (R), W, It, Arg, NZ, A, SA, 2003 F 1, W 2, F 2, 3(R), [Gg(R), SA, Sm(R), U, W, F(R), A(R)], 2004 C, SA, A2, 2005 F, I, It, S, A, NZ, Sm, 2006 W, It, S, F, I, A1, NZ, Arg, SA1(R), 2(R), W2(R), 2007 [US(R), SA1(R), Sm(R), Tg, A, F,SA2], 2008 W, 2009 A, Arg 3, NZ, 2010 W, It, I, S(R), F, A1, 2, NZ, A3, SA, 2011 W2, [Gg, R, S, F]
Moore, B C (Nottingham, Harlequins) 1987 S, [A, J, W], 1988 F, W, S, I 1,2, A 1, 2, Fj, A, 1989 S, I, F, W, R, Fj, 1990 I, F, W, S, Arg 1,2, 1991 W, S, I, F, Fj, A, [NZ, It, F, S, A], 1992 S, I, F, W, SA, 1993 F, W, S, I, NZ, 1994 S, I, F, W, SA 1,2, R, C, 1995 I, F, W, S, [Arg, It, WS (R), A, NZ, F]
Moore, E J (Blackheath) 1883 I, S
Moore, N J N H (Bristol) 1904 W, I, S
Moore, P B C (Blackheath) 1951 W
Moore, W K T (Leicester) 1947 W, I, 1949 F, S, 1950 I, F, S
Mordell, R J (Rosslyn Park) 1978 W
Morfitt, S (W Hartlepool) 1894 W, I, S, 1896 W, I, S
Morgan, B J (Scarlets) 2012 S(R),It(R),W,F,I,SA 1,2
Morgan, J R (Hawick) 1920 W
Morgan, O C (Gloucester) 2007 S,I
Morgan, W G D (Medicals, Newcastle) 1960 W, I, F, S, 1961 SA, W, I, F, S
Morley, A J (Bristol) 1972 SA, 1973 NZ 1, W, I, 1975 S, A 1,2
Morris, A D W (United Services, RN) 1909 A, W, F
Morris, C D (Liverpool St Helens, Orrell) 1988 A, 1989 S, I, F, W, 1992 S, I, F, W, C, SA, 1993 F, W, S, I, 1994 F, W, SA 1,2, R, 1995 S (t), [Arg, WS, A, NZ, F]
Morris, R (Northampton) 2003 W 1, It
Morrison, P H (Cambridge U) 1890 W, S, I, 1891 I
Morse, S (Marlborough N) 1873 S, 1874 S, 1875 S
Mortimer, W (Marlborough N) 1899 W
Morton, H J S (Blackheath) 1909 I, S, 1910 W, I
Moss, F (Broughton) 1885 W, I, 1886 W
Mullan, M J (Worcester) 2010 It(R)
Mullins, A R (Harlequins) 1989 Fj
Mycock, J (Sale) 1947 W, I, S, F, 1948 A
Myers, E (Bradford) 1920 I, S, 1921 W, I, 1922 W, I, F, S, 1923 W, I, S, F, 1924 W, I, F, S, 1925 S, F
Myers, H (Keighley) 1898 I

Nanson, W M B (Carlisle) 1907 F, W
Narraway, L J W (Gloucester) 2008 W,It(R),S(R),NZ1,2, 2009 W(R),I(R)
Nash, E H (Richmond) 1875 I
Neale, B A (Rosslyn Park) 1951 I, F, S
Neale, M E (Blackheath) 1912 F
Neame, S (O Cheltonians) 1879 S, I, 1880 I, S
Neary, A (Broughton Park) 1971 W, I, F, S (2[1C]), P, 1972 W, I, F, S, SA, 1973 NZ 1, W, I, F, S, NZ 2, A, 1974 S, I, F, W, 1975 I, F, W, S, A 1, 1976 A, W, S, I, F, 1977 I, 1978 F (R), 1979 S, I, F, W, NZ, 1980 I, F, W, S
Nelmes, B G (Cardiff) 1975 A 1,2, 1978 W, S, I, NZ
Newbold, C J (Blackheath) 1904 W, I, S, 1905 W, I, S
Newman, S C (Oxford U) 1947 F, 1948 A, W
Newton, A W (Blackheath) 1907 S
Newton, P A (Blackheath) 1882 S
Newton-Thompson, J O (Oxford U) 1947 S, F
Nichol, W (Brighouse R) 1892 W, S
Nicholas, P L (Exeter) 1902 W
Nicholson, B E (Harlequins) 1938 W, I
Nicholson, E S (Leicester) 1935 W, I, S, 1936 NZ, W
Nicholson, E T (Birkenhead Park) 1900 W, I
Nicholson, T (Rockcliff) 1893 I
Ninnes, B F (Coventry) 1971 W
Noon, J D (Newcastle) 2001 C 1,2, US, 2003 W 2, F 2(t+R), 2005 W, F, I, It, S, A, NZ, 2006 W, It, S, F, I, 2006 A1(R), 2, NZ, Arg,

267
ENGLAND

SA1,2, 2007 SA2, F2, [US, SA1], 2008 lt, F, S, I, NZ1(R), 2, Pl, A, SA, NZ3, 2009 lt

Norman, D J (Leicester) 1932 SA, W
North, E H G (Blackheath) 1891 W, I, S
Northmore, S (Millom) 1897 I
Novak, M J (Harlequins) 1970 W, S, F
Novis, A L (Blackheath) 1929 S, F, 1930 W, I, F, 1933 I, S

Oakeley, F E (United Services, RN) 1913 S, 1914 I, S, F
Oakes, R F (Hartlepool R) 1897 W, I, S, 1898 I, S, W, 1899 W, S
Oakley, L F L (Bedford) 1951 W
Obolensky, A (Oxford U) 1936 NZ, W, I, S
Ojo, T O (London Irish) 2008 NZ1,2
Ojomoh, S O (Bath, Gloucester) 1994 I, F, SA 1(R),2, R, 1995 S (R), [Arg, WS, A (t), F], 1996 F, 1998 NZ 1
Old, A G B (Middlesbrough, Leicester, Sheffield) 1972 W, I, F, S, SA, 1973 NZ 2, A, 1974 S, I, F, W, 1975 I, A 2, 1976 S, I, 1978 F
Oldham, W L (Coventry) 1908 S, 1909 A
Olver, C J (Northampton) 1990 Arg 3, 1991 [US], 1992 C
O'Neill, A (Teignmouth, Torquay A) 1901 W, I, S
Openshaw, W E (Manchester) 1879 I
Orwin, J (Gloucester, RAF, Bedford) 1985 R, F, S, I, W, NZ 1,2, 1988 F, W, S, I 1,2, A 1,2
Osborne, R R (Manchester) 1871 S
Osborne, S H (Oxford U) 1905 S
Oti, C (Cambridge U, Nottingham, Wasps) 1988 S, I 1, 1989 S, I, F, W, R, 1990 Arg 1,2, 1991 Fj, A, [NZ, It]
Oughtred, B (Hartlepool R) 1901 S, 1902 W, I, S, 1903 W, I
Owen, J E (Coventry) 1963 W, I, F, S, A, 1964 NZ, 1965 W, I, F, S, 1966 I, S, 1967 NZ
Owen-Smith, H G O (St Mary's Hospital) 1934 W, I, S, 1936 NZ, W, I, S, 1937 W, I, S

Page, J J (Bedford, Northampton) 1971 W, I, F, S, 1975 S
Paice, D J (London Irish) 2008 NZ1(R),2(R)
Pallant, J N (Notts) 1967 I, F, S
Palmer, A C (London Hospital) 1909 I, S
Palmer, F H (Richmond) 1905 W
Palmer, G V (Richmond) 1928 I, F, S
Palmer, J A (Bath) 1984 SA 1,2, 1986 I (R)
Palmer, T P (Leeds, Wasps, Stade Français) 2001 US (R), 2006 Arg(R), SA1,2, 2007 It(R), I(R), F1, W1, 2008 NZ1, 2, Pl(R), A, SA, 2010 F(R), A1, 2, NZ, A3, Sm, SA, 2011 W1, It, F, S, I1, W2, 3(R), I2(R), [Arg(R), Gg, R, S(R), F], 2012 S, It, F(R), I(R), SA 1(R), 2(R), 3
Pargetter, T A (Coventry) 1962 S, 1963 F, NZ 1
Parker, G W (Gloucester) 1938 I, S
Parker, Hon S (Liverpool) 1874 S, 1875 S
Parling, G M W (Leicester) 2012 S(R),It(R),W,F,I,SA 1,2,3
Parsons, E I (RAF) 1939 S
Parsons, M J (Northampton) 1968 W, I, F, S
Patterson, W M (Sale) 1961 SA, S
Pattisson, R M (Blackheath) 1883 I, S
Paul, H (Gloucester) 2002 F(R), 2004 It(t&R), S(R), C, SA, A2
Paul, J E (RIE Coll) 1875 S
Payne, A T (Bristol) 1935 I, S
Payne, C M (Harlequins) 1964 I, F, S, 1965 I, F, S, 1966 W, I, F, S
Payne, J H (Broughton) 1882 S, 1883 W, I, S, 1884 I, 1885 W, I
Payne, T A N (Wasps) 2004 A1, 2006 A1(R), 2(R), 2007 F1, W1, 2008 It, NZ1(R), 2, SA, NZ3, 2009 A 1, 2, A, Arg 3, NZ, 2010 W, It, I, S, F, A1, 2
Pearce, G S (Northampton) 1979 S, I, F, W, 1981 Arg 1,2, 1982 A, S, 1983 F, W, S, I, NZ, 1984 S, SA 2, A, 1985 R, F, S, I, W, NZ 1,2, 1986 W, S, I, F, 1987 I, F, W, S, [A, US, W], 1988 Fj, 1991 [US]
Pears, D (Harlequins) 1990 Arg 1,2, 1992 F (R), 1994 F
Pearson, A W (Blackheath) 1875 I, S, 1876 I, S, 1877 S, 1878 S, I
Peart, T G A H (Hartlepool R) 1964 F, S
Pease, F E (Hartlepool R) 1887 I
Penny, S H (Leicester) 1909 A
Penny, W J (United Hospitals) 1878 I, 1879 S, I
Percival, L J (Rugby) 1891 I, 1892 I, 1893 S
Periton, H G (Waterloo) 1925 W, 1926 W, I, F, S, 1927 W, I, S, F, 1928 A, I, F, S, 1929 W, I, S, F, 1930 W, I, F, S
Perrott, E S (O Cheltonians) 1875 I
Perry, D G (Bedford) 1963 F, S, NZ 1,2, A 1964 NZ, W, I, 1965 W, I, F, S, 1966 W, I, F
Perry, M B (Bath) 1997 A 2, NZ 1, SA, NZ 2, 1998 W, S, I, A 1, NZ 1,2, SA 1, H, It, A 2, 1999 I, F, W, A US, C, [It, NZ, Tg, Fj, SA], 2000 I, F, W, S, SA 1,2, A, SA 3, 2001 W, F (R)
Perry, S A (Bristol) 2006 NZ, Arg, SA1(R), 2(R), 2007 I(R), F1(R), W1(R), SA1(R), 2(R), W2, F2, 3, [US, SA1]
Perry, S V (Cambridge U, Waterloo) 1947 W, I, 1948 A, W, I, S, F

Peters, J (Plymouth) 1906 S, F, 1907 I, S, 1908 W
Phillips, C (Birkenhead Park) 1880 S, 1881 I, S
Phillips, M S (Fylde) 1958 A, I, F, S, 1959 W, I, F, S, 1960 W, I, F, S, 1961 W, 1963 W, I, F, S, NZ 1,2, A, 1964 NZ, W, I, F, S
Pickering, A S (Harrogate) 1907 I
Pickering, R D A (Bradford) 1967 I, F, S, W, 1968 F, S
Pickles, R C W (Bristol) 1922 I, F
Pierce, N (Liverpool) 1898 I, 1903 S
Pilkington, W N (Cambridge U) 1898 S
Pillman, C H (Blackheath) 1910 W, I, F, S, 1911 W, F, I, S, 1912 W, F, 1913 SA, W, F, I, S, 1914 W, I, S
Pillman, R L (Blackheath) 1914 F
Pinch, J (Lancaster) 1896 W, I, 1897 S
Pinching, W W (Guy's Hospital) 1872 S
Pitman, I J (Oxford U) 1922 S
Plummer, K C (Bristol) 1969 W, 1976 S, I, F
Pool-Jones, R J (Stade Francais) 1998 A 1
Poole, F O (Oxford U) 1895 W, I, S
Poole, R W (Hartlepool R) 1896 S
Pope, E B (Blackheath) 1931 W, S, F
Portus, G V (Blackheath) 1908 F, I
Potter, S (Leicester) 1998 A 1(t)
Poulton, R W (later Poulton Palmer) (Oxford U, Harlequins, Liverpool) 1909 F, I, S, 1910 W, 1911 S, 1912 W, I, S, 1913 SA, W, F, I, S, 1914 W, I, S, F
Powell, D L (Northampton) 1966 W, I, 1969 I, F, S, W, 1971 W, I, F, S (2[1C])
Pratten, W E (Blackheath) 1927 S, F
Preece, I (Coventry) 1948 I, S, F, 1949 F, I, S, 1950 W, I, F, S, 1951 W, I, F
Preece, P S (Coventry) 1972 SA, 1973 NZ 1, W, I, F, S, NZ 2, 1975 I, F, W, A 2, 1976 W (R)
Preedy, M (Gloucester) 1984 SA 1
Prentice, F D (Leicester) 1928 I, F, S
Prescott, R E (Harlequins) 1937 W, I, 1938 I, 1939 W, I, S
Preston, N J (Richmond) 1979 NZ, 1980 I, F
Price, H L (Harlequins) 1922 I, S, 1923 W, I
Price, J (Coventry) 1961 I
Price, P L A (RIE Coll) 1877 I, S, 1878 S
Price, T W (Cheltenham) 1948 S, F, 1949 W, I, F, S
Probyn, J A (Wasps, Askeans) 1988 F, W, S, I 1,2, A 1, 2, A, 1989 S, I, R (R), 1990 I, F, W, S, Arg 1,2,3, 1991 W, S, I, F, Fj, A, [NZ, It, F, S, A], 1992 S, I, F, W, 1993 F, W, S, I
Prout, D H (Northampton) 1968 W, I
Pullin, J V (Bristol) 1966 W, 1968 W, I, F, S, 1969 I, F, S, W, SA, 1970 I, W, S, F, 1971 W, I, F, S (2[1C]), P, 1972 W, I, F, S, SA, 1973 NZ 1, W, I, F, S, NZ 2, A, 1974 S, I, F, W, 1975 I, W (R), S, A 1,2, 1976 F
Purdy, S J (Rugby) 1962 S
Pyke, J (St Helens Recreation) 1892 W
Pym, J A (Blackheath) 1912 W, I, S, F

Quinn, J P (New Brighton) 1954 W, NZ, I, S, F

Rafter, M (Bristol) 1977 S, F, W, 1978 F, W, S, I, NZ, 1979 S, I, F, W, NZ, 1980 W(R), 1981 W, Arg 1,2
Ralston, C W (Richmond) 1971 S (C), P, 1972 W, I, F, S, SA, 1973 NZ 1, W, I, F, S, NZ 2 2, A, 1974 S, I, F, W, 1975 I, F, W, S
Ramsden, H E (Bingley) 1898 S, W
Ranson, J M (Rosslyn Park) 1963 NZ 1,2, A, 1964 W, I, F, S
Raphael, J E (OMTs) 1902 W, I, S, 1905 W, S, NZ, 1906 W, S, F
Ravenscroft, J (Birkenhead Park) 1881 I
Ravenscroft, S C W (Saracens) 1998 A 1, NZ 2(R)
Rawlinson, W C W (Blackheath) 1876 S
Redfern, S P (Leicester) 1984 I (R)
Redman, N C (Bath) 1984 A, 1986 S (R), 1987 I, S, [A, J, W], 1988 Fj, 1990 Arg 1,2, 1991 Fj, [It, US], 1993 NZ, 1994 F, W, SA 1,2, 1997 Arg 1, A 1
Redmond, G F (Cambridge U) 1970 F
Redwood, B W (Bristol) 1968 W, I
Rees, D L (Sale) 1997 A 2, NZ 1, SA, NZ 2, 1998 F, W, SA 2(R), 1999 S, I, F, A
Rees, G W (Nottingham) 1984 SA 2(R), A, 1986 I, F, 1987 F, W, S, [A, J, US, W], 1988 S (R), I 1,2, A 1,2, Fj, 1989 W (R), R (R), Fj (R), 1990 Arg 3(R), 1991 Fj, [US]
Rees, T (Wasps) 2007 S(R), It(R), I(R), F1, W1, F3, [US, SA1], 2008 W(R), NZ1, 2, Pl, A, SA, NZ3(R)
Reeve, J S R (Harlequins) 1929 F, 1930 W, I, F, S, 1931 W, I, S, F
Regan, M (Liverpool) 1953 W, I, F, S, 1954 W, NZ, I, S, F, 1956 I, S, F
Regan, M P (Bristol, Bath, Leeds) 1995 SA, WS, 1996 F, W, S, I, It, Arg, 1997 S, I, F, W, A 1, NZ 2(R), 1998 F, 2000 SA 1(t), A(R), Arg, SA 3(t), 2001 It(R), S(R), C 2(R), R, 2003 F 1(t), It(R), W 2,

[Gg(R), Sm], 2004 It(R), I(R), NZ1(R), 2, A1, 2007 SA1,2,W2, F2, 3, [US, SA1, A, F, SA2], 2008 W, It, F
Rendall, P A G (Wasps, Askeans) 1984 W, SA 2, 1986 W, S, 1987 I, F, S, [A, J, W], 1988 F, W, S, I 1,2, A 1,2, A, 1989 S, I, F, W, R, 1990 I, F, W, S, 1991 [It (R)]
Rew, H (Blackheath) 1929 S, F, 1930 F, S, 1931 W, S, F, 1934 W, I, S
Reynolds, F J (O Cranleighans) 1937 S, 1938 I, S
Reynolds, S (Richmond) 1900 W, I, S, 1901 I
Rhodes, J (Castleford) 1896 W, I, S
Richards, D (Leicester) 1986 I, F, 1987 S, [A, J, US, W], 1988 F, W, S, I 1, A 1,2, Fj, A, 1989 S, I, F, W, R, 1990 Arg 3, 1991 W, S, I, F, Fj, A, [NZ, It, US], 1992 S (R), F, W, C, 1993 NZ, 1994 W, SA 1, C, 1995 I, F, W, S, [WS, A, NZ], 1996 F (t), S, I
Richards, E E (Plymouth A) 1929 S, F
Richards, J (Bradford) 1891 W, I, S
Richards, P C (Gloucester, London Irish) 2006 A1, 2,NZ(R), Arg(R), SA1, 2, 2007 [US(R), SA1(R), Tg(R), A(t), F(R), SA2(R)], 2008 NZ2(R)
Richards, S B (Richmond) 1965 W, I, F, S, 1967 A, I, F, S, W
Richardson, J V (Birkenhead Park) 1928 A, W, I, F, S
Richardson, W R (Manchester) 1881 I
Rickards, C H (Gipsies) 1873 S
Rimmer, G (Waterloo) 1949 W, I, 1950 W, 1951 W, I, F, 1952 SA, W, 1954 W, NZ, I, S
Rimmer, L I (Bath) 1961 SA, W, I, F, S
Ripley, A G (Rosslyn Park) 1972 W, I, F, S, SA, 1973 NZ 1, W, I, F, S, NZ 2, A, 1974 S, I, F, W, 1975 I, F, S, A 1,2, 1976 A, W, S
Risman, A B W (Loughborough Coll) 1959 W, I, F, S, 1961 SA, W, I, F
Ritson, J A S (Northern) 1910 F, S, 1912 F, 1913 SA, W, F, I, S
Rittson-Thomas, G C (Oxford U) 1951 W, I, F
Robbins, G L (Coventry) 1986 W, S
Robbins, P G D (Oxford U, Moseley, Coventry) 1956 W, I, S, F, 1957 W, I, F, S, 1958 W, A, I, S, 1960 W, I, F, S, 1961 SA, W, 1962 S
Roberts, A D (Northern) 1911 W, F, I, S, 1912 I, S, F, 1914 I
Roberts, E W (RNE Coll) 1901 W, I, 1905 NZ, 1906 W, I, 1907 S
Roberts, G D (Harlequins) 1907 S, 1908 F, W
Roberts, J (Sale) 1960 W, I, F, S, 1961 SA, W, I, F, S, 1962 W, I, F, S, 1963 W, I, F, S, 1964 NZ
Roberts, R S (Coventry) 1932 I
Roberts, S (Swinton) 1887 W, I
Roberts, V G (Penryn, Harlequins) 1947 F, 1949 W, I, F, S, 1950 I, F, S, 1951 W, I, F, S, 1956 W, I, S, F
Robertshaw, A R (Bradford) 1886 W, I, S, 1887 W, S
Robinson, A (Blackheath) 1889 M, 1890 W, S, I
Robinson, E T (Coventry) 1954 S, 1961 I, F, S
Robinson, G C (Percy Park) 1897 I, S, 1898 I, 1899 W, 1900 I, S, 1901 I, S
Robinson, J T (Sale) 2001 It (R), S (R), F (R), I, A, R, SA, 2002 S, I, F, It, NZ, A, SA, 2003 F 1, W 1, S, I, NZ, A, F 3, [Gg, SA, Sm, U(R), W, F, A], 2004 It, S, I, W, F, C, SA, A2, 2005 W, F, I, 2007 S, It, F1, W1, SA1, W2, F3, [US, SA1, A, F, SA2]
Robinson, J J (Headingley) 1893 S, 1902 W, I, S
Robinson, R A (Bath) 1988 A 2, Fj, A, 1989 S, I, F, W, 1995 SA
Robshaw, C D C (Harlequins) 2009 Arg 2, 2012 S, It, W, F, I, SA 1,2
Robson, A (Northern) 1924 W, I, F, S, 1926 W
Robson, M (Oxford U) 1930 W, I, F, S
Rodber, T A K (Army, Northampton) 1992 S, I, 1993 NZ, 1994 I, F, W, SA 1,2, R, C, 1995 I, F, W, S, [Arg, It, WS (R), A, NZ, F], SA, WS, 1996 W, S (R), I (t), It, Arg, 1997 S, I, F, W, A 1, 1998 H (R), It (R), A 2, SA 2, 1999 S, I, F, W, A, US (R), [NZ (R), Fj (R)]
Rogers, D P (Bedford) 1961 I, F, S, 1962 W, I, F, 1963 W, I, F, S, NZ 1,2, A, 1964 NZ, W, I, F, S, 1965 W, I, F, S, 1966 W, I, F, S, 1967 A, S, W, NZ, 1969 I, F, S, W
Rogers, J H (Moseley) 1890 W, S, I, 1891 S
Rogers, W L Y (Blackheath) 1905 W, I
Rollitt, D M (Bristol) 1967 I, F, S, W, 1969 I, F, S, W, 1975 S, A 1,2
Roncoroni, A D S (West Herts, Richmond) 1933 W, I, S
Rose, W M H (Cambridge U, Coventry, Harlequins) 1981 I, F, 1982 A, S, I, 1987 I, F, W, S, [A]
Rossborough, P A (Coventry) 1971 W, 1973 NZ 2, A, 1974 S, I, 1975 I, F
Rosser, D W A (Wasps) 1965 W, I, F, S, 1966 W
Rotherham, Alan (Richmond) 1883 W, S, 1884 W, S, 1885 W, I, 1886 W, I, S, 1887 W, I, S
Rotherham, Arthur (Richmond) 1898 S, W, 1899 W, I, S
Roughley, D (Liverpool) 1973 A, 1974 S, I
Rowell, R E (Leicester) 1964 W, 1965 W
Rowley, A J (Coventry) 1932 SA
Rowley, H C (Manchester) 1879 S, I, 1880 I, S, 1881 I, W, S, 1882 I, S

Rowntree, G C (Leicester) 1995 S (t), [It, WS], WS, 1996 F, W, S, I, It, Arg, 1997 S, I, F, W, A 1, 1998 A 1, NZ 1, 2, SA 1, H (R), It (R), 1999 US, C, [It (R), Tg, Fj (R)], 2001 C 1,2, US, I(R), A, R, SA, 2002 S, I, F, W, It, 2003 F 1(R), W 1, It, S, I, NZ, F 2, 2004 C, SA, A2, 2005 W, F, I, It, 2006 A1, 2
Royds, P M R (Blackheath) 1898 S, W, 1899 W
Royle, A V (Broughton R) 1889 M
Rudd, E L (Liverpool) 1965 W, I, S, 1966 W, I, S
Russell, R F (Leicester) 1905 NZ
Rutherford, D (Percy Park, Gloucester) 1960 W, I, F, S, 1961 SA, 1965 W, I, F, S, 1966 W, I, F, S, 1967 NZ
Ryalls, H J (New Brighton) 1885 W, I
Ryan, D (Wasps, Newcastle) 1990 Arg 1,2, 1992 C, 1998 S
Ryan, P H (Richmond) 1955 W, I

Sackey, P H (Wasps) 2006 NZ,Arg, 2007 F2,3(R), [SA1, Sm, Tg, A, F, SA2], 2008 W, It, F, S, I, PI, A, SA, NZ3, 2009 It, W, I
Sadler, E H (Army) 1933 I, S
Sagar, J W (Cambridge U) 1901 W, I
Salmon, J L B (Harlequins) 1985 NZ 1,2, 1986 W, S, 1987 I, F, W, S, [A, J, US, W]
Sample, C H (Cambridge U) 1884 I, 1885 I, 1886 S
Sampson, P C (Wasps) 1998 SA 1, 2001 C 1,2
Sanders, D L (Harlequins) 1954 W, NZ, I, S, F, 1956 W, I, S, F
Sanders, F W (Plymouth A) 1923 I, S, F
Sanderson, A (Sale) 2001 R (R), 2002 Arg, 2003 It(t + R), W 2(R), F 2
Sanderson, P H (Sale, Harlequins, Worcester) 1998 NZ 1,2, SA 1, 2001 C 1(R),2(R), US(t+R), 2005 A, NZ, Sm, 2006 A1, 2, NZ, Arg, SA1,2, 2007 SA1(R)
Sandford, J R P (Marlborough N) 1906 I
Sangwin, R D (Hull and E Riding) 1964 NZ, W
Sargent, G A F (Gloucester) 1981 I (R)
Savage, K F (Northampton) 1966 W, I, F, S, 1967 A, I, F, S, W, NZ, 1968 W, F, S
Sawyer, C M (Broughton) 1880 S, 1881 I
Saxby, L E (Gloucester) 1932 SA, W
Scarbrough, D G R (Leeds, Saracens) 2003 W 2, 2007 SA2
Schofield, D F (Sale) 2007 SA1,2(R)
Schofield, J W (Manchester) 1880 I
Scholfield, J A (Preston Grasshoppers) 1911 W
Schwarz, R O (Richmond) 1899 S, 1901 W, I
Scorfield, E S (Percy Park) 1910 F
Scott, C T (Blackheath) 1900 W, I, 1901 W, I
Scott, E K (St Mary's Hospital, Redruth) 1947 W, 1948 A, W, I, S
Scott, F S (Bristol) 1907 W
Scott, H (Manchester) 1955 F
Scott, J P (Rosslyn Park, Cardiff) 1978 F, W, S, I, NZ, 1979 S (R), I, F, W, NZ, 1980 I, F, W, S, 1981 W, S, I, F, Arg 1,2, 1982 I, F, W, 1983 F, W, S, I, NZ, 1984 S, I, F, W, SA 1,2
Scott, J S M (Oxford U) 1958 F
Scott, M T (Cambridge U) 1887 I, 1890 S, I
Scott, W M (Cambridge U) 1889 M
Seddon, R L (Broughton R) 1887 W, I, S
Sellar, K A (United Services, RN) 1927 W, I, S, 1928 A, W, I, F
Sever, H S (Sale) 1936 NZ, W, I, S, 1937 W, I, S, 1938 W, I, S
Shackleton, I R (Cambridge U) 1969 SA, 1970 I, W, S
Sharp, R A W (Oxford U, Wasps, Redruth) 1960 W, I, F, S, 1961 I, F, 1962 W, I, F, 1963 W, I, F, S, 1967 A
Sharples, C D J (Gloucester) 2011 W2(R), 2012 F
Shaw, C H (Moseley) 1906 S, SA, 1907 F, W, I, S
Shaw, F (Cleckheaton) 1898 I
Shaw, J F (RNE Coll) 1898 S, W
Shaw, S D (Bristol, Wasps) 1996 It, Arg, 1997 S, I, F, W, A 1, SA (R), 2000 I, F, W, It, S, SA 1(R),2(R), 2001 C 1(R), 2, US, I, 2003 It (R), W 2, F 2(R), 3(R), 2004 It(t&R), S(R), NZ1, 2, A1, 2005 Sm(R), 2006 W(R), It(R), S(R), F(R), I, 2007 W2,F2,3, [US, SA1, Sm, A, F, SA2], 2008 W, It, F, S, I, A(R), SA(R), 2009 F, S, NZ, 2010 W, It, F, I, A1, 2(R), 3(R), SA(R), 2011 W1(R), It(R), F(R), S(R), I1(R), W2, I2(R), [Gg, R(R), F(R)]
Sheasby, C M A (Wasps) 1996 It, Arg, 1997 W (R), Arg 1(R),2(R), SA (R), NZ 2(t)
Sheppard, A (Bristol) 1981 W (R), 1985 W
Sheridan, A J (Sale) 2004 C(R), 2005 A, NZ, Sm, 2006 W, It, S, F(R), I, NZ, SA1, 2007 W2, F2, [US, SA1, Sm, Tg, A, F, SA2], 2008 W, F, S, I, NZ1, PI, A, 2009 It, W, I, F, S, 2010 NZ, A3, Sm, SA, 2011 W1, F, I2, [Arg]
Sherrard, C W (Blackheath) 1871 S, 1872 S
Sherriff, G A (Saracens) 1966 S, 1967 A, NZ
Shewring, H E (Bristol) 1905 I, NZ, 1906 W, S, F, SA, 1907 F, W, I, S
Shooter, J H (Morley) 1899 I, S, 1900 I, S
Shuttleworth, D W (Headingley) 1951 S, 1953 S

Sibree, H J H (Harlequins) 1908 F, 1909 I, S
Silk, N (Harlequins) 1965 W, I, F, S
Simms, K G (Cambridge U, Liverpool, Wasps) 1985 R, F, S, I, W, 1986 I, F, 1987 I, F, W, [A, J, W], 1988 F, W
Simpson, C P (Harlequins) 1965 W
Simpson, J P M (Wasps) 2011 [Gg(R)]
Simpson, P D (Bath) 1983 NZ, 1984 S, 1987 I
Simpson, T (Rockcliff) 1902 S, 1903 W, I, S, 1904 I, S, 1905 I, S, 1906 S, SA, 1909 F
Simpson-Daniel, J D (Gloucester) 2002 NZ, A, 2003 W 1(t + R), It, 2, 2004 I(R), NZ1, 2005 Sm, 2006 It(R), 2007 SA1(R)
Sims, D (Gloucester) 1998 NZ 1(R),2, SA 1
Skinner, M G (Harlequins) 1988 F, W, S, I 1,2, 1989 Fj, 1990 I, F, W, S, Arg 1,2, 1991 Fj (R), [US, F, S, A], 1992 S, I, F, W
Skirving, B D (Saracens) 2007 SA2
Sladen, G M (United Services, RN) 1929 W, I, S
Sleightholme, J M (Bath) 1996 F, W, S, I, It, Arg, 1997 S, I, F, W, Arg 1,2
Slemen, M A C (Liverpool) 1976 I, F, 1977 S, I, F, W, 1978 F, W, S, I, NZ, 1979 S, I, F, W, NZ, 1980 I, F, W, S, 1981 W, S, I, F, 1982 A, S, I, F, W, 1983 NZ, 1984 S
Slocock, L A N (Liverpool) 1907 F, W, I, S, 1908 F, W, I, S
Slow, C F (Leicester) 1934 S
Small, H D (Oxford U) 1950 W, I, F, S
Smallwood, A M (Leicester) 1920 F, I, 1921 W, I, S, F, 1922 I, S, 1923 W, I, S, F, 1925 I, S
Smart, C E (Newport) 1979 F, W, NZ, 1981 S, I, F, Arg 1,2, 1982 A, S, I, F, W, 1983 F, W, S, I
Smart, S E J (Gloucester) 1913 SA, W, F, I, S, 1914 W, I, S, F, 1920 W, I, S
Smeddle, R W (Cambridge U) 1929 W, I, S, 1931 F
Smith, C C (Gloucester) 1901 W
Smith, D F (Richmond) 1910 W, I
Smith, J V (Cambridge U, Rosslyn Park) 1950 W, I, F, S
Smith, K (Roundhay) 1974 F, W, 1975 W, S
Smith, M J K (Oxford U) 1956 W
Smith, O J (Leicester) 2003 It(R), W 2(R), F 2, 2005 It(R), S(R)
Smith, S J (Sale) 1973 I, F, S, A, 1974 I, F, 1975 W (R), 1976 F, 1977 F (R), 1979 NZ, 1980 I, F, W, S, 1981 W, S, I, F, Arg 1,2, 1982 A, S, I, F, W, 1983 F, W, S
Smith, S R (Richmond) 1959 W, F, S, 1964 F, S
Smith, S T (Wasps) 1985 R, F, S, I, W, NZ 1,2, 1986 W, S
Smith, T H (Northampton) 1951 W
Soane, F (Bath) 1893 S, 1894 W, I, S
Sobey, W H (O Millhillians) 1930 W, F, S, 1932 SA, W
Solomon, B (Redruth) 1910 W
Sparks, R H W (Plymouth A) 1928 I, F, S, 1929 W, I, S, 1931 I, S, F
Speed, H (Castleford) 1894 W, I, S, 1896 S
Spence, F W (Birkenhead Park) 1890 I
Spencer, J (Harlequins) 1966 W
Spencer, J S (Cambridge U, Headingley) 1969 I, F, S, W, SA, 1970 I, W, S, F, 1971 W, I, S (2[1C]), P
Spong, R S (O Millhillians) 1929 F, 1930 W; I, F, S, 1931 F, 1932 SA, W
Spooner, R H (Liverpool) 1903 W
Springman, H H (Liverpool) 1879 S, 1887 S
Spurling, A (Blackheath) 1882 I
Spurling, N (Blackheath) 1886 I, S, 1887 W
Squires, P J (Harrogate) 1973 F, S, NZ 2, A, 1974 S, I, F, W, 1975 I, F, W, S, A 1,2, 1976 A, W, 1977 S, I, F, W, 1978 F, W, S, I, NZ, 1979 S, I, F, W
Stafford R C (Bedford) 1912 W, I, S, F
Stafford, W F H (RE) 1874 S
Stanbury, E (Plymouth A) 1926 W, I, S, 1927 W, I, S, F, 1928 A, W, I, F, S, 1929 W, I, S, F
Standing, G (Blackheath) 1883 W, I
Stanger-Leathes, C F (Northern) 1905 I
Stark, K J (O Alleynians) 1927 W, I, S, F, 1928 A, W, I, F, S
Starks, A (Castleford) 1896 W, I
Starmer-Smith, N C (Harlequins) 1969 SA, 1970 I, W, S, F, 1971 S (C), P
Start, S P (United Services, RN) 1907 S
Steeds, J H (Saracens) 1949 F, S, 1950 I, F, S
Steele-Bodger, M R (Cambridge U) 1947 W, I, S, F, 1948 A, W, I, S, F
Steinthal, F E (Ilkley) 1913 W, F
Stephenson, M (Newcastle) 2001 C 1,2, US
Stevens, C B (Penzance-Newlyn, Harlequins) 1969 SA, 1970 I, W, S, 1971 P, 1972 W, I, F, S, SA, 1973 NZ 1, W, I, F, S, NZ 2, A, 1974 S, I, F, W, 1975 I, F, W, S
Stevens, M J H (Bath, Saracens) 2004 NZ1(R), 2(t), 2005 I, It, S, NZ(R), Sm, 2006 W, It, F, 2007 SA2, W2(R), F2, 3(R); [US(R), SA1, Sm, Tg, A(R), F(R), SA2(R)], 2008 W(R), It, F(R), S(R), I(R), NZ1,

2, PI, A(t&R), SA(R), NZ3(R), 2011 W2, 3(R), I2(R), [Arg(R), Gg, S, F], 2012 S(R), It(R), W(R), F(R), I(R)
Still, E R (Oxford U, Ravenscourt P) 1873 S
Stimpson, T R G (Newcastle, Leicester) 1996 It, 1997 S, I, F, W, A 1, NZ 2(t+R), 1998 A 1, NZ 1,2(R), SA 1(R), 1999 US (R), C (R), 2000 SA 1, 2001 C 1(t),2(R), 2002 W (R), Arg, SA (R)
Stirling, R V (Leicester, RAF, Wasps) 1951 W, I, F, S, 1952 SA, W, S, I, F, 1953 W, I, F, S, 1954 W, NZ, I, S, F
Stoddart, A E (Blackheath) 1885 W, I, 1886 W, I, S, 1889 M, 1890 W, I, 1893 W, S
Stoddart, W B (Liverpool) 1897 W, I, S
Stokes, F (Blackheath) 1871 S, 1872 S, 1873 S
Stokes, L (Blackheath) 1875 I, 1876 S, 1877 I, S, 1878 S, 1879 S, I, 1880 I, S, 1881 I, W, S
Stone, F le S (Blackheath) 1914 F
Stoop, A D (Harlequins) 1905 S, 1906 F, SA, 1907 F, W, 1910 W, I, S, 1911 W, F, I, S, 1912 W, S
Stoop, F M (Harlequins) 1910 S, 1911 F, I, 1913 SA
Stout, F M (Richmond) 1897 W, I, 1898 I, S, W, 1899 I, S, 1903 S, 1904 W, I, S, 1905 W, I, S
Stout, P W (Richmond) 1898 S, W, 1899 W, I, S
Strettle, D (Harlequins, Saracens) 2007 I, F1, W1, 2, 2008 W, NZ1, 2011 I1(R), 2012 S, It, W, I, SA2
Stringer, N C (Wasps) 1982 A (R), 1983 NZ (R), 1984 SA 1 (R), A, 1985 R
Strong, E L (Oxford U) 1884 W, I, S
Sturnham B (Saracens) 1998 A 1, NZ 1(t),2(t)
Summerscales, G E (Durham City) 1905 NZ
Sutcliffe, J W (Heckmondwike) 1889 M
Swarbrick, D W (Oxford U) 1947 W, I, F, 1948 A, W, 1949 I
Swayne, D H (Oxford U) 1931 W
Swayne, J W R (Bridgwater) 1929 W
Swift, A H (Swansea) 1981 Arg 1,2, 1983 F, W, S, 1984 SA 2
Syddall, J P (Waterloo) 1982 I, 1984 A
Sykes, A R V (Blackheath) 1914 F
Sykes, F D (Northampton) 1955 F, S, 1963 NZ 2, A
Sykes, P W (Wasps) 1948 F, 1952 S, I, F, 1953 W, I, F
Syrett, R E (Wasps) 1958 W, A, I, F, 1960 W, I, F, S, 1962 W, I, F

Tait, M J M (Newcastle, Sale) 2005 W, 2006 A1, 2,SA1, 2, 2007 It(R), I(R), F1(R), W1, SA1, 2, W2, [US(R), SA1(R), Sm, Tg, A, F, SA2], 2008 It(t), F(R), S(R), It&R), NZ2, 2009 It(R), W(R), I(R), F(R), S(R), Arg 1(R) ,2(R), NZ(R), 2010 W, It, I, S, F(R), A1(R)
Tallent, J A (Cambridge U, Blackheath) 1931 S, F, 1932 SA, W, 1935 I
Tanner, C C (Cambridge U, Gloucester) 1930 S, 1932 SA, W, I, S
Tarr, F N (Leicester) 1909 A, W, F, 1913 S
Tatham, W M (Oxford U) 1882 S, 1883 W, I, S, 1884 W, I, S
Taylor, A S (Blackheath) 1883 W, I, 1886 W, I
Taylor, E W (Rockcliff) 1892 I, 1893 I, 1894 W, I, S, 1895 W, I, S, 1896 W, I, 1897 W, I, S, 1899 I
Taylor, F (Leicester) 1920 F, I
Taylor, F M (Leicester) 1914 W
Taylor, H H (Blackheath) 1879 S, 1880 S, 1881 I, W, 1882 S
Taylor, J T (W Hartlepool) 1897 I, 1899 I, 1900 I, 1901 W, I, 1902 W, I, S, 1903 W, I, 1905 S
Taylor, P J (Northampton) 1955 W, I, 1962 W, I, F, S
Taylor, R B (Northampton) 1966 W, 1967 I, F, S, W, NZ, 1969 F, S, W, SA, 1970 I, W, S, F, 1971 S (2[1C])
Taylor, W J (Blackheath) 1928 A, W, I, F, S
Teague, M C (Gloucester, Moseley) 1985 F (R), NZ 1, 2, 1989 S, I, F, W, R, 1990 F, W, S, 1991 W, S, I, F, Fj, A, [NZ, It, F, S, A], 1992 SA, 1993 F, W, S, I
Teden, D E (Richmond) 1939 W, I, S
Teggin, A (Broughton R) 1884 I, 1885 W, 1886 I, S, 1887 I, S
Tetley, T S (Bradford) 1876 S
Thomas, C (Barnstaple) 1895 W, I, S, 1899 I
Thompson, P H (Headingley, Waterloo) 1956 W, I, S, F, 1957 W, I, F, S, 1958 W, A, I, F, S, 1959 W, I, F, S
Thompson, S G (Northampton, Brive, Leeds, Wasps) 2002 S, I, F, W, It, Arg, NZ, A, SA, 2003 F 1, W 1, It, S, I, NZ, A, F 2(R), 3, [Gg, SA, Sm(R), W, F, A], 2004 It, S, I, W, F, NZ1, A1(R), C, SA, A2, 2005 W, F, I, It, S, A, NZ, Sm, 2006 W, It, S, F, I(R), 2009 Arg 1(R), A, Arg 3(R), NZ(R), 2010 W(R), It(R), S(R), F(R), A1, 2, NZ, A3(R), Sm(R), SA(R), 2011 W1(R), It(R), F(R), S(R), I1(R), W(R), I2, [Arg, Gg(t&R), R, S, F]
Thomson, G T (Halifax) 1878 S, 1882 I, S, 1883 W, I, S, 1884 I, S, 1885 I
Thomson, W B (Blackheath) 1892 W, 1895 W, I, S
Thorne, J D (Bristol) 1963 W, I, F
Tindall, M J (Bath, Gloucester) 2000 I, F, W, It, S, SA 1,2, A, Arg, SA 3, 2001 W (R), R, SA (R), 2002 S, I, F, W, It, NZ, A, SA, 2003 It, S, I, NZ, A, F 2, [Gg, SA, Sm, W, F(R), A], 2004 W, F, NZ1, 2,

A1, C, SA, A2, 2005 A, NZ, Sm, 2006 W, It, S, F, I(t&R), 2007 S,It,I,F1, 2008 W,NZ1,2, 2009 W,I,F,S, 2010 F,A1,2,NZ,A3,SA, 2011 W1,It,F,S, W3, I2, [Arg, R, S]
Tindall, V R (Liverpool U) 1951 W, I, F, S
Titterrell, A J (Sale) 2004 NZ2(R), C(R), 2005 It(R), S(R), 2007 SA2(R)
Tobin, F (Liverpool) 1871 S
Todd, A F (Blackheath) 1900 I, S
Todd, R (Manchester) 1877 S
Toft, H B (Waterloo) 1936 S, 1937 W, I, S, 1938 W, I, S, 1939 W, I, S
Toothill, J T (Bradford) 1890 S, I, 1891 W, I, 1892 W, I, S, 1893 W, I, S, 1894 W, I
Tosswill, L R (Exeter) 1902 W, I, S
Touzel, C J C (Liverpool) 1877 I, S
Towell, A C (Bedford) 1948 F, 1951 S
Travers, B H (Harlequins) 1947 W, I, 1948 A, W, 1949 F, S
Treadwell, W T (Wasps) 1966 I, F, S
Trick, D M (Bath) 1983 I, 1984 SA 1
Tristram, H B (Oxford U) 1883 S, 1884 W, S, 1885 W, 1887 S
Troop, C L (Aldershot S) 1933 I, S
Tucker, J S (Bristol) 1922 W, 1925 NZ, W, I, S, F, 1926 W, I, F, S, 1927 W, I, S, F, 1928 A, W, I, F, S, 1929 W, I, F, 1930 W, I, F, S, 1931 W
Tucker, W E (Blackheath) 1894 W, I, 1895 W, I, S
Tucker, W E (Blackheath) 1926 I, 1930 W, I
Tuilagi, E M (Leicester) 2011 W2,I2,[Arg,Gg,R,S,F], 2012 W,F,I,SA 1,2,3
Turner, D P (Richmond) 1871 S, 1872 S, 1873 S, 1874 S, 1875 I, S
Turner, E B (St George's Hospital) 1876 I, 1877 I, 1878 I
Turner, G R (St George's Hospital) 1876 S
Turner, H J C (Manchester) 1871 S
Turner, M F (Blackheath) 1948 S, F
Turner, S C (Sale) 2007 W1, SA1,2(R)
Turner-Hall, J (Harlequins) 2012 S(R),It(R)
Turquand-Young, D (Richmond) 1928 A, W, 1929 I, S, F
Twynam, H T (Richmond) 1879 I, 1880 I, 1881 W, 1882<j> I, 1883 I, 1884 W, I, S

Ubogu, V E (Bath) 1992 C, SA, 1993 NZ, 1994 S, I, F, W, SA 1,2, R, C, 1995 I, F, W, S, [Arg, WS, A, NZ, F], SA, 1999 F (R), W (R), A (R)
Underwood, A M (Exeter) 1962 W, I, F, S, 1964 I
Underwood, R (Leicester, RAF) 1984 I, F, W, A, 1985 R, F, S, I, W, 1986 W, I, F, 1987 I, F, W, S, [A, J, W], 1988 F, W, S, I, 1,2, Fj, A, 1989 S, I, F, W, R, Fj, 1990 I, F, W, S, Arg 3, 1991 W, S, I, F, Fj, A, [NZ, It, US, F, S, A], 1992 S, I, F, W, SA, 1993 F, W, S, I, NZ, 1994 S, I, F, W, SA 1,2, R, C, 1995 I, F, W, S, [Arg, It, WS, A, NZ, F], SA, WS, 1996 F, W, S, I
Underwood, T (Leicester, Newcastle) 1992 C, SA, 1993 S, I, NZ, 1994 S, I, W, SA 1,2, R, C, 1995 I, F, W, S, [Arg, It, A, NZ], 1996 Arg, 1997 S, I, F, W, 1998 A 2, SA 2
Unwin, E J (Rosslyn Park, Army) 1937 S, 1938 W, I, S
Unwin, G T (Blackheath) 1898 S
Uren, R (Waterloo) 1948 I, S, F, 1950 I
Uttley, R M (Gosforth) 1973 I, F, S, NZ 2, A, 1974 I, F, W, 1975 F, W, S, A 1,2, 1977 S, I, F, W, 1978 NZ 1979 S, 1980 I, F, W, S

Vainikolo, L P I (Gloucester) 2008 W(R),It,F,S,I
Valentine J (Swinton) 1890 W, 1896 W, I, S
Vanderspar, C H R (Richmond) 1873 S
Van Gisbergen, M C (Wasps) 2005 A(t)
Van Ryneveld, C B (Oxford U) 1949 W, I, F, S
Varley, H (Liversedge) 1892 S
Varndell, T W (Leicester) 2005 Sm(R), 2006 A1,2, 2008 NZ2
Vassall, H (Blackheath) 1881 W, S, 1882 I, S, 1883 W
Vassall, H H (Blackheath) 1908 I
Vaughan, D B (Headingley) 1948 A, W, I, S, 1949 I, F, S, 1950 W
Vaughan-Jones, A (Army) 1932 I, S, 1933 W
Verelst, C L (Liverpool) 1876 I, 1878 I
Vernon, G F (Blackheath) 1878 S, I, 1880 I, S, 1881 I
Vesty, S B (Leicester) 2009 Arg 1(R),2(R)
Vickery, G (Aberavon) 1905 I
Vickery, P J (Gloucester, Wasps) 1998 W, A 1, NZ 1,2, SA 1, 1999 US, C, [It, NZ, Tg, SA], 2000 I, F, W, S, A, Arg (R), SA 3(R), 2001 W, It, S, A, SA, 2002 I, F, Arg, NZ, A, SA, 2003 NZ(R), A, [Gg, SA, Sm(R), U, W, F, A], 2004 It, S, I, W, F, 2005 W(R), F, A, NZ, 2006 SA1(R),2, 2007 S, I, W2, F2(R),3, [US, Tg(R), A, F, SA2], 2008 W, F, S, I, PI(R), A, SA, NZ3, 2009 It, W, I, F, S
Vivyan, E J (Devonport A) 1901 W, 1904 W, I, S
Voyce, A T (Gloucester) 1920 I, S, 1921 W, I, S, F, 1922 W, I, F, S, 1923 W, I, S, F, 1924 W, I, F, S, 1925 NZ, W, I, S, F, 1926 W, I, F, S

Voyce, T M D (Bath, Wasps) 2001 US (R), 2004 NZ2, A1, 2005 Sm, 2006 W(R), It, F(R), I, A1
Vyvyan, H D (Saracens) 2004 C(R)

Wackett, J A S (Rosslyn Park) 1959 W, I
Wade, C G (Richmond) 1883 W, I, S, 1884 W, S, 1885 W, 1886 W, I
Wade, M R (Cambridge U) 1962 W, I, F
Wakefield, W W (Harlequins) 1920 W, F, I, S, 1921 W, I, S, F, 1922 W, I, F, S, 1923 W, I, S, F, 1924 W, I, F, S, 1925 NZ, W, I, S, F, 1926 W, I, F, S, 1927 S, F
Walder, D J H (Newcastle) 2001 C 1,2, US, 2003 W 2(R)
Waldrom, T R (Leicester) 2012 SA 2(R),3
Walker, G A (Blackheath) 1939 W, I
Walker, H W (Coventry) 1947 W, I, S, F, 1948 A, W, I, S, F
Walker, R (Manchester) 1874 S, 1875 I, 1876 S, 1879 S, 1880 S
Wallens, J N S (Waterloo) 1927 F
Walshe, N P J (Bath) 2006 A1(R), 2(R)
Walton, E J (Castleford) 1901 W, I, 1902 I, S
Walton, W (Castleford) 1894 S
Ward, G (Leicester) 1913 W, F, S, 1914 W, I, S
Ward, H (Bradford) 1895 W
Ward, J I (Richmond) 1881 I, 1882 I
Ward, J W (Castleford) 1896 W, I, S
Wardlow, C S (Northampton) 1969 SA (R), 1971 W, I, F, S (2[1C])
Warfield, P J (Rosslyn Park, Durham U) 1973 NZ 1, W, I, 1975 I, F, S
Warr, A L (Oxford U) 1934 W, I
Waters, F H H (Wasps) 2001 US, 2004 NZ2(R), A1(R)
Watkins, J A (Gloucester) 1972 SA, 1973 NZ 1, W, NZ 2, A, 1975 F, W
Watkins, J K (United Services, RN) 1939 W, I, S
Watson, F B (United Services, RN) 1908 S, 1909 S
Watson, J H D (Blackheath) 1914 W, S, F
Watt, D E J (Bristol) 1967 I, F, S, W
Webb, C S H (Devonport Services, RN) 1932 SA, W, I, S, 1933 W, I, S, 1935 S, 1936 NZ, W, I, S
Webb, J M (Bristol, Bath) 1987 [A (R), J, US, W], 1988 F, W, S, I 1,2, A 1,2, A, 1989 S, I, F, W, 1991 Fj, A, [NZ, It, F, S, A], 1992 S, I, F, W, C, SA, 1993 F, W, S, I
Webb, J W G (Northampton) 1926 F, S, 1929 S
Webb, R E (Coventry) 1967 S, W, NZ, 1968 I, F, S, 1969 I, F, S, W, 1972 I, F
Webb, St L H (Bedford) 1959 W, I, F, S
Webber, R W (Wasps) 2012 It(R),W(R),F(R)
Webster, J G (Moseley) 1972 W, I, SA, 1973 NZ 1, W, NZ 2, 1974 S, W, 1975 I, F, W
Wedge, T G (St Ives) 1907 F, 1909 W
Weighill, R H G (RAF, Harlequins) 1947 S, F, 1948 S, F
Wells, C M (Cambridge U, Harlequins) 1893 S, 1894 W, S, 1896 S, 1897 W, S
West, B R (Loughborough Colls, Northampton) 1968 W, I, F, S, 1969 SA, 1970 I, W, S
West, D E (Leicester) 1998 F (R), S (R), 2000 Arg (R), 2001 W, It, S, F (t), C 1,2, US, I (R), A, SA, 2002 F (R), W (R), It (R), 2003 W 2(R), F 2,3(t+R), [U, F(R)]
West, R (Gloucester) 1995 [WS]
Weston, H T F (Northampton) 1901 S
Weston, L E (W of Scotland) 1972 F, S
Weston, M P (Richmond, Durham City) 1960 W, I, F, S, 1961 SA, W, I, F, S, 1962 W, I, F, 1963 W, I, F, S, NZ 1,2, A, 1964 NZ, W, I, F, S, 1965 F, S, 1966 S, 1968 F, S
Weston, W H (Northampton) 1933 I, S, 1934 I, S, 1935 W, I, S, 1936 NZ, W, S, 1937 W, I, S, 1938 W, I, S
Wheatley, A A (Coventry) 1937 W, I, S, 1938 W, S
Wheatley, H F (Coventry) 1936 I, 1937 S, 1938 W, S, 1939 W, I, S
Wheeler, P J (Leicester) 1975 F, W, 1976 A, W, S, I, 1977 S, I, F, W, 1978 F, W, S, I, NZ, 1979 S, I, F, W, NZ, 1980 I, F, W, S, 1981 W, S, I, F, 1982 A, S, I, F, W, 1983 F, S, I, NZ, 1984 S, I, F, W
White, C (Gosforth) 1983 NZ, 1984 S, I, F
White, D F (Northampton) 1947 W, I, S, 1948 I, F, 1951 S, 1952 SA, W, S, I, F, 1953 W, I, S
White, J M (Saracens, Bristol, Leicester) 2000 SA 1,2, Arg, SA 3, 2001 F, C 1,2, US, I, R (R), 2002 S, W, It, 2003 F 1(R), W 2, F 2,3, [Sm, U(R)], 2004 W, F(R), NZ1,2, A1,C, SA, A2, 2005 W, 2006 W(R), It(R), S, F, I, A1,2, NZ, Arg, SA1,2, 2007 S(R), It(R), I(R),F1, W1, 2009 It(R),W(R),I(t&R),F(t&R),S(R),Arg 1(R),2
White-Cooper, W R S (Harlequins) 2001 C 2, US
Whiteley, E C P (O Alleynians) 1931 S, F
Whiteley, W (Bramley) 1896 W
Whitely, H (Northern) 1929 W
Wightman, B J (Moseley, Coventry) 1959 W, 1963 W, I, NZ 2, A
Wigglesworth, H J (Thornes) 1884 I

FIJI

FIJI'S 2012 TEST RECORD

OPPONENTS	DATE	VENUE	RESULT
Japan	5 Jun	A	Won 25–19
Samoa	10 Jun	N	Lost 26–29
Scotland	16 Jun	H	Lost 25–37
Tonga	23 Jun	H	Won 29–17

NEW ERA BEGINS FOR FIJI RUGBY

Getty Images

Waisea Nayacalevu celebrates after scoring a try against France during the Tokyo Sevens.

The fallout from Fiji's disappointing Rugby World Cup 2011 campaign was as widespread as it was swift. The tenure of head coach Samu Domoni was brought to an end after the tournament, as was the contract of High Performance Manager Talemo Waqa.

The Fiji Rugby Union undertook a wide-ranging Board of Enquiry that looked into all aspects of the RWC 2011 campaign and the Development and High Performance programmes that underpinned it. The report from the Board of Enquiry recommended vast changes at all levels of Fiji rugby.

A new CEO from outside the broader rugby family of Fiji was brought in with a mandate for change and so 2012 began with a sense of urgency not seen in the country for some time. As the only team from Oceania not to have achieved direct qualification for RWC 2015, the pressure from an expectant and disappointed rugby public was immense.

The year began on a high note with the Fiji Warriors, as the country's second team are known, embarking on their quest for a fourth consecutive IRB Pacific Rugby Cup title under the watchful eye of new national team coach Inoke Male, who was relishing the opportunity to test his locally-based players against Super Rugby Academy sides in Australia and New Zealand.

Despite a shaky start and an opening 36–24 loss to Queensland A, the Warriors went on an extraordinary run of victories in their remaining five matches in the Australian and New Zealand legs. A feat made all the more remarkable considering the historically poor record of Pacific Island teams against the New Zealand sides, the Warriors having failed to win a match in 2011. The victory margins were close – four points the biggest – as the Warriors beat the Crusader Knights, Blues Development XV and Chiefs Development XV in March to all but wrap up the title.

They needed just one point from the Pacific Islands phase, held in Tonga during October, to realise Male's target. In the end, they didn't even need that as Tonga A's 20–18 win over Samoa A in the opening match handed the Warriors the title, but they still finished the competition in style by beating Samoa A 42–34 and their hosts 25–16 to make it seven wins in a row.

In the interim, attention turned to the Flying Fijians and the IRB Pacific Nations Cup, a chance to banish the demons of RWC 2011 and improve their IRB World Ranking which had dropped to 16th after that tournament.

"The boys have talked it over during our training," revealed Male before the squad headed to Japan. "[The need] to forget last year's performances and to start a new journey, starting with this PNC campaign and to be on the right track for the next World Cup."

Fiji entered the Pacific Nations Cup in June as the lowest ranked team, but with Male at the helm and seven players stepping up from the Warriors side, hopes were high of success. Male reflected the Fijian public's expectations by stating "we are here to rebuild Fiji Rugby."

The campaign started on the best possible note with a 25–19 win over hosts and defending champions Japan in Nagoya, a solid first match in charge for Male. Five days later, in perfect conditions in Tokyo, Fiji took on Samoa but despite establishing a 10–3 lead in the opening 10 minutes they were unable to contain the explosive pace of a rampant Samoan backline. Nemia Kenatale scored twice for the Fijians in the 29–26 loss. "We played some good rugby for the first 20 minutes, but then made too many unforced errors," lamented Male afterwards.

Fiji then put the PNC on the backburner to return home and face a Scotland team brimming with confidence after upsetting Australia. Their arrival, as part of the 2012–2019 IRB Tours and Test schedule, was significant with Scotland the first Tier One Union to tour Fiji since Italy in 2006.

In front of 10,000 people in baking heat at Churchill Park in Lautoka, Fiji unveiled their new challenge the i-Bole – which replaced the Cibi – ahead of a thrilling match against Scotland. Trailing 24–11 at half-time, Fiji launched a comeback with tries from Waisea Nayacalevu and Metuisela Talebula to cut the deficit to 27–25 with 12 minutes to play. There was to be no fairytale ending, though, and Scotland departed with a 37–25 victory.

The final outing in June saw Tonga arrive in Lautoka to complete the Pacific Nations Cup. Determined to atone for their defeats by Samoa and Scotland, Fiji produced a ruthless second-half display to win 29–17 and finish as runners-up to Samoa in the standings.

Fiji had already finished as runners-up to New Zealand in the 2011/12 HSBC Sevens World Series, albeit by just six points. Fiji won three tournaments in Australia, Hong Kong and England, but couldn't prevent New Zealand winning a 10th Series title.

For the Fiji Under 20 team it was always going to be hard to match their performance at the IRB Junior World Championship in Italy, where they finished a best ever sixth. Few, though, expected Fiji to be battling relegation on the final day and edging Italy 19–17 to avoid relegation to the IRB Junior World Rugby Trophy in 2013.

FIJI INTERNATIONAL STATISTICS
MATCH RECORDS UP TO 10 OCTOBER 2012

WINNING MARGIN

Date	Opponent	Result	Winning Margin
10/09/1983	Niue Island	120–4	116
21/08/1969	Solomon Islands	113–13	100
08/09/1983	Solomon Islands	86–0	86
30/08/1979	Papua New Guinea	86–0	86
23/08/1969	Papua New Guinea	88–3	85

MOST POINTS IN A MATCH
BY THE TEAM

Date	Opponent	Result	Points
10/09/1983	Niue Island	120–4	120
21/08/1969	Solomon Islands	113–13	113
23/08/1969	Papua New Guinea	88–3	88
08/09/1983	Solomon Islands	86–0	86
30/08/1979	Papua New Guinea	86–0	86

BY A PLAYER

Date	Player	Opponent	Points
10/09/1983	Severo Koroduadua	Niue Island	36
21/08/1969	Semesa Sikivou	Solomon Islands	27
28/08/1999	Nicky Little	Italy	25

MOST CONVERSIONS IN A MATCH
BY THE TEAM

Date	Opponent	Result	Cons
21/08/1969	Solomon Islands	113–13	19
10/09/1983	Niue Island	120–4	18
23/08/1969	Papua New Guinea	88–3	14

BY A PLAYER

Date	Player	Opponent	Cons
10/09/1983	Severo Koroduadua	Niue Island	18
21/08/1969	Semesa Sikivou	Solomon Islands	12
07/10/1989	Severo Koroduadua	Belgium	10

MOST PENALTIES IN A MATCH
BY THE TEAM

Date	Opponent	Result	Pens
08/07/2001	Samoa	28–17	7

BY A PLAYER

Date	Player	Opponent	Pens
08/07/2001	Nicky Little	Samoa	7
26/05/2000	Nicky Little	Tonga	6
25/05/2001	Nicky Little	Tonga	6
05/10/1996	Nicky Little	Hong Kong	6
08/07/1967	Inoke Tabualevu	Tonga	6

MOST TRIES IN A MATCH
BY THE TEAM

Date	Opponent	Result	Tries
21/08/1969	Solomon Islands	113–13	25
10/09/1983	Niue Island	120–4	21
23/08/1969	Papua New Guinea	88–3	20
18/08/1969	Papua New Guinea	79–0	19
30/08/1979	Papua New Guinea	86–0	18

BY A PLAYER

Date	Player	Opponent	Tries
30/08/1979	Tevita Makutu	Papua New Guinea	6
18/08/1969	George Sailosi	Papua New Guinea	5

MOST DROP GOALS IN A MATCH
BY THE TEAM

Date	Opponent	Result	DGs
02/07/1994	Samoa	20–13	3
12/10/1991	Romania	15–17	3

BY A PLAYER

Date	Player	Opponent	Pens
02/07/1994	Opeti Turuva	Samoa	3
12/10/1991	Tomasi Rabaka	Romania	2

MOST CAPPED PLAYERS

Name	Caps
Nicky Little	71
Jacob Rauluni	50
Joeli Veitayaki	49
Emori Katalau	47
Norman Ligairi	47

LEADING PENALTY SCORERS

Name	Pens
Nicky Little	140
Severo Koroduadua	47
Seremaia Bai	42
Waisale Serevi	27

LEADING TRY SCORERS

Name	Tries
Senivalati Laulau	18
Norman Ligairi	16
Viliame Satala	16
Fero Lasagavibau	16

LEADING DROP GOAL SCORERS

Name	DGs
Opeti Turuva	5
Severo Koroduadua	5
Waisale Serevi	3

LEADING CONVERSION SCORERS

Name	Cons
Nicky Little	117
Severo Koroduadua	56
Waisale Serevi	40

LEADING POINT SCORERS

Name	Points
Nicky Little	670
Severo Koroduadua	268
Seremaia Bai	223
Waisale Serevi	221

FIJI

FIJI INTERNATIONAL PLAYERS
UP TO 10 OCTOBER 2012

A Apimeleki 1924 *Sa, Tg, Tg, Sa*, 1926 *Tg, Tg*
S Aria 1986 *W*, 1988 *Tg, Sa, E, Tg*, 1991 *C, F*, 1993 *Sa, Tg*, 1994 *J*
S Bai 2000 *J, US, C, It*, 2001 *Tg, Sa, Tg, Sa, W, It*, 2004 *Tg, Sa*, 2005 *M, NZ, Tg, Sa, Tg, Sa, W, It*, 2006 *Tg, It, Sa, J*, 2007 *J, C, A, W, SA*, 2009 *Sa, J, S, I*, 2010 *F, W, It*, 2011 *J, NZ, Tg, Nm, SA, Sa, W*
EM Bakaniceva 2010 *J, Tg*
J Bale 2004 *Tg, Sa*, 2005 *M, NZ, Tg, Sa, Tg, Sa, W, It, Sa, J*
P Bale 1995 *C, Sa, Tg, W, I*
S Baleca 1951 *M*, 1952 *A, A*, 1954 *A, A*
DV Baleinadogo 2001 *Tg, Sa, Tg, Sa, C, Sa*, 2002 *Sa, Tg*, 2007 *Sa, J*
K Baleisawani 2004 *Tg, Sa*
N Baleiverata 1988 *Tg, Sa, E*, 1990 *J*
D Baleiwai 1990 *J, HK*, 1991 *Tg, C, F, R*
J Balewai 1926 *Tg, Tg*, 1928 *Tg, Tg, Tg, Sa*, 1932 *Tg, Tg, Tg*
S Banuve 1990 *Tg*
S Baravilala 1934 *Tg, Tg*, 1947 *Tg, Tg*, 1948 *M, M*
M Bari 1995 *Sa, Tg, W, I*, 1996 *Sa, Tg, HK, HK, M*, 1997 *NZ, Coo, Sa*, 1998 *S, US, A, Tg*, 1999 *Ur, F*

G Barley 1964 *W, F*, 1970 *M, C*
I Basiyalo 1994 *J*
S Basiyalo 1976 *I*
A Batibasaga 1967 *Tg*, 1968 *Tg, Tg*, 1969 *W, PNG, SI, PNG*
I Batibasaga 1970 *C*, 1972 *Tg, Tg, A*, 1973 *Tg, E*, 1974 *M, M*, 1976 *I*, 1977 *Tg, Tg*, 1979 *M*
I Batibasaga 1974 *M*
A Batikaciwa 1932 *Tg, Tg, Tg*, 1934 *Tg, Tg, Tg*
E Batimala 1994 *J, J, M, W, Sa, Tg*, 1995 *C, Sa, Tg*, 1996 *HK*, 1998 *S*
J Bibi 1928 *Tg, Tg, Tg, Sa*
PTQ Biu 1999 *Sp, Ur*, 2000 *J, Tg, Sa*, 2001 *It, F*, 2002 *Sa, Tg, Sa, NZ, Tg*, 2003 *CHL*
TM Biumaiwai 1954 *A, A, M, M*
M Black 1996 *SA, Sa, Tg, HK*
S Bobo 2004 *Tg, Sa*, 2005 *M, NZ, Tg, W, Pt*, 2007 *W, SA*, 2010 *A*
R Bogisa 1994 *J, W*, 1995 *C, W*
K Bogiwalu 1924 *Sa, Tg, Tg, Sa*, 1926 *Tg, Tg*
A Boko 2009 *S, I, R*
A Bola 1934 *Tg*
D Bola 1983 *Sa, Niu, Tg*, 1984 *A, Sa, NZ*

E **Bola** 1939 *M*
K **Bola** 2009 *R*, 2010 *Tg, Sa*, 2012 *J, Sa, Tg*
MS **Bola** 2009 *Tg, Sa, J, S, I, R*, 2010 *A, J, Tg, Sa*, 2011 *Tg, Sa*, 2012 *J, Sa, Tg*
IC **Bolakoro** 2009 *Sa*, 2011 *Sa*
FV **Bolavucu** 2009 *Tg, J*
E **Bolawaqatabu** 1963 *Sa, Tg, Sa, Tg*, 1969 *W, PNG, SI, PNG*, 1970 *M, M*, 1972 *Tg, Tg, Tg, A*, 1973 *M, M*
P **Bolea** 2001 *Sa*
P **Bosco** 1968 *Tg, Tg*, 1970 *M, M*, 1972 *Tg, Tg, Tg, A*, 1973 *M, M, Tg, E*, 1977 *Tg, Tg, Tg, BI*, 1979 *M, E*
A **Bose** 1932 *Tg, Tg, Tg*, 1934 *Tg, Tg, Tg*
E **Bose** 1998 *Sa*
K **Bose** 1958 *Tg, Tg*, 1959 *Tg*, 1961 *A, A, A*
V **Bose** 1980 *A*
I **Buadromo** 1970 *C*
VT **Buatava** 2007 *Sa, J, A*, 2010 *A*, 2011 *Tg, Sa, J, NZ, Tg, Tg, Nm, SA, Sa, W*
T **Bucaonadi** 1983 *Tg, Sa*
S **Bueta** 1986 *Tg*
V **Bueta** 1982 *Sa, Sa, E*
V **Buli** 1963 *Sa, Tg, Sa, Tg*
A **Burogolevu** 1954 *A, A*
A **Buto** 2012 *J, Sa, S*
I **Cagilaba** 1974 *M*, 1976 *I*, 1977 *Tg*, 1979 *M, E, F, PNG, Sa*
GK **Cakobau** 1939 *M*
J **Cama** 1987 *NZ*
T **Cama** 1985 *A, A, I, W*, 1987 *Ar, NZ, It, F, Sa, Tg*, 1989 *Tg, Tg*, 1990 *Sa*
A **Camaibau** 1948 *M, M*
J **Campbell** 1994 *J, J, M, W, Sa, Tg*
R **Caucau** 2003 *Ar, CHL, F, S*, 2006 *It, Sa*, 2010 *A*
J **Cavalevu** 1951 *M*, 1952 *A*, 1954 *A, A, M, M, M*
S **Cavu** 1958 *Tg*, 1961 *A*, 1963 *Sa, Tg, Sa, Tg*, 1964 *M, W, F, C*, 1967 *Tg, Tg*, 1968 *NZ*
TGN **Cavubati** 2011 *Tg, J*
VB **Cavubati** 1995 *Sa, Tg*, 1997 *NZ, Tg, Coo, Sa*, 1998 *F*, 1999 *C, US*, 2001 *Sa, C, Sa, It, F*, 2002 *NZ, Tg, W, I, S*, 2004 *Tg, Sa*, 2005 *M, NZ, Tg, Sa, Tg, Sa*
R **Cavubuka** 1985 *Tg*, 1986 *Sa, Tg*
K **Cavuilati** 1948 *M, M*, 1951 *M*, 1952 *A*
ST **Cavuilati** 1974 *NZ, M*, 1976 *A, A*
R **Cavukubu** 1986 *W*
I **Cawa** 1952 *A*, 1957 *M, M*
RI **Cawa** 1928 *Tg, Tg*, 1932 *Tg, Tg*, 1934 *Tg, Tg, Tg*, 1938 *M, M, M*
I **Cerelala** 1980 *NZ, Ar*
M M **Cevalawa** 1948 *M, M*
I **Cobitu** 1947 *Tg, Tg*, 1948 *M, M, M*
S **Dakuiyaco** 2000 *C*
J **Dakuvula** 2010 *J*
J **Damu** 1985 *I, W*, 1986 *W*, 1987 *F*
P **Damu** 2000 *J, Sa, US, C, It*, 2001 *Tg, Sa, Tg, C, Sa*
P **Dau** 1991 *Tg*, 1992 *Tg*
V **Daunibau** 1932 *Tg, Tg, Tg*
S **Daunitutu** 1963 *Sa, Tg, Sa, Tg*, 1964 *M, W, F, C*
J **Daunivucu** 2007 *A, W*, 2009 *Tg, Sa*
I **Daveta** 1932 *Tg, Tg*, 1934 *Tg, Tg, Tg*
W **Daveta Nailago** 2011 *J, Tg, Tg, Nm, SA, Sa, W*, 2012 *J, Sa, S*
M **Davu** 2001 *It, F*
E **Dawai** 1947 *Tg*
L **Dawai** 1947 *Tg, Tg*
O **Dawai** 1954 *A, M, M, M*, 1957 *M, M*, 1958 *Tg, Tg, Tg*, 1959 *Tg*, 1961 *A, A*
A **Delai** 2011 *Tg, Sa, Tg*
Delana 1926 *Tg*
V **Delasau** 2000 *US, C, It*, 2001 *Tg, Tg, Sa, C, Sa, It, F*, 2002 *Sa, NZ*, 2003 *Tg, F, US, J, S*, 2005 *M, NZ, Tg, Sa*, 2007 *J, C, A, W, SA*, 2008 *Sa, M*
A **Dere** 1986 *W*, 1989 *Bel, S, E*, 1990 *J, HK*, 1991 *Tg, E, C, F, R*
I **Derenalagi** 2001 *F*
V **Devo** 1924 *Sa, Tg, Tg, Sa*
GC **Dewes** 2007 *J, A, Tg, J, C, W, SA*, 2008 *Sa, M, Tg*, 2009 *Tg, Sa, J, S, I, R*, 2010 *A, J, Tg, Sa, F, W*, 2011 *Tg, J*, 2012 *J, Tg*
I **Domolailai** 2001 *It, F*, 2005 *M, NZ, Tg, Sa, Sa, W*, 2006 *Tg, It, Sa, J*, 2007 *A*
JU **Domolailai** 2008 *Tg*, 2009 *Tg, Sa, J, S*, 2011 *Tg, Sa, NZ, Tg*, 2012 *Sa, S, Tg*
S **Domoni** 1952 *A*, 1954 *A*, 1957 *M*
SR **Domoni** 1990 *HK*, 1991 *Tg, Tg, E, C, F*
JAR **Dovi** 1938 *M, M, M*
A **Doviverata** 1948 *M*
RAR **Doviverata** 1999 *Sp*, 2000 *J, Tg, Sa, US, C, It*, 2001 *Tg, Sa, Tg, Sa, C, Sa, It, F*, 2002 *Sa, Tg, Sa, NZ, Sa, W, I*, 2003 *Tg, Sa,*

F, US, J, S, 2004 *Tg, Sa*, 2005 *W, It*, 2006 *It, Sa, J*, 2007 *Sa, J, A, Tg*
A **Durusolo** 1928 *Tg, Tg*
A **Eastgate** 1968 *NZ*
J **Edwards** 1988 *Tg*
A **Elder** 1994 *J*
L **Erenavula** 1989 *Tg, Bel, S, E*, 1990 *J, Sa*, 1992 *M*
RS **Fatiaki** 2009 *J*, 2011 *Sa, J, NZ, Tg, Tg, SA, W*
I **Finau** 1980 *A, It, NZ, Ar, Ar*, 1983 *Tg, Sa, SI, Niu, Sa*, 1984 *A, Tg, NZ*, 1985 *Sa, A, I, W*, 1986 *Tg*
S **Fuli** 2004 *Sa*
VT **Gadolo** 2000 *J*, 2002 *Tg, S*, 2003 *Tg, Tg, Ar, CHL, J*, 2005 *M, NZ, Tg, Sa, Tg, Sa, W, Pt, It*, 2007 *J, A, SA*
P **Gale** 1984 *Tg*, 1985 *Sa, Tg, A, A, I, W*, 1987 *Ar, Sa, Tg*, 1988 *Sa, E*
R **Ganilau** 1979 *M, E, Tg*
RP **Ganilau** 1939 *M*
S **Ganilau** 1951 *M*, 1952 *A*
E **Gaunavou** 1961 *A, A, A*
I **Gavidi** 2005 *Pt, It*
R **Gavidi** 1934 *Tg, Tg, Tg*, 1938 *M*
W **Gavidi** 1972 *Tg, Tg, A*, 1973 *M, E*, 1974 *NZ, M, M*, 1976 *A, A*, 1977 *Tg, Tg, Tg, BI*, 1979 *M, E, F*, 1980 *A, It, NZ*
V **Goneva** 2007 *Sa, J, A, Tg*, 2008 *J, Tg*, 2009 *Sa, J, S, I, R*, 2010 *W, It*, 2011 *Tg, Sa, NZ, Tg, Tg, Nm, SA, Sa, W*, 2012 *J, Sa, S, Tg*
A **Gutugutuwai** 1967 *Tg*, 1968 *NZ, Tg*, 1969 *PNG*
S **Gutugutuwai** 1982 *Sa*, 1983 *Tg, Sa, Niu, Tg, Sa*, 1984 *A, Sa, Tg, NZ*, 1985 *Sa, Tg*
R **Howard** 1977 *Tg, Tg, Tg*
APT **Hughes** 1985 *Sa, Tg, A, I, W*, 1986 *Sa, Tg*
P **Hughes** 1973 *Tg, E*
M **Kafoa** 1994 *J, J*
S **Kalou** 2010 *A, J, Tg, Sa, F, W, It*, 2011 *Tg, Sa, NZ, Nm, Sa*
E **Katalau** 1995 *C, Sa, Tg, W, I*, 1996 *SA, Sa, Tg, HK, HK, M*, 1997 *NZ, Tg, Coo, Sa*, 1998 *S, F, US, A*, 1999 *C, US, J, Tg, Sa, M, Ur, It, Nm, C, F, E*, 2000 *J, Tg, Sa, US, C, It*, 2001 *Tg, Tg, Sa, C, It, F*, 2002 *S*, 2003 *Tg, Ar, J*
IC **Katonibau** 2012 *J, Sa, Tg*
E **Katonitabua** 1984 *A, Sa, Tg, Tg, NZ*, 1985 *Sa*
L **Katowale** 1991 *Tg, Tg, C, F*
P **Kean** 1982 *Sa*, 1983 *Tg, SI, Niu*, 1984 *A*
AR **Kenatale** 1988 *Tg*
NS **Kenatale** 2008 *J, Tg*, 2009 *Tg, Sa, J*, 2010 *F, W, It*, 2011 *Tg, Sa, NZ, Tg, Nm, SA, Sa, W*, 2012 *Sa, S*
S **Kepa** 1961 *A*
ILR **Keresoni** 2008 *Tg*, 2009 *Sa, J*, 2010 *J, Sa*, 2011 *J, NZ, Tg, Tg, Nm, W*
KR **Ketedromo** 2010 *J, Tg*, 2012 *J, S, Tg*
P **Kewa Nacuva** 1979 *F, PNG, Sa, Tg*, 1980 *NZ, M, Ar*
K **Kida** 1926 *Tg, Tg, Tg*
L **Kididromo** 1987 *NZ, F*, 1988 *Sa, Tg*
A **Kikau** 1948 *M*
O **Kililoa** 1986 *Sa, Tg*
P **Kina** 1976 *A, A, A*, 1979 *M, E, F*, 1980 *A, It, NZ, M, NZ, Ar, Ar*
E **Kobiti** 1924 *Sa, Tg, Tg, Sa*, 1926 *Tg, Tg, Tg*
O **Koliloa** 1986 *Tg*
Ratu **Komaitai** 1992 *M*, 1993 *S, Tg*
SS **Koniferedi** 2012 *J, S, Tg*
S **Koroduadua** 1982 *S, E*, 1983 *Tg, Sa, Niu, Tg, Sa*, 1985 *Sa, Tg, A, A*, 1987 *Ar, NZ, It, F, Sa, Tg*, 1988 *E, Tg*, 1989 *Sa, Tg, Tg, Bel, S, E*, 1990 *Sa*, 1991 *C, F*
A **Koroi** 1932 *Tg, Tg*, 1934 *Tg*
B **Koroi** 2012 *J, Tg*
L **Koroi** 1992 *Sa, Tg*, 1998 *US, A*
J **Koroibanuve** 1926 *Tg*
S **Koroibanuve** 1924 *Sa, Tg, Tg, Tg, Sa*
STR **Koroilagilagi** 2012 *J, Sa*
A **Koroitamana** 1992 *Tg*
S **Koroitamuda** 1924 *Sa, Tg, Tg, Tg, Sa*
I **Koroiyadi** 2001 *Tg*
A **Kororua** 1938 *M, M, M*
N **Korovata** 1990 *HK*, 1991 *Sa, Tg*
M **Korovou** 1994 *W, Tg*, 1995 *C, Tg*
I **Korovulavula** 1938 *M, M*, 1939 *M*
SK **Koto** 2005 *M, Tg, Sa, Tg, W, It*, 2006 *Tg, It, Sa, J*, 2007 *Sa, J, A, Tg, J, C, W, SA*, 2008 *Sa, M, J, Tg*, 2009 *Tg, Sa, J*, 2011 *J, NZ, Tg, Tg, Nm, SA, Sa, W*
SD **Koyamaibole** 2001 *Tg, Sa, C, Sa, It, F*, 2002 *Sa, Tg, Sa, NZ, Tg, W, I, S*, 2003 *Tg, Tg, Ar, CHL, F, US, J, S*, 2004 *Tg, Sa*, 2005 *M, NZ, Tg, Sa, Sa, W, Pt, It*, 2007 *Tg, J, C, A, W, SA*, 2010 *F, W, It*, 2011 *J, Tg, Tg, SA, Sa*
J **Kubu** 1985 *W*, 1986 *W, Tg, Sa, Tg*, 1987 *NZ, It, F, Sa, Tg*, 1988 *E*
P **Kubuwai** 1991 *Sa, Tg*

J Kuinikoro 1977 *Tg, Tg, Tg, Bl*, 1979 *M, E, PNG, Sa, Tg*, 1980 *A, NZ*
I Kunagogo 1980 *A, NZ, M*
E Kunavore 1963 *Tg, Sa*
M Kunavore 2005 *Sa, Pt, It*, 2006 *It, J*, 2007 *C, A*
W Kunavula 1951 *M*
A Kunawave 1957 *M, M*, 1958 *Tg, Tg, Tg*, 1959 *Tg*
M Kurisaru 1968 *Tg, Tg, Tg*, 1969 *PNG, SI, PNG*, 1970 *M, C*, 1972 *Tg, Tg, Tg*, 1973 *M, Tg, E*, 1976 *A*
A Kuruisaqila 1957 *M*, 1959 *Tg*
R Kuruisiga 1926 *Tg, Tg, Tg*
M Labaibure 1948 *M, M, M*, 1952 *A*, 1954 *A, M, M, M*
E Labalaba 1979 *E, F, PNG, Sa, Tg*, 1980 *M*, 1981 *Tg, Tg, Tg*
P Lagilagi 1939 *M*
S Lala Ragata 1999 *Ur*, 2000 *J, Tg, Sa, US*
A Laqeretabua 1924 *Sa, Tg, Tg, Tg, Sa*, 1926 *Tg, Tg, Tg*, 1928 *Tg, Tg, Tg, Sa*, 1932 *Tg, Tg, Tg*, 1934 *Tg, Tg, Tg*, 1938 *M, M*
F Lasagavibau 1997 *NZ, Tg, Coo, Sa*, 1998 *S, F, US, Sa, Tg*, 1999 *C, US, Tg, Sa, M, Sp, Nm, C, F*, 2001 *It, F*, 2002 *W, I, S*
T Latianara 1976 *I*
T Latianara 2002 *Sa, Tg*
R Latilevu 1970 *C*, 1972 *Tg, Tg*, 1973 *E*, 1974 *NZ*, 1976 *A, A*
S Laulau 1980 *A, It, M, NZ, Ar, Ar*, 1981 *Sa, Sa, Tg, Tg, Tg*, 1982 *Sa, Sa, Sa, Tg*, 1983 *Tg, Sa, SI, Niu, Tg, Sa*, 1984 *A, Sa, Tg, Tg, NZ*, 1985 *Sa, Tg, A, A, I, W*
K Leawere 2002 *S*, 2003 *Tg, Tg, Ar, CHL, F, J*, 2004 *Tg, Sa*, 2005 *W, Pt, It*, 2007 *Sa, A, Tg, J, C, W, SA*, 2008 *Sa, M, J, Tg*, 2009 *Tg, Sa, J*
S Leawere 2003 *Tg, Ar, CHL*, 2006 *Tg, J*
I Ledua 2009 *Tg, Sa, J, S, I, R*
P Lese 1951 *M*
J Levula 1951 *M*, 1952 *A, A*, 1954 *A, A, M, M, M*, 1957 *M, M*, 1958 *Tg, Tg, Tg*, 1959 *Tg*, 1961 *A, A, A*
RWG Lewaravu 2007 *Sa, J, A, J, A, SA*, 2008 *Sa, M*, 2009 *S, I*, 2010 *F, It*, 2011 *Tg, Tg, Nm, SA, W*
I Leweniqila 1984 *Tg*
NAS Ligairi 2000 *Tg, Sa, US, C, It*, 2001 *Sa, Tg, Sa, C, Sa*, 2002 *Sa, Tg, Sa, NZ, Tg, W, I, S*, 2003 *Ar, CHL, F, J, S*, 2004 *Tg, Sa*, 2005 *M, NZ, Tg, Sa, Tg, Sa, W, It*, 2006 *Tg, It, Sa, J*, 2007 *Tg, J, C, A, W, SA*, 2009 *I, R*, 2010 *F, It*
S Ligamamada 1970 *C*, 1977 *Tg*
V Lilidamu 1986 *Tg, Tg*, 1988 *Tg*
L Little 1995 *C, Sa, Tg, W, I*, 1996 *SA, M*, 1997 *Tg, Coo, Sa*, 1998 *S*, 1999 *US, Tg, Sp*
N Little 1996 *SA, Sa, Tg, HK, M*, 1997 *NZ, Tg, Coo, Sa*, 1998 *S, F, US, Sa*, 1999 *C, US, J, Tg, Sa, Sp, It, Nm, C, F, E*, 2000 *J, Tg, Sa, US, C, It*, 2001 *Sa, Tg, Sa, Sa, C, Sa, It, F*, 2002 *Sa, Tg, Sa, NZ, W, I*, 2003 *Tg, Tg, Ar, CHL, F, US, J, S*, 2005 *M, NZ, Tg, Sa, Tg, Sa, It*, 2007 *J, C, W*, 2009 *S, I*, 2011 *Tg, Sa, Tg, SA, Sa, W*
Livai 1926 *Tg*
V Loba 1939 *M*
D Lobendhan 1973 *M, Tg*, 1976 *A*
J Lotawa 2004 *Tg, Sa*, 2006 *Tg, J*
T Lovo 1989 *S, E*, 1990 *HK*, 1991 *Tg, C, F*, 1993 *S, Sa, Tg*
GV Lovobalavu 2007 *J, A, Tg, A, SA*, 2009 *S, I, R*, 2010 *F, W, It*, 2011 *Tg, Nm, Sa, W*
E Lovodua 1958 *Tg, Tg, Tg*, 1961 *A, A, A*, 1963 *Sa, Tg, Sa*, 1964 *M*
S Lovokuru 1986 *W, Sa, Tg*, 1987 *NZ*
I Lutumailagi 1979 *F, PNG*, 1980 *It, NZ, M, Ar, Ar*, 1982 *Tg*
M Luveitasau 2005 *Sa, Tg, Sa, W, It*, 2006 *Tg, It, Sa*, 2007 *A*
WS Luveniyali 2007 *Tg, A*, 2008 *Sa, M, J, Tg*, 2009 *Sa, J*, 2010 *A*, 2011 *Sa, J, Tg, Tg, Nm, SA, Sa*
GDC Ma'afu 2010 *A, J, Tg, Sa, W, It*, 2011 *Sa, NZ, Tg, Tg, Nm, SA, Sa, W*
V Maimuri 2003 *Ar, F, US, J, S*
I Makutu 1976 *A, A, A*
RPN Makutu 2011 *Tg, Sa, J*
T Makutu 1979 *PNG, Sa, Tg*, 1980 *M, NZ, Ar, Ar*, 1981 *Sa, Tg, Tg, Tg*, 1982 *Sa, Sa*
K Malai 1988 *Tg, Sa, Tg*
IM Male 1998 *A*, 1999 *Ur, E*, 2000 *J, Tg, Sa, US, C, It*, 2001 *Tg, Sa, Tg, Sa, C, Sa*
E Malele 1973 *Tg*, 1976 *I*
D Manaseitava 1981 *Sa*, 1983 *Niu, Sa*, 1985 *Sa, Tg*
DT Manu 2009 *S*, 2010 *A, F, W, It*, 2011 *Tg, Sa, NZ, Tg, Nm, SA, Sa*
A Mara 1928 *Tg, Tg, Tg, Sa*
W Masirewa 1995 *Sa, W, I*, 1998 *A*
M Masitabua 1974 *M*
MS Matadigo 2006 *Tg*, 2009 *Tg*, 2011 *Sa, NZ, Tg, SA, W*
E Matalau 1976 *A, A*
S Matalulu 1994 *M, W, Sa*

J Matanatabu 1993 *Sa, Tg*
A Matanibuka 1932 *Tg, Tg, Tg*, 1934 *Tg, Tg, Tg*
A Matanibukaca 2005 *M, NZ, Tg, Tg*
S Matasarasara 1928 *Tg, Tg*
JL Matavesi 2009 *S, I, R*, 2010 *F, W*
NL Matawalu 2010 *J, Tg, Sa*, 2012 *J, S, Tg*
T Matawalu 2005 *Pt*, 2007 *Sa, J*
L Matea 1924 *Sa, Tg, Tg, Sa*
W Mateiwai 1993 *Sa, Tg, Tg*
N Matirawa 1984 *Tg*, 1989 *Tg, Tg, E*
JTF Matson 1999 *M, Ur*
J McLennan 1994 *M, W, Sa, Tg*, 1995 *C*, 1996 *HK*
T Mitchell 1986 *Tg, Tg*, 1987 *It, F, Sa, Tg*, 1988 *Tg, Sa, E, Tg, Tg*
A Mocelutu 1994 *J, J, M, W, Sa, Tg*, 1995 *C, Sa*, 1997 *Tg, Coo, Sa*, 1998 *S, US, Sa, Tg*, 1999 *M, Ur, It, Nm, C, F*, 2001 *Tg*, 2002 *Sa, Tg, Sa, NZ, W, I, S*, 2003 *Tg, Ar, CHL, US, J*
V Mocelutu 1974 *NZ, M, M*
M Mocetadra 2012 *Tg*
S Morrell 2009 *J*
I Mow 2002 *Sa, Tg, Sa, Tg*, 2003 *Tg*
A Mucunabita 1994 *J, J*
J Mucunabitu 1957 *M, M*, 1959 *Tg*, 1964 *M, W, F*, 1968 *NZ, Tg, Tg*
K Murimurivalu 2011 *Tg, Tg, Tg, Nm, SA, Sa*
I Musanamasi 1982 *Sa, Sa, E*, 1983 *SI*
K Musunamasi 1977 *Tg, Tg, Bl*, 1979 *M, E, PNG, Sa*
L Nabaro 1976 *I*
N Nabaro 1957 *M, M*, 1959 *Tg*, 1961 *A, A, A*, 1964 *M*
M Nabati 1985 *A, A, W*
O Nabavu 1926 *Tg, Tg*
K Nabili 1926 *Tg*, 1928 *Tg, Tg, Tg, Sa*
K Nabili 1985 *Tg*
I Nabobo 1976 *I*
G Naborisi 1954 *A*
G Naborisi 1992 *Tg*
I Nabou 1961 *A, A, A*
M Nabuta 1967 *Tg, Tg*, 1968 *NZ, Tg, Tg, Tg*, 1969 *PNG, SI, PNG*
S Nacaka 1981 *Tg*, 1982 *Sa, Tg, S*
F Naceba 1924 *Sa, Tg, Tg, Sa*
I Nacewa 2003 *S*
S Nacolai 1968 *NZ, Tg, Tg*, 1969 *W, SI, PNG*
V Nadaku 1934 *Tg*, 1938 *M, M, M*
A Nadolo 1987 *It, F, Sa, Tg*, 1988 *E, Tg, Tg*, 1989 *Tg, Tg*, 1991 *Sa, Tg, Tg, R*, 1992 *Sa, Tg*, 1993 *S, Sa, Tg, Tg*, 1995 *C, Sa, Tg, I*
J Nadolo 2000 *Tg, Sa, US, C, It*
RND Nadolo 2010 *A, J, Tg*
A Nadredre 1964 *F, C*, 1968 *Tg*
M Nadridri 2004 *Sa*, 2005 *Sa, Tg*
N Nadruku 1988 *Tg, Sa, E, Tg, Tg*, 1989 *Tg, Bel, S, E*, 1990 *J, HK*, 1991 *C, R*
S Nadruku 1981 *Sa, Sa, Tg, Tg*, 1982 *Sa, Sa, Sa, Tg, S, E*, 1983 *SI, Tg*, 1984 *Sa, Tg, NZ*
A Naevo 1996 *HK, HK, M*, 1997 *NZ, Tg, Sa*, 1998 *S, F, US, Sa, Tg*, 1999 *J, Tg, Sa, M, Sp, Ur, It, Nm, C*, 2001 *Tg, Sa, Tg, Sa, C, Sa*, 2002 *W, I, S*, 2003 *Tg, Tg, F, US, S*
RMS Naevo 2006 *Sa, J*, 2007 *J, C, W, SA*, 2008 *Sa, M, J*, 2009 *Tg, Sa*, 2010 *F, W, It*
I Nagatalevu 1939 *M*
A Nagi 2001 *It, F*, 2004 *Tg, Sa*, 2005 *W, Pt, It*, 2006 *Tg, It, Sa, J*
A Nagicu 1996 *HK*
T Nagusa 2008 *Sa, M, J*, 2009 *Tg, I, R*, 2010 *A, J*, 2011 *Tg, J, NZ*
Naibuka 1968 *Tg*
T Naidole 1954 *M*, 1957 *M, M*, 1958 *Tg, Tg, Tg*, 1959 *Tg*
S Naiduki 1979 *PNG, Sa, Tg*
J Naikadawa 2009 *R*, 2010 *A, J, It*, 2011 *J*
AN Naikatini 2012 *J, Sa, S, Tg*
J Naikidi 1982 *S*
M Naikovu 1957 *M, M*, 1958 *Tg, Tg, Tg*
O Naikovu 1947 *Tg, Tg*, 1948 *M*, 1954 *M*
M Nailumu 1976 *I*
J Naisilisili 2010 *Tg, Sa*
K Naisoro 1991 *Sa, Tg, Tg, F, R*
V Naisoro 1938 *M, M, M*
S Naitau 1968 *Tg, Tg*
S Naiteqe 2000 *J, Tg, Sa, US, It*, 2001 *Sa*
T Naitini 1947 *Tg, Tg*
E Naituivau 1990 *Tg, Sa, HK*, 1991 *Tg, E, C, R*, 1992 *M*, 1995 *W, I*, 1996 *SA, Sa, Tg, HK, M*, 1997 *NZ, Tg, Coo, Sa*, 1999 *Nm, E*
E Naituku 1987 *Ar, It*
I Naituku 1988 *Tg, Sa, E, Tg*, 1990 *Sa*, 1993 *S*
R Naituku 1984 *M*
S Naituku 1983 *SI*, 1985 *A, A, I*, 1986 *Sa*, 1987 *Ar, It, F, Sa, Tg*, 1988 *Tg*, 1989 *Tg, Tg, Bel, S, E*, 1990 *J*
A Naituyaga 1997 *NZ, Tg, Coo, Sa*
A Naituyaga 1972 *A*, 1974 *NZ, M, M*, 1976 *A*

279

FIJI

S Naivilawasa 1986 *Tg*, 1987 *Ar, It, F, Tg*, 1988 *Tg, Sa, E, Tg, Tg*, 1989 *Tg, Tg, Bel, S, E*, 1990 *Tg*, 1991 *Sa, Tg, E, C*
L Nakarawa 2009 *I, R*, 2010 *Tg, Sa*, 2011 *Tg, Sa, Tg, Nm, SA, Sa, W*, 2012 *J, Sa, S, Tg*
M Nakauta 1998 *F, US, Sa*, 1999 *Sp, Ur, It, Nm, F, E*
T Nakauta 1987 *Sa, Tg*, 1988 *Tg*
K Nalaga 1986 *Sa*, 1987 *Ar*, 1989 *Tg*
N Nalaga 2009 *S*, 2010 *F, It*, 2011 *J, NZ, Nm, SA, Sa*
K Nalatu 1967 *Tg, Tg*, 1970 *M, M*, 1973 *M, M*
V Nalio 1961 *A*, 1963 *Sa, Tg, Tg*, 1964 *M, W*, 1967 *Tg*, 1968 *NZ*
L Namadila 1973 *E*, 1974 *M*, 1976 *I*, 1980 *It*
R Namoro 1982 *Sa, S, E*, 1983 *Tg, Sa, Sa*, 1984 *A, Sa, Tg, Tg, NZ*, 1985 *Sa, A, A, I, W*, 1986 *W, Tg, Tg*, 1987 *Ar, F*
I Namua 1969 *PNG*
N Nanuku 2005 *Pt*
A Naqaya 2000 *J, Tg*
S Naqelevuki 1967 *Tg, Tg*, 1968 *Tg, Tg, Tg*, 1969 *W, PNG, SI, PNG*, 1970 *M, M*, 1972 *A*
SM Naqelevuki 2008 *Sa, M, J, Tg*, 2010 *Tg, Sa, F*
J Narisia 1972 *A*, 1973 *Tg*
V Narisia 1977 *Tg, Tg, Tg, BI*, 1979 *F, PNG, Sa, Tg*
V Narisia 1990 *J, Tg*
A Nariva 2002 *S*, 2003 *Tg, Tg*
J Narruhn 2002 *Sa, Tg, Sa, NZ, Tg, W, I, S*
P Naruma 1988 *Tg, Sa, E, Tg*, 1989 *Tg, S*, 1990 *Tg, Sa*, 1991 *F, R*, 1992 *Sa, M*, 1993 *S, Sa*
P Nasalo 1968 *Tg, Tg*, 1969 *W*, 1970 *M*
W Nasalo 1974 *NZ*, 1976 *A, A*
S Nasau 1998 *S*
S Nasave 1969 *W, SI*, 1970 *M*, 1972 *Tg, Tg*, 1973 *M, M*, 1974 *NZ, M, M*, 1976 *A, A, A*, 1977 *BI*, 1979 *M, E, F, PNG, Sa, Tg*
R Nasiga 2008 *Tg*, 2010 *A, J, Sa*, 2011 *Sa, J, NZ, Tg, Tg, Sa, W*
S Nasilasila 1996 *HK*
J Nasova 1963 *Sa*, 1964 *M, W, C*, 1967 *Tg, Tg*, 1968 *NZ, Tg, Tg*
K Natoba 2000 *US, C, It*, 2001 *Tg, Tg, Sa*
M Natuilagilagi 1989 *E*, 1990 *Tg*, 1991 *Sa, Tg*, 1992 *Sa, M*, 1993 *Sa, Tg*
S Natuna 1924 *Sa, Tg, Tg, Tg, Sa*, 1928 *Tg, Tg, Tg, Sa*
W Natuna 1982 *Sa, Tg*
J Naucabalavu 1963 *Sa, Tg, Sa, Tg*, 1964 *M, W, F, C*, 1967 *Tg, Tg, Tg*, 1968 *NZ, Tg, Tg*, 1969 *PNG, SI, PNG*, 1970 *M*
J Naucabalavu 1961 *A, A, A*, 1963 *Sa*, 1964 *W, F, C*, 1967 *Tg*
J Naucabalavu 1972 *Tg, Tg, Tg, A*, 1973 *M, E*, 1974 *NZ, M*, 1976 *A, A*, 1980 *A, It*
E Nauga 1992 *M*, 1993 *S*, 1994 *J, J, M, W, Sa*
B Naulago 1985 *Sa, Tg*
S Naureure 2012 *J, Sa, Tg*
S Naurisau 1954 *M*, 1959 *Tg*
M Navugona 1992 *Sa, Tg*
A Nawalu 1954 *A, A, M, M*
P Nawalu 1983 *Tg, SI, Sa*, 1984 *Tg, Tg, NZ*, 1985 *Sa, Tg, A, A, I, W*, 1986 *W*, 1987 *Ar, NZ, It, F, Sa*
P Nayacakalou 1957 *M*
A Nayacalagilagi 1926 *Tg*
K Nayacalevu 1980 *M, NZ*
WN Nayacalevu 2012 *J, Sa, S*
TR Nayate 1979 *M*
I Neivua 2007 *Sa, J, A, Tg, J, C, A, W*
P Nicuvu 1980 *NZ*
E Nima 1947 *Tg, Tg*, 1948 *M*
S Niqara 1996 *M*
AS Niuqila 1983 *Sa, SI, Tg, Sa*, 1984 *A, Sa, Tg, NZ*, 1985 *Sa, Tg, A, A, I, W*, 1986 *W*
M Nukuvou 1947 *Tg, Tg*, 1948 *M, M*, 1952 *A*
R Nyholt 2001 *F*, 2002 *Sa, Tg, Sa, NZ, Tg, W, I*, 2003 *Tg, Ar, CHL, F, US*
M Olsson 1988 *Tg*, 1990 *Tg, Sa, HK*, 1991 *Sa, E, R*
S Ose 1967 *Tg*
S Pe 1951 *M*, 1954 *A, M, M, M*
G Penjueli 1994 *J*
L Peters 2005 *Sa, Tg, Sa*, 2007 *Sa, J*
LD Politini 1982 *Sa, E*, 1983 *Sa, Tg*
JJV Prasad 2004 *Tg, Sa*, 2005 *Tg, Tg, Sa, Pt*, 2007 *Sa, J, A*
E Puamau 1976 *I*
R Qalo 1968 *NZ, Tg*
R Qaraniqio 1972 *A*, 1973 *M, M*, 1974 *NZ, M*, 1976 *I*, 1977 *Tg, Tg, BI*, 1979 *M, E*, 1980 *A, It, NZ*, 1981 *Sa, Sa, Tg, Tg, Tg*
I Qauqau 1999 *Sa*
A Qera 2005 *Sa, Tg, Pt*, 2006 *Tg, It, J*, 2007 *Sa, J, A, J, C, W, SA*, 2008 *Sa*, 2009 *S, I*, 2010 *F, W, It*, 2011 *J, NZ, Tg, Nm, SA, Sa, W*
A Qio 1926 *Tg, Tg, Tg*
I Qio Ravoka 1947 *Tg, Tg*, 1948 *M, M*

AQ Qiodravu 2000 *US, C, It*, 2001 *Tg, Sa, Tg, Sa, C, Sa, It, F*, 2007 *A, Tg, J, C, A, W, SA*
J Qoro 1968 *Tg, Tg*, 1969 *W, PNG, SI, PNG*, 1970 *M, M*, 1972 *Tg, Tg, Tg*, 1973 *M*
J Qoro 1985 *Tg*
M Qoro 1987 *Ar, It, F, Sa*, 1989 *Bel*
N Qoro 1998 *A*, 1999 *C, US, J, Tg, Sa, M, Sp*
JQ Qovu 2005 *M, NZ, Tg, Sa, Tg, Sa, Pt, It*, 2007 *A*, 2010 *A, F, W, It*
S Qurai 1938 *M, M, M*, 1939 *M*
S Rabaka 1992 *Sa, M*, 1993 *Tg*, 1994 *J, J*, 1998 *S, US*, 1999 *C, US, J, Tg, Sa*, 2001 *Tg, Tg, Sa, C, Sa, It, F*, 2002 *Sa, Tg, Sa, NZ, Tg, W, I*, 2003 *Tg, F, J*
T Rabaka 1991 *Sa, Tg, Tg, R*
RS Rabeni 2000 *J*, 2002 *Sa, Tg, Sa, NZ, Tg, W*, 2003 *Tg, Tg, Ar, CHL, F, US, J, S*, 2004 *Tg, Sa*, 2006 *Tg, It, Sa, J*, 2007 *J, C, A, W, SA*, 2009 *Tg*, 2010 *F, It*, 2011 *J*
S Rabici 1926 *Tg*, 1928 *Tg, Tg, Tg*
A Rabitu 1990 *J, Sa*, 1993 *S, Sa, Tg*
S Rabitu 1932 *Tg, Tg*, 1934 *Tg, Tg, Tg*
S Rabonaqica 2008 *J, Tg*
T Rabuli 1972 *Tg*, 1973 *M, Tg, E*, 1974 *M, M*, 1976 *A, A, A*
A Racika 1969 *SI*, 1970 *M, M, C*, 1972 *Tg, Tg, Tg, A*, 1973 *M, M, Tg, E*, 1974 *NZ, M, M*, 1976 *A, A*, 1977 *Tg, Tg, Tg, BI*, 1979 *M, E, F, PNG, Sa, Tg*, 1980 *A, It, NZ*
S Radidi 2008 *M, Tg*, 2010 *A*
U Radike 1959 *Tg*
U Radike 1938 *M, M, M*
A Radrado 1989 *Tg, Tg*
M Radrekusa 1988 *Tg*
I Radrodro 1951 *M*
I Radrodro 1980 *A, It, NZ*
I Radrodro 1957 *M*, 1958 *Tg, Tg, Tg*
J Radrodro 1970 *M, M, C*
J Raikuna 1963 *Sa, Tg*, 1964 *M, C*, 1967 *Tg, Tg*, 1968 *NZ, Tg, Tg, Tg*, 1969 *M, SI, PNG*, 1970 *M*
JR Railomo 2005 *NZ*, 2007 *J, C, A, W, SA*, 2008 *Sa, M, J, Tg*
L Raitilava 1968 *NZ*, 1969 *W, PNG, SI, PNG*, 1972 *Tg, Tg, Tg, A*, 1976 *A, A*
S Raiwalui 1997 *NZ, Tg, Coo, Sa*, 1998 *S, F, US, A, Sa, Tg*, 1999 *C, US, J, Tg, Sa, M, Sp, It, Nm, C, F, E*, 2000 *J, Tg, Sa, US, C, It*, 2001 *Sa, C, Sa*, 2002 *Sa, Tg, Sa, NZ, Tg, W, I, S*, 2006 *Tg, It, Sa, J*
E Rakai 1983 *SI, Tg, Sa*, 1984 *A, Sa, Tg*, 1985 *Sa, Tg, A, A, I, W*, 1986 *W, Sa, Tg*, 1987 *NZ, F*
K Rakoroi 1983 *Tg, SI, Niu, Tg*, 1984 *A, Sa, Tg*, 1985 *A, A, I, W*, 1986 *W, Tg, Sa, Tg*, 1987 *Ar, NZ, It, F, Sa, Tg*
S Ralagi 1951 *M*, 1952 *A, A*, 1954 *A, A*
S Ralawa 1934 *Tg, Tg, Tg*, 1938 *M, M, M*, 1939 *M*
J Ralulu 2008 *Sa, Tg*, 2010 *J, Tg, Sa*, 2012 *S, Tg*
TD Ralumu 1979 *E, F*
T Ranavue 1947 *Tg, Tg*, 1952 *A, A*, 1954 *A, A, M, M, M*
S Rarasea 1961 *A*
V Rarawa 2010 *It*
L Rasala 1994 *J, J*
M Rasari 1988 *Tg, Sa, E, Tg*, 1989 *Bel, S, E*, 1990 *Sa*, 1991 *Sa, Tg*
I Rasila 1992 *Sa, M*, 1998 *S, F, A*, 1999 *C, US, Sp, Ur, E*, 2000 *J, Tg, Sa, US, C, It*, 2001 *Tg, Sa, Tg, Tg, Sa, It*, 2002 *Sa, Tg, Sa, NZ, S*, 2003 *Tg, Tg, Ar, CHL, J, S*
P Rasiosateki 1963 *Sa, Tg*, 1964 *M, W, F, C*
S Rasolea 1984 *Tg, NZ*, 1985 *Sa, Tg, A*
S Rasua 1961 *A, A, A*
J Ratu 1980 *NZ, Ar, Ar*, 1981 *Sa, Tg, Tg*, 1982 *Tg, Sa, S, E*
J Ratu 2009 *S, R*
Q Ratu 1976 *I*, 1977 *Tg, Tg, Tg, BI*
R Ratu 2009 *Sa, J*, 2010 *A, J, Tg, Sa, W*
S Ratu 1968 *Tg*
N Ratudina 1972 *Tg*, 1973 *M, M, E*, 1974 *NZ, M, M*, 1977 *Tg, Tg, Tg, BI*, 1979 *M, F*
E Ratudradra 1980 *A, M, NZ, Ar, Ar*, 1981 *Tg, Tg, Tg*
V Ratudradra 1976 *A, A*, 1977 *Tg, BI*, 1979 *M, E*, 1980 *NZ, M*, 1981 *Sa, Sa*, 1982 *Sa*, 1984 *Tg*
S Ratumaiyali 1947 *Tg*
K Ratumuri 1980 *M*, 1981 *Sa, Sa*
E Ratuniata 2001 *Sa, Tg*, 2002 *Sa, Sa*
I Ratuva 2012 *J, Sa, S*
RARG Ratuva 2005 *M, NZ, Tg, Tg, Sa, W, It*, 2006 *Sa, J*, 2007 *Tg, J, A, W, SA*, 2008 *Sa, M, J, Tg*
N Ratuveilawa 1961 *A*, 1963 *Sa, Tg, Sa, Tg*, 1964 *C*
K Ratuvou 2005 *Sa, W, Pt, It*, 2006 *Tg, It, Sa, J*, 2007 *Tg, J, C, W, SA*, 2008 *Sa, M, J*, 2012 *Sa, S*
SD Raulini 1997 *Sa*
T Raulumi 1973 *M*
J Rauluni 1995 *C, Sa, Tg, W, I*, 1996 *SA, Sa, Tg*, 1997 *NZ, Tg*, 1998

E **Tatawaqa** 1981 *Tg, Tg, Tg,* 1982 *Sa, Sa, Sa, Tg, S*
P **Tatukivei** 1958 *Tg*
E **Tauga** 1994 *Tg*
I **Taukei** 1924 *Sa, Tg, Tg, Tg, Sa,* 1926 *Tg*
I **Tawake** 1986 *W,* 1987 *Sa, Tg,* 1988 *Tg, Tg,* 1990 *J,* 1991 *Tg, E, C, F, R,* 1992 *Sa, Tg, M,* 1993 *S, Sa, Tg,* 1994 *J, J, M, W, Sa, Tg,* 1995 *C, Sa, Tg, W, I,* 1996 *SA, Sa, Tg, HK, M,* 1997 *NZ, Coo, Sa,* 1998 *S, F, US, A,* 1999 *C, US, Tg, Sp, Ur, E*
S **Tawake** 1992 *Sa, M,* 1998 *Sa, Tg,* 1999 *C, US, J, M, It, Nm, C, F, E,* 2002 *Sa, NZ, Tg, W, I, S,* 2003 *CHL*
S **Tawase** 1961 *A, A*
E **Teleni** 1982 *Sa, Sa, S, E,* 1983 *Tg, Sa, Niu, Tg, Sa,* 1984 *A, Sa, Tg,* 1985 *A, A, I, W,* 1986 *W,* 1988 *Tg,* 1989 *Tg, Tg, Bel, S, E*
L **Temani** 1924 *Sa, Tg, Tg, Tg, Sa*
DD **Thomas** 2007 *Tg,* 2008 *M, Tg*
I **Tikoduadua** 1982 *S, E,* 1983 *Sa*
E **Tikoidraubuta** 1992 *Tg*
I **Tikomaimakogai** 1999 *US, J, Tg, Sa, M, Ur, It, Nm, E,* 2000 *J, Tg*
K **Tilalati** 2000 *J, Sa*
A **Toga** 1963 *Tg, Sa, Tg*
S **Toga** 1964 *W, C,* 1967 *Tg, Tg, Tg,* 1968 *NZ, Tg,* 1969 *W, PNG, SI, PNG,* 1970 *C*
A **Tokairavua** 1967 *Tg,* 1970 *M, C,* 1972 *Tg, Tg, Tg, A,* 1973 *M, Tg,* 1977 *Tg, Tg*
J **Toloi** 1994 *M, W, Sa, Tg*
S **Tolotu** 1964 *F*
RDT **Tonawai** 2007 *Tg,* 2010 *Tg, Sa*
J **Tora** 2005 *Tg, Sa, Tg, Sa, Pt,* 2006 *Tg, J*
P **Tora** 1986 *Sa, Tg*
P **Tove** 1951 *M*
TD **Tuapati** 2010 *A, J, Tg, Sa, F, W, It,* 2011 *Tg, Sa, Tg, SA, Sa,* 2012 *Sa, S, Tg*
T **Tubananitu** 1980 *A, It, NZ,* 1981 *Sa, Sa, Tg, Tg, Tg,* 1982 *Sa, Sa, Sa, Tg, S,* 1983 *Niu, Tg, Sa,* 1984 *Tg, NZ,* 1985 *A*
W **Tubu** 1967 *Tg*
P **Tubui** 1981 *Sa, Sa*
S **Tubuna** 1932 *Tg, Tg, Tg*
N **Tubutubu** 1924 *Sa, Tg, Tg, Tg, Sa*
E **Tudia** 1973 *Tg*
P **Tuidraki** 1994 *J, J, M, W, Sa, Tg*
P **Tuidraki** 1932 *Tg, Tg, Tg*
J **Tuikabe** 1999 *US, Sa, Ur,* 2000 *J, Tg, Sa, US, C, It,* 2001 *Tg, Sa, Tg, Sa, C, Sa, It, F*
A **Tuilevu** 1996 *SA, Sa, Tg, HK,* 1997 *Tg, Coo, Sa,* 1998 *S, F, A, Sa,* 2003 *Tg, Tg, Ar, F, US, J, S,* 2004 *Tg*
J **Tuilevu** 2008 *Tg*
W **Tuinagiagia** 1968 *Tg,* 1976 *I*
E **Tuisese** 2001 *F*
I **Tuisese** 1969 *W, SI,* 1970 *M, M, C,* 1972 *Tg, Tg, Tg,* 1973 *E,* 1974 *NZ, M, M,* 1976 *A, A,* 1977 *Tg, Tg, Bl*
I **Tuisese** 2000 *J, Sa*
S **Tuisese** 1958 *Tg,* 1963 *Sa, Tg, Sa, Tg,* 1964 *M, W, F*
W **Tuisese** 1947 *Tg,* 1948 *M, M, M*
A **Tuitavua** 1938 *M, M, M,* 1939 *M,* 1947 *Tg, Tg,* 1948 *M, M, M,* 1952 *A, A,* 1954 *A, A, M, M, M*
E **Tuivunivono** 1993 *Tg*
N **Tuiyau** 1948 *M, M, M*
T **Tukaitabua** 1968 *NZ, Tg, Tg,* 1972 *Tg*
U **Tukana** 1963 *Sa, Tg,* 1964 *M, W, F, C*
T **Tukunia** 1984 *Tg*
W **Turaga** 1986 *Tg*
A **Turagacoko** 1968 *NZ, Tg, Tg,* 1969 *W*
A **Turukawa** 2004 *Sa,* 2005 *Pt,* 2007 *Sa, J, A, Tg*
E **Turuva** 1984 *A,* 1985 *A, I*
O **Turuva** 1990 *HK,* 1991 *E, R,* 1994 *Sa, Tg,* 1995 *C, Sa, Tg,* 1998 *A,* 1999 *C, US*
S **Tuva** 1959 *Tg,* 1961 *A, A, A*
M **Tuvoli** 1951 *M*
S **Tuvula** 1985 *A, I, W,* 1986 *W,* 1987 *Ar, NZ, It*
E **Tuvunivono** 1992 *M,* 1993 *S, Tg,* 1997 *NZ*
T **Uliuviti** 1926 *Tg, Tg, Tg,* 1928 *Tg*
A **Uluinayau** 1996 *SA, Sa, Tg, HK, HK, M,* 1997 *NZ, Tg, Coo, Sa,* 1998 *F, Sa, Tg,* 1999 *C, J, Tg, Sa, Nm, C, F, E,* 2001 *Tg, C, Sa,* 2002 *Sa, Tg, Sa, NZ,* 2003 *Tg, US*
N **Uluiviti** 1957 *M, M,* 1959 *Tg*
N **Uluvula** 1976 *I,* 1979 *M, E, F, PNG, Tg,* 1980 *Ar, Ar,* 1982 *Sa, Sa,* 1983 *Tg, Sa, SI, Sa,* 1984 *A, Tg, NZ,* 1986 *Tg*
J **Vadugu** 1961 *A, A*
I **Vai** 1979 *Tg*
RMT **Vakacegu** 2004 *Sa,* 2007 *Sa, A,* 2008 *Sa, M, J*
F **Vakadrano** 1986 *Tg*
J **Vakalomaloma** 1996 *HK*
S **Vakarua** 1926 *Tg, Tg*
M **Vakatawabai** 1967 *Tg*

S **Valewai** 1948 *M, M, M,* 1951 *M,* 1952 *A, A*
S **Vanini** 1964 *F*
S **Varo** 1982 *Sa,* 1984 *A, Tg, Tg, NZ*
V **Varo** 1970 *C,* 1972 *Tg, Tg, Tg, A,* 1973 *M, Tg*
L **Vasuvulagi** 1989 *S, E,* 1990 *Tg*
AV **Vata** 2005 *It,* 2008 *Sa, J, Tg*
J **Vatubua** 1992 *Tg*
S **Vatubua** 1951 *M,* 1952 *A, A,* 1954 *A, A, M, M, M,* 1958 *Tg, Tg*
W **Vatubua** 1988 *Tg, Tg*
S **Vatudau** 1939 *M*
WNNM **Vatuvoka** 2009 *S, R,* 2011 *J, Tg*
V **Vatuwaliwali** 1980 *M, NZ, Ar, Ar,* 1981 *Tg, Tg, Tg,* 1982 *Sa, Sa, Sa, Tg, S, E,* 1983 *Niu, Tg, Sa*
E **Vavaitamana** 1934 *Tg,* 1938 *M, M, M,* 1947 *Tg, Tg,* 1948 *M, M, M*
E **Vavaitamana** 1934 *Tg, Tg*
V **Vavaitamana** 1932 *Tg, Tg, Tg,* 1934 *Tg, Tg, Tg,* 1938 *M, M, M,* 1939 *M*
J **Veidreyaki** 1976 *A*
A **Veikoso** 1947 *Tg, Tg,* 1948 *M, M, M*
V **Veikoso** 2009 *S, I,* 2010 *A, J, Tg, Sa, F, W, It,* 2011 *Tg, Sa, NZ, Tg, Nm, W,* 2012 *J, S*
J **Veitayaki** 1994 *M, W, Sa, Tg,* 1995 *C, Sa, Tg, W, I,* 1996 *SA, Sa, Tg, HK, HK, M,* 1997 *NZ,* 1998 *S, F, US, Sa, Tg,* 1999 *C, US, J, Tg, Sa, M, Sp, Ur, It, Nm, C, F, E,* 2000 *J, Tg, Sa, US, C, It,* 2001 *Tg,* 2003 *Tg, Tg, Ar, CHL, F, US, J, S*
S **Verevuni** 1992 *Sa, Tg*
J **Vidiri** 1994 *J, J, M, W, Sa, Tg,* 1995 *C*
SN **Viriviri** 1976 *A, A,* 1977 *Tg, Tg, Bl,* 1979 *E, F, PNG, Sa, Tg,* 1980 *NZ, M, NZ, Ar, Ar,* 1981 *Sa, Sa, Tg, Tg,* 1982 *Sa, Sa, S, E*
J **Visei** 1970 *M, C,* 1972 *Tg,* 1973 *M, M, Tg, E,* 1974 *M,* 1976 *I*
N **Vitau** 1994 *J,* 1996 *M*
S **Vodivodi** 1967 *Tg, Tg, Tg*
S **Vola** 1964 *C*
I **Volavola** 1968 *Tg, Tg, Tg,* 1969 *W, PNG, SI, PNG*
L **Volavola** 1976 *I*
M **Volavola** 2005 *W, Pt, It,* 2010 *Tg, Sa*
P **Volavola** 1985 *W,* 1986 *W, Tg, Sa, Tg,* 1987 *NZ, It, Tg,* 1991 *F, R*
S **Vonolagi** 1988 *Tg, Sa, E, Tg, Tg,* 1990 *Tg, Sa,* 1992 *Tg,* 1993 *S, Sa, Tg*
T **Vonolagi** 1989 *Tg, Bel, E,* 1990 *J, HK,* 1991 *Sa, Tg, E, R,* 1992 *M,* 1993 *S, Sa, Tg, Tg*
J **Voreqe** 1938 *M, M,* 1939 *M,* 1947 *Tg*
U **Vosabalavu** 1924 *Sa, Tg, Tg, Tg, Sa*
T **Vosaicake** 1938 *M, M, M,* 1939 *M*
K **Vosailagi** 1979 *F, Sa, Tg,* 1980 *A, It, NZ, M, Ar, Ar,* 1981 *Sa, Sa*
M **Vosanibole** 1991 *Tg, F*
W **Votu** 2012 *J, Sa, S, Tg*
AW **Vuaviri** 2012 *Tg*
E **Vucago** 2006 *Tg,* 2010 *A, J*
L **Vuetaki** 1980 *A, It, Ar*
S **Vuetaki** 1982 *Sa, Sa,* 1983 *SI, Niu, Tg,* 1984 *Sa,* 1985 *Tg*
I **Vuivuda** 1948 *M, M, M*
B **Vukiwai** 1984 *Tg*
J **Vulakoro** 2004 *Tg, Sa,* 2005 *W, Pt*
J **Vulavou** 1989 *Tg*
N **Vuli** 1991 *F, R,* 1992 *Sa, Tg,* 1993 *Tg*
AJ **Vulivuli** 2010 *F, W, It,* 2011 *Tg, Sa, NZ, Tg, Tg, Nm, Sa, W*
R **Vunakece** 1954 *M, M*
M **Vunibaka** 1999 *C, J, M, Sp, It, C, E,* 2000 *Sa, US, C, It,* 2001 *It, F,* 2003 *Tg, F, US, J*
S **Vunivalu** 1987 *Ar, NZ, F*
R **Vuruya** 1951 *M,* 1952 *A*
P **Wadali** 1957 *M*
T **Wainiqolo** 1990 *J, Tg, HK,* 1993 *Tg, Tg*
P **Waisake** 1976 *A,* 1980 *A, It, M*
V **Waka** 1967 *Tg, Tg, Tg*
S **Walisoliso** 1963 *Tg,* 1964 *W, F, C,* 1967 *Tg, Tg, Tg*
P **Waqa** 1926 *Tg,* 1928 *Tg, Sa,* 1932 *Tg, Tg, Tg,* 1934 *Tg, Tg*
J **Waqabitu** 1995 *W, I,* 1996 *Sa,* 1997 *NZ, Coo, Sa,* 1998 *S, F, US, Sa, Tg,* 2000 *J, Tg, Sa,* 2001 *It, F*
A **Waqaliti** 1985 *A*
DM **Waqaniburotu** 2010 *A, J, Tg, Sa,* 2011 *Tg, J, NZ, Tg, Nm, SA*
I **Waqavatu** 1989 *Tg, Tg, Bel, S*
I **Wea** 1938 *M*
J **Wesele** 1934 *Tg,* 1939 *M*
R **Williams** 1994 *W, Sa, Tg,* 1995 *C*
AE **Wise** 2009 *J,* 2010 *A, J*
T **Yacabula** 2002 *Tg, Sa, Tg*
K **Yacalevu** 1980 *Ar,* 1981 *Sa, Sa, Tg, Tg, Tg,* 1982 *Sa, Sa, Sa, Tg, S,* 1983 *SI, Niu*
S **Yalayala** 1983 *Tg, SI, Tg,* 1984 *Sa, Tg, NZ,* 1985 *Sa, Tg,* 1986 *Tg, Sa, Tg*
A **Yalayalatabua** 2007 *Sa, A,* 2008 *J,* 2009 *Sa, J, S, R,* 2010 *J, Tg, Sa*
JNBN **Yanuyanutawa** 2012 *Sa, S, Tg*

FRANCE

FRANCE'S 2012 TEST RECORD

OPPONENTS	DATE	VENUE	RESULT
Italy	4 Feb	H	Won 30–12
Scotland	26 Feb	A	Won 23–17
Ireland	4 Mar	H	Drew 17–17
England	11 Mar	H	Lost 22–24
Wales	17 Mar	A	Lost 16–9
Argentina	16 Jun	A	Lost 23–20
Argentina	23 Jun	A	Won 49–10

LES BLEUS HEADING IN RIGHT DIRECTION, SAYS PELOUS

By Iain Spragg

France unearthed a new star in Wesley Fofana during the RBS Six Nations.

THE COUNTRIES

France's rehabilitation and inevitable rebuilding work in the wake of their heartbreaking defeat to the All Blacks in the Rugby World Cup 2011 Final is firmly on track, according to record-breaking former captain Fabien Pelous.

Les Bleus were devastated after their 8–7 loss to New Zealand – the third time a French side had finished as runners-up in the tournament's history – and after a lacklustre Six Nations campaign and a mixed summer tour of Argentina, it seemed the side's World Cup hangover was lingering.

But Pelous, France's most-capped player with 118 Test appearances between 1995 and 2007 and captain a record 42 times in his career, insists the current team under new head coach Philippe Saint-André is making genuine progress.

"The France team is embarking on a four-year cycle which will bring it to 2015," Pelous said. "The introduction of new players into the squad with the aim of beginning this new cycle is essential. The France team is no exception in this regard, especially since certain players retired after the World Cup. Talented young players such as Wesley Fofana and Yoann Maestri will play an essential part in this process."

France defied expectations to reach the RWC 2011 Final. It was a fractious and controversial campaign under Marc Lièvremont in which they lost to both New Zealand and Tonga in the pool phase as reports of a complete breakdown in the relationship between the coach and his players surfaced.

When Saint-André succeeded Lièvremont at the end of 2011 after their heroic but all-too-familiar disappointment in the final, the clamour was for the new coach to heal the divisions that had threatened to rip the squad apart in New Zealand.

But Pelous, a veteran of the RWC 1999 Final against the Wallabies and the tournaments of 2003 and 2007, believes reports of debilitating disharmony between the players and the coaching staff were misleading.

"The crisis during the World Cup was exaggerated by the media," he said. "It was not so much a crisis in French rugby as a crisis within the France team, which just happened to take place during the long and difficult event which is the World Cup. Lièvremont's departure after the World Cup diffused any resentment which may have surfaced during the event.

"Saint-André was in competition with Fabien Galthié to succeed Lièvremont and both were legitimate candidates. His decision to name Yannick Bru and Patrice Lagisquet as his assistants was without doubt a determining factor in his appointment.

"The feeling in France after the New Zealand game was difficult to describe. Emotions were mixed because despite having had an average World Cup in terms of results and the performances, no France team had ever come so close to winning the title. Despite our poor play during the tournament, the final proved very frustrating for France. We had conflicting feelings of pride for our players and disappointment at having come so close to success."

Saint-André had three months to prepare for his side's Six Nations opener against Italy in Paris and named two uncapped players – Fofana and Maestri – in a 30-man squad for the Championship.

It was evolution rather than revolution in terms of selection and French supporters waited to see how the former Gloucester, Bourgoin, Sale and Toulon coach would adapt to his elevation to Test level.

The early signs were encouraging. France kicked off with a comfortable 30–12 win over the Azzurri with tries from Aurélien Rougerie,

Julien Malzieu, Vincent Clerc and impressive debutant Fofana avenging their shock defeat to Italy 12 months earlier in Rome and getting their campaign off to a perfect start.

France denied Italy a try at the Stade de France and after the team's tribulations in New Zealand, a tentative sense of optimism was reborn.

When they overcame Scotland 23–17 at Murrayfield three weeks later thoughts began to turn to the Championship title. The Scots were looking for a first win over France since their 20–16 triumph back in 2006 while Saint-André opted to keep faith with the same starting XV and replacements for the match.

For the first 56 minutes in Edinburgh, the home side looked capable of registering a rare win as they battled into a 17–13 lead. Scotland started the stronger of the two sides with a seventh-minute score from Stuart Hogg but Fofana's first-half try redressed the balance until Lee Jones scampered over for the home side 16 minutes after the restart.

The visitors were rocking but, just five minutes after the Scots had scored, full back Maxime Médard replied to edge his side ahead, and at the final whistle France were four points to the good and still unbeaten in the competition.

Two wins from two, however, were to prove as good as it got for France in the tournament and in their third outing Les Bleus were held to a 17–17 draw by Ireland in Paris, recovering from a 17–6 half-time deficit thanks to another Fofana try and two penalties from Morgan Parra.

In a match which had to be rearranged due to a frozen pitch in Paris in February, France paid the price for their sluggish first-half display and, although they were the dominant side at the Stade de France in the second period, they had left themselves too much to do.

"We were happy with the Italy result, especially as we were beaten by the same team the year before," Pelous said. "It was a good start for a new team. It was harder against Scotland and then Ireland but, as I have said, the France team is in the process of restructuring and, as with all teams undergoing such a process, performances can vary from match to match. This would explain the differences in performances."

France moved on to the England and Wales games. Saint-André recalled half backs Lionel Beauxis and Julien Dupuy for the clash with the English at the Stade de France and, although the chance of the Grand Slam had evaporated in Paris, Les Bleus remained in genuine contention for the title.

The Anglo-Gallic clash in Paris was a thriller between the old rivals but ultimately it did not go France's way. The visitors stormed into an early lead with tries from Manu Tuilagi and Ben Foden but penalties from Beauxis, Dupuy and substitute Parra saw France come roaring back to within two points. Tom Croft scored England's third try only for Fofana's fourth try in as many appearances on 74 minutes to again cut the deficit.

The home crowd sensed a famous recovery with the match poised at 24–22 but the clock was again against them and the English clung on for the win. As in Dublin, France were punished for their early lethargy and, despite periods of dominance, they were unable to produce 80 minutes of their best rugby.

They concluded the Six Nations against Wales in Cardiff. With the title now beyond their reach, Saint-André made five changes to his starting XV and for long spells of the game at the Millennium Stadium, Les Bleus threatened to deny Warren Gatland's side the prized Grand Slam they were chasing.

An early Dimitri Yachvili penalty saw France score first but Wales registered the only try of the match midway through the first half through Alex Cuthbert and at the break they led 10–3.

A Beauxis penalty on 44 minutes kept the visitors in the hunt and when Yachvili landed his second with eight minutes to play, Wales were protecting a precarious 13–9 advantage. The game hung in the balance but the hosts got the all-important next score with a Leigh Halfpenny penalty to claim a 16–9 win, the title and the Grand Slam.

The result relegated France to fourth behind Ireland on points difference in the final Championship table but although two victories in five outings did not constitute a vintage season by French standards, the two defeats were both by narrow margins and, in the shape of Clermont Auvergne's Fofana, Saint-André had unearthed a real star.

"The game with England in Paris was a very close match," Pelous said. "There was an attempt at a drop goal from Trinh-Duc in the final minute which could have changed the result. Unfortunately, the drop went under the bar.

"The match in Cardiff was dominated by a very assured Welsh team. Wales will be very difficult to deal with in the years to come. This match highlighted the differences which currently exist between the two teams."

Northern hemisphere competition made way for an excursion south of the equator in the summer to play Argentina in two Tests and Saint-André took the decision to rest a raft of key senior players for the trip, naming Pascal Pape as captain in place of Thierry Dusautoir.

In the forwards, there were five newcomers to the set-up in props Antoine Guillamon and Yvan Watremez, hooker Christopher Tolofua and second rows Romain Taofifenua and Christophe Sansom, while in the back division scrum half Maxime Machenaud, centre Geoffrey

Doumayrou, wing Romain Martial and full back Brice Dulin took the tour party's uncapped contingent to nine.

The first Test against the Pumas at the Estadio Olimpico in Córdoba was a tense and closely-contested affair. France surged into the lead with three Parra penalties, and when number 8 Louis Picamoles crashed over on 26 minutes Les Bleus were 14–10 in front.

The second half ebbed and flowed but two further penalties from Parra edged the visitors into a 20–16 lead and France were on the verge of their first win in Argentina since their 37–12 triumph in Buenos Aires 14 years earlier.

They came within three minutes of success but could not close out the match. Pumas wing Manuel Montero was the first to a chip ahead to touch down for the crucial score and the home side claimed a dramatic 23–20 win.

Facing a potential sixth straight defeat to Argentina, Saint-André made six changes for the second Test in Tucumán, handing a Test debut to Agen's Machenaud, and his team responded magnificently to the challenge of beating the Pumas in their own backyard with a record 49–10 victory.

The first of Les Bleus' six tries came after 11 minutes through wing Benjamin Fall and the tourists scored at regular intervals with Yoann Huget (2), Machenaud, Maxime Mermoz and Alexandre Lapandry all crossing to underline France's supremacy.

"It was a brave decision to leave many important players at home but many of them needed a rest after the World Cup," Pelous said. "Let's not forget that most of the players had played around 40 matches in the season. Obviously the result in the first Test was compromised but the objective of introducing new players to the team was achieved.

"It was a tour that had good things. Young players had their first outings in the side while Pascal Pape proved he can lead the team in the absence of Dusautoir."

The end of the Argentina tour brought down the curtain on Saint-André's first season as coach. The Rugby World Cup in New Zealand ensured it was a truncated campaign and, while his modest record of three victories in seven games was far from a resounding success, Pelous insists it was an encouraging start to the Saint-André era.

"You cannot sum up the time after the World Cup solely based on the team's results," he said. "France has made a change of direction and this change is starting to gather speed. I am looking forward to the future of this team and hope that they will continue to progress with the new coach."

FRANCE INTERNATIONAL STATISTICS
MATCH RECORDS UP TO 10 OCTOBER 2012

MOST CONSECUTIVE TEST WINS

10	1931 E, G, 1932 G, 1933 G, 1934 G, 1935 G, 1936 G1, 2, 1937 G, It
8	1998 E, S, I, W, Arg 1, 2, Fj, Arg 3
8	2001 SA3, A, Fj 2002 It, W, E, S, I
8	2004 I, It, W, S, E, US, C, A

MOST CONSECUTIVE TESTS WITHOUT DEFEAT

Matches	Wins	Draws	Period
10	10	0	1931 to 1938
10	8	2	1958 to 1959
10	9	1	1986 to 1987

MOST POINTS IN A MATCH
BY THE TEAM

Pts	Opponents	Venue	Year
87	Namibia	Toulouse	2007
77	Fiji	Saint Etienne	2001
70	Zimbabwe	Auckland	1987
67	Romania	Bucharest	2000
64	Romania	Aurillac	1996
64	Georgia	Marseilles	2007
62	Romania	Castres	1999
62	Romania	Bucharest	2006
61	Fiji	Brisbane	2003
60	Italy	Toulon	1967
59	Romania	Paris	1924
56	Romania	Lens	2003
56	Italy	Rome	2005

BY A PLAYER

Pts	Player	Opponents	Venue	Year
30	D Camberabero	Zimbabwe	Auckland	1987
28	C Lamaison	New Zealand	Twickenham	1999
28	F Michalak	Scotland	Sydney	2003
27	G Camberabero	Italy	Toulon	1967
27	C Lamaison	New Zealand	Marseilles	2000
27	G Merceron	South Africa	Johannesburg	2001
27	J-B Elissalde	Namibia	Toulouse	2007
26	T Lacroix	Ireland	Durban	1995
26	F Michalak	Fiji	Brisbane	2003
25	J-P Romeu	United States	Chicago	1976
25	P Berot	Romania	Agen	1987
25	T Lacroix	Tonga	Pretoria	1995

MOST TRIES IN A MATCH
BY THE TEAM

Tries	Opponents	Venue	Year
13	Romania	Paris	1924
13	Zimbabwe	Auckland	1987
13	Namibia	Toulouse	2007
12	Fiji	Saint Etienne	2001
11	Italy	Toulon	1967
10	Romania	Aurillac	1996
10	Romania	Bucharest	2000

BY A PLAYER

Tries	Player	Opponents	Venue	Year
4	A Jauréguy	Romania	Paris	1924
4	M Celhay	Italy	Paris	1937

MOST CONVERSIONS IN A MATCH
BY THE TEAM

Cons	Opponents	Venue	Year
11	Namibia	Toulouse	2007
9	Italy	Toulon	1967
9	Zimbabwe	Auckland	1987
8	Romania	Wellington	1987
8	Romania	Lens	2003

BY A PLAYER

Cons	Player	Opponents	Venue	Year
11	J-B Elissalde	Namibia	Toulouse	2007
9	G Camberabero	Italy	Toulon	1967
9	D Camberabero	Zimbabwe	Auckland	1987
8	G Laporte	Romania	Wellington	1987

FRANCE

MOST PENALTIES IN A MATCH
BY THE TEAM

Penalties	Opponents	Venue	Year
8	Ireland	Durban	1995
7	Wales	Paris	2001
7	Italy	Paris	2002
6	Argentina	Buenos Aires	1977
6	Scotland	Paris	1997
6	Italy	Auch	1997
6	Ireland	Paris	2000
6	South Africa	Johannesburg	2001
6	Argentina	Buenos Aires	2003
6	Fiji	Brisbane	2003
6	England	Twickenham	2005
6	Wales	Paris	2007
6	England	Twickenham	2007
6	Ireland	Dublin	2011

BY A PLAYER

Penalties	Player	Opponents	Venue	Year
8	T Lacroix	Ireland	Durban	1995
7	G Merceron	Italy	Paris	2002
6	J-M Aguirre	Argentina	Buenos Aires	1977
6	C Lamaison	Scotland	Paris	1997
6	C Lamaison	Italy	Auch	1997
6	G Merceron	Ireland	Paris	2000
6	G Merceron	South Africa	Johannesburg	2001
6	F Michalak	Fiji	Brisbane	2003
6	D Yachvili	England	Twickenham	2005

MOST DROP GOALS IN A MATCH
BY THE TEAM

Drops	Opponents	Venue	Year
3	Ireland	Paris	1960
3	England	Twickenham	1985
3	New Zealand	Christchurch	1986
3	Australia	Sydney	1990
3	Scotland	Paris	1991
3	New Zealand	Christchurch	1994

BY A PLAYER

Drops	Player	Opponents	Venue	Year
3	P Albaladejo	Ireland	Paris	1960
3	J-P Lescarboura	England	Twickenham	1985
3	J-P Lescarboura	New Zealand	Christchurch	1986
3	D Camberabero	Australia	Sydney	1990

CAREER RECORDS

MOST CAPPED PLAYERS

Caps	Player	Career Span
118	F Pelous	1995 to 2007
111	P Sella	1982 to 1995
98	R Ibañez	1996 to 2007
93	S Blanco	1980 to 1991
89	O Magne	1997 to 2007
86	D Traille	2001 to 2011
84	S Marconnet	1998 to 2011
82	I Harinordoquy	2002 to 2012
78	A Benazzi	1990 to 2001
76	A Rougerie	2001 to 2012
75	J Bonnaire	2004 to 2012
74	L Nallet	2000 to 2012
73	Y Jauzion	2001 to 2011
71	J-L Sadourny	1991 to 2001
71	O Brouzet	1994 to 2003
71	C Califano	1994 to 2007
69	R Bertranne	1971 to 1981
69	P Saint-André	1990 to 1997
69	P de Villiers	1999 to 2007
67	C Dominici	1998 to 2007
64	F Galthié	1991 to 2003
63	M Crauste	1957 to 1966
63	B Dauga	1964 to 1972
63	S Betsen	1997 to 2007
63	D Szarzewski	2004 to 2012

MOST CONSECUTIVE TESTS

Tests	Player	Span
46	R Bertranne	1973 to 1979
45	P Sella	1982 to 1987
44	M Crauste	1960 to 1966
35	B Dauga	1964 to 1968

MOST TESTS AS CAPTAIN

Tests	Captain	Span
42	F Pelous	1997 to 2006
41	R Ibanez	1998 to 2007
34	J-P Rives	1978 to 1984
34	P Saint-André	1994 to 1997
31	T Dusautoir	2009 to 2012
25	D Dubroca	1986 to 1988
25	F Galthié	1999 to 2003
24	G Basquet	1948 to 1952
22	M Crauste	1961 to 1966

MOST POINTS IN TESTS

Points	Player	Tests	Career
380	C Lamaison	37	1996 to 2001
373	D Yachvili	61	2002 to 2012
367	T Lacroix	43	1989 to 1997
354	D Camberabero	36	1982 to 1993
274	M Parra	43	2008 to 2012
271	F Michalak	56	2001 to 2012
267	G Merceron	32	1999 to 2003
265	J-P Romeu	34	1972 to 1977
247	T Castaignède	54	1995 to 2007
233	S Blanco	93	1980 to 1991
214	J-B Elissalde	35	2000 to 2008
200	J-P Lescarboura	28	1982 to 1990

MOST CONVERSIONS IN TESTS

Cons	Player	Tests	Career
59	C Lamaison	37	1996 to 2001
51	D Yachvili	61	2002 to 2012
48	D Camberabero	36	1982 to 1993
45	M Vannier	43	1953 to 1961
42	T Castaignède	54	1995 to 2007
41	F Michalak	56	2001 to 2012
40	J-B Elissalde	35	2000 to 2008
36	R Dourthe	31	1995 to 2001
36	G Merceron	32	1999 to 2003
36	M Parra	43	2008 to 2012
32	T Lacroix	43	1989 to 1997
29	P Villepreux	34	1967 to 1972

MOST TRIES IN TESTS

Tries	Player	Tests	Career
38	S Blanco	93	1980 to 1991
33*	P Saint-André	69	1990 to 1997
32	V Clerc	61	2002 to 2012
30	P Sella	111	1982 to 1995
26	E Ntamack	46	1994 to 2000
26	P Bernat Salles	41	1992 to 2001
25	C Dominici	67	1998 to 2007
23	C Darrouy	40	1957 to 1967
23	A Rougerie	76	2001 to 2012

* Saint-André's total includes a penalty try against Romania in 1992

MOST PENALTY GOALS IN TESTS

Penalties	Player	Tests	Career
89	T Lacroix	43	1989 to 1997
85	D Yachvili	61	2002 to 2012
78	C Lamaison	37	1996 to 2001
63	M Parra	43	2008 to 2012
59	D Camberabero	36	1982 to 1993
57	G Merceron	32	1999 to 2003
56	J-P Romeu	34	1972 to 1977
42	F Michalak	56	2001 to 2012
38	J-B Elissalde	35	2000 to 2008
33	P Villepreux	34	1967 to 1972
33	P Bérot	19	1986 to 1989

MOST DROP GOALS IN TESTS

Drops	Player	Tests	Career
15	J-P Lescarboura	28	1982 to 1990
12	P Albaladejo	30	1954 to 1964
11	G Camberabero	14	1961 to 1968
11	D Camberabero	36	1982 to 1993
9	J-P Romeu	34	1972 to 1977

FRANCE

INTERNATIONAL CHAMPIONSHIP RECORDS

RECORD	DETAIL	HOLDER	SET
Most points in season	156	in five matches	2002
Most tries in season	18	in four matches	1998
	18	in five matches	2006
Highest Score	56	56–13 v Italy	2005
Biggest win	51	51 – 0 v Wales	1998
Highest score conceded	49	14–49 v Wales	1910
Biggest defeat	37	0–37 v England	1911
Most appearances	50	P Sella	1983–1995
Most points in matches	217	D Yachvili	2003–2012
Most points in season	80	G Merceron	2002
Most points in match	24	S Viars	v Ireland, 1992
	24	C Lamaison	v Scotland, 1997
	24	J-B Elissalde	v Wales, 2004
Most tries in matches	14	S Blanco	1981–1991
	14	P Sella	1983–1995
Most tries in season	5	P Estève	1983
	5	E Bonneval	1987
	5	E Ntamack	1999
	5	P Bernat Salles	2001
	5	V Clerc	2008
Most tries in match	3	M Crauste	v England, 1962
	3	C Darrouy	v Ireland, 1963
	3	E Bonneval	v Scotland, 1987
	3	D Venditti	v Ireland, 1997
	3	E Ntamack	v Wales, 1999
	3	V Clerc	v Ireland, 2008
Most cons in matches	30	D Yachvili	2003–2012
Most cons in season	11	M Parra	2010
Most cons in match	6	D Yachvili	v Italy, 2003
Most pens in matches	49	D Yachvili	2003–2012
Most pens in season	18	G Merceron	2002
Most pens in match	7	G Merceron	v Italy, 2002
Most drops in matches	9	J-P Lescarboura	1982–1988
Most drops in season	5	G Camberabero	1967
Most drops in match	3	P Albaladejo	v Ireland, 1960
	3	J-P Lescarboura	v England, 1985

MISCELLANEOUS RECORDS

RECORD	HOLDER	DETAIL
Longest Test Career	F Haget	1974 to 1987
	C Califano	1994 to 2007
	S Marconnet	1998 to 2011
Youngest Test Cap	C Dourthe	18 yrs 7 days in 1966
Oldest Test Cap	A Roques	37 yrs 329 days in 1963

CAREER RECORDS OF FRANCE INTERNATIONAL PLAYERS

UP TO 10 OCTOBER 2012

PLAYER BACKS:	DEBUT	CAPS	T	C	P	D	PTS
M Andreu	2010 v W	6	2	0	0	0	10
J Arias	2009 v A	2	0	0	0	0	0
M Bastareaud	2009 v W	9	2	0	0	0	10
L Beauxis	2007 v It	20	1	18	25	3	125
J-M Buttin	2012 v W	2	0	0	0	0	0
V Clerc	2002 SA	61	32	0	0	0	160
Y David	2008 It	4	0	0	0	0	0
J-M Doussain	2011 v NZ	1	0	0	0	0	0
B Dulin	2012 v Arg	2	0	0	0	0	0
J Dupuy	2009 v NZ	8	0	4	10	0	38
F Estebanez	2010 v Fj	8	0	0	0	0	0
B Fall	2009 v Sm	3	2	0	0	0	10
W Fofana	2012 v It	7	4	0	0	0	20
F Fritz	2005 v SA	22	3	0	0	2	21
Y Huget	2010 v Arg	9	2	0	0	0	10
M Machenaud	2012 v Arg	1	1	0	0	0	5
J Malzieu	2008 v S	20	5	0	0	0	25
M Médard	2008 v Arg	30	10	0	0	1	53
M Mermoz	2008 v A	19	2	0	0	0	10
F Michalak	2001 v SA	56	9	41	42	6	271
A Palisson	2008 v A	21	2	0	0	0	10
M Parra	2008 v S	43	2	36	63	1	274
C Poitrenaud	2001 v SA	47	7	0	0	0	35
A Rougerie	2001 v SA	76	23	0	0	0	115
F Trinh-Duc	2008 v S	42	9	2	1	6	70
D Yachvili	2002 v C	61	2	51	85	2	373

FORWARDS:

D Attoub	2006 v R	4	0	0	0	0	0
J Bonnaire	2004 v S	75	6	0	0	0	30
V Debaty	2006 v R	8	0	0	0	0	0
T Domingo	2009 v W	18	1	0	0	0	5
L Ducalcon	2010 v S	10	0	0	0	0	0
T Dusautoir	2006 v R	54	6	0	0	0	30
I Harinordoquy	2002 v W	82	13	0	0	0	65
R Lakafia	2011 v I	3	0	0	0	0	0
A Lapandry	2009 v Sm	8	2	0	0	0	10
W Lauret	2010 v SA	3	0	0	0	0	0
Y Maestri	2012 v It	7	0	0	0	0	0
N Mas	2003 v NZ	53	0	0	0	0	0
L Nallet	2000 v R	74	9	0	0	0	45
B Noirot	2010 v Fj	1	0	0	0	0	0
F Ouedraogo	2007 v NZ	27	1	0	0	0	5
P Papé	2004 v I	42	3	0	0	0	15
L Picamoles	2008 v I	28	2	0	0	0	10
J Pierre	2007 v NZ	27	1	0	0	0	5
J-B Poux	2001 v Fj	42	3	0	0	0	15
C Samson	2012 v Arg	1	0	0	0	0	0
W Servat	2004 v I	49	2	0	0	0	10
D Szarzewski	2004 v C	63	6	0	0	0	30
R Taofifenua	2012 v Arg	1	0	0	0	0	0
C Tolofua	2012 v Arg	2	0	0	0	0	0
Y Watremez	2012 v Arg	1	0	0	0	0	0

FRANCE INTERNATIONAL PLAYERS
UP TO 10 OCTOBER 2012

Note: Years given for International Championship matches are for second half of season; eg 1972 means season 1971–72. Years for all other matches refer to the actual year of the match. Entries in square brackets denote matches played in RWC Finals.

Abadie, A (Pau) 1964 I
Abadie, A (Graulhet) 1965 R, 1967 SA 1,3,4, NZ, 1968 S, I
Abadie, L (Tarbes) 1963 R
Accoceberry, G (Bègles) 1994 NZ 1,2, C 2, 1995 W, E, S, I, R 1, [Iv, S], It, 1996 I, W 1, R, Arg 1, W 2(R), SA 2, 1997 S, It 1
Aguerre, R (Biarritz O) 1979 S
Aguilar, D (Pau) 1937 G
Aguirre, J-M (Bagnères) 1971 A 2, 1972 S, 1973 W, I, J, R, 1974 I, W, Arg 2, R, SA 1, 1976 W (R), E, US, A 2, R, 1977 W, E, S, I, Arg 1,2, NZ 1,2, R, 1978 E, S, I, W, R, 1979 I, W, E, S, NZ 1,2, R, 1980 W, I
Ainciart, E (Bayonne) 1933 G, 1934 G, 1935 G, 1937 G, It, 1938 G 1
Albaladéjo, P (Dax) 1954 E, It, 1960 W, I, It, R, 1961 S, SA, E, W, I, NZ 1,2, A, 1962 S, E, W, I, 1963 S, I, E, W, It, 1964 S, NZ, W, It, I, SA, Fj
Albouy, A (Castres) 2002 It (R)
Alvarez, A-J (Tyrosse) 1945 B2, 1946 B, I, K, W, 1947 S, I, W, E, 1948 I, A, S, W, E, 1949 I, E, W, 1951 S, E, W
Amand, H (SF) 1906 NZ
Ambert, A (Toulouse) 1930 S, I, E, G, W
Amestoy, J-B (Mont-de-Marsan) 1964 NZ, E
André, G (RCF) 1913 SA, E, W, I, 1914 I, W, E
Andreu, M (Castres) 2010 W(R),It,E,SA(R),Arg2,A(R)
Andrieu, M (Nîmes) 1986 Arg 2, NZ 1, R 2, NZ 2, 1987 [R, Z], R, 1988 E, S, I, W, Arg 1,2,3,4, R, 1989 I, W, E, S, NZ 2, B, A 2, 1990 W, E, I (R)
Anduran, J (SCUF) 1910 W
Aqua, J-L (Toulon) 1999 R, Tg, NZ 1(R)
Araou, R (Narbonne) 1924 R
Arcalis, R (Brive) 1950 S, I, 1951 I, E, W
Arias, J (SF) 2009 A(R), 2010 Fj
Arino, M (Agen) 1962 R
Aristouy, P (Pau) 1948 S, 1949 Arg 2, 1950 S, I, E, W
Arlettaz, P (Perpignan) 1995 R 2
Armary, L (Lourdes) 1987 [R], R, 1988 S, I, W, Arg 3,4, R, 1989 W, S, A 1,2, 1990 W, E, S, I, A 1,2,3, NZ 1, 1991 W 2, 1992 S, I, R, Arg 1,2, SA 1,2, Arg, 1993 E, S, I, W, SA 1,2, R 2, A 1,2, 1994 I, W, NZ 1(t),2(t), 1995 I, R 1 [Tg, I, SA]
Arnal, J-M (RCF) 1914 I, W
Arnaudet, M (Lourdes) 1964 I, 1967 It, W
Arotca, R (Bayonne) 1938 R
Arrieta, J (SF) 1953 E, W
Arthapignet, P (see Harislur-Arthapignet)
Artiguste, E (Castres) 1999 WS
Astre, R (Béziers) 1971 R, 1972 I 1, 1973 E (R), 1975 E, S, I, SA 1,2, Arg 2, 1976 A 2, R
Attoub, D (Castres, SF) 2006 R, 2012 W, Arg 1,2
Aucagne, D (Pau) 1997 W (R), S, It 1 (R), A 1, R 2(R), SA 2(R), 1998 S (R), W (R), Arg 2(R), Fj (R), Arg 3, A, 1999 W 1(R), S (R)
Audebert, A (Montferrand) 2000 R, 2002 W (R)
Aué, J-M (Castres) 1998 W (R)
Augé, J (Dax) 1929 S, W
Augras-Fabre, L (Agen) 1931 I, S, W
August, B (Biarritz) 2007 W1(R)

Auradou, D (SF) 1999 E (R), S (R), WS (R), Tg, NZ 1, W 2(R), [Arg (R)], 2000 A (R), NZ 1,2, 2001 S, I, It, W, E (R), SA 1,2, NZ (R), SA 3, A, Fj, 2002 It, E, I (R), C (R), 2003 S (R), It (R), W (R), Arg, 1,2, NZ (R), R (R), E 2(R),3, [J(R), US, NZ] , 2004 I(R), It(R), S(R), E(R)
Averous, J-L (La Voulte) 1975 S, I, SA 1,2, 1976 I, W, E, US, A 1,2, R, 1977 W, E, S, I, Arg 1, R, 1978 E, S, I, 1979 NZ 1,2, 1980 E, S, 1981 A 2
Avril, D (Biarritz) 2005 A1
Azam, O (Montferrand, Gloucester) 1995 R 2, Arg (R), 2000 A (R), NZ 2(R), 2001 SA 2(R), NZ, 2002 E (R), I (R), Arg (R), A 1
Azarete, J-L (Dax, St Jean-de-Luz) 1969 W, R, 1970 S, I, W, R, 1971 S, I, E, SA 1,2, A 1, 1972 E, W, I 2, A 1, R, 1973 NZ, W, I, R, 1974 I, R, SA 1,2, 1975 W

Baby, B (Toulouse, Clermont-Auvergne) 2005 I,SA2(R),A1, 2008 Arg,PI,A3, 2009 I(R),S,W
Bacqué, N (Pau) 1997 R 2
Bader, E (Primevères) 1926 M, 1927 I, S
Badin, C (Chalon) 1973 W, I, 1975 Arg 1
Baillette, M (Perpignan) 1925 I, NZ, S, 1926 W, M, 1927 I, W, G 2, 1929 G, 1930 S, I, E, G, 1931 I, S, E, 1932 G
Baladie, G (Agen) 1945 B 1,2, W, 1946 B, I, K
Ballarin, J (Tarbes) 1924 E, 1925 NZ, S
Baquey, J (Toulouse) 1921 I
Barbazanges, A (Roanne) 1932 G, 1933 G
Barcella, F (Auch, Biarritz) 2008 It,W,Arg, 2009 S, W, It, NZ1, 2, A, SA, NZ3, 2010 Arg1, 2011 I3(R), [J, C(t&R), NZ1(R), Tg(R), E(R), W(R), NZ2(R)]
Barrau, M (Beaumont, Toulouse) 1971 S, E, W, 1972 E, W, A 1,2, 1973 S, NZ, E, I, J, R, 1974 I, S
Barrau, M (Agen) 2004 US,C(R),NZ(R)
Barrère, P (Toulon) 1929 G, 1931 W
Barrière, P (Béziers) 1960 R
Barthe, F (SBUC) 1925 W, E
Barthe, J (Lourdes) 1954 Arg 1,2, 1955 S, 1956 I, W, It, E, Cz, 1957 S, I, E, W, R 1,2, 1958 S, E, A, W, It, I, SA 1,2, 1959 S, E, It, W
Basauri, R (Albi) 1954 Arg 1
Bascou, P (Bayonne) 1914 E
Basquet, G (Agen) 1945 W, 1946 B, I, K, W, 1947 S, I, W, E, 1948 I, A, S, W, E, 1949 S, I, E, W, 1950 S, I, E, W, 1951 S, I, E, W, 1952 S, I, SA, W, E, It
Bastareaud, M (SF) 2009 W,E,It(R),NZ1, 2010 S,I,W,It(R),E
Bastiat, J-P (Dax) 1969 R, 1970 S, I, W, 1971 S, I, SA 2, 1972 S, A 1, 1973 E, 1974 Arg 1,2, SA 2, 1975 W, Arg 1,2, R, 1976 S, I, W, E, A 1,2, R, 1977 W, E, S, I, 1978 E, S, I, W
Baudry, N (Montferrand) 1949 S, I, W, Arg 1,2
Baulon, R (Vienne, Bayonne) 1954 S, NZ, W, E, It, 1955 I, E, W, It, 1956 S, I, W, It, E, Cz, 1957 S, I, It
Baux, J-P (Lannemezan) 1968 NZ 1,2, SA 1,2
Bavozet, J (Lyon) 1911 S, E, W
Bayard, J (Toulouse) 1923 S, W, E, 1924 W, R, US
Bayardon, J (Chalon) 1964 S, NZ, E
Beaurin-Gressier, C (SF) 1907 E, 1908 E
Beauxis, L (SF, Toulouse) 2007 It(R),I(R),W1(R),E1(R),S,W2,

Bourdeu, J R (Lourdes) 1952 S, I, SA, W, E, It, 1953 S, I, E
Bourgarel, R (Toulouse) 1969 R, 1970 S, I, E, R, 1971 W, SA 1,2, 1973 S
Bourguignon, G (Narbonne) 1988 Arg 3, 1989 I, E, B, A 1, 1990 R
Bousquet, A (Béziers) 1921 E, I, 1924 R
Bousquet, R (Albi) 1926 M, 1927 I, S, W, E, G 1, 1929 W, E, 1930 W
Bousses, G (Bourgoin) 2006 S(R)
Boyau, M (SBUC) 1912 I, S, W, E, 1913 W, I
Boyer, P (Toulon) 1935 G
Boyet, B (Bourgoin) 2006 I(R), 2007 NZ1,2, 2008 A1,2(R)
Boyoud, R (Dax) 2008 A1(R),2, 2009 S(R)
Branca, G (SF) 1928 S, 1929 I, S
Branlat, R (RCF) 1906 NZ, E, 1908 W
Bréjassou, R (Tarbes) 1952 S, I, SA, W, E, 1953 W, E, 1954 S, I, NZ, 1955 S, I, E, W, It
Brèthes, R (St Séver) 1960 Arg 2
Bringeon, A (Biarritz O) 1925 W
Brouzet, O (Grenoble, Bègles, Northampton, Montferrand) 1994 S, NZ 2(R), 1995 E, S, I, R 1, [Tg, Iv, E (t)], It, Arg (R), 1996 W 1(R), 1997 R 1, A 1,2, It 2, Arg, SA 1,2, 1998 E, S, I, W, Arg 1,2, Fj, Arg 3, A, 1999 I, W 1, E, S, R, [C (R), Nm, Fj (R), Arg, NZ 2(R), A (R)], 2000 W, E, S, I, It, A, NZ 1(R),2(R), 2001 SA 1,2, NZ, 2002 W, E, S, I, Arg, A 1(R),2, SA, NZ, C, 2003 E 1, S, I, It, W, E 3, [Fj(R),J,S(R),US,I(R)]
Bru, Y (Toulouse) 2001 A (R), Fj (R), 2002 It, 2003 Arg 2, NZ, R, E 2, 3(R), [J, S(R), US, I(t&R), NZ], 2004 I(R), It(R), W(R), S(R), E(R)
Brugnaut, J (Dax) 2008 S,I(R)
Brun, G (Vienne) 1950 E, W, 1951 S, E, W, 1952 S, I, SA, W, E, It, 1953 E, W, It
Bruneau, M (SBUC) 1910 W, E, 1913 SA, E
Brunet, Y (Perpignan) 1975 SA 1, 1977 Arg 1
Bruno, S (Béziers, Sale) 2002 W (R), 2004 A(R),NZ(t&R) 2005 S(R), E, W, I, It, SA1, 2(R), A1(R), 2(R), C, SA3(R), 2006 S(R), I(R), 2007 I(R), E1(R), NZ1, 2, E3(R), W2(R), [Gg, Arg 2(t&R)], 2008 A1, 2
Brusque, N (Pau, Biarritz) 1997 R 2(R), 2002 W, E, S, I, Arg, A 2, SA, NZ, C, 2003 E 2, [Fj,S,I,E,NZ(R)], 2004 I, It, W, S, E, A, Arg, 2005 SA1(R), 2, A1, 2006 S
Buchet, E (Nice) 1980 R, 1982 E, R (R), Arg 1,2
Buisson, H (see Empereur-Buisson)
Buonomo, Y (Béziers) 1971 A 2, 1972 I 1
Burgun, M (RCF) 1909 I, 1910 W, S, I, 1911 S, E, 1912 I, S, 1913 S, E, 1914 E
Bustaffa, D (Carcassonne) 1977 Arg 1,2, NZ 1,2, 1978 W, R, 1980 W, E, S, SA, R
Buttin, J-M (Clermont-Auvergne) 2012 W(R), Arg 1
Buzy, C-E (Lourdes) 1946 K, W, 1947 S, I, W, E, 1948 I, A, S, W, E, 1949 S, I, E, W, Arg 1,2

Caballero, Y (Montauban) 2008 A2(R)
Cabanier, J-M (Montauban) 1963 R, 1964 S, Fj, 1965 S, I, W, It, R, 1966 S, I, E, W, It, R, 1967 S, A, E, It, W, I, SA 1,3, NZ, R, 1968 S, I
Cabannes, L (RCF, Harlequins) 1990 NZ 2(R), 1991 S, I, W 1, E, US 2, W 2, [R, Fj, C, E], 1992 W, E, S, I, R, Arg 2, SA 1,2, 1993 E, S, I, W, R 1, SA 1,2, 1994 E, S, C 1, NZ 1,2, 1995 W, E, S, R 1, [Tg (R), Iv, S, I, SA, E], 1996 E, S, I, W 1, 1997 It 2, Arg, SA 1,2
Cabrol, H (Béziers) 1972 A 1(R),2, 1973 J, 1974 SA 2
Cadenat, J (SCUF) 1910 S, E, 1911 W, I, 1912 W, E, 1913 I
Cadieu, J-M (Toulouse) 1991 R, US 1, [R, Fj, C, E], 1992 W, I, R, Arg 1,2, SA 1
Cahuc, F (St Girons) 1922 S
Califano, C (Toulouse, Saracens, Gloucester) 1994 NZ 1,2, C 2, 1995 W, E, S, I, [Iv, S, I, SA, E], It, Arg, NZ 1,2, 1996 E, S, I, W, R 1, Arg, SA 1,2, 1997 I, W, E, A 1,2, It 2, R 2(R), Arg, SA 1,2, 1998 E, S, I, W, 1999 I, W 1, E (R), S, WS, Tg (R), NZ 1, W 2, [C, Nm, Fj], 2000 W, E, S, I, It, R, A, NZ 1,2(R), 2001 S (R), I (R), It, W, SA 1(R),2(R), NZ, 2003 E 1, S (R), I (R), 2007 NZ1,2
Cals, R (RCF) 1938 G 1
Calvo, G (Lourdes) 1961 NZ 1,3
Camberabero, D (La Voulte, Béziers) 1982 R, Arg 1,2, 1983

E, W, 1987 [R (R), Z, Fj (R), A, NZ], 1988 I, 1989 B, A 1, 1990 W, S, I, R, A 1,2,3, NZ 1,2, 1991 S, I, W 1, E, R, US 1,2, W 2, [R, Fj, C], 1993 E, S, I
Camberabero, G (La Voulte) 1961 NZ 3, 1962 R, 1964 R, 1967 A, E, It, W, I, SA 1,3,4, 1968 S, E, W
Camberabero, L (La Voulte) 1964 R, 1965 S, I, 1966 E, W, 1967 A, E, It, W, I, 1968 S, E, W
Cambré, T (Oloron) 1920 E, W, I, US
Camel, A (Toulouse) 1928 S, A, I, E, G, W, 1929 W, E, G, 1930 S, I, E, G, W, 1935 G
Camel, M (Toulouse) 1929 S, W, E
Camicas, F (Tarbes) 1927 G 2, 1928 S, I, E, G, W, 1929 I, S, W, E
Camo, E (Villeneuve) 1931 I, S, W, E, G, 1932 G
Campaès, A (Lourdes) 1965 W, 1967 NZ, 1968 S, I, E, W, Cz, NZ 1,2, A, 1969 S, W, 1972 R, 1973 NZ
Campan, O (Agen) 1993 SA 1(R),2(R), R 2(R), 1996 I, W 1, R
Candelon, J (Narbonne) 2005 SA1,A1(R)
Cantoni, J (Béziers) 1970 W, R, 1971 S, I, E, W, SA 1,2, R, 1972 S, I 1, 1973 S, NZ, W, I, 1975 W (R)
Capdouze, J (Pau) 1964 SA, Fj, R, 1965 S, I, E
Capendeguy, J-M (Bègles) 1967 NZ, R
Capitani, P (Toulon) 1954 Arg 1,2
Capmau, J-L (Toulouse) 1914 E
Carabignac, G (Agen) 1951 S, I, 1952 SA, W, E, 1953 S, I
Carbonne, J (Perpignan) 1927 W
Carbonneau, P (Toulouse, Brive, Pau) 1995 R 2, Arg, NZ 1,2, 1996 E, S, R (R), Arg 2, W 2, SA 1, 1997 I (R), W, E, S (R), R 1(R), A 1,2, 1998 E, S, I, W, Arg 1,2, Fj, Arg 3, A, 1999 I, W 1, E, S, 2000 W, E, S, 2001 I
Carminati, A (Béziers, Brive) 1986 R 2, NZ 2, 1987 [R, Z], 1988 I, W, Arg 1,2, 1989 I, W, S, NZ 1(R),2, A 2, 1990 S, 1995 It, R 2, Arg, NZ 1,2
Caron, L (Lyon O, Castres) 1947 E, 1948 I, A, W, E, 1949 S, I, E, W, Arg 1
Carpentier, M (Lourdes) 1980 E, SA, R, 1981 S, I, A 1, 1982 E, S
Carrère, C (Toulon) 1966 R, 1967 S, A, E, W, I, SA 1,3,4, NZ, R, 1968 S, I, E, W, Cz, NZ 3, A, R, 1969 S, I, 1970 S, I, W, E, 1971 E, W
Carrère, J (Vichy, Toulon) 1956 S, 1957 E, W, R 2, 1958 S, SA 1,2, 1959 I
Carrère, R (Mont-de-Marsan) 1953 E, It
Casadei, D (Brive) 1997 S, R 1, SA 2(R)
Casaux, L (Tarbes) 1959 I, It, 1962 S
Cassagne, P (Pau) 1957 It
Cassayet-Armagnac, A (Tarbes, Narbonne) 1920 S, E, W, US, 1921 W, E, I, 1922 S, E, W, 1923 S, W, E, I, 1924 S, E, W, R, US, 1925 S, W, 1926 S, I, E, W, M, 1927 I, S, W
Cassiède, M (Dax) 1961 NZ 3, A, R
Castaignède, S (Mont-de-Marsan) 1999 W 2, [C (R), Nm (R), Fj, Arg (R), NZ 2(R), A (R)]
Castaignède, T (Toulouse, Castres, Saracens) 1995 R 2, Arg, NZ 1,2, 1996 E, S, I, W 1, Arg 1,2, 1997 I, A 1,2, It 2, 1998 E, S, I, W, Arg 1,2, Fj, 1999 I, W 1, E, S, R, WS, Tg (R), NZ 1, W 2, [C], 2000 W, E, S, It, 2002 SA, NZ, C, 2003 E 1(R), S (R), It, W, Arg 1, 2005 A2(R),C,Tg,SA3, 2006 It,E,W,R,SA(R), 2007 NZ1,2
Castel, R (Toulouse, Béziers) 1996 I, W 1, W 2, SA 1(R),2, 1997 I (R), W, E (R), S (R), A 1(R), 1998 Arg 3(R), A (R), 1999 W 1(R), E, S
Castets, J (Toulon) 1923 W, E, I
Caujolle, J (Tarbes) 1909 E, 1913 SA, E, 1914 W, E
Caunègre, R (SB) 1938 R, G 2
Caussade, A (Lourdes) 1978 R, 1979 I, W, E, NZ 1,2, R, 1980 W, E, S, 1981 S, I, W, R
Caussarieu, G (Pau) 1929 I
Cayrefourcq, E (Tarbes) 1921 E
Cazalbou, J (Toulouse) 1997 It 2(R), R 2, Arg, SA 2(R)
Cazals, P (Mont-de-Marsan) 1961 NZ 1, A, R
Cazenave, A (Pau) 1927 E, G 1, 1928 S, A, G
Cazenave, F (RCF) 1950 E, 1952 S, 1954 I, NZ, W, E
Cécillon, M (Bourgoin) 1988 I, W, Arg 2,3,4, R, 1989 I, E, NZ 1,2, A 1, 1991 S, I, E (R), R, 1, W 2, [E], 1992 W, E, S, I, R, Arg 1,2, SA 1,2, 1993 E, S, I, W, R 1, SA 1,2, R 2, A 1,2, 1994 I, W, NZ 1(R), 1995 I, R 1, [Tg, S (R), I, SA]

Celaya, M (Biarritz O, SBUC) 1953 E, W, It, 1954 I, E, It, Arg 1,2, 1955 S, I, E, W, It, 1956 S, I, W, It, E, Cz 1957 S, I, E, W, R 2, 1958 S, E, A, W, It, 1959 S, E, 1960 S, E, W, I, R, Arg 1,2,3, 1961 S, SA, E, W, It, I, NZ 1,2,3, A, R

Celhay, M (Bayonne) 1935 G, 1936 G 1, 1937 G, It, 1938 G 1, 1940 B

Cermeno, F (Perpignan) 2000 R

Cessieux, N (Lyon) 1906 NZ

Cester, E (TOEC, Valence) 1966 S, I, E, 1967 W, 1968 S, I, E, W, Cz, NZ 1,3, A, SA 1,2, R, 1969 S, I, E, W, 1970 S, I, W, E, 1971 A 1, 1972 R, 1973 S, NZ, W, I, J, R, 1974 I, W, E, S

Chabal, S (Bourgoin, Sale, Racing-Metro) 2000 S, 2001 SA 1,2, NZ (R), Fj (R), 2002 Arg (R), A 2, SA (R), NZ (t), C (R), 2003 E 1(R), S (R), I (R), Arg 2, NZ (R), E 2(R), 3, [J(R), US, NZ], 2005 S, E, A2(R), Tg, 2007 It, I, E1, NZ1, 2, E2(R), W2, [Arg1(R), Nm, I, NZ(R), E(R), Arg 2(R)], 2008 A1, 2, Arg(R), PI(R), A3, 2009 I, S(R), W, E, It, NZ1(R), 2, SA(R), Sm, NZ3, 2010 W(R), It(R), E(R), Fj(R), Arg2, A, 2011 S(R), I1(R), E, It

Chaban-Delmas, J (CASG) 1945 B 2

Chabowski, H (Nice, Bourgoin) 1985 Arg 2, 1986 R 2, NZ 2, 1989 B (R)

Chadebech, P (Brive) 1982 R, Arg 1,2, 1986 S, I

Champ, E (Toulon) 1985 Arg 1,2, 1986 I, W, E, R 1, Arg 1,2, A, NZ 1, R 2, NZ 2,3, 1987 W, E, S, I, [S, R, Fj, A, NZ], R, 1988 E, S, Arg 1,3,4, R, 1989 W, S, A 1,2, 1990 W, E, NZ 1, 1991 R, US 1, [R, Fj, C, E]

Chapuy, L (SF) 1926 S

Charpentier, G (SF) 1911 E, 1912 W, E

Charton, P (Montferrand) 1940 B

Charvet, D (Toulouse) 1986 W, E, R 1, Arg 1, A, NZ 1,3, 1987 W, E, S, I, [S, R, Z, Fj, A, NZ], R, 1989 E (R), 1990 W, E, 1991 S, I

Chassagne, J (Montferrand) 1938 G 1

Chatau, A (Bayonne) 1913 SA

Chaud, E (Toulon) 1932 G, 1934 G, 1935 G

Chazalet, A (Bourgoin) 1999 Tg

Chenevay, C (Grenoble) 1968 SA 1

Chevallier, B (Montferrand) 1952 S, I, SA, W, E, It, 1953 E, W, It, 1954 S, I, NZ, W, Arg 1, 1955 S, I, E, W, It, 1956 S, I, W, It, E, Cz, 1957 S

Chiberry, J (Chambéry) 1955 It

Chilo, A (RCF) 1920 S, W, 1925 I, NZ

Cholley, G (Castres) 1975 E, S, I, SA 1,2, Arg 1,2, R, 1976 S, I, W, E, A 1,2, R, 1977 W, E, S, I, Arg 1,2, NZ 1,2, R, 1978 E, S, I, W, R, 1979 I, S

Chouly, D (Brive, Perpignan) 2007 NZ1(R),2, 2009 NZ2(R),A(R)

Choy, J (Narbonne) 1930 S, I, E, G, W, 1931 I, 1933 G, 1934 G, 1935 G, 1936 G 2

Cigagna, A (Toulouse) 1995 [E]

Cimarosti, J (Castres) 1976 US (R)

Cistacq, J-C (Agen) 2000 R (R)

Clady, A (Lezignan) 1929 G, 1931 I, S, E, G

Clarac, H (St Girons) 1938 G 1

Claudel, R (Lyon) 1932 G, 1934 G

Clauzel, F (Béziers) 1924 E, W, 1925 W

Clavé, J (Agen) 1936 G 2, 1938 R, G 2

Claverie, H (Lourdes) 1954 NZ, W

Cléda, T (Pau) 1998 E (R), S (R), I (R), W (R), Arg 1(R), Fj (R), Arg 3(R), 1999 I (R), S

Clément, G (RCF) 1931 W

Clément, J (RCF) 1921 S, W, E, 1922 S, E, W, I, 1923 S, W, I

Clemente, M (Oloron) 1978 R, 1980 S, I

Clerc, V (Toulouse) 2002 SA, NZ, C, 2003 E 1, S, I, It (R), W (R), Arg 2, 2004 I, It, W, 2005 SA2, Tg, 2006 SA, 2007 I, W1, E1, S, E2, W2, [Nm, I, Gg(R), NZ, E, Arg 2(R)], 2008 S, I, E, It(t), W, 2009 NZ1, 2, A(R), SA, Sm, NZ3, 2010 S(R), I, SA, Arg1, 2011 S(R), I1(R), E, It, W, I2, 3(R), [J, C, NZ1, Tg, E, W, NZ2], 2012 It, S, I, E

Cluchague, L (Biarritz O) 1924 S, 1925 E

Coderc, J (Chalon) 1932 G, 1933 G, 1934 G, 1935 G, 1936 G 1

Codorniou, D (Narbonne) 1979 NZ 1,2, R, 1980 W, E, S, I, 1981 S, W, E, A 2, 1983 E, S, I, W, A 1,2, 1984 I, W, E, S, NZ 1,2, R, 1985 E, S, I, W, Arg 1,2

Coeurveille, C (Agen) 1992 Arg 1(R),2

Cognet, L (Montferrand) 1932 G, 1936 G 1,2, 1937 G, It

Collazo, P (Bègles) 2000 R

Colombier, J (St Junien) 1952 SA, W, E

Colomine, G (Narbonne) 1979 NZ 1

Comba, F (SF) 1998 Arg 1,2, Fj, Arg 3, 1999 I, W 1, E, S, 2000 A, NZ 1,2, 2001 S, I

Combe, J (SF) 1910 S, E, I, 1911 S

Combes, G (Fumel) 1945 B 2

Communeau, M (SF) 1906 NZ, E, 1907 E, 1908 E, W, 1909 E, W, I, 1910 S, E, I, 1911 S, E, I, 1912 I, S, W, E, 1913 SA, E, W

Condom, J (Boucau, Biarritz O) 1982 R, 1983 E, S, I, W, A 1,2, R, 1984 I, W, E, S, NZ 1,2, R, 1985 E, S, I, W, Arg 1,2, 1986 S, I, W, E, R 1, Arg 1,2, NZ 1, A 2, NZ 2,3, 1987 W, E, S, I, [S, R, Z, A, NZ], R, 1988 E, S, W, Arg 1,2,3,4, R, 1989 I, W, E, S, NZ 1,2, A 1, 1990 I, R, A 2,3(R)

Conilh de Beyssac, J-J (SBUC) 1912 I, S, 1914 I, W, E

Constant, G (Perpignan) 1920 W

Correia, P (Albi) 2008 A2

Coscolla, G (Béziers) 1921 S, W

Costantino, J (Montferrand) 1973 R

Costes, A (Montferrand) 1994 C 2, 1995 R 1, [Iv], 1997 It 1, 1999 WS, Tg (R), NZ 1, [Nm (R), Fj (R), Arg (R), NZ 2(R), A (t&R)], 2000 S (R), I

Costes, F (Montferrand) 1979 E, S, NZ 1,2, R, 1980 W, I

Couffignal, H (Colomiers) 1993 R 1

Coulon, E (Grenoble) 1928 S

Courtiols, M (Bègles) 1991 R, US 1, W 2

Coux, J-F (Bourgoin) 2007 NZ1,2

Couzinet, D (Biarritz) 2004 US,C(R), 2008 A1(R)

Crabos, R (RCF) 1920 S, E, W, I, US, 1921 S, W, E, I, 1922 S, E, W, I, 1923 S, I, 1924 S, I

Crampagne, J (Bègles) 1967 SA 4

Crancée, R (Lourdes) 1960 Arg 3, 1961 S

Crauste, M (RCF, Lourdes) 1957 R 1,2, 1958 S, E, A, W, It, I, 1959 E, It, W, I, 1960 S, E, W, I, It, R, Arg 1,3, 1961 S, SA, E, W, It, I, NZ 1,2,3, A, R, 1962 S, E, W, I, It, R, 1963 S, I, E, W, It, R, 1964 S, NZ, E, W, It, I, SA, Fj, R, 1965 S, I, E, W, It, R, 1966 S, I, E, W, It

Cremaschi, M (Lourdes) 1980 R, 1981 R, NZ 1,2, 1982 W, S, 1983 A 1,2, R, 1984 I, W

Crenca, J-J (Agen) 1996 SA 2(R), 1999 R, Tg, WS (R), NZ 1(R), 2001 SA 1,2, NZ (R), SA 3, A, Fj, 2002 I, W, E, S, I, Arg, A 2, SA, NZ, C, 2003 E 1, S, I, It, W, R, E 2, [Fj, J(t&R), NZ(R)], 2004 I(R), It(R), W(R), S(R), E(R)

Crichton, W H (Le Havre) 1906 NZ, E

Cristina, J (Montferrand) 1979 R

Cussac, P (Biarritz O) 1934 G

Cutzach, A (Quillan) 1929 G

Daguerre, F (Biarritz O) 1936 G 1

Daguerre, J (CASG) 1933 G

Dal Maso, M (Mont-de-Marsan, Agen, Colomiers) 1988 R (R), 1990 NZ 2, 1996 SA 1(R),2, 1997 I, W, E, S, It 1, R 1(R), A 1,2, It 2, Arg, SA 1,2, 1998 W (R), Arg 1(t) (R), Fj (R), 1999 R (R), WS (R), Tg, NZ 1(R), W 2(R), [Nm (R), Fj (R), Arg (R), A (R)], 2000 W, E, S, I, It

Danion, J (Toulon) 1924 I

Danos, P (Toulon, Béziers) 1954 Arg 1,2, 1957 R 2, 1958 S, E, W, It, I, SA 1,2, 1959 S, E, It, W, I, 1960 S, E

Dantiacq, D (Pau) 1997 R 1

Darbos, P (Dax) 1969 R

Darracq, R (Dax) 1957 It

Darrieussecq, A (Biarritz O) 1973 E

Darrieussecq, J (Mont-de-Marsan) 1953 It

Darrouy, C (Mont-de-Marsan) 1957 I, E, W, It, R 1, 1959 E, 1961 R, 1963 S, I, E, W, It, 1964 NZ, E, W, It, I, SA, Fj, R, 1965 S, I, E, It, R, 1966 S, I, E, W, It, R, 1967 S, A, E, It, W, I, SA 1,2,4

Daudé, J (Bourgoin) 2000 S

Daudignon, G (SF) 1928 S

Dauga, B (Mont-de-Marsan) 1964 S, NZ, E, W, It, I, SA, Fj, R, 1965 S, I, E, W, It, R, 1966 S, I, E, W, It, R, 1967 S, A, E, It, W, I, SA 1,2,3,4, NZ, R, 1968 S, I, NZ 1,2,3, A, SA 1,2, R, 1969 S, I, E, R, 1970 S, I, W, E, R, 1971 S, I, E, W, SA 1,2, A 1,2, R, 1972 S, I 1, W

Dauger, J (Bayonne) 1945 B 1,2, 1953 S
Daulouède, P (Tyrosse) 1937 G, It, 1938 G 1, 1940 B
David, Y (Bourgoin, Toulouse) 2008 It, 2009 SA, Sm(R), NZ3(R)
Debaty, V (Perpignan, Clermont-Auvergne) 2006 R(R), 2012 It, S(R), I(R), E(R), W(R), Arg 1(R),2
De Besombes, S (Perpignan) 1998 Arg 1(R), Fj (R)
Decamps, P (RCF) 1911 S
Dedet, J (SF) 1910 S, E, I, 1911 W, I, 1912 S, 1913 E, I
Dedeyn, P (RCF) 1906 NZ
Dedieu, P (Béziers) 1963 E, It, 1964 W, It, I, SA, Fj, R, 1965 S, I, E, W
De Gregorio, J (Grenoble) 1960 S, E, W, I, It, R, Arg 1,2, 1961 S, SA, E, W, It, I, 1962 S, E, W, 1963 S, W, It, 1964 NZ, E
Dehez, J-L (Agen) 1967 SA 2, 1969 R
De Jouvencel, E (SF) 1909 W, I
De Laborderie, M (RCF) 1921 I, 1922 I, 1925 W, E
Delage, C (Agen) 1983 S, I
De Malherbe, H (CASG) 1932 G, 1933 G
De Malmann, R (RCF) 1908 E, W, 1909 E, W, I, 1910 E, I
De Muizon, J J (SF) 1910 I
Delaigue, G (Toulon) 1973 J, R
Delaigue, Y (Toulon, Toulouse, Castres) 1994 S, NZ 2(R), C 2, 1995 I, R 1, [Tg, Iv], It, R 2(R), 1997 It 1, 2003 Arg 1,2, 2005 S, E, W, I, It, A2(R), Tg, SA3(R)
Delmotte, G (Toulon) 1999 R, Tg
Delque, A (Toulouse) 1937 It, 1938 G 1, R, G 2
De Rougemont, M (Toulon) 1995 E (t), R 1(t), [Iv], NZ 1,2, 1996 I (R), Arg 1,2, W 2, SA 1, 1997 E (R), S (R), It 1
Desbrosse, C (Toulouse) 1999 [Nm (R)], 2000 I
Descamps, P (SB) 1927 G 2
Desclaux, F (RCF) 1949 Arg 1,2, 1953 It
Desclaux, J (Perpignan) 1934 G, 1935 G, 1936 G 1,2, 1937 G, It, 1938 G 1, R, G 2, 1945 B 1
Deslandes, C (RCF) 1990 A 1, NZ 2, 1991 W 1, 1992 R, Arg 1,2
Desnoyer, L (Brive) 1974 R
Destarac, L (Tarbes) 1926 S, I, E, W, M, 1927 W, E, G 1,2
Desvouges, R (SF) 1914 W
Detrez, P-E (Nîmes) 1983 A 2(R), 1986 Arg 1(R),2, A (R), NZ1
Devergie, T (Nîmes) 1988 R, 1989 NZ 1,2, B, A 2, 1990 W, E, S, I, R, A 1,2,3, 1991 US 2, W 2, 1992 R (R), Arg 2(R)
De Villiers, P (SF) 1999 W 2, [Arg (R), NZ 2(R), A (R)], 2000 W (R), E (R), S (R), I (R), It (R), NZ 1(R),2, 2001 S, I, It, W, E, SA 1,2, NZ (R), SA 3, A, Fj, 2002 It, W, E, I, SA, NZ, C, 2003 Arg 1,2, NZ (R), 2004 I, It, W, S, E, US, C, NZ, 2005 S, I(R), It(R), SA1(R), 2, A1(R), 2, C, Tg(R), SA3, 2006 S, I, It, E, W, SA, NZ1, 2, Arg, 2007 It, I, E1, S, W2, [Arg1, Nm, I, NZ, E]
Deygas, M (Vienne) 1937 It
Deylaud, C (Toulouse) 1992 R, Arg 1,2, SA 1, 1994 C 1, NZ 1,2, 1995 W, E, S, [Iv (R), S, I, SA], It, Arg
Diarra, L (Montauban) 2008 It
Dintrans, P (Tarbes) 1979 NZ 1,2, R, 1980 E, S, I, SA, R, 1981 S, I, W, E, A 1,2, R, NZ 1,2, 1982 W, E, S, I, R, Arg 1,2, 1983 E, W, A 1,2, R, 1984 I, W, E, S, NZ 1,2, R, 1985 E, S, I, W, Arg 1,2, 1987 [R], 1988 Arg 1,2,3, 1989 W, E, S, 1990 R
Dispagne, S (Toulouse) 1996 I (R), W 1
Dizabo, P (Tyrosse) 1948 A, S, E, 1949 S, I, E, W, Arg 2, 1950 S, I, 1960 Arg 1,2,3
Domec, A (Carcassonne) 1929 W
Domec, H (Lourdes) 1953 W, It, 1954 S, I, NZ, W, E, It, 1955 S, I, E, W, 1956 I, W, It, 1958 E, A, W, It, I
Domenech, A (Vichy, Brive) 1954 W, E, It, 1955 S, I, E, W, 1956 S, I, W, It, E, Cz, 1957 S, I, E, W, It, R 1,2, 1958 S, E, It, 1959 It, 1960 S, E, W, I, It, R, Arg 1,2,3, 1961 S, SA, E, W, It, I, NZ 1,2,3, A, R, 1962 S, E, W, I, It, R, 1963 W, It
Domercq, J (Bayonne) 1912 I, S
Domingo, T (Clermont-Auvergne) 2009 W(R), E(R), It(R), NZ2(R), Sm, 2010 S, I, W, It, E, SA, Arg2, A, 2011 S, I1, E, W, 2012 Arg 2(R)
Dominici, C (SF) 1998 E, S, Arg 1,2, 1999 E, S, WS, NZ 1, W 2, [C, Fj, Arg, NZ 2, A], 2000 W, E, S, R, 2001 I (R), It, W, E, SA 1,2, Fj, 2003 Arg 1, R, E 2,3, [Fj,J,S,I,E], 2004

I, It, W, S, E, A(R), NZ(R), 2005 S, E, W, I, It, 2006 S, I, It, E, W, NZ1, 2(R), Arg, 2007 It, I, W1, E1, S(R), E3, W2(R), [Arg 1, Gg, NZ(R), E(R), Arg 2]
Dorot, J (RCF) 1935 G
Dospital, P (Bayonne) 1977 R, 1980 I, 1981 S, I, W, E, 1982 I, R, Arg 1,2, 1983 E, S, I, W, 1984 E, S, NZ 1,2, R, 1985 E, S, I, W, Arg 1
Dourthe, C (Dax) 1966 R, 1967 S, A, E, W, I, SA 1,2,3, NZ, 1968 W, NZ 3, SA 1,2, 1969 W, 1971 SA 2(R), R, 1972 I 1,2, A 1,2, R, 1973 S, NZ, E, 1974 I, Arg 1,2, SA 1,2, 1975 W, E, S
Dourthe, M (Dax) 2000 NZ 2(t)
Dourthe, R (Dax, SF, Béziers) 1995 R 2, Arg, NZ 1,2, 1996 E, R, 1996 Arg 1,2, W 2, SA 1,2, 1997 W, A 1, 1999 I, W 1,2, [C, Nm, Fj, Arg, NZ 2, A], 2000 W, E, It, R, A, NZ 1,2, 2001 S, I
Doussain, J-M (Toulouse) 2011 [NZ2(R)]
Doussau, E (Angoulême) 1938 R
Droitecourt, M (Montferrand) 1972 R, 1973 NZ (R), E, 1974 E, S, Arg 1, SA 2, 1975 SA 1,2, Arg 1,2, R, 1976 S, I, W, A 1, 1977 Arg 2
Dubertrand, A (Montferrand) 1971 A 1,2, R, 1972 I 2, 1974 I, W, E, SA 2, 1975 Arg 1,2, R, 1976 S, US
Dubois, D (Bègles) 1971 S
Dubroca, D (Agen) 1979 NZ 2, 1981 NZ 2(R), 1982 E, S, 1984 W, E, S, 1985 Arg 2, 1986 S, I, W, E, R 1, Arg 2, A, NZ 1, R 2, NZ 2,3, 1987 W, E, S, I, [S, Z, Fj, A, NZ], R, 1988 E, S, I, W
Ducalcon, L (Castres) 2010 S(R),Fj,Arg2(R), 2011 S(R), It(R), W(R), I2, [C, NZ1, Tg]
Duché, A (Limoges) 1929 G
Duclos, A (Lourdes) 1931 S
Ducousso, J (Tarbes) 1925 S, W, E
Dufau, G (RCF) 1948 I, A, 1949 I, W, 1950 S, E, W, 1951 S, I, E, W, 1952 SA, W, 1953 S, I, E, W, 1954 S, I, NZ, W, E, It, 1955 S, I, E, W, It, 1956 S, I, W, It, 1957 S, I, E, W, It, R 1
Dufau, J (Biarritz) 1912 I, S, W, E
Duffaut, Y (Agen) 1954 Arg 1,2
Duffour, R (Tarbes) 1911 W
Dufourcq, J (SBUC) 1906 NZ, E, 1907 E, 1908 W
Duhard, Y (Bagnères) 1980 E
Duhau, J (SF) 1928 I,1930 I, G, 1931 I, S, W, 1933 G
Dulaurens, C (Toulouse) 1926 I, 1928 S, 1929 W
Dulin, B (Agen) 2012 Arg 1,2
Duluc, A (Béziers) 1934 G
Du Manoir, Y le P (RCF) 1925 I, NZ, S, W, E, 1926 S, 1927 I, S
Dupont, C (Lourdes) 1923 S, W, I, 1924 S, I, W, R, US, 1925 S, 1927 E, G 1,2, 1928 A, G, W, 1929 I
Dupont, J-L (Agen) 1983 S
Dupont, L (RCF) 1934 G, 1935 G, 1936 G 1,2, 1938 R, G 2
Dupouy, A (SB) 1924 W, R
Duprat, B (Bayonne) 1966 E, W, It, R, 1967 S, A, E, SA 2,3, 1968 S, I, 1972 E, W, I 2, A 1
Dupré, P (RCF) 1909 W
Dupuy, J (Leicester, SF) 2009 NZ1,2,A(R),SA,Sm(R),NZ3, 2012 S(R),E
Dupuy, J-V (Tarbes) 1956 S, I, W, It, E, Cz, 1957 S, I, E, W, It, R 2, 1958 S, E, SA 1,2, 1959 S, E, It, W, I, 1960 W, I, It, Arg 1,3, 1961 I, SA, E, NZ 2, R, 1962 S, E, W, I, It, W, It, R, 1964 S
Durand, N (Perpignan) 2007 NZ1,2
Dusautoir, T (Biarritz, Toulouse) 2006 R, SA, NZ1, 2007 E3, W2(R), [Nm, I, NZ, E, Arg 2], 2008 S, I, E, W, Arg, PI, A3, 2009 I, S, W, E, It, NZ1, 2, A, SA, Sm, NZ3, 2010 S, I, W, It, E, SA, Arg1, 2, A, 2011 S, I1, E, It, W, I2, [J, NZ1, Tg, E, W, NZ2], 2012 It, S, I, E, W
Du Souich, C J (see Judas du Souich)
Dutin, B (Mont-de-Marsan) 1968 NZ 2, A, SA 2, R
Dutour, F X (Toulouse) 1911 E, I, 1912 S, W, E, 1913 S
Dutrain, H (Toulouse) 1945 W, 1946 B, I, 1947 E, 1949 I, E, W, Arg 1
Dutrey, J (Lourdes) 1940 B
Duval, R (SF) 1908 E, W, 1909 E, W, 1911 E, W, I

Echavé, L (Agen) 1961 S

Elhorga, P (Agen) 2001 NZ, 2002 A 1,2, 2003 Arg 2, NZ (R), R, [Fj(R),US,I(R),NZ], 2004 I(R),It(R),S,E, 2005 S,E, 2006 NZ2,Arg, 2008 A1
Elissalde, E (Bayonne) 1936 G 2, 1940 B
Elissalde, J-B (La Rochelle, Toulouse) 2000 S (R), R (R), 2003 It (R), W (R), 2004 I, It, W, A, Arg, 2005 SA1, 2(R), A1, 2, SA3, 2006 S, I, It, W(R), NZ1(R), 2, 2007 E2(R), 3, W2(R), [Arg 1(R), Nm, I, Gg(R), NZ, E, Arg 2], 2008 S, I, W, Arg, PI
Elissalde, J-P (La Rochelle) 1980 SA, R, 1981 A 1,2, R
Empereur-Buisson, H (Béziers) 1931 E, G
Erbani, D (Agen) 1981 A 1,2, NZ 1,2, 1982 Arg 1,2, 1983 S (R), I, W, A 1,2, R, 1984 W, E, R, 1985 E, W (R), Arg 2, 1986 S, I, W, E, R 1, Arg 2, NZ 1,2(R),3, 1987 W, E, S, I, [S, R, Fj, A, NZ], 1988 E, S, 1989 I (R), W, E, S, NZ 1, A 2, 1990 W, E
Escaffre, P (Narbonne) 1933 G, 1934 G
Escommier, M (Montelimar) 1955 It
Esponda, J-M (RCF) 1967 SA 1,2, R, 1968 NZ 1,2, SA 2, R, 1969 S, I (R), E
Estebanez, F (Brive, Racing Metro) 2010 Fj,Arg2(R),A(R), 2011 W(R),I3, [J,NZ1(R), Tg(R)]
Estève, A (Béziers) 1971 SA 1, 1972 I 1, E, W, I 2, A 2, R, 1973 S, NZ, E, I, 1974 I, W, E, S, R, SA 1,2, 1975 W, E
Estève, P (Narbonne, Lavelanet) 1982 R, Arg 1,2, 1983 E, S, I, W, A 1,2, R, 1984 I, W, E, S, NZ 1,2, R, 1985 E, S, I, W, 1986 S, I, 1987 [S, Z]
Etcheberry, J (Rochefort, Cognac) 1923 W, I, 1924 S, I, E, W, R, US, 1926 S, I, E, M, 1927 I, S, W, G 2
Etchenique, J-M (Biarritz O) 1974 R, SA 1, 1975 E, Arg 2
Etchepare, A (Bayonne) 1922 I
Etcheverry, M (Pau) 1971 S, I
Eutrope, A (SCUF) 1913 I

Fabre, E (Toulouse) 1937 It, 1938 G 1,2
Fabre, J (Toulouse) 1963 S, I, E, W, It, 1964 S, NZ, E
Fabre, L (Lezignan) 1930 G
Fabre, M (Béziers) 1981 A 1, R, NZ 1,2, 1982 I, R
Failliot, P (RCF) 1911 S, W, I, 1912 I, S, E, 1913 E, W
Fall, B (Bayonne, Racing Métro) 2009 Sm, 2010 S, 2012 Arg 2
Fargues, G (Dax) 1923 I
Fauré, F (Tarbes) 1914 I, W, E
Faure, L (Sale) 2008 S,I,E,A1,PI,A3, 2009 I,E
Fauvel, J-P (Tulle) 1980 R
Favre, M (Lyon) 1913 E, W
Ferrand, L (Chalon) 1940 B
Ferrien, R (Tarbes) 1950 S, I, E, W
Finat, R (CASG) 1932 G, 1933 G
Fite, R (Brive) 1963 W, It
Floch, J (Clermont-Auvergne) 2008 E(R),It,W
Fofana, W (Clermont-Auvergne) 2012 It,S,I,E,W, Arg 1,2(R)
Forest, M (Bourgoin) 2007 NZ1(R),2(R)
Forestier, J (SCUF) 1912 W
Forgues, F (Bayonne) 1911 S, E, W, 1912 I, W, E, 1913 S, SA, W, 1914 I, E
Fort, J (Agen) 1967 It, W, I, SA 1,2,3,4
Fourcade, G (BEC) 1909 E, W
Foures, H (Toulouse) 1951 S, I, E, W
Fournet, F (Montferrand) 1950 W
Fouroux, J (La Voulte) 1972 I 2, R, 1974 W, E, Arg 1,2, R, SA 1,2, 1975 W, Arg 1, R, 1976 S, I, W, E, US, A 1, 1977 W, E, S, I, Arg 1,2, NZ 1,2, R
Francquenelle, A (Vaugirard) 1911 S, 1913 W, I
Fritz, F (Toulouse) 2005 SA1, A2, SA3, 2006 S, I, It, E, W, SA, NZ1, 2, Arg, 2007 It, 2009 I(R), It, NZ2(R), A, 2010 Arg1, 2012 W, Arg 1,2
Froment, R (Castres) 2004 US(R)
Furcade, R (Perpignan) 1952 S

Gabernet, S (Toulouse) 1980 E, S, 1981 S, I, W, E, A 1,2, R, NZ 1,2, 1982 I, 1983 A 2, R
Gachassin, J (Lourdes) 1961 S, I, 1963 R, 1964 S, NZ, E, W, It, I, SA, Fj, 1965 S, I, E, W, It, R, 1966 S, I, E, W, 1967 S, A, It, W, I, 1968 S, I, W, I, NZ, 1968 I, 1969 S, I
Galasso, A (Toulon, Montferrand) 2000 R (R), 2001 E (R)
Galau, H (Toulouse) 1924 S, I, E, W, US

Galia, J (Quillan) 1927 E, G 1,2, 1928 S, A, I, E, W, 1929 I, E, G, 1930 S, I, E, G, W, 1931 S, W, E, G
Gallart, P (Béziers) 1990 R, A 1,2(R),3, 1992 S, I, R, Arg 1,2, SA 1,2, Arg, 1994 I, W, E, 1995 I (t), R 1, [Tg]
Gallion, J (Toulon) 1978 E, S, I, W, 1979 I, W, E, S, NZ 2, R, 1980 W, E, S, I, 1983 A 1,2, R, 1984 I, W, E, S, R, 1985 E, S, I, 1986 Arg 2
Galthié, F (Colomiers, SF) 1991 R, US 1, [R, Fj, C, E], 1992 W, E, S, R, Arg, 1994 I, W, E, 1995 [SA, E], 1996 W 1(R), 1997 I, It 2, SA 1,2, 1998 W (R), Fj (R), 1999 R, WS (R), Tg, NZ 1(R), [Fj (R), Arg, NZ 2, A], 2000 W, E, A, NZ 1,2, 2001 S, It, W, E, SA 1,2, NZ, SA 3, A, Fj, 2002 E, S, I, SA, NZ, C, 2003 E 1, S, Arg 1,2, NZ, R, E 2, [Fj,J,S,I,E]
Galy, J (Perpignan) 1953 W
Garbajosa, X (Toulouse) 1998 I, W, Arg 2(R), Fj, 1999 W 1(R), E, S, WS, NZ 1, W 2, [C, Nm (R), Fj (R), Arg, NZ 2, A], 2000 A, NZ 1,2, 2001 S, I, E, 2002 It (R), W, SA (R), C (R), 2003 E 1, S, I, It, W, E 3
Garuet-Lempirou, J-P (Lourdes) 1983 A 1,2, R, 1984 I, NZ 1,2, R, 1985 E, S, I, W, Arg 1, 1986 S, I, W, E, R 1, Arg 1, NZ 1, R 2, NZ 2,3, 1987 W, E, S, I, [S, R, Fj, A, NZ], 1988 E, S, Arg 1,2, R, 1989 E (R), S, NZ 1,2, 1990 W, E
Gasc, J (Graulhet) 1977 NZ 2
Gasparotto, G (Montferrand) 1976 A 2, R
Gauby, G (Perpignan) 1956 Cz
Gaudermen, P (RCF) 1906 E
Gayraud, W (Toulouse) 1920 I
Gelez, F (Agen) 2001 SA 3, 2002 I (R), A 1, SA, NZ, C (R), 2003 S, I
Geneste, R (BEC) 1945 B 1, 1949 Arg 2
Genet, J-P (RCF) 1992 S, I, R
Gensane, R (Béziers) 1962 S, E, W, I, It, R, 1963 S
Gérald, G (RCF) 1927 E, G 2, 1928 S, 1929 I, S, W, E, G, 1930 S, I, E, G, W, 1931 I, S, E, G
Gérard, D (Bègles) 1999 Tg
Gérintes, G (CASG) 1924 R, 1925 I, 1926 W
Geschwind, P (RCF) 1936 G 1,2
Giacardy, M (SBUC) 1907 E
Gimbert, P (Bègles) 1991 R, US 1, 1992 W, E
Giordani, P (Dax) 1999 E, S
Glas, S (Bourgoin) 1996 S (t), I (R), W 1, R, Arg 2(R), W 2, SA 1,2, 1997 I, W, E, S, It 2(R), R 2, Arg, SA 1,2, 1998 E, S, I, W, Arg 1,2, Fj, Arg 3, A, 1999 W 2, [C,Nm, Arg (R), NZ 2(R), A (t&R)], 2000 I, 2001 SA 1,2, NZ
Gomès, A (SF) 1998 Arg 1,2, Fj, Arg 3, A, 1999 I (R)
Gommes, J (RCF) 1909 I
Gonnet, C-A (Albi) 1921 E, I, 1922 E, W, 1924 S, E, 1926 S, I, E, W, M, 1927 I, S, W, E, G 1
Gonzalez, J-M (Bayonne) 1992 Arg 1,2, SA 1,2, Arg, 1993 R 1, SA 1, R 2, A 1,2, 1994 I, W, E, S, C 1, NZ 1,2, C 2, 1995 W, E, S, I, R 1, [Tg, S, I, SA, E], It, Arg, 1996 E, S, I, W 1
Got, R (Perpignan) 1920 I, US, 1921 S, W, 1922 S, E, W, I, 1924 I, E, W, R, US
Gourdon, J-F (RCF, Bagnères) 1974 S, Arg 1,2, R, SA 1,2, 1975 W, E, S, I, R, 1976 S, I, W, E, 1978 E, S, 1979 W, E, S, R, 1980 I
Gourragne, J-F (Béziers) 1990 NZ 2, 1991 W 1
Goutta, B (Perpignan) 2004 C
Goyard, A (Lyon U) 1936 G 1,2, 1937 G, It, 1938 G 1, R, G
Graciet, R (SBUC) 1926 I, W, 1927 S, G 1, 1929 E, 1930 W
Grandclaude, J-P (Perpignan) 2005 E(R),W(R), 2007 NZ1
Graou, S (Auch, Colomiers) 1992 Arg (R), 1993 SA 1,2, R 2, A 2(R), 1995 R 2, Arg (t), NZ 2(R)
Gratton, J (Agen) 1984 NZ 2, 1985 E, S, I, W, Arg 1,2, 1986 S, NZ 1
Graule, V (Arl Perpignan) 1926 I, E, W, 1927 S, W, 1931 G
Greffe, M (Grenoble) 1968 W, Cz, NZ 1,2, SA 1
Griffard, J (Lyon U) 1932 G, 1933 G, 1934 G
Gruarin, A (Toulon) 1964 W, It, I, SA, Fj, R, 1965 S, I, E, W, It, 1966 S, I, E, W, It, R, 1967 S, A, E, It, W, I, NZ, 1968 S, I
Guélorget, P (RCF) 1931 E, G
Guichemerre, A (Dax) 1920 E, 1921 E, I, 1923 S
Guilbert, A (Toulon) 1975 E, S, I, SA 1,2, 1976 A 1, 1977 Arg 1,2, NZ 1,2, R, 1979 I, W, E

Magois, H (La Rochelle) 1968 SA 1,2, R
Majérus, R (SF) 1928 W, 1929 I, S, 1930 S, I, E, G, W
Malbet, J-C (Agen) 1967 SA 2,4
Maleig, A (Oloron) 1979 W, E, NZ 2, 1980 W, E, SA, R
Mallier, L (Brive) 1999 R, W 2(R), [C (R)], 2000 I (R), It
Malquier, Y (Narbonne) 1979 S
Malzieu, J (Clermont-Auvergne) 2008 S,It,W,Arg,PI,A3, 2009 I,S(R),W,E,It(R), 2010 I(R),W,It(R),E(R),Arg1, 2012 It,S,I,E
Manterola, T (Lourdes) 1955 It, 1957 R 1
Mantoulan, C (Pau) 1959 I
Marcet, J (Albi) 1925 I, NZ, S, W, E, 1926 I, E
Marchal, J-F (Lourdes) 1979 S, R, 1980 W, S, I
Marconnet, S (SF, Biarritz) 1998 Arg 3, A, 1999 I (R), W 1(R), E, S (R), R, Tg, 2000 A, NZ 1,2, 2001 S, I, It (R), W (R), E, 2002 S (R), Arg (R), A 1,2, SA (R), C (R), 2003 E1(R), S, I, It, W, Arg 1(t+R),2, NZ, R, E 2,3(t+R), [S, US(R), I, E, NZ], 2004 I, It, W, S, E, A, Arg, NZ, 2005 S, E, W, I, It, SA1, 2, A1(R), 2(R), C, Tg, SA3(R), 2006 S, I(R), It(R), E, W, R, SA, NZ1, 2(R), Arg(R), 2007 It(R), I, W1(R), 2009 W, E, It, NZ1, A, SA(R), Sm, NZ3, 2010 I(R), 2011 I1(R), E(R), It, I2
Marchand, R (Poitiers) 1920 S, W
Marfaing, M (Toulouse) 1992 R, Arg 1
Marlu, J (Montferrand, Biarritz)) 1998 Fj (R), 2002 S (R), I (R), 2005 E
Marocco, P (Montferrand) 1968 S, I, W, E, R 1, Arg 1,2, A, 1988 Arg 4, 1989 I, 1990 E (R), NZ 1(R), 1991 S, I, W 1, E, US 2, [R, Fj, C, E]
Marot, A (Brive) 1969 R, 1970 S, I, W, 1971 SA 1, 1972 I 2, 1976 A 1
Marquesuzaa, A (RCF) 1958 It, SA 1,2, 1959 S, E, It, W, 1960 S, E, Arg 1
Marracq, H (Pau) 1961 R
Marsh, T (Montferrand) 2001 SA 3, A, Fj, 2002 It, W, E, S, I, Arg, A 2, 2003 [Fj, J, S, I, E, NZ], 2004 C, A, Arg, NZ
Martin, C (Lyon) 1909 I, 1910 W, S
Martin, H (SBUC) 1907 E, 1908 W
Martin, J-L (Béziers) 1971 A 2, R, 1972 S, I 1
Martin, L (Pau) 1948 I, A, S, W, E, 1950 S
Martin, R (SF, Bayonne) 2002 E (t+R), S (R), I (R), 2005 SA1(t&R), 2, A1, 2, C, SA3, 2006 S, I(t&R), R, SA(R), NZ1(R), 2, Arg, 2007 E2, W2, [Arg 1, Gg(R), Arg 2(R)], 2009 NZ2(R), A(R)
Martine, R (Lourdes) 1952 S, I, It, 1953 It, 1954 S, I, NZ, W, E, It, Arg 2, 1955 S, I, W, 1958 A, W, It, I, SA 1,2, 1960 S, E, Arg 3, 1961 S, It
Martinez, A (Narbonne) 2002 A 1, 2004 C
Martinez, G (Toulouse) 1982 W, E, S, Arg 1,2, 1983 E, W
Marty, D (Perpignan) 2005 It,C,Tg, 2006 I, It(R), R(R), NZ1(R), Arg(R), 2007 I, W1, E1, S, E2, [Nm, I, Gg, NZ, E, Arg 2], 2008 S, I, E, 2009 SA(R), Sm, NZ3, 2010 S(R), I(R), W(R), It, E(R), SA, Fj, 2011 W, I2, [J(R), C, E(R)]
Mas, F (Béziers) 1962 R, 1963 S, I, E, W
Mas, N (Perpignan) 2003 NZ, 2005 E, W, I, It, 2007 W1, NZ1, 2(R), E2(R), 3(R), W2, [Nm(R), Gg(R), Arg 2], 2008 S(R), I, E, It, W, Arg(R), PI, A3, 2009 I(R), S, NZ1(R), 2, A(R), SA, Sm(R), NZ3(R), 2010 S, I, W, It, E, SA, Arg1, 2, A, 2011 S, I1, E, It, W, I3, [J, E, W, NZ], 2012 It, S, I, E
Maso, J (Perpignan, Narbonne) 1966 It, 1967 S, R, 1968 S, W, Cz, NZ 1,2,3, A, R, 1969 S, I, W, 1971 SA 1,2, R, 1972 E, W, A 2, 1973 W, I, J, R
Massare, J (PUC) 1945 B 1,2, W, 1946 B, I, W
Massé, A (SBUC) 1908 W, 1909 E, W, 1910 W, S, E, I
Masse, H (Grenoble) 1937 G
Matheu-Cambas, J (Agen) 1945 W, 1946 B, I, K, W, 1947 S, I, W, E, 1948 I, A, S, W, E, 1949 S, I, E, W, Arg 1,2, 1950 E, W, 1951 S, I
Matiu, L (Biarritz) 2000 W, E
Mauduy, G (Périgueux) 1957 It, R 1,2, 1958 S, E, 1961 W, It
Mauran, J (Castres) 1952 SA, W, E, It, 1953 I, E
Mauriat, P (Lyon) 1907 E, 1908 W, E, 1909 W, I, 1910 W, S, E, I, 1911 S, E, W, I, 1912 I, S, 1913 S, SA, W, I
Maurin, G (ASF) 1906 E
Maury, A (Toulouse) 1925 I, NZ, S, W, E, 1926 S, I, E
Mayssonnié, A (Toulouse) 1908 E, W, 1910 W
Mazars, L (Narbonne, Bayonne) 2007 NZ2, 2010 Arg1
Mazas, L (Colomiers, Biarritz) 1992 Arg, 1996 SA 1
Médard, M (Toulouse) 2008 Arg,PI,A3, 2009 I,S,W,E,It,NZ1,

2,A,SA(R),Sm,NZ3, 2010 Fj, 2011 S,I1,It,W,I2(R),3,[J,C(R), NZ1,Tg,E,W,NZ2], 2012 It,S
Mela, A (Albi) 2008 S(R),I,It(R),W(R)
Melville, E (Toulon) 1990 I (R), A 1,2,3, NZ 1, 1991 US 2
Menrath, R (SCUF) 1910 W
Menthiller, Y (Romans) 1964 W, It, SA, R, 1965 E
Merceron, G (Montferrand) 1999 R (R), Tg, 2000 S, I, R, 2001 S (R), W, E, SA 1,2, NZ (R), Fj, 2002 It, W, E, S, I, Arg, A 2, C, 2003 E 1, It (R), W (R), NZ (t+R), R (R), E 3, [Fj(R),J(R),S(R),US,E(R),NZ]
Meret, F (Tarbes) 1940 B
Mericq, S (Agen) 1959 I, 1960 S, E, W, 1961 I
Merle, O (Grenoble, Montferrand) 1993 SA 1,2, R 2, A 1,2, 1994 I, W, E, S, C 1, NZ 1,2, C 2, 1995 W, I, R 1, [Tg, S, I, SA, E], 1996 R, A, Arg (R), NZ 1,2, 1996 E, S, R, Arg, SA 2, 1997 I, W, E, S, It 1, R 1, A 1,2, It 2, R 2, SA 1(R),2
Mermoz, M (Toulouse, Perpignan) 2008 A2, 2009 S(R), NZ2, A, SA, 2010 SA, Arg1(R), 2011 S, I2, [C, NZ1, Tg, E, W, NZ2] 2012 It(R), E(R), Arg 1(R),2
Merquey, J (Toulon) 1950 S, I, E, W
Mesnel, F (RCF) 1986 NZ 2(R),3, 1987 W, E, S, I, [S, Z, Fj, A, NZ], R, 1988 E, Arg 1,2,3,4, R, 1989 I, W, E, S, NZ 1, A 1,2, 1990 E, S, I, A 2,3, NZ 1,2, 1991 S, I, W 1, E, R, US 1,2, W 2, [R, Fj, C, E], 1992 W, E, S, I, SA 1,2, 1993 E (R), W, 1995 I, R 1, [Iv, E]
Mesny, P (RCF, Grenoble) 1979 NZ 1,2, 1980 SA, R, 1981 I, W (R), A 1,2, R, NZ 1,2, 1982 I, Arg 1,2
Meyer, G-S (Périgueux) 1960 S, E, It, R, Arg 2
Meynard, J (Cognac) 1954 Arg 1, 1956 Cz
Mias, L (Mazamet) 1951 S, I, E, W, 1952 I, SA, W, E, It, 1953 S, I, W, It, 1954 S, I, NZ, W, 1957 R 2, 1958 S, E, A, W, I, SA 1,2, 1959 S, It, W, I
Michalak, F (Toulouse, Natal Sharks) 2001 SA 3(R), A, Fj (R), 2002 It, A 1, 2, 2003 It, W, Arg 2(R), NZ, R, E 2, [Fj, J, S, I, E, NZ(R)], 2004 I, W, S, E, A, Arg, NZ, 2005 S(R), E(R),W(R), I(R), It(R), SA1, 2, A 1, 2, C, Tg(R), SA3, 2006 S, I, It, E, W, 2007 E2(R), 3, [Arg1(t&R), Nm, I, NZ(R), E(R), Arg 2], 2009 It(R), 2010 I(R), W(R), 2012 Arg 1(R),2
Mignardi, A (Agen) 2007 NZ1,2
Mignoni, P (Béziers, Clermont-Auvergne)) 1997 R 2(R), Arg (t), 1999 R, WS, NZ 1, W 2(R), [C, Nm], 2002 W, E (R), I (R), Arg, A 2(R), 2005 S, It(R), C(R), 2006 R, 2007 It, I, W1, E1(R), S, E2, 3(R), W2, [Arg 1, Gg, Arg 2(R)]
Milhères, C (Biarritz) 2001 E
Milliand, P (Grenoble) 1936 G 2, 1937 G, It
Millo-Chluski, R (Toulouse) 2005 SA1, 2008 Arg,PI,A3(R), 2009 I(R), S, W(R), NZ1, 2, A, SA, Sm(R), NZ3, 2010 SA, Fj, A(R), 2011 I2, [C]
Milloud, O (Bourgoin) 2000 R (R), 2001 NZ, 2002 W (R), E (R), 2003 It W (R), Arg 1, R (R), E 2(t+R),3, [J, S(R), US, I(R), E(R)], 2004 US, C(R), A, Arg, NZ(R), 2005 S(R), E(R), W(R), SA1, 2(R), A1, 2, C(R), Tg, SA3, 2006 S(R), I, E(R), W(R), NZ1(R), 2, Arg, 2007 It, I(R), W1, E1, S, E2, 3, [Arg 1, I, Gg, NZ, E]
Minjat, R (Lyon) 1945 B 1
Miorin, H (Toulouse) 1996 R, SA 1, 1997 I, W, E, S, It 1, 2000 It (R), R (R)
Mir, J-H (Lourdes) 1967 R, 1968 I
Mir, J-P (Lourdes) 1967 A
Modin, R (Brive) 1987 [Z]
Moga, A-M-A (Bègles) 1945 B 1,2, W, 1946 B, I, K, W, 1947 S, I, W, E, 1948 I, A, S, W, E, 1949 S, I, E, W, Arg 1,2
Mola, U (Dax, Castres) 1997 S (R), 1999 R (R), WS, Tg (R), NZ 1, W 2, [C, Nm, Fj, Arg (R), NZ 2(R), A (R)]
Mommejat, B (Cahors, Albi) 1958 It, I, SA 1,2, 1959 S, E, It, W, I, 1960 S, E, R, 1962 S, E, W, I, It, R, 1963 S, I, W
Moncla, F (RCF, Pau) 1956 Cz, 1957 I, E, W, It, R 1, 1958 SA 1,2, 1959 S, E, It, W, I, 1960 S, E, W, It, R, Arg 1,2,3, 1961 S, SA, E, W, It, I, NZ 1,2,3
Moni, C (Nice, SF) 1996 R, 2000 A, NZ 1,2, 2001 S, I, It, W
Monié, R (Perpignan) 1956 Cz, 1957 E
Monier, R (SBUC) 1911 I, 1912 S
Monniot, M (RCF) 1912 W, E
Montade, A (Perpignan) 1925 I, NZ, S, W, 1926 W
Montanella, B (Auch) 2007 NZ1(R)
Montlaur, P (Agen) 1992 E (R), 1994 S (R)
Moraitis, B (Toulon) 1969 E, W

303

FRANCE

Sella, P (Agen) 1982 R, Arg 1,2, 1983 E, S, I, W, A 1,2, R, 1984 I, W, E, S, NZ 1,2, R, 1985 E, S, I, W, Arg 1,2, 1986 S, I, W, E, R 1, Arg 1,2, A, NZ 1, R 2, NZ 2,3, 1987 W, E, S, I, [S, R, Z (R), Fj, A, NZ], 1988 E, S, I, W, Arg 1,2,3,4, R, 1989 I, W, E, S, NZ 1,2, B, A 1,2, 1990 W, E, S, I, A 1,2,3, 1991 W, 1, E, R, US 1,2, W 2, [Fj, C, E], 1992 W, E, S, I, Arg, 1993 E, S, I, W, R 1, SA 1,2, R 2, A 1,2, 1994 I, W, E, S, C 1, NZ 1,2, C 2, 1995 W, E, S, I, [Tg, S, I, SA, E]
Semmartin, J (SCUF) 1913 W, I
Sénal, G (Béziers) 1974 Arg 1,2, R, SA 1,2, 1975 W
Sentilles, J (Tarbes) 1912 W, E, 1913 S, SA
Serin, L (Béziers) 1928 E, 1929 W, E, G, 1930 S, I, E, G, W, 1931 I, W, E
Serre, P (Perpignan) 1920 S, E
Serrière, P (RCF) 1986 A, 1987 R, 1988 E
Servat, W (Toulouse) 2004 I,It,W,S,E,US,C,A,Arg,NZ 2005 S, E(R), W(R), It(R), SA1(R), 2, 2008 S, I(R), E(R), W(R), 2009 It(R), NZ1, 2, SA, NZ3, 2010 S, I, W, It, E, Arg2, A, 2011 S, I1, E, It, W, [J, C, NZ1(R), Tg, E, W, NZ2], 2012 It, S(R), I(R), E(R), W
Servole, L (Toulon) 1931 I, S, W, E, G, 1934 G, 1935 G
Sicart, N (Perpignan) 1922 I
Sillières, J (Tarbes) 1968 R, 1970 S, I, 1971 S, I, E, 1972 E, W
Siman, M (Montferrand) 1948 E, 1949 S, 1950 S, I, E, W
Simon, S (Bègles) 1991 R, US 1
Simonpaoli, R (SF) 1911 I, 1912 I, S
Sitjar, M (Agen) 1964 W, It, I, R, 1965 It, R, 1967 A, E, It, W, I, SA 1,2
Skrela, D (Colomiers, SF, Toulouse) 2001 NZ, 2007 It,I,W1,E1,2,3(R),W2, [Arg 1,Gg(R),Arg 2], 2008 S(R), I, E(R), W, Arg, PI, A3, 2010 SA(R), Fj(R), 2011 I2(R), 3, [J(R)]
Skrela, J-C (Toulouse) 1971 SA 2, A 1,2, 1972 I 1(R), E, W, I 2, A 1, 1973 W, J, R, 1974 W, E, S, Arg 1, R, 1975 W (R), E, S, I, SA 1,2, Arg 1,2, R, 1976 S, I, W, E, US, A 1,2, R, 1977 W, E, S, I, Arg 1,2, NZ 1,2, R, 1978 E, S, I, W
Soler, M (Quillan) 1929 G
Soro, R (Lourdes, Romans) 1945 B 1,2, W, 1946 B, I, K, 1947 S, I, W, E, 1948 I, A, S, W, E, 1949 S, I, E, W, Arg 1,2
Sorondo, L-M (Montauban) 1946 K, 1947 S, I, W, E, 1948 I Arg 1,2, Fj, 1999 W, E(R), [C (R), Nm (R), Arg, NZ 2, A]
Soulette, C (Béziers, Toulouse) 1997 R 2, 1998 S (R), I (R), W (R), Arg 1,2, Fj, 1999 W, E(R), [C (R), Nm (R), Arg, NZ 2, A]
Soulié, E (CASG) 1920 E, I, US, 1921 S, E, I, 1922 E, W, I
Sourgens, J (Bègles) 1926 M
Sourgens, O (Bourgoin) 2007 NZ2
Souverbie, J-M (Bègles) 2000 R
Spanghero, C (Narbonne) 1971 E, W, SA 1,2, A 1,2, R, 1972 S, E, W, I 2, A 1,2, 1974 I, W, E, S, R, SA 1, 1975 E, S, I
Spanghero, W (Narbonne) 1964 SA, Fj, R, 1965 S, I, E, W, It, R, 1966 S, I, E, W, It, R, 1967 S, A, E, SA 1,2,3,4, NZ, 1968 S, I, E, W, NZ 1,2,3, A, SA 1,2, R, 1969 S, I, W, 1970 R, 1971 E, W, SA 1, 1972 E, I 2, A 1,2, R, 1973 S, NZ, E, W, I
Stener, G (PUC) 1956 S, I, E, 1958 SA 1,2
Struxiano, P (Toulouse) 1913 W, I, 1920 S, E, W, I, US
Sutra, G (Narbonne) 1967 SA 2, 1969 W, 1970 S, I
Swierczinski, C (Bègles) 1969 E, 1977 Arg 2
Szarzewski, D (Béziers, SF) 2004 C(R), 2005 I(R),A1,2, SA3, 2006 S, E(R), W(t&R), R(R), SA, NZ1, 2(R), Arg(R), 2007 It(R), E2 (R), W2, [Arg1(R), Nm, I(R), Gg(R), NZ(R), E(R)], 2008 S(R), I, E, It, W, Arg, PI, A3, 2009 I, S, W, E, It, NZ1(R), 2(R), A, SA(R), Sm, NZ3(R), 2010 S(R) , I(R), W(R), It(R), E(R), SA, Arg1, 2011 I2, 3,[J(R), NZ1, Tg(R), NZ2(R)], 2012 It(R), S, I, E, W(R), Arg 1, 2

Tabacco, P (SF) 2001 SA 1,2, NZ, SA 3, A, Fj, 2003 It (R), W (R), Arg 1, NZ, E 2(R),3, [S(R), US, I(R), NZ], 2004 US, 2005 S
Tachdjian, M (RCF) 1991 S, I, E
Taffary, M (RCF) 1975 W, E, S, I
Taillantou, J (Pau) 1930 I, G, W
Taofifenua, R (Perpignan) 2012 Arg 1(R)
Tarricq, P (Lourdes) 1958 A, W, It, I
Tavernier, H (Toulouse) 1913 I
Téchoueyres, W (SBUC) 1994 E, S, 1995 [Iv]
Terreau, M-M (Bourg) 1945 W, 1946 B, I, K, W, 1947 S, I, W, E, 1948 I, A, W, E, 1949 S, Arg 1,2, 1951 S
Theuriet, A (SCUF) 1909 E, W, 1910 S, 1911 W, 1913 E
Thevenot, M (SCUF) 1910 W, E, I

Thierry, R (RCF) 1920 S, E, W, US
Thiers, P (Montferrand) 1936 G 1,2, 1937 G, It, 1938 G 1,2, 1940 B, 1945 B, 1,2
Thiéry, B (Bayonne, Biarritz) 2007 NZ1,2(R), 2008 A1,2
Thion, J (Perpignan, Biarritz) 2003 Arg 1,2, NZ, R, E 2, [Fj, S, I, E], 2004 A, Arg, NZ 2005 S, E, W, I, It, A2, C, Tg, SA3, 2006 S, I, It, E, W, R(R), SA, 2007 It, I(R), W1, E1, S, E2, 3, W2, [Arg 1, I, Gg, NZ, E, Arg 2], 2008 E(R), It, W, 2009 E, It(R), 2010 Fj, Arg2(R), A, 2011 S(R), I1(R), E(R), It(R)
Tignol, P (Toulouse) 1953 S, I
Tilh, H (Nantes) 1912 W, E, 1913 S, SA, E, W
Tillous-Borde, S (Castres) 2008 A1(R),2,PI(R),A3, 2009 I,S,W(R),E(R)
Tolofua, C (Toulouse) 2012 Arg 1(R),2(R)
Tolot, J-L (Agen) 1987 [Z]
Tomas, J (Clermont-Auvergne, Montpellier) 2008 It(R),A3(R), 2011 W(R)
Tordo, J-F (Nice) 1991 US 1(R), 1992 W, E, S, I, R, Arg 1,2, SA 1, Arg, 1993 E, S, I, W, R 1
Torossian, F (Pau) 1997 R 1
Torreilles, S (Perpignan) 1956 S
Tournaire, F (Narbonne, Toulouse) 1995 It, 1996 I, W 1, R, Arg 1,2(R), W 2, SA 1,2, 1997 I, E, S, It 1, R 1, A 1,2, It 2, R 2, Arg, SA 1,2, 1998 E, S, I, W, Arg 1,2, Fj, Arg 3, A, 1999 I, W 1, E, S, R (R), WS, NZ 1, [C, Nm, Fj, Arg, NZ 2, A], 2000 W, E, S, I, It, A (R)
Tourte, R (St Girons) 1940 B
Traille, D (Pau, Biarritz) 2001 SA 3, A, Fj, 2002 It, W, E, S, I, Arg, A 1,2, SA, NZ, C, 2003 E 1, S, I, It, W, Arg, 1,2, NZ, R, E 2, [Fj(R), J, S(R), US, NZ], 2004 I, It, W, S, E, 2005 S, E, W, It(R), SA1(R), 2, A1(R), 2006 It, E, W, R, SA, NZ1, 2, Arg, 2007 S(R), E2, 3, W2(R), [Arg 1, Nm, I, NZ, E], 2008 S, I, E, It(R), W, A1, PI(R), A3(R), 2009 E(R), It, NZ1, 2, A, SA, Sm(R), NZ3, 2010 Fj, Arg2, A, 2011 S, I1, E(R), It(R), W, I2, [C, NZ1, 2(R)]
Trillo, J (Bègles) 1967 SA 3,4, NZ, R, 1968 S, I, NZ 1,2,3, A, 1969 I, E, W, R, 1970 E, R, 1971 S, I, SA 1,2, A 1,2, 1972 S, A 1,2, R, 1973 S, E
Trinh-Duc, F (Montpellier) 2008 S, I(R), E, It, W(R), A1, 2, 2009 W(R), E, It, NZ1, 2, A, SA, Sm, NZ3, 2010 S, I, W, It, E, SA, Arg1, 2011 S, I1, E, It, W, I2, 3(R), [J, C, NZ1(R), Tg(R), E(R), NZ2(t&R)], 2012 It, S, I, E(R), W(R), Arg 1, 2(R)
Triviaux, R (Cognac) 1931 E, G
Tucco-Chala, M (PUC) 1940 B

Ugartemendia, J-L (St Jean-de-Luz) 1975 S, I

Vaills, G (Perpignan) 1928 A, 1929 G
Valbon, L (Brive) 2004 US, 2005 S(R), 2006 S,E(R), 2007 NZ1(R)
Vallot, C (SCUF) 1912 S
Van Heerden, A (Tarbes) 1992 E, S
Vannier, M (RCF, Chalon) 1953 W, 1954 S, I, Arg 1,2, 1955 S, I, E, W, It, 1956 S, I, W, It, E, 1957 S, I, E, W, It, R 1,2, 1958 S, E, A, W, It, I, 1960 S, E, W, I, It, R, Arg 1,3, 1961 SA, E, W, It, I, NZ 1, A
Vaquer, F (Perpignan) 1921 S, W, 1922 W
Vaquerin, A (Béziers) 1971 R, 1972 S, I 1, A 1, 1973 S, 1974 W, E, S, Arg 1,2, R, SA 1,2, 1975 W, E, S, I, 1976 US, A 1(R),2, R, 1977 Arg 2, 1979 W, E, 1980 S, I
Vareilles, C (SF) 1907 E, 1908 E, W, 1910 S, E
Varenne, F (RCF) 1952 S
Varvier, T (RCF) 1906 E, 1909 E, W, 1911 E, W, 1912 I
Vassal, G (Carcassonne) 1938 R, G 2
Vaysse, J (Albi) 1924 US, 1926 M
Vellat, E (Grenoble) 1927 I, E, G 1,2, 1928 A
Venditti, D (Bourgoin, Brive) 1996 R, SA 1(R),2, 1997 I, W, E, S, R 1, A 1, SA 2, 2000 W (R), E, S, It (R)
Vergé, L (Bègles) 1993 R 1(R)
Verger, A (SF) 1927 W, E, G 1, 1928 I, E, G, W
Verges, S-A (SF) 1906 NZ, E, 1907 E
Vermeulen, E (Brive, Montferrand, Clermont-Auvergne) 2001 SA 1(R),2(R), 2003 NZ, 2006 NZ1,2,Arg, 2007 W1,S(R), 2
Viard, G (Narbonne) 1969 W, 1970 S, R, 1971 S, I
Viars, S (Brive) 1992 W, E, I, R, Arg 1,2, SA 1,2(R), Arg, 1993 R 1, 1994 C 1(R), NZ 1(t), 1995 E (R), [Iv], 1997 R 1(R), A 1(R),2

Vigerie, M (Agen) 1931 W
Vigier, R (Montferrand) 1956 S, W, It, E, Cz, 1957 S, E, W, It, R 1,2, 1958 S, E, A, W, It, I, SA 1,2, 1959 S, E, It, W, I
Vigneau, A (Bayonne) 1935 G
Vignes, C (RCF) 1957 R 1,2, 1958 S, E
Vila, E (Tarbes) 1926 M
Vilagra, J (Vienne) 1945 B 2
Villepreux, P (Toulouse) 1967 It, I, SA 2, NZ, 1968 I, Cz, NZ 1,2,3, A, 1969 S, I, E, W, R, 1970 S, I, W, E, R, 1971 S, I, E, W, A 1,2, R, 1972 S, I 1, E, W, I 2, A 1,2
Viviès, B (Agen) 1978 E, S, I, W, 1980 SA, R, 1981 S, A 1, 1983 A 1(R)
Volot, M (SF) 1945 W, 1946 B, I, K, W
Watremez, Y (Biarritz) 2012 Arg 1
Weller, S (Grenoble) 1989 A 1,2, 1990 A 1, NZ 1

Wolf, J-P (Béziers) 1980 SA, R, 1981 A 2, 1982 E

Yachvili, D (Biarritz) 2002 C (R), 2003 S (R), I, It, W, R (R), E 3, [US,NZ], 2004 I(R), It(R), W(R), S, E, 2005 S(R), E, W, I, It, SA1(R), 2, C, Tg, 2006 S(R), I(R), It(R), E, W, SA, NZ1, 2(R), Arg, 2007 E1, 2008 E(R), It, W(R), A1, 2(R), 2009 NZ1(R), 2(R), A, 2010 It(R), SA(R), Arg1(R), Fj, Arg2(R), A(R), 2011 S(R), I1(R), E, I2, 3(R), [J, C(R), NZ1, Tg, E, W, NZ2], 2012 It, W
Yachvili, M (Tulle, Brive) 1968 E, W, Cz, NZ 3, A, R, 1969 S, I, R, 1971 E, SA 1,2 A 1, 1972 R, 1975 SA 2

Zago, F (Montauban) 1963 I, E

307

FRANCE

Georgia's Irakli Machkhaneli is tackled
by two Russian players during their
European Nations Cup match.

GEORGIA

GEORGIA'S 2012 TEST RECORD

OPPONENTS	DATE	VENUE	RESULT
Spain	11 Feb	A	Lost 25–18
Portugal	25 Feb	H	Won 32–7
Romania	10 Mar	A	Won 19–13
Russia	17 Mar	H	Won 46–0
Ukraine	9 Jun	H	Won 33–3
USA	16 Jun	A	Lost 36–20
Canada	23 Jun	A	Lost 31–12

GEORGIA – NO LONGER THE UNDERDOGS?

By Lúcás Ó'Cealláchain

Getty Images

More and more Georgians are now watching and playing rugby.

Following an impressive showing at their third Rugby World Cup, Georgian rugby has been consistently getting stronger. Georgia looked very comfortable with the Tier One countries in New Zealand and put in strong performances to concern Argentina and especially Scotland, who had to dig deep to put the Lelos away in a closely-fought 15–6 encounter. The performance against his native Scotland will have been especially pleasing for then coach Richie Dixon. Equally impressive was how they dispatched European Nations Cup rivals Romania on rugby's biggest stage 25–9. The victory over Romania was a clear target for Georgia heading into the competition and rather than sitting back and resting on their laurels, they are aiming higher.

The 2011/12 season was all about consolidating Georgia's position as the top team in Europe below the Six Nations, the Lelos having dominated the European Nations Cup for several years now.

Picking up where they left off in the competition spanning two years was always going to be difficult, and a shaky start after RWC 2011 saw

2012 IN PICTURES

Passion: Bradley Davies shows how much the Six Nations victory over Ireland meant to Wales at the final whistle.

Snow slide: Tommaso Benvenuti defies the freezing conditions to score against England.

In hot pursuit: Australia's Rebecca Tavo breaks through the USA defence in the IRB Women's Sevens Challenge Cup in Hong Kong.

Going nuts for Fiji: Fans celebrate Fiji's victory over New Zealand in the final of the Hong Kong Sevens.

Man in the middle: Craig Joubert had the honour of refereeing the first RWC 2015 qualifying match between Mexico and Jamaica.

Hard-hitting: Aurélien Rougerie dislodges the ball in Clermont Auvergne's Heineken Cup quarter-final win over Saracens.

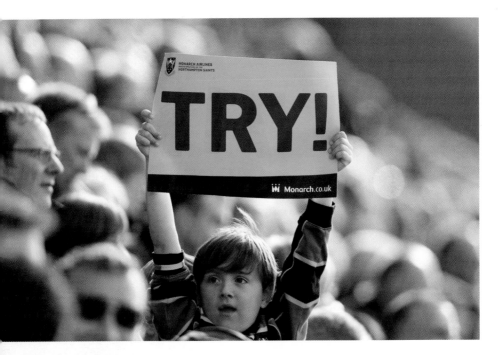

A game for all ages: A young Northampton fan celebrates a try.

Rainstorm: Scotland braved driving rain to beat the Wallabies 9-6 for their first win on Australian soil since 1982.

**RBS 6 Nations
winners:** Wales

**Aviva
Premiership
winners:**
Harlequins

**Heineken
Cup
winners:**
Leinster

**HSBC Sevens
World Series
winners:** New Zealand

**RB Junior World
Championship
winners:**
South Africa

**The Rugby
Championship
winners:**
New Zealand

Giving thanks:
Samoa captain David
Lemi celebrates one of
his tries against Fiji in the
IRB Pacific Nations Cup.

Elation: Japan's Yusuke
Nagae celebrates after
scoring against Tonga.

Rugby mad: An incredible 40,000 people turned up to see Madagascar beat Namibia to win the Africa Cup Division 1B title.

Historic day: The Chiefs perform a haka written for them after winning a maiden Super Rugby title.

Fair play: Kurtley Beale helps New Zealand's Dan Carter to his feet.

Pride: Argentina take to the pitch for their Rugby Championship match against New Zealand at Estadio Ciudad de La Plata.

A growing sport: Tunisia beat Kenya in the CAR Women's Sevens Championship final to qualify for RWC Sevens 2013.

them suffer a surprise 25–18 defeat away to Spain in February. Much of this could be put down to the changing of the guard in Georgian rugby, with a new coach in place – New Zealander Milton Haig having taken over from Dixon – and several new players in the squad.

It didn't take long for normal European service to resume as they put Portugal to the sword later that month with a 32–7 victory at Avchala Stadium in Tbilisi, Haig having recalled several experienced campaigners to the squad to deliver a crucial result. Haig's plans to create a more expansive style of attacking play started to show signs of success and the Lelos defence was strong again. There was plenty of room for improvement in the performance, but the attacking play excited the Georgian fans about what was to come.

A disjointed performance against Romania in Bucharest saw Georgia toil towards victory over a team they had dominated at Rugby World Cup 2011. The game smacked of two teams who knew each other all too well. Smarting from that defeat, a strong Romanian pack matched the Lelos in the set piece and broken play to claw their way back into the game. However, the Romanian backs could not provide the finishing touch and Georgia did just enough to edge the encounter 19–13 with Merab Kvirikashvili instrumental, kicking four penalties and one conversion to guide his team to victory.

The stage was set for a showdown with Russia on 17 March in Tbilisi. This was the first time that the two countries would meet in Georgia since 2008, with previous fixtures being moved to neutral venues in Ukraine and Turkey for political reasons. As a result 25,000 fans turned out to see the match, which was sold out weeks in advance.

The European Nations Cup title was up for grabs and Georgia attacked from the very first minute. Russia have a poor record against Georgia, having won just once in 15 previous meetings, but this was expected to be a tighter affair now that both teams had been to the Rugby World Cup. Nothing could have been further from the truth as Georgia dominated every aspect of play. Following a simple penalty by Kvirikashvili, Mamuka Gorgodze breached the Russian defence with his usual abrasive running. The Lelos were relishing the challenge in front of their home crowd and a further try from second row Giorgi Chkhaidze saw Georgia lead 17–0 at the break.

Sensing that the Russian Bears were shaky, Georgia piled on the pressure in the second half as their dominance of the set piece wore the Russian pack down. The extent of this could be seen when Gorgodze unselfishly had time to pass to a team-mate in the in-goal area for another try. The floodgates opened and one-way traffic resulted in tries for Irakli Abuseridze, Levan Datunashvili and Irakli Machkhaneli (2).

GEORGIA

Combined with the kicking of Kvirikashvili the final score was 46–0 and Georgia had secured their fifth European Nations Cup title with one match left. The attacking play of the Lelos and the resolute defence in the face of a valiant Russian attack will have pleased the home fans and Haig.

A potential banana skin stood in the way of Georgia's party celebrations when they hosted Ukraine in Tbilisi in June in a rescheduled match, but two converted first-half tries from outside centre Merab Sharikadze and second row Bachuki Gujaraidze set the Lelos on their way to victory. The first try, scored as a result of a combination of strong running by Sharikadze and poor defending by Ukraine, came after just four minutes of play. Despite their best efforts, Ukraine could not get a foothold in the game as the Georgians continued to boss proceedings with their forward pack rampant and their backs carving the defence open. Three more tries followed in the second half with the icing on the cake being the effort by right wing Machkhaneli in the final minute, Georgia emerging 33–3 winners after an impressive performance.

Now that the Lelos have cemented their place on the international stage, the question remains as to who can challenge them at this level? End-of-season fixtures against USA and Canada brought defeats, but the goal was to give younger players more match experience and this blooding of younger players indicates the long-term ambitions of the Georgian Rugby Union (GRU).

International success means the GRU can rely on the strong support of the government for the foreseeable future. The government are providing several sites of land free of charge to the Union to develop playing fields and stadia. The number of players in Georgia has more than doubled from 2,600 to 6,156 in the period from 2007 to 2012 and is expected to rise again in the next 12 months after the country successfully hosted the IRB Junior World Rugby Trophy in 2011.

Lasha Khurtsidze, Head of International Public Relations and High Performance at the GRU, says he has every reason to be optimistic about the future. "More and more people come and watch rugby, and more and more people are now playing rugby. It is fair to say that we've nearly got more people willing to play than we can accommodate."

Georgian Rugby Union President George Nijaradze is confident that there is potential to increase it to as many as 30,000 "in six or seven years". But Nijaradze also believes there is more to their progress than that. "The number of players does not itself solve all problems. You can increase the number of players or clubs, but the main thing is to increase the quality. Without the quality, numbers don't work."

The performance of Georgian players abroad, especially in France, has been a major development tool for Georgian rugby. The trend of Georgian players working their way up the French leagues was started over 10 years ago when Frenchman Claude Saurel was at the helm of the national team and it continues to this day. Since then there has been a wave of imports to France, with the majority of Top 14 clubs now keeping Georgian players on their books. Clubs like Toulon, Clermont Auvergne and Montpellier all see the value in the what you see is what you get package Georgian rugby has to offer – hard graft, physical athletes and a no-nonsense approach to the game of rugby.

The crowning glory can be said to be the sight of Gorgodze, or 'Gorgodzilla' as he is also known, playing for the Barbarians in May 2012, becoming the fourth Georgian to don the famous black-and-white jersey. Former basketball player Gorgodze has consistently been among the best foreign players in the Top 14 and French legend Fabien Galthié, his coach at Montpellier, says his work rate is second to none. Gorgodze played a critical part in the Baa-Baas' 29–28 win over Ireland, immense in both attack and defence.

Now Georgia's players are attracting the interest of clubs in the UK as well with the recent signing of number 8 Dimitri Basilaia by Edinburgh. Head coach Michael Bradley is familiar with Basilaia, having spent a stint as a consultant in Georgia before taking over at the Scottish side.

The most telling factor in Georgia's rugby development could be that at RWC 2011 nine of the squad were plying their trade at home in Georgia. With the development of domestic competitions, facilities and government support, that figure may rise even higher in the future. The long-term future of the sport is secure in Georgia and it may only be a matter of time before the Lelos are challenging the bigger nations on the world stage.

GEORGIA

GEORGIA INTERNATIONAL STATISTICS

MATCH RECORDS UP TO 10 OCTOBER 2012

WINNING MARGIN

Date	Opponent	Result	Winning Margin
07/04/2007	Czech Republic	98–3	95
03/02/2002	Netherlands	88–0	88
06/02/2010	Germany	77–3	74
26/02/2005	Ukraine	65–0	65
12/06/2005	Czech Republic	75–10	65

MOST POINTS IN A MATCH
BY THE TEAM

Date	Opponent	Result	Points
07/04/2007	Czech Republic	98–3	98
03/02/2002	Netherlands	88–0	88
06/02/2010	Germany	77–3	77
12/06/2005	Czech Republic	75–10	75

BY A PLAYER

Date	Player	Opponent	Points
06/02/2010	Merab Kvirikashvili	Germany	32
08/03/2003	Pavle Jimsheladze	Russia	23
07/04/2007	Merab Kvirikashvili	Czech Republic	23
12/06/2005	Malkhaz Urjukashvili	Czech Republic	20
28/02/2009	Lasha Malaguradze	Spain	20

MOST TRIES IN A MATCH
BY THE TEAM

Date	Opponent	Result	Tries
07/04/2007	Czech Republic	98–3	16
03/02/2002	Netherlands	88–0	14
23/03/1995	Bulgaria	70–8	11
26/02/2005	Ukraine	65–0	11
12/06/2005	Czech Republic	75–10	11
06/02/2010	Germany	77–3	11

BY A PLAYER

Date	Player	Opponent	Tries
23/03/1995	Pavle Jimsheladze	Bulgaria	3
23/03/1995	Archil Kavtarashvili	Bulgaria	3
12/06/2005	Mamuka Gorgodze	Czech Republic	3
07/04/2007	David Dadunashvili	Czech Republic	3
07/04/2007	Malkhaz Urjukashvili	Czech Republic	3
26/04/2008	Mamuka Gorgodze	Spain	3

MOST CONVERSIONS IN A MATCH
BY THE TEAM

Date	Opponent	Result	Cons
06/02/2010	Germany	77–3	11
03/02/2002	Netherlands	88–0	9
07/04/2007	Czech Republic	98–3	9
12/06/2005	Czech Republic	75–10	7

BY A PLAYER

Date	Player	Opponent	Cons
06/02/2010	Merab Kvirikashvili	Germany	11
03/02/2002	Pavle Jimsheladze	Netherlands	9
07/04/2007	Merab Kvirikashvili	Czech Republic	9
12/06/2005	Malkhaz Urjukashvili	Czech Republic	7

MOST PENALTIES IN A MATCH
BY THE TEAM

Date	Opponent	Result	Pens
08/03/2003	Russia	23–17	6
28/09/2011	Romania	25–9	6
11/06/2010	Scotland A	22–21	5

BY A PLAYER

Date	Player	Opponent	Pens
08/03/2003	Pavle Jimsheladze	Russia	6
28/09/2011	Merab Kvirikashvili	Romania	5
11/06/2010	Irakli Kiasashvili	Scotland A	5

MOST DROP GOALS IN A MATCH
BY THE TEAM

Date	Opponent	Result	DGs
20/10/1996	Russia	29–20	2
21/11/1991	Ukraine	19–15	2
15/07/1992	Ukraine	15–0	2
04/06/1994	Switzerland	22–21	2

BY A PLAYER

Date	Player	Opponent	DGs
15/07/1992	Davit Chavleishvili	Ukraine	2

MOST CAPPED PLAYERS

Player	Caps
Irakli Abuseridze	82
Malkhaz Urjukashvili	69
Gia Labadze	67
Ilia Zedginidze	64

LEADING TRY SCORERS

Player	Tries
Irakli Machkhaneli	21
Mamuka Gorgodze	20
Malkhaz Urjukashvili	18
Tedo Zibzibadze	15

LEADING CONVERSION SCORERS

Player	Cons
Merab Kvirikashvili	77
Pavle Jimsheladze	61
Malkhaz Urjukashvili	45

LEADING PENALTY SCORERS

Player	Pens
Merab Kvirikashvili	51
Pavle Jimsheladze	48
Malkhaz Urjukashvili	45

LEADING DROP GOAL SCORERS

Player	DGs
Kakha Machitidze	4
Nugzar Dzagnidze	3
Pavle Jimsheladze	3
Lasha Malaguradze	3

LEADING POINT SCORERS

Player	Points
Merab Kvirikashvili	343
Pavle Jimsheladze	320
Malkhaz Urjukashvili	318
Nugzar Dzagnidze	105
Irakli Machkhaneli	105

GEORGIA

GEORGIA INTERNATIONAL PLAYERS
UP TO 10 OCTOBER 2012

V Abashidze 1998 *It, Ukr, I*, 1999 *Tg, Tg*, 2000 *It, Mor, Sp*, 2001 *H, Pt, Rus, Sp, R*, 2006 *J*

N Abdaladze 1997 *Cro, De*

I Abuseridze 2000 *It, Pt, Mor, Sp, H, R*, 2001 *H, Pt, Rus, Sp, R*, 2002 *Pt, Rus, Sp, R, I, Rus*, 2003 *Pt, Rus, CZR, R, It, E, Sa, SA*, 2004 *Rus*, 2005 *Pt, Ukr, R*, 2006 *Rus, R, Pt, Ukr, J, R, Sp, Pt, Pt*, 2007 *R, Rus, CZR, Nm, ESp, ItA, Ar, I, Nm, F*, 2008 *Pt, R, Pt, Rus, Sp, S*, 2009 *Ger, Pt, Sp, R, Rus, ArJ, ItA*, 2010 *Pt, Sp, R, Rus, C, US*, 2011 *Ukr, Sp, Pt, R, Rus, S, E, R, Ar*, 2012 *Sp, R, Rus, Ukr, US, C*

V Akhvlediani 2007 *CZR*

K Alania 1993 *Lux*, 1994 *Swi*, 1996 *CZR, CZR, Rus*, 1997 *Pt, Pol, Cro, De*, 1998 *It*, 2001 *H, Pt, Sp, F, SA*, 2002 *H, Pt, Rus, Sp, R, I, Rus*, 2003 *Rus*, 2004 *Pt, Sp*

N Andghuladze 1997 *Pol*, 2000 *It, Pt, Mor, Sp, H, R*, 2004 *Sp, Rus, CZR, R*

D Ashvetia 1998 *Ukr*, 2005 *Pt*, 2006 *R*, 2007 *Sp*

K Asieshvili 2008 *ItA*, 2010 *S, ItA, Nm*, 2012 *Sp*

G Babunashvili 1992 *Ukr, Ukr, Lat*, 1993 *Rus, Pol, Lux*, 1996 *CZR*

Z Bakuradze 1989 *Z*, 1990 *Z*, 1991 *Ukr, Ukr*, 1993 *Rus, Pol*

D Baramidze 2000 *H*

O Barkalaia 2002 *I*, 2004 *Sp, Rus, CZR, R, Ur, CHL, Rus*, 2005 *Pt, Ukr, R, CZR, CHL*, 2006 *Rus, R, Pt, Ukr, J, Bb, R, Sp*, 2007 *Nm, ItA, I, F*, 2008 *Pt, R, Pt, Rus, Sp, ESp, Ur, ItA, S*, 2009 *Ger, Sp, R*

D Basilaia 2008 *Pt, R, Pt, CZR, Rus, Sp, S*, 2009 *Ger, Sp, R, C, US, ItA*, 2011 *Nm, S, E, R*, 2012 *Sp, Pt, R, Rus*

G Begadze 2012 *Pt, R, Rus, Ukr, US*

R Belkania 2004 *Sp*, 2005 *CHL*, 2007 *Sp, Rus*, 2012 *Pt, R, Rus, Ukr, US, C*

G Beriashvili 1993 *Rus, Pol*, 1995 *Ger*

G Berishvili 2011 *Nm, E, R*, 2012 *Sp, Pt, R, Rus, US, C*

M Besselia 1991 *Ukr*, 1993 *Rus, Pol*, 1996 *Rus*, 1997 *Pt*

B Bitsadze 2012 *Ukr, US, C*

D Bolgashvili 2000 *It, Pt, H, R*, 2001 *H, Pt, Rus, Sp, R, F, SA*, 2002 *H, Pt, Rus, I*, 2003 *Pt, Sp, Rus, CZR, R, E, Sa, SA*, 2004 *Rus, Ur, CHL, Rus*, 2005 *CZR*, 2007 *Sp*, 2010 *ItA*

J Bregvadze 2008 *ESp, ItA*, 2009 *C, IrA*, 2010 *Sp, R, S, Nm*, 2011 *Ukr, Sp, R, Rus, Nm, S, E, R, Ar*

G Buguianishvili 1996 *CZR, Rus*, 1997 *Pol*, 1998 *It, Rus, I, R*, 2000 *Sp, H, R*, 2001 *H, F, SA*, 2002 *Rus*

D Chavleishvili 1990 *Z, Z*, 1992 *Ukr, Ukr, Lat*, 1993 *Pol, Lux*

D Chichua 2008 *CZR*

I Chikava 1993 *Pol, Lux*, 1994 *Swi*, 1995 *Bul, Mol, H*, 1996 *CZR, CZR*, 1997 *Pol*, 1998 *I*

R Chikvaidze 2004 *Ur, CHL*

L Chikvinidze 1994 *Swi*, 1995 *Bul, Mol, Ger, H*, 1996 *CZR, Rus*

L Chilachava 2012 *Sp, C*

G Chkhaidze 2002 *H, R, I, Rus*, 2003 *Pt, CZR, It, E, SA, Ur*, 2004 *CZR, R*, 2006 *Pt, Ukr*, 2007 *R, Rus, CZR, Nm, ESp, ItA, Ar, I, Nm, F*, 2008 *R, Pt, CZR, Rus, Sp*, 2009 *Ger, Pt, Sp, R, Rus, ArJ, ItA*, 2010 *Ger, Pt, Sp, R, Rus, C, US*, 2011 *Ukr, Sp, Pt, R, Rus, S, E, R, Ar*, 2012 *Sp, Pt, R, Rus, Ukr, US, C*

S Chkhenkeli 1997 *Pol*

I Chkhikvadze 2005 *CHL*, 2007 *Sp*, 2008 *Pt, R, Pt, CZR, Rus, ESp, Ur, ItA, S*, 2009 *Ger, Sp, ItA*, 2010 *Sp, Rus, S, ItA, Nm, C, US*, 2011 *Pt, Nm, R*, 2012 *Pt*

I Chkonia 2007 *ESp, ItA*

D Dadunashvili 2003 *It, E, SA, Ur*, 2004 *Sp, Rus, CZR, R*, 2005 *CHL*, 2007 *Sp, Rus, CZR, Nm, ItA*, 2008 *Pt, R, Pt, CZR, Rus, Sp, S*, 2009 *C, IrA, US*, 2010 *Sp, S, ItA, Nm*

L Datunashvili 2004 *Sp*, 2005 *Pt, Ukr, R, CZR*, 2006 *Rus, R, Pt, Ukr, J, Bb, CZR, Pt, Pt*, 2007 *R, Rus, Nm, ESp, ItA, I, Nm, F*, 2008 *Pt, Pt*, 2009 *Sp, R, Rus, C, US, ArJ*, 2010 *Ger, Pt, Sp, R, Rus, C, US*, 2011 *Ukr, Sp, Pt, R, Rus, S, E, R, Ar*, 2012 *Sp, Pt, Rus*

V Didebulidze 1991 *Ukr*, 1994 *Kaz*, 1995 *Bul, Mol*, 1996 *CZR*, 1997 *De*, 1999 *Tg*, 2000 *H*, 2001 *H, Pt, Rus, Sp, R, F, SA*, 2002 *H, Pt, Rus, Sp, R, I, Rus*, 2003 *Pt, Sp, Rus, CZR, R, It, E, Sa, SA*, 2004 *Rus*, 2005 *Pt*, 2006 *R, R*, 2007 *R, Sp, Rus, CZR, Nm, ESp, ItA, Ar, Nm, F*

E Dzagnidze 1992 *Ukr, Ukr, Lat*, 1993 *Rus, Pol*, 1995 *Bul, Mol, Ger, H*, 1998 *I*

N Dzagnidze 1989 *Z*, 1990 *Z, Z*, 1991 *Ukr*, 1992 *Ukr, Ukr, Lat*, 1993 *Rus, Pol*, 1994 *Swi*, 1995 *Ger, H*

T Dzagnidze 2008 *ESp*

D Dzneladze 1992 *Ukr, Lat*, 1993 *Lux*, 1994 *Kaz*

P Dzotsenidze 1995 *Ger, H*, 1997 *Pt, Pol*

G Elizbarashvili 2002 *Rus*, 2003 *Sp*, 2004 *CHL*, 2005 *CZR*, 2006 *Pt, Ukr, J, Bb, CZR, Sp, Pt*, 2007 *R, Sp, Rus, I, F*, 2009 *C, IrA*

O Eloshvili 2002 *H*, 2003 *SA*, 2006 *Bb, CZR*, 2007 *Sp, CZR, Nm, ESp, ItA, I, F*

S Essakia 1999 *Tg, Tg*, 2000 *It, Mor, Sp, H*, 2004 *CZR, R*

M Gagnidze 1991 *Ukr, Ukr*

D Gasviani 2004 *Sp, Rus*, 2005 *CZR, CHL*, 2006 *Ukr, J*, 2007 *Rus, CZR*, 2008 *ESp, Ur, ItA, S*

A Ghibradze 1992 *Ukr, Ukr, Lat*, 1994 *Swi*, 1995 *Bul, Mol, Ger*, 1996 *CZR*

D Ghudushauri 1992 *Z*, 1991 *Ukr, Ukr*

L Ghvaberidze 2004 *Pt*

R Gigauri 2006 *Ukr, J, Bb, CZR, Sp, Pt, Pt*, 2007 *R, Nm, ESp, ItA, Ar, Nm, F*, 2008 *Pt, R, Pt, Rus, Sp, ESp, Ur, 2009 C, IrA, US, ArJ, ItA*, 2010 *S, ItA, Nm*, 2011 *Nm, S, E, R*, 2012 *Sp*

A Giorgadze 1996 *CZR*, 1998 *It, Ukr, Rus, R*, 1999 *Tg, Tg*, 2000 *It, Pt, Mor, H, R*, 2001 *H, Pt, Rus, Sp, R, F, SA*, 2002 *H, Pt, Rus, Sp, R, I, Rus*, 2003 *Pt, Sp, Rus, R, It, E, Sa, SA, Ur*, 2005 *Pt, Ukr, R, CZR*, 2006 *Rus, R, Pt, Bb, CZR, Sp, Pt*, 2007 *R, Ar, I, Nm, F*, 2009 *Ger, Pt, Sp, ArJ*, 2010 *Ger, Pt, C, US*, 2011 *Pt, S, Ar*

I Giorgadze 2001 *F, SA*, 2003 *Pt, Sp, Rus, R, It, E, Sa, Ur*, 2004 *Rus*, 2005 *Pt, R, CZR*, 2006 *Rus, R, Pt, Bb, CZR, R, Sp, Pt, Pt*, 2007 *R, Sp, Rus, CZR, Ar, Nm, F*, 2008 *R*, 2009 *Ger, Pt, Sp, Rus*, 2010 *Ger, Sp, R, Rus*, 2011 *Ukr*

M Giorgodze 2003 *Sp, Rus*, 2004 *Pt, Sp, Rus, CZR, R, Ur, CHL, Rus*, 2005 *Pt, Ukr, R, CZR, CHL*, 2006 *Rus, Pt, Bb, CZR, R, Sp, Pt, Pt*, 2007 *Ar, I, Nm*, 2008 *R, Rus, Sp*, 2009 *Ger, Pt, Sp, R, Rus, ArJ*, 2011 *R, Rus, S, E, R, Ar*, 2012 *Pt, R, Rus*

E Gueguchadze 1990 *Z, Z*

L Gugava 2004 *Sp, Rus, CZR, Ur, CHL, Rus*, 2005 *Pt, Ukr*, 2006 *Bb, CZR*, 2009 *C, IrA, US*, 2010 *C, US*, 2011 *Ukr, Sp, Pt, R, Rus, Nm, Ar*, 2012 *Ukr, C*

I Guiorkhelidze 1998 *R*, 1999 *Tg, Tg*

G Guiunashvili 1989 *Z*, 1990 *Z*, 1991 *Ukr, Ukr*, 1992 *Ukr, Ukr, Lat*, 1993 *Rus, Pol, Lux*, 1994 *Swi*, 1996 *Rus*, 1997 *Pt*

K Guiunashvili 1990 *Z, Z*, 1991 *Ukr, Ukr*, 1992 *Ukr, Ukr, Lat*

B Gujaraidze 2008 *ESp*, 2012 *Ukr*

S Gujaraidze 2003 *SA, Ur*

I Gundishvili 2002 *I*, 2003 *Pt, Sp, Rus, CZR*, 2008 *ESp, Ur, ItA*, 2009 *C, US*

D Gurgenidze 2007 *Sp, ItA*

A Gusharashvili 1998 *Ukr*

D Iobidze 1993 *Rus, Pol*

E Iovadze 1993 *Lux*, 1994 *Kaz*, 1995 *Bul, Mol, Ger, H*, 2001 *Sp, F, SA*, 2002 *H, Rus, Sp, R, I*

IRELAND

IRELAND'S 2012 TEST RECORD

OPPONENTS	DATE	VENUE	RESULT
Wales	5 Feb	H	Lost 21–23
Italy	25 Feb	H	Won 42–10
France	5 Mar	A	Drew 17–17
Scotland	10 Mar	H	Won 32–14
England	17 Mar	A	Lost 30–9
New Zealand	9 Jun	A	Lost 42–10
New Zealand	16 Jun	A	Lost 22–19
New Zealand	23 Jun	A	Lost 60–0

MIXED FORTUNES FOR THE IRISH

By Ruaidhri O'Connor

Fly half Johnny Sexton played well as Ireland came close to beating New Zealand in the second Test.

Frustration was the overriding emotion at the end of Ireland's longest season.

It was a campaign where the national side played 17 times, winning just six matches but offering enough glimpses of their abilities that led to disappointment when the team failed to live up to their potential.

Ireland's problems were exacerbated when their results were juxtaposed against Leinster's third Heineken Cup win in four years, achieved the hard way with victory over Clermont Auvergne in an epic semi-final in France and a sensational display in an historic all-Irish final against Ulster.

If the season had ended there, Irish rugby fans could have signed off for the summer basking in the glory of that day. But then Declan Kidney took his charges to New Zealand for a three-Test tour against the world champions and it proved as difficult as it had sounded at the outset.

In keeping with the theme of the season, the tourists came within a last-gasp Dan Carter drop goal of a draw in the second Test in Christchurch, before succumbing to its worst-ever defeat a week later in Hamilton, a 60–0 mauling that left a bitter taste that has lingered going into the new season.

The season began in the aftermath of Rugby World Cup 2011 when the team were welcomed home from New Zealand with open arms thanks to the historic pool stage victory over Australia.

Among the players there was lingering disappointment over the quarter-final exit at the hands of their near neighbours Wales and the RBS Six Nations opener offered a chance for redemption, with Warren Gatland taking his side to the Aviva Stadium for the first time since the old ground got a facelift.

Wales have been getting the upper hand in recent meetings between the sides and they were the better side once again here, but Ireland – despite the absence of captain Brian O'Driscoll who missed the campaign after undergoing shoulder surgery – stayed in touch throughout and Tommy Bowe's try gave them a six-point lead with just over 10 minutes remaining and Wales down to 14 men after Bradley Davies's sin-binning.

But their position of strength wouldn't last, George North crossed for an unconverted try before Wayne Barnes gave a penalty against Stephen Ferris for an alleged tip-tackle, allowing Leigh Halfpenny the opportunity to set the Welsh on their way to the Grand Slam.

"Three teams have had their Grand Slams ended this weekend, and three teams are still in it. That is the nature of it," Kidney said in the aftermath. "We had to defend for 60 per cent-plus of the game, and if you do that then you are going to ask for trouble. There are different aspects of the game I know we can improve on. It is just a case now of getting ready for the next match in six days' time."

That match never materialised as the Stade de France pitch froze over on a bitterly cold night in Paris and the encounter was postponed at the last minute, meaning Ireland and France would have to play four Tests in four weeks to win the Championship.

A 42–10 victory over Italy got Ireland back on track ahead of their return to Paris where they came tantalisingly close to claiming just a second victory in the French capital since 1972. Tommy Bowe's brace of tries saw the visitors lead 17–6 at half-time, but they failed to score after the interval as Wesley Fofana's try hauled Les Bleus back into the tie and they ended up with a 17–17 draw.

Despite avoiding defeat in France for the first time since O'Driscoll's hat-trick in 2000, stand-in skipper Paul O'Connell was unhappy with the result. "There's a big feeling of defeat and an opportunity lost," he said. "We're really disappointed with our second-half performance."

Bowe agreed, saying: "There's a real sense of disappointment in the changing room. We gave ourselves the best opportunity to win. At half-time we were delighted, really excited about the second half, but it turned out to be very disappointing."

That disappointment was put to one side as the team responded by

IRELAND

powering past Scotland thanks to tries from Rory Best, Eoin Reddan, Andrew Trimble and Fergus McFadden.

Buoyed by that 32–14 win, they went to Twickenham for a St Patrick's Day meeting with England that ended in humiliation. Ireland's Achilles heel has long been their lack of depth at prop and, when tighthead prop Mike Ross was forced off with a neck injury before half-time, he was replaced by Tom Court – a loosehead – and the scrum crumbled. England inflicted what Kidney would describe as an "extremely painful" defeat that left Ireland third in the Six Nations table.

"All credit to England, they played well and deserved to win. I know we're better than that, but we were well beaten," he said. "That was always on the cards because we have guys who don't have huge tighthead experience playing for Ireland at the moment. It's something we'll have to work on and bring more Irish guys through."

So, a disappointing Six Nations provided the backdrop for the return of Heineken Cup action and, once again, the European competition restored the good feeling.

Connacht had made their debut in the tournament this season and, although they didn't get out of a pool including Toulouse and Harlequins, their final-day victory over the Aviva Premiership team at the Sportsground gave the province a huge lift.

The other three provinces reached the last eight and the stage was set for an all-Irish quarter-final as Ulster travelled to Munster and claimed a famous 22–16 victory that handed them a first semi-final place since they claimed the trophy in 1999, which they duly won against Edinburgh at the Aviva Stadium.

Leinster saw their way past the Cardiff Blues in Dublin before they squeezed past Clermont on a dramatic day in Bordeaux when the smallest of margins gave Joe Schmidt's charges the narrowest of victories. With a last-gasp lunge, Fofana reached for the line but couldn't ground the ball and the stage was set for an historic day at Twickenham.

Irish fans packed out the old ground on 19 May as Leinster claimed their third title in four years and their second in succession under Schmidt with Sean Cronin, Sean O'Brien and Heinke van der Merwe adding to a penalty try for a 42–14 win on a memorable evening.

"After we won one we talked about not being content with that and trying to create some sort of dynasty and something to be remembered by," a fully-recovered O'Driscoll said. "We're going in the right direction towards doing that, but I know this team will be hungry for more."

A week later, the European champions were denied a double by the Ospreys at the RDS, the second time the Neath-Swansea region had shocked them in the RaboDirect PRO12 final in four years. The Welsh side had also beaten Munster in the semi-final. The Irish province had topped the league table, despite operating without their front-line internationals for much of the season, but in a fitting finale to his club career Shane Williams scored a last-gasp try and Dan Biggar stepped up to deliver a 31–30 shock win.

The club game finished with a dramatic second-ever Ulster Bank All Ireland League title for St Mary's, who defeated leaders Clontarf on the penultimate weekend before sealing the league in front of a packed Templeville Road with a 23–19 victory over third-placed Young Munster to ensure Hugh Hogan lifted the trophy.

The end of the domestic season signalled the beginning of the tour to New Zealand, with an Ireland side shorn of its Leinster players suffering a 29–28 defeat to the Barbarians before taking the long trip south.

The long season had taken its toll and Kidney was missing a host of his first-choice stars for the toughest of tests. Things got off to a difficult start as the world champions blitzed the tourists 42–10 at Eden Park, winning their first outing since claiming the Webb Ellis Cup.

A week later, it was oh, so different as Ireland came out of the blocks with purpose in Christchurch and tore into their opponents with a ferocity that was lacking the previous week.

Conor Murray got over for a try, while Jonathan Sexton's boot sent Ireland in ahead 10–9 at half-time and, although Aaron Smith crossed for a try, the Irish fly half pulled the visitors level with 12 minutes left on the clock. Ireland were on top, but the All Blacks turned the tide in the closing stages and Carter sent over a last-ditch drop goal that rescued a 22–19 win.

New Zealand coach Steve Hansen admitted they "probably shouldn't have won", but a week later there was no doubt about the result as a tired-looking Irish side slipped to their worst-ever defeat in Hamilton.

A 60–0 scoreline left a bitter taste in Rob Kearney's mouth as he reflected on the campaign. "It probably hasn't been that great a season for us. A couple of games could have gone our way. I look at Wales at home and France away, and last week (against New Zealand) as well. All three of them went against us but that's sport and we have to move on."

Although the senior team's results left a disappointing taste in the mouth, the Under 20 side's performances at the IRB Junior World Championship offered some hope. Ireland upset hosts and eventual winners South Africa in their opening match and, although defeat to England denied them a shot at the title, Mike Ruddock's charges responded to beat the English at the second attempt and then France 18–7 to take fifth place.

IRELAND

IRELAND INTERNATIONAL STATISTICS

MATCH RECORDS UP TO 10 OCTOBER 2012

MOST CONSECUTIVE TEST WINS

10 2002 R, Ru, Gg, A, Fj, Arg, 2003 S1, It1, F, W1
8 2003 Tg, Sm, W2, It2, S2, R, Nm, Arg
8 2008 Arg, 2009 F, It, E, S, W, C, US
6 1968 S, W, A, 1969 F, E, S
6 2004 SA, US, Arg, 2005 It, S, E

MOST CONSECUTIVE TESTS WITHOUT DEFEAT

Matches	Wins	Draws	Period
12	11	1	2008 to 2010
10	10	0	2002 to 2003
8	8	0	2003
7	6	1	1968 to 1969
6	6	0	2004 to 2005

MOST POINTS IN A MATCH

BY THE TEAM

Pts	Opponents	Venue	Year
83	USA	Manchester (NH)	2000
78	Japan	Dublin	2000
70	Georgia	Dublin	1998
64	Fiji	Dublin	2002
64	Namibia	Sydney	2003
63	Georgia	Dublin	2002
62	Russia	Rotorua	2011
61	Italy	Limerick	2003
61	Pacific Islands	Dublin	2006
60	Romania	Dublin	1986
60	Italy	Dublin	2000
55	Zimbabwe	Dublin	1991
55	USA	Dublin	2004
55	Canada	Limerick	2008
54	Wales	Dublin	2002
53	Romania	Dublin	1998
53	USA	Dublin	1999
51	Italy	Rome	2007
50	Japan	Bloemfontein	1995

BY A PLAYER

Pts	Player	Opponents	Venue	Year
32	R J R O'Gara	Samoa	Apia	2003
30	R J R O'Gara	Italy	Dublin	2000
26	D G Humphreys	Scotland	Murrayfield	2003
26	D G Humphreys	Italy	Limerick	2003
26	P Wallace	Pacific Islands	Dublin	2006
24	P A Burke	Italy	Dublin	1997
24	D G Humphreys	Argentina	Lens	1999
23	R P Keyes	Zimbabwe	Dublin	1991
23	R J R O'Gara	Japan	Dublin	2000
22	D G Humphreys	Wales	Dublin	2002
21	S O Campbell	Scotland	Dublin	1982
21	S O Campbell	England	Dublin	1983
21	R J R O'Gara	Italy	Rome	2001
21	R J R O'Gara	Argentina	Dublin	2004
21	R J R O'Gara	England	Dublin	2007
20	M J Kiernan	Romania	Dublin	1986
20	E P Elwood	Romania	Dublin	1993
20	S J P Mason	Samoa	Dublin	1996
20	E P Elwood	Georgia	Dublin	1998
20	K G M Wood	USA	Dublin	1999
20	D A Hickie	Italy	Limerick	2003
20	D G Humphreys	USA	Dublin	2004

MOST TRIES IN A MATCH
BY THE TEAM

Tries	Opponents	Venue	Year
13	USA	Manchester (NH)	2000
11	Japan	Dublin	2000
10	Romania	Dublin	1986
10	Georgia	Dublin	1998
10	Namibia	Sydney	2003
9	Fiji	Dublin	2003
9	Russia	Rotorua	2011
8	Western Samoa	Dublin	1988
8	Zimbabwe	Dublin	1991
8	Georgia	Dublin	2002
8	Italy	Limerick	2003
8	Pacific Islands	Dublin	2006
8	Italy	Rome	2007
8	Canada	Limerick	2008
7	Japan	Bloemfontein	1995
7	Romania	Dublin	1998
7	USA	Dublin	1999
7	USA	Dublin	2004
7	Japan	Tokyo	2005

BY A PLAYER

Tries	Player	Opponents	Venue	Year
4	B F Robinson	Zimbabwe	Dublin	1991
4	K G M Wood	USA	Dublin	1999
4	D A Hickie	Italy	Limerick	2003
3	R Montgomery	Wales	Birkenhead	1887
3	J P Quinn	France	Cork	1913
3	E O'D Davy	Scotland	Murrayfield	1930
3	S J Byrne	Scotland	Murrayfield	1953
3	K D Crossan	Romania	Dublin	1986
3	B J Mullin	Tonga	Brisbane	1987
3	M R Mostyn	Argentina	Dublin	1999
3	B G O'Driscoll	France	Paris	2000
3	M J Mullins	USA	Manchester (NH)	2000
3	D A Hickie	Japan	Dublin	2000
3	R A J Henderson	Italy	Rome	2001
3	B G O'Driscoll	Scotland	Dublin	2002
3	K M Maggs	Fiji	Dublin	2002

MOST CONVERSIONS IN A MATCH
BY THE TEAM

Cons	Opponents	Venue	Year
10	Georgia	Dublin	1998
10	Japan	Dublin	2000
9	USA	Manchester (NH)	2000
7	Romania	Dublin	1986
7	Georgia	Dublin	2002
7	Namibia	Sydney	2003
7	USA	Dublin	2004
7	Russia	Rotorua	2011
6	Japan	Bloemfontein	1995
6	Romania	Dublin	1998
6	USA	Dublin	1999
6	Italy	Dublin	2000
6	Italy	Limerick	2003
6	Japan	Tokyo	2005
6	Pacific Islands	Dublin	2006
6	Canada	Limerick	2008

BY A PLAYER

Cons	Player	Opponents	Venue	Year
10	E P Elwood	Georgia	Dublin	1998
10	R J R O'Gara	Japan	Dublin	2000
8	R J R O'Gara	USA	Manchester (NH)	2000
7	M J Kiernan	Romania	Dublin	1986
7	R J R O'Gara	Namibia	Sydney	2003
7	D G Humphreys	USA	Dublin	2004
6	P A Burke	Japan	Bloemfontein	1995
6	R J R O'Gara	Italy	Dublin	2000
6	D G Humphreys	Italy	Limerick	2003
6	D G Humphreys	Japan	Tokyo	2005
6	P Wallace	Pacific Islands	Dublin	2006
6	R J R O'Gara	Russia	Rotorua	2011
6	M J Kiernan	Canada	Dunedin	1987
5	E P Elwood	Romania	Dublin	1999
5	R J R O'Gara	Georgia	Dublin	2002
5	D G Humphreys	Fiji	Dublin	2002
5	D G Humphreys	Romania	Dublin	2005
5	R J R O'Gara	Canada	Limerick	2008
5	J Sexton	Fiji	Dublin	2009

IRELAND

MOST PENALTIES IN A MATCH
BY THE TEAM

Penalties	Opponents	Venue	Year
8	Italy	Dublin	1997
7	Argentina	Lens	1999
6	Scotland	Dublin	1982
6	Romania	Dublin	1993
6	USA	Atlanta	1996
6	Western Samoa	Dublin	1996
6	Italy	Dublin	2000
6	Wales	Dublin	2002
6	Australia	Dublin	2002
6	Samoa	Apia	2003
6	Japan	Osaka	2005

BY A PLAYER

Penalties	Player	Opponents	Venue	Year
8	P A Burke	Italy	Dublin	1997
7	D G Humphreys	Argentina	Lens	1999
6	S O Campbell	Scotland	Dublin	1982
6	E P Elwood	Romania	Dublin	1993
6	S J P Mason	Western Samoa	Dublin	1996
6	R J R O'Gara	Italy	Dublin	2000
6	D G Humphreys	Wales	Dublin	2002
6	R J R O'Gara	Australia	Dublin	2002

MOST DROP GOALS IN A MATCH
BY THE TEAM

Drops	Opponents	Venue	Year
2	Australia	Dublin	1967
2	France	Dublin	1975
2	Australia	Sydney	1979
2	England	Dublin	1981
2	Canada	Dunedin	1987
2	England	Dublin	1993
2	Wales	Wembley	1999
2	New Zealand	Dublin	2001
2	Argentina	Dublin	2004
2	England	Dublin	2005

BY A PLAYER

Drops	Player	Opponents	Venue	Year
2	C M H Gibson	Australia	Dublin	1967
2	W M McCombe	France	Dublin	1975
2	S O Campbell	Australia	Sydney	1979
2	E P Elwood	England	Dublin	1993
2	D G Humphreys	Wales	Wembley	1999
2	D G Humphreys	New Zealand	Dublin	2001
2	R J R O'Gara	Argentina	Dublin	2004
2	R J R O'Gara	England	Dublin	2005

CAREER RECORDS

MOST CAPPED PLAYERS

Caps	Player	Career Span
124	R J R O'Gara	2000 to 2012
120	B G O'Driscoll	1999 to 2012
105	J J Hayes	2000 to 2011
98	P A Stringer	2000 to 2011
92	M E O'Kelly	1997 to 2009
88	D P O'Callaghan	2003 to 2012
85	P J O'Connell	2002 to 2012
82	G T Dempsey	1998 to 2008
72	D G Humphreys	1996 to 2005
72	D P Wallace	2000 to 2011
72	G E A Murphy	2000 to 2011
70	K M Maggs	1997 to 2005
69	C M H Gibson	1964 to 1979
69	G W D'Arcy	1999 to 2012
67	M J Horan	2000 to 2011
65	S H Easterby	2000 to 2008
65	S P Horgan	2000 to 2009
63	W J McBride	1962 to 1975
62	A G Foley	1995 to 2005
62	D A Hickie	1997 to 2007
62	R D Best	2005 to 2012
61	J F Slattery	1970 to 1984
59	P S Johns	1990 to 2000
58	P A Orr	1976 to 1987
58	K G M Wood	1994 to 2003
57	D P Leamy	2004 to 2011
55	B J Mullin	1984 to 1995
54	T J Kiernan	1960 to 1973
54	P M Clohessy	1993 to 2002
52	D G Lenihan	1981 to 1992
51	M I Keane	1974 to 1984

MOST CONSECUTIVE TESTS

Tests	Player	Span
52	W J McBride	1964 to 1975
49	P A Orr	1976 to 1986
43	D G Lenihan	1981 to 1989
39	M I Keane	1974 to 1981
38	P A Stringer	2003 to 2007
37	G V Stephenson	1920 to 1929

MOST TESTS AS CAPTAIN

Tests	Captain	Span
83	B G O'Driscoll	2002 to 2012
36	K G M Wood	1996 to 2003
24	T J Kiernan	1963 to 1973
19	C F Fitzgerald	1982 to 1986
17	J F Slattery	1979 to 1981
17	D G Lenihan	1986 to 1990

MOST POINTS IN TESTS

Points	Player	Tests	Career
1075	R J R O'Gara	124	2000 to 2012
565*	D G Humphreys	72	1996 to 2005
308	M J Kiernan	43	1982 to 1991
296	E P Elwood	35	1993 to 1999
240	B G O'Driscoll	120	1999 to 2012
236	J J Sexton	32	2009 to 2012
217	S O Campbell	22	1976 to 1984
158	T J Kiernan	54	1960 to 1973
145	D A Hickie	62	1997 to 2007
120	T J Bowe	49	2004 to 2012
113	A J P Ward	19	1978 to 1987

* Humphreys's total includes a penalty try against Scotland in 1999

MOST TRIES IN TESTS

Tries	Player	Tests	Career
45	B G O'Driscoll	120	1999 to 2012
29	D A Hickie	62	1997 to 2007
24	T J Bowe	49	2004 to 2012
21	S P Horgan	65	2000 to 2009
19	G T Dempsey	82	1998 to 2008
18	G E A Murphy	72	2000 to 2011
17	B J Mullin	55	1984 to 1995
16	R J R O'Gara	124	2000 to 2012
15	K G M Wood	58	1994 to 2003
15	K M Maggs	70	1997 to 2005
14	G V Stephenson	42	1920 to 1930
12	K D Crossan	41	1982 to 1992
12	D P Wallace	72	2000 to 2011
12	K G Earls	32	2008 to 2012
11	A T A Duggan	25	1963 to 1972
11	S P Geoghegan	37	1991 to 1996
11	A D Trimble	48	2005 to 2012

MOST CONVERSIONS IN TESTS

Cons	Player	Tests	Career
175	R J R O'Gara	124	2000 to 2012
88	D G Humphreys	72	1996 to 2005
43	E P Elwood	35	1993 to 1999
40	M J Kiernan	43	1982 to 1991
27	J J Sexton	32	2009 to 2012
26	T J Kiernan	54	1960 to 1973
16	R A Lloyd	19	1910 to 1920
15	S O Campbell	22	1976 to 1984

MOST PENALTY GOALS IN TESTS

Penalties	Player	Tests	Career
200	R J R O'Gara	124	2000 to 2012
110	D G Humphreys	72	1996 to 2005
68	E P Elwood	35	1993 to 1999
62	M J Kiernan	43	1982 to 1991
57	J J Sexton	32	2009 to 2012
54	S O Campbell	22	1976 to 1984
31	T J Kiernan	54	1960 to 1973
29	A J P Ward	19	1978 to 1987

MOST DROP GOALS IN TESTS

Drops	Player	Tests	Career
15	R J R O'Gara	124	2000 to 2012
8	D G Humphreys	72	1996 to 2005
7	R A Lloyd	19	1910 to 1920
7	S O Campbell	22	1976 to 1984
6	C M H Gibson	69	1964 to 1979
6	B J McGann	25	1969 to 1976
6	M J Kiernan	43	1982 to 1991

IRELAND

INTERNATIONAL CHAMPIONSHIP RECORDS

RECORD	DETAIL	HOLDER	SET
Most points in season	168	in five matches	2000
Most tries in season	17	in five matches	2000
	17	in five matches	2004
	17	in five matches	2007
Highest Score	60	60–13 v Italy	2000
Biggest win	47	60–13 v Italy	2000
Highest score conceded	50	18–50 v England	2000
Biggest defeat	40	6–46 v England	1997
Most appearances	61	R J R O'Gara	2000–2012
Most points in matches	551	R J R O'Gara	2000–2012
Most points in season	82	R J R O'Gara	2007
Most points in match	30	R J R O'Gara	v Italy, 2000
Most tries in matches	25	B G O'Driscoll	2000–2011
Most tries in season	5	J E Arigho	1928
	5	B G O'Driscoll	2000
	5	T J Bowe	2012
Most tries in match	3	R Montgomery	v Wales, 1887
	3	J P Quinn	v France, 1913
	3	E O'D Davy	v Scotland, 1930
	3	S J Byrne	v Scotland, 1953
	3	B G O'Driscoll	v France, 2000
	3	R A J Henderson	v Italy, 2001
	3	B G O'Driscoll	v Scotland, 2002
Most cons in matches	81	R J R O'Gara	2000–2012
Most cons in season	11	R J R O'Gara	2000
	11	R J R O'Gara	2004
Most cons in match	6	R J R O'Gara	v Italy, 2000
Most pens in matches	107	R J R O'Gara	2000–2012
Most pens in season	17	R J R O'Gara	2006
Most pens in match	6	S O Campbell	v Scotland, 1982
	6	R J R O'Gara	v Italy, 2000
	6	D G Humphreys	v Wales, 2002
Most drops in matches	7	R A Lloyd	1910–1920
Most drops in season	2	on several	Occasions
Most drops in match	2	W M McCombe	v France, 1975
	2	E P Elwood	v England, 1993
	2	D G Humphreys	v Wales, 1999
	2	R J R O'Gara	v England, 2005

MISCELLANEOUS RECORDS

RECORD	HOLDER	DETAIL
Longest Test Career	A J F O'Reilly	1955 to 1970
	C M H Gibson	1964 to 1979
Youngest Test Cap	F S Hewitt	17 yrs 157 days in 1924
Oldest Test Cap	J J Hayes	37 yrs 277 days in 2011

CAREER RECORDS OF IRELAND
INTERNATIONAL PLAYERS
UP TO 10 OCTOBER 2012

PLAYER BACKS:	DEBUT	CAPS	T	C	P	D	PTS
T J Bowe	2004 v US	49	24	0	0	0	120
D M Cave	2009 v C	3	0	0	0	0	0
G W D'Arcy	1999 v R	69	7	0	0	0	35
K G Earls	2008 v C	32	12	0	0	0	60
L M Fitzgerald	2006 v PI	23	2	0	0	0	10
F A Jones	2011 v S	3	0	0	0	0	0
R D J Kearney	2007 v Arg	41	7	1	0	0	37
F L McFadden	2011 v It	14	4	0	0	0	20
C Murray	2011 v F	12	1	0	0	0	5
B G O'Driscoll	1999 v A	120	45	0	0	5	240
R J R O'Gara	2000 v S	124	16	175	200	15	1075
T G O'Leary	2007 v Arg	24	3	0	0	0	15
E G Reddan	2006 F	45	2	0	0	0	10
J J Sexton	2009 v Fj	32	1	27	57	2	236
A D Trimble	2005 v A	48	11	0	0	0	55
P R Wallace	2006 v SA	30	2	11	7	0	53
S R Zebo	2012 v NZ	1	0	0	0	0	0

IRELAND

FORWARDS:

R D Best	2005 v NZ	62	7	0	0	0	35
T D Buckley	2007 v Arg	25	2	0	0	0	10
T G Court	2009 v It	29	1	0	0	0	5
S M Cronin	2009 v Fj	21	0	0	0	0	0
S Ferris	2006 v PI	35	2	0	0	0	10
D J Fitzpatrick	2012 v NZ	2	0	0	0	0	0
C E Healy	2009 v A	33	1	0	0	0	5
J P R Heaslip	2006 v PI	50	7	0	0	0	35
C G Henry	2010 v A	2	0	0	0	0	0
S Jennings	2007 v Arg	13	1	0	0	0	5
D P Leamy	2004 v US	57	2	0	0	0	10
R Loughney	2012 v NZ	1	0	0	0	0	0
M P McCarthy	2011 v S	4	0	0	0	0	0
K R McLaughlin	2010 v It	5	0	0	0	0	0
S K O'Brien	2009 v Fj	22	2	0	0	0	10
D P O'Callaghan	2003 v W	88	1	0	0	0	5
P J O'Connell	2002 v W	85	6	0	0	0	30
P O'Mahony	2012 v It	7	0	0	0	0	0
N Ronan	2009 v C	4	0	0	0	0	0
M R Ross	2009 v C	22	0	0	0	0	0
R J Ruddock	2010 v A	1	0	0	0	0	0
D C Ryan	2008 v Arg	21	0	0	0	0	0
D Toner	2010 v Sm	3	0	0	0	0	0
D M Tuohy	2010 v NZ	5	1	0	0	0	5
D A Varley	2010 v A	2	0	0	0	0	0

IRELAND INTERNATIONAL PLAYERS
UP TO 10 OCTOBER 2012

Note: Years given for International Championship matches are for second half of season; eg 1972 means season 1971–72. Years for all other matches refer to the actual year of the match. Entries in square brackets denote matches played in RWC Finals.

Abraham, M (Bective Rangers) 1912 E, S, W, SA, 1914 W

Adams, C (Old Wesley), 1908 E, 1909 E, F, 1910 F, 1911 E, S, W, F, 1912 S, W, SA, 1913 W, F, 1914 F, E, S

Agar, R D (Malone) 1947 F, E, S, W, 1948 F, 1949 S, W, 1950 F, E, W

Agnew, P J (CIYMS) 1974 F (R), 1976 A

Ahearne, T (Queen's Coll, Cork) 1899 E

Aherne, L F P (Dolphin, Lansdowne) 1988 E 2, WS, It, 1989 F, W, E, S, NZ, 1990 E, S, F, W (R), 1992 E, S, F, A

Alexander, R (NIFC, Police Union) 1936 E, S, W, 1937 E, S, W, 1938 E, S, 1939 E, S, W

Allen, C E (Derry, Liverpool) 1900 E, S, W, 1901 E, S, W, 1903 S, W, 1904 E, S, W, 1905 E, S, W, NZ, 1906 E, S, W, SA, 1907 S, W

Allen, G G (Derry, Liverpool) 1896 E, S, W, 1897 E, S, 1898 E, S, 1899 E, W

Allen, T C (NIFC) 1885 E, S 1

Allen, W S (Wanderers) 1875 E

Allison, J B (Edinburgh U) 1899 E, S, 1900 E, S, W, 1901 E, S, W, 1902 E, S, W, 1903 S

Anderson, F E (Queen's U, Belfast, NIFC) 1953 F, E, S, W, 1954 NZ, F, E, S, W, 1955 F, E, S, W

Anderson, H J (Old Wesley) 1903 E, S, 1906 E, S

Anderson, W A (Dungannon) 1984 A, 1985 S, F, W, E, 1986 F, S, R, 1987 E, S, F, W, [W, C, Tg, A], 1988 S, F, W, E 1,2, 1989 F, W, E, NZ, 1990 E, S

Andrews, G (NIFC) 1875 E, 1876 E

Andrews, H W (NIFC) 1888 M, 1889 S, W

Archer, A M (Dublin U, NIFC) 1879 S

Arigho, J E (Lansdowne) 1928 F, E, W, 1929 F, E, S, W, 1930 F, E, S, W, 1931 F, E, S, W, SA

Armstrong, W K (NIFC) 1960 SA, 1961 E

Arnott, D T (Lansdowne) 1876 E

Ash, W H (NIFC) 1875 E, 1876 E, 1877 S

Aston, H R (Dublin U) 1908 E, W

Atkins, A P (Bective Rangers) 1924 F

Atkinson, J M (NIFC) 1927 F, A

Atkinson, J R (Dublin U) 1882 W, S

Bagot, J C (Dublin U, Lansdowne) 1879 S, E, 1880 E, S, 1881 S

Bailey, A H (UC Dublin, Lansdowne) 1934 W, 1935 E, S, W, NZ, 1936 E, S, W, 1937 E, S, W, 1938 E, S

Bailey, N (Northampton) 1952 E

Bardon, M E (Bohemians) 1934 E

Barlow, M (Wanderers) 1875 E

Barnes, R J (Dublin U, Armagh) 1933 W

Barr, A (Belfast Collegians) 1898 W, 1899 S, 1901 E, S

Barry, N J (Garryowen) 1991 Nm 2(R)

Beamish, C E St J (RAF, Leicester) 1933 W, S, 1934 S, W, 1935 E, S, W, NZ, 1936 E, S, W, 1938 W

Beamish, G R (RAF, Leicester) 1925 E, S, W, 1928 F, E, S, W, 1929 F, E, S, W, 1930 F, S, W, 1931 F, E, S, W, SA, 1932 E, S, W, 1933 E, W, S

Beatty, W J (NIFC, Richmond) 1910 F, 1912 F, W

Becker, V A (Lansdowne) 1974 F, W

Beckett, G G P (Dublin U) 1908 E, S, W

Bell, J C (Ballymena, Northampton, Dungannon) 1994 A 1,2, US, 1995 S, It, [NZ, W, F], Fj, 1996 US, S, F, W, E, WS, A, 1997 It 1, F, W, E, S, 1998 Gg, R, SA 3, 1997 W S It (R), A 2, [US (R), A 3(R), R], 2001 R (R), 2003 Tg, Sm, It 2(R)

Bell, R J (NIFC) 1875 E, 1876 E

Bell, W E (Belfast Collegians) 1953 F, E, S, W

Bennett, F (Belfast Collegians) 1913 S

Bent, G C (Dublin U) 1882 W, E

Berkery, P J (Lansdowne) 1954 W, 1955 W, 1956 S, W, 1957 F, E, S, W, 1958 A, E, S

Bermingham, J J C (Blackrock Coll) 1921 E, S, W, F

Best, N A (Ulster) 2005 NZ(R),R, 2006 NZ1,2,A1,SA,A2, 2007 F(R),E(R),S1(R),Arg1, 2(R),S2,It2, [Nm(R),Gg(R),F(R),Arg(t&R]

Best, R D (Ulster) 2005 NZ(R), A(t), 2006 W(R), A1(R), SA, A2, PI(R), 2007 W, F, E, S1, It1, S2(R), It2, [Nm, Gg, Arg(R)], 2008 It, F(R), S(R), W, E, NZ1(R), A, C(R), NZ2, Arg(R), 2009 F(R),It(R),E(R),S,W(R),C,US, 2010 It(R), F(R), E, W, S, SA, Sm(R), NZ2, 2011 It, F1, S1, W, E1, F2, 3, E2(R), [US, A, It, W], 2012 W, It, F, S, E, NZ 1, 2, 3

Best, S J (Belfast Harlequins, Ulster) 2003 Tg (R), W 2, S 2(R), 2003 [Nm(R)], 2004 W(R), US(R), 2005 J1, 2, NZ(R), R, 2006 F(R), W(R), PI(R), 2007 E(R), S1, It1(R), Arg1, 2, S2, It2(R), [Nm(R), Gg(R), F(R)]

Bishop, J P (London Irish) 1998 SA, 1,2, Gg, R, SA 3, 1999 F, W, E, S, It, A 1,2, Arg 1, [US, A 3, Arg 2], 2000 E, Arg, C, 2002 NZ 1,2, Fj, Arg, 2003 W 1, E

Blackham, J C (Queen's Coll, Cork) 1909 S, W, F, 1910 E, S, W

Blake-Knox, S E F (NIFC) 1976 E, S, 1977 F (R)

Blayney, J J (Wanderers) 1950 S

Bond, A T W (Derry) 1894 S, W

Bornemann, W W (Wanderers) 1960 E, S, W, SA

Boss, I J (Ulster, Leinster) 2006 NZ2(R),A1(R),SA(R),A2,PI(R), 2007 F,E(R),Arg1,S2,It2(R), [Gg(R),Arg(R)], 2010 Sm(R), 2011 S2(R),[Ru]

Bowe, T J (Ulster, Ospreys) 2004 US, 2005 J1, 2, NZ, A, R, 2006 It, F, 2007 Arg1, S2, 2008 S, W, E, NZ1, A, C, NZ2, Arg, 2009 F, It, E, S, W, A, SA, 2010 It, F, E, W, S, NZ1, A, SA, Sm, NZ2, Arg, 2011 S1, W, E1, 2, [US, A, It, W], 2012 W, It, F, S, E

Bowen, D St J (Cork Const) 1977 W, E, S

Boyd, C A (Dublin U) 1900 S, 1901 S, W

Boyle, C V (Dublin U) 1935 NZ, 1936 E, S, W, 1937 E, S, W, 1938 W, 1939 W

Brabazon, H M (Dublin U) 1884 E, 1885 S 1, 1886 E

Bradley, M J (Dolphin) 1920 W, F, 1922 E, S, W, F, 1923 E, S, W, F, 1925 F, S, W, 1926 F, E, S, W, 1927 F, E, W

Bradley, M T (Cork Constitution) 1984 A, 1985 S, F, W, E, 1986 F, W, E, S, R, 1987 E, S, F, W, [W, C, Tg, A], 1988 S, F, W, E 1, 1990 W, 1992 NZ 1,2, 1993 S, F, W, E, R, 1994 F, W, E, S, A 1,2, US, 1995 S, F, [NZ]

Bradshaw, G (Belfast Collegians) 1903 W

Bradshaw, R M (Wanderers) 1885 E, S 1,2

Brady, A M (UC Dublin, Malone) 1966 S, 1968 E, S, W

Brady, J A (Wanderers) 1976 E, S

Brady, J R (CIYMS) 1951 S, W, 1953 F, E, S, W, 1954 W, 1956 W, 1957 F, E, S, W

Bramwell, T (NIFC) 1928 F

Brand, T N (NIFC) 1924 NZ

Brennan, J I (CIYMS) 1957 S, W

Brennan, J (St Mary's Coll, Barnhall) 1998 SA 1(R),2(R), 1999 F (R), S (R), It, A 2, Arg 1, [US, A 3], 2000 E (R), 2001 W (R), E (R), Sm (R)

Bresnihan, F P K (UC Dublin, Lansdowne, London Irish) 1966 E, W, 1967 A 1, E, S, W, F, 1968 F, E, S, W, A, 1969 F, E, S, W, 1970 SA, F, E, S, W, 1971 F, E, S, W

Brett, J T (Monkstown) 1914 W

Bristow, J R (NIFC) 1879 E

Brophy, N H (Blackrock Coll, UC Dublin, London Irish) 1957 F, E, 1959 E, S, W, F, 1960 F, SA, 1961 S, W, 1962 E, S, W, 1963 E, W, 1967 E, S, W, F, A 2

Brown, E L (Instonians) 1958 F

Brown, G S (Monkstown, United Services) 1912 S, W, SA

Brown, H (Windsor) 1877 E
Brown, T (Windsor) 1877 E, S
Brown, W H (Dublin U) 1899 E
Brown, W J (Malone) 1970 SA, F, S, W
Brown, W S (Dublin U) 1893 S, W, 1894 E, S, W
Browne, A W (Dublin U) 1951 SA
Browne, D (Blackrock Coll) 1920 F
Browne, H C (United Services and RN) 1929 E, S, W
Browne, W F (United Services and Army) 1925 E, S, W, 1926 S, W, 1927 F, E, S, W, A, 1928 E, S
Browning, D R (Wanderers) 1881 E, S
Bruce, S A M (NIFC) 1883 E, S, 1884 E
Brunker, A A (Lansdowne) 1895 E, W
Bryant, C H (Cardiff) 1920 E, S
Buchanan, A McM (Dublin U) 1926 E, S, W, 1927 S, W, A
Buchanan, J W B (Dublin U) 1882 S, 1884 E, S
Buckley, J H (Sunday's Well) 1973 E, S
Buckley, T D (Munster, Sale) 2007 Arg1(R),2(R), 2008 It(R),F(R),S(R),W(R),E(R), NZ1(R),A(R),C,NZ2(R), 2009 C,US,Fj(R), 2010 E(R),W(R),S(R),NZ1,A,SA,Arg, 2011 S2,F2(R),[US(R),Ru]
Bulger, L Q (Lansdowne) 1896 E, S, W, 1897 E, S, 1898 E, S, W
Bulger, M J (Dublin U) 1888 M
Burges, J H (Rosslyn Park) 1950 F, E
Burgess, R B (Dublin U) 1912 SA
Burke, P A (Cork Constitution, Bristol, Harlequins) 1995 E, S, W (R), It, [J], Fj, 1996 US (R), A, 1997 It 1, S (R), 2001 R (R), 2003 S 1(R), Sm (R)
Burkitt, J C S (Queen's Coll, Cork) 1881 E
Burns, I J (Wanderers) 1980 E (R)
Butler, L G (Blackrock Coll) 1960 W
Butler, N (Bective Rangers) 1920 E
Byers, R M (NIFC) 1928 S, W, 1929 E, S, W
Byrne, E (St Mary's Coll) 2001 It (R), F (R), S (R), W (R), E (R), Sm, NZ (R), 2003 A (R), Sm (R)
Byrne, E M J (Blackrock Coll) 1977 S, F, 1978 F, W, E, NZ
Byrne, J S (Blackrock Coll, Leinster, Saracens) 2001 R (R), 2002 W (R), E (R), S (R), It, NZ 2(R), R, Ru (R), Gg, A, Arg, 2003 S 1, It 1, F, W 1, E, A, Tg, Sm, W 2(R), It 2, S2(R), [R(R),Nm(R)], 2004 F,W,E,It,S,SA1,2,3,Arg, 2005 It,S,E,F,W,NZ,A,R
Byrne, N F (UC Dublin) 1962 F
Byrne, S J (UC Dublin, Lansdowne) 1953 S, W, 1955 F
Byron, W G (NIFC) 1896 E, S, W, 1897 E, S, 1898 E, S, W, 1899 E, S, W

Caddell, E D (Dublin U, Wanderers) 1904 S, 1905 E, S, W, NZ, 1906 E, S, W, SA, 1907 E, S, 1908 S, W
Cagney, S J (London Irish) 1925 W, 1926 F, E, S, W, 1927 F, 1928 E, S, W, 1929 F, E, S, W
Caldwell, R (Ulster) 2009 C(R),US(R)
Callan, C P (Lansdowne) 1947 F, E, S, W, 1948 F, E, S, W, 1949 F, E
Cameron, E D (Bective Rangers) 1891 S, W
Campbell, C E (Old Wesley) 1970 SA
Campbell, E F (Monkstown) 1899 S, W, 1900 E, W
Campbell, K P (Ulster) 2005 J1(R),2(R),R
Campbell, S B B (Derry) 1911 E, S, W, F, 1912 F, E, S, W, SA, 1913 E, S, F
Campbell, S O (Old Belvedere) 1976 A, 1979 A 1,2, 1980 E, S, F, W, 1981 F, W, E, S, SA 1, 1982 W, E, S, F, 1983 S, F, W, E, 1984 F, W
Canniffe, D M (Lansdowne) 1976 W, E
Cantrell, J L (UC Dublin, Blackrock Coll) 1976 A, F, W, E, S, 1981 S, SA 1,2, A
Carey, R W (Dungannon) 1992 NZ 1,2
Carney, B B (Munster) 2007 Arg1,2,S2,It2(R)
Carpendale, M J (Monkstown) 1886 S, 1887 W, 1888 W, S
Carr, N J (Ards) 1985 S, F, W, E, 1986 W, E, S, R, 1987 E, S, W
Carroll, C (Bective Rangers) 1930 F
Carroll, R (Lansdowne) 1947 F, 1950 S, W
Casement, B N (Dublin U) 1875 E, 1876 E, 1879 E
Casement, F (Dublin U) 1906 E, S, W
Casey, J C (Young Munster) 1930 S, 1932 E
Casey, P J (UC Dublin, Lansdowne) 1963 F, E, S, W, NZ, 1964 E, S, W, F, 1965 F, E, S
Casey, R E (Blackrock Coll, London Irish) 1999 [A 3(t), Arg 2(R)], 2000 E, US (R), C (R), 2009 C,US
Cave, D M (Ulster) 2009 C,US, 2012 NZ 1(R)
Chambers, J (Dublin U) 1886 E, S, 1887 E, S, W
Chambers, R R (Instonians) 1951 F, E, S, W, 1952 F, W
Clancy, T P J (Lansdowne) 1988 W, E 1,2, WS, It, 1989 F, W, E, S
Clarke, A T H (Northampton, Dungannon) 1995 Fj (R), 1996 W, E, WS, 1997 F (R), It 2(R), 1998 Gg (R), R

Clarke, C P (Terenure Coll) 1993 F, W, E, 1998 W, E
Clarke, D J (Dolphin) 1991 W, Nm 1,2, [J, A], 1992 NZ 2(R)
Clarke, J A B (Bective Rangers) 1922 S, W, F, 1923 F, 1924 E, S, W
Clegg, R J (Bangor) 1973 F, 1975 E, S, F, W
Clifford, J T (Young Munster) 1949 F, E, S, W, 1950 F, E, S, W, 1951 F, E, SA, 1952 F, S, W
Clinch, A D (Dublin U, Wanderers) 1892 S, 1893 W, 1895 E, S, W, 1896 E, S, W, 1897 E, S
Clinch, J D (Wanderers, Dublin U) 1923 W, 1924 F, E, S, W, NZ, 1925 F, E, S, 1926 E, S, W, 1927 F, 1928 F, E, S, W, 1929 F, E, S, W, 1930 F, E, S, W, SA
Clohessy, P M (Young Munster) 1993 F, W, E, 1994 F, W, E, S, A 1,2, US, 1995 E, S, F, W, 1996 S, F, 1997 It 2, 1998 F (R), W (R), SA 2(R), Gg, R, SA 3, 1999 F, W, E, S, It, A 1,2 Arg 1, [US, A 3(R)], 2000 E, S, It, F, W, Arg, J, SA, 2001 It, F, R, S, W, E, Sm (R), NZ, 2002 W, E, S, F
Clune, J J (Blackrock Coll) 1912 SA, 1913 W, F, 1914 F, E, W
Coffey, J J (Lansdowne) 1900 E, 1901 W, 1902 E, S, W, 1903 E, S, W, 1905 E, S, W, NZ, 1906 E, S, W, SA, 1907 E, 1908 W, 1910 F
Cogan, W St J (Queen's Coll, Cork) 1907 E, S
Collier, S R (Queen's Coll, Belfast) 1883 S
Collins, P C (Lansdowne, London Irish) 1987 [C], 1990 S (R)
Collis, W R F (KCH, Harlequins) 1924 F, W, NZ, 1925 F, E, S, 1926 F
Collis, W S (Wanderers) 1884 W
Collopy, G (Bective Rangers) 1891 S, 1892 S
Collopy, R (Bective Rangers) 1923 E, S, W, F, 1924 F, E, S, W, NZ, 1925 F, E, S, W
Collopy, W P (Bective Rangers) 1914 F, E, S, W, 1921 E, S, W, F, 1922 E, S, W, F, 1923 S, W, F, 1924 F, E, S, W
Combe, A (NIFC) 1875 E
Condon, H C (London Irish) 1984 S (R)
Cook, H G (Lansdowne) 1884 W
Coote, P B (RAF, Leicester) 1933 S
Corcoran, J C (London Irish) 1947 A, 1948 F
Corken, T S (Belfast Collegians) 1937 E, S, W
Corkery, D S (Cork Constitution, Bristol) 1994 A 1,2, US, 1995 E, [NZ, J, W, F], Fj, 1996 US, S, F, W, E, WS, A, 1997 It 1, F, W, E, S, 1998 S, W, E, 1999 A 1(R),2(R)
Corley, H H (Dublin U, Wanderers) 1902 E, S, W, 1903 E, S, W, 1904 E, S
Cormac, H S T (Clontarf) 1921 E, S, W
Corrigan, R (Greystones, Lansdowne, Leinster) 1997 C (R), It 2, 1998 S, F, W, E, SA 3(R), 1999 A 1(R),2(R), [Arg 2], 2002 NZ 1,2, R, Ru, Gg, A, Fj (R), Arg, 2003 S 1, It 1, A, Tg, Sm, W 2, It 2, S 2, [R,Arg,A,F], 2004 F,W,E,It,S,SA1,2,3,Arg, 2005 It,S,E,F,W, J1(R),2(R), 2006 F
Costello, P (Bective Rangers) 1960 F
Costello, R A (Garryowen) 1993 S
Costello, V C P (St Mary's Coll, London Irish) 1996 US, F, W, E. WS (R), 1997 C, It 2(R), 1998 S (R), F, W, E, SA 1,2, Gg, R, SA 3, 1999 F, W, E, S (R), It, A 1, 2002 R (R), A, Arg, 2003 S 1, It 1, F, E, A, It 2, S 2, [R,Arg,F], 2004 F(R),W(R),It(R), S(R)
Cotton, J (Wanderers) 1889 W
Coulter, H H (Queen's U, Belfast) 1920 E, S, W
Court, T G (Ulster) 2009 It(R),W(t),C,US(R),Fj, 2010 It(R),F(t&R),NZ1(R),A(R), SA(R),Sm,NZ2,Arg(R), 2011 It(R),F1(R),S1(R),W(R),E1(R),S2,F3(R),E2(R),[US,A(R), It(R)], 2012 W(R),It(R),F(R),St&R(R),E(R)
Courtney, A W (UC Dublin) 1920 S, W, F, 1921 E, S, W, F
Cox, H L (Dublin U) 1875 E, 1876 E, 1877 E, S
Craig, R G (Queen's U, Belfast) 1938 S, W
Crawford, E C (Dublin U) 1885 E, S 1
Crawford, W E (Lansdowne) 1920 E, S, W, F, 1921 E, S, W, F, 1922 E, S, 1923 E, S, W, F, 1924 F, E, W, NZ, 1925 F, E, S, W, 1926 F, E, S, W, 1927 F, E, S, W
Crean, T J (Wanderers) 1894 E, S, W, 1895 E, S, W, 1896 E, S, W
Crichton, R Y (Dublin U) 1920 E, S, W, F, 1921 F, 1922 E, 1923 W, F, 1924 F, E, S, W, NZ, 1925 E, S
Croker, E W D (Limerick) 1878 E
Cromey, G E (Queen's U, Belfast) 1937 E, S, W, 1938 E, S, W, 1939 E, S, W
Cronin, B M (Garryowen) 1995 S, 1997 S
Cronin, S M (Connacht, Leinster) 2009 Fj(R), 2010 W(R),NZ1,A,Sm,NZ2(R),Arg, 2011 It(R),F1(R),S1(R),W(R),E1(R),S2,[Ru,It(R)], 2012 It(R),F(R),S(R),E(R),NZ 1(R),3(R)
Cronyn, A P (Dublin U, Lansdowne) 1875 E, 1876 E, 1880 S
Crossan, K D (Instonians) 1982 S, 1984 F, W, E, 1985 S, F, W, E, 1986 E, S, R, 1987 E, S, F, W, [W, C, Tg, A], 1988 S, F, W, E 1, WS, It, 1989 W, S, NZ, 1990 E, S, F, W, Arg, 1991 E, S, Nm 2 [Z, J, S], 1992 W

333

Crotty, D J (Garryowen) 1996 A, 1997 It 1, F, W, 2000 C
Crowe, J F (UC Dublin) 1974 NZ
Crowe, L (Old Belvedere) 1950 E, S, W
Crowe, M P (Lansdowne) 1929 W, 1930 E, S, W, 1931 F, S, W, SA, 1932 S, W, 1933 W, S, 1934 E
Crowe, P M (Blackrock Coll) 1935 E, 1938 E
Cullen, L F M (Blackrock Coll, Leinster, Leicester) 2002 NZ 2(R), R (R), Ru (R), Gg (R), A (R), Fj, Arg (R), 2003 S 1(R), It 1(R), F (R), W 1, Tg, Sm, It 2, 2004 US(R), 2005 J1,2,R, 2007 Arg2, 2009 Fj, 2010 It, F, E(R), W(R), 2011 It(R), F1(R), S1(R), W(R), E1(R), S2, F2,[Ru]
Cullen, T J (UC Dublin) 1949 F
Cullen, W J (Monkstown and Manchester) 1920 E
Culliton, M G (Wanderers) 1959 E, S, W, F, 1960 E, S, W, F, SA, 1961 E, S, W, F, 1962 S, F, 1964 E, S, W, F
Cummins, W E A (Queen's Coll, Cork) 1879 S, 1881 E, 1882 E
Cunningham, D McC (NIFC) 1923 E, S, W, 1925 F, E, W
Cunningham, M J (UC Cork) 1955 F, E, S, W, 1956 F, S, W
Cunningham, V J G (St Mary's Coll) 1988 E 2, It, 1990 Arg (R), 1991 Nm 1,2, [Z, J(R)], 1992 NZ 1,2, A, 1993 S, F, W, E, R, 1994 F
Cunningham, W A (Lansdowne) 1920 W, 1921 E, S, W, F, 1922 E, 1923 S, W
Cuppaidge, J L (Dublin U) 1879 E, 1880 E, S
Currell, J (NIFC) 1877 S
Curtis, A B (Oxford U) 1950 F, E, S
Curtis, D M (London Irish) 1991 W, E, S, Nm 1,2, [Z, J, S, A], 1992 W, E, S (R), F
Cuscaden, W A (Dublin U, Bray) 1876 E
Cussen, D J (Dublin U) 1921 E, S, W, F, 1922 E, 1923 E, S, W, F, 1926 F, E, S, W, 1927 F, E

Daly, J C (London Irish) 1947 F, E, S, W, 1948 E, S, W
Daly, M J (Harlequins) 1938 E
Danaher, P P A (Lansdowne, Garryowen) 1988 S, F, W, WS, It, 1989 F, NZ (R), 1990 F, 1992 S, F, NZ 1, A, 1993 S, F, W, E, R, 1994 F, W, E, S, A 1,2, US, 1995 E, S, F, W
D'Arcy, G W (Lansdowne, Leinster) 1999 [R (R)], 2002 Fj (R), 2003 Tg (R), Sm (R), W 2(R), 2004 F, W, E, It, S, SA1, 2005 It, NZ, A, R, 2006 It, F, W, S, E, NZ1, 2, A1, SA, A2, PI(R), 2007 W, F, E, S1, It1, 2, [Nm, Gg, F, Arg], 2008 It, 2009 F(t&R), It(R), S, W, Fj, SA(R), 2010 It, F, E, W, S, NZ1, SA, NZ2, Arg, 2011 It, F1, S1, W, E1, F3, E2, [US, A, It, W], 2012 W, It, F, S, E, NZ 2
Dargan, M J (Old Belvedere) 1952 S, W
Davidson, C T (NIFC) 1921 F
Davidson, I G (NIFC) 1899 E, 1900 S, W, 1901 E, S, W, 1902 E, S, W
Davidson, J C (Dungannon) 1969 F, E, S, W, 1973 NZ, 1976 NZ
Davidson, J W (Dungannon, London Irish, Castres) 1995 Fj, 1996 S, F, W, E, WS, A, 1997 It 1, F, W, E, S, 1998 Gg (R), R (R), SA 3(R), 1999 F, W, E, S, It, A 1,2, [US,R (R), Arg 2], 2000 S (R), W (R), US, C, 2001 It (R), S
Davies, F E (Lansdowne) 1892 S, W, 1893 E, S, W
Davis, J L (Monkstown) 1898 E, S
Davis, W J N (Edinburgh U, Bessbrook) 1890 S, W, E, 1891 E, S, W, 1892 E, S, 1895 S
Davison, W (Belfast Academy) 1887 W
Davy, E O'D (UC Dublin, Lansdowne) 1925 W, 1926 F, E, S, W, 1927 F, E, S, W, A, 1928 F, E, S, W, 1929 F, E, S, W, 1930 F, E, S, W, 1931 F, E, S, W, SA, 1932 E, S, W, 1933 E, W, S, 1934 E
Dawson, A R (Wanderers) 1958 A, E, S, W, F, 1959 E, S, W, F, 1960 F, SA, 1961 E, S, W, F, SA, 1962 S, F, W, 1963 F, E, S, W, NZ, 1964 E, S, F
Dawson, K (London Irish) 1997 NZ, C, 1998 S, 1999 [R, Arg 2], 2000 E, S, It, F, W, J, SA, 2001 R, S, W (R), E (R), Sm, 2002 Fj, 2003 Tg, It 2(R), S 2(R)
Dean, P M (St Mary's Coll) 1981 SA 1,2, A, 1982 W, E, S, F, 1984 A, 1985 S, F, W, E, 1986 F, W, R, 1987 E, S, F, W, [W, A], 1988 S, F, W, E 1,2, WS, It, 1989 F, W, E, S
Deane, E C (Monkstown) 1909 E
Deering, M J (Bective Rangers) 1929 W
Deering, S J (Bective Rangers) 1935 E, S, W, NZ, 1936 E, S, W, 1937 E, S
Deering, S M (Garryowen, St Mary's Coll) 1974 W, 1976 F, W, E, S, 1977 W, E, 1978 NZ
De Lacy, H (Harlequins) 1948 E, S
Delany, M G (Bective Rangers) 1895 W
Dempsey, G T (Terenure Coll, Leinster) 1998 Gg (R). SA 3, 1999 F, E, S, It, A 2, 2000 E (R), S, It, F, W, SA, 2001 It, F, S, W, E, NZ, 2002 W, E, S, It, F, NZ 1,2, R, Ru, Gg, A, Arg, 2003 S 1, E (R), A, Sm, W 2(R), It 2, S 2(R), [R, Nm, Arg, A, F], 2004

F,W, E, It, S, SA1, 2, 3, US(R), Arg, 2005 It(R), S, E, F, W, J1, 2, NZ(R), R(R), 2006 E(R), NZ1(R), 2(t&R), A1, SA, A2(R), PI, 2007 W, F, E, S1, It1, 2, [Nm, Gg, F], 2008 It, F, A(R), NZ2
Dennison, S P (Garryowen) 1973 F, 1975 E, S
Dick, C J (Ballymena) 1961 W, F, SA, 1962 W, 1963 F, E, S, W
Dick, J S (Queen's U, Belfast) 1962 E
Dick, J S (Queen's U, Cork) 1887 E, S, W
Dickson, J A N (Dublin U) 1920 E, W, F
Doherty, A E (Old Wesley) 1974 P (R)
Doherty, W D (Guy's Hospital) 1920 E, S, W, 1921 E, S, W, F
Donaldson, J A (Belfast Collegians) 1958 A, E, S, W
Donovan, T M (Queen's Coll, Cork) 1889 S
Dooley, J F (Galwegians) 1959 E, S, W
Doran, B R W (Lansdowne) 1900 S, W, 1901 E, S, W, 1902 E, S, W
Doran, E F (Lansdowne) 1890 S, W
Doran, G P (Lansdowne) 1899 S, W, 1900 E, S, 1902 S, W, 1903 W, 1904 E
Douglas, A C (Instonians) 1923 F, 1924 E, S, 1927 A, 1928 S
Dowling, I (Munster) 2009 C,US
Downing, A J (Dublin U) 1882 W
Dowse, J C A (Monkstown) 1914 F, S, W
Doyle, J A P (Greystones) 1984 E, S
Doyle, J T (Bective Rangers) 1935 W
Doyle, M G (Blackrock Coll, UC Dublin, Cambridge U, Edinburgh Wands) 1965 F, E, S, W, SA, 1966 F, E, S, W, 1967 A 1, E, S, W, F, A 2, 1968 F, E, S, W, A
Doyle, T J (Wanderers) 1968 E, S, W
Duffy, G W (Harlequins, Connacht) 2004 SA 2(R), 2005 S(R),J1,2, 2007 Arg1,2,S2, [Arg(R)], 2009 C,US
Duggan, A T A (Lansdowne) 1963 NZ, 1964 F, 1966 W, 1967 A 1, S, W, A 2, 1968 F, E, S, W, 1969 F, E, S, W, 1970 SA, F, E, S, W, 1971 F, E, S, W, 1972 F 2
Duggan, W (UC Cork) 1920 S, W
Duggan, W P (Blackrock Coll) 1975 E, S, F, W, 1976 A, F, W, S, NZ, 1977 W, E, S, F, 1978 S, F, W, E, NZ, 1979 E, S, A 1,2, 1980 E, 1981 F, W, E, S, SA 1,2, A, 1982 W, E, S, 1983 S, F, W, E, 1984 F, W, E, S
Duignan, P (Galwegians) 1998 Gg, R
Duncan, W R (Malone) 1984 W, E
Dunlea, F J (Lansdowne) 1989 W, E, S
Dunlop, R (Dublin U) 1889 W, 1890 S, W, E, 1891 E, S, W, 1892 E, S, 1893 W, 1894 W
Dunn, P E F (Bective Rangers) 1923 S
Dunn, T B (NIFC) 1935 NZ
Dunne, M J (Lansdowne) 1929 F, E, S, 1930 F, E, S, W, 1932 E, S, W, 1933 E, W, S, 1934 E, S, W
Dwyer, P J (UC Dublin) 1962 W, 1963 F, NZ, 1964 S, W

Earls, K G (Munster) 2008 C, NZ2(R), 2009 A(R), Fj, SA, 2010 It(R), F, E, W, S, SA(R), NZ2(R), Arg(R), 2011 It, F1, S1, W, E1, F2, 3, E2, [US, A, Ru, It, W], 2012 It, F, S, E, NZ 1, 3
Easterby, S H (Llanelli Scarlets) 2000 S, It, F, W, Arg, US, C, 2001 S, Sm (R), 2002 W, E, S (R), It, F, NZ 1, 2, R, Ru, Gg, 2003 Tg, Sm, It 2, S 2(t+R), [Nm, Arg, A, F], 2004 F, W, E, It, S, SA1, 2, 3, US, Arg, 2005 It, S, E, F, W, NZ, A, 2006 It, F, W, S, E, SA(R), A2(R), PI, 2007 W, F, E, S1, It1, 2, [Nm, Gg, F, Arg], 2008 It, S(R), E(R)
Easterby, W G (Ebbw Vale, Ballynahinch, Llanelli, Leinster) 2000 US, C, 2001 R (R), S, W (R), Sm (R), 2002 W (R), S (R), R (R), Ru (R), Gg (R), Fj, 2003 S 1(R), It 1(R), Tg, Sm 2(R), It 2, S 2(R), [R(R), Nm(R), F(R)], 2004 W(R), It(R), S(R), SA2(R), US, 2005 S(R)
Edwards, H G (Dublin U) 1877 E, 1878 E
Edwards, R W (Malone) 1904 W
Edwards, T (Lansdowne) 1888 M, 1890 S, W, E, 1892 W, 1893 E
Edwards, W V (Malone) 1912 F, E
Egan, J D (Bective Rangers) 1922 S
Egan, J T (Cork Constitution) 1931 F, E, SA
Egan, M S (Garryowen) 1893 E, 1895 S
Ekin, W (Queen's Coll, Belfast) 1888 W, S
Elliott, W J (Bangor) 1979 S
Elwood, E P (Lansdowne, Galwegians) 1993 W, E, R, 1994 F, W, E, S, A 1,2, 1995 F, W, [NZ, W, F], 1996 US, 1997 F, W, E, NZ, C, It 2(R), 1998 F, W, E, SA 1,2, Gg, R, SA 3, 1999 It, Arg 1(R), 1(R), A 3(R), R]
English, M A F (Lansdowne, Limerick Bohemians) 1958 W, F, 1959 E, S, F, 1960 E, S, 1961 S, W, F, 1962 F, W, 1963 E, S, W, NZ
Ennis, F N G (Wanderers) 1979 A 1(R)
Ensor, A H (Wanderers) 1973 W, F, 1974 F, W, E, S, P, NZ, 1975 E, S, F, W, 1976 A, NZ, 1977 E, 1978 S, F, W, E
Entrican, J C (Queen's U, Belfast) 1931 S
Erskine, D J (Sale) 1997 NZ (R), C, It 2

Fagan, G L (Kingstown School) 1878 E
Fagan, W B C (Wanderers) 1956 F, E, S
Farrell, J L (Bective Rangers) 1926 F, E, S, W, 1927 F, E, S, W, A, 1928 F, E, S, W, 1929 F, E, S, W, 1930 F, E, S, W, 1931 F, E, S, W, SA, 1932 E, S, W
Feddis, N (Lansdowne) 1956 E
Feighery, C F P (Lansdowne) 1972 F 1, E, F 2
Feighery, T A 0 (St Mary's Coll) 1977 W, E
Ferris, H H (Queen's Coll, Belfast) 1901 W
Ferris, J H (Queen's Coll, Belfast) 1900 E, S, W
Ferris, S (Ulster) 2006 PI, 2007 Arg1(R),2,S2, 2008 A(R),C,NZ2(R),Arg, 2009 F,It,E, S,W,A,Fj,SA, 2010 F,E,W,S,SA,Sm(R),NZ2,Arg, 2011 F3(R),E2,[US,A,It,W], 2012 W, It,F,S,E
Field, M J (Malone) 1994 E, S, A 1(R), 1995 F (R), W (t), It (R), [NZ(t + R), J], Fj, 1996 F (R), W, E, A (R), 1997 F, W, E, S
Finlay, J E (Queen's Coll, Belfast) 1913 E, S, W, 1920 E, S, W
Finlay, W (NIFC) 1876 E, 1877 E, S, 1878 E, 1879 S, E, 1880 S, 1882 S
Finn, M C (UC Cork, Cork Constitution) 1979 E, 1982 W, E, S, F, 1983 S, F, W, E, 1984 E, S, A, 1986 F, W
Finn, R G A (UC Dublin) 1977 F
Fitzgerald, C C (Glasgow U, Dungannon) 1902 E, 1903 E, S
Fitzgerald, C F (St Mary's Coll) 1979 A 1,2, 1980 E, S, F, W, 1982 W, E, S, F, 1983 S, F, W, E, 1984 F, W, A, 1985 S, F, W, E, 1986 F, W, E, S
Fitzgerald, D C (Lansdowne, De La Salle Palmerston) 1984 E, S, 1986 W, E, S, R, 1987 E, S, F, W, [W, C, A], 1988 S, F, W, E 1, 1989 NZ (R), 1990 E, S, F, W, Arg, 1991 F, W, E, S, Nm 1,2, [Z, S, A], 1992 W, S (R)
Fitzgerald, J (Wanderers) 1884 W
Fitzgerald, J J (Young Munster) 1988 S, F, 1990 S, F, W, 1991 F, W, E, S, [J], 1994 A 1,2
Fitzgerald, L M (Leinster) 2006 PI, 2007 Arg2(R), 2008 W(R),E(R),C,NZ2,Arg, 2009 F,It,E,S,W,A, 2010 SA,Sm,NZ2, 2011 It,F1,S1,W,S2,F2,3(R)
Fitzgibbon, M J J (Shannon) 1992 W, E, S, F, NZ 1,2
Fitzpatrick, D J (Ulster) 2012 NZ 1,3(R)
Fitzpatrick, J M (Dungannon) 1998 SA 1,2 Gg (R), R (R), SA 3, 1999 F (R), W (R), E (R), It, Arg 1 (R), [US (R), A 3, R, Arg 2(t&R)], 2000 S (R), It (R), Arg (R), US, C, SA (t&R), 2001 R (R), 2003 W 1(R), E (R), Tg, W 2(R), It 2(R)
Fitzpatrick, M P (Wanderers) 1978 S, 1980 S, F, W, 1981 F, W, E, S, A, 1985 F (R)
Flannery, J P (Munster) 2005 R(R), 2006 It, F, W, S, E, NZ1, 2, A1,2007 W(R),F(R),E(R),S1(R),It1(R),Arg1,S2,It2(R),[Nm(R), Gg(R), F, Arg], 2008 NZ1, A(R), C, NZ2(R), Arg, 2009 F, It, E, S(R), W, A, Fj, SA, 2010 It, F, 2011 S2(R), F2(R), 3(R), E2, [US(R)]
Flavin, P (Blackrock Coll) 1997 F (R), S
Fletcher, W W (Kingstown) 1882 W, S, 1883 E
Flood, R S (Dublin U) 1925 W
Flynn, M K (Wanderers) 1959 F, 1960 F, 1962 E, S, F, W, 1964 E, S, W, F, 1965 F, E, S, W, SA, 1966 F, E, S, 1972 F 1, E, F 2, 1973 NZ
Fogarty, J (Leinster) 2010 NZ1(R)
Fogarty, T (Garryowen) 1891 W
Foley, A G (Shannon, Munster) 1995 E, S, F, W, It, [J(t + R)], 1996 A, 1997 It 1, E (R), 2000 E, S, It, F, W, Arg, C, J, SA, 2001 It, F, R, S, W, E, Sm, NZ, 2002 W, E, S, It, F, NZ 1,2, R, Ru, Gg, A, Fj, Arg, 2003 S 1, It 1, F, W, E 2, [R,A], 2004 F,W,E,It,S, SA1,2,3,US(R),Arg, 2005 It,S,E,F,W
Foley, B 0 (Shannon) 1976 F, E, 1977 W (R), 1980 F, W, 1981 F, E, S, SA 1,2, A
Forbes, R E (Malone) 1907 E
Forrest, A J (Wanderers) 1880 E, S, 1881 E, S, 1882 W, E, 1883 E, 1885 S 2
Forrest, E G (Wanderers) 1888 M, 1889 S, W, 1890 S, E, 1891 E, 1893 S, W, 1894 E, S, W, 1895 W, 1897 E, S
Forrest, H (Wanderers) 1893 S, W
Fortune, J J (Clontarf) 1963 NZ, 1964 E
Foster, A R (Derry) 1910 E, S, F, 1911 E, S, W, F, 1912 F, E, S, W, 1914 E, S, W, 1921 E, S, W
Francis, N P J (Blackrock Coll, London Irish, Old Belvedere) 1987 [Tg, A], 1988 WS, It, 1989 S, 1990 E, F, W, 1991 E, S, Nm 1,2, [Z, J, S, A], 1992 W, E, S, 1993 F, R, 1994 F, W, E, S, A 1,2, US, 1995 E, [NZ, J, W, F], Fj, 1996 US, S
Franks, J G (Dublin U) 1898 E, S, W
Frazer, E F (Bective Rangers) 1891 S, 1892 S
Freer, A E (Lansdowne) 1901 E, S, W
Fulcher, G M (Cork Constitution, London Irish) 1994 A 2, US, 1995 E (R), S, F, W, It, [NZ, W, F], Fj, 1996 US, S, F, W, E, A, 1997 It 1, W (R), 1998 SA 1(R)

Fulton, J (NIFC) 1895 S, W, 1896 E, 1897 E, 1898 W, 1899 E, 1900 W, 1901 E, 1902 E, S, W, 1903 E, S, W, 1904 E, S
Furlong, J N (UC Galway) 1992 NZ 1,2

Gaffikin, W (Windsor) 1875 E
Gage, J H (Queen's U, Belfast) 1926 S, W, 1927 S, W
Galbraith, E (Dublin U) 1875 E
Galbraith, H T (Belfast Acad) 1890 W
Galbraith, R (Dublin U) 1875 E, 1876 E, 1877 E
Galwey, M J (Shannon) 1991 F, W, Nm 2(R), [J], 1992 E, S, F, NZ 1,2, A, 1993 F, W, E, R, 1994 F, W, E, S, A 1, US (R), 1995 E, 1996 WS, 1998 F (R), 1999 W (R), 2000 E (R), S, It, F, W, Arg, C, 2001 It, F, R, W, E, Sm, NZ, 2002 W, E, S
Ganly, J B (Monkstown) 1927 F, E, S, W, A, 1928 F, E, S, W, 1929 F, S, 1930 F
Gardiner, F (NIFC) 1900 E, S, 1901 E, W, 1902 E, S, W, 1903 E, W, 1904 E, S, W, 1906 E, S, W, 1907 S, W, 1908 S, W, 1909 E, S, F
Gardiner, J B (NIFC) 1923 E, S, W, F, 1924 F, E, S, W, NZ, 1925 F, E, S, W
Gardiner, S (Belfast Albion) 1893 E, S
Gardiner, W (NIFC) 1892 E, S, 1893 E, S, W, 1894 E, S, W, 1895 E, S, W, 1896 E, S, W, 1897 E, S, 1898 W
Garry, M G (Bective Rangers) 1909 E, S, W, F, 1911 E, S, W
Gaston, J T (Dublin U) 1954 NZ, F, E, S, W, 1955 W 1956 F, E
Gavin, T J (Moseley, London Irish) 1949 F, E
Geoghegan, S P (London Irish, Bath) 1991 F, W, E, S, Nm 1, [Z, S, A], 1992 E, S, F, A, 1993 S, F, W, E, R, 1994 F, W, E, S, A 1,2, US, 1995 E, S, F, W, [NZ, J, W, F], Fj, 1996 US, S, W, E
Gibson, C M H (Cambridge U, NIFC) 1964 E, S, W, F, 1965 F, E, S, W, SA, 1966 F, E, S, W, 1967 A 1 E, S, W, F, A 2, 1968 E, S, W, A, 1969 E, S, W, 1970 SA, F, E, S, W, 1971 F, E, S, W, 1972 F 1, E, F 2, 1973 NZ, E, S, W, F, 1974 F, W, E, S, P, 1975 E, S, F, W, 1976 A, F, W, E, S, NZ, 1977 W, E, S, F, 1978 F, W, E, NZ, 1979 S, A 1,2
Gibson, M E (Lansdowne, London Irish) 1979 F, W, E, S, 1981 W (R), 1986 R, 1988 S, F, W, E 2
Gifford, H P (Wanderers) 1890 S
Gillespie, J C (Dublin U) 1922 W, F
Gilpin, F G (Queen's U, Belfast) 1962 E, S, F
Glass, D C (Belfast Collegians) 1958 F, 1960 W, 1961 W, SA
Gleeson, K D (St Mary's Coll, Leinster) 2002 W (R), F (R), NZ 1,2, R, Ru, Gg, A, Arg, 2003 S 1, It 1, F, W 1, E, A, W 2, [R,A,F], 2004 F,W,E,It, 2006 NZ1(R),A1(R), 2007 Arg1,S2(R)
Glennon, B T (Lansdowne) 1993 F (R)
Glennon, J J (Skerries) 1980 E, S, 1987 E, S, F, [W (R)]
Godfrey, R P (UC Dublin) 1954 S, W
Goodall, K G (City of Derry, Newcastle U) 1967 A 1, E, S, W, F, A 2, 1968 F, E, S, W, A, 1969 F, E, S, 1970 SA, F, E, S, W
Gordon, A (Dublin U) 1884 S
Gordon, T G (NIFC) 1877 E, S, 1878 E
Gotto, R P C (NIFC) 1906 SA
Goulding, W J (Cork) 1879 S
Grace, T 0 (UC Dublin, St Mary's Coll) 1972 F 1, E, 1973 NZ, E, S, W, 1974 E, S, P, NZ, 1975 E, S, F, W, 1976 A, F, W, E, S, NZ, 1977 P, E, S, F, 1978 S
Graham, R I (Dublin U) 1911 F
Grant, E L (CIYMS) 1971 F, E, S, W
Grant, P J (Bective Rangers) 1894 S, W
Graves, C R A (Wanderers) 1934 E, S, W, 1935 E, S, W, NZ, 1936 E, S, W, 1937 E, S, 1938 E, S, W
Gray, R D (Old Wesley) 1923 E, S, 1925 F, 1926 F
Greene, E H (Dublin U, Kingstown) 1882 W, 1884 W, 1885 E, S 2, 1886 E
Greer, R (Kingstown) 1876 E
Greeves, T J (NIFC) 1907 E, S, W, 1909 W, F
Gregg, R J (Queen's U, Belfast) 1953 F, E, S, W, 1954 F, E, S, 1955 W, 1957 E, S
Griffin, C S (London Irish) 1951 F, E
Griffin, J L (Wanderers) 1949 S, W
Griffiths, W (Limerick) 1878 E
Grimshaw, C (Queen's U, Belfast) 1969 E (R)
Guerin, B N (Galwegians) 1956 S
Gwynn, A P (Dublin U) 1895 W
Gwynn, L H (Dublin U) 1893 S, 1894 E, S, W, 1897 S, 1898 E, S

Hakin, R F (CIYMS) 1976 W, S, NZ, 1977 W, E, F
Hall, R 0 N (Dublin U) 1884 W
Hall, W H (Instonians) 1923 E, S, W, F, 1924 F, S
Hallaran, C F G T (Royal Navy) 1921 E, S, W, 1922 E, S, W, 1923 E, F, 1924 F, E, S, W, 1925 F, 1926 F, E
Halpin, G F (Wanderers, London Irish) 1990 E, 1991 [J], 1992 E, S, F, 1993 R, 1994 F (R), 1995 It, [NZ, W, F]

Halpin, T (Garryowen) 1909 S, W, F, 1910 E, S, W, 1911 E, S, W, F, 1912 F, E, S

Halvey, E O (Shannon) 1995 F, W, It, [J, W (t), F (R)], 1997 NZ, C (R)

Hamilton, A J (Lansdowne) 1884 W

Hamilton, G F (NIFC) 1991 F, W, E, S, Nm 2, [Z, J, S, A], 1992 A

Hamilton, R L (NIFC) 1926 F

Hamilton, R J (Wanderers) 1893 W

Hamilton, W J (Dublin U) 1877 E

Hamlet, G T (Old Wesley) 1902 E, S, W, 1903 E, S, W, 1904 S, W, 1905 E, S, W, NZ, 1906 SA, 1907 E, S, W, 1908 E, S, W, 1909 E, S, W, F, 1910 E, S, F, 1911 E, S, W, F

Hanrahan, C J (Dolphin) 1926 S, W, 1927 E, S, W, A, 1928 F, E, S, 1929 F, E, S, W, 1930 F, E, S, W, 1931 F, 1932 S, W

Harbison, H T (Bective Rangers) 1984 W (R), E, S, 1986 R, 1987 E, S, F, W

Hardy, G G (Bective Rangers) 1962 S

Harman, G R A (Dublin U) 1899 E, W

Harper, J (Instonians) 1947 F, E, S

Harpur, T G (Dublin U) 1908 E, S, W

Harrison, T (Cork) 1879 S, 1880 S, 1881 E

Harvey, F M W (Wanderers) 1907 W, 1911 F

Harvey, G A D (Wanderers) 1903 E, S, 1904 W, 1905 E, S

Harvey, T A (Dublin U) 1900 W, 1901 S, W, 1902 E, S, W, 1903 E, W

Haycock, P P (Terenure Coll) 1989 E

Hayes, J J (Shannon, Munster) 2000 S, It, F, W, Arg, C, J, SA, 2001 It, F, R, S, W, E, Sm, NZ, 2002 W, E, S, It, F, NZ 1,2, R, Ru, Gg, A, Fj, Arg, 2003 S 1, It 1, F, W 1, E, A, Sm, Arg, A, F], 2004 F, W, E, It, S, SA1, 2, 3, US, Arg, 2005 It, S, E, F, W, NZ, A, R(R), 2006 It, F, W, S, E, NZ1, 2, A1, SA, A2, PI, 2007 W, F, E, S1, It1, S2(R), It2, 2008 It, F, S, W, E, NZ1, A, C(R), NZ2, Arg, 2009 F, It, E, S, W, A, Fj, SA, 2010 It, F, E, W, S, Sm, NZ2(R), 2011 S2(R)

Headon, T A (UC Dublin) 1939 S, W

Healey, P (Limerick) 1901 E, S, W, 1902 E, S, W, 1903 E, S, W, 1904 S

Healy, C E (Leinster) 2009 A, SA, 2010 It, F, E, W, S, NZ1, A, SA, Sm(R), NZ2, Arg, 2011 It, F1, S1, W, E1, F2, 3, E2, [A, Ru, It, W], 2012 W, It, F, S, E, NZ 1, 2, 3

Heaslip, J P R (Leinster) 2006 PI, 2007 Arg1, S2, 2008 It(R), F, S, W, E, NZ1, A, C, NZ2, Arg, 2009 F, It, E, S(R), W, A, Fj, SA, 2010 It, F, E, W, S, NZ1, SA, Sm, NZ2, Arg, 2011 F1, S1, W, E1, F2(R), 3, E2, [US, A, Ru, It, W], 2012 W, It, F, S, E, NZ 1, 2

Heffernan, M R (Cork Constitution) 1911 E, S, W, F

Hemphill, R (Dublin U) 1912 F, E, S, W

Henderson, N J (Queen's U, Belfast, NIFC) 1949 S, W, 1950 F, 1951 F, E, S, W, SA, 1952 F, S, W, E, 1953 F, E, S, W, 1954 NZ, F, E, S, W, 1955 F, E, S, W, 1956 S, W, 1957 F, E, S, W, 1958 A, E, S, W, F, 1959 E, S, W, F

Henderson R A J (London Irish, Wasps, Young Munster) 1996 WS, 1997 NZ, C, 1998 F, W, SA 1(R),2(R), 1999 F (R), E, S (R), It, 2000 S (R), It (R), F, W, Arg, US, J (R), SA, 2001 It, F, 2002 W (R), E (R), F, R (R), Ru (t), Gg (R), 2003 It 1(R),2

Henebrey, G J (Garryowen) 1906 E, S, W, SA, 1909 W, F

Henry, C G (Ulster) 2010 A, 2012 NZ 3(R)

Heron, A G (Queen's Coll, Belfast) 1901 E

Heron, J (NIFC) 1877 S, 1879 E

Heron, W T (NIFC) 1880 E, S

Herrick, R W (Dublin U) 1886 S

Heuston, F S (Kingstown) 1882 W, 1883 E, S

Hewitt, D (Queen's U, Belfast, Instonians) 1958 A, E, S, F, 1959 S, W, F, 1960 E, S, W, F, 1961 E, S, W, F, 1962 S, F, 1965 W

Hewitt, F S (Instonians) 1924 W, NZ, 1925 F, E, S, 1926 E, 1927 E, S, W

Hewitt, J A (NIFC) 1981 SA 1(R),2(R)

Hewitt, T R (Queen's U, Belfast) 1924 W, NZ, 1925 F, E, S, 1926 F, E, S, W

Hewitt, V A (Instonians) 1935 S, W, NZ, 1936 E, S, W

Hewitt, W J (Instonians) 1954 E, 1956 S, 1959 W, 1961 SA

Hewson, F T (Wanderers) 1875 E

Hickie, D A (St Mary's Coll, Leinster) 1997 W, E, S, NZ, C, It 2, 1998 S, F, W, E, SA 1,2, 2000 S, It, F, W, J, SA, 2001 F, R, S, W, E, NZ, 2002 W, E, S, It, F, NZ, Gg, A, 2003 S 1, It 1, F, W 1, E, It 2, S 2, [R,Nm,Arg,A], 2004 SA3,Arg, 2005 It, S, E, F, W, 2006 A2, PI, 2007 W, F, E, S1, It1, 2, [Nm, Gg, Arg]

Hickie, D J (St Mary's Coll) 1971 F, W, 1972 F 1, E

Higgins, J A D (Civil Service) 1947 S, W, A, 1948 F, S, W

Higgins, W W (NIFC) 1884 E, S

Hillary, M F (UC Dublin) 1952 E

Hingerty, D J (UC Dublin) 1947 F, E, S, W

Hinton, W P (Old Wesley) 1907 W, 1908 E, S, W, 1909 E, S, 1910 E, S, W, F, 1911 E, S, W, 1912 F, E, W

Hipwell, M L (Terenure Coll) 1962 E, S, 1968 F, A, 1969 F (R), S (R), W, 1971 F, E, S, W, 1972 F 2

Hobbs, T H M (Dublin U) 1884 S, 1885 E

Hobson, E W (Dublin U) 1876 E

Hogan, N A (Terenure Coll, London Irish) 1995 E, W, [J, W, F], 1996 F, W, E, WS, 1997 F, W, E, It 2

Hogan, P (Garryowen) 1992 F

Hogan, T (Munster, Leinster) 2005 J1(R),2(R), 2007 It1(R),Arg1

Hogg, W (Dublin U) 1885 S 2

Holland, J J (Wanderers) 1981 SA 1,2, 1986 W

Holmes, G W (Dublin U) 1912 SA, 1913 E, S

Holmes, L J (Lisburn) 1889 S, W

Hooks, K J (Queen's U, Belfast, Ards, Bangor) 1981 S, 1989 NZ, 1990 F, W, Arg, 1991 F

Horan, A K (Blackheath) 1920 E, W

Horan, M J (Shannon, Munster) 2000 US (R), 2002 Fj, Arg (R), 2003 S 1(R), It 1(R), F, W 1, E, A, Sm, It 2, S 2, [R, Nm, Arg(t&R), A(R), F(R)], 2004 It(R), S(R), SA1(R), 2(t&R), 3(R), US, 2005 It(R), S(R), E(R), F(R), W(R), J1, 2, NZ, A, R, 2006 It, W, S, E, NZ1, 2, A1, SA, A2(R), 2007 W, F, E, It1, 2, [Nm, Gg, F,Arg], 2008 It, F, S, W, E, NZ1, A, C, NZ2, Arg, 2009 F, It, E, S, W, 2010 S2(R)

Horgan, A P (Cork Const, Munster) 2003 Sm, W 2, S 2, 2004 F(R), 2005 J1,2,NZ

Horgan, S P (Lansdowne, Leinster) 2000 S, It, W, Arg, C, J, SA (R), 2001 It, S, W, E, NZ, 2002 S, It, F, A, Fj, Arg, 2003 S 1, [R,Nm,Arg,A,F], 2004 F,W,E,It,S,SA1,2,3,US, Arg, 2005 It,S,E,NZ,A,R, 2006 It,F,W,S,E,NZ1,2,A1,SA,A2,PI, 2007 F,E,S1,It1, [Gg,F, Arg], 2008 S(R),W,E,NZ1,A,C(R), 2009 Fj

Houston, K J (Oxford U, London Irish) 1961 SA, 1964 S, W, 1965 F, E, SA

Howe, T G (Dungannon, Ballymena, Ulster) 2000 US, J, SA, 2001 It, F, R, Sm, 2002 It (R), 2003 Tg, W 2, 2004 F,W,E,SA2

Hughes, R W (NIFC) 1878 E, 1880 E, S, 1881 S, 1882 E, S, 1883 E, S, 1884 E, S, 1885 E, 1886 E

Humphreys, D G (London Irish, Dungannon, Ulster) 1996 F, W, E, WS, 1997 E (R), S, It 2, 1998 S, E (R), SA 2(t + R), R (R), 1999 F, E, NZ, 2002 Arg 1, [US, A 3, Arg 2], 2000 E, S (R), F t&R), W (R), Arg, US (R), C, J (R), SA (R), 2001 It (R), R S (R), W, E, NZ, 2002 W, E, S, It, F, NZ (t+R), Ru (R), Gg (R), Fj, 2003 S 1, It 1, F, W 1, E, A, W 2, It 2, S 2(R), [R, Arg, A(R), F(R)], 2004W(R), It(R), S(R), SA2(R), US, 2005 S(R), W(R), J1, 2, NZ(R), A(R), R

Hunt, E W F de Vere (Army, Rosslyn Park) 1930 F, 1932 E, S, W, 1933 E

Hunter, D V (Dublin U) 1885 S 2

Hunter, L M (Civil Service) 1968 W, A

Hunter, W R (CIYMS) 1962 E, S, W, F, 1963 F, E, S, 1966 F, E, S, 1958 A, E, S, W, F

Hurley, D (Munster) 2009 US(t&R)

Hurley, H D (Old Wesley, Moseley) 1995 Fj (t), 1996 WS

Hutton, S A (Malone) 1967 S, W, F, A 2

Ireland J (Windsor) 1876 E, 1877 E

Irvine, H A S (Collegians) 1901 S

Irwin, D G (Queen's U, Belfast, Instonians) 1980 F, W, E, S, SA 1, 2, 1982 W, 1983 S, F, W, E, 1984 F, W, 1987 [Tg, A (R)], 1989 F, W, E, S, NZ, 1990 E, S

Irwin, J W S (NIFC) 1938 E, S, 1939 E, S, W

Irwin, S T (Queen's Coll, Belfast) 1900 E, S, W, 1901 E, W, 1902 E, S, W, 1903 S

Jack, H W (UC Cork) 1914 S, W, 1921 W

Jackman, B J (Leinster) 2005 J1(R),2(R), 2007 Arg1(R),2(R), 2008 It(R),F,S,W(R), E(R)

Jackson, A R V (Wanderers) 1911 E, S, W, F, 1913 W, F, 1914 F, E, S, W

Jackson, F (NIFC) 1923 E

Jackson, H W (Dublin U) 1877 E

Jameson, J S (Lansdowne) 1888 M, 1889 S, W, 1891 W, 1892 E, W, 1893 S

Jeffares, E W (Wanderers) 1913 E, S

Jennings, S (Leicester, Leinster) 2007 Arg 2, 2008 NZ1(R),A,C,NZ2(R), 2010 E(R), W(R),NZ1(R),A, 2011 F3,[US,Ru(R)], 2012 S(R)

Johns, P S (Dublin U, Dungannon, Saracens) 1990 Arg, 1992 NZ 1,2, A, 1993 S, F, W, E, R, 1994 F, W, E, S, A 1,2, US, 1995 E, S, W, It, [NZ, J, W, F], 1996 US, S, F, WS, 1997 It 1(R), F, W, E, S, NZ, C, It 2, 1998 S, F, W, E, SA 1,2, Gg, R, SA 3, 1999 F, W, E, S, It, A 1,2, Arg 1, [US, A 3, R], 2000 F (R), J

Johnston, J (Belfast Acad) 1881 S, 1882 S, 1884 S, 1885 S 1,2, 1886 E, 1887 E, S, W
Johnston, M (Dublin U) 1880 E, S, 1881 E, S, 1882 E, 1884 E, S, 1886 E
Johnston, R (Wanderers) 1893 E, W
Johnston, R W (Dublin U) 1890 S, W, E
Johnston, T J (Queen's Coll, Belfast) 1892 E, S, W, 1893 E, S, 1895 E
Johnstone, W E (Dublin U) 1884 W
Johnstone-Smyth, T R (Lansdowne) 1882 E
Jones, F A (Munster) 2011 S2(R),F2(R),3

Kavanagh, J R (UC Dublin, Wanderers) 1953 F, E, S, W, 1954 NZ, S, W, 1955 F, E, 1956 E, S, W, 1957 F, E, S, W, 1958 A, E, S, W, 1959 E, S, W, F, 1960 E, S, W, F, SA, 1961 E, S, W, F, SA, 1962 F
Kavanagh, P J (UC Dublin, Wanderers) 1952 E, 1955 W
Keane, K P (Garryowen) 1998 E (R)
Keane, M I (Lansdowne) 1974 F, W, E, S, P, NZ, 1975 E, S, F, W, 1976 A, F, W, E, S, NZ, 1977 W, E, S, F, 1978 S, F, W, E, NZ, 1979 F, W, E, S, A 1,2, 1980 E, S, F, W, 1981 F, W, E, S, 1982 W, E, S, F, 1983 S, F, W, E, 1984 F, W, E, S
Kearney, R D J (Leinster) 2007 Arg 2, 2008 It(R), F, S, W, E, NZ1, A, C, NZ2, Arg, 2009 F, It, E, S, W, A, Fj, SA, 2010 It, F, W(R), S(R), NZ1, A, SA, NZ2, 2011 S2, F2, [A, Ru, It, W], 2012 W, It, F, S, E, NZ 1, 2, 3
Kearney, R K (Wanderers) 1982 F, 1984 A, 1986 F, W
Keatley, I J (Connacht) 2009 C,US
Keeffe, E (Sunday's Well) 1947 F, E, S, W, A, 1948 F
Kelly, H C (NIFC) 1877 E, S, 1878 E, 1879 S, 1880 E, S
Kelly, J C (UC Dublin) 1962 F, W, 1963 F, E, S, W, NZ, 1964 E, S, W, F
Kelly, J P (Cork Constitution) 2002 It, NZ 1,2, R, Ru, Gg, A (R), 2003 It 1, F, A, Tg, Sm, It 2, [R(R),Nm(R),A(R),F]
Kelly, S (Lansdowne) 1954 S, W, 1955 S, 1960 W, F
Kelly, W (Wanderers) 1884 S
Kennedy, A G (Belfast Collegians) 1956 F
Kennedy, A P (London Irish) 1986 W, E
Kennedy, F (Wanderers) 1880 E, 1881 E, 1882 W
Kennedy, F A (Wanderers) 1904 E, W
Kennedy, H (Bradford) 1938 S, W
Kennedy, J M (Wanderers) 1882 W, 1884 W
Kennedy, K W (Queen's U, Belfast, London Irish) 1965 F, E, S, W, SA, 1966 F, E, W, 1967 A 1, E, S, W, F, A 2, 1968 F, A, 1969 F, E, S, W, 1970 SA, F, E, S, W, 1971 F, E, S, W, 1972 F 1, E, F 2, 1973 NZ, E, S, W, F, 1974 F, W, E, S, P, NZ, 1975 F, W
Kennedy, T J (St Mary's Coll) 1978 NZ, 1979 F, W, E (R), A 1,2, 1980 E, S, F, W, 1981 SA 1,2, A
Kenny, P (Wanderers) 1992 NZ 2(R)
Keogh, F S (Bective Rangers) 1964 W, F
Keon, J J (Limerick) 1879 E
Keyes, R P (Cork Constitution) 1986 E, 1991 [Z, J, S, A], 1992 W, E, S
Kidd, F W (Dublin U, Lansdowne) 1877 E, S, 1878 E
Kiely, M D (Lansdowne) 1962 W, 1963 F, E, S, W
Kiernan, M J (Dolphin, Lansdowne) 1982 W (R), E, S, F, 1983 S, F, W, E, 1984 E, S, A, 1985 S, F, W, E, 1986 F, W, E, S, R, 1987 E, S, F, W, [W, C, A], 1988 S, F, W, E 1,2, WS, 1989 F, W, E, S, 1990 E, S, F, W, Arg, 1991 F
Kiernan, T J (UC Cork, Cork Const) 1960 E, S, W, F, SA, 1961 E, S, W, F, SA, 1962 E, W, 1963 F, S, W, NZ, 1964 E, S, 1965 F, E, S, W, SA, 1966 F, E, S, W, 1967 A 1, E, S, W, F, A 2, 1968 F, E, S, W, A, 1969 F, E, S, W, 1970 SA, F, E, S, W, 1971 F, 1972 F 1, E, F 2, 1973 NZ, E, S
Killeen, G V (Garryowen) 1912 E, S, W, 1913 E, S, W, F, 1914 E, S, W
King, H (Dublin U) 1883 E, S
Kingston, T J (Dolphin) 1987 [W, Tg, A], 1988 S, F, W, E 1, 1990 F, W, 1991 [J], 1993 F, W, E, R, 1994 F, W, E, S, 1995 F, W, It, [NZ, J (R), W, F], Fj, 1996 US, S, F
Knox, J H (Dublin U, Lansdowne) 1904 W, 1905 E, S, W, NZ, 1906 E, S, W, 1907 W, 1908 S
Kyle, J W (Queen's U, Belfast, NIFC) 1947 F, E, S, W, A, 1948 F, E, S, W, 1949 F, E, S, W, 1950 F, E, S, W, 1951 F, E, S, W, SA, 1952 F, S, W, E, 1953 F, E, S, W, 1954 NZ, F, 1955 F, E, W, 1956 F, E, W, 1957 F, E, S, W, 1958 A, E, S

Lambert, N H (Lansdowne) 1934 S, W
Lamont, R A (Instonians) 1965 F, E, SA, 1966 F, E, S, W, 1970 SA, F, E, S, W
Landers, M F (Cork Const) 1904 W, 1905 E, S, W, NZ
Lane, D J (UC Cork) 1934 S, W, 1935 E, S

Lane, M F (UC Cork) 1947 W, 1949 F, E, S, W, 1950 F, E, S, W, 1951 F, S, W, SA, 1952 F, S, 1953 F, E
Lane, P (Old Crescent) 1964 W
Langan, D J (Clontarf) 1934 W
Langbroek, J A (Blackrock Coll) 1987 [Tg]
Lavery, P (London Irish) 1974 W, 1976 W
Lawlor, P J (Clontarf) 1951 S, SA, 1952 F, S, W, E, 1953 F, 1954 NZ, E, S, 1956 F, E
Lawlor, P J (Bective Rangers) 1935 E, S, W, 1937 E, S, W
Lawlor, P J (Bective Rangers) 1990 Arg, 1992 A, 1993 S
Leahy, K T (Wanderers) 1992 NZ 1
Leahy, M W (UC Cork) 1964 W
Leamy, D P (Munster) 2004 US, 2005 It, J2, NZ, A, R, 2006 It, F, W, S, E, NZ1 2, 2, A1, SA, A2, PI(R), 2007 W, F, E, S1, It1, 2, [Nm, Gg, F, Arg], 2008 It, F, S, W, E, NZ1, A, 2009 F(R), It (t&R), E(R), S, W(R), C, US, A(t&R), Fj, 2010 Sm, NZ2(R), Arg(R), 2011 It, S1(R), W(R), E1(R), S2,F2, E2(R), [US(R), Ru(R), It(R), W(R)]
Lee, S (NIFC) 1891 E, S, W, 1892 E, S, W, 1893 E, S, W, 1894 E, S, W, 1895 E, W, 1896 E, S, W, 1897 E, 1898 E
Le Fanu, V C (Cambridge U, Lansdowne) 1886 E, S, 1887 E, W, 1888 S, 1889 W, 1890 E, 1891 E, 1892 E, S, W
Lenihan, D G (UC Cork, Cork Const) 1981 A, 1982 W, E, S, F, 1983 S, F, W, E, 1984 F, W, E, S, A, 1985 S, F, W, E, 1986 F, W, E, S, R, 1987 E, S, F, W, [W, C, Tg, A], 1988 S, F, W, E 1,2, WS, It, 1989 F, W, E, S, NZ, 1990 S, F, W, Arg, 1991 Nm 2, [Z, S, A], 1992 W
L'Estrange, L P F (Dublin U) 1962 E
Levis, F H (Wanderers) 1884 E
Lewis, K P (Leinster) 2005 J2(R), 2007 Arg1,2(R)
Lightfoot, E J (Lansdowne) 1931 F, E, S, W, SA, 1932 E, S, W, 1933 E, W, S
Lindsay, H (Dublin U, Armagh) 1893 E, S, W, 1894 E, S, W, 1895 E, 1896 E, S, W, 1898 E, S, W
Little, T J (Bective Rangers) 1898 W, 1899 S, W, 1900 S, W, 1901 E, S
Lloyd, R A (Dublin U, Liverpool) 1910 E, S, 1911 E, S, W, F, 1912 F, E, S, W, SA, 1913 E, S, W, F, 1914 F, E, 1920 E, F
Longwell, G W (Ballymena) 2000 J (R), SA, 2001 F (R), R, S (R), Sm, NZ (R), 2002 W (R), E (R), S (R), It, F, NZ 1,2, R, Ru, Gg, A, Arg, 2003 S 1, It 1, F, E, A, It 2, 2004 It(R)
Loughney, R (Connacht) 2012 NZ 1(R)
Lydon, C T J (Galwegians) 1956 S
Lyle, R K (Dublin U) 1910 W, F
Lyle, T R (Dublin U) 1885 E, S 1,2, 1886 E, 1887 E, S
Lynch, J F (St Mary's Coll) 1971 F, E, S, W, 1972 F 1, E, F 2, 1973 NZ, E, S, W, 1974 F, W, E, S, P, NZ
Lynch, L M (Lansdowne) 1956 S
Lytle, J H (NIFC) 1894 E, S, W, 1895 W, 1896 E, S, W, 1897 E, S, 1898 E, S, 1899 S
Lytle, J N (NIFC) 1888 M, 1889 W, 1890 E, 1891 E, S, 1894 E, S, W
Lyttle, V J (Collegians, Bedford) 1938 E, 1939 E, S

McAleese, D R (Ballymena) 1992 F
McAllan, G H (Dungannon) 1896 S, W
Macauley, J (Limerick) 1887 E, S
McBride, W D (Malone) 1988 W, E 1, WS, It, 1989 S, 1990 F, W, Arg, 1993 S, F, W, E, R, 1994 W, E, S, A 1(R), 1995 S, F, [NZ, W, F], Fj (R), 1996 W, E, WS, A, 1997 It 1(R), F, W, E, S
McBride, W J (Ballymena) 1962 E, S, F, W, 1963 F, E, S, W, NZ, 1964 E, S, F, 1965 F, E, S, W, SA, 1966 F, E, S, W, 1967 A 1, E, S, W, F, A 2, 1968 F, E, S, W, A, 1969 F, E, S, W, 1970 SA, F, E, S, W, 1971 F, E, S, W, 1972 F 1, E, F 2, 1973 NZ, E, S, W, F, 1974 F, W, E, S, P, NZ, 1975 E, S, F, W
McCahill, S A (Sunday's Well) 1995 Fj (t)
McCall, B W (London Irish) 1985 F (R), 1986 E, S
McCall, M C (Bangor, Dungannon, London Irish) 1992 NZ 1(R),2, 1994 W, 1996 E (R), A, 1997 It 1, NZ, C, It 2, 1998 S, E, SA 1,2
McCallan, B (Ballymena) 1960 E, S
McCarten, R J (London Irish) 1961 E, W, F
McCarthy, E A (Kingstown) 1882 W
McCarthy, J S (Dolphin) 1948 F, E, S, W, 1949 F, E, S, W, 1950 W, 1951 F, E, S, W, SA, 1952 F, S, W, E, 1953 F, E, S, 1954 W, 1955 F, E, W, 1955 F, E
McCarthy, M P (Connacht) 2011 S2,F3(R), 2012 S(R),E(R)
McCarthy, P D (Cork Const) 1992 NZ 1,2, A, 1993 S, R (R)
MacCarthy, St G (Dublin U) 1882 W
McCarthy, T (Cork) 1898 W
McClelland, T A (Queen's U, Belfast) 1921 E, S, W, F, 1922 E, W, F, 1923 E, S, W, F, 1924 F, E, S, W, NZ
McClenahan, R O (Instonians) 1923 E, S, W

McClinton, A N (NIFC) 1910 W, F
McCombe, W McM (Dublin U, Bangor) 1968 F, 1975 E, S, F, W
McConnell, A A (Collegians) 1947 A, 1948 F, E, S, W, 1949 F, E
McConnell, G (Derry, Edinburgh U) 1912 F, E, 1913 W, F
McConnell, J W (Lansdowne) 1913 S
McCormac, F M (Wanderers) 1909 W, 1910 W, F
McCormick, W J (Wanderers) 1930 E
McCoull, H C (Belfast Albion) 1895 E, S, W, 1899 E
McCourt, D (Queen's U, Belfast) 1947 A
McCoy, J J (Dungannon, Bangor, Ballymena) 1984 W, A, 1985 S, F, W, E, 1986 F, 1987 [Tg], 1988 E 2, WS, It, 1989 F, W, E, S, NZ
McCracken, H (NIFC) 1954 W
McCullen, A (Lansdowne) 2003 Sm
McCullough, M T (Ulster) 2005 J1,2,NZ(R),A(R)
McDermott, S J (London Irish) 1955 S, W
Macdonald, J A (Methodist Coll, Belfast) 1875 E, 1876 E, 1877 S, 1878 E, 1879 S, 1880 E, 1881 S, 1882 E, S, 1883 E, S, 1884 E, S
McDonald, J P (Malone) 1987 [C], 1990 E (R), S, Arg
McDonnell, A C (Dublin U) 1889 W, 1890 S, W, 1891 E
McDowell, J C (Instonians) 1924 F, NZ
McFadden, F L (Leinster) 2011 It, F1, S2, F2(R), E2(R), [Ru], 2012 W, It(R), F(R), S(R), E(R), NZ 1, 2, 3
McFarland, B A T (Derry) 1920 S, W, F, 1922 W
McGann, B J (Lansdowne) 1969 F, E, S, W, 1970 SA, F, E, S, W, 1971 F, E, S, W, 1972 F 1, E, F 2, 1973 NZ, E, S, W, 1976 F, W, E, S, NZ
McGowan, A N (Blackrock Coll) 1994 US
McGown, T M W (NIFC) 1899 E, S, 1901 S
McGrath, D G (UC Dublin, Cork Const) 1984 S, 1987 [W, C, Tg, A]
McGrath, N F (Oxford U, London Irish) 1934 W
McGrath, P J (UC Cork) 1965 E, S, W, SA, 1966 F, E, S, W, 1967 A 1, A 2
McGrath, R J M (Wanderers) 1977 W, E, F (R), 1981 SA 1,2, A, 1982 W, E, S, F, 1983 S, F, W, E, 1984 F, W
McGrath, T (Garryowen) 1956 W, 1958 F, 1960 E, S, W, F, 1961 SA
McGuinness, C D (St Mary's Coll) 1997 NZ, C, 1998 F, W, E, SA 1,2, Gg, R (R), SA 3, 1999 F, W, E, S
McGuire, E P (UC Galway) 1963 E, S, W, NZ, 1964 E, S, W, F
MacHale, S (Lansdowne) 1965 F, E, S, W, SA, 1966 F, E, S, W, 1967 S, W, F
McHugh, M (St Mary's Coll) 2003 Tg
McIldowie, G (Malone) 1906 SA, 1910 E, S, W
McIlrath, J A (Ballymena) 1976 A, F, NZ, 1977 W, E
McIlwaine, E H (NIFC) 1895 S, W
McIlwaine, E N (NIFC) 1875 E, 1876 E
McIlwaine, J E (NIFC) 1897 E, S, 1898 E, S, W, 1899 E, W
McIntosh, L M (Dublin U) 1884 S
MacIvor, C V (Dublin U) 1912 F, E, S, W, 1913 E, S, F
McIvor, S C (Garryowen) 1996 A, 1997 It 1, S (R)
McKay, J W (Queen's U, Belfast) 1947 F, E, S, W, A, 1948 F, E, S, W, 1949 F, E, S, W, 1950 F, E, S, W, 1951 F, E, S, W, SA, 1952 F
McKee, W D (NIFC) 1947 A, 1948 F, E, S, W, 1949 F, E, S, W, 1950 F, E, 1951 SA
McKeen, A J W (Lansdowne) 1999 [R (R)]
McKelvey, J M (Queen's U, Belfast) 1956 F, E
McKenna, P (St Mary's Coll) 2000 Arg
McKibbin, A R (Instonians, London Irish) 1977 W, E, S, 1978 S, F, W, E, NZ, 1979 F, W, E, S, 1980 E, S
McKibbin, C H (Instonians) 1976 S (R)
McKibbin, D (Instonians) 1950 F, E, S, W, 1951 F, E, S, W
McKibbin, H R (Queen's U, Belfast) 1938 W, 1939 E, S, W
McKinney, S A (Dungannon) 1972 F 1, E, F 2, 1973 W, F, 1974 F, E, S, P, NZ, 1975 E, S, 1976 A, F, W, E, S, NZ, 1977 W, E, S, 1978 S (R), F, W, E
McLaughlin, J H (Derry) 1887 E, S, 1888 W, S
McLaughlin, K R (Leinster) 2010 It, 2011 S2(R), 2012 NZ 1(R),2,3
McLean, R E (Dublin U) 1881 S, 1882 W, E, S, 1883 E, S, 1884 E, S, 1885 E, S 1
Maclear, B (Cork County, Monkstown) 1905 E, S, W, NZ, 1906 E, S, W, SA, 1907 E, S, W
McLennan, A C (Wanderers) 1977 F, 1978 S, F, W, E, NZ, 1979 F, W, E, S, 1980 E, F, 1981 F, W, E, S, SA 1,2
McLoughlin, F M (Northern) 1976 A
McLoughlin, G A J (Shannon) 1979 F, W, E, S, A 1,2, 1980 E, 1981 SA 1,2, 1982 W, E, S, F, 1983 S, F, W, E, 1984 F
McLoughlin, R J (UC Dublin, Blackrock Coll, Gosforth) 1962 E, S, F, 1963 E, S, W, NZ, 1964 E, S, W, 1965 F, E, S, W, SA, 1966 F, E, S, W, 1971 F, E, S, W, 1972 F 1, E, F 2, 1973 NZ, E, S, W, F, 1974 F, W, E, S, P, NZ, 1975 E, S, F, W

McMahon, L B (Blackrock Coll, UC Dublin) 1931 E, SA, 1933 E, 1934 E, 1936 E, S, W, 1937 E, S, W, 1938 E, S
McMaster, A W (Ballymena) 1972 F 1, E, F 2, 1973 NZ, E, S, W, F, 1974 F, E, S, P, 1975 F, W, 1976 A, F, W, NZ
McMordie, J (Queen's Coll, Belfast) 1886 S
McMorrow, A (Garryowen) 1951 W
McMullen, A R (Cork) 1881 E, S
McNamara, V (UC Cork) 1914 E, S, W
McNaughton, P P (Greystones) 1978 S, F, W, E, 1979 F, W, E, S, A 1,2, 1980 E, S, F, W, 1981 F
MacNeill, H P (Dublin U, Oxford U, Blackrock Coll, London Irish) 1981 F, W, E, S, A, 1982 W, E, S, F, 1983 S, F, W, E, 1984 F, W, E, A, 1985 S, F, W, E, 1986 F, W, E, S, R, 1987 E, S, F, W, [W, C, Tg, A], 1988 S (R), E 1,2
McQuilkin, K P (Bective Rangers, Lansdowne) 1996 US, S, F, 1997 F (t & R), S
MacSweeney, D A (Blackrock Coll) 1955 S
McVicker, H (Army, Richmond) 1927 E, S, W, A, 1928 F
McVicker, J (Collegians) 1924 F, E, S, W, NZ, 1925 F, E, S, W, 1926 F, E, S, W, 1927 F, E, S, W, A, 1928 W, 1930 F
McVicker, S (Queen's U, Belfast) 1922 E, S, W, F
McWeeney, J P J (St Mary's Coll) 1997 NZ
Madden, M N (Sunday's Well) 1955 E, S, W
Magee, A M (Louis) (Bective Rangers, London Irish) 1895 E, S, W, 1896 E, S, W, 1897 E, S, 1898 E, S, W, 1899 E, S, W, 1900 E, S, W, 1901 E, S, W, 1902 E, S, W, 1903 E, S, W, 1904 W
Magee, J T (Bective Rangers) 1895 E, S
Maggs, K M (Bristol, Bath, Ulster) 1997 NZ (R), C, It 2, 1998 S, F, W, E, SA 1,2, Gg, R (R), SA 3, 1999 F, W, E, S, It, A 1,2, Arg 1, [US, A 3, Arg 2], 2000 E, F, Arg, US (R), C, 2001 It (R), F (R), R, S (R), W, E, Sm, NZ, 2002 W, E, S, R, Ru, Gg, A, Fj, Arg, 2003 S 1, It 1, F, W 1, E, A, W 2, S 2, [R,Nm,Arg,A,F], 2004 F,W(R),E(R),It(R),S(R),SA1(R),2, US, 2005 S,F,W,J1
Maginiss, R M (Dublin U) 1875 E, 1876 E
Magrath, R M (Cork Constitution) 1909 S
Maguire, J F (Cork) 1884 S
Mahoney, J (Dolphin) 1923 E
Malcomson, G L (RAF, NIFC) 1935 NZ, 1936 E, S, W, 1937 E, S, W
Malone, N G (Oxford U, Leicester) 1993 S, F, 1994 US (R)
Mannion, N P (Corinthians, Lansdowne, Wanderers) 1988 WS, It, 1989 F, W, E, S, NZ, 1990 E, S, F, W, Arg, 1991 Nm 1(R),2, [J], 1993 S
Marshall, B D E (Queen's U, Belfast) 1963 E
Mason, S J P (Orrell, Richmond) 1996 W, E, WS
Massey-Westropp, R H (Limerick, Monkstown) 1886 E
Matier, R N (NIFC) 1878 E, 1879 S
Matthews, P M (Ards, Wanderers) 1984 A, 1985 S, F, W, E, 1986 R, 1987 E, S, F, W, [W, Tg, A], 1988 S, F, W, E 1,2, WS, It, 1989 F, W, E, S, NZ, 1990 E, S, 1991 F, W, E, S, Nm 1 [Z, S, A], 1992 W, E, S
Mattsson, J (Wanderers) 1948 E
Mayne, R B (Queen's U, Belfast) 1937 W, 1938 E, W, 1939 E, S, W
Mayne, R H (Belfast Academy) 1888 W, S
Mayne, T (NIFC) 1921 E, S, F
Mays, K M A (UC Dublin) 1973 NZ, E, S, W
Meares, A W D (Dublin U) 1899 S, W, 1900 E, W
Megaw, J (Richmond, Instonians) 1934 W, 1938 E
Millar, A (Kingstown) 1880 E, S, 1883 E
Millar, H J (Monkstown) 1904 W, 1905 E, S, W
Millar, S (Ballymena) 1958 F, 1959 E, S, W, F, 1960 E, S, W, F, SA, 1961 E, S, W, F, SA, 1962 E, S, F, 1963 F, E, S, W, 1964 F, 1968 F, E, S, W, A, 1969 F, E, S, W, 1970 SA, F, E, S, W
Miller, W H J (Queen's U, Belfast) 1951 E, S, W, 1952 S, W
Miller, E R P (Leicester, Tererure Coll, Leinster) 1997 It 1, F, W, E, NZ, It 2, 1998 S, W (R), Gg, R, 1999 F, W, E, S, Arg 1(R), [US (R), A 3(t&R), Arg 2(R)], 2000 US, C (R), SA, 2001 R, W, E, Sm, NZ, 2002 E, S, It (R), Fj, 2003 W 1(t+R), Tg, Sm, It 2, S 2, [Nm, Arg(R), A(t&R), F(R)], 2004 SA3(R), US, Arg(R), 2005 It(R), S(R), F(R), W(R), J1(R), 2
Miller, F H (Wanderers) 1886 S
Milliken, R A (Bangor) 1973 E, S, W, F, 1974 F, W, E, S, P, NZ, 1975 E, S, F, W
Millin, T J (Dublin U) 1925 W
Minch, J B (Bective Rangers) 1912 SA, 1913 E, S, 1914 E, S
Moffat, J (Belfast Academy) 1888 W, S, M, 1889 S, 1890 S, W, 1891 S
Moffatt, J E (Old Wesley) 1904 S, 1905 E, S, W
Moffett, J W (Ballymena) 1961 E, S
Molloy, M G (UC Galway, London Irish) 1966 F, E, 1967 A 1, E,

S, W, F, A 2, 1968 F, E, S, W, A, 1969 F, E, S, W, 1970 F, E, S, W, 1971 F, E, S, W, 1973 F, 1976 A
Moloney, J J (St Mary's Coll) 1972 F 1, E, F 2, 1973 NZ, E, S, W, F, 1974 F, W, E, S, P, NZ, 1975 E, S, F, W, 1976 S, 1978 S, F, W, E, 1979 A 1,2, 1980 S, W
Moloney, L A (Garryowen) 1976 W (R), S, 1978 S (R), NZ
Molony, J U (UC Dublin) 1950 S
Monteith, J D E (Queen's U, Belfast) 1947 E, S, W
Montgomery, A (NIFC) 1895 S
Montgomery, F P (Queen's U, Belfast) 1914 E, S, W
Montgomery, R (Cambridge U) 1887 E, S, W, 1891 E, 1892 W
Moore, C M (Dublin U) 1887 S, 1888 W, S
Moore, D F (Wanderers) 1883 E, S, 1884 E, W
Moore, F W (Wanderers) 1884 W, 1885 E, S 2, 1886 S
Moore, H (Windsor) 1876 E, 1877 S
Moore, H (Queen's U, Belfast) 1910 S, 1911 W, F, 1912 F, E, S, W, SA
Moore, T A P (Highfield) 1967 A 2, 1973 NZ, E, S, W, F, 1974 F, W, E, S, P, NZ
Moore, W D (Queen's Coll, Belfast) 1878 E
Moran, F G (Clontarf) 1936 E, 1937 E, S, W, 1938 S, W, 1939 E, S, W
Morell, H B (Dublin U) 1881 E, S, 1882 W, E
Morgan, G J (Clontarf) 1934 E, S, W, 1935 E, S, W, NZ, 1936 E, S, W, 1937 E, S, W, 1938 E, S, W, 1939 E, S, W
Moriarty, C C H (Monkstown) 1899 W
Moroney, J C M (Garryowen) 1968 W, A, 1969 F, E, S, W
Moroney, R J M (Lansdowne) 1984 F, W, 1985 F
Moroney, T A (UC Dublin) 1964 W, 1967 A 1, E
Morphy, E McG (Dublin U) 1908 E
Morris, D P (Bective Rangers) 1931 W, 1932 E, 1935 E, S, W, NZ
Morrow, J W R (Queen's Coll, Belfast) 1882 S, 1883 E, S, 1884 E, W, 1885 S 1,2, 1886 E, S, 1888 S
Morrow, R D (Bangor) 1986 F, E, S
Mortell, M (Bective Rangers, Dolphin) 1953 F, E, S, W, 1954 NZ, F, E, S, W
Morton, W A (Dublin U) 1888 S
Mostyn, M R (Galwegians) 1999 A 1, Arg 1, [US, A 3, R, Arg 2]
Moyers, L W (Dublin U) 1884 W
Moylett, M M F (Shannon) 1988 E 1
Mulcahy, W A (UC Dublin, Bective Rangers, Bohemians) 1958 A, E, S, W, F, 1959 E, S, W, F, 1960 E, S, W, SA, 1961 E, S, W, SA, 1962 E, S, F, W, 1963 F, E, S, W, NZ, 1964 E, S, W, F, 1965 F, E, S, W, SA
Muldoon, J (Connacht) 2009 C,US, 2010 NZ1
Mullan, B (Clontarf) 1947 F, E, S, W, 1948 F, E, S, W
Mullane, J P (Limerick Bohemians) 1928 W, 1929 F
Mullen, K D (Old Belvedere) 1947 F, E, S, W, A, 1948 F, E, S, W, 1949 F, E, S, W, 1950 F, E, S, W, 1951 F, E, S, W, SA, 1952 F, S, W
Mulligan, A A (Wanderers) 1956 F, E, 1957 F, E, S, W, 1958 A, E, S, F, 1959 E, S, W, F, 1960 E, S, W, F, SA, 1961 W, F, SA
Mullin, B J (Dublin U, Oxford U, Blackrock Coll, London Irish) 1984 A, 1985 S, W, E, 1986 F, W, E, S, R, 1987 E, S, F, W, [W, C, Tg, A], 1988 S, F, W, E 1,2, WS, It, 1989 F, W, E, S, NZ, 1990 E, S, W, Arg, 1991 F, W, E, S, Nm 1,2, [J, S, A], 1992 W, E, S, 1994 US, 1995 E, S, F, W, It, [NZ, J, W, F]
Mullins, M J (Young Munster, Old Crescent) 1999 Arg 1(R), [R], 2000 E, S, It, Arg (t&R), US, C, 2001 It, R, W (R), E (R), Sm (R), NZ (R), 2003 Tg, Sm
Murphy, B J (Munster) 2007 Arg 1(R),2, 2009 C,US
Murphy, C J (Lansdowne) 1939 E, S, W, 1947 F, E
Murphy, G E A (Leicester) 2000 US, C (R), J, 2001 R, S, Sm, 2002 W, E, NZ 1,2, Fj, 2003 S 1(R), It 1, F, W 1, E, A, W 2, It 2(R), S 2, 2004 It,S,SA1,3,US,Arg, 2005 It,S,E, F,W,NZ,A,R, 2006 It,F,W,S,E,NZ1,2,A1(R),SA(R),A2, 2007 W(t&R),F,Arg1(t&R),2, S2,It2, [Nm(R),Arg], 2008 It,F,S,E,NZ1(R),A(R),Arg, 2009 F(R),It(R),S(R),W(R), 2010 E,W,S,NZ1(R),A(R),Arg, 2011 E2,[US,Ru(R)]
Murphy, J G M W (London Irish) 1951 SA, 1952 S, W, E, 1954 NZ, 1958 W
Murphy, J J (Greystones) 1981 SA 1, 1982 W (R), 1984 S
Murphy, J N (Greystones) 1992 A
Murphy, K J (Cork Constitution) 1990 E, S, F, W, Arg, 1991 F, W (R), S (R), 1992 S, F, NZ 2(R)
Murphy, N A A (Cork Constitution) 1958 A, E, S, W, F, 1959 E, S, W, F, 1960 E, S, W, F, SA, 1961 E, S, W, 1962 E, 1963 NZ, 1964 E, S, W, F, 1965 F, E, S, W, SA, 1966 F, E, S, W, 1967 A 1, E, S, W, F, 1969 F, E, S, W
Murphy, N F (Cork Constitution) 1930 E, W, 1931 F, E, S, W, SA, 1932 E, S, W, 1933 E
Murphy-O'Connor, J (Bective Rangers) 1954 E

Murray, C (Munster) 2011 F2(R),E2(R),[US,A(R),It,W], 2012 W,It,F,NZ 1,2,3
Murray, H W (Dublin U) 1877 S, 1878 E, 1879 E
Murray, J B (UC Dublin) 1963 F
Murray, P F (Wanderers) 1927 F, 1929 F, E, S, 1930 F, E, S, W, 1931 F, E, S, W, SA, 1932 E, S, W, 1933 E, W, S
Murtagh, C W (Portadown) 1977 S
Myles, J (Dublin U) 1875 E

Nash, L C (Queen's Coll, Cork) 1889 S, 1890 W, E, 1891 E, S, W
Neely, M R (Collegians) 1947 F, E, S, W
Neill, H J (NIFC) 1885 E, S 1,2, 1886 S, 1887 E, S, W, 1888 W, S
Neill, J McF (Instonians) 1926 F
Nelson, J E (Malone) 1947 A, 1948 E, S, W, 1949 F, E, S, W, 1950 F, E, S, W, 1951 F, E, W, 1954 F
Nelson, R (Queen's Coll, Belfast) 1882 S, 1883 S, 1886 S
Nesdale, R P (Newcastle) 1997 W, E, S, NZ (R), C, 1998 F (R), W (R), Gg, SA 3(R), 1999 It, A 2(R), [US (R), R]
Nesdale, T J (Garryowen) 1961 F
Neville, W C (Dublin U) 1879 S, E
Nicholson, P C (Dublin U) 1900 E, S, W
Norton, G W (Bective Rangers) 1949 F, E, S, W, 1950 F, E, S, W, 1951 F, E, S
Notley, J R (Wanderers) 1952 F, S
Nowlan, K W (St Mary's Coll) 1997 NZ, C, It 2

O'Brien, B (Derry) 1893 S, W
O'Brien, B A P (Shannon) 1968 F, E, S
O'Brien, D J (London Irish, Cardiff, Old Belvedere) 1948 E, S, W, 1949 F, E, S, W, 1950 F, E, S, W, 1951 F, E, S, W, SA, 1952 F, S, W, E
O'Brien, K A (Broughton Park) 1980 E, 1981 SA 1(R), 2
O'Brien, S K (Leinster) 2009 Fj(R), SA(R), 2010 It(R), Sm, 2011 It, F1, S1, W, E1, F2, 3, [A, Ru, It, W], 2012 W, It, F, E, NZ 1, 2, 3
O'Brien-Butler, P E (Monkstown) 1897 S, 1898 E, S, 1899 S, W, 1900 E
O'Callaghan, C T (Carlow) 1910 W, F, 1911 E, S, W, F, 1912 F
O'Callaghan, D P (Cork Const, Munster) 2003 W 1(R), Tg (R), Sm (R), W 2(R), It2(R), [R(R), A(t&R)], 2004 F(t&R), W, It, S(t&R), SA2(R), US, 2005 It(R), S(R), W(R), NZ, A, R, 2006 It(R), F(R), W, S(R), E(R), NZ1, 2, A1, SA, A2, PI(R), 2007 W, F, E, S1, It1, 2, [Nm, Gg, F,Arg], 2008 It, F, S, W, E, NZ1, A, C, NZ2, Arg, 2009 F, It, E, S, W, A, Fj(R), SA, 2010 E, W, S, NZ1, A, SA, Sm, NZ2, Arg, 2011 It, F1, S1, W, E1, F2, 3, E2, [US, A, Ru, It, W], 2012 W, It, F, S, E, NZ 1(R), 2(R), 3(R)
O'Callaghan, M P (Sunday's Well) 1962 W, 1964 E, F
O'Callaghan, P (Dolphin) 1967 A 1, E, A 2, 1968 F, E, S, W, 1969 F, E, S, W, 1970 SA, F, E, S, W, 1976 F, W, E, S, NZ
O'Connell, K D (Sunday's Well) 1994 F, E (t)
O'Connell, P (Bective Rangers) 1913 W, F, 1914 F, E, S, W
O'Connell, P J (Young Munster, Munster) 2002 W, It (R), F (R), NZ 1, 2003 E, A (R), Tg, Sm, W 2, S 2, [R, Nm, Arg, A, F], 2004 F, W, E, S, SA1, 2, 3, US, Arg, 2005 It, S, E, F, W, 2006 It, F, S, E, NZ1, 2, A1, SA, A2, PI, 2007 W, F, E, S1, 2, It2, [Nm, Gg, F,Arg], 2008 S(R), W, E, NZ1, A, C, NZ2, Arg, 2009 F, It, E, S, W, A, Fj, SA, 2010 It, F, E, W, S, 2011 It, F1, S1, W, E1,F2(R), 3, E2, [US, A, It, W], 2012 W, It, F
O'Connell, W J (Lansdowne) 1955 F
O'Connor, H S (Dublin U) 1957 F, E, S, W
O'Connor, J (Garryowen) 1895 S
O'Connor, J H (Bective Rangers) 1888 M, 1890 S, W, E, 1891 E, S, 1892 E, W, 1893 E, S, 1894 E, S, W, 1895 E, 1896 E, S, W
O'Connor, J H (Wasps) 2004 SA3,Arg, 2005 S, E, F, W, J1, NZ, A, R, 2006 W(R), E(t&R)
O'Connor, J J (Garryowen) 1909 F
O'Connor, J J (UC Cork) 1933 S, 1934 E, S, W, 1935 E, S, W, NZ, 1936 S, W, 1938 S
O'Connor, P J (Lansdowne) 1887 W
O'Cuinneagain, D (Sale, Ballymena) 1998 SA 1,2, Gg (R), R (R), SA 3, 1999 F, W, E, S, It, A 1,2, Arg 1, [US, A 3, R, Arg 2], 2000 E, It (R)
Odbert, R V M (RAF) 1928 F
O'Donnell, R C (St Mary's Coll) 1979 A 1,2, 1980 S, F, W
O'Donoghue, P J (Bective Rangers) 1955 F, E, S, W, 1956 W, 1957 F, E, 1958 A, E, S, W
O'Driscoll, B G (Blackrock Coll, Leinster) 1999 A 1,2, Arg 1, [US, A 3, R (R), Arg 2], 2000 E, S, It, F, W, J, SA, 2001 F, S, W, E, Sm, NZ, 2002 W, E, S, It, F, NZ 1,2, R, Ru, Gg, A, Fj, Arg, 2003 S 1, It 1, F, W 1, E, A, F, It 2, S 2, [R, Nm, Arg, A, F], 2004 W, E, It, S, SA1, 2, 3, US, Arg, 2005 It, E, F, W, 2006 It, F, W, S, E, NZ1, 2, A1, SA, A2, PI, 2007 W, E, S1, It1, S2, [Nm, Gg, F,

IRELAND

ITALY

ITALY'S 2012 TEST RECORD

OPPONENTS	DATE	VENUE	RESULT
France	4 Feb	A	Lost 30–12
England	11 Feb	H	Lost 15–19
Ireland	25 Feb	A	Lost 42–10
Wales	10 Mar	A	Lost 24–3
Scotland	17 Mar	H	Won 13–6
Argentina	9 Jun	A	Lost 37–22
Canada	15 Jun	A	Won 25–16
USA	23 Jun	A	Won 30–10

ITALY ON THE RIGHT PATH TO LONG-TERM GOAL

With Sergio Parisse

Sergio Parisse salutes the crowd after Italy's narrow loss to England in the snow in Rome.

A new era dawned in Italian rugby in 2012 with former Perpignan coach Jacques Brunel having taken over from Nick Mallett after a disappointing Rugby World Cup 2011 in New Zealand which saw the Azzurri miss out on their target of a first-ever quarter-final appearance. The players had shed tears on the pitch in Dunedin as former Springbok coach Mallett's reign came to an end, but were soon embracing the new philosophy of the Frenchman.

Italy, under Mallett, had relied on an organised defence, a solid scrum and kicking game, but Brunel had a different approach, a desire to see the Azzurri play a more expansive, attacking style of rugby. This new philosophy was evident in his first match in charge, the RBS Six Nations opener against France, but while the enthusiasm was there the execution was not yet perfected and so there was to be no repeat of Italy's memorable victory in Rome a year earlier, Les Bleus winning 30–12.

Brunel was also not afraid to give young players a chance as part of the new approach, an example being wing Giovanbattista Venditti who made his Test debut at the Stade de France and would end his first Championship with two tries, including the only try in the Azzurri's vital win over Scotland on the final day to avoid another Six Nations wooden spoon.

Italy were, in the words of Brunel after the French loss, "on an interesting path" and it was one which would inevitably involve many twists and turns in the coming months. One disappointment along the way for captain Sergio Parisse was the manner of the defeat away to Ireland at the end of February.

The two sides had met in the pool stages of Rugby World Cup 2011 with Ireland running out 36–6 winners at Otago Stadium to end Italy's dreams of a first appearance in the knockout stages. Parisse admits that Ireland had simply been "better than us and played a better game" that day but that "not one of us gave up until the final whistle". Italy's inspirational number 8 was not able to say the same when the two sides met five months later at the Aviva Stadium when Ireland ran out 42–10 winners.

"It was a very disappointing defeat," admitted Parisse, who had scored the try that levelled the score at 10–10 late in the first half. "Even if the final score looks similar to that in Dunedin, the game was completely different. We performed pretty well in the first half, but when Ireland came back early in the second half and scored some points we gave up from a mental point of view. That's something Italy can't afford, whoever the opponent is. At half-time, when we assembled in the locker room, we were confident we could bring the game home, but we failed to approach the second half and Ireland showed why they are a great team, again."

The manner of defeat put a damper on a personal milestone for Parisse, the then 28-year-old captaining the Azzurri for a record-breaking 38th time. "I would prefer to have celebrated in a different way, but I'm proud of the goal I achieved. I'll always be grateful to Nick Mallett for appointing me when he took over from [Pierre] Berbizier in 2007.

"I was a very young captain then, as Marco Bortolami was before me, and skippering the team helped me in developing and growing both on and off the field. Nick gave me his confidence and I always tried to repay him by playing at my best and helping him in keeping the team together, even in the most difficult situations."

There was little time for Italy to regroup before welcoming Scotland to Rome for the wooden spoon decider, both sides eager to claim their first win of the 2012 Championship. A crowd of 72,357 packed into the Stadio Olimpico – the second highest of all time for a rugby international in Italy – and showed their growing passion for the sport.

"We have played twice in the Olimpico so far in 2012 – we will face New Zealand there on 17 November – and all of us will remember those two games for many reasons," explained Parisse.

"In February we faced England under the snow, a very unusual scenario in Rome. The stadium was sold out, but almost 20,000 fans unfortunately missed the game due to the weather, and as players we missed a great chance to beat England for the first time in our history. The fans were great, most of them only reached the stadium just ahead of kick-off to face the snow and freezing cold conditions. We missed a great opportunity, we were leading at half-time and we were at 15–6 a few minutes into the second half.

"We had to win, but we lost. England were maybe not at their best but the crowd were fantastic. We made too many mistakes, our half backs took some wrong decisions and the game turned in England's favour. Sometimes heart and passion can't be enough and that was the case here, which was a great shame."

A month later, with conditions the complete opposite as the sun shone on the Eternal City, Italy reproduced the same passion but this time got the result, dominating the Scottish scrum to win 13–6.

"It was the right payback for our fans and for us as well, the ideal conclusion to Jacques' first Six Nations as our coach. We fought and performed well right from the kick-off, the lineouts were the best of our whole Six Nations campaign and the fans were, once more, a key factor. Everybody deserved to win on that day, one player in particular."

That player was Fabio Ongaro who was retiring from international rugby at the end of the Championship and tighthead prop Martin Castrogiovanni summed up the contribution of the 34-year-old to Italian rugby by immediately handing him his RBS Man of the Match medal.

"Fabio played a few more RaboDirect PRO12 games before retiring from rugby at the end of the season and is now team manager for the new Italian franchise team, the Zebre. Fabio is our most capped hooker in Italian rugby, a guy who gave an enormous contribution to our national team and a great friend of mine. The night before the Scotland game I dreamt we would beat Scotland and Fabio would leave the field celebrated by the whole team ... and so it was to be."

The Six Nations was over for another year with Italy having lost four and won one match under Brunel and attention now started to turn to their tour of the Americas in June with Test matches scheduled against Argentina, Canada and USA. A trip they would ultimately make without their inspirational leader after Parisse suffered a serious hamstring injury while playing for Stade Français in the climax of the Top 14 regular season. Parisse initially retained his place in the 30-man squad named by Brunel, but failed to recover in time to lead the Azzurri challenge.

"It was an important experience for the team, that is the most important thing. We left Italy with seven uncapped guys, six of them made their debut in the Test arena on that tour, and it was a good opportunity for Jacques to see some young talented players at the highest level.

"Jacques put the emphasis on a young team, just as was the case in 2002 when Castrogiovanni, Bortolami, myself and many others played our first Tests. We lost to Argentina but we won two games against tough Canada and USA teams and the youngsters had a great experience and will have grown in confidence.

"Many young, talented players are coming through the FIR Academy system, playing their club rugby in both the RaboDirect PRO12 and the Heineken Cup. It is crucial for our rugby that more and more young Italian players are reaching the top level of the game in order to develop the national team, to create a strong, positive internal competition for places."

The future potential for Italian rugby was also being highlighted in Romania where the newly-formed Italia Emergenti impressed at the IRB Nations Cup in early June, beating the national teams of Russia and Portugal before losing narrowly to their hosts in the winner-takes-all encounter on the final day to miss out on the title. There was a setback, though, at the IRB Junior World Championship in South Africa where Italy's Under 20s were hit by injuries to several key players and subsequently relegated to the IRB Junior World Rugby Trophy in 2013.

The Azzurri will finish 2012 with Tests against Tonga, New Zealand and Australia in November and Parisse is confident that under Brunel the team will continue to evolve. "We're developing our rugby, we know which areas of the game Italy must improve and Jacques is working hard with us in this sense. We believe he is doing a great job. He is an ambitious coach and we want to grow, to develop and become a better team. We share his vision, we appreciate the rugby he is trying to make us play, but we know it will take time before we will perform as he and we want to, playing the rugby he wants us to play. It won't be a quick process, but we are on the right path."

ITALY INTERNATIONAL STATISTICS

MATCH RECORDS UP TO 10 OCTOBER 2012

WINNING MARGIN

Date	Opponent	Result	Winning Margin
18/05/1994	Czech Republic	104–8	96
07/10/2006	Portugal	83–0	83
17/06/1993	Croatia	76–11	65
19/06/1993	Morocco	70–9	61
02/03/1996	Portugal	64–3	61

MOST POINTS IN A MATCH
BY THE TEAM

Date	Opponent	Result	Points
18/05/1994	Czech Republic	104–8	104
07/10/2006	Portugal	83–0	83
17/06/1993	Croatia	76–11	76
19/06/1993	Morocco	70–9	70

BY A PLAYER

Date	Player	Opponent	Points
10/11/2001	Diego Dominguez	Fiji	29
05/02/2000	Diego Dominguez	Scotland	29
01/07/1983	Stefano Bettarello	Canada	29
21/05/1994	Diego Dominguez	Netherlands	28
20/12/1997	Diego Dominguez	Ireland	27

MOST TRIES IN A MATCH
BY THE TEAM

Date	Opponent	Result	Tries
18/05/1994	Czech Republic	104–8	16
07/10/2006	Portugal	83–0	13
18/11/1998	Netherlands	67–7	11
17/06/1993	Croatia	76–11	11

BY A PLAYER

Date	Player	Opponent	Tries
19/06/1993	Ivan Francescato	Morocco	4
10/10/1937	Renzo Cova	Belgium	4

MOST CONVERSIONS IN A MATCH
BY THE TEAM

Date	Opponent	Result	Cons
18/05/1994	Czech Republic	104–8	12
19/06/1993	Morocco	70–9	10
17/06/1993	Croatia	76–11	9
07/10/2006	Portugal	83–0	9

BY A PLAYER

Date	Player	Opponent	Cons
18/05/1994	Luigi Troiani	Czech Republic	12
19/06/1993	Gabriel Filizzola	Morocco	10
17/06/1993	Luigi Troiani	Croatia	9

MOST PENALTIES IN A MATCH
BY THE TEAM

Date	Opponent	Result	Pens
01/10/1994	Romania	24–6	8
27/11/2010	Fiji	24–16	8
10/11/2001	Fiji	66–10	7

BY A PLAYER

Date	Player	Opponent	Pens
01/10/1994	Diego Dominguez	Romania	8
27/11/2010	Mirco Bergamasco	Fiji	8
10/11/2001	Diego Dominguez	Fiji	7

MOST DROP GOALS IN A MATCH
BY THE TEAM

Date	Opponent	Result	DGs
07/10/1990	Romania	29–21	3
05/02/2000	Scotland	34–20	3
11/07/1973	Transvaal	24–28	3

BY A PLAYER

Date	Player	Opponent	DGs
05/02/2000	Diego Dominguez	Scotland	3
11/07/1973	Rocco Caligiuri	Transvaal	3

MOST CAPPED PLAYERS

Player	Caps
Alessandro Troncon	101
Andrea Lo Cicero	95
Marco Bortolami	94
Mauro Bergamasco	92
Sergio Parisse	88
Martin Castrogiovanni	88

LEADING TRY SCORERS

Player	Tries
Marcello Cuttitta	25
Paolo Vaccari	22
Manrico Marchetto	21
Carlo Checchinato	21
Alessandro Troncon	19

LEADING CONVERSION SCORERS

Player	Cons
Diego Dominguez	127
Luigi Troiani	57
Stefano Bettarello	46
David Bortolussi	35
Ramiro Pez	33

LEADING PENALTY SCORERS

Player	Pens
Diego Dominguez	209
Stefano Bettarello	106
Luigi Troiani	57
Ramiro Pez	52
Mirco Bergamasco	49

LEADING DROP GOAL SCORERS

Player	DGs
Diego Dominguez	19
Stefano Bettarello	15
Ramiro Pez	6

LEADING POINT SCORERS

Player	Points
Diego Dominguez	983
Stefano Bettarello	483
Luigi Troiani	294
Ramiro Pez	260
Mirco Bergamasco	256

ITALY

ITALY INTERNATIONAL PLAYERS
UP TO 10 OCTOBER 2012

E Abbiati 1968 *WGe*, 1970 *R*, 1971 *Mor*, *F*, 1972 *Pt*, *Sp*, *Sp*, *Yug*, 1973 *Pt*, *ETv*, 1974 *Leo*
A Agosti 1933 *Cze*
M Aguero 2005 *Tg*, *Ar*, *Fj*, 2006 *Fj*, 2007 *Ur*, *Ar*, *I*, *Pt*, 2008 *A*, *Ar*, *Pl*, 2009 *A*, 2010 *I*, *E*, *S*, *F*, *W*
A Agujari 1967 *Pt*
E Aio 1974 *WGe*
G Aiolfi 1952 *Sp*, *Ger*, *F*, 1953 *F*, 1955 *Ger*, *F*
A Alacevich 1939 *R*
A Albonico 1934 *R*, 1935 *F*, 1936 *Ger*, *R*, 1937 *Ger*, *R*, *Bel*, *Ger*, *F*, 1938 *Ger*
N Aldorvandi 1994 *Sp*, *CZR*, *H*
M Alfonsetti 1994 *F*
E Allevi *Sp*, 1933 *Cze*
V Ambron 1962 *Ger*, *R*, 1963 *F*, 1964 *Ger*, *F*, 1965 *F*, *Cze*, 1966 *F*, *Cze*, *R*, 1967 *Pt*, *R*, 1968 *F*, *WGe*, *Yug*, 1969 *Bul*, *Sp*, *Bel*, 1970 *Mad*, *Mad*, *R*, 1971 *Mor*, 1972 *Sp*, *Sp*
R Ambrosio 1987 *NZ*, *USS*, *Sp*, 1988 *F*, *R*, *A*, *I*, 1989 *R*, *Sp*, *Ar*, *Z*, *USS*
B Ancillotti 1978 *Sp*, 1979 *F*, *Pol*, *R*
E Andina 1952 *F*, 1955 *F*
C Angelozzi 1979 *E*, *Mor*, 1980 *Coo*

A Angioli 1960 *Ger*, *F*, 1961 *Ger*, *F*, 1962 *F*, *Ger*, *R*, 1963 *F Yug*, 1973 *Pt*, *ETv*, 1974 *Leo*
A Angrisiani 1979 *Mor*, *F*, *Pol*, *USS*, *Mor*, 1980 *Coo*, 1984 *Tun*
S Annibal 1980 *Fj*, *Coo*, *Pol*, *Sp*, 1981 *F*, *WGe*, 1982 *R*, *E*, *WGe*, 1983 *F*, *USS*, *Sp*, *Mor*, *F*, *A*, 1984 *F*, 1985 *F*, *Z*, *Z*, 1986 *Tun*, *F*, *Pt*, 1990 *F*
JM Antoni 2001 *Nm*, *SA*
C Appiani 1976 *Sp*, 1977 *Mor*, *Pol*, *Sp*, 1978 *USS*
S Appiani 1985 *R*, 1986 *Pt*, 1988 *A*, 1989 *F*
O Arancio 1993 *Rus*, 1994 *CZR*, *H*, *A*, *A*, *R*, *W*, *F*, 1995 *S*, *I*, *Sa*, *E*, *Ar*, *F*, *R*, *NZ*, *SA*, 1996 *W*, *Pt*, *W*, *A*, *E*, *S*, 1997 *I*, *I*, 1998 *S*, *Ar*, *E*, 1999 *F*, *W*, *I*, *SA*, *E*, *NZ*
D Armellin 1965 *Cze*, 1966 *Ger*, 1968 *Pt*, *WGe*, *Yug*, 1969 *Bul*, *Sp*, *Bel*, *F*
A Arrigoni 1949 *Cze*
G Artuso 1977 *Pol*, *R*, 1978 *Sp*, 1979 *F*, *E*, *NZ*, *Mor*, 1980 *F*, *R*, *JAB*, 1981 *F*, 1982 *F*, *E*, *Mor*, 1983 *F*, *R*, *USS*, *C*, *C*, 1984 *USS*, 1985 *R*, *EngB*, *USS*, *R*, 1986 *Tun*, *F*, *Tun*, 1987 *Pt*, *F*, *R*, *NZ*
E Augeri 1962 *F*, *Ger*, *R*, 1963 *F*
A Autore 1961 *Ger*, *F*, 1962 *F*, 1964 *Ger*, 1966 *Ger*, 1968 *Pt*, *WGe*, *Yug*, 1969 *Bul*, *Sp*, *Bel*, *F*
L Avigo 1959 *F*, 1962 *F*, *Ger*, *R*, 1963 *F*, 1964 *Ger*, *F*, 1965 *F*, *Cze*, 1966 *Ger*, *R*
R Aymonod 1933 *Cze*, 1934 *Cat*, *R*, 1935 *F*
A Azzali 1981 *WGe*, 1982 *F*, *R*, *WGe*, 1983 *F*, *R*, *USS*, *Sp*, *Mor*, *F*, 1984 *F*, *Mor*, *R*, 1985 *R*, *EngB*, *Sp*
S Babbo 1996 *Pt*

A **Bacchetti** 2009 *I, S*
A **Balducci** 1929 *Sp*
F **Baraldi** 1973 *Cze, Yug,* 1974 *Mid, Sus, Oxo,* 1975 *E, Pol, H, Sp,* 1976 *F, R, A,* 1977 *F, Mor, Cze*
R **Baraldi** 1971 *R*
A **Barattin** 1996 *A, E*
S **Barba** 1985 *R, EngB,* 1986 *E, A,* 1987 *Pt, F, R, Ar, Fj,* 1988 *R, USS, A,* 1990 *F, Pol, Sp, H, R, USS,* 1991 *F, R, Nm, Nm, US, E, USS,* 1992 *Sp, F, R, R, S,* 1993 *Sp, F, Cro, Mor, Sp*
RJ **Barbieri** 2006 *J, Fj, Pt,* 2007 *Ur, Ar, I,* 2008 *SA,* 2010 *Ar, A, Fj,* 2011 *E, W, F, S, S, A,* 2012 *F, E, I, W, S, Ar, C, US*
G **Barbini** 1978 *USS*
M **Barbini** 2002 *NZ, Sp, Ar, A,* 2003 *I, NZ,* 2004 *F, I, R, J, NZ, US,* 2005 *W, E,* 2007 *I*
N **Barbini** 1953 *Ger, R,* 1954 *Sp, F,* 1955 *Ger, F, Sp, Cze,* 1956 *Ger,* 1957 *Ger,* 1958 *R,* 1960 *Ger, F*
F **Bargelli** 1979 *E, Sp, Mor, F, Pol, USS, NZ, Mor,* 1980 *F, R, Fj, Sp,* 1981 *F, R*
S **Barilari** 1948 *Cze,* 1953 *Ger, R*
M **Baroni** 1999 *F, W, I, SA, SA,* 2000 *C*
V **Barzaghi** 1929 *Sp,* 1930 *Sp,* 1933 *Cze*
JL **Basei** 1979 *E, Sp, Mor, F, Pol, USS, NZ, Mor,* 1980 *F, R, Fj, JAB, Coo, USS,* 1981 *R*
A **Battagion** 1948 *F, Cze*
F **Battaglini** 1948 *F*
M **Battaglini** 1940 *R, Ger,* 1951 *Sp,* 1953 *F, R*
A **Becca** 1937 *R,* 1938 *Ger,* 1939 *R,* 1940 *Ger*
E **Bellinazzo** 1958 *R,* 1959 *F,* 1960 *Ger, F,* 1961 *Ger, F,* 1962 *F, Ger,* 1964 *Ger, F,* 1966 *F, Ger, R,* 1967 *F*
A **Benatti** 2001 *Fj, SA, Sa,* 2002 *W,* 2003 *NZ*
A **Benettin** 2012 *C*
C **Bentivoglio** 1977 *Pol*
T **Benvenuti** 2010 *Ar, A, Fj,* 2011 *W, F, S, J, S, A, Rus, US, I,* 2012 *F, E, I, W, S, Ar, C, US*
D **Beretta** 1993 *S*
A **Bergamasco** 1973 *Bor, Tva,* 1977 *Pol,* 1978 *USS*
M **Bergamasco** 1998 *H, E,* 1999 *SA, E,* 2000 *S, W, I, E, F, C,* 2001 *I, E, F, S, W, Fj, SA, Sa,* 2002 *F, S, W, I, E, NZ, Sp, A,* 2003 *W, I, S, I, Geo, NZ, Tg, W,* 2004 *J, C, NZ,* 2005 *I, W, Ar, A, Ar, Fj,* 2006 *I, E, F, J, Fj, Pt, Rus, A, Ar, C,* 2007 *F, S, W, J, NZ, R, Pt, S,* 2008 *I, E, W, Ar, A, PI,* 2009 *E, I, S, W, F, A, NZ, NZ, SA, Sa,* 2010 *I, E, S, F, W,* 2011 *J, Rus, US, I,* 2012 *E, Ar, C, US*
M **Bergamasco** 2002 *F, S, W, Ar, A,* 2003 *W, I, E, F, S, S, Geo, NZ, C,* 2004 *E, F, S, I, W,* 2005 *I, W, S, Tg, Ar, Fj,* 2006 *I, E, F, W, S, J, Fj, Pt, Rus, A, Ar, C,* 2007 *F, E, S, W, I, J, I, NZ, R, S,* 2008 *I, E, W, F, S, A, Ar, PI,* 2009 *E, I, S, W, F, A, NZ, NZ, SA, Sa,* 2010 *I, E, S, F, W, SA, Ar, A, Fj,* 2011 *I, E, W, F, S, S, A, US, I,* 2012 *W, S*
L **Bernabo** 1970 *Mad, Mad, R,* 1972 *Sp, Sp*
V **Bernabò** 2004 *US,* 2005 *Tg, Fj,* 2007 *E, S, W, I, Ur, Ar, J, I, NZ, R,* 2010 *W, SA,* 2011 *I, E, W, S*
F **Berni** 1985 *R, Sp, Z, Z,* 1986 *E, A,* 1987 *R, NZ,* 1988 *A,* 1989 *F*
D **Bertoli** 1967 *R*
V **Bertolotto** 1936 *Ger, R,* 1937 *Ger, R,* 1942 *R,* 1948 *F*
O **Bettarello** 1958 *F,* 1959 *F,* 1961 *Ger*
R **Bettarello** 1953 *Ger, R*
S **Bettarello** 1979 *Pol, E, Sp, F, NZ, Mor,* 1980 *F, R, Fj, JAB, Coo, Pol, USS, Sp,* 1981 *F, R, USS, WGe,* 1982 *F, R, E, WGe, Mor,* 1983 *F, R, USS, C, Sp, Mor, F, A,* 1984 *F, Mor, R, Tun, USS,* 1985 *F, R, EngB, Sp, Z, USS, R,* 1986 *Tun, F, Pt, E, A, Tun, USS,* 1987 *R, USS, Sp,* 1988 *USS, A*
L **Bettella** 1969 *Sp, Bel, F*
R **Bevilacqua** 1937 *Bel, Ger, F,* 1938 *Ger,* 1939 *Ger, R,* 1940 *R, Ger,* 1942 *R*
C **Bezzi** 2003 *W, I, E, F, S, I, NZ, W,* 2004 *US,* 2005 *Ar, A*
G **Biadene** 1958 *R,* 1959 *F*
G **Bigi** 1930 *Sp,* 1933 *Cze*
M **Bimbati** 1989 *Z*
M **Birtig** 1998 *H,* 1999 *F*
F **Blessano** 1975 *F, R, Pol, H, Sp,* 1976 *F, R, J,* 1977 *F, Mor, Pol, R, Cze, R, Sp,* 1978 *F, Ar, Sp,* 1979 *F, Pol, R*
L **Boccaletto** 1969 *Bul, Bel, F,* 1970 *Cze, Mad, Mad, R,* 1971 *F, R,* 1972 *Pt, Sp, Sp,* 1975 *E*
S **Boccazzi** 1985 *Z,* 1988 *USS*

R **Bocchino** 2010 *I, F, W, SA, A, Fj,* 2011 *J, S, A, Rus, US, I,* 2012 *Ar, US*
M **Bocconelli** 1967 *R*
M **Bollesan** 1963 *F,* 1964 *F,* 1965 *F,* 1966 *F, Ger,* 1967 *F, Pt,* 1968 *Pt, WGe, Yug,* 1969 *Bul, Sp, Bel, F,* 1970 *Cze, Mad, Mad, R,* 1971 *Mor, F, R,* 1972 *Pt, Pt, Sp, Sp, Yug, A,* 1974 *Pt, Mid, Sus, Oxo, WGe, Leo,* 1975 *F, Sp, Cze*
A **Bona** 1972 *Sp, Yug,* 1973 *Rho, WTv, Bor, NEC, Nat, ETv, Leo, FS, Tva, Cze, Yug, A,* 1974 *Pt, WGe, Leo,* 1975 *F, Sp, R, Cze, E, Pol, H, Sp,* 1976 *F, R, J, A, Sp,* 1977 *F, Mor,* 1978 *Ar, USS, Sp,* 1979 *F, Sp, Mor, F, Pol, USS, NZ, Mor,* 1980 *F, R, Fj, JAB, Pol, Sp,* 1981 *F*
L **Bonaiti** 1979 *R,* 1980 *Pol*
G **Bonati** 1939 *Ger, R*
S **Bonetti** 1972 *Yug,* 1973 *Rho, WTv, Bor, NEC, Nat, ETv, Leo, FS, Tva,* 1974 *Pt, Mid, Sus, Oxo, Leo,* 1975 *F, Sp, R, Cze, E, Pol, H, Sp,* 1976 *R, J, A, Sp,* 1977 *F, Mor, R, Sp,* 1978 *F,* 1979 *F,* 1980 *USS*
S **Bonfante** 1936 *Ger, R*
G **Bonino** 1949 *F*
M **Bonomi** 1988 *F, R,* 1990 *Sp, H, R, USS,* 1991 *F, R, Nm, Nm, E, NZ, USS,* 1992 *R, R,* 1993 *Cro, Mor, Sp, F, S,* 1994 *Sp, R, H, A, A, W,* 1995 *S, I, Sa, F, Ar, R, NZ,* 1996 *W*
S **Bordon** 1990 *R, USS,* 1991 *Nm, USS,* 1992 *F, R,* 1993 *Sp, F, Pt, Rus, F,* 1994 *R, A, A, R, W, F,* 1995 *I, E, Ar, F, Ar, NZ, SA,* 1996 *W, A, E,* 1997 *I, F*
L **Borsetto** 1977 *Pol*
V **Borsetto** 1948 *F, Cze*
M **Bortolami** 2001 *Nm, SA, Fj, SA, Sa,* 2002 *F, S, W, I, E, NZ, Sp, R, Ar, A,* 2003 *W, I, E, S, Geo, Tg, C,* 2004 *E, F, S, I, W, R, J, C, NZ,* 2005 *I, W, S, E, F, Ar, Ar, A, Tg, Ar, Fj,* 2006 *I, E, F, W, S, J, Fj, Pt, Rus, A, Ar, C,* 2007 *F, S, W, I, J, I, NZ, R, Pt,* 2008 *W, F, S, A, Ar, PI,* 2009 *E, S, W, F, A, A, NZ,* 2010 *I, E, S, F, W, SA, SA,* 2011 *J, A, Rus, I,* 2012 *F, E, I, W, S, Ar*
G **Bortolini** 1933 *Cze,* 1934 *Cat*
D **Bortolussi** 2006 *J, Fj, Pt, Rus, Ar, C,* 2007 *Ur, Ar, J, I, NZ, R, Pt, S,* 2008 *I, E*
L **Boscaino** 1967 *Pt*
L **Bossi** 1940 *R, Ger*
T **Botes** 2012 *F, E, I, W, S*
A **Bottacchiara** 1991 *NZ, USS,* 1992 *Sp, F, R, R*
G **Bottacin** 1956 *Cze*
O **Bottonelli** 1929 *Sp,* 1934 *R,* 1935 *Cat, F,* 1937 *Ger,* 1939 *Ger*
L **Bove** 1948 *Cze,* 1949 *F, Cze*
O **Bracaglia** 1939 *R*
M **Braga** 1958 *R*
L **Bricchi** 1929 *Sp,* 1930 *Sp,* 1933 *Cze*
L **Brighetti** 1934 *Cat*
A **Brunelli** 1969 *Bel,* 1970 *Mad,* 1971 *F*
M **Brunello** 1988 *I,* 1989 *F,* 1990 *F, Sp, H, R, USS,* 1993 *Pt*
S **Brusin** 1957 *Ger*
KS **Burton** 2007 *Ur, Ar,* 2009 *A, NZ,* 2011 *I, E, W, F, S,* 2012 *F, E, I, W, S, Ar, C, US*
P **Buso** 2008 *W*
G **Busson** 1957 *Ger,* 1958 *R,* 1959 *F,* 1960 *Ger, F,* 1961 *Ger, F,* 1962 *F, Ger,* 1963 *F*
F **Caccia-Dominioni** 1935 *F,* 1937 *Ger*
C **Caione** 1995 *R,* 1996 *Pt,* 1997 *F, R,* 1998 *Rus, Ar, H, E,* 1999 *F, S, SA, Ur, Sp, Fj, Tg, NZ,* 2000 *Sa, Fj, C, R, NZ,* 2001 *I, E, S, Fj*
R **Caligiuri** 1969 *F,* 1973 *Pt, Rho, WTv, NEC, Nat, ETv, Leo, FS, Tva,* 1975 *E, Pol, H, Sp,* 1976 *F, R, J, A, Sp,* 1978 *F, Ar, USS, Sp,* 1979 *F, Pol, R*
A **Caluzzi** 1970 *R,* 1971 *Mor, F,* 1972 *Pt, Pt, Sp, Sp,* 1973 *Pt,* 1974 *Oxo, WGe, Leo*
P **Camiscioni** 1975 *E,* 1976 *R, J, A, Sp,* 1977 *F,* 1978 *F*
M **Campagna** 1933 *Cze,* 1934 *Cat,* 1936 *Ger, R,* 1937 *Ger, R, Bel,* 1938 *Ger*
GJ **Canale** 2003 *S, Geo, NZ, Tg, C, W,* 2004 *S, I, W, R, J, C,* 2005 *I, Ar, Ar, A, Tg, Ar, Fj,* 2006 *I, E, F, W, S, A, Ar, C,* 2007 *F, E, S, W, J, I, R, Pt, S,* 2008 *I, E, W, F, S, A,* 2009 *E, I, S, W, F, A, NZ, NZ, SA,* 2010 *I, E, S, F, W, SA, SA, Ar, A, Fj,* 2011 *I, E, W, F, S, J, S, A, Rus, US, I,* 2012 *F, E, I, W, S*

354

JF **Montauriol** 2009 *E, A*
G **Morelli** 1988 *I*, 1989 *F, R*
G **Morelli** 1976 *F*, 1982 *F, R, Mor*, 1983 *R, C, Sp, A, USS*, 1984 *Mor, R, USS*, 1985 *R, EngB, Z, Z, USS, R*, 1986 *Tun, F, E, A, Tun, USS*, 1987 *F, NZ*
G **Morelli** 1981 *WGe*, 1982 *R, E, Mor*, 1983 *USS*, 1984 *F*
A **Moreno** 1999 *Tg, NZ*, 2002 *F, S*, 2008 *Ar*
A **Moretti** 1997 *R*, 1998 *Rus*, 1999 *Ur, Sp, Tg, NZ*, 2002 *E, NZ, Sp, R, Ar, A*, 2005 *Ar*
U **Moretti** 1933 *Cze*, 1934 *R*, 1935 *Cat*, 1937 *R, Ger, F*, 1942 *R*
A **Morimondi** 1930 *Sp*, 1933 *Cze*, 1934 *Cat*, 1935 *Cat*
LE **Morisi** 2012 *E, US*
A **Moscardi** 1993 *Pt*, 1995 *R*, 1996 *S*, 1998 *Ar, H, E*, 1999 *F, S, W, I, SA, SA, Ur, Fj, E, Tg, NZ*, 2000 *S, W, I, E, F, Sa, Fj, C, R, NZ*, 2001 *I, E, F, S, W, Nm, SA, Ur, Ar, Fj, SA, Sa*, 2002 *F, S, W, I, E*
A **Muraro** 2000 *C, R, NZ*, 2001 *I, E, Nm, SA, Ur, Ar, Fj, SA, Sa*, 2002 *F*
E **Nathan** 1930 *Sp*
G **Navarini** 1957 *Ger*, 1958 *R*
M **Nicolosi** 1982 *R*
C **Nieto** 2002 *E*, 2005 *Ar, Ar, A, Tg, Ar, Fj*, 2006 *I, E, F, W, J, Fj, A, Ar, C*, 2007 *F, S, W, I, Ar*, 2008 *E, F, S, SA, Ar, A, Ar, Pl*, 2009 *E, I, S, W, F*
A **Nisti** 1929 *Sp*, 1930 *Sp*
L **Nitoglia** 2004 *C, NZ, US*, 2005 *I, W, S, E, F, Ar, Tg, Ar, Fj*, 2006 *I, E, F, W, S*
F **Ongaro** 2000 *C*, 2001 *Nm, SA, Ur, Ar*, 2002 *Ar, A*, 2003 *E, F, S, I, Geo, NZ, Tg, C, W*, 2004 *E, F, S, I, W, R, J, C, NZ, US*, 2005 *I, W, S, E, F, Tg, Ar, Fj*, 2006 *I, E, F, W, S, J, Fj, Pt, Rus, Ar, C*, 2007 *F, S, Ur, Ar, I, NZ, S*, 2008 *F, S, SA, Ar, A, Ar, Pl*, 2009 *E, I, NZ, SA, Sa*, 2010 *I, E, S, F, W, SA, SA, Ar, A, Fj*, 2011 *I, E, S, Rus, US, I*, 2012 *S*
C **Orlandi** 1992 *S*, 1993 *Sp, F, Mor, F, Rus, F, S*, 1994 *Sp, CZR, H, A, A, R, W*, 1995 *S, I, Sa, E, Ar, F, Ar, R, NZ, SA*, 1996 *W, Pt, W, A, E, S*, 1997 *I, F, F, Ar, R, SA, I*, 1998 *S, W*, 2000 *W, F*
S **Orlando** 2004 *E, S, W, C, NZ, US*, 2005 *E, F, Ar, A*, 2006 *J*, 2007 *Ur, Ar, Pt*
L **Orquera** 2004 *C, NZ, US*, 2005 *I, W, S, E, F, Ar, Tg*, 2008 *A, Ar*, 2009 *W, F*, 2010 *Ar, A, Fj*, 2011 *I, E, W, F, S, J, S, A, US, I*
A **Osti** 1981 *F, R, USS*, 1982 *E, Mor*, 1983 *R, C, A, USS*, 1984 *R, USS*, 1985 *F*, 1986 *Tun*, 1988 *R*
S **Pace** 2001 *SA, Sa*, 2005 *Fj*
S **Pace** 1977 *Mor*, 1984 *R, Tun*
P **Pacifici** 1969 *Bul, Sp, F*, 1970 *Cze, Mad, Mad, R*, 1971 *Mor, F*
R **Paciucci** 1937 *R, Ger, F*
F **Paganelli** 1972 *Sp*
S **Palmer** 2002 *Ar, A*, 2003 *I, E, F, S, S, NZ, C, W*, 2004 *I, R*
P **Paoletti** 1972 *Pt, Sp, Yug*, 1973 *Pt, Rho, WTv, Bor, NEC, Nat, ETv, Leo, FS, Tva*, 1974 *Mid, Oxo, WGe, Leo*, 1975 *F, Sp*, 1976 *R*
T **Paoletti** 2000 *S, W, I, E, F, Sa, C, R, NZ*, 2001 *F, Nm, Ur, Ar, Fj, SA*
G **Paolin** 1929 *Sp*
S **Parisse** 2002 *NZ, Sp, R, Ar, A*, 2003 *S, I, Geo, NZ, Tg, C, W*, 2004 *E, F, S*, 2005 *I, W, S, E, F, Ar, Ar, A, Tg, Ar, Fj*, 2006 *I, E, F, W, S, Fj, Pt, Rus, Ar, C*, 2007 *F, E, S, W, I, J, I, NZ, R, Pt, S*, 2008 *I, E, W, F, S, Ar, A, Ar, Pl*, 2009 *E, I, S, W, F, A, A, NZ, NZ, SA*, 2010 *SA, SA, Ar, A, Fj*, 2011 *I, E, W, F, S, J, S, A, Rus, US, I*, 2012 *F, E, I, W, S*
E **Parmiggiani** 1942 *R*, 1948 *Cze*
P **Paselli** 1929 *Sp*, 1930 *Sp*, 1933 *Cze*
E **Passarotto** 1975 *Sp*
E **Patrizio** 2007 *Ur*, 2008 *F, S, SA*
R **Pavan** 2008 *SA*
A **Pavanello** 2007 *Ar*, 2009 *SA, Sa*, 2012 *E, I, Ar, C, US*
E **Pavanello** 2002 *R, Ar, A*, 2004 *R, J, C, NZ, US*, 2005 *Ar, A*
P **Pavesi** 1977 *Pol*, 1979 *Mor*, 1980 *USS*
M **Pavin** 1980 *USS*, 1986 *F, Pt, E, A, Tun, USS*, 1987 *Ar*
R **Pedrazzi** 2001 *Nm, Ar*, 2002 *F, S, W*, 2005 *S, E, F*
P **Pedroni** 1989 *Z, USS*, 1990 *F, Pol, R*, 1991 *F, R, Nm*, 1993

Rus, F, 1994 *Sp, R, CZR, H*, 1995 *I, Sa, E, Ar, F, Ar, R, NZ, SA*, 1996 *W, W*
G **Peens** 2002 *W, I, E, NZ, Sp, R, Ar, A*, 2003 *E, F, S, S, I, Geo, NZ*, 2004 *NZ*, 2005 *E, F, Ar, Ar, A*, 2006 *Pt, A*
L **Pelliccione** 1983 *Sp, Mor, F*
L **Pelliccione** 1977 *Pol*
M **Percudani** 1952 *F*, 1954 *F*, 1955 *Ger, Sp, F, Cze*, 1956 *Cze*, 1957 *F*, 1958 *R*
F **Perrini** 1955 *Sp, F, Cze*, 1956 *Ger, F, Cze*, 1957 *F*, 1958 *F*, 1959 *F*, 1962 *R*, 1963 *F*
F **Perrone** 1951 *Sp*
AR **Persico** 2000 *S, W, E, F, Sa, Fj*, 2001 *F, S, W, Nm, SA, Ur, Ar, Fj, SA, Sa*, 2002 *F, S, W, I, E, NZ, Sp, R, Ar, A*, 2003 *W, I, E, F, S, I, Geo, Tg, C, W*, 2004 *E, F, S, I, W, R, J, C, NZ*, 2005 *I, W, S, E, F, Ar, Ar, Tg, Ar*, 2006 *I, E*
J **Pertile** 1994 *R*, 1995 *Ar*, 1996 *W, A, E, S*, 1997 *I, F, SA*, 1998 *Rus*, 1999 *S, W, I, SA, SA*
S **Perugini** 2000 *I, F, Sa, Fj*, 2001 *S, W, Nm, SA, Ur, Ar*, 2002 *W, I*, 2003 *W, S, Geo, NZ, Tg, W*, 2004 *E, F, I, W, C, NZ, US*, 2005 *I, W, S, E, F*, 2006 *I, E, F, W, S, Pt, Rus*, 2007 *F, E, S, W, I, J, I, NZ, Pt, S*, 2008 *I, E, W, F, S, A, Ar, Pl*, 2009 *E, I, S, W, F, A, A, NZ, NZ, SA, Sa*, 2010 *I, E, S, F, W, SA, SA, Ar, Fj*, 2011 *I, E, W, F, S, Rus, US, I*
L **Perziano** 1993 *Pt*
M **Perziano** 2000 *NZ*, 2001 *F, S, W, Nm, SA, Ur, Ar, Fj, SA*
V **Pesce** 1988 *I*, 1989 *R*
P **Pescetto** 1956 *Ger, Cze*, 1957 *F*
G **Petralia** 1984 *F*
R **Pez** 2000 *Sa, Fj, C, R, NZ*, 2001 *I*, 2002 *S, W, E, A*, 2003 *I, E, F, S, S, Geo*, 2005 *Ar, A, Tg, Ar, Fj*, 2006 *I, E, F, W, S, J, Fj, Pt, Rus, A, Ar*, 2007 *F, E, S, W, I, J, R, S*
M **Phillips** 2002 *F, S, W, I, E*, 2003 *W, I, E, F, S, S, I, NZ, W*
G **Pianna** 1934 *R*, 1935 *Cat, F*, 1936 *Ger, R*, 1938 *Ger*
A **Piazza** 1990 *USS*
F **Piccini** 1963 *F*, 1964 *Ger*, 1966 *F*
S **Picone** 2004 *I, W*, 2005 *F*, 2006 *E, F, S, J, Pt, Rus, Ar, C*, 2008 *E, W, F, S, SA, Ar*, 2009 *NZ, SA, Sa*, 2010 *I, SA, SA*
F **Pietroscanti** 1987 *USS, Sp*, 1988 *A, I*, 1989 *F, R, Sp, Ar, Z, USS*, 1990 *F, Pol, R, H*, 1991 *Nm, Nm*, 1992 *Sp, F, R*, 1993 *Sp, Mor, Sp, F, Rus, F*
F **Pignotti** 1968 *WGe, Yug*, 1969 *Bul, Sp, Bel*
C **Pilat** 1997 *I*, 1998 *S, W*, 2000 *E, Sa*, 2001 *I, W*
MJ **Pini** 1998 *H, E*, 1999 *F, Ur, Fj, E, Tg, NZ*, 2000 *S, W, I, F*
M **Piovan** 1973 *Pt*, 1974 *Pt, Mid, Sus, Oxo*, 1976 *A*, 1977 *F, Mor, R*, 1979 *F*
R **Piovan** 1996 *Pt*, 1997 *R*, 2000 *R, NZ*
M **Piovene** 1995 *NZ*
E **Piras** 1971 *R*
M **Pisaneschi** 1948 *Cze*, 1949 *Cze*, 1953 *F, Ger, R*, 1954 *Sp, F*, 1955 *Ger, F, Sp, F, Cze*
F **Pitorri** 1948 *Cze*, 1949 *F*
M **Pitorri** 1973 *NEC*
G **Pivetta** 1979 *R, E, Mor*, 1980 *Coo*, 1981 *R, USS, WGe*, 1982 *F, R, WGe, Mor*, 1983 *F, USS, C, Sp, Mor, F, USS*, 1984 *F, Mor, R, Tun*, 1985 *F, R, Sp, Z, Z*, 1986 *Pt*, 1987 *Sp*, 1989 *R, Sp*, 1990 *F, Pol, R, Sp, R, USS*, 1991 *F, R, Nm, Nm, US, E, NZ, USS*, 1992 *Sp, F, R, R*, 1993 *Cro, Mor, Sp*
M **Platania** 1994 *F*, 1995 *F, R*, 1996 *Pt*
I **Ponchia** 1955 *F, Sp, F, Cze*, 1956 *F*, 1957 *Ger*, 1958 *F*
E **Ponzi** 1973 *Cze, A*, 1974 *WGe*, 1975 *F, Sp, R, Cze, E, Pol, H, Sp*, 1976 *F, R, J, A, Sp*, 1977 *F, Mor, Pol, R*
G **Porcellato** 1989 *R*
G **Porzio** 1970 *Cze, Mad, Mad*
C **Possamai** 1970 *Cze, Mad, Mad*
W **Pozzebon** 2001 *I, E, F, S, W, Nm, SA, Ur, Ar, Fj, SA, Sa*, 2002 *NZ, Sp*, 2004 *R, J, C, NZ, US*, 2005 *W, E*, 2006 *C*
A **Pratichetti** 2012 *C*
C **Pratichetti** 1988 *R*, 1990 *Pol*
M **Pratichetti** 2004 *NZ*, 2007 *E, W, I, Ur, Ar, I, Pt*, 2008 *SA, Ar, Ar, Pl*, 2009 *E, I, S, W, F, A, NZ, SA*, 2010 *W, SA*, 2011 *J, Rus*
G **Preo** 1999 *I*, 2000 *I, E, Sa, Fj, R, NZ*
P **Presutti** 1974 *Mid, Sus, Oxo*, 1977 *Pol, Cze, R, Sp*, 1978 *F*

T Tedeschi 1948 *F*
G Testoni 1937 *Bel*, 1938 *Ger*, 1942 *R*
C Tinari 1980 *JAB, Coo, Pol, USS, Sp*, 1981 *USS, WGe*, 1982 *F, WGe*, 1983 *R, USS, C, C, Sp, Mor, A, USS*, 1984 *Mor, R*
M Tommasi 1990 *Pol*, 1992 *R, S*, 1993 *Pt, Cro, Sp, F*
G Toniolatti 2008 *A*, 2009 *E, I, A, NZ*, 2011 *J, Rus, US*, 2012 *W, S, Ar, C*
C Torresan 1980 *F, R, Fj, Coo, Pol, USS*, 1981 *R, USS*, 1982 *R, Mor*, 1983 *C, F, A, USS*, 1984 *F, Mor, Tun, USS*, 1985 *Z, Z, USS*
F Tozzi 1933 *Cze*
P Travagli 2004 *C, NZ*, 2008 *I, E, W, F, S, Ar, Pl*
L Travini 1999 *SA, Ur, Sp, Fj*, 2000 *I*
F Trebbi 1933 *Cze, Cze*
F Trentin 1979 *Mor, F, Pol, USS*, 1981 *R*
M Trevisiol 1988 *F, USS, A, I*, 1989 *F, Ar, USS*, 1994 *R*
M Trippiteli 1979 *Pol*, 1980 *Pol, Sp*, 1981 *F, R*, 1982 *F, E, WGe*, 1984 *Tun*
LR Troiani 1985 *R*, 1986 *Tun, F, Pt, A, USS*, 1987 *Pt, F*, 1988 *R, USS, A, I*, 1989 *Sp, Ar, Z, USS*, 1990 *F, Pol, R, Sp, H, R, USS*, 1991 *F, R, Nm, Nm, US, E*, 1992 *Sp, F, R, R, S*, 1993 *Sp, F, Cro, Rus, F*, 1994 *Sp, CZR, A, A, F*, 1995 *S, E, Ar*
A Troncon 1994 *Sp, R, CZR, H, A, A, R, W, F*, 1995 *S, I, Sa, E, Ar, F, Ar, R, NZ, SA*, 1996 *W, W, A, E, S*, 1997 *I, F, F, Ar, SA, I*, 1998 *S, W, Rus, Ar, H, E*, 1999 *F, S, W, I, Ur, Sp, Fj, E, Tg, NZ*, 2000 *S, W, I, E, F, R, NZ*, 2001 *I, F, Nm, SA, Ur, Ar, Fj, SA, Sa*, 2002 *F, S, W, I, E, Sp, R, Ar, A*, 2003 *W, I, E, F, S, S, I, Geo, NZ, Tg, C, W*, 2004 *R, J*, 2005 *I, W, S, E, F*, 2007 *F, E, S, W, I, J, I, NZ, R, Pt, S*
G Troncon 1962 *F, Ger, R*, 1963 *F*, 1964 *Ger, F*, 1965 *Cze*, 1966 *F, R*, 1967 *F*, 1968 *Yug*, 1972 *Pt*
L Turcato 1952 *Sp, Ger, F*, 1953 *Ger, R*
M Turcato 1949 *F*, 1951 *Sp*
P Vaccari 1991 *Nm, Nm, US, E, NZ, USS*, 1992 *Sp, F, R, R, S*, 1993 *Mor, Sp, F, Rus, F, S*, 1994 *Sp, R, CZR, H, A, A, R, W, F*, 1995 *I, Sa, E, Ar, F, Ar, R, NZ, SA*, 1996 *W, W, E, S*, 1997 *I, F, F, Ar, R, SA, I*, 1998 *S, W, Ar*, 1999 *Ur, Sp, E, Tg, NZ*, 2001 *Fj*, 2002 *F, S, Ar, A*, 2003 *W, I, E, F, S*
V Vagnetti 1939 *R*, 1940 *R*
F Valier 1968 *Yug*, 1969 *F*, 1970 *Cze, R*, 1971 *Mor, R*, 1972 *Pt*
L Valtorta 1957 *Ger*, 1958 *F*
C Van Zyl 2011 *J, S, A, Rus, US, I*, 2012 *F, W*
G Venditti 2012 *F, E, I, S, Ar, C, US*
O Vene 1966 *F*
E Venturi 1983 *C*, 1985 *EngB, Sp*, 1986 *Tun, Pt*, 1988 *USS, A*, 1989 *F, R, Sp, Ar, USS*, 1990 *F, Pol, R, Sp, H, R, USS*, 1991 *F, R, NZ, USS*, 1992 *Sp, F, R*, 1993 *Sp, F*
P Vezzani 1973 *Yug*, 1975 *F, Sp, R, Cze, E, Pol, H, Sp*, 1976 *F*
F Vialetto 1972 *Yug*
V Viccariotto 1948 *F*

S Vigliano 1937 *R, Bel, Ger, F*, 1939 *R*, 1942 *R*
L Villagra 2000 *Sa, Fj*
E Vinci I 1929 *Sp*
P Vinci II 1929 *Sp*, 1930 *Sp*, 1933 *Cze*
F Vinci III 1929 *Sp*, 1930 *Sp*, 1934 *Cat, R*, 1935 *Cat, F*, 1936 *Ger, R*, 1937 *Ger, R, Ger, F*, 1939 *Ger, R*, 1940 *Ger*
P Vinci IV 1929 *Sp*, 1930 *Sp*, 1933 *Cze, Cze*, 1934 *Cat, R*, 1935 *Cat, F*, 1937 *Ger, Bel, Ger, F*, 1939 *Ger*
A Visentin 1970 *R*, 1972 *Pt, Sp*, 1973 *Rho, WTv, Bor, NEC, Nat, ETv, Leo, FS, Tva, Cze, Yug, A*, 1974 *Pt, Leo*, 1975 *F, Sp, R, Cze*, 1976 *R*, 1978 *Ar*
G Visentin 1935 *Cat, F*, 1936 *R*, 1937 *Ger, Bel, Ger, F*, 1938 *Ger*, 1939 *Ger*
T Visentin 1996 *W*
W Visser 1999 *I, SA, SA*, 2000 *S, W, I, F, C, R, NZ*, 2001 *I, E, F, S, W, Nm, SA, Ur, Ar, Fj, SA, Sa*
F Vitadello 1985 *Sp*, 1987 *Pt*
C Vitelli 1973 *Cze, Yug*, 1974 *Pt, Sus*
I Vittorini 1969 *Sp*
RMS Vosawai 2007 *J, I, NZ, R, Pt*, 2010 *W, SA*, 2011 *W*, 2012 *S*
RS Wakarua 2003 *Tg, C, W*, 2004 *E, F, S, W, J, C, NZ*, 2005 *Fj*
F Williams 1995 *SA*
M Zaffiri 2000 *Fj, R, NZ*, 2001 *W*, 2003 *S*, 2005 *Tg, Fj*, 2006 *W, S, C*, 2007 *E, S, W, I*
R Zanatta 1954 *Sp, F*
G Zanchi 1953 *Ger, R*, 1955 *Sp, Cze*, 1957 *Ger*
A Zanella 1977 *Mor*
M Zanella 1976 *J, Sp*, 1977 *R, Pol, Cze*, 1978 *Ar*, 1980 *Pol, USS*
E Zanetti 1942 *R*
F Zani 1960 *Ger, F*, 1961 *Ger, F*, 1962 *F, R*, 1963 *F*, 1964 *F*, 1965 *F*, 1966 *Ger, R*
G Zani 1934 *R*
A Zanni 2005 *Tg, Ar, Fj*, 2006 *F, W, S, Pt, Rus, A, Ar, C*, 2007 *S, W, I, Ur, I, NZ*, 2008 *I, E, W, F, S, SA, Ar, A, Pl*, 2009 *E, I, S, W, F, A, A, NZ, NZ, SA, Sa*, 2010 *I, E, S, F, W, SA, SA, Ar, A, Fj*, 2011 *I, E, W, F, S, J, S, A, Rus, US, I*, 2012 *F, E, I, W, S, Ar, C, US*
C Zanoletti 2001 *Sa*, 2002 *E, NZ, R, Ar, A*, 2005 *A*
G Zanon 1981 *F, R, USS, WGe*, 1982 *R, E, WGe, Mor*, 1983 *F, R, USS, C, C, Sp, Mor, F, A, USS*, 1984 *F, Mor, R, USS*, 1985 *F, R, EngB, Sp, Z, Z, USS*, 1986 *USS*, 1987 *R, Ar, USS*, 1989 *Sp, Ar*, 1990 *F, Pol, R, Sp, H, R, USS*, 1991 *Nm, US, E*
M Zingarelli 1973 *A*
N Zisti 1999 *E, NZ*, 2000 *E, F*
G Zoffoli 1936 *Ger, R*, 1937 *Ger, R, Ger*, 1938 *Ger*, 1939 *R*
S Zorzi 1985 *R*, 1986 *Tun, F*, 1988 *F, R, USS*, 1992 *R*
A Zucchelo 1956 *Ger, F*
C Zucchi 1952 *Sp*, 1953 *F*
L Zuin 1977 *Cze*, 1978 *Ar, USS, Sp*, 1979 *F, Pol, R*

JAPAN

JAPAN'S 2012 TEST RECORD

OPPONENTS	DATE	VENUE	RESULT
Kazakhstan	28 Apr	A	Won 87–0
UAE	5 May	H	Won 106–3
Korea	12 May	A	Won 52–8
Hong Kong	19 May	H	Won 67–0
Fiji	5 Jun	H	Lost 19–25
Tonga	10 Jun	H	Lost 20–24
Samoa	17 Jun	H	Lost 26–27

BRAVE BLOSSOMS FOCUS ON LONG-TERM GOALS

By Rich Freeman

THE COUNTRIES

Takamichi Sasaki carries the ball forward as Japan beat Hong Kong by 67–0 in the Asian 5 Nations.

Japan's international season began with a new coach. It almost ended the same way.

The Brave Blossoms' failure to win two games at Rugby World Cup 2011 had seen the Japan Rugby Football Union and John Kirwan agree that the New Zealander would not seek an extension of his contract.

Conservative elements within the JRFU made it no secret that they blamed Japan's poor campaign on there being too many 'foreigners' within the national set-up and pushed for a Japanese coach.

But Eddie Jones – who led Suntory Sungoliath to the domestic double of Top League and All-Japan Championship – was eventually named Kirwan's successor with Masahiro Kunda the new assistant coach as

Japan started rebuilding towards Rugby World Cup 2015 with a squad based around young locally born players.

Just four players from Rugby World Cup 2011 made it into Jones's first squad – though others would later return from overseas sabbaticals, injuries and retirement – as Japan opened their season with an 87–0 win over Kazakhstan in the HSBC Asian 5 Nations, with veteran wing Hirotoki Onozawa grabbing a hat-trick of tries.

But the high standards expected by the new coach were already evident.

"It was a so-so performance but it is going to take a little time to get used to this new style of rugby," said new Japan captain Toshiaki Hirose.

The following week, the future of Japanese rugby was on display as Yoshikazu Fujita became the youngest player at 18 years, seven months and 27 days to play for the Brave Blossoms. The teenager didn't let the occasion get to him, running in six tries as Japan thrashed the United Arab Emirates 106–3.

"I think he enjoyed himself," Jones said of the former Higashi Fukuoka High School standout. "But then if I scored six tries in my first Test match I would be happy too."

However, Jones was quick to point out that Fujita still has a long way to go.

"He is a long way from the finished product, but he has potential. If he works hard then he is going to be a very good player for Japan."

Matches against Korea are never easy given the history between the two countries, but Jones's third game in charge saw his team leave Seoul with another bonus-point win. Onozawa again grabbed a hat-trick to move fourth on the all-time list of Test try scorers as the Brave Blossoms won 52–8.

Hong Kong had talked themselves up prior to the start of the A5N, but the following week Japan produced their most clinical performance to date, running in 11 tries in a 67–0 win to claim the silverware and make it 20 bonus-point wins from as many games in the five-year history of the tournament.

"I can't fault the players' attitude at all," Jones said. "They are learning really quickly and working very hard. That was our best performance of the Asian 5 Nations. We had the game won by half-time. We played with a fair bit of discipline and control and I'm really pleased with the growth of the team."

Japan then entered the IRB Pacific Nations Cup in early June as the reigning champions and with home advantage, but Jones was careful to remind his players they had longer-term goals.

"It would be nice to retain the trophy, but I want this team to be at its absolute peak in September 2015 for the next Rugby World Cup. If that means losing a few battles to win the war, then so be it."

A 25–19 loss to Fiji in Nagoya set the tone for the rest of the tournament, as missed tackles and handling errors saw Japan lose a game they could have won.

The Brave Blossoms then went down 24–20 to Tonga – a much closer margin of defeat than at Rugby World Cup 2011, but a loss all the same before the Japan leg of the tournament ended with a humdinger.

The final game at Tokyo's Prince Chichibu Memorial Rugby Ground saw Japan burst out of the blocks to take a 16–0 lead against Samoa, only for the visitors to respond with 27 unanswered points of their own.

A magnificent fight-back saw Japan close to within a point, but Ryan Nicholas missed a last-minute conversion, handing the game and the PNC title to Samoa.

Following such a sterling performance against the PNC champions, Jones and his squad had high hopes of finishing the season in style against the French Barbarians, but it wasn't to be.

Jones ripped into his squad after it lost the first game 40–21, saying they had shown no heart and passion.

When a journalist questioned Jones's selection policy, the Australian responded: "Before, when Kirwan was the coach, everyone was complaining about the number of foreigners. Now we're trying to develop Japanese players and you're complaining about it. If you think I am responsible for the performance, I'll resign tonight. And I mean it."

Jones made wholesale changes for the second game but to no avail as Japan lost 51–18, though he was far happier with the performance and the future.

"Sometimes you just get beaten by a better team. This year we have tried to develop a style of play that'll give us a competitive edge. We just don't have the consistency yet to play at a high level all the time."

Jones's run-in with certain members of the fourth estate was in marked contrast to the relationship between the two parties during the course of the domestic season.

His mix of high-profile imports and locally produced players saw Suntory produce a style of rugby that drew nothing but praise. Springbok scrum half Fourie du Preez and former Australia flanker George Smith both played huge roles as Suntory lost just one game during the regular season.

Smith scored a hat-trick of tries in the Top League final as Suntory dethroned Panasonic Wild Knights with a comprehensive 47–28 victory, and then played another blinder to help his side beat the same opposition to wrap up the domestic season with a 21–9 win in the final of the All-Japan Championship.

"Three weeks ago Fourie du Preez told me he had never worked with a harder-working team. And he has won three Super Rugby competitions and one World Cup," said Jones, who will be hoping his Brave Blossoms show a similar work ethic over the next four years.

Getty Images

Hitoshi Ono wins lineout ball during the IRB Pacific Nations Cup match against Tonga.

JAPAN

JAPAN INTERNATIONAL STATISTICS

MATCH RECORDS UP TO 10 OCTOBER 2012

WINNING MARGIN

Date	Opponent	Result	Winning Margin
06/07/2002	Chinese Taipei	155–3	152
27/10/1998	Chinese Taipei	134–6	128
21/07/2002	Chinese Taipei	120–3	117
13/05/2011	United Arab Emirates	111–0	111
03/05/2008	Arabian Gulf	114–6	108

MOST POINTS IN A MATCH
BY THE TEAM

Date	Opponent	Result	Points
06/07/2002	Chinese Taipei	155–3	155
27/10/1998	Chinese Taipei	134–6	134
21/07/2002	Chinese Taipei	120–3	120
03/05/2008	Arabian Gulf	114–6	114
13/05/2011	United Arab Emirates	111–0	111

BY A PLAYER

Date	Player	Opponent	Points
21/07/2002	Toru Kurihara	Chinese Taipei	60
06/07/2002	Daisuke Ohata	Chinese Taipei	40
16/06/2002	Toru Kurihara	Korea	35
08/05/1999	Keiji Hirose	Tonga	34
28/04/2012	Ayumu Goromaru	Kazakhstan	32

MOST TRIES IN A MATCH
BY THE TEAM

Date	Opponent	Result	Tries
06/07/2002	Chinese Taipei	155–3	23
27/10/1998	Chinese Taipei	134–6	20
21/07/2002	Chinese Taipei	120–3	18
03/05/2008	Arabian Gulf	114–6	18
13/05/2011	United Arab Emirates	111–0	17

BY A PLAYER

Date	Player	Opponent	Tries
06/07/2002	Daisuke Ohata	Chinese Taipei	8
21/07/2002	Toru Kurihara	Chinese Taipei	6
08/05/2005	Daisuke Ohata	Hong Kong	6
05/05/2012	Yoshikazu Fujita	United Arab Emirates	6

MOST CONVERSIONS IN A MATCH
BY THE TEAM

Date	Opponent	Result	Cons
06/07/2002	Chinese Taipei	155–3	20
27/10/1998	Chinese Taipei	134–6	17
21/07/2002	Chinese Taipei	120–3	15

BY A PLAYER

Date	Player	Opponent	Cons
21/07/2002	Toru Kurihara	Chinese Taipei	15
06/07/2002	Andy Miller	Chinese Taipei	12
13/05/2011	James Arlidge	United Arab Emirates	12

MOST PENALTIES IN A MATCH
BY THE TEAM

Date	Opponent	Result	Pens
08/05/1999	Tonga	44–17	9
08/04/1990	Tonga	28–16	6

BY A PLAYER

Date	Player	Opponent	Pens
08/05/1999	Keiji Hirose	Tonga	9
08/04/1990	Takahiro Hosokawa	Tonga	6

MOST DROP GOALS IN A MATCH
BY THE TEAM

Date	Opponent	Result	DGs
15/09/1998	Argentina	44–29	2

BY A PLAYER

Date	Player	Opponent	DGs
15/09/1998	Kensuke Iwabuchi	Argentina	2

MOST CAPPED PLAYERS

Name	Caps
Yukio Motoki	79
Hirotoki Onozawa	74
Takeomi Ito	61
Hitoshi Ono	61
Daisuke Ohata	58

LEADING TRY SCORERS

Name	Tries
Daisuke Ohata	69
Hirotoki Onozawa	51
Terunori Masuho	28
Takashi Kikutani	25

LEADING CONVERSION SCORERS

Name	Cons
James Arlidge	78
Keiji Hirose	77
Toru Kurihara	71
Ryan Nicholas	53

LEADING PENALTY SCORERS

Name	Pens
Keiji Hirose	76
Toru Kurihara	35
James Arlidge	28
Takahiro Hosokawa	24

LEADING DROP GOAL SCORERS

Name	DGs
Kyohei Morita	5

LEADING POINT SCORERS

Name	Points
Keiji Hirose	413
Toru Kurihara	347
Daisuke Ohata	345
James Arlidge	286
Hirotoki Onozawa	255

JAPAN INTERNATIONAL PLAYERS

UP TO 10 OCTOBER 2012

T Adachi 1932 *C, C*
M Aizawa 1984 *Kor*, 1986 *US, C, S, E, Kor*, 1987 *A, NZ, NZ*, 1988 *OU, Kor*
H Akama 1973 *F*, 1975 *A, W*, 1976 *S, E, It, Kor*, 1977 *S*
T Akatsuka 1994 *Fj*, 1995 *Tg, NZ*, 2005 *Sp*, 2006 *HK, Kor*
J Akune 2001 *W, C*
M Amino 2000 *Kor, C*, 2003 *Rus, AuA, Kor, E, E, S, Fj, US*
E Ando 2006 *AG, Kor, Geo, Tg, Sa, JAB, Fj*, 2007 *HK, Fj, Tg, Sa, JAB, It*
D Anglesey 2002 *Tg, Tai, Tai*
T Aoi 1959 *BCo, BCo, OCC*, 1963 *BCo*
S Aoki 1989 *S*, 1990 *Fj*, 1991 *US, C*, 1993 *W*
Y Aoki 2007 *Kor, AuA, JAB*, 2008 *Kor, Kaz, HK, AuA, Tg, Fj, Sa, US, US*, 2009 *Kaz, Sin, Sa, JAB, Tg, Fj*, 2011 *Sa, Tg, US, NZ*
S Arai 1959 *BCo, BCo*
R Arita 2012 *Kaz, ARE, Kor, HK, Fj, Tg, Sa*
JA Arlidge 2007 *Kor*, 2008 *Kor, AG, Kaz, HK, AuA, Tg, Fj, M, Sa*, 2009 *Sa, JAB, Tg, Fj, C, C*, 2010 *Kor, AG, Kaz, HK, Fj, Sa, Tg, Sa, Rus*, 2011 *Kaz, ARE, Tg, It, F, Tg, C*
G Aruga 2006 *HK, Kor*, 2007 *Kor, HK, AuA, Sa, JAB, It, Fj, C*, 2008 *Kor, HK*, 2009 *C, C*, 2011 *ARE, Fj*
K Aruga 1974 *NZU*, 1975 *A, A, W, W*, 1976 *S, E, It, Kor*
R Asano 2003 *AuA, AuA, F, Fj*, 2005 *Ar, HK, Kor, R, C, I, I, Sp*, 2006 *Kor, Geo, Tg, It, HK, Kor*, 2007 *HK, Kor*
M Atokawa 1969 *HK*, 1970 *Tha, BCo*, 1971 *E, E*
H Atou 1976 *BCo*
T Baba 1932 *C*
GTM Bachop 1999 *C, Tg, Sa, Fj, Sp, Sa, W, Ar*
I Basiyalo 1997 *HK, US, US, C, HK*
D Bickle 1996 *HK, HK, C, US, US, C*

KCC Chang 1930 *BCo*, 1932 *C, C*
T Chiba 1930 *BCo*
M Chida 1980 *Kor*, 1982 *HK, C, C, Kor*, 1983 *W*, 1984 *F, F, Kor*, 1985 *US, I, I, F, F*, 1986 *US, C, S, E, Kor*, 1987 *US, E*
H Daimon 2004 *S, W*
K Endo 2004 *It*, 2006 *AG, Kor, Geo, Tg, It, JAB, Fj*, 2007 *HK, Fj, Tg, AuA, Sa, It, Fj, W, C*, 2008 *AuA, Tg, Fj, M, US, US*, 2009 *C, C*, 2010 *Kor, AG, Kaz, HK, Fj, Sa, Tg, Sa, Rus*, 2011 *ARE, Sa, Tg, It, F, Tg, C*
J Enomoto 2005 *Sp*
R Enomoto 1959 *BCo, BCo*
B Ferguson 1993 *W*, 1994 *Fj, Fj, HK, Kor*, 1995 *Tg, Tg, R, W, I, NZ*, 1996 *HK, HK, C, US, US, C*
K Fijii 2000 *Sa*
S Fuchigami 2000 *I*, 2002 *Rus, Tai*, 2003 *US, Rus*
A Fuji 1959 *BCo, BCo*
A Fujii 1956 *AuUn*
J Fujii 2012 *Kaz, ARE, Kor, HK, Fj, Sa*
M Fujii 1930 *BCo*
M Fujikake 1993 *W*, 1994 *HK*, 1995 *Tg*
T Fujimoto-Kamohara 1969 *HK*, 1970 *BCo*, 1971 *E, E*, 1972 *HK*, 1973 *W*
N Fujita 2010 *Kor, AG, Kaz, Rus*, 2011 *HK, ARE, SL, Fj, It, US, F, NZ, Tg, C*
T Fujita 1980 *H, F*, 1983 *W*, 1984 *F, F, Kor*, 1985 *US, I, I, F, F*, 1986 *US, C, S, E*, 1987 *US, E, A, NZ, NZ*, 1989 *S*, 1990 *Fj, Tg, Kor, Sa*, 1991 *US, US, I*
Y Fujita 2012 *ARE*
M Fujiwara 1973 *W*, 1974 *NZU*, 1975 *A, A, W, W*, 1976 *S, E, It*, 1977 *S*, 1978 *F, Kor*, 1979 *HK, E*, 1980 *H, F*

T **Kitagawa** 2005 *Sp*, 2006 *AG, Kor, Tg, Sa, JAB*, 2008 *Kor, AG, Kaz, HK, AuA, Tg, Fj, M, Sa, US, US*, 2009 *Kaz, Kor, Sa, JAB, Tg, Fj, C, C*, 2010 *Kor, AG, HK, Fj, Sa, Tg, Sa, Rus*, 2011 *HK, Sa, Fj, It, F, NZ, Tg, C*
T **Kitagawa** 2006 *HK*, 2007 *HK, A*
Y **Kitagawa** 2007 *Kor*, 2009 *HK, Kor, Sin, JAB*, 2011 *NZ*
T **Kitahara** 1978 *Kor*, 1979 *HK*
H **Kitajima** 1963 *BCo*
T **Kitano** 1930 *BCo*, 1932 *C, C*
S **Kitaoka** 1959 *BCo*
T **Kizu** 2009 *C*, 2010 *AG*, 2011 *HK, Kaz, ARE, Sa, Fj*, 2012 *Kaz, ARE, Kor, HK, Fj, Tg, Sa*
H **Kobayashi** 1983 *W*, 1984 *F, Kor*, 1985 *I, F*, 1986 *Kor*
I **Kobayashi** 1975 *A, A, W, W*, 1976 *BCo, S, E, It, Kor*, 1977 *S, 1978 F, Kor*, 1979 *HK, E, E*
K **Kobayashi** 1959 *BCo, BCo*
K **Koizumi** 1997 *US, C, HK*, 2000 *Fj, US, Tg, Sa, C*, 2001 *W, C, 2002 Tg, Tai*
J **Komura** 1992 *HK*, 1998 *Kor*, 2000 *Kor, C*
GN **Konia** 2003 *US, AuA, AuA, F, Fj, US*
K **Konishi** 1986 *US, Kor*
Y **Konishi** 1980 *F, Kor*, 1982 *HK, Kor*, 1983 *W*, 1984 *F, F, Kor, 1985 US, I, I, F, F*, 1986 *US, C, S, E, Kor*, 1987 *NZ*
M **Koshiyama** 1984 *F, F, Kor*, 1985 *US, I, I*, 1986 *C, Kor*, 1987 *NZ, NZ*
T **Kouda** 1988 *Kor*
O **Koyabu** 1974 *SL*
K **Kubo** 2000 *I*, 2001 *Kor, W, Sa, C*, 2002 *Rus, Kor, Tai, Kor, Kor, 2003 US, Rus, E, F, Fj*, 2004 *Kor, C, It*
K **Kubota** 2004 *S, R, W*
T **Kudo-Nakayama** 1979 *E*
T **Kumagae** 2004 *Kor, Rus, C, It, S, R, W*, 2005 *Ur, Ar, Kor, R, C, I, I, Sp*, 2006 *AG, Kor, Geo, It, Sa, Fj*, 2007 *HK, Fj, AuA, Sa, A*
N **Kumagai** 1977 *S*, 1978 *F*, 1979 *HK*
M **Kunda** 1990 *Sa, US, Kor*, 1991 *C, HK, S, I, Z*, 1992 *HK*, 1993 *HK, C*, 1997 *HK, C, US*, 1998 *C, HK, HK, US, C, Ar, Kor, HK, Kor*, 1999 *Sa, Fj, US, Sp, Sa, W, Ar*
S **Kurihara** 1986 *S, E*, 1987 *E*
S **Kurihara** 1974 *SL*
T **Kurihara** 2000 *Fj, US, Tg, Sa, Kor, C*, 2001 *Kor, W, W, Sa, C, 2002 Rus, Tg, Kor, Kor, Tai*, 2003 *US, Rus, AuA, AuA, E, E, S, F, Fj, US*
M **Kurokawa** 1998 *Tai, HK, Kor*, 2000 *Fj, Tg, Sa, Kor, C*
T **Kurosaka** 1970 *BCo*, 1974 *SL*, 1975 *A, A, W, W*
M **Kusatsu** 1963 *BCo*
T **Kusumi** 2007 *A, W*, 2008 *Kor*
E **Kutsuki** 1985 *F*, 1986 *US, C, S, E*, 1987 *US, E, A, NZ, NZ*, 1989 *S*, 1990 *Fj, Tg, Kor, Sa, US, Kor*, 1991 *US, US, C, HK, S, I, Z, 1992 HK*, 1993 *W*, 1994 *Fj, Fj, HK*
Y **Kuwazuru** 2012 *ARE, Kor, HK*
S **Latu** 1987 *US, A, NZ, NZ*, 1989 *S*, 1990 *Fj, Tg, Kor, Sa, US, Kor*, 1991 *US, C, HK, S, I, Z*, 1992 *HK, 1993 Ar, Ar*, 1994 *Fj, Fj, HK, Kor*, 1995 *Tg, Tg, R, W, I, NZ*
ST **Latu** 1993 *W*, 1994 *Fj, Fj, HK, Kor*, 1995 *Tg, R, W, I*
MG **Leitch** 2008 *US, US*, 2009 *Kaz, HK, Kor, Sa, JAB, C, C*, 2010 *HK, Fj, Tg, Rus*, 2011 *HK, ARE, Tg, Fj, It, F, NZ, Tg, C*, 2012 *Kaz, Kor, HK, Fj*
CED **Loamanu** 2005 *Ur, HK*, 2007 *Kor, Fj, Tg, Sa, JAB, It, Fj, W, C*, 2008 *AuA, Tg, Fj, M, Sa*
ET **Luaiufi** 1990 *Fj, Kor, US, Kor*, 1991 *US, US, C, HK, S, I, Z*
T **Madea** 1991 *US, C, HK*, 1995 *Tg*
P **Mafileo** 2008 *US*
S **Makabe** 2009 *C*, 2010 *Kaz*, 2012 *Kaz, ARE, Kor, HK, Fj, Tg, Sa*
HAW **Makiri** 2005 *Ur, Ar, HK, Kor, R, I, I*, 2006 *AG, Tg, Sa, JAB*, 2007 *Kor, Tg, AuA, Sa, JAB, It, A, Fj, W, C*, 2008 *AuA, Tg, Fj, M, Sa*
M **Mantani** 1969 *HK*, 1970 *Tha, BCo*, 1971 *E, E*, 1972 *HK*
G **Marsh** 2007 *AuA, Sa, JAB*
T **Masuho** 1991 *US, C, HK, S, I, Z*, 1993 *Ar, Ar*, 1994 *Fj, Fj, Kor*, 1995 *Tg, W*, 1996 *HK, C, US, US, C*, 1997 *HK, C, US, C, HK*, 1998 *C, US, HK, US, C, Ar, Kor, Tai, HK*, 1999 *C, US, Sp, Sa, 2000 Fj, US, Tg, Sa, Kor, C*, 2001 *Kor, W, Sa, C*
Y **Masutome** 1986 *Kor*
K **Matsubara** 1930 *BCo*
T **Matsubara** 1932 *C, C*
Y **Matsubara** 2004 *Kor, Rus, C, It*, 2005 *Sp*, 2006 *AG, Kor, Geo, Tg, It, Sa, JAB, Fj, Kor*, 2007 *Kor, Fj, Tg, Sa, JAB, It, Fj, W, C*
T **Matsuda** 1992 *HK*, 1993 *W*, 1994 *Fj, HK, Kor*, 1995 *Tg, R, W, I, NZ*, 1996 *HK, C, US, US, C, Kor*, 1998 *US, HK, HK, US, C, Ar, Kor, HK, Kor*, 1999 *C, S, Fj, US, Sp, Sa, Ar*, 2001 *Kor, Tai, W*, 2003 *US, AuA, Kor, E, S, Fj, US*
J **Matsumoto** 1977 *S*, 1978 *F*, 1980 *H*, 1982 *C, C*

T **Matsunaga** 1985 *F, F*
Y **Matsunobu** 1963 *BCo*
H **Matsuo** 2003 *AuA, AuA, Kor, E, E*
K **Matsuo** 1986 *US, C, S, E, Kor*, 1987 *E, NZ*, 1988 *Kor*, 1990 *Tg, Kor, Sa, US*, 1991 *US, HK, S, I, Z*, 1993 *Ar, Ar*, 1994 *Fj, Fj, HK, 1995 Tg*
Y **Matsuo** 1974 *SL*, 1976 *BCo, E, It, Kor*, 1977 *S*, 1979 *HK, E, E, 1982 HK, C, C*, 1983 *OCC, W*, 1984 *F, F, Kor*
S **Matsuoka** 1963 *BCo*, 1970 *Tha*
K **Matsushita** 2008 *US, US*, 2010 *AG, HK, Fj, Sa, Tg*
F **Mau** 2004 *Rus, C, It, S, R, W*
AF **McCormick** 1996 *HK, HK, US*, 1997 *HK, C, US, US, C, HK*, 1998 *C, US, HK, Ar, Kor, Tai, HK*, 1999 *C, Tg, Sa, Fj, US, Sp, Sa, W, Ar*
R **Miki** 1999 *Sp*, 2002 *Tg, Tai, Kor, Tai, Kor*, 2004 *S, R, W*
A **Miller** 2002 *Rus, Kor, Tai, Kor, Tai*, 2003 *Kor, S, F, Fj, US*
S **Miln** 1998 *C, US, HK, HK, US*
Y **Minamikawa** 1976 *BCo*, 1978 *F, Kor*, 1979 *HK, E, E*, 1980 *H, F, Kor*, 1982 *HK, C, C, Kor*
M **Mishima** 1930 *BCo*, 1932 *C, C*
T **Miuchi** 2002 *Rus, Kor, Kor, Tai, Kor*, 2003 *US, Rus, AuA, Kor, E, E, S, F, Fj, US*, 2004 *Rus, C, It, S, R, W*, 2005 *Ur, Ar, HK, Kor, R, C, I, I*, 2006 *HK, Kor*, 2007 *Kor, HK, Fj, Tg, Sa, It, Fj, W, C*, 2008 *Kor, AG, Kaz, HK, AuA, Tg, Fj, Sa*
S **Miura** 1963 *BCo*
K **Miyai** 1959 *BCo, BCo*, 1963 *BCo*
K **Miyaji** 1969 *HK*
K **Miyajima** 1959 *BCo, BCo*
H **Miyaji-Yoshizawa** 1930 *BCo*
T **Miyake** 2005 *Sp*, 2006 *Sa, JAB, Fj*
K **Miyamoto** 1986 *S, E*, 1987 *US, E, A*, 1988 *Kor*, 1991 *I*
K **Miyata** 1971 *E, E*, 1972 *HK*
M **Miyauchi** 1975 *W*, 1976 *It, Kor*
K **Mizobe** 1997 *C*
K **Mizoguchi** 1997 *C*
K **Mizube** 1997 *HK*
H **Mizuno** 2004 *R*, 2005 *HK, Kor, R, C, I*, 2006 *AG, Geo, Tg, It, Sa, JAB*
M **Mizutani** 1970 *Tha*, 1971 *E*
N **Mizuyama** 2008 *Tg, M, Sa, US*
Y **Mochizuki** 2012 *Kaz, ARE, Kor, HK, Fj, Tg, Sa*
S **Mori** 1974 *NZU, SL*, 1975 *A, A, W, W*, 1976 *BCo, S, E, It, Kor*, 1977 *S*, 1978 *F*, 1979 *HK, E, E, CU*, 1980 *NZU, H, F, Kor*, 1981 *AuUn*
K **Morikawa** 2012 *ARE*
K **Morioka** 1959 *BCo*
K **Morita** 2004 *C, It*, 2005 *Ur, Ar, Kor, R, C, I*
A **Moriya** 2006 *Tg, It, Sa, JAB, Fj*, 2008 *AG, Kaz*
Y **Motoki** 1991 *US, US, C*, 1992 *HK*, 1993 *Ar, Ar*, 1994 *Fj, Fj, Kor*, 1995 *Tg, Tg, R, W, I, NZ*, 1996 *HK, HK, C, US, US, C, Kor*, 1997 *HK, C, US, US, C, HK*, 1998 *C, US, HK, US, C, Ar, Kor, HK, Kor*, 1999 *C, Tg, Sa, Fj, US, Sp, Sa, W, Ar*, 2001 *W, W, Sa, C*, 2002 *Rus, Tg, Kor, Tai, Kor, Tai, Kor*, 2003 *Kor, E, E, S, Fj, US*, 2004 *Kor, Rus, C, It, S, R, W*, 2005 *Ur, Ar, HK, Kor, R, C, I, I*
M **Motoyoshi** 2001 *Tai*
S **Mukai** 1985 *I, I, F*, 1986 *US, C, E, Kor*, 1987 *US, A, NZ, NZ*
M **Mukoyama** 2004 *Kor, C, It, S, R, W*
K **Muraguchi** 1976 *S, Kor*
D **Murai** 1985 *I, I, F, F*, 1987 *E*
K **Murata** 1963 *BCo*
W **Murata** 1991 *US, S*, 1995 *Tg, NZ*, 1996 *HK, HK, C, US, US, C, Kor*, 1997 *HK, C, US, US, HK*, 1998 *HK, HK, US, C, Ar, Kor, Kor*, 1999 *US, W*, 2001 *W, W, Sa*, 2002 *Rus, Tg, Kor, Tai, Kor, Tai*, 2003 *US, AuA, E*, 2005 *Ur, Ar, Kor, I, I*
Y **Murata** 1971 *E, E*, 1972 *HK*, 1973 *W*, 1974 *NZU, SL*
Y **Nagae** 2012 *Kaz, ARE, Kor, HK, Fj, Tg, Sa*
M **Nagai** 1988 *Kor*
Y **Nagatomo** 1993 *W*, 1994 *Fj, HK*, 1995 *Tg*, 1996 *US, US*, 1997 *C*
Y **Nagatomo** 2010 *Kor, AG, Kaz*, 2012 *Kaz, ARE, Kor, HK, Fj, Sa*
T **Naito** 1934 *AuUn*
M **Nakabayashi** 2005 *HK, Kor, R, I*
T **Nakai** 2005 *Ur, HK, C, I, I, Sp*, 2006 *AG, Kor, Geo, Tg, It, Fj*
T **Nakamichi** 1996 *HK, HK, US, US, C*, 1998 *Ar, Kor*, 1999 *C, Sa, Fj, Sp, W, Ar*, 2000 *Fj, US, Tg*
N **Nakamura** 1998 *C, US, HK, HK, US, C, Ar, Kor, Tai, HK*, 1999 *C, Tg, Sa, Fj, US, Sp, W, Ar*
S **Nakamura** 2009 *Kaz, Sin*, 2010 *AG, Kaz, HK, Fj*
S **Nakashima** 1989 *S*, 1990 *Fj, Tg, Kor, Sa, US*, 1991 *US, US, C, HK, S*
T **Nakayama** 1976 *BCo*, 1978 *F*, 1979 *E*, 1980 *H*, 1982 *C, C*
Y **Nakayama** 2008 *Kor, AG, Kaz, HK, Tg, M*, 2009 *HK, Kor, Sin, Tg, Fj*

S **Tanaka** 1959 *BCo, BCo*
N **Tanifuji** 1979 *HK, E, E,* 1982 *C, C,* 1983 *W,* 1984 *F, Kor,* 1985 *US*
Y **Tanigawa** 1969 *HK*
I **Taniguchi** 2010 *Rus,* 2011 *Kaz, SL, Sa, Tg, Fj, US, F, NZ, Tg*
T **Taniguchi** 2006 *Tg, It, JAB,* 2008 *Kor, Kaz, HK, AuA, Tg, Fj, M, Sa, US*
H **Tanuma** 1996 *Kor,* 1997 *HK, C, US, US, HK,* 1998 *C, US, HK,* 1999 *Sa, Fj, US, Sp, Sa, W, Ar,* 2000 *Fj, US, Tg, Sa, Kor, C, I,* 2001 *Kor, Tai, W, W, Sa, C,* 2002 *Kor,* 2003 *AuA, E, F*
J **Tarrant** 2009 *Kaz, HK, Kor, Sa, JAB, Tg, Fj*
H **Tatekawa** 2012 *Kaz, ARE, Kor, HK, Fj, Tg, Sa*
M **Tatsukawa** 2000 *Sa*
T **Taufa** 2009 *Kaz, Kor, Sin, Sa, JAB, Tg, Fj, C, C,* 2010 *Kor, AG, Kaz, HK, Fj, Sa, Tg, Sa,* 2011 *HK, Kaz, ARE, SL, C*
N **Taumoefolau** 1985 *F, F,* 1986 *US, C, S, E, Kor,* 1987 *US, E, A, NZ,* 1988 *Kor,* 1989 *S,* 1990 *Fj*
T **Terai** 1969 *HK,* 1970 *Tha,* 1971 *E, E,* 1972 *HK,* 1973 *W, F,* 1974 *NZU,* 1975 *A, W, W,* 1976 *S, E, It, Kor*
S **Teramura** 1930 *BCo*
LM **Thompson** 2007 *HK, Fj, Tg, Sa, JAB, It, Fj, W, C,* 2008 *M, Sa, US, US,* 2009 *Kaz, Kor, Sa, Tg, Fj,* 2010 *Kor, AG, Kaz, HK, Fj, Sa, Tg, Sa, Rus,* 2011 *HK, Kaz, SL, Sa, Tg, It, US, F, Tg, C*
R **Thompson** 1998 *C, US, HK, HK, US, C*
Z **Toba-Nakajima** 1930 *BCo,* 1932 *C*
K **Todd** 2000 *Fj, Sa, I*
H **Tominaga** 1959 *BCo, BCo*
K **Tomioka** 2008 *US, US,* 2009 *Kor, Sin, Sa, JAB*
T **Tomioka** 2005 *I, I*
T **Toshi** 1932 *C, C*
H **Toshima** 1980 *H, F,* 1982 *HK, C, C,* 1984 *F, F, Kor*
M **Toyoda** 2008 *US*
N **Toyoda** 1982 *HK*
S **Toyoda** 1974 *SL*
T **Toyoda** 1978 *Kor*
M **Toyota** 2009 *Sin, Sa, Tg, Fj,* 2010 *Kor, AG, Kaz, HK*
K **Toyoyama** 1976 *BCo,* 1979 *E, E,* 1980 *H*
M **Toyoyama** 2000 *Fj, US, Sa, C,* 2001 *Kor, W, W, Sa, C,* 2002 *Rus, Kor, Tai, Kor, Tai,* 2003 *US, Rus, AuA, Kor, E, E, S, Fj, US*
H **Tsuboi** 2012 *Kaz, ARE*
M **Tsuchida** 1985 *F*
T **Tsuchiya** 1956 *AuUn,* 1959 *BCo, BCo*
E **Tsuji** 1980 *Kor,* 1982 *Kor*
T **Tsuji** 2003 *S, Fj, US,* 2005 *HK, R, C,* 2006 *Kor*
Y **Tsujimoto** 2001 *Kor*
K **Tsukagoshi** 2002 *Kor,* 2005 *Ur, Ar, HK, Kor, R, C, I, I*
S **Tsukda** 2001 *Kor, C,* 2002 *Tg, Tai, Kor, Tai, Kor,* 2003 *AuA, E*
T **Tsuyama** 1976 *BCo, Kor*
H **Tui** 2012 *Tg, Sa*
P **Tuidraki** 1997 *HK, C,* 1998 *C, US, HK, HK, US, C, Tai,* 1999 *Tg, Sa, Fj, Sa, W, Ar,* 2000 *I,* 2001 *Tai, W, W*
A **Tupuailai** 2009 *C, C,* 2010 *Kor, AG, Kaz, HK, Fj, Sa, Tg, Sa, Rus,* 2011 *HK, Kaz, SL, It, US, F, NZ, Tg, C*
K **Uchida** 2012 *Kaz, ARE*
M **Uchida** 1969 *HK*
A **Ueda** 1975 *W,* 1978 *Kor,* 1979 *E, E*
T **Ueda** 2011 *HK, Kaz, ARE, SL, US, NZ*
S **Ueki** 1963 *BCo*
R **Ueno** 2011 *SL*
N **Ueyama** 1973 *F,* 1974 *NZU, SL,* 1975 *A, A, W, W,* 1976 *BCo, E, It, Kor,* 1978 *F,* 1980 *Kor*
H **Ujino** 1976 *BCo,* 1977 *S,* 1978 *F, Kor,* 1979 *HK, E, E,* 1980 *H, Kor,* 1982 *HK, Kor*
R **Umei** 1958 *NZ23, NZ23, NZ23*
Y **Uryu** 2000 *Sa,* 2001 *Kor*
T **Usuzuki** 2011 *ARE, SL, Sa, Fj, It, US, NZ*
S **Vatuvei** 2010 *Kor, AG, Kaz, Sa,* 2011 *US, NZ, Tg, C*
K **Wada** 1997 *HK, US, US, C, HK*
K **Wada** 2010 *AG, Kaz, Fj, Tg, Rus*

S **Wada** 1930 *BCo*
T **Wada** 1975 *A,* 1976 *S,* 1979 *E, E*
J **Washington** 2005 *Ur, Ar, HK, Kor, R, C, I*
M **Washiya** 2000 *Kor, C*
H **Watanabe** 1990 *Sa*
T **Watanabe** 2002 *Kor*
Y **Watanabe** 1996 *HK, HK,* 1998 *C, US, HK, Ar, Kor, Tai, HK,* 1999 *C, Tg, US, Sp, Sa,* 2000 *Fj, US,* 2003 *Rus, AuA, AuA, E, S,* 2004 *Kor,* 2005 *HK, R, C,* 2007 *HK, Fj, Tg, Sa, JAB, A, W*
SJ **Webb** 2008 *AG, Kaz, HK, AuA, Tg, Fj, M, US, US,* 2009 *Kaz, Kor, Sa, Tg, Fj, C, C,* 2010 *Kor, Kaz, HK, Fj, Sa, Tg,* 2011 *HK, Kaz, ARE, SL, Sa, Tg, Fj, It, US, F, NZ, Tg, C*
IM **Williams** 1993 *W*
MC **Williams** 2011 *Sa, Fj, US, F, NZ, C*
T **Yagai** 1930 *BCo*
T **Yajima** 1978 *Kor,* 1979 *E*
K **Yamada** 1963 *BCo*
K **Yamaguchi** 1936 *NZU*
T **Yamaguchi** 2009 *R, W*
Y **Yamaguchi** 1970 *Tha, BCo,* 1971 *E, E,* 1972 *HK*
E **Yamamoto** 2001 *Kor, W,* 2002 *Tg, Kor*
I **Yamamoto** 1973 *W*
M **Yamamoto** 2002 *Rus, Kor, Tai, Kor,* 2003 *Rus, AuA, AuA, Kor, E, E, Fj, US,* 2004 *Kor, Rus, C, S, R, W,* 2006 *Sa, JAB, Fj,* 2007 *HK, Fj, AuA, JAB, A*
M **Yamamoto** 2004 *C, S, W,* 2006 *HK, Kor,* 2007 *HK, Fj, Tg, AuA, Sa*
T **Yamamoto** 1988 *Kor,* 1989 *S,* 1990 *Fj*
R **Yamamura** 2002 *Tg, Tai, Tai,* 2003 *AuA, F,* 2004 *Kor, Rus, C, It, S, R, W,* 2005 *Ur, Ar, HK, Kor, R, C, I, I, Sp,* 2006 *Kor, Geo, It, Sa, JAB, Fj, HK, Kor,* 2007 *Kor, Tg, AuA, Sa, JAB, It, A, Fj, W, C*
R **Yamanaka** 2010 *AG*
T **Yamaoka** 2004 *It, S, R, W,* 2005 *Sp,* 2006 *AG, Kor, Geo, Tg, It, Sa, JAB, Fj*
H **Yamashita** 2009 *Kaz, HK, Kor, Sin, Sa, JAB, Tg, Fj,* 2012 *Kor, HK, Fj, Tg, Sa*
O **Yamashita** 1974 *SL*
M **Yasuda** 1984 *F*
N **Yasuda** 2000 *Kor, I*
Y **Yasue** 2009 *HK, Kor*
T **Yasui** 1976 *S, E,* 1977 *S,* 1978 *F,* 1979 *HK, E*
K **Yasumi** 1986 *C,* 1987 *US, NZ*
Y **Yatomi** 2006 *Kor,* 2007 *HK, Fj, Tg, AuA, Sa, JAB, A, Fj,* 2009 *Kaz, Kor, JAB, C*
O **Yatsuhashi** 1996 *US, C,* 1998 *US, HK, HK, US, C, Ar, Tai, Kor,* 2000 *Kor, C*
A **Yokoi** 1969 *HK,* 1970 *Tha, NZU, BCo,* 1971 *E,* 1972 *AuUn, AuUn, HK,* 1973 *W, E, F,* 1974 *NZU*
A **Yoshida** 1995 *R, W, I, NZ,* 1996 *C, US, C, Kor,* 1997 *US, HK,* 1999 *Sa,* 2000 *Fj, US, Tg, Sa, Kor, C*
H **Yoshida** 2001 *Sa, C,* 2002 *Tg, Tai,* 2004 *R, W,* 2006 *AG, Kor, Geo, Tg, Sa, JAB, Fj, HK, Kor*
H **Yoshida** 2008 *AG, Kaz, M,* 2009 *Kaz, HK, Sin*
J **Yoshida** 1973 *W, F*
M **Yoshida** 1974 *NZU,* 1975 *A, A, W,* 1976 *BCo, S, E, It, Kor,* 1977 *S,* 1978 *F, W*
T **Yoshida** 2002 *Tg, Tai, Kor,* 2003 *E*
T **Yoshida** 2007 *Kor, Fj, Tg, Sa, It, Fj, W, C,* 2008 *Kor, Kaz, AuA, Tg, M, Sa, US,* 2009 *Kor, Sa, JAB, C, C,* 2010 *AG, HK, Sa,* 2011 *US, NZ*
Y **Yoshida** 1988 *Kor,* 1989 *S,* 1990 *Fj, Tg, Kor, Sa, US, Kor,* 1991 *US, US, C, HK, S, I, Z,* 1992 *HK,* 1993 *Ar, W,* 1994 *Fj, Fj, HK, Kor,* 1995 *Tg, R, I, NZ,* 1996 *HK*
K **Yoshinaga** 1986 *Kor,* 1987 *US, A, NZ,* 1990 *Sa*
K **Yoshino** 1973 *W*
T **Yoshino** 1985 *US, I, I, F, F,* 1986 *Kor,* 1987 *NZ*
H **Yuhara** 2010 *Kor, AG, HK, Fj, Rus,* 2011 *HK, ARE, SL, NZ*

BE PART OF THE
IRB WOMEN'S SEVENS
WORLD SERIES

AMSTERDAM
17-18 May 2013

4

HOUSTON
1-2 Feb 2013

2

DUBAI **1**
30 Nov - 1 Dec 2012

3

GUANGZHOU
30-31 Mar 2013

www.irb.com

 @irbwomens

 www.facebook.com/irbsevens

NAMIBIA

NAMIBIA'S 2012 TEST RECORD

OPPONENTS	DATE		VENUE
Senegal	4 Jul	N	Won 20–18
Madagascar	8 Jul	A	Lost 57–54

ENCOURAGING SIGNS FOR NAMIBIAN RUGBY

By Andrew Poolman

Namibia contest lineout ball against Senegal in their
Rugby World Cup 2015 qualifier in Madagascar.

THE COUNTRIES

It **proved to** be a tumultuous but ultimately encouraging year on and off the pitch for Namibian rugby and although the senior side were in action just twice in 2012 after their appearance at Rugby World Cup 2011 in New Zealand, the Under 19s claimed the Confédération Africaine de Rugby (CAR) title in September to suggest a bright future for the Welwitschias.

It was a year in which Namibian rugby underwent a major political overhaul with the election of a new president and the subsequent appointment of a new head coach as the Union's focus shifted to the qualifying campaign for RWC 2015 in England and what they hoped would be a fifth successive appearance in the tournament.

Windhoek lawyer Bradley Basson was the man to replace Buks Bock as NRU president while former Test prop Danie Vermeulen was unveiled as the new coach, succeeding Johan Diergaardt after his contract expired, and with the management and coaching restructuring completed, Namibia prepared for the Africa Cup in Madagascar in July.

The four-team tournament featuring the Welwitschias, the hosts, Senegal and Morocco doubled up as the first phase of World Cup qualifying in Africa with the Division 1B winners promoted to Division 1A in 2013.

The Namibians, who had been relegated to the Africa Cup's second tier after a financial crisis meant they were unable to send a team to the 1A competition in Kenya in 2011, began the competition against Senegal in Antananarivo.

A crowd of 35,000 packed the Mahamasina Stadium for the clash and it was a pulsating affair from which Vermeulen's new-look side, featuring just nine of the players from the World Cup squad, dramatically emerged 20–18 winners.

The Senegalese drew first blood with two early Aldric Folliot penalties but the Welwitschias hit back on 25 minutes when fly half Theuns Kotze went over for the first try of the match. Four further successful penalties for Senegal, however, saw Namibia trail 18–10 late into the second half and a defeat which would have abruptly ended their World Cup hopes loomed.

They did not give up. Full back Justin Nel scampered over for a try converted by Kotze with eight minutes to play and then, with just three minutes on the clock, the fly half landed a crucial drop goal to make the score 20–18. There was still time for a late drop goal attempt by the Senegalese but it drifted wide and Namibia had the crucial victory.

"Our scrums were good though while the backline looked dangerous, especially in the second half," said team manager William Steenkamp. "But we made far too many unforced errors with too many handling errors and knock-ons."

The victory came at a cost with flanker and captain Tinus du Plessis suffering a broken arm and debutant centre Anthony Jevu ruled out with a broken collarbone, so Vermeulen turned to number 8 Pieter-Jan van Lill to lead the side in the final against Madagascar.

To describe the match as entertaining and high scoring would be an understatement and it needed extra-time to separate the two sides in front of a crowd of 40,000 in Antananarivo.

Madagascar raced into a 19–0 lead with three tries inside the first 20 minutes and, despite a brief Namibian rally, the home side were 29–14 in front at the break. The second half was even more spectacular as the Welwitschias stormed back into the match with five tries but Madagascar refused to crumble and found two more scores to level the match at 43–43 after 80 minutes and force the contest into two additional, 10-minute halves.

Namibia seemed to be edging towards a famous victory when Kotze landed a late penalty to make it 54–50 to the visitors but the home side delivered the coup de grace in the 100th minute of the game with a converted try to seal an unbelievable 57–54 triumph.

NAMIBIA

It was a sensational climax to a remarkable match and although Namibia were stunned by the result, they left Madagascar safe in the knowledge they were still in the mix to qualify for RWC 2015.

"This was the strangest match I have ever been involved in as a coach," Vermeulen admitted. "We lost because we did not stick to our plan of keeping possession of the ball – and when we did this for 33 minutes of the second half we scored 29 unanswered points.

"I have to add that Madagascar plays a type of rugby that suits them perfectly and with such a home crowd behind them, it lifted their performance by 40 per cent above their potential."

A month later, the next generation of Namibian players headed to Zimbabwe to compete in the CAR Under 19 Championship and led by hooker Gerhard Lotter, the junior Welwitschias swept all before them in the tournament in Harare.

Tunisia were dispatched 44–7 and Kenya defeated 39–11 to set up a deciding match with the hosts at Prince Edward School. A charge-down led to Namibia's first try for Ethan Beukes and the visitors were to remain in front throughout the match and, although Zimbabwe dominated the closing 15 minutes, Namibia were still convincing 44–23 winners.

Number 8 Wian Conradie scored twice while GD Orlam, Donovan Kandjii, Gerhard Lotter and Deslee Beukes all crossed as the Welwitschias' fast and expansive game plan reaped rewards. Victory ended Zimbabwe's three-year reign as champions and booked Namibia's place at the IRB Junior World Rugby Trophy 2013 in Chile.

"These are exciting times for Namibian rugby as this is our fourth win over Zimbabwe this year," said coach Jood Opperman. "We have beaten them from the Under 13s all the way to the Under 19s. We are slowly regaining our status as the continent's leading side in age-grade rugby and credit to the Union for all their support.

"We played well from the ruck and the changes that were made to the technical team have paid off. Zimbabwe had a lot of gaps in their play and we took advantage of that but I am happy with the win and we have to prepare very seriously for the Junior World Rugby Trophy."

In Sevens rugby, Namibia were in action in September in Morocco in the CAR men's qualifying tournament for Rugby World Cup Sevens 2013, but their dreams of booking their place in the showpiece event in Moscow were dashed.

Drawn to face Tunisia, Zimbabwe and Ivory Coast in the pool stages, the Namibians were unable to record a victory but did finish the tournament in style, beating Zambia 22–10 in the semi-final of the Bowl competition before exacting revenge on the Ivorians with a 24–7 triumph in the final.

NAMIBIA INTERNATIONAL STATISTICS

MATCH RECORDS UP TO 10 OCTOBER 2012

WINNING MARGIN

Date	Opponent	Result	Winning Margin
15/06/2002	Madagascar	112–0	112
21/04/1990	Portugal	86–9	77
27/05/2006	Kenya	82–12	70
26/05/2007	Zambia	80–10	70

MOST POINTS IN A MATCH
BY THE TEAM

Date	Opponent	Result	Points
15/06/2002	Madagascar	112–0	112
21/04/1990	Portugal	86–9	86
31/08/2003	Uganda	82–13	82
27/05/2006	Kenya	82–12	82

BY A PLAYER

Date	Player	Opponent	Points
06/07/1993	Jaco Coetzee	Kenya	35
26/05/2007	Justinus van der Westhuizen	Zambia	33
27/06/2009	Chrysander Botha	Cote D'Ivoire	29
21/04/1990	Moolman Olivier	Portugal	26
15/06/2002	Riaan van Wyk	Madagascar	25

MOST TRIES IN A MATCH
BY THE TEAM

Date	Opponent	Result	Tries
15/06/2002	Madagascar	112–0	18
21/04/1990	Portugal	86–9	16
17/10/1999	Germany	79–13	13

BY A PLAYER

Date	Player	Opponent	Tries
21/04/1990	Gerhard Mans	Portugal	6
15/06/2002	Riaan van Wyk	Madagascar	5
16/05/1992	Eden Meyer	Zimbabwe	4
16/08/2003	Melrick Africa	Kenya	4

MOST CONVERSIONS IN A MATCH
BY THE TEAM

Date	Opponent	Result	Cons
15/06/2002	Madagascar	112–0	11
21/04/1990	Portugal	86–9	11
31/08/2003	Uganda	82–13	11
27/05/2006	Kenya	82–12	11

BY A PLAYER

Date	Player	Opponent	Cons
21/04/1990	Moolman Olivier	Portugal	11
27/05/2006	Morne Schreuder	Kenya	11
26/05/2007	Justinus van der Westhuizen	Zambia	9
31/08/2003	Rudi van Vuuren	Uganda	8
04/07/1993	Jaco Coetzee	Arabian Gulf	8

MOST PENALTIES IN A MATCH
BY THE TEAM

Date	Opponent	Result	Pens
22/06/1991	Italy	33–19	5
23/01/1998	Portugal	36–19	5
30/06/1990	France A	20–25	5
28/11/2009	Tunisia	22–10	5
15/06/2011	Portugal	29–23	5

BY A PLAYER

Date	Player	Opponent	Pens
22/06/1991	Jaco Coetzee	Italy	5
23/01/1998	Rudi van Vuuren	Portugal	5
30/06/1990	Shaun McCulley	France A	5
28/11/2009	Emile Wessels	Tunisia	5
15/06/2011	Theuns Kotze	Portugal	5

MOST DROP GOALS IN A MATCH
BY THE TEAM

Date	Opponent	Result	DGs
10/09/2011	Fiji	25–49	3

BY A PLAYER

Date	Player	Opponent	Pens
10/09/2011	Theuns Kotze	Fiji	3

NAMIBIA

MOST CAPPED PLAYERS

Name	Caps
Hugo Horn	35
Eugene Jantjies	34
Herman Lindvelt	33
Johnnie Redelinghuys	32

LEADING PENALTY SCORERS

Name	Pens
Jaco Coetzee	46
Emile Wessels	21
Morne Schreuder	18
Rudi van Vuuren	14

LEADING TRY SCORERS

Name	Tries
Gerhard Mans	27
Eden Meyer	21
Melrick Africa	12

LEADING DROP GOAL SCORERS

Name	DGs
Theuns Kotze	4
Jaco Coetzee	3
Eugene Jantjies	2

LEADING CONVERSIONS SCORERS

Name	Cons
Jaco Coetzee	82
Morne Schreuder	36
Rudi van Vuuren	26

LEADING POINTS SCORERS

Name	Points
Jaco Coetzee	340
Morne Schreuder	146
Gerhard Mans	118
Rudi van Vuuren	109
Chrysander Botha	107

THE COUNTRIES

NAMIBIA INTERNATIONAL PLAYERS

UP TO 10 OCTOBER 2012

MJ Africa 2003 *Sa, Ken, Uga, Ar, I, A,* 2005 *Mad, Mor,* 2006 *Ken, Tun, Ken, Tun, Mor, Mor,* 2007 *Za, Geo, R, Uga, SA, I, F, Ar, Geo*

W Alberts 1991 *Sp, Pt, It, It, Z, Z, I, I, Z, Z, Z,* 1995 *Z,* 1996 *Z, Z*

H Amakali 2005 *Mad*

J Augustyn 1991 *Z,* 1998 *Iv, Mor, Z*

RS Bardenhorst 2007 *Geo, R*

J Barnard 1990 *Z, Pt, W, W, F, F,* 1991 *Sp, Pt, It, It, Z, Z, I, I, Z, Z, Z,* 1992 *Z, Z*

D Beukes 2000 *Z, Ur,* 2001 *Z, Z*

E Beukes 1990 *Z, F, WGe*

J Beukes 1994 *Z, Mor,* 1995 *Z*

AJ Blaauw 1996 *Z, Z,* 1997 *Tg,* 1998 *Pt, Tun, Z, Iv, Mor, Z,* 1999 *Z, Fj, F, C, Ger,* 2000 *Z, Z, Ur,* 2001 *It,* 2003 *Ar, I, A, R,* 2004 *Mor*

ML Blom 2010 *Sp,* 2011 *Pt, Geo,* 2012 *Sen, Mad*

J Bock 2005 *Mad, Mor,* 2009 *Iv, Iv,* 2010 *R, Geo, Pt*

JH Bock 2005 *Mad, Mor,* 2006 *Ken, Tun, Ken, Tun, Mor, Mor,* 2007 *Za, R, SA, I, F, Ar, Geo,* 2009 *Pt, Tun,* 2010 *R, Geo,* 2011 *R, Pt, Geo, SA*

J Booysen 2003 *Sa, Ken, Ar, A,* 2007 *Uga*

M Booysen 1993 *W, AG, Z,* 1994 *Rus, Z, HK,* 1996 *Z, Z*

LW Botes 2006 *Ken, Mor,* 2007 *Za, Geo, R, Uga, SA, F*

CA Botha 2008 *Z,* 2009 *Iv, Iv, Pt, Tun, Tun,* 2010 *Rus, R, Geo, Pt, Sp,* 2011 *R, Pt, Geo, Fj, Sa, SA, W,* 2012 *Sen, Mad*

HP Botha 2000 *Z, Z, Ur*

AC Bouwer 2012 *Sen, Mad*

H Breedt 1998 *Tun, Z*

H Brink 1992 *Z, Z,* 1993 *W, Ken, Z,* 1994 *Rus, Z, Iv, Mor, HK*

J Britz 1996 *Z*

E Buitenbag 2010 *Rus*

B Buitendag 1990 *W, W, F, F, WGe,* 1991 *Sp, Pt, It, It, Z, I, I, Z, Z, Z,* 1992 *Z, Z,* 1993 *W, AG, Ken, Z*

J Burger 2004 *Za, Ken, Z, Mor,* 2006 *Tun, Tun, Mor, Mor,* 2007 *Za, Geo, R, SA, I, F, Ar, Geo,* 2008 *Z,* 2009 *Iv, Iv, Pt, Tun, Tun,* 2010 *R, Geo, Pt,* 2011 *Fj, Sa, SA, W*

B Calitz 1992 *Z*

C Campbell 2008 *Z*

DJ Coetzee 1990 *Pt, W, F, F, WGe,* 1991 *Sp, Pt, It, It, Z, Z, I, I, Z, Z, Z,* 1992 *Z, Z,* 1993 *W, AG, Ken, Z,* 1994 *Z, Iv, Mor, HK,* 1995 *Z, Z*

JC Coetzee 1990 *W*

M Couw 2006 *Ken*

B Cronjé 1994 *Rus*

HDP Dames 2011 *Fj, Sa, SA, W,* 2012 *Sen, Mad*

J Dames 1998 *Tun, Z*

D de Beer 2000 *Z*

S de Beer 1995 *Z,* 1997 *Tg,* 1998 *Tun, Z, Iv, Mor, Z,* 1999 *Ger*

AD de Klerk 2009 *Iv, Iv*

CJ De Koe 2010 *Geo, Pt, Sp*

DP De La Harpe 2010 *Rus, R, Geo, Pt, Sp,* 2011 *R, Pt, Geo, Fj, Sa, SA, W*

RCA De La Harpe 2011 *R, Pt, Geo, Fj, SA, W*

SC De La Harpe 2010 *Sp*

H de Waal 1990 *Z, Pt*

N de Wet 2000 *Ur*

R Dedig 2004 *Mor, Za, Ken, Z, Mor*

CJH Derks 1990 *Z, Pt, W, W, F, F, WGe,* 1991 *Sp, Pt, It, It, Z, Z, I, I, Z, Z, Z,* 1992 *Z, Z,* 1993 *W, AG, Z,* 1994 *Rus, Z, Iv, Mor, HK*

J Deysel 1990 *Z, Pt, W, W,* 1991 *Sp, Pt, It, It, Z, Z, I, I, Z, Z, Z,* 1992 *Z*

V Dreyer 2002 *Z,* 2003 *Ar, I*

J Drotsky 2006 *Ken,* 2008 *Sen*

AJ Du Plessis 2010 *Pt, Sp*

I du Plessis 2005 *Mor,* 2009 *Tun*

M du Plessis 2001 *Z,* 2005 *Mor*

N du Plessis 1993 *Ken,* 1994 *Rus,* 1995 *Z*

O Du Plessis 2008 *Sen*

T Du Plessis 2006 *Ken, Tun, Mor, Mor,* 2007 *Geo, R, Uga, SA, I, F, Ar, Geo,* 2008 *Sen, Z,* 2009 *Iv, Iv, Pt, Tun, Tun,* 2010 *R, Geo, Pt, Sp,* 2011 *R, Pt, Geo, Fj, SA, W,* 2012 *Sen*

P du Plooy 1992 *Z, Z,* 1994 *Z, Mor, HK*

S du Rand 2007 *Geo, R, Uga*

JA Du Toit 2007 *Za, Geo, R, Uga, SA, I, F, Geo,* 2008 *Sen, Z,* 2009 *Pt, Tun, Tun,* 2010 *Rus, R, Geo, Pt, Sp,* 2011 *R, Pt, Geo, Sa, SA, W*

N du Toit 2002 *Tun,* 2003 *Sa, Ar, I, A, R*

V du Toit 1990 *Pt, W, W, F*

JH Duvenhage 2000 *Z, Z,* 2001 *It, Z, Z,* 2002 *Mad,* 2003 *Sa, Uga, Ar, I, R,* 2007 *Za, R, Uga*

A Engelbrecht 2000 *Z*

J Engelbrecht 1990 *WGe,* 1994 *Rus, Z, Iv, Mor, HK,* 1995 *Z, Z*

N Engelbrecht 1996 *Z*

H Engels 1990 *F, WGe*

E Erasmus 1997 *Tg*

G Esterhuizen 2008 *Sen, Z*

SF Esterhuizen 2008 *Z,* 2009 *Iv, Iv, Pt, Tun, Tun,* 2010 *Rus, R, Geo, Pt, Sp,* 2011 *R, Pt,* 2012 *Sen, Mad*

N Esterhuyse 2006 *Ken, Tun, Mor,* 2007 *Za, Geo, R, Uga, SA, I, F, Ar, Geo,* 2008 *Z,* 2009 *Iv, Iv, Pt, Tun, Tun,* 2010 *Rus, R, Geo, Pt, Sp,* 2011 *R, Pt, Geo, Fj, Sa, SA, W*

D Farmer 1997 *Tg,* 1998 *Pt, Iv, Mor, Z,* 1999 *Z, Fj, Ger*

F Fisch 1999 *Z, Ger*

TR Forbes 2010 *Rus*

HH Franken 2011 *Sa,* 2012 *Sen, Mad*

S Furter 1999 *Z, Fj, F, C, Ger,* 2001 *It,* 2002 *Mad, Z, Tun, Tun,* 2003 *Sa, Ken, Uga, Ar, I, A, R,* 2004 *Mor,* 2006 *Ken, Tun, Ken*

E Gaoab 2005 *Mad, Mor*

I Gaya 2004 *Za, Ken*

J Genis 2000 *Z, Z, Ur,* 2001 *Z*

N Genis 2006 *Mor*

R Gentz 2001 *It*

R Glundeung 2006 *Ken*

CJ Goosen 1991 *Sp, Pt, It, It,* 1993 *W*

D Gouws 2000 *Z, Z, Ur,* 2001 *It, Z, Z*

T Gouws 2003 *Ken, Uga,* 2004 *Za, Ken,* 2006 *Ken, Tun*

A Graham 2001 *It, Z, Z,* 2002 *Mad, Tun,* 2003 *Ken, Uga, I,* 2004 *Mor*

A Greeff 1997 *Tg*

D Grobelaar 2008 *Z*

DP Grobler 2001 *Z,* 2002 *Mad, Tun, Tun,* 2003 *Sa, Ken, Uga, Ar, I, A, R,* 2004 *Mor, Za, Ken, Z, Mor,* 2006 *Ken, Tun, Ken,* 2007 *Za, Geo, R, SA, Ar*

HJ Grobler 1990 *Z, Pt, W, W, F, F, WGe,* 1991 *Sp, Pt, It, It, Z, Z, I, I, Z, Z,* 1992 *Z, Z*

T Grünewald 1990 *Z*

D Grunschloss 2003 *A, R*

F Hartung 1996 *Z, Z*

RJ Herridge 2009 *Pt, Tun, Tun*

L Holtzhausen 1997 *Tg,* 1998 *Pt, Tun, Z, Iv, Mor, Z,* 1999 *Ger*

F Horn 2005 *Mad, Mor*, 2006 *Ken*
H Horn 1997 *Tg*, 1998 *Pt, Iv, Mor, Z*, 1999 *Z, Fj, F, C, Ger*, 2001 *It*, 2002 *Mad, Z, Tun*, 2003 *Sa*, 2007 *Za, Geo, R, Uga, SA, I, F, Ar, Geo*, 2008 *Sen, Z*, 2009 *Iv, Iv, Tun, Tun*, 2010 *Rus*, 2011 *Fj, Sa, SA, W*
K Horn 1997 *Tg*, 1998 *Pt*
Q Hough 1995 *Z, Z*, 1998 *Pt, Tun, Z, Iv, Mor, Z*, 1999 *Z, Fj, F, C*
P Human 2012 *Sen, Mad*
D Husselman 1993 *AG*, 1994 *Z, Mor*, 2002 *Mad, Z, Tun*, 2003 *Sa, Ar, I, A*
JJ Husselman 2004 *Za, Ken*
E Isaacs 1993 *Ken*, 1994 *Iv*
P Isaacs 2000 *Z, Z, Ur*, 2001 *Z, Z*, 2003 *A*, 2005 *Mad, Mor*
E Izaacs 1998 *Pt*, 1999 *Z, Ger*, 2000 *Z, Z, Ur*, 2001 *It, Z, Z*, 2002 *Mad, Z, Tun, Tun*, 2003 *Sa, Ken, Ar, A, R*
M Jacobs 1999 *Z, Fj, F, Ger*
E Jansen 2006 *Ken*
EA Jantjies 2006 *Ken, Tun, Ken, Tun*, 2007 *Za, Geo, R, Uga, SA, I, F, Ar, Geo*, 2008 *Sen, Z*, 2009 *Iv, Iv, Pt, Tun, Tun*, 2010 *Rus, R, Geo, Pt, Sp*, 2011 *R, Pt, Geo, Fj, Sa, SA, W*, 2012 *Sen, Mad*
R Jantjies 1994 *HK*, 1995 *Z, Z*, 1996 *Z*, 1998 *Pt, Tun, Iv, Mor, Z*, 1999 *Z, Fj, F, C*, 2000 *Z, Z*
M Jeary 2003 *Uga*, 2004 *Za, Mor*
R Jeary 2000 *Z, Ur*
D Jeffrey 1990 *F*
J Jenkins 2002 *Mad, Tun*, 2003 *Ken*
AJ Jevu 2012 *Sen*
D Kamonga 2004 *Mor, Za, Ken, Z, Mor*, 2007 *Uga, Geo*
M Kapitako 2000 *Z, Z*, 2001 *It, Z, Z*, 2003 *Uga*, 2004 *Za*, 2006 *Tun*
HI Kasera 2012 *Mad*
M Katjiuanjo 2005 *Mad, Mor*
M Kazombiaze 2006 *Ken, Tun*
U Kazombiaze 2006 *Ken, Tun, Mor, Mor*, 2007 *Za, Uga, SA, I, F, Ar, Geo*, 2008 *Sen, Z*, 2009 *Iv, Iv, Pt, Tun, Tun*, 2010 *Rus, Geo*, 2011 *W*
R Kitshoff 2010 *Pt, Sp*, 2011 *R, Pt, Geo, Fj, Sa, SA, W*
DPW Koen 2006 *Tun*
HVW Koll 2009 *Pt, Tun*, 2010 *Rus, R, Geo, Pt, Sp*, 2011 *R, Pt, Geo, Fj, Sa, SA, W*, 2012 *Sen, Mad*
A Kotze 1991 *Sp, Z, Z, I, I*, 1993 *W, AG, Z*
D Kotze 1993 *W, AG, Ken, Z*, 1994 *Rus, HK*
J Kotze 1995 *Z, Z*, 1996 *Z, Z*, 2000 *Z, Z*, 2001 *It, Z, Z*, 2002 *Mad, Z, Tun, Tun*, 2004 *Za, Ken, Z, Mor*
P Kotze 2001 *It*
P Kotze 1996 *Z*
TAW Kotze 2011 *Pt, Fj, Sa, SA, W*, 2012 *Sen, Mad*
L Kotzee 2008 *Z*
JL Kruger 2001 *It, Z, Z*
R Kruger 2003 *Ken, Uga*, 2005 *Mad, Mor*
R Kruger 2004 *Mor, Za, Ken, Mor*
SO Lambert 2000 *Z, Ur*, 2001 *It, Z, Z*, 2003 *Ken, Uga*, 2004 *Mor*, 2005 *Mad*, 2006 *Ken, Tun, Ken*
B Langenhoven 2007 *SA, I, F, Ar, Geo*, 2008 *Sen, Z*, 2009 *Pt, Tun, Tun*, 2010 *Rus*
R Larson 2011 *Fj, Sa, W*
G Lensing 2002 *Mad, Z, Tun, Tun*, 2003 *Sa, Ar, I, A, R*, 2004 *Mor*, 2006 *Ken, Mor, Mor*, 2007 *R, SA, I, F, Ar, Geo*, 2009 *Iv, Iv, Tun, Tun*
C Lesch 2005 *Mad, Mor*
HD Lindvelt 1998 *Iv, Z*, 1999 *F, C, Ger*, 2001 *It, Z, Z*, 2002 *Mad, Z, Tun, Tun*, 2003 *Sa, Ken, Uga, Ar, I, A*, 2004 *Mor, Za, Ken, Z, Mor*, 2006 *Ken, Tun, Ken, Mor, Mor*, 2007 *Za, Geo, SA, F, Ar*
J Lombaard 1996 *Z*
H Loots 1990 *Z*
J Losper 2005 *Mor*
SJ Losper 1990 *Z, Pt, W, W, F, F, WGe*, 1991 *Sp, Pt, It, It, Z, Z, I, I, Z, Z, Z*
TC Losper 2007 *Za, Geo, R, Uga, SA, I, F*, 2008 *Sen*, 2011 *Geo, W*
W Lötter 1990 *Z*
RC Loubser 1999 *F*, 2005 *Mad, Mor*
O Louw 1993 *Ken, Z*, 1994 *Z, Iv*, 1996 *Z*
M MacKenzie 2004 *Mor*, 2006 *Ken, Tun*, 2007 *Uga, I, F, Ar*

B Malgas 1991 *Z, Z, Z*, 1993 *W, AG, Ken, Z*, 1994 *Rus, Z, Iv, Mor, HK*, 1995 *Z, Z*, 1996 *Z*
G Mans 1990 *Z, Pt, W, W, F*, 1991 *Sp, Pt, It, Z, Z, I, I, Z, Z*, 1992 *Z, Z*, 1993 *W, AG, Ken, Z*, 1994 *Rus, Z, Iv, Mor, HK*
C Marais 2010 *Pt, Sp*, 2011 *Fj, SA*
M Marais 1992 *Z*, 1993 *W, AG, Z*
W Maritz 1990 *Z*, 1991 *Z, Z, I, I, Z, Z, Z*
S McCulley 1990 *W, W, F, WGe*
E Meyer 1991 *Sp, Pt, It, It, Z, Z, I, I, Z, Z, Z*, 1992 *Z, Z*, 1993 *W*, 1994 *Z, Iv, Mor, HK*, 1995 *Z, Z*, 1996 *Z*
H Meyer 2004 *Za, Ken, Z, Mor*
JM Meyer 2003 *Ken, Uga, Ar, I, R*, 2006 *Ken, Tun, Tun, Mor, Mor*, 2007 *Uga, SA, I, F, Ar, Geo*
P Meyer 2005 *Mad*
DA Mouton 1999 *Z, Fj, Ger*, 2000 *Z, Z, Ur*, 2002 *Mad, Z, Tun*, 2003 *Sa, Ken, Uga, Ar, I, A, R*, 2004 *Mor*, 2005 *Mad, Mor*, 2006 *Tun, Ken, Tun, Mor*, 2007 *Ar*, 2008 *Sen*
H Mouton 2000 *Z*
P Mouton 2005 *Mad, Mor*
H Neethling 1993 *Ken*
G Nel 2006 *Mor, Mor*
JA Nel 2012 *Sen, Mad*
S Nell 2000 *Z, Z*
J Nienaber 1998 *Pt, Tun, Z, Mor, Z*
J Nieuwenhuis 2007 *Za, Geo, R, Uga, SA, I, F, Geo*, 2008 *Sen, Z*, 2009 *Iv, Iv, Tun, Tun*, 2010 *R, Geo, Sp*, 2011 *R, Pt, Geo, Fj, SA, W*
EB O'Callaghan 2010 *R, Geo, Pt, Sp*, 2011 *R, Pt, Geo, Fj, Sa, SA, W*
J Olivier 1999 *Z, Fj, Ger*, 2000 *Z, Z, Ur*
M Olivier 1990 *Pt, F*
LT Oosthuizen 1990 *Z, Pt, W, W, F, F, WGe*
J Opperman 1999 *Z, Fj, F, C, Ger*
T Opperman 2002 *Mad, Z*
WJ Otto 1993 *AG, Z*, 1994 *Rus*
R Pedro 1998 *Z*, 1999 *Ger*, 2000 *Ur*, 2001 *It, Z, Z*, 2003 *Sa, Ken, Uga, Ar, I, A, R*, 2004 *Mor*
DG Philander 2008 *Sen*, 2009 *Iv, Iv, Pt, Tun, Tun*, 2010 *Rus*, 2011 *R, Pt, Geo, W*
F Pienaar 2006 *Ken*
D Pieters 2008 *Sen*
L Plaath 2001 *It, Z, Z*
CJ Powell 2001 *It, Z, Z*, 2002 *Mad, Z, Tun, Tun*, 2003 *Sa, Ken, Uga, Ar, I, R*, 2004 *Mor, Ken, Z, Mor*, 2006 *Ken, Tun, Tun, Mor, Mor*, 2007 *Za, Geo, R, Ar, Geo*
JH Redelinghuys 2006 *Ken, Tun, Mor*, 2007 *Za, Geo, R, Uga, SA, I, F, Ar, Geo*, 2008 *Sen, Z*, 2009 *Iv, Iv, Pt, Tun, Tun*, 2010 *Rus, R, Geo, Pt, Sp*, 2011 *R, Pt, Geo, Fj, Sa, SA, W*, 2012 *Sen, Mad*
C Redlinghaus 2001 *It*
H Reinders 1996 *Z*
G Rich 1993 *W*
C Roets 1995 *Z*
P Rossouw 2004 *Za, Ken, Z, Mor*, 2005 *Mad, Mor*, 2006 *Mor, Mor*, 2007 *Za, Geo, R*
A Samuelson 1995 *Z*, 1996 *Z, Z*, 1997 *Tg*, 1998 *Pt, Tun, Z, Iv, Mor, Z*, 1999 *Z, Fj, F, C, Ger*
M Schreuder 2002 *Mad, Z, Tun, Tun*, 2003 *Sa, Ken, Uga, I, A, R*, 2004 *Mor, Za, Ken, Z, Mor*, 2006 *Ken, Ken*, 2007 *Ar, Geo*
C Schumacher 1995 *Z*
JH Senekal 1998 *Iv, Mor, Z*, 1999 *Z, Fj, F, C, Ger*, 2002 *Mad, Z*, 2003 *Sa, Ken, Uga, Ar, I, A, R*, 2005 *Mad*, 2006 *Ken, Mor, Mor*, 2007 *Geo, R, Uga, I, Ar, Geo*
A Skinner 1990 *Z, Pt, W, W, F, F, WGe*
G Smit 1990 *F*
C Smith 2012 *Sen, Mad*
E Smith 1998 *Tun, Iv, Mor, Z*, 1999 *Fj, F, C*, 2002 *Mad*
P Smith 1993 *Ken*, 1994 *Iv*, 1995 *Z, Z*
S Smith 1990 *Pt, W, W, F*, 1992 *Z, Z*, 1993 *W, AG, Ken, Z*, 1994 *Rus, Z, Iv, Mor, HK*, 1996 *Z*
W Smith 2002 *Mad, Z, Tun*
D Snyders 2003 *Uga*, 2005 *Mad*
H Snyman 1990 *F, F*, 1991 *Sp, Pt, It, It, Z, Z, I, I, Z, Z, Z*, 1992 *Z, Z*, 1993 *W, AG, Ken, Z*, 1994 *Z, Iv, Mor, HK*, 1995 *Z, Z*, 1996 *Z, Z*

M **Snyman** 1994 *Rus, Z, Iv, Mor, HK*
D **Spangenberg** 2005 *Mad, Mor*
A **Steenkamp** 1994 *Iv, Mor*
C **Steenkamp** 2007 *Uga*
T **Steenkamp** 1992 *Z, Z*, 1993 *Ken*, 1994 *Rus, Iv*, 1995 *Z*, 1996 *Z*, 1998 *Pt, Tun, Z*
P **Steyn** 1996 *Z, Z*, 1997 *Tg*, 1998 *Pt, Tun, Z, Iv, Mor*, 1999 *Z, Fj, F, C*
A **Stoop** 1990 *Z, Pt, W*, 1991 *Sp, Pt, It, It, Z, I, I, Z*
L **Stoop** 1994 *Iv*
L **Stoop** 2012 *Sen, Mad*
H **Stroh** 2012 *Mad*
G **Suze** 2005 *Mad*
CI **Swanepoel** 2012 *Sen, Mad*
N **Swanepoel** 2003 *Ken, Ar, I, A, R*, 2004 *Mor, Za, Ken, Z, Mor*
H **Swart** 1995 *Z*, 1996 *Z*, 1997 *Tg*, 1998 *Pt, Tun, Z*
JL **Swart** 1990 *F, WGe*
BM **Swartz** 1990 *W, W, F, F, WGe*
R **Theart** 1998 *Pt*
J **Theron** 1998 *Iv, Mor, Z*, 1999 *Fj, F, C, Ger*, 2004 *Mor*
RHR **Thompson** 2004 *Za, Ken, Mor*, 2005 *Mad*, 2006 *Ken, Tun, Ken, Tun, Mor, Mor*
D **Tredoux** 2001 *Z*
L **van Coller** 1993 *AG, Ken*, 1994 *Rus, Iv*
GE **van der Berg** 2005 *Mor*, 2006 *Ken, Tun, Tun, Mor*
L **van der Linde** 2006 *Tun*
A **van der Merwe** 1990 *Pt, W, W, F, F, WGe*, 1991 *Sp, Pt, It, It, Z, I, I, Z, Z, Z*, 1992 *Z, Z*
D **van der Merwe** 1990 *WGe*
S **van der Merwe** 1997 *Tg*, 1998 *Iv, Mor, Z*, 1999 *Z, Fj, F, C*, 2002 *Z, Tun, Tun*, 2003 *Sa, Ken, Ar, I, A, R*, 2004 *Za, Ken, Z, Mor*, 2006 *Tun, Mor*
J **van der Westhuizen** 2007 *Za, Geo*
L **van Dyk** 1998 *Tun, Z, Iv, Mor, Z*, 1999 *Fj, F, C, Ger*, 2002 *Mad*
JA **van Lill** 2002 *Mad, Tun, Tun*, 2003 *Sa, Ar, I, A, R*, 2004 *Mor*, 2006 *Tun*, 2007 *Za*
PJ **Van Lill** 2006 *Ken*, 2008 *Sen, Z*, 2009 *Iv, Pt, Tun, Tun*, 2010 *Rus, R, Geo, Pt, Sp*, 2011 *R, Pt, Geo, Fj, Sa, SA*, 2012 *Sen, Mad*
RE **Van Neel** 2010 *Rus*, 2011 *Sa*
F **van Rensburg** 1995 *Z*, 1996 *Z, Z*, 1997 *Tg*, 1998 *Tun, Z*, 1999 *Z, Fj, F, C, Ger*, 2000 *Z*, 2001 *It, Z, Z*
SJ **van Rensburg** 1998 *Z, Iv, Mor, Z*, 1999 *Z, Fj, F, Ger*, 2000 *Z, Ur*
SL **Van Rooi** 2003 *Uga, A*, 2004 *Mor*, 2005 *Mor*
A **van Rooyen** 1991 *Sp, Pt, It, It, I*, 1992 *Z, Z*

M **van Rooyen** 1996 *Z*, 1998 *Pt, Tun, Z, Mor, Z*, 1999 *Z, F, C*
C **van Schalkwyk** 1993 *AG, Z*
A **Van Tonder** 1995 *Z*
CJ **van Tonder** 2002 *Tun*, 2003 *Sa, Ken, Uga, I, A, R*, 2004 *Mor, Za, Ken, Z, Mor*, 2006 *Ken, Ken*, 2007 *Za*
JH **Van Tonder** 2004 *Mor, Ken, Z, Mor*, 2006 *Ken, Tun*, 2007 *Uga, SA, I, F, Ar, Geo*, 2008 *Z*, 2009 *Iv, Iv, Pt, Tun*
N **van Vuuren** 1993 *AG*
RJ **van Vuuren** 1997 *Tg*, 1998 *Pt, Tun, Z*, 1999 *Z, Ger*, 2000 *Z, Z, Ur*, 2002 *Mad, Z*, 2003 *Ken, Uga, R*
A **van Wyk** 1993 *W, Ken*, 1994 *Iv, HK*
D **Van Wyk** 2011 *R, Pt, Geo, Fj, Sa, SA, W*
G **van Wyk** 1999 *Z, Fj, F, C*, 2000 *Z, Z, Ur*, 2001 *It*
L **van Wyk** 2004 *Mor*
M **Van Wyk** 2009 *Iv, Iv, Pt*, 2010 *Rus, Geo, Pt*, 2011 *R, Pt, Geo*
R **van Wyk** 2002 *Mad, Z, Tun, Tun*, 2003 *Sa*, 2004 *Mor, Za, Ken, Z, Mor*
R **van Wyk** 2004 *Za, Ken, Z, Mor*
J **van Zyl** 2008 *Sen*
R **van Zyl** 1997 *Tg*, 1998 *Tun, Z, Iv, Mor, Z*
WP **Van Zyl** 2007 *SA, I, F, Ar, Geo*, 2008 *Z*, 2009 *Iv, Iv, Pt, Tun, Tun*, 2010 *R, Geo, Pt, Sp*, 2011 *Fj, Sa, SA, W*
M **Venter** 2003 *Uga*, 2004 *Mor*, 2008 *Z*, 2009 *Iv, Iv, Pt, Tun, Tun*, 2010 *Rus*
D **Vermaak** 1998 *Z*
JJ **Vermaak** 1990 *Pt*, 1994 *Rus*, 1996 *Z*
A **Vermeulen** 2010 *Rus*
B **Vermeulen** 1995 *Z*
D **Vermeulen** 1996 *Z, Z*, 1997 *Tg*, 1998 *Pt*
G **Vermeulen** 1991 *Z*
M **Visser** 2007 *Za, Geo, R, Uga, SA, Ar, Geo*, 2009 *Iv, Iv, Pt, Tun, Tun*, 2010 *Rus, R, Geo, Pt, Sp*, 2011 *SA*
CW **Viviers** 2010 *Sp*, 2011 *R, Pt, Geo*
P **von Wielligh** 1991 *It, Z*, 1992 *Z*, 1993 *AG, Z*, 1994 *Iv, Mor*, 1995 *Z*, 1996 *Z*
B **Walters** 2009 *Pt*
GAE **Walters** 2008 *Z*, 2009 *Iv*, 2010 *R, Geo, Pt, Sp*
W **Wentzel** 1991 *Sp, Z, Z*
E **Wessels** 2002 *Tun, Tun*, 2003 *Sa, Ar, I, A, R*, 2006 *Tun, Mor, Mor*, 2007 *SA, I, F*, 2009 *Iv, Pt, Tun, Tun*, 2010 *Rus*
LP **Winkler** 2008 *Z*, 2009 *Iv, Iv*, 2010 *Rus, R, Geo*, 2011 *R, Pt, Geo, Fj, Sa*
RC **Witbooi** 2004 *Za, Z*, 2005 *Mor*, 2006 *Ken, Tun, Ken*, 2007 *Za, Geo, R, Uga, I, F, Geo*, 2008 *Sen*
J **Wohler** 2005 *Mad, Mor*
J **Zaayman** 1997 *Tg*, 1998 *Pt, Tun, Z, Iv, Mor, Z*, 1999 *Z, Fj, F, C, Ger*

All Black captain Richie McCaw holds aloft the Bledisloe Cup.

NEW ZEALAND

NEW ZEALAND'S 2012 TEST RECORD

OPPONENTS	DATE	VENUE	RESULT
Ireland	9 Jun	H	Won 42–10
Ireland	16 Jun	H	Won 22–19
Ireland	23 Jun	H	Won 60–0
Australia	18 Aug	A	Won 27–19
Australia	25 Aug	H	Won 22–0
Argentina	8 Sep	H	Won 21–5
South Africa	15 Sep	H	Won 21–11
Argentina	29 Sep	A	Won 54–15
South Africa	6 Oct	A	Won 32–16

DOMINANT ALL BLACKS REMAIN UNBEATEN

By Iain Spragg

Hosea Gear evades the desperate lunge of Jean de Villiers in their Rugby Championship encounter.

New Zealand began 2012 as the reigning world champions after a long-awaited World Cup triumph on home soil and the All Blacks proved unfazed by their undisputed status as the number one side, despatching Ireland in their three-Test summer series before claiming the inaugural Rugby Championship title with an unblemished record.

The All Blacks were dormant for seven months after lifting the Webb Ellis Cup in Auckland but there was no evidence of either complacency or over-confidence when they returned to the fray to face Ireland in June, while their performances in The Rugby Championship merely underlined their supremacy both home and away in the southern hemisphere.

They were pushed perilously close by the Irish in Christchurch and made to dig deep by the Australians in Sydney but nine wins in nine Tests ultimately told its own story and allayed any fears that the All

Blacks might struggle to recapture the irresistible form that saw them end the country's 24-year wait for World Cup glory.

It was a new era on the pitch for the All Blacks with the advent of The Rugby Championship in place of the Tri-Nations and it was also a new era in the dugout as Steve Hansen succeeded Graham Henry as coach.

Henry stood down after eight years at the helm days after his side had beaten France in the Rugby World Cup Final and by December the New Zealand Rugby Union opted for continuity when they promoted Hansen from assistant to head coach on an initial two-year deal.

"No words can explain how humbling it is to be given the opportunity to be the All Blacks coach," Hansen said after his appointment. "From a coaching point of view, in this sport it's the greatest honour you can receive. It comes with a huge amount of responsibility.

"All I can say is I'm a passionate New Zealander, passionate about New Zealand rugby and passionate about the All Black jersey and its legacy. I look forward to the next two years and achieving things with this team and enhancing that legacy. My aim will be to leave the team in a better shape than how I found it."

Hansen subsequently named former Chiefs coach Ian Foster as his new assistant and Brian McLean as his defensive coordinator while his first side to play Ireland in Auckland in early June featured three debutants in wing Julian Savea, scrum half Aaron Smith and second row Brodie Retallick.

The Irish had not beaten New Zealand in 24 previous attempts and although the opening quarter of the match saw Dan Carter edge opposite number Johnny Sexton in a battle of the boots, the All Blacks pulled away effortlessly in the final hour and a Savea hat-trick gave New Zealand a 42–10 win and Hansen the perfect start to his new career.

The second Test a week later saw the All Blacks playing in Christchurch for the first time since the 2011 earthquake but hopes of an emotional and victorious return nearly failed to materialise as the tourists came dramatically close to claiming an historic win.

Scrum half Smith scored New Zealand's only try early in the second half but a Sexton penalty on 68 minutes levelled the scores at 19–19 and, with Israel Dagg sin-binned minutes later, the result hung in the balance until Carter's last-gasp drop goal sealed victory for the 14-man All Blacks.

Criticism in the New Zealand press of the performance evidently stung the team and they were simply unstoppable in the third Test in Hamilton, running in nine unanswered tries including braces for Sonny Bill Williams and Sam Cane as Ireland were ruthlessly demolished 60–0 to conclude the tour.

"We have introduced a group of young men to the All Black jersey and by and large we are pretty happy with how they have performed." Hansen said. "Aaron Cruden ran the team as if he had been there for years, then Beauden Barrett came in and did the same. Sam Cane was also outstanding tonight."

The Rugby Championship and an opening fixture against Australia in Sydney was next on the agenda but an error-strewn performance from the Wallabies ensured the All Blacks were rarely tested as they recorded a 27–19 success.

Dagg scored the first try of the match after 12 minutes. Cory Jane added the second 20 minutes later and, although Australia replied before the break through Nathan Sharpe, the second half was almost exclusively a duel between Carter and Berrick Barnes and the home side never seriously threatened to overhaul their visitors.

The return fixture a week later in Auckland was equally comfortable. Another Dagg effort proved the only try of the match but what New Zealand may have lacked going forward, they more than made up for with their superb defence, denying the Australians a single point in a 22–0 victory, the first time they had shut-out the Wallabies in 50 years.

Early September saw newcomers Argentina arrive in Wellington and the Pumas took to their task with relish in the early exchanges, taking a surprise 12th-minute lead courtesy of a Rodrigo Roncero try. The lead lasted a little over 10 minutes when Cruden landed his second penalty of the game but Argentina did not crumble and New Zealand had to wait until the 66th minute before they crossed the whitewash through Savea. Jane added a second late on and Hansen's men emerged with a hard-fought 21–5 victory.

"In our first half we tried to play way too much rugby for the conditions," the coach conceded. "We tried to move the ball at times we should have held on to it. Our ball security wasn't that great. But part of that was the intensity the Argentineans brought.

"They're a welcome addition to this competition. In years to come we're going to look back on this first year and say this is the beginning of something new. They're only going to get better and better and they're a very good side at the moment. They're probably one of the best defensive teams in the world."

The All Blacks met South Africa seven days later in Dunedin but it was not to be a classic between the reigning and recently deposed world champions. An early try from Dagg was cancelled out by Bryan Habana's effort seven minutes into the second half and had Springboks fly half Morné Steyn enjoyed a better game with the boot, South Africa may have pushed New Zealand closer. Instead substitute Aaron Smith stretched the lead with a second All Black try on the hour and the home side ground out a 21–11 win.

New Zealand made the trip to Argentina for the fifth match of the competition knowing victory over the Pumas would seal the title, and while the South Americans were always in touch in their clash in Wellington, they were blown away in Buenos Aires as the All Blacks produced their best performance of the tournament.

Scrum half Martín Landajo went over the Argentineans in the seventh minute but it was a fleeting moment of hope for the home side as Aaron Smith replied eight minutes later to spark an All Black onslaught.

Wing Jane helped himself to a hat-trick while Savea scored a brace, and at the final whistle New Zealand had won 54–15 to claim the inaugural Rugby Championship title, adding to the 10 Tri Nations crowns they had already amassed.

"The goal is to put last year behind us but we've got the tag of world champions and we want to play like that," said captain Richie McCaw. "To secure The Rugby Championship this year was a big goal and it's nice to be able to do that. But I think a better performance today is what the guys are pretty happy with. Rather than scoreboard-wise, it was the manner in which we did it which was satisfying."

Pride rather than silverware was at stake when New Zealand touched down in South Africa to end their campaign but there was absolutely no sign of the champions easing off in Soweto as the All Blacks strove to complete a southern hemisphere campaign without defeat for a fifth time.

The Springboks, however, were out of the blocks fastest with an early Habana try. Second row Sam Whitelock and then Aaron Smith replied in the first half for New Zealand but the visitors' resolve was put to the test when substitute fly half Elton Jantjies landed two penalties and the home side found themselves 16–12 ahead at the break.

The All Blacks' unbeaten record in 2012 was in real danger but scores from the midfield pairing of Ma'a Nonu and Conrad Smith calmed what nerves may have been jangling and with South Africa unable to further trouble the scoreboard, New Zealand were 32–16 victors.

This was McCaw's 100th Test victory – the first player to ever reach this milestone – and extended the All Blacks' unbeaten sequence which had begun in the pool stages of RWC 2011 to 16 matches, just two wins short of equalling the record of 18 set by Lithuania between 2006 and 2010.

"We are getting better," insisted Hansen after the game. "We don't want to get ahead of ourselves. We'll enjoy the moment for what it is, a great victory against a great opponent. Come Monday, the feet will be back on the floor.

"We know we have some very talented players, but so have a lot of other teams. The difference between us and them is that we are perhaps getting our preparation right during the week and ensuring that our players have the best chance to perform on the Saturday."

NEW ZEALAND

NEW ZEALAND INTERNATIONAL STATISTICS

MATCH RECORDS UP TO 10 OCTOBER 2012

MOST CONSECUTIVE TEST WINS

17 1965 SA 4, 1966 BI 1,2,3,4, 1967 A,E,W,F,S, 1968 A 1,2, F 1,2,3, 1969 W 1,2
16 2011 Tg, J, F, C, Arg, A, F, 2012 I 1,2,3, A1,2, Arg1, SA1, Arg2, SA2
15 2005 A 1, SA 2, A 2, W,I E,S, 2006 I 1,2, Arg, A 1, SA 1, A 2, 3, SA 2
15 2009 A 3, 4, W,It E,F 3, 2010 I 1, W 1,2, SA 1, 2, A 1, 2, SA 3, A 3
12 1988 A 3, 1989 F 1,2, Arg 1,2, A,W,I, 1990 S 1,2, A 1,2

MOST CONSECUTIVE TESTS WITHOUT DEFEAT

Matches	Wins	Draws	Period
23	22	1	1987 to 1990
17	17	0	1965 to 1969
17	15	2	1961 to 1964
16	16	0	2011 to 2012
15	15	0	2005 to 2006
15	15	0	2009 to 2010

MOST POINTS IN A MATCH
BY THE TEAM

Pts	Opponents	Venue	Year
145	Japan	Bloemfontein	1995
108	Portugal	Lyons	2007
102	Tonga	Albany	2000
101	Italy	Huddersfield	1999
101	Samoa	N Plymouth	2008
93	Argentina	Wellington	1997
91	Tonga	Brisbane	2003
91	Fiji	Albany	2005
85	Romania	Toulouse	2007
83	Japan	Hamilton	2011
79	Canada	Wellington	2011
76	Italy	Marseilles	2007
74	Fiji	Christchurch	1987
73	Canada	Auckland	1995
71	Fiji	Albany	1997
71	Samoa	Albany	1999

BY A PLAYER

Pts	Player	Opponents	Venue	Year
45	S D Culhane	Japan	Bloemfontein	1995
36	T E Brown	Italy	Huddersfield	1999
33	C J Spencer	Argentina	Wellington	1997
33	A P Mehrtens	Ireland	Dublin	1997
33	D W Carter	British/Irish	Wellington	2005
33	N J Evans	Portugal	Lyons	2007
32	T E Brown	Tonga	Albany	2000
30	M C G Ellis	Japan	Bloemfontein	1995
30	T E Brown	Samoa	Albany	2001
29	A P Mehrtens	Australia	Auckland	1999
29	A P Mehrtens	France	Paris	2000
29	L R MacDonald	Tonga	Brisbane	2003
29	D W Carter	Canada	Hamilton	2007

MOST TRIES IN A MATCH
BY THE TEAM

Tries	Opponents	Venue	Year
21	Japan	Bloemfontein	1995
16	Portugal	Lyons	2007
15	Tonga	Albany	2000
15	Fiji	Albany	2005
15	Samoa	N Plymouth	2008
14	Argentina	Wellington	1997
14	Italy	Huddersfield	1999
13	U S A	Berkeley	1913
13	Tonga	Brisbane	2003
13	Romania	Toulouse	2007
13	Japan	Hamilton	2011
12	Italy	Auckland	1987
12	Fiji	Christchurch	1987
12	Canada	Wellington	2011

BY A PLAYER

Tries	Player	Opponents	Venue	Year
6	M C G Ellis	Japan	Bloemfontein	1995
5	J W Wilson	Fiji	Albany	1997
4	D McGregor	England	Crystal Palace	1905
4	C I Green	Fiji	Christchurch	1987
4	J A Gallagher	Fiji	Christchurch	1987
4	J J Kirwan	Wales	Christchurch	1988
4	J T Lomu	England	Cape Town	1995
4	C M Cullen	Scotland	Dunedin	1996
4	J W Wilson	Samoa	Albany	1999
4	J M Muliaina	Canada	Melbourne	2003
4	S W Sivivatu	Fiji	Albany	2005
4	Z R Guildford	Canada	Wellington	2011

MOST CONVERSIONS IN A MATCH
BY THE TEAM

Cons	Opponents	Venue	Year
20	Japan	Bloemfontein	1995
14	Portugal	Lyons	2007
13	Tonga	Brisbane	2003
13	Samoa	N Plymouth	2008
12	Tonga	Albany	2000
11	Italy	Huddersfield	1999
10	Fiji	Christchurch	1987
10	Argentina	Wellington	1997
10	Romania	Toulouse	2007
9	Canada	Melbourne	2003
9	Italy	Marseilles	2007
9	Ireland	N Plymouth	2010
9	Japan	Hamilton	2011
8	Italy	Auckland	1987
8	Wales	Auckland	1988
8	Fiji	Albany	1997
8	Italy	Hamilton	2003
8	Fiji	Albany	2005
8	Canada	Wellington	2011

BY A PLAYER

Cons	Player	Opponents	Venue	Year
20	S D Culhane	Japan	Bloemfontein	1995
14	N J Evans	Portugal	Lyons	2007
12	T E Brown	Tonga	Albany	2000
12	L R MacDonald	Tonga	Brisbane	2003
11	T E Brown	Italy	Huddersfield	1999
10	G J Fox	Fiji	Christchurch	1987
10	C J Spencer	Argentina	Wellington	1997
9	D W Carter	Canada	Melbourne	2003
9	C R Slade	Japan	Hamilton	2011
8	G J Fox	Italy	Auckland	1987
8	G J Fox	Wales	Auckland	1988
8	A P Mehrtens	Italy	Hamilton	2002

MOST DROP GOALS IN A MATCH
BY THE TEAM

Drops	Opponents	Venue	Year
3	France	Christchurch	1986

BY A PLAYER

Drops	Player	Opponents	Venue	Year
2	O D Bruce	Ireland	Dublin	1978
2	F M Botica	France	Christchurch	1986
2	A P Mehrtens	Australia	Auckland	1995

MOST PENALTIES IN A MATCH
BY THE TEAM

Pens	Opponents	Venue	Year
9	Australia	Auckland	1999
9	France	Paris	2000
7	Western Samoa	Auckland	1993
7	South Africa	Pretoria	1999
7	South Africa	Wellington	2006
7	Australia	Auckland	2007
7	Argentina	Auckland	2011
6	British/Irish Lions	Dunedin	1959
6	England	Christchurch	1985
6	Argentina	Wellington	1987
6	Scotland	Christchurch	1987
6	France	Paris	1990
6	South Africa	Auckland	1994
6	Australia	Brisbane	1996
6	Ireland	Dublin	1997
6	South Africa	Cardiff	1999
6	Scotland	Murrayfield	2001
6	South Africa	Christchurch	2004
6	Australia	Sydney	2004
6	South Africa	Dunedin	2008
6	Australia	Tokyo	2009

BY A PLAYER

Pens	Player	Opponents	Venue	Year
9	A P Mehrtens	Australia	Auckland	1999
9	A P Mehrtens	France	Paris	2000
7	G J Fox	Western Samoa	Auckland	1993
7	A P Mehrtens	South Africa	Pretoria	1999
7	D W Carter	South Africa	Wellington	2006
7	D W Carter	Australia	Auckland	2007
7	P A T Weepu	Argentina	Auckland	2011
6	D B Clarke	British/Irish Lions	Dunedin	1959
6	K J Crowley	England	Christchurch	1985
6	G J Fox	Argentina	Wellington	1987
6	G J Fox	Scotland	Christchurch	1987
6	G J Fox	France	Paris	1990
6	S P Howarth	South Africa	Auckland	1994
6	A P Mehrtens	Australia	Brisbane	1996
6	A P Mehrtens	Ireland	Dublin	1997
6	A P Mehrtens	South Africa	Cardiff	1999
6	A P Mehrtens	Scotland	Murrayfield	2001
6	D W Carter	South Africa	Dunedin	2008
6	D W Carter	Australia	Tokyo	2009

NEW ZEALAND

THE COUNTRIES

MOST CAPPED PLAYERS

Caps	Player	Career Span
112	R H McCaw	2001 to 2012
100	J M Muliaina	2003 to 2011
99	K F Mealamu	2002 to 2012
92	S B T Fitzpatrick	1986 to 1997
91	D W Carter	2003 to 2012
91	T D Woodcock	2002 to 2012
81	J W Marshall	1995 to 2005
79	I D Jones	1990 to 1999
75	A J Williams	2002 to 2012
74	J F Umaga	1997 to 2005
72	M A Nonu	2003 to 2012
71	A K Hore	2002 to 2012
70	A P Mehrtens	1995 to 2004
68	J T Rokocoko	2003 to 2010
67	C R Jack	2001 to 2007
66	G M Somerville	2000 to 2008
65	P A T Weepu	2004 to 2012
63	J J Kirwan	1984 to 1994
63	J T Lomu	1994 to 2002
62	R M Brooke	1992 to 1999
62	D C Howlett	2000 to 2007
62	R So'oialo	2002 to 2009
62	C G Smith	2004 to 2012
60	C W Dowd	1993 to 2000
60	J W Wilson	1993 to 2001
59	A D Oliver	1997 to 2007
59	B C Thorn	2003 to 2011
58	G W Whetton	1981 to 1991
58	Z V Brooke	1987 to 1997
58	C M Cullen	1996 to 2002
57	B T Kelleher	1999 to 2007
56	O M Brown	1992 to 1998
56	L R MacDonald	2000 to 2008
55	C E Meads	1957 to 1971
55	F E Bunce	1992 to 1997
55	M N Jones	1987 to 1998

MOST CONSECUTIVE TESTS

Tests	Player	Span
63	S B T Fitzpatrick	1986 to 1995
51	C M Cullen	1996 to 2000
49	R M Brooke	1995 to 1999
41	J W Wilson	1996 to 1999
40	G W Whetton	1986 to 1991

MOST TESTS AS CAPTAIN

Tests	Captain	Span
75	R H McCaw	2004 to 2012
51	S B T Fitzpatrick	1992 to 1997
30	W J Whineray	1958 to 1965
23	R D Thorne	2002 to 2007
22	T C Randell	1998 to 2002
21	J F Umaga	2004 to 2005
19	G N K Mourie	1977 to 1982
18	B J Lochore	1966 to 1970
17	A G Dalton	1981 to 1985

MOST POINTS IN TESTS

Points	Player	Tests	Career
1342	D W Carter	91	2003 to 2012
967	A P Mehrtens	70	1995 to 2004
645	G J Fox	46	1985 to 1993
291	C J Spencer	35	1997 to 2004
245	D C Howlett	62	2000 to 2007
236	C M Cullen	58	1996 to 2002
234	J W Wilson	60	1993 to 2001
230	J T Rokocoko	68	2003 to 2010
207	D B Clarke	31	1956 to 1964
201	A R Hewson	19	1981 to 1984
185	J T Lomu	63	1994 to 2002
185*	J F Umaga	74	1997 to 2005

Umaga's haul includes a penalty try

CAREER RECORDS

MOST CONVERSIONS IN TESTS

Cons	Player	Tests	Career
237	D W Carter	91	2003 to 2012
169	A P Mehrtens	70	1995 to 2004
118	G J Fox	46	1985 to 1993
49	C J Spencer	35	1997 to 2004
43	T E Brown	18	1999 to 2001
33	D B Clarke	31	1956 to 1964
32	S D Culhane	6	1995 to 1996

MOST PENALTY GOALS IN TESTS

Penalties	Player	Tests	Career
235	D W Carter	91	2003 to 2012
188	A P Mehrtens	70	1995 to 2004
128	G J Fox	46	1985 to 1993
43	A R Hewson	19	1981 to 1984
41	C J Spencer	35	1997 to 2004
38	D B Clarke	31	1956 to 1964
24	W F McCormick	16	1965 to 1971

MOST TRIES IN TESTS

Tries	Player	Tests	Career
49	D C Howlett	62	2000 to 2007
46	C M Cullen	58	1996 to 2002
46	J T Rokocoko	68	2003 to 2010
44	J W Wilson	60	1993 to 2001
37	J T Lomu	63	1994 to 2002
37*	J F Umaga	74	1997 to 2005
35	J J Kirwan	63	1984 to 1994
34	J M Muliaina	100	2003 to 2011
29	D W Carter	91	2003 to 2012
29	S W Sivivatu	45	2005 to 2011
24	J W Marshall	81	1995 to 2005
24	M A Nonu	72	2003 to 2012
23	C G Smith	62	2004 to 2012
20	F E Bunce	55	1992 to 1997
20*	R H McCaw	112	2001 to 2012

Umaga and McCaw's hauls each include a penalty try

MOST DROP GOALS IN TESTS

Drops	Player	Tests	Career
10	A P Mehrtens	70	1995 to 2004
7	G J Fox	46	1985 to 1993
6	D W Carter	91	2003 to 2012
5	D B Clarke	31	1956 to 1964
5	M A Herewini	10	1962 to 1967
5	O D Bruce	14	1976 to 1978

387

RUGBY CHAMPIONSHIP (FORMERLY TRI-NATIONS) RECORDS

RECORD	DETAIL	HOLDER	SET
Most points in season	184	in six matches	2010
Most tries in season	22	in six matches	2010
Highest Score	55	55-35 v S Africa (h)	1997
Biggest win	39	54-15 v Argentina (a)	2012
Highest score conceded	46	40-46 v S Africa (a)	2000
Biggest defeat	21	7-28 v Australia (a)	1999
Most appearances	45	R H McCaw	2002 to 2012
Most points in matches	519	D W Carter	2003 to 2012
Most points in season	99	D W Carter	2006
Most points in match	29	A P Mehrtens	v Australia (h) 1999
Most tries in matches	16	C M Cullen	1996 to 2002
Most tries in season	7	C M Cullen	2000
Most tries in match	3	J T Rokocoko	v Australia (a) 2003
	3	D C Howlett	v Australia (h) 2005
	3	C S Jane	v Argentina (a) 2012
Most cons in matches	69	D W Carter	2003 to 2012
Most cons in season	14	D W Carter	2006
Most cons in match	4	C J Spencer	v S Africa (h) 1997
	4	A P Mehrtens	v Australia (a) 2000
	4	A P Mehrtens	v S Africa (a) 2000
	4	C J Spencer	v S Africa (a) 2003
	4	D W Carter	v S Africa (a) 2006
	4	D W Carter	v Australia (a) 2008

NEW ZEALAND

RECORD	DETAIL	HOLDER	SET
	4	D W Carter	v Australia (a) 2010
Most pens in matches	113	D W Carter	2003 to 2012
Most pens in season	21	D W Carter	2006
Most pens in match	9	A P Mehrtens	v Australia (h) 1999

MISCELLANEOUS RECORDS

RECORD	HOLDER	DETAIL
Longest Test Career	E Hughes/C E Meads	1907–21/1957–71
Youngest Test Cap	J T Lomu	19 yrs 45 days in 1994
Oldest Test Cap	E Hughes	40 yrs 123 days in 1921

CAREER RECORDS OF NEW ZEALAND INTERNATIONAL PLAYERS

UP TO 10 OCTOBER 2012

PLAYER BACKS :	DEBUT	CAPS	T	C	P	D	PTS
B J Barrett	2012 v I	2	0	3	1	0	9
D W Carter	2003 v W	91	29	237	235	6	1342
A W Cruden	2010 v I	16	1	7	7	1	43
I J A Dagg	2010 v I	21	11	1	0	0	57
S R Donald	2008 v E	23	1	15	21	0	98
T E Ellison	2009 v It	3	0	0	0	0	0
H E Gear	2008 v A	12	6	0	0	0	30
Z R Guildford	2009 v W	10	6	0	0	0	30
C S Jane	2008 v A	38	14	0	0	0	70
R D Kahui	2008 v E	17	10	0	0	0	50
L T C Masaga	2009 v It	1	0	0	0	0	0
A S Mathewson	2010 v A	4	0	0	0	0	0
M A Nonu	2003 v E	72	24	0	0	0	120
R M N Ranger	2010 v W	3	1	0	0	0	5
S J Savea	2012 v I	5	6	0	0	0	30
A L Smith	2012 v I	9	4	0	0	0	20
B R Smith	2009 v It	8	1	0	0	0	5
C G Smith	2004 v It	62	23	0	0	0	115
B J Stanley	2010 v I	3	0	0	0	0	0
P A T Weepu	2004 v W	65	7	10	16	0	103
S Williams	2010 v E	19	6	0	0	0	30

FORWARDS :

A F Boric	2008 v E	24	2	0	0	0	10
S J Cane	2012 v I	3	2	0	0	0	10
W W V Crockett	2009 v It	7	1	0	0	0	5
A P de Malmanche	2009 v It	5	0	0	0	0	0
T J S Donnelly	2009 v A	15	0	0	0	0	0
H T P Elliot	2010 v S	3	0	0	0	0	0
C C Faumuina	2012 v Arg	3	0	0	0	0	0
B J Franks	2010 v I	21	1	0	0	0	5
O T Franks	2009 v It	40	0	0	0	0	0
J M R A Hoeata	2011 v Fj	3	0	0	0	0	0
A K Hore	2002 v E	71	7	0	0	0	35
T D Latimer	2009 v F	5	0	0	0	0	0
R H McCaw	2001 v I	112	20*	0	0	0	100
K F Mealamu	2002 v W	99	12	0	0	0	60
L J Messam	2008 v S	16	2	0	0	0	10
K J Read	2008 v S	44	7	0	0	0	35
B A Retallick	2012 v I	9	0	0	0	0	0
L Romano	2012 v I	7	0	0	0	0	0
A J Thomson	2008 v I	28	6	0	0	0	30
V V J Vito	2010 v I	16	2	0	0	0	10
G B Whitelock	2009 v It	1	1	0	0	0	5
S L Whitelock	2010 v I	34	4	0	0	0	20
A J Williams	2002 v E	75	7	0	0	0	35
T D Woodcock	2002 v W	91	8	0	0	0	40

NB McCaw's figures include a penalty try awarded against Ireland in 2008.

NEW ZEALAND

NEW ZEALAND INTERNATIONAL PLAYERS
UP TO 10 OCTOBER 2012

Entries in square brackets denote matches played in RWC Finals.

Abbott, H L (Taranaki) 1906 F

Afoa, I F (Auckland) 2005 I,S, 2006 E(R), 2008 I1, SA2, A1(R), 2(R), SA3(R), A3(R), S, I2(t&R), W(R), E3(R), 2009 F1(R), 2(R), It1, SA2(R), A2(R), SA3(R), A3(R), 4(R), It2(R), E(R), 2010 SA3(R), A3(R), 4(R), E(R), S(R), I2(R), W3(R), 2011 Fj(R), SA1(R), 2, A2(R), [J(R), Arg(R)]

Aitken, G G (Wellington) 1921 SA 1,2

Alatini, P F (Otago) 1999 F 1(R), [It, SA 3(R)], 2000 Tg, S 1, A 1, SA 1, A 2, SA 2, It, 2001 Sm, Arg 1, F, SA 1, A 1, SA 2, A 2

Allen, F R (Auckland) 1946 A 1,2, 1947 A 1,2, 1949 SA 1,2

Allen, M R (Taranaki, Manawatu) 1993 WS (t), 1996 S 2 (t), 1997 Arg 1(R),2(R), SA 2(R), A 3(R), E 2, W (R)

Allen, N H (Counties) 1980 A 3, W

Alley, G T (Canterbury) 1928 SA 1,2,3

Anderson, A (Canterbury) 1983 S, E, 1984 A 1,2,3, 1987 [Fj]

Anderson, B L (Wairarapa-Bush) 1986 A 1

Anesi, S R (Waikato) 2005 Fj(R)

Archer, W R (Otago, Southland) 1955 A 1,2, 1956 SA 1,3

Argus, W G (Canterbury) 1946 A 1,2, 1947 A 1,2

Arnold, D A (Canterbury) 1963 I, W, 1964 E, F

Arnold, K D (Waikato) 1947 A 1,2

Ashby, D L (Southland) 1958 A 2

Asher, A A (Auckland) 1903 A

Ashworth, B G (Auckland) 1978 A 1,2

Ashworth, J C (Canterbury, Hawke's Bay) 1978 A 1,2,3, 1980 A 1,2,3, 1981 SA 1,2,3, 1982 A 1,2, 1983 BI 1,2,3,4, A, 1984 F 1,2, A 1,2,3, 1985 E 1,2, A

Atiga, B A C (Auckland) 2003 [Tg(R)]

Atkinson, H (West Coast) 1913 A 1

Avery, H E (Wellington) 1910 A 1,2,3

Bachop, G T M (Canterbury) 1989 W, I, 1990 S 1,2, A 1,2,3, F 1,2, 1991 Arg 1,2, A 1,2, [E, US, C, A, S], 1992 Wld 1, 1994 SA 1,2,3, A, 1995 C, [I, W, S, E, SA], A 1,2

Bachop, S J (Otago) 1994 F 2, SA 1,2,3, A

Badeley, C E O (Auckland) 1921 SA 1,2

Baird, J A S (Otago) 1913 A 2

Ball, N (Wellington) 1931 A, 1932 A 2,3, 1935 W, 1936 E

Barrett, B J (Taranaki) 2012 I 3(R),Arg1(R)

Barrett, J (Auckland) 1913 A 2,3

Barry, E F (Wellington) 1934 A 2

Barry, L J (North Harbour) 1995 F 2

Bates, S P (Waikato) 2004 It(R)

Batty, G B (Wellington, Bay of Plenty) 1972 W, S, 1973 E 1, I, F, E 2, 1974 A 1,3, I, 1975 S, 1976 SA 1,2,3,4, 1977 BI 1

Batty, W (Auckland) 1930 BI 1,3,4, 1931 A

Beatty, G E (Taranaki) 1950 BI 1

Bell, R H (Otago) 1951 A 3, 1952 A 1,2

Bellis, E A (Wanganui) 1921 SA 1,2,3

Bennet, R (Otago) 1905 A

Berghan, T (Otago) 1938 A 1,2,3

Berry, M J (Wairarapa-Bush) 1986 A 3(R)

Berryman, N R (Northland) 1998 SA 2(R)

Bevan, V D (Wellington) 1949 A 1,2, 1950 BI 1,2,3,4

Birtwistle, W M (Canterbury) 1965 SA 1,2,3,4, 1967 E, W, S

Black, J E (Canterbury) 1977 F 1, 1979 A, 1980 A 3

Black, N W (Auckland) 1949 SA 3

Black, R S (Otago) 1914 A 1

Blackadder, T J (Canterbury) 1998 E 1(R),2, 2000 Tg, S 1,2, A 1, SA 1, A 2, SA 2, F 1,2, It

Blair, C (Canterbury) 2001 S (R), Arg 2, 2002 E, W

Blake, A W (Wairarapa) 1949 A 1

Blowers, A F (Auckland) 1996 SA 2(R),4(R), 1997 I, E 1(R), W (R), 1999 F 1(R), SA 1, A 1(R), SA 2, A 2(R), [It]

Boggs, E G (Auckland) 1946 A 2, 1949 SA 1

Bond, J G (Canterbury) 1949 A 2

Booth, E E (Otago) 1906 F, 1907 A 1,3

Boric, A F (North Harbour) 2008 E1(R), 2(R), SA2, A2(R), SA3(R), Sm, A3(R), 4(R), S, E3(R), 2009 It2, E(R), F3(R), 2010 I1, W1, A3(R), E(R), S(R), I2, W3(R), 2011 [Tg(R), J(R), F1(R), C(R)]

Boroevich, K G (Wellington) 1986 F 1, A 1, F 3(R)

Botica, F M (North Harbour) 1986 F 1, A 1, 2, 3, F 2, 3, 1989 Arg 1(R)

Bowden, N J G (Taranaki) 1952 A 2

Bowers, R G (Wellington) 1954 I, F

Bowman, A W (Hawke's Bay) 1938 A 1,2,3

Braid, D J (Auckland) 2002 W, 2003 [C(R),Tg], 2008 A1, 2010 S(R),W3(R)

Braid, G J (Bay of Plenty) 1983 S, E

Bremner, S G (Auckland, Canterbury) 1952 A 2, 1956 SA 2

Brewer, M R (Otago, Canterbury) 1986 F 1, A 1,2,3, F 2,3, 1988 A 1, 1989 A, W, I, 1990 S 1,2, A 1,2,3, F 1,2, 1992 I 2, A 1, 1994 F 1,2, SA 1,2,3, A, 1995 C, [I, W, E, SA], A 1,2

Briscoe, K C (Taranaki) 1959 BI 2, 1960 SA 1,2,3,4, 1963 I, W, 1964 E, S

Brooke, R M (Auckland) 1992 I 2, A 1,2,3, SA, 1993 BI 1,2,3, A, WS, 1994 SA 2,3, 1995 C, [J, S, E, SA], A 1,2, It, F 1,2, 1996 WS, S 1,2, A 1, SA 1, A 2, SA 2, A 3, I, E 1, W, E 2, 1998 E 1,2, A 1, SA 1, A 2, SA 2, A 3, 1999 WS, F 1, SA 1, A 1, SA 2, A 2, [Tg, E, It (R), S, F 2]

Brooke, Z V (Auckland) 1987 [Arg], 1989 Arg 2(R), 1990 A 1,2,3, F 1(R), 1991 Arg 2, A 1,2, [E, It, C, A, S], 1992 A 2,3, SA, 1993 BI 1,2,3(R), WS (R), S, E, 1994 F 2, SA 1,2,3, A, 1995 [J, S, E, SA], A 1,2, It, F 1,2, 1996 WS S 1,2, A 1, SA 1, A 2, SA 2,3,4,5, 1997 Arg 1,2, A 1, SA 1, A 2, SA 2, A 3, I, E 1, W, E 2

Brooke-Cowden, M (Auckland) 1986 F 1, A 1, 1987 [W]

Broomhall, S R (Canterbury) 2002 SA 1(R),2(R), E, F

Brown, C (Taranaki) 1913 A 2,3

Brown, O M (Auckland) 1992 I 2, A 1,2,3, SA, 1993 BI 1,2,3, A, S, E, 1994 F 1,2, SA 1,2,3, A, 1995 C, [I, W, S, E, SA], A 1,2, It, F 1,2, 1996 WS, S 1,2, A 1, SA 1, A 2, SA 2,3,4,5, 1997 Fj, Arg 1,2, A 1, SA 1, A 2, SA 2, A 3, I, E 1, W, E 2, 1998 E 1,2, A 1, SA 1, A 2, SA 2

Brown, R H (Taranaki) 1955 A 3, 1956 SA 1,2,3,4, 1957 A 1,2, 1958 A 1,2,3, 1959 BI 1,3, 1961 F 1,2,3, 1962 A 1

Brown, T E (Otago) 1999 WS, F 1(R), SA 1(R), A 1(R),2(R), [E (R), It, S (R)], 2000 Tg, S 2(R), A 1(R), SA 1(R), A 2(R), 2001 Sm, Arg 1(R), F, SA 1, A 1

Brownlie, C J (Hawke's Bay) 1924 W, 1925 E, F

Brownlie, M J (Hawke's Bay) 1924 I, W, 1925 E, F, 1928 SA 1,2,3,4

Bruce, J A (Auckland) 1914 A 1,2

Bruce, O D (Canterbury) 1976 SA 1,2,4, 1977 BI 2,3,4, F 1,2, 1978 A 1,2, I, W, E, S

Bryers, R F (King Country) 1949 A 1

Budd, T A (Southland) 1946 A 2, 1949 A 2

Bullock-Douglas, G A H (Wanganui) 1932 A 1,2,3, 1934 A 1,2

Bunce, F E (North Harbour) 1992 Wld 1, 2, 3, I 1,2, A 1,2,3, SA, 1993 BI 1,2,3, A, WS, S, E, 1994 F 1,2, SA 1,2,3, A, 1995 C, [I, W, S, E, SA], A 1,2, It, F 1,2, 1996 WS, S 1,2, A1, SA 1, A 2, SA 2, 3, 4, 5, 1997 Fj, Arg 1,2, A 1, SA 1, A 2, SA 2, A 3, I, E 1, W, E 2

Burgess, G A J (Auckland) 1981 SA 2

Burgess, G F (Southland) 1905 A

Burgess, R E (Manawatu) 1971 BI 1,2,3, 1972 A 3, W, 1973 I, F

Burke, P S (Taranaki) 1955 A 1, 1957 A 1,2

Burns, P J (Canterbury) 1908 AW 2, 1910 A 1,2,3, 1913 A 3

Bush, R G (Otago) 1931 A

Bush, W K (Canterbury) 1974 A 1,2, 1975 S, 1976 I, SA, 2,4, 1977 BI 2,3,4(R), 1978 I, W, 1979 A

Buxton, J B (Canterbury) 1955 A 3, 1956 SA 1

Cain, M J (Taranaki) 1913 US, 1914 A 1,2,3
Callesen, J A (Manawatu) 1974 A 1,2,3, 1975 S
Cameron, D (Taranaki) 1908 AW 1,2,3
Cameron, L M (Manawatu) 1980 A 3, 1981 SA 1(R),2,3, R
Cane, S J (Bay of Plenty) 2012 I 2(R),3,Arg2(R)
Carleton, S R (Canterbury) 1928 SA 1,2,3, 1929 A 1,2,3
Carrington, K R (Auckland) 1971 BI 1,3,4
Carter, D W (Canterbury) 2003 W, F, A 1(R), [It, C, Tg, SA(R), F(R)], 2004 E1, 2, PI, A1, SA1, A2, It, W, F, 2005 Fj, BI1, 2, SA1, A1, W, E, 2006 Arg, A1, SA1, A2, 3, SA2, 3, E, F1, 2, W, 2007 F1, C, SA1, A1, SA2, A2, [It, S, F], 2008 I1, E1, 2, SA1, 2, A1, 2, SA3, Sm, A3, 4, S(R), I2, W, E3, 2009 A2, SA3, A3, 4, W, E, F3, 2010 I1, W1, 2, SA1, 2, A1, 2, SA3, A4, E, S, I2, W3, 2011 Fj(R), SA1, A1, 2, [Tg, F1], 2012 I 1, 2, A1, 2, Arg2, SA2
Carter, M P (Auckland) 1991 A 2, [It, A], 1997 Fj (R), A 1(R), 1998 E 2(R), A 2
Casey, S T (Otago) 1905 S, I, E, W, 1907 A 1,2,3, 1908 AW 1
Cashmore, A R (Auckland) 1996 S 2(R), 1997 A 2(R)
Catley, E H (Waikato) 1946 A 1, 1947 A 1,2, 1949 SA 1,2,3,4
Caughey, T H C (Auckland) 1932 A 1,3, 1934 A 1,2, 1935 S, I, 1936 E, A 1, 1937 SA 3
Caulton, R W (Wellington) 1959 BI 2,3,4, 1960 SA 1,4, 1961 F 2, 1963 E 1,2, I, W, 1964 E, S, F, A 1,2,3
Cherrington, N P (North Auckland) 1950 BI 1
Christian, D L (Auckland) 1949 SA 4
Clamp, M (Wellington) 1984 A 2,3
Clark, D W (Otago) 1964 A 1,2
Clark, W H (Wellington) 1953 W, 1954 I, E, S, 1955 A 1,2, 1956 SA 2,3,4
Clarke, A H (Auckland) 1958 A 3, 1959 BI 4, 1960 SA 1
Clarke, D B (Waikato) 1956 SA 3,4, 1957 A 1,2, 1958 A 1,3, 1959 BI 1,2,3,4, 1960 SA 1,2,3,4, 1961 F 1,2,3, 1962 A 1,2,3,4,5, 1963 E 1,2, I, W, 1964 E, S, F, A 1,2,3
Clarke, E (Auckland) 1992 Wld 2,3, I 1,2, 1993 BI 1,2, S (R), E, 1998 SA 2, A 3
Clarke, I J (Waikato) 1953 W, 1955 A 1,2,3, 1956 SA 1,2,3,4, 1957 A 1,2, 1958 A 1,3, 1959 BI 1,2, 1960 SA 2,4, 1961 F 1,2,3, 1962 A 1,2,3, 1963 E 1,2
Clarke, R L (Taranaki) 1932 A 2,3
Cobden, D G (Canterbury) 1937 SA 1
Cockerill, M S (Taranaki) 1951 A 1,2,3
Cockroft, E A P (South Canterbury) 1913 A 3, 1914 A 2,3
Codlin, B W (Counties) 1980 A 1,2,3
Collins, A H (Taranaki) 1932 A 2,3, 1934 A 1
Collins, J (Wellington) 2001 Arg 1, 2003 E (R), W, F, SA 1, A 1, SA 2, A 2, [It, W, SA, A, F], 2004 E2(R), Arg, PI(R), A1(R), SA1, It, F, 2005 Fj, BI1, 2, 3, SA1, A1, SA2, W, E, 2006 Arg, A1, 2, 3, SA2(R), 3, F1, 2, W, 2007 F2, C, SA1, A1, SA2(R), A2, [It, Pt, R, F]
Collins, J L (Poverty Bay) 1964 A 1, 1965 SA 1,4
Colman, J T H (Taranaki) 1907 A 1,2, 1908 AW 1,3
Connor, D M (Auckland) 1961 F 1,2,3, 1962 A 1,2,3,4,5, 1963 E 1,2, 1964 A 2,3
Conway, R J (Otago, Bay of Plenty) 1959 BI 2,3,4, 1960 SA 1,3,4, 1965 SA 1,2,3,4
Cooke, A E (Auckland, Wellington) 1924 I, W, 1925 E, F, 1930 BI 1, 2, 3, 4
Cooke, R J (Canterbury) 1903 A
Cooksley, M S B (Counties, Waikato) 1992 Wld 1, 1993 BI 2,3(R), A, 1994 F 1,2,3, SA 1,2, A, 2001 A 1(R), SA 2(t&R)
Cooper, G J L (Auckland, Otago) 1986 F 1, A 1,2, 1992 Wld 1,2,3, I 1
Cooper, M J A (Waikato) 1992 I 2, SA (R), 1993 BI 1(R),3(t), WS (t), S, 1994 F 1,2
Corner, M M N (Auckland) 1930 BI 2,3,4, 1931 A, 1934 A 1, 1936 E
Cossey, R R (Counties) 1958 A 1
Cottrell, A I (Canterbury) 1929 A 1,2,3, 1930 BI 1,2,3,4, 1931 A, 1932 A 1,2,3
Cottrell, W D (Canterbury) 1968 A 1,2, F 2,3, 1970 SA 1, 1971 BI 1,2,3,4
Couch, M B R (Wairarapa) 1947 A 1, 1949 A 1,2
Coughlan, T D (South Canterbury) 1958 A 1
Cowan, Q J (Southland) 2004 It(R), 2005 W(R), I(R), S(R), 2006 I1(R), SA1(R), A2(R), SA2(R), 3, 2008 E1(R), 2(R), SA1(R), A1(t&R), 2, SA3, Sm, A3, 4, I2, W, E3, 2009 F1, 2, A1, SA2, A2, SA3, A3, 4, W(R), It2(R), E, F3, 2010 I1, W1, 2, SA1, 2(R), A1, SA3, A3, 4, S, W3, 2011 Fj, SA1, 2, [Tg, J(R), C, Arg(R)]
Creighton, J N (Canterbury) 1962 A 4
Cribb, R T (North Harbour) 2000 S 1,2, A 1, SA 1, A 2, SA 2, F 1,2, It, 2001 Sm, F, SA 1, A 1, SA 2, A 2

Crichton, S (Wellington) 1983 S, E
Crockett, W W V (Canterbury) 2009 It1, W, It2, 2011 Fj, SA1, A1, 2012 A2
Cross, T (Canterbury) 1904 BI, 1905 A
Crowley, K J (Taranaki) 1985 E 1,2, A, Arg 1,2, 1986 A 3, F 2,3, 1987 [Arg], 1990 S 1,2, A 1,2,3, F 1,2, 1991 Arg 1,2, [A]
Crowley, P J B (Auckland) 1949 SA 3,4, 1950 BI 1,2,3,4
Cruden, A W (Manawatu) 2010 I1(R), W1(R), 2(R), SA2(R), A1(R), 3, 2011 [Arg(R), A, F2], 2012 I 1(R), 3, A2(R), Arg1, SA1, Arg2(R), SA2(R)
Culhane, S D (Southland) 1995 [J], It, F 1,2, 1996 SA 3,4
Cullen C M (Manawatu, Central Vikings, Wellington) 1996 WS, S 1,2, A 1, SA 1, A 2, SA 2,3,4,5, 1997 Fj, Arg 1,2, A 1, SA 1, A 2, SA 2, A 3, I, E 1, W, E 2, 1998 E 1,2, A 1, SA 1, A 2, SA 2, A 3, [It(R), SA, F 2, SA 3], 2000 Tg, S 1,2, A 1, SA 1, A 2, SA 2, F 1,2, It, 2001 A 2(R), 2002 It, Fj, A 1, SA 1, A 2, F
Cummings, W (Canterbury) 1913 A 2,3
Cundy, R T (Wairarapa) 1929 A 2(R)
Cunningham, G R (Auckland) 1979 A, S, E, 1980 A 1,2
Cunningham, W (Auckland) 1905 S, I, 1906 F, 1907 A 1,2,3, 1908 AW 1,2,3
Cupples, L F (Bay of Plenty) 1924 I, W
Currie, C J (Canterbury) 1978 I, W
Cuthill, J E (Otago) 1913 A 1, US

Dagg, I J A (Hawke's Bay) 2010 I1, W1, SA2(R), A1(R), SA3(R), A3, 2011 SA2, [Tg, F1, C, A, F2], 2012 I 1, 2, 3, A1, 2, Arg1, SA1, Arg2, SA2
Dalley, W C (Canterbury) 1924 I, 1928 SA 1,2,3,4
Dalton, A G (Counties) 1977 F 2, 1978 A 1,2,3, I, W, E, S, 1979 F 1,2, S, 1981 S 1,2, SA 1,2,3, R, F 1,2, 1982 A 1,2,3, 1983 BI 1, 2, 3, 4, A, 1984 F 1,2, A 1, 2, 3, 1985 E 1,2, A
Dalton, D (Hawke's Bay) 1935 I, W, 1936 A 1,2, 1937 SA 1,2,3, 1938 A 1,2
Dalton, R A (Wellington) 1947 A 1,2
Dalzell, G N (Canterbury) 1953 W, 1954 I, E, S, F
Davie, M G (Canterbury) 1983 E (R)
Davies, W A (Auckland, Otago) 1960 SA 4, 1962 A 4,5
Davis, K (Auckland) 1952 A 2, 1953 W, 1954 I, E, S, F, 1955 A 2, 1958 A 1,2,3
Davis, L J (Canterbury) 1976 I, 1977 BI 3,4
Davis, W L (Hawke's Bay) 1967 A, E, W, F, S, 1968 A 1,2, F 1, 1969 W 1,2, 1970 SA 2
Deans, I B (Canterbury) 1988 W 1,2, A 1,2,3, 1989 F 1,2, Arg 2, A
Deans, R G (Canterbury) 1905 S, I, E, W, 1908 AW 3
Deans, R M (Canterbury) 1983 S, E, 1984 A 1(R),2,3
Delamore, G W (Wellington) 1949 SA 4
Delany, M P (Bay of Plenty) 2009 It 2
De Malmanche, A P (Waikato) 2009 It1(R), A3(R) 2010 I1(R), W1(R), 2(R)
Dermody, C (Southland) 2006 I1,2,E(R)
Devine, S J (Auckland) 2002 E, W 2003 E (R), W, F, SA 1, A 1(R), [C, SA(R), F]
Dewar, H (Taranaki) 1913 A 1, US
Diack, E S (Otago) 1959 BI 2
Dick, J (Auckland) 1937 SA 1,2, 1938 A 3
Dick, M J (Auckland) 1963 I, W, 1964 E, S, F, 1965 SA 3, 1966 BI 4, 1967 A, E, W, F, 1969 W 1,2, 1970 SA 1,4
Dixon, M J (Canterbury) 1954 I, E, S, F, 1956 SA 1,2,3,4, 1957 A 1,2
Dobson, R L (Auckland) 1949 A 1
Dodd, E H (Wellington) 1905 A
Donald, A J (Wanganui) 1983 S, E, 1984 F 1,2, A 1,2,3
Donald, J G (Wairarapa) 1921 SA 1,2
Donald, Q (Wairarapa) 1924 I, W, 1925 E, F
Donald, S R (Waikato) 2008 E1(R), 2(R), A2(R), SA3(R), Sm(R), A3(R), 4, S, I2(R), 2009 F1, 2, A1, SA1, 2, A2(R), SA3, A4(R), It2(R), E(R) A4(R), S(R), W3(R), 2011[F2(R)]
Donaldson, M W (Manawatu) 1977 F 1,2, 1978 A 1,2,3, I, E, S, 1979 F 1,2, A, S (R), 1981 SA 3(R)
Donnelly, T J S (Otago) 2009 A3,4,W(R),It2,E,F3, 2010 W2,SA1,2,A1,2,SA3,A3,4,I2
Dougan, J P (Wellington) 1972 A 1, 1973 E 2
Dowd, C W (Auckland) 1993 BI 1,2,3, A, WS, S, E, 1994 SA 1(R), 1995 C, [I, W, J, E, SA], A 1,2, F1, 2, 1996 WS, S 1,2, A 1, SA 1, A 2, SA 2,3,4,5, 1997 Fj, Arg 1,2, A 1, SA 1, A 2, SA 2, A 3, I, E 1, W, 1998 E 1,2, A 1, SA 1, A 2,3(R), 1999 SA 2(R), A 2(R), [Tg (R), E, It, S, F 2, SA 3], 2000 Tg, S 1(R),2(R), A 1(R), SA 1(R), A 2(R)

Harper, E T (Canterbury) 1904 BI, 1906 F
Harding, S (Otago) 2002 Fj
Harris, P C (Manawatu) 1976 SA 3
Hart, A H (Taranaki) 1924 I
Hart, G F (Canterbury) 1930 BI 1, 2, 3, 4, 1931 A, 1934 A 1, 1935 S, I, W, 1936 A 1,2
Harvey, B A (Wairarapa-Bush) 1986 F 1
Harvey, I H (Wairarapa) 1928 SA 4
Harvey, L R (Otago) 1949 SA 1,2,3,4, 1950 BI 1,2,3,4
Harvey, P (Canterbury) 1904 BI
Hasell, E W (Canterbury) 1913 A 2,3
Hayman, C J (Otago) 2001 Sm (R), Arg 1, F (R), A 1(R), SA 2(R), A 2(R), 2002 F (t), W, 2004 E1, 2, PI, A1, 2, SA2, It, W(R), F, 2005 BI1, SA1, A1, SA2, A2, W, E, 2006 I1, 2, A1, SA2, A2, SA3, E, F1, 2, W, 2007 F1, 2, SA1, A1, SA2, A2, [It, Pt(R), S, F]
Hayward, H O (Auckland) 1908 AW 3
Hazlett, E J (Southland) 1966 BI 1,2,3,4, 1967 A, E
Hazlett, W E (Southland) 1928 SA 1, 2, 3, 4, 1930 BI 1, 2, 3, 4
Heeps, T R (Wellington) 1962 A 1,2,3,4,5
Heke, W R (North Auckland) 1929 A 1,2,3
Hemi, R C (Waikato) 1953 W, 1954 I, E, S, F, 1955 A 1,2,3, 1956 SA 1,3,4, 1957 A 1,2, 1959 BI 1,3,4
Henderson, P (Wanganui) 1949 SA 1,2,3,4, 1950 BI 2,3,4
Henderson, P W (Otago) 1991 Arg 1, [C], 1992 Wld 1,2,3, I 1, 1995 [J]
Herewini, M A (Auckland) 1962 A 5, 1963 I, 1964 S, F, 1965 SA 4, 1966 BI 1,2,3,4, 1967 A
Hewett, D N (Canterbury) 2001 I (R), S (R), Arg 2, 2002 It (R), I 1, 2, A 1, SA 1, A 2, SA 2, 2003 E, F, SA 1, A 1, SA 2, A 2, [It, Tg(R), W, SA, A, F]
Hewett, J A (Auckland) 1991 [It]
Hewitt, N J (Southland) 1995 [I (t), J], 1996 A 1(R), 1997 SA 1(R), I, E 1, W, E 2, 1998 E 2(t + R)
Hewson, A R (Wellington) 1981 S 1,2, SA 1, 2, 3, R, F 1, 2, 1982 A 1,2,3, 1983 BI 1, 2, 3, 4, 1984 F 1, 2, A 1
Higginson, G (Canterbury, Hawke's Bay) 1980 W, 1981 S 1, SA 1, 1982 A 1,2, 1983 A
Hill, D W (Waikato) 2006 I2(R)
Hill, S F (Canterbury) 1955 A 3, 1956 SA 1,3,4, 1957 A 1,2, 1958 A 3, 1959 BI 1,2,3,4
Hines, G R (Waikato) 1980 A 3
Hobbs, M J B (Canterbury) 1983 BI 1,2,3,4, A, S, E, 1984 F 1,2, A 1,2,3, 1985 E 1,2, A, Arg 1,2, 1986 A 2,3, F 2,3
Hoeata, J M R A (Taranaki) 2011 Fj,SA1(R),2(R)
Hoeft, C H (Otago) 1998 E 2(t + R), A 2(R), SA 2, A 3, 1999 WS, F 1, SA 1, A 1,2, [Tg,E, S, F 2, SA 3(R)], 2000 S 1,2, A 1, SA 1, A 2, SA 2, 2001 Sm, Arg 1, F, SA 1, A 1, SA 2, A 2, 2003 W, [C, F(R)]
Holah, M R (Waikato) 2001 Sm, Arg 1(t&R), F (R), SA 1(R), A 1(R), SA 2(R), A 2(R), 2002 It, I 2(R), A 2(t), E, F, W (R), 2003 W, F (R), A 1(R), SA 2, [It(R), C, Tg(R), W(R), SA(t&R), A(R), F(t&R)], 2004 E1(R), 2, Arg(R), PI, A1, SA1, A2, SA2, 2005 BI3(R), A1(R), 2006 I1, SA3(R)
Holder, E C (Buller) 1934 A 2
Hook, L S (Auckland) 1929 A 1,2,3
Hooper, J A (Canterbury) 1937 SA 1,2,3
Hopkinson, A E (Canterbury) 1967 S, 1968 A 2, F 1,2,3, 1969 W 2, 1970 SA 1,2,3
Hore, A (Taranaki) 2002 E, F, 2004 E1(t), 2(R), Arg, A1(t), 2005 W(R), I(R), S(R), 2006 I2(R), Arg(R), A1(R), SA1(R), A2(R), SA3, E(R), F2(R), W(R), 2007 F1(R), C, SA2(R), [Pt, S(R), R(R), F(R)], 2008 I1, E1, 2, SA1, 2, A1, 2, SA3, Sm, A3, 4, 2009 F1, A1, SA1, 2, A2, SA3, A3, 4, W, E, F3, 2010 S(R), I2(R), W3(R), 2011 Fj, SA1, A1, SA2(R), A2(R), [Tg, J, F1(R), C, Arg(R), A(R), F2(R)], 2012 I 1, 2, 3, A1(R), 2(R), Arg1(R), SA1, Arg2, SA2
Hore, J (Otago) 1930 BI 2,3,4, 1932 A 1,2,3, 1934 A 1,2, 1935 S, 1936 E
Horsley, R H (Wellington) 1960 SA 2,3,4
Hotop, J (Canterbury) 1952 A 1,2, 1955 A 3
Howarth, S P (Auckland) 1994 SA 1,2,3, A
Howlett, D C (Auckland) 2000 Tg (R), F 1,2, It, 2001 Sm, Arg 1(R), F (R), SA 1, A 1,2, I, S, Arg 2, 2002 It, I 1,2(R), Fj, A 1, SA 1, A 2, SA 2, E, F, W, 2003 E, F, W, F, SA 1, A 1, SA 2, A 2, [It, C(R), Tg, W, SA, A, F], 2004 E1, A1, SA1, SA2, SA2, W, F, 2005 Fj, BI1, 2, 3, A1, SA1, 2, 2006 I1, 2, SA1, A3, SA3, 2007 F2(R), C, SA2, A2, [It, S, R(R)]
Hughes, A M (Auckland) 1949 A 1,2, 1950 BI 1,2,3,4
Hughes, E (Southland, Wellington) 1907 A 1, 2, 3, 1908 AW 1, 1921 SA 1,2

Hunter, B A (Otago) 1971 BI 1,2,3
Hunter, J (Taranaki) 1905 S, I, E, W, 1906 F, 1907 A 1,2,3, 1908 AW 1,2,3
Hurst, I A (Canterbury) 1973 I, F, E 2, 1974 A 1,2

Ieremia, A (Wellington) 1994 SA 1,2,3, 1995 [J], 1996 SA 2(R),5(R), 1997 A 1(R), SA 1(R), A 2, SA 2, A 3, I, E 1, 1999 WS, F 1, SA 1, A 1, SA 2, A 2, [Tg, E, S, F 2, SA 3], 2000 Tg, S 1,2, A 1,2, SA 2
Ifwersen, K D (Auckland) 1921 SA 3
Innes, C R (Auckland) 1989 W, I, 1990 A 1, 2, 3, F 1,2, 1991 Arg 1, 2, A 1,2, [E, US, It, C, A, S]
Innes, G D (Canterbury) 1932 A 2
Irvine, I B (North Auckland) 1952 A 1
Irvine, J G (Otago) 1914 A 1,2,3
Irvine, W R (Hawke's Bay, Wairarapa) 1924 I, W, 1925 E, F, 1930 BI 1
Irwin, M W (Otago) 1955 A 1,2, 1956 SA 1, 1958 A 2, 1959 BI 3,4, 1960 SA 1

Jack, C R (Canterbury, Tasman) 2001 Arg 1(R), SA 1(R),2, A 2, I, S, Arg 2, 2002 I 1,2, A 1, SA 1, A 2, SA 2, 2003 E, W, F, SA 1, A 1, SA 2(R), A 2, [It, C, SA, A, F], 2004 E1, 2, Arg, PI, A1, SA1, A2, SA2, It, W, F, 2005 Fj(R), BI1, 2, 3, SA1, A1, SA2, A2, W, E, S, 2006 I1, 2, A1, SA1, A2, 3, SA2(R), 3, E, F2, 2007 F1, 2, A1, SA2, A2, [It, Pt, S(R), R(R), F(R)]
Jackson, E S (Hawke's Bay) 1936 A 1,2, 1937 SA 1,2,3, 1938 A 3
Jaffray, J L (Otago, South Canterbury) 1972 A 2, 1975 S, 1976 I, SA 1, 1977 BI 2, 1979 F 1,2
Jane, C S (Wellington) 2008 A4(R),S(R), 2009 F1, 2, It1(R), A1, SA3(R), A3, 4, W, It2, F3, 2010 I1, W1, 2, SA1, 2, A1, 2, SA3, A3, 4, I2, 2011 SA1, 2(R), A2, [Tg(R), J, F1, Arg, A, F2], 2012 A1, 2, Arg1, SA1, Arg2, SA2
Jarden, R A (Wellington) 1951 A 1,2, 1952 A 1,2, 1953 W, 1954 I, E, S, F, 1955 A 1,2,3, 1956 SA 1,2,3,4
Jefferd, A C R (East Coast) 1981 S 1,2, SA 1
Jessep, E M (Wellington) 1931 A, 1932 A 1
Johnson, L M (Wellington) 1928 SA 1,2,3,4
Johnston, W (Otago) 1907 A 1,2,3
Johnstone, B R (Auckland) 1976 SA 2, 1977 BI 1,2, F 1,2, 1978 I, W, E, S, 1979 F 1,2, S, E
Johnstone, C R (Canterbury) 2005 Fj(R),BI2(R),3(R)
Johnstone, P (Otago) 1949 SA 2,4, 1950 BI 1,2,3,4, 1951 A 1,2,3
Jones, I D (North Auckland, North Harbour) 1990 S 1,2, A 1,2,3, F 1,2, 1991 Arg 1,2, A 1,2, [E, US, It, C, A, S], 1992 Wld 1,2,3, I 1,2, A 1,2,3, SA, 1993 BI 1,2(R),3, WS, S, E, 1994 F 1,2, SA 1,3, A, 1995 C, [I, W, S, E, SA], A 1,2, It, F 1,2, 1996 WS, S 1,2, A 1, SA 1, A 2, SA 2,3,4,5, 1997 Fj, Arg 1,2, A 1, SA 1, A 2, SA 2,3, I, E 1, W, 1998 E 1,2, A 1, SA 1, A 2,3(R), 1999 F 1(R), [It, S (R)]
Jones, M G (North Auckland) 1973 E 2
Jones, M N (Auckland) 1987 [It, Fj, S, F], A, 1988 W 1,2, A 2,3, 1989 F 1,2, Arg 1,2, 1990 F 1,2, 1991 Arg 1,2, A 1,2, [E, US, S], 1992 Wld 1,3, I 2, A 1,3, SA, 1993 BI 1,2,3, A, WS, 1994 SA 3(R), A, 1995 A 1(R), 2, F 1,2, 1996 WS, S 1,2, A 1, A 2, SA 2,3,4,5, 1997 Fj, 1998 E 1, SA 1, A 2
Jones, P F H (North Auckland) 1954 E, S, 1955 A 1,2, 1956 SA 3,4, 1958 A 1,2,3, 1959 BI 1, 1960 SA 1
Joseph, H T (Canterbury) 1971 BI 2,3
Joseph, J W (Otago) 1992 Wld 2,3(R), I 1, A 1(R),3, SA, 1993 BI 1,2,3, A, WS, S, E, 1994 SA 2(t), 1995 C, [I, W, J (R), S, SA (R)]

Kahui, R D (Waikato) 2008 E2,A1,2,SA3,Sm,A3,S,W, 2010 W1(R),2,SA1(R), 2011 SA2,[Tg,J,F1,A,F2]
Kaino, J (Auckland) 2006 I1(R),2, 2008 I1, E1, SA1, 2, A1, 2, SA3, Sm, A3, 4, I2, W, E3, 2009 F2, It1, A1, SA1, 2, A2, SA3, W, E(R), F3, 2010 I1, W2, SA1, 2, A1, 2, SA3, A3(R), 4, E, I2, W3, 2011 Fj(R), SA1, A1, SA2, [Tg, J, F1, C, Arg, A, F2]
Karam, J F (Wellington, Horowhenua) 1972 W, S, 1973 E 1, I, F, 1974 A 1,2,3, I, 1975 S
Katene, T (Wellington) 1955 A 2
Kearney, J C (Otago) 1947 A 2, 1949 SA 1,2,3
Kelleher, B T (Otago, Waikato) 1999 WS (R), SA 1(R), A 2(R), [Tg (R), E, It, F 2], 2000 S 1, A 1(R),2(R), It (R), 2001 Sm, F (R), A 1(R), SA 2, A 2, I, S, 2002 It 1, I 2(R), Fj, SA 1(R), 2(R), 2003 F (R), [A(R)], 2004 Arg, PI(R), SA1(R), 2(R), It, W(R), F, 2005 Fj, BI1(R), 2, 3, SA1, W, E, 2006 I1, 2, A1, 2, 3, SA3(R), E, F1(R), 2, W, 2007 F2, C, SA1, A1, 2, [It, S, F]

THE COUNTRIES

Kelly, J W (Auckland) 1949 A 1,2
Kember, G F (Wellington) 1970 SA 4
Ketels, R C (Counties) 1980 W, 1981 S 1,2, R, F 1
Kiernan, H A D (Auckland) 1903 A
Kilby, F D (Wellington) 1932 A 1,2,3, 1934 A 2
Killeen, B A (Auckland) 1936 A 1
King, R M (Waikato) 2002 W
King, R R (West Coast) 1934 A 2, 1935 S, I, W, 1936 E, A 1,2, 1937 SA 1,2,3, 1938 A 1,2,3
Kingstone, C N (Taranaki) 1921 SA 1,2,3
Kirk, D E (Auckland) 1985 E 1,2, A, Arg 1, 1986 F 1, A 1,2,3, F 2,3, 1987 [It, Fj, Arg, S, W, F], A
Kirkpatrick, I A (Canterbury, Poverty Bay) 1967 F, 1968 A 1(R),2, F 1,2,3, 1969 W 1,2, 1970 SA 1,2,3,4, 1971 BI 1,2,3,4, 1972 A 1,2,3, W, S, 1973 E 1, I, F, E 2, 1974 A 1,2,3, I 1975 S, 1976 I, SA 1,2,3,4, 1977 BI 1,2,3,4
Kirton, D E (Otago) 1967 E, W, F, S, 1968 A 1,2, F 1,2,3, 1969 W 1,2, 1970 SA 2,3
Kirwan, J J (Auckland) 1984 F 1,2, 1985 E 1,2, A, Arg 1,2, 1986 F 1, A 1,2,3, F 2,3, 1987 [It, Fj, Arg, S, W, F], A, 1988 W 1,2, A 1,2,3, 1989 F 1,2, Arg 1,2, A, 1990 S 1,2, A 1,2,3, F 1,2, 1991 Arg 2, A 1,2, [E, It, C, A, S], 1992 Wld 1,2(R),3, I 1,2, A 1,2,3, SA, 1993 BI 2,3, A, WS, 1994 F 1,2, SA 1,2,3
Kivell, A L (Taranaki) 1929 A 2,3
Knight, A (Auckland) 1934 A 1
Knight, G A (Manawatu) 1977 F 1,2, 1978 A 1, 2, 3, E, S, 1979 F 1,2, A, 1980 A 1,2,3, W, 1981 S 1, 2, SA 1,3, 1982 A 1,2,3, 1983 BI 1, 2, 3, 4, A, 1984 F 1, 2, A 1, 2, 3, 1985 E 1, 2, A, 1986 A 2,3
Knight, L G (Poverty Bay) 1977 BI 1,2,3,4, F 1,2
Koteka, T T (Waikato) 1981 F 2, 1982 A 3
Kreft, A J (Otago) 1968 A 2
Kronfeld, J A (Otago) 1995 C, [I, W, S, E, SA], A 1,2(R) 1996 WS, S 1,2, A 1, SA 1, A 2, 3,4,5, 1997 Fj, Arg 1,2, A 1, SA 1, A 2, SA 2, A 3, I (R), E 1, W, E 2, 1998 E 1,2, A 1, SA 1,2 A 3, 1999 WS, F 1, SA 1, A 1, SA 2, A 2, [Tg, E, S, F 2, SA 3], 2000 Tg, S 1(R),2, A 1(R), SA 1, A 2, SA 2
Laidlaw, C R (Otago, Canterbury) 1964 F, A 1, 1965 SA 1, 2, 3, 4, 1966 BI 1, 2, 3, 4, 1967 E, W, S, 1968 A 1, 2, F 1, 2, 1970 SA 1, 2, 3
Laidlaw, K F (Southland) 1960 SA 2,3,4
Lambert, K K (Manawatu) 1972 S (R), 1973 E 1, I, F, E 2, 1974 I, 1976 SA 1,3,4, 1977 BI 1,4
Lambourn, A (Wellington) 1934 A 1,2, 1935 S, I, W, 1936 E, 1937 SA 1,2,3, 1938 A 3
Larsen, B P (North Harbour) 1992 Wld 2,3, I 1, 1994 F 1,2, SA 1,2,3, A (t), 1995 [I, W, J, E(R)], It, F 1, 1996 S 2(t), SA 4(R)
Latimer, T D (Bay of Plenty) 2009 F1(R), 2, It1, 2, F3(R)
Lauaki, S T (Waikato) 2005 Fj(R), BI1(R), 2(R), 3, A2, I, S, 2007 [It(R), Pt, S(R), R], 2008 E1(R), 2(R), SA1(R), 2(R), A1(R), Sm(R)
Laulala, C D E (Canterbury) 2004 W, 2006 I2
Le Lievre, J M (Canterbury) 1962 A 4
Lee, D D (Otago) 2002 E (R), F
Lendrum, R N (Counties) 1973 E 2
Leonard, B G (Waikato) 2007 F1(R), 2(R), SA2(R), A2(R), [It(R), Pt, S(R), R(R), F(R)], 2009 It1, SA1, A3(R), W
Leslie, A R (Wellington) 1974 A 1, 2, 3, I, 1975 S, 1976 I, SA 1, 2, 3, 4
Leys, E T (Wellington) 1929 A 3
Lilburne, H T (Canterbury, Wellington) 1928 SA 3,4, 1929 A 1,2,3, 1930 BI 1,4, 1931 A, 1932 A 1, 1934 A 2
Lindsay, D F (Otago) 1928 SA 1,2,3
Lineen, T R (Auckland) 1957 A 1,2, 1958 A 1,2,3, 1959 BI 1,2,3,4, 1960 SA 1,2,3
Lister, T N (South Canterbury) 1968 A 1,2, F 1, 1969 W 1,2, 1970 SA 1,4, 1971 BI 4
Little, P F (Auckland) 1961 F 2,3, 1962 A 2,3,5, 1963 I, W, 1964 E, S, F
Little, W K (North Harbour) 1990 S 1,2, A 1,2,3, F 1,2, 1991 Arg 1,2, A 1, [It, S], 1992 Wld 1,2,3, I 1,2, A 1,2,3, SA, 1993 BI 1, WS (R), 1994 SA 2(R), A, 1995 C, [I, W, S, E, SA], A 1,2, It, F 1,2, 1996 S 2, A 1, SA 1, A 2, SA 2,3,4,5, 1997 W, E 2, 1998 E 1, A 1, SA 1, A 2
Loader, C J (Wellington) 1954 I, E, S, F
Lochore, B J (Wairarapa) 1964 E, S, 1965 SA 1,2,3,4, 1966 BI 1,2,3,4, 1967 A, E, W, F, S, 1968 A 1, F 2,3, 1969 W 1,2, 1970 SA 1,2,3,4, 1971 BI 3
Loe, R W (Waikato, Canterbury) 1987 [It, Arg], 1988 W 1,2, A 1,2,3, 1989 F 1,2, Arg 1,2, A, W, I, 1990 S 1,2, A 1,2,3, F 1,2,

1991 Arg 1,2, A 1,2, [E, It, C, A, S], 1992 Wld 1,2,3, I 1, A 1,2,3, SA, 1994 F 1,2, SA 1,2,3, A, 1995 [J, S, SA (R)], A 2(t), F 2(R)
Lomu, J T (Counties Manukau, Wellington) 1994 F 1,2, 1995 [I, W, S, E, SA], A 1,2, It, F 1,2, 1996 WS, S 1, A 1, SA 1, A 2, 1997 E 1, W, E 2, 1998 E 1,2, A 1(R), SA 1, A 2, SA 2, A 3, 1999 WS (R), SA 1(R), A 1(R), SA 2(R), A 2(R), [Tg, E, It, S, F 2, SA 3], 2000 Tg, S 1,2, A 1, SA 1, A 2, SA 2, F 1, 2001 Arg 1, F, SA 1, A 1, SA 2, A 2, I, S, Arg 2, 2002 It (R), I 1(R),2, Fj, SA 1(R), E, F, W
Long, A J (Auckland) 1903 A
Loveridge, D S (Taranaki) 1978 W, 1979 S, E, 1980 A 1,2,3, W, 1981 S 1,2, SA 1,2,3, R, F 1,2, 1982 A 1,2,3, 1983 BI 1,2,3,4, A, 1985 Arg 2
Lowen, K R (Waikato) 2002 E
Lucas, F W (Auckland) 1924 I, 1925 F, 1928 SA 4, 1930 BI 1,2,3,4
Lunn, W A (Otago) 1949 A 1,2
Lynch, T W (South Canterbury) 1913 A 1, 1914 A 1,2,3
Lynch, T W (Canterbury) 1951 A 1,2,3

McAlister, C L (North Harbour) 2005 BI3, SA1(R), A1(R), SA2(R), A2(R), 2006 I1, 2, SA1(R), A3, SA2, F1, W, 2007 F2, C, SA1(R), A1, SA2, A2, [It, S, R, F], 2009 F1(R), 2(R), It1, SA1(R), 2(R), A2, It2, F3(R)
McAtamney, F S (Otago) 1956 SA 2
McCahill, B J (Auckland) 1987 [Arg, S (R), W (R)], 1989 Arg 1(R),2(R), 1991 A 2, [E, US, C, A]
McCaw, R H (Canterbury) 2001 I, S, Arg 2, 2002 I 1,2, A 1, SA 1, A 2, SA 2, 2003 E, F, SA 1, A 1,2, [It, C(R), Tg(R), W, SA, A, F], 2004 E1, Arg, It, W, F, 2005 Fj, BI1, 2, SA1, A1, SA2, A2, W(R), I, S, 2006 I1, 2, A1, SA1, A2, 3, SA2, 3, E, F1, 2, W, 2007 F1, 2, C(R), SA1, A1, SA2, A2, [It, S, R(R), F], 2008 I1, E1, 2, A2, SA3, A3, 4, S(R), I2, W, E3, 2009 A1, SA1, 2, A2, SA3, A3, 4, W, E, F3, 2010 I1, W1, 2, SA1, 2, A1, 2, SA3, A3, 4, E, S, I2, W3, 2011 Fj, SA1, A1, 2, [Tg, F1, Arg, A, F2], 2012 I 1, 2, 3, A1, 2, Arg1, SA1, Arg2, SA2
McCaw, W A (Southland) 1951 A 1,2,3, 1953 W, 1954 F
McCool, M J (Wairarapa-Bush) 1979 A
McCormick, W F (Canterbury) 1965 SA 4, 1967 E, W, F, S, 1968 A 1,2, F 1,2,3, 1969 W 1,2, 1970 SA 1,2,3, 1971 BI 1
McCullough, J F (Taranaki) 1959 BI 2,3,4
McDonald, A (Otago) 1905 S, I, E, W, 1907 A 1, 1908 AW 1, 1913 A 1, US
Macdonald, A J (Auckland) 2005 W(R),S
Macdonald, H H (Canterbury, North Auckland) 1972 W, S, 1973 E 1, I, F, E 2, 1974 I, 1975 S, 1976 I, SA 1,2,3
MacDonald, L R (Canterbury) 2000 S 1(R),2(R), SA 1(t),2(R), 2001 Sm, Arg 1, F, SA 1(R), A 1(R), SA 2, A 2, I, S, 2002 I 1,2, Fj (R), A 2(R), SA 2, 2003 A 2(R), [It(R), C, Tg, W, SA, A, F], 2005 BI1, 2(R), SA1, 2, A2, W(R), I, E(R), S(R), 2006 Arg, A1, SA1, A2, 3(R), SA2, F1, 2, 2007 F1, 2, C(R), SA1(R), [It, Pt(R), S, F], 2008 I1(R), E1(R), 2, SA1(R), 2(R)
McDonnell, J M (Otago) 2002 It, I 1(R),2(R), Fj, SA 1(R), A 2(R), E, F
McDowell, S C (Auckland, Bay of Plenty) 1985 Arg 1,2, 1986 A 2,3, F 2,3, 1987 [It, Fj, S, W, F], A, 1988 W 1,2, A 1,2,3, 1989 F 1,2, Arg 1,2, A, W, I, 1990 S 1,2, A 1,2,3, F 1,2, 1991 Arg 1,2, A, [E, US, It, C, A, S], 1992 Wld 1,2,3, I 1 2
McEldowney, J T (Taranaki) 1977 BI 3,4
MacEwan, I N (Wellington) 1956 SA 2, 1957 A 1,2, 1958 A 1, 2, 3, 1959 BI 1, 2, 3, 1960 SA 1, 2, 3, 4, 1961 F 1, 2, 3, 1962 A 1, 2, 3, 4
McGrattan, B (Wellington) 1983 S, E, 1985 Arg 1,2, 1986 F 1, A 1
McGregor, A J (Auckland) 1913 A 1, US
McGregor, D (Canterbury, Southland) 1903 A, 1904 BI, 1905 E, W
McGregor, N P (Canterbury) 1924 W, 1925 E
McGregor, R W (Auckland) 1903 A, 1904 BI
McHugh, M J (Auckland) 1946 A 1,2, 1949 SA 3
McIntosh, D N (Wellington) 1956 SA 1,2, 1957 A 1,2
McKay, D W (Auckland) 1961 F 1,2,3, 1963 E 1,2
McKechnie, B J (Southland) 1977 F 1,2, 1978 A 2(R),3, W (R), E, S, 1979 A, 1981 SA 1(R), F 1
McKellar, G F (Wellington) 1910 A 1,2,3
McKenzie, R J (Wellington) 1913 A 1, US, 1914 A 2,3
McKenzie, R McC (Manawatu) 1934 A 1, 1935 S, 1936 A 1, 1937 SA 1,2,3, 1938 A 1,2,3
McLachlan, J S (Auckland) 1974 A 2
McLaren, H C (Waikato) 1952 A 1
McLean, A L (Bay of Plenty) 1921 SA 2,3

2011 Fj, SA1, A1, 2, [Tg, J, F1, Arg, A, F2], 2012 A1, 2, Arg1, SA1, Arg2, SA2
Norton, R W (Canterbury) 1971 BI 1,2,3,4, 1972 A 1,2,3, W, S, 1973 E 1, I, F, E 2, 1974 A 1,2,3, I, 1975 S, 1976 I, SA 1,2,3,4, 1977 BI 1,2,3,4

O'Brien, J G (Auckland) 1914 A 1
O'Callaghan, M W (Manawatu) 1968 F 1,2,3
O'Callaghan, T R (Wellington) 1949 A 2
O'Donnell, D H (Wellington) 1949 A 2
O'Halloran, J D (Wellington) 2000 It (R)
Old, G H (Manawatu) 1981 SA 3, R (R), 1982 A 1(R)
O'Leary, M J (Auckland) 1910 A 1,3, 1913 A 2,3
Oliver, A D (Otago) 1997 Fj (t), 1998 E 1,2, A 1, SA 1, A 2, SA 2, A 3, 1999 WS, F 1, SA 1, A 1, SA 2, A 2, [Tg, E, S, F 2, SA 3(R)], 2000 Tg (R), S 1,2, A 1, SA 1, A 2, SA 2, F 1,2, It, 2001 Sm, Arg 1, F, SA 1, A 1, SA 2, A 2, I, S, Arg 2, 2003 E, F, 2004 It,F, 2005 W,S, 2006 Arg, SA1, 2, 3(R), F1, W, 2007 F2, SA1, A1, 2, [It(R), Pt(R), S, F]
Oliver, C J (Canterbury) 1929 A 1,2, 1934 A 1, 1935 S, I, W, 1936 E
Oliver, D J (Wellington) 1930 BI 1,2
Oliver, D O (Otago) 1954 I, F
Oliver, F J (Southland, Otago, Manawatu) 1976 SA 4, 1977 BI 1, 2, 3, 4, F 1,2, 1978 A 1, 2, 3, I, W, E, S, 1979 F 1,2, 1981 SA 2
O'Neill, K J (Canterbury) 2008 SA2(R)
Orr, R W (Otago) 1949 A 1
Osborne, G M (North Harbour) 1995 C, [I, W, J, E, SA], A 1,2, F 1(R),2, 1996 SA 2,3,4,5, 1997 Arg 1(R), A 2,3, I, 1999 [It]
Osborne, W M (Wanganui) 1975 S, 1976 SA 2(R),4(R), 1977 BI 1,2,3,4, F 1(R),2, 1978 I, W, E, S, 1980 W, 1982 A 1,3
O'Sullivan, J M (Taranaki) 1905 S, I, E, W, 1907 A 3
O'Sullivan, T P A (Taranaki) 1960 SA 1, 1961 F 1, 1962 A 1,2

Page, J R (Wellington) 1931 A, 1932 A 1,2,3, 1934 A 1,2
Palmer, B P (Auckland) 1929 A 2, 1932 A 2,3
Parker, J H (Canterbury) 1924 I, W, 1925 E
Parkhill, A A (Otago) 1937 SA 1,2,3, 1938 A 1,2,3
Parkinson, R M (Poverty Bay) 1972 A 1,2,3, W, S, 1973 E 1,2
Paterson, A M (Otago) 1908 AW 2,3, 1910 A 1,2,3
Paton, H (Otago) 1910 A 1,3
Pene, A R B (Otago) 1992 Wld 1(R),2,3, I 1,2, A 1,2(R), 1993 BI 3, A, WS, S, E, 1994 F 1,2(R), SA 1(R)
Phillips, W J (King Country) 1937 SA 2, 1938 A 1,2
Philpott, S (Canterbury) 1991 [It (R), S (R)]
Pickering, E A R (Waikato) 1958 A 2, 1959 BI 1,4
Pierce, M J (Wellington) 1985 E 1,2, A, Arg 1, 1986 A 2, 3, F 2,3, 1987 [It, Arg, S, W, F], A, 1988 W 1, 2, A 1, 2, 3, 1989 F 1, 2, Arg 1, 2, A, W, I
Pokere, S T (Southland, Auckland) 1981 SA 3, 1982 A 1, 2, 3, 1983 BI 1, 2, 3, 4, A, S, E, 1984 F 1, 2, A 2, 3, 1985 E 1, 2, A
Pollock, H R (Wellington) 1932 A 1,2,3, 1936 A 1,2
Porter, C G (Wellington) 1925 F, 1929 A 2,3, 1930 BI 1,2,3,4
Preston, J P (Canterbury, Wellington) 1991 [US, S], 1992 SA (R), 1993 BI 2,3, A, WS, 1996 SA 4(R), 1997 I (R), E 1(R)
Procter, A C (Otago) 1932 A 1
Purdue, C A (Southland) 1905 A
Purdue, E (Southland) 1905 A
Purdue, G B (Southland) 1931 A, 1932 A 1,2,3
Purvis, G H (Waikato) 1991 [US], 1993 WS
Purvis, N A (Otago) 1976 I

Quaid, C E (Otago) 1938 A 1,2

Ralph, C S (Auckland, Canterbury) 1998 E 2, 2002 It, I 1,2, A 1, SA 1, A 2, SA 2, 2003 E, A 1(R), [C,Tg,SA(R),F(t&R)]
Ranby, R M (Waikato) 2001 Sm (R)
Randell, T C (Otago) 1997 Fj, Arg 1,2, A 1, SA 1, A 2, SA 2, A 3, I, E 1, W, E 2, 1998 E 1,2, A 1, SA 1, A 2, SA 2, A 3, 1999 WS, F 1, SA 1, A 1, SA 2, A 2, [Tg, E, It, S, F 2, SA 3], 2000 Tg, S 1,2(R), A 1, SA 1, A 2, SA 2, F 2(R), It (R), 2001 Arg 1, F, SA 1, A 1, SA 2, A 2, 2002 It, Fj, E, F, A, E
Ranger, R M N (Northland) 2010 W2(R),SA2,A3(R)
Rangi, R E (Auckland) 1964 A 2,3, 1965 SA 1,2,3,4, 1966 BI 1,2,3,4
Rankin, J G (Canterbury) 1936 A 1,2, 1937 SA 2
Rawlinson, G P (North Harbour) 2006 I1, 2(R), SA2, 2007 SA1
Read, K J (Canterbury) 2008 S, I2(R), E3(R), 2009 F1, 2, It1, A1(R), SA1(R), 2(R), A2, SA3, A3, 4(R), W, E, F3, 2010 I1, W1, 2,

SA1, 2, A1, 2, SA3, A3, 4, E, S, I2, W3, 2011 A1, 2, [C, Arg, A, F2], 2012 I 1, 2, A1, 2, Arg1, SA1, Arg2, SA2
Reedy, W J (Wellington) 1908 AW 2,3
Reid, A R (Waikato) 1952 A 1, 1956 SA 3,4, 1957 A 1,2
Reid, H R (Bay of Plenty) 1980 A 1,2, W, 1983 S, E, 1985 Arg 1,2, 1986 A 2,3
Reid, K H (Wairarapa) 1929 A 1,3
Reid, S T (Hawke's Bay) 1935 S, I, W, 1936 E, A 1,2, 1937 SA 1,2,3
Reihana, B T (Waikato) 2000 F 2, It
Reside, W B (Wairarapa) 1929 A 1
Retallick, B A (Bay of Plenty) 2012 I1, 2, 3(R), A1(R), 2(R), Arg1, SA1(R), Arg2(t&R), SA2
Rhind, P K (Canterbury) 1946 A 1,2
Richardson, J (Otago, Southland) 1921 SA 1,2,3, 1924 I, W, 1925 E, F
Rickit, H (Waikato) 1981 S 1,2
Riechelmann, C C (Auckland) 1997 Fj (R), Arg 1(R), A 1(R), SA 2(t), I (R), E 2(t)
Ridland, A J (Southland) 1910 A 1,2,3
Roberts, E J (Wellington) 1914 A 1,2,3, 1921 SA 2,3
Roberts, F (Wellington) 1905 S, I, E, W, 1907 A 1,2,3, 1908 AW 1,3, 1910 A 1,2,3
Roberts, R W (Taranaki) 1913 A 1, US, 1914 A 1,2,3
Robertson, B J (Counties) 1972 A 1,3, S, 1973 E 1, I, F, 1974 A 1,2,3, I, 1976 I, SA 1,2,3,4, 1977 BI 1,3,4, F 1,2, 1978 A 1,2,3, W, E, S, 1979 F 1,2, A, 1980 A 2,3, W, 1981 S 1,2
Robertson, D J (Otago) 1974 A 1,2,3, I, 1975 S, 1976 I, SA 1,3,4, 1977 BI 1
Robertson, S M (Canterbury) 1998 A 2(R), SA 2(R), A 3(R), 1999 [It (R)], 2000 Tg (R), S 1,2(R), A 1, SA 1(R),2(R), F 1,2, It, 2001 I, S, Arg 2, 2002 I 1,2, Fj (R), A 1, SA 1, A 2, SA 2
Robilliard, A C C (Canterbury) 1928 SA 1,2,3,4
Robinson, C E (Southland) 1951 A 1,2,3, 1952 A 1,2
Robinson, K J (Waikato) 2002 E, F (R), W, 2004 E1,2,PI, 2006 E,W, 2007 SA2,A2, [R, F]
Robinson, M D (North Harbour) 1998 E 1(R), 2001 S (R), Arg 2
Robinson, M P (Canterbury) 2000 S 2, SA 1, 2002 It, I 2, A 1, SA 1, E (t&R), F, W (R)
Rokocoko, J T (Auckland) 2003 E, W, F, SA 1, A 1, SA 2, A 2, [It, W, SA, A, F], 2004 E1, 2, Arg, PI, A1, SA1, A2, SA2, It, W, F, 2005 SA1(R), A1, SA2, A2, W, E(R), S, 2006 I1, 2, A1, 2, SA3, E, F1, 2, 2007 F1, 2, SA1, A1, SA2, A2, [Pt, R, F], 2008 S, I2, W, E3, 2009 F1, 2, It1, SA1, 2, A2, SA3, A3, 2010 I1, W1, SA1, A1, 2, SA3, A4, E
Rollerson, D L (Manawatu) 1980 W, 1981 S 2, SA 1,2,3, R, F 1(R),2
Romano, L (Canterbury) 2012 I 3, A1, 2, Arg1, SA1, Arg2, SA2(R)
Roper, R A (Taranaki) 1949 A 2, 1950 BI 1,2,3,4
Ross, I B (Canterbury) 2009 F1, 2, It1, A1, SA1, 2, A2, SA3
Rowley, H C B (Wanganui) 1949 A 2
Rush, E J (North Harbour) 1995 [W (R), J], It, F 1,2, 1996 S 1(R),2, A 1(t), SA 1(R)
Rush, X J (Auckland) 1998 A 3, 2004 E1, 2, PI, A1, SA1, A2, SA2
Rutledge, L M (Southland) 1978 A 1, 2, 3, I, W, E, S, 1979 F 1, 2, A, 1980 A 1, 2, 3
Ryan, J (Wellington) 1910 A 2, 1914 A 1,2,3
Ryan, J A C (Otago) 2005 Fj, BI3(R), A1(R), SA2(R), A2(R), W, S, 2006 F1, W(R)

Sadler, B S (Wellington) 1935 S, I, W, 1936 A 1,2
Salmon, J L B (Wellington) 1981 R, F 1, 2(R)
Savage, L T (Canterbury) 1949 SA 1,2,4
Savea, S J (Wellington) 2012 I 1, 2, Arg1, SA1, Arg2
Saxton, C K (South Canterbury) 1938 A 1,2,3
Schuler, K J (Manawatu, North Harbour) 1990 A 2(R), 1992 A 2, 1995 [I (R), J]
Schuster, N J (Wellington) 1988 A 1,2,3, 1989 F 1,2, Arg 1,2, A, W, I
Schwalger, J E (Wellington) 2007 C, 2008 I1(R)
Scott, R W H (Auckland) 1946 A 1,2, 1947 A 1,2, 1949 SA 1,2,3,4, 1950 BI 1,2,3,4, 1953 W, 1954 I, E, S, F
Scown, A I (Taranaki) 1972 A 1,2,3, W (R), S
Scrimshaw, G (Canterbury) 1928 SA 1
Seear, A (Otago) 1977 F 1, 2, 1978 A 1, 2, 3, I, W, E, S, 1979 F 1, 2, A
Seeling, C E (Auckland) 1904 BI, 1905 S, I, E, W, 1906 F, 1907 A 1,2, 1908 AW 1,2,3
Sellars, G M V (Auckland) 1913 A 1, US
Senio, K (Bay of Plenty) 2005 A2(R)
Shaw, M W (Manawatu, Hawke's Bay) 1980 A 1,2,3(R), W, 1981

Tonu'u, O F J (Auckland) 1997 Fj (R), A 3(R), 1998 E 1,2, SA 1(R)

Townsend, L J (Otago) 1955 A 1,3

Tremain, K R (Canterbury, Hawke's Bay) 1959 BI 2,3,4, 1960 SA 1,2,3,4, 1961 F 2,3 1962 A 1,2,3, 1963 E 1,2, I, W, 1964 E, S, F, A 1,2,3, 1965 SA 1,2,3,4, 1966 BI 1,2,3,4, 1967 A, E, W, S, 1968 A 1, F 1,2,3

Trevathan, D (Otago) 1937 SA 1,2,3

Tuck, J M (Waikato) 1929 A 1,2,3

Tuiali'i, M M (Auckland) 2004 Arg,A2(R),SA2(R),It,W, 2005 I,E(R),S(R), 2006 Arg

Tuigamala, V L (Auckland) 1991 [US, It, C, S], 1992 Wld 1,2,3, I 1, A 1,2,3, SA, 1993 BI 1,2,3, A, WS, S, E

Tuitavake, A S M (North Harbour) 2008 I1,E1,A1,2(R),Sm,S

Tuitupou, S (Auckland) 2004 E1(R),2(R),Arg,SA1(R),A2(R),SA2, 2006 Arg,SA1,2(R)

Turner, R S (North Harbour) 1992 Wld 1,2(R)

Turtill, H S (Canterbury) 1905 A

Twigden, T M (Auckland) 1980 A 2,3

Tyler, G A (Auckland) 1903 A, 1904 BI, 1905 S, I, E, W, 1906 F

Udy, D K (Wairarapa) 1903 A

Umaga, J F (Wellington) 1997 Fj, Arg 1,2, A 1, SA 1,2, 1999 WS, F 1, SA 1, A 1, SA 2, A 2, [Tg, E, S, F 2, SA 3], 2000 Tg, S 1,2, A 1, SA 1, A 2, SA 2, F 1,2, It, 2001 Sm, Arg 1, F, SA 1, A 1, SA 2, A 2, I, S, Arg 2, 2002 I 1, Fj, SA 1(R), A 2, SA 2, E, F, W, 2003 E, W, F, SA 1, A 1, SA 2, A 2, [It], 2004 E1, 2, Arg,PI, A1, SA1, A2, SA2, It, F, 2005 Fj,BI1, 2, 3, SA1, A1, SA2, A2, W, E, S

Urbahn, R J (Taranaki) 1959 BI 1,3,4

Urlich, R A (Auckland) 1970 SA 3,4

Uttley, I N (Wellington) 1963 E 1,2

Vidiri, J (Counties Manukau) 1998 E 2(R), A 1

Vincent, P B (Canterbury) 1956 SA 1,2

Vito, V V J (Wellington) 2010 I1(R), W1, A1(R), 2(R), SA3(R), A3, 2011 SA2(R), A2(R), [Tg, J, C, Arg(R), A(R)], 2012 I 1, A2(R), Arg1

Vodanovich, I M H (Wellington) 1955 A 1, 2, 3

Wallace, W J (Wellington) 1903 A, 1904 BI, 1905 S, I, E, W, 1906 F, 1907 A 1,2,3, 1908 AW 2

Waller, D A G (Wellington) 2001 Arg 2(t)

Walsh, P T (Counties) 1955 A 1, 2, 3, 1956 SA 1, 2, 4, 1957 A 1,2, 1958 A 1,2,3, 1959 BI 1, 1963 E 2

Ward, R H (Southland) 1936 A 2, 1937 SA 1,3

Waterman, A C (North Auckland) 1929 A 1,2

Watkins, E L (Wellington) 1905 A

Watt, B A (Canterbury) 1962 A 1,4, 1963 E 1,2, W, 1964 E, S, A 1

Watt, J M (Otago) 1936 A 1,2

Watt, J R (Wellington) 1958 A 2, 1960 SA 1,2,3,4, 1961 F 1,3, 1962 A 1,2

Watts, M G (Taranaki) 1979 F 1,2, 1980 A 1,2,3(R)

Webb, D S (North Auckland) 1959 BI 2

Weepu, P A T (Wellington, Auckland) 2004 W, 2005 SA1(R), A1, SA2, A2, I, E(R), S, 2006 Arg, A1(R), SA1, A3(R), SA2, F1, Sm(R), A3(R), 2007 F1, C(R), SA1(R), A1(R), SA2, 2008 A2(R), SA3(R), It1(R), A1(R), SA1(R), 2(R), 2010 I1(R), W1(R), 2(R), SA1(R), 2, A1(R), 2, SA3(R), A3, 2011 Fj(R), SA1(R), A1, SA2(R), A2, [Tg(R), J(R), F1, C(R), Arg, A, F2], 2012 I 1(R), 2(R), 3(R), A1(R), 2(R), Arg1(R), SA1, Arg2(R), SA2(R)

Wells, J (Wellington) 1936 A 1,2

West, A H (Taranaki) 1921 SA 2,3

Whetton, A J (Auckland) 1984 A 1(R),3(R), 1985 A (R), Arg 1(R), 1986 A 2, 1987 [It, Fj, Arg, S, W, F], A, 1988 W 1,2, A 1,2,3, 1989 F 1,2, Arg 1,2, A, 1990 S 1,2, A 1,2,3, F 1,2, 1991 Arg 1, [E, US, It, C, A]

Whetton, G W (Auckland) 1981 SA 3, R, F 1,2, 1982 A 3, 1983 BI 1,2,3,4, 1984 F 1,2, A 1,2,3, 1985 E 1,2, A, Arg 2, 1986 A 2,3, F 2,3, 1987 [It, Fj, Arg, S, W, F], A, 1988 W 1,2, A 1,2,3, 1989 F 1,2, Arg 1,2, A, W, I, 1990 S 1,2, A 1,2,3, F 1,2, 1991 Arg 1,2, A 1,2, [E, US, It, C, A, S]

Whineray, W J (Canterbury, Waikato, Auckland) 1957 A 1,2, 1958 A 1,2,3, 1959 BI 1,2,3,4, 1960 SA 1,2,3,4, 1961 F 1,2,3, 1962 A 1,2,3,4,5, 1963 E 1,2, I, W, 1964 E, S, F, 1965 SA 1,2,3,4

White, A (Southland) 1921 SA 1, 1924 I, 1925 E, F

White, H L (Auckland) 1954 I, E, F, 1955 A 3

White, R A (Poverty Bay) 1949 A 1,2, 1950 BI 1,2,3,4, 1951 A 1,2,3, 1952 A 1,2, 1953 W, 1954 I, E, S, F, 1955 A 1,2,3, 1956 SA 1,2,3,4

White, R M (Wellington) 1946 A 1,2, 1947 A 1,2

Whitelock, G B (Canterbury) 2009 It1(R)

Whitelock, S L (Canterbury) 2010 I1(R), W1(R), 2(R), SA1(R), 2(R), A1(R), 2(R), SA3(R), A4(R), E, S, I2(R), W3, 2011 Fj(R), SA1, A1(R), SA2, A2, [Tg(R), J, F1, C, Arg, A, F2], 2012 I 1, 2, 3, A1, 2, Arg1(R), SA1, Arg2, SA2

Whiting, G J (King Country) 1972 A 1,2, S, 1973 E 1, I, F

Whiting, P J (Auckland) 1971 BI 1,2,4, 1972 A 1,2,3, W, S, 1973 E 1, I, F, 1974 A 1,2,3, I, 1976 I, SA 1,2,3,4

Williams, A J (Auckland, Tasman) 2002 E, F, W, 2003 E, W, F, SA 1, A 1, SA 2, A 2, [Tg, W, SA, A, F], 2004 SA1(R), A2, It(R), W, F(R), 2005 Fj, BI1, 2, 3, SA1, A1, SA2, A2, I, E(R), 2006 Arg, A1(R), SA1, A2, 3(R), SA2, 3, F1, 2, W, 2007 F1, 2, [It, Pt, S, F], 2008 I1, E1, 2, SA1, A2, A1, 2, SA3, Sm, A3, 4, S, I2, W, E3, 2011 Fj, SA1, A1, SA2, A2(R), [Tg, J(R), F1(R), C, Arg(R), A(R), F2(R)], 2012 I 1(R), 2(R)

Williams, B G (Auckland) 1970 SA 1,2,3,4, 1971 BI 1,2,4, 1972 A 1,2,3, W, S, 1973 E 1, I, F, E 2, 1974 A 1,2,3, I, 1975 S, 1976 I, SA 1,2,3,4, 1977 BI 1,2,3,4, F 1, 1978 A 1,2,3, I (R), W, E, S

Williams, G C (Wellington) 1967 E, W, F, S, 1968 A 2

Williams, P (Otago) 1913 A 1

Williams, S (Canterbury) 2010 E, S, I2(R), W3, 2011 SA1(R), A1(R), SA2, [Tg, J(R), F1(R), C, Arg, A(R), F2(R)], 2012 I 1, 2, 3, A1, 2

Williment, M (Wellington) 1964 A 1, 1965 SA 1,2,3, 1966 BI 1,2,3,4, 1967 A

Willis, R K (Waikato) 1998 SA 2, A 3, 1999 SA 1(R), A 1(R), SA 2(R), A 2(R), [Tg (R), E(R), It, F 2(R), SA 3], 2002 SA 1(R)

Willis, T E (Otago) 2002 It, Fj, SA 2(R), A 2, SA 2

Willocks, C (Otago) 1946 A 1,2, 1949 SA 1,3,4

Wilson, B W (Otago) 1977 BI 3,4, 1978 A 1,2,3, 1979 F 1,2, A 1,2,3,4

Wilson, D D (Canterbury) 1954 E, S

Wilson, H W (Otago) 1949 A 1, 1950 BI 4, 1951 A 1,2,3

Wilson, J W (Otago) 1993 S, E, 1994 A, 1995 C, [I, J, S, E, SA], A 1,2, It, F 1, 1996 WS, S 1,2, A 1, SA 1, A 2, SA 2,3,4,5, 1997 Fj, Arg 1,2, A 1, SA 1, A 2, SA 2, A 3, I, E 1, W, E 2, 1998 E 1,2, A 1, SA 1, A 2, SA 2, A 3, 1999 WS, F 1, SA 1, A 1, SA 2, A 2, [Tg, E, It, S, F 2, SA 3], 2001 Sm, Arg 1, F, SA 1, A 1, SA 2

Wilson, N A (Wellington) 1908 AW 1,2, 1910 A 1,2,3, 1913 A 2,3, 1914 A 1,2,3

Wilson, N L (Otago) 1951 A 1,2,3

Wilson, R G (Canterbury) 1979 S, E

Wilson, S S (Wellington) 1977 F 1,2, 1978 A 1,2,3, I, W, E, S, 1979 F 1,2, A, S, E, 1980 A 1, W, 1981 S 1,2, SA 1,2,3, R, F 1,2, 1982 A 1,2,3, 1983 BI 1, 2, 3, 4, A, S, E

Witcombe, D J C (Auckland) 2005 Fj, BI1(R), 2(R), SA1(R), A1(R)

Wolfe, T N (Wellington, Taranaki) 1961 F 1,2,3, 1962 A 2,3, 1963 E 1

Wood, M E (Canterbury, Auckland) 1903 A, 1904 BI

Woodcock, T D (North Harbour) 2002 W, 2004 E1(t&R), 2(t&R), Arg, W, F, 2005 Fj, BI1, 2, 3, SA1, A1, SA2, A2, W(R), I, E, 2006 Arg, A1, 2, 3, SA2(R), 3, E, F1, 2, W(R), 2007 F1, 2, SA1, A1, SA2, A2, [It, Pt(R), S, F], 2008 E2(R),S A1, 2, A1, 2, SA3, Sm, A3, 4, I2, W, E3, 2009 F1, 2, It1(R), A1, SA1, 2, A2, SA3, A3, 4, E, F3, 2010 W1(R), 2, SA1, 2, A1, 2, SA3, A3, 4, E, S, I2, W3, 2011 SA2, A2, [Tg, J, F1, C, Arg, A, F2], 2012 I 1, 2, 3, A1, Arg1, SA1, Arg2, SA2

Woodman, F A (North Auckland) 1981 SA 1,2, F 2

Wrigley, E (Wairarapa) 1905 A

Wright, T J (Auckland) 1986 F 1, A 1, 1987 [Arg], 1988 W 1,2, A 1,2,3, 1989 F 1,2, Arg 1,2, A, W, I, 1990 S 1,2, A 1,2,3, F 1,2, 1991 Arg 1,2, A 1,2, [E, US, It, S]

Wulf, R N (North Harbour) 2008 E2,SA1,2,Sm(R)

Wylie, J T (Auckland) 1913 A 1, US

Wyllie, A J (Canterbury) 1970 SA 2, 3, 1971 BI 2, 3, 4, 1972 W, S, 1973 E 1, I, F, E 2

Yates, V M (North Auckland) 1961 F 1,2,3

Young, D (Canterbury) 1956 SA 2, 1958 A 1,2,3, 1960 SA 1,2,3,4, 1961 F 1,2,3, 1962 A 1,2,3,5, 1963 E 1,2, I, W, 1964 E, S, F

ROMANIA

ROMANIA'S 2012 TEST RECORD

OPPONENTS	DATE	VENUE	RESULT
Portugal	4 Feb	H	Won 15–7
Russia	25 Feb	A	Won 25–0
Georgia	10 Feb	H	Lost 13–19
Spain	17 Feb	A	Lost 13–12
Ukraine	31 Mar	H	Won 71–0
Uruguay	8 Jun	H	Won 29–9

ROMANIA END LONG WAIT FOR SILVERWARE

By Chris Thau

Florin Surugiu is tackled during Romania's Nations Cup match against Emerging Italy.

Romania's year has been something of a rollercoaster, from the lows of returning home from Rugby World Cup 2011 without a win, through an inconsistent and disappointing climax to the European Nations Cup 2012 to the high of winning the IRB Nations Cup for the first time.

A new coaching team was appointed after RWC 2011, where Romania had given Scotland an almighty scare in their opening match, with former captain and number 8 Harry Dumitras taking over as head coach. Former captain Marius Tincu, who won the last of his 54 Test caps in March 2012, is the new forwards coach with former centre Eugen Apjok, head coach of domestic champions CSM Baia Mare, as backs coach.

The first task of the new coaching triumvirate was to prepare Romania for the second phase of the European Nations Cup, a seven-tier competition which spans two years with teams in each division playing each other home and away.

"We had a mixed season, which started with a laboured 15–7 win over Portugal, followed by a satisfying 25–0 defeat of Russia away in Sochi," admitted Dumitras, who played 48 Tests for Romania between 1984 and 1993. "We started to believe that the new game plan we were trying to implement was paying dividends when disaster struck. We lost 13–19 to Georgia at home, a match we could and should have won.

"It was a catastrophe from a coach's point of view. Instead of maintaining the approach we used against Russia, playing a wide, fast-flowing game, the boys somehow felt they had to take revenge for the defeat at RWC 2011 and took the Georgians on up front, which was exactly the opposite of what we agreed to do. That is clearly not the way to defeat Georgia, but the instincts are sometimes more powerful than the rational approach. It was terrible.

"After the loss to Georgia, we felt that we had no more chance of winning the competition so I decided to experiment by bringing in new players for the match again Spain. That's when the aberration against Spain happened, not that I wish to deny Spain any plaudits. They were better than us on the day and deserved to win [13–12]."

Romania ended their European Nations Cup 2012 campaign with an emphatic 71–0 victory over Ukraine, who were relegated from Division 1A, to finish as runners-up, albeit 10 points adrift of champions Georgia following a record of won six, lost four over the two years.

A new defence coach in Neil Kelly, the former Wakefield, Featherstone Rovers and Dewsbury player and coach, was another important cog in Dumitras's management team. Kelly, who was Namibia's defence coach at RWC 2011 and has previously worked with the Wales Rugby League team, has been encouraged by what he has seen, but knows it will take time to truly reap the rewards.

"We are making progress, but it will take time. I am very encouraged by the commitment and physicality of the players. We are trying to adopt an easily understandable defence pattern, working slowly, step by step," explained Kelly.

The progress was evident in June when Romania hosted the IRB Nations Cup for the sixth successive year. The Oaks, attempting to play a more expansive game than their traditional forward-orientated style, began with a 29–9 defeat of Uruguay in Bucharest with new Romanian Prime Minister Victor Ponta an interested spectator, and then survived an Argentina Jaguars fight-back to prevail 23–21 and make their final match against Emerging Italy a title decider.

Dorin Manole scored all of Romania's points in a first half that ended with them leading the young Italians 10–3, but the fly half was also guilty of missing three penalty attempts. Fortunately the misses didn't prove costly with Romania winning 17–13, although they endured a nervous finish after Alberto Chiesa's try five minutes from time.

"This was a dream that became reality," admitted Dumitras amid the celebrations at the Stadionul National Arcul de Triumf. "It is the first trophy Romanian rugby has won since the European Nations Cup in 2006. This was achieved by a group of determined players who strongly believed in this dream. We have almost forgotten what is like to lift a trophy and tonight we are about to learn it again."

Another pleasing aspect of the Nations Cup success for Dumitras was the fact that more than half of the squad were fringe players or newcomers who were not involved in RWC 2011, suggesting that the future could once again be bright for Romanian rugby.

Lynn Howells, the Romanian Rugby Federation's (FRR) new director of rugby, certainly believes the coaching team has the right blend to bring more success in the years to come. "Harry is a quality coach and we became good friends," said Howells, the former Pontypridd, Edinburgh and Wales coach. "It is a definite advantage that Romania has got a Romanian coach, but mind you Marius is quite superb and I foresee a great future for him.

"Eugen, who is very knowledgeable, is doing a fine job, not to mention the new defence coach Neil Kelly whose contribution has been tremendous. It is a highly effective team and the fact that we won the IRB Nations Cup just proves that the potential is there."

Romania will hope this potential continues to develop through the November Test window when they face Japan and USA, and into the European Nations Cup, with Division 1A – involving Georgia, Romania, Russia, Portugal, Spain and newcomers Belgium – to once again provide the region's two direct qualified teams for RWC 2015. The team ranked third come the tournament's climax in 2014 will face a play-off for the right to represent Europe in the Répechage, a route Romania successfully negotiated to become the 20th and final qualifier for RWC 2011 in New Zealand.

"This (qualification) is our main objective and we have already been planning ahead," admitted former national coach Peter Ianusevici, who has rejoined the Federation as technical director after 20 years in charge of German rugby. The appointment of Ianusevici, who coached Romania at RWC 1991, was the last act of FRR president and former Romania captain Alin Petrache before he stepped down to become Secretary of State for Sport and is expected to add fresh impetus.

ROMANIA INTERNATIONAL STATISTICS

MATCH RECORDS UP TO 10 OCTOBER 2012

WINNING MARGIN

Date	Opponent	Result	Winning Margin
21/09/1976	Bulgaria	100–0	100
19/03/2005	Ukraine	97–0	97
13/04/1996	Portugal	92–0	92
17/11/1976	Morocco	89–0	89
19/04/1996	Belgium	83–5	78

MOST POINTS IN A MATCH
BY THE TEAM

Date	Opponent	Result	Points
21/09/1976	Bulgaria	100–0	100
19/03/2005	Ukraine	97–0	97
13/04/1996	Portugal	92–0	92
17/11/1976	Morocco	89–0	89

BY A PLAYER

Date	Player	Opponent	Points
05/10/2002	Ionut Tofan	Spain	30
13/04/1996	Virgil Popisteanu	Portugal	27
04/02/2001	Petre Mitu	Portugal	27
13/04/1996	Ionel Rotaru	Portugal	25

MOST TRIES IN A MATCH
BY THE TEAM

Date	Opponent	Result	Tries
17/11/1976	Morocco	89–0	17
21/10/1951	East Germany	64–26	16
19/03/2005	Ukraine	97–0	15
16/04/1978	Spain	74–3	14

BY A PLAYER

Date	Player	Opponent	Tries
30/04/1972	Gheorghe Rascanu	Morocco	5
18/10/1986	Cornel Popescu	Portugal	5
13/04/1996	Ionel Rotaru	Portugal	5

MOST CONVERSIONS IN A MATCH
BY THE TEAM

Date	Opponent	Result	Cons
13/04/1996	Portugal	92–0	12
19/03/2005	Ukraine	97–0	11
04/10/1997	Belgium	83–13	10

BY A PLAYER

Date	Player	Opponent	Cons
13/04/1996	Virgil Popisteanu	Portugal	12
04/10/1997	Serban Guranescu	Belgium	10
19/03/2005	Marin Danut Dumbrava	Ukraine	8
22/03/2008	Florin Adrian Vlaicu	Czech Republic	8

MOST PENALTIES IN A MATCH
BY THE TEAM

Date	Opponent	Result	Pens
15/06/2010	Argentina Jaguars	24–8	7
14/05/1994	Italy	26–12	6
04/02/2001	Portugal	47–0	6

BY A PLAYER

Date	Player	Opponent	Pens
14/05/1994	Neculai Nichitean	Italy	6
04/02/2001	Petre Mitu	Portugal	6

MOST DROP GOALS IN A MATCH
BY THE TEAM

Date	Opponent	Result	DGs
29/10/1967	West Germany	27–5	4
14/11/1965	West Germany	9–8	3
17/10/1976	Poland	38–8	3
03/10/1990	Spain	19–6	3

BY A PLAYER

Date	Player	Opponent	DGs
29/10/1967	Valeriu Irimescu	West Germany	3
17/10/1976	Alexandru Dumitru	Poland	3

ROMANIA

404

MOST CAPPED PLAYERS

Player	Caps
Cristian Petre	91
Adrian Lungu	77
Romeo Stefan Gontineac	77
Lucian Mihai Sirbu	77
Gabriel Brezoianu	72

LEADING TRY SCORERS

Player	Tries
Petre Motrescu	33
Gabriel Brezoianu	28
Florica Murariu	27

LEADING CONVERSIONS SCORERS

Player	Cons
Danut Dumbrava	69
Florin Vlaicu	59
Petre Mitu	53
Ionut Tofan	52

LEADING PENALTY SCORERS

Player	Pens
Danut Dumbrava	70
Neculai Nichitean	53
Petre Mitu	53
Ionut Tofan	46

LEADING DROP GOAL SCORERS

Player	DGs
Alexandru Dumitru	14
Neculai Nichitean	10
Valeriu Irimescu	10
Gelu Ignat	8

LEADING POINTS SCORERS

Player	Points
Marin Danut Dumbrava	369
Petre Mitu	335
Ionut Tofan	322
Florin Vlaicu	267
Neculai Nichitean	257

THE COUNTRIES

UP TO 10 OCTOBER 2012

A Achim 1974 *Pol*, 1976 *Pol, Mor*
M Adascalitei 2007 *Rus*, 2009 *Pt, Ur, F, ItA*, 2012 *Ukr, Ur*
Ailenei 2012 *Ukr*
M Aldea 1979 *USS, W, Pol, F*, 1980 *It, USS, I, F*, 1981 *It, Sp, USS, S, NZ, F*, 1982 *WGe, It, USS, Z, Z, F*, 1983 *Mor, WGe, It, USS, Pol, W, USS, F*, 1984 *It, S, F*, 1985 *E, USS*
C Alexandrescu 1934 *It*
N Anastasiade 1927 *Cze*, 1934 *It*
V Anastasiade 1939 *It*
I Andrei 2003 *W, I, Ar, Nm*, 2004 *CZR, Pt, Sp, Rus, Geo, It, W, J, CZR*, 2005 *Rus, US, S, Pt*, 2006 *CZR*, 2007 *Pt*, 2008 *Sp, Pt, Rus*
I Andriesi 1937 *It, H, Ger*, 1938 *F, Ger*, 1939 *It*, 1940 *It*
E Apjok 1996 *Bel*, 2000 *It*, 2001 *Pt*
AM Apostol 2011 *Nm, E*, 2012 *Rus, Geo, Sp*
D Armasel 1924 *F, US*
A Atanasiu 1970 *It, F*, 1971 *It, Mor, F*, 1972 *Mor, Cze, WGe*, 1973 *Sp, Mor, Ar, Ar, WGe*, 1974 *Pol*
I Bacioiu 1976 *USS, Bul, Pol, F, Mor*
N Baciu 1964 *Cze, EGe*, 1967 *It, F*, 1968 *Cze, Cze, F*, 1969 *Pol, WGe, F*, 1970 *It*, 1971 *It, Mor, F*, 1972 *Mor, Cze, WGe*, 1973 *Ar, Ar*, 1974 *Cze, EGe*
VC Badalicescu 2012 *Pt*
B Balan 2003 *Pt, Sp, Geo*, 2004 *W*, 2005 *Rus, Ukr, J, US, S, Pt*, 2006 *Geo, Pt, Ukr, Rus, F, Geo, Sp, S*, 2007 *Sp, ESp, ItA, Nm, It, S, Pt, NZ*, 2009 *Fj*, 2010 *Ger, Rus, Ur, Ur*, 2011 *Pt*
D Balan 1983 *F*
PV Balan 1998 *H, Pol, Ukr, Ar, Geo, I*, 1999 *F, S, A, US, I*, 2000 *Mor, H, Pt, Sp, Geo, F, It*, 2001 *Pt, Sp, H, Rus, Geo, I, E*, 2002 *Pt, Sp, H, Rus, Geo, Sp, S*, 2003 *CZR, F, W, I, Nm*, 2004 *It, W, J, CZR*, 2005 *Geo, C, I*, 2006 *Geo, Pt, F, Geo, Sp, S*, 2007 *Geo*, 2009 *Ur, F*
L Balcan 1963 *Bul, EGe, Cze*
F Balmus 2000 *Mor, H, Pt*
S Bals 1927 *F, Ger, Cze*
G Baltaretu 1965 *WGe, F*
C Barascu 1957 *F*
M Baraulea 2004 *CZR, Pt, Geo*
A Barbu 1958 *WGe, It*, 1959 *EGe, Pol, Cze, EGe*, 1960 *F*
A Barbuliceanu 2008 *Rus, ESp*, 2009 *Sp, Pt, Rus, Geo, Pt*
S Bargaunas 1971 *It, Mor*, 1972 *F*, 1974 *Cze*, 1975 *It*
S Barsan 1934 *It*, 1936 *F, It*, 1937 *It, H, F, Ger*, 1938 *F, Ger*, 1939 *It*, 1940 *It*, 1942 *It*
RC Basalau 2007 *Pt*, 2008 *Geo, Pt, Rus, CZR, Ur, Rus, ESp*, 2010 *ItA, Tun*
CD Beca 2009 *Sp, Ger, Rus, Geo, Pt*, 2011 *Pt*
E Beches 1979 *It, Sp, USS*, 1982 *WGe, It*, 1983 *Pol*
M Bejan 2001 *I, W*, 2002 *Pt*, 2003 *Geo, CZR*, 2004 *It*
C Beju 1936 *F, It, Ger*
G Bentia 1919 *US, F*, 1924 *F, US*
V Bezarau 1995 *Ar, F, It*
R Bezuscu 1985 *It*, 1987 *F*
G Bigiu 2007 *Pt*, 2008 *Geo, Sp, Pt, Rus, CZR, Ur, Rus*
M Blagescu 1952 *EGe, EGe*, 1953 *It*, 1955 *Cze*, 1957 *F, Cze, Bel, F*
G Blasek 1937 *It, H, F, Ger*, 1940 *It*, 1942 *It*
A Bogheanu 1980 *Mor*
D Boldor 1988 *It, Sp, US, USS, USS, W*, 1989 *It, E, Sp, Z*
A Boroi 1975 *Sp*
P Bors 1975 *JAB*, 1976 *Sp*, 1977 *It*, 1980 *It, USS, I, Pol, F*, 1981 *It, Sp, USS, S, NZ, F*, 1982 *WGe*, 1983 *Mor, WGe, It, USS*, 1984 *It*
IC Botezatu 2009 *Ger, Rus, Geo, ItA*, 2010 *Ger, Rus, Ukr, Ukr, Nm, ArJ*, 2011 *Pt*, 2012 *Ur*
D Bozian 1997 *Bel*, 1998 *H, Pol, Ukr*

V Brabateanu 1919 *US, F*
M Braga 1970 *It, F*
C Branescu 1994 *It, E*, 1997 *F*
I Bratulescu 1927 *Ger, Cze*
G Brezoianu 1996 *Bel*, 1997 *F*, 1998 *H, Pol, Ukr, Ar, Geo, I*, 1999 *F, S, A, US, I*, 2000 *H, Pt, Sp, Geo, F, It*, 2001 *Sp, Rus, Geo, I, W, E*, 2002 *Pt, Sp, H, Rus, Geo, I, It, Sp, W, S, S*, 2003 *Pt, Sp, Rus, Geo, CZR, F, W, I, A, Ar, Nm*, 2005 *Rus, Ukr, J, US, S, Pt, C, I*, 2006 *CZR, Pt, Ukr, Rus, F, Geo, Sp, S*, 2007 *Geo, Sp, CZR, ESp, ItA, Nm, It, S, NZ*
V Brici 1991 *NZ*, 1992 *USS, F, It*, 1993 *Tun, F, Sp, I*, 1994 *Sp, Ger, Rus, It, W, It, E*, 1995 *F, S, J, J, SA, A*, 1996 *Pt, F*, 1997 *WalA, F*
TE Brinza 1990 *It, USS*, 1991 *C*, 1992 *It, Ar*, 1993 *Pt, Tun, F, F, I*, 1994 *Sp, Ger, It, W, It, E*, 1995 *F, S, J, J, SA, A*, 1996 *Pt, F, Pol*, 1997 *WalA, F, W, Ar, F, It*, 1998 *Ukr*, 1999 *A, US, I*, 2000 *H, Geo*, 2002 *H*
I Bucan 1976 *Bul*, 1977 *Sp*, 1978 *Cze*, 1979 *F*, 1980 *It, USS, I, Pol, F*, 1981 *It, Sp, USS, S, NZ, F*, 1982 *WGe, It, USS, Z, Z, F*, 1983 *Mor, WGe, It, USS, Pol, W, USS, F*, 1984 *It, S, F, Sp*, 1985 *E, Tun, USS, USS, It*, 1986 *Pt, S, F, Pt*, 1987 *It, USS, Z, S, USS, F*
M Bucos 1972 *Mor, Cze, WGe*, 1973 *Sp*, 1975 *JAB, Pol, F*, 1976 *H, It, Sp, USS, Bul, Pol, F, Mor*, 1977 *Sp, It, F, Pol, It, F*, 1978 *Pol, F*, 1979 *W*, 1980 *It, Mor*
P Buda 1953 *It*, 1955 *Cze*, 1957 *F, Cze*
C Budica 1974 *Cze, EGe, Cze*
SS Burcea 2006 *F*, 2007 *ESp, ItA, Nm, Rus, Pt*, 2008 *Geo, Pt, CZR, Ur, Rus, ESp*, 2009 *Sp, Ger, Rus, Geo, Pt, ItA, Fj*, 2010 *Ger, Rus, Ukr, Ukr, Nm, ArJ, ItA, Tun, Ur, Ur*, 2011 *Rus, ArJ, Ukr, S, E*
M Burghelea 1974 *Cze, EGe, F*, 1975 *It*
S Burlescu 1936 *F, It, Ger*, 1938 *F, Ger*, 1939 *It*
M Butugan 2003 *It*
VN Calafeteanu 2004 *J*, 2005 *Ukr*, 2006 *CZR, Pt, Ukr, F, Sp, S*, 2007 *Geo, Sp, CZR, ESp, ItA, Nm, It, S, Pt, NZ*, 2008 *Geo, Sp, Pt, CZR*, 2009 *Ger, Geo, Pt, Ur, F, ItA, ItA, Fj*, 2010 *Ger, Rus, Tun, Ur, Ur*, 2011 *Pt, Geo, Sp, Nm, ArJ, Ar, E, Geo*, 2012 *Pt, Rus, Geo, Sp, Ukr, Ur*
A Caligari 1951 *EGe*, 1953 *It*
S Caliman 1958 *EGe*, 1960 *Pol, EGe, Cze*
P Calistrat 1940 *It*, 1942 *It*
Ion Camenita 1939 *It*
ME Capatana 2012 *Ukr*
CF Caplescu 2007 *Sp, CZR, Rus, Pt*, 2008 *Rus, CZR, Ur*
C Capmare 1983 *Pol*, 1984 *It*
N Capusan 1960 *F*, 1961 *Pol, Cze, EGe, F*, 1962 *Cze, EGe, Pol, It*
R Capusan 1963 *Bul, EGe, Cze*
G Caracostea 1919 *US, F*
G Caragea 1980 *I, Pol, F*, 1981 *It, Sp, USS, S, NZ, F*, 1982 *WGe, It, USS, Z, Z, F*, 1983 *Mor, WGe, It, USS, Pol, W, F*, 1984 *F, Sp*, 1985 *E, Tun*, 1986 *S, F, Tun, Tun, Pt, F, I*, 1988 *It, Sp, US, USS, USS, W*, 1989 *E*
C Carp 1989 *Z, Sa, USS*
D Carpo 2008 *Sp, Pt, Rus, CZR, Ur, Rus, ESp*, 2009 *Sp, Ger, Rus, Geo, Pt, Ur, F*, 2010 *Ger, Rus, Geo, Pt, Sp, ArJ, ItA, Tun, Ur, Ur*, 2011 *Pt, Rus, Geo, Sp, Nm, ArJ, Ukr, S, Ar, Geo*, 2012 *Pt, Rus, Geo*
GA Catuna 2009 *ItA*, 2012 *Pt*
I Cazan 2010 *ItA, Tun, Ur*, 2011 *Pt, Rus, Geo, Sp, Nm, ArJ, S, Ar, E*
G Celea 1963 *EGe*
D Chiriac 1999 *S, A, I*, 2001 *H*
G Chiriac 1996 *Bel*, 2001 *Pt, Rus*, 2002 *Sp, H, Rus, Geo, I, Sp, W, S, S*, 2003 *Rus, Geo, F, W, I, A, Ar, Nm*

R Chiriac 1952 *EGe*, 1955 *Cze*, 1957 *F, Bel, F*, 1958 *Sp, WGe*, 1960 *F*, 1961 *Pol, EGe, Cze, EGe, F*, 1962 *Cze, EGe, Pol, It, F*, 1963 *Bul, EGe, Cze, F*, 1964 *Cze, EGe, WGe, F*

M Chiricencu 1980 *It, Pol*

S Chirila 1989 *Sp, S*, 1990 *F, H, Sp, It, USS*, 1991 *It*

V Chirita 1999 *S*

G Cilinca 1993 *Pt*

N Cioarec 1974 *Pol*, 1976 *It*, 1979 *Pol*

P Ciobanel 1961 *Pol, EGe, Cze, EGe, F*, 1962 *Cze, EGe, Pol, It, F*, 1963 *F*, 1964 *Cze, EGe, WGe, F*, 1965 *WGe, F*, 1966 *Cze, It, F*, 1967 *F*, 1968 *Cze, Cze, F*, 1969 *Pol, WGe, Cze, F*, 1970 *F*, 1971 *F*

I Ciobanu 1952 *EGe*

M Ciobanu 1949 *Cze*, 1951 *EGe*

R Cioca 1994 *Sp, Ger, Rus, It, It, E*, 1995 *S*, 1996 *Bel*

I Ciofu 2000 *It*, 2003 *Pt*

ML Ciolacu 1998 *Ukr, Ar, Geo, I*, 1999 *F*, 2001 *Sp, H, Rus, Geo, W, E*

S Ciorascu 1988 *US, USS, USS, F, W*, 1989 *It, E, Sp, Z, Sa, USS, S*, 1990 *It, F, H, Sp, USS*, 1991 *It, NZ, S, F, C, Fj*, 1992 *Sp, It, Ar*, 1994 *Ger, Rus, It, W*, 1995 *F, S, J, C, SA, A*, 1996 *F*, 1997 *F, It*, 1999 *F*

M Ciornei 1972 *WGe, F*, 1973 *Ar, Ar, WGe, F*, 1974 *Mor, Pol, EGe, F, Cze*, 1975 *It, Sp*

SE Ciuntu 2007 *NZ, Rus, Pt*, 2008 *Geo, Sp, Pt, Rus, CZR, Ur, ESp*, 2009 *Sp, Ger, Rus, Geo, Pt, Ur, F, ItA, Fj*, 2010 *Ger, Rus, Geo, Pt, Sp, Ukr, Ukr, Nm, ArJ, ItA, Tun*, 2011 *Ukr, S, E, Geo*

C Cocor 1940 *It*, 1949 *Cze*

M Codea 1998 *Ukr*, 2001 *E*

L Codoi 1980 *I, Pol*, 1984 *F*, 1985 *Tun, USS*

C Cojocariu 1990 *It, F, H, Sp, It, USS*, 1991 *It, NZ, F, S, F, C, Fj*, 1992 *Sp, It, USS, F, Ar*, 1993 *Pt, F, F, I*, 1994 *Sp, Ger, Rus, It, W, It, E*, 1995 *F, S, J, J, C, SA, A, Ar, F, It*, 1996 *F*

L Colceriu 1991 *S, Fj*, 1992 *Sp, It, It*, 1993 *I*, 1994 *Sp, Ger, Rus, It, W, It*, 1995 *F, J, J, C, SA, A*, 1997 *WalA, F, W, Bel, Ar, F, It*, 1998 *Pol, Ukr*

D Coliba 1987 *USS, F*

M Coltuneac 2002 *Sp, W, S*

T Coman 1984 *Sp*, 1986 *F, Tun, Tun, I*, 1988 *Sp, US, USS, USS*, 1989 *It*, 1992 *F*

C Constantin 2001 *Pt*, 2002 *Geo, W*

F Constantin 1972 *Mor, Cze, WGe*, 1973 *Ar, Ar, WGe*, 1980 *Mor*, 1982 *It*

I Constantin 1971 *Mor*, 1972 *WGe*, 1973 *Ar, Ar, WGe, F*, 1974 *Mor, Pol, Sp, F, Cze*, 1975 *It, Sp, JAB, Pol, F*, 1976 *H, It, Sp, USS, Bul, Pol*, 1977 *It, F*, 1978 *Pol, F*, 1979 *It, Sp, USS, W, Pol, F*, 1980 *It, USS, I, Pol, F*, 1981 *It, Sp, USS, S, NZ, F*, 1982 *WGe, It, USS, Z, Z*, 1983 *WGe, USS, 1985 It*

L Constantin 1983 *USS, F*, 1984 *It, S, F, Sp*, 1985 *E, It, Tun, USS, USS, It*, 1986 *Pt, S, F, Tun, Tun, Pt, F, I*, 1987 *It, USS, Z, F, S, USS, F*, 1991 *It, NZ, F*

LT Constantin 1985 *USS*

S Constantin 1980 *Mor*, 1982 *Z, Z*, 1983 *Pol, W, USS, F*, 1984 *S, F*, 1985 *USS*, 1986 *Pt, S, F, Tun*, 1987 *It, Z, S*

T Constantin 1992 *USS, F, It*, 1993 *Pt, F, Sp*, 1996 *Pt*, 1997 *It*, 1999 *F, US, I*, 2000 *Pt, Sp, Geo, F*, 2002 *Rus, Geo*

T Constantin 1985 *USS*

N Copil 1985 *USS, It*, 1986 *S*

D Coravu 1968 *F*

N Cordos 1958 *EGe*, 1961 *EGe*, 1963 *Bul, Cze*, 1964 *Cze, EGe*

V Cornel 1977 *F*, 1978 *Cze, Sp*

G Corneliu 1980 *Mor, USS*, 1982 *WGe, It, Z, Z*, 1986 *Tun, Pt, F*, 1993 *I*, 1994 *W*

G Corneliu 1976 *USS, Bul*, 1977 *F*, 1979 *It*, 1981 *S*, 1982 *Z*

M Corneliu 1979 *USS*

F Corodeanu 1997 *WalA, F, W*, 1998 *H, Pol, Ar, Geo*, 1999 *F, S, A, US, I*, 2000 *H, Rus, Geo*, 2001 *Pt, Sp, Rus, Geo, It, Sp, W, S, S*, 2003 *Sp*, 2005 *Geo, J, US, S, Pt, C, I*, 2006 *Geo, CZR, Pt, Geo, Sp, S*, 2007 *Geo, ItA, Nm, It, S, Pt, NZ*, 2008 *Ur, Rus, ESp*, 2009 *Sp, Ger, Rus, Pt*

Coste 2007 *Pt*, 2008 *Geo, Sp, Pt, Rus, CZR, Ur*, 2009 *Sp, Rus, Geo, Pt, F*, 2010 *Ukr*, 2012 *Pt, Rus, Geo, Ur*

L Costea 1994 *E*, 1995 *S, J, J, Ar, F*, 1997 *WalA, F*

L Coter 1957 *F, Cze*, 1959 *EGe, Pol, Cze*, 1960 *F*

F Covaci 1936 *Ger*, 1937 *H, F, Ger*, 1940 *It*, 1942 *It*

C Cratunescu 1919 *US, F*

N Crissoveloni 1936 *F, It*, 1937 *H, F, Ger*, 1938 *F, Ger*

S Cristea 1973 *Mor*

C Cristoloveanu 1952 *EGe*

G Crivat 1938 *F, Ger*

V Csoma 1983 *WGe*

D Curea 2005 *Rus, Ukr, J, US, S, Pt*

V Daiciulescu 1966 *Cze, F*, 1967 *It, Pol*, 1968 *F*, 1969 *Pol, F*, 1970 *F*, 1971 *F*

A Damian 1934 *It*, 1936 *F, It, Ger*, 1937 *It*, 1938 *F, Ger*, 1939 *It*, 1949 *Cze*

M Danila 2012 *Ukr*

G Daraban 1969 *Cze*, 1972 *Mor, Cze, WGe, F*, 1973 *Sp, Mor, Ar, Ar*, 1974 *Cze, EGe, F, Cze*, 1975 *It, Sp, JAB, Pol, F*, 1976 *H, It, Sp, USS, Bul, Pol, F, Mor*, 1977 *Sp, It, F*, 1978 *Cze, Sp, Pol, F*, 1982 *F*, 1983 *Mor, WGe, It, USS, W*

CR Dascalu 2006 *Ukr, F, Geo, Sp, S*, 2007 *Sp, CZR, ESp, NZ, Rus, Pt*, 2008 *Geo, Rus, Ur, Rus, ESp*, 2009 *Sp, Rus, Geo, Ur, ItA, ItA*, 2010 *Ger, Geo, Sp, Ukr, Ukr, Nm*, 2011 *Pt, Rus, Geo*

V David 1984 *Sp*, 1986 *Pt, S, F, Tun*, 1987 *USS, Z, F*, 1992 *USS*

S Demci 1998 *Ar*, 2001 *H, Rus, Geo, I, W*

R Demian 1959 *EGe*, 1960 *F*, 1961 *Pol, EGe, Cze, EGe, F*, 1962 *Cze, Pol, It, F*, 1963 *Bul, EGe, Cze, F*, 1964 *WGe, F*, 1965 *WGe, F*, 1966 *Cze, It, F*, 1967 *It, Pt, Pol, WGe, F*, 1968 *Cze, F, WGe, F*, 1971 *It, Mor*

E Denischi 1949 *Cze*, 1952 *EGe, EGe*

I Diaconu 1942 *It*

C Diamandi-Telu 1938 *Ger*, 1939 *It*

ND Dima 1999 *A, US, I*, 2000 *H, Pt, Geo, F, It*, 2001 *Sp, H, Rus, Geo, W, E*, 2002 *Pt, Sp, Rus, W, S, S*, 2004 *CZR, Pt, Sp, Rus, Geo*, 2009 *ItA, ItA*, 2010 *Ger, Geo, Pt, Sp, Nm, ArJ, Ur, Ur*, 2011 *Geo, Sp, Nm, Ukr*

TI Dimofte 2004 *It, W, CZR*, 2005 *C, I*, 2006 *Geo, CZR, Pt, Ukr, Rus, Pt, Geo, Sp, S*, 2007 *ESp, ItA, Nm, It, S, Pt, NZ, Rus, Pt*, 2008 *Geo, Sp, Pt, Rus, CZR, Ur, Rus, ESp*, 2009 *Sp, Ger, Rus, Geo, Sp, Pt, Rus, CZR, Ur, Rus, ESp*, 2010 *Ger, Rus, Geo, Pt, Sp, Ukr, Ukr, Nm, ItA, Tun, Ur, Ur*, 2011 *Sp, Nm, ArJ, Ukr, S, Ar, Geo*

C Dinescu 1934 *It*, 1936 *F, It, Ger*, 1937 *It, H, F, Ger*, 1938 *F, Ger*, 1940 *It*, 1942 *It*

IC Dinis 2012 *Pt, Rus, Geo, Sp, Ukr, Ur*

C Dinu 1965 *WGe, F*, 1966 *Cze, It, F*, 1967 *It, Pt, Pol, WGe*, 1968 *F*, 1969 *Pol, WGe, Cze, F*, 1970 *It, F*, 1971 *Mor, F*, 1972 *Mor, Cze, WGe, F*, 1973 *Sp, Mor, Ar, Ar, WGe, F*, 1974 *Mor, Pol, Sp, Cze, F, Cze*, 1975 *It, Sp*, 1976 *H, It, Sp, Pol, F, Mor*, 1977 *Sp, It, F, Pol, It, F*, 1978 *Sp, Pol, F*, 1979 *Sp, USS, W, Pol*, 1980 *I, Pol, F*, 1981 *It, Sp, USS, NZ, F*, 1982 *F*, 1983 *Mor, WGe, It, USS*

F Dinu 2000 *Mor, H*

G Dinu 1990 *It, F, H, Sp, It, USS*, 1991 *It, S, F, C, Fj*, 1992 *Sp, It, USS, F, It*, 1993 *F*

G Dinu 1975 *Pol*, 1979 *It, Sp*, 1983 *Pol, USS*

F Dobre 2001 *E*, 2004 *W, CZR*, 2007 *Pt*, 2008 *CZR*, 2012 *Rus, Ukr, Ur*

I Dobre 1951 *EGe*, 1952 *EGe*, 1953 *It*, 1955 *Cze*, 1957 *Cze, Bel, F*, 1958 *Sp*

I Doja 1986 *Tun, Pt, F, I*, 1988 *F, W*, 1989 *Sp, Z, Sa, S*, 1990 *It*, 1991 *It, NZ, F, C*, 1992 *Sp*

V Doja 1997 *Bel*, 1998 *Pol, Geo, I*

A Domocos 1989 *Z, Sa, USS*

I Dorutiu 1957 *Cze, Bel, F*, 1958 *Sp, WGe*

A Draghici 1919 *US*

C Dragnea 1995 *F*, 1996 *Pol*, 1997 *WalA, F, Bel, Ar, F, It*, 1998 *H, Pol*, 1999 *F*, 2000 *F*

I Dragnea 1985 *Tun*

S Dragnea 2002 *S*

M Dragomir 1996 *Bel*, 1997 *Bel*, 1998 *H, Pol, Ukr, Geo, I*, 2001 *I, W, E*

M Dragomir 2001 *H, Geo*, 2002 *I*

V Dragomir 1964 *Cze, EGe*, 1966 *It*, 1967 *Pol, WGe*

G Dragomirescu 1919 *F*

G Dragomirescu-Rahtopol 1963 *Bul, EGe, Cze, F*, 1964 *Cze, EGe, WGe, F*, 1965 *WGe, F*, 1966 *Cze*, 1967 *It, Pt, Pol,*

ROMANIA

G Ignat 1986 *Pt, S, F, Tun,* 1988 *It, Sp, US, USS, USS, F, W,* 1989 *It, E, Sp, S,* 1990 *It, F, H, Sp,* 1991 *It, NZ,* 1992 *Sp, It, USS, F*
V Ilca 1987 *F*
I Ilie 1952 *EGe, EGe,* 1953 *It,* 1955 *Cze,* 1957 *F, Cze, Bel, F,* 1958 *It,* 1959 *EGe*
M Iliescu 1961 *EGe,* 1963 *Bul, EGe, Cze, F,* 1965 *WGe, F,* 1967 *WGe*
T Ioan 1937 *H, F, Ger*
V Ioan 1927 *Ger, Cze,* 1937 *It*
A Ion 2012 *Sp, Ukr*
F Ion 1991 *S,* 1992 *Sp,* 1993 *F*
G Ion 1984 *Sp,* 1986 *F, I,* 1988 *USS, F, W,* 1989 *It, E, Sp, Sa, USS, S,* 1990 *It, F, H, Sp, It, USS,* 1991 *It, NZ, F, S, F, C, Fj,* 1992 *Sp, It, USS, F, Ar,* 1993 *Pt, F, Sp, F,* 1994 *Sp, Rus, It, W, It,* 1997 *WalA*
P Ion 2003 *Ar,* 2004 *It,* 2005 *Rus, Ukr, J, US, S,* 2006 *Geo, CZR, Pt, Ukr, Rus, F, Geo, S,* 2007 *Geo, Sp, CZR, ESp, ItA, Pt, NZ, Rus,* 2008 *Geo, Sp, Rus, Ur, Rus, ESp,* 2009 *Sp, Ger, Rus, Geo, Pt, Ur, F, ItA, ItA, Fj,* 2010 *Ger, Rus, Geo, Pt,* 2011 *ArJ, Ukr, S, Ar, E, Geo,* 2012 *Geo, Sp*
V Ion 1980 *Mor, USS,* 1982 *Z, Z, F,* 1983 *Mor, It, USS, W, USS, F,* 1984 *S,* 1985 *It,* 1987 *It, USS, Z, F, S*
A Ionescu 1958 *EGe, It,* 1959 *EGe, Pol, Cze,* 1960 *Pol, EGe, Cze,* 1961 *Pol, Cze, EGe, F,* 1962 *EGe, It, F,* 1963 *F,* 1964 *Cze, EGe, F,* 1965 *WGe,* 1966 *Cze, It, F*
D Ionescu 1949 *Cze,* 1951 *EGe,* 1952 *EGe, EGe,* 1953 *It,* 1955 *Cze,* 1957 *F, Cze, F,* 1958 *Sp, It*
G Ionescu 1934 *It,* 1936 *F, It, Ger,* 1937 *It, F,* 1938 *F, Ger,* 1940 *It,* 1942 *It*
G Ionescu 1949 *Cze*
M Ionescu 1972 *Mor,* 1976 *USS, Bul, Pol, F,* 1977 *It, F, Pol, It, F,* 1978 *Cze, Sp, Pol, F,* 1979 *It, Sp, USS, W, Pol, F,* 1980 *I,* 1981 *NZ,* 1983 *USS*
R Ionescu 1968 *Cze, Cze,* 1971 *F*
S Ionescu 1936 *It, Ger,* 1937 *It*
V Ionescu 1993 *Tun, F,* 1994 *Ger, Rus,* 1998 *Ukr*
V Ionescu 1992 *It*
F Ionita 1974 *Sp,* 1978 *Pol, F*
P Iordachescu 1957 *F, Cze, Bel, F,* 1958 *Sp, WGe, EGe, It,* 1959 *EGe, Pol, Cze, EGe,* 1960 *Pol, EGe, Cze,* 1961 *EGe,* 1963 *F,* 1964 *Cze, EGe, WGe,* 1965 *WGe, F,* 1966 *Cze*
M Iordan 1980 *Mor*
P Iordanescu 1949 *Cze*
V Iorgulescu 1967 *WGe,* 1968 *Cze, F,* 1969 *Pol, WGe, Cze,* 1970 *It, F,* 1971 *F,* 1973 *Ar, Ar*
V Irimescu 1960 *F,* 1961 *Pol, Cze, EGe, F,* 1962 *Cze, EGe, Pol, It, F,* 1963 *F,* 1964 *F,* 1965 *WGe, F,* 1966 *Cze, It, F,* 1967 *It, Pt, Pol, WGe, F,* 1968 *Cze, EGe, F,* 1969 *Pol, WGe, Cze, F,* 1970 *It, F,* 1971 *F*
I Irimia 1936 *F, It, Ger,* 1937 *It, H, Ger,* 1938 *F, Ger,* 1939 *It,* 1940 *It*
G Irisescu 1993 *Sp*
A Iulian 2003 *CZR*
VM Ivan 2010 *Geo, Pt, Sp, Ukr, Ukr, Tun*
I Ivanciuc 1991 *Fj,* 1994 *E,* 1995 *J, C, SA, A*
I Jipescu 1927 *F*
C Kramer 1955 *Cze,* 1958 *Sp, WGe, It,* 1960 *Pol, EGe, Cze*
T Krantz 1940 *It,* 1942 *It*
C Kurtzbauer 1939 *It*
C Lapusneanu 1934 *It*
MA Lazar 2008 *CZR, Ur, Rus, ESp,* 2009 *Geo,* 2010 *Geo, Pt, Sp, Tun, Ur, Ur,* 2011 *Rus, Sp, Nm, ArJ, Ukr, S, Ar, Geo,* 2012 *Pt, Rus, Geo, Sp*
MV Lemnaru 2009 *Sp, Rus,* 2010 *Ur, Ur,* 2011 *Rus, Geo, Sp, ArJ, S, Ar, Geo,* 2012 *Pt, Rus, Geo, Sp, Ukr, Ur*
G Leonte 1984 *S, F,* 1985 *E, It, USS,* 1987 *It, USS, Z, S, USS, F,* 1988 *It, Sp, US, USS, USS, F, W,* 1989 *It, E, Sp, Z, Sa, USS, S,* 1990 *It, F, H, Sp, It,* 1991 *It, NZ, F, S, F, C,* 1992 *USS, F, It, Ar,* 1993 *Tun, F, Sp, F, I,* 1994 *Sp, Ger, Rus, It, W, It,* 1995 *F, S, J, J, C, SA, A*
M Leuciuc 1987 *F*
T Luca 1995 *Ar, F, It,* 1996 *F*
V Lucaci 1996 *Bel*
V Lucaci 2009 *Fj,* 2010 *Sp, Ukr,* 2011 *Pt, Sp,* 2012 *Pt, Rus, Geo, Ukr, Ur*
A Lungu 1980 *It, USS,* 1981 *It, Sp, USS, S, NZ, F,* 1982

WGe, It, USS, Z, Z, F, 1983 *Mor, WGe, It, USS, Pol, W, USS, F,* 1984 *It, S, F, Sp,* 1985 *E, It, Tun, USS, USS, It,* 1986 *Pt, S, F, Tun, Tun, Pt, F, I,* 1987 *It, USS, Z, F, S, USS, F,* 1988 *It, Sp, US, USS, USS, F, W,* 1989 *It, E, Sp, Z, Sa, USS, S,* 1990 *It, F, It,* 1991 *It, NZ, F, S, F, C, Fj,* 1992 *Sp, It, USS, F, Ar,* 1995 *A*
R Lungu 2002 *Pt, H, It, Sp, W, S,* 2003 *Pt*
A Lupu 2006 *S*
C Lupu 1998 *Pol, I,* 1999 *F,* 2000 *Mor, It,* 2001 *Pt, H, Rus, W,* 2002 *H, Rus*
S Luric 1951 *EGe,* 1952 *EGe, EGe,* 1953 *It,* 1955 *Cze*
V Luscal 1958 *Sp, WGe, EGe*
F Macaneata 1983 *USS*
M Macovei 2006 *Ukr, Rus,* 2007 *Geo, Rus, Pt,* 2008 *Geo, Rus, CZR, Ur, Rus, ESp,* 2009 *Rus, Geo, ItA,* 2010 *Ger, Geo, Sp, Ukr,* 2011 *Pt, Geo, Nm, Ukr, S, Ar, E, Geo,* 2012 *Pt, Rus, Geo, Sp, Ukr, Ur*
V Maftei 1995 *Ar, F, It,* 1996 *Bel,* 1997 *WalA, W, F,* 1998 *Ar,* 2001 *Pt, Sp, H, Geo, I,* 2002 *Pt, Sp, Rus, Geo, I, It, Sp, S,* 2003 *Pt, Geo, CZR, F, W, I, A, Ar, Nm,* 2004 *Pt, Sp, Rus, Geo, W, J, CZR,* 2005 *Rus, Geo, Ukr, C, I,* 2006 *CZR*
G Malancu 1976 *H, It, USS, Bul*
A Man 1988 *US*
A Man 1985 *USS, USS*
D Manoileanu 1949 *Cze*
DG Manole 2009 *Ger,* 2012 *Rus, Geo, Sp, Ur*
G Manole 1959 *Pol,* 1960 *Pol, EGe, Cze*
AV Manta 1996 *Bel,* 1997 *F,* 1998 *Ar, Geo, I,* 2000 *F,* 2001 *Pt, Sp, Rus, Geo,* 2002 *Sp, H, Rus, I, It, Sp,* 2003 *Pt, Rus,* 2005 *C, I,* 2006 *Geo, CZR, Pt, Geo,* 2007 *It, S, NZ,* 2009 *Pt, Ur, F, ItA,* 2010 *Rus, Pt, Ukr, Tun, Ur, Ur*
H Manu 1919 *US, F,* 1927 *F, Ger*
N Marascu 1919 *US, F,* 1924 *F, US,* 1927 *F, Cze*
A Marasescu 1927 *F, Ger,* 1936 *It, Ger*
E Marculescu 1936 *F, It, Ger,* 1937 *It,* 1939 *It,* 1940 *It*
A Marghescu 1980 *Pol,* 1981 *It,* 1983 *W, USS, F,* 1984 *S, F, Sp,* 1985 *E*
I Marica 1972 *WGe, F,* 1973 *Sp, Mor, WGe, F,* 1974 *Mor, Sp, Cze, EGe, F, Cze,* 1975 *It, Sp*
A Marin 1978 *Cze, Sp, Pol,* 1979 *F,* 1980 *Pol,* 1982 *USS,* 1983 *Pol,* 1984 *Sp,* 1985 *USS, It,* 1986 *Pt,* 1987 *USS, Z*
A Marin 2008 *CZR*
N Marin 1991 *Fj,* 1992 *Sp, It,* 1993 *F, I,* 1995 *Ar, F, It*
A Marinache 1949 *Cze,* 1951 *EGe,* 1952 *EGe, EGe,* 1955 *Cze,* 1957 *F, Bel, F,* 1960 *F,* 1961 *Pol, EGe, Cze, EGe, F,* 1962 *Cze, Pol*
V Marinescu 1967 *Pt, WGe,* 1968 *Cze,* 1969 *Cze, F*
F Marioara 1994 *E,* 1996 *Pol,* 1998 *Geo, I*
S Maris 2010 *Ukr, Ukr, Nm, ArJ, ItA, Tun*
V Mariscaru 2011 *Rus, Geo*
A Mateescu 1959 *EGe, Cze, EGe,* 1960 *Pol, EGe, Cze,* 1962 *EGe, Pol,* 1963 *Bul, EGe, Cze,* 1964 *Cze, EGe,* 1965 *WGe, F,* 1966 *F,* 1970 *It, F,* 1973 *Sp, WGe, F,* 1974 *Mor, Pol, Sp*
A Mateiescu 1934 *It,* 1936 *F, Ger*
R Mavrodin 1998 *Geo, I,* 1999 *F, A, US, I,* 2000 *H, Pt, Sp, Geo, F, It,* 2002 *Pt, Sp, H, I, It, Sp, W,* 2003 *I, A, Ar, Nm,* 2004 *Pt, Sp, Rus, Geo, W, J, CZR,* 2005 *Rus, J, US, S, Pt,* 2006 *Ukr, Rus, F, Geo, Sp, S,* 2007 *Geo, ESp, ItA, Nm, It, S, Pt, NZ,* 2009 *Ur*
F Maxim 2007 *Rus*
G Mazilu 1958 *Sp, WGe,* 1959 *EGe, Pol, Cze*
S Mehedinti 1951 *EGe,* 1953 *It*
C Melinte 1958 *EGe, It*
P Mergisescu 1960 *Pol, EGe, Cze*
C Mersoiu 2000 *Mor, Pt,* 2001 *I,* 2002 *S, S,* 2003 *Pt, Sp, Geo, CZR, F, W,* 2004 *CZR, Pt, Sp, Rus, It, W, J, CZR,* 2005 *Rus, Geo, Ukr, I,* 2006 *CZR, Pt, Geo, Sp,* 2007 *Geo, Sp, CZR, Rus, Pt,* 2008 *Geo, Sp, Pt, Rus, CZR, Ur, Rus, ESp,* 2009 *Geo*
A Miclescu 1971 *Mor*
S Mihailescu 1919 *F,* 1924 *F, US,* 1927 *F*
D Mihalache 1973 *Mor*
M Mihalache 2007 *Pt,* 2008 *Geo, Sp, Rus*
V Mihalascu 1967 *Pol, WGe*
A Mitocaru 1992 *Ar,* 1993 *Pt, Sp, F*
P Mitu 1996 *Bel, Pol,* 1997 *W, Bel, Ar, It,* 1998 *H, Pol, Ukr,*

Ar, Geo, I, 1999 F, S, A, US, I, 2000 H, Pt, Sp, Geo, It, 2001 Pt, Sp, H, Rus, 2002 Pt, Sp, H, Rus, Geo, Sp, W, S, S, 2003 Geo, 2005 I, 2006 Geo, 2009 Sp, Ger, Rus, Pt
M Miu 2003 Pt, Sp
V Mladin 1955 Cze, 1957 Bel, F, 1958 Sp, WGe, It, 1959 EGe, 1960 F
S Mocanu 1996 Bel, 1998 H, Pol, Ukr, 2000 Mor, Pt
T Moldoveanu 1937 F, Ger, 1938 F, Ger, 1939 It, 1940 It
O Morariu 1984 Sp, 1985 Tun
V Morariu 1952 EGe, EGe, 1953 It, 1955 Cze, 1957 F, Cze, Bel, F, 1959 EGe, 1960 F, 1961 Pol, Cze, EGe, F, 1962 Cze, EGe, Pol, It, F, 1963 F, 1964 WGe, F
C Moscu 1934 It, 1937 It
M Mot 1980 Mor, 1982 It, USS, Z, 1985 It, It, 1986 F, Tun, 1988 US, USS
M Motoc 1988 US, 1989 S
P Motrescu 1973 Mor, Ar, Ar, 1974 Mor, Pol, Sp, Cze, 1975 JAB, Pol, F, 1976 H, It, Sp, Bul, Pol, F, Mor, 1977 Sp, It, F, Pol, It, F, 1978 Cze, Sp, Pol, F, 1979 It, Sp, USS, W, Pol, 1980 It, Mor
B Munteanu 2000 It
IC Munteanu 1940 It, 1942 It
M Munteanu 1973 WGe, F, 1974 Mor, Sp, Cze, EGe, F, Cze, 1975 It, Sp, JAB, Pol, F, 1976 H, It, Sp, Pol, Mor, 1978 Pol, F, 1979 It, Sp, W, Pol, 1980 It, I, Pol, F, 1981 It, Sp, USS, S, NZ, F, 1982 F, 1983 Mor, WGe, It, USS, Pol, W, USS, F, 1984 It, S, F, 1985 USS, 1986 S, Tun, Pt, F, 1988 It, Sp
T Munteanu 2003 CZR, 2004 CZR
F Murariu 1976 H, USS, Bul, Pol, F, Mor, 1977 Sp, It, F, Pol, It, F, 1978 Cze, Sp, Pol, F, 1979 It, Sp, USS, W, Pol, F, 1980 It, I, Pol, F, 1981 USS, NZ, 1982 USS, Z, Z, F, 1983 Mor, WGe, It, USS, Pol, W, F, 1984 It, S, F, Sp, 1985 E, It, Tun, USS, USS, It, 1986 Pt, S, F, Tun, 1987 It, USS, Z, S, USS, F, 1988 It, Sp, US, USS, USS, F, W, 1989 It, E, Sp, Z
D Musat 1974 Sp, Cze, EGe, Cze, 1975 It, JAB, Pol, F, 1976 Mor, 1980 Mor
M Nache 1980 Mor
M Nagel 1958 EGe, 1960 Pol, EGe, Cze
R Nanu 1952 EGe, EGe, 1953 It, 1955 Cze, 1957 F, Bel, F
V Nastase 1985 Tun, USS, 1986 Tun, Pt, F, I
D Neaga 1988 It, Sp, USS, F, W, 1989 It, E, Sp, Z, Sa, USS, S, 1990 It, F, H, Sp, USS, 1991 It, F, S, F, C, Fj, 1993 Tun, F, Sp, I, 1994 Sp, Ger, Rus, It, W, It, E, 1995 F, S, J, J, C, 1996 Pt, F
I Neagu 1972 Mor, Cze
E Necula 1987 It, F
P Nedelcovici 1924 F
C Nedelcu 1964 Cze, EGe
M Nedelcu 1993 Pt, Tun, F, 1994 Sp, It, 1995 Ar, F, It
V Nedelcu 1996 Pol, 1997 WalA, F, W, Ar, F, 1998 H, Pol, Ukr, Ar, 2000 H, 2001 I, W, E, 2002 Rus, Geo
I Negreci 1994 E, 1995 F, J, C, SA, A, Ar, F, It
I Nemes 1924 F, US, 1927 Ger, Cze
N Nere 2006 CZR, 2007 CZR, Rus, Pt, 2008 Sp, Pt, Rus, 2009 Sp, Rus, Geo, Pt, 2011 Pt, Rus, Geo, Sp, Nm, E
I Niacsu 2012 Sp, Ukr
G Nica 1964 Cze, EGe, WGe, 1966 It, F, 1967 Pol, F, 1969 Pol, WGe, Cze, F, 1970 It, F, 1971 It, Mor, F, 1972 Mor, Cze, WGe, F, 1973 Sp, Mor, Ar, Ar, WGe, F, 1974 Mor, Pol, Sp, Cze, EGe, F, Cze, 1975 It, Sp, JAB, Pol, F, 1976 H, It, Sp, USS, Bul, Pol, F, Mor, 1977 Sp, It, F, Pol, It, F, 1978 Pol, F
N Nichitean 1990 It, Sp, It, USS, 1991 It, F, F, C, Fj, 1992 USS, It, Ar, 1993 Pt, Tun, F, Sp, 1994 Sp, Ger, Rus, It, W, It, 1995 F, S, J, J, C, 1997 WalA, F
G Nicola 1927 F, Ger, Cze
C Nicolae 2003 Pt, Rus, 2006 Sp, 2007 ItA, Nm, F, Rus, 2009 Geo, Pt, Ur, F, ItA, Fj, 2010 Pt, Ukr, Nm, ArJ, Tun, Ur, 2011 Pt, Nm, ArJ, Ukr, E
M Nicolae 2003 I, A
N Nicolau 1940 It
M Nicolescu 1969 Pol, WGe, Cze, F, 1971 It, Mor, F, 1972 Mor, Cze, WGe, F, 1973 Sp, Mor, Ar, Ar, WGe, F, 1974 Mor, Cze, EGe, F, Cze, 1975 It, Sp, Pol, F

P Niculescu 1958 It, 1959 EGe, Cze
V Niculescu 1938 F, Ger
F Nistor 1986 Tun
V Nistor 1959 EGe, Pol, EGe
M Oblomenco 1967 It, Pt, WGe, F
G Olarasu 2000 Mor, H
M Olarasu 2000 Mor
V Onutu 1967 It, Pt, Pol, WGe, F, 1968 Cze, 1969 F, 1971 It, Mor
N Oprea 2000 It, 2001 Pt, Sp, H, Rus, Geo, I, W, E
F Opris 1986 F, Tun, Tun, Pt, F, I, 1987 F
G Oprisor 2004 W, J, CZR, 2005 Rus, Ukr, J, US, S, Pt
T Oroian 1988 F, W, 1989 It, E, Sp, Z, USS, 1990 Sp, It, 1993 Pt, Tun, F, Sp, I, 1994 Sp, Ger, Rus, It, W, It, E, 1995 F, S, J, J, C
M Ortelecan 1972 Mor, Cze, WGe, F, 1974 Pol, 1976 It, Sp, USS, Bul, F, 1977 Sp, It, F, Pol, It, F, 1978 Cze, Sp, 1979 F, 1980 USS
A Palosanu 1952 EGe, EGe, 1955 Cze, 1957 F, Cze
E Pana 1937 F, Ger
M Paraschiv 1975 Sp, JAB, Pol, F, 1976 H, It, Sp, USS, Bul, F, Mor, 1977 Sp, It, Pol, F, 1978 Cze, Sp, Pol, F, 1979 It, Sp, W, 1980 It, I, F, 1981 It, USS, S, NZ, F, 1982 WGe, It, USS, Z, Z, F, 1983 Mor, WGe, It, USS, Pol, W, USS, F, 1984 It, S, F, 1985 E, It, Tun, USS, USS, It, 1986 Pt, S, Tun, 1987 It, USS, Z, F, S, USS, F
G Parcalabescu 1940 It, 1942 It, 1949 Cze, 1951 EGe, 1952 EGe, EGe, 1953 It, 1955 Cze, 1957 Cze, Bel, F, 1958 It, 1959 EGe, Pol, Cze, 1960 Pol, EGe, Cze
G Pasache 2001 E
V Pascu 1983 It, Pol, W, USS, F, 1984 It, 1985 USS, 1986 Pt, S, F, Tun, I, 1987 F, 1988 It
C Patrichi 1993 Pt, Tun
A Pavlovici 1972 Mor, Cze
A Penciu 1955 Cze, 1957 F, Cze, Bel, F, 1958 Sp, WGe, EGe, It, 1959 EGe, Pol, Cze, EGe, 1960 F, 1961 Pol, Cze, Cze, EGe, F, 1962 Cze, EGe, Pol, It, F, 1963 Bul, Cze, F, 1964 WGe, F, 1965 WGe, F, 1966 It, F, 1967 F
I Peter 1973 Sp, Mor
AA Petrache 1998 H, Pol, 1999 F, S, A, US, I, 2000 Mor, H, Pt, Sp, Geo, F, 2001 W, E, 2002 Pt, Sp, H, Rus, I, It, Sp, W, S, S, 2003 Pt, Sp, Rus, 2004 It, W, J, CZR
CC Petre 2001 E, 2002 Pt, Sp, H, Rus, Geo, I, It, Sp, W, S, S, 2003 Pt, Rus, Geo, CZR, F, W, I, A, Ar, Nm, 2004 CZR, Pt, Sp, Rus, Geo, It, W, J, CZR, 2005 Rus, Geo, Ukr, J, US, S, Pt, C, I, 2006 Geo, CZR, Pt, Ukr, Rus, F, Geo, Sp, S, 2007 Geo, Sp, CZR, ESp, ItA, Nm, It, S, Pt, NZ, 2008 Sp, Rus, 2009 Ger, Pt, Ur, F, ItA, ItA, 2010 Ger, Rus, Geo, Pt, Sp, Tun, Ur, Ur, 2011 Pt, Rus, Geo, Sp, Nm, ArJ, Ukr, S, Ar, E, Geo, 2012 Pt, Rus, Geo, Sp, Ur
SA Petrichei 2002 I, S, S, 2003 Sp, Rus, Geo, CZR, F, W, I, Ar, Nm, 2004 Pt, Sp, Rus, Geo, 2007 ESp, Nm, 2009 Ur, ItA, ItA, Fj
P Petrisor 1985 It, 1987 USS
H Peuciulescu 1927 F
M Picoiu 2001 Pt, H, 2002 Pt, Sp, H, Rus, I, It, Sp, W
A Pilotschi 1985 It, Tun, 1987 S
C Pinghert 1996 Bel
I Pintea 1974 Pol, 1976 Pol, F, Mor, 1977 Sp, It, F, Pol, It, F, 1979 It, Sp, USS, W, Pol, F, 1980 It, USS
D Piti 1987 USS, F, 1988 It, Sp, US, 1991 S
T Pllotschi 2011 Sp
Plumea 1927 Ger
S Podarescu 1979 Pol, F, 1980 USS, 1982 WGe, It, USS, F, 1983 Mor, WGe, USS, F, 1984 It, 1985 E, It
C Podea 2001 Geo, I, 2002 I, It, Sp, W, S, 2003 Pt, Sp, Rus, F, A
R Polizu 1919 US
A Pop 1970 It, 1971 It, Mor, 1972 Mor, Cze, F, 1973 WGe, F, 1974 Mor, Pol, Sp, EGe, F, Cze, 1975 It, Sp, JAB, Pol, F
D Popa 1993 Tun, F, Sp
I Popa 1934 It, 1936 F, It, Ger, 1937 H, F, 1938 F, Ger, 1939 It, 1940 It, 1942 It
M Popa 1962 EGe
N Popa 1952 EGe
V Poparlan 2007 Nm, Pt, 2008 Geo, Sp, Pt, Ur, Rus, ESp,

2009 *Sp, Ger, Rus, Geo*, 2011 *Pt, Rus, Geo, Sp, ArJ, Ukr, S, Ar, E, Geo*, 2012 *Ukr*
A Popean 1999 *S*, 2001 *Pt, H*
C Popescu 1986 *Tun, Pt, F*
CD Popescu 1997 *Bel*, 2003 *CZR, F, W, I, A, Ar, Nm*, 2004 *CZR, Pt, Sp, Rus, Geo, J, CZR*, 2005 *Rus, S, Pt, C*, 2006 *CZR, Ukr, Rus, F, Geo, Sp, S*, 2007 *Geo, Sp, CZR, ESp, ItA, Nm, It, Pt*, 2009 *Ur, F, ItA* 2010 *Geo, Pt, Sp, Ukr, Ukr, ArJ, ItA, Tun, Ur, Ur*, 2011 *Pt, Rus, ArJ*
I Popescu 1958 *EGe*
I Popescu 2001 *Pt, Sp, H, Rus, Geo*
C Popescu-Colibasi 1934 *It*
V Popisteanu 1996 *Pt, F, Pol*
F Popovici 1973 *Sp, Mor*
N Postolache 1972 *WGe, F*, 1973 *Sp, Mor, WGe, F*, 1974 *Mor, Pol, Sp, EGe, F, Cze*, 1975 *It, Sp, Pol, F*, 1976 *H, It*
C Preda 1961 *Pol, Cze*, 1962 *EGe, F*, 1963 *Bul, EGe, Cze, F*, 1964 *Cze, EGe, WGe, F*
NF Racean 1988 *USS, USS, F, W*, 1989 *It, E, Z, Sa, USS*, 1990 *H, Sp, It, USS*, 1991 *NZ, F, F, C, Fj*, 1992 *Sp, It, USS, F, It, Ar*, 1993 *Pt, Tun, F, Sp*, 1994 *Ger, Rus, It, W*, 1995 *F, S, J, J, C, SA, A*
A Radoi 2008 *CZR*, 2009 *ItA, Fj*, 2010 *Sp, Ukr, Ukr, Nm, ArJ, ItA, Tun*, 2011 *Geo, Sp, ArJ, Ukr*, 2012 *Rus, Sp, Ukr, Ur*
M Radoi 1995 *F*, 1996 *Pt, Pol*, 1997 *WalA, F, W, Bel, Ar, F, It*, 1998 *H, Pol, Ukr*
P Radoi 1980 *Mor*
T Radu 1991 *NZ*
C Raducanu 1985 *It*, 1987 *It, USS, Z, F, S*, 1989 *It, E, Sp, Z*
A Radulescu 1980 *USS, Pol*, 1981 *It, Sp, USS, S, F*, 1982 *WGe, It, USS, Z, Z*, 1983 *Pol, W, USS, F*, 1984 *It, S, F, Sp*, 1985 *E, USS*, 1988 *It, Sp, US, USS, USS, F, W*, 1989 *It, E, Sa, USS*, 1990 *It, F, H, Sp, It, USS*
T Radulescu 1958 *Sp, WGe*, 1959 *EGe, Pol, Cze, EGe*, 1963 *Bul, EGe, Cze*, 1964 *F*, 1965 *WGe, F*, 1966 *Cze*
D Rascanu 1972 *WGe, F*
G Rascanu 1966 *It, F*, 1967 *It, Pt, Pol, WGe, F*, 1968 *Cze, Cze, F*, 1969 *Pol, WGe, Cze, F*, 1970 *It, F*, 1971 *It, Mor, F*, 1972 *Mor, Cze, WGe, F*, 1974 *Sp*
CA Ratiu 2003 *CZR*, 2005 *J, USS, S, Pt, C, I*, 2006 *CZR, Pt, Ukr, Rus, F, Geo, Sp, S*, 2007 *Sp, CZR, ESp, It, S, Pt, NZ, Rus, Pt*, 2009 *Geo, Pt*, 2010 *Sp*, 2011 *Nm, ArJ, Ukr, E*, 2012 *Ur*
I Ratiu 1992 *It*
S Rentea 2000 *Mor*
I Roman 1976 *Bul*
M Rosca 2012 *Ukr*
C Rosu 1993 *I*
I Rotaru 1995 *J, J, C, Ar, It*, 1996 *Pt, F, Pol*, 1997 *W, Bel, Ar, F*
L Rotaru 1999 *F, A, I*
N Rus 2007 *Rus*
VS Rus 2007 *Rus, Pt*, 2008 *Geo, Pt, Rus*, 2009 *F, ItA, Fj*, 2012 *Ur*
M Rusu 1959 *EGe*, 1960 *F*, 1961 *Pol, Cze*, 1962 *Cze, EGe, Pol, It, F*, 1963 *Bul, EGe, Cze, F*, 1964 *WGe, F*, 1965 *WGe, F*, 1966 *Cze, It, F*, 1967 *It, Pt, Pol*
V Rusu 1960 *Pol, EGe, Cze*, 1961 *EGe, F*, 1962 *Cze, EGe, Pol, It, F*, 1964 *Cze, EGe, WGe, F*, 1965 *WGe*, 1966 *It, F*, 1967 *WGe*, 1968 *Cze*
I Sadoveanu 1939 *It*, 1942 *It*
AA Salageanu 1995 *Ar, F, It*, 1996 *Pt, F, Pol*, 1997 *W, Bel, F*
V Samuil 2000 *It*, 2001 *Pt, E*, 2002 *Pt, Sp, Geo*
C Sasu 1989 *Z*, 1991 *It, NZ, F, S, F, C, Fj*, 1993 *I*
C Sauan 1999 *S, A, US, I*, 2000 *It*, 2002 *Geo, I, It, Sp*, 2003 *Pt, Rus, Geo, CZR, F, W, I, A, Ar, Nm*, 2004 *CZR, Pt, Sp, Rus, Geo, It, W, J, CZR*, 2005 *Rus, Geo, Ukr, J, US, S, Pt*, 2006 *Rus*, 2007 *Geo*
G Sava 1989 *Z, S*, 1990 *H, Sp, It, USS*, 1991 *It, F, S, F, C*, 1992 *Sp*
I Sava 1959 *EGe, Pol, Cze, EGe*, 1960 *F*, 1961 *Pol, EGe, Cze, EGe, F*, 1962 *Cze, Pol, It, F*
C Scarlat 1976 *H, Sp*, 1977 *F*, 1978 *Cze, Sp*, 1979 *It, Sp, USS, W, Pol, F*, 1980 *It, USS*, 1982 *USS*
R Schmettau 1919 *US, F*

V Sebe 1960 *Pol, EGe, Cze*
I Seceleanu 1992 *It, USS, F, It, Ar*, 1993 *Pt, Tun, F, Sp, F*
S Seceleanu 1986 *Pt, F, I*, 1990 *It*
E Septar 1996 *Bel, Pol*, 1997 *WalA, W*, 1998 *Pol, Ukr, I*, 1999 *F, S, A, US, I*, 2000 *It*
B Serban 1989 *Sa, USS, S*, 1990 *It*, 1992 *It, USS*
C Serban 1964 *Cze, EGe, WGe*, 1967 *Pol*, 1968 *Cze, F*, 1969 *Pol, WGe, Cze, F*, 1970 *It, F*, 1971 *It, Mor, F*, 1972 *F*, 1973 *WGe, F*, 1974 *Mor*
M Serbu 1967 *It*
E Sfetescu 1924 *F, US*, 1927 *Cze*
E Sfetescu 1934 *It*, 1936 *F, Ger*, 1937 *It*
G Sfetescu 1927 *F, Ger*
M Sfetescu 1924 *F, US*, 1927 *Ger, Cze*
N Sfetescu 1927 *F, Ger, Cze*
G Simion 1998 *H*
G Simion 1919 *US*
I Simion 1976 *H, It, Sp*, 1979 *Pol, F*, 1980 *F*
ML Sirbe 2008 *CZR*, 2010 *Ukr, Ukr, Nm, ArJ, Tun*, 2011 *Pt, Nm*, 2012 *Ur*
L Sirbu 1996 *Pt*, 2000 *Mor, H, Pt, Geo*, 2001 *H, Rus, Geo, I, W, E*, 2002 *Pt, Sp, H, Rus, I, It, S, S*, 2003 *Pt, Sp, CZR, F, W, I, A, Ar, Nm*, 2004 *Pt, Sp, Rus, Geo, It, W, CZR*, 2005 *Rus, Geo, Ukr, J, US, S, Pt, C*, 2006 *Geo, Pt, Ukr, Rus, F, Geo, Sp*, 2007 *Geo, ItA, It, S, Pt, NZ*, 2009 *Ur, F, ItA, ItA, Fj*, 2010 *Ger, Rus, Geo, Pt, Sp, Nm, ArJ, ItA, Ur, Ur*, 2011 *Rus, Nm, Ukr, S, E*
M Slobozeanu 1936 *F*, 1937 *H, F, Ger*, 1938 *F, Ger*
OS Slusariuc 1993 *Tun*, 1995 *J, J, C*, 1996 *Pt, F*, 1997 *Bel, Ar, F*, 1998 *H, Ar, Geo, I*, 1999 *F, S, A*
S Soare 2001 *I, W*, 2002 *Geo*
S Soare 1924 *F, US*
M Socaciu 2000 *It*, 2001 *I, W, E*, 2002 *It, W, S, S*, 2003 *Pt, Sp, Rus, Geo, CZR, F, W, I, A, Nm*, 2004 *CZR, Pt, Sp, Rus, Geo, It, W, J, CZR*, 2005 *Rus, Geo, Ukr, J, US, Pt, C, I*, 2006 *CZR*
S Socol 2001 *Sp, H, Rus, Geo*, 2002 *Pt, It, Sp, W*, 2003 *Sp, Rus, Geo, F, W, I, A, Ar, Nm*, 2004 *CZR, Pt, Sp, Rus, Geo, 2005 Rus, Geo, Ukr, C, I*, 2006 *Geo, CZR, Pt, Ukr, Rus, F, Geo, Sp, S*, 2007 *Geo, Sp, CZR, It, S, Pt, NZ*, 2009 *Ur, F, ItA, Fj*, 2010 *Ger, Rus, Geo, Pt, Sp, Ukr, Ukr, Nm, ArJ, ItA, Ur, Ur*, 2011 *Rus, Geo*
N Soculescu 1949 *Cze*, 1951 *EGe*, 1952 *EGe, EGe*, 1953 *It*, 1955 *Cze*
N Soculescu 1927 *Ger*
V Soculescu 1927 *Cze*
GL Solomie 1992 *Sp, F, It, Ar*, 1993 *Pt, Tun, F, Sp, F, I*, 1994 *Sp, Ger, W, It, E*, 1995 *F, S, J, J, C, SA, A, Ar, F, It*, 1996 *Pt, F, Pol*, 1997 *WalA, F, W, Bel, Ar, F, It*, 1998 *H, Pol, Ukr, Ar, Geo, I*, 1999 *S, A, US, I*, 2000 *Sp, F, It*, 2001 *Sp, H, Rus*
C Stan 1990 *H, USS*, 1991 *It, F, S, F, C, Fj*, 1992 *Sp, It, It, Ar*, 1996 *Pt, Bel, F, Pol*, 1997 *WalA, F, W, Bel*, 1998 *Ar, Geo*, 1999 *F, S, A, US, I*
A Stanca 1996 *Pt, Pol*
R Stanca 1997 *F*, 2003 *Sp, Rus*, 2009 *Geo, Pt*
A Stanciu 1958 *EGe, It*
G Stanciu 1958 *EGe, It*
C Stanescu 1957 *Bel*, 1958 *WGe*, 1959 *EGe*, 1960 *F*, 1961 *Pol, EGe, Cze*, 1962 *Cze, It, F*, 1963 *Bul, EGe, Cze, F*, 1964 *WGe, F*, 1966 *Cze, It*
C Stefan 1951 *EGe*, 1952 *EGe*
E Stoian 1927 *Cze*
E Stoica 1973 *Ar, Ar*, 1974 *Cze*, 1975 *Sp, Pol, F*, 1976 *Sp, USS, Bul, F, Mor*, 1977 *Sp, It, F, Pol, It, F*, 1978 *Cze, Sp, Pol, F*, 1979 *It, Sp, USS, W, Pol, F*, 1980 *It, USS, I, Pol, F*, 1981 *It, Sp, USS, S, NZ, F*, 1982 *WGe, It, USS, Z, Z, F*
G Stoica 1963 *Bul, Cze*, 1964 *WGe*, 1966 *It, F*, 1967 *Pt, F*, 1968 *Cze, Cze, F*, 1969 *Pol*
I Stroe 1986 *Pt*
E Suciu 1976 *Bul, Pol*, 1977 *It, F, It*, 1979 *USS, Pol, F*, 1981 *Sp*
M Suciu 1968 *F*, 1969 *Pol, WGe, Cze*, 1970 *It, F*, 1971 *It, Mor, F*, 1972 *Mor, F*
O Sugar 1983 *It*, 1989 *Z, Sa, USS, S*, 1991 *NZ, F*
K Suiogan 1996 *Bel*
F Surugiu 2008 *Ur, Rus, ESp*, 2010 *Ukr, Ukr, Nm, ArJ, ItA,*

Russia's Vladimir Ostroushko makes a break against Portugal during the IRB Hong Kong Sevens.

RUSSIA

RUSSIA'S 2012 TEST RECORD

OPPONENTS	DATE	VENUE	RESULT
Portugal	11 Feb	A	Won 33–32
Romania	25 Feb	H	Lost 0–25
Ukraine	10 Mar	H	Won 38–19
Georgia	17 Mar	A	Lost 0–46
Spain	19 May	H	Won 41–37
Uruguay	12 Jun	N	Won 19–33

RUSSIAN EVOLUTION

By Lúcás Ó'Ceallacháin

Russian Sevens players celebrate winning the Bowl competition in the Glasgow Sevens.

THE COUNTRIES

Since their historic debut at Rugby World Cup 2011 in New Zealand, Russian rugby has entered a new phase of accelerated development. The Russian team impressed in New Zealand with their attacking style which showed their ability to score tries even against top opposition.

Ultimately, they will have been disappointed not to win their Rugby World Cup 'final' against USA, but the season afterwards has been all about evolution as the coaching team has changed considerably. Following the tournament, head coach Nikolai Nerush returned to the VVA club in Russia and backs coach Henry Paul moved over to spearhead the national Sevens programme. Former forwards coach Kingsley Jones has stepped in as head coach with a new coaching team around him as they look to rebuild a strong national team for a tilt at qualification for England 2015. With all of the movement sideways, in and out, one direction is clear – Russian rugby is moving forward.

Rugby World Cup 2011 served as a springboard for several of the national team to move on to clubs overseas. Back row cum second row

Andrey Ostrikov moved to Sale Sharks, where he was reunited with former Russia director of rugby Steve Diamond. Wing Vasily Artemyev secured a move to Northampton Saints and has impressed in his first season, the 'Red Bullet' scoring three tries on his debut against Saracens in the Anglo Welsh Cup. Russia's best performer at Rugby World Cup 2011, number 8 Victor Gresev, was snapped up by Wasps on a short-term contract, as was hooker Vladislav Korshunov. Eye-catching performances from wings Vladimir Ostroushko and Denis Simplekevich sparked interest from several European clubs, but they remain committed to Russian clubs. There was even a training stint for fly half Yury Kushnarev with the Melbourne Rebels.

With so much change at national team level it was always going to be difficult to maintain the form that had guided Russia to Rugby World Cup 2011 and they struggled with the transition this season. Playing in the European Nations Cup in winter while the domestic season is in shutdown is a perennial problem for the Russian Bears, but this year was tougher than ever. The Rugby World Cup was also a severe disruption for all the teams in the European Nations Cup, dissecting the competition which runs over two seasons.

Russia finished in fourth spot, cementing their place in the top level of the European Nations Cup 2014 which will be a relief, but they will of course be looking to push on in the season to come. Picking up where they left off in a competition almost 12 months previously was never going to be easy, and in February the Bears narrowly defeated Los Lobos of Portugal 33–32 before suffering a heavy 25–0 defeat to Romania in southern Russia. After the heady heights and adoring fans in New Zealand, this was a case of being brought back down to earth with a bump.

A scrappy performance against Ukraine at home saw them do just enough to win 38–19, but it was the hammering that Georgia dished out at the Vake Stadium that will hang over Russia until next season's competition. A 46–0 drubbing is never welcome by the proud Bears, but especially from Georgia. Both teams have now taken part in Rugby World Cups, but Georgia are going from strength to strength with their big-match experience showing. The question of who can stop them at this level remains unanswered and Russia will have to do a lot better than their final fixture, a shaky 41–37 victory over Spain in Moscow in May, if they are going to knock them off their perch.

The IRB Nations Cup in Romania a few weeks later provided a welcome opportunity for Jones and his team to exorcise some performance demons. The Bears can be happy with their victory over Uruguay at the Stadionul National Arcul de Triumf in Bucharest, where they also lost to the Argentina Jaguars (33–9) and Emerging Italy (33–17). It's

416

clear that Russia need more of these games in order to be competitive, but they are developing an attacking style which is exciting to watch. The tournament was also used to blood some new young players, including hooker Stanislav Selskiy and scrum half Alexey Scherban.

The future of the national team looks bright as Russia's age grade sides continued to gain match experience at the major international competitions on a European and global level. In November 2011 at the European Championships, the Under 19 team secured their spot in the IRB Junior World Rugby Trophy 2012 with excellent performances against Spain (15–8) and the Netherlands (45–8) to reach the final against Georgia. Russia lost the final 20–12, but no doubt this group of players will have plenty of opportunities to renew their rivalry in the years to come.

Russia would finish eighth at the IRB Junior World Rugby Trophy despite some strong performances throughout the tournament in Salt Lake City, USA. Defeats by Chile, Tonga and USA meant Russia were left to fight it out with Zimbabwe for seventh spot, with the Young Sables coming out on top 22–10. The pathway to the national team is a proven one, with Simplikevich earning their spurs on this stage before stepping up to the Bears. Names to watch out for in future are German Godlyuk, already capped at Test level, and Danil Chegodaev.

Another key element to the Russian player pathway has been the Sevens circuit, and Russia is falling in love with that version of the game ahead of hosting Rugby World Cup Sevens 2013 in Moscow next June. The men's team impressed as always in the HSBC Sevens World Series, claiming their first piece of silverware with victory in the Bowl final at the Glasgow Sevens. On the European front, several of the Fifteens players continued to hop between the long and short versions of the Game, securing a third-place finish for the men in the FIRA-AER Grand Prix Sevens event in Moscow. The women were not to be outdone and also finished third after a convincing win over France. The Sevens programmes are reaching a peak at just the right time with Rugby World Cup Sevens just around the corner and Rio 2016 a few years further away.

The preparations for Rugby World Cup 2011 caused considerable disruption in the domestic season with key breaks built into the season to accommodate the international players. This spirit of cooperation by the clubs was put to one side when they faced each other on the field of play and Enisei STM of Krasnoyarsk were ruthless in their pursuit of the Russian Super League title – their first since 2007 – including a 104–0 rout of Spartak from Moscow, a 17-match unbeaten run, the best defence (conceding only four tries all season) and scoring a total of 98 tries in 18 matches.

With the bulk of the national side being made up of players from VVA and the Moscow region, the final was a tense shootout between the two Krasnoyarsk clubs, Enisei STM and Krasniy Yar. In the end it was a battle between two New Zealand fly halves with Enisei's Ryan Bambry gaining the upper hand over John Dodd of Krasniy Yar over the two legs of the final, which Enisei won 19–15 and 21–15. There was some consolation for Yar as they took the Russian Cup and the Russian Sevens titles. Dodd beat Bambry to the top scorer honour with 185 to 164 points, but Enisei STM's Kazakhstan international back row Anton Rudoy topped the try-scoring charts with 11 tries.

RUSSIA INTERNATIONAL STATISTICS

MATCH RECORDS UP TO 10 OCTOBER 2012

WINNING MARGIN

Date	Opponent	Result	Winning Margin
13/05/2000	Denmark	104–7	97
16/04/2000	Germany	89–6	83
11/06/2005	Ukraine	72–0	72
25/05/1995	Norway	66–0	66
18/09/1999	Ukraine	71–5	66

MOST POINTS IN A MATCH
BY THE TEAM

Date	Opponent	Result	Points
13/05/2000	Denmark	104–7	104
16/04/2000	Germany	89–6	89
17/02/2002	Netherlands	73–10	73
15/05/1999	Poland	72–13	72
11/06/2005	Ukraine	72–0	72

BY A PLAYER

Date	Player	Opponent	Points
16/04/2000	Konstantin Rachkov	Germany	29
15/05/1999	Konstantin Rachkov	Poland	27
16/02/2003	Konstantin Rachkov	Spain	27
02/06/2002	Werner Pieterse	Netherlands	25
19/07/2003	Konstantin Rachkov	USA A	25

MOST CONVERSIONS IN A MATCH
BY THE TEAM

Date	Opponent	Result	Cons
18/09/1999	Ukraine	71–5	8
15/05/1999	Poland	72–13	8
13/05/2000	Denmark	104–7	8

BY A PLAYER

Date	Player	Opponent	Cons
15/05/1999	Konstantin Rachkov	Poland	8
13/05/2000	Konstantin Rachkov	Denmark	8
16/04/2000	Konstantin Rachkov	Germany	7

MOST PENALTIES IN A MATCH
BY THE TEAM

Date	Opponent	Result	Pens
16/02/2003	Spain	52–19	6
19/07/2003	USA A	30–21	6
08/03/2008	Spain	42–16	6

BY A PLAYER

Date	Player	Opponent	Pens
16/02/2003	Konstantin Rachkov	Spain	6
19/07/2003	Konstantin Rachkov	USA A	6
20/10/1996	Sergey Boldakov	Georgia	5
25/05/1993	Viktor Yakovlev	Georgia	5
19/05/2012	Yury Kushnarev	Spain	5

MOST TRIES IN A MATCH
BY THE TEAM

Date	Opponent	Result	Tries
13/05/2000	Denmark	104–7	17
16/04/2000	Germany	89–6	15
02/10/1997	Poland	70–26	12

BY A PLAYER

Date	Player	Opponent	Tries
18/09/1999	Sergey Sergeev	Ukraine	4
13/05/2000	Andrey Kuzin	Denmark	4
21/04/2007	Igor Galinovskiy	Czech Republic	4

MOST DROP GOALS IN A MATCH
BY THE TEAM

Date	Opponent	Result	DGs
08/03/2003	Georgia	17–23	2

BY A PLAYER

Date	Player	Opponent	DGs
08/03/2003	Konstantin Rachkov	Georgia	2

MOST CAPPED PLAYERS

Name	Caps
Andrey Kuzin	78
Alexander Khrokin	75
Vyacheslav Grachev	73
Vladislav Korshunov	59

LEADING TRY SCORERS

Name	Tries
Vyacheslav Grachev	31
Andrey Kuzin	25
Konstantin Rachkov	16
Alexander Gvozdovsky	15
Alexander Zakarlyuk	14

LEADING CONVERSION SCORERS

Name	Cons
Konstantin Rachkov	54
Yury Kushnarev	45
Vladimir Simonov	25
Victor Motorin	24

LEADING PENALTY SCORERS

Name	Pens
Yury Kushnarev	76
Konstantin Rachkov	47
Vladimir Simonov	21

LEADING DROP GOAL SCORERS

Name	DGs
Konstantin Rachkov	6
Werner Pieterse	2

LEADING POINT SCORERS

Name	Points
Yury Kushnarev	348
Konstantin Rachkov	347
Vladimir Simonov	178
Vyacheslav Grachev	155
Andrey Kuzin	125

THE COUNTRIES

UP TO 10 OCTOBER 2012

D Akulov 2003 *Pt, J, CZR, USAA,* 2004 *Sp, Geo, R, J, Geo,* 2005 *R, CZR, Pt, CZR*
A Andreev 2008 *ItA*
D Antonov 2011 *ItA, US, US, It, I,* 2012 *Pt, R, Ukr, Geo, Sp, Ur, ArJ*
V Artemyev 2009 *Pt, R, Geo, Ger, C,* 2010 *Nm, Pt, Sp, R, Ger, Geo, US, E, Ur, ArJ, ArJ, J,* 2011 *Sp, Pt, R, Ukr, Geo, C, ItA, US, US, It, I, A,* 2012 *Sp*
V Ashurka 1993 *Geo,* 1994 *Nm, Ger, R, H*
O Azarenko 1999 *Ukr, Pol,* 2002 *Geo, Sp, Sp,* 2003 *CZR,* 2006 *Ukr, It*
M Babaev 2006 *Pt,* 2007 *Sp, CZR, Pt, R,* 2008 *Pt, CZR, ItA, R, Ur, Sp,* 2009 *Pt, R, Geo, Ger, S, ItA, C,* 2010 *Nm, Pt, Sp, R, Ger, Geo, US, E, Ur,* 2011 *Sp, Pt, R, Geo, ItA, US, I, A,* 2012 *Pt, R, Ukr, Geo, ?, Ur, ArJ*
V Balashov 1996 *CZR,* 1997 *Tun, Mor, Ukr, Cro,* 1998 *Sp, It, De*
P Baranovsky 1992 *Bel, F,* 1993 *Mor,* 1994 *F, Swe,* 1995 *Pol, Nor, De,* 1997 *Ukr, Pol*
S Bazhenov 2008 *ItA, Ur, Sp,* 2009 *Ur, C*
S Belousov 2006 *Ukr, Ukr, It,* 2007 *Geo,* 2008 *CZR, Ur*
R Bikbov 1993 *Mor, Geo, Pol,* 1994 *Nm, Sp, Ger, R, F, H,* 1996 *Geo, CZR,* 1997 *Tun, Mor, Ukr, Pol, Cro,* 1998 *Sp, It, De, Geo,* 1999 *Ukr, Pol, CZR, Ukr,* 2000 *De,* 2001 *H, Pt,* 2002 *H, Geo, CZR,* 2003 *J*
V Bogdanov 1992 *Ger*
S Boldanov 1992 *Bel, F,* 1996 *Mor, Geo*
V Boltenkov 2010 *ArJ,* 2011 *C,* 2012 *Pt, R, Geo*
V Bondarev 1993 *It,* 1994 *Nm, R*
S Borisov 1992 *Bel, F, Ger,* 1993 *Mor, Pol, It,* 1994 *Nm, Sp, Ger, F, H,* 1995 *Tun, Bel, Pol, F,* 1996 *Sp, Mor,* 2001 *Sp, H, R*
V Botvinnikov 2008 *Pt, Sp, Geo, CZR, ItA, R, Ur, Sp,* 2009 *Pt, S, ItA, Ur, C,* 2010 *Ger, Geo, E, Ur,* 2011 *US, It, A,* 2012 *Pt, R, Ukr, ?*
C Breytenbach 2002 *Geo, R*
S Budnikov 1996 *CZR,* 1997 *Tun, Mor, Cro,* 2000 *Ger, De,* 2002 *Sp, H, Geo, R, Pt, CZR, H*
P Butenko 2012 *Ukr, Geo, ?, ArJ*
A Bychkov 1992 *Bel, F,* 1996 *Geo,* 1997 *Mor*
A Bykanov 2003 *J,* 2005 *R, CZR, Ukr, CZR,* 2006 *Geo,* 2011 *C, ItA, I*
A Byrnes 2011 *US, It, I, A,* 2012 *?, Ur*
A Chebotaryov 1992 *Bel, F, Ger,* 1994 *F*
V Chernykh 1997 *Cro,* 1998 *It*
A Chernyshev 2008 *Pt, Sp, Geo, CZR, ItA, R, Ur,* 2011 *ItA, US*
A Chupin 1999 *CZR, Ukr,* 2001 *R, Pt,* 2002 *H, CZR, H,* 2003 *CZR*
K Djincharadze 1995 *Tun, Bel, Pol,* 1997 *Pol*
D Dyatlov 1996 *CZR,* 1997 *Tun, Mor, Cro,* 1998 *Sp, It, De, Geo,* 1999 *Ukr, Pol, CZR, Ukr,* 2000 *De,* 2001 *R, Pt,* 2002 *Sp, H,* 2003 *CZR, USAA,* 2004 *Sp, R, J, US*
I Dymchenko 1994 *Swe,* 1995 *Nor, De,* 1996 *Sp,* 1997 *Pol,* 2002 *H, Geo, R, CZR, J, I, Geo,* 2003 *Sp, Geo, R, Pt,* 2004 *J, US*
A Emelyanov 1992 *Bel, F*
A Epimakhov 1998 *Sp,* 1999 *Ukr, Pol, CZR,* 2000 *De*
D Eskin 1998 *De*
A Evdokimov 1993 *Mor,* 1994 *Swe,* 1995 *Nor, De,* 1999 *CZR, Ukr,* 2000 *Ger, De,* 2001 *Sp*
A Fatakhov 2005 *CZR,* 2006 *Pt, Ukr, R, ArA, ItA, Ukr, Ukr, It, Pt,* 2007 *Sp, Geo, CZR,* 2008 *ItA, Ur,* 2009 *R, Geo, Ger, S, ItA, Ur, C,* 2010 *Nm, Sp, R, Ger, Geo, US, E, Ur, ArJ,*

J, 2011 *Sp, Pt, R, Ukr, Geo, US, It, I, A,* 2012 *Pt, Ukr, Geo, Sp, ?, Ur, ArJ*
V Fedchenko 2002 *Sp, H, Geo, R, Pt, I, Geo, Sp, Sp,* 2003 *Sp, Geo, R, J, USAA,* 2004 *Sp, Geo, R, Pt, Geo,* 2006 *Pt, ArA, ItA, Pt,* 2007 *CZR, R,* 2008 *Pt, Sp, R, Geo, CZR*
V Fedorov 1994 *Swe,* 1995 *De*
R Fedotov 2004 *J, US*
I Frantsuzov 1992 *Bel,* 1993 *Geo*
I Galinovskiy 2006 *Ukr, Ukr,* 2007 *Sp, Geo, CZR, Pt,* 2008 *Pt, Sp, R, Geo,* 2009 *ItA, Ur,* 2010 *ArJ,* 2011 *Sp, Pt, R, Ukr, Geo, C*
A Garbuzov 2005 *R, CZR, Pt, Ukr, CZR,* 2006 *Geo, Pt, Ukr, R, Pt, ArA, ItA,* 2007 *Sp, Geo, Pt, R,* 2008 *Pt, Sp, R, Geo, CZR,* 2009 *Pt, Geo, Ger, C,* 2010 *Nm,* 2011 *Sp, Pt, R, Ukr, Geo, C, ItA, US, US, It, I, A,* 2012 *Pt, R, Geo, Sp*
N Gasanov 2008 *CZR,* 2012 *Ukr, Geo*
D Gerasimov 2008 *Sp,* 2009 *Pt, R, S, Ur,* 2010 *US, E,* 2012 *Pt, R, Geo, ?, ArJ*
G Godlyuk 2012 *Ukr*
V Grachev 1993 *It,* 1994 *Nm, Sp, Ger, F, Swe, H,* 1995 *Tun, Bel, Pol, F,* 1996 *Sp, Mor, Geo, CZR,* 1997 *Tun, Mor, Ukr, Pol, Cro,* 1998 *Sp, It, Geo,* 1999 *Ukr, Pol, CZR, Ukr,* 2000 *Ger, De,* 2001 *Sp, H, Geo,* 2002 *Sp, H, Geo, R, Pt, J, I, Geo, Sp,* 2003 *Sp, Geo, R, Pt, J, USAA,* 2004 *Sp, Geo, R, Pt, Geo,* 2005 *R, CZR, Pt,* 2006 *Geo, Pt, R, Pt, ArA, ItA, It,* 2007 *Geo,* 2008 *Geo,* 2011 *Ukr, Geo, C, ItA, US, US, It, A*
V Gresev 2006 *It,* 2007 *Geo, CZR, Pt,* 2008 *Pt, Geo, CZR, Sp,* 2009 *Pt, R, Geo, Ger, S, ItA, Ur, C,* 2010 *Nm, Pt, Sp, R, Geo, US, E, Ur, ArJ, ArJ, J,* 2011 *Sp, Pt, R, Geo, C, ItA, US, US, It, I, A,* 2012 *Pt, Geo, Sp, ?, Ur, ArJ*
A Gvozdovsky 2005 *R, CZR, CZR,* 2006 *Geo, Pt, Ukr, R, Pt, ArA,* 2007 *Sp, Geo, CZR, Pt, R,* 2008 *Pt, R, Geo, CZR, Sp,* 2009 *Pt, R, Geo, Ger, S, ItA, Ur, C,* 2010 *Nm, Pt, Sp, R*
J Hendriks 2002 *Geo, Pt, CZR, J, H, I, Geo, Sp, Sp*
V Ignatev 2006 *R, Pt, ArA, ItA, Ukr, Ukr,* 2007 *CZR, Pt,* 2008 *R, Ur*
A Igretsov 2006 *Pt, Ukr, Ukr,* 2007 *CZR, Pt,* 2012 *R, Sp*
V Ilarionov 2001 *H, Pt,* 2002 *Sp, H, Pt, CZR,* 2003 *Geo, R, Pt*
P Ilvovsky 1998 *Sp, It, Geo,* 1999 *Ukr, Pol, CZR, Ukr*
S Kashcheev 1993 *Mor,* 1995 *Tun, De,* 1996 *Sp, Mor, Geo, CZR,* 1997 *Tun, Mor, Cro,* 1998 *It, De,* 1999 *Ukr, Pol, CZR, Ukr, Geo,* 2000 *Ger, De,* 2001 *Geo, R, Pt*
A Kazantsev 2003 *USAA,* 2004 *R, Pt, J, US, Geo,* 2005 *R, CZR, Pt, Ukr*
V Kazydub 1992 *Bel*
I Khokhlov 1994 *Nm, R,* 1995 *F,* 1996 *Sp, Mor, Geo, CZR,* 1997 *Ukr, Cro,* 1998 *It, De, Geo,* 1999 *Ukr, Pol, CZR, Ukr*
A Khrokin 1994 *Swe,* 1995 *Nor, De,* 2000 *Ger,* 2002 *Sp, CZR, J, I, Geo, Sp, Sp,* 2003 *Sp, Geo, R, Pt, J, CZR, USAA,* 2004 *Sp, Geo, R, Pt, J, US, Geo,* 2005 *R, Pt, Ukr, CZR,* 2006 *Geo, Pt, Ukr, R, ArA, ItA, Ukr, It, Pt,* 2007 *Sp, Geo, CZR, Pt,* 2008 *Pt, Sp, R, Geo, ItA, R, Ur, Sp,* 2009 *Pt, R, Geo, Ger, C,* 2010 *Nm, Pt, Sp, R, Ger, Geo, US, E, Ur, ArJ, ArJ, J,* 2011 *Sp, Pt, Ukr, Geo, It, I*
A Khvorostyanoy 2008 *Pt, CZR*
E Kiselev 1994 *Nm, Sp, H*
M Kiselev 2007 *CZR*
N Kiselev 1993 *Geo, Pol,* 1994 *Nm, Sp, Ger,* 1995 *F,* 1996 *Mor, Geo, CZR,* 1997 *Tun,* 1998 *Sp, It, De*
S Klimenko 1992 *F,* 1994 *Ger, R, H,* 2001 *Sp, H, Geo, R*

I **Klyuchnikov** 2003 *Geo, J, USAA,* 2004 *Sp, R, Pt, J, Geo,* 2005 *Pt, Ukr, CZR,* 2006 *Geo, Ukr, ArA, Ukr, Ukr, It,* 2007 *Sp, Geo, R,* 2008 *Pt, Sp, R, Geo, Sp,* 2009 *Pt, R, Geo, Ger, S, ItA, Ur, C,* 2010 *Nm, Pt, Sp, R, Ger, Geo, E, Ur, ArJ, ArJ, J,* 2011 *Sp, Pt, R, Ukr, Geo, C, ItA, US, US, It,* 2012 *Sp*
O **Kobzev** 2005 *R, CZR, Ukr,* 2006 *Geo, Ukr, Ukr,* 2007 *CZR, Pt,* 2008 *Sp, CZR, ItA, R, Ur, Sp,* 2010 *ArJ, J*
V **Kobzev** 2008 *R, Ur*
R **Kochetov** 1992 *Ger*
A **Komarov** 1994 *Swe,* 1995 *Nor, De*
K **Kopeshkin** 2012 *Ukr*
A **Korobeynikov** 1996 *Sp,* 2002 *Sp, H, Geo, R, Pt, CZR, J, H, I, Geo, Sp, Sp,* 2003 *Sp, Geo, R, Pt, J, CZR, USAA,* 2004 *Sp, Geo, R, Pt, J, US, Geo,* 2005 *Pt, CZR,* 2006 *Ukr, R, Pt, ArA, ItA, Pt,* 2007 *Pt,* 2008 *Pt, Sp, CZR,* 2009 *C,* 2010 *Nm, Sp, R, Ger, Geo, US, E, Ur, ArJ, ArJ, J*
V **Korshunov** 2002 *H, Sp,* 2003 *R, Pt, J,* 2004 *Sp, Geo, R, J, US, Geo,* 2005 *Pt, Ukr, CZR,* 2006 *Geo, Pt, Ukr, R, Pt, ArA, It, Pt,* 2007 *Pt, R,* 2008 *Pt, Sp, R, Geo, ItA, R, Sp,* 2009 *Pt, R, Geo, Ger, C,* 2010 *Nm, Pt, Sp, R, Ger, Geo, US, E, Ur, ArJ, ArJ, J,* 2011 *Sp, R, Ukr, Geo, C, ItA, US, US, It, A,* 2012 *Sp*
Y **Koshelev** 2002 *H*
E **Kosolapov** 1992 *Bel, F,* 2000 *De*
I **Kotov** 2012 *?, Ur, ArJ*
Y **Krasnobaev** 1993 *It,* 1997 *Ukr, Pol,* 1998 *Sp, It, De, Geo,* 2000 *De,* 2001 *Sp, R, Pt*
S **Krechun** 1997 *Ukr, Pol, Cro,* 1998 *Sp,* 1999 *Ukr, Pol, CZR, Ukr*
A **Krinitsa** 1994 *Swe*
S **Kryksa** 1993 *Geo, Pol, It,* 1994 *Nm, Sp, Ger, R, F, H,* 1995 *Tun, Bel, Pol, F,* 1996 *Sp, Mor, Geo, CZR*
K **Kulemin** 2006 *Pt, R, Pt,* 2007 *Sp, Pt,* 2008 *R, Geo, Sp,* 2009 *Pt, R, Geo,* 2010 *Pt, Sp, R,* 2012 *R, Ukr, Geo, Sp*
I **Kuperman** 1993 *Geo, Pol*
I **Kurashov** 2006 *Ukr,* 2007 *CZR*
K **Kushnarev** 2004 *J, Geo,* 2005 *Pt, Ukr, CZR,* 2006 *Geo, Ukr, Pt, ArA, ItA, Ukr,* 2007 *Sp, Geo, Pt, R,* 2008 *Pt, Sp, R, ItA, R, Ur,* 2009 *Ger, S, Ur,* 2010 *Ger, Geo, US, E, Ur, ArJ, J,* 2011 *Pt, R*
V **Kushnarev** 1992 *Bel, F*
Y **Kushnarev** 2005 *CZR,* 2006 *Geo, Pt, ArA, ItA, Ukr, Ukr, It,* 2007 *Sp, Geo, CZR, Pt, R,* 2008 *Pt, Sp, R, Geo, CZR, Sp,* 2009 *Pt, R, Geo, Ger, S, ItA, Ur, C,* 2010 *Nm, Pt, Sp, R, Ger, Geo, US, E, Ur,* 2011 *Sp, Pt, R, Ukr, Geo, C, ItA, US, US, It, A,* 2012 *Pt, R, Ukr, Geo, Sp*
A **Kuzin** 1997 *Tun, Mor, Cro,* 1998 *Sp, It, De, Geo,* 1999 *Ukr, Pol, CZR, Ukr,* 2000 *Ger, De,* 2001 *Sp, H, Geo, R,* 2002 *H, Geo, R, Pt, J, I, Geo, Sp,* 2003 *Sp, Geo, R, USAA,* 2004 *Sp, Geo, Pt,* 2005 *Pt, Ukr, CZR,* 2006 *Geo, Pt, Ukr, R, ArA, ItA, Ukr, It, Pt,* 2007 *Sp, Geo, CZR,* 2009 *Pt, R, Geo, Ger, S, ItA, C,* 2010 *Nm, Sp, R, Ger, Geo, US, E, Ur, ArJ, ArJ, J,* 2011 *Sp, Pt, R, Ukr, It, I, A*
S **Kuzmenko** 2002 *Sp, Sp,* 2005 *Ukr,* 2008 *R, Ur*
L **Kuzmin** 1998 *Geo*
P **Kvernadze** 2012 *R, Ukr, Geo, ?, Ur, ArJ*
D **Loskutov** 2004 *R, US, Geo,* 2005 *R*
A **Lubkov** 2003 *CZR,* 2005 *R, CZR*
A **Lugin** 2004 *US,* 2005 *R, CZR,* 2008 *ItA, R, Ur, Sp,* 2009 *S, ItA, Ur*
S **Lysko** 1994 *Swe*
K **Maglakelidze** 2009 *S, ItA, Ur,* 2010 *Nm, Pt, Sp, R, E, ArJ,* 2011 *Sp, Pt, R*
A **Makovetskiy** 2010 *Nm, Ger, Geo, US, E, Ur, ArJ, J,* 2011 *Ukr, C, US, US, It, A,* 2012 *Pt, R, Ukr, Geo, Sp, ?, Ur, ArJ*
A **Malinin** 1993 *Pol,* 1994 *Ger, H*
D **Malyakin** 2005 *R*
R **Mamin** 1998 *De, Geo,* 1999 *Pol*
D **Mananikov** 1994 *F,* 1995 *Pol*
V **Marchenko** 1992 *Bel, F,* 1997 *Tun, Mor, Ukr, Pol,* 1999 *Ukr,* 2001 *Sp, H, R, Pt,* 2006 *Ukr, Pt, Ukr, Ukr, It, Pt,* 2007 *Sp, Geo, Pt, R,* 2008 *Pt, Sp, ItA, R, Ur,* 2009 *R, Ger*
E **Matveev** 2007 *CZR, R,* 2008 *Geo, CZR, Sp,* 2009 *Pt, R, Geo, Ger, S, ItA, C,* 2010 *Nm, Pt, Sp, R, Ger, Geo, US, E, Ur, ArJ, ArJ, J,* 2011 *Sp, R, Ukr, Geo, I, A,* 2012 *Pt, R*

N **Medkov** 2007 *CZR,* 2010 *Ger, E, Ur, ArJ, J,* 2012 *R*
G **Minadze** 2009 *ItA,* 2010 *Ger, US*
I **Mironov** 1992 *F*
E **Mochnev** 1993 *Geo, Pol*
V **Motorin** 1999 *Ukr, Pol, CZR, Ukr,* 2001 *Sp, H, Geo,* 2002 *Sp, CZR, J, I, Geo,* 2003 *Sp, J, CZR, USAA,* 2004 *Sp, R, Geo,* 2006 *Pt, ArA, ItA, Ukr, Ukr, It, Pt,* 2007 *Sp, CZR, Pt, R,* 2008 *Pt, Sp, R, Geo, CZR, ItA, R, Sp,* 2009 *Pt, Ger, S*
I **Naumenko** 2002 *H,* 2003 *CZR,* 2007 *Sp, Geo, CZR*
V **Negodin** 1993 *Geo, Pol, It,* 1994 *Nm, Sp, R,* 1995 *F,* 1996 *Geo, CZR,* 1997 *Pol, Cro,* 1998 *Sp, It, De, Geo,* 1999 *Ukr, Pol, CZR,* 2001 *Geo*
Y **Nikolaev** 1993 *Pol, It,* 1994 *Nm, Sp, R,* 1997 *Tun, Ukr, Pol,* 1998 *It*
I **Nikolaychuk** 1993 *Mor, Geo, Pol, It,* 1994 *Nm, Sp, Ger, R, F, H,* 1995 *Tun, Bel, Pol, F,* 1996 *Sp, Mor, Geo, CZR,* 1997 *Tun, Mor, Pol,* 1998 *Sp, It, De, Geo,* 1999 *Ukr, Pol, CZR, Ukr,* 2000 *Ger, De,* 2001 *Sp, H, Geo, R, Pt,* 2002 *H, Geo, R, J, CZR, USAA,* 2005 *CZR*
I **Novikov** 1994 *Nm, Sp, R, H*
P **Novikov** 2004 *Geo,* 2005 *Pt, Ukr, CZR,* 2006 *Geo, Pt, Ukr, R, Pt, ArA*
S **Novoselov** 1997 *Pol,* 2000 *Ger,* 2001 *H,* 2003 *CZR,* 2004 *R, J,* 2006 *Ukr, Pt, ArA, ItA,* 2007 *Sp, Pt, R*
A **Ostrikov** 2008 *Pt, Sp, R, Geo,* 2009 *Pt, R, Geo, Ger,* 2010 *Pt, Sp, R,* 2011 *Sp, Pt, R, Geo*
V **Ostroushko** 2006 *It, Pt,* 2007 *Geo,* 2009 *ItA, Ur,* 2010 *Ger, ArJ, ArJ, J,* 2011 *Sp, Pt, R, Ukr, Geo, C, US, US, It, I, A,* 2012 *Pt, R, Sp*
A **Otrokov** 2012 *Ukr, Geo, ?, Ur, ArJ*
A **Panasenko** 2004 *Geo,* 2005 *Pt, CZR,* 2006 *Geo, Ukr, R,* 2007 *Sp, Geo, Pt, R,* 2008 *Geo, CZR, Sp,* 2009 *R, S, ItA, Ur, C,* 2010 *Nm, Ger, Geo, US, ArJ, J,* 2011 *Ukr, C, ItA, US*
S **Patlasov** 1997 *Tun, Mor, Ukr, Cro,* 1998 *Sp, It, Geo,* 1999 *Ukr*
S **Perepyolkin** 1993 *It*
A **Petrovetz** 1996 *CZR,* 1997 *Pol*
W **Pieterse** 2002 *Pt, CZR, J, H, I, Sp, Sp*
A **Podshibiakin** 1995 *Nor, De*
D **Polovykh** 2006 *Ukr, Ukr*
S **Popov** 2003 *CZR,* 2004 *Sp, J,* 2005 *Ukr, CZR,* 2006 *Ukr, ArA, ItA, Ukr, It,* 2007 *Geo,* 2010 *US, J,* 2011 *Ukr, Geo, C, US, US, I, A,* 2012 *Sp, ?, Ur, ArJ*
V **Postnikov** 1995 *Nor, De*
I **Povesma** 2007 *Pt, R*
I **Prishchepenko** 2003 *USAA,* 2004 *Sp, Geo, R,* 2005 *CZR,* 2006 *Geo, Pt, Ukr, R, Pt, ArA, ItA, Ukr, Ukr, It,* 2007 *Sp, Geo, CZR, R,* 2008 *Pt, Sp, R,* 2009 *R, Geo, Ger,* 2010 *ArJ, ArJ, J,* 2011 *R, Ukr, Geo, C, ItA, US, US, It, I, A*
E **Pronenko** 2009 *Pt, S, ItA, Ur, C,* 2010 *Nm, Pt, Sp, R, Ger, Geo, US, E, Ur, ArJ, ArJ, J,* 2011 *Sp, Pt, R,* 2012 *?, Ur, ArJ*
A **Protasov** 2002 *H*
K **Rachkov** 1997 *Pol, Cro,* 1998 *Sp, It, De, Geo,* 1999 *Ukr, Pol, CZR, Ukr,* 2000 *Ger, De,* 2001 *H, Geo, R, Pt,* 2002 *Sp, H, Geo, R, Pt, I, Geo,* 2003 *Sp, Geo, R, J, CZR, USAA,* 2004 *Sp, Geo,* 2006 *Pt, R, It, Pt,* 2011 *Sp, R, Ukr, Geo, US, It, I, A*
A **Rechnev** 2001 *H, R, Pt,* 2003 *Pt,* 2004 *Geo,* 2005 *CZR,* 2006 *Geo, Ukr, Ukr, Ukr*
Y **Rechnev** 2003 *J,* 2004 *Sp, Geo, R, Pt, J, US, Geo,* 2006 *Pt, ArA, ItA,* 2007 *Sp*
R **Romak** 2001 *Pt,* 2002 *Sp, H, Geo, R, Pt, CZR, J, H, I, Geo, Sp, Sp,* 2003 *Sp, Geo, USAA,* 2004 *Sp, Geo, R, Pt, J, US, Geo,* 2005 *R, CZR, Pt, Ukr, CZR,* 2006 *Geo, Pt, Ukr, R, ArA, ItA, Ukr, Pt*
S **Romanov** 1992 *Bel, F, Ger,* 1994 *Ger, F, H,* 1995 *Tun, Pol, F*
O **Rudenok** 1995 *Tun, Bel, Pol,* 1996 *Sp*
A **Ryabov** 2011 *ItA,* 2012 *Pt, R, Ukr, Geo, Sp, ?, ArJ*
R **Sagdeev** 2002 *Pt, CZR, J, H, Sp,* 2004 *Geo,* 2005 *Pt, Ukr*
A **Sarychev** 1999 *Ukr, Pol, CZR,* 2000 *De,* 2001 *Sp, H, R,* 2002 *Sp, Sp,* 2003 *Geo, R, Pt, J, CZR, USAA,* 2004 *Sp, Geo, R, Pt, J,* 2005 *R, CZR, Pt,* 2006 *Pt, Ukr, Ukr, Pt*
S **Selskiy** 2012 *?*
A **Sergeev** 1992 *Ger,* 1993 *Mor,* 1995 *Tun, Bel, F,* 1996 *Mor,*

RUSSIA

Alafoti Faosiliva in action during the Tokyo Sevens match between Samoa and Scotland.

Getty Images

SAMOA

SAMOA'S 2012 TEST RECORD

OPPONENTS	DATE	VENUE	RESULT
Tonga	5 Jun	N	Won 20–18
Fiji	10 Jun	N	Won 29–26
Japan	17 Jun	A	Won 27–26
Scotland	23 Jun	H	Lost 16–17

SUCCESS COMES QUICKLY FOR NEW-LOOK SAMOA

THE COUNTRIES

Getty Images

Sakaria Taulafo powers through a tackle by Tonga's Viliami Faingaa during their Pacific Nations Cup match in Nagoya.

Samoa followed up a good performance at Rugby World Cup 2011 in New Zealand by winning the IRB Pacific Nations Cup title for the second time in three years, achieving success despite changes off the field with a new coaching team at the helm.

The performance of Manu Samoa over the past two years has seen significant improvement with the average losing margins against Tier One opposition shrinking from 40 points to less than a converted try. This included an historic win over the Wallabies in Australia which raised hopes of achieving a first RWC quarter-final since 1995.

Samoa ultimately performed well at RWC 2011 and narrowly lost their Pool D encounters with South Africa (13–5) and Wales (17–10), meaning their quarter-final dreams were over.

The Samoa Rugby Union subsequently faced criticism off the field by senior players and the public, which resulted in an independent review of the campaign and auditing of all fundraising generated for the Union for participation at the Rugby World Cup. While the reports highlighted that there was no impropriety, it did identify a number of issues and provided a road map for the future.

One of the highly praised aspects of the RWC 2011 campaign was the Manu Samoa coaching team. Unfortunately, as a result of the good performances in New Zealand, a number of the coaching staff were recruited by teams around the world. Assistant coach Brian 'Aussie' McLean was recruited by the All Blacks and Tom Coventry went to Super Rugby side the Chiefs, trainer David Edgar to Japanese club Suntory and kicking coach Scott Wisemantel to Japan.

This loss of coaching talent and knowledge put the Union in a difficult position which was further compounded by an ageing national squad and a number of senior players retiring. The future was looking a little bleak.

In April, the Union went into the market for a new head coach and Stephen Betham, the Samoa Sevens coach who had led the country to the HSBC Sevens World Series title in 2009/10, was duly appointed. With Betham's appointment confirmed, the next step was the recruitment of Darryl Suasua and Greg Smith as assistant coaches and Sami Leota as team manager. Coventry and Mike Casey return for the Tests in November, with Marcus Agnew as performance analyst.

With such a large turnover of coaching staff it would have been understandable had 2012 been primarily a building year, but the Union set two major goals of winning the Pacific Nations Cup and defeating Scotland in Apia.

Only a month into his new role, Betham selected his first squad for the Pacific Nations Cup in Japan, one which featured only 12 players from the Manu Samoa squad for RWC 2011. The other 18 had either played in the IRB Pacific Rugby Cup or national Sevens programmes, while 13 had graduated from Samoa's Licenced Training Centre (LTC).

Betham admitted his new-look side were on a "real learning curve" after they capitalised on two Tongan errors to win their first PNC 2012 match 20–18 at the Mizuho Park Rugby Ground in Nagoya on 5 June, and the margin was only slightly bigger five days later in Tokyo when new captain David Lemi crossed twice in a tight 29–26 win over Fiji.

Only Japan could therefore prevent Samoa from repeating their PNC success of 2010, but few expected what was to follow at the Prince Chichibu Memorial Rugby Ground in Tokyo on 17 June. Japan raced into a 16–0 lead only for Samoa to score 27 unanswered points to turn the match on its head. Samoa, though, still had to withstand a tremendous fight-back by their hosts to edge a thrilling encounter 27–26.

There was no chance for Betham and his players to celebrate, though, as a week later they welcomed Scotland for their first Test on Samoan soil.

SAMOA

Samoa dominated proceedings for 77 minutes at Apia Park, but a late try by debutant Rob Harley enabled Scotland to snatch a 17–16 victory.

Interestingly, the Samoa team that day showed nine changes from the experienced line-up that had beaten Australia just under a year earlier. Only one of their outside backs played in both matches, while three of their backs against Scotland boasted just 15 caps between them. So, although the Test was heartbreakingly lost, it confirmed that Samoa is developing a squad with strength in depth.

With Betham elevated to Manu Samoa coach, his assistant Tausa Faamaoni Lalomilo took charge for the final two rounds of the HSBC Sevens World Series in May. Samoa finished fourth overall in the 2011/12 Series with one Cup success in Las Vegas. They were also runners up in Tokyo and London to cap off a good season. A number of senior players have since retired and the Samoa Sevens programme is now in a development phase with young, emerging players getting an opportunity after time in the LTC.

With the luxury of having already qualified directly for Rugby World Cup Sevens 2013 in Moscow by virtue of reaching the semi-finals at Dubai 2009, Samoa were able to send a young squad to the Oceania Sevens Championship in Australia – the regional men's qualifier – in late August to gain valuable experience. Lalomilo returned home "really proud of my boys" after they narrowly lost 12–7 to Australia in the final.

As part of their preparations for the IRB Junior World Championship 2012, the Samoan Under 20s squad travelled to Australia for a warm-up match with their hosts, one of three warm-up matches in total. Samoa led 19–12 at half-time, but their set piece was found wanting and Australia ran out comfortable 62–19 winners.

Set piece frailty was evident at JWC 2012 in South Africa with Samoa hampered by a number of injuries to tight five players in the build up. Samoa failed to score a try in the pool stages, losing heavily to New Zealand and Wales, but then turned the tables on Fiji on day four with a four-try burst to ensure their place at the 2013 tournament in France. They ended with a heavy loss to Scotland to finish 10th in the standings.

Off the field, the High Performance Unit (HPU) conducted a national planning forum in September, resulting in the LTC programme being restructured for 2013. As a result, the programme will service 120 players annually, including the provision of 24 scholarships for women. The integration of a women's programme, headed by former Samoan international Stan Toomalatai – a veteran of RWC 1991 and RWC 1995, in the HPU and LTC programme stems directly from the Samoa Rugby Union's intention to have both men's and women's teams qualify for the 2016 Olympic Games in Rio de Janeiro.

SAMOA INTERNATIONAL STATISTICS

MATCH RECORDS UP TO 10 OCTOBER 2012

SAMOA

WINNING MARGIN

Date	Opponent	Result	Winning Margin
11/07/2009	PNG	115–7	108
08/04/1990	Korea	74–7	67
18/07/2009	PNG	73–12	61
10/06/2000	Japan	68–9	59
29/06/1997	Tonga	62–13	49

MOST POINTS IN A MATCH
BY THE TEAM

Date	Opponent	Result	Points
11/07/2009	PNG	115–7	115
08/04/1990	Korea	74–7	74
18/07/2009	PNG	73–12	73
10/06/2000	Japan	68–9	68
29/06/1997	Tonga	62–13	62

BY A PLAYER

Date	Player	Opponent	Points
11/07/2009	Gavin Williams	PNG	30
29/05/2004	Roger Warren	Tonga	24
03/10/1999	Silao Leaega	Japan	23
08/04/1990	Andy Aiolupo	Korea	23
08/07/2000	Toa Samania	Italy	23

MOST TRIES IN A MATCH
BY THE TEAM

Date	Opponent	Result	Tries
11/07/2009	PNG	115–7	17
08/04/1990	Korea	74–7	13
18/07/2009	PNG	73–12	11

BY A PLAYER

Date	Player	Opponent	Tries
28/05/1991	Tupo Fa'amasino	Tonga	4
10/06/2000	Elvis Seveali'i	Japan	4
02/07/2005	Alesana Tuilagi	Tonga	4
11/07/2009	Esera Lauina	PNG	4

MOST CONVERSIONS IN A MATCH
BY THE TEAM

Date	Opponent	Result	Cons
11/07/2009	PNG	115–7	15
18/07/2009	PNG	73–12	9
08/04/1990	Korea	74–7	8

BY A PLAYER

Date	Player	Opponent	Cons
11/07/2009	Gavin Williams	PNG	10
18/07/2009	Titi Jnr Esau	PNG	9
08/04/1990	Andy Aiolupo	Korea	8

MOST PENALTIES IN A MATCH
BY THE TEAM

Date	Opponent	Result	Pens
29/05/2004	Tonga	24–14	8

BY A PLAYER

Date	Player	Opponent	Pens
29/05/2004	Roger Warren	Tonga	8

MOST DROP GOALS IN A MATCH
BY THE TEAM

1 on 11 Occasions

BY A PLAYER

1 on 11 Occasions

MOST CAPPED PLAYERS

Name	Caps
Brian Lima	65
To'o Vaega	60
Semo Sititi	59
Opeta Palepoi	42
Mahonri Schwalger	40

LEADING PENALTY SCORERS

Name	Pens
Darren Kellett	35
Earl Va'a	31
Silao Leaega	31
Roger Warren	29
Andy Aiolupo	24

LEADING TRY SCORERS

Name	Tries
Brian Lima	31
Semo Sititi	17
Afato So'oialo	15
To'o Vaega	15
Alesana Tuilagi	15
Mahonri Schwalger	40

LEADING DROP GOAL SCORERS

Name	DGs
Darren Kellet	2
Roger Warren	2
Steve Bachop	2
Tusi Pisi	2

LEADING POINT SCORERS

Name	Points
Earl Va'a	184
Andy Aiolupo	172
Silao Leaega	160
Darren Kellett	155
Brian Lima	150

LEADING CONVERSION SCORERS

Name	Cons
Andy Aiolupo	35
Earl Va'a	33
Silao Leaega	26
Tanner Vili	21
Gavin Williams	18

UP TO 10 OCTOBER 2012

A'ati 1932 *Tg*
V Afatia 2012 *Tg*
JT Afoa 2010 *Tg, J*
Agnew 1924 *Fj, Fj*
S Ah Fook 1947 *Tg*
F Ah Long 1955 *Fj*
Ah Mu 1932 *Tg*
T Aialupo 1986 *W*
F Aima'asu 1981 *Fj, 1982 Fj, Fj, Fj, Tg, 1988 Tg, Fj*
AA Aiolupo 1983 *Tg, 1984 Fj, Tg, 1985 Fj, Tg, Tg, 1986 Fj, Tg,*
1987 *Fj, Tg, 1988 Tg, Fj, I, W, 1989 Fj, WGe, Bel, R, 1990*
Kor, Tg, J, Tg, Fj, 1991 W, A, Ar, S, 1992 Tg, Fj, 1993 Tg,
Fj, NZ, 1994 Tg, W, A
A Aiono 2009 *PNG, 2010 J, I, E, S, 2011 Tg, 2012 Tg, S*
Aitofele 1924 *Fj, Fj*
P Alalatoa 1986 *W*
V Alalatoa 1988 *I, W, 1989 Fj, 1991 Tg, W, A, Ar, S, 1992 Tg,*
Fj
P Alauni 2009 *PNG*
R Ale 1997 *Tg, Fj, 1999 J, Ar, W, S*
A Alelupo 1994 *Fj*
T Aleni 1982 *Tg, 1983 Tg, 1985 Tg, 1986 W, Fj, Tg, 1987 Fj,*
S Alesana 1979 *Tg, Fj, 1980 Tg, 1981 Fj, 1982 Fj, Tg, 1983*
Tg, Fj, 1984 Fj, Tg, 1985 Fj, Tg
T Allen 1924 *Fj, Fj*
K Anufe 2009 *Tg, 2012 Tg, Fj, J*
L Aoelua 2008 *NZ*
T Aoese 1981 *Fj, Fj, 1982 Fj, Fj, Fj, Tg, 1983 Tg*
J Apelu 1985 *Tg*
F Asi 1963 *Fj, Fj, Tg*
F Asi 1975 *Tg*
L Asi 2010 *J*
SP Asi 1999 *S, 2000 Fj, J, Tg, C, It, US, W, S, 2001 Tg, Fj, NZ,*
Fj, Tg, Fj
Atiga 1924 *Fj*
S Ati'ifale 1979 *Tg, 1980 Tg, 1981 Fj, Fj*
J Atoa 1975 *Tg, 1981 Fj*
F Autagavaia 2012 *Tg, Fj, J, S*
WO Avei 2011 *J, Tg, SA, 2012 Tg, Fj, J, S*
SJ Bachop 1991 *Tg, Fj, W, A, Ar, S, 1998 Tg, Fj, 1999 J, C,*
F, NZ, US, Fj, J, Ar, W, S
C Betham 1955 *Fj*
ML Birtwistle 1991 *Fj, W, A, Ar, S, 1993 Fj, NZ, 1994 Tg, W,*
Fj, A, 1996 I
W Brame 2009 *J, Fj*
FE Bunce 1991 *W, A, Ar, S*
CH Capper 1924 *Fj*
J Cavanagh 1955 *Fj, Fj, Fj*
J Clarke 1997 *Tg, 1998 A, 1999 US, Fj, J*
A Collins 2005 *S, Ar*
A Cortz 2007 *Fj*
G Cowley 2005 *S, Ar, 2006 J, Tg*
T Cowley 2000 *J, C, It*
D Crichton 2012 *Tg, Fj, J, S*
L Crichton 2006 *Fj, Tg, 2007 Fj, SA, J, Tg, SA, Tg, E, US*
O Crichton 1988 *Tg*
O Crichton 1955 *Fj, Fj, Fj, 1957 Tg, Tg*
T Curtis 2000 *Fj, J, Tg, C, It, US*
H Ekeroma 1972 *Tg*
G Elisara 2003 *I, Nm*
S Enari 1975 *Tg*
S Epati 1972 *Tg*
T Esau 2009 *PNG, PNG, F, It*
K Ese 1947 *Tg*
S Esera 1981 *Fj*
L Eves 1957 *Tg, Tg*
H Fa'afili 2008 *Fj, Tg, J, 2009 J, Tg, Fj, PNG, W, F, It*
T Fa'afou 2007 *Fj*
P Fa'alogo 1963 *Fj*
Fa'amaile 1947 *Tg*
T Fa'amasino 1988 *W, 1989 Bel, R, 1990 Kor, Tg, J, Tg, Fj,*
1991 *Tg, Fj, A, 1995 It, Ar, E, SA, Fj, Tg, 1996 NZ, Tg, Fj*
JS Fa'amatuainu 2005 *S, Ar, 2008 Fj, J, 2009 J, Tg, Fj, PNG,*

W, F, It, 2011 *Tg*
S Fa'aofo 1990 *Tg*
Fa'asalele 1957 *Tg, Tg*
F Fa'asau 1963 *Fj, Tg*
M Faasavalu 2002 *SA, 2003 I, Nm, Ur, Geo, E, SA, 2011 J, Fj,*
A, Nm, W, Fj, SA, 2012 Fj, J, S
V Faasua 1987 *Fj, 1988 Tg, Fj, W*
S Fa'asua 2000 *W*
F Fa'asuaga 1947 *Tg*
L Fa'atau 2000 *Fj, Tg, C, US, 2001 I, It, 2002 Fj, Tg, Fj, Tg,*
SA, 2003 I, Ur, E, SA, 2004 Tg, S, Fj, 2005 A, Tg, Tg, Fj, S,
E, Ar, 2006 J, Fj, Tg, 2007 Fj, SA, J, Tg, SA, US
F Fagasoaia 2010 *J*
K Faiva'ai 1998 *Tg, Fj, A, 1999 J, C, Tg, NZ, US, Fj*
L Falaniko 2010 *Tg, Fj, 1991 Tg, 1993 Tg, Fj, NZ, 1995 SA, It,*
Ar, E, SA, Fj, Tg, S, E, 1996 NZ, 1999 US, Fj, W, S
E Fale 2008 *Tg*
S Fale 1955 *Fj*
S Fanolua 1990 *Tg, Fj, 1991 Tg, Fj*
TL Fanolua 1996 *NZ, Fj, 1997 Tg, 1998 Tg, Fj, A, 1999 W, S,*
2000 *J, Tg, C, It, US, 2001 Tg, Fj, NZ, Fj, Tg, J, Fj, 2002 Fj,*
2003 *Nm, Ur, Geo, E, 2005 A, Tg, Fj, Fj*
R Fanuatanu 2003 *I, Geo*
M Faoagali 1999 *J, C*
A Faosiliva 2006 *J, Tg, 2008 Tg, NZ, 2010 Tg, J, Fj, 2012 Tg,*
Fj, J
DS Farani 2005 *Tg, Fj, S, E, Ar, 2006 J, Fj, Tg*
J Fatialofa 2009 *F*
M Fatialofa 1996 *Tg*
PM Fatialofa 1988 *I, W, 1989 Bel, R, 1990 Kor, Tg, J, 1991 Tg,*
Fj, W, A, Ar, S, 1992 Tg, Fj, 1993 Tg, Fj, NZ, 1994 Tg, W, Fj,
A, 1995 SA, It, Ar, E, SA, Fj, Tg, S, E, 1996 NZ, Fj
Fatu 1947 *Tg*
E Feagai 1963 *Fj, Tg*
S Feagai 1963 *Fj, Fj*
D Feaunati 2003 *Nm, Ur, Geo, E, SA*
I Fea'unati 1996 *I, 1997 Tg, 1999 Tg, NZ, Fj, Ar, 2000 Fj, J,*
Tg, C, It, US, 2006 Fj, Tg
M Fepuleai 1957 *Tg*
V Fepuleai 1988 *W, 1989 Fj, WGe, R*
I Fesuiai'i 1985 *Fj, Tg*
JA Filemu 1995 *S, E, 1996 NZ, Tg, Fj, I, 1997 Fj, 1999 J, C,*
Tg, F, NZ, 2000 Fj, J, Tg, C, It, US, 2001 Tg, Fj, Tg, J
F Fili 2003 *I, Nm, 2009 W, F, 2011 Tg*
F Filisoa 2005 *Tg*
T Fong 1983 *Tg, Fj, 1984 Fj, Tg, 1986 W, Fj, Tg, 1987 Fj, Tg*
K Fotuali'i 2010 *J, I, E, S, 2011 A, Nm, W, Fj, SA, 2012 J, S*
S Fretton 1947 *Tg*
Fruean 1932 *Tg*
J Fruean 1972 *Tg, 1975 Tg*
S Fruean 1955 *Fj, Fj*
P Fualau 2012 *Tg, Fj*
P Fuatai 1988 *Tg, Fj, 1989 Fj, WGe, R*
S Fuatai 1972 *Tg*
T Fuga 1999 *F, NZ, US, 2000 Fj, J, Tg, C, It, US, 2007 SA, Tg*
ES Fuimaono Sapolu 2005 *S, E, Ar, 2006 Fj, Tg, 2007 SA, E,*
US, 2008 Fj, Tg, J, 2009 J, Fj, PNG, PNG, F, It, 2011 Fj, A,
Nm, W, Fj, SA
T Galuvao 2007 *Tg*
N George 2004 *Tg, Fj*
C Glendinning 1999 *J, C, Tg, F, NZ, US, Fj, J, W, S, 2000 Fj,*
J, Tg, C, It, US, 2001 Tg, Fj, NZ, Fj, Tg, Fj
A Grey 1957 *Tg, Tg*
I Grey 1985 *Fj, Tg*
P Grey 1975 *Tg, 1979 Tg, Fj, 1980 Tg*
G Harder 1995 *SA, It, Ar, SA*
Hellesoe 1932 *Tg*
B Helleur 2011 *Tg, A*
J Helleur 2010 *Tg, J, Fj, J*
M Hewitt 1955 *Fj, Fj*
J Huch 1982 *Fj, Fj, 1986 Fj, Tg*
J Hunt 1957 *Tg, Tg*
A Ieremia 1992 *Tg, Fj, 1993 Tg, Fj, NZ*

I **Imo** 1924 *Fj*
T **Imo** 1955 *Fj, Fj, Fj*, 1957 *Tg, Tg*
A **Ioane** 1957 *Tg, Tg, Tg*
E **Ioane** 1990 *Tg, Fj*, 1991 *Tg, Fj, S*
T **Iona** 1975 *Tg*
T **Iosua** 2006 *J*, 2011 *J, Fj, Tg*
Iupati 1924 *Fj*
M **Iupeli** 1988 *Tg, Fj, I, W*, 1989 *Fj, WGe, R*, 1993 *Tg, NZ*, 1994 *Tg, W, Fj, A*, 1995 *SA, E*
S **Iuta** 1947 *Tg*
T **Jensen** 1987 *Tg*, 1989 *Bel*
CAI **Johnston** 2005 *A, Tg, Fj, S, E, Ar*, 2006 *Fj, Tg*, 2007 *SA, J, Tg, SA, Tg, E, US*, 2008 *Fj, J*, 2009 *J, Tg, Fj, PNG, W, F, It*, 2010 *J, Fj, E, S*, 2011 *Tg, A, Nm, W, Fj, SA*, 2012 *J, S*
JVI **Johnston** 2008 *Tg, J*, 2011 *Tg*, 2012 *Fj*
MN **Jones** 1986 *W*
S **Kalapu** 1957 *Tg*
D **Kaleopa** 1990 *Kor, Tg, J*, 1991 *A*, 1992 *Fj*, 1993 *Tg, Fj*
S **Kaleta** 1994 *Tg, W*, 1995 *S, E*, 1996 *NZ*, 1997 *Tg, Fj*
T **Kali** 1975 *Tg*
L **Kamu** 1955 *Fj, Fj, Fj*
MG **Keenan** 1991 *W, A, Ar*, 1992 *Tg, Fj*, 1993 *NZ*, 1994 *Tg, W, Fj, A*
JR **Keil** 2010 *J, J*
F **Kelemete** 1984 *Fj, Tg*, 1985 *Tg*, 1986 *W*
DK **Kellet** 1993 *Tg, Fj, NZ*, 1994 *Tg, W, Fj, A*, 1995 *It, Ar, Fj, Tg, S, E*
DA **Kerslake** 2005 *Tg, Fj, Tg, E*, 2006 *J, Tg*, 2007 *Fj, SA, J, Tg*
A **Koko** 1999 *J*
R **Koko** 1983 *Tg, Fj, Fj*, 1984 *Fj, Tg*, 1985 *Fj, Tg, Tg*, 1986 *W, Fj, Tg*, 1987 *Fj, Tg*, 1988 *Tg, Fj, I, W*, 1989 *WGe, R*, 1993 *Tg, NZ*, 1994 *Tg*
M **Krause** 1984 *Tg*, 1986 *W*
H **Kruse** 1963 *Fj, Fj, Tg*
JA **Kuoi** 1987 *Fj, Tg*, 1988 *I, W*, 1990 *Kor, Tg*
B **Laban** 1955 *Fj*, 1957 *Tg, Tg*
SL **Lafaiali'i** 2001 *Tg, Fj, NZ, Tg*, 2002 *Fj, Tg, Fj, Tg, SA*, 2003 *I, Nm, Ur, Geo, E, SA*, 2004 *S, Fj*, 2005 *A, S, E*, 2007 *Fj, J, Tg, Tg, US*
I **Laga'aia** 1975 *Tg*, 1979 *Tg, Fj*
F **Lalomilo** 2001 *I, It*
PR **Lam** 1991 *W, Ar, S*, 1994 *W, Fj, A*, 1995 *SA, Ar, E, SA, Fj, Tg, S, E*, 1996 *NZ, Tg, Fj, I*, 1997 *Tg, Fj*, 1998 *Tg, Fj, A*, 1999 *J, C, Tg, F, NZ, US, Fj, J, Ar, W, S*
F **Lameta** 1990 *Tg, Fj*
S **Lameta** 1982 *Fj*
G **Latu** 1994 *Tg, W, Fj, A*, 1995 *SA, Ar, E, SA, Fj, Tg*
E **Lauina** 2008 *Fj, Tg, J, NZ*, 2009 *J, Tg, Fj, PNG, PNG*
M **Lautau** 1985 *Fj*
T **Lavea** 2010 *I, E, S*, 2011 *J, Fj, Nm, W*
FH **Lavea Levi** 2007 *Fj, SA, J, Tg*, 2008 *Fj, J, NZ*, 2009 *J, Tg, Fj, PNG, W, F, It*, 2010 *Tg, J, Fj, I, E, S*, 2011 *J, Fj, Tg, A, Fj*
S **Leaega** 1997 *Tg, Fj*, 1999 *J, J, Ar, W, S*, 2001 *Tg, Fj, NZ, Fj, Tg, Fj, I, It*, 2002 *Fj, Tg, SA*
K **Lealamanua** 2000 *Fj, J, Tg, C, It*, 2001 *NZ, Fj, Tg, J, Fj*, 2002 *Fj, Tg, Fj, Tg, SA*, 2003 *I, Nm, Ur, Geo, E, SA*, 2004 *Tg, S, Fj*, 2005 *S, E*, 2007 *SA, Tg, E, US*
GE **Leaupepe** 1995 *SA, Ar, E, Fj, Tg, S, E*, 1996 *NZ, Tg, Fj, I*, 1997 *Tg, Fj*, 1998 *Tg, A*, 1999 *J, C, Tg, F, NZ, US, Fj, J, Ar, W*, 2005 *A*
S **Leaupepe** 1979 *Tg, Fj*, 1980 *Tg*
P **Leavai** 1990 *J*
A **Leavasa** 1979 *Tg, Fj*, 1980 *Tg*
P **Leavasa** 1955 *Fj, Fj, Fj*, 1957 *Tg, Tg, Tg*
PL **Leavasa** 1993 *Tg, Fj*, 1995 *It, Ar, E, S, E*, 1996 *NZ, Tg, Fj, I*, 1997 *Tg, Fj*, 2002 *Tg, Fj, SA*
S **Leavasa** 1955 *Fj, Fj, Fj*, 1957 *Tg*
T **Leiasamaivao** 1993 *Tg, NZ*, 1994 *Tg, W, Fj*, 1995 *It, Ar, E, SA, S, E*, 1996 *NZ, Tg, Fj, I*, 1997 *Tg, Fj*
N **Leleimalefaga** 2007 *Fj, US*
F **Lemalu** 2012 *Tg, Fj, J, S*
S **Lemalu** 2003 *Ur, Geo, E*, 2004 *Tg, S, Fj*, 2008 *Tg, J, NZ*, 2010 *J, I*, 2011 *Fj, Tg*
S **Lemamea** 1988 *I, W*, 1989 *Fj, WGe, Bel, R*, 1990 *J*, 1992 *Tg, Fj*, 1995 *E, SA, Fj, Tg*
D **Lemi** 2004 *Tg, S, Fj*, 2005 *Tg, Fj, Tg, Fj*, 2007 *Fj, SA, J, Tg, SA, Tg, E, US*, 2008 *Fj, Tg, J*, 2009 *W, F, It*, 2010 *Tg, J, Fj, I, E, S*, 2011 *Fj, Tg, SA*, 2012 *Tg, Fj, J, S*
DA **Leo** 2005 *A, Tg, Fj, Tg, Fj, S, E, Ar*, 2006 *J, Fj, Tg*, 2007 *SA, J, Tg, SA, Tg, E*, 2008 *Tg, J*, 2009 *J, Fj, PNG, PNG*, 2010 *S*, 2011 *J, Fj, A, Nm, W, Fj, SA*
J **Leota** 2011 *Fj, Tg*

M **Leota** 2000 *Fj, Tg, C*
P **Leota** 1990 *Kor, Tg, J*
T **Leota** 1997 *Tg, Fj*, 1998 *Tg, Fj, A*, 1999 *J, C, Tg, F, Fj, J, Ar, W, S*, 2000 *Fj, J*, 2001 *Tg, Fj, NZ, Fj, J, Fj*, 2002 *Fj, Tg, Fj, Tg, SA*, 2003 *I*, 2005 *A*
A **Le'u** 1987 *Fj, Tg*, 1989 *WGe, R*, 1990 *Kor, J, Tg, Fj*, 1993 *Tg, Fj, NZ*, 1996 *I*
T **Leupolu** 2001 *I, It*, 2002 *Fj, Tg, Fj, Tg, SA*, 2003 *I, Nm, SA*, 2004 *Tg, S, Fj*, 2005 *Ar*
R **Levasa** 2008 *NZ*, 2009 *J, PNG*, 2010 *J, Fj*
A **Liaina** 1963 *Fj, Fj, Tg*
S **Liaina** 1963 *Fj, Fj, Tg*
P **Lilomaiava** 1993 *NZ*
BP **Lima** 1991 *Tg, Fj, W, A, Ar, S*, 1992 *Tg, Fj*, 1993 *Fj, NZ*, 1994 *Tg, W, Fj, A*, 1995 *SA, It, Ar, E, SA, Fj, Tg, S, E*, 1996 *NZ, Tg, Fj*, 1997 *Fj*, 1998 *Tg, Fj, A*, 1999 *Tg, F, NZ, US, J, Ar, W, S*, 2000 *C, It, US*, 2001 *Fj, Tg, Fj, I, It*, 2002 *Fj, Tg*, 2003 *I, Nm, Ur, Geo, E, SA*, 2004 *Tg, S, Fj*, 2005 *A, Fj*, 2006 *J, Fj*, 2007 *Fj, Tg, SA, E*
F **Lima** 1981 *Fj*
M **Lima** 1982 *Fj, Fj*
M **Lome** 1957 *Tg, Tg, Tg*, 1963 *Fj*
M **Luafalealo** 1999 *J*, 2000 *It, US*, 2001 *Tg, Fj, NZ, Fj, J, Fj*
E **Lua'iufi** 1987 *Fj, Tg*, 1988 *Tg, Fj*
Lui 1932 *Tg*
LS **Lui** 2004 *Fj*, 2005 *Tg, Fj, Ar*, 2006 *J, Tg*, 2007 *Tg, Tg, E, US*, 2009 *J, Tg, Fj, PNG, PNG, W, F*, 2010 *Tg, J, Fj, J*, 2012 *Tg, Fj, J, S*
M **Lupeli** 1993 *Fj*
A **Macdonald** 1924 *Fj, Fj*, 1932 *Tg*
M **Magele** 2009 *PNG*
T **Magele** 1988 *Tg*
U **Mai** 2008 *Tg, J, NZ*, 2009 *J, Fj, PNG, PNG, W, F, It*, 2010 *Tg, J, Fj*, 2011 *J, Fj, Tg*
F **Mailei** 1963 *Fj, Tg*
F **Malele** 1979 *Tg, Fj*, 1980 *Tg*
J **Maligi** 2000 *W, S*
P **Maligi** 1982 *Fj, Tg*, 1983 *Tg, Fj*, 1984 *Fj, Tg*, 1985 *Fj, Tg, Tg*, 1986 *Fj, Tg*
L **Malo** 1979 *Fj*
J **Mamea** 2000 *W, S*
L **Mano** 1988 *Fj, I, W*
C **Manu** 2002 *Fj, Tg, Tg, SA*
S **Mapusua** 2006 *J, Fj, Tg*, 2007 *SA, J, Tg, Tg, E, US*, 2009 *Tg, Fj, W, F, It*, 2010 *I, E, S*, 2011 *J, A, Nm, W, Fj, SA*
P **Mareko** 1979 *Fj*
K **Mariner** 2005 *Ar*
BF **Masoe** 2012 *Tg, Fj, J, S*
M **Mata'afa** 1947 *Tg*
P **Matailina** 1957 *Tg, Tg, Tg*
O **Matauiau** 1996 *Tg, Fj*, 1999 *Ar, W, S*, 2000 *It, W, S*
K **Mavaega** 1985 *Tg*
M **McFadyen** 1957 *Tg*
K **McFall** 1983 *Fj*
J **Meafou** 2007 *Tg, SA, E*, 2008 *NZ*
L **Mealamu** 2000 *W, S*
I **Melei** 1972 *Tg*
C **Meredith** 1932 *Tg*
J **Meredith** 2001 *I, It*, 2002 *Fj, Tg, Fj, Tg, SA*, 2003 *I, Nm, Ur, Geo, E, SA*, 2004 *Tg, S, Fj*, 2005 *A, Tg, Fj, Fj*
J **Meredith** 1963 *Fj, Fj, Tg*
O **Meredith** 1947 *Tg*
A **Mika** 2000 *S*
D **Mika** 1994 *W, A*
MAN **Mika** 1995 *SA, It, Ar, E, SA, S, E*, 1997 *Tg, Fj*, 1999 *Tg, F, NZ, J, Ar, W*
S **Mika** 2004 *Fj*, 2005 *A, Tg, Fj, Tg, Fj*
S **Mikaele** 2008 *NZ*, 2009 *PNG, PNG*, 2010 *J*
P **Misa** 2000 *W, S*
S **Moala** 2008 *Fj*
F **Moamanu** 1989 *WGe*
S **Moamanu** 1985 *Fj*, 1986 *Fj, Tg*
M **Moke** 1990 *Kor, Tg, J, Tg, Fj*
P **Momoisea** 1972 *Tg, Tg*
H **Moors** 1924 *Fj, Fj*
R **Moors** 1994 *Tg*
Mose 1932 *Tg*
S **Motoi** 1984 *Fj*
F **Motusagu** 2000 *Tg, It*, 2005 *A*
R **Muagututia** 2010 *J*
L **Mulipola** 2009 *PNG*, 2010 *J*, 2011 *J, Fj, Tg, SA*, 2012 *Tg, Fj, J, S*
L **Mulipola** 2009 *F, It*

TDL Tagaloa 1990 *Kor, Tg, J, Tg, Fj,* 1991 *W, A, Ar, S*
S Tagicakibau 2003 *Nm, Ur, Geo, E, SA,* 2004 *Tg, S, Fj,* 2005 *S, E, Ar,* 2007 *Tg,* 2009 *J, Tg, Fj,* 2011 *J, Fj, A, Nm, W, Fj*
Tagimanu 1924 *Fj*
I Taina 2005 *Tg, Fj, Tg, Fj, S*
F Taiomaivao 1989 *Bel*
F Talapusi 1979 *Tg, Fj,* 1980 *Tg*
F Talapusi 2005 *A, Fj, Tg, Fj*
Tamalua 1932 *Tg*
F Tanoa'i 1996 *Tg, Fj*
S Tanuko 1987 *Tg*
P Tapelu 2002 *SA*
V Tasi 1981 *Fj,* 1982 *Fj, Fj, Fj, Tg,* 1983 *Tg, Fj,* 1984 *Fj, Tg*
J Tatupu 2010 *J*
S Tatupu 1990 *Tg,* 1993 *Tg, Fj, NZ,* 1995 *It, Ar, E, SA, Fj, Tg*
N Tauafao 2005 *A, Tg, Fj, Tg, Fj, S, Ar,* 2007 *Fj,* 2008 *Fj, Tg, J, NZ,* 2009 *J, Fj, PNG, PNG*
S Taulafo 2009 *W, F, It,* 2010 *Tg, Fj, I, E, S,* 2011 *J, A, Nm, W, Fj, SA,* 2012 *Tg, Fj, J, S*
I Tautau 1985 *Fj, Tg,* 1986 *W*
A Tavana 2012 *Tg*
T Tavita 1984 *Fj, Tg*
E Taylor 2011 *J, Fj*
HL Tea 2008 *Fj, Tg, J, NZ,* 2009 *PNG*
I Tekori 2007 *SA, J, SA, Tg, E, US,* 2009 *Tg, Fj, W, F,* 2010 *Tg, J, Fj, I, E, S,* 2011 *J, Nm, W, SA,* 2012 *J, S*
AT Telea 1995 *S, E,* 1996 *NZ, Tg, Fj*
E Telea 2008 *Fj*
S Telea 1989 *Bel*
A Teo 1947 *Tg*
F Teo 1955 *Fj*
V Teo 1957 *Tg, Tg*
KG Thompson 2007 *Fj, SA, Tg, SA, Tg, E, US,* 2008 *Tg, J,* 2009 *W, F, It,* 2010 *Tg, Fj, I, E, S,* 2011 *A, Nm, W, Fj, SA,* 2012 *J, S*
H Thomson 1947 *Tg*
A Tiatia 2001 *Tg, Fj, NZ, Fj, Tg, J, Fj*
R Tiatia 1972 *Tg*
S Tilialo 1972 *Tg*
MM Timoteo 2009 *Tg, F, It,* 2012 *Tg, Fj*
F Tipi 1998 *Fj, A,* 1999 *J, C, F, NZ, Fj*
F Toala 1998 *Fj,* 1999 *J, C, S,* 2000 *W, S*
L Toelupe 1979 *Fj*
P Toelupe 2008 *Fj, J, NZ*
T Tofaeono 1989 *Fj, Bel*
A Toleafoa 2000 *W, S,* 2002 *Tg, SA*
K Toleafoa 1955 *Fj, Fj*
PL Toleafoa 2006 *J, Fj*
K Tole'afoa 1998 *Tg, A,* 1999 *Ar*
F Toloa 1979 *Tg,* 1980 *Tg*
R Tolufale 2008 *NZ,* 2009 *PNG*
J Tomuli 2001 *I, It,* 2002 *Fj, Tg, Fj, Tg, SA,* 2003 *I, Nm, Ur, Geo, E, SA,* 2006 *J*
L Tone 1998 *Tg, Fj, A,* 1999 *J, C, Tg, F, NZ, US, J, Ar, W, S,* 2000 *Fj, J, Tg, C, It, US, S,* 2001 *NZ, Fj, Tg, J, Fj*
S Tone 2000 *W*
Toni 1924 *Fj*
OFJ Tonu'u 1992 *Tg,* 1993 *Tg, Fj, NZ*
F To'omalatai 1989 *Bel*
PS To'omalatai 1985 *Fj, Tg,* 1986 *W, Fj, Tg,* 1988 *Tg, Fj, I, W,* 1989 *Fj, WGe, Bel, R,* 1990 *Kor, Tg, J, Tg, Fj,* 1991 *Tg, Fj, W, A, Ar, S,* 1992 *Tg, Fj,* 1993 *Fj,* 1994 *A,* 1995 *Fj*
O Treviranus 2009 *J, Tg, Fj, PNG, PNG, W, F, It,* 2010 *J, Fj, J, I, E, S,* 2011 *Fj, Tg, Nm, W, SA*
Tualai 1924 *Fj, Fj*
I Tualaulelei 1963 *Fj, Fj, Tg*
F Tuatagaloa 1957 *Tg*
K Tuatagaloa 1963 *Fj, Fj, Tg,* 1972 *Tg*
V Tuatagaloa 1963 *Fj, Tg*
Tufele 1924 *Fj*
D Tuiavi'l 2003 *I, Nm, Ur, E, SA*
T Tuifua 2011 *J, Fj, A, Nm, Fj, SA*
G Tuigamala 2012 *Tg, Fj*
VL Tuigamala 1996 *Fj, I,* 1997 *Tg, Fj,* 1998 *Tg, Fj, A,* 1999 *F,*

NZ, US, Fj, J, Ar, W, S, 2000 *Fj, J, Tg, US,* 2001 *J, Fj, I, It*
AF Tuilagi 2005 *Tg, Fj, Tg, Fj, S, Ar,* 2006 *J, Tg,* 2007 *Fj, SA, J,* 2008 *Tg, J,* 2009 *W*
AT Tuilagi 2002 *Fj, Tg, SA,* 2005 *A, Tg, Fj, Tg, Fj, S, E,* 2007 *SA, J, Tg, SA, Tg, E, US,* 2010 *I, E, S,* 2011 *J, A, Nm, W, Fj, SA*
F Tuilagi 1992 *Tg,* 1994 *W, Fj, A,* 1995 *SA, SA, Fj,* 2000 *W, S,* 2001 *Fj, NZ, Tg,* 2002 *Fj, Tg, Fj, Tg, SA*
H Tuilagi 2002 *Fj, Tg, Fj, Tg,* 2007 *SA, E,* 2008 *J,* 2009 *W, F, It*
T Tuisaula 1947 *Tg*
R Tuivaiti 2004 *Fj*
A Tunupopo 1963 *Fj*
P Tupa'i 2005 *A, Tg, S, E, Ar*
A Tupou 2008 *NZ,* 2009 *PNG*
S Tupuola 1982 *Fj, Fj, Fj, Tg,* 1983 *Tg, Fj,* 1985 *Tg,* 1986 *Fj, Tg,* 1987 *Fj, Tg,* 1988 *W,* 1989 *R*
P Tu'uau 1972 *Tg, Tg,* 1975 *Tg*
D Tyrrell 2000 *Fj, J, C,* 2001 *It,* 2002 *Fj, Tg, SA,* 2003 *I, Nm, Ur, Geo, E, SA*
S Uati 1988 *Tg, Fj*
T Ugapo 1988 *Tg, Fj, I, W,* 1989 *Fj, WGe, Bel*
U Ulia 2004 *Tg, S, Fj,* 2005 *Ar,* 2006 *J, Fj, Tg,* 2007 *Fj, Tg, Tg, US*
J Ulugia 1985 *Fj, Tg*
M Umaga 1995 *SA, It, Ar, E, SA,* 1998 *Tg, Fj, A,* 1999 *Tg, F, NZ, US, Fj*
A Utu'utu 1979 *Tg, Fj*
L Utu'utu 1975 *Tg*
E Va'a 1996 *I,* 1997 *Fj,* 1998 *A,* 1999 *Tg, NZ, Fj, J, W, S,* 2001 *Tg, Fj, NZ, Fj, Tg, J, Fj, I,* 2002 *Fj, Tg, Fj, Tg, SA,* 2003 *I, Nm, Ur, Geo, E, SA*
JH Va'a 2005 *A, Fj, Tg, Fj, S, E, Ar,* 2006 *Fj, Tg,* 2007 *SA, J, Tg, SA,* 2009 *J, Tg, Fj, W, It*
M Vaea 1991 *Tg, Fj, W, A, Ar, S,* 1992 *Fj,* 1995 *S*
K Vaega 1982 *Fj, Tg,* 1983 *Fj*
TM Vaega 1986 *W,* 1989 *WGe, Bel, R,* 1990 *Kor, Tg, J, Tg, Fj,* 1991 *Tg, Fj, W, A, Ar, S,* 1992 *Tg, Fj,* 1993 *Tg, Fj, NZ,* 1994 *Tg, W, Fj, A,* 1995 *SA, It, Ar, E, SA, Fj, Tg, S, E,* 1996 *NZ, Tg, Fj, I,* 1997 *Tg,* 1998 *Fj, A,* 1999 *J, C, F, NZ, Fj, J, Ar, W, S,* 2000 *Fj, J, Tg, C, It, US,* 2001 *Tg, J, Fj, I*
A Vaeluaga 2000 *W, S,* 2001 *Tg, Fj, Tg, J, Fj, I,* 2007 *SA, J, SA, E, US*
F Vagaia 1972 *Tg*
K Vai 1987 *Fj, Tg,* 1989 *Bel*
TS Vaifale 1989 *R,* 1990 *Kor, Tg, J, Tg, Fj,* 1991 *Tg, Fj, W, Ar, S,* 1992 *Tg, Fj,* 1993 *NZ,* 1994 *Tg, W, Fj, A,* 1995 *SA, It, SA, Fj, S, E,* 1996 *NZ, Tg,* 1997 *Tg, Fj*
S Vaili 2001 *I, It,* 2002 *Fj, Tg, Fj, Tg,* 2003 *Geo,* 2004 *Tg, S, Fj*
L Vailoaloa 2005 *A,* 2011 *J, Fj, Tg*
S Vaisola Sefo 2007 *US*
T Veiru 2000 *W, S*
M Vili 1957 *Tg*
M Vili 1975 *Tg*
T Vili 1999 *C, Tg, US, Ar,* 2000 *Fj, J, Tg, C, It, US,* 2001 *Tg, Fj, J, Fj, I, It,* 2003 *Ur, Geo, E, SA,* 2004 *Tg, S, Fj,* 2005 *A, Tg, Fj, S, E,* 2006 *J, Fj, Tg*
K Viliamu 2001 *I, It,* 2002 *Fj, SA,* 2003 *I, Ur, Geo, E, SA,* 2004 *S*
T Viliamu 1947 *Tg*
Visesio 1932 *Tg*
FV Vitale 1994 *W, Fj, A,* 1995 *Fj, Tg*
F Vito 1972 *Tg,* 1975 *Tg*
M von Dincklage 2004 *S*
R Warren 2004 *Tg, S,* 2005 *Tg, Fj, Tg, Fj, S, Ar,* 2008 *Fj, Tg, J, NZ*
S Wendt 1955 *Fj, Fj, Fj*
AF Williams 2009 *J, Fj, PNG, PNG, F, It,* 2010 *J, J*
DR Williams 1988 *I, W,* 1995 *SA, It, E*
G Williams 2007 *Fj, SA, SA, Tg,* 2008 *Tg, J,* 2009 *J, Tg, Fj, PNG, PNG, W, It,* 2010 *J, I, E*
H Williams 2001 *Tg, Tg, J*
PB Williams 2010 *Tg, J, Fj, I, E, S,* 2011 *A, Nm, W, Fj, SA,* 2012 *Fj, J, S*
P Young 1988 *I,* 1989 *Bel*

SCOTLAND

SCOTLAND'S 2012 TEST RECORD

OPPONENTS	DATE	VENUE	RESULT
England	4 Feb	H	Lost 6–13
Wales	12 Feb	A	Lost 27–13
France	26 Feb	H	Lost 17–23
Ireland	10 Mar	A	Lost 32–14
Italy	17 Mar	A	Lost 13–6
Australia	5 Jun	A	Won 9–6
Fiji	16 Jun	A	Won 37–25
Samoa	23 Jun	A	Won 17–16

FINE MARGINS – THE TALE OF SCOTLAND'S SEASON

By Chris Paterson

Getty Images

Scotland players celebrate a first win over the Wallabies on Australian soil in 30 years.

Fine margins – that was the story of Scotland's fortunes on the international stage during the 2011/12 season.

Scotland, under the leadership of head coach Andy Robinson, played 14 internationals from August 2011 until June 2012 and ended with a 50 per cent win/loss ratio. Five of the defeats were by seven points or fewer, while four of the victories were by nine points or fewer. A typical roller-coaster season, then, as we sought for that elusive companion, consistency.

We began with the massive disappointment of failing to qualify for the quarter-finals of a Rugby World Cup for the first time. We'd had really consistent preparations and had opened our pool campaign with two victories against Romania (34–24) and Georgia (15–6) in the wind and rain of Invercargill in New Zealand's deep south. But in our last two pool games we lost to Argentina (13–12) and England (16–12) in the last few minutes in agonisingly close-run contests.

On a personal level I had always set goals and it had been my ambition to play in the Rugby World Cup for a fourth time, a record for a Scot. I had never said anything in public, but I thought that if I got to the World Cup I'd probably like to finish at the World Cup. I was pretty happy with my form at the World Cup and I remember speaking to our attack coach Gregor Townsend in the changing room at Eden Park in Auckland after the England game thinking, "I want to go on."

If the RBS Six Nations had followed on from the Rugby World Cup in a matter of weeks then I may well have done. But in the interim I picked up a couple of injuries and thought about it and decided that it was the right time to bow out from international rugby.

I still feel really comfortable with my decision. I remember speaking to the former Scotland scrum half Bryan Redpath and he said to me: "You'll know when it's time to retire." I didn't believe him at the time. I thought you just want to play forever, but he was spot on. I played my last game for Edinburgh against Treviso at Murrayfield in May and I'm now involved in an ambassadorial role for Scottish Rugby, doing some coaching at elite and community level and some PR activity around the country.

For the first time since 1999 then I was a spectator for Scotland's Six Nations campaign. Ahead of the matches the climate was really positive. You need to take strength from your domestic scene and, at that point, Edinburgh Rugby were going well in the Heineken Cup and Glasgow Warriors had found their form after a slow start in the RaboDirect PRO12.

So I don't believe we were over-hyped going into the Six Nations. Everyone who had been involved in Rugby World Cup 2011 was determined to put that disappointment right and we all knew that a good start in the Six Nations makes a massive impact on your overall performance in the Championship.

Our first game was against England at Murrayfield, and it was something of a fresh start for them too after the World Cup. The game at international level now tends to operate on four-year cycles. We'd seen a few changes after the World Cup with myself and Nathan Hines retiring, and Simon Danielli and Dan Parks also went on to retire from international rugby during the course of the season.

From the outside looking in I thought the England coach Stuart Lancaster did really well getting his team together in such a short period of time. The match was a typical Calcutta Cup arm wrestle with just the one try in the game for England's fly half Charlie Hodgson off a charge-down.

We could take encouragement from the performance of the Edinburgh Rugby back-row forward David Denton, who, in his first Scotland start, was named Man of the Match against England, but the bounce that would have come from a winning start was not to be for us as we lost 13–6.

SCOTLAND

A 27–13 defeat away to Wales at the Millennium Stadium followed although, again, there were some signs of encouragement, especially in the debut of the Hawick-raised full back Stuart Hogg.

Hoggy and another of our Six Nations debutants, Lee Jones, both scored really good tries against France at Murrayfield in game three but while the performance was good it was the same end result, a 23–17 loss.

That defeat was probably the turning point of our Six Nations campaign and not in a good sense. The majority of supporters recognised in the games against England, Wales and France the good in what we were trying to do. But in terms of results we suffered three defeats in a row and I think our displays against Ireland and Italy in the closing two games of the Championship reflected that. We went into our shell a little bit and suffered our two poorest performances.

The Six Nations is such an intense, in-your-face tournament. A good start leads to a good tournament and, generally, the opposite is true. With five defeats for Scotland there was really nowhere to hide.

There were changes to our coaching team after the Championship. Our attack coach Gregor Townsend and defence coach Graham Steadman left the national management team, Gregor moving to Glasgow Warriors as head coach and Steady joining Newcastle Falcons.

Scott Johnson, with a wealth of international experience from Australia, the United States and Wales, joined as senior assistant coach and, with effect from the November Tests, Matt Taylor takes up the reins as defence coach, joining us from the Queensland Reds.

But back to last season. In times gone by, post-Six Nations when players had returned to their clubs you frequently saw a drop-off in some performances. This time around there was a strong desire from players who were hurting at what had gone before on the international stage and felt they had a chance to show what they and their clubs could achieve.

In Edinburgh Rugby's case that was in the Heineken Cup; in Glasgow Warriors' the RaboDirect PRO12. Edinburgh had won five of six pool games in the Heineken Cup, including that incredible 48–47 win against Racing Métro at Murrayfield.

There was an element of Wimbledon's crazy gang about the way Edinburgh played, but it's that very approach that gave us the chance to beat anyone. The challenge for Edinburgh is to do that consistently.

When we beat London Irish at Murrayfield in our final pool game and learned that we would face Toulouse at home in the quarter-final it certainly captured the imagination of the supporters.

We attracted just shy of 40,000 people to Murrayfield that day – a UK record for a Heineken Cup quarter-final. Cup rugby against such an illustrious team proved a huge draw and there was a lot to be excited about in our win that day. Greig Laidlaw led the charge and some of our young players, Tom Brown, Grant Gilchrist, David Denton and Matt Scott, showed that they could perform in that environment.

Edinburgh's Heineken Cup campaign ended at the semi-final stage with a defeat to Ulster. Glasgow also fell at that hurdle in the RaboDirect PRO12 play-off but, again, it was a close-run thing before Leinster accounted for them.

Glasgow developed the happy knack of churning out wins through the quality of their decision-making and being really difficult to beat, especially in front of their vocal home support.

Domestic season done and dusted, it was time to focus on Scotland's summer tour to Australia, Fiji and Samoa. It finished very much the reverse of the Six Nations – performances could have been better in some of the games but we were on the right side of the results, winning three out of three.

On the tour Scotland won two of the games by, as near as damn it, the last kick of the match – beating Australia 9–6 and Samoa 17–16. Greig Laidlaw continued to grow in stature as both a fly half and goal-kicker and we saw some of our younger players demonstrate that they were ready and able to step up.

You expect a Scotland side to be courageous and, in conditions that were far removed from the sun-kissed image we have of Australia, they displayed guts galore as they posted back-to-back wins against the Wallabies, but Scotland's first on Australian soil in 30 years.

Tim Visser marked his qualification for Scotland with a try brace on his debut against Fiji in the 37–25 win. His Edinburgh Rugby team-mate Matt Scott, who had been called in as 23rd man to make his debut against Ireland during the Six Nations, started every Test on the tour and won the coaches' recognition as most improved player.

The player of the tour was Alasdair Strokosch. "Stroker" had missed three of the Six Nations games through injury but he was back to his uncompromising hard-man best, knocking people back in the tackle, on this tour. Just ask Joe Ansbro!

Tom Brown and the Glasgow forward trio, Ryan Grant, Tom Ryder and Robert Harley, also made their debuts on the tour and the morale at its conclusion, as Scotland moved into the top 10 of the IRB World Rankings once again, was that we could look forward to the future with some confidence.

So, the tour was a success, but we know we have to improve performances if we are to continue this trend in the next 12 months.

SCOTLAND

SCOTLAND INTERNATIONAL STATISTICS

MATCH RECORDS UP TO 10 OCTOBER 2012

MOST CONSECUTIVE TEST WINS

6	1925 F, W, I, E, 1926 F, W
6	1989 Fj, R, 1990 I, F, W, E

MOST CONSECUTIVE TESTS WITHOUT DEFEAT

Matches	Wins	Draws	Period
9	6*	3	1885 to 1887
6	6	0	1925 to 1926
6	6	0	1989 to 1990
6	4	2	1877 to 1880
6	5	1	1983 to 1984

* includes an abandoned match

MOST POINTS IN A MATCH

BY THE TEAM

Pts	Opponents	Venue	Year
100	Japan	Perth	2004
89	Ivory Coast	Rustenburg	1995
65	USA	San Francisco	2002
60	Zimbabwe	Wellington	1987
60	Romania	Hampden Park	1999
56	Portugal	Saint Etienne	2007
55	Romania	Dunedin	1987
53	USA	Murrayfield	2000
51	Zimbabwe	Murrayfield	1991
49	Argentina	Murrayfield	1990
49	Romania	Murrayfield	1995

BY A PLAYER

Pts	Player	Opponents	Venue	Year
44	A G Hastings	Ivory Coast	Rustenburg	1995
40	C D Paterson	Japan	Perth	2004
33	G P J Townsend	USA	Murrayfield	2000
31	A G Hastings	Tonga	Pretoria	1995
27	A G Hastings	Romania	Dunedin	1987
26	K M Logan	Romania	Hampden Park	1999
24	B J Laney	Italy	Rome	2002
24	D A Parks	Argentina	Tucumán	2010
23	G Ross	Tonga	Murrayfield	2001
22	G D Laidlaw	Fiji	Lautoka	2012
21	A G Hastings	England	Murrayfield	1986
21	A G Hastings	Romania	Bucharest	1986
21	C D Paterson	Wales	Murrayfield	2007
21	D A Parks	South Africa	Murrayfield	2010

MOST TRIES IN A MATCH

BY THE TEAM

Tries	Opponents	Venue	Year
15	Japan	Perth	2004
13	Ivory Coast	Rustenburg	1995
12	Wales	Raeburn Place	1887
11	Zimbabwe	Wellington	1987
10	USA	San Francisco	2002
9	Romania	Dunedin	1987
9	Argentina	Murrayfield	1990

BY A PLAYER

Tries	Player	Opponents	Venue	Year
5	G C Lindsay	Wales	Raeburn Place	1887
4	W A Stewart	Ireland	Inverleith	1913
4	I S Smith	France	Inverleith	1925
4	I S Smith	Wales	Swansea	1925
4	A G Hastings	Ivory Coast	Rustenburg	1995

MOST CONVERSIONS IN A MATCH

BY THE TEAM

Cons	Opponents	Venue	Year
11	Japan	Perth	2004
9	Ivory Coast	Rustenburg	1995
8	Zimbabwe	Wellington	1987
8	Romania	Dunedin	1987
8	Portugal	Saint Etienne	2007

BY A PLAYER

Cons	Player	Opponents	Venue	Year
11	C D Paterson	Japan	Perth	2004
9	A G Hastings	Ivory Coast	Rustenburg	1995
8	A G Hastings	Zimbabwe	Wellington	1987
8	A G Hastings	Romania	Dunedin	1987

MOST PENALTIES IN A MATCH

BY THE TEAM

Penalties	Opponents	Venue	Year
8	Tonga	Pretoria	1995
7	Wales	Murrayfield	2007
6	France	Murrayfield	1986
6	Italy	Murrayfield	2005
6	Ireland	Murrayfield	2007
6	Italy	Saint Etienne	2007
6	Argentina	Tucumán	2010
6	South Africa	Murrayfield	2010

BY A PLAYER

Penalties	Player	Opponents	Venue	Year
8	A G Hastings	Tonga	Pretoria	1995
7	C D Paterson	Wales	Murrayfield	2007
6	A G Hastings	France	Murrayfield	1986
6	C D Paterson	Italy	Murrayfield	2005
6	C D Paterson	Ireland	Murrayfield	2007
6	C D Paterson	Italy	Saint Etienne	2007
6	D A Parks	Argentina	Tucumán	2010
6	D A Parks	South Africa	Murrayfield	2010

MOST DROP GOALS IN A MATCH

BY THE TEAM

Drops	Opponents	Venue	Year
3	Ireland	Murrayfield	1973
2	on several	occasions	

BY A PLAYER

Drops	Player	Opponents	Venue	Year
2	R C MacKenzie	Ireland	Belfast	1877
2	N J Finlay	Ireland	Glasgow	1880
2	B M Simmers	Wales	Murrayfield	1965
2	D W Morgan	Ireland	Murrayfield	1973
2	B M Gossman	France	Parc des Princes	1983
2	J Y Rutherford	New Zealand	Murrayfield	1983
2	J Y Rutherford	Wales	Murrayfield	1985
2	J Y Rutherford	Ireland	Murrayfield	1987
2	C M Chalmers	England	Twickenham	1995
2	D A Parks	Wales	Cardiff	2010
2	D A Parks	Argentina	Tucumán	2010

CAREER RECORDS

MOST CAPPED PLAYERS

Caps	Player	Career Span
109	C D Paterson	1999 to 2011
87	S Murray	1997 to 2007
83	M R L Blair	2002 to 2012
82	G P J Townsend	1993 to 2003
77	J P R White	2000 to 2009
77	N J Hines	2000 to 2011
75	G C Bulloch	1997 to 2005
71	S B Grimes	1997 to 2005
70	K M Logan	1992 to 2003
68	S F Lamont	2004 to 2012
67	D A Parks	2004 to 2012
66	S M Taylor	2000 to 2009
65	S Hastings	1986 to 1997
64	A F Jacobsen	2002 to 2012
62	C P Cusiter	2004 to 2012
61	A G Hastings	1986 to 1995
61	G W Weir	1990 to 2000
61	T J Smith	1997 to 2005
61	R W Ford	2004 to 2012
60	C M Chalmers	1989 to 1999
60	B W Redpath	1993 to 2003
59	H F G Southwell	2004 to 2011
53	A R Henderson	2001 to 2008
52	J M Renwick	1972 to 1984
52	C T Deans	1978 to 1987
52	A G Stanger	1989 to 1998
52	A P Burnell	1989 to 1999
51	A R Irvine	1972 to 1982
51	G Armstrong	1988 to 1999

MOST CONSECUTIVE TESTS

Tests	Player	Span
49	A B Carmichael	1967 to 1978
44	C D Paterson	2004 to 2008
40	H F McLeod	1954 to 1962
37	J M Bannerman	1921 to 1929
35	A G Stanger	1989 to 1994

MOST TESTS AS CAPTAIN

Tests	Captain	Span
25	D M B Sole	1989 to 1992
21	B W Redpath	1998 to 2003
20	A G Hastings	1993 to 1995
19	J McLauchlan	1973 to 1979
19	J P R White	2005 to 2008
16	R I Wainwright	1995 to 1998
15	M C Morrison	1899 to 1904
15	A R Smith	1957 to 1962
15	A R Irvine	1980 to 1982

SCOTLAND

440

MOST POINTS IN TESTS

Points	Player	Tests	Career
809	C D Paterson	109	1999 to 2011
667	A G Hastings	61	1986 to 1995
273	A R Irvine	51	1972 to 1982
266	D A Parks	67	2004 to 2012
220	K M Logan	70	1992 to 2003
210	P W Dods	23	1983 to 1991
166	C M Chalmers	60	1989 to 1999
164	G P J Townsend	82	1993 to 2003
141	B J Laney	20	2001 to 2004
123	D W Hodge	26	1997 to 2002
106	A G Stanger	52	1989 to 1998

MOST PENALTY GOALS IN TESTS

Penalties	Player	Tests	Career
170	C D Paterson	109	1999 to 2011
140	A G Hastings	61	1986 to 1995
61	A R Irvine	51	1972 to 1982
55	D A Parks	67	2004 to 2012
50	P W Dods	23	1983 to 1991
32	C M Chalmers	60	1989 to 1999
29	K M Logan	70	1992 to 2003
29	B J Laney	20	2001 to 2004
21	M Dods	8	1994 to 1996
21	R J S Shepherd	20	1995 to 1998

MOST TRIES IN TESTS

Tries	Player	Tests	Career
24	I S Smith	32	1924 to 1933
24	A G Stanger	52	1989 to 1998
22	C D Paterson	109	1999 to 2011
17	A G Hastings	61	1986 to 1995
17	A V Tait	27	1987 to 1999
17	G P J Townsend	82	1993 to 2003
15	I Tukalo	37	1985 to 1992
13	K M Logan	70	1992 to 2003
12	A R Smith	33	1955 to 1962

MOST DROP GOALS IN TESTS

Drops	Player	Tests	Career
17	D A Parks	67	2004 to 2012
12	J Y Rutherford	42	1979 to 1987
9	C M Chalmers	60	1989 to 1999
7	I R McGeechan	32	1972 to 1979
7	G P J Townsend	82	1993 to 2003
6	D W Morgan	21	1973 to 1978
5	H Waddell	15	1924 to 1930

MOST CONVERSIONS IN TESTS

Cons	Player	Tests	Career
90	C D Paterson	109	1999 to 2011
86	A G Hastings	61	1986 to 1995
34	K M Logan	70	1992 to 2003
26	P W Dods	23	1983 to 1991
25	A R Irvine	51	1972 to 1982
19	D Drysdale	26	1923 to 1929
17	B J Laney	20	2001 to 2004
15	D W Hodge	26	1997 to 2002
15	D A Parks	67	2004 to 2012
14	F H Turner	15	1911 to 1914
14	R J S Shepherd	20	1995 to 1998

THE COUNTRIES

INTERNATIONAL CHAMPIONSHIP RECORDS

RECORD	DETAIL	HOLDER	SET
Most points in season	120	in four matches	1999
Most tries in season	17	in four matches	1925
Highest Score	38	38–10 v Ireland	1997
Biggest win	28	31–3 v France	1912
	28	38–10 v Ireland	1997
Highest score conceded	51	16–51 v France	1998
Biggest defeat	40	3–43 v England	2001
Most appearances	53	C D Paterson	2000–2011
Most points in matches	403	C D Paterson	2000–2011
Most points in season	65	C D Paterson	2007
Most points in match	24	B J Laney	v Italy, 2002
Most tries in matches	24	I S Smith	1924–1933
Most tries in season	8	I S Smith	1925
Most tries in match	5	G C Lindsay	v Wales, 1887
Most cons in matches	34	C D Paterson	2000–2011
Most cons in season	11	K M Logan	1999
Most cons in match	5	F H Turner	v France, 1912
	5	J W Allan	v England, 1931
	5	R J S Shepherd	v Ireland, 1997
Most pens in matches	99	C D Paterson	2000–2011
Most pens in season	16	C D Paterson	2007
Most pens in match	7	C D Paterson	v Wales, 2007
Most drops in matches	9	D A Parks	2004–2012
Most drops in season	5	D A Parks	2010
Most drops in match	2	on several	Occasions

MISCELLANEOUS RECORDS

RECORD	HOLDER	DETAIL
Longest Test Career	W C W Murdoch	1935 to 1948
Youngest Test Cap	N J Finlay	17 yrs 36 days in 1875*
Oldest Test Cap	J McLauchlan	37 yrs 210 days in 1979
* C Reid, also 17 yrs 36 days on debut in 1881, was a day *older* than Finlay, having lived through an extra leap-year day.		

SCOTLAND

CAREER RECORDS OF SCOTLAND INTERNATIONAL PLAYERS

UP TO 10 OCTOBER 2012

PLAYER BACKS:	DEBUT	CAPS	T	C	P	D	PTS
J A A Ansbro	2010 v SA	11	3	0	0	0	15
M R L Blair	2002 v C	83	7	0	0	0	35
T G Brown	2012 v A	1	0	0	0	0	0
C P Cusiter	2004 v W	62	3	0	0	0	15
J E Cuthbert	2011 v I	1	0	0	0	0	0
N J de Luca	2008 v F	35	1	0	0	0	5
M B Evans	2008 v C	30	3	0	0	0	15
A Grove	2009 v Fj	3	0	0	0	0	0
S W Hogg	2012 v W	7	1	0	0	0	5
R J H Jackson	2010 v NZ	13	0	2	2	2	16
L Jones	2012 v E	4	1	0	0	0	5
G D Laidlaw	2010 v NZ	10	2	8	15	0	71
R P Lamont	2005 v W	29	6	0	0	0	30
S F Lamont	2004 v Sm	68	8	0	0	0	40
R G M Lawson	2006 v A	30	0	0	0	0	0
G A Morrison	2004 v A	35	3	0	0	0	15
D A Parks	2004 v W	67	4	15	55	17	266
M C M Scott	2012 v I	4	0	0	0	0	0
H F G Southwell	2004 v Sm	59	8	0	0	0	40
T J W Visser	2012 v Fj	2	2	0	0	0	10
D Weir	2012 v F	2	0	1	0	0	2

FORWARDS:

J A Barclay	2007 v NZ	39	2	0	0	0	10
J W Beattie	2006 v R	16	3	0	0	0	15
K D R Brown	2005 v R	49	4	0	0	0	20
G D S Cross	2009 v W	14	0	0	0	0	0
D K Denton	2011 v I	6	0	0	0	0	0
A G Dickinson	2007 v NZ	24	1	0	0	0	5
R W Ford	2004 v A	61	2	0	0	0	10
R Grant	2012 v A	3	0	0	0	0	0
R J Gray	2010 v F	24	1	0	0	0	5
D W H Hall	2003 v W	37	1	0	0	0	5
J L Hamilton	2006 v R	39	1	0	0	0	5
R Harley	2012 v Sm	1	1	0	0	0	5
A F Jacobsen	2002 v C	64	0	0	0	0	0
E D Kalman	2012 v W	2	0	0	0	0	0
A D Kellock	2004 v A	44	1	0	0	0	5
S Lawson	2005 v R	34	2	0	0	0	10
M J Low	2009 v F	15	0	0	0	0	0
S J MacLeod	2004 v A	24	0	0	0	0	0
E A Murray	2005 v R	47	2	0	0	0	10
R M Rennie	2008 v I	19	0	0	0	0	0
T P Ryder	2012 v Fj	2	0	0	0	0	0
A K Strokosch	2006 v A	28	1	0	0	0	5
R J Vernon	2009 v Fj	20	0	0	0	0	0
J Welsh	2012 v It	1	0	0	0	0	0

SCOTLAND

SCOTLAND INTERNATIONAL PLAYERS
UP TO 10 OCTOBER 2012

Note: Years given for International Championship matches are for second half of season; eg 1972 means season 1971–72. Years for all other matches refer to the actual year of the match. Entries in square brackets denote matches played in RWC Finals.

Abercrombie, C H (United Services) 1910 I, E, 1911 F, W, 1913 F, W
Abercrombie, J G (Edinburgh U) 1949 F, W, I, 1950 F, W, I, E
Agnew, W C C (Stewart's Coll FP) 1930 W, I
Ainslie, R (Edinburgh Inst FP) 1879 I, E, 1880 I, E, 1881 E, 1882 I, E
Ainslie, T (Edinburgh Inst FP) 1881 E, 1882 I, E, 1883 W, I, E, 1884 W, I, E, 1885 W, I 1,2
Aitchison, G R (Edinburgh Wands) 1883 I
Aitchison, T G (Gala) 1929 W, I, E
Aitken, A I (Edinburgh Inst FP) 1889 I
Aitken, G G (Oxford U) 1924 W, I, E, 1925 F, W, I, E, 1929 F
Aitken, J (Gala) 1977 E, I, F, 1981 F, W, E, I, NZ 1,2, R, A, 1982 E, I, F, W, 1983 F, W, E, NZ, 1984 W, E, I, F, R
Aitken, R (London Scottish) 1947 W
Allan, B (Glasgow Acads) 1881 I
Allan, J (Edinburgh Acads) 1990 NZ 1, 1991, W, I, R, [J, I, WS, E, NZ]
Allan, J L (Melrose) 1952 F, W, I, 1953 W
Allan, J L F (Cambridge U) 1957 I, E
Allan, J W (Melrose) 1927 F, 1928 I, 1929 F, W, I, E, 1930 F, E, 1931 F, W, I, E, 1932 SA, W, I, 1934 I, E
Allan, R C (Hutchesons' GSFP) 1969 I
Allardice, W D (Aberdeen GSFP) 1947 A, 1948 F, W, I, 1949 F, W, I, E
Allen, H W (Glasgow Acads) 1873 E
Anderson, A H (Glasgow Acads) 1894 I
Anderson, D G (London Scottish) 1889 I, 1890 W, I, E, 1891 W, E, 1892 W, E
Anderson, E (Stewart's Coll FP) 1947 I, E
Anderson, J W (W of Scotland) 1872 E
Anderson, T (Merchiston Castle School) 1882 I
Angus, A W (Watsonians) 1909 W, 1910 F, W, E, 1911 W, I, 1912 F, W, I, E, SA, 1913 F, W, 1914 E, 1920 F, W, I, E
Ansbro, J A (Northampton, London Irish) 2010 SA,Sm, 2011 F,W,E,It1,I2,[R,E], 2012 A,Sm
Anton, P A (St Andrew's U) 1873 E
Armstrong, G (Jedforest, Newcastle) 1988 A, 1989 W, E, I, F, Fj, R, 1990 I, F, W, E, NZ 1,2, Arg, 1991 F, W, E, I, R, [J, I, WS, E, NZ], 1993 I, F, W, E, 1994 E, I, 1996 NZ, 1,2, A, 1997 W, SA (R), 1998 It, I, F, W, E, SA (R), 1999 W, E, I, F, Arg, R, [SA, U, Sm, NZ]
Arneil, R J (Edinburgh Acads, Leicester and Northampton) 1968 I, E, A, 1969 F, W, I, E, SA, 1970 F, W, I, E, A, 1971 F, W, I, E (2[1C]), 1972 F, W, E, NZ
Arthur, A (Glasgow Acads) 1875 E, 1876 E
Arthur, J W (Glasgow Acads) 1871 E, 1872 E
Asher, A G G (Oxford U) 1882 I, 1884 W, I, E, 1885 W, 1886 I, E
Auld, W (W of Scotland) 1889 W, 1890 W
Auldjo, L J (Abertay) 1878 E

Bain, D McL (Oxford U) 1911 E, 1912 F, W, E, SA, 1913 F, W, I, E, 1914 W, I
Baird, G R T (Kelso) 1981 A, 1982 E, I, F, W, A 1,2, 1983 I, F, W, E, NZ, 1984 W, E, I, F, A, 1985 I, W, E, 1986 F, W, E, I, R, 1987 E, 1988 I
Balfour, A (Watsonians) 1896 W, I, E, 1897 E
Balfour, L M (Edinburgh Acads) 1872 E
Bannerman, E M (Edinburgh Acads) 1872 E, 1873 E
Bannerman, J M (Glasgow HSFP) 1921 F, W, I, E, 1922 F, W, I, E, 1923 F, W, I, E, 1924 F, W, I, E, 1925 F, W, I, E, 1926 F, W, I, E, 1927 F, W, I, E, A, 1928 F, W, I, E, 1929 F, W, I, E
Barclay, J A (Glasgow Warriors) 2007 [NZ], 2008 F,W,Arg 2,NZ,SA,C, 2009 W,F,It,I, Fj,A, 2010 F,W,It,E,I,Arg 1,2,NZ,SA,Sm, 2011 F,W,I1,E,It1,2,[R,Arg,E], 2012 E(R), W(R),F,I,It,A,Fj
Barnes, I A (Hawick) 1972 W, 1974 F (R), 1975 E (R), NZ, 1977 I, F, W
Barrie, R W (Hawick) 1936 E
Bearne, K R F (Cambridge U, London Scottish) 1960 F, W
Beattie, J A (Hawick) 1929 F, W, 1930 W, 1931 F, W, I, E, 1932 SA, W, I, E, 1933 W, E, I, 1934 I, E, 1935 W, I, E, NZ, 1936 W, I, E
Beattie, J R (Glasgow Acads) 1980 I, F, W, E, 1981 F, W, E, I, 1983 F, W, E, NZ, 1984 E (R), R, A, 1985 I, 1986 F, W, E, I, R, 1987 I, F, W, E
Beattie, J W (Glasgow Warriors) 2006 R,PI, 2007 F, 2008 Arg 1, 2009 Fj,A,Arg, 2010 F,W,It,E,I,Arg 1,2, 2011 I1,2
Beattie, R S (Newcastle, Bristol) 2000 NZ 1,2(R), Sm (R), 2003 E(R), It(R), I 2, [J(R), US,Fj]
Bedell-Sivright, D R (Cambridge U, Edinburgh U) 1900 W, 1901 W, I, E, 1902 W, I, E, 1903 W, I, 1904 W, I, E, 1905 NZ, 1906 W, I, E, SA, 1907 W, I, E, 1908 W, I
Bedell-Sivright, J V (Cambridge U) 1902 W
Begbie, T A (Edinburgh Wands) 1881 I, E
Bell, D L (Watsonians) 1975 I, F, W, E
Bell, J A (Clydesdale) 1901 W, I, E, 1902 W, I, E
Bell, L H I (Edinburgh Acads) 1900 E, 1904 W, I
Berkeley, W V (Oxford U) 1926 F, 1929 F, W, I
Berry, C W (Fettesian-Lorettonians) 1884 I, E, 1885 W, I 1, 1887 I, W, E, 1888 W, I
Bertram, D M (Watsonians) 1922 F, W, I, E, 1923 F, W, I, E, 1924 W, I, E
Beveridge, G (Glasgow) 2000 NZ 2(R), US (R), Sm (R), 2002 Fj(R), 2003 W 2, 2005 R(R)
Biggar, A G (London Scottish) 1969 SA, 1970 F, I, E, A, 1971 F, W, I, E (2[1C]), 1972 F, W
Biggar, M A (London Scottish) 1975 I, F, W, E, 1976 W, E, I, 1977 I, F, W, 1978 I, F, W, E, NZ, 1979 W, E, I, F, NZ, 1980 I, F, W, E
Birkett, G A (Harlequins, London Scottish) 1975 NZ
Bishop, J M (Glasgow Acads) 1893 I
Bisset, A A (RIE Coll) 1904 W
Black, A W (Edinburgh U) 1947 F, W, 1948 E, 1950 W, I, E
Black, W P (Glasgow HSFP) 1948 F, W, I, E, 1951 E
Blackadder, W F (W of Scotland) 1938 E
Blaikie, C F (Heriot's FP) 1963 I, E, 1966 E, 1968 A, 1969 F, W, I, E
Blair, M R L (Edinburgh, Brive) 2002 C, US, 2003 F(t+R), W 1(R), SA 2(R), It 2, I 2, [US], 2004 W(R), E(R), It(R), F(R), I(R), Sm(R), A1(R), 3(R), J(R), A4(R), SA(R), 2005 I(t&R), It(R), W(R), E, R, Arg, Sm(R), NZ(R), 2006 F, W, E, I, It(R), SA 1, 2, R, PI(R), A, 2007 I2, SA, [Pt, R, It, Arg], 2008 F, W, I, E, It, Arg 1, 2, NZ, SA, C, 2009 W, F, It, I, E, Fj(R), 2010 W(R), It(R), I(R), Arg 1(R), 2(R), NZ, Sm(R), 2011 F(R), W(R), I1, E(R), It1(R), 2, [R, Arg(R), E], 2012 E(R),W(R), F, I, It, A, Fj, Sm(R)
Blair, P C B (Cambridge U) 1912 SA, 1913 F, W, I, E
Bolton, W H (W of Scotland) 1876 E
Borthwick, J B (Stewart's Coll FP) 1938 W, I
Bos, F H ten (Oxford U, London Scottish) 1959 E, 1960 F, W, SA, 1961 F, SA, W, I, E, 1962 F, W, I, E, 1963 F, W, I, E
Boswell, J D (W of Scotland) 1889 W, I, 1890 W, I, E, 1891 W, I, E, 1892 W, I, E, 1893 I, E, 1894 I, E
Bowie, T C (Watsonians) 1913 I, E, 1914 I, E
Boyd, G M (Glasgow HSFP) 1926 E
Boyd, J L (United Services) 1912 E, SA
Boyle, A C W (London Scottish) 1963 F, W, I

Cowie, W L K (Edinburgh Wands) 1953 E

Cownie, W B (Watsonians) 1893 W, I, E, 1894 W, I, E, 1895 W, I, E

Crabbie, G E (Edinburgh Acads) 1904 W

Crabbie, J E (Edinburgh Acads, Oxford U) 1900 W, 1902 I, 1903 W, I, 1904 E, 1905 W

Craig, A (Orrell, Glasgow) 2002 C, US, R, SA, Fj, 2003 I 1, F(R), W 1(R), E, It 1, SA 1,2, W 2, I 2, [J,US,F], 2004 A3(R), 2005 F,I,It,W,E

Craig, J B (Heriot's FP) 1939 W

Craig, J M (West of Scotland, Glasgow) 1997 A, 2001 W (R), E (R), It

Cramb, R I (Harlequins) 1987 [R(R)], 1988 I, F, A

Cranston, A G (Hawick) 1976 W, E, I, 1977 E, W, 1978 F (R), W, E, NZ, 1981 NZ 1,2

Crawford, J A (Army, London Scottish) 1934 I

Crawford, W H (United Services, RN) 1938 W, I, E, 1939 W, E

Crichton-Miller, D (Gloucester) 1931 W, I, E

Crole, G B (Oxford U) 1920 F, W, I, E

Cronin, D F (Bath, London Scottish, Bourges, Wasps) 1988 I, F, W, E, A, 1989 W, E, I, F, Fj, R, 1990 I, F, W, E, NZ 1,2, 1991 F, W, E, I, R, [Z], 1992 A 2, 1993 I, F, W, E, NZ, 1995 C, I, F, [Tg, F, NZ], WS, 1996 NZ 1,2, A, It, 1997 F (R), 1998 I, F, W, E

Cross, G D S (Edinburgh) 2009 W, 2010 E(R), 2011 I1(t&R),E(R),It1,I2,[R,Arg], 2012 E(R),W,F,I,It,Fj(R)

Cross, M (Merchistonians) 1875 E, 1876 E, 1877 I, E, 1878 E, 1879 I, E, 1880 I, E

Cross, W (Merchistonians) 1871 E, 1872 E

Cumming, R S (Aberdeen U) 1921 F, W

Cunningham, G (Oxford U) 1908 W, I, 1909 W, E, 1910 F, I, E, 1911 E

Cunningham, R F (Gala) 1978 NZ, 1979 W, E

Currie, L R (Dunfermline) 1947 A, 1948 F, W, I, 1949 F, W, I, E

Cusiter, C P (Borders, Perpignan, Glasgow Warriors) 2004 W, E, It, F, I, Sm, A1, 2, 3, J, A4, SA, 2005 F, I, It, W, Arg(R), Sm, NZ, 2006 F(R), W(R), E(R), I(R), It, R(R), PI, 2007 E, W, It, I1, F(R), I2(R), [R(R), NZ, It(R), Arg(R)], 2008 F(R), W(R), I(R), 2009 W(R), F(R), It(R), I(R), E(R), Fj, A, Arg, 2010 F, W, It, E, I, 2011 It2(R), [R(R), E(R)], 2012 E, W, F(R), It, A(R), Fj(R), Sm

Cuthbert, J E (Bath) 2011 I2(R)

Cuthbertson, W (Kilmarnock, Harlequins) 1980 I, 1981 W, E, I, NZ 1,2, R, A, 1982 E, I, F, W, A 1,2, 1983 I, F, W, NZ, 1984 W, E, A

Dalgleish, A (Gala) 1890 W, E, 1891 W, I, 1892 W, 1893 W, 1894 W, I

Dalgleish, K J (Edinburgh Wands, Cambridge U) 1951 I, E, 1953 F, W

Dall, A K (Edinburgh) 2003 W 2(R)

Dallas, J D (Watsonians) 1903 E

Danielli, S C J (Bath, Borders, Ulster) 2003 It 2, W 2, [J(R), US, Fj, A], 2004 W, E, It, F, I, 2005 F, I, 2008 W(R), It, Arg 1, 2009 F, It, I, E, Fj, A, 2010 It, E(R), I(R), Arg 2, 2011 I1(R), E, It1, 2, [R,E]

Davidson, J A (London Scottish, Edinburgh Wands) 1959 E, 1960 I, E

Davidson, J N G (Edinburgh U) 1952 F, W, I, E, 1953 F, W, 1954 F

Davidson, J P (RIE Coll) 1873 E, 1874 E

Davidson, R S (Royal HSFP) 1893 E

Davies, D S (Hawick) 1922 F, W, I, E, 1923 F, W, I, E, 1924 F, E, 1925 W, I, E, 1926 F, W, I, E, 1927 F, W, I

Dawson, J C (Glasgow Acads) 1947 A, 1948 F, W, 1949 F, W, I, 1950 F, W, I, E, 1951 F, W, I, E, SA, 1952 F, W, I, E, 1953 E

Deans, C T (Hawick) 1978 F, W, E, NZ, 1979 W, E, I, F, NZ, 1980 I, F, 1981 F, W, E, I, NZ 1,2, R, A, 1982 E, I, F, W, A 1,2, 1983 I, F, W, E, NZ, 1984 W, E, I, F, A, 1985 I, F, W, E, 1986 F, W, E, I, R, 1987 I, F, W, [F, Z, R, NZ]

Deans, D T (Hawick) 1968 E

Deas, D W (Heriot's FP) 1947 F, W

De Luca, N J (Edinburgh) 2008 F, W, I(t&R), Arg 2(R), NZ, SA, C, 2009 F(R), It(R), I(R), E(R), Fj(R), A(R), Arg(R), 2010 It(R), E, I, Arg 1, 2(R), 2011 F, W, I1, E(R), It1(R), I2(R), It2, [Gg, Arg, E(R)], 2012 E, W, F(R), It, A, Fj

Denton, D K (Edinburgh) 2011 I2(R), 2012 E,W,F,I,It

Dewey, R E (Edinburgh, Ulster) 2006 R, 2007 E(R), W, It, I1, F, I2, SA, [Pt, R, NZ(R), It, Arg]

Dick, L G (Loughborough Colls, Jordanhill, Swansea) 1972 W (R), E, 1974 W, E, I, F, 1975 I, F, W, E, NZ, A, 1976 F, 1977 E

Dick, R C S (Cambridge U, Guy's Hospital) 1934 W, I, E, 1935 W, I, E, NZ, 1936 W, I, E, 1937 W, 1938 W, I, E

Dickinson, A G (Gloucester, Sale) 2007 [NZ], 2008 E(R),It(R),Arg 1(R),2(t&R),NZ(R), SA(R),C(R), 2009 W(t&R),F,It(R),I,E, 2010 F,W,It(R),I(R),Arg 2(R),NZ(t&R), 2011 I2(R),It2,[R(R),Arg(R),E(R)]

Dickson, G (Gala) 1978 NZ, 1979 W, E, I, F, NZ, 1980 W, 1981 F, 1982 W (R)

Dickson, M R (Edinburgh U) 1905 I

Dickson, W M (Blackheath, Oxford U) 1912 F, W, E, SA, 1913 F, W, I

Di Rollo, M P (Edinburgh) 2002 US (R), 2005 R,Arg,Sm,NZ, 2006 F,E,I,It,SA 1,2, R,PI

Dobson, J (Glasgow Acads) 1911 E, 1912 F, W, I, E, SA

Dobson, J D (Glasgow Acads) 1910 I

Dobson, W G (Heriot's FP) 1922 W, I, E

Docherty, J T (Glasgow HSFP) 1955 F, W, 1956 E, 1958 F, W, A, I, E

Dods, F P (Edinburgh Acads) 1901 I

Dods, J H (Edinburgh Acads) 1895 W, I, E, 1896 W, I, E, 1897 I, E

Dods, M (Gala, Northampton) 1994 I (t), Arg 1,2, 1995 WS, 1996 I, F, W, E

Dods, P W (Gala) 1983 I, F, W, E, NZ, 1984 W, E, I, F, R, A, 1985 I, F, W, E, 1989 W, E, I, F, 1991 I (R), R, [Z, NZ (R)]

Donald, D G (Oxford U) 1914 W, I

Donald, R L H (Glasgow HSFP) 1921 W, I, E

Donaldson, W P (Oxford U, W of Scotland) 1893 I, 1894 I, 1895 E, 1896 I, E, 1899 I

Don-Wauchope, A R (Fettesian-Lorettonians) 1881 E, 1882 E, 1883 W, 1884 W, I, E, 1885 W, I 1,2, 1886 W, I, E, 1888 I

Don-Wauchope, P H (Fettesian-Lorettonians) 1885 I 1,2, 1886 W, 1887 I, W, E

Dorward, A F (Cambridge U, Gala) 1950 F, 1951 SA, 1952 W, I, E, 1953 F, W, E, 1955 F, 1956 I, E, 1957 F, W, I, E

Dorward, T F (Gala) 1938 W, I, E, 1939 I, E

Douglas, B A F (Borders) 2002 R, SA, Fj, 2003 I 1, F, W 1, E, It 1, SA 1, 2, It 2, W 2, [J, US(t&R), F(R), Fj, A], 2004 W, E, It, F, I, Sm, A1, 2, 3, A4(R), SA(R), 2005 F, I(R), It(R), W(R), E(R), R, Arg, NZ, 2006 W, E, I, It, SA 1, 2(R)

Douglas, G (Jedforest) 1921 W

Douglas, J (Stewart's Coll FP) 1961 F, SA, W, I, E, 1962 F, W, I, E, 1963 F, W, I

Douty, P S (London Scottish) 1927 A, 1928 F, W

Drew, D (Glasgow Acads) 1871 E, 1876 E

Druitt, W A H (London Scottish) 1936 W, I, E

Drummond, A H (Kelvinside Acads) 1938 W, I

Drummond, C W (Melrose) 1947 F, W, I, E, 1948 F, I, E, 1950 F, W, I, E

Drybrough, A S (Edinburgh Wands, Merchistonians) 1902 I, 1903 I

Dryden, R H (Watsonians) 1937 E

Drysdale, D (Heriot's FP) 1923 F, W, I, E, 1924 F, W, I, E, 1925 F, W, I, E, 1926 F, W, I, E, 1927 F, W, I, E, A, 1928 F, W, I, E, 1929 F

Duff, P L (Glasgow Acads) 1936 W, I, 1938 W, I, E, 1939 W

Duffy, H (Jedforest) 1955 F

Duke, A (Royal HSFP) 1888 W, I, 1889 W, I, 1890 W, I

Dunbar, J P A (Leeds) 2005 F(R), It(R)

Duncan, A W (Edinburgh U) 1901 W, I, E, 1902 W, I, E

Duncan, D D (Oxford U) 1920 F, W, I, E

Duncan, M D F (W of Scotland) 1986 F, W, E, R, 1987 I, F, W, E, [F, Z, R, NZ], 1988 I, F, W, E, A, 1989 W

Duncan, M M (Fettesian-Lorettonians) 1888 W

Dunlop, J W (W of Scotland) 1875 E

Dunlop, Q (W of Scotland) 1971 E (2[1C])

Dykes, A S (Glasgow Acads) 1932 E

Dykes, J C (Glasgow Acads) 1922 F, E, 1924 I, 1925 F, W, I, 1926 F, W, I, E, 1927 F, W, I, E, A, 1928 F, I, 1929 F, W, I

Dykes, J M (Clydesdale, Glasgow HSFP) 1898 I, E, 1899 W, E, 1900 W, I, 1901 W, I, E, 1902 E

Edwards, D B (Heriot's FP) 1960 I, E, SA

Edwards, N G B (Harlequins, Northampton) 1992 E, I, F, W, A 1, 1994 W

Elgie, M K (London Scottish) 1954 NZ, I, E, W, 1955 F, W, I, E

Elliot, C (Langholm) 1958 E, 1959 F, 1960 F, 1963 E, 1964 F, NZ, W, I, E, 1965 F, W, I

Elliot, M (Hawick) 1895 W, 1896 E, 1897 I, E, 1898 I, E

Elliot, T (Gala) 1905 E
Elliot, T (Gala) 1955 W, I, E, 1956 F, W, I, E, 1957 F, W, I, E, 1958 W, A, I
Elliot, T G (Langholm) 1968 W, A, 1969 F, W, 1970 E
Elliot, W I D (Edinburgh Acads) 1947 F, W, E, A, 1948 F, W, I, E, 1949 F, W, I, E, 1950 F, W, I, E, 1951 F, W, I, E, SA, 1952 F, W, I, E, 1954 NZ, I, E, W
Ellis, D G (Currie) 1997 W, E, I, F
Emslie, W D (Royal HSFP) 1930 F, 1932 I
Eriksson, B R S (London Scottish) 1996 NZ 1, A, 1997 E
Evans, H L (Edinburgh U) 1885 I 1,2
Evans, M B (Glasgow Warriors, Castres) 2008 C(R), 2009 W(R), F, It, I, E, 2010 F, W(t&R), It, E, I, Arg 1, 2, NZ, Sm(R), 2011 F, W, I1, E, It2, [R, Gg, Arg, E], 2012 E, W, I, It, Fj, Sm(R)
Evans, T H (Glasgow Warriors) 2008 Arg 1,NZ,SA, 2009 F,It,I,E,Arg, 2010 F,W
Ewart, E N (Glasgow Acads) 1879 E, 1880 I, E

Fahmy, E C (Abertillery) 1920 F, W, I, E
Fairley, I T (Kelso, Edinburgh) 1999 It, I (R), [Sp (R)]
Fasson, F H (London Scottish, Edinburgh Wands) 1900 W, 1901 W, I, 1902 W, E
Fell, A N (Edinburgh U) 1901 W, I, E, 1902 W, E, 1903 W, E
Ferguson, J H (Gala) 1928 W
Ferguson, W G (Royal HSFP) 1927 A, 1928 F, W, I, E
Fergusson, E A J (Oxford U) 1954 F, NZ, I, E, W
Finlay, A B (Edinburgh Acads) 1875 E
Finlay, J F (Edinburgh Acads) 1871 E, 1872 E, 1874 E, 1875 E, 1880 I, E, 1881 I, E
Finlay, N J (Edinburgh Acads) 1875 E, 1876 E, 1878 E, 1879 I, E, 1880 I, E, 1881 I, E
Finlay, R (Watsonians) 1948 E
Fisher, A T (Waterloo, Watsonians) 1947 I, E
Fisher, C D (Waterloo) 1975 NZ, A, 1976 W, E, I
Fisher, D (W of Scotland) 1893 I
Fisher, J P (Royal HSFP, London Scottish) 1963 E, 1964 F, NZ, W, I, E, 1965 F, W, I, E, SA, 1966 F, W, I, E, A, 1967 F, W, I, E, NZ, 1968 F, W, I, E
Fleming, C J N (Edinburgh Wands) 1896 I, E, 1897 I
Fleming, G R (Glasgow Acads) 1875 E, 1876 E
Fletcher, H N (Edinburgh U) 1904 E, 1905 W
Flett, A B (Edinburgh U) 1901 W, I, E, 1902 W, I
Forbes, J L (Watsonians) 1905 W, 1906 I, E
Ford, D St C (United Services, RN) 1930 I, E, 1931 E, 1932 W, I
Ford, J R (Gala) 1893 I
Ford, R W (Borders, Glasgow, Edinburgh) 2004 A3(R), 2006 W(R), E(R), PI(R), A(R), 2007 E(R), W(R), It(R), I1(R), F, I2, SA, [Pt(R), R, It, Arg], 2008 F, W, I, E, Arg 1, 2, NZ, SA, C, 2009 W, F, It, I, E, Fj, A, Arg, 2010 F, W, It, E, I, Arg 1, 2, NZ, SA, Sm, 2011 F, W, I1, E, It1, I2, [R, Gg, Arg, E], 2012 E, W, F, I, It, A, Fj, Sm
Forrest, J E (Glasgow Acads) 1932 SA, 1935 E, NZ
Forrest, J G S (Cambridge U) 1938 W, I, E
Forrest, W T (Hawick) 1903 W, I, E, 1904 W, I, E, 1905 W, I
Forsayth, H H (Oxford U) 1921 F, W, I, E, 1922 W, I, E
Forsyth, I W (Stewart's Coll FP) 1972 NZ, 1973 F, W, I, E, P
Forsyth, J (Edinburgh U) 1871 E
Foster, R A (Hawick) 1930 W, 1932 SA, I, E
Fox, J (Gala) 1952 F, W, I, E
Frame, J N M (Edinburgh U, Gala) 1967 NZ, 1968 F, W, I, E, 1969 W, I, E, SA, 1970 F, W, I, E, A, 1971 F, W, I, E (2[1C]), 1972 F, W, E, 1973 P (R)
France, C (Kelvinside Acads) 1903 I
Fraser, C F P (Glasgow U) 1888 W, 1889 W
Fraser, J W (Edinburgh Inst FP) 1881 E
Fraser, R (Cambridge U) 1911 F, W, I, E
French, J (Glasgow Acads) 1886 W, 1887 I, W, E
Frew, A (Edinburgh U) 1901 W, I, E
Frew, G M (Glasgow HSFP) 1906 SA, 1907 W, I, E, 1908 W, I, E, 1909 W, I, E, 1910 F, W, I, 1911 I, E
Friebe, J P (Glasgow HSFP) 1952 E
Fullarton, I A (Edinburgh) 2000 NZ 1(R),2, 2001 NZ (R), 2003 It 2(R), I 2(t), 2004 Sm(R), A1(R),2
Fulton, A K (Edinburgh U, Dollar Acads) 1952 F, 1954 F
Fyfe, K C (Cambridge U, Sale, London Scottish) 1933 W, E, 1934 E, 1935 W, I, E, NZ, 1936 W, I, 1939 I

Gallie, G H (Edinburgh Acads) 1939 W
Gallie, R A (Glasgow Acads) 1920 F, W, I, E, 1921 F, W, I, E
Gammell, W B B (Edinburgh Wands) 1977 I, F, W, 1978 W, E

Geddes, I C (London Scottish) 1906 SA, 1907 W, I, E, 1908 W, E
Geddes, K I (London Scottish) 1947 F, W, I, E
Gedge, H T S (Oxford U, London Scottish, Edinburgh Wands) 1894 W, I, E, 1896 E, 1899 W, E
Gedge, P M S (Edinburgh Wands) 1933 I
Gemmill, R (Glasgow HSFP) 1950 F, W, I, E, 1951 F, W, I
Gibson, W R (Royal HSFP) 1891 I, E, 1892 W, I, E, 1893 W, I, E, 1894 W, I, E, 1895 W, I, E
Gilbert-Smith, D S (London Scottish) 1952 E
Gilchrist, J (Glasgow Acads) 1925 F
Gill, A D (Gala) 1973 P, 1974 W, E, I, F
Gillespie, J I (Edinburgh Acads) 1899 E, 1900 W, E, 1901 W, I, E, 1902 W, I, 1904 I, E
Gillies, A C (Watsonians) 1924 W, I, E, 1925 F, W, E, 1926 F, W, 1927 F, W, I, E
Gilmour, H R (Heriot's FP) 1998 Fj
Gilray, C M (Oxford U, London Scottish) 1908 E, 1909 W, E, 1912 I
Glasgow, I C (Heriot's FP) 1997 F (R)
Glasgow, R J C (Dunfermline) 1962 F, W, I, E, 1963 I, E, 1964 I, E, 1965 W, I
Glen, W S (Edinburgh Wands) 1955 W
Gloag, L G (Cambridge U) 1949 F, W, I, E
Godman, P J (Edinburgh) 2005 R(R), Sm(R), NZ(R), 2006 R, PI(R), A(t&R), 2007 W, It, 2008 Arg 2, NZ, SA, C, 2009 W, F, It, I, E, Fj, A, Arg, 2010 F, W(R), E(R)
Goodfellow, J (Langholm) 1928 W, I, E
Goodhue, F W J (London Scottish) 1890 W, I, E, 1891 W, I, E, 1892 W, I, E
Gordon, R (Edinburgh Wands) 1951 W, 1952 F, W, I, E, 1953 W
Gordon, R E (Royal Artillery) 1913 F, W, I
Gordon, R J (London Scottish) 1982 A 1,2
Gore, A C (London Scottish) 1882 I
Gossman, B M (W of Scotland) 1980 W, 1983 F, W
Gossman, J S (W of Scotland) 1980 E (R)
Gowans, J J (Cambridge U, London Scottish) 1893 W, 1894 W, E, 1895 W, I, E, 1896 I, E
Gowlland, G C (London Scottish) 1908 W, 1909 W, E, 1910 F, W, I, E
Gracie, A L (Harlequins) 1921 F, W, I, E, 1922 F, W, I, E, 1923 F, W, I, E, 1924 F
Graham, G (Newcastle) 1997 A (R), SA (R), 1998 I, F (R), W (R), 1999 F (R), Arg (R), R, [SA, U, Sm, NZ (R)], 2000 I (R), US, A, Sm, 2001 I (R), Tg (R), Arg (R), NZ (R), 2002 E (R), It (R), I (R), F (R), W (R)
Graham, I N (Edinburgh Acads) 1939 I, E
Graham, J (Kelso) 1926 I, E, 1927 F, W, I, E, A, 1928 F, W, I, E, 1930 I, E, 1932 SA, W
Graham, J H S (Edinburgh Acads) 1876 E, 1877 I, E, 1878 E, 1879 I, E, 1880 I, E, 1881 I, E
Grant, D (Hawick) 1965 F, E, SA, 1966 F, W, I, E, A, 1967 F, W, I, E, NZ, 1968 F
Grant, D M (East Midlands) 1911 W, I
Grant, M L (Harlequins) 1955 F, 1956 F, W, 1957 F
Grant, R (Glasgow Warriors) 2012 A,Fj,Sm
Grant, T O (Hawick) 1960 I, E, SA, 1964 F, NZ, W
Grant, W St C (Craigmount) 1873 E, 1874 E
Gray, C A (Nottingham) 1989 W, E, I, F, Fj, R, 1990 I, F, W, E, NZ 1,2, Arg, 1991 F, W, E, I, [J, I, WS, E, NZ]
Gray, D (W of Scotland) 1978 E, 1979 I, F, NZ, 1980 I, F, W, E, 1981 F
Gray, G L (Gala) 1935 NZ, 1937 W, I, E
Gray, R J (Glasgow Warriors, Sale) 2010 F(R), W(R), I(R), NZ, SA, Sm, 2011 F, I1, E, It1, I2, It2(R), [R, Gg(R), Arg, E], 2012 E, W, F, I, It, A, Fj, Sm
Gray, S D (Borders, Northampton) 2004 A3, 2008 NZ(R), SA(R), C(R), 2009 W(R), It(R), I(R), E
Gray, T (Northampton, Heriot's FP) 1950 E, 1951 F, E
Greenlees, H D (Leicester) 1927 A, 1928 F, W, 1929 I, E, 1930 E
Greenlees, J R C (Cambridge U, Kelvinside Acads) 1900 I, 1902 W, I, E, 1903 W, I, E
Greenwood, J T (Dunfermline and Perthshire Acads) 1952 F, 1955 F, W, I, E, 1956 F, W, I, E, 1957 F, W, E, 1958 F, W, A, I, E, 1959 F, W, I
Greig, A (Glasgow HSFP) 1911 I
Greig, L L (Glasgow Acads, United Services) 1905 NZ, 1906 SA, 1907 W, 1908 W, I
Greig, R C (Glasgow Acads) 1893 W, 1897 I
Grieve, C F (Oxford U) 1935 W, 1936 E

SCOTLAND

Grieve, R M (Kelso) 1935 W, I, E, NZ, 1936 W, I, E
Grimes, S B (Watsonians, Newcastle) 1997 A (t+R), 1998 I (R), F (R), W (R), E (R), Fj, A 1, 2, 1999 W (R), E, It, I, F, Arg, R, [SA, U, Sm (R), NZ (R)], 2000 It, I, F (R), W, US, A, Sm (R), 2001 F (R), W (R), E (R), It, I (R), Tg, Arg, NZ, 2002 E, It, I, F (R), W (R), C, US, R, SA, Fj, 2003 I 1, F, W 1, E(R), It 1(R), W 2, I 2, [J, US, F, Fj, A], 2004 W, E, It, F, I, Sm, A1, J, A4, SA, 2005 F, I, It, W, E(R)
Grove, A (Worcester) 2009 Fj,A,Arg
Gunn, A W (Royal HSFP) 1912 F, W, I, SA, 1913 F

Hall, A J A (Glasgow) 2002 US (R)
Hall, D W H (Edinburgh, Edinburgh Rugby, Glasgow Warriors) 2003 W 2(R), 2005 R(R), Arg, Sm(R), NZ(R), 2006 F, E, I, It(R), SA 1(R), 2, R, PI, A, 2007 E, W, It, I1, F(R), 2008 Arg 2(R), NZ(R), SA(R), C(R), 2009 W(R), F(R), It(R), I(R), E(R), Fj(R), A(R), Arg(R), 2010 SA(R), Sm(R), 2011 F(R), I2(R), It2(R), [Arg(R)]
Hamilton, A S (Headingley) 1914 W, 1920 F
Hamilton, C P (Newcastle) 2004 A2(R), 2005 R,Arg,Sm,NZ
Hamilton, H M (W of Scotland) 1874 E, 1875 E
Hamilton, J L (Leicester, Edinburgh, Gloucester) 2006 R(R), A(R), 2007 E, W, It(R), I1(R), F(R), I2, SA, [R, NZ(R), It, Arg], 2008 F, W, I(R), NZ, SA, C, 2009 W, F, I, E, 2010 W, It, E, I, Arg 1, 2, NZ, Sm(R), 2011 I2, [Gg, Arg], 2012 E, W, F, I, It
Hannah, R S M (W of Scotland) 1971 I
Harley, R (Glasgow Warriors) 2012 Sm(R)
Harrower, P R (London Scottish) 1885 W
Hart, J G M (London Scottish) 1951 SA
Hart, T M (Glasgow U) 1930 W, I
Hart, W (Melrose) 1960 SA
Harvey, L (Greenock Wands) 1899 I
Hastie, A J (Melrose) 1961 W, I, E, 1964 I, E, 1965 E, SA, 1966 F, W, I, E, A, 1967 F, W, I, NZ, 1968 F, W
Hastie, I R (Kelso) 1955 F, 1958 F, E, 1959 F, W, I
Hastie, J D H (Melrose) 1938 W, I, E
Hastings, A G (Cambridge U, Watsonians, London Scottish) 1986 F, W, E, I, R, 1987 I, F, W, E, [F, Z, R, NZ], 1988 I, F, W, E, A, 1989 Fj, R, 1990 I, F, W, E, NZ 1,2, Arg, 1991 F, W, E, I, [J, I, WS, E, NZ], 1992 E, I, F, W, A 1, 1993 I, F, W, E, NZ, 1994 W, E, I, F, SA, 1995 C, I, F, W, E, R, [Iv, Tg, F, NZ]
Hastings, S (Watsonians) 1986 F, W, E, I, R, 1987 I, F, W, [R], 1988 I, F, W, A, 1989 W, E, I, F, Fj, R, 1990 I, F, W, E, NZ 1,2, Arg, 1991 F, W, E, I, [J, Z, I, WS, E, NZ], 1992 E, I, F, W, A 1,2, 1993 I, F, W, E, NZ, 1994 E, I, F, SA, 1995 W, E, R (R), [Tg, F, NZ], 1996 I, F, W, E, NZ 2, It, 1997 W, E (R)
Hay, B H (Boroughmuir) 1975 NZ, A, 1976 F, 1978 I, F, W, E, NZ, 1979 W, E, I, F, NZ, 1980 I, F, W, E, 1981 F, W, E, I, NZ 1,2
Hay, J A (Hawick) 1995 WS
Hay-Gordon, J R (Edinburgh Acads) 1875 E, 1877 I, E
Hegarty, C B (Hawick) 1978 I, F, W, E
Hegarty, J J (Hawick) 1951 F, 1953 F, W, I, E, 1955 F
Henderson, A R (Glasgow Warriors) 2001 I (R), Tg (R), NZ (R), 2002 It, I, US (R), 2003 SA 1,2, It 2, I 2, [US, F, Fj, A], 2004 W, E(t&R), It(R), F, I, Sm, A1, 2, 3, J, A4, SA, 2005 W(R), R, Arg, Sm, NZ, 2006 F, W, E, I, It, SA 1, 2, PI, A, 2007 E, It(R), I1(R), F, I2, SA, [NZ, It(R), Arg(R)], 2008 F, W, I, It(R)
Henderson, B C (Edinburgh Wands) 1963 E, 1964 F, I, E, 1965 F, W, I, E, 1966 F, W, I, E
Henderson, F W (London Scottish) 1900 W, I
Henderson, I C (Edinburgh Acads) 1939 I, E, 1947 F, W, E, A, 1948 I, E
Henderson, J H (Oxford U, Richmond) 1953 F, W, I, E, 1954 F, NZ, I, E, W
Henderson, J M (Edinburgh Acads) 1933 W, E, I
Henderson, J Y M (Watsonians) 1911 E
Henderson, M M (Dunfermline) 1937 W, I, E
Henderson, N F (London Scottish) 1892 I
Henderson, R G (Newcastle Northern) 1924 I, E
Hendrie, K G P (Heriot's FP) 1924 F, W, I
Hendry, T L (Clydesdale) 1893 W, I, E, 1895 I
Henriksen, E H (Royal HSFP) 1953 I
Hepburn, D P (Woodford) 1947 A, 1948 F, W, I, E, 1949 F, W, I, E
Heron, G (Glasgow Acads) 1874 E, 1875 E
Hill, C C P (St Andrew's U) 1912 F, I
Hilton, D I W (Bath, Glasgow) 1995 C, I, F, W, E, R, [Tg, F, NZ], WS, 1996 I, F, W, E, NZ 1,2, A, It, 1997 W, A, SA, 1998 It, I (R), F, W, E, A 1,2, SA, (R) 1999 W (R), E (R), It (R), I (R), F,

R (R), [SA (R), U (R), Sp], 2000 It (R), F (R), W (R), 2002 SA(R)
Hines, N J (Edinburgh, Glasgow, Perpignan, Leinster, Clermont-Auvergne) 2000 NZ 2(R), 2002 C, US, R(R), SA(R), Fj(R), 2003 W 1(R), E, It 1, SA 1,2, It 2, W 2(R), I 2, [US, F(R), Fj, A], 2004 E(R), It(R), F(R), I(R), A3, J, A4, SA, 2005 F(R), I(R), It(R), W(R), E, 2006 E(R), I, It, SA 1, 2, R, PI, 2007 W(R), It, I1, F, I2, SA, [Pt, R, It, Arg], 2008 F, W, I, E, It, NZ, SA, C, 2009 I(R), E(R), Fj, A, Arg, 2010 F, It(R), E(R), NZ(R), SA, Sm, 2011 F, W, I1(R), E, It1, 2, [R(R), Gg, Arg(R), E(R)]
Hinshelwood, A J W (London Scottish) 1966 F, W, I, E, A, 1967 F, W, I, E, NZ, 1968 F, W, I, E, A, 1969 F, W, I, SA, 1970 F, W
Hinshelwood, B G (Worcester) 2002 C (R), R(R), SA(R), Fj, 2003 It 2, [J, US(R), Fj(R), A(R)], 2004 W, E, It, Sm, A1, 2, J, A4, SA, 2005 It(R)
Hodge D W (Watsonians, Edinburgh) 1997 F (R), A, SA (t+R), 1998 A 2(R), SA, 1999 W, Arg, R, [Sp, Sm (R)], 2000 F (R), W, E, NZ 1,2, US (R), Sm (R), 2001 F (R), W, E, It, I (R), 2002 E, W (R), C, US
Hodgson, C G (London Scottish) 1968 I, E
Hogg, A (Edinburgh) 2004 W, E(R), It, F(R), I, Sm, A1, 2, 3, J, A4, SA, 2005 F, I, It, W, E, R, Arg, Sm, NZ, 2006 F, W, E, I, It, SA 1, 2, 2007 E(R), W(R), It(R), I1(R), F, I2, SA(t&R), [Pt, R, It, Arg], 2008 W(R), I, E, It, Arg 1, 2, NZ, SA, 2009 W
Hogg, C D (Melrose) 1992 A 1,2, 1993 NZ (R), 1994 Arg 1,2
Hogg, C D (Boroughmuir) 1978 F (R), W (R)
Hogg, S W (Glasgow Warriors) 2012 W(R),F,I,It,A,Fj,Sm
Holmes, S D (London Scottish) 1998 It, I, F
Holms, W F (RIE Coll) 1886 W, E, 1887 I, E, 1889 W, I
Horsburgh, G B (London Scottish) 1937 W, I, E, 1938 W, I, E, 1939 W, I, E
Howie, D D (Kirkcaldy) 1912 F, W, I, E, SA, 1913 F, W
Howie, R A (Kirkcaldy) 1924 F, W, I, E, 1925 W, I, E
Hoyer-Millar, G C (Oxford U) 1953 I
Huggan, J L (London Scottish) 1914 E
Hume, J (Royal HSFP) 1912 F, 1920 F, 1921 F, W, I, E, 1922 F
Hume, J W G (Oxford U, Edinburgh Wands) 1928 I, 1930 F
Hunter, F (Edinburgh U) 1882 I
Hunter, I G (Selkirk) 1984 I (R), 1985 F (R), W, E
Hunter, J M (Cambridge U) 1947 F
Hunter, M D (Glasgow High) 1974 F
Hunter, W J (Hawick) 1964 F, NZ, W, 1967 F, W, I, E
Hutchison, W R (Glasgow HSFP) 1911 E
Hutton, A H M (Dunfermline) 1932 I
Hutton, J E (Harlequins) 1930 E, 1931 F

Inglis, H M (Edinburgh Acads) 1951 F, W, I, E, SA, 1952 W, I
Inglis, J M (Selkirk) 1952 E
Inglis, W M (Cambridge U, Royal Engineers) 1937 W, I, E, 1938 W, I, E
Innes, J R S (Aberdeen GSFP) 1939 W, I, E, 1947 A, 1948 F, W, I, E
Ireland, J C H (Glasgow HSFP) 1925 W, I, E, 1926 F, W, I, E, 1927 F, W, I, E
Irvine, A R (Heriot's FP) 1972 NZ, 1973 F, W, I, E, P, 1974 W, E, I, F, 1975 I, F, W, E, NZ, A, 1976 F, W, E, I, 1977 E, I, F, W, 1978 I, F, E, NZ, 1979 W, E, I, F, NZ, 1980 I, F, W, E, 1981 F, W, E, I, NZ 1,2, R, A, 1982 E, I, F, W, A 1,2
Irvine, D R (Edinburgh Acads) 1878 E, 1879 I, E
Irvine, R W (Edinburgh Acads) 1871 E, 1872 E, 1873 E, 1874 E, 1875 E, 1876 E, 1877 I, E, 1878 E, 1879 I, E, 1880 I, E
Irvine, T W (Edinburgh Acads) 1885 I 1,2, 1886 W, I, E, 1887 I, E, 1888 W, I, 1889 I
Jackson, R J H (Glasgow Warriors) 2010 NZ(R), Sm(R), 2011 F(R), I1, E, It1, I2, It2(R), [R, Arg, E], 2012 I(R), It(R)
Jackson, K L T (Oxford U) 1933 W, E, I, 1934 W
Jackson, T G H (Army) 1947 F, W, E, A, 1948 F, W, I, E, 1949 F, W, I, E
Jackson, W D (Hawick) 1964 I, 1965 E, SA, 1968 A, 1969 F, W, I, E
Jacobsen, A F (Edinburgh) 2002 C (R), US, 2003 I 2, 2004 It, F, I, A3, J, A4, SA, 2005 R, Arg(R), Sm, 2006 R(R), PI(R), A(R), 2007 E(R), W(R), It(t&R), I1(R), F(R), I2, SA(R), [Pt], 2008 F, W, I, E, It, Arg 1, 2, NZ, SA, C, 2009 W, F, It, Fj, A, Arg, 2010 F(R), W(R), It, E, I, Arg 1, 2, NZ, SA, Sm, 2011 F, W, I1, I2, E, [Gg, Arg, E], 2012 E, W, F, I
Jamieson, J (W of Scotland) 1883 W, I, E, 1884 W, I, E, 1885 W, I 1,2
Jardine, I C (Stirling County) 1993 NZ, 1994 W, E (R), Arg 1,2,

1995 C, I, F, [Tg, F (t & R), NZ (R)], 1996 I, F, W, E, NZ 1,2, 1998 Fj

Jeffrey, J (Kelso) 1984 A, 1985 I, E, 1986 F, W, E, I, R, 1987 I, F, W, E, [F, Z, R], 1988 I, W, A, 1989 W, E, I, F, Fj, R, 1990 I, F, W, E, NZ 1,2, Arg, 1991 F, W, E, I, [J, I, WS, E, NZ]

Johnston, D I (Watsonians) 1979 NZ, 1980 I, F, W, E, 1981 R, A, 1982 E, I, F, W, A 1,2, 1983 I, F, W, NZ, 1984 W, E, I, F, R, 1986 F, W, E, I, R

Johnston, H H (Edinburgh Collegian FP) 1877 I, E

Johnston, J (Melrose) 1951 SA, 1952 F, W, I, E

Johnston, W C (Glasgow HSFP) 1922 F

Johnston, W G S (Cambridge U) 1935 W, I, 1937 W, I, E

Joiner, C A (Melrose, Leicester) 1994 Arg 1,2, 1995 C, I, F, W, E, R, [Iv, Tg, F, NZ], 1996 I, F, W, E, NZ 1, 1997 SA, 1998 It, I, A 2(R), 2000 NZ 1(R),2, US (R)

Jones, L (Edinburgh) 2012 E,W,F,I

Jones, P M (Gloucester) 1992 W (R)

Junor, J G (Glasgow Acads) 1876 E, 1877 I, E, 1878 E, 1879 E, 1881 I

Kalman, E D (Glasgow Warriors) 2012 W(R),F(R)

Keddie, R R (Watsonians) 1967 NZ

Keith, G J (Wasps) 1968 F, W

Keller, D H (London Scottish) 1949 F, W, I, E, 1950 F, W, I

Kellock, A D (Edinburgh, Glasgow Warriors) 2004 A3(t&R), 2005 R(R), Arg(R), Sm(R), NZ(R), 2006 F, W, E, It(R), SA 1(R), 2, PI(R), A, 2007 E, 2008 Arg 1(t&R), 2(R), 2009 It, Fj, A, Arg, 2010 F, W, It, E, I, Arg 1, 2, 2011 F, W, It, E, It1, I2(R), It2, [R, E], 2012 E(R), W(R), F(R), I(R), It(R), A, Fj, Sm

Kelly, R F (Watsonians) 1927 A, 1928 F, W, E

Kemp, J W Y (Glasgow HSFP) 1954 W, 1955 F, W, I, E, 1956 F, W, I, E, 1957 F, W, I, E, 1958 F, W, A, I, E, 1959 F, W, I, E, 1960 F, W, I, E, SA

Kennedy, A E (Watsonians) 1983 NZ, 1984 W, E, A

Kennedy, F (Stewart's Coll FP) 1920 F, W, I, E, 1921 E

Kennedy, N (W of Scotland) 1903 W, I, E

Ker, A B M (Kelso) 1988 W, E

Ker, H T (Glasgow Acads) 1887 I, W, E, 1888 I, 1889 W, 1890 I, E

Kerr, D S (Heriot's FP) 1923 F, W, 1924 F, 1926 I, E, 1927 W, I, E, 1928 I, E

Kerr, G (Leeds, Borders, Glasgow, Edinburgh) 2003 I 1(R), F(R), W 1(R), E(R), SA 1, 2, W 2, [J(R), US, F], 2004 W(R), E(R), It(R), F(R), I(R), J, A4, SA, 2005 F, I, It, W, E, Arg, Sm(R), NZ, 2006 F, W, E, I, It, SA 1, 2, PI, A, 2007 E, W, It, I1, F, SA, [Pt(R), R, NZ(R), It, Arg], 2008 F(R), W(R), I(R)

Kerr, G C (Old Dunelmians, Edinburgh Wands) 1898 I, E, 1899 I, W, E, 1900 W, I, E

Kerr, J M (Heriot's FP) 1935 NZ, 1936 I, E, 1937 W, I

Kerr, R C (Glasgow) 2002 C, US, 2003 W 2

Kerr, W (London Scottish) 1953 E

Kidston, D W (Glasgow Acads) 1883 W, E

Kidston, W H (W of Scotland) 1874 E

Kilgour, I J (RMC Sandhurst) 1921 F

King, J H F (Selkirk) 1953 F, W, E, 1954 E

Kininmonth, P W (Oxford U, Richmond) 1949 F, W, I, E, 1950 F, W, I, E, 1951 F, W, I, E, SA, 1952 F, W, I, 1954 F, NZ, I, E, W

Kinnear, R M (Heriot's FP) 1926 F, W, I

Knox, J (Kelvinside Acads) 1903 W, I, E

Kyle, W E (Hawick) 1902 W, I, E, 1903 W, I, E, 1904 W, I, E, 1905 W, I, E, NZ, 1906 W, I, E, 1908 E, 1909 W, I, E, 1910 W

Laidlaw, A S (Hawick) 1897 I

Laidlaw, F A L (Melrose) 1965 F, W, I, E, SA, 1966 F, W, I, E, A, 1967 F, W, I, E, NZ, 1968 F, W, I, A, 1969 F, W, I, E, SA, 1970 F, W, I, A, 1971 F, W, I

Laidlaw, G D (Edinburgh) 2010 NZ(R), 2011 I2(R), 2012 E(R),W,F,I,It,A,Fj,Sm

Laidlaw, R J (Jedforest) 1980 I, F, W, E, 1981 F, W, E, I, NZ 1,2, R, A, 1982 E, I, F, W, A 1,2, 1983 I, F, W, E, NZ, 1984 W, E, I, F, R, A, 1985 I, F, 1986 F, W, E, I, R, 1987 I, F, W, E, [F, R, NZ], 1988 I, F, W, E

Laing, A D (Royal HSFP) 1914 W, I, E, 1920 F, W, I, 1921 F

Lambie, I K (Watsonians) 1978 NZ (R), 1979 W, E, NZ

Lambie, L B (Glasgow HSFP) 1934 W, I, E, 1935 W, I, E, NZ

Lamond, G A W (Kelvinside Acads) 1899 W, E, 1905 E

Lamont, R P (Glasgow, Sale, Toulon, Glasgow Warriors) 2005 W,E,R,Arg,Sm, 2007 E(R),I1(R),F(R),I2,SA, [Pt,R,It,Arg], 2008

F,I,E,SA,C, 2009 Fj,A,Arg, 2010 W,NZ, 2011 It2,[Gg], 2012 E,W,F

Lamont, S F (Glasgow, Northampton, Llanelli Scarlets) 2004 Sm,A1,2,3,J,A4,SA, 2005 F,I,It,W,E,R,Arg,Sm,NZ, 2006 F,W,E,I,It,SA1,R,PI,A, 2007 E,W,It,I1,F,I2,[Pt,R,It,Arg], 2008 NZ, 2009 W,Fj,A,Arg, 2010 F,W,It,E,I,Arg 1,2,NZ,SA,Sm, 2011 F(R),W(R),I1,E, It1,I2,[R,Gg,Arg,E], 2012 E,W,F,I,It,A,Fj(R),Sm

Laney, B J (Edinburgh) 2001 NZ, 2002 E, It, I, F, W, C, US, R, SA, Fj, 2003 I 1, F, SA 2(R), It 2(R), W 2, 2004 W,E,It,I(R)

Lang, D (Paisley) 1876 E, 1877 I

Langrish, R W (London Scottish) 1930 F, 1931 F, W, I

Lauder, W (Neath) 1969 I, E, SA, 1970 F, W, I, A, 1973 F, 1974 W, E, I, F, 1975 I, F, NZ, A, 1976 F, 1977 E

Laughland, I H P (London Scottish) 1959 F, 1960 F, W, I, E, 1961 SA, W, I, E, 1962 F, W, I, E, 1963 F, W, I, 1964 F, NZ, W, I, E, 1965 F, W, I, E, SA, 1966 F, W, I, E, 1967 E

Lawrie, J R (Melrose) 1922 F, W, I, E, 1923 F, W, I, E, 1924 W, I, E

Lawrie, K G (Gala) 1980 F (R), W, E

Lawson, A J M (Edinburgh Wands, London Scottish) 1972 F (R), E, 1973 F, 1974 W, E, 1976 E, I, 1977 E, 1978 NZ, 1979 W, E, I, F, NZ, 1980 W (R)

Lawson, R G M (Gloucester) 2006 A(R), 2007 E(R),W(R),It(R),I1(R),F,SA(R), [Pt(R), NZ(R)], 2008 E(R),Arg 1(R),2(R),NZ(R),SA(R),C(R), 2009 A(R),Arg(R), 2010 E(R), Arg 1,2,SA,Sm, 2011 F,W,I1(R),E,It1,I2,[Gg,Arg]

Lawson, S (Glasgow, Sale, Gloucester) 2005 R,Arg(R),Sm,NZ, 2006 F(R),W,I(R),It,SA 1,2(R),R(R), 2007 [Pt,R(R),NZ,Arg(R)], 2008 It(R), 2010 F(R),W(R),E(R),I(R),Arg1(R), 2(R),NZ(R), 2011 W(R),I1(R),E(R),It1(R),2,[R(R)], 2012 E(R),W(R),F(R),Fj(R),Sm(R)

Lawther, T H B (Old Millhillians) 1932 SA, W

Ledingham, G A (Aberdeen GSFP) 1913 F

Lee, D J (London Scottish, Edinburgh) 1998 I (R), F, W, E, Fj, A 1,2, SA, 2001 Arg, 2004 It(R),F,I(R)

Lees, J B (Gala) 1947 I, A, 1948 F, W, E

Leggatt, H T O (Watsonians) 1891 W, I, E, 1892 W, I, 1893 W, E, 1894 I, E

Lely, W G (Cambridge U, London Scottish) 1909 I

Leslie, D G (Dundee HSFP, W of Scotland, Gala) 1975 I, F, W, E, NZ, A, 1976 F, W, E, I, 1978 NZ, 1980 E, 1981 W, E, I, NZ 1,2, R, A, 1982 E, 1983 I, F, W, E, 1984 W, E, I, F, R, 1985 F, W, E

Leslie, J A (Glasgow, Northampton) 1998 SA, 1999 W, E, It, I, F, [SA], 2000 It, F, W, US, A, Sm, 2001 F, W, E, It, I, Tg, Arg, NZ, 2002 F, W

Leslie, M D (Glasgow, Edinburgh) 1998 SA (R), 1999 W, E, It, I, F, R, [SA, U, Sm, NZ], 2000 It, I, F, W, E, NZ 1,2, 2001 F, W, E, It, 2002 It (R), I, F, W, R, SA, Fj(R), 2003 I 1, F, SA 1(R), 2 (R), It 2(R), W 2, [J(R),US(R)]

Liddell, E H (Edinburgh U) 1922 F, W, I, 1923 F, W, I, E

Lind, H (Dunfermline) 1928 I, 1931 F, W, I, E, 1932 SA, W, E, 1933 W, E, I, 1934 W, I, E, 1935 I, 1936 E

Lindsay, A B (London Hospital) 1910 I, 1911 I

Lindsay, G C (London Scottish) 1884 W, 1885 I 1, 1887 W, E

Lindsay-Watson, R H (Hawick) 1909 I

Lineen, S R P (Boroughmuir) 1989 W, E, I, F, Fj, R, 1990 I, F, W, E, NZ 1,2, Arg, 1991 F, W, E, I, R, [J, Z, I, E, NZ], 1992 E, I, F, W, A 1,2

Little, A W (Hawick) 1905 W

Logan, K M (Stirling County, Wasps) 1992 A 2, 1993 E (R), NZ (t), 1994 W, E, I, F, Arg 1,2, SA, 1995 C, I, F, W, E, R, [Iv, Tg, F, NZ], WS, 1996 W (R), NZ 1,2, A, 1997 W, E, I, F, A, 1998 I, F, SA, 1999 W, E, It, I, F, Arg, R, [SA, U, Sm, NZ], 2000 It, I, F, Sm, 2001 F, W, E, It, 2002 I (R), F (R), W, 2003 I 1, F, W 1, E, It 1, SA 1,2, It 2, I 2, [J,US(R),F,Fj,A]

Logan, W R (Edinburgh U, Edinburgh Wands) 1931 E, 1932 SA, W, I, 1933 W, E, I, 1934 W, I, E, 1935 W, I, E, NZ, 1936 W, I, E, 1937 W, I, E

Longstaff, S L (Dundee HSFP, Glasgow) 1998 F (R), W, E, Fj, A 1,2 1999 It (R), I, Arg (R), R, [U (R), Sp], 2000 It, I, NZ 1

Lorraine, H D B (Oxford U) 1933 W, E, I

Loudoun-Shand, E G (Oxford U) 1913 E

Low, M J (Glasgow Warriors) 2009 F(R),E(R),Fj,A,Arg, 2010 F,Arg 1,2,SA(R),Sm(R), 2011 F(R),W(R),I1,E,It2

Lowe, J D (Heriot's FP) 1934 W

Lumsden, I J M (Bath, Watsonians) 1947 F, W, A, 1949 F, W, I, E

Lyall, G G (Gala) 1947 A, 1948 F, W, I, E

Lyall, W J C (Edinburgh Acads) 1871 E

Mather, C G (Edinburgh, Glasgow) 1999 R (R), [Sp, Sm (R)], 2000 F (t), 2003 [F,Fj,A], 2004 W,E,F

Maxwell, F T (Royal Engineers) 1872 E

Maxwell, G H H P (Edinburgh Acads, RAF, London Scottish) 1913 I, E, 1914 W, I, E, 1920 W, E, 1921 F, W, I, E, 1922 F, E

Maxwell, J M (Langholm) 1957 I

Mayer, M J M (Watsonians, Edinburgh) 1998 SA, 1999 [SA (R), U, Sp, Sm, NZ], 2000 It, I

Mein, J (Edinburgh Acads) 1871 E, 1872 E, 1873 E, 1874 E, 1875 E

Melville, C L (Army) 1937 W, I, E

Menzies, H F (W of Scotland) 1893 W, I, 1894 W, E

Metcalfe, G H (Glasgow Hawks, Glasgow) 1998 A 1,2, 1999 W, E, It, I, F, Arg, R, [SA, U, Sm, NZ], 2000 It, I, F, W, E, 2001 I, Tg, 2002 E, It, I, F, W (R), C, US, 2003 I 1, F, W 1, E, It 1, SA 1,2, W 2, I 2, [US,F,Fj,A]

Metcalfe, R (Northampton, Edinburgh) 2000 E, NZ 1,2, US (R), A (R), Sm, 2001 F, W, E

Methuen, A (London Scottish) 1889 W, I

Michie, E J S (Aberdeen U, Aberdeen GSFP) 1954 F, NZ, I, E, 1955 W, I, E, 1956 F, W, I, E, 1957 F, W, I, E

Millar, J N (W of Scotland) 1892 W, I, E, 1893 W, 1895 I, E

Millar, R K (London Scottish) 1924 I

Millican, J G (Edinburgh U) 1973 W, I, E

Milne, C J B (Fettesian-Lorettonians, W of Scotland) 1886 W, I, E

Milne, D F (Heriot's FP) 1991 [J(R)]

Milne, I G (Heriot's FP, Harlequins) 1979 I, F, NZ, 1980 I, F, 1981 NZ 1,2, R, A, 1982 E, I, F, W, A 1,2, 1983 I, F, W, E, NZ, 1984 W, E, I, F, A, 1985 F, W, E, 1986 F, W, E, I, R, 1987 I, F, W, E, [F, Z, NZ], 1988 A, 1989 W, 1990 NZ 1,2

Milne, K S (Heriot's FP) 1989 W, E, I, F, Fj, R, 1990 I, F, W, E, NZ 2, Arg, 1991 F, W (R), E, [Z], 1992 E, I, F, W, A 1, 1993 I, F, W, E, NZ, 1994 W, E, I, F, SA, 1995 C, I, F, W, E, [Tg, F, NZ]

Milne, W M (Glasgow Acads) 1904 I, E, 1905 W, I

Milroy, E (Watsonians) 1910 W, 1911 E, 1912 W, I, E, SA, 1913 F, W, I, E, 1914 I, E

Mitchell, G W E (Edinburgh Wands) 1967 NZ, 1968 F, W

Mitchell, J G (W of Scotland) 1885 W, I 1,2

Moffat, J S D (Edinburgh, Borders) 2002 R, SA, Fj(R), 2004 A3

Moir, C C (Northampton) 2000 W, E, NZ 1

Moncreiff, F J (Edinburgh Acads) 1871 E, 1872 E, 1873 E

Monteith, H G (Cambridge U, London Scottish) 1905 E, 1906 W, I, E, SA, 1907 W, I, 1908 E

Monypenny, D B (London Scottish) 1899 I, W, E

Moodie, A R (St Andrew's U) 1909 E, 1910 F, 1911 F

Moore, A (Edinburgh Acads) 1990 NZ 2, Arg, 1991 F, W, E

Morgan, D W (Stewart's-Melville FP) 1973 W, I, E, P, 1974 I, F, 1975 I, F, W, E, NZ, A, 1976 F, W, 1977 I, F, W, 1978 I, F, W, E

Morrison, G A (Glasgow Warriors) 2004 A1(R),2(R),3,J(R),A4(R),SA(R), 2008 W(R), E,It,Arg 1,2, 2009 W,F,It,I,E,Fj,A, 2010 F,W,It,E,I,Arg 1,2,NZ,SA,Sm, 2011 I2,It2, [Gg,Arg], 2012 F,I,It

Morrison, I R (London Scottish) 1993 I, F, W, E, 1994 W, SA, 1995 C, I, F, W, E, R, [Tg, F, NZ]

Morrison, M C (Royal HSFP) 1896 W, I, E, 1897 I, E, 1898 I, E, 1899 I, W, E, 1900 W, E, 1901 W, I, E, 1902 W, I, E, 1903 W, I, 1904 W, I, E

Morrison, R H (Edinburgh U) 1886 W, I, E

Morrison, W H (Edinburgh Acads) 1900 W

Morton, D S (W of Scotland) 1887 I, W, E, 1888 W, I, 1889 W, I, 1890 I, E

Mowat, J G (Glasgow Acads) 1883 W, E

Mower, A L (Newcastle) 2001 Tg, Arg, NZ, 2002 It, 2003 I 1, F, W 1, E, It 1, SA 1,2, W 2, I 2

Muir, D E (Heriot's FP) 1950 F, W, I, E, 1952 W, I, E

Munnoch, N M (Watsonians) 1952 F, W, I

Munro, D S (Glasgow High Kelvinside) 1994 W, E, I, F, Arg 1,2, 1997 W (R)

Munro, P (Oxford U, London Scottish) 1905 W, I, E, NZ, 1906 W, I, E, SA, 1907 I, E, 1911 F, W, I

Munro, R (St Andrew's U) 1871 E

Munro, S (Ayr, W of Scotland) 1980 I, F, 1981 F, W, E, I, NZ 1,2, R, 1984 W

Munro, W H (Glasgow HSFP) 1947 I, E

Murdoch, W C W (Hillhead HSFP) 1935 E, NZ, 1936 W, I, 1939 E, 1948 F, W, I, E

Murray, C A (Hawick, Edinburgh) 1998 E (R), Fj, A 1,2, SA, 1999 W, E, It, I, F, Arg, [SA, U, Sp, Sm, NZ], 2000 NZ 2, US, A, Sm, 2001 F, W, E, It (R), Tg, Arg

Murray, E A (Glasgow, Northampton, Newcastle) 2005 R(R), 2006 R,PI,A, 2007 E,W,It,I1,F,I2,SA, [Pt,R,It,Arg], 2008 F,W,I,E,It,Arg 1,2,NZ,SA,C, 2009 It,I,E, 2010 W,It,E,I,NZ,SA,Sm, 2011 F,W,It1(R),2(R),[Gg,E], 2012 E,I(R),It(R),A,Fj,Sm

Murray, G M (Glasgow Acads) 1921 I, 1926 W

Murray, H M (Glasgow U) 1936 W, I

Murray, K T (Hawick) 1985 I, F, W

Murray, R O (Cambridge U) 1935 W, E

Murray, S (Bedford, Saracens, Edinburgh) 1997 A, SA, 1998 It, Fj, A 1,2, SA, 1999 W, E, It, I, F, Arg, R, [SA, U, Sm, NZ], 2000 It, I, F, W, E, NZ 1, US, A, Sm, 2001 F, W, E, It, I, Tg, Arg, NZ, 2002 E, It, I, F, W, R, SA, 2003 I 1, F, W 1, E, It 1, SA 1,2, W 2, [J, F, A(R)], 2004 W, E, It, F, I, Sm, A1, 2, 2005 F, I, It, W, E, R, Arg, Sm, NZ, 2006 F, W, I, It, SA1, R, PI, A, 2007 E(t&R), W, It, I1, F, SA(R), [Pt, NZ]

Murray, W A K (London Scottish) 1920 F, I, 1921 F

Mustchin, M L (Edinburgh) 2008 Arg 1,2,NZ(R),SA(R),C(R)

Napier, H M (W of Scotland) 1877 I, E, 1878 E, 1879 I, E

Neill, J B (Edinburgh Acads) 1963 E, 1964 F, NZ, W, I, E, 1965 F

Neill, R M (Edinburgh Acads) 1901 E, 1902 I

Neilson, G T (W of Scotland) 1891 W, I, E, 1892 W, E, 1893 W, 1894 W, I, 1895 W, I, E, 1896 W, I, E

Neilson, J A (Glasgow Acads) 1878 E, 1879 E

Neilson, R T (W of Scotland) 1898 I, E, 1899 I, W, 1900 I, E

Neilson, T (W of Scotland) 1874 E

Neilson, W (Merchiston Castle School, Cambridge U, London Scottish) 1891 W, E, 1892 W, I, E, 1893 I, E, 1894 E, 1895 W, I, E, 1896 I, 1897 I, E

Neilson, W G (Merchistonians) 1894 E

Nelson, J B (Glasgow Acads) 1925 F, W, I, E, 1926 F, W, I, E, 1927 F, W, I, E, 1928 I, E, 1929 F, W, I, E, 1930 F, W, I, E, 1931 F, W, I

Nelson, T A (Oxford U) 1898 E

Nichol, J A (Royal HSFP) 1955 W, I, E

Nichol, S A (Selkirk) 1994 Arg 2(R)

Nicol, A D (Dundee HSFP, Bath, Glasgow) 1992 E, I, F, W, A 1,2, 1993 NZ, 1994 W, 1997 A, SA, 2000 I (R), F, W, E, NZ 1,2, 2001 F, W, E, I (R), Tg, Arg, NZ

Nimmo, C S (Watsonians) 1920 E

Ogilvy, C (Hawick) 1911 I, E, 1912 I

Oliver, G H (Hawick) 1987 [Z], 1990 NZ 2(R), 1991 [Z]

Oliver, G K (Gala) 1970 A

Orr, C E (W of Scotland) 1887 I, E, W, 1888 W, I, 1889 W, I, 1890 W, I, E, 1891 W, I, E, 1892 W, I, E

Orr, H J (London Scottish) 1903 W, I, E, 1904 W, I

Orr, J E (W of Scotland) 1889 I, 1890 W, I, E, 1891 W, I, E, 1892 W, I, E, 1893 I, E

Orr, J H (Edinburgh City Police) 1947 F, W

Osler, F L (Edinburgh U) 1911 F, W

Park, J (Royal HSFP) 1934 W

Parks, D A (Glasgow Warriors, Cardiff Blues) 2004 W(R), E(R), F(R), I, Sm(t&R), A1, 2, 3, J, A4, SA, 2005 F, I, It, W, R, Arg, Sm, NZ, 2006 F, W, E, I, It(R), SA1, PI, A, 2007 E, I1, F, I2(R), SA(R), [Pt, R, NZ(R), It, Arg], 2008 F, W, I(R), E(R), It, Arg 1, 2(R), NZ(R), SA(t), C(R), 2010 W, It, E, I, Arg 1, 2, NZ, SA, Sm, 2011 F, W, I1(R), E(R), It1(R), 2, [R(R), Gg, Arg(R), E(R)], 2012 E

Paterson, C D (Edinburgh, Gloucester) 1999 [Sp], 2000 F, W, E, NZ 1,2, US, A, Sm, 2001 F, W, E, It, I, NZ, 2002 E, It, I, F, W, C, US, R, SA, Fj, 2003 I 1, F, W, I 1, SA 1,2, E (R), W 2(R), I 2, [J, US, F, Fj, A], 2004 W, E, It, F, I, Sm, A3, J, A4, SA, 2005 F, I, It, W, E, R, Arg, Sm, NZ, 2006 F, W, E, I, It, SA 1, 2, R(R), PI, A, 2007 E, W, It, I1, F, I2, SA, [Pt(R), R, NZ, It, Arg], 2008 F(R), W, I, E, It, Arg 1, 2, NZ, SA, 2009 W(R), F(R), It(t&R), I, E, Fj(R), A(R), Arg(R), 2010 F, W, SA(R), 2011 I1, E, It1, I2, [R, Gg(R), Arg, E]

Paterson, D S (Gala) 1969 SA, 1970 I, E, A, 1971 F, W, I, E (2[1C]), 1972 W

Paterson, G Q (Edinburgh Acads) 1876 E

Paterson, J R (Birkenhead Park) 1925 F, W, I, E, 1926 F, W, I, E, 1927 F, W, I, E, A, 1928 F, W, I, E, 1929 F, W, I, E

Patterson, D (Hawick) 1896 W

Patterson, D W (West Hartlepool) 1994 SA, 1995 [Tg]

Pattullo, G L (Panmure) 1920 F, W, I, E

Paxton, I A M (Selkirk) 1981 NZ 1,2, R, A, 1982 E, I, F, W, A

Scott, T (Langholm, Hawick) 1896 W, 1897 I, E, 1898 I, E, 1899 I, W, E, 1900 W, I, E

Scott, T M (Hawick) 1893 E, 1895 W, I, E, 1896 W, E, 1897 I, E, 1898 I, E, 1900 W, I

Scott, W P (W of Scotland) 1900 I, E, 1902 I, E, 1903 W, I, E, 1904 W, I, E, 1905 W, I, E, NZ, 1906 W, I, E, SA, 1907 W, I, E

Scoular, J G (Cambridge U) 1905 NZ, 1906 W, I, E, SA

Selby, J A R (Watsonians) 1920 W, I

Shackleton, J A P (London Scottish) 1959 E, 1963 F, W, 1964 NZ, W, 1965 I, SA

Sharp, A V (Bristol) 1994 E, I, F, Arg 1,2 SA

Sharp, G (Stewart's FP, Army) 1960 F, 1964 F, NZ, W

Shaw, G D (Sale) 1935 NZ, 1936 W, 1937 W, I, E, 1939 I

Shaw, I (Glasgow HSFP) 1937 I

Shaw, J N (Edinburgh Acads) 1921 W, I

Shaw, R W (Glasgow HSFP) 1934 W, I, E, 1935 W, I, E, NZ, 1936 W, I, E, 1937 W, I, E, 1938 W, I, E, 1939 W, I, E

Shedden, D (W of Scotland) 1972 NZ, 1973 F, W, I, E, P, 1976 W, E, I, 1977 I, F, W, 1978 I, F, W

Shepherd, R J S (Melrose) 1995 WS, 1996 I, F, W, E, NZ 1,2, A, It, 1997 W, E, I, F, SA, 1998 It, I, W (R), Fj (t), A 1,2

Shiel, A G (Melrose, Edinburgh) 1991 [I (R), WS], 1993 I, F, W, E, NZ, 1994 Arg 1,2, SA, 1995 R, [Iv, F, NZ], WS, 2000 I, NZ 1(R),2

Shillinglaw, R B (Gala, Army) 1960 I, E, SA, 1961 F, SA

Simmers, B M (Glasgow Acads) 1965 F, W, 1966 A, 1967 F, W, I, 1971 F (R)

Simmers, W M (Glasgow Acads) 1926 W, I, E, 1927 F, W, I, E, A, 1928 F, W, I, E, 1929 F, W, I, E, 1930 F, W, I, E, 1931 F, W, I, E, 1932 SA, W, I, E

Simpson, G L (Kirkcaldy, Glasgow) 1998 A 1,2, 1999 Arg (R), R, [SA, U, Sm, NZ], 2000 It, I, NZ 1(R), 2001 I, Tg (R), Arg (R), NZ

Simpson, J W (Royal HSFP) 1893 I, E, 1894 W, I, E, 1895 W, I, E, 1896 W, I, 1897 E, 1899 W, E

Simpson, R S (Glasgow Acads) 1923 I

Simson, E D (Edinburgh U, London Scottish) 1902 E, 1903 W, I, E, 1904 W, I, E, 1905 W, I, E, NZ, 1906 W, I, E, 1907 W, I, 1911 I

Simson, J T (Watsonians) 1905 NZ, 1909 W, I, E, 1910 F, W, 1911 I

Simson, R F (London Scottish) 1911 E

Sloan, A T (Edinburgh Acads) 1914 W, 1920 F, W, I, E, 1921 F, W, I, E

Sloan, D A (Edinburgh Acads, London Scottish) 1950 F, W, E, 1951 W, I, E, 1953 F

Sloan, T (Glasgow Acads, Oxford U) 1905 NZ, 1906 W, SA, 1907 W, E, 1908 W, 1909 I

Smeaton, P W (Edinburgh Acads) 1881 I, 1883 I, E

Smith, A R (Oxford U) 1895 W, I, E, 1896 W, I, 1897 I, E, 1898 I, E, 1900 I, E

Smith, A R (Cambridge U, Gosforth, Ebbw Vale, Edinburgh Wands) 1955 W, I, E, 1956 F, W, I, E, 1957 F, W, I, E, 1958 F, W, A, I, 1959 F, W, I, E, 1960 F, W, I, E, SA, W, I, E, 1962 F, W, I, E

Smith, C J (Edinburgh) 2002 C, US (R), 2004 Sm(t&R), A1(R), 2(R), 3(R), J(R), 2005 Arg(R), Sm, NZ(R), 2006 F(R), W(R), E(R), I(R), It(R), SA 1(R), 2, R(R), 2007 I2(R), [R(R), NZ, It(R), Arg(R)], 2008 E(R), It(R)

Smith, D W C (London Scottish) 1949 F, W, I, E, 1950 F, W, I, 1953 I

Smith, E R (Edinburgh Acads) 1879 I

Smith, G K (Kelso) 1957 I, E, 1958 F, W, A, 1959 F, W, I, E, 1960 F, W, I, E, 1961 F, SA, W, I, E

Smith, H O (Watsonians) 1895 W, 1896 W, I, E, 1898 I, E, 1899 W, I, E, 1900 E, 1902 E

Smith, I R (Gloucester, Moseley) 1992 E, I, W, A 1,2, 1994 E (R), I, Arg 1,2, 1995 [Iv], WS, 1996 I, F, W, E, NZ 1,2, A, It, 1997 E, I, F, A, SA

Smith, I S (Oxford U, Edinburgh U) 1924 W, I, E, 1925 F, W, I, E, 1926 F, W, I, E, 1927 F, W, I, E, 1929 F, W, I, E, 1930 F, W, I, 1931 F, W, I, E, 1932 SA, W, I, E, 1933 W, E, I

Smith, I S G (London Scottish) 1969 SA, 1970 F, W, I, E, 1971 F, W, I

Smith, M A (London Scottish) 1970 W, I, E, A

Smith, R T (Kelso) 1929 F, W, I, E, 1930 F, W, I, E

Smith, S H (Glasgow Acads) 1877 I, 1878 E

Smith, T J (Gala) 1983 E, NZ, 1985 I, F

Smith, T J (Watsonians, Dundee HSFP, Glasgow, Brive,

Northampton) 1997 E, I, F, 1998 SA, 1999 W, E, It, I, Arg, R, [SA, U, Sm, NZ], 2000 It, I, F, W, E, NZ 1,2, US, A, Sm, 2001 F, W, E, It, I, Tg, Arg, NZ, 2002 E, It, I, F, W, R, SA, 2003 I 1, F, W 1, E, It 1,2, [J,US,F,Fj,A], 2004 W,E,Sm,A1,2,2005 F,I,It,W,E

Sole, D M B (Bath, Edinburgh Acads) 1986 F, W, 1987 I, F, W, E, [F, Z, R, NZ], 1988 I, F, W, E, A, 1989 W, E, I, F, Fj, R, 1990 I, F, W, E, NZ 1,2, Arg, 1991 F, W, E, I, R, [J, I, WS, E, NZ], 1992 E, I, F, W, A 1,2

Somerville, D (Edinburgh Inst FP) 1879 I, 1882 I, 1883 W, I, E, 1884 W

Southwell, H F G (Edinburgh, Stade Français) 2004 Sm(t&R),A1,2,3(R),J,A4,SA,2005 F,I,It,W,E,R(R),Arg(R),Sm(R),NZ, 2006 F,W,E,I,It,SA 1,2, 2006 R,PI(t&R),A(R), 2007 E,W,It,I1,SA(R), [Pt(R),R(R),NZ,It(R),Arg(R)], 2008 F(R),W,I,E,It,Arg 2,NZ(R),SA(R), 2009 W,F,It,E(R), 2010 F(R),It,E,I,Arg 1,2,NZ,SA,Sm, 2011 F,W

Speirs, L M (Watsonians) 1906 SA, 1907 W, I, E, 1908 W, I, E, 1910 F, W, E

Spence, K M (Oxford U) 1953 I

Spencer, E (Clydesdale) 1898 I

Stagg, P K (Sale) 1965 F, W, E, SA, 1966 F, W, I, E, A, 1967 F, W, I, E, NZ, 1968 F, W, I, E, A, 1969 F, W, I (R), SA, 1970 F, W, I, E, A

Stanger, A G (Hawick) 1989 Fj, R, 1990 I, F, W, E, NZ 1,2, Arg, 1991 F, W, E, I, R, [J, Z, I, WS, E, NZ], 1992 E, I, F, W, A 1,2, 1993 I, F, W, E, NZ, 1994 W, E, I, F, SA, 1995 R, [Iv], 1996 NZ 2, A, It, 1997 W, E, I, F, A, SA, 1998 It, I (R), F, W, E

Stark, D A (Boroughmuir, Melrose, Glasgow Hawks) 1993 I, F, W, E, 1996 NZ 2(R), It (R), 1997 W (R), E, SA

Steel, J F (Glasgow) 2000 US, A, 2001 I, Tg, NZ

Steele, W C C (Langholm, Bedford, RAF, London Scottish) 1969 E, 1971 F, W, I, E (2[1C]), 1972 F, W, E, NZ, 1973 F, W, I, E, 1975 I, F, W, E, NZ (R), 1976 W, E, I, 1977 E

Stephen, A E (W of Scotland) 1885 W, 1886 I

Steven, P D (Heriot's FP) 1984 A, 1985 F, W, E

Steven, R (Edinburgh Wands) 1962 I

Stevenson, A K (Glasgow Acads) 1922 F, 1923 F, W, E

Stevenson, A M (Glasgow U) 1911 F

Stevenson, G D (Hawick) 1956 E, 1957 F, 1958 F, W, A, I, E, 1959 W, I, E, 1960 W, I, E, SA, 1961 F, SA, W, I, E, 1963 F, W, I, 1964 E, 1965 F

Stevenson, H J (Edinburgh Acads) 1888 W, I, 1889 W, I, 1890 W, I, E, 1891 W, I, E, 1892 W, I, E, 1893 I, E

Stevenson, L E (Edinburgh U) 1888 W

Stevenson, R C (London Scottish) 1897 I, E, 1898 E, 1899 I, W, E

Stevenson, R C (St Andrew's U) 1910 F, I, E, 1911 F, W, I

Stevenson, W H (Glasgow Acads) 1925 F

Stewart, A K (Edinburgh U) 1874 E, 1876 E

Stewart, A M (Edinburgh Acads) 1914 W

Stewart, B D (Edinburgh Acads, Edinburgh) 1996 NZ 2, A, 2000 NZ 1,2

Stewart, C A R (W of Scotland) 1880 I, E

Stewart, C E B (Kelso) 1960 W, 1961 F

Stewart, J (Glasgow HSFP) 1930 F

Stewart, J L (Edinburgh Acads) 1921 I

Stewart M J (Northampton) 1996 It, 1997 W, E, I, F, A, SA, 1998 It, I, F, W, Fj (R), 2000 It, I, F, W, E, NZ 1(R), 2001 F, W, E, It, I, Tg, Arg, NZ, 2002 E, It, I, F, W, C, US, R(R)

Stewart, M S (Stewart's Coll FP) 1932 SA, W, I, 1933 W, E, I, 1934 W, I, E

Stewart, W A (London Hospital) 1913 F, W, I, 1914 W

Steyn, S S L (Oxford U) 1911 E, 1912 I

Strachan, G M (Jordanhill) 1971 E (C) (R), 1973 W, I, E, P

Strokosch, A K (Edinburgh, Gloucester) 2006 A(R), 2008 I, E, It, Arg 1, 2, C, 2009 F, It, I, E, Fj, A, Arg, 2010 It(R), Arg 1(R), 2(R), 2011 It(R), I2, [Gg, Arg, E], 2012 E, W, A, Fj, Sm

Stronach, R S (Glasgow Acads) 1901 W, E, 1905 W, I, E

Stuart, C D (W of Scotland) 1909 I, 1910 F, W, I, E, 1911 I, E

Stuart, L M (Glasgow HSFP) 1923 F, W, I, E, 1924 F, 1928 E, 1930 I, E

Suddon, N (Hawick) 1965 W, I, E, SA, 1966 A, 1968 E, A, 1969 F, W, I, 1970 I, E, A

Sutherland, W R (Hawick) 1910 W, E, 1911 F, E, 1912 F, W, E, SA, 1913 F, W, I, E, 1914 W

Swan, J S (Army, London Scottish, Leicester) 1953 E, 1954 F, NZ, I, E, W, 1955 F, W, I, E, 1956 F, W, I, E, 1957 F, W, 1958 F

[J,US(R),F,Fj(R),A], 2004 W(R),E,It,F,I,Sm,A1,2,J(R),A4(R), SA, 2005 F, I, E, Arg, Sm, NZ, 2006 F, W, E, I, It, SA 1, 2, R, 2007 I2, SA, [Pt, R, It, Arg], 2008 F, W, E(R), It(R), NZ, SA, 2009 W, F, It, I, E, Fj(R), A(R), Arg(R)

White, T B (Edinburgh Acads) 1888 W, I, 1889 W

Whittington, T P (Merchistonians) 1873 E

Whitworth, R J E (London Scottish) 1936 I

Whyte, D J (Edinburgh Wands) 1965 W, I, E, SA, 1966 F, W, I, E, A, 1967 F, W, I, E

Will, J G (Cambridge U) 1912 F, W, I, E, 1914 W, I, E

Wilson, A W (Dunfermline) 1931 F, I, E

Wilson, A W (Glasgow) 2005 R(R)

Wilson, G A (Oxford U) 1949 F, W, E

Wilson, G R (Royal HSFP) 1886 E, 1890 W, I, E, 1891 I

Wilson, J H (Watsonians) 1953 I

Wilson, J S (St Andrew's U) 1931 F, W, I, E, 1932 E

Wilson, J S (United Services, London Scottish) 1908 I, 1909 W

Wilson, R (London Scottish) 1976 E, I, 1977 E, I, F, 1978 I, F, 1981 R, 1983 I

Wilson, R L (Gala) 1951 F, W, I, E, SA, 1953 F, W, E

Wilson, R W (W of Scotland) 1873 E, 1874 E

Wilson, S (Oxford U, London Scottish) 1964 F, NZ, W, I, E, 1965 W, I, E, SA, 1966 F, W, I, A, 1967 F, W, I, E, NZ, 1968 F, W, I, E

Wood, A (Royal HSFP) 1873 E, 1874 E, 1875 E

Wood, G (Gala) 1931 W, I, 1932 W, I, E

Woodburn, J C (Kelvinside Acads) 1892 I

Woodrow, A N (Glasgow Acads) 1887 I, W, E

Wotherspoon, W (W of Scotland) 1891 I, 1892 I, 1893 W, E, 1894 W, I, E

Wright, F A (Edinburgh Acads) 1932 E

Wright, H B (Watsonians) 1894 W

Wright, K M (London Scottish) 1929 F, W, I, E

Wright, P H (Boroughmuir) 1992 A 1,2, 1993 F, W, E, 1994 W, 1995 C, I, F, W, E, R, [Iv, Tg, F, NZ], 1996 W, E, NZ 1

Wright, R W J (Edinburgh Wands) 1973 F

Wright, S T H (Stewart's Coll FP) 1949 E

Wright, T (Hawick) 1947 A

Wyllie, D S (Stewart's-Melville FP) 1984 A, 1985 W (R), E, 1987 I, F, [F, Z, R, NZ], 1989 R, 1991 R, [J (R), Z], 1993 NZ (R), 1994 W (R), E, I, F

Young, A H (Edinburgh Acads) 1874 E

Young, E T (Glasgow Acads) 1914 E

Young, R G (Watsonians) 1970 W

Young, T E B (Durham) 1911 F

Young, W B (Cambridge U, London Scottish) 1937 W, I, E, 1938 W, I, E, 1939 W, I, E, 1948 E

455

SCOTLAND

Ruan Pienaar kicks the ball upfield during The Rugby Championship.

SOUTH AFRICA

SOUTH AFRICA'S 2012 TEST RECORD

OPPONENTS	DATE	VENUE	RESULT
England	9 Jun	H	Won 22–17
England	16 Jun	H	Won 36–27
England	23 Jun	H	Drew 14–14
Argentina	18 Aug	H	Won 27–6
Argentina	25 Aug	A	Drew 16–16
Australia	8 Sep	A	Lost 26–19
New Zealand	15 Sep	A	Lost 21–11
Australia	29 Sep	H	Won 31–8
New Zealand	6 Oct	H	Lost 16–32

SPRINGBOKS BEGIN REBUILDING PROCESS

By Iain Spragg

Morné Steyn scores a try against England in the first Test under new coach Heyneke Meyer.

South Africa enjoyed fluctuating fortunes in Heyneke Meyer's first season as Springbok head coach, claiming a series victory over England in the summer but failing to make a serious impression on the inaugural Rugby Championship later in the year.

Meyer replaced Peter de Villiers in the wake of South Africa's disappointing Rugby World Cup 2011 campaign in New Zealand but after his side had overpowered England in the first two of their three Tests, they were unable to replicate that dominance in The Rugby Championship and recorded just two wins in six games to finish a distant and disappointing third in the final table.

A lacklustre Tri-Nations challenge in 2011, followed by the side's World Cup exit in the quarter-finals to Australia, meant South African expectations were uncharacteristically muted when Meyer was unveiled in January and the new coach caught the cautious mood of the nation when he spoke at his first press conference.

"It would be easy to promise the world, but I need to plan very thoroughly," he said. "I want to get the support of everyone behind the team and to do that I have to pick the best possible team. I don't want to make promises I can't keep. It's truly humbling but also a huge honour and responsibility because the Springboks carry the hopes and dreams of the whole country.

"Having been involved with the Blue Bulls for so long, I've experienced first hand how passionate South African rugby supporters are. I know the importance of rugby in the South African psyche and will do everything in my power to ensure the Springboks remain among the pacesetters of world rugby."

Meyer's first squad contained nine uncapped players as England touched down in South Africa for the first time since 2007 and following the retirement of John Smit, Stormers centre Jean de Villiers was named as the new captain.

Three uncapped players – second rows Eben Etzebeth and Juandre Kruger and flanker Marcell Coetzee – made Meyer's starting XV for the first Test and it was to be a winning start for the new coach as his team outscored the visitors two tries to one to post a 22–17 win in Durban.

Two early penalties from England fly half Owen Farrell initially put the home side on the back foot but when Morné Steyn dived over in the corner seven minutes into the second half, South Africa established an advantage they did not relinquish and a second try from de Villiers was enough to dampen the tourists' challenge.

Meyer made minimal changes for the second Test in Johannesburg, with Pat Lambie at full back for the injured Zane Kirchner the only difference in the starting XV, and for the first 50 minutes of the contest a repeat performance seemed assured as Willem Alberts, Bismarck du Plessis and Francois Hougaard crossed to establish a commanding 28–10 lead.

England rallied, however, with two tries from Ben Youngs to close the gap to just four points after 64 minutes and the Springboks were eventually indebted to the brilliance of JP Pietersen, who sparked and then finished a sweeping move that brought South Africa their fourth try and a 36–27 win.

"In the first half we played Super Rugby rugby and it was great to watch," Meyer said. "But to put two performances like that together for 80 minutes is tough. We will learn a lot from games like that."

With the series victory confirmed, Meyer's team prepared for the third Test targeting a 10th successive win against the English but they were denied in a rain-soaked Port Elizabeth by a gutsy performance by the team in white.

England drew first blood with a 10th-minute try from scrum half

Danny Care but three Steyn penalties before the break redressed the balance while the pivotal moment came on the hour when Pietersen danced over. Farrell attempted a speculative last-gasp drop goal to steal the match but it missed and at the final whistle it was all square at 14–14.

"All credit to England, I thought they adapted much better than us to the conditions," Meyer said after only the second ever draw between the two countries. "They kicked it behind us one or two times and defended for their lives. It is no use making excuses. They had a great game and we didn't adapt well. Our guys need to learn. A lot of these guys haven't played in these conditions at Test level."

With a new-look England side in their own phase of rebuilding under a new coach, Meyer knew The Rugby Championship would prove a far sterner test of his side's credentials and overall it was to be an underwhelming campaign.

The Springboks kicked off against Argentina in Cape Town and there were no real alarms for the home team as the South Africa back row in particular, ably supported by the boot of Steyn, asserted their authority. Kirchner, Coetzee and Bryan Habana ran in the three tries and South Africa claimed a 27–6 win to start the new tournament in perfect style.

Seven days later the Springboks were in Argentina for the return fixture, and in their own backyard the Pumas were an altogether tougher nut to crack.

Centre Santiago Fernández scored for Argentina after 16 minutes and, although Steyn kept the visitors in contention with three successful penalties, South Africa still needed a slice of luck to escape from Mendoza with a 16–16 draw, Frans Steyn charging down a clearance after 64 minutes for a vital, if fortuitous, try.

"It was a tough game, a frustrating game," de Villiers admitted. "We couldn't get momentum and we conceded too many penalties. We need to play better. We need to change from our mistakes. I think that is the big thing. We are a young team but we are representing our country and that's a lot of responsibility. We need to learn from these mistakes and play better next time against Australia."

The clash with the Wallabies in Perth in early September did not result in the improvements the captain wanted. The early signs were good with Habana crossing after 19 minutes but the Springboks were unable to protect their 13–6 advantage at the break as the second half unfolded and tries from Scott Higginbotham and Ben Alexander earned the Australians a 26–19 triumph.

South Africa's season was rapidly unravelling and the task did not get any easier when they faced the All Blacks in Dunedin in the fourth instalment of the tournament.

The final scoreline of 21–11 to New Zealand was not what Meyer had hoped for but a much-improved performance from his troops did at least provide proof the team was heading in the right direction. South Africa, however, needed a victory and they had to wait a fortnight until it arrived.

It came in Pretoria against Australia and as soon as Kirchner went over midway through the first half, the Springboks looked in total control. Habana helped himself to a hat-trick to take his superb career tally of Test tries to 46 while Francois Louw added a fifth and South Africa, if not their coach, were able to celebrate a comprehensive 31–8 victory.

"We have very high standards and there were three more tries that we should have scored," Meyer said. "It's great to come home and win. We haven't beaten the Aussies for some time but we have to start taking those opportunities. We would like to score more tries next week against New Zealand but we are aware of the challenge of playing the world champions.

"They're the world champions and one of the reasons for that is their defence. It's going to be really difficult to create and score against them. We will need to be more patient with ball in hand, more tactically astute. If we get scoring opportunities, we will need to make them count."

In the early exchanges against the All Blacks in Soweto, Meyer's side did exactly that. Two missed penalties from fly half Johan Goosen were disappointing but his profligacy was forgotten in the 12th minute when de Villiers seized on a loose ball in midfield and sent Habana speeding away for the opening try of the match. Goosen converted and a subsequent penalty saw the Springboks race into a 10–0 lead.

It was inevitable New Zealand would respond and the catalyst for their comeback was a try from Sam Whitelock after 25 minutes. Three further New Zealand scores followed either side of the break and in the second half South Africa could only reply with two penalties as the newly crowned Rugby Championship champions came out 32–16 winners.

"We are improving but we came up against a quality side in New Zealand today," said de Villiers. "We know that they have a good defensive system but we just kept chipping away at them. It was a very similar game to the first match in Dunedin. We had our opportunities but we were not able to capitalise."

Defeat condemned South Africa to third behind Australia in the table with Argentina in fourth. It meant Meyer had recorded four wins, three losses and two draws in his first nine Tests at the helm and the coach was keen to emphasise the positives of the Springboks' new era.

"Although we're still the second-best team in the world," he said before the IRB World Rankings updated and South Africa fell to third, "we still have a long way to go. There's a huge difference between second and first."

SOUTH AFRICA INTERNATIONAL STATISTICS

MATCH RECORDS UP TO 10 OCTOBER 2012

MOST CONSECUTIVE TEST WINS

17 1997 A2,It, F 1,2, E,S, 1998 I 1,2,W 1,E 1, A 1,NZ 1,2, A 2, W 2, S, I 3
15 1994 Arg 1,2, S, W 1995 WS, A, R, C, WS, F, NZ, W, It, E, 1996 Fj

MOST CONSECUTIVE TESTS WITHOUT DEFEAT

Matches	Wins	Draws	Period
17	17	0	1997 to 1998
16	15	1	1994 to 1996
15	12	3	1960 to 1963

MOST POINTS IN A MATCH
BY THE TEAM

Pts	Opponents	Venue	Year
134	Uruguay	E London	2005
105	Namibia	Cape Town	2007
101	Italy	Durban	1999
96	Wales	Pretoria	1998
87	Namibia	Albany	2011
74	Tonga	Cape Town	1997
74	Italy	Port Elizabeth	1999
72	Uruguay	Perth	2003
68	Scotland	Murrayfield	1997
64	USA	Montpellier	2007
63	Argentina	Johannesburg	2008
62	Italy	Bologna	1997
61	Australia	Pretoria	1997

BY A PLAYER

Pts	Player	Opponents	Venue	Year
35	P C Montgomery	Namibia	Cape Town	2007
34	J H de Beer	England	Paris	1999
31	P C Montgomery	Wales	Pretoria	1998
31	M Steyn	N Zealand	Durban	2009
30	T Chavhanga	Uruguay	E London	2005
29	G S du Toit	Italy	Port Elizabeth	1999
29	P C Montgomery	Samoa	Paris	2007
28	G K Johnson	W Samoa	Johannesburg	1995
26	J H de Beer	Australia	Pretoria	1997
26	P C Montgomery	Scotland	Murrayfield	1997
26	M Steyn	Italy	East London	2010
25	J T Stransky	Australia	Bloemfontein	1996
25	C S Terblanche	Italy	Durban	1999

MOST TRIES IN A MATCH
BY THE TEAM

Tries	Opponents	Venue	Year
21	Uruguay	E London	2005
15	Wales	Pretoria	1998
15	Italy	Durban	1999
15	Namibia	Cape Town	2007
12	Tonga	Cape Town	1997
12	Uruguay	Perth	2003
12	Namibia	Albany	2011
11	Italy	Port Elizabeth	1999
10	Ireland	Dublin	1912
10	Scotland	Murrayfield	1997

BY A PLAYER

Tries	Player	Opponents	Venue	Year
6	T Chavhanga	Uruguay	E London	2005
5	C S Terblanche	Italy	Durban	1999
4	C M Williams	W Samoa	Johannesburg	1995
4	P W G Rossouw	France	Parc des Princes	1997
4	C S Terblanche	Ireland	Bloemfontein	1998
4	B G Habana	Samoa	Paris	2007
4	J L Nokwe	Australia	Johannesburg	2008

MOST CONVERSIONS IN A MATCH
BY THE TEAM

Cons	Opponents	Venue	Year
13	Italy	Durban	1999
13	Uruguay	E London	2005
12	Namibia	Cape Town	2007
12	Namibia	Albany	2011
9	Scotland	Murrayfield	1997
9	Wales	Pretoria	1998
9	Argentina	Johannesburg	2008
8	Italy	Port Elizabeth	1999
8	USA	Montpellier	2007
7	Scotland	Murrayfield	1951
7	Tonga	Cape Town	1997
7	Italy	Bologna	1997
7	France	Parc des Princes	1997
7	Italy	Genoa	2001
7	Samoa	Pretoria	2002
7	Samoa	Brisbane	2003
7	England	Bloemfontein	2007
7	Italy	East London	2010

BY A PLAYER

Cons	Player	Opponents	Venue	Year
12	P C Montgomery	Namibia	Cape Town	2007
9	P C Montgomery	Wales	Pretoria	1998
9	A D James	Argentina	Johannesburg	2008
8	P C Montgomery	Scotland	Murrayfield	1997
8	G S du Toit	Italy	Port Elizabeth	1999
8	G S du Toit	Italy	Durban	1999
7	A O Geffin	Scotland	Murrayfield	1951
7	J M F Lubbe	Tonga	Cape Town	1997
7	H W Honiball	Italy	Bologna	1997
7	H W Honiball	France	Parc des Princes	1997
7	A S Pretorius	Samoa	Pretoria	2002
7	J N B van der Westhuyzen	Uruguay	E London	2005
7	P C Montgomery	England	Bloemfontein	2007

MOST PENALTIES IN A MATCH
BY THE TEAM

Pens	Opponents	Venue	Year
8	Scotland	Port Elizabeth	2006
8	N Zealand	Durban	2009
7	France	Pretoria	1975
7	France	Cape Town	2006
7	Australia	Cape Town	2009
6	Australia	Bloemfontein	1996
6	Australia	Twickenham	1999
6	England	Pretoria	2000
6	Australia	Durban	2000
6	France	Johannesburg	2001
6	Scotland	Johannesburg	2003
6	N Zealand	Bloemfontein	2009
6	Australia	Bloemfontein	2010

BY A PLAYER

Pens	Player	Opponents	Venue	Year
8	M Steyn	N Zealand	Durban	2009
7	P C Montgomery	Scotland	Port Elizabeth	2006
7	P C Montgomery	France	Cape Town	2006
7	M Steyn	Australia	Cape Town	2009
6	G R Bosch	France	Pretoria	1975
6	J T Stransky	Australia	Bloemfontein	1996
6	J H de Beer	Australia	Twickenham	1999
6	A J J van Straaten	England	Pretoria	2000
6	A J J van Straaten	Australia	Durban	2000
6	P C Montgomery	France	Johannesburg	2001
6	L J Koen	Scotland	Johannesburg	2003
6	M Steyn	Australia	Bloemfontein	2010

SOUTH AFRICA

Drops	Opponents	Venue	Year
MOST DROP GOALS IN A MATCH BY THE TEAM			
5	England	Paris	1999
4	England	Twickenham	2006
3	S America	Durban	1980
3	Ireland	Durban	1981
3	Scotland	Murrayfield	2004

Drops	Player	Opponents	Venue	Year
MOST DROP GOALS IN A MATCH BY A PLAYER				
5	J H de Beer	England	Paris	1999
4	A S Pretorius	England	Twickenham	2006
3	H E Botha	S America	Durban	1980
3	H E Botha	Ireland	Durban	1981
3	J N B van der Westhuyzen	Scotland	Murrayfield	2004
2	B L Osler	N Zealand	Durban	1928
2	H E Botha	NZ Cavaliers	Cape Town	1986
2	J T Stransky	N Zealand	Johannesburg	1995
2	J H de Beer	N Zealand	Johannesburg	1997
2	P C Montgomery	N Zealand	Cardiff	1999
2	F P L Steyn	Australia	Cape Town	2007

CAREER RECORDS

THE COUNTRIES

MOST CAPPED PLAYERS

Caps	Player	Career Span
111	J W Smit	2000 to 2011
110	V Matfield	2001 to 2011
102	P C Montgomery	1997 to 2008
89	J H van der Westhuizen	1993 to 2003
83	B G Habana	2004 to 2012
81	J de Villiers	2002 to 2012
80	J P du Randt	1994 to 2007
77	M G Andrews	1994 to 2001
76	J P Botha	2002 to 2011
73	C J van der Linde	2002 to 2011
69	J H Smith	2003 to 2010
69	J Fourie	2003 to 2011
68	S W P Burger	2003 to 2011
66	A G Venter	1996 to 2001
64	B J Paulse	1999 to 2007
63	D J Rossouw	2003 to 2011
62	P F du Preez	2004 to 2011
60	R Pienaar	2006 to 2012
54	A-H le Roux	1994 to 2002
53	F P L Steyn	2006 to 2012
52	J C van Niekerk	2001 to 2010
51	P A van den Berg	1999 to 2007
50	P J Spies	2006 to 2012
47	J T Small	1992 to 1997
47	E R Januarie	2005 to 2010
46	B W du Plessis	2007 to 2012
45	J-P R Pietersen	2006 to 2012

MOST POINTS IN TESTS

Points	Player	Tests	Career
893	P C Montgomery	102	1997 to 2008
486	M Steyn	41	2009 to 2012
312	H E Botha	28	1980 to 1992
240	J T Stransky	22	1993 to 1996
235	B G Habana	83	2004 to 2012
221	A J J van Straaten	21	1999 to 2001
190	J H van der Westhuizen	89	1993 to 2003
181	J H de Beer	13	1997 to 1999
171	A S Pretorius	31	2002 to 2007
160	J Fourie	69	2003 to 2011
156	H W Honiball	35	1993 to 1999
154	A D James	42	2001 to 2011
145	L J Koen	15	2000 to 2003
135*	B J Paulse	64	1999 to 2007
132	F P L Steyn	53	2006 to 2012
130	P J Visagie	25	1967 to 1971

* includes a penalty try

MOST TRIES IN TESTS

Tries	Player	Tests	Career
47	B G Habana	83	2004 to 2012
38	J H van der Westhuizen	89	1993 to 2003
32	J Fourie	69	2003 to 2011
27*	B J Paulse	64	1999 to 2007
25	P C Montgomery	102	1997 to 2008
21	P W G Rossouw	43	1997 to 2003
20	J T Small	47	1992 to 1997
20	J de Villiers	81	2002 to 2012
19	D M Gerber	24	1980 to 1992
19	C S Terblanche	37	1998 to 2003
14	C M Williams	27	1993 to 2000
14	J-P R Pietersen	45	2006 to 2012

* includes a penalty try

MOST CONSECUTIVE TESTS

Tests	Player	Span
46	J W Smit	2003 to 2007
39	G H Teichmann	1996 to 1999
28	V Matfield	2008 to 2010
26	A H Snyman	1996 to 1998
26	A N Vos	1999 to 2001
25	S H Nomis	1967 to 1972
25	A G Venter	1997 to 1999
25	A-H le Roux	1998 to 1999

MOST TESTS AS CAPTAIN

Tests	Captain	Span
83	J W Smit	2003 to 2011
36	G H Teichmann	1996 to 1999
29	J F Pienaar	1993 to 1996
22	D J de Villiers	1965 to 1970
18	C P J Krigé	1999 to 2003
17	V Matfield	2007 to 2011
16	A N Vos	1999 to 2001
15	M du Plessis	1975 to 1980
12	R B Skinstad	2001 to 2007
11	J F K Marais	1971 to 1974

MOST DROP GOALS IN TESTS

Drops	Player	Tests	Career
18	H E Botha	28	1980 to 1992
8	J H de Beer	13	1997 to 1999
8	A S Pretorius	31	2002 to 2007
8	M Steyn	41	2009 to 2012
6	P C Montgomery	102	1997 to 2008
5	J D Brewis	10	1949 to 1953
5	P J Visagie	25	1967 to 1971
4	B L Osler	17	1924 to 1933

MOST CONVERSIONS IN TESTS

Cons	Player	Tests	Career
153	P C Montgomery	102	1997 to 2008
59	M Steyn	41	2009 to 2012
50	H E Botha	28	1980 to 1992
38	H W Honiball	35	1993 to 1999
33	J H de Beer	13	1997 to 1999
31	A S Pretorius	31	2002 to 2007
30	J T Stransky	22	1993 to 1996
26	A D James	42	2001 to 2011
25	G S du Toit	14	1998 to 2006
23	A J J van Straaten	21	1999 to 2001
23	L J Koen	15	2000 to 2003
22	R Pienaar	60	2006 to 2012
20	P J Visagie	25	1967 to 1971

MOST PENALTY GOALS IN TESTS

Penalties	Player	Tests	Career
148	P C Montgomery	102	1997 to 2008
103	M Steyn	41	2009 to 2012
55	A J J van Straaten	21	1999 to 2001
50	H E Botha	28	1980 to 1992
47	J T Stransky	22	1993 to 1996
31	L J Koen	15	2000 to 2003
28	A D James	42	2001 to 2011
27	J H de Beer	13	1997 to 1999
25	H W Honiball	35	1993 to 1999
25	A S Pretorius	31	2002 to 2007
23	G R Bosch	9	1974 to 1976
21	F P L Steyn	53	2006 to 2012
19	P J Visagie	25	1967 to 1971

SOUTH AFRICA

RUGBY CHAMPIONSHIP (FORMERLY TRI-NATIONS) RECORDS

RECORD	DETAIL		SET
Most points in season	158	in six matches	2009
Most tries in season	18	in four matches	1997
Highest Score	61	61-22 v Australia (h)	1997
Biggest win	45	53-8 v Australia (h)	2008
Highest score conceded	55	35-55 v N Zealand (a)	1997
Biggest defeat	49	0-49 v Australia (a)	2006
Most appearances	44	V Matfield	2001 to 2011
Most points in matches	232	M Steyn	2009 to 2012
Most points in season	95	M Steyn	2009
Most points in match	31	M Steyn	v N Zealand (h), 2009
Most tries in matches	14	B G Habana	2005 to 2012
Most tries in season	7	B G Habana	2012
Most tries in match	4	J L Nokwe	v Australia (h) 2008
Most cons in matches	26	P C Montgomery	1997 to 2008
Most cons in season	12	J H de Beer	1997
Most cons in match	6	J H de Beer	v Australia (h),1997
Most pens in matches	57	M Steyn	2009 to 2012
Most pens in season	23	M Steyn	2009
Most pens in match	8	M Steyn	v N Zealand (h), 2009

MISCELLANEOUS RECORDS

RECORD	HOLDER	DETAIL
Longest Test Career	J P du Randt	1994-2007
Youngest Test Cap	A J Hartley	18 yrs 18 days in 1891
Oldest Test Cap	J N Ackermann	37 yrs 34 days in 2007

UP TO 10 OCTOBER 2012

PLAYER	Debut	Caps	T	C	P	D	Pts
BACKS :							
G G Aplon	2010 v W	17	5	0	0	0	25
B A Basson	2010 v W	6	0	0	0	0	0
J L de Jongh	2010 v W	12	3	0	0	0	15
J de Villiers	2002 v F	81	20	0	0	0	100
P F du Preez	2004 v I	62	13	0	0	0	65
J J Engelbrecht	2012 v Arg	1	0	0	0	0	0
J Fourie	2003 v U	69	32	0	0	0	160
J L Goosen	2012 v A	4	0	1	2	0	8
B G Habana	2004 v E	83	47	0	0	0	235
F Hougaard	2009 v It	24	4	0	0	0	20
E T Jantjies	2012 v A	2	0	0	2	0	6
Z Kirchner	2009 v BI	21	3	0	0	0	15
P Lambie	2010 v I	17	0	3	0	0	6
C McLeod	2011 v NZ	1	0	0	0	0	0
L N Mvovo	2010 v S	7	1	0	0	0	5
O M Ndungane	2008 v It	9	2	0	0	0	10
W Olivier	2006 v S	37	1	0	0	0	5
R Pienaar	2006 v NZ	60	6	22	17	0	125
J-P R Pietersen	2006 v A	45	14	0	0	0	70
F P L Steyn	2006 v I	53	10	5	21	3	132
M Steyn	2009 v BI	41	7	59	103	8	486
J J Taute	2012 v A	2	0	0	0	0	0
FORWARDS :							
W S Alberts	2010 v W	17	4	0	0	0	20
A Bekker	2008 v W	29	1	0	0	0	5
P M Cilliers	2012 v Arg	4	0	0	0	0	0
M C Coetzee	2012 v E	9	1	0	0	0	5
K R Daniel	2010 v I	5	0	0	0	0	0
J R Deysel	2009 v It	4	0	0	0	0	0
B W du Plessis	2007 v A	46	6	0	0	0	30
J N du Plessis	2007 v A	39	1	0	0	0	5
E Etzebeth	2012 v E	8	0	0	0	0	0
M D Greyling	2011 v A	3	0	0	0	0	0
A J Hargreaves	2010 v W	4	0	0	0	0	0
A F Johnson	2011 v A	3	0	0	0	0	0
R Kankowski	2007 v W	20	1	0	0	0	5

SOUTH AFRICA

P J J Kruger	2012 v E	5	0	0	0	0	0
W Kruger	2011 v A	4	0	0	0	0	0
C R Liebenberg	2012 v Arg	5	0	0	0	0	0
L-F P Louw	2010 v W	14	3	0	0	0	15
G Mostert	2011 v NZ	2	0	0	0	0	0
T Mtawarira	2008 v W	41	2	0	0	0	10
C V Oosthuizen	2012 v E	2	0	0	0	0	0
U J Potgieter	2012 v E	3	0	0	0	0	0
P J Spies	2006 v A	50	7	0	0	0	35
G J Stegmann	2010 v I	6	0	0	0	0	0
J A Strauss	2008 v A	18	0	0	0	0	0
P R van der Merwe	2010 v F	20	1	0	0	0	5
D J Vermeulen	2012 v A	4	0	0	0	0	0

THE COUNTRIES

SOUTH AFRICA
INTERNATIONAL PLAYERS
UP TO 10 OCTOBER 2012
Entries in square brackets denote matches played in RWC Finals.

Ackermann, D S P (WP) 1955 BI 2,3,4, 1956 A 1,2, NZ 1,3, 1958 F 2
Ackermann, J N (NT, BB, N) 1996 Fj, A 1, NZ 1, A 2, 2001 F 2(R), It 1, NZ 1(R), A 1, 2006 I, E1,2, 2007 Sm, A2
Aitken, A D (WP) 1997 F 2(R), E, 1998 I 2(R), W 1(R), NZ 1,2(R), A 2(R)
Alberts, W S (NS) 2010 W2(R), S(t&R), E(R), 2011 NZ2, [W(R), Fj(R), Nm, Sm (t&R), A(t&R)], 2012 E1, 2, Arg1, 2, A1, NZ1, A2, NZ2
Albertyn, P K (SWD) 1924 BI 1,2,3,4
Alexander, F A (GW) 1891 BI 1,2
Allan, J (N) 1993 A 1(R), Arg 1,2(R), 1994 E 1,2, NZ 1,2,3, 1996 Fj, A 1, NZ 1, A 2, NZ 2
Allen, P B (EP) 1960 S
Allport, P H (WP) 1910 BI 2,3
Anderson, J W (WP) 1903 BI 3
Anderson, J H (WP) 1896 BI 1,3,4
Andrew, J B (Tvl) 1896 BI 2
Andrews, E P (WP) 2004 I1 ,2, W1(t&R), PI, NZ1, A1, NZ2, A2, W2, I3, E, 2005 F1,A2, NZ2(t), Arg(R), F3(R), 2006 S1, 2, F, A1(R), NZ1(t), 2007 A2(R), NZ2(R)
Andrews, K S (WP) 1992 E, 1993 F 1,2, A 1(R), 2,3, Arg 1(R), 2, 1994 NZ 3
Andrews, M G (N) 1994 E 2, NZ 1,2,3, Arg 1,2, S, W, 1995 WS, [A, WS, F, NZ], W, It, E, 1996 Fj, A 1, NZ 1, A 2, NZ 2,3,4,5, Arg 1,2, F 1,2, W, 1997 Tg (R), BI 1,2, NZ 1, A 1, NZ 2, A 2, It, F 1,2, E, S, 1998 I 1,2, W 1, E 1, A 1, NZ 1,2, A 2, W 2, S, I 3, E 2, 1999 NZ 1,2(R), A 2(R), [S, U, E, A 3, NZ 3], 2000 A 2, NZ 2, A 3, Arg, I, W, E 3, 2001 F 1,2, It 1, NZ 1, A 1,2, NZ 2, F 3, E
Antelme, J G M (Tvl) 1960 NZ 1,2,3,4, 1961 F
Apsey, J T (WP) 1933 A 4,5, 1938 BI 2
Aplon, G G (WP) 2010 W1, F, It 1, 2, NZ1(R), 2(R), A1, NZ3, A3(R), I, W2, S, E, 2011 A1, 2(R), [Nm], 2012 E3
Ashley, S (WP) 1903 BI 2
Aston, F T D (Tvl) 1896 BI 1,2,3,4
Atherton, S (N) 1993 Arg 1,2, 1994 E 1,2, NZ 1,2,3, 1996 NZ 2
Aucamp, J (WT) 1924 BI 1,2

Baard, A P (WP) 1960 I
Babrow, L (WP) 1937 A 1,2, NZ 1,2,3
Badenhorst, C (OFS) 1994 Arg 2, 1995 WS (R)
Bands, R E (BB) 2003 S 1,2, Arg (R), A 1, NZ 1, A 2, NZ 2, [U,E,Sm(R),NZ(R)]
Barnard, A S (EP) 1984 S Am 1,2, 1986 Cv 1,2
Barnard, J H (Tvl) 1965 S, A 1,2, NZ 3,4
Barnard, R W (Tvl) 1970 NZ 2(R)
Barnard, W H M (NT) 1949 NZ 4, 1951 W
Barry, D W (WP) 2000 C, E 1,2, A 1(R), NZ 1, A 2, 2001 F 1,2, US (R), 2002 W 2, Arg, Sm, NZ 1, A 1, NZ 2, A 2, 2003 A 1, NZ 1, A 2, [U, E, Sm, NZ], 2004 PI, NZ1, A1, NZ2, A2, W2, I3, E, Arg(t), 2005 F1, 2, A1, NZ2, W(R), F3(R), 2006 F
Barry, J (WP) 1903 BI 1,2,3
Bartmann, W J (Tvl, N) 1986 Cv 1,2,3,4, 1992 NZ, A, F, 1,2
Basson, B A (GW, BB) 2010 W1(R),It 1(R),I,W2, 2011 A1,NZ1
Bastard, W E (N) 1937 A 1, NZ 1,2,3, 1938 BI 1,3
Bates, A J (WT) 1969 E, 1970 NZ 1,2, 1972 E
Bayvel, P C R (Tvl) 1974 BI 2,4, F 1,2, 1975 F 1,2, 1976 NZ 1,2,3,4
Beck, J J (WP) 1981 NZ 2(R), 3(R), US
Bedford, T P (N) 1963 A 1,2,3,4, 1964 W, F, 1965 I, A 1,2, 1968 BI 1,2,3,4, F 1,2, 1969 A 1,2,3, S, E, 1970 I, W, 1971 F 1,2
Bekker, A (WP) 2008 W1, 2(R), It(R), NZ1(R), 2(t&R), A1(t&R), Arg(R), NZ3, A2,3, W3(R) ,S(R), E(R), 2009 BI 1(R), 2(R), NZ2(R), A1(R), 2(R), F(t&R), It, 2010 It2, NZ1(R), 2(R), Arg1, 2, NZ1(t&R), A2, NZ2
Bekker, H J (WP) 1981 NZ 1,3
Bekker, H P J (NT) 1952 E, F, 1953 A 1,2,3,4, 1955 BI 2,3,4, 1956 A 1,2, NZ 1,2,3,4
Bekker, M J (NT) 1960 S
Bekker, R P (NT) 1953 A 3,4
Bekker, S (NT) 1997 A 2(t)
Bennett, R G (Border) 1997 Tg (R), BI 1(R), 3, NZ 1, A 1, NZ 2
Bergh, W F (SWD) 1931 W, I, 1932 E, S, 1933 A 1,2,3,4,5, 1937 A 1,2, NZ 1,2,3, 1938 BI 1,2,3
Bestbier, A (OFS) 1974 F 2(R)

Garvey, A C (N) 1996 Arg 1,2, F 1,2, W, 1997 Tg, BI 1,2,3(R), A 1(t), It, F 1,2, E, S, 1998 I 1,2, W 1, E1, A 1, NZ 1,2 A 2, W 2, S, I 3, E 2, 1999 [Sp]

Geel, P J (OFS) 1949 NZ 3

Geere, V (Tvl) 1933 A 1,2,3,4,5

Geffin, A O (Tvl) 1949 NZ 1,2,3,4, 1951 S, I, W

Geldenhuys, A (EP) 1992 NZ, A, F 1,2

Geldenhuys, S B (NT) 1981 NZ 2,3, US, 1982 S Am 1,2, 1989 Wld 1,2

Gentles, T A (WP) 1955 BI 1,2,4, 1956 NZ 2,3, 1958 F 2

Geraghty, E M (Bor) 1949 NZ 4

Gerber, D M (EP, WP) 1980 S Am 3,4, F, 1981 I 1,2, NZ 1,2,3, US, 1982 S Am 1,2, 1984 E 1,2, S Am 1,2, 1986 Cv 1,2,3,4, 1992 NZ, A, F 1,2, E

Gerber, H J (WP) 2003 S 1,2

Gerber, M C (EP) 1958 F 1,2, 1960 S

Gericke, F W (Tvl) 1960 S

Germishuys, J S (OFS, Tvl) 1974 BI 2, 1976 NZ 1,2,3,4, 1977 Wld, 1980 S Am 1,2, BI 1,2,3,4, S Am 3,4, F, 1981 I 1,2, NZ 2,3, US

Gibbs, B (GW) 1903 BI 2

Goosen, C P (OFS) 1965 NZ 2

Goosen, J L (FS) 2012 A1(R),NZ1(R),A2,NZ2

Gorton, H C (Tvl) 1896 BI 1

Gould, R L (N) 1968 BI 1,2,3,4

Grant, P J (WP) 2007 A2(R),NZ2(R), 2008 W1(t&R),It(R),A1(R)

Gray, B G (WP) 1931 W, 1932 E, S, 1933 A 5

Greeff, W W (WP) 2002 Arg (R), Sm, NZ 1, A 1, NZ 2, A 2, F, S, E, 2003 [U,Gg]

Greenwood, C M (WP) 1961 I

Greyling, M D (BB) 2011 A1,NZ1, 2012 NZ1(R)

Greyling, P J F (OFS) 1967 F 1,2,3,4, 1968 BI 1, F 1,2, 1969 A 1,2,3,4, S, E, 1970 I, W, NZ 1,2,3,4, 1971 F 1,2, A 1,2,3, 1972 E

Grobler, C J (OFS) 1974 BI 4, 1975 F 1,2

Guthrie, F H (WP) 1891 BI 1,3, 1896 BI 1

Habana, B G (GL, BB, WP) 2004 E(R),S,Arg, 2005 U, F1, 2, A1, 2, 3, NZ1, A4, NZ2, Arg, W, F3, 2006 S2, F, A1, NZ1, A2, NZ2, 3, I, E1, 2, 2007 E1, 2, S, [Sm, E1, Tg(R), US, Fj, Arg, E2], W, 2008 W1, 2, It, NZ1, A1, NZ3, W3, S, E, 2009 BI 1, 2, NZ1, 2, A1, 2, 3, NZ3, F, It, I, 2010 F, It 1, 2, NZ1, 2, A1, NZ3, A2, 3, I, W2, 2011 A2, NZ2, [W, Nm, Sm, A], 2012 E1, 2, 3, Arg1, 2, A1, NZ1, A2, NZ2

Hahn, C H L (Tvl) 1910 BI 1,2,3

Hall, D B (GL) 2001 F 1,2, NZ 1, A 1,2, NZ 2, It 2, E, US, 2002 Sm, NZ 1,2, A 2

Halstead, T M (N) 2001 F 3, It 2, E, US (R), 2003 S 1,2

Hamilton, F (EP) 1891 BI 1

Hargreaves, A J (NS) 2010 W1(R),It 1(R), 2011 A1,NZ1

Harris, T A (Tvl) 1937 NZ 2,3, 1938 BI 1,2,3

Hartley, A J (WP) 1891 BI 3

Hattingh, H (NT) 1992 A (R), F 2(R), E, 1994 Arg 1,2

Hattingh, L B (OFS) 1933 A 2

Heatlie, B H (WP) 1891 BI 2,3, 1896 BI 1,4, 1903 BI 1,3

Hendricks, M (Bol) 1998 I 2(R), W 1(R)

Hendriks, P (Tvl) 1992 NZ, A, 1994 S, W, 1995 [A, R, C], 1996 A 1, NZ 1, A 2, NZ 2,3,4,5

Hepburn, T B (WP) 1896 BI 4

Heunis, J W (NT) 1981 NZ 3(R), US, 1982 S Am 1,2, 1984 E 1,2, S Am 1,2, 1986 Cv 1,2,3,4, 1989 Wld 1,2

Hill, R A (R) 1960 W, I, 1961 I, A 1,2, 1962 BI 4, 1963 A 3

Hills, W G (NT) 1992 F 1,2, E, 1993 F 1,2, A 1

Hirsch, J G (EP) 1906 I, 1910 BI 1

Hobson, T E C (WP) 1903 BI 3

Hoffman, R S (Bol) 1953 A 3

Holton, D N (EP) 1960 S

Honiball, H W (N) 1993 A 3(R), Arg 2, 1995 WS (R), 1996 Fj, A 1, NZ 5, Arg 1,2, F 1,2, W, 1997 Tg, BI 1,2,3(R), NZ 1(R), A 1(R), NZ 2, A 2, It, F 1,2, E 1,998 W 1(R), E, I A 1, NZ 1,2, A 2, W 2, S, I 3, E 2, 1999 [A 3(R), NZ 3]

Hopwood, D J (WP) 1960 S, NZ 3, 4, W, 1961 E, S, F, I, A 1,2, 1962 BI 1, 2, 3, 4, 1963 A 1,2,4, 1964 W, F, 1965 S, NZ 3,4

Hougaard, D J (BB) 2003 [U(R), E(R), Gg, Sm, NZ], 2007 Sm, A2, NZ2

Hougaard, F (BB) 2009 It(R), 2010 A1(R), NZ3, A2, 3, W2(R),

S, E(t&R), 2011 A2(t), NZ2(R), [W(R), Fj(R), Nm, Sm(R), A(R)], 2012 E1, 2, 3, Arg1, 2, A1, NZ1, A2, NZ2

Howe, B F (Bor) 1956 NZ 1,4

Howe-Browne, N R F G (WP) 1910 BI 1,2,3

Hugo, D P (WP) 1989 Wld 1,2

Human, D C F (WP) 2002 W 1,2, Arg (R), Sm (R)

Hurter, M H (NT) 1995 [R, C], W, 1996 Fj, A 1, NZ 1,2,3,4,5, 1997 NZ 1,2, A 2

Immelman, J H (WP) 1913 F

Jackson, D C (WP) 1906 I, W, E

Jackson, J S (WP) 1903 BI 2

Jacobs, A A (Falcons, NS) 2001 It 2(R), US, 2002 W 1(R), Arg, Sm (R), NZ 1(t+R), A 1(R), F, S, E (R), 2008 W1, 2, NZ1, 2, Arg, NZ3, A2, 3, W3, S, E, 2009 BI 1, 2, NZ2(R), A1(R), 2(R), 3(R), NZ3(R), F, It, 2010 I(R), E(R), 2011 A1(R), NZ1

James, A D (N, Bath, GL) 2001 F 1,2, NZ 1, A 1,2, NZ 2, 2002 F (R), S, E, 2006 NZ1, A2, NZ2, 3(R), E1, 2007 E1, 2, A1, NZ1, Nm, S, [Sm, E1, US, Fj, Arg, E2], 2008 W1, 2, NZ1, 2, A1, Arg, NZ3, A2, 3, 2010 It1, 2(R), NZ1(R), A1(R), 2(R), 2011 A2, [W(R)]

Jansen, E (OFS) 1981 NZ 1

Jansen, J S (OFS) 1970 NZ 1, 2, 3, 4, 1971 F 1, 2, A 1, 2, 3, 1972 E

Jantjes, C A (GL, WP) 2001 It 1, A 1,2, NZ 2, F 3, It 2, E, US, 2005 Arg,W, 2007 W(R), 2008 W1, 2, It, NZ1, 2(R), A1, Arg, NZ3(R), A2, 3, W3, S, E

Jantjies, E T (GL) 2012 A2(R),NZ2(R)

Januarie, E R (GL, WP) 2005 U, F2, A1, 2, 3(R), NZ1, A4, NZ2, 2006 S1(R), 2(R), F(R), A1, I, E1, 2, 2007 E1, 2, Sm, Nm(R), [Sm(R), Tg], W, 2008 W2, It, NZ1, 2, A1, Arg, NZ3(R), A2(R), 3(R), W3(R), S, E, 2009 BI 1(R), NZ1(R), 2(R), A1(R), 2(R), NZ3(R), 2010 W1, F, It 1, 2, NZ1, 2, 3(R)

Jennings, C B (Bor) 1937 NZ 1

Johnson, A F (FS) 2011 A1, NZ1(t&R), 2(t&R)

Johnson, G K (Tvl) 1993 Arg 2, 1994 NZ 3, Arg 1, 1995 WS, [R, C, WS]

Johnstone, P G A (WP) 1951 S, I, W, 1952 E, F, 1956 A 1, NZ 1, 2, 4

Jones, C H (Tvl) 1903 BI 1,2

Jones, P S T (WP) 1896 BI 1,3,4

Jordaan, N (BB) 2002 E (R)

Jordaan, R P (NT) 1949 NZ 1,2,3,4

Joubert, A J (OFS, N) 1989 Wld 1(R), 1993 A 3, Arg 1, 1994 E 1,2, NZ 1,2(R), 3, Arg 2, S, W, 1995 [A, C, WS, F, NZ], W, It, E, 1996 Fj, A 1, NZ 1,3,4,5, Arg 1,2, F 1,2, W, 1997 Tg, BI 1,2, A 2

Joubert, M C (Bol, WP) 2001 NZ 1, 2002 W 1,2, Arg (R), Sm, NZ 1, A1, NZ 2, A 2, F (R), 2003 S 2, Arg, A 1, 2004 I1, 2, W1, PI, NZ1, A1, NZ2, A2, W2, I3, E, S, Arg, 2005 U, F1, 2, A1

Joubert, S J (WP) 1906 I, W, E

Julies, W (Bol, SWD, GL) 1999 [Sp], 2004 I1, 2, W1, S, Arg, 2005 A2(R), 3(t), 2006 F(R), 2007 Sm, [Tg]

Kahts, W J H (NT) 1980 BI 1, 2, 3, S Am 3, 4, F, 1981 I 1,2, NZ 2, 1982 S Am 1,2

Kaminer, J (Tvl) 1958 F 2

Kankowski, R (NS) 2007 W, 2008 W2(R), It, A1(R), W3(R), S(R), E(R), 2009 BI3, NZ3(R), F, It, 2010 W1(R), It 1(R), NZ2(R), A1, 3(R), S, 2011 A1(R), NZ1(R), 2012 E3(R)

Kayser, D J (EP, N) 1999 It 2(R), A 1(R), NZ 2, A 2, [S, Sp (R), U, E, A 3], 2001 It 1(R), NZ 1(R), A 2(R), NZ 2(R)

Kebble, G R (N) 1993 Arg 1,2, 1994 NZ 1(R), 2

Kelly, E W (GW) 1896 BI 3

Kempson, R B (N, WP, Ulster) 1998 I 2(R), W 1, E 1, A 1, NZ 1,2 A 2, W 2, S, I 3, E 2, 1999 It 1,2, W, 2000 C, E 1,2, A 1, NZ 1, A 2,3, Arg, I, W, E 3, 2001 F 1,2(R), NZ 1, A 1,2, NZ 2, 2003 S 1(R),2(R), Arg, A 1(R), NZ 1, A 1,2

Kenyon, B J (Bor) 1949 NZ 4

Kipling, G (GW) 1931 W, I, 1932 E, S, 1933 A 1,2,3,4,5

Kirchner, Z (BB) 2009 BI 3, F, It, I, 2010 W1(R), F, It1, NZ1, 2, A1, I, W2(R), S, E, 2012 E1, Arg1, 2, A1, NZ1, A2, NZ2

Kirkpatrick, A I (GW) 1953 A 2, 1956 NZ 2, 1958 F 1, 1960 S, NZ 1,2,3,4, W, I, 1961 E, S, F

Knight, A S (Tvl) 1912 S, I, W, 1913 E, F

U, F1, 2, A1, 2, 3, NZ1, A4, NZ2, Arg, W, F3, 2006 S1, 2, F, A1, NZ1, A2, NZ2, 2007 E1, 2, Sm(R), A1, NZ1, Nm, S, [Sm, E1, Tg(R), US, Fj, Arg, E2], 2008 W1(R), 2(R), NZ1(R), 2, Arg(R), NZ3, A2(R), 3(R)

Moolman, L C (NT) 1977 Wld, 1980 S Am 1,2, Bl 1,2,3,4, S Am 3,4, F, 1981 I 1,2, NZ 1,2,3, US, 1982 S Am 1,2, 1984 S Am 1,2, 1986 Cv 1,2,3,4

Mordt, R H (Z-R, NT) 1980 S Am 1,2, Bl 1,2,3,4, S Am 3,4, F, 1981 I 2, NZ 1,2,3, US, 1982 S Am 1,2, 1984 S Am 1,2

Morkel, D A (Tvl) 1903 Bl 1

Morkel, D F T (Tvl) 1906 I, E, 1910 Bl 1,3, 1912 S, I, W, 1913 E, F

Morkel, H J (WP) 1921 NZ 1

Morkel, H W (WP) 1921 NZ 1,2

Morkel, J A (WP) 1921 NZ 2,3

Morkel, J W H (WP) 1912 S, I, W, 1913 E, F

Morkel, P G (WP) 1912 S, I, W, 1913 E, F, 1921 NZ 1,2,3

Morkel, P K (WP) 1928 NZ 4

Morkel, W H (WP) 1910 Bl 3, 1912 S, I, W, 1913 E, F, 1921 NZ 1,2,3

Morkel, W S (Tvl) 1906 S, I, W, E

Moss, C (N) 1949 NZ 1,2,3,4

Mostert, G (Stade Français) 2011 NZ1,A2(R)

Mostert, P J (WP) 1921 NZ 1,2,3, 1924 Bl 1,2,4, 1928 NZ 1,2,3,4, 1931 W, I, 1932 E, S

Mtawarira, T (NS) 2008 W2, It, A1(R), Arg, NZ3, A2, 3, W3, S, E, 2009 Bl 1, 2, 3, NZ1, 2, A1, 2, 3, NZ3, F, It(R), I, 2010 I, W2, S, E, 2011 A2, NZ2(R), [W, Fj(R), Nm(R), Sm], 2012 E1, 2, 3, Arg1, 2, A1, NZ1, A2, NZ2

Muir, D J (WP) 1997 It, F 1,2, E, S

Mujati, B V (WP) 2008 W1, It(R), NZ1(R), 2(t), A1(R), Arg(R), NZ3(R), A2(R), 3, W3(t), S(R), E(R)

Mulder, J C (Tvl, GL) 1994 NZ 2,3, S, W, 1995 WS, [A, WS, F, NZ], W, It, E, 1996 Fj, A 1, NZ 1, A 2, NZ 2,5, Arg 1,2, F 1,2, W, 1997 Tg, Bl 1, 1999 It 1(R),2, W, NZ 1, 2000 C(R), A 1, E 3, 2001 F 1, It 1

Muller, G H (WP) 1969 A 3,4, S, 1970 W, NZ 1,2,3,4, 1971 F 1,2, 1972 E, 1974 Bl 1,3,4

Muller, G J (NS, Ulster) 2006 S1(R), NZ1(R), A2, NZ2, 3, A3, I(R), E1, 2, 2007 E1(R), 2(R), Sm(R), A1(R), NZ1(R), A2, NZ2, Nm(R), [Sm(R), E1(R), Fj(t&R), Arg(t&R)], W, 2009 Bl 3, 2011 [W(R)]

Muller, G P (GL) 2003 A 2, NZ 2, [E,Gg(R),Sm,NZ]

Muller, H L (OFS) 1986 Cv 4(R), 1989 Wld 1(R)

Muller, H S V (Tvl) 1949 NZ 1,2,3,4, 1951 S, I, W, 1952 E, F, 1953 A 1,2,3,4

Muller, L J (N) 1992 NZ, A

Muller, P G (N) 1992 NZ, A, F 1,2, E, 1993 F 1,2, A 1,2,3, Arg 1,2, 1994 E 1,2, NZ 1, S, W, 1998 I 1,2, W 1, E 1, A 1, NZ 1,2, A 2, 1999 It 1, W, NZ 1, A 1, [Sp, E, A 3, NZ 3]

Murray, W M (N) 2007 Sm,A2,NZ2

Mvovo, L N (NS) 2010 S,E, 2011 A1,NZ1, 2012 Arg1,2,A1(R)

Myburgh, F R (EP) 1896 Bl 1

Myburgh, J L (NT) 1962 Bl 1, 1963 A 4, 1964 W, F, 1968 Bl 1,2,3, F 1,2, 1969 A 1,2,3,4, E, 1970 I, W, NZ 3,4

Myburgh, W H (WT) 1924 Bl 1

Naude, J P (WP) 1963 A 4, 1965 A 1,2, NZ 1,3,4, 1967 F 1,2,3,4, 1968 Bl 1,2,3,4

Ndungane, A Z (BB) 2006 A1,2,NZ2,3,A3, E1,2, 2007 E2,Nm(R), [US],W(R)

Ndungane, O M (NS) 2008 It, NZ1, A3, 2009 Bl 3, A3, NZ3, 2010 W1, 2011 NZ1(R), [Fj]

Neethling, J B (WP) 1967 F 1,2,3,4, 1968 Bl 4, 1969 S, 1970 NZ 1,2

Nel, J A (Tvl) 1960 NZ 1,2, 1963 A 1,2, 1965 A 2, NZ 1,2,3,4, 1970 NZ 3,4

Nel, J J (WP) 1956 A 1,2, NZ 1,2,3,4, 1958 F 1,2

Nel, P A R O (Tvl) 1903 Bl 1,2,3

Nel, P J (N) 1928 NZ 1,2,3,4, 1931 W, I, 1932 E, S, 1933 A 1,3,4,5, 1937 A 1,2, NZ 2,3

Nimb, C F (WP) 1961 I

Nokwe, J L (FS) 2008 Arg,A2,3, 2009 Bl 3

Nomis, S H (Tvl) 1967 F 4, 1968 Bl 1,2,3,4, F 1,2, 1969 A 1,2,3,4, S, E, 1970 I, W, NZ 1,2,3,4, 1971 F 1,2, A 1,2,3, 1972 E

Nykamp, J L (Tvl) 1933 A 2

Ochse, J K (WP) 1951 I, W, 1952 E, F, 1953 A 1,2,4

Oelofse, J S A (Tvl) 1953 A 1,2,3,4

Oliver, J F (Tvl) 1928 NZ 3,4

Olivier, E (WP) 1967 F 1,2,3,4, 1968 Bl 1,2,3,4, F 1,2, 1969 A 1,2,3,4, S, E

Olivier, J (NT) 1992 F 1,2, E, 1993 F 1,2 A 1,2,3, Arg 1, 1995 W, It (R), E, 1996 Arg 1,2, F 1,2, W

Olivier, W (BB) 2006 S1(R), 2, F, A1, NZ1, A2, NZ2(R), 3, A3, I(R), E1, 2, 2007 E1, 2, NZ1(R), A2, NZ2, [E1(R), Tg, Arg(R)], W(R), 2009 Bl 3, NZ1(R), 2(R), F(R), It(R), I, 2010 F, It2(R), NZ1, 2, A1, 2011 A1, NZ1(R), 2012 E1(t), 2(R), 3

Olver, E (EP) 1896 Bl 1

Oosthuizen, C V (FS) 2012 E1(t&R),NZ2(R)

Oosthuizen, J J (WP) 1974 Bl 1, F 1,2, 1975 F 1,2, 1976 NZ 1,2,3,4

Oosthuizen, O W (NT, Tvl) 1981 I 1(R), 2, NZ 2,3, US, 1982 S Am 1,2, 1984 E 1,2

Osler, B L (WP) 1924 Bl 1,2,3,4, 1928 NZ 1,2,3,4, 1931 W, I, 1932 E, S, 1933 A 1,2,3,4,5

Osler, S G (WP) 1928 NZ 1

Otto, K (NT, BB) 1995 [R, C (R), WS (R)], 1997 Bl 3, NZ 1, A 1, NZ 2, It, F 1,2, E, S, 1998 I 1,2, W 1, E 1, A 1, NZ 1,2, A 2, W 2, S, I 3, E 2, 1999 It 1, W, NZ 1, A 1, [S (R), Sp, U, E, A 3, NZ 3], 2000 C, E 1,2, A 1

Oxlee, K (N) 1960 NZ 1,2,3,4, W, I, 1961 S, A 1,2, 1962 Bl 1,2,3,4, 1963 A 1,2,4, 1964 W, 1965 NZ 1,2

Pagel, G L (WP) 1995 [A (R), R, C, NZ (R)], 1996 NZ 5(R)

Parker, W H (EP) 1965 A 1,2

Partridge, J E C (Tvl) 1903 Bl 1

Paulse, B J (WP) 1999 It 1,2, NZ 1, A 1,2(R), [S (R), Sp, NZ 3], 2000 C, E 1,2, A 1, NZ 1, A 2, NZ 2, A 3, Arg, W, E 3, 2001 F 1,2, It 1, NZ 1, A 1, NZ 2, F 3, It 2, E, 2002 W 1,2, Arg, Sm (R), A 1, NZ 2, A 2, F, S, E, 2003 [Gg], 2004 I1, 2, W1, Pl, NZ1, A2, NZ2, W2, I3, E, 2005 A2, 3, NZ1, A4, F3, 2006 S1, 2, A1(R), NZ1, 3(R), A3(R), 2007 A2, NZ2

Payn, C (N) 1924 Bl 1,2

Pelser, H J M (Tvl) 1958 F 1, 1960 NZ 1,2,3,4, W, I, 1961 F, I, A 1,2

Pfaff, B D (WP) 1956 A 1

Pickard, J A J (WP) 1953 A 3,4, 1956 NZ 2, 1958 F 2

Pienaar, J F (Tvl) 1993 F 1,2, A 1,2,3, Arg 1,2, 1994 E 1,2, NZ 2,3, Arg 1,2, S, W, 1995 WS, [A, C, WS, F, NZ], W, It, E, 1996 Fj, A 1, NZ 1, A 2, NZ 2

Pienaar, R (NS, Ulster) 2006 NZ2(R), 3(R), A3(R), I(t), E1(R), 2007 E1(R), 2(R), Sm(R), A1, NZ1, A2, NZ2, Nm(R), S(R), [E1(t&R), Tg, US(R), Arg(R)], W, 2008 W1(R), It(R), NZ2(R), A1(R), 3(R), W3, S, E, 2009 Bl 1, 2, 3(R), NZ1, A1(R), 2, 3, It(R), I(R), 2010 W1,F(R), It 1(R), 2(R), NZ1(R), 2(R), A1, I, W2, S(R), E, 2011 A1, NZ1, [Fj(R), Nm(R)], 2012 E1(R), 2(R), 3(R), Arg1(R), 2(R), A1, NZ1(R)

Pienaar, Z M J (OFS) 1980 S Am 2(R), Bl 1,2,3,4, S Am 3,4, F, 1981 I 1,2, NZ 1,2,3

Pietersen, J-P R (NS) 2006 A3, 2007 Sm, A1, NZ1, A2, NZ2, Nm, S, [Sm, E1, Tg, US(R), Fj, Arg, E2], W, 2008 NZ2, A1, Arg, NZ3, A2, W3, S, E, 2009 Bl 1, 2, NZ1, 2, A1, 2, F, It, I, 2010 NZ3, A2, 3, 2011 A2, NZ2, [W, Fj, Sm, A], 2012 E1, 2, 3

Pitzer, G (NT) 1967 F 1, 2, 3, 4, 1968 Bl 1, 2, 3, 4, F 1,2, 1969 A 3,4

Pope, C F (WP) 1974 Bl 1,2,3,4, 1975 F 1,2, 1976 NZ 2,3,4

Potgieter, D J (BB) 2009 I(t), 2010 W1,F(t&R),It 1,2(R),A1(R)

Potgieter, H J (OFS) 1928 NZ 1,2

Potgieter, H L (OFS) 1977 Wld

Potgieter, U J (BB) 2012 E3,Arg1(R),2

Powell, A W (GW) 1896 Bl 3

Powell, J M (GW) 1891 Bl 2, 1896 Bl 3, 1903 Bl 1,2

Prentis, R B (Tvl) 1980 S Am 1,2, Bl 1,2,3,4, S Am 3,4, F, 1981 I 1,2

Pretorius, A S (GL) 2002 W 1, 2, Arg, Sm, NZ 1, A 1, NZ 2, F, S (R), E, 2003 NZ 1(R), A 1, 2005 A2, 3, NZ1, A4, NZ2, Arg, 2006 NZ2(R), 3, A3, I, E1(t&R), 2, 2007 S(R), [Sm(R), E1(R), Tg, US(R), Arg(R)], W

Pretorius, J C (GL) 2006 I, 2007 NZ2

Pretorius, N F (Tvl) 1928 NZ 1,2,3,4

Prinsloo, J (Tvl) 1958 F 1,2

Prinsloo, J (NT) 1963 A 3

Prinsloo, J P (Tvl) 1928 NZ 1
Putter, D J (WT) 1963 A 1,2,4

Raaff, J W E (GW) 1903 Bl 1,2, 1906 S, W, E, 1910 Bl 1
Ralepelle, M C (BB) 2006 NZ2(R), E2(R), 2008 E(t&R), 2009 Bl 3, NZ1(R), 2(R), A2(R), NZ3(R), 2010 W1(R), F(R), It 1, 2(R), NZ1(R), 2(R), A1(R), 2(R), 3(R), W2(R), 2011 A1(R), NZ1(R), [Nm(R)]
Ras, W J de Wet (OFS) 1976 NZ 1(R), 1980 S Am 2(R)
Rautenbach, S J (WP) 2002 W 1(R),2(t+R), Arg (R), Sm, NZ 1(R), A 1, NZ 2(R), A 2(R), 2003 [U(R), Gg, Sm, NZ], 2004 W1, NZ1(R)
Reece-Edwards, H (N) 1992 F 1,2, 1993 A 2
Reid, A (WP) 1903 Bl 3
Reid, B C (Bor) 1933 A 4
Reinach, J (OFS) 1986 Cv 1,2,3,4
Rens, I J (Tvl) 1953 A 3,4
Retief, D F (NT) 1955 Bl 1,2,4, 1956 A 1,2, NZ 1,2,3,4
Reyneke, H J (WP) 1910 Bl 3
Richards, A R (WP) 1891 Bl 1,2,3
Richter, A (NT) 1992 F 1,2, E, 1994 E 2, NZ 1,2,3, 1995 [R, C, WS (R)]
Riley, N M (ET) 1963 A 3
Riordan, C A (Tvl) 1910 Bl 1,2
Robertson, I W (R) 1974 F 1,2, 1976 NZ 1,2,4
Rodgers, P H (NT, Tvl) 1989 Wld 1,2, 1992 NZ, F 1,2
Rogers, C D (Tvl) 1984 E 1,2, S Am 1,2
Roos, G D (WP) 1910 Bl 2,3
Roos, P J (WP) 1903 Bl 3, 1906 I, W, E
Rosenberg, W (Tvl) 1955 Bl 2,3,4, 1956 NZ 3, 1958 F 1
Rossouw, C L C (Tvl, N) 1995 WS, [R, WS, F, NZ], 1999 NZ 2(R), A 2(t), [Sp, NZ 3(R)]
Rossouw, D H (WP) 1953 A 3, 4
Rossouw, D J (BB) 2003 [U, Gg, Sm(R), NZ], 2004 E(R), S, Arg, 2005 U, F1, 2, A1, W(R), F3(R), 2006 S1, 2, F, A1, I, E1, 2, 2007 E1, Sm, A1(R), NZ1, S, [Sm, E1, Tg, Fj, Arg, E2], 2008 W1(t&R), NZ3(R), A3(R), S(R), E, 2009 Bl 1(R), 2(R), NZ1(R), 2(R), A1(R), 3(R), NZ3(R), F(R, It, I, 2010 W1, F, NZ1, 2, A1, NZ3(t&R), A2(R), 3, 2011 A1, NZ1, A2, NZ2(t&R), [W, Fj, Nm, Sm, A]
Rossouw, P W G (WP) 1997 Bl 2,3, NZ 1, A 1, NZ 2(R), A 2(R), It, F 1,2, E, S, 1998 I 1,2, W 1, E 1, A 1, NZ 1,2, A 2, W 2, S, I 3, E 2, 1999 It 1, W, NZ 1, A 1(R), NZ 2, A 2, [S, U, E, A 3], 2000 C, E 1,2, A 2, Arg (R), I, W, 2001 F 3, US, 2003 Arg
Rousseau, W P (WP) 1928 NZ 3,4
Roux, F du T (WP) 1960 W, 1961 A 1,2, 1962 Bl 1,2,3,4, 1963 A 2, 1965 A 1,2, NZ 1,2,3,4, 1968 Bl 3,4, F 1,2 1969 A 1,2,3,4, 1970 I, NZ 1,2,3,4
Roux, J P (Tvl) 1994 E 2, NZ 1,2,3, Arg 1, 1995 [R, C, F (R)], 1996 A 1(R), NZ 1, A 2, NZ 3
Roux, O A (NT) 1969 S, E, 1970 I, W, 1972 E, 1974 Bl 3,4
Roux, W G (BB) 2002 F (R), S, E
Russell, R B (MP, N) 2002 W 1(R), 2, Arg, A 1(R), NZ 2(R), A 2, F, E (R), 2003 Arg (R), A 1(R), NZ 1, A 2(R), 2004 I2(t&R), W1, NZ1(R), W2(R), Arg(R), 2005 U(R), F2(R), A1(t), Arg(R), W(R), 2006 F

Samuels, T A (GW) 1896 Bl 2,3,4
Santon, D (Bol) 2003 A 1(R), NZ 1(R), A 2(t), [Gg(R)]
Sauermann, J T (Tvl) 1971 F 1,2, A 1, 1972 E, 1974 Bl 1
Schlebusch, J J J (OFS) 1974 Bl 3,4, 1975 F 2
Schmidt, L U (NT) 1958 F 2, 1962 Bl 2
Schmidt, U L (NT, Tvl) 1986 Cv 1,2,3,4, 1989 Wld 1,2, 1992 NZ, A, 1993 F 1,2, A 1,2,3, 1994 Arg 1,2, S, W
Schoeman, J (WP) 1963 A 3,4, 1965 I, S, A 1, NZ 1,2
Scholtz, C P (WP, Tvl) 1994 Arg 1, 1995 [R, C, WS]
Scholtz, H (FS) 2002 A 1(R), NZ 2(R), A 2(R), 2003 [U(R),Gg]
Scholtz, H H (WP) 1921 NZ 1,2
Schutte, P J W (Tvl) 1994 S, W
Scott, P A (Tvl) 1896 Bl 1,2,3,4
Sendin, W D (GW) 1921 NZ 2
Sephaka, L D (GL) 2001 US, 2002 Sm, NZ 1, A 1, NZ 2, A 2, F, 2003 S 1,2, A 1, NZ 1, A 2(t+R), NZ 2, [U, E(t&R), Gg], 2005 F2, A1, 2(R), W, 2006 S1(R), NZ3 (t&R), A3(R), I
Serfontein, D J (WP) 1980 Bl 1,2,3,4, S Am 3,4, F, 1981 I 1,2, NZ 1, 2, 3, US, 1982 S Am 1,2, 1984 E 1,2, S Am 1,2

Shand, R (GW) 1891 Bl 2,3
Sheriff, A R (Tvl) 1938 Bl 1,2,3
Shimange, M H (FS, WP) 2004 W1(R), NZ2(R), A2(R), W2(R), 2005 U(R), A1(R), 2(R), Arg(R), 2006 S1(R)
Shum, E H (Tvl) 1913 E
Sinclair, D J (Tvl) 1955 Bl 1,2,3,4
Sinclair, J H (Tvl) 1903 Bl 1
Skene, A L (WP) 1958 F 2
Skinstad, R B (WP, GL, N) 1997 E (t), 1998 W 1(R), E 1(t), NZ 1(R),2(R), A 2(R), W 2(R), S, I 3, E 2, 1999 [S, Sp (R), U, E, A 3], 2001 F 1(R), 2(R), It 1, NZ 1, A 1,2, NZ 2, F 3, It 2, E, 2002 W 1,2, Arg, Sm, NZ 1, A 1, NZ 2, A 2, 2003 Arg (R), 2007 E2(t&R), Sm, NZ1, A2, [E1(R), Tg, US(R), Arg(R)]
Slater, J T (EP) 1924 Bl 3,4, 1928 NZ 1
Smal, G P (WP) 1986 Cv 1,2,3,4, 1989 Wld 1,2
Small, J T (Tvl, N, WP) 1992 NZ, A, F 1,2, E, 1993 F 1,2, A 1,2,3, Arg 1,2, 1994 E 1,2, NZ 1,2,3(t), Arg 1, 1995 WS, [A, R, F, NZ], W, It, E (R), 1996 Fj, A 1, NZ 1, A 2, NZ 2, Arg 1,2, F 1,2, W, 1997 Tg, Bl 1, NZ 1(R), A 1(R), NZ 2, A 2, It, F 1,2, E, S
Smit, F C (WP) 1992 E
Smit, J W (NS, Clermont-Auvergne) 2000 C (t), A 1(R), NZ 1(t+R), A 2(R), NZ 2(R), A 3(R), Arg, I, W, E 3, 2001 F 1,2, It 1, NZ 1(R), A 1(R),2(R), NZ 2(R), F 3(R), It 2, E, US (R), 2003 [U(R), E(t&R), Gg, Sm, NZ], 2004 I1, 2, W1, PI, NZ1, A1, NZ2, A2, W2, I3, E, S, Arg, 2005 U, F1, 2, A1, 2, 3, NZ1, A4, NZ2, Arg, W, F3, 2006 S1, 2, F, A1, NZ1, A2, NZ2, 3, A3, I, E1, 2, 2007 E1, 2, Sm, A1, [Sm, E1, Tg(R), US, Fj, Arg, E2], W, 2008 W1, 2, NZ1, W3, S, E, 2009 Bl 1, 2, 3, NZ1, 2, A1, 2, 3, NZ3, F, It, I, 2010 W1, F, It 2, NZ1, 2, A1, NZ3, A2, 3, 2011 A1, NZ1, A2, NZ2(t&R), [W, Fj, Nm, Sm(R), A]
Smith, C M (OFS) 1963 A 3,4, 1964 W, F, 1965 A 1,2, NZ 2
Smith, C W (GW) 1891 Bl 2, 1896 Bl 2,3
Smith, D (GW) 1891 Bl 2
Smith D J (Z-R) 1980 Bl 1,2,3,4
Smith, G A C (EP) 1938 Bl 3
Smith, J H (FS) 2003 S 1(R),2(R), A 1, NZ 1, A 2, NZ 2, [U, E, Sm, NZ], 2004 W2, 2005 U(R), F2(R), A2, 3, NZ1, A4, NZ2, Arg, W, F3, 2006 S1, 2, F, A1, NZ1, A2, I, E2, 2007 E1, 2, A1, Nm, S, [Sm, E1, Tg(t&R), US, Fj, Arg, E2], W, 2008 W1, 2, It, NZ1, 2, A1, Arg, NZ3, A2, 3, W3, S, 2009 Bl 1, 2, 3, NZ1, 2, A1, 2, 3, 2010 NZ3, A2, 3, I, W2, S, E
Smith, P F (GW) 1997 S (R), 1998 I 1(t),2, W 1, NZ 1(R),2(R), A 2(R), W 2, 1999 NZ 2
Smollan, F C (Tvl) 1933 A 3,4,5
Snedden, R C D (GW) 1891 Bl 2
Snyman, A H (NT, BB, N) 1996 NZ 3, 4, Arg 2(R), W (R), 1997 Tg, Bl 1,2,3, NZ 1, A 1, NZ 2, A 2, It, F 1,2, E, S, 1998 I 1,2, W 1, E 1, A 1, NZ 1,2, A 2, W 2, S, I 3, E 2, 1999 NZ 2, 2001 NZ 2, F 3, US, 2002 W 1, 2003 S 1, NZ 1, 2006 S1,2
Snyman, D S L (WP) 1972 E, 1974 Bl 1,2(R), F 1,2, 1975 F 1,2, 1976 NZ 2,3, 1977 Wld
Snyman, J C P (OFS) 1974 Bl 2,3,4
Sonnekus, G H H (OFS) 1974 Bl 3, 1984 E 1,2
Sowerby, R S (N) 2002 Sm (R)
Spies, J J (NT) 1970 NZ 1,2,3,4
Spies, P J (BB) 2006 A1, NZ2, 3, A3, I, E1, 2007 E1(R), 2, A1, 2008 W1, 2, A1, Arg, NZ3, A2, 3, W3, S, E, 2009 Bl 1, 2, 3(R), NZ1, 2, A1, 2, 3, NZ3, 2010 F, It 1, 2, NZ1, A1, NZ3, A2, 3, I, W2, E, 2011 A2, NZ2, [W, Fj, Nm, Sm, A], 2012 E1, 2, 3
Stander, J C J (OFS) 1974 Bl 4(R), 1976 NZ 1, 2, 3, 4
Stapelberg, W P (NT) 1974 F 1,2
Starke, J J (WP) 1956 NZ 4
Starke, K T (WP) 1924 Bl 1,2,3,4
Steenekamp, J G A (Tvl) 1958 F 1
Steenkamp, G G (FS, BB) 2004 S,Arg, 2005 U, F2(R), A2, 3, NZ1(R), A4(R), 2007 E1(R), 2,A1, [Tg, Fj(R)], 2008 W1, 2(R), NZ1, 2, A1, W3(R), S(R), 2009 Bl 1(R), 3(R), 2010 F, It 1, 2,NZ1, 2, A1, NZ3, A2, 3, 2011 A2(R), NZ2, [W(R), Fj, Nm, Sm(R), A]
Stegmann, A C (WP) 1906 S, I
Stegmann, G J (BB) 2010 I,W2,S,E, 2011 A1,NZ1
Stegmann, J A (Tvl) 1912 S, I, W, 1913 E, F

Stewart, C (WP) 1998 S, I 3, E 2
Stewart, D A (WP) 1960 S, 1961 E, S, F, I, 1963 A 1,3,4, 1964 W, F, 1965 I
Steyn, F P L (NS, Racing Metro) 2006 I,E1,2, 2007 E1(R), 2(R), Sm, A1(R), NZ1(R), S, [Sm(R), E1, Tg(R), US, Fj, Arg, E2], W, 2008 W2(R), It, NZ1(R), 2(R), A1, NZ3(R), A2(R), W3(R), S(R), E(R), 2009 BI 1, 2, 3(t&R), NZ1, 2, A1, 2(R), 3(R), NZ3, 2010 W1, A2, 3, W2, S, E, 2011 A2, [W, Fj, Nm, Sm], 2012 E1, 2, Arg1, 2, A1, NZ1
Steyn, M (BB) 2009 BI 1(t&R), 2(R), 3, NZ1(R), 2, A1, 2, 3, NZ3, F, It, I, 2010 F, It 1, 2, NZ1, 2, A1, NZ3, A2, 3, I, W2, S, E, 2011 A1, NZ1, A2(R), NZ2, [W, Fj, Nm, Sm, A], 2012 E1, 2, 3, Arg1, 2, A1, NZ1
Stofberg, M T S (OFS, NT, WP) 1976 NZ 2, 3, 1977 Wld, 1980 S Am 1, 2, BI 1, 2, 3, 4, S Am 3, 4, F, 1981 I 1, 2, NZ 1,2, US, 1982 S Am 1, 2, 1984 E 1, 2
Strachan, L C (Tvl) 1932 E, S, 1937 A 1, 2, NZ 1, 2, 3, 1938 BI 1, 2, 3
Stransky, J T (N, WP) 1993 A 1, 2, 3, Arg 1, 1994 Arg 1, 2, 1995 WS, [A, R (t), C, F, NZ], W, It, E, 1996 Fj (R), NZ 1, A 2, NZ 2, 3, 4, 5(R)
Straeuli, R A W (Tvl) 1994 NZ 1, Arg 1,2, S, W, 1995 WS, [A, WS, NZ (R)], E (R)
Strauss, C P (WP) 1992 F 1,2, E, 1993 F 1,2, A 1,2,3, Arg 1,2, 1994 E 1, NZ 1,2, Arg 1,2
Strauss, J A (WP) 1984 S Am 1,2
Strauss, J A (FS) 2008 A1(R), Arg(R), NZ3(R), A2(R), 3(R), 2009 F(R), It, 2010 S(R), E(R), 2012 E1(R),2(R),3(R),Arg1(R),2,A1, NZ1,A2,NZ2
Strauss, J H P (Tvl) 1976 NZ 3,4, 1980 S Am 1
Strauss, S S F (GW) 1921 NZ 3
Strydom, C F (OFS) 1955 BI 3, 1956 A 1,2, NZ 1,4, 1958 F 1, 1959 J 1(R), 1993 F 2, A 1, 2, 3, Arg 1,2, 1994 E 1, 1995 [A, C, F, NZ], 1996 A 2(R), NZ 2(R), 3, 4, W (R), 1997 Tg, BI 1, 2, 3, A 2
Strydom, L J (NT) 1949 NZ 1,2
Styger, J J (OFS) 1992 NZ (R), A, F 1,2, E, 1993 F 2(R), A 3(R)
Suter, M R (N) 1965 I, S
Swanepoel, W (OFS, GL) 1997 BI 3(R), A 2(R), F 1(R), 2, E, S, 1998 I 2(R), W 1(R), E 2(R), 1999 It 1,2(R), W, A 1, [Sp, NZ 3(t)], 2000 A 1, NZ 1, A 2, NZ 2, A 3
Swart, J (WP) 1996 Fj, NZ 1(R), A 2, NZ 2,3,4,5, 1997 BI 3(R), It, S (R)
Swart, J J N (SWA) 1955 BI 1
Swart, I S (Tvl) 1993 A 1,2,3, Arg 1, 1994 E 1,2, NZ 1,3, Arg 2(R), 1995 WS, [A, WS, F, NZ], W, 1996 A 2

Taberer, W S (GW) 1896 BI 2
Taute, J J (GL) 2012 A2,NZ2
Taylor, O B (N) 1962 BI 1
Terblanche, C S (Bol, N) 1998 I 1,2, W 1, E 1, A 1, NZ 1,2, A 2, W 2, S, I 3, E 2, 1999 It 1(R),2, W, A 1, NZ 2(R), [Sp, E, A 3(R), NZ 3], 2000 E 3, 2002 W 1,2, Arg, Sm, NZ 1, A 1,2(R), 2003 S 1,2, Arg, A 1, NZ 1, A 2, NZ 2, [Gg]
Teichmann, G H (N) 1995 W, 1996 Fj, A 1, NZ 1, A 2, NZ 2,3,4,5, Arg 1,2, F 1,2, W, 1997 Tg, BI 1,2,3, NZ 1, A 1, NZ 2, A 2, It, F 1,2 E, S, 1998 I 1,2, W 1, E 1, A 1, NZ 1,2, A 2, W 2, S, I 3, E 2, 1999 It 1, W, NZ 1
Theron, D F (GW) 1996 A 2(R), NZ 2(R), 5, Arg 1,2, F 1,2, W, 1997 BI 2(R), 3, NZ 1(R), A 1, NZ 2(R)
Theunissen, D J (GW) 1896 BI 3
Thompson, G (WP) 1912 S, I, W
Tindall, J C (WP) 1924 BI 1, 1928 NZ 1,2,3,4
Tobias, E G (SARF, Bol) 1981 I 1,2, 1984 E 1,2, S Am 1,2
Tod, N S (N) 1928 NZ 2
Townsend, W H (N) 1921 NZ 1
Trenery, W E (GW) 1891 BI 2
Tromp, H (NT) 1996 NZ3,4, Arg 2(R), F 1(R)
Truter, D R (WP) 1924 BI 2,4
Truter, J T (N) 1963 A 1, 1964 F, 1965 A 2
Turner, F G (EP) 1933 A 1,2,3, 1937 A 1,2, NZ 1,2,3, 1938 BI 1,2,3
Twigge, R J (NT) 1960 S
Tyibilika, S (N) 2004 S,Arg, 2005 U,A2,Arg, 2006 NZ1,A2,NZ2

Ulyate, C A (Tvl) 1955 BI 1,2,3,4, 1956 NZ 1,2,3

Uys, P de W (NT) 1960 W, 1961 E, S, I, A 1,2, 1962 BI 1,4, 1963 A 1,2, 1969 A 1(R), 2
Uys, P J (Pumas) 2002 S

Van Aswegen, H J (WP) 1981 NZ 1, 1982 S Am 2(R)
Van Biljon, L (N) 2001 It 1(R), NZ 1, A 1,2, NZ 2, F 3, It 2(R), E (R), US, 2002 F (R), S, E (R), 2003 NZ 2(R)
Van Broekhuizen, H D (WP) 1896 BI 4
Van Buuren, M C (Tvl) 1891 BI 1
Van de Vyver, D F (WP) 1937 A 2
Van den Berg, D S (N) 1975 F 1,2, 1976 NZ 1,2
Van den Berg, M A (WP) 1937 A 1, NZ 1,2,3
Van den Berg, P A (WP, GW, N) 1999 It 1(R),2, NZ 2, A 2, [S, U (t+R), E (R), A 3(R), NZ 3(R)], 2000 E 1(R), A 1, NZ 1, A 2, NZ 2(R), A 3(t+R), Arg, I, W, E 3, 2001 F 1(R),2, A 2(R), NZ 2(R), US, 2004 NZ1, 2005 U, F1, 2, A1(R), 2(R), 3(R), 4(R), Arg(R), F3(R), 2006 S2(R), A1(R), NZ1, A2(R), NZ2(R), A3(R), I, E1(R), 2(R), 2007 Sm, A2(R), NZ2, Nm(t&R), S(R), [Tg, US], W(R)
Van den Bergh, E (EP) 1994 Arg 2(t & R)
Van der Linde, A (WP) 1995 It, E, 1996 Arg 1(R), 2(R), F 1(R), W (R), 2001 F 3(R)
Van der Linde, C J (FS, Leinster, WP, GL) 2002 S (R), E(R), 2004 I1(R), 2(R), PI(R), A1(R), NZ2(t&R), A2(R), W2(R), I3(R), E(t&R), S, Arg, 2005 U, F1(R), 2, A1(R), 3, NZ1, A4, NZ2, Arg, W, F3, 2006 S2(R), F(R), A1, NZ1, A2, NZ2, I, E1, 2, 2007 E1(R), 2, A1(R), NZ1(R), A2, NZ2, Nm, S, [Sm, E1(R), Tg, US(R), Arg, E2], W, 2008 W1(t&R), It, NZ1, 2, A1, Arg, NZ3, A2, 2009 F(R), I(t), 2010 W1, It1(R), NZ2, A1(t&R), NZ3(R), A2(R), 3(R), I(R), W2(R), S(R), E(R), 2011 A1(t&R), NZ1(R), 2(R), [Nm]
Van der Merwe, A J (Bol) 1955 BI 2, 3, 4, 1956 A 1, 2, NZ 1, 2, 3, 4, 1958 F 1, 1960 S, NZ 2
Van der Merwe, A V (WP) 1931 W
Van der Merwe, B S (NT) 1949 NZ 1
Van der Merwe, H S (NT) 1960 NZ 4, 1963 A 2,3,4, 1964 F
Van der Merwe, H S (GL) 2007 W(t+R)
Van der Merwe, J P (WP) 1970 W
Van der Merwe, P R (SWD, WT, GW) 1981 NZ 2,3, US, 1986 Cv 1,2, 1989 Wld 1
Van der Merwe, P R (BB) 2010 F(R), It 2(R), A1(R), NZ3, A2, 3(R), I(R), W2(R), S(R), E(R), 2011 A1, 2012 E1(R), 2(R), 3(R), Arg1(R), 2(R), A1(R), NZ1, A2(R), NZ2(R)
Vanderplank, B E (N) 1924 BI 3,4
Van der Schyff, J H (GW) 1949 NZ 1, 2, 3, 4, 1955 BI 1
Van der Watt, A E (WP) 1969 S (R), E, 1970 I
Van der Westhuizen, J C (WP) 1928 NZ 2,3,4, 1931 I
Van der Westhuizen, J H (WP) 1931 I, 1932 E, S
Van der Westhuizen, J H (NT, BB) 1993 Arg 1,2, 1994 E 1,2(R), Arg 2, S, W, 1995 WS, [A, C (R), WS, F, NZ], W, It, E, 1996 Fj, A 1,2(R), NZ 2,3(R), 4,5, Arg 1,2, F, W, 1997 Tg, BI 1,2,3, NZ 1, A 1, NZ 2, A, It, F 1, 1998 I 1,2, W 1, E 1, A 1, NZ 1,2, A 2, W 2, S, I 3, E 2, 1999 NZ 2, A 2, [S, Sp (R), U, E, A 3, NZ 3], 2000 C, E 1,2, A 1(R), NZ 1(R), A 2(R), Arg, I, W, E 3, 2001 F 1,2, It 1(R), NZ 1, A 1,2, NZ 2, F 3, It 2, E, US (R), 2003 S 1,2, A 1, NZ 1, A 2(R), NZ 2, [U,E,Sm,NZ]
Van der Westhuyzen, J N B (MP, BB) 2000 NZ 2(R), 2001 It 1(R), 2003 S 1(R), 2, Arg, A 1, 2003 [E, Sm, NZ], 2004 I1, 2, W1, PI, NZ1, A1, NZ2, A2, W2, I3, E, S, Arg, 2005 U, F1, 2, A1, 4(R), NZ2(R), 2006 S1, 2, F, A1
Van Druten, N J V (Tvl) 1924 BI 1,2,3,4, 1928 NZ 1,2,3,4
Van Heerden, A J (Tvl) 1921 NZ 1,3
Van Heerden, F J (WP) 1994 E 1,2(R), NZ 3, 1995 It, E, 1996 NZ 5(R), Arg 1(R),2(R), 1997 Tg, BI 2(t+R),3(R), NZ 1(R),2(R), 1999 [Sp]
Van Heerden, J L (NT, Tvl) 1974 BI 3,4, F 1,2, 1975 F 1,2, 1976 NZ 1,2,3,4, 1977 Wld, 1980 BI 1,3,4, S Am 3,4, F
Van Heerden, J L (BB) 2003 S 1,2, A 1, NZ 1, A 2(t), 2007 A2, NZ2, S(R), [Sm(R), E1, Tg, US, Fj(R),E2(R)]
Van Jaarsveld, C J (Tvl) 1949 NZ 1
Van Jaarsveldt, D C (R) 1960 S
Van Niekerk, J A (WP) 1928 NZ 4
Van Niekerk, J C (GL, WP, Toulon) 2001 NZ 1(R), A 1(R), NZ 2(t+R), F 3(R), It2, US, 2002 W 1(R),2(R), Sm, NZ 1, A 1, NZ 2, A 2, F, S, E, 2003 A 2, NZ 2, [U, E, Gg, Sm], 2004 NZ1(R), A1(t), NZ2, A2, W2, I3, E, S, Arg(R), 2005

U(R), F2(R), A1(R), 2, 3, NZ1, A4, NZ2, 2006 S1, 2, F, A1, NZ1(R), A2(R), 2008 It(R), NZ1, 2, Arg(R), A2(R), 2010 W1
Van Reenen, G L (WP) 1937 A 2, NZ 1
Van Renen, C G (WP) 1891 BI 3, 1896 BI 1,4
Van Renen, W (WP) 1903 BI 1,3
Van Rensburg, J T J (Tvl) 1992 NZ, A, E, 1993 F 1, 2, A 1, 1994 NZ 2
Van Rooyen, G W (Tvl) 1921 NZ 2,3
Van Ryneveld, R C B (WP) 1910 BI 2,3
Van Schalkwyk, D (NT) 1996 Fj (R), NZ 3,4,5, 1997 BI 2,3, NZ 1, A 1
Van Schoor, R A M (R) 1949 NZ 2,3,4, 1951 S, I, W, 1952 E, F, 1953 A 1,2,3,4
Van Straaten, A J J (WP) 1999 It 2(R), W, NZ 1(R), A 1, 2000 C, E 1,2, NZ 1, A 2, NZ 2, A 3, Arg (R), I (R), W, E 3, 2001 A 1,2, NZ 2, F 3, It 2, E
Van Vollenhoven, K T (NT) 1955 BI 1,2,3,4, 1956 A 1,2, NZ 3
Van Vuuren, T F (EP) 1912 S, I, W, 1913 E, F
Van Wyk, C J (Tvl) 1951 S, I, W, 1952 E, F, 1953 A 1,2,3,4, 1955 BI 1
Van Wyk, J F B (NT) 1970 NZ 1,2,3,4, 1971 F 1,2, A 1,2,3, 1972 E, 1974 BI 1,3,4, 1976 NZ 3,4
Van Wyk, S P (WP) 1928 NZ 1,2
Van Zyl, B P (WP) 1961 I
Van Zyl, C G P (OFS) 1965 NZ 1,2,3,4
Van Zyl, D J (WP) 2000 E 3(R)
Van Zyl, G H (WP) 1958 F 1, 1960 S, NZ 1,2,3,4, W, I, 1961 E, S, F, I, A 1,2, 1962 BI 1,3,4
Van Zyl, H J (Tvl) 1960 NZ 1,2,3,4, I, 1961 E, S, I, A 1,2
Van Zyl, P J (Bol) 1961 I
Veldsman, P E (WP) 1977 Wld
Venter, A G (OFS) 1996 NZ 3,4,5, Arg 1,2, F 1,2, W, 1997 Tg, BI 1,2,3, NZ 1, A 1, NZ 2, It, F 1,2, E, S, 1998 I 1,2, W 1, E 1, A 1, NZ 1,2, A 2, W 2, S (R), I 3(R), E 2(R), 1999 It 1,2(R), W (R), NZ 1, A 1, NZ 2, A 2, [S, U, E, A 3, NZ 3], 2000 C, E 1,2, A 1, NZ 1, A 2, NZ 2, A 3, Arg, I, W, E 3, 2001 F 1, It 1, NZ 1, A 1,2, NZ 2, F 3(R), It 2(R), E (t+R), US (R)
Venter, A J (N) 2000 W (R), E 3(R), 2001 F 3, It 2, E, US, 2002 W 1,2, Arg, NZ 1(R),2, A 2, F, S (R), E, 2003 Arg, 2004 PI,NZ1,A1,NZ2(R),A2,I3,E, 2006 NZ3,A3
Venter, B (OFS) 1994 E 1,2, NZ 1,2,3, Arg 1,2, 1995 [R, C, WS (R), NZ (R)], 1996 A 1, NZ 1, A 2, 1999 A 2, [S, U]
Venter, F D (Tvl) 1931 W, 1932 S, 1933 A 3
Vermeulen, D J (WP) 2012 A1,NZ1,A2,NZ2
Versfeld, C (WP) 1891 BI 3
Versfeld, M (WP) 1891 BI 1,2,3
Vigne, J T (Tvl) 1891 BI 1,2,3
Viljoen, J F (GW) 1971 F 1,2, A 1,2,3, 1972 E
Viljoen, J T (N) 1971 A 1,2,3
Villet, J V (WP) 1984 E 1,2
Visagie, I J (WP) 1999 It 1, W, NZ 1, A 1, NZ 2, A 2, [S, U, E, A 3, NZ 3], 2000 C, E 2, A 1, NZ 1, A 2, NZ 2, A 3, 2001 NZ 1, A 1,2, NZ 2, F 3, It 2(R), E (t+R), US, 2003 S 1(R),2(R), Arg

Visagie, P J (GW) 1967 F 1,2,3,4, 1968 BI 1,2,3,4, F 1,2, 1969 A 1,2,3,4, S, E, 1970 NZ 1,2,3,4, 1971 F 1,2, A 1,2,3
Visagie, R G (OFS, N) 1984 E 1,2, S Am 1,2, 1993 F 1
Visser, J de V (WP) 1981 NZ 2, US
Visser, M (WP) 1995 WS (R)
Visser, P J (Tvl) 1933 A 2
Viviers, S S (OFS) 1956 A 1,2, NZ 2,3,4
Vogel, M L (OFS) 1974 BI 2(R)
Von Hoesslin, D J B (GW) 1999 It 1(R),2, W (R), NZ 1, A 1(R)
Vos, A N (GL) 1999 It 1(t+R),2, NZ 1(R), 2(R), A 2, [S (R), Sp, E (R), A 3(R), NZ 3], 2000 C, E 1,2, A 1, NZ 1, A 2, NZ 2, A 3, Arg, I, W, E 3, 2001 F 1,2, It 1, NZ 1, A 1,2, NZ 2, F 3, It 2, E, US

Wagenaar, C (NT) 1977 Wld
Wahl, J J (WP) 1949 NZ 1
Walker, A P (N) 1921 NZ 1,3, 1924 BI 1,2,3,4
Walker, H N (OFS) 1953 A 3, 1956 A 2, NZ 1,4
Walker, H W (Tvl) 1910 BI 1,2,3
Walton, D C (N) 1964 F, 1965 I, S, NZ 3,4, 1969 A 1,2, E
Wannenburg, P J (BB) 2002 F (R), E, 2003 S 1,2, Arg, A 1(t+R), NZ 1(R), 2004 I1,2, W1, PI(R), 2006 S1(R), F, NZ2(R), 3, A3, 2007 Sm(R), NZ1(R), A2, NZ2
Waring, F W (WP) 1931 I, 1932 E, 1933 A 1,2,3,4,5
Watson, L A (WP) 2007 Sm, 2008 W1, 2, It, NZ1(R), 2(R), Arg, NZ3(R), A2(R), 3(t&R)
Wegner, N (WP) 1993 F 2, A 1, 2, 3
Wentzel, M van Z (Pumas) 2002 F (R), S
Wessels, J J (WP) 1896 BI 1,2,3
Whipp, P J M (WP) 1974 BI 1,2, 1975 F 1, 1976 NZ 1, 3, 4, 1980 S Am 1,2
White, J (Bor) 1931 W, 1933 A 1, 2, 3, 4, 5, 1937 A 1,2, NZ 1,2
Wiese, J J (Tvl) 1993 F 1, 1995 WS, [R, C, WS, F, NZ], W, It, E, 1996 NZ 3(R), 4(R), 5, Arg 1,2, F 1,2, W
Willemse, A K (GL) 2003 S 1,2, NZ 1, A 2, NZ 2, [U,E,Sm,NZ], 2004 W2, I3, 2007 E1, 2(R), Sm, A1, NZ1, Nm, S(R), [Tg]
Williams, A E (GW) 1910 BI 1
Williams, A P (WP) 1984 E 1,2
Williams, C M (WP, GL) 1993 Arg 2, 1994 E 1,2 NZ 1,2,3, Arg 1,2, S, W, 1995 WS, [WS, F, NZ], It, E, 1998 A 1(t), NZ 1(t), 2000 C (R), E 1(t),2(R), A 1(R), NZ 2, A 3, Arg, I, W (R)
Williams, D O (WP) 1937 A 1,2, NZ 1,2,3, 1938 BI 1,2,3
Williams, J G (NT) 1971 F 1,2, A 1,2,3, 1972 E, 1974 BI 1,2,4, F 1,2, 1976 NZ 1,2
Wilson, L G (WP) 1960 NZ 3,4, W, I, 1961 E, F, I, A 1,2, 1962 BI 1,2,3,4, 1963 A 1,2,3,4, 1964 W, F, 1965 I, S, A 1,2, NZ 1,2,3,4
Wolmarans, B J (OFS) 1977 Wld
Wright, G D (EP, Tvl) 1986 Cv 3,4, 1989 Wld 1,2, 1992 F 1,2, E
Wyness, M R K (WP) 1962 BI 1,2,3,4, 1963 A 2

Zeller, W C (N) 1921 NZ 2,3

Zimerman, M (WP) 1931 W, I, 1932 E, S

TONGA

TONGA'S 2012 TEST RECORD

OPPONENTS	DATE	VENUE	RESULT
Samoa	5 Jun	N	Lost 20–18
Japan	10 Jun	A	Won 24–20
Fiji	23Jun	A	Lost 29–17

TIME OF SIGNIFICANT CHANGE FOR TONGA

Alipate Fatafehi is congratulated after scoring a try during the IRB Pacific Nations Cup match against Japan.

Having parted ways with their Rugby World Cup 2011 coaching team of Isitola Maka and his assistant John McKee, and with a new administration at the helm following the handover by the interim administration to a newly-formed Tonga Rugby Union, 2012 was always going to be a period of significant change.

Tonga, though, had high expectations despite the enormity of these changes. After finishing 2011 with their highest ever IRB World Ranking of ninth and their famous win over France still fresh in the minds of the Tonga Rugby Union and fans alike, the optimism was perhaps well justified. Having directly qualified for the next Rugby World Cup – a feat Tonga have only managed to do once before – by finishing third in their pool in New Zealand, the Union were now in a position where they could plan for England 2015 with certainty.

The IRB Pacific Rugby Cup marked the beginning of the four-year cycle to RWC 2015. Competing against the Academy sides from Super Rugby franchises in Australia and New Zealand, the PRC provides Fiji, Samoa and Tonga with a competition platform to expose their best locally-based players against the futures stars of Super Rugby.

Tonga A's tour of Australia in late February proved a disappointing one with losses to both the Junior Waratahs (27–11) and Queensland A (23–8). They were robbed of a chance to finish the Australian tour on a high after their match against the Brumby Runners was cancelled due to bad weather. This meant they headed to New Zealand, tradition-ally the toughest of the two Australasian legs, bottom of the table behind Fiji Warriors and Samoa A.

True to form, New Zealand proved to be a formidable tour for Tonga A and they were comprehensively beaten by the Blues Development XV (40–3), Crusader Knights (58–6) and the Highlanders Development XV (62–8). Without a win in the first two elements of the competition, Tonga A's title dreams were over before they hosted the final leg in Nuku'alofa in October. There were still opportunities, though, to impress the new coaching team and be selected for the European tour in November when Tonga face Italy, USA and Scotland. Home advantage proved a tonic with Tonga A edging Samoa A 20–18 to break their duck and hand Fiji Warriors the title, before ending the competition with a 25–16 loss to the champions.

Tonga entered the IRB Pacific Nations Cup in June confident of going one better than last year when they came agonisingly close to claiming a first title, ultimately finishing second behind Japan who scored a bonus point win over Fiji, with a try in the last minute, to deny them.

Yet to finalise a permanent coaching structure, Tonga went to the PNC in Japan with an interim coaching team, headed up by their RWC 2011 assistant coach and former Wallaby Toutai Kefu.

With three locally-based players stepping up to the national squad after playing in the PRC earlier in the year, and a host of players returning after RWC 2011 – including fly half Kurt Morath – expectations were high.

However, an opening 20–18 loss to Samoa in Nagoya had the Tongan camp reeling. In an error-strewn performance Tonga had led 9–6 at the break courtesy of three Morath penalties, but conceded two tries to slip to defeat. Morath was Tonga's only point scorer with six penalties, taking him past Fiji's Taniela Rawaqa to become the leading point-scorer in PNC history.

"Obviously we are very disappointed with the result," admitted Kefu afterwards. "But you saw the game, we didn't deserve to win."

Despite an horrendous record against Japan in the competition, having won just one of six matches against the Brave Blossoms, Tonga went into their second match in Tokyo with confidence having won the last meeting between the two sides 31–18 at RWC 2011.

Kefu knew that Tonga needed to "cut down our errors" if they were to repeat that victory in Whangarei, but while they outscored their hosts by three tries to two to win 24–20 it wasn't the convincing win their coach had been hoping for.

"It's good to get the win but whether we played well or not [I don't know]," Kefu said afterwards.

Two weeks later, after Fiji's one-off Test with Scotland, Tonga headed to Lautoka for the final PNC match of 2012. Samoa had already been crowned champions after beating Japan a week earlier, so the Churchill Park encounter would determine the runners-up.

Leading at the break for the third time in the tournament, thanks to three Morath penalties, Tonga conceded three second-half tries to lose 29–17. It was a ruthless performance by a Fijian backline that grew in confidence with every minute of the second half.

After the Pacific Nations Cup, the Tonga Rugby Union set about appointing a full-time coaching team to lead the Ikale Tahi into RWC 2015. Mana Otai, Tonga's captain at RWC 1995, was named head coach in September with his first challenge being the November tour to Europe.

It was also a bittersweet year for the Tonga Sevens team. Having beaten Australia to claim third spot at the 2011 Oceania Sevens Championship, Tonga qualified for the Gold Coast, Wellington and Hong Kong rounds of the 2011/12 HSBC Sevens World Series.

After shocking Kenya in the Bowl quarter-finals on the Gold Coast, Tonga then lost 24–15 to Argentina. However, this tournament was only a taste of what was to come in Wellington in February 2012.

Tonga shocked the Sevens world with a stellar performance in Wellington, a tournament where teams from the Pacific Islands have often enjoyed great results at the expense of more fancied opponents. With wins over Argentina, Fiji and a draw against RWC Sevens champions Wales, Tonga reached the Cup quarter-finals where they duly lost to England. They bounced back to beat France 15–7 before losing 24–0 to South Africa in the Plate Final, but the performances in Wellington gave Tonga renewed confidence ahead of Hong Kong, where they would vie for one of three new core team places on the 2012/13 World Series.

Hong Kong, though, would prove a bitter disappointment. An unexpected 26–7 pool loss to their hosts set Tonga on a difficult path in the knockout stages, where a 19–7 loss to Spain in the qualifying quarter-final ended their hopes of becoming a core team.

Having missed out on core team status, Tonga were keen to avoid a repeat when it came to the Oceania regional qualifier for RWC Sevens 2013 in August. They arrived in Australia, though, reeling from the death of coach 'Otenili Pifeleti earlier that month and were then humbled 14–7 by American Samoa in the pool stages. That defeat acted as a wake-up call for Tonga, although they had to survive a fight-back from Papua New Guinea to win 17–15 in the quarter-finals. They then lost 24–7 to eventual champions Australia but crucially edged Cook Islands 19–17 in the third place play-off to qualify for RWC Sevens 2013.

Winning that play-off also secured Tonga's entry into the Gold Coast and Wellington rounds of the 2012/13 HSBC Sevens World Series and the pre-qualifying tournament in Hong Kong for teams hoping to gain core team status for 2013/14. They headed to the opening round in Australia with another man at the helm, former Fiji Sevens assistant coach Etuate Waqa having been unveiled as the new Tonga Sevens coach in September.

There was also disappointment for Tonga at the IRB Junior World Rugby Trophy in June. They had travelled with one goal – to win the title and return to the Junior World Championship from where they had been relegated in 2011. The team enjoyed huge support from the large Tongan community in Salt Lake City, but an opening 22–11 loss to USA on day one derailed their title hopes. Wins over Chile and Russia followed, but Tonga ultimately faced Georgia for third place and a 31–29 victory was cold comfort for a team with title expectations.

TONGA INTERNATIONAL STATISTICS

MATCH RECORDS UP TO 10 OCTOBER 2012

WINNING MARGIN

Date	Opponent	Result	Winning Margin
21/03/2003	Korea	119–0	119
08/07/2006	Cook Islands	90–0	90
01/01/1979	Solomon Islands	92–3	89
10/02/2007	Korea	83–3	80
15/03/2003	Korea	75–0	75

MOST CONVERSIONS IN A MATCH

BY THE TEAM

Date	Opponent	Result	Cons
21/03/2003	Korea	119–0	17
08/07/2006	Cook Islands	90–0	10

BY A PLAYER

Date	Player	Opponent	Cons
21/03/2003	Pierre Hola	Korea	17
08/07/2006	Fangatapu Apikotoa	Cook Islands	9
10/02/2007	Fangatapu Apikotoa	Korea	9
06/12/2002	Pierre Hola	Papua New Guinea	9
05/07/1997	Kusitafu Tonga	Cook Islands	9

MOST POINTS IN A MATCH
BY THE TEAM

Date	Opponent	Result	Points
21/03/2003	Korea	119–0	119
01/01/1979	Solomon Islands	92–3	92
08/07/2006	Cook Islands	90–0	90
06/12/2002	Papua New Guinea	84–12	84
10/02/2007	Korea	83–3	83

BY A PLAYER

Date	Player	Opponent	Points
21/03/2003	Pierre Hola	Korea	39
10/02/2007	Fangatapu Apikotoa	Korea	28
04/05/1999	Sateki Tuipulotu	Korea	27
21/03/2003	Benhur Kivalu	Korea	25
06/12/2002	Pierre Hola	Papua New Guinea	24

MOST TRIES IN A MATCH
BY THE TEAM

Date	Opponent	Result	Tries
21/03/2003	Korea	119–0	17
08/07/2006	Cook Islands	90–0	14
10/02/2007	Korea	83–3	13
24/06/2006	Cook Islands	77–10	13

BY A PLAYER

Date	Player	Opponent	Tries
21/03/2003	Benhur Kivalu	Korea	5
08/06/2011	Viliame Iongi	USA	4

MOST PENALTIES IN A MATCH
BY THE TEAM

Date	Opponent	Result	Pens
05/06/2012	Samoa	18–20	6
10/11/2001	Scotland	20–43	5
28/06/2008	Samoa	15–20	5
13/07/2011	Samoa	29–19	5
19/08/2011	Fiji	32–20	5

BY A PLAYER

Date	Player	Opponent	Pens
05/06/2012	Kurt Morath	Samoa	6
13/07/2011	Kurt Morath	Samoa	5
19/08/2011	Kurt Morath	Fiji	5

MOST DROP GOALS IN A MATCH
BY THE TEAM

1 on 8 Occasions

BY A PLAYER

1 on 8 Occasions

MOST CAPPED PLAYERS

Name	Caps
'Elisi Vunipola	41
Benhur Kivalu	38
Pierre Hola	37
Manu Vunipola	35
Aleki Lutui	33

LEADING TRY SCORERS

Name	Tries
Siua Taumalolo	12
Fepikou Tatafu	11
Benhur Kivalu	10

LEADING CONVERSIONS SCORERS

Name	Cons
Pierre Hola	65
Kurt Morath	34
Sateki Tuipulotu	33
Fangatapu Apikotoa	31

LEADING PENALTY SCORERS

Name	Pens
Kurt Morath	51
Pierre Hola	35
Sateki Tuipulotu	32

LEADING DROP GOAL SCORERS

Name	DGs
Pierre Hola	3

LEADING POINTS SCORERS

Name	Points
Pierre Hola	289
Kurt Morath	226
Sateki Tuipulotu	190
Siua Taumalolo	108

TONGA INTERNATIONAL PLAYERS
UP TO 10 OCTOBER 2012

I Afeaki 1995 *F, S, Iv*, 1997 *Fj*, 2001 *S, W*, 2002 *J, Fj, Sa, Fj*, 2003 *Kor, Kor, I, Fj, Fj, It, C*, 2004 *Sa, Fj*, 2005 *It*, 2007 *Sa, SA, E*
P Afeaki 1983 *Fj, Sa*
S Afeaki 2002 *Fj, Sa, Fj, PNG, PNG*, 2003 *Kor, Kor, I, Fj, It, W, NZ*
V Afeaki 1997 *Sa*, 2002 *Sa, Fj*
JL Afu 2008 *J, Sa, Fj*, 2009 *Fj, Sa, J*, 2011 *US*, 2012 *Sa, J, Fj*
T Afu Fifita 1924 *Fj, Fj, Fj*
A Afu Fungavaka 1982 *Sa*, 1984 *Fj, Fj*, 1985 *Fj*, 1986 *W, Fj, Fj*, 1987 *C, W, I, Sa, Fj*
S 'Aho 1974 *S, W*
T Ahoafi 2007 *AuA, Sa*
P Ahofono 1990 *Sa*
K Ahota'e'iloa 1999 *Sa, F, Fj*, 2000 *C, Fj, J*
M Ahota'e'iloa 2010 *Sa, Fj, J*
S Aisake 1934 *Fj*
M Akau'ola 1934 *Fj*
P 'Ake 1926 *Fj, Fj, Fj*
A Alatini 2001 *S*, 2002 *J, Sa, Fj*, 2003 *I, Fj*
M Alatini 1969 *M*, 1972 *Fj, Fj*, 1973 *M, A, A, Fj*, 1974 *S, W, C*, 1975 *M*, 1977 *Fj*
PF Alatini 1995 *Sa*
S Alatini 1994 *Sa, Fj*, 1998 *Sa, Fj*, 2000 *NZ, US*
S Alatini 1977 *Fj*, 1979 *NC, M, E*
T Alatini 1932 *Fj*
V 'Alipate 1967 *Fj*, 1968 *Fj, Fj, Fj*, 1969 *M*
A Amone 1987 *W, I, Sa, Fj*
A Amore 1988 *Fj*
T Anitoni 1995 *J, Sa, Fj*, 1996 *Sa, Fj*
V Anitoni 1990 *Sa*
F Apikotoa 2004 *Sa, Fj*, 2005 *Fj, Sa, Fj, Sa, It, F*, 2006 *Coo, Coo*, 2007 *Kor, AuA, J, JAB*, 2008 *J, Sa, Fj*, 2009 *Fj, J*, 2010 *Fj, CHL*
T Apitani 1947 *Fj, Fj*
S Asi 1987 *C*
T Asi 1996 *Sa*
H 'Asi 2000 *C*
S Ata 1928 *Fj*
S Atiola 1987 *Sa, Fj*, 1988 *Fj, Fj*, 1989 *Fj, Fj*, 1990 *Fj, J*
H Aulika 2011 *Fj, Fj, C, J, F*
K Bakewa 2002 *PNG, PNG*, 2003 *Fj*
O Beba 1932 *Fj, Fj, Fj*
O Blake 1983 *M, M*, 1987 *Sa, Fj*, 1988 *Sa, Fj, Fj*
T Bloomfield 1973 *M, A, A, Fj*, 1986 *W*
D Briggs 1997 *W*
J Buloka 1932 *Fj, Fj*
D Edwards 1998 *A*, 1999 *Geo, Geo, Kor, US, Sa, F, Fj, C, NZ, It, E*
T Ete'aki 1984 *Fj*, 1986 *W, Fj, Fj*, 1987 *C, W, I*, 1990 *Fj, J, Sa, Kor, Sa*, 1991 *Sa*
U Fa'a 1994 *Sa, W*, 1995 *J*, 1998 *Sa, A, Fj*
L Fa'aoso 2004 *Sa, Fj*, 2005 *Fj, Sa, Fj, Sa*, 2007 *US, E*, 2009 *Pt*, 2011 *Fj, J, Fj*
P Fa'apoi 1963 *Fj*
V Fa'aumu 1986 *Fj, Fj*
V Faingaa 2012 *Sa, Fj*
OHL Faingaanuku 2011 *US*, 2012 *Fj*
T Fainga'anuku 1999 *NZ, It*, 2000 *C, Fj, J, NZ*, 2001 *Fj, Sa, Fj, Sa*
S Faka 'osi'folau 1997 *Z, Nrn, SA, Fj, Sa, Coo, W*, 1998 *A, Fj*, 1999 *Geo, Kor, Fj*, 2001 *Sa*
DAT Fakafanua 2010 *CHL*, 2012 *Sa*
P Fakalelu 2005 *It*, 2006 *Coo, Coo*, 2009 *Sa, J*

J Fakalolo 1926 *Fj, Fj, Fj*
P Fakana 1963 *Fj, Fj*
F Fakaongo 1993 *S, Fj*, 1995 *Iv, Sa, Fj*, 2000 *Fj, J, NZ, Sa*, 2001 *S, W*, 2002 *J, Fj, Sa*
V Fakatou 1998 *Sa, A, Fj*, 1999 *Kor, NZ*
V Fakatulolo 1975 *M*
S Fakaua 2005 *Sa*
P Faka'ua 1967 *Fj, Fj, Fj*, 1968 *Fj, Fj, Fj*, 1969 *M, M*, 1972 *Fj*
N Fakauho 1977 *Fj, Fj*
P Fakava 1988 *Sa, Fj*
FP Faletau 1999 *Geo, Kor, Kor, J, US, Sa, F, Fj, C*
K Faletau 1988 *Sa, Fj*, 1989 *Fj, Fj*, 1990 *Sa*, 1991 *Fj*, 1992 *Fj*, 1997 *Nm, SA, Fj, Sa, Coo, W*, 1999 *Sa, F, Fj, C*
M Fanga'uta 1982 *Fj*
K Fangupo 2009 *Pt*
MU Fangupo 2009 *Sa, J*, 2010 *J, CHL*
F Faotusa 1990 *Sa*
LAHN Fatafehi 2009 *Fj, Sa, Pt*, 2010 *Sa, Fj, J*, 2011 *Fj, NZ, C, J, F*, 2012 *Sa, J, Fj*
IT Fatani 1992 *Fj*, 1993 *Sa, S, Fj, A, Fj*, 1997 *Fj, Coo*, 1999 *Geo, Kor, Kor, J, US, Sa, F, Fj, C, NZ, It, E*, 2000 *C, Fj, J, NZ, Sa, US*
O Faupula 1924 *Fj, Fj, Fj*
SLJ Faupula 2010 *CHL*
AOM Feao 2010 *Sa, Fj*
S Fe'ao 1995 *F, S*
SL Fekau 1983 *M, M*
K Feke 1988 *Fj, Fj*, 1989 *Fj*, 1990 *Fj, Sa*
SH Fekitoa 2010 *Sa, J*
T Feleola 1934 *Fj*
M Felise 1987 *W, I*
I Fenukitau 1993 *Sa, S, Fj, A, Fj*, 1994 *Sa, Fj*, 1995 *J, J, F, S*, 2002 *J, Fj, Sa*, 2003 *It, W, NZ, C*
Fetu'ulele 1967 *Fj*
K Fielea 1987 *C, W, I, Sa, Fj*, 1990 *J, Sa, Kor, Sa*, 1991 *Sa*
L Fifita 1934 *Fj*
P Fifita 1983 *Fj*
P Fifita 2003 *C*
S Fifita 1974 *S, W, C*, 1975 *M*
T Fifita 1984 *Fj, Fj*, 1986 *W, Fj, Fj*, 1987 *C, W, I*, 1991 *Sa, Fj, Fj*
T Fifita 2001 *Fj, Fj*, 2003 *Fj*, 2006 *J*, 2008 *J*
V Fifita 1982 *Fj*
V Fifita 2005 *F*
F Filikitonga 1990 *Fj, Sa*
L Fililava 1960 *M*
M Filimoehala 1968 *Fj*, 1974 *W, C*, 1975 *M, M*
OAML Filipine 2000 *C*, 2006 *J, Fj, Coo, Sa*, 2007 *US, SA*, 2008 *J*
M Filise 1986 *Fj, Fj*
T Filise 2001 *Fj, Fj, S, W*, 2002 *Sa, Fj*, 2004 *Sa, Fj*, 2005 *Fj, Sa, Fj, Sa*, 2007 *Fj, Sa, E*, 2011 *NZ, J*
S Filo 2004 *Sa, Fj*
I Finau 1987 *Sa, Fj*, 1990 *Fj, J, Sa*
M Finau 1974 *NC, M, E, Sa*, 1980 *Sa*, 1984 *Fj*
M Finau 2007 *AuA*, 2008 *J*, 2009 *Fj, J*, 2010 *J, CHL*
S Finau 1998 *Sa*, 1999 *Geo, Sa, F, Fj, C, E*, 2001 *Fj, Fj, S*, 2005 *It, F*
S Finau 1989 *Fj*, 1990 *Fj, J, Sa, Kor, Sa*
S Finau 1924 *Fj, Fj, Fj*, 1926 *Fj, Fj, Fj*
T Finau 1967 *Fj*
T Finau 1924 *Fj, Fj, Fj*
V Finau 1987 *Sa, Fj*
I Fine 2007 *Kor, AuA, JAB, Sa*

V Vaka'uta 1959 *Fj*, 1960 *M*
V Vake 1932 *Fj*
VL Vaki 2001 *Fj, Sa, Fj, Sa, S, W*, 2002 *J, Fj, Sa, Sa, Fj, PNG*, 2003 *I, Fj, Fj, It, W, NZ, C*, 2005 *Fj, Sa, It, F*, 2006 *JAB, Coo, Sa, Coo*, 2007 *US, Sa, SA, E*, 2008 *Fj*
Valeli 1947 *Fj*
F Valu 1973 *M, A, A, Fj*, 1974 *S, W, C*, 1975 *M, M*, 1977 *Fj, Fj, Fj*, 1979 *NC, M, E, Sa, Fj*, 1980 *Sa*, 1981 *Fj*, 1983 *Fj, Sa, M, M*, 1987 *C, W, I*
V Vanisi 1969 *M, M*
L Vano 1986 *Fj*
A Vasi 1993 *Fj*
I Vave 1973 *A, A, Fj*, 1974 *S, C*
T Vave 1993 *A*
M Vea 1992 *Fj*
S Veehala 1987 *Sa, Fj*, 1988 *Fj, Fj*, 1989 *Fj*, 1990 *J, Kor*, 1991 *Sa, Fj, Fj*
J Vikilani 1932 *Fj, Fj*
T Vikilani 1992 *Fj*, 1994 *Sa, W*
T Viliame 1979 *M*
O Vitelefi 1986 *W*
F Vuna 1977 *Fj, Fj, Fj*, 1979 *NC, M, Sa*, 1981 *Fj*

V Vuni 1932 *Fj, Fj, Fj*, 1934 *Fj*
A Vunipola 1982 *Fj*
E Vunipola 1990 *Fj, Kor*, 1993 *Sa, S, Fj, A, Fj*, 1994 *Sa, W*, 1995 *J, J, F, S, Iv*, 1996 *Sa, Fj*, 1997 *Z*, 1999 *Geo, Geo, Kor, Kor, J, F, Fj, NZ, It, E*, 2000 *C, Fj, J, NZ, Sa, US*, 2001 *Fj, Sa, Fj, Sa, S*, 2004 *Sa, Fj*, 2005 *F*
F Vunipola 1988 *Fj*, 1991 *Sa, Fj, Fj*, 1994 *Sa, W, Fj*, 1995 *J, J, F, S, Iv, Sa, Fj*, 1996 *Sa, Fj*, 1997 *SA, Fj*, 1999 *Geo, Kor, Kor, Fj, C, NZ, E*, 2000 *NZ, Sa, US*, 2001 *Sa*
K Vunipola 1982 *Sa, Fj*, 1983 *Fj, Sa, M, M*
M Vunipola 1987 *W, Sa*, 1988 *Sa, Fj, Fj, Fj*, 1989 *Fj, Fj*, 1990 *Kor*, 1991 *Fj, Fj*, 1992 *Sa*, 1993 *Sa, S, Fj, A, Fj*, 1994 *Sa, W*, 1995 *J, J, F, S, Sa, Fj*, 1996 *Sa, Fj*, 1997 *Nm, SA, Coo*, 1999 *Geo, Kor, Kor, US, Fj*
S Vunipola 1977 *Fj*, 1981 *Fj*, 1982 *Sa*
V Vunipola 1982 *Fj*
VS Vunipola 2004 *Sa, Fj*, 2005 *It*
S Vunipoli 1960 *M*, 1963 *Fj*
B Woolley 1998 *Sa, Fj*, 1999 *Geo, Geo, Kor, J, US, Sa, C, It*

USA

USA'S 2012 TEST RECORD

OPPONENTS	DATE	VENUE	RESULT
Canada	9 Jun	A	Lost 28–25
Georgia	16 Jun	H	Won 36–20
Italy	23 Jun	H	Lost 10–30

ELITE CONTRACTS PAVE WAY FOR EXCITING NEW ERA

By Ian Gilbert

Bongarts / Getty Images

The game in the USA is making great strides, and losing 30–10 to Italy was no disgrace.

The start of 2012 ushered in a landmark for USA rugby: the union's first contracted professionals.

The elevation of Sevens to the Olympic programme from 2016 has galvanised support for the abbreviated game in several countries, the States included. In January, the first men's and women's squads were selected to enter the elite training programme near San Diego, California.

USA's elite players largely juggle rugby with their careers – or head overseas to play – but this development allows the Sevens exponents to concentrate on rugby.

As Nigel Melville, the chief executive of USA Rugby, says: "That means our players are now full-time – men's and women's – with full-time training, full-time support and coaching and an increasing number of competitions."

USA sport is a tough market, with rugby competing for attention against domestic giants like American football, basketball, baseball and ice hockey. But Americans revere their Olympians, and the lustre of possible gold could rub off to the extent that athletes are attracted to rugby. This doesn't mean just those with obvious attributes for the game, such as American footballers, but also sprinters, for instance.

"It's about identifying athletes who play seven-a-side and looking at every opportunity," says Melville.

Todd Clever, captain of the Eagles' Test XV, has also played for the Sevens team and acknowledges the importance of the Olympic angle.

"The biggest thing is getting people interested in watching rugby, so right now we have NBC picking up the broadcast," he says. "Olympic sport means a lot more kids watching rugby and a growing interest; Olympic sport means that at the Olympic training facilities in San Diego they have the Olympic fever of training, living and eating rugby."

Away from Sevens, the USA national side had a substantial break after Rugby World Cup 2011, regrouping in June for Tests against Canada, Georgia and Italy. This hiatus affords the mainly amateur players some respite after the sacrifices made in their life outside rugby.

"A lot of these guys are so dedicated towards that [World Cup] goal they devote four years to making a World Cup team, so there's quite a big turnaround after the World Cup," says Clever.

New national coach Mike Tolkin, who took over from Eddie O'Sullivan, ended the month with a ledger of won one, lost two, but the outlook was brighter than might appear the case.

Neighbours Canada shaded a tough battle 28–25, the 36–20 win over Georgia was payback for a narrow defeat in 2010, and losing 30–10 to Six Nations side Italy was no disgrace.

Clever was upbeat about the Eagles' mid-year report card: "I'd definitely give them a higher rating than our performance would suggest. We've got a good group of core guys, and I'm happy with it and looking forward."

The Canada game was Tolkin's first in charge, having been defensive coach at the World Cup, while Andrew Durutalo, Will Holder, Luke Hume and Taylor Mokate (as a replacement) made their debuts.

"Canada was our first time playing together with a new coach and new pattern and bringing in a lot of new guys," said Clever.

"A lot of guys were stepping up – it's a big step up from university or domestic to international rugby – and it was very frustrating losing to Canada by such a close margin in a game we could have had."

Canada in many ways remain a benchmark for the USA – the competition has been regular and intense over the years, though the Eagles have won only a quarter of the 48 fixtures.

"We're always within grasp of them – it's a good rivalry and always going to be tough," Clever said.

And 2012 was the year the Eagles of the future came of age, the Under 20s beating Japan in a nail-biting IRB Junior World Rugby Trophy final on home soil in Salt Lake City.

The USA clung on in the face of determined last-ditch attacks to prevail 37–33. As champions, they will now compete in the IRB Junior World Championship in France in 2013.

Their success illustrates the effectiveness of USA Rugby's defined "pathways", which are intended to help talented youngsters progress from raw beginner through age group and varsity honours to the national team.

Clever, who came through the age group set-up, said: "We're getting more kids playing rugby at a younger age and better athletes picking up a rugby ball."

The non-contact "Rookie Rugby" scheme is heading towards a million participants, and Melville observed: "A lot of kids are picking up a rugby ball for the first time and recognising rugby as an Olympic sport."

The next challenge to take the game forward will be a professional league, something that is high on Melville's agenda. "We've moved forward – we're reaching an exciting stage," he says. "We've made a lot of progress."

In the meantime, several of the team earn a living playing overseas; Clever's rugby CV includes South African Super Rugby franchise the Lions and he is now with Japanese club NTT Shining Arcs.

But for the other Eagles players, economic reality means trying to juggle a career – or putting their work ambitions on hold – while they try to maintain the standards needed for Test rugby. While domestic league game attendances are increasing, sponsorship and broadcast rights will be key to any professional league.

Meanwhile, the women's Sevens squad is already among the world's best, winning the Plate final at the IRB Women's Sevens Challenge Cup at Twickenham in May, then losing to Canada in the final of the Amsterdam Sevens.

The 15-a-side team are already looking towards Women's Rugby World Cup 2014 in Paris, conducting an ambitious trial competition mid-year in Colorado for the top 100 players.

The men's domestic season saw New York Athletic Club claim their fourth Super League title in eight years by beating Old Puget Sound Beach of Seattle. Eagles scrum half Mike Petri captained his club side to a 32–29 victory, while his national team-mate, back row Louis Stanfill, was Man of the Match.

In the women's National Championship, the Midwest Thunderbirds posted a resounding 48–8 victory over Mid-Atlantic to become the USA Rugby Women's All-star champions.

USA INTERNATIONAL STATISTICS
MATCH RECORDS UP TO 10 OCTOBER 2012

WINNING MARGIN

Date	Opponent	Result	Winning Margin
01/07/2006	Barbados	91–0	91
06/07/1996	Japan	74–5	69
07/11/1989	Uruguay	60–3	57
12/03/1994	Bermuda	60–3	57

MOST POINTS IN A MATCH
BY THE TEAM

Date	Opponent	Result	Points
01/07/2006	Barbados	91–0	91
06/07/1996	Japan	74–5	74
17/05/2003	Japan	69–27	69
12/04/2003	Spain	62–13	62
08/04/1998	Portugal	61–5	61

BY A PLAYER

Date	Player	Opponent	Points
07/11/1989	Chris O'Brien	Uruguay	26
31/05/2004	Mike Hercus	Russia	26
01/07/2006	Mike Hercus	Barbados	26
12/03/1994	Chris O'Brien	Bermuda	25
06/07/1996	Matt Alexander	Japan	24

MOST TRIES IN A MATCH
BY THE TEAM

Date	Opponent	Result	Tries
01/07/2006	Barbados	91–0	13
17/05/2003	Japan	69–27	11
07/11/1989	Uruguay	60–3	11
06/07/1996	Japan	74–5	11

BY A PLAYER

Date	Player	Opponent	Tries
11/05/1924	Dick Hyland	Romania	5
06/07/1996	Vaea Anitoni	Japan	4
07/06/1997	Brian Hightower	Japan	4
08/04/1998	Vaea Anitoni	Portugal	4
11/05/1924	John Patrick	Romania	4

MOST CONVERSIONS IN A MATCH
BY THE TEAM

Date	Opponent	Result	Cons
01/07/2006	Barbados	91–0	13
07/11/1989	Uruguay	60–3	8
06/07/1996	Japan	74–5	8

BY A PLAYER

Date	Player	Opponent	Cons
01/07/2006	Mike Hercus	Barbados	13
06/07/1996	Matt Alexander	Japan	8
07/11/1989	Chris O'Brien	Uruguay	7
17/05/2003	Mike Hercus	Japan	7

MOST PENALTIES IN A MATCH
BY THE TEAM

Date	Opponent	Result	Pens
18/09/1996	Canada	18–23	6

BY A PLAYER

Date	Player	Opponent	Pens
18/09/1996	Matt Alexander	Canada	6
21/09/1996	Matt Alexander	Uruguay	5
02/10/1993	Chris O'Brien	Australia	5
20/10/2003	Mike Hercus	Scotland	5
22/05/1999	Kevin Dalzell	Fiji	5
09/06/1984	Ray Nelson	Canada	5

MOST DROP GOALS IN A MATCH
BY THE TEAM

Date	Opponent	Result	DGs
27/11/2010	Georgia	17–19	2

BY A PLAYER

1 on 18 Occasions

USA

MOST CAPPED PLAYERS

Name	Caps
Mike MacDonald	67
Luke Gross	62
Alec Parker	57
Dave Hodges	53

LEADING TRY SCORERS

Name	Tries
Vaea Anitoni	26
Paul Emerick	16
Todd Clever	11
Philip Eloff	10
Riaan van Zyl	10

LEADING CONVERSIONS SCORERS

Name	Cons
Mike Hercus	90
Matt Alexander	45
Chris O'Brien	24
Nese Malifa	17

LEADING PENALTY SCORERS

Name	Pens
Mike Hercus	76
Matt Alexander	55
Mark Williams	35

LEADING DROP GOAL SCORERS

Name	DGs
Mike Hercus	4

LEADING POINTS SCORERS

Name	Points
Mike Hercus	465
Matt Alexander	286
Chris O'Brien	144
Mark Williams	143
Vaea Anitoni	130

USA INTERNATIONAL PLAYERS
UP TO 10 OCTOBER 2012

M Alexander 1995 *C*, 1996 *I*, *C*, *HK*, *J*, *HK*, *J*, *Ar*, *C*, *Ur*, 1997 *W*, *C*, *HK*, *J*, *J*, *HK*, *C*, *W*, *W*, 1998 *Pt*, *Sp*, *J*, *HK*, *C*
AE Allen 1912 *A*
S Allen 1996 *J*, 1997 *HK*, *J*, *J*, *C*, *W*, *W*
T Altemeier 1978 *C*
D Anderson 2002 *S*
B Andrews 1978 *C*, 1979 *C*
VN Anitoni 1992 *C*, 1994 *C*, *Ar*, *Ar*, *I*, 1995 *C*, 1996 *I*, *C*, *C*, *HK*, *J*, *HK*, *J*, *Ar*, *C*, *Ur*, 1997 *W*, *C*, *J*, *HK*, *C*, *W*, *W*, 1998 *Pt*, *Sp*, *J*, *HK*, *C*, *C*, *J*, *HK*, *Fj*, *Ar*, *C*, *Ur*, 1999 *Tg*, *Fj*, *J*, *C*, *Sa*, *E*, *I*, *R*, *A*, 2000 *Fj*, *Sa*
J Arrell 1912 *A*
D Asbun 2012 *Geo*, *It*
S Auerbach 1976 *A*
CA Austin 1912 *A*, 1913 *NZ*
M Aylor 2006 *IrA*, *M*, *C*, *Bar*, *Ur*, 2007 *S*, *C*, *Sa*, *SA*, 2008 *IrA*
A Bachelet 1993 *C*, *A*, 1994 *Ber*, *C*, *Ar*, *Ar*, *I*, 1995 *C*, 1996 *I*, *C*, *C*, *HK*, *J*, *HK*, *J*, *Ar*, *C*, 1997 *W*, *C*, *HK*, *J*, *J*, *HK*, *C*, *W*, *W*, 1998 *Pt*, *Sp*, *J*, *HK*, *C*, *C*, *J*
R Bailey 1979 *C*, 1980 *NZ*, 1981 *C*, *SA*, 1982 *C*, 1983 *C*, *A*, 1987 *Tun*, *C*, *J*, *E*
B Barnard 2006 *IrA*, *M*, *Bar*, *C*
JI Basauri 2007 *S*, *E*, *Tg*, 2008 *Ur*, *J*, *J*, 2010 *Pt*, *Geo*, 2011 *Tg*, *Rus*, *C*, *A*
D Bateman 1982 *C*, *E*, 1983 *A*, 1985 *J*, *C*
P Bell 2006 *IrA*, *M*, *C*, *Bar*, *C*, *Ur*, *Ur*
W Bernhard 1987 *Tun*
CM Biller 2009 *I*, *W*, *Geo*, *C*, *C*, 2010 *Rus*, *Pt*, *Geo*, 2011 *Tg*, *Rus*, *C*, *C*, *J*, *I*, *Rus*, *It*, 2012 *C*, *Geo*, *It*
TW Billups 1993 *C*, *A*, 1994 *Ber*, *C*, *Ar*, *Ar*, *I*, 1995 *C*, 1996 *I*, *C*, *C*, *HK*, *HK*, *J*, *Ar*, *C*, *Ur*, 1997 *W*, *C*, *HK*, *HK*, *W*, *W*, 1998 *Pt*, *Sp*, *J*, *HK*, *C*, *C*, *J*, *HK*, *Fj*, *Ar*, *C*, *Ur*, 1999 *Tg*, *Fj*, *J*, *C*, *Sa*, *E*, *I*, *R*, *A*
RR Blasé 1913 *NZ*
A Blom 1998 *Sp*, *J*, *HK*, *C*, *C*, *HK*, *Fj*, *Ar*, *Ur*, 1999 *Sa*, 2000 *J*, *C*, *I*
H Bloomfield 2007 *E*, *Tg*, *SA*, 2008 *E*, *C*
R Bordley 1976 *A*, *F*, 1977 *C*, *E*, 1978 *C*
J Boyd 2008 *IrA*, 2009 *I*
S Bracken 1994 *Ar*, 1995 *C*
G Brackett 1976 *A*, *F*, 1977 *E*
N Brendel 1983 *A*, 1984 *C*, 1985 *J*, *C*, 1987 *Tun*, *E*
D Briley 1979 *C*, 1980 *W*, *C*, *NZ*
J Buchholz 2001 *C*, 2002 *S*, 2003 *Sp*, *EngA*, *Ar*, *Fj*, *J*, *F*, 2004 *C*
B Burdette 2006 *Ur*, *Ur*, 2007 *E*, *S*, *C*, *E*, *Tg*, *Sa*, *SA*
J Burke 2000 *C*, *I*
JR Burke 1990 *C*, *J*, 1991 *J*, *J*, *S*, *C*, *F*, *NZ*, 1992 *C*
J Burkhardt 1983 *C*, 1985 *C*
E Burlingham 1980 *NZ*, 1981 *C*, *SA*, 1982 *C*, *E*, 1983 *C*, *A*, 1984 *C*, 1985 *C*, 1986 *J*, 1987 *Tun*, *C*, *J*, *E*
C Campbell 1993 *C*, *A*, 1994 *Ber*, *C*, *Ar*
D Care 1998 *Pt*, *J*, *C*
M Carlson 1987 *W*, *C*
DB Carroll 1913 *NZ*, 1920 *F*, *F*
L Cass 1913 *NZ*
M Caulder 1984 *C*, 1985 *C*, 1989 *C*
R Causey 1977 *C*, 1981 *C*, *SA*, 1982 *C*, 1984 *C*, 1986 *J*, 1987 *E*
W Chai 1993 *C*
R Chapman 2011 *J*
D Chipman 1976 *A*, 1978 *C*
JE Clark 1979 *C*, 1980 *C*
P Clark 1924 *R*

J Clarkson 1986 *J*, 1987 *Tun*, *C*, *J*, *E*
J Clayton 1999 *C*, *R*, *A*, 2000 *J*, *C*, *I*, *Fj*, *Tg*, *Sa*, *S*, *W*
N Cleveland 1924 *R*, *F*
TS Clever 2003 *Ar*, 2005 *C*, *R*, *W*, *AraA*, *C*, 2006 *IrA*, *M*, *C*, *Bar*, *C*, *Ur*, 2007 *E*, *S*, *C*, *E*, *Tg*, *Sa*, *SA*, 2008 *E*, *IrA*, *C*, *Ur*, *J*, *J*, 2009 *Geo*, *C*, *C*, *Ur*, *Ur*, 2010 *Pt*, *Geo*, 2011 *Tg*, *Rus*, *C*, *C*, *I*, *Rus*, *It*, 2012 *C*, *Geo*, *It*
R Cooke 1979 *C*, 1980 *W*, *C*, *NZ*, 1981 *C*, *SA*
B Corcoran 1989 *Ur*, *Ar*, 1990 *Ar*
J Coulson 1999 *A*
M Crick 2007 *E*, *S*, *C*, 2008 *E*, *IrA*, *C*, *Ur*, *J*, *J*
R Crivellone 1983 *C*, 1986 *C*, 1987 *C*
K Cross 2003 *Sp*, *Sp*, *J*, *C*, *EngA*, *EngA*, *Ar*, *C*, *Fj*, *S*, 2004 *C*, *Rus*
C Culpepper 1977 *E*, 1978 *C*
C Curtis 1997 *C*, *HK*, *J*, 1999 *Sa*, 2001 *Ar*
P Dahl 2009 *I*, *W*
B Daily 1989 *Ur*, *Ar*, 1990 *Ar*, *C*, *A*, *J*, 1991 *J*, *J*, *S*, *F*, *F*, *It*
K Dalzell 1996 *Ur*, 1998 *Sp*, *C*, *HK*, *C*, *Ur*, 1999 *Tg*, *Fj*, *J*, *C*, *Sa*, *E*, *I*, *R*, *A*, 2000 *J*, *C*, *I*, *Fj*, *Tg*, *Sa*, *S*, *W*, 2001 *C*, *E*, *SA*, 2002 *S*, *C*, *C*, *CHL*, *Ur*, 2003 *Sp*, *Sp*, *J*, *C*, *EngA*, *C*, *Ur*, *Fj*, *S*, *J*, *F*
PJ Danahy 2009 *Ur*, 2010 *Rus*, 2011 *Tg*, *Rus*, *J*, *A*
WP Darsie 1913 *NZ*
G Davis 1920 *F*
G De Bartolo 2008 *E*, *C*, *Ur*, *J*, *J*, 2009 *W*
D de Groot 1924 *F*
MG de Jong 1990 *C*, 1991 *J*, *J*, *S*, *C*, *F*, *F*, *It*, *E*
M Deaton 1983 *A*, 1984 *C*, 1985 *J*
M Delai 1996 *I*, *HK*, *J*, 1997 *HK*, 1998 *HK*, 2000 *J*, *C*, *I*, *Fj*, *Tg*, *Sa*, *S*, *W*, 2001 *C*, *Ar*, *Ur*
RH Devereaux 1924 *R*, *F*
D Dickson 1986 *J*, 1987 *A*
G Dixon 1924 *R*, *F*
C Doe 1920 *F*, *F*, 1924 *R*, *F*
C Doherty 1987 *W*
D Dorsey 2001 *SA*, 2002 *S*, *C*, *C*, *CHL*, *Ur*, *CHL*, *Ur*, 2003 *Sp*, *Sp*, *J*, *C*, *EngA*, *Ar*, *C*, *Ur*, *Fj*, *S*, *J*, *F*, 2004 *C*, *Rus*, *C*, *F*
G Downes 1992 *HK*
BG Doyle 2008 *E*, *IrA*, *C*, 2012 *C*, *Geo*, *It*
R Duncanson 1977 *E*
A Durutalo 2012 *C*, *It*
P Eloff 2000 *J*, *C*, *I*, *Fj*, *Tg*, *Sa*, *S*, *W*, 2001 *C*, *Ar*, *Ur*, *E*, *SA*, 2002 *S*, *C*, *CHL*, *Ur*, 2003 *Sp*, *Sp*, *J*, *C*, *EngA*, *C*, *Ur*, *Fj*, *S*, *J*, *F*, 2006 *Bar*, *C*, *Ur*, *Ur*, 2007 *Tg*, *Sa*, *SA*
PL Emerick 2003 *Sp*, *EngA*, *Ar*, *C*, *Ur*, *Fj*, *S*, *J*, 2004 *C*, *F*, *I*, *It*, 2005 *C*, *R*, *W*, *AraA*, *C*, 2006 *C*, *Bar*, *C*, *Ur*, *Ur*, 2007 *S*, *C*, *E*, 2008 *E*, *IrA*, *C*, *Ur*, *J*, *J*, 2009 *Geo*, *C*, *C*, *Ur*, *Ur*, 2010 *Rus*, *Pt*, *Geo*, 2011 *Tg*, *Rus*, *C*, *C*, *J*, *I*, *Rus*, *It*, 2012 *C*, *Geo*, *It*
TV Enosa 2011 *Tg*, *Rus*, *C*, *C*, *J*, *A*
BE Erb 1912 *A*
C Erskine 2006 *C*, *Ur*, *Ur*, 2007 *E*, *Tg*, *Sa*, *SA*, 2008 *Ur*, *J*, *J*
V Esikia 2006 *IrA*, *M*, *Bar*, *C*, *Ur*, *Ur*, 2007 *E*, *E*, *Tg*, *Sa*, *SA*, 2008 *E*, *IrA*
J Everett 1984 *C*, 1985 *J*, 1986 *J*, 1987 *Tun*, *J*, *E*
W Everett 1985 *J*, 1986 *J*, *C*
M Fabling 1995 *C*
M Fanucchi 1979 *C*, 1980 *W*
R Farley 1989 *I*, *Ur*, *Ar*, 1990 *Ar*, *C*, *A*, *J*, 1991 *J*, *J*, *S*, *C*, *F*, *F*, *It*, *E*, 1992 *C*
P Farner 1999 *Tg*, *Fj*, *J*, *C*, 2000 *J*, *C*, *I*, *Fj*, *Tg*, *Sa*, *S*, *W*, 2002 *C*, *C*, *CHL*, *Ur*, *CHL*, *Ur*
L Farrish 1924 *F*
D Fee 2002 *C*, *C*, *CHL*, *Ur*, *CHL*, *Ur*, 2003 *Sp*, *Sp*, *J*, *C*,

F, It, NZ, 1993 A, 1994 Ber, C, Ar, Ar, I, 1996 HK, J, Ar, C,
Ur, 1997 C, HK, J, J, HK, W, W, 1998 J, HK, C, C, J, HK
M Liscovitz 1977 C, E, 1978 C
THA Liufau 2012 It
R Lockerem 1996 C, Ur
J Lombard 1977 C, E, 1979 C
C Long 2003 Sp
J Lopez 1978 C
I Loveseth 1983 A
RA Lumkong 1994 Ber, C, Ar, Ar, I, 1996 C, C, HK, J, HK,
J, Ar, C, Ur, 1997 W, 1998 Pt, Sp, J, HK, C, C, J, HK, Fj,
C, Ur, 1999 E, R, A
D Lyle 1994 I, 1995 C, 1996 I, C, C, HK, J, HK, J, 1997 W,
C, HK, J, J, HK, C, W, W, 1999 Tg, Fj, J, C, Sa, E, I, R,
2000 S, W, 2001 C, Ar, E, SA, 2002 CHL, Ur, 2003 Sp,
Sp, J, C, EngA, C, Ur, Fj, S, J, F
MS MacDonald 2000 Fj, 2001 C, Ar, Ur, E, SA, 2002 S, C,
C, CHL, Ur, CHL, Ur, 2003 Sp, Sp, J, C, EngA, EngA, C,
Ur, Fj, S, J, F, 2004 C, Rus, F, I, It, 2005 C, R, W, ArA, C,
2006 IrA, C, Bar, C, Ur, Ur, 2007 S, C, E, Tg, Sa, SA, 2008
E, IrA, C, Ur, J, J, 2009 I, W, Geo, C, C, 2010 Pt, Geo,
2011 C, J, I, Rus, It, 2012 C, It
C Mackay 2008 J, 2009 I, W
A Magleby 2000 W, 2001 Ar, Ur, E
A Malifa 2009 I, W, Geo, C
VL Malifa 2007 E, S, C, E, SA, 2008 IrA, C, Ur, J, J, 2009
Ur, Ur, 2010 Rus, Pt, Geo, 2011 Tg, Rus, C, C, J, I, A, It
P Malloy 1995 C
C Manelli 1924 R, F
L Manga 1986 J, 1989 Ar, 1991 J, C, NZ, E, 1992 HK, C
M Mangan 2005 C, R, W, ArA, C, 2006 IrA, M, C, Bar, C,
Ur, 2007 E, S, C, E, Tg, SA
S Manoa 2010 Geo
J McBride 1998 Pt, Sp, C, Fj, Ar, C, Ur, 2000 J, C, I, Tg, Sa
BR McClenahan 2009 W, Ur, 2011 A
T McCormack 1989 Ur, Ar, 1990 Ar, C
G McDonald 1989 I, 1996 I, C
A McGarry 2002 S, CHL
JL McKim 1912 A, 1913 NZ
M McLeod 1997 J, HK, C
C Meehan 1920 F, F
T Meek 2006 IrA, M, C, Bar
H Mexted 2006 Bar, Ur, Ur, 2007 E, S, C, E, Sa
J Meyersieck 1982 C, 1983 C, A, 1985 J, 1986 C
J Mickel 1986 C
K Miles 1982 C, E
C Miller 2002 CHL, Ur
MM Mitchell 1913 NZ
M Moeakiola 2007 E, Tg, Sa, SA, 2008 E, IrA, C, Ur, J, J,
2009 I, W, Geo, C, C, Ur, Ur, 2010 Rus, Pt, Geo, 2011 Tg,
Rus, C, I, Rus, It
T Mokate 2012 C, Geo, It
E Momson 1912 A
B Monroe 1985 C
A Montgomery 1986 C, 1987 W, C, 1988 C, 1989 I, C
LM Morris 1912 A
B Morrison 1979 C, 1980 W
C Morrow 1997 W, C, HK, C, W, W, 1998 Pt, C, C, 1999
Tg, C, E
T Moser 1980 W
N Mottram 1990 Ar, J, 1991 J, S, C, F, NZ, E, 1992 C
F Mounga 1998 C, J, HK, Fj, C, Ur, 1999 Sa, E, I, R, A, 2003
Sp, J, 2004 F, I, It, 2005 R, 2007 E, C, Sa
J Muldoon 1920 F, F
D Murphy 1976 F
J Naivalu 2000 Sa, S, W, 2001 C, Ur, E, 2004 C, Rus, C, F
J Naqica 2001 E, SA, 2002 S, C, C, CHL, Ur, 2003 Ar
J Nash 2006 M, C
RB Nelson 1983 C, A, 1984 C, 1985 C, 1986 J, 1987 C, J,
A, E, 1988 R, USS, 1989 I, Ur, Ar, 1990 Ar, C, A, J, 1991
J, S, C, F, F, It, E
T Ngwenya 2007 E, Tg, Sa, SA, 2008 IrA, C, Ur, J, J, 2009
Geo, C, C, Ur, Ur, 2010 Rus, Pt, Geo, 2011 C, C, I, Rus, It
C Nicolau 2002 C, 2003 J, C, EngA
S Niebauer 1976 A, 1979 C, 1980 W, C, NZ, 1981 C, SA,
1982 C, E
D Niu 1999 Tg, Fj, J, C, E, I, R, A

RM Noble 1912 A
CP O'Brien 1988 C, R, USS, 1989 I, C, Ur, Ar, 1990 Ar, A,
J, 1991 S, C, F, F, NZ, E, 1992 HK, 1993 C, A, 1994 Ber
T O'Brien 1980 NZ, 1983 C, A
M O'Donnell 1976 F
C Okezie 1979 C, 1980 C, NZ, 1981 C, 1982 C, E
JT O'Neill 1920 F, F, 1924 R, F
M Ording 1976 A, F, 1977 E, 1978 C
M Ormsby 1983 C
A Osborne 2007 C
C Osentowski 2004 It, 2005 C, R, W, 2006 IrA, M, C, Bar,
C, Ur, Ur, 2007 E, S, C, E, Tg, Sa, SA
K Oxman 1976 A
S Paga 1998 C, C, 1999 C, Sa, E, I, R, A, 2002 CHL, Ur,
CHL, Ur, 2003 J, 2004 C, Rus, F
TD Palamo 2007 SA, 2008 J
MJ Palefau 2005 C, R, W, ArA, C, 2006 IrA, M, C, 2007 E,
S, 2008 E
AF Paoli 1982 E, 1983 C, 1985 J, 1986 J, C, 1987 C, J, A,
W, C, 1988 C, R, USS, 1989 I, C, Ur, Ar, 1991 J, F, It
AJ Parker 1996 HK, J, HK, J, Ar, C, Ur, 1997 W, 1998 Pt,
Sp, J, HK, C, C, J, HK, Fj, 1999 Fj, C, Sa, E, I, R, A, 2002
CHL, Ur, CHL, Ur, 2003 Sp, Sp, C, EngA, C, Ur, Fj, S, F,
2004 C, Rus, C, I, It, 2005 W, 2006 C, Ur, Ur, 2007 E, Tg,
Sa, SA, 2008 Ur, J, 2009 Geo, C, C, Ur, Ur
D Parks 1980 C
E Parthmore 1977 E
J Paterson 2011 J, I, Rus, It, 2012 C, Geo, It
J Patrick 1920 F, 1924 R, F
DT Payne 2007 S, SA
SB Peart 1912 A, 1913 NZ
J Peter 1987 W, C
T Petersen 1993 C
MZ Petri 2007 SA, 2008 E, IrA, C, Ur, J, J, 2009 I, W, Geo,
C, C, Ur, Ur, 2010 Rus, Pt, Geo, 2011 Tg, Rus, C, C, J, I,
Rus, A, It, 2012 C, Geo, It
A Petruzzella 2004 C, F, I, 2005 W, ArA, C, 2006 IrA, M,
Bar
MD Pidcock 1991 C, NZ, E
ST Pittman 2008 Ur, J, 2009 Geo, C, C, 2010 Rus, Pt, Geo,
2011 Tg, Rus, C, C, J, I, Rus, A, It, 2012 C, Geo, It
M Purcell 1980 W, 1981 C, SA, 1982 C, E, 1983 C, A, 1984
C, 1986 J, C, 1987 Tun, C, J, E
TJ Purpura 2010 Rus
J Pye 2005 ArA, C
P Quinn 2007 E, 2008 Ur, J, J
JA Ramage 1913 NZ
RR Randell 1993 A, 1994 Ber, C, Ar, I, 1995 C, 1996 I, HK,
J, Ar, C, 1997 C
J Raven 1998 C, J
E Reed 1999 A, 2001 Ur, E, SA, 2002 S, C, C
AM Ridnell 1987 A, 1988 C, R, USS, 1991 J, S, C, F, F, It,
NZ, E, 1992 HK, 1993 C
C Righter 1920 F
J Rissone 1996 I, C, C, HK, Ur
WL Rogers 1924 F
R Rosser 2006 Ur, Ur
VR Rouse 2010 Rus
D Rowe 2005 R, W
A Russell 2006 C, Ur
A Ryland 2005 C, R, W, C
R Samaniego 1992 HK
AM Sanborn 1912 A
L Sanft 1996 J
J Santos 1995 C, 1996 C, C, HK
A Satchwell 2002 S, 2003 Ur
A Saulala 1997 C, HK, C, W, W, 1998 Pt, Sp, HK, C, J, HK,
1999 Tg, Fj, J, C, Sa, E, A, 2000 Fj, Tg
M Saunders 1987 Tun, C, J, A, E, W, C, 1988 C, R, USS,
1989 I, C
MH Sawicki 1990 Ar, J, 1991 J, F, NZ
MA Scharrenberg 1993 A, 1994 Ber, C, Ar, Ar, 1995 C, 1996
I, J, HK, J, Ar, C, Ur, 1997 W, C, HK, J, J, HK, C, W, W,
1998 Pt, Sp, J, HK, C, C, Ar, C, Ur, 1999 Tg, Fj, J, C, Sa,
I, R, A
KL Schaupp 1912 A
J Scheitlin 1979 C

498

CJ Schlereth 1993 C, 1994 I, 1998 J
G Schneeweis 1976 A, 1977 E
B Schoener 2006 IrA, M, C
RS Scholz 1920 F, F, 1924 R, F
E Schram 1993 A, 1994 Ber, C, Ar, Ar, 1996 J, Ar
J Schraml 1991 C, 1992 HK, 1993 C
K Schubert 2000 J, C, I, Fj, Tg, Sa, 2001 C, Ar, Ur, E, SA, 2002 S, C, C, CHL, Ur, CHL, Ur, 2003 Sp, Sp, J, C, EngA, Ar, C, Ur, Fj, S, J, F, 2004 C, Rus, C, F, I, It, 2005 C, R, W, ArA, C, 2006 IrA, M, C, Bar, C, 2008 IrA, C
RE Schurfeld 1992 HK, C, 1993 A, 1994 Ber, C
T Scott 1976 F
BH Scully 2011 Rus, C, C, J, I, Rus, A, It
T Selfridge 1976 A, F, 1977 C, 1980 W, C
D Shanagher 1980 NZ, 1981 C, SA, 1982 C, E, 1984 C, 1985 J, 1986 J, 1987 W
RC Shaw 2008 IrA, C
P Sheehy 1991 NZ, E, 1992 HK, C
M Sherlock 1977 C
MM Sherman 2003 EngA, Ar, F, 2004 Rus, 2005 C, W, ArA
W Shiflet 1983 C, A, 1985 J, 1987 A
K Shuman 1997 HK, J, J, W, 1998 J, HK, C, C, J, Ar, 1999 Tg, Fj, J, E, I, R, A, 2000 J, C, I, Fj, Tg, Sa, S, W, 2001 Ar, Ur, E, SA
M Siano 1989 I, C, Ur, Ar
L Sifa 2008 Ur, J, 2009 I, W, Ur, Ur, 2010 Rus, 2011 A
MK Sika 1993 C, A, 1994 Ber, C, Ar, Ar, I, 1996 C, C, J, HK, J, Ar, C, Ur, 1997 J, W
S Sika 2003 Fj, J, F, 2004 C, F, I, It, 2005 W, C, 2006 IrA, M, 2007 S, C, E, Tg, Sa, SA, 2008 IrA, C, Ur, 2009 Geo, C
C Slaby 2008 E, C
C Slater 1920 F, F, 1924 F
N Slater 1924 R
H Smith 2008 Ur, J, J, 2009 I, W, Geo, C, C, Ur, Ur, 2010 Geo, 2011 C, C, J, I, Rus, A, It
M Smith 1988 C
T Smith 1980 C, 1981 C, SA, 1982 E
WL Smith 1912 A
B Smoot 1992 C
J Sprague 2009 Ur, Ur
M Stanaway 1997 C, HK, J, C, 1998 HK
LE Stanfill 2005 C, 2006 C, 2007 E, S, C, E, Tg, Sa, SA, 2008 E, IrA, 2009 I, W, Geo, C, C, Ur, Ur, 2010 Rus, Pt, Geo, 2011 Tg, Rus, C, C, J, I, Rus, A, It, 2012 C, Geo, It
D Steinbauer 1992 C, 1993 C
J Stencel 2006 C
D Stephenson 1976 A, F, 1977 C
I Stevens 1998 C
P Still 2000 S, W, 2001 C, Ar, Ur, E, SA
HR Stolz 1913 NZ
W Stone 1976 F
D Straehley 1983 C, 1984 C
G Sucher 1998 C, J, HK, Fj, C, Ur, 1999 Tg, Fj, J, C, Sa, E, I, R, A
A Suniula 2008 J, 2010 Rus, Pt, Geo, 2011 Tg, Rus, C, C, J, I, Rus, It, 2012 C, Geo, It
RPJ Suniula 2009 I, W, C, C, 2011 Tg, C, C, J, I, Rus, It, 2012 Geo, It
B Surgener 2001 SA, 2002 C, Ur, 2003 Sp, EngA, EngA, 2004 C, F, I, It, 2005 W
E Swanson 1976 A
C Sweeney 1976 A, F, 1977 C, E
M Swiderski 1976 A
K Swiryn 2009 I, W, C, C, Ur, Ur, 2010 Pt, Geo, 2011 Tg, Rus, C, J, A
B Swords 1980 W, C, NZ
KR Swords 1985 J, C, 1986 C, 1987 Tun, C, J, A, W, C, 1988 C, R, USS, 1989 I, C, Ur, Ar, 1990 Ar, C, A, J, 1991 J, J, S, C, F, F, It, NZ, E, 1992 C, 1993 C, A, 1994 Ber, C, Ar, Ar
TK Takau 1994 Ar, Ar, I, 1996 C, C, HK, J, HK, 1997 C, HK, J, HK, W, W, 1998 Sp, HK, C, C, J, HK, Ur, 1999 E, I, R, A
R Tardits 1993 A, 1994 Ber, C, Ar, Ar, I, 1995 C, 1996 I, C, C, J, Ar, 1997 W, C, 1998 Sp, HK, Fj, 1999 Tg, Fj, J, C, Sa, I, R
J Tarpoff 2002 S, C, C, CHL, 2003 Sp, Sp, C, EngA, EngA, 2006 IrA, M, C, Bar

R Templeton 1920 F
P Thiel 2009 Ur, Ur, 2010 Rus, Pt, Geo, 2011 Tg, C, C, J, I, A, It
C Tilden Jr 1920 F, F
M Timoteo 2000 Tg, 2001 C, Ar, Ur, SA, 2002 S, C, C, CHL, Ur, CHL, 2003 Sp, Sp, J, EngA, Ar, C, F, 2004 C, Rus, C, F, I, It, 2005 C, R, 2006 IrA, M, C, Bar, 2012 It
AEO Tuilevuka 2006 IrA, M, C, 2009 I, W, Geo, C, Ur, Ur, 2010 Rus
STV Tuilevuka 2010 Pt
A Tuipulotu 2004 C, Rus, C, I, It, 2005 C, R, W, 2006 C, Bar, C, Ur, Ur, 2007 E, S, C, Tg, Sa, 2008 E
CE Tunnacliffe 1991 F, NZ, E, 1992 HK
E Turkington 1924 R
JC Urban 1913 NZ
TD Usasz 2009 I, W, Geo, C, C, Ur, Ur, 2010 Rus, Pt, Geo, 2011 Tg, Rus, C, C, J, I, Rus, A, It
Vaka 1987 C
AC Valentine 1924 R, F
JL Van Der Giessen 2008 E, C, Ur, J, J, 2009 I, W, Geo, C, C, Ur, Ur, 2010 Rus, Pt, 2011 Tg, Rus, C, C, I, Rus, It
M van der Molen 1992 C
R van Zyl 2003 Sp, Sp, J, C, EngA, C, Ur, Fj, S, J, F, 2004 C, F
Vidal 1920 F
F Viljoen 2004 Rus, C, F, I, It, 2005 C, R, W, ArA, C, 2006 IrA, M, C, Ur, Ur, 2007 E, S, C
T Vinick 1986 C, 1987 A, E
J Vitale 2006 C, Ur, 2007 E, 2008 IrA
BG Vizard 1986 J, C, 1987 Tun, C, J, A, E, W, C, 1988 C, R, USS, 1989 I, C, 1990 C, A, 1991 J, J, S, C, F, It
C Vogl 1996 C, C, 1997 W, C, HK, J, J, HK, C, 1998 HK, Fj, Ar
G Voight 1913 NZ
H von Schmidt 1920 F
J Waasdorp 2003 J, EngA, Ar, Ur, J, F, 2004 C, Rus, C, F, I, It, 2005 C, ArA, C
D Wack 1976 F, 1977 C, 1978 C, 1980 C
B Waite 1976 F
J Walker 1996 I, C, HK, J, Ar, C, Ur, 1997 W, J, HK, C, W, W, 1998 Sp, J, HK, C, C, J, HK, Ar, C, Ur, 1999 Tg, J
D Wallace 1920 F
L Walton 1980 C, NZ, 1981 C, SA
A Ward 1980 NZ, 1983 C
B Warhurst 1983 C, A, 1984 C, 1985 J, C, 1986 J, 1987 Tun, C, J
M Waterman 1992 C
J Welch 2008 J, J, 2009 I, Geo, C
G Wells 2000 J, C, I, Fj, Tg, Sa, S, W, 2001 C, Ar, Ur, E
T Whelan 1982 E, 1987 C, 1988 C, R, USS
EA Whitaker 1990 J, 1991 F, F, It, NZ
B Wiedemer 2007 E, 2008 E, IrA, C
L Wilfley 2000 I, Tg, W, 2001 Ar, Ur, SA, 2002 S, C, C, CHL, Ur, CHL, Ur, 2003 Sp, Sp, C, EngA, EngA, S
JP Wilkerson 1991 E, 1993 A, 1994 C, 1996 C, Ur, 1997 W, C, HK, J, J, C, W, W, 1998 Pt, Sp, J, HK
A Williams 1924 R
B Williams 1988 C, R, USS, 1989 C, 1992 C
C Williams 1990 C, A, J, 1991 J, S, C
D Williams 2004 C, Rus, C, F, I, It, 2005 ArA, 2006 Ur, Ur, 2007 E, C
MA Williams 1987 W, C, 1988 C, R, USS, 1989 I, Ur, Ar, 1990 Ar, C, A, 1991 J, J, F, F, It, NZ, E, 1992 HK, 1994 C, Ar, Ar, I, 1996 I, C, C, HK, 1997 W, 1998 Fj, Ar, Ur, 1999 Tg, J, C, Sa, E, I
G Wilson 1978 C, 1980 W, C, 1981 C, SA
J Winston 1920 F
H Wrenn 1920 F, F
M Wyatt 2003 Ar, C, Ur, J, F, 2004 C, Rus, C, F, I, It, 2005 W, ArA, C, 2006 C
CT Wyles 2007 E, S, C, E, Tg, Sa, SA, 2008 E, IrA, C, Ur, J, J, 2009 I, W, Geo, C, C, Ur, Ur, 2010 Rus, Pt, Geo, 2011 Rus, A, It, 2012 C, Geo, It
D Younger 2000 J, C, I, Fj
S Yungling 1997 HK, W
R Zenker 1987 W, C

WALES

WALES' 2011/12 TEST RECORD

OPPONENTS	DATE	VENUE	RESULT
Australia	3 Dec	H	Lost 18–24
Ireland	5 Feb	A	Won 23–21
Scotland	12 Feb	H	Won 27–13
England	25 Feb	A	Won 19–12
Italy	10 Mar	H	Won 24–3
France	17 Mar	H	Won 16–9
Australia	9 Jun	A	Lost 27–19
Australia	16 Jun	A	Lost 25–23
Australia	23 Jun	A	Lost 20–19

A GRAND SLAM YEAR

By Iain Spragg

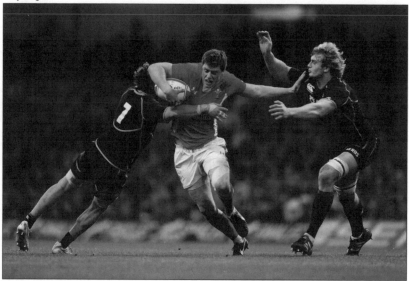

Rhys Priestland tries to break through the challenge of Scotland duo Ross Rennie and Richie Gray.

THE COUNTRIES

I**f the story** of Wales' Rugby World Cup campaign was ultimately one of desperate disappointment after their narrow semi-final defeat to France in Auckland, it was the subsequent Six Nations which offered redemption as Warren Gatland's side exacted their revenge against Les Bleus in Cardiff to claim a third Grand Slam in eight years.

The team's subsequent failure to claim the scalp of Australia on their summer tour, despite giving the Wallabies palpitations in all three Tests, was certainly frustrating for a country striving for a rare success in the southern hemisphere, but the abiding memory of the response to their dramatic Rugby World Cup exit remained their domination of the Championship.

The silverware was secured after France were beaten 16–9 at the Millennium Stadium in March courtesy of an Alex Cuthbert try and the boot of Leigh Halfpenny and, almost five months to the day after they had gone down 9–8 at Eden Park, Wales had a cathartic victory to celebrate.

"Our loss to France spurred us on today to get revenge and it's a great achievement for us," admitted prop Gethin Jenkins, who took over the captaincy in the second half after Sam Warburton was forced off through injury. "We knew France were going to be good. They've played well all Championship and it was up to us to perform on the day.

"Our defence stood out and we managed to grind out a win. The atmosphere was unbelievable and it's great for us to win another Grand Slam, but the occasion didn't quite get to us as they would have hoped. The coaches gave us freedom to go out and play. We're quite a close group and the World Cup obviously brought us tighter."

The transformation from the nearly men in New Zealand to northern hemisphere champions began when Gatland unveiled his squad for the Six Nations. Six uncapped players were included, but the team to face Ireland on the opening day at the Aviva Stadium had a reassuringly familiar feel as the side looked to return to winning ways.

For much of an enthralling clash in Dublin, however, it seemed it would be Ireland who would emerge victorious. The home side led from the third minute after an early Johnny Sexton penalty, and after 75 minutes Wales were trailing 21–20 despite a brace of tries from Jonathan Davies.

The clock was on Ireland's side, but they paid the ultimate price for a late moment of indiscipline when Stephen Ferris was yellow carded for a tip tackle on Ian Evans and Halfpenny gratefully converted the resulting penalty to secure a 23–21 win.

Eight days later they welcomed Scotland to Cardiff. Wales were not, in truth, at their best for the full 80 minutes of the match, but a devastating 14-minute salvo early in the second half and tries from Cuthbert and Halfpenny (2) destroyed Scottish resistance. The home side recorded a 27–13 victory and they were one match away from a 20th Triple Crown.

England at Twickenham stood in their way. Wales were buoyed by the return of Warburton and second row Alun Wyn Jones from injury and the scene was set for the 123rd installment of one of Test rugby's fiercest rivalries.

It was a match that turned decisively on two pivotal moments. The first came in the 75th minute with the two teams locked at 12–12 when replacement centre Scott Williams ripped the ball from Courtney Lawes on halfway and collected his own chip ahead for the first try of the contest.

The other arrived in the dying seconds as silence descended while the TMO took several minutes to decide whether England wing David Strettle had grounded the ball for what could prove to be a match-saving score. The verdict was no try and Wales were 19–12 winners.

WALES

"We ignored everything that was said in the media about us being favourites and all that rubbish," said Man of the Match Warburton. "We didn't listen to it at all because we knew this was going to be the toughest test we'd had so far. You never come to Twickenham and have an easy game, as history tells you.

"It was one hell of a game, really tough. There were times when the boys had to pick me up off the floor and vice versa. England really threw everything at us, especially at the end, and they're an absolute nightmare to play when that situation happens and they very nearly went over."

There were few alarms for Gatland's charges as they dismissed Italy 24–3 at the Millennium Stadium in early March and only France could now deny Wales an 11th Grand Slam.

The build-up to the match was dominated by a row over the Millennium Stadium's retractable roof. With rain forecast, the visitors wanted the stadium open to the elements while Wales were eager to play in the dry, but the French prevailed and as the two teams ran out onto the pitch the Cardiff sky was clearly visible.

In the end, the worries about the weather proved a red herring. France produced arguably their strongest display of the Championship but once Cuthbert had powered over for the only try of the match midway through the first half, Wales were in charge and did not surrender their advantage.

Three penalties from Halfpenny, added to his conversion of the try, kept the French at bay and the capacity crowd in the Millennium Stadium erupted when South African referee Craig Joubert blew his whistle for full-time.

"It has all been about honesty and hard work," Gatland said after the match. "These guys have been a real credit to themselves, Wales and Welsh rugby in how they have prepared themselves. They are excellent professionals and they make our job as coaches easy as they do more than what we expect and what is required. When you have players doing that and looking after themselves and doing all the extras it goes a long way to making us coaches look good.

"We have accepted the tag of favourites which has not always sat well on our shoulders in the past. For a young side they have coped incredibly well and I think it can be good for us as a team over the next two or three years. We have been down in games during this tournament and we have learnt how to win ugly and in the past that may not have happened.

"Our big aim is to be consistent in beating the southern hemisphere sides and we have a young enough side that over the next few years hopefully we can do that."

The opportunity to achieve that elusive, highly-prized triumph south of the equator was just around the corner in the shape of Australia, the reigning Tri-Nations champions. Wales had beaten the Wallabies just once previously Down Under – a 19–16 triumph in Sydney in 1969 – but buoyed by their Grand Slam success, as well as their performances in the World Cup, hopes were high of ending the 43-year drought.

The team warmed up with a 30–21 win over the Barbarians in Cardiff but preparations were hampered by the news that Gatland could not join the squad after breaking bones in both feet after a fall at his home in New Zealand. Gatland's assistant Rob Howley was pressed into action as caretaker head coach and Wales headed to Australia on a mission which they believed was far from impossible.

The first Test in Brisbane was a vibrant encounter but, despite shaking off their jetlag in the second half at the Suncorp Stadium, Wales left their fightback too late to avoid a 27–19 reverse and a first defeat in 2012.

Tries from Scott Higginbotham and Will Genia helped the Wallabies to a 20–6 lead but a Cuthbert try and two Halfpenny penalties reduced the arrears to a single point before a Pat McCabe score saw the home side pull away. Wales still had chances to get back in contention but ultimately fluffed their lines.

A morale-boosting midweek win over the Brumbies before the second Test helped ease the pain of defeat but the tour was now all about the match in Melbourne and the opportunity to level the series.

Wales drew first blood with a George North try after just two minutes and although Australia eased into a 13–7 lead at half-time, the visitors came powering back after the break and they were back in front after 42 minutes when Jonathan Davies collected a Welsh hack up field for a second try.

The remainder of the match was a battle of the boots as Halfpenny traded penalties with Berrick Barnes, and with time almost up Wales were on the brink of a famous 23–22 win. A collapsed maul and the referee's decision to award the Wallabies a penalty, however, put pay to that and replacement fly half Mike Harris stepped up to slot a nerveless effort from the left-hand touchline and break Welsh hearts.

"In international rugby there's a fine margin between winning and losses," said Howley as he reflected on the final 25–23 scoreline. "We were quite clinical when we had the ball and took our opportunities, but we just gave them one too many opportunities to get that kick at goal with discipline in certain areas.

"I said to the guys they could take great heart from their performance. I thought we defended well, the first half in particular, when we needed to. We got off our line very quickly and made our tackles.

"In the second half through our defence we got our try and in just two minutes probably towards the end made a couple of wrong decisions and it's cost us the game. We'll be better for that, but it's hard to swallow."

The third and final Test was almost as agonising as a string of unforced errors denied the tourists the chance to avoid a series whitewash.

There was never more than three points difference between the two sides until the 64th minute when Ryan Jones crashed over under the posts. Halfpenny made no mistake with the straightforward conversion and Wales were 16–12 up.

The lead lasted three minutes. Centre Rob Horne finished off a massive Australian overlap to give the home side renewed hope and, although Halfpenny briefly restored the visitors' supremacy with his fourth penalty of the match, the Wallabies once again snatched victory from the jaws of defeat with Barnes's fourth penalty six minutes from time.

The loss made it just two wins in their last 40 attempts against the three southern hemisphere giants home and away and left the Six Nations champions to reflect on what might, perhaps should, have been as they boarded their flight back to Wales.

"I am just absolutely gutted," admitted flanker Dan Lydiate. "We had our chances but fair play to Australia, they had chances and took them well. They kicked their points.

"We're getting closer, but it was our last chance today and it wasn't good enough. Too many errors on our part, but credit to the Aussies, they're a good team. These games are won and lost by one or two points, but we'll get there and we'll look forward to the autumn series back at our place."

On the domestic scene there was success for the Ospreys, who gave Shane Williams the perfect send-off by beating Leinster to win the RaboDirect PRO12 title. At club level, Pontypridd extracted revenge over Llanelli with a 15–13 victory in the Principality Premiership Grand Final at Sardis Road, a reverse of the result between the two sides 12 months earlier.

Ponty had been hot favourites to win the title in 2011 but were upset by Llanelli in the final and made no mistake at the second time of asking to become Welsh club champions for the first time since 1997.

The Wales Sevens side, meanwhile, finished eighth in the overall standings of the 2011/12 HSBC Sevens World Series, the second highest ranked of the European sides behind England. Paul John's side performed particularly well in Australia and South Africa, winning the Plate at both events. They will hope to better that in 2012/13, a season which will climax with their RWC Sevens title defence in Moscow from 28–30 June.

WALES INTERNATIONAL STATISTICS

MATCH RECORDS UP TO 10 OCTOBER 2012

MOST CONSECUTIVE TEST WINS

11	1907 I, 1908 E, S, F, I, A, 1909 E, S, F, I, 1910 F
10	1999 F1, It, E, Arg 1, 2, SA, C, F2, Arg 3, J
8	1970 F, 1971 E, S, I, F, 1972 E, S, F
8	2004 J, 2005 E, It, F, S, I, US, C

MOST CONSECUTIVE TESTS WITHOUT DEFEAT

Matches	Wins	Draws	Period
11	11	0	1907 to 1910
10	10	0	1999 to 1999
8	8	0	1970 to 1972
8	8	0	2004 to 2005

MOST POINTS IN A MATCH

BY THE TEAM

Pts	Opponents	Venue	Year
102	Portugal	Lisbon	1994
98	Japan	Cardiff	2004
81	Romania	Cardiff	2001
81	Namibia	New Plymouth	2011
77	USA	Hartford	2005
72	Japan	Cardiff	2007
70	Romania	Wrexham	1997
66	Romania	Cardiff	2004
66	Fiji	Hamilton	2011
64	Japan	Cardiff	1999
64	Japan	Osaka	2001
61	Canada	Cardiff	2006
60	Italy	Treviso	1999
60	Canada	Toronto	2005
58	Fiji	Cardiff	2002
57	Japan	Bloemfontein	1995
55	Japan	Cardiff	1993

BY A PLAYER

Pts	Player	Opponents	Venue	Year
30	N R Jenkins	Italy	Treviso	1999
29	N R Jenkins	France	Cardiff	1999
28	N R Jenkins	Canada	Cardiff	1999
28	N R Jenkins	France	Paris	2001
28	G L Henson	Japan	Cardiff	2004
27	N R Jenkins	Italy	Cardiff	2000
27	C Sweeney	USA	Hartford	2005
26	S M Jones	Romania	Cardiff	2001
24	N R Jenkins	Canada	Cardiff	1993
24	N R Jenkins	Italy	Cardiff	1994
24	G L Henson	Romania	Wrexham	2003
23	A C Thomas	Romania	Wrexham	1997
23	N R Jenkins	Argentina	Llanelli	1998
23	N R Jenkins	Scotland	Murrayfield	2001
22	N R Jenkins	Portugal	Lisbon	1994
22	N R Jenkins	Japan	Bloemfontein	1995
22	N R Jenkins	England	Wembley	1999
22	S M Jones	Canada	Cardiff	2002
22	J W Hook	England	Cardiff	2007
22	D R Biggar	Canada	Toronto	2009
22	S L Halfpenny	Scotland	Cardiff	2012

WALES

MOST TRIES IN A MATCH
BY THE TEAM

Tries	Opponents	Venue	Year
16	Portugal	Lisbon	1994
14	Japan	Cardiff	2004
12	Namibia	New Plymouth	2011
11	France	Paris	1909
11	Romania	Wrexham	1997
11	Romania	Cardiff	2001
11	USA	Hartford	2005
11	Japan	Cardiff	2007
10	France	Swansea	1910
10	Japan	Osaka	2001
10	Romania	Cardiff	2004
9	France	Cardiff	1908
9	Japan	Cardiff	1993
9	Japan	Cardiff	1999
9	Japan	Tokyo	2001
9	Canada	Toronto	2005
9	Canada	Cardiff	2006
9	Fiji	Hamilton	2011

BY A PLAYER

Tries	Player	Opponents	Venue	Year
4	W Llewellyn	England	Swansea	1899
4	R A Gibbs	France	Cardiff	1908
4	M C R Richards	England	Cardiff	1969
4	I C Evans	Canada	Invercargill	1987
4	N Walker	Portugal	Lisbon	1994
4	G Thomas	Italy	Treviso	1999
4	S M Williams	Japan	Osaka	2001
4	T G L Shanklin	Romania	Cardiff	2004
4	C L Charvis	Japan	Cardiff	2004

MOST CONVERSIONS IN A MATCH
BY THE TEAM

Cons	Opponents	Venue	Year
14	Japan	Cardiff	2004
11	Portugal	Lisbon	1994
11	USA	Hartford	2005
10	Romania	Cardiff	2001
9	Namibia	New Plymouth	2011
9	Fiji	Hamilton	2011
8	France	Swansea	1910
8	Japan	Cardiff	1999
8	Romania	Cardiff	2004
8	Canada	Cardiff	2006
7	France	Paris	1909
7	Japan	Osaka	2001
7	Japan	Cardiff	2007

BY A PLAYER

Cons	Player	Opponents	Venue	Year
14	G L Henson	Japan	Cardiff	2004
11	N R Jenkins	Portugal	Lisbon	1994
11	C Sweeney	U S A	Hartford	2005
10	S M Jones	Romania	Cardiff	2001
8	J Bancroft	France	Swansea	1910
8	N R Jenkins	Japan	Cardiff	1999
8	J Hook	Canada	Cardiff	2006
7	S M Jones	Japan	Osaka	2001
7	S M Jones	Romania	Cardiff	2004
6	J Bancroft	France	Paris	1909
6	G L Henson	Romania	Wrexham	2003
6	C Sweeney	Canada	Toronto	2005
6	S M Jones	Namibia	New Plymouth	2011

MOST PENALTIES IN A MATCH
BY THE TEAM

Penalties	Opponents	Venue	Year
9	France	Cardiff	1999
8	Canada	Cardiff	1993
7	Italy	Cardiff	1994
7	Canada	Cardiff	1999
7	Italy	Cardiff	2000
6	France	Cardiff	1982
6	Tonga	Nuku'alofa	1994
6	England	Wembley	1999
6	Canada	Cardiff	2002
6	England	Cardiff	2009
6	Canada	Toronto	2009
6	New Zealand	Cardiff	2010

BY A PLAYER

Penalties	Player	Opponents	Venue	Year
9	N R Jenkins	France	Cardiff	1999
8	N R Jenkins	Canada	Cardiff	1993
7	N R Jenkins	Italy	Cardiff	1994
7	N R Jenkins	Canada	Cardiff	1999
7	N R Jenkins	Italy	Cardiff	2000
6	G Evans	France	Cardiff	1982
6	N R Jenkins	Tonga	Nuku'alofa	1994
6	N R Jenkins	England	Wembley	1999
6	S M Jones	Canada	Cardiff	2002
6	D R Biggar	Canada	Toronto	2009
6	S M Jones	New Zealand	Cardiff	2010

MOST DROP GOALS IN A MATCH
BY THE TEAM

Drops	Opponents	Venue	Year
3	Scotland	Murrayfield	2001
2	Scotland	Swansea	1912
2	Scotland	Cardiff	1914
2	England	Swansea	1920
2	Scotland	Swansea	1921
2	France	Paris	1930
2	England	Cardiff	1971
2	France	Cardiff	1978
2	England	Twickenham	1984
2	Ireland	Wellington	1987
2	Scotland	Cardiff	1988
2	France	Paris	2001

BY A PLAYER

Drops	Player	Opponents	Venue	Year
3	N R Jenkins	Scotland	Murrayfield	2001
2	J Shea	England	Swansea	1920
2	A Jenkins	Scotland	Swansea	1921
2	B John	England	Cardiff	1971
2	M Dacey	England	Twickenham	1984
2	J Davies	Ireland	Wellington	1987
2	J Davies	Scotland	Cardiff	1988
2	N R Jenkins	France	Paris	2001

CAREER RECORDS 507

MOST CAPPED PLAYERS

Caps	Player	Career Span
104	S M Jones	1998 to 2011
100	Gareth Thomas	1995 to 2007
100	M E Williams	1996 to 2012
94	C L Charvis	1996 to 2007
92	G O Llewellyn	1989 to 2004
90	G D Jenkins	2002 to 2012
87	N R Jenkins	1991 to 2002
87	S M Williams	2000 to 2011
83	A R Jones	2003 to 2012
76	D J Peel	2001 to 2011
72	I C Evans	1987 to 1998
70	T G L Shanklin	2001 to 2010
68	W M Phillips	2003 to 2012
67	J J Thomas	2003 to 2011
67	R P Jones	2004 to 2012
66	A-W Jones	2006 to 2012
65	J W Hook	2006 to 2012
64	I M Gough	1998 to 2010
59	R Howley	1996 to 2002
58	G R Jenkins	1991 to 2000
57	D J Jones	2001 to 2009
55	J P R Williams	1969 to 1981
54	R N Jones	1986 to 1995
53	G O Edwards	1967 to 1978
53	I S Gibbs	1991 to 2001
52	L S Quinnell	1993 to 2002
52	M Taylor	1994 to 2005
51	D Young	1987 to 2001
51	H Bennett	2003 to 2012

MOST CONSECUTIVE TESTS

Tests	Player	Span
53	G O Edwards	1967 to 1978
43	K J Jones	1947 to 1956
39	G Price	1975 to 1983
38	T M Davies	1969 to 1976
33	W J Bancroft	1890 to 1901

MOST TESTS AS CAPTAIN

Tests	Captain	Span
28	I C Evans	1991 to 1995
28	R P Jones	2008 to 2012
22	R Howley	1998 to 1999
22	C L Charvis	2002 to 2004
21	Gareth Thomas	2003 to 2007
19	J M Humphreys	1995 to 2003
18	A J Gould	1889 to 1897
16	S K Warburton	2011 to 2012
14	D C T Rowlands	1963 to 1965
14	W J Trew	1907 to 1913

WALES

MOST POINTS IN TESTS

Points	Player	Tests	Career
1049	N R Jenkins	87	1991 to 2002
917	S M Jones	104	1998 to 2011
346	J W Hook	65	2006 to 2012
304	P H Thorburn	37	1985 to 1991
290	S M Williams	87	2000 to 2011
211	A C Thomas	23	1996 to 2000
200	Gareth Thomas	100	1995 to 2007
182	S L Halfpenny	35	2008 to 2012
166	P Bennett	29	1969 to 1978
157	I C Evans	72	1987 to 1998

MOST PENALTY GOALS IN TESTS

Penalties	Player	Tests	Career
235	N R Jenkins	87	1991 to 2002
186	S M Jones	104	1998 to 2011
70	P H Thorburn	37	1985 to 1991
61	J W Hook	65	2006 to 2012
36	P Bennett	29	1969 to 1978
35	S P Fenwick	30	1975 to 1981
35	S L Halfpenny	35	2008 to 2012
32	A C Thomas	23	1996 to 2000
22	G Evans	10	1981 to 1983

MOST TRIES IN TESTS

Tries	Player	Tests	Career
58	S M Williams	87	2000 to 2011
40	Gareth Thomas	100	1995 to 2007
33	I C Evans	72	1987 to 1998
22	C L Charvis	94	1996 to 2007
20	G O Edwards	53	1967 to 1978
20	T G R Davies	46	1966 to 1978
20	T G L Shanklin	70	2001 to 2010
18	G R Williams	44	2000 to 2005
17	R A Gibbs	16	1906 to 1911
17	J L Williams	17	1906 to 1911
17	K J Jones	44	1947 to 1957

MOST DROP GOALS IN TESTS

Drops	Player	Tests	Career
13	J Davies	32	1985 to 1997
10	N R Jenkins	87	1991 to 2002
8	B John	25	1966 to 1972
7	W G Davies	21	1978 to 1985
6	S M Jones	104	1998 to 2011
4	J W Hook	65	2006 to 2012

MOST CONVERSIONS IN TESTS

Cons	Player	Tests	Career
153	S M Jones	104	1998 to 2011
130	N R Jenkins	87	1991 to 2002
43	P H Thorburn	37	1985 to 1991
43	J W Hook	65	2006 to 2012
38	J Bancroft	18	1909 to 1914
30	A C Thomas	23	1996 to 2000
29	G L Henson	33	2001 to 2011
25	C Sweeney	35	2003 to 2007
20	W J Bancroft	33	1890 to 1901
20	I R Harris	25	2001 to 2004

RECORD	DETAIL	HOLDER	SET
Most points in season	151	in five matches	2005
Most tries in season	21	in four matches	1910
Highest Score	49	49–14 v France	1910
Biggest win	39	47–8 v Italy	2008
Highest score conceded	60	26–60 v England	1998
Biggest defeat	51	0–51 v France	1998
Most appearances	51	M E Williams	1998–2010
Most points in matches	467	S M Jones	2000–2011
Most points in season	74	N R Jenkins	2001
Most points in match	28	N R Jenkins	v France, 2001
Most tries in matches	22	S M Williams	2000–2011
Most tries in season	6	M C R Richards	1969
	6	S M Williams	2008
Most tries in match	4	W Llewellyn	v England, 1899
	4	M C R Richards	v England, 1969
Most cons in matches	69	S M Jones	2000–2011
Most cons in season	12	S M Jones	2005
Most cons in match	8	J Bancroft	v France, 1910
Most pens in matches	100	S M Jones	2000–2011
Most pens in season	16	P H Thorburn	1986
	16	N R Jenkins	1999
Most pens in match	7	N R Jenkins	v Italy, 2000
Most drops in matches	8	J Davies	1985–1997
Most drops in season	5	N R Jenkins	2001
Most drops in match	3	N R Jenkins	v Scotland, 2001

WALES

MISCELLANEOUS RECORDS

RECORD	HOLDER	DETAIL
Longest Test Career	M E Williams	1996 to 2012
Youngest Test Cap	T W J Prydie	18 yrs 25 days in 2010
Oldest Test Cap	T H Vile	38 yrs 152 days in 1921

CAREER RECORDS OF WALES INTERNATIONAL PLAYERS

UP TO 10 OCTOBER 2012

PLAYER BACKS:	DEBUT	CAPS	T	C	P	D	PTS
M A Beck	2012 v A	3	0	0	0	0	0
D R Biggar	2008 v C	10	0	9	12	0	54
A M Bishop	2008 v SA	16	0	0	0	0	0
A G Brew	2007 v I	9	3	0	0	0	15
L M Byrne	2005 v NZ	46	10	0	0	0	50
A C G Cuthbert	2011 v A	9	4	0	0	0	20
C D Czekaj	2005 v C	9	2	0	0	0	10
J J V Davies	2009 v C	29	8	0	0	0	40
S L Halfpenny	2008 v SA	35	11	11	35	0	182
W T M Harries	2010 v NZ	3	0	0	0	0	0
J W Hook	2006 v Arg	65	13	43	61	4	346
T James	2007 v E	10	2	0	0	0	10
T D Knoyle	2010 v NZ	7	0	0	0	0	0
G P North	2010 v SA	24	11	0	0	0	55
W M Phillips	2003 v R	68	8	0	0	0	40
R Priestland	2011 v S	18	1	12	8	0	53
T W J Prydie	2010 v It	4	1	0	0	0	5
R S Rees	2010 v E	9	1	0	0	0	5
J H Roberts	2008 v S	44	5	0	0	0	25
H R Robinson	2012 v Bb	1	1	0	0	0	5
M L Stoddart	2007 v SA	8	5	0	0	0	25
A R Warren	2012 v Bb	1	0	0	0	0	0
R Webb	2012 v It	3	0	0	0	0	0
L B Williams	2012 v Bb	1	0	0	0	0	0
L D Williams	2011 v Arg	8	2	0	0	0	10
M S Williams	2011 v Bb	14	5	0	0	0	25
S M Williams	2000 v F	87	58	0	0	0	290
FORWARDS:							
S A Andrews	2011 v Bb	2	0	0	0	0	0
H Bennett	2003 v I	51	0	0	0	0	0
R J Bevington	2011 v Bb	7	0	0	0	0	0
L C Charteris	2004 v SA	37	0	0	0	0	0
B S Davies	2009 v S	36	0	0	0	0	0
I R Evans	2006 v Arg	23	1	0	0	0	5
T T Faletau	2011 v Bb	17	2	0	0	0	10
I A R Gill	2010 v I	3	0	0	0	0	0
R M Hibbard	2006 v Arg	17	0	0	0	0	0

THE COUNTRIES

P James	2003 v R	37	0	0	0	0	0	**511**
G D Jenkins	2002 v R	90	4	0	0	0	20	
A R Jones	2003 v E	83	2	0	0	0	10	
A-W Jones	2006 v Arg	66	7	0	0	0	35	
Rhodri P Jones	2012 v Bb	1	0	0	0	0	0	
Ryan P Jones	2004 v SA	67	3*	0	0	0	15	
D J Lydiate	2009 v Arg	27	0	0	0	0	0	
C Mitchell	2009 v C	11	0	0	0	0	0	
K J Owens	2011 v Nm	7	0	0	0	0	0	
A T Powell	2008 v SA	23	1	0	0	0	5	
L Reed	2012 v S	1	0	0	0	0	0	
M Rees	2005 v US	54	2	0	0	0	10	
A C Shingler	2012 v S	2	0	0	0	0	0	
J C Tipuric	2011 v Arg	6	0	0	0	0	0	
J Turnbull	2011 v S	4	0	0	0	0	0	
S K Warburton	2009 v US	30	2	0	0	0	10	
M E Williams	1996 v Bb	100	14	0	0	1	73	

* Ryan Jones's figures include a penalty try awarded against Canada in 2006

WALES INTERNATIONAL PLAYERS
UP TO 10 OCTOBER 2012

Note: Years given for International Championship matches are for second half of season; eg 1972 means season 1971–72. Years for all other matches refer to the actual year of the match. Entries in square brackets denote matches played in RWC Finals.

Ackerman, R A (Newport, London Welsh) 1980 NZ, 1981 E, S, A, 1982 I, F, E, S, 1983 S, I, F, R, 1984 S, I, F, E, A, 1985 S, I, F, E, Fj
Alexander, E P (Llandovery Coll, Cambridge U) 1885 S, 1886 E, S, 1887 E, I
Alexander, W H (Llwynypia) 1898 I, E, 1899 E, S, I, 1901 S, I
Allen, A G (Newbridge) 1990 F, E, I
Allen, C P (Oxford U, Beaumaris) 1884 E, S
Andrews, F (Pontypool) 1912 SA, 1913 E, S, I
Andrews, F G (Swansea) 1884 E, S
Andrews, G E (Newport) 1926 E, S, 1927 E, F, I
Andrews, S A (Cardiff Blues) 2011 Bb(R),A
Anthony, C T (Swansea, Newport, Gwent Dragons) 1997 US 1(R),2(R), C (R), Tg (R), 1998 SA 2, Arg, 1999 S, I (R), 2001 J 1,2, I (R), 2002 I, F, It, E, S, 2003 R (R)
Anthony, L (Neath) 1948 E, S, F
Appleyard, R C (Swansea) 1997 C, R, Tg, NZ, 1998 It, E (R), S, I, F
Arnold, P (Swansea) 1990 Nm 1, 2, Bb, 1991 E, S, I, F 1, A, [Arg, A], 1993 F (R), Z 2, 1994 Sp, Fj, 1995 SA, 1996 Bb (R)
Arnold, W R (Swansea) 1903 S
Arthur, C S (Cardiff) 1888 I, M, 1891 E
Arthur, T (Neath) 1927 S, F, I, 1929 E, S, F, I, 1930 E, S, I, F, 1931 E, S, F, I, SA, 1933 E, S
Ashton, C (Aberavon) 1959 E, S, I, 1960 E, S, I, 1962 I
Attewell, S L (Newport) 1921 E, S, F

Back, M J (Bridgend) 1995 F (R), E (R), S, I
Badger, O (Llanelli) 1895 E, S, I, 1896 E
Baker, A (Neath) 1921 I, 1923 E, S, F, I
Baker, A M (Newport) 1909 S, F, 1910 S
Bancroft, J (Swansea) 1909 E, S, F, I, 1910 F, E, S, I, 1911 E, F, I, 1912 E, S, I, 1913 I, 1914 E, S, F

Bancroft, W J (Swansea) 1890 S, E, I, 1891 E, S, I, 1892 E, S, I, 1893 E, S, I, 1894 E, S, I, 1895 E, S, I, 1896 E, S, I, 1897 E, 1898 I, E, 1899 E, S, I, 1900 E, S, I, 1901 E, S, I
Barlow, T M (Cardiff) 1884 I
Barrell, R J (Cardiff) 1929 S, F, I, 1933 I
Bartlett, J D (Llanelli) 1927 S, 1928 E, S
Bassett, A (Cardiff) 1934 I, 1935 E, S, I, 1938 E, S
Bassett, J A (Penarth) 1929 E, S, F, I, 1930 E, S, I, 1931 E, S, F, I, SA, 1932 E, S, I
Bateman, A G (Neath, Richmond, Northampton) 1990 S, I, Nm 1,2, 1996 SA, 1997 US, S, F, E, R, NZ, 1998 It, E, S, I, 1999 S, Arg 1,2, SA, C, [J, A (R)], 2000 It, E, S, I, Sm, US, SA, 2001 E (R), It (t), R, I, Art (R), Tg
Bater, J (Ospreys) 2003 R (R)
Bayliss, G (Pontypool) 1933 S
Bebb, D I E (Carmarthen TC, Swansea) 1959 E, S, I, F, 1960 E, S, I, F, SA, 1961 E, S, I, F, 1962 E, S, F, I, 1963 E, F, NZ, 1964 E, S, F, SA, 1965 E, S, I, F, 1966 F, A, 1967 S, I, F, E
Beck, M A (Ospreys) 2012 A 1(R),2,3
Beckingham, G (Cardiff) 1953 E, S, 1958 F
Bennett, A M (Cardiff) 1995 [NZ] SA, Fj
Bennett, H (Ospreys) 2003 I 2(R), S, 2(R), [C(R), Tg(R)], 2004 S(R), F(R), Arg 1(R),2, SA1(R), 2006 Arg 2,PI(R), 2007 E2, [J(R)], SA, 2008 E, S, It(R), F, 2009 S(R), E(R), F(R), It, I(R), NZ(R), Sm, Arg(R), A(R), 2010 E(R), S(R), F, I(R), It(R), NZ1(R), 2(R), A(R), SA2(R), Fj, NZ3(R), 2011 Bb, E2, 3(R), Arg(R), [SA, Sm, Fj, I, F, A], A, 2012 I, S
Bennett, I (Aberavon) 1937 I
Bennett, I (Cardiff Harlequins) 1891 E, S, 1892 S, I
Bennett, P (Llanelli) 1969 F (R), 1970 SA, S, F, 1972 S (R), NZ, 1973 E, S, I, F, A, 1974 S, I, F, E, 1975 S (R), I, 1976 E, S, I, F, 1977 I, F, E, S, 1978 E, S, I, F

Bergiers, R T E (Cardiff Coll of Ed, Llanelli) 1972 E, S, F, NZ, 1973 E, S, I, F, A, 1974 E, 1975 I
Bevan, G W (Llanelli) 1947 E
Bevan, J A (Cambridge U) 1881 E
Bevan, J C (Cardiff, Cardiff Coll of Ed) 1971 E, S, I, F, 1972 E, S, F, NZ, 1973 E, S
Bevan, J D (Aberavon) 1975 F, E, S, A
Bevan, S (Swansea) 1904 I
Bevington, R J (Ospreys) 2011 Bb, E2(R), 3(R), Arg(R), [Nm(R), A(R)], A(R)
Beynon, B (Swansea) 1920 E, S
Beynon, G E (Swansea) 1925 F, I
Bidgood, R A (Newport) 1992 S, 1993 Z 1,2, Nm, J (R)
Biggar, D R (Ospreys) 2008 C(R), 2009 C,US(R),Sm, 2010 NZ1(R),2,A(R),Fj, 2011 A(R), 2012 Bb
Biggs, N W (Cardiff) 1888 M, 1889 I 1892 I, 1893 E, S, I, 1894 E, I
Biggs, S H (Cardiff) 1895 E, S, 1896 S, 1897 E, 1898 I, E, 1899 S, I, 1900 I
Birch, J (Neath) 1911 S, F
Birt, F W (Newport) 1911 E, S, 1912 E, S, I, SA, 1913 E
Bishop, A M (Ospreys) 2008 SA2(R),C,A(R), 2009 S(R), C, US, Arg(R), A(R), 2010 I(R), It(R), NZ1, A, SA2(t), Fj, NZ3(R), 2012 Bb
Bishop, D J (Pontypool) 1984 A
Bishop, E H (Swansea) 1889 S
Blackmore, J H (Abertillery) 1909 E
Blackmore, S W (Cardiff) 1987 I, [Tg (R), C, A]
Blake, J (Cardiff) 1899 E, S, I, 1900 E, S, I, 1901 E, S, I
Blakemore, R E (Newport) 1947 E
Bland, A F (Cardiff) 1887 E, S, I, 1888 S, I, M, 1890 S, E, I
Blyth, L (Swansea) 1951 SA, 1952 E, S
Blyth, W R (Swansea) 1974 E, 1975 S (R), 1980 F, E, S, I
Boobyer, N (Llanelli) 1993 Z 1(R),2, Nm, 1994 Fj, Tg, 1998 F, 1999 It (R)
Boon, R W (Cardiff) 1930 S, F, 1931 E, S, F, I, SA, 1932 E, S, I, 1933 E, I
Booth, J (Pontymister) 1898 I
Boots, J G (Newport) 1898 I, E, 1899 I, 1900 E, S, I, 1901 E, S, I, 1902 E, S, I, 1903 E, S, I, 1904 E
Boucher, A W (Newport) 1892 E, S, I, 1893 E, S, I, 1894 E, 1895 E, S, I, 1896 E, I, 1897 E
Bowcott, H M (Cardiff, Cambridge U) 1929 S, F, I, 1930 E, 1931 E, S, 1933 E, I
Bowdler, F A (Cross Keys) 1927 A, 1928 E, S, I, F, 1929 E, S, F, I, 1930 E, 1931 SA, 1932 E, S, I, 1933 I
Bowen, B (S Wales Police, Swansea) 1983 R, 1984 S, I, F, E, 1985 Fj, 1986 E, S, I, F, Fj, Tg, WS, 1987 [C, E, NZ], US, 1988 E, S, I, F, WS, 1989 S, I
Bowen, C A (Llanelli) 1896 E, S, I, 1897 E
Bowen, D H (Llanelli) 1883 E, 1886 E, S, 1887 E
Bowen, G E (Swansea) 1887 S, I, 1888 S, I
Bowen, W (Swansea) 1921 S, F, 1922 E, S, I, F
Bowen, Wm A (Swansea) 1886 E, S, 1887 E, S, I, 1888 M, 1889 S, I, 1890 S, E, I, 1891 E, S
Brace, D O (Llanelli, Oxford U) 1956 E, S, I, F, 1957 E, 1960 S, I, F, 1961 I
Braddock, K J (Newbridge) 1966 A, 1967 S, I
Bradshaw, K (Bridgend) 1964 E, S, I, F, SA, 1966 E, S, I, F
Brew, A G (Newport Gwent Dragons, Ospreys) 2007 I(R),A2,E2, 2010 Fj, 2011 Bb, Arg(R), [Nm], 2012 Bb
Brew, N R (Gwent Dragons) 2003 R
Brewer, T J (Newport) 1950 E, 1955 E, S
Brice, A B (Aberavon) 1899 E, S, I, 1900 E, S, I, 1901 E, S, I, 1902 E, S, I, 1903 E, S, I, 1904 E, S, I
Bridges, C J (Neath) 1990 Nm 1,2, Bb, 1991 E (R), I, F 1, A
Bridie, R H (Newport) 1882 I
Britton, G R (Newport) 1961 S
Broster, B G J (Saracens) 2005 US(R),C
Broughton, A S (Treorchy) 1927 A, 1929 S
Brown, A (Newport) 1921 I
Brown, J (Cardiff) 1925 I
Brown, J A (Cardiff) 1907 E, S, I, 1908 E, S, F, 1909 E
Brown, M (Pontypool) 1983 R, 1986 E, S, Fj (R), Tg, WS
Bryant, D J (Bridgend) 1988 NZ 1,2, WS, R, 1989 S, I, F, E
Bryant, J (Celtic Warriors) 2003 R (R)
Buchanan, D A (Llanelli) 1987 [Tg, E, NZ, A], 1988 I
Buckett, I M (Swansea) 1994 Tg, 1997 US 2, C
Budgett, N J (Ebbw Vale, Bridgend) 2000 S, I, Sm (R), US, SA, 2001 J 1(R),2, 2002 I, F, It, E, S
Burcher, D H (Newport) 1977 I, F, E, S
Burgess, R C (Ebbw Vale) 1977 I, F, E, S, 1981 I, F, 1982 F, E, S
Burnett, R (Newport) 1953 E
Burns, J (Cardiff) 1927 F, I
Burns, L B (Newport Gwent Dragons) 2011 Bb(R), E2(R), 3, [Sm(R), Nm, Fj(R), A(R)]

Bush, P F (Cardiff) 1905 NZ, 1906 E, SA, 1907 I, 1908 E, S, 1910 S, I
Butler, E T (Pontypool) 1980 F, E, S, I, NZ (R), 1982 S, 1983 E, S, I, F, R, 1984 S, I, F, E, A
Byrne, L M (Llanelli Scarlets, Ospreys, Clermont-Auvergne) 2005 NZ(R), Fj, SA, 2006 E(t&R), S(t&R), I, It, F, Arg 1, 2, PI, 2007 F1, A1, E2, 2008 E, S, It, I, F, SA3, NZ, A, 2009 S, E, F, It, I, 2010 E, S, F, I, It, SA1, NZ1, 2, SA2, Fj, NZ3, 2011 E1(R), S, It, I, F, Arg, [Nm,Fj]

Cale, W R (Newbridge, Pontypool) 1949 E, S, I, 1950 E, S, I, F
Cardey, M D (Llanelli) 2000 S
Carter, A J (Newport) 1991 E, S
Cattell, A (Llanelli) 1883 E, S
Challinor, C (Neath) 1939 E
Charteris, L C (Newport Gwent Dragons) 2004 SA2(R), R, 2005 US, C, NZ(R), Fj, 2007 SA(R), 2008 C,NZ(R), 2009 S(R), F(R), It, I(R), US(R), NZ, Sm, Arg, A, 2010 E, F(R), I, It, 2011 Bb, E2(R), 3, [SA, Sm, Nm(R), Fj, I, F, A], 2012 It(R), F(R), A, I, 2(R), 3(t&R)
Charvis, C L (Swansea, Tarbes, Newcastle, Newport Gwent Dragons) 1996 A 3(R), SA, 1997 US, S, I, F, 1998 It (R), E, S, I, F, Z, 2(R), SA 1,2, Arg, 1999 S, I, F 1, It, E, Arg 1, SA, F 2, [Arg 3, A], 2000 F, It (R), E, S, I, Sm, US, SA, 2001 E, S, F, It, R, I, Arg, Tg, A, 2002 E (R), S, SA 1,2, R, Fj, C, NZ, 2003 It, E (R), S 1(R), I 1, F,A, NZ, E 2, S 2, [C, Tg, It, NZ, E], 2004 S, F, E, It, Arg 1, 2, SA1, 2, R, NZ, J, 2005 US, C, NZ, SA, A, 2006 E, S, I, It, 2007 A1, 2, E2, Arg(R), F2(R), [C(t&R), A, J, Fj], SA
Clapp, T J S (Newport) 1882 I, 1883 E, S, 1884 E, S, I, 1885 E, S, 1886 S, 1887 E, S, I, 1888 S, I
Clare, J (Cardiff) 1883 E
Clark, S S (Neath) 1882 I, 1887 I
Cleaver, W B (Cardiff) 1947 E, S, F, I, A, 1948 E, S, F, I, 1949 I, 1950 E, S, I, F
Clegg, B G (Swansea) 1979 F
Clement, A (Swansea) 1987 US (R), 1988 E, NZ 1, WS (R), R, 1989 NZ, 1990 S (R), I (R), Nm 1,2, 1991 S (R), A (R), F 2, [WS, A], 1992 I, F, E, S, 1993 I (R), F, J, C, 1994 S, I, F, Sp, C (R), Tg, WS, It, SA, 1995 F, E, [J, NZ, I]
Clement, W H (Llanelli) 1937 E, S, I, 1938 E, S, I
Cobner, T J (Pontypool) 1974 S, I, F, E, 1975 F, E, S, I, A, 1976 E, S, 1977 F, E, S, 1978 E, S, I, F, A 1
Cockbain, B J (Celtic Warriors, Ospreys) 2003 R, [C, It, NZ, E], 2004 S, I, F, E, Arg 1, 2, SA2, NZ, 2005 E, It, F, S, I, US, C(R), NZ, Fj, 2007 F1(t&R), A1
Coldrick, A P (Newport) 1911 E, S, I, 1912 E, S, F
Coleman, E O (Newport) 1949 E, S, I
Coles, F C (Pontypool) 1960 S, I, F
Collins, J E (Aberavon) 1958 A, E, S, F, 1959 E, S, I, F, 1960 E, 1961 F
Collins, R G (S Wales Police, Cardiff, Pontypridd) 1987 E (R), I, [I, E, NZ], US, 1988 E, S, I, F, R, 1990 E, S, I, 1991 A F 2, [WS], 1994 C, Fj, Tg, WS, R, It, SA, 1995 F, E, S, I
Collins, T J (Mountain Ash) 1923 I
Conway-Rees, J (Llanelli) 1892 S, 1893 E, 1894 E
Cook, T (Cardiff) 1949 S, I
Cooper, G J (Bath, Celtic Warriors, Newport Gwent Dragons, Gloucester, Cardiff Blues) 2001 It, J 1, 2, 2003 E 1, S1, I1, F(R), A, NZ, E2, [C, Tg, It(t&R), NZ, E], 2004 S, I, F, E, It, R(R), NZ(R), J, 2005 E(R), It(R), F(R), NZ(R), Fj, SA, A, 2006 E(R), PI(R), 2007 A1(R), E2, [J(R)], 2008 SA1, 2, 3, NZ, A, 2009 C, US(R), NZ, Arg, 2010 E, S
Cooper, V L (Llanelli) 2002 C, 2003 I 2(R), S 2
Cope, W (Cardiff, Blackheath) 1896 S
Copsey, A H (Llanelli) 1992 I, F, E, S, A, 1993 E, S, I, J, C, 1994 E (R), Pt, Sp (R), Fj, Tg, WS (R)
Cornish, F H (Cardiff) 1897 E, 1898 I, E, 1899 I
Cornish, R A (Cardiff) 1923 E, S, 1924 E, 1925 E, S, F, 1926 E, S, I, F
Coslett, T K (Aberavon) 1962 E, S, F
Cowey, B T V (Welch Regt, Newport) 1934 E, S, I, 1935 E
Cresswell, B R (Newport) 1960 E, S, I, F
Cummins, W (Treorchy) 1922 E, S, I, F
Cunningham, L J (Aberavon) 1960 E, S, I, F, 1962 E, S, F, I, 1963 NZ, 1964 E, S, I, F, SA
Cuthbert, A G C (Cardiff Blues) 2011 A(R), 2012 I,S,E,It,F,A 1,2,3
Czekaj, C D (Cardiff Blues) 2005 C, 2006 Arg 1(R), 2007 I,S,A1,2, 2009 C, 2010 A(R), SA2(R)

Dacey, M (Swansea) 1983 E, S, I, F, R, 1984 S, I, F, E, A, 1986 Fj, Tg, WS, 1987 F (R), [Tg]
Daniel, D J (Llanelli) 1891 S, 1894 E, S, I, 1898 I, E, 1899 E, I
Daniel, L T D (Newport) 1970 S
Daniels, P C T (Cardiff) 1981 A, 1982 I
Darbishire, G (Bangor) 1881 E
Dauncey, F H (Newport) 1896 E, S, I
Davey, C (Swansea) 1930 F, 1931 E, S, F, I, SA, 1932 E, S, I, 1933 E, S, 1934 E, S, I, 1935 E, S, I, NZ, 1936 S, 1937 E, I, 1938 E, I

513

WALES

Herrerá, R C (Cross Keys) 1925 S, F, I, 1926 E, S, I, F, 1927 E
Hiams, H (Swansea) 1912 I, F
Hibbard, R M (Ospreys) 2006 Arg 1(R),2(R), 2007 A1(R),2(R), 2008 SA1(R),2,C, 2009 C,US(R), 2011 E1(R),S(R),It(R),I(R),F(R),Arg, 2012 Bb(R), A 2(R)
Hickman, A (Neath) 1930 E, 1933 S
Hiddlestone, D D (Neath) 1922 E, S, I, F, 1924 NZ
Hill, A F (Cardiff) 1885 S, 1886 E, S, 1888 S, I, M, 1889 S, 1890 S, I, 1893 E, S, I, 1894 E, S, I
Hill, S D (Cardiff) 1993 Z 1,2, Nm, 1994 I (R), F, SA, 1995 F, SA, 1996 A 2, F 2(R), It, 1997 E
Hinam, S (Cardiff) 1925 I, 1926 E, S, I, F
Hinton, J T (Cardiff) 1884 I
Hirst, G L (Newport) 1912 S, 1913 S, 1914 E, S, F, I
Hodder, W (Pontypool) 1921 E, S, F
Hodges, J J (Newport) 1899 E, S, I, 1900 E, S, I, 1901 E, S, 1902 E, S, I, 1903 E, S, I, 1904 E, S, 1905 E, S, I, NZ, 1906 E, S, I
Hodgson, G T R (Neath) 1962 I, 1963 E, S, I, F, NZ, 1964 E, S, I, F, SA, 1966 S, I, F, 1967 I
Hollingdale, B G (Swansea) 1912 SA, 1913 E
Hollingdale, T H (Neath) 1927 A, 1928 E, S, I, F, 1930 E
Holmes, T D (Cardiff) 1978 A 2, NZ, 1979 S, I, F, E, 1980 F, E, S, I, NZ, 1981 A, 1982 I, F, E, 1983 E, S, I, F, 1984 E 1985 S, I, F, E, Fj
Hook, J W (Ospreys, Perpignan) 2006 Arg 1(R), 2, A(R), PI, C, NZ(R), 2007 I, S, F1, It, E1, A1, 2, Arg, F2, [C, A(R), J, Fj], SA, 2008 E, S, It(R), I(R), F, SA1(R), 2, 3(R), C, NZ(R), 2009 S(R), F(R), It, NZ, Sm, Arg, A, 2010 E, S, F, I, It, SA1, A, SA2, Fj, NZ3, 2011 E1, S, It, I, F, E3, Arg, [SA, Sm, I(R), F, A], 2012 I(R), S(R), It(R), Bb, A1(R), 3(R)
Hopkin, W H (Newport) 1937 S
Hopkins, K (Cardiff, Swansea) 1985 E, 1987 F, E, S, [Tg, C (R)], US
Hopkins, P L (Swansea) 1908 A, 1909 E, I, 1910 E
Hopkins, R (Maesteg) 1970 E (R)
Hopkins, T (Swansea) 1926 E, S, I, F
Hopkins, W J (Aberavon) 1925 E, S
Horsman, C L (Worcester) 2005 NZ(R),Fj,SA,A, 2006 PI, 2007 I,F1,It,E1,A2(R),E2,F2, [J,Fj]
Howarth, S P (Sale, Newport) 1998 SA 2, Arg, 1999 S, I, F 1, It, E, Arg 1,2, SA, C, F 2, [Arg 3, J, Sm, A], 2000 F, It, E
Howells, B (Llanelli) 1934 E
Howells, W G (Llanelli) 1957 E, S, I, F
Howells, W H (Swansea) 1888 S, I
Howley, R (Bridgend, Cardiff) 1996 E, S, I, F 1, A 1,2, Bb, F 2, It, A 3, SA, 1997 US, S, I, F, E, Tg (R), NZ, 1998 It, E, S, I, F, Z, SA 2, Arg, 1999 S, I, F 1, It, E, Arg 1,2, SA, C, F 2, [Arg 3, J, Sm, A], 2000 F, It, E, Sm, US, SA, 2001 E, S, F, R, I, Arg, Tg, A, 2002 I, F, It, E, S
Hughes, D (Newbridge) 1967 NZ, 1969 NZ 2, 1970 SA, S, E, I
Hughes, G (Penarth) 1934 E, S, I
Hughes, H (Cardiff) 1887 S, 1889 S
Hughes, K (Cambridge U, London Welsh) 1970 I, 1973 A, 1974 S
Hullin, W G (Cardiff) 1967 S
Humphreys, J M (Cardiff, Bath) 1995 [NZ, I], SA, Fj, 1996 It, E, S, I, F 1, A 1,2, Bb, It, A 3, SA, 1997 S, I, F, E, Tg (R), NZ (R), 1998 It (R), E (R), S (R), I (R), F (R), SA 2, Arg, 1999 S, Arg 2(R), SA (R), C, [J (R)], 2003 E 1, I 1
Hurrell, R J (Newport) 1959 F
Hutchinson, F O (Neath) 1894 I, 1896 S, I
Huxtable, R (Swansea) 1920 F, I
Huzzey, H V P (Cardiff) 1898 I, E, 1899 E, S, I
Hybart, A J (Cardiff) 1887 E

Ingledew, H M (Cardiff) 1890 I, 1891 E, S
Isaacs, I (Cardiff) 1933 E, S

Jackson, T H (Swansea) 1895 E
James, C R (Llanelli) 1958 A, F
James, D (Swansea) 1891 I, 1892 S, I, 1899 E
James, D M (Cardiff) 1947 A, 1948 E, S, F, I
James, D R (Treorchy) 1931 F, I
James, D R (Bridgend, Pontypridd, Llanelli Scarlets) 1996 A 2(R), It, A 3, SA, 1997 I, Tg (R), 1998 F (R), Z, SA 1,2, Arg, 1999 S, I, F 1, It, E, Arg 1,2, SA, F 2, [Arg 3, Sm, A], 2000 F, It (R), I (R), Sm (R), US, SA, 2001 E, S, F, It, R, I, 2002 I, F, It, E, S (R), NZ(R), 2005 SA,A, 2006 I,F, 2007 E2,Arg, [J]
James, E (Swansea) 1890 S, 1891 I, 1892 S, I, 1899 E
James, J B (Bridgend) 1968 E
James, P (Ospreys) 2003 R, 2009 NZ,Sm,Arg,A, 2010 E,S,F,I,It(t& R),SA1,NZ1,2,A(R),SA2,Fj,NZ3(R), 2011 I,S,It,I,F,Bb,E2,3,Arg,[S A,Sm,Fj(R),F(R),A], 2012 I(R),S(R),It(R),Bb(t&R),A 1(R),3(R)
James, T (Cardiff Blues, Wasps) 2007 E2,Arg(R),F2(R), [J] 2009 C,US,Sm,Arg(R),A(R), 2010 E,NZ3
James, T O (Aberavon) 1935 I, 1937 S
James, W (Gloucester) 2007 E2,Arg(R),F2(R), [J]

James, W J (Aberavon) 1983 E, S, I, F, R, 1984 S, 1985 S, I, F, E, Fj, 1986 E, S, I, F, Fj, Tg, WS, 1987 E, S, I
James, W P (Aberavon) 1925 E, S
Jarman, H (Newport) 1910 E, S, I, 1911 E
Jarrett, K S (Newport) 1967 E, 1968 E, S, 1969 S, I, F, E, NZ 1,2, A
Jarvis, L (Cardiff) 1997 R (R)
Jeffery, J J (Cardiff Coll of Ed, Newport) 1967 NZ
Jenkin, A M (Swansea) 1895 I, 1896 E
Jenkins, A E (Llanelli) 1920 E, S, F, I, 1921 S, F, 1922 F, 1923 E, S, F, I, 1924 NZ, 1928 S, I
Jenkins, D M (Treorchy) 1926 E, S, I, F
Jenkins, D R (Swansea) 1927 A, 1929 E
Jenkins, E (Newport) 1910 S, I
Jenkins, E M (Aberavon) 1927 S, F, I, A, 1928 E, S, I, F, 1929 F, 1930 E, S, I, F, 1931 E, S, F, I, SA, 1932 E, S, I
Jenkins, G D (Pontypridd, Celtic Warriors, Cardiff Blues) 2002 R, NZ(R), 2003 E 1(R), S 1(R), I 1, F, A, NZ, I 2(R), E 2, [C, Tg, It(R), NZ(R), E(R)], 2004 S(R), I(R), F, E, It, Arg (R), SA1, 2(R), R, NZ, J, 2005 E, It, F, S, I, 2006 E(R), S(R), I(R), It(R), F(R), A, C, NZ(R), 2007 I, S(R), F1, It, E1, 2(R), Arg(R), F2(R), [C, A, J(R), Fj], SA, 2008 E(R), S, It, I, F, SA1, 2, 3, NZ, A, 2009 S, E, F, It(R), I, NZ, Sm, Arg, A, 2010 S(R), It, A, NZ3, 2011 [Sm(R), Nm, Fj, I, F, A], A, 2012 S, E, It, I, F, A 1, 2, 3
Jenkins, G R (Pontypool, Swansea) 1991 F 2, [WS (R), Arg, A], 1992 I, F, E, S, A, 1993 C, 1994 E, I, F, Pt, Sp, C, Tg, WS, R, It, SA, 1995 F, E, S, I, [J], SA (R), Fj (t), 1996 E (R), 1997 US, US 1, C, 1998 S, I, F, Z, SA 1(R), 1999 I (R), F 1, It, E, Arg 1,2, SA, F 2, [Arg 3, J, Sm, A], 2000 F, It, E, S, I, Sm, US, SA
Jenkins, J C (London Welsh) 1906 SA
Jenkins, J L (Aberavon) 1923 S, F
Jenkins, L H (Mon TC, Newport) 1954 I, 1956 E, S, I, F
Jenkins, N R (Pontypridd, Cardiff) 1991 E, S, I, F 1, 1992 I, F, E, S, 1993 E, S, I, F, Z 1,2, Nm, J, C, 1994 S, I, F, E, Pt, Sp, C, Tg, WS, R, It, SA, 1995 F, E, S, I, [J, NZ, I], SA, Fj, 1996 F 1, A 1,2, Bb, F 2, It, A 3, SA, 1997 S, I, F, E, Tg, NZ, 1998 It, E, S, I, F, SA 2, Arg, 1999 S, I, F 1, It, E, Arg 1,2, SA, F, [Arg 3, J, Sm, A], 2000 F, It, E, (R), Sm (R), US (R), SA, 2001 E, S, F, It, 2002 SA 1(R),2(R), R
Jenkins, V G J (Oxford U, Bridgend, London Welsh) 1933 E, I, 1934 S, I, 1935 E, S, NZ, 1936 E, S, I, 1937 E, 1938 E, S, 1939 E
Jenkins, W J (Cardiff) 1912 I, F, 1913 S, I
John, B (Llanelli, Cardiff) 1966 A, 1967 S, NZ, 1968 E, S, I, F, 1969 S, I, F, E, NZ 1,2, A, 1970 SA, S, E, I, 1971 E, S, I, F, 1972 E, S, F
John, D A (Llanelli) 1925 I, 1928 E, S, I
John, D E (Llanelli) 1923 F, I, 1928 E, S, I
John, E R (Neath) 1950 E, S, I, F, 1951 E, S, I, F, 1952 E, S, I, F, 1953 E, S, I, F, NZ, 1954 E
John, G (St Luke's Coll, Exeter) 1954 E, F
John, J H (Swansea) 1926 E, S, I, F, 1927 E, S, F, I
John, P (Pontypridd) 1994 Tg, 1996 Bb (t), 1997 US (R), US 1,2, C, R, Tg, 1998 Z 2(R), SA 1
John, S C (Llanelli, Cardiff) 1995 S, I, 1997 E (R), Tg, NZ (R), 2000 F (R), E (R), Sm (R), SA (R), 2001 E (R), S (R), Tg (R), A, 2002 I, F, It (R), S (R)
Johnson, T A W (Cardiff) 1921 E, F, I, 1923 E, S, F, 1924 E, S, NZ, 1925 E, S, F
Johnson, W D (Swansea) 1953 E
Jones , A E (SEE Emyr)
Jones, A H (Cardiff) 1933 E, S
Jones, A M (Llanelli Scarlets) 2006 E(t&R),S(R)
Jones, A R (Ospreys) 2003 E2(R), S2, [C(R), Tg(R)), It, NZ, E], 2004 S, I, Arg 1, 2, R, NZ, J(t&R), 2005 E, It, F, S, I, US,N Z, Fj(R), SA(t&R), A(R), 2006 E, S, I, It, F, Arg 1, 2, A, PI(R), C, NZ, 2007 S, It(R), E1(R), A1, Arg, [C, A], 2008 E, S, I, F, SA1, 3, NZ, A, 2009 S, E, F, I, 2010 E, S, F, I, It, SA1, NZ1, 2, A, SA2, Fj, NZ3, 2011 F, Arg, [SA, Sm, Fj(R), F], 2012 I, S, E, It, F, A 1, 2, 3
Jones, A W (Mountain Ash) 1905 I
Jones, A-W (Ospreys) 2006 Arg 1, 2, PI, C(R), NZ(R), 2007 I, S, F1, It, E1, 2, Arg, F2, [C, A, J, Fj], SA, 2008 E, S, I, F, SA1, 2, 3, NZ, A, 2009 S, E, F, I, It, NZ, Sm, Arg, A, 2010 E, S, SA1(R), NZ1, 2, A, SA2, NZ3, 2011 E, S, It, I, F, Bb(R), Arg, [SA, Sm, Nm, Fj(R), I, F, A(R)], 2012 E, It, F, Bb, A1(R), 2, 3
Jones, B J (Newport) 1960 I, F
Jones, B L (Devonport Services, Llanelli) 1950 E, S, I, F, 1951 E, S, SA, 1952 E, I, F
Jones, C (Harlequins) 2007 A1(R),2
Jones, C W (Cambridge U, Cardiff) 1934 E, S, I, 1935 E, S, I, NZ, 1936 E, S, I, 1938 E, S, I
Jones, C W (Bridgend) 1920 E, S, F
Jones, C (Aberavon) 1897 E
Jones, D (Treherbert) 1902 E, S, I, 1903 E, S, I, 1905 E, S, I, NZ, 1906 E, S, SA

Llewellyn, P D (Swansea) 1973 I, F, A, 1974 S, E
Llewellyn, W (Llwynypia) 1899 E, S, I, 1900 E, S, I, 1901 E, S, I, 1902 E, S, I, 1903 I, 1904 E, S, I, 1905 E, S, I, NZ
Llewelyn, D B (Newport, Llanelli) 1970 SA, S, E, I, F, 1971 E, S, I, F, 1972 E, S, F, NZ
Lloyd, A (Bath) 2001 J 1
Lloyd, D J (Bridgend) 1966 E, S, I, F, A, 1967 S, I, F, E, 1968 S, I, F, 1969 S, I, F, E, NZ 1, A, 1970 F, 1972 E, S, F, 1973 E, S
Lloyd, D P M (Llanelli) 1890 S, E, 1891 E, I
Lloyd, E (Llanelli) 1895 S
Lloyd, G L (Newport) 1896 I, 1899 S, I, 1900 E, S, 1901 E, S, 1902 S, I, 1903 E, S, I
Lloyd, R (Pontypool) 1913 S, F, I, 1914 E, S, F, I
Lloyd, T (Maesteg) 1953 I, F
Lloyd, T J (Neath) 1909 F, 1913 F, I, 1914 E, S, F, I
Loader, C D (Swansea) 1995 SA, Fj, 1996 F 1, A 1,2, Bb, F 2, It, A 3, SA, 1997 US, S, I, F, E, US 1, R, Tg, NZ
Lockwood, T W (Newport) 1887 E, S, I
Long, E C (Swansea) 1936 E, S, I, 1937 E, S, 1939 S, I
Luscombe, H N (Newport Gwent Dragons, Harlequins) 2003 S 2(R), 2004 Arg 1,2,SA1,2,R,J, 2005 E,It,S(t&R), 2006 E,S,I,It,F, 2007 I
Lydiate, D J (Newport Gwent Dragons) 2009 Arg(R), A, 2010 A, Fj, NZ3, 2011 E1, S, It, I, F, Bb, E2, 3, Arg, [SA, Sm, I, F, A], A, 2012 S, E, It, F, A 1,2,3
Lyne, H S (Newport) 1883 S, 1884 E, S, I, 1885 E

McBryde, R C (Swansea, Llanelli, Neath, Llanelli Scarlets) 1994 Fj, SA (t), 1997 US 2, 2000 I (R), 2001 E, S, F, It, R, I, Arg, Tg, A, 2002 I, F, It, E, S (R), SA 1,2, C, NZ, 2003 A, NZ, E 2, S 2, [C,It,NZ,E], 2004 I,E,It, 2005 It(R),F(R),S(R),I(R)
McCall, B E W (Welch Regt, Newport) 1936 E, S, I
McCarley, A (Neath) 1938 E, S, I
McCusker, R J (Scarlets) 2010 SA1(R),NZ1(R),2(R)
McCutcheon, W M (Swansea) 1891 S, 1892 E, S, 1893 E, S, I, 1894 E
McIntosh, D L M (Pontypridd) 1996 SA, 1997 E (R)
Madden, M (Llanelli) 2002 SA 1(R), R, Fj(R), 2003 I 1(R), F(R)
Maddock, H T (London Welsh) 1906 E, S, I, 1907 E, S, 1910 F
Maddocks, K (Neath) 1957 E
Main, D R (London Welsh) 1959 E, S, I, F
Mainwaring, H J (Swansea) 1961 F
Mainwaring, W T (Aberavon) 1967 S, I, F, E, NZ, 1968 E
Major, W C (Maesteg) 1949 F, 1950 S
Male, B O (Cardiff) 1921 F, 1923 S, 1924 S, I, 1927 E, S, F, I, 1928 S, I, F
Manfield, L (Mountain Ash, Cardiff) 1939 S, I, 1947 A, 1948 E, S, F, I
Mann, B B (Cardiff) 1881 E
Mantle, J T (Loughborough Colls, Newport) 1964 E, SA
Margrave, F L (Llanelli) 1884 E, S
Marinos, A W N (Newport, Gwent Dragons)) 2002 I (R), F, It, E, S, SA 1,2, 2003 R
Marsden-Jones, D (Cardiff) 1921 E, 1924 NZ
Martin, A J (Aberavon) 1973 A, 1974 S, I, 1975 F, E, S, I, A, 1976 E, S, I, F, 1977 I, F, E, S, 1978 E, S, I, F, A 1,2, NZ, 1979 S, I, F, E, 1980 F, E, S, I, NZ, 1981 I, F
Martin, W J (Newport) 1912 I, F, 1919 NZA
Mason, J E (Pontypridd) 1988 NZ 2(R)
Mathews, Rev A A (Lampeter) 1886 S
Mathias, R (Llanelli) 1970 F
Matthews, C M (Bridgend) 1939 I
Matthews, J (Cardiff), 1947 E A, 1948 E, S, F, 1949 E, S, I, F, 1950 E, S, I, F, 1951 E, S, I, F
May, P S (Llanelli) 1988 E, S, I, F, NZ 1,2, 1991 [WS]
Meek, N N (Pontypool) 1993 E, S, I
Meredith, A (Devonport Services) 1949 E, S, I
Meredith, B V (St Luke's Coll, London Welsh, Newport) 1954 I, F, S, 1955 E, S, I, F, 1956 E, S, I, F, 1957 E, S, I, F, 1958 A, E, S, I, 1959 E, S, I, F, 1960 E, S, F, SA, 1961 E, S, I, 1962 S, E, F, I
Meredith, C C (Neath) 1953 S, NZ, 1954 E, I, F, S, 1955 E, S, I, F, 1956 E, I, 1957 E, S
Meredith, J (Swansea) 1888 S, I, 1890 S, E
Merry, J A (Pill Harriers) 1912 I, F
Michael, G M (Swansea) 1923 E, S, F
Michaelson, R C B (Aberavon, Cambridge U) 1963 E
Millar, W H (Mountain Ash) 1896 I, 1900 E, S, I, 1901 E, S, I
Mills, F M (Swansea, Cardiff) 1892 E, S, I, 1893 E, S, I, 1894 E, S, I, 1895 E, S, I, 1896 E
Mitchell, C (Ospreys, Exeter) 2009 C(R),US(R),Sm(R), 2010 NZ2(R), 2011 E1,S,It,I,E2,3,[Nm]
Moon, R H StJ B (Llanelli) 1993 F, Z 1,2, Nm, J, C, 1994 S, I, F, E, Sp, C, Fj, WS, R, It, SA, 1995 E (R), 2000 S, I, Sm (R), US (R), 2001 E (R), S (R)
Moore, A P (Cardiff) 1995 [J], SA, Fj, 1996 It

Moore, A P (Swansea) 1995 SA (R), Fj, 1998 S, I, F, Z, SA 1, 1999 C, 2000 S, I, US (R), 2001 E (R), S, F, It, J 1,2, R, I, Arg, Tg, A, 2002 F, It, E, S
Moore, S J (Swansea, Moseley) 1997 C, R, Tg
Moore, W J (Bridgend) 1933 I
Morgan, C H (Llanelli) 1957 I, F
Morgan, C I (Cardiff) 1951 I, F, SA, 1952 E, S, I, 1953 S, I, F, NZ, 1954 E, I, S, 1955 E, S, I, F, 1956 E, S, I, F, 1957 E, S, I, F, 1958 E, S, I, F
Morgan, C S (Cardiff Blues) 2002 I, F, It, E, S, SA 1,2, R(R), 2003 F, 2005 US
Morgan, D (Swansea) 1885 S, 1886 E, S, 1887 E, S, I, 1889 I
Morgan, D (Llanelli) 1895 I, 1896 E
Morgan, D E (Llanelli) 1920 I, 1921 E, S, F
Morgan, D R R (Llanelli) 1962 E, S, F, I, 1963 E, S, I, F, NZ
Morgan, E (Swansea) 1914 E, S, F, I
Morgan, E (London Welsh) 1902 E, S, I, 1903 I, 1904 E, S, I, 1905 E, S, I, NZ, 1906 E, S, I, SA, 1908 F
Morgan, F L (Llanelli) 1938 E, S, I, 1939 E
Morgan, G R (Newport) 1984 S
Morgan, H J (Abertillery) 1958 E, S, I, F, 1959 I, F, 1960 E, 1961 E, S, I, F, 1962 E, S, I, F, 1963 S, I, F, 1965 E, S, I, F, 1966 E, S, I, F, A
Morgan, H P (Newport) 1956 E, S, I, F
Morgan, J L (Llanelli) 1912 SA, 1913 E
Morgan, K A (Pontypridd, Swansea, Newport Gwent Dragons) 1997 US 1,2, C, R, NZ, 1998 S, I, F, 2001 J 1,2, R, I, Arg, Tg, A, 2002 I, F, It, E, S, SA 1,2, 2003 E 1, S 1, [C,It], 2004 J(R), 2005 E(R),It(R),F,S,I,US,C,NZ,Fj, 2006 A,PI, NZ, 2007 I,S,It,E1,Arg,F2, [C,A(R),J]
Morgan, M E (Swansea) 1938 E, S, I, 1939 E
Morgan, N H (Newport) 1960 S, I, F
Morgan, P E J (Aberavon) 1961 E, S, F
Morgan, P J (Llanelli) 1980 S (R), I, NZ (R), 1981 I
Morgan, S (Cardiff Blues) 2007 A2(R)
Morgan, T (Llanelli) 1889 I
Morgan, W G (Cambridge U) 1927 F, I, 1929 E, S, F, I, 1930 I, F
Morgan, W I (Swansea) 1908 A, 1909 E, S, F, I, 1910 F, E, S, I, 1911 E, F, I, 1912 S
Morgan, W L (Cardiff) 1910 S
Moriarty, R D (Swansea) 1981 A, 1982 I, F, E, S, 1983 E, 1984 S, I, F, E, 1985 S, I, F, 1986 Fj, Tg, WS, 1987 [I, Tg, C (R), E, NZ, A]
Moriarty, W P (Swansea) 1986 I, F, Fj, Tg, WS, 1987 F, E, S, I, [I, Tg, C, E, NZ, A], US, 1988 E, S, I, F, NZ 1
Morley, J C (Newport) 1929 E, S, F, I, 1930 E, I, 1931 E, S, F, I, SA, 1932 E, S, I
Morris, D R (Neath, Swansea, Leicester) 1998 Z, SA 1(R),2(R), 1999 S, I, It (R), 2000 US, SA, 2001 E, S, F, It, Arg, Tg, A, 2004 Arg 1(R),2(R),SA1(R)
Morris, G L (Swansea) 1882 I, 1883 E, S, 1884 E, S
Morris, H T (Cardiff) 1951 F, 1955 I, F
Morris, J I T (Swansea) 1924 E, S
Morris, M S (S Wales Police, Neath) 1985 S, I, F, 1990 I, Nm 1,2, Bb, 1991 I, F 1, [WS (R)], 1992 E
Morris, R R (Swansea, Bristol) 1933 S, 1937 S
Morris, S (Cross Keys) 1920 E, S, F, I, 1922 E, S, I, F, 1923 E, S, F, I, 1924 E, S, F, NZ, 1925 E, S, F
Morris, W (Llanelli) 1896 S, I, 1897 E
Morris, W D (Neath) 1967 F, E, 1968 E, S, I, F, 1969 S, I, F, E, NZ 1,2, A, 1970 SA, S, E, I, F, 1971 E, S, I, F, 1972 E, S, F, NZ, 1973 E, S, I, A, 1974 S, I, F, E
Morris, W G H (Abertillery) 1919 NZA, 1920 F, 1921 I
Morris, W J (Newport) 1965 S, 1966 F
Morris, W J B (Pontypool) 1963 S, I
Moseley, K (Pontypool, Newport) 1988 NZ 2, R, 1989 S, I, 1990 F, 1991 F 2, [WS, Arg, A]
Murphy, C D (Cross Keys) 1935 E, S, I
Mustoe, L (Cardiff) 1995 Fj, 1996 A 1(R),2, 1997 US 1,2, C, R (R), 1998 E (R), I (R), F (R)

Nash, D (Ebbw Vale) 1960 SA, 1961 E, S, I, F, 1962 F
Newman, C H (Newport) 1881 E, 1882 I, 1883 E, S, 1884 E, S, 1885 E, S, 1886 E, 1887 E
Nicholas, D L (Llanelli) 1981 E, S, I, F
Nicholas, T J (Cardiff) 1919 NZA
Nicholl, C B (Cambridge U, Llanelli) 1891 I, 1892 E, S, I, 1893 E, S, I, 1894 E, S, 1895 E, S, I, 1896 E, S, I
Nicholl, D W (Llanelli) 1894 I
Nicholls, E G (Cardiff) 1896 S, I, 1897 E, 1898 I, E, 1899 E, S, I, 1900 S, I, 1901 E, S, I, 1902 E, S, I, 1903 I, 1904 E, S, 1905 I, NZ, 1906 E, S, I, SA
Nicholls, F E (Cardiff Harlequins) 1892 I
Nicholls, H C W (Cardiff) 1958 I
Nicholls, S H (Cardiff) 1888 M, 1889 S, I, 1891 S

WALES

Sweet-Escott, R B (Cardiff) 1891 S, 1894 I, 1895 I

Tamplin, W E (Cardiff) 1947 S, F, I, A, 1948 E, S, F
Tanner, H (Swansea, Cardiff) 1935 NZ, 1936 E, S, I, 1937 E, S, I, 1938 E, S, I, 1939 E, S, I, 1947 E, S, F, I, 1948 E, S, F, I, 1949 E, S, I, F
Tarr, D J (Swansea, Royal Navy) 1935 NZ
Taylor, A R (Cross Keys) 1937 I, 1938 I, 1939 E
Taylor, C G (Ruabon) 1884 E, S, I, 1885 E, S, 1886 E, S, 1887 E, I
Taylor, H T (Cardiff) 1994 Pt, C, Fj, Tg, WS (R), R, It, SA, 1995 E, S, [J, NZ, I], SA, Fj, 1996 It, E, S, I, F 1, A 1,2, It, A 3
Taylor, J (London Welsh) 1967 S, I, F, E, NZ, 1968 I, F, 1969 S, I, F, E, NZ 1, A, 1970 F, 1971 E, S, I, F, 1972 E, S, F, NZ, 1973 E, S, I, F
Taylor, M (Pontypool, Swansea, Llanelli Scarlets, Sale) 1994 SA, 1995 F, E, SA (R), 1998 Z, SA 1,2, Arg, 1999 I F 1, It, E, Arg 1,2, SA, F 2, [Arg 3, J, Sm, A], 2000 F, It, E, S, Sm, US, 2001 E, S, F, It, 2002 S, SA 1,2, 2003 E 1, S 1, I 1, F, A, NZ, E 2, [C(R),Tg,NZ,E], 2004 F,E,It,R(R), 2005 I,US,C,NZ Sm, US, SA (R)
Thomas, A C (Bristol, Swansea) 1996 It, E, S, I, F 2(R), SA, 1997 US, S, I, F, US 1,2, C, R, NZ (t), 1998 It, E, S (R), Z, SA 1, 2000 Sm, US, SA (R)
Thomas, A R F (Newport) 1963 NZ, 1964 E
Thomas, A G (Swansea, Cardiff) 1952 E, S, I, F, 1953 S, I, F, 1954 E, I, F, 1955 S, I, F
Thomas, B (Neath, Cambridge U) 1963 E, S, I, F, NZ, 1964 E, S, I, F, SA, 1965 E, 1966 E, S, I, 1967 NZ, 1969 S, I, F, E, NZ 1,2
Thomas, B M G (St Bart's Hospital) 1919 NZA, 1921 S, F, I, 1923 F, 1924 E
Thomas, C J (Newport) 1888 I, M, 1889 S, I, 1890 S, E, I, 1891 E, I
Thomas, C R (Bridgend) 1925 E, S
Thomas, D J (Swansea) 1904 E, 1908 A, 1910 E, S, I, 1911 E, S, F, I, 1912 E
Thomas, D J (Swansea) 1930 S, I, 1932 E, S, I, 1933 E, S, 1934 E, 1935 E, S, I
Thomas, D L (Neath) 1937 E
Thomas, D L (Aberavon) 1961 I
Thomas, E (Newport) 1904 S, I, 1909 S, F, I, 1910 F
Thomas, E J R (Mountain Ash) 1906 SA, 1908 F, I, 1909 S
Thomas, G (Newport) 1888 M, 1890 I, 1891 S
Thomas, G (Bridgend, Cardiff, Celtic Warriors, Toulouse, Cardiff Blues) 1995 [J, NZ, I], SA, Fj, 1996 F 1, A 1,2, Bb, F 2, It, A 3, 1997 US, S, I, F, E, US 1,2, C, R, NZ, 1998 It, E, S, I, F, SA 2, Arg, 1999 F 1(R), It, E, Arg 2, SA, F 2, [Arg 3, J (R), Sm, A], 2000 F, It, E, S, I, US (R), SA, 2001 E, F, It, J 1,2, R, Arg, Tg, A, 2002 E, R, Fj, C, NZ, 2003 It, E 1, S 1, I 1, F, I 2, E 2, [C, It, NZ(R), E], 2004 S, I, F, E, It, SA2, R, NZ, 2005 E, It, F, NZ, SA, A, 2006 E, S, A, C, 2007 It(t&R), E1, A1, 2, E2, Arg, Fj, [C(R), A, Fj] 2007 I(t&R),A1,2, 2010 NZ1,2
Thomas, H H M (Llanelli) 1912 F
Thomas, H W (Swansea) 1912 SA, 1913 E
Thomas, H W (Neath) 1936 E, S, I, 1937 E, S, I
Thomas, I (Brynethin) 1924 E
Thomas, I D (Ebbw Vale, Llanelli Scarlets) 2000 Sm, US (R), SA (R), 2001 J 1,2, R, I, Arg (R), Tg, 2002 It, E, S, SA 1,2, Fj, C, NZ, 2003 It, E 1, S 1, I 1, F, A, NZ, E 2, [Tg,NZ,E], 2004 I,F, 2007 A1,2,E2
Thomas, J D (Llanelli) 1954 I
Thomas, J J (Swansea, Ospreys) 2003 A, NZ(R), E 2(R), R, [It(R), NZ, E], 2004 S(t&R), I, F, E, Arg 2(R), SA1(R), R(t&R), J, 2005 E(R), It, F(R), S(R), US, C, NZ, 2006 It(R), F(R), A, PI(R), C, NZ, 2007 S(R), F1(R), It(R), E1(R), A1, 2, Arg, F2, [C, A], SA, 2008 E, S, It, I, F, SA1, 2, 2009 It, Sm(R), Arg(R), A(R), 2010 E(R), S, F, I, It, SA1, NZ1, 2, A, SA2, Fj, NZ3(R), 2011 E1(R), S(R), I(R), F(R), Arg(R)
Thomas, L C (Cardiff) 1885 E, S
Thomas, M C (Newport, Devonport Services) 1949 F, 1950 E, S, I, F, 1951 E, S, I, F, SA, 1952 E, S, I, F, 1953 E, 1956 E, S, I, F, 1957 E, S, 1958 E, S, I, F, 1959 I, F
Thomas, N (Bath) 1996 SA (R), 1997 US 1(R),2, C (R), R, Tg, NZ, 1998 Z, SA 1
Thomas, N (Swansea) 1900 E, S, I, 1901 E
Thomas, R (Pontypool) 1909 F, I, 1911 S, F, 1912 E, S, SA, 1913 E
Thomas, R C C (Swansea) 1949 F, 1952 I, F, 1953 S, I, F, NZ, 1954 E, I, F, S, 1955 S, I, 1956 E, S, I, 1957 E, 1958 A, E, S, I, F, 1959 E, S, I, F
Thomas, R L (London Welsh) 1889 S, I, 1890 I, 1891 E, S, I, 1892 E
Thomas, R M (Newport Gwent Dragons) 2006 Arg 2(R), 2007 E2(R), SA, 2008 It, SA2, C, 2009 It

Thomas, S (Llanelli) 1890 S, E, 1891 I
Thomas, S G (Llanelli) 1923 E, S, F, I
Thomas, T R (Cardiff Blues) 2005 US(R),C,NZ(R),Fj,SA,A, 2006E,S,I,It,F,PI,C(R),NZ, 2007 I,S,F1(R),It(R),E1(R),2(R),F2(R), [C(R),A(R),J,Fj(R)],SA(R), 2008 SA2(R)
Thomas, W D (Llanelli) 1966 A, 1968 S, I, F, 1969 E, NZ 2, A, 1970 SA, S, E, I, F, 1971 E, S, I, F, 1972 E, S, F, NZ, 1973 E, S, I, F, 1974 E
Thomas, W G (Llanelli, Waterloo, Swansea) 1927 E, S, F, I, 1929 E, 1931 E, S, SA, 1932 E, S, I, 1933 E, S, I
Thomas, W H (Llandovery Coll, Cambridge U) 1885 S, 1886 E, S, 1887 E, S, 1888 S, I, 1890 E, I, 1891 S, I
Thomas, W J (Cardiff) 1961 F, 1963 F
Thomas, W J L (Llanelli, Cardiff) 1995 SA, Fj, 1996 It, E, S, I, F 1, 1996 Bb (R), 1997 US
Thomas, W L (Newport) 1894 S, 1895 E, I
Thomas, W T (Abertillery) 1930 E
Thompson, J F (Cross Keys) 1923 E
Thorburn, P H (Neath) 1985 F, E, Fj, 1986 E, S, I, F, 1987 F, [I, Tg, C, E, NZ, A], US, 1988 S, I, F, WS, R (R), 1989 S, I, F, E, NZ, 1990 F, E, S, I, Nm 1,2, Bb, 1991 E, S, I, F 1, A
Tipuric, J C (Ospreys) 2011 Arg(R),A(R), 2012 I(R),It,Bb, A 3(R)
Titley, M H (Bridgend, Swansea) 1983 R, 1984 S, I, F, E, A, 1985 S, I, Fj, 1986 F, Fj, Tg, WS, 1990 F, E
Towers, W H (Swansea) 1887 I, 1888 M
Travers, G (Pill Harriers, Newport) 1903 E, S, I, 1905 E, S, I, NZ, 1906 E, S, I, SA, 1907 E, S, I, 1908 E, S, F, I, A, 1909 E, S, I, 1911 S, F, I
Travers, W H (Newport) 1937 S, I, 1938 E, S, I, 1939 E, S, I, 1949 E, S, I, F
Treharne, E (Pontypridd) 1881 E, 1883 E
Trew, W J (Swansea) 1900 E, S, I, 1901 E, S, 1903 S, 1905 S, 1906 S, 1907 E, S, 1908 E, S, F, I, A, 1909 E, S, F, I, 1910 F, E, S, 1911 E, S, F, I, 1912 S, 1913 S, F
Trott, R F (Cardiff) 1948 E, S, F, I, 1949 E, S, I, F
Truman, W H (Llanelli) 1934 E, 1935 E
Trump, L C (Newport) 1912 E, S, I, F
Turnbull, B R (Cardiff) 1925 I, 1927 E, S, 1928 E, F, 1930 S
Turnbull, J (Scarlets) 2011 S(R),Bb(R),E3(R), 2012 Bb
Turnbull, M J L (Cardiff) 1933 E, I
Turner, P (Newbridge) 1989 I (R), F, E

Uzzell, H (Newport) 1912 E, S, I, F, 1913 S, F, I, 1914 E, S, F, I, 1920 E, S, F, I
Uzzell, J R (Newport) 1963 NZ, 1965 E, S, I, F

Vickery, W E (Aberavon) 1938 E, S, I, 1939 E
Vile, T H (Newport) 1908 E, S, 1910 I, 1912 I, F, SA, 1913 E, 1921 S
Vincent, H C (Bangor) 1882 I
Voyle, M J (Newport, Llanelli, Cardiff) 1996 A 1(t), F 2, 1997 E, US 1,2, C, Tg, NZ, 1998 It, E, S, I, F, Arg (R), 1999 S (R), I (t), It (R), SA (R), F 2(R), [J, A (R)], 2000 F (R)

Wakeford, J D M (S Wales Police) 1988 WS, R
Waldron, R G (Neath) 1965 E, S, I, F
Walker, N (Cardiff) 1993 I, F, J, 1994 S, F, E, Pt, Sp, 1995 F, E, 1997 US 1,2, C, R (R), Tg, NZ, 1998 E
Waller, P D (Newport) 1908 A, 1909 E, S, F, I, 1910 F
Walne, N J (Richmond, Cardiff) 1999 It (R), E (R), C
Walters, N (Llanelli) 1902 E
Wanbon, R (Aberavon) 1968 E
Warburton, S (Cardiff Blues) 2009 US(R),Sm,A(R), 2010 S(R), I(R), It, SA1, A, NZ3, 2011 E1, S, It, I, F, Bb, E2, 3, [SA, Sm, Nm, Fj, I, F], A, 2012 I, E, F, A 1, 2, 3
Ward, W S (Cross Keys) 1934 S, I
Warlow, D J (Llanelli) 1962 I
Warren, A R (Scarlets) 2012 Bb(R)
Waters, D R (Newport) 1986 E, S, I, F
Waters, K (Newbridge) 1991 [WS]
Watkins, D (Newport) 1963 E, S, I, F, NZ, 1964 E, S, I, F, SA, 1965 E, S, I, F, 1966 E, S, I, F, 1967 I, F, E
Watkins, E (Neath) 1924 E, S, I, F
Watkins, E (Blaina) 1926 S, I, F
Watkins, E V (Cardiff) 1935 NZ, 1937 S, I, 1938 E, S, I, 1939 E, S
Watkins, H V (Llanelli) 1904 S, I, 1905 E, S, I, 1906 E
Watkins, I J (Ebbw Vale) 1988 E (R), S, I, F, NZ 2, R, 1989 S, I, F, E
Watkins, L (Oxford U, Llandaff) 1881 E
Watkins, M J (Newport) 1984 I, F, E, A
Watkins, M J (Llanelli Scarlets) 2003 It(R), E 1(R), S 1(R), I 1(R), R, S 2, 2005 US(R), C(R), Fj, SA(R), A, 2006 E, S, I, It, F, Arg 1, 2(R)
Watkins, S J (Newport, Cardiff) 1964 S, I, F, 1965 E, S, I, F, 1966 E, S, I, F, A, 1967 S, I, F, E, NZ, 1968 E, S, 1969 S, I, F, E, NZ 1, 1970 E, I

522

RUGBY CONTINUES TO BLOSSOM AROUND THE WORLD

By Karen Bond

AFP/Getty Images

The Belgian pack drives forward against Poland en route to winning Division 1B of the European Nations Cup 2012.

THE COUNTRIES

Wales may have dominated the headlines in Europe with their Grand Slam success, but at the same time teams from across the continent were battling for honours in the European Nations Cup as the competition spanning two years drew to a climax.

Georgia were once again crowned champions of Division 1A after winning nine of their 10 matches, the exception being a 25–18 loss in Spain in their first match after again impressing on the Rugby World Cup stage in New Zealand.

The Lelos, under new coach Milton Haig, were pushed hard by traditional rivals Romania in winning 19–13 in March, but a week later they ran riot before 25,000 fans to beat Russia 46–0 in the first meeting between the two sides in Georgia since 2008.

Georgia ultimately finished 10 points clear of Romania in the standings, but when the top tier of the European Nations Cup 2014 kicks off in February it will have a new member in its ranks after Belgium won Division 1B to replace the relegated Ukraine.

Belgium have missed promotion in the last two tournaments through points differential or a solitary point, but now will join Division 1A for a tournament that will provide the Europe 1 and Europe 2 qualifiers to RWC 2015.

"It is going to be a pretty tough test," then Belgium Rugby president Dany Roelands said at the time. "We will meet five nations who have already played in the World Cup, at least once each of them. That will be very challenging for our players and the staff.

"The longer-term ambition for the Union is to stay in the top tier and try to qualify for future Rugby World Cups. I think that is the ambition of any nation, to participate at the highest level of the game and that is definitely what we are working for in Belgium."

Georgia and Belgium were not the only ones celebrating an ENC title in 2012 with Sweden (2A), Switzerland (2B), Israel (2C) and Cyprus (2D) all earning promotion as champions. Cyprus' story is worth mentioning, having gone 15 matches unbeaten since their international debut in 2007. They also ran riot in winning Division 2D, scoring 266 points in four matches against Bulgaria, Greece, Luxembourg and Finland in 2011/12 and conceding just 20.

A nation who can only dream at this stage of replicating Cyprus' start on the international stage are Afghanistan, although the strides they have made in the last 12 months have been equally important. They have gone from counting players on one hand to playing their first official Sevens match against a United Arab Emirates team and also holding a first ever competitive 15-a-side match under the auspices of the Afghanistan Rugby Federation between two clubs, Kabul United RFC and Khurasan RFC. Their journey is only just beginning but the statement "we play for each other and we love to play rugby" by a member of that Sevens squad shows they are in it for the long haul.

The Philippines are certainly one side who have been on a steep upward curve over the last four or five years, climbing from the bottom tier of the HSBC Asian 5 Nations in 2008 to earn their place at the elite table in 2013 by beating Singapore 37–20, Chinese Taipei 34–12 and Sri Lanka 28–18 on home soil in a Division I tournament which also marked the start of Rugby World Cup 2015 qualifying in Asia. Coach Expo Mejia said afterwards that they had "started something here in the Philippines and we plan to build on that", although they know that facing five-time Asian 5 Nations champions Japan, Korea, Hong Kong and UAE will not be an easy task.

The Volcanoes were not the only nation to enjoy success on a regional level as the RWC 2015 qualifying process kicked into gear in five of the six IRB Regional Associations this year, the exception being Oceania which will not embark on the road to England until 2013.

While they will be covered in greater detail in the Road to Rugby World Cup 2015 article earlier in the Yearbook, there were still plenty of highlights around the world worthy of mention, not least an amazing 40,000 crowd that packed into the Mahamasina Stadium in Antananarivo to see Namibia and hosts Madagascar play out an entertaining and high-scoring 57–54 encounter in the Africa Cup Division 1B final in July.

The crowd certainly got their money's worth with a match that swung one way then the other and even went to extra-time with the sides locked at 43–43 at the final whistle. Madagascar's victory earns them a place alongside champions Zimbabwe, Kenya and Uganda in the top tier of the Africa Cup next year and shows the potential for the sport's growth across the continent.

"Rugby is growing rapidly all around the world and we now have more than 5.5 million men, women and children playing the Game," said IRB vice chairman Oregan Hoskins who was in attendance with the Webb Ellis Cup in the capital city of a country where rugby is the number one sport. "Africa has been at the forefront of that growth with a 33 per cent increase in participation since 2007 – the largest rate of growth of all the regions over the period."

While the crowds may have not been as huge as they were in Madagascar, there were also record attendances set for a rugby match in Mexico and Hungary this year, both occasions with the Webb Ellis Cup in attendance. Mexico had the huge honour of hosting the first qualifier for RWC 2015 and Hungary the first in Europe six months later, but the enthusiasm was the same for the Game that continues to reach out to new and exciting frontiers.

The England squad will have learnt a lot from their tough tour to South Africa.

ENGLAND TO SOUTH AFRICA 2012

TOUR PARTY

FULL BACKS: MN Brown (Harlequins), BJ Foden (Northampton Saints), DAV Goode (Saracens), *NJ Abendanon (Bath Rugby)
THREEQUARTERS: CJ Ashton (Northampton Saints), G Lowe (Harlequins), UCC Monye (Harlequins), D Strettle (Saracens), C Wade (London Wasps), AO Allen (Leicester Tigers), BM Barritt (Saracens), JBA Joseph (London Irish), EM Tuilagi (Leicester Tigers), J Turner-Hall (Harlequins), *J May (Gloucester Rugby)
HALF BACKS: OA Farrell (Saracens), TGAL Flood (Leicester Tigers), CC Hodgson (Saracens), DS Care (Harlequins), LAW Dickson (Northampton Saints), BR Youngs (Leicester Tigers), *K Dickson (Harlequins)
FORWARDS: J Gray (Harlequins), DM Hartley (Northampton Saints), LA Mears (Bath Rugby), T Youngs (Leicester Tigers), DR Cole (Leicester Tigers), AR Corbisiero (London Irish), PPL Doran-Jones (Northampton Saints), R Harden (Gloucester Rugby), JWG Marler (Harlequins), M Mullan (Worcester Warriors), MJ Botha (Saracens), G Kitchener (Leicester Tigers), J Gibson (London Irish), TP Palmer (Stade Français), GMW Parling (Leicester Tigers), G Robson (Harlequins), CDC Robshaw (Harlequins), PDA Dowson (Northampton Saints), C Fearns (Bath Rugby), JAW Haskell (Otago Highlanders), TA Johnson (Exeter Chiefs), BJ Morgan (Scarlets), TR Waldrom (Leicester Tigers)
* Replacement on tour
HEAD COACH: S Lancaster

9 June, King's Park, Durban, South Africa 22 (2T 4PG) England 17 (1T 4PG)

SOUTH AFRICA: Z Kirchner (Blue Bulls); J-PR Pietersen (Sharks), J de Villiers (Western Province)(capt), FPL Steyn (Sharks), BG Habana (Western Province); M Steyn (Blue Bulls), F Hougaard (Blue Bulls); T Mtawarira (Sharks), BW du Plessis (Sharks), JN du Plessis (Sharks), E Etzebeth (Western Province), PJJ Kruger (Blue Bulls), MC Coetzee (Sharks), PJ Spies (Blue Bulls), WS Alberts (Sharks)
SUBSTITUTIONS: W Olivier (Blue Bulls) for Habana (temp 31–40 mins); P Lambie (Sharks) for Kirchner (40 mins); CV Oosthuizen (Cheetahs) for J du Plessis (temp 48–58 mins) & for Mtawarira (58 mins); R Pienaar (Ulster) for Hougaard (56 mins); PR van der Merwe (Blue Bulls) for Etzebeth (58 mins); JA Strauss (Cheetahs) for B du Plessis (65 mins); KR Daniel (Sharks) for Coetzee (72 mins)
SCORERS: *Tries:* M Steyn, De Villiers *Penalty Goals:* M Steyn (4)
ENGLAND: Brown; Ashton, Tuilagi, Barritt, Foden; Farrell, B Youngs; Marler, Hartley, Cole, Botha, Parling, Johnson, Morgan, Robshaw (capt)
SUBSTITUTIONS: Flood for Barritt (53 mins); Palmer for Botha (58 mins); Dowson for Morgan (61 mins); L Dickson & Doran-Jones for B Youngs & Marler (72 mins); Mears for Hartley (75 mins); Joseph for Brown (77 mins)
SCORERS: *Try:* Foden *Penalty Goals:* Farrell (4)
REFEREE: SR Walsh (Australia)

13 June, GWK Park, Kimberley, South Africa Barbarians South 26 (3G 1T) England 54 (4G 4T 2PG)

SOUTH AFRICA BARBARIANS SOUTH: *Tries:* J Engelbrecht, H Franklin, N Nelson, N Dukisa *Conversions:* E Watts (3)
ENGLAND: *Tries:* Wade (3), Waldrom (2), Lowe, Kitchener, Care *Conversions:* Hodgson (4) *Penalty Goals:* Hodgson (2)
REFEREE: JI Kaplan (South Africa)

16 June, Ellis Park, Johannesburg, South Africa 36 (2G 2T 3PG 1DG) England 27 (3G 2PG)

SOUTH AFRICA: P Lambie (Sharks); J-PR Pietersen (Sharks), J de Villiers (Western Province)(capt), FPL Steyn (Sharks), BG Habana (Western Province); M Steyn (Blue Bulls), F Hougaard (Blue Bulls); T Mtawarira (Sharks), BW du Plessis (Sharks), JN du Plessis (Sharks), E Etzebeth (Western Province), PJJ Kruger (Blue Bulls), MC Coetzee (Sharks), PJ Spies (Blue Bulls), WS Alberts (Sharks)
SUBSTITUTIONS: W Olivier (Blue Bulls) for Lambie (44 mins); KR Daniel (Sharks) for Alberts (52 mins); R Pienaar (Ulster) for Hougaard (57 mins); W Kruger (Blue Bulls) for J du Plessis (58 mins); JA Strauss (Cheetahs) for B du Plessis (60 mins); PR van der Merwe (Blue Bulls) for PJJ Kruger (61 mins)
SCORERS: *Tries:* Alberts, B du Plessis, Hougaard, Pietersen *Conversions:* M Steyn (2) *Penalty Goals:* M Steyn (3) *Drop Goal:* M Steyn
ENGLAND: Foden; Ashton, Joseph, Tuilagi, Strettle; Flood, B Youngs; Marler, Hartley, Cole, Botha, Parling, Johnson, Morgan, Robshaw (capt)
SUBSTITUTIONS: Palmer for Botha (43 mins); Waldrom for Morgan (46 mins); Corbisiero for Cole (temp 49–55 mins) & for Marler (55 mins); Farrell for Strettle (59 mins); Mears & L Dickson for Hartley & B Youngs (74 mins), Goode for Joseph (77 mins)
SCORERS: *Tries:* B Youngs (2), Flood *Conversion:* Flood (3) *Penalty Goals:* Flood (2)
REFEREE: AC Rolland (Ireland)

19 June, Olen Park, Potchefstroom, South Africa Barbarians North 31 (4G 1PG) England 57 (7G 1T 1PG)

SOUTH AFRICA BARBARIANS NORTH: *Tries:* S Venter (2), J Engelbrecht, D Scholtz *Conversions:* JC Roos (4) *Penalty Goal:* JC Roos
ENGLAND: *Tries:* Abendanon (3), May (2), Morgan, Allen, Penalty try *Conversions:* Hodgson (7) *Penalty Goal:* Hodgson
REFEREE: M Lawrence (South Africa)

23 June, Nelson Mandela Bay Stadium, Port Elizabeth, South Africa 14 (3PG 1T) England 14 (3PG 1T)

SOUTH AFRICA: GG Aplon (Western Province); J-PR Pietersen (Sharks), J de Villiers (Western Province)(capt); BG Habana (Western Province), M Steyn (Blue Bulls), F Hougaard (Blue Bulls); T Mtawarira (Sharks), BW du Plessis (Sharks), JN du Plessis (Sharks), E Etzebeth (Western Province), PJJ Kruger (Blue Bulls), UJ Potgeiter (Blue Bulls), PJ Spies (Blue Bulls), MC Coetzee (Sharks)
SUBSTITUTIONS: R Pienaar (Ulster) for Hougaard (49 mins); R Kankowski (Sharks) & PR van der Merwe (Blue Bulls) for Potgeiter & Etzebeth (54 mins); JA Strauss (Cheetahs) for B du Plessis (62 mins); W Kruger (Blue Bulls) for J du Plessis (75 mins)
SCORERS: *Try:* Pietersen *Penalty Goals:* M Steyn (3)

ENGLAND: Goode; Ashton, Joseph, Tuilagi, Foden; Flood, Care; Marler, Hartley (capt), Cole, Palmer, Parling, Johnson, Waldrom, Haskell

SUBSTITUTIONS: Farrell for Flood (12 mins); Barritt for Farrell (temp 26–35 mins) & for Joseph (62 mins); Mears for Johnson (temp 54–60 mins); Botha & Dowson for Palmer & Johnson (64 mins)
SCORERS: *Try:* Care *Penalty Goals:* Farrell (2), Flood
REFEREE: SR Walsh (Australia)

WALES v BARBARIANS & TO AUSTRALIA 2012

OVERALL SQUAD & TOUR PARTY

FULL BACKS: SL Halfpenny (Cardiff Blues), LB Williams (Scarlets)
THREEQUARTERS: AG Brew (Newport Gwent Dragons), ACG Cuthbert (Cardiff Blues), WTM Harries (Newport Gwent Dragons), GP North (Scarlets), HR Robinson (Cardiff Blues), MA Beck (Ospreys), AM Bishop (Ospreys), JJV Davies (Scarlets), MS Williams (Scarlets), AR Warren (Scarlets)
HALF BACKS: DR Biggar (Ospreys), JW Hook (USA Perpignan), R Priestland (Scarlets), WM Phillips (Aviron Bayonnais), R Webb (Ospreys), LD Williams (Cardiff Blues)
FORWARDS: RM Hibbard (Ospreys), KJ Owens (Scarlets), M Rees (Scarlets), RJ Bevington (Ospreys), IAR Gill (Saracens), P James (Ospreys), GD Jenkins (Cardiff Blues), AR Jones (Ospreys), Rhodri P Jones (Scarlets), LC Charteris (Newport Gwent Dragons), BS Davies (Cardiff Blues), IR Evans (Ospreys), AW Jones (Ospreys), DJ Lydiate (Newport Gwent Dragons), JC Tipuric (Ospreys), J Turnbull (Scarlets), S Warburton (Cardiff Blues), ME Williams (Cardiff Blues), TT Faletau (Newport Gwent Dragons), Ryan P Jones (Ospreys), AC Shingler (Scarlets), *GL Delve (Melbourne Rebels)
* Replacement on tour
CARETAKER HEAD COACH: R Howley

2 June, Millennium Stadium, Cardiff, Wales 30 (3G 3PG) Barbarians 21 (3G)

WALES: LB Williams; Robinson, Bishop, Hook, Brew: Biggar, LD Williams; Gill, M Rees (capt), Rhodri P Jones, A-W Jones, I Evans, Turnbull, Ryan P Jones, Tipuric
SUBSTITUTIONS: P James for Robinson (temp 35–40 mins) & Rhodri Jones (40 mins); ME Wiliams for A-W Jones (45 mins); Webb & Shingler for LD Williams & Ryan Jones (51 mins); Warren for Biggar (61 mins); Harries & Hibbard for Robinson & M Rees (68 mins)
SCORERS: *Tries:* Robinson, Hook, Brew *Conversions:* Hook (3) *Penalty Goals:* Hook (3)
BARBARIANS: JM Muliaina (New Zealand); I Nacewa (Fiji), CDE Lualua (New Zealand), MJ Tindall (England); SM Williams (Wales); SR Donald (New Zealand), RS Rees (Wales); DJ Jones (Wales), B August (France), JW Smit (South Africa)(capt), MR O'Driscoll (Ireland), MD Chisholm (Australia), L-F P Louw (South Africa), JW Beattie (Scotland), M Gorgodze (Georgia)
SUBSTITUTIONS: AP de Malmanche (New Zealand) & A van Zyl (South Africa) for August & M O'Driscoll (40 mins); NS Tialata (New Zealand) & S Tagicakibau (Samoa) for Smit & Tindall (46 mins); A Qera (Fiji) for Gorgodze (56 mins); RGM Lawson (Scotland) for R Rees (57 mins); C Heymans (France) for Muliaina (66 mins)
SCORERS: *Tries:* Donald (2), R Rees *Conversions:* Donald (3)
REFEREE: AC Rolland (Ireland)

9 June, Suncorp Stadium, Brisbane, Australia 27 (3G 1PG 1DG) Wales 19 (1G 4PG)

AUSTRALIA: AP Ashley-Cooper (NSW Waratahs); KC Vuna (Melbourne Rebels), RG Horne (NSW Waratahs), PJ McCabe (Brumbies), DAN Ioane (Queensland Reds); BS Barnes (NSW Waratahs), SW Genia (Queensland Reds); BA Robinson (NSW Waratahs), SUT Polota-Nau (NSW Waratahs), SM Kepu (NSW Waratahs), RA Simmons (Queensland Reds), NC Sharpe (Western Force), S Higginbotham (Queensland Reds), WL Palu (NSW Waratahs), DW Pocock (Western Force)(capt)
SUBSTITUTIONS: AS Faingaa (Queensland Reds) for Vuna (temp 50–55 mins) & Horne (71 mins); ST Moore (Brumbies) for Polota-Nau (55 mins); BE Alexander (Brumbies) & M Hooper (Brumbies) for Robinson & Palu (59 mins); DA Dennis (NSW Waratahs) for Sharpe (64 mins)
SCORERS: *Tries:* Higginbotham, Genia, McCabe *Conversions:* Barnes (3) *Penalty Goals:* Barnes *Drop Goal:* Barnes
WALES: Halfpenny; Cuthbert, JJV Davies, MS Williams, North; Priestland, Phillips; Jenkins, Owens, AR Jones, BS Davies, Charteris, Lydiate, Faletau, Warburton (capt)
SUBSTITUTIONS: Hook for North (28 mins); Ryan Jones, AW Jones & Rees for Faletau, Charteris & Owens (51 mins); Beck for MS Williams (55 mins); James for AR Jones (74 mins)
SCORERS: *Try:* Cuthbert *Conversion:* Halfpenny *Penalty Goals:* Halfpenny (4)
REFEREE: C Joubert (South Africa)

16 June, Etihad Stadium, Melbourne, Australia 25 (1G 6PG) Wales 23 (2G 3PG)

AUSTRALIA: AP Ashley-Cooper (NSW Waratahs); KC Vuna (Melbourne Rebels), RG Horne (NSW Waratahs), PJ McCabe (Brumbies), DAN Ioane (Queensland Reds); BS Barnes (NSW Waratahs), SW Genia (Queensland Reds); BA Robinson (NSW Waratahs), SUT Polota-Nau (NSW Waratahs), SM Kepu (NSW Waratahs), RA Simmons (Queensland Reds), NC Sharpe (Western Force), S Higginbotham (Queensland Reds), WL Palu (NSW Waratahs), DW Pocock (Western Force)(capt)
SUBSTITUTIONS: ST Moore (Brumbies) for Polota-Nau (50 mins); DA Dennis (NSW Waratahs) for Palu (64 mins); BE Alexander (Brumbies) for Robinson (64 mins); M Hooper (Brumbies) for Simmons (69 mins); AS Faingaa (Queensland Reds) for Vuna (70 mins); MJ Harris (Queensland Reds) for Barnes (73 mins)
SCORERS: *Try:* Horne *Conversion:* Barnes *Penalty Goals:* Barnes (5), Harris
WALES: Halfpenny; Cuthbert, JJV Davies, Beck, North; Priestland, Phillips; Jenkins, Rees, AR Jones, BS Davies, Charteris, Lydiate, Ryan Jones, Warburton (capt)
SUBSTITUTIONS: Webb for Phillips (65 mins); Hibbard for Rees (66 mins); Charteris for AW Jones (67 mins)
SCORERS: *Tries:* North, JJV Davies *Conversions:* Halfpenny (2) *Penalty Goals:* Halfpenny (3)
REFEREE: CJ Pollock (New Zealand)

23 June, Allianz Stadium, Sydney, Australia 20 (1T 5PG) Wales 19 (1G 4PG)

AUSTRALIA: KJ Beale (Melbourne Rebels); AP Ashley-Cooper (NSW Waratahs), RG Horne (NSW Waratahs), PJ McCabe (Brumbies), DAN Ioane (Queensland Reds); BS Barnes (NSW Waratahs), SW Genia (Queensland Reds); BA Robinson (NSW Waratahs), SUT Polota-Nau (NSW Waratahs), SM Kepu (NSW Waratahs), S Timani (NSW Waratahs), NC Sharpe (Western Force), S Higginbotham (Queensland Reds), WL Palu (NSW Waratahs), DW Pocock (Western Force)(capt)
SUBSTITUTIONS: AS Faingaa (Queensland Reds) for McCabe (22 mins); BE Alexander (Brumbies), ST Moore (Brumbies) & DA Dennis (NSW Waratahs) for Kepu, Polota-Nau & Higginbotham (56 mins); RA Simmons (Queensland Reds) for Timani (72 mins)
SCORERS: *Try:* Horne *Penalty Goals:* Barnes (5)
WALES: Halfpenny; Cuthbert, JJV Davies, Beck, North; Priestland, Phillips; Jenkins, Rees, AR Jones, BS Davies, AW Jones, Lydiate, Ryan Jones, Warburton (capt)
SUBSTITUTIONS: Tipuric for Warburton (28 mins); James for Jenkins (40 mins); Charteris for Ryan Jones (temp 49–56 mins) & for AW Jones (65 mins); MS Williams & Owens for Beck & Rees (65 mins); Hook for Priestland (69 mins)
SCORERS: *Try:* Ryan Jones *Conversion:* Halfpenny *Penalty Goals:* Halfpenny (4)
REFEREE: C Joubert (South Africa)

SCOTLAND TO AUSTRALIA & PACIFIC ISLANDS 2012

TOUR PARTY

FULL BACKS: SW Hogg (Glasgow), TG Brown (Edinburgh)
THREEQUARTERS: MB Evans (Castres Olympique), SF Lamont (Scarlets), TJW Visser (Edinburgh), JAA Ansbro (London Irish), NJ de Luca (Edinburgh), A Grove (Worcester Warriors), MCM Scott (Edinburgh), *A Dunbar (Glasgow)
HALF BACKS: GD Laidlaw (Edinburgh), D Weir (Glasgow), MRL Blair (Edinburgh), CP Cusiter (Glasgow)
FORWARDS: RW Ford (Edinburgh), D Hall (Glasgow), S Lawson (Gloucester Rugby), GDS Cross (Edinburgh), R Grant (Glasgow), EA Murray (Newcastle Falcons), J Welsh (Glasgow), *M Low (Glasgow), RJ Gray (Glasgow), AD Kellock (Glasgow), RJ Harley (Glasgow), TP Ryder (Edinburgh), RM Rennie (Edinburgh), JA Barclay (Glasgow), AK Strokosch (Gloucester Rugby), *S McInally (Edinburgh), RJ Vernon (Sale Sharks)
* Replacement on tour
HEAD COACH: RA Robinson

5 June, Hunter Stadium, Newcastle, Australia 6 (2PG) Scotland 9 (3PG)

AUSTRALIA: LJ Morahan (Queensland Reds); J Tomane (Brumbies), AS Faingaa (Queensland Reds), MJ Harris (Queensland Reds), DAN Ioane (Queensland Reds); BS Barnes (NSW Waratahs), SW Genia (Queensland Reds); JA Slipper (Queensland Reds), ST Moore (Brumbies), DP Palmer (Brumbies), S Timani (NSW Waratahs), NC Sharpe (Western Force), DA Dennis (NSW Waratahs), S Higginbotham (Queensland Reds), DW Pocock (Western Force)(capt)

SUBSTITUTIONS: RA Simmons (Queensland Reds) for Timani (54 mins); M Hooper (Brumbies) for Dennis (64 mins); BE Alexander (Brumbies) for Palmer (69 mins)

SCORER: *Penalty Goals:* Harris (2)

SCOTLAND: Hogg; SF Lamont, De Luca, Scott, Ansbro; Laidlaw, Blair; Grant, Ford (capt), Murray, Gray, Kellock, Strokosch, Barclay, Rennie

SUBSTITUTIONS: T Brown for S Lamont (38 mins); Cusiter for Blair (63 mins)

SCORER: *Penalty Goals:* Laidlaw (3)

REFEREE: J Peyper (South Africa)

16 June, Churchill Park, Lautoka, Fiji 25 (2G 1T 2PG) Scotland 37 (4G 3PG)

FIJI: S Koniferedi (Nadroga); W Nayacalevu (Melbourne Rebels), V Goneva (Leicester Tigers), A Buto (RC Grenoble), W Votu (Exeter Chiefs); J Ralulu (Nadroga), N Matawalu (Suva); J Yanuyanutawa (Brumbies), V Veikoso (Suva), S Somoca (Nadroga), A Naikatani (Toyota), L Nakarawa (Tailevu), I Ratuva (Nadroga), NE Talei (Edinburgh)(capt), RMM Ravulo (North Harbour)

SUBSTITUTIONS: JU Domolailai (RC Auch) for Ravulo (18 mins); WD Nailago (Naitasiri) for Yanuyanutawa (58 mins); K Ratuvou (Saracens) for Buto (59 mins); M Talebula (Lautoka) & TD Tuapati (Woodlands) for Koniferedi & Veikoso (60 mins); K Ketedromo (Nadi) & NS Kenatale (Otago) for Ratuva & Matawalu (68 mins)

SCORERS: *Tries:* Domolailai, Nayacalevu, Talebula *Conversions:* Ralulu (2) *Penalty Goals:* Ralulu (2)

SCOTLAND: Hogg; M Evans, De Luca, Scott, Visser; Laidlaw, Blair; Grant, Ford (capt), Murray, Gray, Kellock, Strokosch, Barclay, Rennie

SUBSTITUTIONS: Cusiter for Blair (55 mins); Vernon for Barclay (59 mins); S Lamont for M Evans (64 mins); Cross for Murray (68 mins); Weir & S Lawson for Laidlaw & Ford (78 mins); Ryder for Gray (79 mins)

SCORERS: *Tries:* Visser (2), Penalty try, Laidlaw *Conversions:* Laidlaw (4) *Penalty Goals:* Laidlaw (3)

REFEREE: J Peyper (South Africa)

23 June, Apia Park, Apia, Samoa 16 (1G 2PG 1DG) Scotland 17 (2G 1PG)

SAMOA: F Autagavaia (Vailoa); P Perez (Vaimoso), F Otto (Bristol Rugby), PB Williams (Stade Français), D Lemi (Glasgow)(capt); T Pisi (Wellington), KF Fotouali'i (Ospreys); S Taulafo (London Wasps), TT Paulo (ASM Clermont Auvergne), CAI Johnston (Stade Toulousain), F Lemalu (Papatoetoe), D Crichton (Counties Manakau), B Masoe (Papatoetoe), KG Thompson (Waikato), M Fa'asavalu (Harlequins)

SUBSTITUTIONS: L Lui (Moata'a) for Otto (35 mins); L Mulipola (Leicester Tigers) & J Tekori (Castres Olympique) for Johnston & Crichton (40 mins); A Aiono (Leuleumoega) for Masoe (55 mins); WO Avei (Begles-Bordeaux) for Paulo (64 mins); JI Su'a (Tasman) for Fotouali'i (79 mins)

SCORERS: *Try:* Pisi *Conversion:* Pisi *Penalty Goals:* Pisi 2 *Drop Goal:* Pisi

SCOTLAND: Hogg; S Lamont, Ansbro, Scott, Visser; Laidlaw, Cusiter; Grant, Ford (capt), Murray, Gray, Kellock, Strokosch, Vernon, Rennie

SUBSTITUTIONS: Blair for Cusiter (40 mins); M Evans for Ansbro (54 mins); Harley for Vernon (62 mins); S Lawson for Ford (64 mins); Ryder for Kellock (68 mins)

SCORERS: *Tries:* Ansbro, Harley *Conversions:* Laidlaw (2) *Penalty Goal:* Laidlaw

REFEREE: J Peyper (South Africa)

IRELAND TO NEW ZEALAND 2012

TOUR PARTY

FULL BACK: RDJ Kearney (Leinster)

THREEQUARTERS: KG Earls (Munster), FL McFadden (Leinster), A Trimble (Ulster), SR Zebo (Munster), DM Cave (Ulster), GWD D'Arcy (Leinster), BG O'Driscoll (Leinster), *PW Wallace (Ulster)

HALF BACKS: RJR O'Gara (Munster), JJ Sexton (Leinster), P Marshall (Ulster), C Murray (Munster), EG Reddan (Leinster)

FORWARDS: RD Best (Ulster), SM Cronin (Leinster), M Sherry (Munster), DJ Fitzpatrick (Ulster), CE Healy (Leinster), R Loughney (Connacht), MR Ross (Leinster), B Wilkinson (Connacht), DP O'Callaghan (Munster), DC Ryan (Munster), DM Tuohy (Ulster), CG Henry (Ulster), KR McLaughlin (Leinster), M McCarthy (Connacht), SK O'Brien (Leinster), P O'Mahony (Munster), JPR Heaslip (Leinster),

* Replacement on tour

HEAD COACH: D Kidney

9 June, Eden Park, Auckland, New Zealand 42 (4G 1T 3PG) Ireland 10 (1G 1PG)

NEW ZEALAND: IJA Dagg (Hawke's Bay); ZR Guildford (Hawke's Bay), CG Smith (Wellington), SB Williams (Canterbury), SJ Savea (Wellington); DW Carter (Canterbury), AL Smith (Manawatu); TD Woodcock (North Harbour) AK Hore (Taranaki), OT Franks (Canterbury), BA Retallick (Bay of Plenty), SL Whitelock (Canterbury), VVJ Vito (Wellington), KJ Read (Canterbury), RH McCaw (Canterbury)(capt)

SUBSTITUTIONS: AJ Thomson (Otago) for Vito (46 mins); AJ Williams (Auckland) & BR Smith (Otago) for Retallick & Guildford (52 mins); PAT Weepu (Auckland) for AL Smith (57 mins); HTP Elliot (Hawke's Bay) & BJ Franks (Tasman) for Hore & OT Franks (61 mins); AW Cruden (Manawatu) for Savea (67 mins)

SCORERS: *Tries:* Savea (3), Thomson, CG Smith *Conversions:* Carter (4) *Penalty Goals:* Carter (3)

IRELAND: Kearney; McFadden, O'Driscoll (capt), Earls, Zebo; Sexton, Murray; Healy, Best, Fitzpatrick, Tuohy, Ryan, O'Mahony, Heaslip, O'Brien

SUBSTITUTIONS: Loughney for Fitzpatrick (55 mins); O'Gara for Sexton (59 mins); Reddan, O'Callaghan & McLaughlin for Murray, Tuohy & O'Mahony (61 mins); Cronin for Healy (71 mins); Cave for Earls (72 mins)

SCORERS: *Try*: McFadden *Conversion:* Sexton *Penalty Goal:* Sexton

REFEREE: N Owens (Wales)

16 June, Rugby League Park, Christchurch, New Zealand 22 (1G 4PG 1DG) Ireland 19 (1G 1PG)

NEW ZEALAND: IJA Dagg (Hawke's Bay); ZR Guildford (Hawke's Bay), CG Smith (Wellington), SB Williams (Canterbury), SJ Savea (Wellington); DW Carter (Canterbury), AL Smith (Manawatu); TD Woodcock (North Harbour) AK Hore (Taranaki), OT Franks (Canterbury), BA Retallick (Bay of Plenty), SL Whitelock (Canterbury), AJ Thomson (Otago), KJ Read (Canterbury), RH McCaw (Canterbury)(capt)

SUBSTITUTIONS: SJ Cane (Bay of Plenty) for Read (40 mins); BJ Franks (Tasman) for OT Franks (57 mins); PAT Weepu (Auckland) & AJ Williams (Auckland) for AL Smith & Retallick (64 mins); BR Smith (Otago) for Savea (73 mins)

SCORERS: *Try*: AL Smith *Conversion:* Carter *Penalty Goals:* Carter (4) *Drop Goal:* Carter

IRELAND: Kearney; McFadden, O'Driscoll (capt), D'Arcy, Trimble; Sexton, Murray; Healy, Best, Ross, Tuohy, Ryan, McLaughlin, Heaslip, O'Brien

SUBSTITUTIONS: O'Gara for D'Arcy (50 mins); O'Callaghan for Tuohy (58 mins); O'Mahony for McLaughlin (61 mins); Reddan for Murray (64 mins)

SCORERS: *Try*: Murray *Conversion:* Sexton *Penalty Goals:* Sexton (4)

REFEREE: N Owens (Wales)

23 June, Waikato Stadium, Hamilton, New Zealand 60 (6G 3T 1PG) Ireland 0

NEW ZEALAND: IJA Dagg (Hawke's Bay); BR Smith (Otago), CG Smith (Wellington), SB Williams (Canterbury), HE Gear (Wellington); AW Cruden (Manawatu); AL Smith (Manawatu); TD Woodcock (North Harbour), AK Hore (Taranaki), OT Franks (Canterbury), L Romano (Canterbury), SL Whitelock (Canterbury), LJ Messam (Waikato Chiefs), RH McCaw (Canterbury)(capt), SJ Cane (Bay of Plenty)

SUBSTITUTIONS: BJ Barrett (Taranaki) for Cruden (24 mins); KF Mealamu (Auckland) for Hore (40 mins); BA Retallick (Bay of Plenty) for Whitelock (56 mins); TE Ellison (Otago) for CG Smith (58 mins); PAT Weepu (Auckland) for AL Smith (60 mins); AJ Thomson (Otago) for Cane (69 mins); BJ Franks (Tasman) for Woodcock (73 mins)

SCORERS: *Tries*: Cane (2), SB Williams (2), BR Smith, Gear, Messam, Dagg, Thomson *Conversions:* Barrett (3), Cruden (2), Dagg *Penalty Goal:* Barrett

IRELAND: Kearney; McFadden, O'Driscoll (capt), P Wallace, Earls; Sexton, Murray; Healy, Best, Ross, Tuohy, Ryan, McLaughlin, O'Mahony, O'Brien

SUBSTITUTIONS: Trimble for Earls (temp 50–54 & from 64 mins); Henry & O'Gara for McLaughlin & P Wallace (54 mins); O'Callaghan for Tuohy (55 mins); Fitzpatrick & Reddan for Ross & Murray (58 mins); Cronin for Best (68 mins)

REFEREE: R Poite (France)

ITALY TO ARGENTINA & NORTH AMERICA 2012

TOUR PARTY

FULL BACKS: A Benettin (Aironi), G Toniolatti (Aironi)

THREEQUARTERS: T Benvenuti (Treviso), G Venditti (Aironi), L McLean (Treviso), L Morisi (Parma Crociati), A Pratichetti (Treviso), R Quartaroli (Aironi), A Sgarbi (Treviso)

HALF BACKS: R Bocchino (Prato), K Burton (Treviso), E Gori (Treviso), T Tebaldi (Aironi)
FORWARDS: T D'Apice (Aironi), C Festuccia (Parma Crociati), D Giazzon (Rovigo), M Castrogiovanni (Leicester Tigers), A de Marchi (Aironi), M Rizzo (Treviso), L Romano (Aironi), M Bortolami (Aironi), J Furno (Aironi), M Fuser (Mogliano), A Pavanello (Treviso), R Barbieri (Treviso), Mauro Bergamasco (Aironi), S Favaro (Aironi), F Minto (Treviso), A Zanni (Treviso) S Parisse (Stade Français)
HEAD COACH: J Brunel

531

9 June, Estadio Bicentenario, San Juan, Argentina 37 (4G 3PG) Italy 22 (2G 1T 1PG)

ARGENTINA: J Tuculet (Sale Sharks); B Agulla (SU Agen), G Ascarate (Natacion y Gimnasia, Tucumán); F Contepomi (Stade Français)(capt), AO Gosio (Newman); I Mieres (Exeter Chiefs), M Landajo (CA San Isidro); R Roncero (Stade Français), E Guinazu (Biarritz Olympique), FA Gómez Kodela (Biarritz Olympique), E Lozada (Edinburgh), JA Farias Cabello (Tucumán), G Fessia (unattached), L Senatore (Gimnasia y Esgrima, Rosario), T Leonardi (San Isidro Club)
SUBSTITUTIONS: T de la Vega (Club Universitario Buenos Aires) for Fessia (53 mins); M Montero (Pucura) & NA Tetaz Chaparro (Stade Français) for B Agulla & Gomez Kodela (62 mins); B Postiglioni (La Plata) for Guinazu (65 mins); S Guzmán (Tucumán) for Macome (71 mins); T Cubelli (Belgrano Athletic) for Landajo (74 mins)
SCORERS: *Tries*: Leonardi, Roncero, Senatore, F Contepomi *Conversions:* F Contepomi (4) *Penalty Goals:* F Contepomi (3)
ITALY: Toniolatti; Venditti, Quartaroli, Sgarbi, Benvenuti; Burton, Gori; De Marchi, Festuccia, Castrogiovanni, Bortolami (capt), A Pavanello, Zanni, Barbieri, Mauro Bergamasco
SUBSTITUTIONS: Furno for Bortolami (47 mins); Favaro for Barbieri (56 mins); Bocchino, Giazzon & Romano for Burton, Festuccia & De Marchi (65 mins)
SCORERS: *Tries*: Penalty try, Gori, Mauro Bergamasco *Conversions:* Burton, Bocchino *Penalty Goal:* Burton
REFEREE: J Garces (France)

16 June, BMO Stadium, Toronto, Canada 16 (1G 3PG) Italy 25 (1G 6PG)

CANADA: J Pritchard (Bedford Blues): C Trainor (British Columbia), DTH van der Merwe (Glasgow), M Scholtz (Ontario Blues), P Mackenzie (London Welsh): M Evans (Cornish Pirates), S White (unattached); H Buydens (Prairie Wolf Pack), M Pletch (Ontario Blues), J Marshall (RC Aurillac), J Sinclair (London Irish), T Hotson (London Scottish), T Ardron (Ontario Blues), A Carpenter (Plymouth Albion)(capt), C O'Toole (The Rock)
SUBSTITUTIONS: T Dolezel (Ontario Blues) for Buydens (16 mins); E Fairhurst (British Columbia) & A Tiedemann (Prairie Wolf Pack) for White & Pletch (58 mins); C Hearn (The Rock) for Scholtz (62 mins); N Dala (Praire Wolf Pack) for Ardron (67 mins); J Phelan (The Rock) for Hotson (75 mins)
SCORERS: *Try*: Trainor *Conversion:* Pritchard *Penalty Goals:* Pritchard (3)
ITALY: Benetin; Venditti, A Pratichetti, Sgarbi, Benvenuti; Burton, Tebaldi, Rizzo, D'Apice, Castrogiovanni (capt), Furno, A Pavanello, Zanni, Barbieri, Favaro
SUBSTITUTIONS: Toniolatti for Benetin (temp 3–7 mins & 65 mins); Gori for Tebaldi (57 mins); Fuser for Furno (61 mins); Festuccia for D'Apice (67 mins); Mauro Bergamasco for Fuser (75 mins); Romano for Rizzo (79 mins)
SCORERS: *Try*: D'Apice *Conversion:* Burton *Penalty Goals:* Burton (6)
REFEREE: D Pearson (England)

23 June, BBVA Compass Stadium, Houston, USA 10 (1G 1PG) Italy 30 (3G 3PG)

USA: C Wyles (Saracens); J Paterson (Glendale Raptors), P Emerick (London Wasps), A Suniula (Cornish Pirates), L Hume (Old Blue); R Suniula (Chicago Griffins), M Petri (New York AC); S Pittman (London Welsh), C Biller (Northampton Saints), E Fry (Old Boys University), L Stanfill (New York AC), B Doyle (New York AC), T Mokate (Old Boys University), T Clever (NTT Shining Arcs)(capt), S LaValla (Stade Français)
SUBSTITUTIONS: C Hawley (USA Sevens) & M MacDonald (Leeds Carnegie) for Paterson & Fry (40 mins); A Durutallo (Old Puget Sound) for LaValla (temp 55–56 mins) & Mokate (64 mins); W Holder (US Military Academy), T Liufau (RC Nevers) & D Asbun (Oxford University) for R Suniula, Doyle & Biller (67 mins); M Timoteo (Golden Gate) for Petri (76 mins)
SCORERS: *Try*: Emerick *Conversion:* Wyles *Penalty Goal:* Wyles
RED CARDS: A Suniula (44 mins), Emerick (66 mins)
ITALY: McLean; Venditti, Quartaroli, Morisi, Benvenuti; Bocchino, Gori; De Marchi, Festuccia, Castrogiovanni (capt), A Pavanello, Furno, Zanni, Barbieri, Mauro Bergamasco
SUBSTITUTIONS: Rizzo & Sgarbi for Venditti & De Marchi (42 mins); Venditti for Quataroli (49 mins); Favaro & Giazzon for Mauro Bergamasco & Festuccia (54 mins); Tebaldi for Gori (62 mins); D'Apice for Barbieri

MAJOR TOURS

(73 mins); Burton for Bocchino (75 mins)
SCORERS: *Tries:* Festuccia, Gori, Burton *Conversions:* Bocchino (2), Burton *Penalty Goals:* Bocchino (3)
REFEREE: J Garces (France)

FRANCE TO ARGENTINA 2012

TOUR PARTY

FULL BACK: B Dulin (SU Agen)
THREEQUARTERS: J-M Buttin (ASM Clermont Auvergne), Y Huget (Aviron Bayonnais), B Fall (Racing Métro, Paris), R Martial (Castres Olympique), M Mermoz (USA Perpignan), W Fofana (ASM Clermont Auvergne), F Fritz (Stade Toulousain)
HALF BACKS: F Michalak (Sharks), F Trinh-Duc (Montpellier-Herault RC), M Machenaud (SU Agen), M Parra (ASM Clermont Auvergne)
FORWARDS: C Tolofua (Stade Toulousain), D Szarzewski (Stade Français), D Attoub (Stade Français), V Debaty (ASM Clermont Auvergne), A Guillamon (Lyon OU), Y Watremez (Biarritz Olympique), *T Domingo (ASM Clermont Auvergne), Y Maestri (Stade Toulousain), C Samson (RC Toulon), P Pape (Stade Français), R Taofifuena (USA Perpignan), A Lapandry (ASM Clermont Auvergne), W Lauret (Biarritz Olympique), F Ouedraogo (Montpellier-Herault RC), L Picamoles (Biarritz Olympique)
* Replacement on tour
MANAGER / HEAD COACH: PG Saint-Andre

16 June, Estadio Mario Alberto Kempes, Cordoba, Argentina 23 (2G 3PG) France 20 (1T 5PG)

ARGENTINA: R Miralles (Duendes); B Agulla (SU Agen), J Tuculet (Sale Sharks), F Contepomi (Stade Français)(capt), M Montero (Pucura); I Mieres (Exeter Chiefs), M Landajo (CA San Isidro); E Guinazu (Biarritz Olympique), B Postiglioni (La Plata), FN Tetaz Chaparro (Stade Français), B Macome (Tucumán), E Lozada (Edinburgh), JA Farias Cabello (Tucumán), T Leonardi (San Isidro Club) T de la Vega (Club Universitario Buenos Aires)
SUBSTITUTIONS: B Urdapilleta (Harlequins) for Mirallas (40 mins); T Cubelli (Belgrano Athletic) for Landajo (49 mins); A Bordoy (RC Pau), P Henn (CA Brive) & R Baez (Liceo) for Postiglioni, Tetaz Chaparro & Lozada (57 mins); R Bruno (Jockey Club, Cordoba) for Macome (66 mins)
SCORERS: *Tries:* B Agulla, Montero *Conversions:* F Contepomi (2) *Penalty Goals:* F Contepomi (3)
FRANCE: Dulin; Huget, Fofana, Fritz, Buttin; Trinh-Duc, Parra; Watremez, Szarzewski, Attoub, Pape (capt), Maestri, Lauret, Picamoles, Ouedraogo
SUBSTITUTIONS: Debaty for Watremez (40 mins); Michalak for Trinh-Duc (59 mins); Tolofua & Lapandry for Szarzewski & Picamoles (67 mins); Taofifuena for Maestri (75 mins); Mermoz for Fritz (78 mins)
SCORERS: *Try:* Picamoles *Penalty Goals:* Parra (5)
REFEREE: G Clancy (Ireland)

23 June, Estadio Jose Fierro, Tucumán, Argentina 10 (1G 1PG) France 49 (5G 3PG 1T)

ARGENTINA: J Tuculet (Sale Sharks); F Barrea (Cordoba Athletic), AO Gosio (Newman), F Contepomi (Stade Français)(capt), M Montero (Pucura); B Urdapilleta (Harlequins), T Cubelli (Belgrano Athletic); E Guinazu (Biarritz Olympique), A Bordoy (RC Pau), FT Gómez Kodela (Biarritz Olympique), JA Farias Cabello (Tucumán), E Lozada (Edinburgh), T de la Vega (Club Universitario Buenos Aires), L Sentatore (Gimnasia y Esgrima, Rosario), T Leonardi (San Isidro Club)
SUBSTITUTIONS: B Macome (Tucumán) for Farias Cabello (30 mins); G Ascarete (Natacion y Gimnasia, Tucumán) for Tuculet (40 mins); B Postiglioni (La Plata) for Bordoy (55 mins); R Baez (Liceo) for Senatore (59 mins)
SCORERS: *Try:* De la Vega *Conversion:* F Contepomi *Penalty Goal:* F Contepomi
FRANCE: Dulin; Huget, Fritz, Mermoz, Fall; Michalak, Machenaud; Debaty, Szarzewski, Attoub, Pape (capt), Maestri, Lapandry, Picamoles, Ouedraogo
SUBSTITUTIONS: Domingo & Samson for Attoub & Maestri (48 mins); Tolofua for Szarzewski (57 mins); Fofana for Fall (62 mins); Lauret for Picamoles (64); Trinh-Duc & Parra for Michalak & Machenaud (70 mins)
SCORERS: *Tries:* Huget (2), Fall, Machenaud, Mermoz, Lapandry *Conversions:* Michalak (5) *Penalty Goals:* Michalak (3)
REFEREE: G Clancy (Ireland)

The Combined Teams

GATLAND HONOURED BY LIONS APPOINTMENT

Getty Images

Warren Gatland is unveiled as the Lions head coach for the 2013 tour to Australia.

On 4 September 2012, at Iron Monger's Hall in London, Warren Gatland was confirmed as the next British & Irish Lions head coach. The tour Down Under in 2013 represents the 125th year of Lions touring but only the fourth dedicated tour to Australia, as the Lions often stopped in Australia on the way to New Zealand.

Nonetheless, they have played the Wallabies 20 times and lead 15–5 in wins. However, three of the losses have come on the last two tours. In 1989 the Lions won the series 2–1 but in 2001 that was reversed by the Wallabies who are the current holders of the Tom Richards Trophy, **535** named after the only player to have played for both teams.

Gatland, a New Zealander by birth, is the current national coach of Wales and most people's choice for the job. He will be on secondment from the Welsh Rugby Union and was delighted to have been selected.

"It is a huge honour to be selected as the Lions coach and I would regard it as one of the highlights of my career. I am well aware of the history and importance of the Lions as a Rugby entity. I was lucky enough to play against the Lions for Waikato in 1993 and remember that as one of my playing highlights. Having been involved in South Africa in 2009 was also a massive privilege.

"I realised in South Africa that for a player being selected for the Lions and playing in a Test match was the pinnacle of his career. The same applies to the coaches and all the management. For me this is a huge recognition and, more importantly, a massive responsibility to represent and uphold the values and history of the Lions. Therefore I am very proud of this appointment."

In 2009 the Lions went tantalisingly close to beating the Springboks and it opened Gatland's eyes to the challenges that face the tourists every four years. "I learnt how tough it is to mould a team together in such a short period to take on one of the three top nations in the world away from home. We need to make all the squad members feel very much a part of the tour and that they all have an opportunity to be selected for the Tests.

"Again in 2013 it will be a challenge to get the team up to speed in such a short time . . . getting to know each other, learn play calls and the game plan, setting goals, and establishing team ethos is crucial in the first few weeks. This is made harder as the week before the first tour game the RaboDirect PRO12 and the Aviva Premiership finals take place in the UK. There are bound to be a number of players involved in these games which will hamper preparations.

"Some key staff have already been appointed, but over the next few months I will be putting together the coaching team and back room staff. When this is done I will look at dates for pre-selection meetings. It is important I have a viewing schedule to get around all the teams in order to give the players the best chance of impressing.

"I am currently in the planning stage of doing this. The important games will be the November Internationals, 2013 Six Nations and the knockout stages of the various domestic and European competitions. We will probably announce the touring squad in April 2013 but I want to leave it as long as possible so that we are certain that players are free of injury and are in form.

BRITISH & IRISH LIONS

"Australia will be a tough challenge. You can never underestimate their ability and resolve to achieve results, often when it is least expected. They produce exceptional athletes who always exude self-belief and confidence. They have often been one of the most expansive teams and are not afraid to take risks.

"That said I believe we have the talent to go there and win, and the tour is also a chance for northern hemisphere rugby to earn respect for its ability and playing style."

AUSTRALIA V BRITISH & IRISH LIONS TEST RESULTS

DATE	RESULT	VENUE
24/06/1899	Australia 13–3 British & Irish Lions	Sydney
22/07/1899	Australia 0–11 British & Irish Lions	Brisbane
05/08/1899	Australia 10–11 British & Irish Lions	Sydney
12/08/1899	Australia 0–13 British & Irish Lions	Sydney
02/07/1904	Australia 0–17 British & Irish Lions	Sydney
23/07/1904	Australia 3–17 British & Irish Lions	Brisbane
30/07/1904	Australia 0–16 British & Irish Lions	Sydney
30/08/1930	Australia 6–5 British & Irish Lions	Sydney
19/08/1950	Australia 6–19 British & Irish Lions	Brisbane
26/08/1950	Australia 3–24 British & Irish Lions	Sydney
06/06/1959	Australia 6–17 British & Irish Lions	Brisbane
13/06/1959	Australia 3–24 British & Irish Lions	Sydney
28/05/1966	Australia 8–11 British & Irish Lions	Sydney
04/06/1966	Australia 0–31 British & Irish Lions	Brisbane
01/07/1989	Australia 30–12 British & Irish Lions	Sydney
08/07/1989	Australia 12–9 British & Irish Lions	Brisbane
15/07/1989	Australia 18–19 British & Irish Lions	Sydney
30/06/2001	Australia 13–29 British & Irish Lions	Brisbane
07/07/2001	Australia 35–14 British & Irish Lions	Melbourne
14/07/2001	Australia 29–23 British & Irish Lions	Sydney

THE COMBINED TEAMS

BRITISH & IRISH LIONS INTERNATIONAL STATISTICS

MATCH RECORDS UP TO 10 OCTOBER 2012

MOST CONSECUTIVE TEST WINS

6	1891	SA 1,2,3,	1896 SA 1,2,3
3	1899	A 2,3,4	
3	1904	A 1,2,3	
3	1950	A 1,2,	1955 SA 1
3	1974	SA 1,2,3	

MOST CONSECUTIVE TESTS WITHOUT DEFEAT

Matches	Wins	Draws	Period
6	6	0	1891 to 1896
6	4	2	1971 to 1974

MOST POINTS IN A MATCH
BY THE TEAM

Pts	Opponents	Venue	Year
31	Australia	Brisbane	1966
29	Australia	Brisbane	2001
28	S Africa	Pretoria	1974
28	S Africa	Johannesburg	2009
26	S Africa	Port Elizabeth	1974
25	S Africa	Cape Town	1997
25	Argentina	Cardiff	2005
25	S Africa	Pretoria	2009
24	Australia	Sydney	1950
24	Australia	Sydney	1959

BY A PLAYER

Pts	Player	Opponents	Venue	Year
20	J P Wilkinson	Argentina	Cardiff	2005
20	S M Jones	S Africa	Pretoria	2009
18	A J P Ward	S Africa	Cape Town	1980
18	A G Hastings	N Zealand	Christchurch	1993
18	J P Wilkinson	Australia	Sydney	2001
17	T J Kiernan	S Africa	Pretoria	1968
16	B L Jones	Australia	Brisbane	1950

MOST TRIES IN A MATCH
BY THE TEAM

Tries	Opponents	Venue	Year
5	Australia	Sydney	1950
5	S Africa	Johannesburg	1955
5	Australia	Sydney	1959
5	Australia	Brisbane	1966
5	S Africa	Pretoria	1974

BY A PLAYER

Tries	Player	Opponents	Venue	Year
2	A M Bucher	Australia	Sydney	1899
2	W Llewellyn	Australia	Sydney	1904
2	C D Aarvold	N Zealand	Christchurch	1930
2	J E Nelson	Australia	Sydney	1950
2	M J Price	Australia	Sydney	1959
2	M J Price	N Zealand	Dunedin	1959
2	D K Jones	Australia	Brisbane	1966
2	T G R Davies	N Zealand	Christchurch	1971
2	J J Williams	S Africa	Pretoria	1974
2	J J Williams	S Africa	Port Elizabeth	1974
2	T Croft	S Africa	Durban	2009
2	S M Williams	S Africa	Johannesburg	2009

MOST CONVERSIONS IN A MATCH
BY THE TEAM

Cons	Opponents	Venue	Year
5	Australia	Brisbane	1966
4	S Africa	Johannesburg	1955
3	Australia	Sydney	1950
3	Australia	Sydney	1959
3	Australia	Brisbane	2001
3	S Africa	Durban	2009

BY A PLAYER

Cons	Player	Opponents	Venue	Year
5	S Wilson	Australia	Brisbane	1966
4	A Cameron	S Africa	Johannesburg	1955
3	J P Wilkinson	Australia	Brisbane	2001
3	S M Jones	S Africa	Durban	2009

BRITISH & IRISH LIONS

MOST PENALTIES IN A MATCH
BY THE TEAM

Pens	Opponents	Venue	Year
6	N Zealand	Christchurch	1993
6	Argentina	Cardiff	2005
5	S Africa	Pretoria	1968
5	S Africa	Cape Town	1980
5	Australia	Sydney	1989
5	S Africa	Cape Town	1997
5	S Africa	Durban	1997
5	S Africa	Pretoria	2009

BY A PLAYER

Pens	Player	Opponents	Venue	Year
6	A G Hastings	N Zealand	Christchurch	1993
6	J P Wilkinson	Argentina	Cardiff	2005
5	T J Kiernan	S Africa	Pretoria	1968
5	A J P Ward	S Africa	Cape Town	1980
5	A G Hastings	Australia	Sydney	1989
5	N R Jenkins	S Africa	Cape Town	1997
5	N R Jenkins	S Africa	Durban	1997
5	S M Jones	S Africa	Pretoria	2009

MOST DROP GOALS IN A MATCH
BY THE TEAM

Drops	Opponents	Venue	Year
2	S Africa	Port Elizabeth	1974

BY A PLAYER

Drops	Player	Opponents	Venue	Year
2	P Bennett	S Africa	Port Elizabeth	1974

CAREER RECORDS

MOST CAPPED PLAYERS

Caps	Player	Career
17	W J McBride	1962 to 1974
13	R E G Jeeps	1955 to 1962
12	C M H Gibson	1966 to 1971
12	G Price	1977 to 1983
10	A J F O'Reilly	1955 to 1959
10	R H Williams	1955 to 1959
10	G O Edwards	1968 to 1974

MOST CONSECUTIVE TESTS

Tests	Player	Career
15	W J McBride	1966 to 1974
12	C M H Gibson	1966 to 1971
12	G Price	1977 to 1983

MOST TESTS AS CAPTAIN

Tests	Captain	Career
6	A R Dawson	1959
6	M O Johnson	1997 to 2001

MOST POINTS IN TESTS

Points	Player	Tests	Career
67	J P Wilkinson	6	2001 to 2005
66	A G Hastings	6	1989 to 1993
53	S M Jones	6	2005 to 2009
44	P Bennett	8	1974 to 1977
41	N R Jenkins	4	1997 to 2001
35	T J Kiernan	5	1962 to 1968
30	S Wilson	5	1966
30	B John	5	1968 to 1971

MOST TRIES IN TESTS

Tries	Player	Tests	Career
6	A J F O'Reilly	10	1955 to 1959
5	J J Williams	7	1974 to 1977
4	W Llewellyn	4	1904
4	M J Price	5	1959

MOST CONVERSIONS IN TESTS

Cons	Player	Tests	Career
7	J P Wilkinson	6	2001 to 2005
7	S M Jones	6	2005 to 2009
6	S Wilson	5	1966
4	J F Byrne	4	1896
4	C Y Adamson	4	1899
4	B L Jones	3	1950
4	A Cameron	2	1955

MOST PENALTY GOALS IN TESTS			
Penalties	Player	Tests	Career
20	A G Hastings	6	1989 to 1993
16	J P Wilkinson	6	2001 to 2005
13	N R Jenkins	4	1997 to 2001
12	S M Jones	6	2005 to 2009
11	T J Kiernan	5	1962 to 1968
10	P Bennett	8	1974 to 1977
7	S O Campbell	7	1980 to 1983

MOST DROP GOALS IN TESTS			
Drops	Player	Tests	Career
2	P F Bush	4	1904
2	D Watkins	6	1966
2	B John	5	1968 to 1971
2	P Bennett	8	1974 to 1977
2	C R Andrew	5	1989 to 1993

SERIES RECORDS

RECORD	HOLDER	DETAIL
Most team points		79 in S Africa 1974
Most team tries		10 in S Africa 1955 & 1974
Most points by player	N R Jenkins	41 in S Africa 1997
Most tries by player	W Llewellyn	4 in Australia 1904
	J J Williams	4 in S Africa 1974

MAJOR TOUR RECORDS

RECORD	DETAIL	YEAR	PLACE
Most team points	842	1959	Australia, NZ & Canada
Most team tries	165	1959	Australia, NZ & Canada
Highest score & biggest win	116–10	2001	v W Australia President's XV
Most individual points	188 by B John	1971	Australia & N Zealand
Most individual tries	22 by A J F O'Reilly	1959	Australia, NZ & Canada
Most points in match	37 by A G B Old	1974 v SW Districts	Mossel Bay, S Africa
Most tries in match	6 by D J Duckham	1971 v W Coast/Buller	Greymouth, N Zealand
	6 by J J Williams	1974 v SW Districts	Mossel Bay, S Africa

MISCELLANEOUS RECORDS

RECORD	HOLDER	DETAIL
Longest Test Career	W J McBride	13 seasons, 1962–1974
Youngest Test Cap	A J F O'Reilly	19 yrs 91 days in 1955
Oldest Test Cap	N A Back	36 yrs 160 days in 2005

BRITISH & IRISH LIONS

BRITISH & IRISH LIONS INTERNATIONAL PLAYERS
UP TO 10 OCTOBER 2012

From 1891 onwards.

* Indicates that the player was uncapped at the time of his first Lions Test but was subsequently capped by his country.

Aarvold, C D (Cambridge U, Blackheath and England) 1930 NZ 1,2,3,4, A
Ackerman, R A (London Welsh and Wales) 1983 NZ 1,4 (R)
Ackford, P J (Harlequins and England) 1989 A 1,2,3
Adamson, C Y (Durham City) 1899 A 1,2,3,4
Alexander, R (NIFC and Ireland) 1938 SA 1,2,3
Andrew, C R (Wasps and England) 1989 A 2,3, 1993 NZ 1,2,3
Arneil, R J (Edinburgh Acads and Scotland) 1968 SA 1,2,3,4
Archer, H A (Guy's H and *England) 1908 NZ 1,2,3
Ashcroft, A (Waterloo and England) 1959 A 1, NZ 2
Aston, R L (Cambridge U and England) 1891 SA 1,2,3,4
Ayre-Smith, A (Guy's H) 1899 A 1,2,3,4

Back, N A (Leicester and England) 1997 SA 2(R),3, 2001 A 2,3, 2005 NZ 1
Bainbridge, S J (Gosforth and England) 1983 NZ 3,4
Baird, G R T (Kelso and Scotland) 1983 NZ 1,2,3,4
Baker, A M (Newport and Wales) 1910 SA 3
Baker, D G S (Old Merchant Taylors' and England) 1955 SA 3,4
Balshaw, I R (Bath and England) 2001 A 1(R),2(R),3(R)
Bassett, J A (Penarth and Wales) 1930 NZ 1,2,3,4, A
Bateman, A G (Richmond and Wales) 1997 SA 3(R)
Bayfield, M C (Northampton and England) 1993 NZ 1,2,3
Beamish, G R (Leicester, RAF and Ireland) 1930 NZ 1,2,3,4,A
Beattie, J R (Glasgow Acads and Scotland) 1983 NZ 2(R)
Beaumont, W B (Fylde and England) 1977 NZ 2,3,4, 1980 SA 1,2,3,4
Bebb, D I E (Swansea and Wales) 1962 SA 2,3, 1966 A 1,2, NZ 1,2,3,4
Bedell-Sivright, D R (Cambridge U and Scotland) 1904 A 1
Bell, S P (Cambridge U) 1896 SA 2,3,4
Belson, F C (Bath) 1899 A 1
Bennett, P (Llanelli and Wales) 1974 SA 1,2,3,4, 1977 NZ 1,2,3,4
Bentley, J (Newcastle and England) 1997 SA 2,3
Bevan, J C (Cardiff Coll of Ed, Cardiff and Wales) 1971 NZ 1
Bevan, T S (Swansea and Wales) 1904 A 1,2,3, NZ
Black, A W (Edinburgh U and Scotland) 1950 NZ 1,2
Black, B H (Oxford U, Blackheath and England) 1930 NZ 1,2,3,4, A
Blakiston, A F (Northampton and England) 1924 SA 1,2,3,4
Bowcott, H M (Cambridge U, Cardiff and Wales) 1930 NZ 1,2,3,4, A
Bowe, T J (Ospreys and Ireland) 2009 SA 1,2,3
Boyd, C A (Dublin U and *Ireland) 1896 SA 1
Boyle, C V (Dublin U and Ireland) 1938 SA 2,3
Brand, T N (NIFC and *Ireland) 1924 SA 1,2
Bresnihan, F P K (UC Dublin and Ireland) 1968 SA 1,2,4
Bromet, E (Cambridge U) 1891 SA 2,3
Bromet, W E (Oxford U and England) 1891 SA 1,2,3
Brophy, N H (UC Dublin and Ireland) 1962 SA 1,4
Brown, G L (W of Scotland and Scotland) 1971 NZ 3,4, 1974 SA 1,2,3, 1977 NZ 2,3,4
Bucher, A M (Edinburgh Acads and Scotland) 1899 A 1,3,4
Budge, G M (Edinburgh Wands and Scotland) 1950 NZ 4
Bulger, L Q (Lansdowne and Ireland) 1896 SA 1,2,3,4
Bulloch, G C (Glasgow and Scotland) 2001 A l(t), 2005 NZ 3(R)

Burcher, D H (Newport and Wales) 1977 NZ 3
Burnell, A P (London Scottish and Scotland) 1993 NZ 1
Bush, P F (Cardiff and *Wales) 1904 A 1,2,3, NZ
Butterfield, J (Northampton and England) 1955 SA 1,2,3,4
Byrne, J F (Moseley and England) 1896 SA 1,2,3,4
Byrne, J S (Leinster and Ireland) 2005 Arg, NZ 1,2(R),3
Byrne, L M (Ospreys and Wales) 2009 SA 1

Calder, F (Stewart's-Melville FP and Scotland) 1989 A 1,2,3
Calder, J H (Stewart's-Melville FP and Scotland) 1983 NZ 3
Cameron, A (Glasgow HSFP and Scotland) 1955 SA 1,2
Campbell, S O (Old Belvedere and Ireland) 1980 SA 2(R),3,4, 1983 NZ 1,2,3,4
Campbell-Lamerton, M J (Halifax, Army and Scotland) 1962 SA 1,2,3,4, 1966 A 1,2, NZ 1,3
Carey, W J (Oxford U) 1896 SA 1,2,3,4
Carleton, J (Orrell and England) 1980 SA 1,2,4, 1983 NZ 2,3,4
Carling, W D C (Harlequins and England) 1993 NZ 1
Catt, M J (Bath and England) 1997 SA 3
Cave, W T C (Cambridge U and *England) 1903 SA 1,2,3
Chalmers, C M (Melrose and Scotland) 1989 A 1
Chapman, F E (Westoe, W Hartlepool and *England) 1908 NZ 3
Charvis, C L (Swansea and Wales) 2001 A 1(R),3(R)
Clarke, B B (Bath and England) 1993 NZ 1,2,3
Clauss, P R A (Oxford U and Scotland) 1891 SA 1,2,3
Cleaver, W B (Cardiff and Wales) 1950 NZ 1,2,3
Clifford, T (Young Munster and Ireland) 1950 NZ 1,2,3, A 1,2
Clinch, A D (Dublin U and Ireland) 1896 SA 1,2,3,4
Cobner, T J (Pontypool and Wales) 1977 NZ 1,2,3
Colclough, M J (Angoulême and England) 1980 SA 1,2,3,4, 1983 NZ 1,2,3,4
Collett, G F (Cheltenham) 1903 SA 1,2,3
Connell, G C (Trinity Acads and Scotland) 1968 SA 4
Cookson, G (Manchester) 1899 A 1,2,3,4
Cooper, G J (Newport Gwent Dragons and Wales) 2005 Arg
Corry, M E (Leicester and England) 2001 A 1,2(t+R),3, 2005 Arg, NZ 1,2(R),3(R)
Cotton, F E (Loughborough Colls, Coventry and England) 1974 SA 1,2,3,4, 1977 NZ 2,3,4
Coulman, M J (Moseley and England) 1968 SA 3
Cove-Smith, R (Old Merchant Taylors' and England) 1924 SA 1,2,3,4
Cowan, R C (Selkirk and Scotland) 1962 SA 4
Crean, T J (Wanderers and Ireland) 1896 SA 1,2,3,4
Croft, T R (Leicester and England) 2009 SA 1,2,3(t&R)
Cromey, G E (Queen's U, Belfast and Ireland) 1938 SA 3
Crowther, S N (Lennox) 1904 A 1,2,3, NZ
Cueto, M J (Sale and England) 2005 NZ 3
Cunningham, W A (Lansdowne and Ireland) 1924 SA 3
Cusiter, C P (Borders and Scotland) 2005 Arg (R)

Dallaglio, L B N (Wasps and England) 1997 SA 1,2,3
Dancer, G T (Bedford) 1938 SA 1,2,3
D'Arcy, G W (Leinster and Ireland) 2005 Arg
Davey, J (Redruth and England) 1908 NZ 1
Davidson, I G (NIFC and Ireland) 1903 SA 1
Davidson, J W (London Irish and Ireland) 1997 SA 1,2,3
Davies, C (Cardiff and Wales) 1950 NZ 4

Davies, D M (Somerset Police and Wales) 1950 NZ 3,4, A 1
Davies, D S (Hawick and Scotland) 1924 SA 1,2,3,4
Davies, H J (Newport and Wales) 1924 SA 2
Davies, T G R (Cardiff, London Welsh and Wales) 1968 SA 3, 1971 NZ 1,2,3,4
Davies, T J (Llanelli and Wales) 1959 NZ 2,4
Davies, T M (London Welsh, Swansea and Wales) 1971 NZ 1,2,3,4, 1974 SA 1,2,3,4
Davies, W G (Cardiff and Wales) 1980 SA 2
Davies, W P C (Harlequins and England) 1955 SA 1,2,3
Dawes, S J (London Welsh and Wales) 1971 NZ 1,2,3,4
Dawson, A R (Wanderers and Ireland) 1959 A 1,2, NZ 1,2,3,4
Dawson, M J S (Northampton, Wasps and England) 1997 SA 1,2,3, 2001 A 2(R),3, 2005 NZ 1(R),3(R)
Dibble, R (Bridgwater Albion and England) 1908 NZ 1,2,3
Dixon, P J (Harlequins and England) 1971 NZ 1,2,4
Dobson, D D (Oxford U and England) 1904 A 1,2,3, NZ
Dodge, P W (Leicester and England) 1980 SA 3,4
Dooley, W A (Preston Grasshoppers and England) 1989 A 2,3
Doran, G P (Lansdowne and Ireland) 1899 A 1,2
Down, P J (Bristol and *England) 1908 NZ 1,2,3
Doyle, M G (Blackrock Coll and Ireland) 1968 SA 1
Drysdale, D (Heriot's FP and Scotland) 1924 SA 1,2,3,4
Duckham, D J (Coventry and England) 1971 NZ 2,3,4
Duggan, W P (Blackrock Coll and Ireland) 1977 NZ 1,2,3,4
Duff, P L (Glasgow Acads and Scotland) 1938 SA 2,3

Easterby, S H (Llanelli Scarlets and Ireland) 2005 NZ 2,3
Edwards, G O (Cardiff and Wales) 1968 SA 1,2, 1971 NZ 1,2,3,4, 1974 SA 1,2,3,4
Edwards, R W (Malone and Ireland) 1904 A 2,3, NZ
Ellis, H A (Leicester and England) 2009 SA 3(R)
Evans, G (Maesteg and Wales) 1983 NZ 3,4
Evans, G L (Newport and Wales) 1977 NZ 2,3,4
Evans, I C (Llanelli and Wales) 1989 A 1,2,3, 1993 NZ 1,2 3, 1997 SA 1
Evans, R T (Newport and Wales) 1950 NZ 1,2,3,4, A 1,2
Evans, T P (Swansea and Wales) 1977 NZ 1
Evans, W R (Cardiff and Wales) 1959 A 2, NZ 1,2,3
Evers, G V (Moseley) 1899 A 2,3,4

Farrell, J L (Bective Rangers and Ireland) 1930 NZ 1,2,3,4,A
Faull, J (Swansea and Wales) 1959 A 1, NZ 1,3,4
Fenwick, S P (Bridgend and Wales) 1977 NZ 1,2,3,4
Fitzgerald, C F (St Mary's Coll and Ireland) 1983 NZ 1,2,3,4
Fitzgerald, L M (Leinster and Ireland) 2009 SA 2
Flutey, W A (Wasps and England) 2009 SA 3
Ford, R W (Edinburgh and Scotland) 2009 SA 3(R)
Foster, A R (Queen's U, Belfast and Ireland) 1910 SA 1,2
Francombe, J S (Manchester) 1899 A 1

Gabe, R T (Cardiff and Wales) 1904 A 1,2,3, NZ
Gibbs, I S (Swansea and Wales) 1993 NZ 2,3, 1997 SA 1,2 3
Gibbs, R A (Cardiff and Wales) 1908 NZ 1,2
Gibson, C M H (Cambridge U, NIFC and Ireland) 1966 NZ 1,2,3,4, 1968 SA 1(R),2,3,4, 1971 NZ 1,2,3,4
Gibson, G R (Northern and England) 1899 A 1,2,3,4
Gibson, T A (Cambridge U and *England) 1903 SA 1,2,3
Giles, J L (Coventry and England) 1938 SA 1,3
Gillespie, J I (Edinburgh Acads and Scotland) 1903 SA 1,2,3
Gould, J H (Old Leysians) 1891 SA 1
Gravell, R W R (Llanelli and Wales) 1980 SA 1(R),2,3,4
Graves, C R A (Wanderers and Ireland) 1938 SA 1,3
Gray, H G S (Scottish Trials) 1899 A 1,2
Greenwood, J T (Dunfermline and Scotland) 1955 SA 1,2,3,4
Greenwood, W J H (Harlequins and England) 2005 NZ 1(R),3
Greig, L L (US and *Scotland) 1903 SA 1,2,3
Grewcock, D J (Bath and England) 2001 A 1,2,3, 2005 Arg, NZ 1(R)
Grieve, C F (Oxford U and Scotland) 1938 SA 2,3
Griffiths, G M (Cardiff and Wales) 1955 SA 2,3,4
Griffiths, V M (Newport and Wales) 1924 SA 3,4
Guscott, J C (Bath and England) 1989 A 2,3, 1993 NZ 1,2,3, 1997 SA 1,2,3

Hall, M R (Bridgend and Wales) 1989 A 1
Hammond, J (Cambridge U, Blackheath) 1891 SA 1,2,3, 1896 SA 2,4
Hancock, P F (Blackheath and England) 1891 SA 1,2,3, 1896 SA 1,2,3,4
Hancock, P S (Richmond and *England) 1903 SA 1,2,3
Handford, F G (Manchester and England) 1910 SA 1,2,3
Harding, A F (London Welsh and Wales) 1904 A 1,2,3, NZ, 1908 NZ 1,2,3
Harding, R (Cambridge U, Swansea and Wales) 1924 SA 2,3,4
Harris, S W (Blackheath and England) 1924 SA 3,4
Harrison, E M (Guy's H) 1903 SA 1
Hastings, A G (London Scottish, Watsonians and Scotland) 1989 A 1,2,3, 1993 NZ 1,2,3
Hastings, S (Watsonians and Scotland) 1989 A 2,3
Hay, B H (Boroughmuir and Scotland) 1980 SA 2,3,4
Hayes, J J (Munster and Ireland) 2005 Arg, 2009 SA 3(R)
Hayward, D J (Newbridge and Wales) 1950 NZ 1,2,3
Healey, A S (Leicester and England) 1997 SA 2(R),3(R)
Heaslip, J P R (Leinster and Ireland) 2009 SA 1,2,3
Henderson, N J (Queen's U, Belfast, NIFC and Ireland) 1950 NZ3
Henderson, R A J (Wasps and Ireland) 2001 A 1,2,3
Henderson, R G (Northern and Scotland) 1924 SA 3,4
Hendrie, K G P (Heriot's FP and Scotland) 1924 SA 2
Henson, G L (Neath-Swansea Ospreys and Wales) 2005 NZ 2
Hewitt, D (Queen's U, Belfast, Instonians and Ireland) 1959 A 1,2, NZ 1,3,4, 1962 SA 4
Hickie, D A (Leinster and Ireland) 2005 Arg
Higgins, R (Liverpool and England) 1955 SA 1
Hill, R A (Saracens and England) 1997 SA 1,2, 2001 A 1,2, 2005 NZ 1
Hind, G R (Guy's H and *England) 1908 NZ 2,3
Hinshelwood, A J W (London Scottish and Scotland) 1966 NZ 2,4, 1968 SA 3
Hodgson, J McD (Northern and *England) 1930 NZ 1,3
Holmes, T D (Cardiff and Wales) 1983 NZ 1
Hopkins, R (Maesteg and Wales) 1971 NZ 1(R)
Horgan, S P (Leinster and Ireland) 2005 Arg (R),NZ 1(R),2(R),3(R)
Horrocks-Taylor, J P (Leicester and England) 1959 NZ 3
Horton, A L (Blackheath and England) 1968 SA 2,3,4
Howard, W G (Old Birkonians) 1938 SA 1
Howie, R A (Kirkcaldy and Scotland) 1924 SA 1,2,3,4
Howley, R (Cardiff and Wales) 2001 A 1,2
Hulme, F C (Birkenhead Park and England) 1904 A 1

Irvine, A R (Heriot's FP and Scotland) 1974 SA 3,4, 1977 NZ 1,2,3,4, 1980 SA 2,3,4
Irwin, D G (Instonians and Ireland) 1983 NZ 1,2,4
Isherwood, G A M (Old Alleynians, Sale) 1910 SA 1,2,3

Jackett, E J (Falmouth, Leicester and England) 1908 NZ 1,2,3
Jackson, F S (Leicester) 1908 NZ 1
Jackson, P B (Coventry and England) 1959 A 1,2, NZ 1,3,4
James, D R (Llanelli and Wales) 2001 A 1,2,3
Jarman, H (Newport and Wales) 1910 SA 1,2,3
Jarman, J W (Bristol and *England) 1899 A 1,2,3,4
Jeeps, R E G (Northampton and *England) 1955 SA 1,2,3,4, 1959 A 1,2, NZ 1,2,3, 1962 SA 1,2,3,4
Jenkins, G D (Cardiff Blues and Wales) 2005 NZ 1,2,3, 2009 SA 1,2,3
Jenkins, N R (Pontypridd, Cardiff and Wales) 1997 SA 1,2,3, 2001 A 2(R)
Jenkins, V G J (Oxford U, London Welsh and Wales) 1938 SA 1
John, B (Cardiff and Wales) 1968 SA 1, 1971 NZ 1,2,3,4
John, E R (Neath and Wales) 1950 NZ 1,2,3,4, A 1,2
Johnson, M O (Leicester and England) 1993 NZ 2,3, 1997 SA 1,2,3, 2001 A 1,2,3
Johnston, R (Wanderers and Ireland) 1896 SA 1,2,3
Jones, A R (Ospreys and Wales) 2009 SA 1(R),2
Jones, A-W (Ospreys and Wales) 2009 SA 1,2(R),3(R)
Jones, B L (Devonport Services, Llanelli and Wales) 1950 NZ 4, A 1,2

O'Reilly, A J F (Old Belvedere and Ireland) 1955 SA 1,2,3,4, 1959 A 1,2, NZ 1,2,3,4
Oldham, W L (Coventry and England) 1908 NZ 1
Orr, P A (Old Wesley and Ireland) 1977 NZ 1
O'Shea, J P (Cardiff and Wales) 1968 SA 1
Owen, M J (Newport Gwent Dragons and Wales) 2005 Arg

Parker, D S (Swansea and Wales) 1930 NZ 1,2,3,4, A
Pask, A E I (Abertillery and Wales) 1962 SA 1,2,3, 1966 A 1,2, NZ 1,3,4
Patterson, C S (Instonians and Ireland) 1980 SA 1,2,3
Patterson, W M (Sale and *England) 1959 NZ 2
Paxton, I A M (Selkirk and Scotland) 1983 NZ 1,2,3,4
Pedlow, A C (CIYMS and Ireland) 1955 SA 1,4
Peel, D J (Llanelli Scarlets and Wales) 2005 NZ 1,2,3
Perry, M B (Bath and England) 2001 A 1,2,3
Phillips, W M (Ospreys and Wales) 2009 SA 1,2,3
Pillman, C H (Blackheath and England) 1910 SA 2,3
Piper, O J S (Cork Const and Ireland) 1910 SA 1
Poole, H (Cardiff) 1930 NZ 3
Popplewell, N J (Greystones and Ireland) 1993 NZ 1,2,3
Preece, I (Coventry and England) 1950 NZ 1
Prentice, F D (Leicester and England) 1930 NZ 2, A
Price, B (Newport and Wales) 1966 A 1,2, NZ 1,4
Price, G (Pontypool and Wales) 1977 NZ 1,2,3,4, 1980 SA 1,2,3,4, 1983 NZ 1,2,3,4
Price, M J (Pontypool and Wales) 1959 A 1,2, NZ 1,2,3
Prosser, T R (Pontypool and Wales) 1959 NZ,4
Pullin, J V (Bristol and England) 1968 SA 2,3,4, 1971 NZ 1,2,3,4

Quinnell, D L (Llanelli and *Wales) 1971 NZ. 3, 1977 NZ 2,3, 1980 SA 1,2
Quinnell, L S (Llanelli and Wales) 2001 A 1,2,3

Ralston, C W (Richmond and England) 1974 SA 4
Reed, A I (Bath and Scotland) 1993 NZ 1
Rees, H E (Neath and *Wales) 1977 NZ 4
Rees, M (Llanelli Scarlets and Wales) 2009 SA 1(R),2,3
Reeve, J S R (Harlequins and England) 1930 NZ 1,3,4, A
Regan, M P (Bristol and England) 1997 SA 3
Reid, T E (Garryowen and Ireland) 1955 SA 2,3
Renwick, J M (Hawick and Scotland) 1980 SA 1
Rew, H (Blackheath, Army and England) 1930 NZ 1,2,3,4
Reynolds, F J (Old Cranleighans and England) 1938 SA 1,2
Richards, D (Leicester and England) 1989 A 1,2,3, 1993 NZ 1,2,3
Richards, D S (Swansea and Wales) 1980 SA 1
Richards, M C R (Cardiff and Wales) 1968 SA 1,3,4
Richards, T J (Bristol and Australia) 1910 SA 1,2
Rimmer, G (Waterloo and England) 1950 NZ 3
Ringland, T M (Ballymena and Ireland) 1983 NZ 1
Risman, A B W (Loughborough Colls and England) 1959 A 1,2, NZ 1,4
Ritson, J A S (Northern and *England) 1908 NZ 1
Robbie, J C (Greystones and Ireland) 1980 SA 4
Roberts, J H (Cardiff Blues and Wales) 2009 SA 1,2
Robins, J D (Birkenhead Park and Wales) 1950 NZ 1,2,3, A 1,2
Robins, R J (Pontypridd and Wales) 1955 SA 1,2,3,4
Robinson, J T (Sale and England) 2001 A 1,2,3, 2005 NZ 1,2
Rodber, T A K (Northampton and England) 1997 SA 1,2
Rogers, D P (Bedford and England) 1962 SA 1,4
Rogers, R J (Bath) 1904 NZ
Rotherham, A (Cambridge U and *England) 1891 SA 1,2,3
Rowlands, K A (Cardiff and Wales) 1962 SA 1,2,4
Rowntree, G C (Leicester and England) 2005 Arg, NZ 2(t+R),3(R)
Rutherford, D (Gloucester and England) 1966 A 1
Rutherford, J Y (Selkirk and Scotland) 1983 NZ 3

Saunders, S M (Guy's H) 1904 A 1,2
Savage, K F (Northampton and England) 1968 SA 1,2,3,4
Scotland, K J F (Cambridge U, Heriot's FP and Scotland) 1959 A 1,2, NZ 1,3,4
Scott, W P (West of Scotland and Scotland) 1903 SA 1,2,3

Sealy, J (Dublin U and *Ireland) 1896 SA 1,2,3,4
Sharp, R A W (Oxford U, Redruth and England) 1962 SA 3,4
Shaw, S D (Wasps and England) 2009 SA 2,3
Sheridan, A J (Sale and England) 2009 SA 2(t&R),3
Simpson, C (Cambridge U) 1891 SA 1
Skrimshire, R T (Newport and Wales) 1903 SA 1,2,3
Slattery, J F (Blackrock Coll and Ireland) 1974 SA 1,2,3,4
Slemen, M A C (Liverpool and England) 1980 SA 1
Smith, A R (Edinburgh Wands, London Scottish and Scotland) 1962 SA 1,2,3
Smith, D F (Richmond and England) 1910 SA 1,2,3
Smith, D W C (London Scottish and Scotland) 1950 A 1
Smith, G K (Kelso and Scotland) 1959 A 1,2, NZ 1,3
Smith, I S (Oxford U, London Scottish and Scotland) 1924 SA 1,2
Smith, O J (Leicester and England) 2005 Arg
Smith, T J (Watsonians, Northampton and Scotland) 1997 SA 1,2,3, 2001 A 1,2,3
Smith, T W (Leicester) 1908 NZ 2,3
Smyth, R S (Dublin U and Ireland) 1903 SA 1,2,3
Smyth, T (Malone, Newport and Ireland) 1910 SA 2,3
Sole, D M B (Edinburgh Acads and Scotland) 1989 A 1,2,3
Spong, R S (Old Millhillians and England) 1930 NZ 1,2,3,4, A
Spoors, J A (Bristol) 1910 SA 1,2,3
Squire, J (Newport, Pontypool and Wales) 1977 NZ 4, 1980 SA 1,2,3,4, 1983 NZ 1
Squires, P J (Harrogate and England) 1977 NZ 1
Stagg, P K (Oxford U, Sale and Scotland) 1968 SA 1,3,4
Stanger-Leathes, C F (Northern and *England) 1904 A 1
Steele, W C C (Bedford, RAF and Scotland) 1974 SA 1,2
Stephens, I (Bridgend and Wales) 1983 NZ 1
Stephens, J R G (Neath and Wales) 1950 A 1,2
Stevenson, R C (St Andrew's U and Scotland) 1910 SA 1,2,3
Stimpson, T R G (Newcastle and England) 1997 SA 3(R)
Stout, F M (Gloucester and England) 1899 A 1,2,3,4, 1903 SA 1,2,3
Surtees, A A (Cambridge U) 1891 SA 1,2,3
Swannell, B I (Northampton and *Australia) 1899 A 2,3,4, 1904 A 1,2,3, NZ

Tait, A V (Newcastle and Scotland) 1997 SA 1,2
Tanner, H (Swansea and Wales) 1938 SA 2
Taylor, A R (Cross Keys and Wales) 1938 SA 1,2
Taylor, J (London Welsh and Wales) 1971 NZ 1,2,3,4
Taylor, R B (Northampton and England) 1968 SA 1,2,3,4
Teague, M C (Gloucester, Moseley and England) 1989 A 2,3, 1993 NZ 2(t)
Tedford, A (Malone and Ireland) 1903 SA 1,2,3
Telfer, J W (Melrose and Scotland) 1966 A 1,2, NZ 1,2,4, 1968 SA 2,3,4
Thomas, G (Toulouse and Wales) 2005 NZ 1,2,3
Thomas, M C (Devonport Services, Newport and Wales) 1950 NZ 2,3, A 1, 1959 NZ 1
Thomas, R C C (Swansea and Wales) 1955 SA 3,4
Thomas, W D (Llanelli and *Wales) 1966 NZ 2,3, 1968 SA 3(R),4, 1971 NZ 1,2,4 (R)
Thompson, C E K (Lancashire) 1899 A 2,3,4
Thompson, R (Cambridge U) 1891 SA 1,2,3
Thompson, R H (Instonians, London Irish and Ireland) 1955 SA 1,2,4
Thompson, S G (Northampton and England) 2005 Arg (R), NZ 1(R),2
Timms, A B (Edinburgh U and Scotland) 1899 A 2,3,4
Todd, A F (Blackheath and *England) 1896 SA 1,2,3,4
Townsend, G P J (Northampton and Scotland) 1997 SA 1,2
Trail, D H (Guy's H) 1904 A 1,2,3, NZ
Travers, W H (Newport and Wales) 1938 SA 2,3
Tucker, C C (Shannon and Ireland) 1980 SA 3,4
Turner, J W C (Gala and Scotland) 1968 SA 1,2,3,4

Underwood, R (RAF, Leicester and England) 1989 A 1,2,3, 1993 NZ 1,2,3
Underwood, T (Newcastle and England) 1997 SA 3
Unwin, E J (Rosslyn Park, Army and England) 1938 SA 1,2
Uttley, R M (Gosforth and England) 1974 SA 1,2,3,4

Vassall, H H (Blackheath and England) 1908 NZ 1,2,3
Vickery, P J (Gloucester, Wasps and England) 2001 A 1,2,3, 2009 SA 1,3
Vile, T H (Newport and *Wales) 1904 A 2,3, NZ
Voyce, A T (Gloucester and England) 1924 SA 3,4

Waddell, G H (Cambridge U, London Scottish and Scotland) 1962 SA 1,2
Waddell, H (Glasgow Acads and Scotland) 1924 SA 1,2,4
Wainwright, R I (Watsonians and Scotland) 1997 SA 3
Walker, E F (Lennox) 1903 SA 2,3
Walker, S (Instonians and Ireland) 1938 SA 1,2,3
Wallace, D P (Munster and Ireland) 2009 SA 1,2,3(R)
Wallace, Jos (Wanderers and Ireland) 1903 SA 1,2,3
Wallace, P S (Saracens and Ireland) 1997 SA 1,2,3
Wallace, W (Percy Park) 1924 SA 1
Waller, P D (Newport and Wales) 1910 SA 1,2,3
Ward, A J P (Garryowen and Ireland) 1980 SA 1
Waters, J A (Selkirk and Scotland) 1938 SA 3
Watkins, D (Newport and Wales) 1966 A 1,2, NZ 1,2,3,4
Watkins, S J (Newport and Wales) 1966 A 1,2, NZ 3
Webb, J (Abertillery and Wales) 1910 SA 1,2,3
Welsh, W B (Hawick and Scotland) 1930 NZ 4
Weston, M P (Richmond, Durham City and England) 1962 SA 1,2,3,4, 1966 A 1,2
Wheeler, P J (Leicester and England) 1977 NZ 2,3,4, 1980 SA 1,2,3,4
White, D B (London Scottish and Scotland) 1989 A 1
White, J M (Leicester and England) 2005 Arg (R),NZ 1,2,3
Whitley, H (Northern and *England) 1924 SA 1,3,4
Whittaker, T S (Lancashire) 1891 SA 1,2,3
Wilkinson, J P (Newcastle and England) 2001 A 1,2,3, 2005 Arg, NZ 1,2
Willcox, J G (Oxford U, Harlequins and England) 1962 SA 1,2,4
Williams, B L (Cardiff and Wales) 1950 NZ 2,3,4, A 1,2
Williams, C (Swansea and Wales) 1980 SA 1,2,3,4
Williams, D (Ebbw Vale and Wales) 1966 A 1,2, NZ 1,2,4

Williams, D B (Cardiff and *Wales) 1977 NZ 1,2,3
Williams, J F (London Welsh and Wales) 1908 NZ 3
Williams, J J (Llanelli and Wales) 1974 SA 1,2,3,4, 1977 NZ 1,2,3
Williams, J L (Cardiff and Wales) 1908 NZ 1,2
Williams, J P R (London Welsh and Wales) 1971 NZ 1,2,3,4, 1974 SA 1,2,3,4
Williams, M E (Cardiff Blues and Wales) 2005 NZ 3(R), 2009 SA 1(R),2(R),3
Williams, R H (Llanelli and Wales) 1955 SA 1,2,3,4, 1959 A 1,2, NZ 1,2,3,4
Williams, S H (Newport and *England) 1910 SA 1,2,3
Williams, S M (Ospreys and Wales) 2005 Arg, NZ 2, 2009 SA 2(R),3
Williams, W O G (Swansea and Wales) 1955 SA 1,2,3,4
Willis, W R (Cardiff and Wales) 1950 NZ 4, A 1,2
Wilson, S (London Scottish and Scotland) 1966 A 2, NZ 1,2,3,4
Windsor, R W (Pontypool and Wales) 1974 SA 1,2,3,4, 1977 NZ 1
Winterbottom, P J (Headingley, Harlequins and England) 1983 NZ 1,2,3,4, 1993 NZ, 1,2,3
Wood, B G M (Garryowen and Ireland) 1959 NZ 1,3
Wood, K B (Leicester) 1910 SA 1,3
Wood, K G M (Harlequins and Ireland) 1997 SA 1,2, 2001 A 1,2,3
Woodward, C R (Leicester and England) 1980 SA 2,3
Worsley, J P R (Wasps and England) 2009 SA3
Wotherspoon, W (Cambridge U and Scotland) 1891 SA 1

Young, A T (Cambridge U, Blackheath and England) 1924 SA 2
Young, D (Cardiff and Wales) 1989 A 1,2,3
Young, J (Harrogate, RAF and Wales) 1968 SA 1
Young, J R C (Oxford U, Harlequins and England) 1959 NZ 2
Young, R M (Queen's U, Belfast, Collegians and Ireland) 1966 A 1,2, NZ 1, 1968 SA 3

BARBARIANS BEATEN BUT UNBOWED

By Iain Spragg

Getty Images

Barbarians wing Shane Williams tries to evade his Wales team-mate Martyn Williams.

The Barbarians marked their 120th season in 2010/11 by claiming the scalps of South Africa, England and Wales, but found the 2011/12 campaign an altogether sterner assignment, winning just once in four outings against Test opposition.

The solitary victory came against Ireland at Kingsholm in May, but losses to England and Wales either side of the fixture, coupled with the team's heavy defeat to Australia six months earlier, meant it was not to be a vintage season for the Baa-Baas in terms of results.

They began the campaign in October against the South of Scotland in the Bill McLaren Foundation Match and, despite tries from Ulster's Mike McComish and Rugby Lions' Leigh Hinton in the opening half hour, the home side rallied to record a 22–15 win.

A fortnight later the Barbarians faced the Wallabies at Twickenham looking for their first triumph over the Australians since a 19–7 victory at the Arms Park in 1976, but Graham Henry's side never threatened to emulate their predecessors' famous feat. A late score from Wigan Warriors' Sam Tomkins, playing his first game of rugby union, gave Barbarians supporters something to cheer but the final 60–11 scoreline did not ultimately flatter the Wallabies.

The busy late May and early June fixture list kicked off with a 40–7 win over Loughborough Students at Holywell Park. It was followed by the encounter with England at Twickenham and, although the match ended in a 57–26 defeat, the side rediscovered its scoring touch with a brace of tries from All Black Mils Muliaina and further five-pointers from England's Mike Tindall and Samoan Pelu Taele.

There was, however, little time to reflect on the match and just two days later the Barbarians faced Ireland in Gloucester. In their two previous outings they had played on the back foot, but first-half tries from Iain Balshaw, Cornelius van Zyl and Paul Sackey finally put the Baa-Baas in the driving seat and, although Ireland fought back after the break, a fourth try from Tindall and a late penalty from Felipe Contepomi were enough to secure a 29–28 victory.

The season ended against Wales in Cardiff, but there was no repeat of the success in the Millennium Stadium 12 months earlier despite tries from half backs Stephen Donald and Richie Rees in the first 40 minutes which established a 14–13 half-time advantage. A second try from New Zealander Donald after the restart seemed to have sealed victory, but Wales hit back with scores from James Hook and Aled Brew to emerge 31–20 winners.

Elsewhere, the French Barbarians embarked on a two-match tour of Japan in June and recorded back-to-back victories against the Brave Blossoms at the Prince Chichibu Memorial Rugby Ground in Tokyo.

Coached by Labit Laurent and Laurent Travers and captained by Les Bleus hooker William Servat, the French Barbarians began the first match with a try from Benjamin Lapeyre as early as the second minute and ultimately won 40–21. They were in even more dominant form four days later when the two teams met again with Castres fly half Pierre Bernard contributing 22 points in a 51–18 victory.

The South African Barbarians were also in action in 2012 as England toured the Rainbow Nation and, although they were beaten twice by the men in white, they scored eight tries in the two matches and were disgraced in neither contest.

The SA Barbarians South were the first to tackle the tourists in Kimberley and tries from JJ Engelbrecht, Hannes Franklin, Norman Nelson and substitute Ntabeni Dukisa gave the home supporters ample entertainment despite England's 54–26 win.

Six days later it was the turn of the SA Barbarians North to cross swords with the English, and in another high-scoring encounter the home side drew first blood in Potchefstroom with a try from Engelbrecht.

A brace from Shaun Venter gave them further reward for their endeavour and, although England proved too strong as the match unfolded, Deon Scholtz scored a fourth try late on in a 57–31 reverse.

RESULTS

11/10/2011	Barbarians	15–22	South of Scotland
26/11/2011	Barbarians	11–60	Australia
09/05/2012	Barbarians	40–7	Loughborough Students
27/05/2012	Barbarians	26–57	England
29/05/2012	Barbarians	29–28	Ireland
02/06/2012	Barbarians	21–30	Wales
13/06/2012	South African Barbarians South	26–54	England
19/06/2012	South African Barbarians North	31–57	England
20/06/2012	French Barbarians	40–21	Japan
24/06/2012	French Barbarians	51–18	Japan

THE BARBARIANS

The crowd look on as Clermont Auvergne and Leinster packs scrummage during their Heineken Cup match.

Getty Images

Elite Competitions

Alesana Tuilagi in action for Leicester Tigers in the Aviva Premiership.

Getty Images

QUINS SEAL MAIDEN TITLE

By Paul Morgan

Getty Images

Harlequins skipper Chris Robshaw lifts the Aviva Premiership trophy.

The **2011/12 Aviva** Premiership campaign will be remembered as a season of new beginnings. New champions, in Harlequins, and a new side emerging from the RFU Championship, London Welsh, to take their place at the top table of English rugby.

Harlequins captain Chris Robshaw lifted the Aviva Premiership trophy at Twickenham in May after a gruelling season, the Londoners becoming English champions for the first time in their history.

No one could begrudge the Quins their first title as they had led the table almost from start to finish, finally winning the Aviva Premiership Final 30-23 after a tense and dramatic clash with Leicester Tigers at the home of English rugby in front of an 81,779 crowd.

At the other end of the table the Newcastle Falcons fought relegation to the bitter end, before finally going down by one point, despite winning their final match against London Wasps, who finished one place above them in the final table.

Newcastle's demotion to the RFU Championship wasn't confirmed on the final day of the season as initially the Rugby Football Union rejected Championship winners London Welsh's application for promotion after their stadium failed the minimum standards set by the Union.

But the Exiles – as they had done on the field – fought hard against the decision and finally emerged triumphant from an RFU Appeal to take their place in the Aviva Premiership for the 2012/13 season, moving their home matches from Old Deer Park to the Kassam Stadium in Oxford.

Harlequins, to their credit, came to Twickenham, where many have resorted to a safety-first performance, refusing to abandon their free-flowing style in the final, and such adventure was rewarded with the silverware they coveted.

Tries in each half by wing Tom Williams and Robshaw – accompanied by 20 points from fly half Nick Evans's trusty right boot – saw Quins become the sixth different club to be crowned Premiership champions after Newcastle Falcons, Leicester Tigers, London Wasps, Sale Sharks and Saracens.

Evans kicked six penalties and a conversion, eclipsing his 19-year-old opposite number George Ford, whose 13-point haul included conversions of both Leicester tries by flanker Steve Mafi and centre Anthony Allen.

Leicester produced everything in their armoury to wrest the title away from Quins, scoring 10 unanswered points during the final quarter, but the Londoners had already done enough to deliver the perfect send-off for England captain Robshaw and many of his teammates who departed on a three-Test tour to South Africa soon after.

Robshaw deservedly took Man of the Match honours, and it was hard to question whether there had been a more influential player on the English rugby stage over the course of a season which had also seen the flanker captain England to second place in the RBS Six Nations.

The final victory completed a remarkable road to redemption for one of the most famous club teams in world rugby. Three years before they had become embroiled in the 'Bloodgate' saga, when they were found to have cheated in a Heineken Cup quarter-final by faking a blood substitution. But that was long forgotten as the players went on their unforgettable lap of honour at Twickenham.

Even amid those celebrations Robshaw was quick to remember the supporters who had stuck by Quins through thick and thin, immediately dedicating their first English title to them.

It was a remarkable journey for Harlequins, who have risen from the wreckage of the biggest scandal to hit English rugby to champions in the space of three years.

"The fans gave us a guard of honour coming in and it was emotional for myself and the other players who have been at the club for eight years now," Robshaw said. "Of course we have had our highs and lows, a bit of drama. It is nice to repay them."

Harlequins director of rugby Conor O'Shea has overseen the club's rise, which included winning the 2011 Amlin Challenge Cup and notable away victories at Munster and Toulouse.

Quins topped the Premiership table from the third week of the regular season and they completed a deserved win against Leicester Tigers in the final, with Danny Care and Joe Marler among their outstanding players.

"A couple of years ago this team said it wanted to create a different chapter in Quins history," O'Shea reflected. "It is a massive tribute to Dean [Richards, their former director of rugby], for putting so many of the structures in place, and a lot of people at the club, including the owners.

"It's a very special day for the club. I'm so proud of the effort of those players."

It was almost inevitable that Harlequins faced Leicester in that final as the Tigers had made their eighth successive Premiership Final appearance. But the most consistent English club in the professional era were left to contemplate another defeat at the final hurdle.

"We just needed to be a bit more composed," said director of rugby Richard Cockerill. "We will be better for the experience, but this wasn't a learning experience. We came here to win.

"We didn't and that was disappointing. That is sport. Someone has to lose and it is us, again. It is back-to-back finals. We are the only side that has been here eight times on the trot.

"It is not OK to come to a final and lose. We came here to win. We have lost back-to-back finals – but we have been in them, which is more than most sides.

"The Quins have been top of the league for most of the season and they played well today. In the end they probably deserved to win."

Saracens, the 2011 champions, were knocked out in the semi-finals by Leicester. Northampton also departed the competition at this stage after defeat against Quins. Both sides, though, had turned in some world-class displays to reach the final four.

Saracens didn't end the 2011/12 season without having set a new world-record attendance for a club rugby match when 83,761 people watched the Aviva Premiership encounter against Harlequins at Wembley in April.

The bumper crowd beat the previous world record of 82,208 fans that watched the Leinster versus Munster Heineken Cup semi-final in May 2009, as well as topping the recent Premiership record attendance of 82,000 at the Harlequins versus Saracens fixture in December 2011.

If Quins earned the plaudits for lifting the title it was Exeter Chiefs who were taken to the hearts of Premiership rugby, finishing in the top five for the first time in their history and qualifying for the Heineken Cup.

Sale Sharks also made it into the Heineken Cup but perhaps more significantly they left Edgeley Park in Stockport to play home matches at the modern Salford City Stadium, creating a big milestone in the proud history of the North West's premier club.

In London, Saracens also said farewell to their ground-sharing arrangement with Watford FC to take up residence in a brand new state-of-the-art stadium at the old Barnet Copthall Athletics Stadium. They will move into the Allianz Park in February 2013. The club predict that Allianz Park will become a unique venue for Premiership rugby, athletics and community sport. Incorporating an artificial turf pitch and an indoor training area, the new stadium will become a genuine community sports hub, used every day of the year and made available free of charge to local schools.

There was good news off the pitch to end the season with, the Premiership recording a 1.1 per cent season-on-season rise in attendances across the season, confirming an average attendance of 12,572, compared to 12,433 in 2010/11. This shows a remarkable rise in the last 12 years as back in the 1999/2000 season the average Premiership attendance was 5,476, a growth of 130 per cent.

"Facilities are the key to this rise. Compare our stadiums now to the way they were 12 years ago and many clubs are unrecognisable," said Premiership Rugby chief executive Mark McCafferty. "We've also managed to increase the number of sell outs, year on year, from 22 to 28 and it was only two months ago that Saracens and Harlequins set a new world record for a club game when 83,761 came to Wembley to watch their Aviva Premiership Rugby match. The Aviva Premiership Rugby final was a triumph as well with 81,779 packed into Twickenham. Everyone involved in Aviva Premiership Rugby, and all our partners, should be very proud."

September 3: **London Irish** 24–29 **Harlequins, Leicester Tigers** 28–30 **Exeter Chiefs, Worcester Warriors** 17–12 **Sale Sharks, Saracens** 15–20 **London Wasps, Newcastle Falcons** 9–22 **Bath Rugby;** September 4: **Northampton Saints** 26–24 **Gloucester Rugby;** September 9, **Harlequins** 26–13 **Northampton Saints. Sale Sharks** 30–29 **London Irish;** September 10: **Exeter Chiefs** 32–15 **Newcastle Falcons, Gloucester Rugby** 29–8 **Worcester Warriors, Bath Rugby** 26–28 **Saracens;** September 11: **London Wasps** 35–29 **Leicester Tigers;** September 17: **Harlequins** 42–6 **Gloucester Rugby, London Wasps** 18–29 **Sale Sharks, Northampton Saints** 13–14 **London Irish, Newcastle Falcons** 26–27 **Leicester Tigers, Bath Rugby** 23–19 **Exeter Chiefs;** September 18: **Saracens** 18–6 **Worcester Warriors;** September 23: **Sale Sharks** 29–21 **Northampton Saints;** September 24: **Leicester Tigers** 25–50 **Saracens, Gloucester Rugby** 23–6 **Bath Rugby, London Irish** 46–29 **Newcastle Falcons, Worcester Warriors** 15–17 **Harlequins;** September 25: **Exeter Chiefs** 21–11 **London Wasps;** September 30: **Worcester Warriors** 12–3 **Northampton Saints;** October 1: **Gloucester Rugby** 33–30 **London Irish, Exeter Chiefs** 13–17 **Saracens, Harlequins** 48–41 **Sale Sharks, Bath Rugby** 26–25 **Leicester Tigers;** October 2: **Newcastle Falcons** 15–10 **London Wasps;** October 8: **Northampton Saints** 33–3 **Exeter Chiefs, Sale Sharks** 13–11 **Gloucester Rugby, Leicester Tigers** 18–27 **Harlequins;** October 9: **London Irish** 42–24 **Worcester Warriors, London Wasps** 27–24 **Bath Rugby, Saracens** 25–5 **Newcastle Falcons;** October 28: **Sale Sharks** 13–34 **Leicester Tigers, Worcester Warriors** 12–14 **London Wasps;** October 29: **London Irish** 12–13 **Bath Rugby, Harlequins** 19–13 **Exeter Chiefs, Northampton Saints** 44–15 **Newcastle Falcons, Gloucester Rugby** 17–19 **Saracens;** November 4: **Newcastle Falcons** 16–16 **Worcester Warriors;** November 5, **Bath Rugby** 13–26 **Harlequins, Exeter Chiefs** 19–24 **Gloucester Rugby, Leicester Tigers** 24–24 **London Irish;** November 6: **London Wasps** 13–24 **Northampton Saints, Saracens** 23–10 **Sale Sharks;** November 25: **Sale Sharks** 23–30 **Exeter Chiefs, Worcester Warriors** 16–7 **Bath Rugby;** November 26: **Gloucester Rugby** 14–19 **Leicester Tigers, London Irish** 21–17 **London Wasps, Northampton Saints** 30–8 **Saracens;** November 27: **Harlequins** 39–8 **Newcastle Falcons;** December 2: **Newcastle Falcons** 26–25 **Gloucester Rugby;** December 3: **Bath Rugby** 13–16 **Sale Sharks, Leicester Tigers** 30–25 **Northampton Saints, Exeter Chiefs** 15–9 **Worcester Warriors;** December 4: **Saracens** 15–11 **London Irish, London Wasps** 16–22 **Harlequins;** December 24: **Northampton Saints** 22–13 **Bath Rugby;** December 26: **Sale Sharks** 27–19 **Newcastle Falcons, Gloucester Rugby** 39–10 **London Wasps;** December 27: **London Irish** 29–22 **Exeter Chiefs, Worcester Warriors** 13–32 **Leicester Tigers, Harlequins** 11–19 **Saracens;** December 31: **Newcastle Falcons** 14–32 **Northampton Saints, Exeter Chiefs** 9–11 **Harlequins;** January 1: **Bath Rugby** 30–3 **London Irish, London Wasps** 0–6 **Worcester Warriors, Saracens** 15–15 **Gloucester Rugby, Leicester Tigers** 28–23 **Sale Sharks;** January 6: **Northampton Saints** 24–3 **Harlequins;** January 7: **Worcester Warriors** 21–15 **Gloucester Rugby, Newcastle Falcons** 10–16 **Exeter Chiefs, Leicester Tigers** 29–11 **London Wasps;** January 8: **London Irish** 21–19 **Sale Sharks, Saracens** 26–19 **Bath Rugby;** February 10: **Sale Sharks** 15–12 **Worcester Warriors;** February 11: **Harlequins** 30–13 **London Irish, Bath Rugby** 30–24 **Newcastle Falcons, Gloucester Rugby** 27–24 **Northampton Saints, Exeter Chiefs** 19–11 **Leicester Tigers;** February 12: **London Wasps** 17–22 **Saracens;** February 18: **Bath Rugby** 11–14 **Gloucester Rugby, London Wasps** 12–15 **Exeter Chiefs, Newcastle Falcons** 19–10 **London Irish, Northampton Saints** 24–17 **Sale Sharks, Harlequins** 16–14 **Worcester Warriors;** February 19: **Saracens** 19–20 **Leicester Tigers;** February 24: **Sale Sharks** 46–34 **London Wasps, Worcester Warriors** 16–11 **Saracens;** February 25: **Leicester Tigers** 42–15 **Newcastle Falcons, Exeter Chiefs** 9–12 **Bath Rugby, Gloucester Rugby** 29–23 **Harlequins;** February 26: **London Irish** 23–30 **Northampton Saints;** March 2: **Newcastle Falcons** 9–9 **Harlequins;** March 3: **Bath Rugby** 36–17 **Worcester Warriors, Exeter Chiefs** 37–12 **Sale Sharks, London Wasps** 18–13 **London Irish;** March 4, **Leicester Tigers** 36–3 **Gloucester Rugby, Saracens** 18–12 **Northampton Saints;** March 23: **Sale Sharks** 9–45 **Saracens, Worcester Warriors** 19–9 **Newcastle Falcons;** March 24: **Harlequins** 14–6 **Bath Rugby, Gloucester Rugby** 27–28 **Exeter Chiefs, Northampton Saints** 32–15 **London Wasps;** March 25: **London Irish** 32–41

Leicester Tigers; March 30: **Leicester Tigers** 43–13 **Worcester Warriors, Newcastle Falcons** 22–19 **Sale Sharks**; March 31: **Exeter Chiefs** 18–11 **London Irish, Saracens** 19–24 **Harlequins, Bath Rugby** 6–26 **Northampton Saints**; April 1: **London Wasps** 26–24 **Gloucester Rugby**; April 13: **Sale Sharks** 16–9 **Bath Rugby**; April 14: **Northampton Saints** 21–35 **Leicester Tigers, Gloucester Rugby** 20–29 **Newcastle Falcons, London Irish** 19–28 **Saracens, Worcester Warriors** 26–31 **Exeter Chiefs, Harlequins** 33–17 **London Wasps**; April 20: **Newcastle Falcons** 3–9 **Saracens**; April 21: **Bath Rugby** 17–12 **London Wasps, Gloucester Rugby** 19–24 **Sale Sharks, Worcester Warriors** 16–25 **London Irish, Harlequins** 33–43 **Leicester Tigers**; April 22: **Exeter Chiefs** 15–18 **Northampton Saints**; May 5: **Leicester Tigers** 28–3 **Bath Rugby, London Irish** 52–18 **Gloucester Rugby, London Wasps** 10–14 **Newcastle Falcons, Northampton Saints** 42–14 **Worcester Warriors, Sale Sharks** 10–24 **Harlequins, Saracens** 40–22 **Exeter Chiefs**

	P	W	D	L	F	A	BP	PTS
Harlequins	22	17	1	4	526	389	5	75
Leicester Tigers	22	15	1	6	647	475	12	74
Saracens	22	16	1	5	489	350	7	73
Northampton Saints	22	14	0	8	539	374	9	65
Exeter Chiefs	22	12	0	10	436	421	11	59
Sale Sharks	22	10	0	12	453	538	9	49
London Irish	22	8	1	13	514	516	12	46
Bath Rugby	22	9	0	13	365	412	8	44
Gloucester Rugby	22	8	1	13	456	507	10	44
Worcester Warriors	22	7	1	14	322	448	6	36
London Wasps	22	6	0	16	363	502	9	33
Newcastle Falcons	22	6	2	14	351	529	4	32

ELITE COMPETITIONS

SEMI-FINALS

12 May, Twickenham Stoop, London

HARLEQUINS 25 (1G 6PG) NORTHAMPTON SAINTS 23 (1T 6PG)

HARLEQUINS: M Brown; T Williams, G Lowe, J Turner-Hall, S Smith; N Evans, K Dickson; J Marler, J Gray, J Johnston, O Kohn, G Robson, M Fa'asavalu, C Robshaw (captain), N Easter

SUBSTITUTIONS: T Guest for Fa'asavalu (68 mins); M Hopper for Smith (69 mins)

SCORERS: *Try:* Marler *Conversion:* Evans *Penalty Goals:* Evans (6)

NORTHAMPTON: B Foden; V Artemyev, G Pisi, J Downey, P Diggin; R Lamb, L Dickson (captain); S Tonga'uiha, A Long, B Mujati, M Sorenson, C Day, J Craig, P Dowson, R Wilson

SUBSTITUTIONS: P Doran-Jones for Mujati (57 mins); R McMillan for Long (62 mins); A Waller for Tonga'uiha (65 mins); T Harrison for Craig (65 mins); B Nutley for Wilson (77 mins)

SCORERS: *Tries:* Dickson *Penalty Goals:* Lamb (6)

YELLOW CARD: R Wilson

REFEREE: A Small

12 May 2012, Welford Road, Leicester

LEICESTER 24 (1G 1T 4PG) SARACENS 15 (5PG)

LEICESTER: G Murphy (captain); H Agulla, M Tuilagi, A Allen, A Tuilagi; G Ford, B Youngs; M Ayerza, G Chuter, D Cole; G Skivington, G Parling; S Mafi, C Newby, T Waldrom

SUBSTITUTION: M Castrogiovanni for Cole (58 mins)

SCORERS: *Tries:* Tuilagi, Mafi *Conversion:* Ford *Penalty Goals:* Ford (4)

SARACENS: A Goode; D Strettle, O Farrell, B Barritt, C Wyles; C Hodgson, N De Kock; R Gill, S Brits, M Stevens; S Borthwick (captain), M Botha; J Wray, W Fraser, E Joubert

SUBSTITUTIONS: C Nieto for Stevens (62 mins); G Kruis for Botha; J Short for Strettle (66 mins); A Powell for Barritt (78 mins); J Smit for Gill; J George for Brits (78 mins)

SCORERS: *Penalty Goals:* Farrell (5)

REFEREE: D Pearson

AVIVA PREMIERSHIP

FINAL

HARLEQUINS 30 (1G 1T 6PG) LEICESTER TIGERS 23 (2G 3PG)

HARLEQUINS: M Brown; T Williams, G Lowe, J Turner-Hall, U Monye; N Evans, D Care; J Marler, J Gray, J Johnston, O Kohn, G Robson, M Fa'asavalu, C Robshaw (captain), N Easter

SUBSTITUTIONS: T Guest for Fa'asavalu (72 mins); R Clegg for Evans (76 mins)

SCORERS: *Tries:* Williams, Robshaw *Conversion:* Evans *Penalty Goals:* Evans (6)

LEICESTER: G Murphy (captain); H Agulla, M Tuilagi, A Allen, A Tuilagi; G Ford, B Youngs; M Ayerza, G Chuter, D Cole, G Skivington, G Parling, S Mafi, J Salvi, T Waldrom

SUBSTITUTIONS: M Castrogiovanni for Cole (55 mins); T Youngs for Chuter (61 mins); L Mulipola for Agulla (73 mins); G Kitchener for Skivington (73 mins); S Hamilton for Ayerza (73 mins); B Twelvetrees for Ford (73 mins);

SCORERS: *Tries:* Mafi, Allen *Conversions:* Ford (2) *Penalty Goals:* Ford (3)

YELLOW CARD: Waldrom (38 mins)

REFEREE: W Barnes

TOULOUSE TRIUMPHANT AGAIN

by Iain Spragg

Toulouse hold aloft the Bouclier de Brennus for the third time in five years.

The unerringly accurate boot of Luke McAlister ensured Toulouse continued their recent stranglehold on the Top 14 as the New Zealander kicked all his side's points in an 18–12 win over Toulon in Paris, a result which handed the club a record 19th Bouclier de Brennus and further underlined the Red and Blacks' status as the most successful club in the history of French rugby.

Six penalties from McAlister proved decisive as Toulouse eventually overcame the spirited challenge of Toulon, the nouveau riche of the French game, in front of a 79,612-strong crowd at the Stade de France to give Guy Noves' defending champions a third domestic crown in five seasons and their fourth title triumph since the turn of the century.

Toulon, in contrast, were searching for their first league silverware for 20 years, but four penalties from former England fly half Jonny Wilkinson were not quite enough to stop the Toulouse juggernaut in its tracks as Bernard Laporte's team paid a heavy price for failing to gain parity up front.

For Noves, victory completed a personal hat-trick of final triumphs over Rugby Club Toulonnais after featuring as a player for Toulouse in a 36–22 win in 1985 and then working on the club's coaching staff four years later when they beat Toulon in the Parc des Princes for a second time.

"I look at the young players and the whole of my staff enjoying it and being rewarded for their hard work," said Noves after his team had lifted the trophy. "We're used to very good things and we want to repeat them.

"But it was tough until the final whistle today. We could have lost at the end and conceded a converted try. I'm a little disappointed because it wasn't a beautiful final but with finals, well, you have to win them and that's it."

It was certainly no great surprise that Toulouse reached the final for a second successive season. The defending champions after their 15-10 win over Montpellier in 2011, Noves' team were once again in convincing form throughout the 26 games of the regular Top 14 campaign and, despite suffering a surprising loss to Bayonne at the Stade Jean Duager on the opening day, they were beaten just five more times over the next nine months and eventually finished top of the table to guarantee themselves home advantage in the semi-finals.

Clermont, the 2010 champions, finished level with Toulouse on 87 points but garnered fewer bonus points in the process. This placed Les Jaunards second, but they still went through to the last four automatically and were spared the inconvenience of playing an extra game at the truncated quarter-final stage of the competition.

That fate fell to the next four sides in the final table and the semi-final line-up was decided after Castres had despatched Montpellier 31–15 at the Stade Ernest Wallon and Toulon defeated Racing Métro 17–13 at the Stade Mayol 24 hours later.

The first semi-final saw Toulouse cross swords with Castres and, although the clash at the Stadium de Toulouse did not yield a try from either side, it was not lacking in incident and tension and, had the visitors been able to capitalise on the home team's early indiscipline, then the result could have been different.

The closing stages of the first half saw yellow cards for Toulouse centre Florian Fritz and wing Timoci Matanavou, as well as a spectacular try-saving tackle from Vincent Clerc on centre Max Evans, but Castres accumulated only six points while they enjoyed their numerical advantage.

Toulouse were 15–12 up at the break but once they were restored to their full complement in the second period they began to dominate, pulling away with three McAlister penalties – taking his tally for the match to six – and Castres were condemned to a 24–15 defeat.

The second semi-final between Clermont and Toulon at the same venue the following day also failed to produce a try but was arguably even more dramatic as the result hung in the balance until the final kick of the match.

The first half saw Wilkinson and Clermont's Morgan Parra trade penalties and they continued what seemed increasingly like a personal duel throughout the second period, with Parra landing a 73rd-minute shot at goal to level the scores at 12–12.

Thoughts inevitably began to turn to the prospect of extra-time, but when Wilkinson responded four minutes later with his fifth penalty to give Toulon a three-point advantage it appeared as though the contest was finally over.

Parra, however, had one last chance from distance in the dying seconds and, although his effort was on target, it fell agonisingly short and Toulon could begin celebrating a 15–12 triumph.

The day of the final itself did not begin well for Toulouse when Noves' starting XV was blighted by injury and at the 11th hour he was forced to withdraw prop Jean-Baptiste Poux and wing Yves Donguy – drafting in Gurthro Steenkamp and Matanavou – but the late changes proved a mere distraction rather than a disaster for the defending champions.

The pattern of the game was established early on when Wilkinson was on target with a penalty in the opening minute, but Toulon's lead lasted all of two minutes before McAlister returned the favour. The New Zealander then put Toulouse in front on 21 minutes but two further successful kicks from the English No.10 and another from the Kiwi saw the two teams retreat to the dressing room at half-time locked at 9–9.

It became 12–12 soon after the restart, but tempers flared shortly after when hooker William Servat, playing his last game for Toulouse, and his opposite number Sébastien Bruno were both sin-binned. The balance decisively swung in the favour of Noves' side when prop Davit Kubriashvili was yellow carded just after the hour for repeated infringements at the scrum, and Toulon never fully recovered.

While Kubriashvili watched disconsolately from the bench, McAlister duly slotted his fifth and sixth penalties of the match to take his team 18–12 clear and, although Toulon created two presentable chances in the closing stages to reduce the arrears, the Toulouse defence held firm and the Bouclier de Brennus was theirs again.

"Congratulations to Toulouse," said Laporte, who had only replaced Philippe Saint-Andre as head coach in September. "They finished the season in top position and I cannot argue with the result. When you are dominated as we were at the scrum, it would have been a remarkable feat to have won.

"There are always regrets but if you had told me when I arrived at the club last year that we would be playing in a Top 14 final, I would have been happy. The players have had a great season and they deserve credit for that. They have shown pride in the team and the community and they did not give up, even when we were down to 14 men."

Victory, however, was a fairytale end to the glittering career of former France hooker Servat, a loyal servant to Toulouse for 13 years and a five-time Top 14 champion with the club.

"To finish with the title is amazing," Servat said after the match. "I dread to think how it would have felt if the result had been different. I tried to play the game like a final because it was important to play for the whole group and not for myself. I feel a lot of happiness, a lot of pride to have participated in so many great things with the club. This group of players are really extraordinary."

TOP 14 2011/12 RESULTS

26 August, 2011: **Bayonne** 18 **Toulouse** 13, **Brive** 19 **Agen** 20, **Clermont** 22 **Lyon** 13, **Perpignan** 25 **Castres** 6, **Racing** 30 **Montpellier** 22, **Stade Français** 41 **Bordeaux** 20. 27 August: **Toulon** 30 **Biarritz** 5. 3 September: **Biarritz** 9 **Agen** 9, **Castres** 35 **Stade Français** 10, **Montpellier** 12 **Brive** 28, **Racing** 47 **Perpignan** 23, **Toulon** 0 **Clermont** 17, **Bordeaux** 18 **Bayonne** 6. 4 September: **Lyon** 9 **Toulouse** 19. 9 September: **Agen** 24 **Lyon** 18, **Bayonne** 12 **Toulon** 12, **Biarritz** 18 **Castres** 23, **Clermont** 34 **Bordeaux** 6, **Perpignan** 12 **Brive** 9, **Stade Français** 19 **Montpellier** 19. 10 September: **Toulouse** 41 **Racing** 36. 16 September: **Bordeaux** 16 **Toulon** 27, **Brive** 12 **Lyon** 15, **Castres** 30 **Agen** 11, **Perpignan** 19 **Montpellier** 12, **Stade Français** 33 **Bayonne** 18, **Toulouse** 24 **Biarritz** 0. 17 September: **Racing** 11 **Clermont** 22. 23 September: **Biarritz** 24 **Perpignan** 29, **Castres** 30 **Brive** 24, **Clermont** 19 **Bayonne** 13, **Montpellier** 16 **Bordeaux** 20, **Racing** 25 **Lyon** 12, **Agen** 23 **Toulouse** 24. 24 September: **Toulon** 34 **Stade Français** 8. 30 September: **Bayonne** 27 **Racing** 23, **Bordeaux** 11 **Biarritz** 13, **Lyon** 16 **Castres** 18, **Perpignan** 12 **Agen** 19, **Stade Français** 28 **Brive** 17, **Montpellier** 19 **Toulon** 6. 1 October: **Toulouse** 22 **Clermont** 9. 14 October: **Bayonne** 17

Montpellier 26, Bordeaux 22 Racing 18, Brive 32 Biarritz 7, Clermont 29 Agen 13, Castres 24 Toulouse 3. 15 October: Toulon 38 Perpignan 0. 16 October: Lyon 18 Stade Français 6. 21 October: Perpignan 3 Clermont 39. 22 October: Agen 37 Stade Français 13, Biarritz 15 Lyon 15, Brive 30 Bayonne 10, Montpellier 16 Castres 21, Toulouse 56 Bordeaux 6, Racing 9 Toulon 16. 28 October: Castres 19 Racing 23. 29 October: Bayonne 18 Perpignan 16, Clermont 41 Biarritz 0, Toulon 18 Brive 3, Toulouse 18 Stade Français 15, Agen 18 Montpellier 12. 4 November: Brive 12 Racing 18. 5 November: Toulouse 21 Perpignan 17, Bordeaux 24 Castres 9, Stade Français 37 Clermont 16. 25 November: Bayonne 15 Lyon 9, Racing 28 Biarritz 9, Perpignan 16 Stade Français 35. 26 November: Brive 9 Toulouse 9, Montpellier 29 Clermont 23, Castres 22 Toulon 22, Agen 24 Bordeaux 15. 29 November: Biarritz 21 Bayonne 19. 30 November: Lyon 10 Montpellier 30. 2 December: Bordeaux 16 Brive 12. 3 December: Toulouse 33 Toulon 12, Clermont 33 Castres 16, Stade Français 29 Racing 3. 4 December: Agen 37 Bayonne 18, Lyon 19 Perpignan 12, Biarritz 23 Montpellier 30. 13 December: Toulon 34 Agen 12. 23 December: Brive 6 Clermont 9, Bayonne 16 Castres 16, Perpignan 38 Bordeaux 13, Stade Français 23 Biarritz 10, Toulon 20 Lyon 15, Racing 26 Agen 8, Montpellier 25 Toulouse 45. 30 December: Toulouse 30 Bayonne 15. 31 December: Montpellier 29 Racing 14, Agen 19 Brive 9, Bordeaux 39 Stade Français 6, Castres 33 Perpignan 6, Lyon 6 Clermont 6, Biarritz 25 Toulon 6. 6 January, 2012: Agen 6 Biarritz 15. 7 January: Bayonne 20 Bordeaux 27, Brive 9 Montpellier 23, Stade Français 38 Castres 21, Toulouse 51 Lyon 10, Perpignan 14 Racing 14. 8 January: Clermont 25 Toulon 19. 27 January: Montpellier 38 Stade Français 6. 28 January: Brive 17 Perpignan 9, Castres 29 Biarritz 23, Lyon 19 Agen 11, Toulon 50 Bayonne 10, Racing 13 Toulouse 19, Bordeaux 10 Clermont 17. 3 February: Bordeaux 31 Lyon 10. 10 February: Montpellier 22 Perpignan 11, Biarritz 15 Toulouse 20. 11 February: Bayonne 26 Stade Français 20, Toulon 44 Bordeaux 7, Clermont 31 Racing 13. 17 February: Perpignan 25 Biarritz 6. 18 February: Bayonne 22 Clermont 22, Bordeaux 26 Montpellier 30, Brive 13 Castres 15, Lyon 22 Racing 33, Toulouse 21 Agen 10, Stade Français 19 Toulon 19. 24 February: Lyon 9 Brive 22. 2 March: Agen 23 Castres 12, Toulon 19 Montpellier 6. 3 March: Agen 22 Perpignan 17, Biarritz 38 Bordeaux 13, Brive 25 Stade Français 9, Racing 22 Bayonne 21, Clermont 35 Toulouse 5, Castres 6 Lyon 6. 9 March: Racing 22 Bordeaux 13. 10 March: Toulouse 34 Castres 27, Agen 20 Clermont 29, Biarritz 26 Brive 11, Montpellier 37 Bayonne 26, Stade Français 40 Lyon 19, Perpignan 22 Toulon 22. 23 March: Bordeaux 18 Toulouse 17. 24 March: Castres 27 Montpellier 18, Clermont 29 Perpignan 23, Lyon 17 Biarritz 34, Stade Français 53 Agen 27, Toulon 32 Racing 20, Bayonne 19 Brive 12. 30 March: Racing 27 Castres 16. 31 March: Biarritz 15 Clermont 14, Brive 14 Toulon 9, Lyon 24 Bordeaux 13, Montpellier 44 Agen 18, Perpignan 47 Bayonne 9. 13 April: Stade Français 18 Toulouse 22, Perpignan 25 Toulouse 10. 14 April: Agen 22 Toulon 13, Clermont 25 Stade Français 9, Montpellier 43 Lyon 12, Racing 40 Brive 19, Bayonne 24 Biarritz 19, Castres 44 Bordeaux 20. 20 April: Clermont 22 Montpellier 9. 21 April: Bordeaux 29 Agen 15, Lyon 19 Bayonne 20, Stade Français 35 Perpignan 31, Toulouse 30 Brive 21, Biarritz 22 Racing 13, Toulon 25 Castres 25. 4 May: Montpellier 21 Biarritz 16. 5 May: Toulon 25 Toulouse 22, Bayonne 31 Agen 10, Brive 9 Bordeaux 23, Castres 30 Clermont 19, Perpignan 34 Lyon 22, Racing 19 Stade Français 13. 12 May: Agen 25 Racing 22, Biarritz 16 Stade Français 5, Bordeaux 37 Perpignan 29, Castres 31 Bayonne 29, Clermont 57 Brive 14, Lyon 5 Toulon 29, Toulouse 20 Montpellier 13.

FINAL TABLE

	P	W	D	L	F	A	BP	PTS
Toulouse	26	19	1	6	629	448	9	87
Clermont	26	19	2	5	644	364	7	87
Toulon	26	14	5	7	581	393	7	73
Castres	26	14	4	8	585	522	5	69
Montpellier	26	14	1	11	601	505	9	67
Racing Metro	26	13	1	12	569	538	10	64
Stade Français	26	11	2	13	568	588	10	58
Bordeaux	26	12	0	14	493	619	5	53
Biarritz	26	10	2	14	424	518	8	52
Agen	26	12	1	13	479	573	2	52
Perpignan	26	9	2	15	515	578	9	49
Bayonne	26	9	3	14	479	619	6	48
Brive	26	7	1	18	408	488	12	42
Lyon	26	5	3	18	369	591	5	31

Matthew Lewis/Getty Images

Toulon managed to overcome Clermont in a closely-fought semi-final.

ELITE COMPETITIONS

25 May, 2012
Castres 31 Montpellier 15
26 May, 2012
Toulon 17 Racing Metro 13

SEMI-FINALS

2 June, Stadium de Toulouse, Toulouse

TOULOUSE 24 (7PG 1DG) CASTRES 15 (4PG 1DG)

TOULOUSE: C Poitrenaud; V Clerc, F Fritz, L McAlister, T Matanavou; L Beauxis, J-M Doussain; J-P Poux, W Servat, C Johnston, Y Maestri, P Albacete, J Bouilhou, T Dusautoir (captain), L Picamoles

SUBSTITUTIONS: G Steenkamp for Poux (40 mins); L Burgess for Doussain (53 mins); Y David for Beauxis (53 mins); R Millo-Chluski for Maestri (63 mins); Y Jauzion for Poitrenaud (72 mins); G Lamboley for Bouilhou (72 mins); Y Montes for Johnston (72 mins); C Tolofua for Servat (77 mins)

SCORERS: *Penalty Goals:* McAlister (6), Beauxis *Drop Goal:* Beauxis

YELLOW CARDS: F Fritz (32 mins); T Matanavou (36 mins)

CASTRES: R Teulet; R Martial, M Evans, R Cabannes, M Andreu; P Bernard, T Lacrampe; Y Forestier, M Bonello, L Ducalcon, M Rolland, J Tekori, I Diarra, Y Caballero, C Masoe (captain)

SUBSTITUTIONS: S Taumoepeau for Ducalcon (54 mins); M-A Rallier for Bonello (54 mins); K Wihongi for Forestier (54 mins); R Kockott for Lacrampe (56 mins); R Capo Ortega for Rolland (62 mins); T Sanchou for Martial (68 mins); S Baikeinuku for Cabannes (68 mins); J Bornman for Diarra (71 mins)

SCORERS: *Penalty Goals:* Bernard (3) Teulet *Drop Goal:* Bernard

REFEREE: J Garces (France)

TOP 14

3 June, Stadium de Toulouse, Toulouse

CLERMONT AUVERGNE 12 (4PG)
TOULON 15 (5PG)

CLERMONT AUVERGNE: J-M Buttin; S Nakaitaci, A Rougerie (captain), W Fofana, S Sivivatu; B James, M Parra; T Domingo, B Kayser, D Zirakashvili, J Cudmore, N Hines, J Bardy, A Lapandry

SUBSTITUTIONS: E Vermeulen for Bardy (43 mins); T Paulo for Kayser (52 mins); J Pierre for Cudmore (56 mins); D Skrela for James (57 mins); V Debaty for Domingo (57 mins); L Byrne for Buttin (67 mins); D Kotze for Zirakashvili (67 mins)

SCORERS: *Penalty Goals:* Parra (4)

TOULON: L Rooney; A Palisson, M Bastareaud, M Giteau, D Smith; J Wilkinson, S Tillous-Borde; E Roberts, S Bruno, D Kubriashvili, B Botha, S Shaw, J van Niekerk (captain), S Armitage, JM Fernandez Lobbe

SUBSTITUTIONS: J Orioli for Bruno (50 mins); L Emmanuelli for Roberts (55 mins); C Samson for Shaw (56 mins); P Gunther for van Niekerk (68 mins); B Lapeyre for Palisson (71 mins)

SCORERS: *Penalty Goals:* Wilkinson (5)

REFEREE: P Gauzere (France)

FINAL

9 June, Stade de France, Paris

TOULOUSE 18 (6PG) TOULON (4PG) 12

TOULOUSE: C Poitrenaud; V Clerc, Y David, F Fritz, T Matanavou; L McAlister, J-M Doussain; G Steenkamp, W Servat, C Johnston, Y Maestri, P Albacete, J Bouilhou, T Dusautoir (captain), L Picamoles

SUBSTITUTIONS: L Burgess for Doussain (50 mins); C Tolofua for Bouilhou (temp 53 to 62 mins); Y Jauzion for David (61 mins); Y Nyanga Kabasele for Bouilhou (68 mins); L Beauxis for McAlister (70 mins); D Human for Steenkamp (76 mins); G Lamboley for Maestri (76 mins)

SCORERS: *Penalty Goals:* McAlister (6)

YELLOW CARD: W Servat (51 mins)

TOULON: B Lapeyre; A Palisson, M Bastareaud, M Giteau, D Smith; J Wilkinson, S Tillous-Borde; E Roberts, S Bruno, D Kubriashvili, B Botha, S Shaw, J van Niekerk (captain), S Armitage, JM Fernandez Lobbe

SUBSTITUTIONS: M Ivaldi for van Niekerk (temp 53 to 62 mins); C Samson for Shaw (61 mins); Ivaldi for van Niekerk (68 mins); P Gunther for Bruno (68 mins); L Chilachava for Gunther (70 mins); Gunther for Kubriashvili (73 mins); L Emmanuelli for Roberts (74 mins)

SCORERS: *Penalty Goals:* Wilkinson (4)

YELLOW CARDS: S Bruno (51 mins); D Kubriashvili (63 mins)

REFEREE: R Poite (France)

WILLIAMS SIGNS OFF IN STYLE

by Iain Spragg

INPHO

Shane Williams of the Ospreys holds aloft the RaboDirect PRO12 trophy.

Shane Williams scored a fairytale farewell try for the Ospreys in the final of the RaboDirect PRO12 against Leinster to clinch a thrilling 31-30 win in Dublin and crown the Welsh region champions for a record fourth time.

Playing his final competitive game for the Ospreys before departing for Japan after nine years on the wing, Williams raced over for his second try of the match two minutes before full-time to snatch a dramatic win for Steve Tandy's side at the RDS Arena and in the process deny the Irish province an unprecedented PRO12 and Heineken Cup double.

In a repeat of the 2010 final, which the Welshmen won 17–12, the

Ospreys once again proved too strong for Leinster in front of a partisan Dublin crowd but left it late to clinch victory in a match in which they trailed for 52 of the 80 minutes of play.

Leinster seemed to have prevailed when wing Isa Nacewa went over just after the hour to establish a 30–21 lead, but Williams's late try, which required confirmation from the TMO before it was awarded, a superb conversion from wide on the right from fly half Dan Biggar and some dogged defence were enough to give the Ospreys a second title in three years.

"I think it is testament to the team, the whole group and backroom staff and everyone involved in the organisation," said Tandy after lifting the first silverware of his short four-month reign as the Ospreys head coach.

"The team have been fantastic since I have taken over, and in fairness the boys were relentless. We probably thought we were out of the game today, but the guys dug deep. Some things were a bit frantic out there but we stuck with what we were trying to achieve. I think it is great for the Ospreys and what a great way to finish the season."

Ironically, the campaign began in early September with an opening day meeting at the Liberty Stadium between the two eventual finalists and, in sharp contrast to the final itself, the clash proved a one-side affair as the Ospreys cantered to a comfortable 27–3 victory with a brace of tries from scrum half Rhys Webb and further scores from wing Hanno Dirksen and flanker Justin Tipuric.

The Welsh side completed the league double over their Irish rivals in March with a narrow 23–22 triumph in Dublin, but Leinster proved far more consistent over the course of the whole campaign and lost just three times in 26 outings to top the table, 10 points clear of Tandy's team in second. They were joined in the knockout phase by third-placed Munster and Glasgow, who were looking to become the first Scottish side to claim the title.

The first semi-final pitted the Ospreys against three-time champions Munster in Swansea. Most neutrals predicted a tense and tight encounter at the Liberty Stadium, but it was actually a surprisingly one-sided affair.

Munster struck first when fly half Ian Keatley scored a try after just three minutes, but the remaining 77 minutes were one-way traffic as the Ospreys comprehensively dismantled the visitors, scoring five tries to record a thumping 45–10 win.

The star of the show was Biggar with the first Ospreys' try in the rout, and he also contributed 20 points with the boot, while Kahn Fotuali'i, Dirksen, Andrew Bishop and Webb also crossed for the home side.

"I thought it was a great performance and to beat Munster is always good," Tandy said. "I thought the defence was key as Munster did put us under pressure, but we turned the ball over and when we did that we did execute and secure the points.

"Even when we were two or three tries up still the defence didn't want to give Munster any easy points and made them work for everything. It was a really good night for us. I thought the supporters were unbelievable, but we can't get ahead of ourselves as we have a final now to hopefully go and win."

The following day Leinster welcomed Glasgow to the RDS and a cagey, cautious first half yielded a modest 12 points as three penalties from fly half Johnny Sexton to a single effort from opposite number Duncan Weir gave Joe Schmidt's home side a 9–3 advantage.

The second half, however, was more expansive and Leinster seemed to have settled the contest when wing Dave Kearney raced over for the first try of the game on 66 minutes. Sexton successfully converted to make it 19–3 to the Irish side, but Glasgow refused to buckle and late scores from substitute hooker Dougie Hall and full back Stuart Hogg reduced the arrears to four points. Had there been time left after Hogg's score, the Scottish side may have completed a miraculous escape.

"They never gave up and the defensive effort on the line was outstanding," said Glasgow head coach Sean Lineen after his side's 19–15 loss. "You can't keep soaking up and soaking up the tackles and it told in the end. We will take some consolation that the guys never gave up and came back to score a couple of tries, but as I say, it was too little, too late.

"We are out of the competition, and the guys are really disappointed there. We didn't really do it any justice in the first half and we kept giving them the ball back."

The stage was now set for the final, and Leinster went into the match just eight days after beating Ulster 42–14 in the Heineken Cup Final, with Schmidt's team on the verge of becoming the first team ever to win the PRO12 and be crowned European champions in the same season.

A capacity crowd of more than 18,000 crammed into the RDS to witness Leinster's attempt to make history, but it was the Ospreys who were quickest out of the blocks with an early Biggar penalty. Sexton replied with the boot minutes later, but it was not long before the first try of the contest, hooker Sean Cronin bulldozing over in the 22nd minute to put Leinster in the driving seat.

A second Leinster try from Nacewa before the break twisted the knife and, although the referee yellow carded loosehead Heinke van der Merwe just before the end of the half, when the whistle sounded the home side enjoyed an important, if not impregnable, 17–9 lead.

The Ospreys were under the cosh but, with the luxury of a man advantage as the match restarted, they struck. Full back Richard Fussell made the initial break and, although he was hauled down short, centre Ashley Beck was on hand to collect the offload and speed over.

The rest of the match ebbed and flowed. Two further Sexton penalties eased Leinster back out in front but when Williams squeezed in at the corner after 59 minutes, the Welsh side thought they were back in business only to see Nacewa wriggle over for his second try. Sexton converted and Leinster were nine points to the good.

The clock seemed to be Leinster's friend, but the sin-binning of substitute prop Nathan White on 72 minutes proved critical. Biggar punished Irish indiscipline with his fourth penalty, but the real body blow came six minutes later when Williams was on the end of a flowing Ospreys attack wide right, ducking out of Rob Kearney's attempted tackle for the score. Welsh supporters held their breath as they waited for the television match official to verify the try, but when the call came through and Biggar held his nerve to slot the difficult conversion, the Ospreys were champions again.

"I am pretty gutted, obviously," admitted Schmidt after the game. "We knew that it was going to be tough, and we had to be in front in the back half of the game. The yellow cards mean you have to overwork a little bit. We fell off a couple of tight tackles and maybe just didn't have things bounce our way.

"I thought it was a superb kick by Dan Biggar from the edge, and it was pretty much the same thing he did to us last time to get a one-point win here in March. There was always going to be a little bit of fatigue. I think you get more fatigue when you are down to 14 men twice in the half."

Schmidt's disappointment was in sharp contrast to Williams's joy, and the Wales legend probably could not have enjoyed a more emotional send-off had the 35-year-old written the script himself.

His second and pivotal try in the final took his career tally for the Ospreys to 57 in 141 competitive appearances and, having played a major role in the team's three previous Celtic League triumphs, it was fitting he would say goodbye to the region after a fourth success in the competition.

"I will never forget this day," he said. "I've had a great time with the Ospreys, and what a fantastic way to hang my boots up. We've shown that we can compete with the likes of Leinster. They are probably the best European side ever, but we can come to the RDS and play a full-strength side and come away with a victory under pressure. That's the sign of a good team.

"I enjoy success, of course, like anybody else. The one you remember is the latest one and this is a great way for me to finish."

RABODIRECT PRO12 2011/12 RESULTS

2 September 2011: **Ospreys** 27 **Leinster** 3, **Ulster** 28 **Glasgow** 14, **Edinburgh** 15 **Blues** 38. 3 September: **Treviso** 9 **Connacht** 11, **Munster** 20 **Dragons** 12. 4 September: **Scarlets** 32 **Aironi** 9. 9 September: **Glasgow** 12 **Munster** 23, **Leinster** 31 **Dragons** 10. 10 September: **Aironi** 19 **Ulster** 25, **Connacht** 13 **Scarlets** 11, **Ospreys** 26 **Edinburgh** 19. 11 September: **Blues** 33 **Treviso** 18. 16 September: **Ulster** 20 **Blues** 3, **Edinburgh** 19 **Connacht** 14. 17 September: **Treviso** 27 **Ospreys** 32, **Leinster** 19 **Glasgow** 23, **Dragons** 23 **Aironi** 14, **Munster** 35 **Scarlets** 12. 23 September: **Blues** 13 **Munster** 18, **Connacht** 17 **Dragons** 13, **Glasgow** 13 **Treviso** 15. 24 September: **Aironi** 25 **Edinburgh** 19, **Scarlets** 10 **Leinster** 15. 25 September: **Ospreys** 32 **Ulster** 14. 30 September: **Dragons** 22 **Ulster** 9, **Edinburgh** 29 **Munster** 14, **Ospreys** 26 **Connacht** 21. 1 October: **Treviso** 20 **Scarlets** 10, **Leinster** 26 **Aironi** 7, **Blues** 13 **Glasgow** 34. 7 October: **Scarlets** 33 **Edinburgh** 17, **Ulster** 12 **Treviso** 23, **Glasgow** 24 **Dragons** 19. 8 October: **Aironi** 26 **Blues** 37, **Leinster** 30 **Connacht** 20, **Munster** 35 **Ospreys** 17. 28 October: **Glasgow** 28 **Ospreys** 17, **Edinburgh** 28 **Leinster** 36, **Munster** 18 **Aironi** 6. 29 October: **Treviso** 50 **Dragons** 24, **Scarlets** 24 **Ulster** 17, **Connacht** 20 **Blues** 26. 4 November: **Leinster** 24 **Munster** 19. 5 November: **Aironi** 6 **Glasgow** 18, **Treviso** 11 **Edinburgh** 22, **Ulster** 22 **Connacht** 3, **Ospreys** 9 **Scarlets** 9. 24 November: **Blues** 38 **Aironi** 0. 25 November: **Scarlets** 22 **Dragons** 12, **Glasgow** 17 **Ulster** 9. 26 November: **Treviso** 20 **Leinster** 30, **Connacht** 6 **Ospreys** 17, **Munster** 34 **Edinburgh** 17. 2 December: **Ulster** 24 **Scarlets** 17, **Connacht** 13 **Treviso** 15, **Edinburgh** 50 **Aironi** 10, **Leinster** 52 **Blues** 9. 3 December: **Ospreys** 19 **Munster** 13. 4 December: **Dragons** 14 **Glasgow** 14. 23 December: **Aironi** 27 **Treviso** 13, **Blues** 28 **Dragons** 9. 26 December: **Scarlets** 22 **Ospreys** 14, **Leinster** 42 **Ulster** 13, **Edinburgh** 23 **Glasgow** 23, **Munster** 24 **Connacht** 9. 30 December: **Dragons** 6 **Scarlets** 10, **Ulster** 33 **Munster** 17. 31 December: **Treviso** 37 **Aironi** 14. 1 January, 2012: **Connacht** 13 **Leinster** 15, **Glasgow** 17 **Edinburgh** 12, **Ospreys** 17 **Blues** 12. 6 January: **Dragons** 21 **Ospreys** 20, **Edinburgh** 20 **Ulster** 42. 7 January: **Aironi** 20 **Connacht** 6, **Blues** 19 **Leinster** 23, **Scarlets** 16 **Glasgow** 14, **Munster** 29 **Treviso** 11. 9 February: **Glasgow** 19 **Scarlets** 9, **Leinster** 42 **Treviso** 8. 10 February: **Ulster** 30 **Dragons** 12, **Blues** 22 **Connacht** 15, **Edinburgh** 14 **Ospreys** 15. 17 February: **Blues** 21 **Ulster** 14, **Ospreys** 23 **Aironi** 7, **Leinster** 16 **Scarlets** 13. 18 February: **Treviso** 14 **Munster** 35, **Connacht** 13 **Glasgow** 13, **Dragons** 21 **Edinburgh** 10. 23 February: **Scarlets** 34 **Treviso** 20. 24 February: **Munster** 16 **Blues** 13, **Ulster** 15 **Ospreys** 14, **Connacht** 26 **Edinburgh** 13. 25 February: **Glasgow** 10 **Leinster** 10. 26 February: **Aironi** 9 **Dragons** 10. 2 March: **Aironi** 6 **Leinster** 22, **Ospreys** 20 **Glasgow** 26, **Ulster** 38 **Edinburgh** 16, **Scarlets** 38 **Connacht** 10. 3 March: **Treviso** 13 **Blues** 20, **Dragons** 14 **Munster** 24. 11 March: **Aironi** 21 **Munster** 17. 15 March: **Dragons** 18 **Blues** 14. 23 March: **Leinster** 22 **Ospreys** 23, **Edinburgh** 15 **Dragons** 29, **Glasgow** 29 **Aironi** 6. 24 March: **Treviso** 23 **Ulster** 27, **Blues** 14 **Scarlets** 26, **Connacht** 16 **Munster** 20. 30 March: **Ulster** 45 **Aironi** 7, **Dragons** 19 **Connacht** 27, **Glasgow** 31 **Blues** 3, **Edinburgh** 26 **Scarlets** 23. 31 March: **Ospreys** 41 **Treviso** 10, **Munster** 9 **Leinster** 18. 13 April: **Dragons** 32 **Treviso** 33, **Leinster** 54 **Edinburgh** 13. 14 April: **Connacht** 26 **Ulster** 21, **Blues** 12 **Ospreys** 33, **Munster** 35 **Glasgow** 29. 15 April: **Aironi** 23 **Scarlets** 26. 20 April: **Ospreys** 31 **Dragons** 12, **Ulster** 8 **Leinster** 16. 21 April: **Connacht** 19 **Aironi** 16, **Scarlets** 20 **Munster** 20. 22 April: **Treviso** 8 **Glasgow** 13, **Blues** 38 **Edinburgh** 13. 5 May: **Aironi** 11 **Ospreys** 18, **Dragons** 18 **Leinster** 22, **Edinburgh** 44 **Treviso** 21, **Glasgow** 24 **Connacht** 3, **Munster** 36 **Ulster** 8, **Scarlets** 29 **Blues** 20.

FINAL TABLE

	P	W	D	L	F	A	BP	PTS
Leinster	22	18	1	3	568	326	7	**81**
Ospreys	22	16	1	8	491	337	5	**71**
Munster	22	14	1	7	489	367	9	**67**
Glasgow	22	13	4	5	445	321	5	**65**
Scarlets	22	12	2	8	446	373	10	**62**
Ulster	22	12	0	10	474	424	8	**56**
Blues	22	10	0	12	446	460	10	**50**
Connacht	22	7	1	14	321	433	7	**37**
Dragons	22	7	1	14	370	474	6	**36**
Treviso	22	7	0	15	419	558	8	**36**
Edinburgh	22	6	1	15	454	588	6	**32**
Aironi	22	4	0	18	289	551	6	**22**

ELITE COMPETITIONS

SEMI-FINALS

11 May, Liberty Stadium, Swansea

OSPREYS 45 (4G 1T 4PG) MUNSTER 10 (1G 1PG)

OSPREYS: R Fussell; H Dirksen, A Bishop, A Beck, S Williams; D Biggar, K Fotuali'i; P James, R Hibbard, A Jones, AW Jones (captain), I Evans, R Jones, J Tipuric, J Bearman

SUBSTITUTIONS: R Bevington for James (56 mins); R Webb for Fotuali'i (56 mins); S Baldwin for Hibbard (61 mins); A Jarvis for A Jones (65 mins); J King for AW Jones (69 mins); T Isaacs for Dirksen (71 mins); M Morgan for Biggar (72 mins)

SCORERS: *Tries:* Biggar, Fotuali'i, Dirksen, Bishop, Webb *Conversions:* Biggar (4) *Penalty Goals:* Biggar (4)

MUNSTER: J Murphy; I Dineen, K Earls, L Mafi, S Zebo; I Keatley, C Murray; W du Preez, M Sherry, BJ Botha; D O'Callaghan, M O'Driscoll, D Ryan, T O'Donnell, P O'Mahony (captain)

SUBSTITUTIONS: R O'Gara for Murphy (24 mins); Dave O'Callaghan for Donncha O'Callaghan (53); T O'Leary for Murray (56 mins); D Barnes for Keatley (69 mins); D Fogarty for Sherry (69 mins); S Archer for Botha (74 mins); D Kilcoyne for Du Preez (74 mins)

SCORERS: *Try:* Keatley *Conversion:* Keatley *Penalty Goal:* Keatley

REFEREE: A Rolland (Ireland).

12 May, RDS, Dublin

LEINSTER 19 (1G 4PG) GLASGOW 15 (1G 1T 1PG)

LEINSTER: I Nacewa; F McFadden, E O'Malley, G D'Arcy, D Kearney; J Sexton, E Reddan; C Healy, R Strauss, M Ross, B Thorn, D Toner, S O'Brien, S Jennings, J Heaslip (captain)

SUBSTITUTIONS: A Conway for O'Malley (49 mins); H van der Merwe for Healy (51 mins); K McLaughlin for O'Brien (55 mins); S Cronin for Strauss (57 mins); L Cullen for Toner (57 mins); N White for Ross (65 mins)

SCORERS: *Try:* D Kearney *Conversion:* Sexton *Penalty Goals:* Sexton (4)

GLASGOW: S Hogg; F Aramburu, A Dunbar, G Morrison, DTH van der Merwe; D Weir, C Cusiter; R Grant, P MacArthur, M Cusack, R Gray, A Kellock, R Harley, C Fusaro, J Barclay

SUBSTITUTIONS: M Low for Cusack (47 mins); D Hall for MacArthur (55 mins); R Jackson for Weir (57 mins); T Ryder for Gray (57 mins); P Murchie for Morrison (65 mins); J Welsh for Grant (66 mins); H Pyrgos for Cusiter (69 mins); J Beattie for Harley (77)

SCORERS: *Tries:* Hall, Hogg *Conversion:* Jackson *Penalty Goal:* Weir

YELLOW CARD: A Dunbar (28 mins)

REFEREE: G Clancy (Ireland)

RABODIRECT PRO12

FINAL

LEINSTER 30 (3G 3PG) OSPREYS 31 (2G 1T 4PG)

LEINSTER: R Kearney; F McFadden, B O'Driscoll, G D'Arcy, I Nacewa; J Sexton, E Reddan; H van der Merwe, S Cronin, M Ross, L Cullen (captain), D Toner, K McLaughlin, S Jennings, J Heaslip

SUBSTITUTIONS: N White for Ross (14 mins): B Thorn for Cullen (45 mins); R Strauss for Cronin (52 mins); D Ryan for Jennings (74 mins)

SCORERS: *Tries:* Cronin, Nacewa (2) *Conversions:* Sexton (3) *Penalty Goals:* Sexton (3)

YELLOW CARDS: H van der Merwe (40 mins); N White (72 mins)

OSPREYS: R Fussell; H Dirksen, A Bishop, A Beck, S Williams; D Biggar, R Webb; P James, R Hibbard, A Jones, AW Jones (captain), I Evans, R Jones, J Tipuric, J Bearman

SUBSTITUTIONS: K Fotuali'i for Webb (55 mins); R Bevington for James (66 mins); J King for Evans (66 mins); S Baldwin for Hibbard (74 mins); A Jarvis for A Jones (74 mins)

SCORERS: *Tries:* Beck, S Williams (2) *Conversions:* Biggar (2) *Penalty Goals:* Biggar (4)

REFEREE: R Poite (France)

DEFENDING THE TITLE

By Rob Kearney

Getty Images

Leinster players celebrate their successful defence of the Heineken Cup.

They say it is even harder to defend a title than it is to win the trophy the first time around and, speaking from experience, I think that's probably true. It took a massive collective effort to win the Heineken Cup in 2011, but I'd have to say it was an even greater challenge to everyone involved with the squad to repeat the feat 12 months later.

Our 42–14 winning scoreline against Ulster in the final at Twickenham might have looked comfortable enough, but it didn't really reflect the intensity of the match and it definitely doesn't tell you anything about the campaign as a whole. We had some narrow escapes en route to the final, some huge battles and it was far from plain sailing from our opening group game against Montpellier all the way to the final.

We knew that as defending champions we were there to be shot at. It comes with the territory, and we had to dig very deep because teams wanted to take the Leinster scalp. You have to raise the intensity of your game in that situation and you cannot afford to have an off day.

I didn't realise until after the final that we had become the first team to win the Heineken Cup without losing a game. It wasn't a record we were conscious of before kick-off, but looking back it's definitely a source of pride because a lot of good teams tried very hard to knock us off our perch.

The first good team was Montpellier in our opening group game in France and, although we came away with a 16–16 draw, we were definitely lucky to escape with a share of the points. Johnny Sexton kicked a penalty with the last kick of the game to level up the scores, but in all honesty Montpellier would have been worthy winners if Johnny had missed it. We shot ourselves in the first half with a blocked kick that gifted them a try, but their back row, and in particular Mamuka Gorgodze, were absolute monsters. It was definitely points gained rather than dropped.

Our next big test came against Bath at the Rec and although I felt we created some decent chances, one of which I butchered, we weren't clinical enough. We left a few scores out there, while they got the only try of the match through Matt Banahan, and on another day it could have been 18–13 to Bath rather than the other way around.

A week later Bath came to the Aviva Stadium for the return fixture, but I was surprised because this time they didn't really turn up. We beat them 52–27 and, after winning 26–13 against Glasgow in Scotland, we knew we had qualified for the quarter-finals. It was relief all round because Glasgow hasn't been our happiest hunting ground and to reach the knockout stages with a group game to spare temporarily dispelled a bit of pressure.

We drew Cardiff in Dublin in the quarter-finals and, unluckily for them, I felt we produced our strongest performance of the season. I said earlier that final scorelines can sometimes be misleading, but I thought we were good value for our 34–3 win against the Blues.

It was all built on a devastating performance from the front row, and Cian Healy in particular, and with such a great platform up front we were able to cut loose. We scored four tries and I was very happy to get two. In truth, I ran a grand total of about two metres for them, but a try is still a try.

It was Clermont in Bordeaux in the semi-final, and we were all aware that they were going to be our biggest test so far. We also knew that it was their centenary season, so they desperately wanted to break their Heineken Cup duck to mark the milestone, and with the power and flair in their squad we were expecting a massive physical and psychological battle.

We got exactly what we expected. Clermont were definitely up for it and, although we eventually scraped through 19–15, the final 10 minutes of the match were maybe the toughest of my career as they camped on our line looking for the try to take them into the lead.

It was brutal rugby. They kept coming at us and, in all honesty, if the game had lasted five more minutes Clermont would have won, and at times like that it's as much about heart as it is fitness. We had to put our bodies on the line to keep them out.

That attitude was summed up by Gordon D'Arcy with a desperate tackle on Wesley Fofana at the death to dislodge the ball just as he looked certain to score a match-winning try. Gordon is the kind of player who comes up with the big plays when it really matters, and that was right up there with anything he's done before.

Facing Ulster in the final definitely made the build-up to the final different to 2009 and 2011. The country was gripped by the prospect of an all-Ireland final, but we consciously tried to remove that aspect from our preparations because we felt we needed to be clinical and professional and not get swept away by the emotion that was building up.

We spoke in the build-up about our two PRO12 victories over Ulster earlier in the season, but we used both results as a warning rather than any indication of superiority. We knew they had fielded under-strength teams for both games and we knew they would be much stronger opponents at Twickenham.

The atmosphere in London was incredible. I'm not sure exactly how many of the record crowd of more than 80,000 were actually Irish, but the noise was amazing and gave us a huge lift.

The match itself was close for the first hour. We got the two first-half tries from Sean O'Brien and Cian Healy, but when Dan Tuohy went over for Ulster after 60 minutes they cut our advantage to 10 points and it was game on.

Luckily for us, the clock was our friend by this stage, and Ulster had to chase the game. They knew they had to pull a few rabbits out of the hat and, as they were forced to take risks, we knew the opportunities would come and we got the tries from Heinke van der Merwe and Sean Cronin to put the game to bed.

Almost as soon as the final whistle blew, people began to ask how our 2012 win compared to beating Northampton in 2011 and Leicester

HEINEKEN CUP

in 2009. I'm not really sure how they rate in terms of importance, but they were certainly contrasting in terms of style.

The Leicester game was tight, with not many scoring opportunities, the Saints final will probably go down as one of the greatest fight-backs in the history of the competition, while the win over Ulster brought five tries. I suppose it all comes down to personal taste.

Personally, my favourite has to be the Ulster match simply because I was involved for the full 80 minutes. I watched the Leicester game from the bench at Murrayfield, coming on for the final 10 minutes, and I missed the drama of the second half against Northampton because of injury. I was struggling with a back injury in the week before Ulster and only passed fit on the Tuesday, so it was a huge relief to play. It's a squad game these days, but every player wants to be involved in the big matches and I'm no different. Missing a Heineken Cup final is a really horrible experience.

Looking back at the tournament, I think it was another hugely competitive season, and perhaps the stand-out performance was Edinburgh's progress through to the semi-finals, the first time a Scottish side had reached the last four. The sign of a healthy competition is seeing new teams reaching the latter stages, and Edinburgh's success was good news for Scottish rugby as well as the Heineken Cup. Their head coach Michael Bradley is an Irishman and, while I'm sure he wanted his team to make the final, I think he can be proud of the progress the club have made since he took the job.

In terms of individual performances over the season, I'd have to single out Ruan Pienaar for Ulster. The Springbok scrum half pulled all the right strings for Ulster and was absolutely awesome. He's a great competitor with a superb rugby brain and deserves a lot of credit for his consistency and impact.

I was also impressed by the Clermont trio of Fofana, Morgan Parra and Sitiveni Sivivatu. Fofana had an incredible breakthrough season for Clermont in Europe and France in the Six Nations, and he's a big, big talent. Like Pienaar for Ulster, Parra is the little general of the Clermont side and a box of tricks while Sivivatu remains one of the hardest players to handle in the competition.

It's no secret that I've got huge respect for Clermont, and I think the biggest compliment I can pay them is the fact I'm not overly enthused by the prospect of facing them again in the group stage of the 2012/13 Heineken Cup.

But no one at Leinster expects things to be easy in this competition. When you set yourself high standards, you know the opposition will raise their game as well. That's what makes the Heineken Cup such a tough but brilliant tournament, and we'll be ready for the new set of challenges.

HEINEKEN CUP 2011/12 RESULTS

ROUND ONE

11 November 2011

Harlequins 25 Connacht 17

Racing 20 Cardiff 26

12 November 2011

Aironi 12 Leicester 28

Ospreys 28 Biarritz 21

London Irish 19 Edinburgh 20

Ulster 16 Clermont 11

Montpellier 16 Leinster 16

Munster 23 Northampton 21

Scarlets 31 Castres 23

13 November 2011

Glasgow 26 Bath 21

Toulouse 21 Gloucester 17

Saracens 42 Treviso 17

ROUND TWO

18 November 2011

Cardiff 26 London Irish 18

Edinburgh 48 Racing 47

Clermont 54 Aironi 3

Northampton 23 Scarlets 28

19 November 2011

Treviso 26 Ospreys 26

Connacht 10 Toulouse 36

Biarritz 15 Saracens 10

Leicester 20 Ulster 9

Castres 24 Munster 27

Gloucester 9 Harlequins 28

20 November 2011

Leinster 38 Glasgow 13

Bath 16 Montpellier 13

ROUND THREE

9 December 2011	
Ulster 31 Aironi 10	Harlequins 20 Toulouse 21
Cardiff 25 Edinburgh 8	

10 December 2011	
Treviso 30 Biarritz 26	Racing 14 London Irish 34
Castres 41 Northampton 22	Scarlets 14 Munster 17
Connacht 10 Gloucester 14	Saracens 31 Ospreys 26

11 December 2011	
Bath 13 Leinster 18	Clermont 30 Leicester 12
Glasgow 20 Montpellier 15	

ROUND FOUR

16 December 2011	
Biarritz 29 Treviso 12	Ospreys 13 Saracens 16
Edinburgh 19 Cardiff 12	

17 December 2011	
Aironi 20 Ulster 46	Gloucester 23 Connacht 19
Leicester 23 Clermont 19	Montpellier 13 Glasgow 13
London Irish 19 Racing 25	Leinster 52 Bath 27

18 December 2011	
Munster 19 Scarlets 13	Toulouse 24 Harlequins 31
Northampton 45 Castres 0	

ROUND FIVE

13 January 2012	
Ospreys 44 Treviso 17	Ulster 41 Leicester 7
Racing 24 Edinburgh 27	

14 January 2012	
Montpellier 24 Bath 22	Munster 26 Castres 10
Aironi 0 Clermont 82	Toulouse 24 Connacht 3
Scarlets 17 Northampton 29	Harlequins 20 Gloucester 14
London Irish 15 Cardiff 22	

15 January 2012	
Glasgow 16 Leinster 23	Saracens 20 Biarritz 16

ROUND SIX

20 January 2012	
Connacht 9 **Harlequins** 8	**Gloucester** 34 **Toulouse** 24

21 January 2012	
Bath 23 **Glasgow** 18	**Leicester** 33 **Aironi** 6
Leinster 25 **Montpellier** 3	**Castres** 13 **Scarlets** 16
Clermont 19 **Ulster** 15	**Northampton** 36 **Munster** 51

22 January 2012	
Treviso 20 **Saracens** 26	**Cardiff** 36 **Racing** 30
Biarritz 36 **Ospreys** 5	**Edinburgh** 34 **London Irish** 11

POOL TABLES

POOL ONE

	P	W	D	L	F	A	BP	PTS
Munster	6	6	0	0	163	118	1	25
Scarlets	6	3	0	3	119	124	3	15
Northampton	6	2	0	4	176	160	4	12
Castres	6	1	0	5	111	167	3	7

POOL FOUR

	P	W	D	L	F	A	BP	PTS
Clermont	6	6	4	2	215	69	4	20
Ulster	6	4	0	2	158	87	4	20
Leicester	6	4	0	2	123	117	1	17
Aironi	6	0	0	6	51	274	0	0

POOL TWO

	P	W	D	L	F	A	BP	PTS
Edinburgh	6	5	0	1	156	138	2	22
Cardiff	6	5	0	1	145	110	1	21
London Irish	6	1	0	5	116	139	5	9
Racing	6	1	0	5	160	190	5	9

POOL FIVE

	P	W	D	L	F	A	BP	PTS
Saracens	6	5	0	1	145	107	2	22
Biarritz	6	3	0	3	143	105	6	18
Ospreys	6	2	1	3	142	147	3	13
Treviso	6	1	1	3	102	167	0	6

POOL THREE

	P	W	D	L	F	A	BP	PTS
Leinster	6	5	0	1	172	88	2	24
Glasgow	6	2	1	3	106	133	2	12
Bath	6	2	0	4	122	151	3	11
Montpellier	6	1	2	3	84	112	2	10

POOL SIX

	P	W	D	L	F	A	BP	PTS
Toulouse	6	4	0	2	150	105	2	18
Harlequins	6	4	0	2	122	94	1	17
Gloucester	6	3	0	3	111	122	3	15
Connacht	6	1	0	5	68	130	2	6

HEINEKEN CUP

QUARTER-FINALS

7 April 2012	
Edinburgh 19 Toulouse 14	Leinster 34 Cardiff 3
8 April 2012	
Munster 16 Ulster 22	Saracens 3 Clermont 22

SEMI-FINALS

28 April, Aviva Stadium, Dublin

ULSTER 22 (1G 5PG) EDINBURGH 19 (1G 4PG)

ULSTER: S Terblanche; A Trimble, D Cave, P Wallace, C Gilroy; P Jackson, R Pienaar; T Court, R Best, D Fitzpatrick, J Muller (captain), D Tuohy, S Ferris, W Faloon, P Wannenburg

SUBSTITUTIONS: A Macklin for Fitzpatrick (65 mins); R Diack for Faloon (73 mins); P McAllister for Court (77 mins); L Stevenson for Ferris (77 mins)

SCORERS: *Try:* Wannenburg *Conversion:* Pienaar *Penalty Goals:* Pienaar (5)

YELLOW CARD: S Terblanche (28 mins)

EDINBURGH: T Brown; L Jones, N De Luca, M Scott, T Visser; G Laidlaw (captain), M Blair; A Jacobsen, R Ford, G Cross, G Gilchrist, S Cox, D Denton, R Rennie, N Talei

SUBSTITUTIONS: R Grant for Rennie (56 mins); J Thompson for Jones (70 mins); J Gilding for Cross (73 mins); K Traynor for Jacobsen (77 mins)

SCORERS: *Try:* Thompson *Conversion:* Laidlaw *Penalty Goals:* Laidlaw (4)

REFEREE: R Poite (France)

CLERMONT AUVERGNE 15 (5PG)
LEINSTER 19 (1G 3PG 1DG)

CLERMONT: L Byrne; S Sivivatu, A Rougerie (captain), W Fofana, J Malzieu; B James, M Parra; L Faure, B Kayser, D Zirakashvili, J Cudmore, N Hines, J Bonnaire, A Lapandry, E Vermeulen

SUBSTITUTIONS: J-M Buttin for Malzieu (12 mins); R King for Byrne (22 mins); V Debaty for Faure (48 mins); J Bardy for Vermeulen (55 mins); J Pierre for Hines (57 mins); D Kotze for Zirakashvili (59 mins); T Paulo for Kayser (64 mins)

SCORERS: *Penalty Goals:* James (5)

LEINSTER: R Kearney; I Nacewa, B O'Driscoll, G D'Arcy, L Fitzgerald; J Sexton, I Boss; C Healy, R Strauss, M Ross, L Cullen (captain), B Thorn, S O'Brien, S Jennings, J Heaslip

SUBSTITUTIONS: E Reddan for Boss (53 mins); H Van der Merwe for Healy (56 mins); F McFadden for Fitzgerald (64 mins); S Cronin for Strauss (64 mins); K McLaughlin for Jennings (64 mins)

SCORERS: *Try:* Healy *Conversion:* Sexton *Penalty Goals:* Sexton *Drop Goal:* Sexton

REFEREE: W Barnes (England)

FINAL

LEINSTER 42 (4G 1T 3PG) ULSTER 14 (1T 3PG)

LEINSTER: R Kearney; F McFadden, B O'Driscoll, G D'Arcy, I Nacewa; J Sexton, E Reddan; C Healy, R Strauss , L Cullen (captain), B Thorn, K McLaughlin, S O'Brien, J Heaslip

SUBSTITUTIONS: D Toner for Cullen (58 mins); H Van der Merwe for Healy (62 mins); S Jennings for McLaughlin (62 mins); S Cronin for Strauss (67 mins); N White for Ross (69 mins); I Madigan for Sexton (74 mins); I Boss for Reddan (74 mins)

SCORERS: *Tries:* O'Brien, Healy, Penalty, Van der Merwe, Cronin *Conversions:* Sexton (3), McFadden *Penalty Goals:* Sexton (3)

ULSTER: S Terblanche; A Trimble, D Cave, P Wallace, C Gilroy; P Jackson, R Pienaar; T Court, R Best, J Afoa, J Muller (captain), D Tuohy, S Ferris, C Henry (W Faloon 67), P Wannenburg

SUBSTITUTIONS: I Humphreys for Jackson (40 mins); W Faloon for Henry (67 mins); P Marshall for Humphreys (70 mins); D Fitzpatrick for Afoa (74 mins); P McAllister for Court (75 mins); A D'Arcy for Cave (77 mins); L Stevenson for Tuohy (77 mins)

SCORERS: *Try:* Tuohy *Penalty Goals:* Pienaar (3)

YELLOW CARD: S Terblanche (72 mins)

REFEREE: N Owens (Wales)

James Hook of Perpignan during their Amlin Challenge Cup match against Exeter Chiefs.

YACHVILI SEALS FIRST EUROPEAN TRIUMPH

by Iain Spragg

Stu Forster/Getty Images

Biarritz celebrate a hard-fought victory over Toulon in the Amlin Challenge Cup Final.

French sides dominated the Amlin Challenge Cup as Biarritz Olympique triumphed 21–18 over Top 14 rivals Toulon in a dramatic final in London, lifting a European trophy for the first time in the club's history.

The semi-finalists were all French clubs, but it was Biarritz who were eventually crowned champions after a titanic struggle at The Stoop was decided by a late penalty from scrum half Dimitri Yachvili which sealed victory for Patrice Lagisquet's side. The win, however, was not without controversy as Yachvili could have been sin-binned moments before his seventh and pivotal penalty in the 73rd minute for a tap tackle on opposite number Sébastien Tillous-Borde, but he stayed on the pitch and Biarritz were victorious.

"It has been a very hard season and that is why we are very happy tonight," Yachvili said. "We never gave up and we deserved to win."

Biarritz were joined in the last eight by Toulon, Stade Français, Brive, Exeter Chiefs, Harlequins, London Wasps and Scarlets, after being knocked out of the Heineken Cup, but it was a clean sweep for the Top 14 sides and the semi-finals at the end of April became an exclusively Gallic affair.

The first match saw Toulon tackle Stade Français at the Stade Félix Mayol and, although they took an early lead with a Steffon Armitage try, the home side were outscored two tries to one by the Parisians and had to rely on a dramatic last-gasp drop goal from Jonny Wilkinson to secure a 32–29 victory.

In contrast, the second semi-final between Biarritz and Brive at Parc des Sports Aguilera was more straightforward for the home side and, once captain Damien Traille had crashed over for the only try of the match in the first half, the writing was on the wall. Brive did not trouble the scorers while Yachvili contributed 14 points with the boot and at the final whistle Biarritz were comfortable 19–0 winners.

Spectators hoping for 80 minutes of running rugby in the final at The Stoop were ultimately disappointed as in slippery conditions the game became an attritional battle of forward power and, ultimately, a contest between the prolific left boots of Yachvili and Wilkinson.

The French scrum half drew first blood in the fourth minute with the opening penalty of the match, but the English fly half replied within seven minutes, and at the break Biarritz had established a precarious 12–9 advantage.

The crucial phase of the match came early in the second half when prop Carl Hayman and flanker Armitage both saw yellow. Toulon's indiscipline proved costly as Yachvili punished both indiscretions with three points and he was also on hand to calmly land Biarritz's match-winning penalty late on to make it 21–18.

There was, however, still time for Toulon to mount one last foray into opposition territory but as the forwards attempted to manufacture a position for Wilkinson to drop a goal and take the match into extra time, they conceded a penalty and Biarritz were champions.

"This is fantastic," admitted captain Imanol Harinordoquy after collecting the trophy. "The season has been very hard but we've won a title. Normally it's Jonny Wilkinson who gives us a hard life but this time Dimitri gave Toulon a hard time."

ROUND ONE

10 November, 2011

Toulon 53 **Padova** 22   **Worcester** 14 **Stade Français** 23

11 November, 2011

Perpignan 15 **Exeter** 12

12 November, 2011

Cavalieri 3 **Dragons** 33   **Rovigo** 10 **Bayonne** 43

La Vila 10 **A2gen** 50   **Newcastle** 27 **Lyon** 19

Brive 26 **Sale** 18   **Bordeaux** 14 **Wasps** 47

13 November, 2011

Bucharest 34 **Crociati** 7

ROUND TWO

17 November, 2011

Bayonne 20 **Bordeaux** 3   **Dragons** 27 **Perpignan** 13

18 November, 2011

Stade Français 49 **Bucharest** 3   **Sale** 59 **La Vila** 6

19 November, 2011

Padova 3 **Newcastle** 34   **Exeter** 68 **Cavalieri** 0

Crociati 3 **Worcester** 34   **Lyon** 19 **Toulon** 26

20 November, 2011

Wasps 38 **Rovigo** 7   **Agen** 8 **Brive** 29

ROUND THREE

8 December, 2011

Agen 14 **Sale** 29   **Newcastle** 6 **Toulon** 3

9 December, 2011

Perpignan 54 **Cavalieri** 20

10 December, 2011

Rovigo 7 **Bordeaux** 31   **Crociati** 0 **Stade Français** 57

La Vila 18 **Brive** 47   **Lyon** 31 **Padova** 16

Bayonne 19 **Wasps** 11

11 December, 2011

Bucharest 13 **Worcester** 24   **Exeter** 18 **Dragons** 6

ROUND FOUR

15 December, 2011

Bordeaux 15 **Rovigo** 10   **Brive** 38 **La Vila** 13

Stade Français 45 **Crociati** 3   **Wasps** 25 **Bayonne** 11

17 December, 2011

Cavalieri 13 **Perpignan** 30   **Padova** 3 **Lyon** 43

Worcester 57 **Bucharest** 13   **Toulon** 36 **Newcastle** 10

18 December, 2011	
Sale 41 **Agen** 21	**Dragons** 19 **Exeter** 23

ROUND FIVE

12 January, 2012

Bordeaux 6 **Bayonne** 12

13 January, 2012

Brive 50 **Agen** 13

14 January, 2012

Bucharest 13 **Stade Français** 34	**Cavalieri** 10 **Exeter** 50
Rovigo 11 **Wasps** 32	**La Vila** 10 **Sale** 69
Worcester 55 **Crociati** 10	**Perpignan** 27 **Dragons** 13

15 January, 2012

Newcastle 43 **Padova** 0	**Toulon** 29 **Lyon** 10

ROUND SIX

19 January, 2012

Agen 62 **La Vila** 7	**Sale** 9 **Brive** 19

21 January, 2012

Crociati 13 **Bucharest** 26	**Lyon** 21 **Newcastle** 13
Padova 6 **Toulon** 50	**Dragons** 45 **Cavalieri** 16
Exeter 31 **Perpignan** 14	**Stade Français** 33 **Worcester** 10

22 January, 2012

Bayonne 92 **Rovigo** 6	**Wasps** 36 **Bordeaux** 13

FINAL TABLES

POOL ONE

	P	W	D	L	F	A	BP	PTS
Stade Français	6	6	0	0	241	43	5	29
Worcester	6	4	0	2	194	95	4	20
Bucharest	6	2	0	4	102	184	2	10
Crociati	6	0	0	6	36	251	0	0

POOL FOUR

	P	W	D	L	F	A	BP	PTS
Exeter	6	5	0	1	202	64	3	23
Perpignan	6	4	0	2	153	112	2	18
Dragons	6	3	0	3	139	100	3	15
Cavalieri	6	0	0	6	62	280	0	0

POOL TWO

	P	W	D	L	F	A	BP	PTS
Toulon	6	5	0	1	197	73	5	25
Newcastle	6	4	0	2	133	82	2	18
Lyon	6	3	0	3	143	114	2	14
Padova	6	0	0	6	50	254	0	0

POOL FIVE

	P	W	D	L	F	A	BP	PTS
Brive	6	6	0	0	209	79	3	27
Sale	6	4	0	2	225	96	4	20
Agen	6	2	0	4	168	166	2	10
La Vila	6	0	0	6	64	325	0	0

POOL THREE

	P	W	D	L	F	A	BP	PTS
Wasps	6	5	0	1	189	75	4	24
Bayonne	6	5	0	1	197	61	2	22
Bordeaux	6	2	0	4	82	132	2	10
Rovigo	6	0	0	6	51	251	1	1

QUARTER-FINALS

5 April, 2012
Stade Français 27 Exeter 17
6 April, 2012
Toulon 37 Harlequins 8
7 April, 2012
Wasps 23 Biarritz 26
8 April, 2012
Brive 15 Scarlets 11

SEMI-FINALS

27 April, Stade Félix Mayol, Toulon

TOULON 32 (1T 7PG 2DG) STADE FRANCAIS 29 (2G 3PG 2DG)

TOULON: B Lapeyre; A Palisson, G Messina, M Giteau, D Smith; J Wilkinson, S Tillous-Borde; L Emmanuelli, J-C Orioli, D Kubriashvili, C Samson, D Schofield, P Gunther, S Armitage, J van Niekerk (captain)

SUBSTITUTIONS: C Hayman for Kubriashvili (49 mins); E Lewis-Roberts for Emmanuelli (51 mins); J Sata for Schofield (60 mins); S Brun for Orioli (60 mins); J El Abd for Gunther (79 mins)

SCORERS: *Try:* Armitage *Penalty Goals:* Wilkinson (7) *Drop Goals:* Wilkinson (2)

STADE FRANCAIS: H Bonneval; P Sackey, M Turinui, G Smith, J Arias; J Plisson, J Fillol (captain); S Wright, A de Malmanche, D Attoub, T Palmer, A Flanquart, A Burban, P Rabadan, D Lyons

SUBSTITUTIONS: L Sempere for de Malmanche (51 mins); S Parisse for Rabadan (52 mins); O Milloud for Wright (54 mins); J Dupuy for Fillol (60 mins); D Camara for Lyons (73 mins)

SCORERS: *Tries:* Bonneval, Turinui *Conversions:* Plisson (2) *Penalty Goals:* Plisson (3) *Drop Goals:* Plisson (2)

YELLOW CARD: J Arias (69 mins)

REFEREE: A Rolland (Ireland)

AMLIN CHALLENGE CUP

28 April, Parc des Sports Aguilera, Biarritz

BIARRITZ 19 (1G 4PG) BRIVE 0

BIARRITZ: I Balshaw; T Ngwenya, D Haylett-Petty, D Traille (captain), B Baby; M Bosch, D Yachvili; S Marconnet, A Heguy, E van Staden, J Thion, M Carizza, B Guyot, T Gray, R Lakafia

SUBSTITUTIONS: E Lund for Carizza (30 mins); FG Koleda for Marconnet (40 mins); Y Watremez for van Staden (51 mins); B August for Heguy (60 mins); C Gimenez for Haylett-Petty (65 mins); M Lund for Guyot (66 mins); J-P Barraque for Balshaw (67 mins); J Peyrelongue for Yachvili (72 mins)

SCORERS: *Try:* Traille *Conversion:* Yachvili *Penalty Goals:* Yachvili (2)

BRIVE: M Atayi; R Cooke, R Swanepoel, J Noon, S Galala; M Belie, A Figuerola; J Poirot, I Natriashvili, A Barozzi, R Uys, O Caisso, S Azoulai (captain), V Forgues, A Claassen

SUBSTITUTIONS: S Geraghty for Noon (temp 13 to 24 mins); A Mignardi for Belie (13 mins); P Luafutu for Forgues (51 mins); J Le Devedec for Uys (51 mins); P Barnard for Barozzi (temp 56 to 62 mins); V Lacombe for Natriashvili (56 mins); P Henn for Poirot (62 mins)

RED CARD: A Barozzi (80 mins)

REFEREE: G Clancy (Ireland)

FINAL

18 May, The Stoop, London, Twickenham

TOULON 18 (5PG 1DG) BIARRITZ 21 (7PG)

TOULON: B Lapeyre; A Palisson, M Bastareaud, M Giteau, D Smith; J Wilkinson, S Tillous-Borde; E Lewis-Roberts, S Bruno, C Hayman, C Samson, K Chesney, P Gunther, S Armitage, J van Niekerk (captain)

SUBSTITUTIONS: J-C Orioli for Bruno (51 mins); D Schofield for Chesney (58 mins)

SCORERS: *Penalty Goals:* Wilkinson (5) *Drop Goal:* Wilkinson

YELLOW CARDS: C Hayman (46 mins), S Armitage (53 mins)

BIARRITZ: I Balshaw; T Ngwenya, J-P Barraque, D Traille, D Haylett-Petty; J Peyrelongue, D Yachvili; Y Watremez, A Heguy, E van Staden, J Thion, P Taele, W Lauret, B Guyot, I Harinordoquy (captain)

SUBSTITUTIONS: S Marconnet for Watremez (41 mins); T Gray for Guyot (50 mins); B Augus for Heguy (69 mins); E Lund for Thion (71 mins); M Bosch for Peyrelongue (72 mins)

SCORERS: *Penalty Goals:* Yachvili (7)

REFEREE: W Barnes (England)

SUPERUGBY

HARD WORK KEY TO CHIEFS' MAIDEN TITLE

By Chiefs coach Dave Rennie

Getty Images

Aaron Cruden breaks through a tackle in the Super Rugby Final.

A **question I** have been asked a lot is what we were looking for when we put the squad together, and selection was probably the most important part of our success in the end. We based our squad

592 selection on work ethic and character. We had a strong understanding of the young talent across the country as well as experienced players who could help nurture their development. Our prior working relationships saw us recruit a large number of players from outside of our franchise who we believed would lift the expectation and performance of the Chiefs. We did a lot of homework around their character. Ultimately what we wanted were hard-working good buggers.

We believed that the people would get behind us regardless of the result if we emptied out the tank every week. A lot of people thought we were a little light to measure up, but we were pretty happy we had a group who would work bloody hard for each other and that was going to be crucial for any success.

We placed a high expectation on accountability and stripped things back to the bone. We placed a massive emphasis on leadership and selected a group who we believed would model quality standards and values. We had some really good experienced players around the young guys, people like Kane Thompson and Mahonri Schwalger and others who have been here quite a while, like Tanerau Latimer, Liam Messam, Craig Clarke, Richard Kahui and Lelia Masaga. These guys are very passionate about the Chiefs jersey. And with Aaron Cruden and Sonny Bill Williams we had a couple of big performers in key positions.

The co-captain scenario created a bit of confusion within the media. They were concerned about who the ref was going to talk to, who would do the toss and who would lead the team out. They were incidentals. We chose two captains because it suited us. Both Craig and Liam have different strengths and are great foils for each other. And while Craig wore the 'C' on game day, they both shared responsibility for the role throughout the week.

Creating a culture where guys wanted to play for each other was crucial. We have been lucky this year with the Rugby World Cup and having quite a big void before Christmas meant we were able to have a five-week camp. We were able to get a lot of rugby specific conditioning into them, but it also gave us a lot of time to create a culture. We trained throughout the franchise while engaging with the communities. From Waiuku and Raglan to Te Kuiti and Taupo. The boys had to hitchhike over 200km from Hamilton to Ohope Beach on the East coast. This saw them complete a range of challenges in Hamilton, Cambridge, Tauranga, Mt Maunganui, Rotorua, Te Puke and Whakatane. This was the first time most of the boys had hitchhiked and was a great way to associate with our people. We even attended Christmas parades in Hamilton, Pukekohe, Tauranga, Otorohanga and Matamata. If we wanted people to get behind us we needed to show interest in them.

We focused on the historical side of this region, the Kingitanga movement which filtered through our themes and awards throughout the year. This allowed us to understand the origins of this franchise. Our players bought into it big time. We had Pa wars, inter-Marae miniteam games with the shield up for grabs each week. We used Waiata (songs) to back up speakers and had a haka written for us, which was about who we are, who we represent and what we wanted to be. This haka, performed after the final, highlighted how close this team is.

The season began against the Highlanders and that was a game we had control of with 20 minutes to go, but we didn't close it out and they came back strong and probably outmuscled us in the last quarter. Looking back now, maybe that was the making of us and our season. We learned a lot from that game, although we lost a few players as well – Ben Afeaki, Toby Smith, Brendon Leonard and Masaga – to long-term injuries. That was a blow and some people wrote off our chances. But that just highlighted the character of our team and we won the next nine. We showed that we had really good depth and the players took confidence from that. It also gave some of the young guys opportunities earlier than we anticipated, but they fronted up big time with help from the experienced guys around them. There was a real emphasis on doing all the little things really well, not just training and playing but reviews and previews, one-on-ones, all those little things and I guess the culture and camaraderie built up.

Without a doubt in that run the Crusaders was an important game. They had lost the week before so were pretty motivated. We had just beaten the Blues and the boys got up again and performed pretty clinically. Our set piece was strong and we had a lot of physicality and intensity in everything we did. They are a very strong side and tough to beat so we took a lot of confidence from that and we won a few more tight ones. We won all three games on tour which added to our belief.

The loss to the Reds was a good wake-up call for us. We played pretty well for 39 minutes, but they got four quick tries and we weren't good enough across the board. Sometimes these sorts of games force you to have a good look at yourself and what things need to be better. It certainly gave us coaches an opportunity to challenge the players and for them to challenge each other.

The bye week gave us chance to regroup and front up against the Bulls. That was probably a crucial game, and if we had lost we could have drifted back to the pack and had a tough run home. The Bulls played pretty well and it was a hell of an arm wrestle. It was important we then got five points against the Blues to ensure we would be top of the table going into the international break.

We had a review and then we gave the boys two weeks off to freshen up mentally and physically, although they all had set goals and had to come back fitter and stronger than when they left. We tested them on an array of things and they were in really good physical shape. We came out of the June window in pretty good nick, pretty fresh and the boys were charged.

We had a close battle against the Highlanders, a game we had under control but made a bit tight because we didn't put them away. Then it was the Crusaders and they had their backs to the wall. If they had lost they could have been battling to make the top six. They were pretty motivated and able to stifle our set piece. We played with a lot of character, defended pretty well and hung in and had an opportunity to steal a draw at the end.

We went to the Hurricanes pretty confident a win would be enough to qualify first as the Stormers hadn't scored a lot of tries over the season, but we were pretty average. We had already qualified and I'm not sure if that was an issue, but I'm not making excuses as the Hurricanes had had a good season and are a bloody good side but we lacked a bit of edge.

Those two defeats forced us to take a hard look at things. We did a full season review of everything that we did really well early in the year and what was different in the last couple of games. Little things we had been doing well but perhaps not paid enough attention to detail to lately. We had a bit of fun, we did a lot of hard work, a bit of team building and those two weeks were really crucial to us going into the semi-final with the Crusaders.

Maybe if we had held on and beaten the Hurricanes then we would have thought we didn't play bad, we still won and might have brushed over things. We had a fantastic review. The players were great. We had real clarity on the areas that needed to be better. When you lose key games you can sulk or try to take lessons from it and that is one great thing about this group, that they are able to refocus quickly.

To be honest we had got beaten up by the Crusaders a couple of weeks earlier and we knew we couldn't afford to be bullied again. Our players made that statement early on. We wanted to be aggressive in everything we did and that attitude really set us up. The Crusaders are a very good side, full of All Blacks and fantastic players with a lot of semi-final and final experience.

If we got on the wrong side again our season was finished and it would have been a hell of a disappointment to have lost three in a row. Our players got up big time and it was an amazingly intense game of footy, the sort you see at Test level and that was fitting for a semi-final.

The second semi-final kicked off at 3am our time, and I wasn't remotely surprised the Sharks won that game against the Stormers. They had been the form South African side in the previous couple of months and had already beaten the Stormers. We were hopeful they would get up, but we had prepared to travel.

The fact we turned up to our planned training session knowing we didn't have to travel meant we could have a really good review of the Crusaders match and to be able to sleep in your own beds all week was great, as was the chance to play in front of our own supporters and sponsors. It also meant we could have the whole squad there and be part of the preparations, something we couldn't have done if we'd had to travel to Cape Town.

We were pretty average in the first 20 minutes of the final, we lacked a bit of intensity with and without the ball and we weren't able to turn pressure into points. The second 20 was much better and we were able to gain momentum. Our intensity was way better in the second half and we were camped in their half. The conditions weren't the greatest, but we still wanted to move the ball and find space in behind them.

Much has been made of the Sharks' travel in the knockout stages. To spend that much time travelling you focus more on recovery and less on training. We were able to force them to make a lot of tackles in that first half and it told on them later. It was a bloody tough assignment for them, but we got the benefits of being consistent over the season and finishing in the top two.

Playing before a sell-out crowd was amazing. Waikato Stadium is a great place to play. It is only a small crowd, 25,000, but they are right on the edge of the pitch which makes for a brilliant atmosphere. They are really vocal and people around here have been pretty patient, and it was nice to be able to win it here in front of them and all our friends and families. It was really terrific to see the whole squad celebrate together. It was a very special occasion, a lot of hard work from a lot of people to realise a dream.

With team success comes individual honours. It was great to see both Liam Messam and Hika Elliot play against Ireland alongside new All Blacks Brodie Retallick and Sam Cane. Ben Tameifuna was a squad member, and although he didn't get game time he has a big future. With Richard Kahui injured, Sonny Bill and Aaron were World Cup winners re-selected. All played with distinction. They also dominated the Awards dinner with Aaron winning the Supporters' Player of the Year, Sonny the Player's Player of the Year and Brodie the Coaches' Player of the Year.

We've already started planning for next year. Not too many sides

SUPER RUGBY

have backed up in the history of Super Rugby and that makes it tough. A key thing for us is not being satisfied with what we have achieved. We want to be better and it's such a tough competition that we will need to be. Putting ourselves into a position where we can play in the play-offs again is crucial. We won't be able to sneak up on anyone and there will be a few people gunning for us, but we're determined to raise the bar even higher.

Getty Images

Sonny Bill Williams won the Players' Player of the Year Award after an impressive season with the Chiefs.

ELITE COMPETITIONS

24 February: **Blues** 18 **Crusaders** 19, **Brumbies** 19 **Force** 17. 25 February: **Bulls** 18 **Sharks** 13, **Chiefs** 19 **Highlanders** 23, **Waratahs** 21 **Reds** 25. 26 February: **Stormers** 39 **Hurricanes** 26, **Lions** 27 **Cheetahs** 25. 2 March: **Chiefs** 29 **Blues** 14, **Rebels** 19 **Waratahs** 35. 3 March: **Lions** 28 **Hurricanes** 30, **Highlanders** 27 **Crusaders** 24, **Reds** 35 **Force** 20. 4 March: **Cheetahs** 19 **Bulls** 51, **Stormers** 15 **Sharks** 12. 9 March: **Crusaders** 19 **Chiefs** 24. 10 March: **Force** 19 **Hurricanes** 46, **Brumbies** 24 **Cheetahs** 23, **Highlanders** 18 **Waratahs** 17, **Reds** 11 **Rebels** 6. 11 March: **Sharks** 32 **Lions** 20, **Bulls** 23 **Blues** 29. 16 March: **Chiefs** 29 **Brumbies** 22. 17 March: **Stormers** 27 **Blues** 17, **Hurricanes** 17 **Highlanders** 19, **Waratahs** 20 **Force** 21. 18 March: **Sharks** 27 **Reds** 22, **Rebels** 26 **Cheetahs** 33. 23 March: **Blues** 25 **Hurricanes** 26, **Rebels** 30 **Force** 29. 24 March: **Waratahs** 34 **Sharks** 30, **Crusaders** 28 **Cheetahs** 21, **Brumbies** 33 **Highlanders** 26. 25 March: **Bulls** 61 **Reds** 8, **Lions** 19 **Stormers** 24. 30 March: **Highlanders** 43 **Rebels** 12. 31 March: **Hurricanes** 38 **Cheetahs** 47, **Chiefs** 30 **Waratahs** 13, **Brumbies** 26 **Sharks** 29m **Force** 45 **Reds** 19. 1 April: **Lions** 13 **Crusaders** 23, **Stormers** 20 **Bulls** 17. 5 April: **Rebels** 34 **Blues** 23. 6 April: **Hurricanes** 42 **Sharks** 18, **Reds** 20 **Brumbies** 13, **Force** 12 **Chiefs** 20. 7 April: **Highlanders** 6 **Stormers** 21. 8 April: **Cheetahs** 26 **Lions** 5, **Bulls** 32 **Crusaders** 30. 13 April: **Blues** 23 **Sharks** 29, **Force** 18 **Waratahs** 23. 14 April: **Crusaders** 31 **Stormers** 24, **Brumbies** 37 **Rebels** 6. 15 April: **Cheetahs** 33 **Chiefs** 39, **Lions** 18 **Bulls** 32. 20 April: **Highlanders** 30 **Blues** 27, **Reds** 13 **Stormers** 23. 21 April: **Hurricanes** 14 **Crusaders** 42, **Waratahs** 30 **Rebels** 21. 22 April: **Sharks** 12 **Chiefs** 18, **Bulls** 36 **Brumbies** 34. 27 April: **Blues** 11 **Reds** 23. 28 April: **Lions** 20 **Brumbies** 34, **Chiefs** 33 **Hurricanes** 14, **Force** 3 **Stormers** 17. 29 April: **Cheetahs** 33 **Highlanders** 36, **Waratahs** 33 **Crusaders** 37. 4 May: **Hurricanes** 35 **Blues** 19, **Rebels** 35 **Bulls** 41. 5 May: **Chiefs** 34 **Lions** 21, **Brumbies** 23 **Waratahs** 6. 6 May: **Sharks** 28 **Highlanders** 16, **Cheetahs** 17 **Force** 13, **Crusaders** 15 **Reds** 11. 11 May: **Blues** 25 **Lions** 3, **Waratahs** 24 **Bulls** 27. 12 May: **Highlanders** 20 **Hurricanes** 26, **Rebels** 28 **Crusaders** 19. 13 May: **Sharks** 53 **Force** 11, **Stormers** 16 **Cheetahs** 14, **Reds** 42 **Chiefs** 27. 18 May: **Hurricanes** 25 **Brumbies** 37. 19 May: **Highlanders** 16 **Bulls** 11. 26 May: **Hurricanes** 66 **Rebels** 24, **Blues** 20 **Highlanders** 27, **Brumbies** 12 **Reds** 13, **Force** 17 **Lions** 11. 27 May: **Cheetahs** 35 **Waratahs** 34, **Sharks** 25 **Stormers** 20. 1 June: **Crusaders** 51 **Highlanders** 18, **Rebels** 19 **Brumbies** 27. 2 June: **Blues** 34 **Chiefs** 41, **Waratahs** 12 **Hurricanes** 33. 3 June: **Bulls** 14 **Stormers** 19. 29 June: **Highlanders** 21 **Chiefs** 27, **Rebels** 17 **Reds** 32. 30 June: **Crusaders** 22 **Hurricanes** 23, **Force** 17 **Brumbies** 28. 1 July: **Stormers** 27 **Lions** 17, **Bulls** 40 **Cheetahs** 24. 6 July: **Chiefs** 21 **Crusaders** 28, **Reds** 19 **Highlanders** 13. 7 July: **Sharks** 32 **Bulls** 10, **Blues** 32 **Force** 9, **Waratahs** 15–19 **Brumbies**. 8 July: **Cheetahs** 6 **Stormers** 13, **Lions** 37 **Rebels** 32. 13 July: **Hurricanes** 28 **Chiefs** 25. 14 July: **Brumbies** 16 **Blues** 30, **Crusaders** 38 **Force** 24, **Reds** 32 **Waratahs** 16. 15 July: **Stormers** 26 **Rebels** 21, **Sharks** 34 **Cheetahs** 15, **Bulls** 37 **Lions** 20.

SUPER RUGBY

FINAL TABLE

	P	W	D	L	BYE	F	A	BP	PTS
Stormers	16	14	0	2	2	350	254	2	66
Chiefs	16	12	0	4	2	444	358	9	61
Reds	16	11	0	5	2	359	347	6	58
Crusaders	16	11	0	5	2	485	343	9	61
Bulls	16	10	0	6	2	472	369	11	59
Sharks	16	10	0	6	2	436	348	11	59
Brumbies	16	10	0	6	2	404	331	10	58
Hurricanes	16	10	0	6	2	489	429	9	57
Highlanders	16	9	0	7	2	359	385	6	50
Cheetahs	16	5	0	11	2	391	458	10	38
Waratahs	16	4	0	12	2	346	407	11	35
Blues	16	4	0	12	2	359	430	8	32
Rebels	16	4	0	12	2	362	520	8	32
Force	16	3	0	13	2	306	440	7	27
Lions	16	3	0	13	2	317	460	5	25

PLAY-OFFS

21 July	
Crusaders 28–13 **Bulls**	Reds 17–30 **Sharks**

ELITE COMPETITIONS

27 July, Waikato Stadium, Hamilton

CHIEFS 20 (2G 2PG) CRUSADERS 17 (1T 4PG)

CHIEFS: R Robinson; T Nanai-Williams, A Horrell, SB Williams, A Tikoirotuma; A Cruden, T Kerr-Barlow; S Taumalolo, M Schwalger, B Tameifuna, C Clarke (captain), B Retallick, L Messam, T Latimer, K Thompson

SUBSTITUTIONS: S Cane for Thompson (60 mins), B Afeaki for Tameifuna (60 mins)

SCORERS: *Tries:* Messam, Taumalolo *Conversions:* Cruden (2) *Penalty Goals:* Cruden (2)

CRUSADERS: I Dagg; A Whitelock, R Fruean, R Crotty, Z Guildford; D Carter, A Ellis; W Crockett, C Flynn, B Franks, L Romano, S Whitelock, G Whitelock, M Todd, R McCaw (captain)

SUBSTITUTIONS: T Donnelly for Romano (16 mins), Q MacDonald for Flynn (temp 21 to 27 mins), O Franks for B Franks (54 mins)

SCORERS*: Tries:* Crotty *Penalty Goals:* Carter (4)

REFEREE: C Joubert (South Africa)

28 July, Newlands Stadium, Cape Town

STORMERS 19 (1G 4PG) SHARKS 26 (2G 1PG 2DG)

STORMERS: J Pietersen; G Aplon, J de Jongh, J de Villiers (captain), B Habana; P Grant, D Duvenage; S Kitshoff, T Liebenberg, B Harris, E Etzebeth, A Bekker, S Kolisi, R Elstadt, D Fourie

SUBSTITUTIONS: G van den Heever for Pietersen (57 mins), F Malherbe for Harris (60 mins), L Schreuder for Duvenage (68 mins), DK Steenkamp for Bekker (70 mins), D Armand for Liebenberg (76 mins), D Carstens for Kitshoff (76 mins)

SCORERS: *Tries:* Aplon *Conversion:* Grant *Penalty Goals:* Grant (4)

SHARKS: R Viljoen; L Ludik, JP Pietersen, T Whitehead, L Mvovo; F Michalak, C McLeod; T Mtawarira, B du Plessis, J du Plessis, W Alberts, A Bresler, K Daniel (captain), M Coetzee, R Kankowski

SUBSTITUTIONS: S Sykes for Alberts (57 mins), W Herbst for J du Plessis (60 mins), M Bosman for Whitehead (68 mins), J Botes for Coetzee (70 mins), J Deysel for R Kankowski (73 mins)

SCORERS: *Tries:* Ludik, Pietersen *Conversions:* Michalak (2) *Penalty Goal:* Michalak *Drop Goals:* Michalak

REFEREE: S Walsh (Australia)

SUPER RUGBY

FINAL

4 August, Waikato Stadium, Hamilton

CHIEFS 37 (4G 3PG) SHARKS 6 (2PG)

CHIEFS: R Robinson; T Nanai-Williams, A Horrell, SB Williams, A Tikoirotuma; A Cruden, T Kerr-Barlow; S Taumalolo, M Schwalger, B Tameifuna, C Clarke (captain), B Retallick, L Messam, T Latimer, K Thompson

SUBSTITUTIONS: S Cane for Thompson (58 mins), L Masaga for Nanai-Williams (58 mins), B Leonard for Kerr-Barlow (68 mins), H Elliot for Schwalger (68 mins), B Afeaki for Tameifuna (68 mins), M Fitzgerald for Retallick (72 mins), J Willison for Robinson (72 mins)

SCORERS: *Tries:* Nanai-Williams, Thompson, Masaga, Williams *Conversions:* Cruden (4) *Penalty Goals:* Cruden (3)

SHARKS: P Lambie; L Ludik, JP Pietersen, P Jordaan, L Mvovo; F Michalak, C McLeod; T Mtawarira, B du Plessis; J du Plessis, W Alberts, A Bresler, K Daniel (captain), M Coetzee, R Kankowski

SUBSTITUTIONS: J Deysel for Kankowski (52 mins), S Sykes for Alberts (52 mins), W Herbst for J du Plessis (52 mins), J Botes for Coetzee (62 mins), M Bosman for Pietersen (63 mins), C Burden for B du Plessis (72 mins), R Viljoen for Michalak (72 mins)

SCORERS: *Penalty Goals:* Michalak (2)

REFEREE: S Walsh (Australia)

Referees

Emirates

ENSURING THE BEST POSSIBLE STANDARDS

By James Fitzgerald

Jöel Jutge ticks off England's Martin Corry during the 2007 RBS 6 Nations.

I t is nothing new to suggest that there is considerable pressure on the man in the middle of any given Test match.

Set against a backdrop of an evolving and considerable Law book, ever-increasing public, coach and media scrutiny the role of the match official is an integral part of Rugby. It takes a certain character to excel as a referee on the big stage week-in, week-out just as it does to perform as a player or coach.

The IRB is committed to promoting the highest-possible standards of officiating across Fifteens and Sevens in order that the world's best referees are fully prepared for an ever evolving environment, the demands of elite level refereeing and that we arrive at Rugby World Cup 2015 and the Rio 2016 Olympic Games with competition for places and a strong group of match officials.

In 2012, the IRB embarked on an innovative programme to achieve just that. A restructured and more streamlined selection process of match officials was announced, overseen by an expert committee with the aim of ensuring consistency and accuracy of performance in international Rugby.

Frenchman Joël Jutge was appointed IRB High Performance Match Official Manager. The 46-year-old succeeds Paddy O'Brien, the New Zealander who carried out the role with great success for eight years. Jutge joined the International Rugby Board in early September at what is an exciting time for the Game as it continues to experience unprecedented growth.

A vastly experienced former referee who took charge of 35 Tests between 1996 and 2007, Jutge was selected on the panel for two Rugby World Cups, in 2003 in Australia and 2007 in France.

His final appointment as an international referee turned out to be the RWC 2007 quarter-final between Argentina and Scotland at the Stade de France as a persistent knee injury forced him to call time on his career with the whistle.

"I am thrilled to be appointed to this role at such an exciting time for the Game and its growth," Jutge said at the time of his appointment. "I am passionate about rugby and officiating and excited about the IRB's vision of ensuring that the structures continue to be in place to allow our top referees to shine on the world's biggest stages, while providing the platform for our best young talent to prove themselves."

Thankfully for the global Game, O'Brien has not been lost to Rugby, having taken on the exciting challenge of overseeing the development of IRB Rugby Sevens match officials ahead of the sport's Olympic Games debut at Rio 2016.

"I am looking forward to using the experience gained through my years working with the FFR to work within a strong IRB Referee Selection Committee alongside Paddy O'Brien to strengthen relationships with stakeholders and add further momentum to our commitment to

MATCH OFFICIALS

driving forward match official standards across both forms of the Game," added Jutge.

Since retiring from refereeing in 2009, Jutge has channelled his passion for the Game and refereeing into identifying and nurturing the best up-and-coming match official talent in France in his role as Referee Manager for the Fédération Française de Rugby (FFR). Under his guidance, France has delivered a number of referees for international duty with Romain Poite, Jérôme Garces, Pascal Gauzere and Mathieu Raynal all due to take charge of Tests in November.

IRB Chairman Bernard Lapasset was pleased with the appointment. "This is a key appointment for the IRB in what is a hugely important area of the Game and Joël brings with him vast experience, great knowledge and expertise as well as enormous respect within the international Rugby family. This is an excellent opportunity."

The Frenchman has now joined the selection committee, which is chaired by IRB Council Member and former Scotland international John Jeffrey and also comprises former elite referees Lyndon Bray, Tappe Henning (both SANZAR), Donal Courtney and Clayton Thomas (both 6 Nations). They meet four times a year to make selections for the next international window with all performances reviewed as part of the next round of appointments.

"These are exciting times for rugby worldwide and Joël's appointment underscores the IRB's commitment to ensuring that the best and fittest officials are appointed to our showcase events and matches, while working with our Unions to guide the next generation who are knocking on the door," said Jeffrey.

The Game's governing body has also recently unveiled two female referee panels, one for Fifteens and one for Sevens as preparations continue towards Rugby World Cup Sevens 2013 and Women's Rugby World Cup 2014.

The panels are supported by a development pathway that standardises and structures performance management and preparations, while also giving the world's top female referees opportunities to take charge of men's and women's international matches.

This programme is managed by IRB Referee Development Consultant Bernd Gabbei, who works closely with Jutge to develop and implement structured performance programmes specifically targeted at raising female refereeing standards globally.

REFEREES

THE NEW LAW TRIALS EXPLAINED

By James Fitzgerald

Getty Images

The scrum area is one of the Law amendments currently being trialled.

Rugby is an ever evolving sport and as such it is important the Laws of the Game keep pace with how it is being played. For this reason a number of important Law amendments are currently being trialled that will hopefully improve rugby for players and spectators alike.

In addition to proposed Law changes, one of the principal differences is a revised scrum engagement sequence that brings with it the unanimous backing of the International Rugby Board's expert Scrum Steering Group.

The trial, which incorporates the sequence "crouch, touch, set" has been in place from the start of this season in each hemisphere and forms one part of the IRB's ongoing commitment to improving the scrum phase of the Game.

The group examined the results of extensive testing of engagement sequence variations in live and machine environments in a trial driven by the IRB Scrum Forces Project that is run by the University of Bath in conjunction with the Rugby Football Union.

"Most people accept the scrum is currently a problematic area of the Game, accounting for roughly 17 per cent of match time in elite Rugby and with more than 50 per cent of scrums resulting in collapses or resets," said IRB Rugby Committee chairman and former New Zealand captain Graham Mourie.

"The IRB is committed to addressing these issues and has tasked the specialist steering group to identify the causes and to identify solutions. This is a positive first step but it should be noted that we must wait for the outcomes of the three-year Scrum Forces Project before we can take a holistic approach to the scrum."

The IRB-funded Scrum Forces Project is currently halfway through its three-year ground-breaking study of forces in the set scrum. The steering group, comprising some of the foremost experts on scrummaging in the modern Game, was established in 2011 to oversee the research of the project run by the University of Bath in conjunction with the RFU and to identify solutions for current scrum issues.

The other Law trials feature five proposed amendments. This initiative, which follows an extensive consultation and analysis process, also includes the formation of a fully consultative Laws Representative Group comprising technical representatives from the top Unions as well as representatives of the IRB Rugby Committee.

The five Law amendments being trialled are:

Law 16

16.7 (ruck): The ball has to be played within five seconds of it being at the back of a ruck with a warning from the referee to "use it". Sanction – scrum.

Law 19

19.2 (b) (quick throw-in): For a quick throw in, the player may be anywhere outside the field of play between the line of touch and the player's goal line.

19.4 (who throws in): When the ball goes into touch from a knock-on, the non-offending team will be offered the choice of a lineout at the point the ball crossed the touch line; or a scrum at the place of the knock-on. The non-offending team may exercise this option by taking a quick throw-in.

*20.4 (g) (forming a scrum): The referee will call "crouch" then "touch".
The front rows crouch and using their outside arm; each prop touches
the point of the opposing prop's outside shoulder. The props then
withdraw their arms. The referee will then call "set" when the front
rows are ready. The front rows may then set the scrum.*

Law 21

*21.4 Penalty and free-kick options and requirements: Lineout alterna-
tive. A team awarded a penalty or a free-kick at a lineout may choose
a further lineout, they throw in. This is in addition to the scrum option
above.*

"We have a collective responsibility to ensure that the Game is as enjoyable to play, officiate and watch as possible at every level," said IRB
Chairman Bernard Lapasset.

"Rugby is currently in good health with participation growing around
the world, but there is collective responsibility to ensure that a structured
process can be implemented to allow for global analysis and to monitor
trends relating to the shape and character of the Game."

Meanwhile, the IRB and its Member Unions have underscored their
commitment to consistent and accurate match officiating by sanctioning
and supporting two trials that have seen the powers of the television
match official (TMO) extended for the current season of the Aviva
Premiership in England and the Absa Currie Cup in South Africa.

England's premier domestic competition provides the backdrop for
an extended protocol that now allows the TMO to be consulted on
potential infringements prior to a try being scored and potential acts of
foul play.

A different set of protocols is being used in the Currie Cup which
allows referees to consult with the TMO for potential infringements up
to two phases before the try is scored.

The trials will be subject to extensive evaluation and Union, player
and match official consultation to allow the IRB Rugby Committee to
determine a protocol that improves the efficiency of the TMO role
without adversely impacting on the character of the Game.

LAWS OF THE GAME

REFEREE BIOGRAPHIES

November is a busy month packed full of internationals, the majority of them in Europe. We profile the 19 officials appointed by the International Rugby Board to referee a Test.

Getty Images

WAYNE BARNES (RFU)
DOB: 20/04/1979   Tests: 41

A barrister by profession, Wayne has been on the referee panel for the last two Rugby World Cups, having taken charge of his first Test during the IRB Pacific Nations Cup in 2006. The Englishman was the referee the last time New Zealand lost a Test match, the 2011 Tri-Nations decider with Australia.

Getty Images

GEORGE CLANCY (IRFU)
DOB: 12/01/1977   Tests: 25

The Irishman had the honour of refereeing the opening match of Rugby World Cup 2011 between New Zealand and Tonga, his first appearance at the showpiece tournament. George refereed his first Test in September 2006 between Uruguay and USA, while his most recent was New Zealand v South Africa in The Rugby Championship.

Getty Images

JÉRÔME GARCES (FFR)
DOB: 24/10/1973   Tests: 9

Selected as an assistant referee and reserve referee for Rugby World Cup 2011, Jérôme has since made his refereeing debut in the RBS Six Nations after taking charge of Italy v England in a snow-hit Rome. The Frenchman was also an assistant referee twice in The Rugby Championship.

Image SA

GREG GARNER (RFU)
DOB: 26/06/1980   Tests: 5

One of the newer referees on the international stage, Greg takes charge of his first Test involving a Tier One nation in November when Italy host Tonga in Brescia. He has refereed at the last two Junior World Championships, taking charge of the 2012 title decider in South Africa.

PASCAL GAUZERE (FFR)

DOB: 23/04/1977   Tests: 5

The Frenchman made his Test debut in March 2010 with the Russia-Germany encounter, which was sandwiched between his two Junior World Championships. He refereed the JWC 2010 final in Argentina and his most recent appointment in the middle was in the IRB Pacific Nations Cup in June.

Martin Seras Lima

LEIGHTON HODGES (WRU)

DOB: 25/11/1975   Tests: 1

The Welshman takes charge of the first Test in the November window between Russia and USA, five months after officiating in his second Junior World Championship. His only previous Test as a referee was Ukraine v Romania in August 2011.

Image SA

GLEN JACKSON (NZRU)

DOB: 23/10/1975   Tests: 0

The former New Zealand Maori only ended his playing career in May 2010, but is on a fast track to the top and takes charge of his first Test on 10 November with England v Fiji at Twickenham. He gained valuable experience at JWC 2012 and was assistant referee twice in The Rugby Championship.

Image SA

CRAIG JOUBERT

DOB: 08/11/1977   Tests: 38

The South African had the honour of refereeing the RWC 2011 Final and then five months later the opening match of the 2015 qualifying process between Mexico and Jamaica. The most experienced of his country's officials in action in November, he refereed his first Test in 2003 involving Namibia and Uganda.

Getty Images

JOHN LACEY (IRFU)

DOB: 12/10/1973   Tests: 3

Another match official with two Junior World Championships behind him, John refereed his first Test in March 2010 but it was this year's IRB Pacific Nations Cup in Japan that yielded his other Tests. The Irishman has been utilised as an assistant referee 10 times, including twice in The Rugby Championship.

Getty Images

REFEREE BIOGRAPHIES

Martin Seras Lima

JOAQUÍN MONTES (URU)
DOB: 23/06/1979   Tests: 5

With experience of a Junior World Championship and Junior World Rugby Trophy behind him, Joaquin has refereed five Tests in the last 12 months, his most recent being the Rugby World Cup 2015 qualifier between Paraguay and Bermuda in September 2012.

Getty Images

NIGEL OWENS (WRU)
DOB: 18/06/1971   Tests: 41

A veteran of two Rugby World Cups, Nigel took charge of his first Test, between Portugal and Georgia, in February 2003 and nearly a decade later he remains among the Game's top match officials. Off the pitch he is a television presenter and stand-up comedian in his native Wales.

Image SA

FRANCISCO PASTRANA (UAR)
DOB: 13/09/1979   Tests: 4

A veteran of four Junior World Rugby Trophy or Junior World Championships since 2009, Francisco will take charge of two matches in the IRB International Rugby Series in Colwyn Bay, Wales. The Argentinean official has refereed four Tests, three of them involving Uruguay.

Getty Images

JACO PEYPER (SARU)
DOB: 13/05/1980   Tests: 7

The South African cut his teeth at two Junior World Championships and was given the honour of refereeing the 2011 final. A month later he refereed his first Test between Kenya and Zimbabwe with The Rugby Championship encounter between Argentina and New Zealand in La Plata his most recent appointment with the whistle.

Getty Images

ROMAIN POITE
DOB: 14/09/1975   Tests: 23

One of four Frenchman taking charge of matches in November, Romain refereed his first Test in November 2006 between Morocco and Namibia. He was a member of the RWC 2011 panel, four years after operating as a fourth or fifth official at France 2007.

MATHIEU RAYNAL

DOB: 09/08/1981   Tests: 3

Another up-and-coming match official who has honed his
skills at the last two Junior World Championships, Mathieu
has refereed three Tests involving six different teams. That
will become eight on 24 November when he takes charge
of Scotland v Tonga in Aberdeen.

Image SA

ALAIN ROLLAND (IRFU)

DOB: 22/08/1966   Tests: 63

A former scrum half capped three times by Ireland, Alain
made his debut as an international referee with Wales v
Romania in September 2001 and has refereed at three
Rugby World Cups, having the honour of taking charge of
the 2007 final.

Getty Images

JUAN SYLVESTRE (UAR)

DOB: 25/03/1982   Tests: 0

A newcomer to the international stage, Juan has just
returned from the IRB Americas Rugby Championship in
Canada, where he took charge of two matches. The
Argentinean official will referee the Uruguay v Portugal
encounter in Montevideo on 11 November.

STEVE WALSH (ARU)

DOB: 28/03/1972   Tests: 49

Steve will join the select club of officials to have refereed
50 Tests when he takes charge of France's battle with
Argentina on 17 November, ironically the two sides he
refereed in his first Test back in June 1998. A touch judge
at RWC 1999, the New Zealander has been on the referee
panel for the three subsequent tournaments.

Getty Images

LOURENS VAN DER MERWE (SARU)

DOB: 03/02/1977   Tests: 1

Lourens has had a whirlwind year, from taking charge of
four matches at the Junior World Championship in his
native South Africa to refereeing his first Test between
Botswana and Swaziland in June and then being assistant
referee for the three Bledisloe Cup encounters in 2012.

Image SA

REFEREE BIOGRAPHIES

INTERNATIONAL REFEREES

DISMISSALS IN MAJOR INTERNATIONAL MATCHES

Up to 10 October 2012 in major international matches. These cover all matches for which the eight senior members of the International Board have awarded caps, and also all matches played in Rugby World Cup final stages.

A E Freethy	sent off	C J Brownlie (NZ)	E v NZ	1925
K D Kelleher	sent off	C E Meads (NZ)	S v NZ	1967
R T Burnett	sent off	M A Burton (E)	A v E	1975
W M Cooney	sent off	J Sovau (Fj)	A v Fj	1976
N R Sanson	sent off	G A D Wheel (W)	W v I	1977
N R Sanson	sent off	W P Duggan (I)	W v I	1977
D I H Burnett	sent off	P Ringer (W)	E v W	1980
C Norling	sent off	J-P Garuet (F)	F v I	1984
K V J Fitzgerald	sent off	H D Richards (W)	NZ v W	*1987
F A Howard	sent off	D Codey (A)	A v W	*1987
K V J Fitzgerald	sent off	M Taga (Fj)	Fj v E	1988
O E Doyle	sent off	A Lorieux (F)	Arg v F	1988
B W Stirling	sent off	T Vonolagi (Fj)	E v Fj	1989
B W Stirling	sent off	N Nadruku (Fj)	E v Fj	1989
F A Howard	sent off	K Moseley (W)	W v F	1990
F A Howard	sent off	A Carminati (F)	S v F	1990
F A Howard	sent off	A Stoop (Nm)	Nm v W	1990
A J Spreadbury	sent off	A Benazzi (F)	A v F	1990
C Norling	sent off	P Gallart (F)	A v F	1990
C J Hawke	sent off	F E Mendez (Arg)	E v Arg	1990
E F Morrison	sent off	C Cojocariu (R)	R v F	1991
J M Fleming	sent off	P L Sporleder (Arg)	WS v Arg	*1991
J M Fleming	sent off	M G Keenan (WS)	WS v Arg	*1991
S R Hilditch	sent off	G Lascubé (F)	F v E	1992
S R Hilditch	sent off	V Moscato (F)	F v E	1992
D J Bishop	sent off	O Roumat (Wld)	NZ v Wld	1992
E F Morrison	sent off	J T Small (SA)	A v SA	1993
I Rogers	sent off	M E Cardinal (C)	C v F	1994
I Rogers	sent off	P Sella (F)	C v F	1994
D Mené	sent off	J D Davies (W)	W v E	1995
S Lander	sent off	F Mahoni (Tg)	F v Tg	*1995
D T M McHugh	sent off	J Dalton (SA)	SA v C	*1995
D T M McHugh	sent off	R G A Snow (C)	SA v C	*1995
D T M McHugh	sent off	G L Rees (C)	SA v C	*1995
J Dumé	sent off	G R Jenkins (W)	SA v W	1995
W J Erickson	sent off	V B Cavubati (Fj)	NZ v Fj	1997
W D Bevan	sent off	A G Venter (SA)	NZ v SA	1997
C Giacomel	sent off	R Travaglini (Arg)	F v Arg	1997

W J Erickson	sent off	D J Grewcock (E)	NZ v E	1998
S R Walsh	sent off	J Sitoa (Tg)	A v Tg	1998
R G Davies	sent off	M Giovanelli (It)	S v It	1999
C Thomas	sent off	T Leota (Sm)	Sm v F	1999
C Thomas	sent off	G Leaupepe (Sm)	Sm v F	1999
S Dickinson	sent off	J-J Crenca (F)	NZ v F	1999
E F Morrison	sent off	M Vunibaka (Fj)	Fj v C	*1999
A Cole	sent off	D R Baugh (C)	C v Nm	*1999
W J Erickson	sent off	N Ta'ufo'ou (Tg)	E v Tg	*1999
P Marshall	sent off	B D Venter (SA)	SA v U	*1999
P C Deluca	sent off	W Cristofoletto (It)	F v It	2000
J I Kaplan	sent off	A Troncon (It)	It v I	2001
R Dickson	sent off	G Leger (Tg)	W v Tg	2001
P C Deluca	sent off	N J Hines (S)	US v S	2002
P D O'Brien	sent off	M C Joubert (SA)	SA v A	2002
P D O'Brien	sent off	J J Labuschagne (SA)	E v SA	2002
S R Walsh	sent off	V Ma'asi (Tg)	Tg v I	2003
N Williams	sent off	S D Shaw (E)	NZ v E	2004
S J Dickinson	sent off	P C Montgomery (SA)	W v SA	2005
S M Lawrence	sent off	L W Moody (E)	E v Sm	2005
S M Lawrence	sent off	A Tuilagi (Sm)	E v Sm	2005
S R Walsh	sent off	S Murray (S)	W v S	2006
J I Kaplan	sent off	H T-Pole (Tg)	Sm v Tg	*2007
A C Rolland	sent off	J Nieuwenhuis (Nm)	F v Nm	*2007
N Owens	sent off	N Nalaga (Pl)	F v Pl	2008
W Barnes	sent off	J P R Heaslip (I)	NZ v I	2010
C Joubert	sent off	D A Mitchell (A)	A v NZ	2010
N Owens	sent off	P B Williams (Sm)	SA v Sm	*2011
A C Rolland	sent off	S K Warburton (W)	W v F	*2011

Matches in World Cup final stages

INTERNATIONAL

Referee Alain Rolland gives a red card to Sam Warburton during the Rugby World Cup 2011 semi-final.

AFP/Getty Images